Christian Writers' Market Guide 2001

Christian Writers' Market Guide 2001

THE REFERENCE TOOL FOR THE CHRISTIAN WRITER

SALLY E. STUART

SHAW

WATERBROOK
PRESS

Christian Writers' Market Guide 2001
A SHAW BOOK
Published by WaterBrook Press
2375 Telstar Dr., Suite 160
Colorado Springs, CO 80920
A division of Random House, Inc.

ISSN 1080-3955

ISBN 0-87788-189-8

Printed in the United States of America
2001

10 9 8 7 6 5 4 3 2 1

CONTENTS

Indicates a new category this year

III. PERIODICALS

VI. INDEXES AND GLOSSARY

INTRODUCTION

We have survived the year 2000, and it looks as if it is time to move into the twenty-first Century with this 16th edition of the market guide. If you are reading this, you have already noticed our brand new cover design. You have probably also noted that the guide has been getting larger every year. This year is no exception. Please note that the market guide is just one of several writing resource books available from Harold Shaw Publishers, now an imprint of WaterBrook Press. It is exciting to see them committed to the needs of the Christian writer.

I have not made a lot of internal format changes this year, but you will find the preferred Bible version listed for book publishers as well as periodical publishers. One of the most helpful changes will be found in the periodical section where I have indicated the paying markets with a dollar sign ($) in front of the listing. In the book section, you will also find an indication of which publishers are now doing e-books. E-books are also included in the topical listings for books, so you can identify them more quickly. Of course, there are even more publishers who have e-mail or Websites, as well as some changes in those who had them previously.

Even more publishers are making guidelines available by e-mail or on their Websites, saving the writer untold time and money by not having to send for them the conventional way. Check the publishers' individual listings to see which ones do. All of this is changing how we do our market research, making it much easier and less time-consuming to learn a great deal more about the publishers and publications we want to write for. Keep in mind that you can easily access all those publishers with e-mail or links through my Website at http://www.stuartmarket.com.

I have found it interesting this year that more publishers are wholeheartedly embracing the advantages of e-mail. Many who said last year that they did not want e-mail queries or submissions are now saying they prefer them. Many of them—many more than previously—used e-mail to update their listings. That also accounts for the fact that we have even more updated listings that usual.

Again this year the number of periodical publishers dropped while the number of book publishers expanded. In this 2001 edition, you will find 695 publications, including 64 new ones. The book publishers have jumped from about 330 last year to over 370 this year, with 72 new. Some of the old publishers or publications have ceased publishing or closed their doors to freelancers, but the number of new publishers continues to grow. I encourage you to seek out some possible new markets from these lists. This edition has the most markets ever—about 1150 total.

Since a number of publishers are now making assignments only, it is even more important that you establish a reputation in your areas of interest and expertise. Once you have acquired a number of credits in a given field, write to some of those assignment-only editors, giving those credits, and ask for an assignment. In general, you will be better off striving to get some of those assignments, instead of hoping to fill one of the small slots left for unsolicited material.

There are no new topics this year, but if you have some you'd like to see included, please let me know for future editions. One place you will see some expansion and reorganization this year is in the Resources for Writers section. There are new and much clearer divisions, which will make things easier to find. Check the Table of Contents for a new list of the divisions included. Every section has new resources for you to pursue.

Our agent list continues to grow slowly, with a total of 90 this year (20 new). The list of Christian agents, and secular agents who are willing to handle Christian books, continues to grow. But as I have said before, it is crucial that you carefully check out agents before signing a contract or committing to work with them.

See the introduction to the agent section for some tips on how to do that. Do not assume that because they are listed I can personally vouch for them. I do not have the time or resources to check out each one thoroughly; that is your job. Because the number of agents is still limited, I have included a few agents who charge fees, but the prevailing consensus is that agents should not charge fees, other than actual office expenses (such as long-distance phone calls and photocopying). You will need to decide if any such fees are acceptable in your situation.

It is a good idea each year to study the market analysis sections of this book for more insight into what's happening in the industry. As with any new reference book, I suggest you spend some quality time becoming familiar with its contents and structure. Discover the supplementary lists available throughout the book. Read through the glossary and spend a few minutes learning terms you are not familiar with. Review the lists of writers' groups and conferences and mark those you might be interested in pursuing during the coming months. The denominational listing and corporate-family listings will help you start making the important connection between periodicals and book publishers associated with different denominations or publishing groups. With so many publishers being bought out or merging, it will help keep you up-to-date with the new members of these often growing families.

Be sure to carefully study the "How to Use This Book" section. It will save you a lot of time and frustration in trying to understand the meaning of all the notations in the primary listings, and it's full of helpful hints. Remember to send for sample copies (or catalog) and guidelines for any of these publishers or periodicals you are not familiar with. Then study those carefully before submitting anything to that publisher. I've noticed that publishers who make their guidelines available on their Website often include a great deal more information than you get in the usual guidelines sheet.

Editors tell me repeatedly that they are looking for writers who understand them, their periodical or publishing house, and most of all, their unique approach to the marketplace. One of the biggest complaints I've gotten from publishers over the years is that the material they receive routinely is not appropriate for their needs. However, I don't remember receiving even one such complaint this year, so I hope that is an indication that you are all doing a better job of marketing. With a little time and effort, you can fulfill all their expectations, distinguish yourself as a professional, and sell what you write.

Again, I wish you well as you embark on this exciting road to publication, whether for the first time or as a long-time veteran. And as I remind you every year, each of you has been given a specific mission in the field of writing. You and I often feel inadequate to the task, but I learned a long time ago that the writing assignments God has given me cannot be written quite as well by anyone else.

Sally E. Stuart
1647 SW Pheasant Dr.
Aloha, OR 97006
(503)642-9844 (Please call after 9 A.M. Pacific time.)
Fax (503)848-3658
E-mail: stuartcwmg@aol.com
Website: http://www.stuartmarket.com

P.S. For information on how to receive the market guide automatically every year and freeze the price at $24.99, plus postage, for future editions, or for information on getting the guide at a discounted group rate or getting books on consignment for your next seminar or conference, contact me at the address or numbers above. Note that this market guide usually comes out during January or February of each year.

HOW TO USE THIS BOOK

The purpose of this market guide is to make your marketing job easier and more targeted. However, it will serve you well only if you put some time and effort into studying its contents and using it as a springboard for discovering and becoming an expert on those publishers best suited to your writing topics and style.

Below you will find information on its general set-up and instructions for its use. In order to help you become more of an expert on marketing, I am including an explanation of each entry in the alphabetical listings for both the book section and the periodical section. Be sure to study these before trying to use this book.

1. Spend some time initially getting acquainted with the contents and set-up of this resource book. You cannot make the best use of it until you know exactly what it has to offer.

2. Study the contents pages, where you will find listings of all the periodical and book topics. When selecting a topic, be sure to check related topics as well. Some cross-referencing will often be helpful. For example, if you have a novel that deals with doctor-assisted suicide, you might find the list for adult novels and the list for controversial issues and see which publishers are on both lists. Those would be good potential markets. In the topical sections you will find a letter "R" following publishers that accept reprints (pieces that have been printed in other publications, but for which you retain the rights).

3. The primary/alphabetical listings for book and periodical publishers contain those publishers who answered the questionnaire and those who did not. The listings preceded by an asterisk (*) are those publishers who didn't respond and whose information I was unable to update from other sources. Those with a number symbol (#) were updated from their printed guidelines or other current sources. Since the information in those two groups was not verified by the publisher, you are encouraged to send for sample copies or catalogs and writer's guidelines before submitting to them or get that information by e-mail or on their Websites. A plus sign (+) indicates a new listing.

4. In each **book publisher listing** you will find the following information (as available) in this format:

  a) Name of publisher
  b) Address, phone and fax numbers, e-mail address, Website
  c) Denomination or affiliation
  d) Name of editor—This may include the senior editor's name, followed by the name of another editor to whom submissions should be sent. In a few cases, several editors are named with the type of books each is responsible for. Address to appropriate editor.
  e) Sometimes a statement of purpose
  f) Sometimes a list of imprint names
  g) Number of inspirational/religious titles published per year

h) Number of submissions received annually

i) Percentage of books from first-time authors

j) In the past, it has indicated only those publishers who do not accept manuscripts through agents. If it said nothing about agents, you could assume they did accept manuscripts through agents. Starting this year, some listings will indicate whether they accept, prefer, require, or don't accept manuscripts through agents.

k) The percentage of books from freelance authors they subsidy publish (if any). This does not refer to percentage paid by author. If percentage of subsidy is over 50%, the publisher will be listed in a separate section under Subsidy Publishers.

l) Whether they reprint out-of-print books from other publishers

m) Preferred manuscript length in words or pages; if pages, it refers to double-spaced, manuscript pages.

n) Average amount of royalty, if provided. If royalty is a percentage of wholesale or net, it is based on price paid by bookstores or distributors. If it is on retail price, it is based on cover price of the book.

o) Average amount paid for advances. Whether a publisher pays an advance or not is noted in the listing; if they did not answer the question, there is no mention of it.

p) Whether they make any outright purchases and amount paid. In this kind of sale, an author is paid a flat fee and receives no royalties.

q) Average first printing (number of books usually printed for a first-time author)

r) Average length of time between acceptance of a manuscript and publication of the work

s) Whether they consider simultaneous submissions. This means you can send a query or complete manuscript simultaneously to more than one publisher, as long as you advise everyone involved that you are doing so.

t) Length of time it should take them to respond to a query/proposal or to a complete manuscript (when two lengths of time are given, the first generally refers to a query and the latter to a complete manuscript). Give them a one-month grace period beyond that and then send a polite follow-up letter if you haven't heard from them.

u) Whether a publisher "accepts," "prefers," or "requires" the submission of an ACCEPTED manuscript on disk (do not send your unsolicited manuscripts/submissions on disk). Most publishers now do accept or require that books be sent on a computer disk (usually along with a hard copy), but since each publisher's needs are different, that information will be supplied to you by the individual publisher when the time comes. This section also indicates if they will accept submissions by e-mail.

v) This year it will indicate what Bible version they prefer.

w) Availability and cost for writer's guidelines and book catalogs—If the listing says "guidelines," it means they are available for a #10 (business-sized) SASE with a first-class stamp. The cost of the catalog (if any), the size of envelope, and amount of postage are given, if specified (affix stamps to envelope; don't send loose). Tip: If postage required is more than $1.24, I suggest you put $1.24 in postage on the envelope and clearly mark it "Special Standard

Mail." (That is enough for up to 1 pound.) (Please note that if the postage rates increase this year, this amount may change. Check with your local post office.) If the listing says "free catalog," it means you need only request it; they do not ask for payment or SASE. Note: If sending for both guidelines and catalog, it is not necessary to send two envelopes; guidelines will be sent with catalog. If guidelines are available by e-mail or Website, that will be indicated.

x) Nonfiction Section—Preference for query letter, book proposal, or complete manuscript, and if they accept phone, fax, or e-queries (if it does not say they accept them, assume they do not; this reference applies to fiction as well as nonfiction). If they want a query letter, send just a letter describing your project. If they want a query letter/proposal, you can add a chapter-by-chapter synopsis and the number of sample chapters indicated. If not specified, send one to three chapters. This is often followed by a quote from them about their needs or what they don't want to see.

y) Fiction Section—Same information as nonfiction section

z) Special Needs—If they have specific topics they need that are not included in the subject listings, they are indicated here.

aa) Ethnic Books—Usually specifies which ethnic groups they target or any particular needs

bb) Also Does—Indicates which publishers also publish booklets, pamphlets or tracts. This year also includes e-books.

cc) Photos—Indicates if they accept freelance photos for book covers. If interested, contact them for details or photography guidelines.

dd) Tips—Specific tips provided by the editor/publisher.

Note: At the end of some listings you will find an indication that the publisher receives mailings of book proposals from The Writer's Edge (see Editorial Services/Illinois for an explanation of that service) and/or First Edition (see index).

5. In each **periodical listing** you will find the following information (as available) in this format:

a) Name of periodical

b) Address, phone, fax, e-mail address, Website

c) Denomination or affiliation

d) Name of editor and editor to submit to (if different)

e) Theme of publication—This will help you understand their particular slant.

f) Format of publication, frequency of publication, number of pages and size of circulation—Tells whether magazine, newsletter, journal, tabloid, newspaper, or take-home paper. Frequency of publication indicates quantity of material needed. Number of pages usually indicates how much material they can use. Circulation indicates the amount of exposure your material will receive and often indicates how well they might pay or the probability that they will stay in business.

g) Subscription rate—Amount given is for a one-year subscription in the country of origin. I suggest you subscribe to at least one of your primary markets every year to become better acquainted with its specific focus.

h) Date established—Included only if 1997 or later

i) Openness to freelance; percentage freelance written. Again this year this information has been expanded to indicate the percentage of unsolicited freelance and the percentage of assigned. Since not all publishers have responded to this question, some will still give the two percentages combined or indicate only the unsolicited number. If they buy only a small percentage, it often means they are open but receive little that is appropriate. The percentage freelance written indicates how great your chances are of selling to them. When you have a choice, choose those with the higher percentage, but only if you have done your homework and know they are an appropriate market for your material.

j) Preference for query or complete manuscript also tells if they want a cover letter with complete manuscripts and whether they will accept phone, fax, or e-mail queries. (If it does not mention cover letters or phone, fax, or e-mail queries, assume they do not accept them.)

k) Payment schedule, payment on acceptance (they pay when the piece is accepted) or publication (they pay when it is published), and rights purchased. (See glossary for definitions of different rights.)

l) If a publication does not pay, or pays in copies or subscription, that is indicated in bold, capital letters.

m) If a publication is not copyrighted, that is indicated. That means you should ask for your copyright notice to appear on your piece when they publish it, so your rights will be protected.

n) Preferred word lengths and average number of manuscripts purchased per year (in parentheses)

o) Response time—The time they usually take to respond to your query or manuscript submission (add at least two weeks for delays for mailing).

p) Seasonal material (also refers to holiday)—If sending holiday or seasonal material, it should reach them at least the specified length of time in advance.

q) Acceptance of simultaneous submissions and reprints—If they accept simultaneous submissions, it means they will look at submissions (usually timely topic or holiday material) sent simultaneously to several publishers. Best to send to non-overlapping markets (such as denominational), and be sure to always indicate that it is a simultaneous submission. Reprints are pieces you have sold previously, but to which you hold the rights (which means you sold only first or one-time rights to the original publisher and the rights reverted to you as soon as they were published).

r) If they accept, prefer or require submissions on disk or by e-mail. Many now prefer an e-mail submission, rather than on disk. Most will want a query or hard copy first. If it does not say they prefer or require disks, you should wait and see if they ask for them. If they accept an e-mail submission, it will indicate whether they want it as an attached file or copied into the message. If it says they accept e-mail submissions, but doesn't indicate a preference, it means they will take it either way.

s) Average amount of kill fee, if they pay one (see glossary for definition)

t) Whether or not they use sidebars (see glossary for definition), and whether they use them regularly or sometimes

u) Their preferred Bible version is indicated. The most popular version is the NIV (New International Version). If no version is indicated, they usually have no preference. See glossary for Bible Versions list.

v) Availability and cost for writer's guidelines, theme list, and sample copies—If the listing says "Guidelines," it means they are available for a #10 SASE (business-sized) with a first-class stamp. Many will now have guidelines available by e-mail or Website, and the listing will indicate that. The cost for a sample copy, the size of envelope, and number of stamps required are given, if specified (affix stamps to envelope; don't send loose). Tip: If postage required is more than $1.24, I suggest you put $1.24 in postage on the envelope and clearly mark it "Special Standard Mail." (That is enough for up to one pound). If the listing says "free sample copy," it means you need only to request them; they do not ask for payment or SASE. Note: If sending for both guidelines and sample copy, it is not necessary to send two envelopes; guidelines will be sent with sample copy. If a listing doesn't mention guidelines or sample copy, they probably don't have them.

w) "Not in topical listings" means the publisher has not supplied a list of topics they are interested in. Send for their guidelines to determine topics used.

x) Poetry—Name of poetry editor (if different). Average number of poems bought each year. Types of poetry; number of lines. Payment rate. Maximum number of poems you may submit at one time.

y) Fillers—Name of fillers editor (if different). Types of fillers accepted; word length. Payment rate.

z) Columns/Departments—Name of column editor. Names of columns in the periodical (information in parentheses gives focus of column); word length requirements. Payment rate. Be sure to see sample before sending ms or query. Most columns require a query.

aa) Special Issues or Needs—Indicates topics of special issues they have planned for the year, or unique topics not included in regular subject listings

bb) Ethnic—Any involvement they have in the ethnic market

cc) Contest—Information on contests they sponsor or how to obtain that information. See Contest section at back of book for full list of contests.

dd) Tips—Tips from the editor on how to break into this market or how to be successful as an author.

ee) At the end of some listings you will find a notation as to where that particular periodical placed in the Top 50+ Christian Periodical list in 2000, and/or their place in previous years. This list is compiled annually to indicate the most writer-friendly publications. To receive a complete listing, plus a prepared analysis sheet and writer's guidelines for the top 50 of those markets, send $25 (includes postage) to: Sally Stuart, 1647 SW Pheasant Dr., Aloha, OR 97006, or call (503)642-9844 for more information.

Some listings also include EPA winners. These awards are made annually by the Evangelical Press Association (a trade organization for Christian periodicals).

6. It is important that you adhere closely to the guidelines set out in these listings. If a publisher asks for a query only, do not send a complete manuscript. Following these guidelines will mark you as a professional.

7. If your manuscript is completed, select the proper topical listing and target audience, and make up a list of possible publishers. Check first to see which ones will accept a complete manuscript (if you want to send it to those that require a query, you will have to write a query letter or book proposal to send first). Please do not assume that your manuscript will be appropriate for all those on the list. Read the primary listing for each and if you are not familiar with a publisher, read their writer's guidelines and study one or more sample copies or book catalog. (The primary listings contain information on how to get these.) Be sure the slant of your manuscript fits the slant of the publisher.

8. If you have an idea for an article, short story, or book but you have not written it yet, a reading of the appropriate topical listing will help you decide on a possible slant or approach. Select some publishers to whom you might send a query about your idea. If your idea is for an article, do not overlook the possibility of writing on the same topic for a number of different periodicals listed under that topic, either with the same target audience or another from the list that indicates an interest. For example, you could write on money management for a general adult magazine, a teen magazine, a women's publication, or one for pastors. Each would require a different slant, but you would get a lot more mileage from that idea.

9. If you do not have an idea, simply start reading through the topical listings or the primary listings. They are sure to trigger any number of book or magazine ideas you could go to work on.

10. If you run into words or terms you are not familiar with, check the glossary at the back of the book for definitions.

11. If you need someone to look at your material to evaluate it or to give it a thorough editing, look up the section on Editorial Services and find someone to send it to for such help. That often will make the difference between success or failure in publishing.

12. If you are a published author with other books to your credit, you may be interested in finding an agent. Unpublished authors generally don't need or won't be able to find an agent. However, some agents will consider unpublished authors (their listing will indicate that), but you must have a completed manuscript before you approach an agent (see agent list). Christian agents are at a premium, so realize it will be hard to find an agent unless you have had some success in book writing. The agent list also includes secular agents who handle religious/inspirational material.

13. Check the Group list to find a group to join in your area. Go to the Conference list to find a conference you might attend this year. Attending a conference every year or two is almost essential to your success as a writer.

14. **ALWAYS SEND AN SASE WITH EVERY QUERY OR MANUSCRIPT**, unless your cover letter indicates that you do not want it returned. If that is the case, send a #10 SASE for their acceptance or rejection.

15. **DO NOT RELY SOLELY ON THE INFORMATION PROVIDED IN THIS MARKET GUIDE.** It is just that—a guide—and is not intended to be complete by itself. It is important to your success as a freelance writer that you learn how to use writer's guidelines and study book catalogs or sample copies before submitting to any publisher. Be a professional!

ADDITIONAL RESOURCES TO HELP WITH YOUR WRITING AND MARKETING

1. **Sally Stuart's Guide to Getting Published**—At last, the author of the Christian Writers' Market Guide has compiled all the information you need to understand and function in the world of Christian publishing. Takes you through all the steps needed to be successful as a freelance writer. Serves as both a text and a reference book. One of the most important and useful resources you'll ever find for your writing library. $21, postpaid.

2. **2001 Top 50+ Christian Periodical Publishers Packet**—Includes a list of the Top 50+ "writer-friendly" periodicals, preprepared analysis sheets, and publisher's guidelines for each of the top 50, and a master form for analyzing your own favorite markets. Saves more than $40 in postage and 25-30 hours of work. $25, postpaid. New packet every year.

3. **The 2001 Christian Writers' Market Guide on computer disk**—in ASCII Text on $3\frac{1}{2}$" HD disk, for quick marketing reference. This is currently in text form as it appears in the book, not in a database. $30 postpaid.

4. **A Market Plan for More Sales**—A step-by-step plan to help you be successful in marketing. Includes 5 reproducible forms. $5 postpaid.

5. **The Complete Guide to Christian Writing and Speaking**—A how-to handbook for beginning and advanced writers and speakers written by the 19 members of the editorial staff of *The Christian Communicator.* Special! $6.50, postpaid (regularly $13).

6. **The Complete Guide to Writing for Publication**—Written by top experts in the field. Contains chapters on various genres of fiction, marketing tips, and writing for children, plus everything you wanted to know about writing for publication. $18 postpaid.

7. **New! WriterSpeaker.Com**—A friendly guide to Internet research and marketing. Plus how to set up and promote your own Website. $18 postpaid.

8. **New! Effective Magazine Writing**—Gives a clear understanding of each step of the magazine writing process. From the former editor of *Decision* magazine. $14 postpaid.

9. **New! How to Write What You Love—and Make a Living at It**—Discusses how to find a distinctive style, make time to write, negotiate contracts, contact agents, secure copyrights, and make multiple sales. $16 postpaid.

10. **The Complete Guide to Writing & Selling the Christian Novel**—This guide not only gives you the how-to for writing excellent fiction, it gives insight into how to successfully sell it, and specifically how to make it Christian without being preachy. $18 postpaid.

11. **Permissions Packet**—A compilation of over 16 pages of information directly from publishers on how and when to ask permission to quote from other people's material or from Bible paraphrases. Information not available elsewhere in printed form. $6 postpaid.

12. **Electronic Research Sites and How to Use Them**—This manual is a must-have for any writer wanting to pursue electronic research. It not only lists all the best research sites on the Web, it also includes a copy of the home page for each one so you know exactly what each site has to offer. $13 postpaid.

13. **Copyright Law, What You Don't Know Can Cost You**—Answers all

the questions about rights and copyright law that affect you as a writer. Simple Q & A format followed by the actual wording of the law. Includes reproducible copyright forms & instructions. $18 postpaid.

14. **Write on Target, A Five-Phase Program for Nonfiction Writers,** by Dennis Hensley & Holly Miller—The craft of writing, the nuts and bolts, finding your niche, selling your manuscript, and mapping your future success as a writer. $15 postpaid.

15. **100 Plus Motivational Moments for Writers and Speakers**—A devotional book specifically for writers and speakers written by successful writers and speakers. $13 postpaid.

16. **You Can Do It! A Guide to Christian Self-Publishing** (revised edition) by Athena Dean. Dean shares insider self-publishing secrets for the Christian market. Takes you step-by-step through the project, including actual budgets and current cost estimates. $13 postpaid.

17. **2001 Internet Directory of Christian Publishers**—A handy listing of over 825 Christian publishers who have Websites or e-mail addresses. Note: Since this list is growing daily and is too long to maintain in a booklet format, it now comes on 8½ x 11 sheets, 3-hole punched to put in a looseleaf notebook. $9.50 postpaid.

18. **A Savvy Approach to Book Sales, Marketing Advice to Get the Buzz Going**—by Elaine Wright Colvin. A wealth of information on how to promote your self-published book, as well as many ideas for the author wanting to boost the sales of a book from a royalty publisher. $13 postpaid.

19. The following resources are all 8-page, 8½ x 11 booklets on areas of specific interest, as indicated:

a) **Keeping Track of Your Periodical Manuscripts**—These pages can be duplicated to keep track of every step involved in sending out your periodical manuscripts to publishers. $5 postpaid.

b) **Keeping Track of Your Book Manuscripts**—A similar booklet summarizing the steps in tracking a book manuscript from idea to publication. $5 postpaid.

c) **How to Submit a Book Proposal to a Publisher**—Contains all you need to know to present a professional-looking book proposal to a publishing house (includes a sample book proposal). $5 postpaid.

d) **How to Submit an Article or Story to a Publisher**—Shows how to write a query, prepare a professional-looking manuscript, and more. $5 postpaid.

e) **How to Write That Sure-Sell Magazine Article**—Contains a 3-step writing plan for articles, a list of article types, 12 evaluation questions, sample manuscript page, and more. $5 postpaid.

f) **How to Write a Picture Book**—An inside look at how to write, format, and lay out a children's picture book, with tips for those all-important finishing touches. $5 postpaid.

g) **How to Write Daily Devotionals That Inspire**—Includes the basic format and patterns for daily devotionals, marketing tips, 12 evaluation questions, and polishing. $5 postpaid.

h) **How to Write Personal Experience Articles**—Includes how to write

a query letter/sample, components of personal experience article, interviewing tips, and more. $5 postpaid.

20. The following resources are all 8½ x 5½ booklets, 12-20 pages, on areas of specific interest, as indicated:

    a) **The Art of Researching the Professional Way**—$5 postpaid.

    b) **Interviewing the Professional Way**—$5 postpaid.

    c) **The Professional Way to Write Dialogue**—$5 postpaid.

    d) **The Professional Way to Create Characters**—$5 postpaid.

    e) **Writing Junior Books the Professional Way (for ages 8-12)**—$5 postpaid.

    f) **Writing for Young Adults the Professional Way**—$5 postpaid.

    g) **How to Develop a Professional Writers' Group**—$5 postpaid.

    h) **Preparing for a Writing Conference**—$5 postpaid

Note: Any of the above $5 booklets may be purchased at 2 for $9, 4 for $17, 6 for $25, 8 for $33, 10 for $40, 12 for $48, or all 16 for $62.

To order any of the above resources, send a list of what you want with your check or money order to: Sally E. Stuart, 1647 SW Pheasant Dr., Aloha OR 97006, (503)642-9844. Fax: (503)848-3658, stuartcwmg@aol.com.

21. **The Writer's Edge**—A service that links book writers and Christian publishers. The writer fills out a book information form and sends that along with 3 sample chapters, a synopsis, and a check for $59. The writer receives a brief critique of the manuscript or, if the manuscript is accepted by The Writer's Edge, a synopsis of the manuscript will appear in a newsletter that goes to more than 55 Christian publishers who use The Writer's Edge as a screening tool for unsolicited manuscripts. Writer's Edge now also considers previously published books. *For further information, send an SASE to The Writer's Edge, PO Box 1266, Wheaton, IL 60189, or obtain an application by e-mail at writersedge@usa.net or from one of their Websites: http://members.xoom.com/WRITERSEDGE, or http://writersedge.tripod.com. The Writer's Edge cannot be reached by phone.*

RESOURCES FOR WRITERS

Below you will find a variety of resources that will help you as you carry out your training or work as a freelance writer. In addition to the resources here, also check out the separate listings for groups, conferences, editorial services, and contests. You are encouraged to spend some time checking out these resources, as they represent a wealth of knowledge and contacts that will help you be more successful in this business of writing and publishing. Note: This section has been reorganized from last year to make categories of resources easier to locate. Always check the most specific category first.

CONNECTING WITH OTHER WRITERS

+CHRISTIAN WEBRING. Webring for Christian authors and poets at: http://christianwebrings.org/rings/capstone.

+CHRISTIAN WRITERS' GROUP (CWG). A discussion group for published or aspiring, born-again writers. Purposes: To share ideas, tips, conference/seminar information, encouragement, support, and prayer requests. Editors/publishers also welcome. To join, go to: http://www.onelist.com/subscribe/CWG, or e-mail: CWG-subscribe@onelist.com. List owner: Lisa Wiener. Co-Moderator: Rev. Dennis Wenzel. Group Website: http://members.truepath.com/CWG. Membership (300) open.

CHRISTIAN WRITER'S WORKSHOP. Http://www.billyates.com/cww. This is an interactive Christian writers' group that meets twice a week on the Internet for discussion and has a weekly newsletter that comes by e-mail. Part of the Writers Club on AOL (http://www.writersclub.com). To find the club at 10:00 ET on Tuesday nights, go to workshop chat room at http://chat.writersclub.com; for the Thursday night chat, 9 pm ET, go to Writer's Workshop chat room of the Writers Club on AOL (keyword=writers). To sign up for the newsletter, contact Bill Yates, e-mail: WTYates @aol.com.

*CHURCH WRITERS GROUP. Leader: Mary Spagnuolo, The Amy Foundation. Offers critiques of your manuscripts online. Anyone interested in joining can e-mail Mary at: amyfoundation@mail.serve.com.

INTERNATIONAL@WRITERS CLUB. Provides writers worldwide with a host of services and opportunities with a base for networking, job opportunities, and invaluable writing resources. Membership is $35/year. For more information, visit their Website at: http://members.tripod.com/awriters/iwc.htm.

INTERNET FOR CHRISTIANS. A book by Quentin J. Schultze, Gospel Films, Inc., $12.95. Available at your local Christian bookstore. Author also offers a free newsletter, Internet for Christians. To subscribe, send the message "SUBSCRIBE" and your e-mail address to: ifc-request@gospelcom.

net. Website: http://www.gospelcom.net/ifc (includes hyperlinks to all listed sites).

KINGDOM WRITERS. Leader: Marilyn Phemister (marilyp@larned.com). An e-mail critique group and fellowship for Christian writers. You may submit work for critique, and critique the works of others in return. To subscribe, send a blank e-mail message to: KingdomWriters-subscribe@ egroups.com. Website: http://www.angelfire.com/ks/kingwrit/index.html. Membership (60 & growing) open.

WOMEN WHO MINISTER TO WOMEN. Moderating an e-mail loop for advanced women authors and speakers. Http://www.righttotheheart.org. Or e-mail info@righttotheheart.com.

+WRITING 4 HIM. A critique list for all types of writing where you can get your manuscripts critiqued. To join, go to: http://www.egroups.com/ group/writing_4_him.htm. For a list of guidelines, go to: http://susette williams.com/writing_4_him.htm. Offers additional resources.

YAHOO CHRISTIAN WRITERS CLUB. Http://clubs.yahoo.com/clubs/ christianwritersclub.

FIND: BOOKS

+BOOK SEARCH. To find the best price on a book you are looking for—they search 27 stores in 18 seconds—go to: http://www.acses.com. Provides a printout in order by lowest price.

BOOK WIRE. Http://www.bookwire.com. The most complete listing of book resources on the Web.

CHRISTIAN BOOK DISTRIBUTORS (CBD). Http://www.christianbook.com. Check out what's selling in the marketplace. Books can be found by publisher, author or subject.

+COMPETING BOOK RESEARCH. Http://www.writerswrite.com/books/ booklinks. A source for finding information on competing books to include in your book proposal. Contains over 400 categorized links to best book-related sites on the Web.

+MOUNTAINVIEW FREE BOOK SEARCH, Mountainview Books, PO Box 129, Hopeland PA 17533. Fax (717)627-2493. E-mail: tctc@ptd.net. E-mail the book title and author (if you have it). They will search and get back to you within two weeks. They will e-mail you the price, and you decide whether to buy it—no obligation.

FIND: INFORMATION

+ASK-AN-EXPERT PAGE. Http://www.K12Science.org/askanexpert.html. Also see: http://www.askanexpert.com, or http://www.askjeeves.com.

+BIOGRAPHICAL INFORMATION. Http://www.biography.com. Short biographies on over 20,000 personalities.

***CHRISTIAN INFORMATION MINISTRY/RESEARCH SERVICE.** Provides fee-based custom research and information retrieval for authors, churches, individuals, publishers, ministries, speakers; primarily topics pertaining to the Bible, theology and Christian living. Basic research fee is $35/hr, plus expenses, such as photocopying and shipping. Cecil R. Price, Th.M., PO Box 141055, Dallas TX 75214. (214)827-0057. E-mail: cecil_ r_price@ acd.org. Also ask about The Booklet Book, a listing of practical resources for busy Christians.

INFORMATION PLEASE. Http://www.InfoPlease.com. This 50-year-old print resource is now available on the Internet.

INTERNET RESEARCH RESOURCES. Http://www.dailyplanit.com/resources. htm. Designed to put a library reference room at your fingertips; links to a broad range of resources.

+MAG PORTAL. Http://MagPortal.com. This site lets you search for articles online simultaneously, without having to visit each magazine's Website individually.

+STATISTICS SOURCE. Http://nilesonline.com/data.

FIND: QUOTES

BARTLETT'S FAMILIAR QUOTATIONS. Http://www.bartleby.com. Just enter the word or words and it gives you the quotations.

JOURNALISM QUOTES. Http://www.schindler.org/quote.htm.

QUOTATIONS. Http://www.itools.com/find-it. Hit "Research It," then "Quota-tions." Search by topic, author, etc., including Bible quotations. Also: http://www.quotationspage.com; http://www.quoteland.com; http://www. aphids.com/quotes/index.shtml; http://business.virgin.net/mark.fryer/intro. html.

FREELANCE JOBS

+COUNCIL FOR INTERNATIONAL EXCHANGE OF SCHOLARS. The Fulbright Scholar Program for faculty and professionals is offering more than 73 awards in communications and journalism for lecturing and/or doing research abroad during the coming academic year. For details, go to: http://www.iie.org/cies.

+CREATIVE FREELANCERS. Http://www.freelancers.com.

+FREELANCE WRITING: WEBSITE FOR TODAY'S WORKING WRITER. Job Bank at: http://www.freelancewriting.com/fjb.html.

+HIRE MINDS. Http://www.hireminds.com.

+JOBSWARM. Http://www.JobSwarm.com/50476569-2593. Lists all kinds of freelance writing opportunities and gives you the opportunity to bid on the jobs.

+JOURNALISM JOBS. Http://www.journalismjobs.com.

+MONIQUE'S NEWS JOBS. Http://www.newsjobs.net.

+NETREAD. Http://www.netread.com/jobs/jobs.

+POWER PROSE. Http://www.powerprose.com/library/writers.asp.

+REPORTERS/WRITERS/EDITORS. Http://www.newslink.org/joblink.html.

+SUN OASIS JOBS. Http://www.sunoasis.com/intern.html.

+WRITER ONLINE BUYS REPRINTS. Writer Online is developing and pro-moting a fee-based reprint service, wherein publishers and readers can buy, collect, and reprint articles on the craft and marketing of writing. Http://www.novalearn.com/wol/Archive.htm.

+**WRITERS WRITE.** Http://www.writerswrite.com. Several links, including job listings.

+**WRITING EMPLOYMENT CENTER.** Http://www.poewar.com/jobs.htm.

GROUPS/ORGANIZATIONS OF INTEREST

AMERICAN BOOKSELLERS ASSOCIATION. Http://www.bookweb.org.

AMERICAN CHRISTIAN WRITERS, PO Box 110390, Nashville TN 37222. (800)21-WRITE. Website: http://www.ecpa.org/ACW. Reg Forder, director. Ministry with a goal to provide full service to Christian writers and speakers. Publishes two writers' periodicals, operates two correspondence schools, hosts three dozen conferences each year, offers a critique service and book publishing division, and has a mail-order learning center that offers thousands of books, cassette tapes, and software programs for writers.

AMERICAN SELF-PUBLISHING ASSOCIATION. Offers monthly newsletter; dues $45/year. For free sample, e-mail: ASPublish@aol.com. Website: http://www.booksamerica.com/AmericanSelfPublisher. Address: PO Box 232233, Sacramento CA 95823.

AMERICAN SOCIETY OF JOURNALISTS AND AUTHORS, 1501 Broadway, Ste. 302, New York NY 10036. (212)997-0947. Fax (212)768-7414. E-mail: execdir@asja.org. Website: http://www.asja.org.

THE AMY FOUNDATION sponsors the Amy Writing Awards, which is a call to present spiritual truth reinforced with biblical references in secular, non-religious publications. First prize is $10,000 with a total of $34,000 given annually. The Amy Writing Awards is designed to recognize creative, skillful writing that presents in a sensitive, thought-provoking manner a biblical position on issues affecting the world today. To be eligible, submitted articles must be published in a secular, non-religious publication and must be reinforced with at least one passage of Scripture. For details on The Amy Writing Awards and a copy of last year's winning entries, contact: The Amy Foundation, PO Box 16091, Lansing MI 48901-6091. (517)323-6233. Website: http://www.amyfound.org.

+**AP NEWSWIRE.** Http://www.ap.org.

ASSOCIATED CHURCH PRESS, PO Box 7, Riverdale MD 20738-0007, or PO Box 21749, Washington DC 20009-9749. (301)403-8900. Fax (301)779-4681. E-mail: jroos@erols.com. Website: http://www.thelutheran.org/acp. Joe Roos, executive director.

+**ASSOCIATION OF AMERICAN PUBLISHERS.** Http://www.publishers.org.

THE ASSOCIATION OF AUTHOR'S REPRESENTATIVES, INC. Http://www.bookwire.com/AAR. Includes a list of agents who don't charge fees (except for office expenses).

AUTHOR'S GUILD. (212)563-5904.

R. R. BOWKER, 121 Chanlon Rd., New Providence NJ 07974, (908)464-6800. Toll-free: (888)269-5372. E-mail: info@bowker.com. Website: http://www.bowker.com/standards/home/isbn. This company issues International

Standard Book Numbers (ISBN), Standard Account Numbers (SAN), and Advanced Book Information forms. Forms can be printed off their Website.

CANADIAN CHURCH PRESS, 28 Flerimac Rd., West Hill ON M1E 4A9 Canada. L. June Steveson, pres.

CATHOLIC PRESS ASSOCIATION, 3555 Veterans Memorial Hwy., Unit O, Ronkonkoma NY 11779. (631)471-4730x15. Fax (631)471-4804. E-mail: cathjour@aol.com. Website: http://www.catholicpress.org. Owen McGovern, exec. dir.; Felicia M. Morales, publications ed.

CBA (formerly Christian Booksellers Assn.), PO Box 62000, Colorado Springs CO 80962-2000. (800)252-1950. E-mail: webmaster@cba-intl.org. Website: http://www.cbaonline.org. Bill Anderson, president.

*CHRISTIAN AFRICAN-AMERICAN BOOKSELLERS ASSN. Twice a year produces a black-consumer catalog. President: Mark Ribbins. (216)921-3530.

CHRISTIAN NEWSPAPER ASSOCIATION, 7317 Cahill Rd., Ste. 201, Minneapolis MN 55439. Karen Beard, exec. dir. (952)562-1234. E-mail: Kbeard46@ hotmail.com. Website: www.christiannewsassoc.com.

+CHRISTIAN WRITERS FELLOWSHIP INTL. Sandy Brooks, 1624 Jefferson Davis Rd., Clinton SC 29325-6401. (864)697-6035. E-mail: cwfi@cwfi-on-line.org. To contact Sandy Brooks personally: sandybrooks@cwfi-online. org. Website: http://www.cwfi-online.org. No meetings, but offers market consultations, critique service, writers' books and conference workshop tapes. Connects writers living in the same area and helps start writers' groups.

EDITORIAL FREELANCERS ASSN. Http://www.the-efa.org.

EP NEWS, 7317 Cahill Rd., Ste. 201, Minneapolis MN55439. Doug Trouten, dir. (952)562-1234. E-mail: editor@mcchronicle.com.

EVANGELICAL CHRISTIAN PUBLISHERS ASSN. (ECPA), 1969 E. Broadway Rd., Ste. 2, Tempe AZ 85282. (602)966-3998. Fax (602)966-1944. E-mail: Jkusy @ecpa.org. Website: http://www.ecpa.org. Doug Ross, pres./CEO. Trade organization of more than 200 Christian book publishers around the world. Offers a submission service on the Internet, called First Edition, where your book proposal can be reviewed by the Christian publishers who are members of this association. Cost is $79. Visit their Website for additional information.

EVANGELICAL PRESS ASSN., 314 Dover Rd., Charlottesville VA 22901. (804)973-5941. Fax (804)973-2710. E-mail: 74473.272@compuserve. com. Website: http://www.epassoc.org. Ronald E. Wilson, director. Trade association for Christian periodicals and associate members (open to writers).

FIRST EDITION. See Evangelical Christian Publishers Assn. listing above.

+FREEDOM FORUM ONLINE. Http://www.freedomforum.org. News about free press.

ICHRISTIAN.COM. The largest e-commerce business site for Christian books and merchandise. Sells Christian-oriented merchandise, offers private chat rooms, free e-mail and downloadable study aids. Http://www. iChristian.com.

+**INDEPENDENT PUBLISHERS FOR CHRIST**, PO Box 280349, Lakewood CO 80228. Fax (303)793-0838. Offers help for those who want to publish their book independently.

INTERNATIONAL CHRISTIAN WRITERS, Stanley C. Baldwin, director, 12900 SE Nixon, Milwaukie OR 97222 (include SASE for reply). E-mail: SCBaldwin@juno.com. A point of contact for writers around the world. Prayer Fellowship: Joyce Tomanek, e-mail: neh8_10_@alltel.net. Networking: Susan Peel, e-mail: suepeel@your-office.com.

+**INTERNATIONAL JOURNALISTS' NETWORK.** Http://www.ijnet.org.

INTERNATIONAL WOMEN'S WRITING GUILD. (212)737-7536. Website: http://www.iwwg.com.

LITERATURE MINISTRY PRAYER FELLOWSHIP. Contact: Ethel Herr, 731 Lakefair Dr., Sunnyvale CA 94089. (408)734-4707. E-mail: ethel@mylawfirm.com. Sends out a prayer letter three times a year that lists prayer concerns of members, broken down to facilitate daily prayer. Send letter or e-mail to join group (no cost) and ask for deadline for next letter.

NATIONAL RELIGIOUS BROADCASTERS, 7839 Ashton Ave., Manassas VA 20109. (703)330-7000. Website: http://www.nrb.com. Request information on the Directory of Religious Media. E. Brandt Gustavson, pres./pub.

NATIONAL SPEAKERS ASSN., 1500 S. Priest Dr., Tempe AZ 85281. (480) 968-2552. Fax (480)968-0911. Website: http://www.nsaspeaker.org. Convention and training for professional speakers. Puts out the Professional Speaker's Magazine. Info on Website.

NATIONAL WRITERS UNION (East), 113 University Pl. 6th Fl., New York NY 10003-4527. (212)254-0279. Fax (212)254-0673. E-mail: nwu@nwu.org. Website: http://www.nwu.org. Trade union for freelance writers in all genres publishing in U.S. markets. See Website for list of local groups.

+**NATIONAL WRITERS UNION (West),** #101, 337—17th St., Oakland CA 94612. (510)839-0110. Fax (510)839-6079. E-mail: nwu@nwu.org. Website: http://www.nwu.org. Trade union for freelance writers in all genres publishing in U.S. markets.

+**NEWSPAPER ASSN. OF AMERICA.** Http://www.naa.org.

+**PAINTED ROCK WRITERS AND READERS COLONY.** Http://www.painted rock.com.

PEN AMERICAN CENTER, 568 Broadway, New York NY 10012 (212)334-1660. Website: http://www.pen.org. Poets, playwrights, editors, essayists, and novelists.

PUBLISHERS WEEKLY is the international news magazine and trade journal for the secular book publishing and bookselling industry. Website: http://www.publishersweekly.com.

RELIGION NEWS SERVICE, 1101 Connecticut Ave. NW, Ste 350, Washington DC 20036. (202)463-8777. Toll-free (800)767-6781. Fax (202)463-0033. E-mail: info@religionnews.com. Website: http://www.religionnews.com.

SMALL PUBLISHERS ASSN. OF NORTH AMERICA, Box 1306, Buena Vista CO 81211. (719)395-4790. Fax (719)395-8374. E-mail: Span@SPANnet. org. Website: http://www.SPAN net.org. A nonprofit professional trade association for independent presses, self-publishers and authors. See Website for membership benefits.

WRITERS GUILD OF AMERICA EAST, 555 W 57th St., New York NY 10019. (212)767-7800. Website: http://www.wgaeast.org.
WRITERS GUILD OF AMERICA WEST, 7000 W 3rd St., Los Angeles CA 90048. (323)782-4532. Toll-free (800)548-4532. Website: http://www.wga. org.
WRITERS INFORMATION NETWORK, PO Box 11337, Bainbridge Island WA 98110. (206)842-9103. E-mail: writersinfonetwork@juno.com. Website: http://www.bluejaypub.com/win. Newsletter, seminars, editorial services.
WRITERS' UNION OF CANADA, 40 Wellington St. East, 3rd Fl., Toronto ON M5E 1C7 Canada. (416)703-8982. Fax (416)703-0826. E-mail: twuc@the-wire.com. Website: http://www.writersunion.ca.

ILLUSTRATION SOURCES

+CARTOONWORKS. Provides cartoon illustrations for articles. Contact: Ron Wheeler, 9818 Summit, Kansas City MO 64114. Phone/fax (816)941-9221; e-mail: ron@cartoonworks.com. See latest portfolio additions at http://www.cartoonworks.com.
+ILLUSTRATION BY C.E. ELLICOTT. Christian artist who designs book covers. Offers a discount to self-published or e-published authors. Http://pages.prodigy.net/cellic/art.htm.
+ILLUSTRATION BY RIVER DIAZ. Christian artist who designs book covers. Http://members.xoom.com/riverdiaz.
MAZZOCCHI GROUP GRAPHIC DESIGN, 58690 S. US 131, PO Box 68, Three Rivers MI 49093. (616)273-7070. Fax (616)273-7026. E-mail: omega777@net-link.net. Specializes in custom, full-color designs for the book cover of your self-published book. Designed by a Christian artist with over 20 years experience. Guidelines available.
PHOTOSOURCEBANK. PhotoSource Intl., Rohn Engh, director, Pine Lake Farm, 1910—35th Rd., Osceola WI 54020. (715)248-3800. Fax (715)248-7394. E-mail: web@photosource.com. Http://www.photosource.com. For an informational message, call: (715)248-1512. Good source of stock photos, and an opportunity for you to post a description of the photos you have for sale on this Website.
+STOCK PHOTOS. Medici@iname.com.

LANGUAGE/VOCABULARY

+ACRONYM AND ABBREVIATION LIST. Http://www.ucc.ie/info/net/acronyms/index.html.
BABELFISH TRANSLATIONS. Type anything in English and it will translate it into either Spanish, French, Portuguese, Italian, or German—or the other way around. Http://babelfish.altavista.com/translate.dyn.
+BRITISH SPEAK. Http://pages.prodigy.com/NY/NYC/britspk/main.html. British terminology.
+CLICHÉ FINDER. Http://www.westegg.com/cliche.
+THE DIALECTIZER. Website: http://www.rinkworks.com/dialect. Converts English to Redneck, Jive, Cockney, Elmer Fuddish, Swedish, or Pig Latin.

A WORD A DAY. Http://www.wordsmith.org/awad/index.html. This is the Website for the mailing list by the same name. At the Website you can sign up to get a new word and its definition sent each day.

+WORD POLICE. Http://www.theatlantic.com/unbound/wordpolice/six.

LEGAL CONCERNS

+ASJA CONTRACTS WATCH. Free e-newsletter from the American Society of Journalists and Authors that keeps writers up to date on latest contract development. To subscribe, send the following message from the address you want added to the list: To: ASJA- Manager@silverquick.com; Subject: Contracts Watch; Text of message: Join ASJACW-list.

COPYRIGHT AND PUBLISHING LAW ATTORNEY. Randolph Law Offices, 160 E. Niagara St., Tonawanda NY 14150. (716)693-5669. Fax (716)693-5683. E-mail: sallie@authorlaw.com. Website: http://www.authorlaw.com. Offers full legal services to writers at affordable rates.

COPYRIGHT LAW—LIBRARY OF CONGRESS COPYRIGHT OFFICE, 101 Independence Ave. SE, Washington DC 20559-6000. (202)707-3000. Website: http://lcweb.loc.gov/copyright. You may call or write for forms, or get them from the Website. Also check out this copyright information site: http://www.benedict.com.

COPYRIGHT PIRACY. Http://www.sharpwriter.com/content/piracy.htm.

+CREDITING INTERNET RESEARCH. Http://www.mla.org/style/sources.htm.

FAIR BUSINESS PRACTICES BRANCH, COMPETITION BUREAU, INDUS-TRY CANADA, 50 Victoria St., Hull QB K1A 0C9 Canada. (819)997-4282 or (800)348-5358. E-mail: compbureau@ic-gc.ca. Website: http://competition.ic-gc-ca. Contact about illegal or unethical behavior by an agent or publisher in Canada. You also might notify or contact The Canadian Author's Assn. at (705)653-0323.

THE FEDERAL TRADE COMMISSION, BUREAU OF CONSUMER PROTEC-TION, CRC-240, Washington DC 20580. (877)382-4357. (202)326-2676. Fax (202)326- 2050. Website: http://www.ftc.gov. Lydia Parnes, Deputy Director. Contact about illegal or unethical behavior by an agent or publisher in the U.S.

FREEDOM OF INFORMATION ACT BY THE SOCIETY OF PROFESSIONAL JOURNALISTS. Http://spj.org/foia/index.htm.

+INTELLECTUAL PROPERTY LAW. Http://www.intelproplaw.com. Look up copyrights or connect to legal reference sites.

*LITNET: LEGAL & LITIGATION SUPPORT SERVICES DIRECTORY. Http://www.litnet.com. The most comprehensive Web directory of legal and litigation support service providers.

+PERMISSIONS CONTACTS. Http://www.publist.com. Lists over 150,000 publications with basic information, including who to contact for permissions.

UNITED STATES POSTAL INSPECTION SERVICE, 475 L'Enfant Plaza West SW, Washington DC 20260-2166. Manager, Fraud and Prohibited Mailings. Contact about incidents of potential mail fraud.

*VOLUNTEER LAWYERS FOR THE ARTS. (212)319-2787.

Note: If you are the victim of fraud or have questions/concerns about an agent or publisher, contact the Better Business Bureau in their town, as well as their local attorney general or their state attorney general's office of consumer protection. You can also contact the Better Business Bureau online to see if a certain company has any complaints on file at: http://www.bbb.org.

MARKET SOURCES

*AMERICA'S LARGEST NEWSPAPERS, 14 Hickory Ave., Takoma Park MD 20912. A computerized list of the 120 largest daily newspapers with the names of over 700 key editors. Available on disk or hard copy.

CANADIAN MAGAZINE PUBLISHERS ASSN., 130 Spadina Ave., Ste. 202, Toronto ON M5V 2L4 Canada. (416)504-0274. Fax (416)504-0437. E-mail: cmpainfo@cmpa.ca. Http://www.cmpa.ca.

CHRISTIAN WRITERS' MARKET GUIDE WEBSITE. Http://www.stuartmarket. com. Sally Stuart's Website with information on the latest guide, links to the Websites or e-mail of all the Christian publishers or publications that have them. Lots more in the works.

GILA QUEEN'S GUIDE TO MARKETS. A market newsletter for writers and artists. Secular. Http://www.gilaqueen.com. Kathy Ptacek, ed., PO Box 97, Newton NJ 07860. (973)579-1537. Fax (973)579-6441. E-mail: GilaQueen @worldnet.att.

+LINKS TO FOREIGN MAGAZINES & NEWSPAPERS. Http://dir.yahoo.com/ News_and_Media/By_Region/countries; http://www.cmpa.ca/ maghome.html (Canadian); http://www.vicnet.net.au/~ozlit (Australian); http://www.news directory.com/news/magazine/society.

+LITERARY MARKETPLACE. Http://www.literarymarketplace.com. General market guide put out by R.R. Bowker, 121 Chanlon Rd., PO Box 31, New Providence NJ 07974-9903. (908)464-6800. Toll free (888)269-5372. Cost $189.95.

+PATHWAYS CHRISTIAN WRITERS RESOURCES. Http://www.angelfire. com/ca4/Pathways. From Australia, this site lists 112 Christian publishers, some in Australia and England, plus links to other writer's site and how-to help.

+PUBLISHER'S CATALOGS. Http://www.lights.com/publisher. Includes over 6,000 publishers. Search by publisher's name or city; takes you to the publisher's Website.

+PUBLISHERS MARKETING ASSOCIATION ONLINE. Http://pma-online. org. Lists basic contact information on hundreds of publishers.

+PUBLIST. Http://www.publist.com. List over 150,000 publications with basic contact information.

+ROSEDOG.COM. Http://www.rosedog.com. Connects writers, agents and publishers at no cost to any of them.

+WEB-ZINE ARTICLE DISTRIBUTION SITES. Http://www.meer.net/~johnl/ e-zine-list; http://www.ideamarketers.com; http://www.EzineArticles.com. A way to help establish your name as an "expert" in a particular field.

WRITER'S DIGEST WEBSITE. Http://www.writersdigest.com. Lots of writer's helps, including copies of writer's guidelines you can print right off the site. Website for guidelines: http://www.writersdigest.com/guidelines/index.htm.

WRITERS GUIDELINES DATABASES. Http://mav.net/guidelines/religious.shtml. Site where you can print out guidelines.

WRITER'S RELIEF, INC., 245 Teaneck Rd., #3, Ridgefield Park NJ 07660. (201)641-3003. Fax (201)641-1253. E-mail: Ronnie@wrelief.com. Website: http://www.wrelief.com. An author's submission service, handling your manuscript submissions for an hourly rate of $35-50 (plus postage and copying), or a flat fee after completing review. Prepares manuscripts, proofreads, writes query and cover letters, tracks submissions, keeps records, etc.

YAHOO'S LIST OF CHRISTIAN PUBLICATIONS ON THE WEB. Go to the search engine Yahoo: Society and Culture: Religion: Christian.

PROMOTION & SELF-PROMOTION

*ADVOCATE MEDIA GROUP, 10820 Nelle Ave. NE, Albuquerque NM 87111-3941. Contact: Shelly Simone. AMG is an all-inclusive media marketing company that promotes authors, musicians, and other product producers through their nationally syndicated TV & radio show, *Interviews & Reviews,* as well as their nationally circulated *Interviews & Reviews* magazine. Specializes in generating TV and radio exposure in the Christian marketplace.

AUTHORLINK! Includes a place to advertise and sell self-published books. Http://www.authorlink.com.

*BOOK MARKETING UPDATE is a newsletter for book writers that guarantees to get you national publicity and more book sales (at least $25,000 worth), or your money back. Contact: Bradley Communications Corp., 135 E. Plumstead Ave., PO Box 1206, Lansdowne PA 19050-8206. (800) 784-4359x432. Fax (610)284-3704.

BOOKWIRE. This is an author tour database for Internet browsers. Lets general public and industry professionals know about authors touring in their area. For more information or to list your tour, contact Roger Williams at roger.williams@bookwire.com, or call him at (212)982-7008. Website: http://www.bookwire.com.

CHRISTIANBOOKREVIEWER.COM. A place to have your book—even a self-published book—reviewed. This is a Website where bookstores and libraries can go to get brief reviews of all the latest Christian books. For details contact: Jerry Luquire, Brentwood Media Group, 4000 Beallwood Ave., Columbus GA 31904. (800)334-8861. E-mail: Brentwood@aol.com. Website: http://www.ChristianBookReviewer.com.

CLASS PROMOTIONAL SERVICES, LLC. PO Box 66810, Albuquerque NM 87193. (800)433-6633 or (505)899-4283. Fax (505)899-9282. E-mail: CLASSmrktng@aol.com. Website: http://www.classervices.com. Contact: Kim Garrison. A complete promotions agency catering to the Christian marketplace with top quality advertising and publicity campaigns. CLASS Promotional Services is a division of Christian Leaders, Authors & Speakers Services, which provides resources, training, and promotion for Christian authors and speakers. See Website for details.

*COFFEEHOUSE BOOKSTORE is a cyberstore for self-published Christian writers, artists and musicians. For $20/mo (plus a small origination/set-up fee) CoffeeHouse will design and host your site, advertise to the Christian community through magazines, conferences and other media, register and update regularly with major Web search engines and maintain your site with appropriate links. There are no commissions or fees to pay on product sales. You sell your products and keep all profits. For more information, call (888)896-4568. Fax (503)637-3765. E-mail: coffeebooks@integrityonline.com. Website under construction.

DIRECTORY OF RELIGIOUS MEDIA. Put out by the National Religious Broadcasters, it has nearly 4,300 entries of station contacts, products and services. Cost to non-members is $79.95. Contact: Valerie Fraedrich, 7839 Ashton Ave., Manassas VA 20109. (703)330-7000x516. E-mail: vfraedrich@nrb.org. Website: http://www.nrb.org/directory.htm.

+GUEST FINDER. A place to get noticed for possible interviews, plus tips on being a better guest. Http://www.guestfinder.com.

+INTERNET PUBLICITY RESOURCES. Http://marketing.tenagra.com/pubnet.

+MARKETING TIP OF THE WEEK NEWSLETTER. Http://bookmarket.com. Plus other helps for promoting your book.

THE MIDWEST BOOK REVIEW. 278 Orchard Dr., Oregon WI 53575. (608) 835-7937. E-mail: mbr@execpc.com. Website: http://www.execpc.com/~MBR/bookwatch. James Cox, editor-in-chief. Send copy of your book to be reviewed for library resource newsletters, etc.

+RADIO-TV INTERVIEW REPORT, PO Box 1206, Lansdown PA 19050-8206. 800-989-1400. Authors pay to have their profile included in this publication that goes to radio and TV producers who are looking for talk-show guests.

+A SAVVY APPROACH TO BOOK SALES, Marketing Advice to Get the Buzz Going, by Elaine Wright Colvin. $13 postpaid from Stuart Marketplace, 1647 SW Pheasant Dr., Aloha OR 97006.

#THE WRITE CONNECTION/MARY HAMPTON, 8305 SE Lorry Ave., Vancouver WA 98664-2208. Offers help in promoting your published book. Will help you develop a marketing plan to help get the best exposure for you and your book. Send a SASE for details.

REFERENCE TOOLS

A WEB OF ON-LINE DICTIONARIES. http://www.yourdictionary.com. Linked to more than 600 dictionaries in 150 different languages.

+ENCYCLOPEDIA BRITANNICA. Http://www.britannica.com. Free.

+FREE INTERNET ENCYCLOPEDIA. Http://clever.net/cam/encyclopedia.html.

+GROLIER'S NEW BOOK OF KNOWLEDGE ONLINE. Http://my.grolier.com/multi.asp.

+ONELOOK DICTIONARIES. Http://www.onelook.com. Definitions from over 500 dictionaries.

+OXFORD ENGLISH DICTIONARY. Http://www.oed.com.

+REFERENCE BOOKS ONLINE. Http://www.xrefer.com. Searches 25 reference books simultaneously.

RESEARCH & RESOURCES FOR WRITERS. Http://www.fontayne.com/linkresource.html. Links to lots of great sites, such as Bartlett's Familiar Quotations, other quotation resources, grammar/style notes, a rhyming dictionary, speech writing resources, etc.

+ROGET'S ONLINE THESAURUS. Http://www.thesaurus.com.

+WEBSTER'S HYPERTEXT DICTIONARY. Http://m-w.com/netdict.htm.

+WORLD BOOK ONLINE. Http://www.worldbook.com.

RESEARCH: BIBLE

+BIBLE ANSWER MACHINE. Http://BibleAnswerMachine.ww7.com.

BIBLE PROPHECY. Http://www.armageddonbooks.com. Links to every Bible Prophecy site on the Web.

+ONEPLACE.COM. Http://www.oneplace.com. Provides Bible study tools, such as words in Greek or Hebrew, or Strong's Concordance.

UNBOUND BIBLE. A collection of searchable Bibles, consisting of seven English versions, Greek and Hebrew versions, four ancient versions, and 17 other languages. Http://unbound.biola.edu.

RESEARCH: LIBRARIES

+GREAT LIBRARIES ON THE WEB. Http://www.ipl.org/svcs/greatlibs.

+LIBRARYSPOT. Http://www.libraryspot.com. A free gateway to more than 5,000 libraries worldwide.

+PROJECT BARTLEBY. Http://www.bartleby.com. The most comprehensive public reference library ever published on the Web.

WATERBORO PUBLIC LIBRARY WEBSITE. Information on copyright laws, resources for publishing online, or resources for business, technical and science writing. Http://www.waterboro.lib.me.us/writing.htm.

RESEARCH: NEWS

+AMERICAN NEWS SERVICE. Http://www.americannews.com.

CHRISTIAN SCIENCE MONITOR NEWS SITE. Http://www.csmonitor.com.

EPA NEWS SERVICE. c/o Doug Trouten, Minnesota Christian Chronicle, 7317 Cahill Rd., Minneapolis MN 55439. (952)562-1234.

INDUSTRY NEWS SITE. Http://www.mediacentral.com.

+NEWSPAPER DIRECTORY. Http://www.newsd.com.

NEWSROOM HOMEPAGE AT ASSIGNMENTEDITOR.COM. Connect to virtually any newspaper in the world, check news wires, access maps and people finders, etc. Http://assignmenteditor.com.

+NEWS STORY RESEARCH. Http://www.newstream.com. Offers keyword searches on news stories. Search for specific news items: http://www.newstrawler.com.

+NEWS STORY SOURCES. Http://www.ap.org; http://www.slate.com/code/todayspapers/todayspapers.asp; http://dailynews.yahoo.com; http://nt.excite.com; http://www.newsbot.com; http://www.newshub.com; http://totalnews.com; http://www.newsindex.com; http://www.newshunt.com; http://fullcoverage.yahoo.com; http://www.all-links.com/newscentral.

USA WEEKEND. Links to over 500 newspapers, listed by state. Http://www.usaweekend.com/partners/partners_links/index.html.

RESOURCES: CHILDREN'S WRITING

+CATALOG OF BOOKS & TOOLS FOR CHILDREN'S WRITERS. E-mail: cbi@autobots.net.

THE CHILDREN'S BOOK COUNCIL. Http://www.cbcbooks.org. Go to the Authors/Illustrators Page for marketing information and beginner instruction for writers and illustrators of children's books, plus lots of good links.

CHILDREN'S WRITING RESOURCE CENTER. A Website sponsored by Children's Book Insider (a newsletter for children's writers). Http://www.write4kids.com. Offers market news, tutorials, FAQ, files to download, surveys, and links to other resources for children's writers. CBI offers other resources, including a complete children's writing course for under $20.

+CHILDREN'S WRITING UPDATE. E-zine. To subscribe, mailto: join-cw update@mh.databack.com.

GLORY PRESS/PROF. DICK BOHRER, M.S., M.A. (teacher 39 yrs, editor 11 yrs, author of 16 books), PO Box 624, West Linn OR 97068. (503)638-7711. E-mail: glorypress@juno.com. Offers a writing course called 21 Ways to Write Stories for Christian Kids. Counsels his students on all their writing. References: gude@juno.com, k&kyoung@stic.net, asrduff@aol.com.

+HEDGEHOPPER. Http://homestead.com/Hedgehopping/index.html. For beginning children's writers.

+HOW TO WRITE PICTURE BOOKS. Free E-books for children's writers. Http://www.write4kids.com/ebooks.html.

INSTITUTE OF CHILDREN'S LITERATURE. Website includes information about their writing programs and writing aptitude test; also a chat room and other resources for writers. Http://www.InstituteChildrensLit.com. Contact information: 93 Long Ridge Rd., West Redding CT 06896. (203)792-8600, (800)243-9645. Fax (203)792-8406. E-mail: information services@InstituteChildrensLit.com.

+LANGUAGE ARTS FOR KIDS. Http://kidslangarts.about.com. Resources for children's writers. Features on children who write and children's writers.

+SECRETS OF WRITING FOR KIDS. Free report for beginners. Mailto: writing4kids@autobots.net.

THE SOCIETY OF CHILDREN'S BOOK WRITERS AND ILLUSTRATORS, 8271 Beverly Blvd., Los Angeles CA 90048, (323)782-1010, fax (323)782-1892, e-mail: membership@scbwi.org, http://www.scbwi.org. This is the professional organization for children's book writers.

+TRENDS IN CHILDREN'S PUBLISHING. Http://www.underdown.org/trends.htm.

+VERLA KAY'S WEBSITE FOR CHILDREN'S WRITERS. Http://www.verlakay.com.

RESOURCES: FICTION WRITING

AT-HOME WRITING WORKSHOPS. Director: Marlene Bagnull, Litt.D., Write His Answer Ministries, 316 Blanchard Rd., Drexel Hill PA 19026. E-mail: mbagnull@aol.com. Website: http://www.writehisanswer.com. Fiction, 10 units, $255. Units may also be purchased individually for $30-34.

+CHARACTER NAME SOURCES. Site for names and their origins: http://www.kabalarians.com; http://www.babynames.com; http://www.census.gov/genealogy/names; http://censuslinks.com/directory; http://www.parentsoup.com/babyname; http://www.dibonsmith.com/menu.htm; http://www.goodnames4u.com.

CRIME MYSTERY WRITING/FORENSIC SITES. Http://flash.lakeheadu.ca/~pals/forensics; http://forensics.to; http://www.visualexpert.com; http://www.poisonlab.com; http://www.tritechusa.com.

+ENOVEL.COM. Website: http://www.enovel.com. A new electronic publisher that will publish your novel in a downloadable format for free.

FAITH, HOPE & LOVE is the inspirational chapter of Romance Writers of America. Dues for the chapter are $20/yr, but you must also be a member of RWA to join (dues $70/yr). Chapter offers these services: online list service for members, a Website, 20-pg bimonthly newsletter, annual contest, connects critique partners by mail or e-mail, and latest romance market information. To join, contact RWA National Office, 3707 FM 1960 West, Ste. 550, Houston TX 77068. (281)440-6885. Fax (281)440-7510. Website: http://www.rwanational.com. Or go to FHL Website: http://www.robinleehatcher.com/FHL. Over 150 members.

+FICTION & SCI-FI/FANTASY EGROUPS. Go to: http://egroups.com. Type into box: Christian_fic2 (for genre fiction), or ChristSF (for science fiction and Christianity). A Christian fantasy site at: http://www.christianfantasy.com. Christian sci-fi site at: http://www.christian-fandom.org/christian-fandom.

+FICTION FIX NEWSLETTER, The Nuts and Bolts of Crafting Better Fiction. Http://www.coffeehouseforwriters.com/news.html. To subscribe, send a blank e-mail to: FictionFix-subscribe@topica.com.

+FICTION WRITING CLASSES (F2K). Http://fiction.4-writers.com/creative-writing-classes.shtml.

FICTION WRITERS CONNECTION. Website: http://www.fictionwriters.com. Helpful instruction for fiction and nonfiction writers; free critiquing. Also hosts chat nights. E-mail: Bcamenson@fictionwriters.com, for details.

INSPIRATIONAL ROMANCE. Http://members.aol.com/inspirlvg. Includes links to publishers of inspirational romances.

MYSTERY WRITERS OF AMERICA. Http://www.mysterynet.com. (212)888-8171.

+MYSTERY WRITERS SITES OF INTEREST. Http://www.cluelass.com; http://www.crime.org; http://www.svn.net/mikekell/crimewriter.html; http://crime.about.com; http://www.mayhem.net; http://www.MurderMustAdvertise.com. To join the e-mail group for Murder Must Advertise, go to: http://www.onelist.com/community/MurderMustAdvertise, or send e-mail to: MurderMustAdvertise-subscribe@onelist.com.

+NOVEL CONTEST. Http://www.authorlink.com.

+NOVEL PRO. Website: http://novelcode.com/html/novelpro.htm. Software that helps organize ideas, work on pieces of the story without getting lost, brainstorm creation of characters and scenes, etc. Cost is $29.95. Order on Website.

+ROMANCE WRITERS MESSAGE BOARD. Romance Writers 4 Him. Http://www.InsideTheWeb.com/mbs.cgi/mb1057088.

+ROMANCE WRITERS OF AMERICA, 3707 fm 1960 West, Ste. 555, Houston TX 77068. (281)440-6885. E-mail: info@rwanational.com. Website: http://www.rwanational.com.

+ROMANCE WRITERS SITE. Http://www.eHarlequin.com.

SCIENCE FICTION AND FANTASY WRITERS OF AMERICA, Box 171, Unity ME 04988-0171. E-mail: execdir@sfwa.org. Website: http://www.sfwa.org. (207)861-8078.

+SCIENCE FICTION LANGUAGE. Http://www.sfwa.org/members/elgin/SHE_Excerpts01.html#lsf; http://www.suzettehadenelgin.com; http://www.langmaker.com.

+SCIENCE FICTION SITE. Ralan Conley's SpecFic & Humor Webstravaganza. Http://www.ralan.com.

+SHORT MYSTERY FICTION SOCIETY. Http://www.thewindjammer.com/smfs.

+SPECULATIVE FICTION LINKS. Spicy Green Iguana, Inc. Http://members.aol.com/mhatv/index.html.

+STORYCRAFT STORY DEVELOPMENT SOFTWARE. Guides writers through the entire process of writing novels, screenplays, teleplays, plays and short stories. To order, go to: http://www.storycraft-soft.com.

+WEBSITES OF CHRISTIAN FICTION AUTHORS. Connect to over 60 sites at: http://www.deehenderson.com.

WESTERN WRITERS OF AMERICA. Rita Cleary, WWA Membership, 20 Cove Woods Rd., Oyster Bay NY 11771.

+WRITER'S BLOCKS 2.0. Http://www.writersblocks.com. Organize story elements for your fiction.

WRITER'S DIGEST WORKSHOPS. Writer's Digest School, 1507 Dana Ave., Cincinnati OH 45207. (800)759-0963. Novel Writing Workshop, or Writing & Selling Short Stories. This is a secular course, but you may request a Christian instructor.

RESOURCES: POETRY WRITING

ACADEMY OF AMERICAN POETS, 584 Broadway, Ste. 1208, New York NY 10012-3250, (212)274-0343, Fax (212)274-9427, http://www.poets.org.
+ALBANY POETRY WORKSHOP. Http://www.sonic.net/poetry/albany.
+ALL POETS: POETRY FOR EVERYONE. Website: http://www.allpoets.com. Good resource site for poets. Post your poetry or short story and get feedback. Sponsors a poetry contest.
+CYBERKEATS' INTERACTIVE POETRY PAGE. Http://www.geocities.com/SoHo/Lofts/3307.
+HOW TO WRITE HAIKU. Http://www.selendy.com/haiku.
+INKSPOT SITE FOR POETS. Http://www.inkspot.com/ss/genres/poetry.html.
POETRY SOCIETY OF AMERICA. (212)254-9628.
POETRY WRITING SESSIONS. Mary Harwell Sayler, PO Box 730, DeLand FL 32721-0730. Encourages Christian poets to write poems, then revise with purpose and style. Seven study units address poetry content, theme, language, rhyme, rhythm, traditional patterns, and free verse forms. Complete course, including instructor's evaluation of assignments is $275. Or order Session One with notebook for $50 (subsequent units $40 each). Instructional tapes and critique service also available.
POETS & WRITERS. (212)226-3586. Website: http://www.pw.org. Publishing advice, conference list, grants and awards, literary links, news from the writing world, and resources.
+RHYMING DICTIONARY. Http://www.WriteExpress.com/online.html.
+UNIVERSITY OF BUFFALO POETRY LINKS. Http://wings.buffalo.edu/epc/connects/poetrywebs.html.

RESOURCES: SCREENWRITING/SCRIPTWRITING

+ARTICLES ON SCREENWRITING. Http://www.novalearn.com/wol/Glatzer5a.htm.
ART WITHIN. A Christian-based performing art troupe looking for scripts that will appeal to a secular audience. Scripts must be written for a Broadway/off-Broadway production (not written for the church market), with a Christian theme interwoven. Contact: Art Within, Bryan Coley, Artistic Director, 1940 Minnewil Ln., Marietta GA 30068, (707)565-8804. E-mail: bryan.coley@mindspring.com. Website: http://www.artwithin.org.
***CHRISTIAN DRAMA NORTHWEST.** An e-mail group for those interested in drama. To join, send an e-mail to: Dramanw-subscribe@egroups.com.
+CHRISTIANS IN HOLLYWOOD. A publication for Christians interested in breaking into Hollywood. Contact: Victorya Rogers Communications, PMB #241, 9899 Santa Monica Blvd., Beverly Hills CA 90212. E-mail: victorya@victorya.com.
COLLABORATOR SOFTWARE/SERVICES FOR SCREEN WRITERS AND NOVELISTS. Http://www.collaborator.com.
+THE COMPLETE BOOK OF SCRIPTWRITING. By J. Michael Straczynski, Writer's Digest Books.

+**THE DRAMA IMPROVEMENT CONFERENCE.** Greater Portland Area, October. Contact: Judy Straalsund, PO Box 19844, Portland OR 97280-0844. (503)245-6919. Fax (503)244-5421. E-mail: tapestry@teleport.com. Website: http://www.tapestrytheatre.org. Special track for teen actors. Geared to all Christian dramatists, and features workshops, performances, networking, forums and a book table. Playwrights are encouraged to attend.

THE DRAMATISTS GUILD, 1501 Broadway, Ste. 701, New York NY 10036. (212)398-9366. Website: http://www.dramaguild.com. Professional association of playwrights, composers, and lyricists.

SAMUEL FRENCH, INC., 45 W. 25th St., New York NY 10010-2751. (212) 206-8990. Fax (212)206-1429. Agent for religious/inspirational stage plays. See listing under Agents.

GENESIS CREATIVE GROUP, 28126 Peacock Ridge, Ste. 104, Rancho Palos Verdes CA 90275. (310)541-9232. Fax (310)541-9532. E-mail: KenRUnger @aol.com. Agent: Ken Unger. Agent/packager who handles screenplays, TV/Movie scripts. See full listing in agent section.

+**GETTING YOUR ACTS TOGETHER,** by Frank V. Priore. A complete step-by-step guide on how to write and sell a full-length play for the school market. Send $14.95, plus $2 postage to: Toad Hall, RR 2 Box 16B, Laceyville PA 18623.

GRIZZLY ADAMS PRODUCTIONS, Box 1987, Loveland CO 80539. (970)667-4509. Fax (970)613-1083. E-mail: tvguy@compuserve.com, or balsiger@verinet.com. Website: http://www.amazingfilms.com. Producers of network television and home movies, including Christian films.

HOLLYWOOD CREATIVE DIRECTORY, 3000 W. Olympic Blvd., Ste. 2525, Santa Monica CA 90404. (310)315-4815, or (800)815-0503. Website: http://www.hcdonline.com. Comes out 3 times a year. Lists production companies and staff (the ones who option or buy screenplays for production). Also check your local newsstand for copies of *The Hollywood Reporter* and *Daily Variety* newspapers.

*****ILLINOIS/CHICAGO SCREENWRITING COMPETITION.** This is a biennial event sponsored by the Chicago and Illinois Film Offices to support and promote local screenwriters. It is offered exclusively to resident writers who have completed a feature length script set in Illinois. Winners receive $2000 each, and their scripts are sent to a select group of production companies and Hollywood producers and studios. Current competition started in January 2001. Call (312)814-8711 for an application.

+**MARKET INSIGHT FOR PLAYWRIGHTS.** Each issue features listings for contests, theaters and development programs. Http://www.booklocker. com/newsletters/playwright.html.

+**MOVIEBYTES.COM.** Http://www.moviebytes.com. Screenwriting contests and markets online.

+**PROPER FORMATTING FOR SCRIPTS.** Http://www.inteleye.com. Revises and formats theatrical screenplays for a fee. Payment is $150-250 for up to 120 pgs, plus .50/page over 120.

SCREENPLAY SYSTEMS, INC., 150 E. Olive Ave., Ste. 203, Burbank CA

91502. Software for writing screenplays. (800)84-STORY. Fax (818)843-8364. Website: http://www.screenplay.com.

+SCREEN TALK. Http://www.screentalk.org.

SCREENWRIGHT: THE CRAFT OF SCREENWRITING, by Charles Deemer. To read an excerpt and order this book go to: http://www.booklocker. com/bookpages/charlesdeemer01.html.

SCREENWRITERS & PLAYWRIGHTS HOME PAGE. Http://www.teleport. com/~cdeemer/scrwriter.html.

SCRIPTWRITERS NETWORK. Http://scriptwritersnetwork.com. Also see: http://www.screenwriters.com.screennet.html; and http://www.screenwriter. com/main.html.

SCRIPTWRITING RECOMMENDED BOOKS. *Making a Good Script Great,* by Linda Seger; *Writing Screenplays That Sell,* by Michael Hauge; *Story,* by Robert McKee; *The Writer's Journey*, by Chris Vogler; *Writing Treatments That Sell,* by Ken Atchity. Also a formatting program: *Final Draft.*

SELLING TO HOLLYWOOD. Http://www.sellingtohollywood.com. Information for scriptwriters and announcement of a scriptwriters conference. Next conference is August 2001 in Los Angeles.

+SPIRITUAL THEATER INTERNATIONAL. Looking for new play submissions. Send plays to: Spiritual Theater Intl., PO Box 538, Littleton CO 80160. Attn: New Play Submissions. Must include a copy of their submission form (on Website): http://www.spiritualtheater.com/release.htm

STORIE ARTS, INC., 407 S. Vail Ave., Arlington Heights IL 60005-1847. (888)291-6752. E-mail: gsilagi@yahoo.com. Website under construction. Contact: Guy Silagi. A Christian film/video company looking for original scripts to be produced as film shorts, half-hour shows for broadcast/video or feature-length films. Producing for various markets including youth, comedy and drama.

+WORDPLAY. Website: http://www.wordplayer.com. Articles and advice on writing for the screen, Q & A, bulletin board, and more for the aspiring screenwriter.

+THE WRITERS STORE. Http://www.writersstore.com. Essentials for writers and filmmakers.

RESOURCES: SONGWRITING

THE CHRISTIAN MEDIA DIRECTORY. Easy-to-use guide to the Christian music, film, and video business. 21st Century Edition on CD-ROM. Christian Media, PO Box 448, Jacksonville OR 97530. (541)899-8888. E-mail: James@christianmedianetwork.com. Website: http://www.christianmedia network.com. Also has The Christian Artist Survival Guide, How to Produce, Manufacture, Distribute & Promote an Independent Christian Record, $33.45, incl. postage.

CHRISTIAN MUSIC ONLINE. Website: http://www.cmo.com.

+CHRISTIAN PUBLISHER.COM. Http://www.christianpublisher.com. Distributes original Christian music CDs and tapes. See information on Website.

CHRISTIAN SONGWRITERS WEB RING. Http://web2.airmail.net/cots/ webring.htm. Chat room, discussion group, subscribe to mailing list.

THE DRAMATISTS GUILD, 1501 Broadway, Ste. 701, New York NY 10036. (212)398-9366. Fax (212)944-0420. Http://www.dramaguild.com. Professional association of playwrights, composers, and lyricists.

+E-MAIL GROUP FOR SONGWRITERS. Http://www.kadu.org. To join list write to: kadu-discuss@xc.org.

+FINDING A COLLABORATOR. Helpful article at: http://www.writersdigest. com/newsletter/song writing.htm.

+INSIDE TRACK TO GETTING STARTED IN CHRISTIAN MUSIC. Book from Harvest House Publishers, $17.99.

*MARANATHA! MUSIC, NEW SONG REVIEW. This group offers critiquing and coaching for new songwriters by seasoned professionals. Charges $30 per song. This is an independent critique—not for publishing. Send SASE for submission guidelines to: Maranatha! Music New Song Review, PO Box 1077, Dana Point CA 92629-5077.

THE NASHVILLE SONGWRITERS ASSOCIATION INTERNATIONAL, 1701 West End Ave., 3rd Floor, Nashville TN 37203. Conducts seminars from Maine to Florida.

*THE NATIONAL ACADEMY OF RECORDING ARTS AND SCIENCES, 3402 Pico Blvd., Santa Monica CA 90405. Presents the Grammy Awards. Also engages in professional educational activities, such as seminars; provides scholarships; offers associate memberships.

*PERFORMING RIGHTS SOCIETIES. These three groups collect royalties due their members from radio, TV, and concert performances. The three societies are: ASCAP, 6430 Sunset Blvd., Hollywood CA 90028; BMI, 6255 Sunset Blvd., Hollywood CA 90028; and SESAC, 9000 Sunset Blvd., Hollywood CA 90069.

+RESOURCES & CONTESTS. Http://www.musesmuse.com.

+RHYMING DICTIONARY. Http://www.WriteExpress.com/online.html.

*THE SONGWRITERS GUILD, 1222—16th Ave. S., Ste. 25, Nashville TN 37212. Protects the rights of songwriters.

THE SONGWRITER'S MARKET. For more information on the Songwriter's Market Guide put out by Writer's Digest, visit this Website: http://www. writersdigest.com/marketbooks/2000songs.html.

+SONGWRITING LINKS. Http://www.lyricist.com.

SEARCH ENGINES

+BALDEY.COM. Http://www.baldey.com. A new meta-search engine. Combines the top findings from a number of other search engines. Will search in English or 14 other languages.

METOR SEARCH ENGINE. Http://www.metor.com. A new, more comprehensive search engine with both general and specific collections of sites.

+PILOT SEARCH. Good literary search engine: http://www.pilot-search.com.

SEARCH ENGINES. Http://www.711.net. This site connects you to 12 search engines. Also check out: http://www.google.com.

SERVICES FOR WRITERS

Note: Check out these services before hiring any of them. Their listing here in no way indicates an endorsement.

*COFFEEHOUSE BOOKSTORE is a cyberstore for self-published Christian writers, artists and musicians. For $20/mo (plus a small origination/set-up fee) CoffeeHouse will design and host your site, advertise to the Christian community through magazines, conferences and other media, register and update regularly with major Web search engines and maintain your site with appropriate links. There are no commissions or fees to pay on product sales. You sell your products and keep all profits. For more information, call (888)896-4568. Fax (503)637-3765. E-mail: coffeebooks@ integrityonline.com. Website under construction.

CORRESPONDENCE COURSE FOR MANUSCRIPT EDITING. The University of Wisconsin offers a correspondence course in manuscript editing for those wanting to do editing on a professional level or for writers wanting to improve their personal editing skills. Reasonable cost. Contact: University of Wisconsin Learning Innovations, 505 S. Rosa Rd., Ste 200, Madison WI 53719. (800)442-6460. Ask about Manuscript Editing C350 - A52.

CORNERSTONE INDEXING/SHIRLEY WARKENTIN, 1862 Tenaya Ave., Clovis CA 93611. (559)322-2145. E-mail: indexer@juno.com. Website: http://homestead.juno.com/indexer. Writes subject and Scripture indexes for nonfiction books from a Christian perspective, conforming to publisher specifications.

FAX SERVICES WHEN YOU DON'T HAVE A FAX. You can now receive faxes through an existing e-mail address. Check out these sites: http://www.efax.com (totally free); and http://www.faxaway.com (not free, but offers free trial).

+FREE INTERNET ACCESS. Guide to free Internet Service Providers for US and foreign countries. Http://www.hereontheweb.com/freeinternet.htm.

JUNO OFFERS FREE E-MAIL SERVICE. This service is free (if you qualify) and an easy solution for those who want an e-mail address and the ability to correspond with others by e-mail, but don't need or want additional access to the Internet. There is no obligation for requesting the software or trying it out. E-mail your request to: signup@juno.com, or call (800)654-5866. This service is advertiser supported, and membership is limited to the US for now (although you can communicate with e-mail users in other countries). You may sign up at their Website: http://dl. www.juno.com/dynoget/taga.

LOGOS RESEARCH SYSTEMS, 715 SE Fidalgo Ave., Oak Harbor WA 98277-4049. (360)679-6575. Toll-free: (800)875-6467. Fax (360)675-8169. E-mail: info@logos.com. Website: http://www.logos.com. Offers electronic publishing solutions for academic and reference book publishers; converts books to CD-ROMs.

MAIL.COM OFFERS FREE E-MAIL. Set up a free, personalized e-mail address that you can access anytime and anywhere. All you need is an Internet connection and a Web browser. Http://www.mail.com/mailcom/signup_1.jhtml?sr=mc.us.mk.247em/03.

+**MANUSCRIPT BOXES.** To obtain rugged boxes for mailing manuscripts, contact: Papyrus Place, 2216 Dundee Rd., Louisville KY 40205, or e-mail: info@papyrusplace.com.

MANUSCRIPT MARKETING/WILLIAM KERCHER. West Coast writers: PO Box 1474, Gresham OR 97030. (503)887-4779. Fax (503)492-4104. E-mail: wkerch@easystreet.com. A manuscript service for fiction and non-fiction writers. Avoid the confusion and frustration trying to pick the right agent or publisher. They will submit a clean and complete package to agents or publishers who are actively seeking manuscripts.

+**SCORE** (Service Corps of Retired Executives) offers free advice to small businesses by e-mail. Go to: http://www.score.org.

+**STAMPS.COM.** Free software for printing your postage on your computer. Http://www.stamps.com/mysoftware.

WEB PAGE DEVELOPMENT/RESOURCES

+**CREATING AND PROMOTING YOUR WEB SITE,** by Ernst S. Sibberson. Website: http://www.bluejaypub.com/BJPbookshelf/creating.htm. Cost $7.95, plus $3 shipping. BlueJay Publications, PO Box 522, Sandusky OH 44870.

DOMAIN NAMES. To see if the domain name you want to use is already in use, go to: http://www.networksolutions.com/cgi-bin/whois/whois. If your Internet service provider cannot host your domain, find a good hosting service, such as Westhost at: http://www.westhost.com. To register your domain name, go to: http://www.networksolutions.com.

+**FREE COUNTERS.** Website: http://www.superstats.com, or http://www.thecounter.com.

+**FREE FILL-IN FORMS.** Website: http://www.bravenet.com/samples/email forms.php.

+**FREE GREETING CARDS.** Website: http://associates.123greetings.com.

+**FREE GUESTBOOK.** Website: http://homepagetools.com/guestbook.

+**FREE ONLINE CUSTOMER SERVICE.** Website: http://humanclick.com.

+**FREE POLLS.** Website: http://apps3.vantagenet.com/site/poll.asp.

+**FREE WEB-BASED E-MAIL SERVICE.** Website: http://www.zzn.com.

HELPFUL WEBSITES. Http://www.BigNoseBird.com; http://www.hotwired.com/webmonkey. Free Websites that offer downloads of the language and free CGI scripts.

HOMESTEAD WEB SERVER. Http://www.homestead.com/SparrowsNest/Home.html.

HOW TO PROMOTE YOUR WEBSITE. Http://www.wilsonweb.com.

MAINTAINING YOUR WEBSITE. Http://www.workz.com/Build/Vendors/home.asp.

MEDIA BUILDER. Offers free fonts and Web graphics to use on your Web page: http://www.mediabuilder.com.

OURCHURCH.COM. Free Christian Web server; easy to use. Http://www. OurChurch.com.

POOR RICHARD'S WEBSITE. Http://www.poorrichard.com. Information on setting up your own Website, including almost 800 links to related sites, and examples of free and low-cost Website utilities.

TRUEPATH: CHRIST-CENTERED WEB HOSTING. One of the easiest places to create a free Web page: http://www.truepath.com. You can use their graphics and editor or just upload your own created page. They don't put banners on your page, just pop up advertising you can click off. Also check out: http://www.ilovejesus.com.

WEBSITE WORKSTATION. Http://www.davesite.com/webstation. All kinds of advice on Website design, etc.

+WEB-ZINE ARTICLE DISTRIBUTION SITES. Http://www.meer.net/ ~johnl/e-zine-list; http://www.ideamarketers.com; http://www.Ezine Articles.com. Free articles to put on your Web page.

WEBSITES OF INTEREST TO WRITERS: GENERAL

+ABSOLUTE WRITE. Http://www.absolutewrite.com. Good links, market info, and Q&As.

ACW PRESS: RESOURCES FOR THE CHRISTIAN WRITER. Http://www. acwpress.com/links.htm. Links to lots of great resources.

AMERICAN CHRISTIAN WRITERS. Http://www.ECPA.ORG/ACW.

AMERICAN JOURNALISM REVIEW'S NEWS LINK. Http://www.newslink. org. Links more than 60 Websites including The Freedom Forum, Pulitzer Prizes, American Society of Magazine Editors, American Society of Newspaper Editors, Newsletter Publishers Assn., and the Committee to Protect Journalists.

+CHRISTIAN MINISTRY LINKS. Http://www.CrossSearch.com. Links to over 40 Christian ministries.

+CLAY TABLETS. Http://www.dingir.org/tablets. Links to a variety of writing sites, including contests.

+DENOMINATIONAL THEOLOGY. Http://apu.edu/~bstone/theology/trad. html. Check out the theology of various denominations.

+EXPERTS. Http://www.experts.com. A diverse source of experts, academic and otherwise. Also: http://www.profnet.com.

+E-ZINES. Http://www.zinebook.com, or http://www.meer.net/~johnl/e-zine-list.

+FEDWORLD INFORMATION NETWORK. Http://www.fedworld.gov. Source of federal reports for your research.

+FREELANCE SUCCESS. Http://www.freelancesuccess.com.

+FREELANCE WRITING: WEBSITE FOR TODAY'S WORKING WRITER. Website: http://www.freelancewriting.com. Links to all kinds of resources, including a Job Bank and current contests.

+GEOGRAPHIC NAMES & PLACES. Http://www.mit.edu/geo. Gives statistics and background information on a city you may want to include in an article or novel.

INKSPOT, THE WRITER'S RESOURCE. Http://www.inkspot.com. A comprehensive writing resource full of market information, tips on improving your writing, articles, interviews with professional authors and editors, networking opportunities, and a guide to the best resources for writers on the Web.

+IUNIVERSE.COM/AUTHOR TOOLKIT. Http://www/iuniverse.com/author toolkit/default.asp.

THE LITTFIN PRATT AGENCY/VALINDA LITTFIN/LONNI COLLINS PRATT, 518 W. Nepessing, Ste. A, Lapeer MI 48446. (810)245-8572. Fax (810) 664-1267. E-mail: vlittfin@expression.org. Website: http://www.littfinpratt. com. Links to major publishing periodicals; free publicity workshop; samples of actual press kit components.

+PAGE ONE LITERARY NEWSLETTER. Http://www.pageonelit.com.

+PHONE BOOK SEARCH USA. Http://www.switchboard.com; or http://www.contractjobs.com/tel.

+POSTAGE RATES WORLDWIDE. Http://www.geocities.com/wallstreet/exchange/1161/index.htm. International postage rates.

+PUBLIC OPINION POLLS. Http://www.pollingreport.com. Add substance to your articles with the latest opinion poll results.

SHARP WRITER. A site with quick references and lots of useful writer's links. Http://www.sharpwriter.com.

+TIME ZONE CONVERTER. Http://www.timezoneconverter.com.

TOURBUS. Http://www.TOURBUS.com. A newsletter about what's happening on the Internet, including information on current Internet viruses and hoaxes.

WRITERLADY. How-to articles and links for writers, plus much more.

+WRITERSPEAKER.COM. Http://www.writerspeaker.com. Offers all kinds of help for the writer or speaker, including a free newsletter.

WRITE TOOLS. Professional writing and editing services. A one-stop reference site for writers and editors. Http://www.writetool.com.

WEBSITES OF INTEREST: SPECIALTY TOPICS

+CARTOONING. Http://www.cartoon.org. Click on Advice, for information on getting started.

CHRISTIAN COMICS INTERNATIONAL. Http://members.aol.com/ChriCom. Nate Butler can be reached by e-mail at: ChrisCom@aol.com. For a list of 20 different Christian comics, cartoons, and related paperback or hardback books (can be ordered on the spot), go to http://users.aol.com/ChriCom/buybooks.html. Another contact person for writers interested in scripting a comic or other aspects of comic ministry is: Len Cowan, 519—164th Pl. SE, Bothell WA 98012, e-mail: clcowan@xc.org.

+CHRISTIAN HISTORY. Http://www.christianhistory.net, or http://www.gospelcom.net/chi/index.html.

CLOTHING OF PAST ERAS. Covers everything from ancient Greece to the Middle Ages to the 1950s. Http://members.aol.com/nebula5/tcpinfo2.html#history.

+GREETING CARD WRITER MAGAZINE. PO Box 43523, Cincinnati OH

45243-0523. E-mail: editor@greetingcardwriter.com. Http://www.greeting cardwriter.com. Latest marketing information, interviews with editors and writers in the field, plus articles for beginners and the more advanced.

+HISTORY CHANNEL. Http://www.historychannel.com. Historical research by topic, time, event, etc. Also: http://www.historynet.com.

HOMESCHOOLING. Http://www.learnathome.com; http://www.homeschool headquarters.com; http://www.hsrc.com; http://homeschool.crosswalk. com. For writers in home school market.

+JOIN HANDS. If writing for pastors, Christian education leaders, or music directors, you may find some helpful resources at http://www.joinhands. com.

PARENT SOUP. Http://www.parentsoup.com. For writers of parenting articles. Also: http://www.Nappaland.com.

+PASTORAL WRITING RESOURCES. Website: http://www.pastors.com.

+TRAVELWRITERS.COM. Resource for travel writers. Contact info on over 800 travel publications. Free market news and press trip announcements. Http://www.travelwriters.com.

+WOMEN'S WRITING RESOURCES. Women's Ministry Institute site: http:// www.wministute.org; http://www.womensministry.net.

WRITERS' SOFTWARE

AMERICAN CHRISTIAN WRITERS SOFTWARE FOR WRITERS, PO Box 110390, Nashville TN 37222. (800)21-WRITE. Send a #10 SASE/1 stamp for an 8-page catalog of software (mostly shareware) of special interest to writers.

*BESTSELLER: A SUBMISSION TRACKING SOFTWARE FOR WRITERS. For a demo copy send $12 US or $17.50 CAN; for complete program, send $73.95 US or $99.45 CAN (prices include postage) to: Salt Spring Island Software, 137 McPhillips Ave., Salt Spring Island BC, V8K 2T6 Canada. For more information call (604)537-4339.

+NOVEL PRO. Website: http://novelcode.com/html/novelpro.htm. Software that helps organize ideas, work on pieces of the story without getting lost, brainstorm creation of characters and scenes, etc. Cost is $29.95. Order on Website.

+S.A.M.M. A manuscript tracking freeware program. Download at http://www.sandbaggers.8m.com/samm.htm.

SOFTWARE DREAMPACK FOR WRITERS. Dreampack offers 57 separate writer's programs for $19.95. Categories include Accessories, Brain Trainers, Skill Improvement, Writing Support, Organizers, Diversions, Learning Programs, Reference, Self-care, and more. Details at: http:// www.novalearn.com/dp.

+STORYCRAFT STORY DEVELOPMENT SOFTWARE. Guides writers through the entire process of writing novels, screenplays, teleplays, plays and short stories. To order, go to: http://www.storycraft-soft.com.

+WRITE PRO. Http://www.writepro.com.

+WRITER'S BLOCKS 2.0. Http://www.writersblocks.com. Organize story elements for your fiction.

WRITING INSTRUCTION: CASSETTE TAPES

THE CHRISTIAN COMMUNICATOR MANUSCRIPT CRITIQUE SERVICE CASSETTE HANDS-ON COURSE. For information contact: Susan Titus Osborn, 3133 Puente St., Fullerton CA 92835-1952. (714) 990-1532. E-mail: Susanosb@aol.com. Website: http://www.christiancommunicator.com. Offers basic writing course available by cassette. Includes 6 lessons on 12 cassettes, handouts, and critiqued assignments. Cost for entire course: $150, by the lesson: $30. Completion of entire course entitles you to one unit of Continuing Education Credit (CEU) from Pacific Christian College of Hope International University for an additional $30.

CHRISTIAN WRITERS LEARNING CENTER. Over 1,000 cassette tapes to choose from. Cost is $5-6 each, depending on quantity. Send SASE for list of topics to: American Christian Writers, PO Box 110390, Nashville TN 37222. (800)21-WRITE.

CREATIVE CHRISTIAN MINISTRIES. Tapes on a variety of topics for Christian writers (recorded at past writers' conferences by top writer/speakers). $4.95 ea.; or order five tapes and select one, of your choice, absolutely free. Also other resources available to help you become an effective, productive writer. Send SASE for free Writer's Catalog: Creative Christian Ministries, PO Box 12624, Roanoke VA 24027. (540)342-7511. E-mail: ccmbbr@juno.com. Website: http://www.EquippingForMinistry.org.

WRITE HIS ANSWER MINISTRIES. Director: Marlene Bagnull, Litt.D., 316 Blanchard Rd., Drexel Hill PA 19026. E-mail: mbagnull@aol.com. Website: http://www.writehisanswer.com. Tapes on 20+ topics, $5 ea. Topics include: Taking the Pain Out of Marketing; Writing Manuscripts That Sell and Touch Lives; Turning Personal Experience into Print; and Self-Publishing. Tapes of Marlene's 8½ hour Christian Writers Seminar (emphasis on writing for periodicals) are $26.95 or 6½ hour Book Writers Symposium are $22.95 and include handouts.

WRITING INSTRUCTION: CORRESPONDENCE COURSES

AMERICAN SCHOOL OF CHRISTIAN WRITING. This division of American Christian Writers offers a 3-year, 36-lesson correspondence course that covers the entire field of Christian writing. Students may purchase full course or selected portions. Several payment plans available. For lesson list and enrollment forms contact: American Christian Writers, PO Box 110390, Nashville TN 37222. (800)21-WRITE. Website: http://www.ecpa.org/acw.

ASSOCIATED WRITING PROGRAMS, Tallwood House MSN 113, George Mason University, Fairfax VA 22030. (703)993-4301. Fax (703)993-4302. E-mail: awp@gmu.edu.

AT-HOME WRITING WORKSHOPS. Director: Marlene Bagnull, Litt.D., Write His Answer Ministries, 316 Blanchard Rd., Drexel Hill PA 19026. E-mail: mbagnull@aol.com. Website: http://www.writehisanswer.com. Offers 3 courses of study with 6-10 study units in each. (1) Putting Your Best Foot Forward (lays foundation for your writing ministry), 6 units, $170; (2)

Nonfiction (articles, tracts, curriculum, devotionals, how-tos, etc., plus planning a nonfiction book and book proposal), 10 units, $272; (3) Fiction, 10 units, $255. Units may also be purchased individually for $30-34.

CHRISTIAN WRITERS GUILD. Director: Norman B. Rohrer, 65287 Fern Ln., Hume CA 93628. (559)335-2333. Offers a 3-year home study course: Discover Your Possibilities in Writing. Includes an introduction to writing, article writing, short inspirational pieces, and fiction, plus a number of additional benefits. Send for your free Starter Kit. Cost for 3-year course is $995. Offers several payment plans and a $195 discount for full payment up front. Special scholarship through the Christian Writers' Market Guide: Instead of paying $150 down payment, you may pay $25 down, plus $15/month for the next 27 months as you study. Ask about the CWMG special when you request your starter kit.

CHRISTIAN WRITERS INSTITUTE CORRESPONDENCE COURSES. This 55-year-old institution, founded by veteran publisher Robert Walker, is a division of American Christian Writers. Offers six, 1-year courses with an assigned instructor/mentor. Writing assignments are given with a goal of having a publishable manuscript by the end of each course. Two payment plans available. Contact: Christian Writers Institute, PO Box 110390, Nashville TN 37222. (800)21-WRITE. Website: http://www.ecpa.org/ACW.

CORRESPONDENCE COURSE FOR MANUSCRIPT EDITING. The University of Wisconsin offers a correspondence course in manuscript editing for those wanting to do editing on a professional level or for writers wanting to improve their personal editing skills. Reasonable cost. Contact: University of Wisconsin Learning Innovations, 505 S. Rosa Rd., Ste. 200, Madison WI 53719. (800)442-6460. Ask about Manuscript Editing C350-A52.

GLORY PRESS/PROF. DICK BOHRER, M.S., M.A. (teacher 39 yrs, editor 11 yrs, author of 16 books), PO Box 624, West Linn OR 97068. (503)638-7711. E-mail: glorypress@juno.com. Offers a writing course based on his 228-page text, How to Write What YOU Think. Cost of book $25. Then you pay him $1 per page as you write the assignments in the text. To enroll, send $25 with a short Christian testimony. Also offers courses entitled How to Write Features Like a Pro, and 21 Ways to Write Stories for Christian Kids. Counsels his students on all their writing. References: gude@juno.com, k&kyoung@stic.net, asrduff@aol.com.

+THE INSTITUTE OF CHILDREN'S LITERATURE, 93 Long Ridge Rd., West Redding CT 06896-0811. Secular.

+LONG RIDGE WRITERS GROUP, 91 Long Ridge Rd., West Redding CT 06896-1123. Secular correspondence course, but you may request a Christian instructor.

*RIGHTEOUS WRITING. Intensive writing course covering research, library strategy, note taking, cultivating a topic, outlining, polishing, avoiding pitfalls, approaching editors, copyrighting, marketing, and more. Contact: Dr. Kenneth Gentry, PO Box 388, Placentia CA 92871. E-mail: KennethGentry@compuserve.com.

WRITER'S DIGEST WORKSHOPS. Writer's Digest School, 1507 Dana Ave., Cincinnati OH 45207. (800)759-0963. Offers courses in Writing & Selling Nonfiction Articles; Novel Writing Workshop; Writing & Selling Short

Stories; and Writing Your Life Stories. This is a secular course, but you may request a Christian instructor.

THE WRITING ACADEMY SEMINAR. Sponsors year-round correspondence writing program and annual seminar in various locations. Contact: Inez Schneider, New Member Coordinator, 4010 Singleton Rd., Rockford IL 61114. (815)877-9675. E-mail: patty@wams.org. Website: http://www. wams.org.

WRITING SERVICES INSTITUTE (WSI)/MARSHA L. DRAKE, #109—4351 Rumble St., Burnaby BC V5J 2A2 Canada. Phone/fax (604)321-3555. E-mail: write@telus.net. Website: http://www3.telus.net/WRITE. Offers several correspondence courses: Write for Fun and Profit; Write for Success; Write Fiction from Plot to Print; Write with Power; and Write for You: Magazine Article Writing. Write for details and information on correspondence courses.

WRITING INSTRUCTION: E-MAIL/INTERNET COURSES

THE CHRISTIAN COMMUNICATOR MANUSCRIPT CRITIQUE SERVICE E-MAIL HANDS-ON COURSE. For information contact: Susan Titus Osborn, 3133 Puente St., Fullerton CA 92835-1952. (714)990-1532. E-mail: Susanosb@aol.com. Website: http://www.christiancommunicator. com. Offers basic writing course available by e-mail. Includes 6 lessons online, handouts, and critiqued assignments. Cost for entire course: $120, by the lesson: $25. Completion of entire course entitles you to one unit of Continuing Education Credit (CEU) from Pacific Christian College of Hope International University for an additional $30.

+COFFEEHOUSE FOR WRITERS. Http://www.coffeehouse4writers.com/ courses.html. Offers a variety of 4-week writing workshops for $50. List of offerings is on Website.

EPISTLEWORKS CREATIONS/JOANN RENO WRAY, 812 W Glenwood St., Broken Arrow OK 74011-6419. (918)451-4017. Fax (918)451-4417. E-mail: jaw@webzone.net. Offers e-mail classes on the following topics: Writing and Marketing Devotionals (6 Lessons $30); How to Self-Edit and Write with Concision (6 Lessons $30); Laughing All the Way—Writing the Humor Article (8 Lessons $45). Other classes planned. Check Website at http://epistleworks.com. Extensive Page of research, writing, conference info, & magazine writers guidelines links found at http://epistleworks. com/WritersBooks.html.

LIFE WRITE. Free 9-lesson writing course. Http://LifeWrite.com.

THE LITTFIN PRATT AGENCY/VALINDA LITTFIN/LONNI COLLINS PRATT, 518 W. Nepessing, Ste. A, Lapeer MI 48446. (810)245-8572. Fax (810) 664-1267. E-mail: vlittfin@expression.org. Website: http://www.littfin pratt.com. Offers mentoring programs for serious new or intermediate writers (must have access to e-mail). Choose Beginning Career Mentoring (12-14 wks) or Intermediate Career Mentoring (6-8 wks). Send for application information and details by e-mail only.

NOVELCRAFT ONLINE CLASSES. Courses for writers, $25-40 or $60. Http:// www.noveladvice.com.

ONLINELEARNING.NET/UCLA EXTENSION. Offers an extensive selection of writing courses called The Writers' Program. Call (800)784-8436, ext. 350. Website: http://www.onlinelearning.net.

+SIMPLE STEPS TO LANDING PROFITABLE ASSIGNMENTS. Shows aspiring writers how to get an editor's attention without spending hours, days and weeks on a manuscript. Download this self-directed course for just $24.95. Http://www.dougschmidt.com.

*WRITERS CLUB UNIVERSITY COURSE CATALOG. Http://www.writersclub. com/wcu/toc.cfm.

+WRITERS ONLINE WORKSHOPS. Includes introductory, intermediate and advanced workshops in a variety of genres: novels, nonfiction, poetry, screenplays, memoirs and more. Go to: http://www.WritersOnlineWork shops.com. Address: PO Box 12915, Cincinnati OH 45212-0915. Sponsored by Writer's Digest.

+WRITERS ON THE NET. Http://www.writers.com. Online classes and a Writing Tips section.

+THE WRITING SCHOOL HOME PAGE. Http://www.mythbreakers.com/ writingschool.

WRITING INSTRUCTION: MISCELLANEOUS HELPS

THE ART OF WRITING. Http://www.artofwritingzine.com. Includes interesting tips and information on writing, plus several helpful links.

CARTOONING. Http://www.cartoon.org. Website for the International Museum of Cartoon Art. Includes information on how to become a cartoonist. Click on "Advice."

+COLUMBIA GUIDE TO ONLINE STYLE. Http://www.columbia.edu/cu/ cup/cgos/idx_basic.html.

THE ECLECTIC WRITER. How-to articles for writers. Http://www.eclectics. com/writing/writing.html.

EEI PRESS. Offers reference books for writers, professional editors, and proofreaders. Visit their Website: http://www.eeicom.com/press, or for a catalog, send to 66 Canal Center Plaza, Ste. 200, Alexandria VA 22314-5507, or call (703)683-0683, toll-free (800)683-8380. Fax (703)683-4915. E-mail: press@eeicommunications.com.

FREELANCE WRITING. Http://www.suite101.com/topics/page.cfm/1639. Practical helps for freelancers, such as how to write a query letter.

+GLOSSARY OF WRITING TERMS. Http://www.writersdigest.com/news letter/nsswm99glossary.html.

+THE GRAMMAR LADY. Http://www.grammarlady.com.

+GUIDE TO GRAMMAR AND WRITING. Http://webster.commnet.edu/HP/ pages/darling/grammar.htm.

+MANUSCRIPT FORMAT. For a sample and instructions on format for an article or a book, go to: http://www.shunn.net/format.html, or http://www. sfwa.org/writing/format_betancourt.htm.

PARADIGM ONLINE WRITING ASSISTANT. Http://www.powa.org.

+PROFESSIONAL WRITING DEGREE. Taylor University Fort Wayne has initiated the country's first "Professional Writing" major at an accredited

Christian University. The four-year bachelor of arts program includes free-lance writing, fiction, business and technical writing, journalism, scriptwriting, public relations, editorial and opinion writing, TV and radio news broadcasting, speech writing, and academic research writing. Write to Office of Admissions, TUFW, 1025 W. Rudisill Blvd., Fort Wayne IN 46807. (219)465-2111.

RENSSELEAR WRITING CENTER ONLINE HANDOUTS. Http://www.rpi.edu/web/writingcenter/handouts.html. Includes 12, one-page handouts on Basic Prose Styles, and 18 handouts on Basic Punctuation and Mechanics.

+SALLY STUART'S GUIDE TO GETTING PUBLISHED. This book tells you everything you need to know about how to write for publication and get published. $21 postpaid from Stuart Marketplace, 1647 SW Pheasant Dr., Aloha OR 97006. Website: Http://www.stuartmarket.com.

STYLE AND PROOFREADING HELPS. Http://www.proofread.com, or http://www.theslot.com.

WRITING UPDATE FROM WRITER'S DIGEST. This is a periodic, free, e-mail newsletter from the editors at Writer's Digest that includes up-to-date writing-related news and tips. To subscribe, contact: newsletter-manager@fwpubs.com, with "Subscribe WD Newsletter" in the message box, or sign up at their Website: http://www.writersdigest.com.

+YOUNG AUTHOR EDITION OF WRITING SMARTER NOT HARDER, by Colleen Reese. A how-to book for elementary-school-age children. Great for children's writing classes or home schoolers. To order a copy, send $7.95, plus $1.50 shipping to: Kaleidoscope Press, 2507—94th Ave. E., Edgewood WA 98371, or call 253-848-1116. Writing Smarter Not Harder (for jr. high through adults) is also available for the same price.

TOPICAL/SUBJECT LISTINGS OF BOOK PUBLISHERS

One of the most difficult aspects of marketing is trying to determine which publishers might be interested in the book you want to write. This topical listing was designed to help you do just that.

First, look up your topic of interest in the following lists. If you don't find the specific topic, check the list of topics in the table of contents, find any related topics, and pursue those. Once you have discovered which publishers are interested in a particular topic, the next step is to secure writer's guidelines and book catalogs from those publishers. Don't assume, just because a particular publisher is listed under your topic, that it would automatically be interested in your book. It is your job to determine whether your approach to the subject will fit within the unique scope of that publisher's catalog. It is also helpful to visit a Christian bookstore to actually see some of the books produced by each publisher you are interested in pursuing.

Note, too, that the primary listings for each publisher indicate what the publisher prefers to see—a query, book proposal, or complete manuscript.

R—Indicates which publishers reprint out-of-print books from other publishers.

An asterisk (*) following a topic indicates it is a new topic this year.

APOLOGETICS

ACU Press
Alba House—R
Ambassador-Emerald—R
Baker Books—R
Baptist Pub. House
Bethany House
Black Forest—R
Brentwood—R
Bridge-Logos
Broadman & Holman
Canadian Institute—R
Canon Press—R
Canticle Books—R
Christian Publications
Christian Univ Press—R
College Press—R
Conciliar Press—R
Concordia
Crossway Books
Dry Bones Press—R
Eerdmans Publishing—R
Essence Publishing—R
Gospel Publishing—R
Guardian Books—R
Hendrickson—R
Hensley Publishing—R
Holy Cross—R
Huntington House—R
Inkling Books—R
InterVarsity Press
Kregel—R
Lightwave Publishing
Longwood—R
Lutterworth Press
Magnus Press—R
Master Books
Master Design—R
McDougal Publishing—R
Messianic Jewish—R
Multnomah
Novalis—R
Oregon Catholic Press—R
Our Sunday Visitor—R
Oxford University
P & R Publishing
Pickwick Publications—R
Promise Publishing
Quintessential Books—R
Read 'N Run —R
Regnery—R
Revell
Review and Herald

Rose Publishing
Son-Rise
Still Waters Revival—R
TEACH Services—R
Tekna Books
Trinity Foundation—R
Tyler Press—R
Univ Press of America—R
Vital Issues Press—R
World Bible—R
Zondervan

ARCHAEOLOGY

Baker Books—R
BIBAL Press
Black Forest—R
Brentwood—R
Christopher Publishing
College Press—R
Conciliar Press—R
Doubleday
Eerdmans Publishing—R
Electric Works—R
Encounter Books—R
Essence Publishing—R
Facts on File

Greenwood Publishing
Guardian Books—R
Hendrickson—R
Huntington House—R
Longwood—R
Lutterworth Press
Master Design—R
Monument Press
New Leaf Press—R
Oxford University
Promise Publishing
Ragged Edge—R
Read 'N Run—R
Review and Herald
Trinity Press Intl.—R
Tyler Press—R
Univ/Ottawa Press
Univ Press of America—R
World Bible—R
Yale Univ Press—R
Zondervan

AUTOBIOGRAPHY

Ambassador-Emerald—R
Bethany House
Black Forest—R
Blue Dolphin
Bookwrights Press
Brentwood—R
Christopher Publishing
Cladach Publishing
Doubleday
Eerdmans Publishing—R
Encounter Books—R
Essence Publishing—R
Fairway Press—R
Friends United Press—R
Greenwood Publishing
Guardian Books—R
Guernica Editions—R
Hearth Publishing—R
Liguori Publications
Living Books for All
Longwood—R
Lowenbrown Publishing
Lutterworth Press
Master Design—R
Messianic Jewish—R
Novalis—R
Openbook—R
Paraclete Press—R
Paragon House—R
Promise Publishing
Providence House—R
Quixote Publications
RBC Publishing
Read 'N Run —R

Regnery—R
Review and Herald
Rising Star Press
Son-Rise
Southern Baptist Press—R
Still Waters Revival—R
Tekna Books
Tyler Press—R
VESTA—R
Vital Issues Press—R
West Coast Paradise—R
Zondervan

BIBLE/BIBLICAL STUDIES

Abingdon Press—R
ACU Press
Alba House—R
Ambassador-Emerald—R
AMG Publishers—R
Baker Books—R
Baptist Pub. House
Bethany House
BJU Press—R
Black Forest—R
Boyd, R.H.
Brentwood—R
Bridge Resources
Broadman & Holman
Canticle Books—R
Chalice Press
Chariot Victor
Christian Ed Pub.
Christian Publications
Christopher Publishing
City Bible Publishing
Cladach Publishing
College Press—R
Conciliar Press—R
Contemporary Drama Service
Cornell Univ Press—R
Creation House
Cross Cultural—R
Crossway Books
CSS Publishing
Doubleday
Dry Bones Press—R
Eden Publishing
Editores Betania-Caribe
Eerdmans Publishing—R
Electric Works—R
Essence Publishing—R
Fairway Press—R
Forward Movement
Geneva Press
Goetz Publishing, B.J.
Gospel Publishing—R
Greenwood Publishing

Guardian Books—R
Harcourt Religion
HarperSanFrancisco
Hendrickson—R
Hensley Publishing —R
Holy Cross—R
Huntington House—R
Inkling Books—R
Intl. Awakening Press—R
InterVarsity Press
Judson Press—R
Kregel—R
Libros Liguori
Lightwave Publishing
Living Books for All
Logion Press
Loizeaux (commentary)
Longwood—R
Lowenbrown Publishing
Lutterworth Press
Magnus Press—R
Master Design—R
McDougal Publishing—R
Mercer University Press
Messianic Jewish—R
Morehouse—R
Mt. Olive College Press
New City Press—R
New Hope—R
Northstone—R
Omega House—R
Oregon Catholic Press—R
Our Sunday Visitor—R
Oxford University
P & R Publishing
Pauline Books
Paulist Press
Pickwick Publications—R
Promise Publishing
Providence House—R
Ragged Edge—R
Rainbow/Legacy Press—R
Read 'N Run—R
Resource Publications
Revell
Review and Herald
St. Anthony Messenger—R
Shaw Pub., Harold—R
Sheed & Ward—R
Shining Star
Smyth & Helwys
Son-Rise
Southern Baptist Press—R
Starburst Publishers
TEACH Services—R
Tekna Books
Thomas More—R
Toccoa Falls

Trinity Foundation—R
Trinity Press Intl.—R
Troista Books
Tyler Press—R
United Church Pub.
Univ Press of America—R
VESTA—R
Vital Issues Press—R
Wadsworth—R
Westminster John Knox
Wood Lake Books—R
World Bible—R
Yale Univ Press—R
Zondervan

BIBLE COMMENTARY

Alba House—R
Ambassador-Emerald—R
AMG Publishers—R
Baptist Pub. House
BJU Press—R
Bridge-Logos
Canon Press—R
City Bible Publishing
College Press—R
Conciliar Press—R
Editores Betania-Caribe
Encounter Books—R
Forward Movement
Greenwood Publishing
Guardian Books—R
Hendrickson—R
Inkling Books—R
Kregel—R
Living Books for All
Longwood—R
Lutterworth Press
Master Design—R
New Canaan
New City Press—R
Novalis—R
Oregon Catholic Press—R
Pickwick Publications—R
Promise Publishing
Providence House—R
Read 'N Run—R
Review and Herald
Starburst Publishers
Trinity Foundation—R
Westminster John Knox
WinePress—R
World Bible—R

BIOGRAPHY

Ambassador Books
Ambassador-Emerald—R

Baptist Pub. House
Bethany House
BJU Press—R
Black Forest—R
Blue Dolphin
Bookwrights Press
Brentwood—R
Bridge-Logos
Canon Press—R
Christian Publications
Christopher Publishing
Cladach Publishing
Conciliar Press—R
Cornell Univ. Press—R
Cross Cultural—R
Daybreak Books
Dimension Books—R
Doubleday
Eerdmans Publishing—R
Eerdmans/Young Readers
Encounter Books—R
Essence Publishing—R
Facts on File
Fairway Press—R
Greenwood Publishing
Guardian Books—R
Hay House
Hearth Publishing—R
ICS Publications—R
Inkling Books—R
Intl. Awakening Press—R
Kaleidoscope Press—R
Lifetime Book—R
Liguori Publications
Living Books for All
Longwood—R
Lowenbrown Publishing
Lutterworth Press
Master Design—R
McDougal Publishing—R
Mercer University Press
Messianic Jewish—R
Morrow and Co., Wm.
Mt. Olive College Press
New Hope—R
Northfield
Novalis—R
Openbook—R
Oxford University
Pacific Press
Paraclete Press—R
Paragon House—R
Promise Publishing
Providence House—R
Quintessential Books—R
Quixote Publications
RBC Publishing
Read 'N Run—R

Regnery—R
Review and Herald
Rising Star Press
Shaw Pub., Harold—R
Son-Rise
Southern Baptist Press—R
Still Waters Revival—R
Summit Pub. Group—R
TEACH Services—R
Tekna Books
Toccoa Falls
Troista Books
Tyler Press—R
United Church Pub.
VESTA—R
Vital Issues Press—R
West Coast Paradise—R
Yale Univ Press—R
YWAM Publishing—R
Zondervan

BOOKLETS

Accent Books & Videos
Canon Press
Christian Publications
Concordia
Cross Way Pub.
Elim Books
Essence Publishing
Forward Movement
Found/Religious Freedom
Fruit-Bearer Pub.
Good Book
Good News Publishers
Gospel Publishing
Guardian Books
Hearth Publishing
Huntington House
Intl. Awakening Press
InterVarsity Press
Jireh Publishing
Kindred Productions
Libros Liguori
Lightwave Publishing
Liguori Publications
Living Books for All
Longwood
Lowenbrown Publishing
Messianic Jewish
Our Sunday Visitor
Paradise Research
Partnership Book Services
Review and Herald
St. Anthony Messenger Press
Trinity Foundation
Tyler Press
Vital Issues Press

West Coast Paradise
WinePress
Word For Word Publishing

CANADIAN/FOREIGN

Canadian Inst. For Law
CERDIC Publications
Creative Bound
Essence Publishing
Guardian Books
Guernica Editions
Hunt Publishing, John
Inheritance Publications
Kindred Productions
Lightwave Publishing
Living Books for All
Lutterworth Press
Northstone Publishing
Novalis
Openbook Publishers
Skysong Press
Still Waters Revival
United Church Pub. Hs
Univ. of Ottawa Press
Verbinum
VESTA Publications
West Coast Paradise
Windflower Communications
Wood Lake Books

CELEBRITY PROFILES

Black Forest—R
Blue Dolphin
Bridge-Logos
Christopher Publishing
Encounter Books—R
Essence Publishing—R
Frederick Fell—R
Guardian Books—R
Judson Press—R
Liguori Publications
Longwood—R
New Leaf Press—R
Promise Publishing
Penguin Putnam
Read 'N Run—R
Shaw Pub., Harold—R
Zondervan

CHILDREN'S EASY READERS

Abingdon Press—R
Ambassador Books
BJU Press—R
Black Forest—R
Blessing Our World

Conciliar Press—R
Concordia
Eerdmans/Young Readers
Essence Publishing—R
Guardian Books—R
Henry Holt
HOHM Press
Hunt Publishing, John
Inkling Books—R
Lightwave Publishing
Liguori Publications
Longwood—R
Lutterworth Press
Master Design—R
Moody Press
Pacific Press
RBC Publishing
Read 'N Run—R
Waldman House
ZonderKidz

CHILDREN'S PICTURE BOOKS

Abingdon Press—R
Ambassador Books
Art Can Drama—R
BJU Press—R
Blessing Our World
Boyds Mills Press—R
Candy Cane Press
Chariot Victor
Compradore
Conciliar Press—R
Concordia
CSS Publishing
Devoted to You Books
Eden Publishing (some)
Eerdmans/Young Readers
Essence Publishing—R
Fairway Press—R
Focus Publishing
Guardian Books—R
Henry Holt
HOHM Press
Hunt Publishing, John
Kaleidoscope Press—R
Lightwave Publishing
Liguori Publications
Longwood—R
Lowenbrown Publishing
Lutterworth Press
Messianic Jewish—R
Moody Press
Morehouse—R
National Baptist—R
Novalis—R
Pauline Books

Paulist Press
Penguin Putnam
RBC Publishing
Reader's Digest Children's
Read 'N Run —R
St. Anthony Messenger—R
Son-Rise
Vital Issues Press—R
Waldman House
ZonderKidz

CHRISTIAN EDUCATION

Abingdon Press—R
ACU Press
Baker Books—R
BJU Press—R
Black Forest—R
Boyd, R.H.
Brentwood—R
Bridge-Logos
Bristol House—R
Broadman & Holman
Canon Press—R
Chalice Press
Chariot Victor
Christian Ed Pub.
Christopher Publishing
College Press—R
Contemporary Drama Service
Crossway Books
CSS Publishing
Educational Ministries
Eerdmans Publishing—R
Encounter Books—R
Essence Publishing—R
Fairway Press—R
Geneva Press
Goetz Publishing, B.J.
Gospel Publishing—R
GROUP Publishing—R
Group's FaithWeaver
Guardian Books—R
Harcourt Religion
Holy Cross—R
Hunt Publishing, John
Lightwave Publishing
Liturgical Press
Logion Press
Logos Productions
Longwood—R
Lowenbrown Publishing
Lutterworth Press
Master Books
Master Design—R
McDougal Publishing—R
Meriwether—R
National Baptist—R

New Canaan
New Hope—R
New Leaf Press—R
Novalis—R
Omega House—R
Openbook—R
Oregon Catholic Press—R
P & R Publishing
Perigee Books
Providence House—R
Ragged Edge—R
Rainbow/Legacy Press—R
Rainbow/Rainbow Books—R
Religious Education
Resource Publications
Rose Publishing
Smyth & Helwys
Southern Baptist Press—R
Standard
Still Waters Revival—R
Trinity Foundation—R
Tyler Press—R
United Church Press
United Church Pub.
Vital Issues Press—R
Westminster John Knox
Wood Lake Books—R
Zondervan

CHRISTIAN HOME SCHOOLING

AMG Publishers—R
Art Can Drama—R
Baker Books—R
BJU Press—R
Black Forest—R
Brentwood—R
Bridge-Logos
Canon Press—R
Christian Publications
Crossway Books
Eden Publishing
Eerdmans Publishing—R
Encounter Books—R
Essence Publishing—R
Fairway Press—R
Focus Publishing
Guardian Books—R
Harcourt Religion
Hensley Publishing —R
Hunt Publishing, John
Huntington House—R
Inkling Books—R
Kaleidoscope Press—R
Longwood—R
Master Design—R
McDougal Publishing—R

Omega House—R
Oregon Catholic Press—R
Promise Publishing
Providence House—R
Rainbow/Legacy Press—R
Rainbow/Rainbow Books—R
Review and Herald
Saint Mary's Press—R
Shaw Pub., Harold—R
Son-Rise
Standard
Still Waters Revival—R
TEACH Services—R
Tyler Press—R
Vital Issues Press—R
Windflower—R
YWAM Publishing—R
Zondervan

CHRISTIAN LIVING

Abingdon Press—R
Albury Publishing—R
Ambassador-Emerald—R
AMG Publishers—R
Baker Books—R
Baptist Pub. House
Barbour Publishing
Beacon Hill Press
Bethany House
BJU Press—R
Black Forest—R
Brentwood—R
Bridge-Logos
Bristol House—R
Broadman & Holman
Canon Press—R
Canticle Books—R
Chalice Press
Chariot Victor
Chosen Books
Christian Publications
Christopher Publishing
City Bible Publishing
Cladach Publishing
College Press—R
Compradore
Creation House
Crossway Books
CSS Publishing
DCTS Publishing—R
Dimensions for Living—R
Doubleday
Eerdmans Publishing—R
Electric Works—R
Encounter Books—R
Essence Publishing—R
Fairway Press—R

Friends United Press—R
Gesher—R
Gospel Publishing—R
Guardian Books—R
HarperSanFrancisco
Haworth Press—R
Hearth Publishing—R
Hendrickson—R
Hensley Publishing —R
Holy Cross—R
Honor Books
Horizon House—R
Howard Publishing
Hunt Publishing, John
Huntington House—R
Impact Christian Books—R
InterVarsity Press
James Russell
Jireh Publishing
Judson Press—R
Kindred Productions
Kregel—R
Libros Liguori
Life Cycle Books—R
Lillenas
Liturgical Press
Living Books for All
Longwood—R
Lowenbrown Publishing
Lutterworth Press
Magnus Press—R
McDougal Publishing—R
Moody Press
Multnomah
New City Press—R
New Leaf Press—R
Omega House—R
Openbook—R
Oregon Catholic Press—R
Our Sunday Visitor—R
P & R Publishing
Paraclete Press—R
Perigee Books
Promise Publishing
Providence House—R
Quintessential Books—R
Ragged Edge—R
Rainbow/Legacy Press—R
Read 'N Run —R
Revell
Review and Herald
Rising Star Press
Shaw Pub., Harold—R
Sheed & Ward—R
Shining Star
Small Helm Press—R
Smyth & Helwys
Son-Rise

Standard
Starburst Publishers
Still Waters Revival—R
Tekna Books
Thomas More—R
Troista Books
Tyler Press—R
United Church Press
United Church Pub.
Vital Issues Press—R
Wellness
West Coast Paradise—R
Western Front—R
Westminster John Knox
Zondervan

CHRISTIAN SCHOOL BOOKS

Art Can Drama—R
Baker Books—R
Black Forest—R
Canon Press—R
Christian Publications
ETC Publications
Fairway Press—R
Guardian Books—R
Hunt Publishing, John
Huntington House—R
Inkling Books—R
Kaleidoscope Press—R
Longwood—R
Lowenbrown Publishing
Lutterworth Press
Master Design—R
New Canaan
Son-Rise
Southern Baptist Press—R
Troista Books
Tyler Press—R
Westminster John Knox
Windflower—R
Wordsmiths

CHURCH LIFE

ACU Press
Alban Institute
Albury Publishing—R
Art Can Drama—R
Baker Books—R
Baptist Pub. House
Bethany House
Black Forest—R
Brentwood—R
Bridge-Logos
Bristol House—R
Broadman & Holman

Canon Press—R
Chalice Press
Christian Publications
Christopher Publishing
City Bible Publishing
Concordia
Crossway Books
CSS Publishing
DCTS Publishing—R
Eerdmans Publishing—R
Essence Publishing—R
Fairway Press—R
Forward Movement
Friends United Press—R
Gesher—R
Gospel Publishing—R
Greenwood Publishing
GROUP Publishing—R
Guardian Books—R
HarperSanFrancisco
Hendrickson—R
Holy Cross—R
Hunt Publishing, John
Impact Christian Books—R
InterVarsity Press
Judson Press—R
Kregel—R
Libros Liguori
Lillenas
Living Books for All
Longwood—R
Master Design—R
McDougal Publishing—R
Moody Press
Morehouse—R
Multnomah
New Leaf Press—R
Novalis—R
Openbook—R
OSL Publications—R
Our Sunday Visitor—R
P & R Publishing
Ragged Edge—R
Rainbow/Legacy Press—R
Read 'N Run —R
Review and Herald
Rising Star Press
Sheed & Ward—R
Smyth & Helwys
Tekna Books
Troista Books
Tyler Press—R
United Church Press
United Church Pub.
Vital Issues Press—R
Westminster John Knox
Wood Lake Books—R
Zondervan

CHURCH RENEWAL

Alba House—R
Alban Institute
Ambassador-Emerald—R
Baker Books—R
Bethany House
Black Forest—R
Brentwood—R
Bridge-Logos
Bristol House—R
Broadman & Holman
Chosen Books
Christian Publications
City Bible Publishing
Concordia
Crossway Books
CSS Publishing
Dimension Books—R
Eerdmans Publishing—R
Essence Publishing—R
Fairway Press—R
Forward Movement
Geneva Press
Gospel Publishing—R
GROUP Publishing—R
Guardian Books—R
HarperSanFrancisco
Hendrickson—R
Holy Cross—R
Hunt Publishing, John
Impact Christian Books—R
Intl. Awakening Press—R
InterVarsity Press
Judson Press—R
Kregel—R
Libros Liguori
Longwood—R
Lowenbrown Publishing
Lutterworth Press
Master Design—R
McDougal Publishing—R
Moody Press
Multnomah
Omega House—R
Oregon Catholic Press—R
OSL Publications—R
Our Sunday Visitor—R
P & R Publishing
Pastor's Choice
Ragged Edge—R
Read 'N Run —R
Review and Herald
Rising Star Press
Sheed & Ward—R
Smyth & Helwys
Southern Baptist Press—R
Tekna Books

Thomas More—R
Troista Books
Tyler Press—R
United Church Press
United Church Pub.
Vital Issues Press—R
Westminster John Knox
Wood Lake Books—R
Zondervan

CHURCH TRADITIONS

Black Forest—R
Bridge-Logos
Canon Press—R
Conciliar Press—R
Concordia
Cross Cultural—R
CSS Publishing
Eerdmans Publishing—R
Encounter Books—R
Essence Publishing—R
Forward Movement
Geneva Press
Greenwood Publishing
Guardian Books—R
HarperSanFrancisco
Holy Cross—R
Hunt Publishing, John
Inkling Books—R
Liguori Publications
Longwood—R
Lutterworth Press
Morehouse—R
Novalis—R
Oregon Catholic Press—R
OSL Publications—R
Our Sunday Visitor—R
Paraclete Press—R
RBC Publishing
Read 'N Run —R
Rising Star Press
Tekna Books
Thomas More—R
Troista Books
United Church Pub.
Univ Press of America—R
Westminster John Knox
Wood Lake Books—R

CONTROVERSIAL ISSUES

Accent Books
Ambassador-Emerald—R
Ambassador House
Baker Books—R
Black Forest—R
Blue Dolphin

Brentwood—R
Bridge-Logos
Canon Press—R
Canticle Books—R
CERDIC Publications
Chalice Press
Christian Publications
Conari Press—R
Conciliar Press—R
Cross Cultural—R
Encounter Books—R
Essence Publishing—R
Found/Religious Freedom
Frederick Fell—R
Grace House Press—R
Greenwood Publishing
Guardian Books—R
HarperSanFrancisco
Haworth Press—R
Hay House
Hendrickson—R
Hunt Publishing, John
Huntington House—R
Inkling Books—R
Innisfree Press
InterVarsity Press
Jireh Publishing
Kregel—R
Lillenas
Lowenbrown Publishing
Lutterworth Press
Magnus Press—R
Monument Press
Multnomah
Novalis—R
P & R Publishing
Pilgrim Press
Quintessential Books—R
RBC Publishing
Read 'N Run—R
Regnery—R
Rising Star Press
Still Waters Revival—R
Tekna Books
Trinity Foundation—R
Troista Books
Tyler Press—R
United Church Pub.
Vital Issues Press—R
Westminster John Knox
Zondervan

COOKBOOKS

Ambassador-Emerald—R
Black Forest—R
Brentwood—R
Christopher Publishing

Conari Press—R
Countryman, J.
Crane Hill—R
Daybreak Books
Doubleday
Eden Publishing
Fairway Press—R
Grace House Press—R
Guardian Books—R
Hearth Publishing—R
Huntington House—R
Liguori Publications
Longwood—R
Morrow & Company, Wm.
Mt. Olive College Press
Omega House—R
Pacific Press
Perigee Books
Providence House—R
Rainbow/Legacy Press—R
Read 'N Run—R
Review and Herald
Son-Rise
Southern Baptist Press—R
Starburst Publishers
Summit Pub. Group—R
TEACH Services—R
Tekna Books
Tyler Press—R

COUNSELING AIDS

Baker Books—R
Baptist Pub. House
Bethany House
Black Forest—R
Brentwood—R
Bridge-Logos
Christopher Publishing
Conari Press—R
Crossroad Publishing—R
Dimension Books—R
Eden Publishing
Eerdmans Publishing—R
Essence Publishing—R
Fairway Press—R
Gospel Publishing—R
Grace House Press—R
Guardian Books—R
Harcourt Religion
Haworth Press—R
InterVarsity Press
Judson Press—R
Kaleidoscope Press—R
Kregel—R
Life Cycle Books—R
Longwood—R
Lutterworth Press

New Leaf Press—R
Novalis—R
P & R Publishing
Pastor's Choice
Providence House—R
Read 'N Run —R
Resource Publications
Shaw Pub., Harold—R
Son-Rise
Southern Baptist Press—R
Tekna Books
Tyler Press—R
United Church Pub.
Upper Room Books
WhiteStone Circle
Zondervan

CREATION SCIENCE

Albury Publishing—R
Black Forest—R
Christopher Publishing
Crossway Books
Electric Works—R
Essence Publishing—R
Guardian Books—R
Hendrickson—R
Huntington House—R
Inkling Books—R
InterVarsity Press
Kaleidoscope Press—R
Kregel—R
Lightwave Publishing
Longwood—R
P & R Publishing
Pacific Press
Promise Publishing
Review and Herald
Rose Publishing
Starburst Publishers
Tekna Books
Zondervan

CULTS/OCCULT

Albury Publishing—R
Ambassador-Emerald—R
Baker Books—R
Bethany House
Black Forest—R
Bridge-Logos
Conciliar Press—R
CSS Publishing
Essence Publishing—R
Greenwood Publishing
Guardian Books—R
Hendrickson—R
Huntington House—R

Impact Christian Books—R
InterVarsity Press
Kregel—R
Longwood—R
Lutterworth Press
Monument Press
New Leaf Press—R
Open Court—R
P & R Publishing
Promise Publishing
Read 'N Run—R
Rose Publishing
Son-Rise
Tekna Books
Tyler Press—R
Vital Issues Press—R
Wood Lake Books—R
Zondervan

CURRENT/SOCIAL ISSUES

Accent Books
Ambassador-Emerald—R
Baker Books—R
Baptist Pub. House
Baylor University Press
Beacon Hill Press
Bethany House
Black Forest—R
Blue Dolphin
Brentwood—R
Bridge-Logos
Bristol House—R
Canon Press—R
Chalice Press
Christian Media—R
Christian Publications
Christopher Publishing
Conari Press—R
Cornell Univ. Press—R
Cross Cultural—R
Crossroad Publishing—R
Crossway Books
Dry Bones Press—R
Eden Publishing
Eerdmans Publishing—R
Encounter Books—R
Essence Publishing—R
Fairway Press—R
Frederick Fell—R
Geneva Press
Grace House Press—R
Greenwood Publishing
Guardian Books—R
Haworth Press—R
Hay House
Hendrickson—R
Horizon House—R

Howard Publishing
Huntington House—R
Inkling Books—R
InterVarsity Press
Judson Press—R
Kregel—R
Libros Liguori
Life Cycle Books—R
Liguori Publications
Lillenas
Longwood—R
Lowenbrown Publishing
Loyola Press
Lutterworth Press
Multnomah
New Hope—R
New World Library
Openbook—R
Oxford University
P & R Publishing
Paragon House—R
Paulist Press
PREP Publishing—R
Promise Publishing
Quintessential Books—R
Ragged Edge—R
RBC Publishing
Read 'N Run—R
Regnery—R
Rising Star Press
Shaw Pub., Harold—R
Small Helm Press—R
Smyth & Helwys
Son-Rise
Starburst Publishers
Still Waters Revival—R
Tekna Books
Tyler Press—R
United Church Pub.
Univ/Ottawa Press
VESTA—R
Vital Issues Press—R
West Coast Paradise—R
Western Front—R
Wood Lake Books—R
Zondervan

CURRICULUM

Art Can Drama—R
Black Forest—R
Boyd, R.H. (VBS)
Christian Ed Pub.
Cross Cultural—R
CSS Publishing
Educational Ministries
Encounter Books—R
Facts on File

Family Hope Services
Greenwood Publishing
Gospel Publishing—R
Group's FaithWeaver
Logos Productions
Longwood—R
Master Books
Master Design—R
Openbook—R
Providence House—R
Rainbow/Legacy Press—R
Rainbow/Rainbow Books—R
Rose Publishing
Smyth & Helwys
Standard
Tekna Books
Through the Bible Pub.
Tyler Press—R
United Church Press
Wellness
Westminster John Knox
Wonder Time (mag.)
Wood Lake Books—R

DEATH/DYING

Abingdon Press—R
ACTA Publications
Alba House—R
Albury Publishing—R
Black Forest—R
Blue Dolphin
Bridge-Logos
Broadman & Holman
Christopher Publishing
Conari Press—R
Cross Cultural—R
Crossroad Publishing—R
CSS Publishing
Daybreak Books
Eden Publishing
Eerdmans Publishing—R
Electric Works—R
Encounter Books—R
Essence Publishing—R
Fairway Press—R
Forward Movement
Gilgal Publications
Grace House Press—R
Greenwood Publishing
Guardian Books—R
HarperSanFrancisco
Haworth Press—R
Hay House
Hendrickson—R
Hunt Publishing, John
InterVarsity Press
Kregel—R

Life Cycle Books—R
Liguori Publications
Lillenas
Liturgy Training
Longwood—R
Lutterworth Press
Master Design—R
Moody Press
Novalis—R
OSL Publications—R
Paraclete Press—R
Perigee Books
Promise Publishing
Rainbow/Legacy Press—R
Read 'N Run—R
Review and Herald
Sheed & Ward—R
Smyth & Helwys
Tekna Books
Thomas More—R
United Church Press
Upper Room Books
Westminster John Knox
WhiteStone Circle
Wood Lake Books—R
Zondervan

DEVOTIONAL BOOKS

ACTA Publications
ACU Press
Alba House—R
Albury Publishing—R
Ambassador-Emerald—R
AMG Publishers—R
Baptist Pub. House
Barbour Publishing
Black Forest—R
Boyd, R.H.
Brentwood—R
Bridge-Logos
Broadman & Holman
Chariot Victor
Christian Publications
Christopher Publishing
Cladach Publishing
College Press—R
Conari Press—R
Concordia
Contemporary Drama Service
Countryman, J.
Cross Cultural—R
Crossroad Publishing—R
Crossway Books
CSS Publishing
DCTS Publishing—R
Dimensions for Living—R
Doubleday

Eerdmans Publishing—R
Essence Publishing—R
Fairway Press—R
Forward Movement
Friends United Press—R
Geneva Press
Gesher—R
Gilgal Publications
Gospel Publishing—R
Grace House Press—R
Guardian Books—R
HarperSanFrancisco
Hendrickson—R
Hensley Publishing —R
Honor Books
Howard Publishing
Hunt Publishing, John
Impact Christian Books—R
Inkling Books—R
James Russell
Jireh Publishing
Judson Press—R
Kregel—R
Libros Liguori
Lightwave Publishing
Liguori Publications
Living Books for All
Longwood—R
Lutterworth Press
Master Design—R
McDougal Publishing—R
Morehouse—R
New Leaf Press—R
Novalis—R
Openbook—R
Pacific Press
Pauline Books
Promise Publishing
Providence House—R
Rainbow/Legacy Press—R
Read 'N Run—R
Revell
Review and Herald
St. Anthony Messenger—R
Saint Mary's Press—R
Shaw Pub., Harold—R
Sheed & Ward—R
Smyth & Helwys
Son-Rise
Standard (for kids)
Starburst Publishers
TEACH Services—R
Tekna Books
Thomas More—R
Toccoa Falls
Troista Books
Tyler Press—R
United Church Press

United Church Pub.
Upper Room Books
Wesleyan Publishing House
West Coast Paradise—R
Westminster John Knox
WhiteStone Circle
Wood Lake Books—R
World Bible—R
Zondervan

DISCIPLESHIP

ACU Press
Albury Publishing—R
Ambassador-Emerald—R
Baker Books—R
Baptist Pub. House
Beacon Hill Press
Bethany House
Black Forest—R
Brentwood—R
Bridge-Logos
Bristol House—R
Broadman & Holman
Chalice Press
Chariot Victor
Chosen Books
Christian Publications
College Press—R
Concordia
Creation House
Crossway Books
CSS Publishing
DCTS Publishing—R
Eerdmans Publishing—R
Essence Publishing—R
Fairway Press—R
Forward Movement
Gesher—R
Gospel Publishing—R
GROUP Publishing—R
Guardian Books—R
HarperSanFrancisco
Hendrickson—R
Horizon House—R
Howard Publishing
Hunt Publishing, John
Inkling Books—R
InterVarsity Press
Judson Press—R
Kregel—R
Libros Liguori
Lightwave Publishing
Liguori Publications
Lillenas
Living Books for All
Logos Productions
Longwood—R

Lowenbrown Publishing
Lutterworth Press
Master Design—R
McDougal Publishing—R
Messianic Jewish—R
Moody Press
Multnomah
New Hope—R
New Leaf Press—R
New World Library
Novalis—R
Omega House—R
OSL Publications—R
P & R Publishing
Promise Publishing
Quintessential Books—R
Rainbow/Legacy Press—R
Read 'N Run —R
Review and Herald
Sheed & Ward—R
Smyth & Helwys
Southern Baptist Press—R
Standard
Tekna Books
Thomas More—R
Toccoa Falls
Tyler Press—R
Upper Room Books
Vital Issues Press—R
Wesleyan Publishing House
West Coast Paradise—R
Wood Lake Books—R
YWAM Publishing—R
Zondervan

DIVORCE

Albury Publishing—R
Baker Books—R
Bethany House
Black Forest—R
Brentwood—R
Bridge-Logos
Broadman & Holman
Eden Publishing
Essence Publishing—R
Faith One
Forward Movement
Gilgal
Greenwood Publishing
Guardian Books—R
Haworth Press—R
Hay House
Huntington House—R
InterVarsity Press
Liguori Publications
Lillenas
Longwood—R

Lowenbrown Publishing
Lutterworth Press
Novalis—R
P & R Publishing
Perigee Books
PREP Publishing—R
Promise Publishing
Read 'N Run —R
Regnery—R
Southern Baptist Press—R
Tekna Books
Tyler Press—R
Vital Issues Press—R
Wood Lake Books—R
Zondervan

DOCTRINAL

ACU Press
Alba House—R
Albury Publishing—R
Ambassador-Emerald—R
Baker Books—R
Beacon Hill Press
Bethany House
Black Forest—R
Brentwood—R
Bridge-Logos
Broadman & Holman
Canon Press—R
Canticle Books—R
Christian Publications
Christian Univ Press—R
City Bible Publishing
College Press—R
Concordia
Cross Cultural—R
CSS Publishing
Eerdmans Publishing—R
Essence Publishing—R
Fairway Press—R
Forward Movement
Friends United Press—R
Geneva Press
Gospel Publishing—R
Greenwood Publishing
Guardian Books—R
Hearth Publishing—R
Hendrickson—R
Impact Christian Books—R
Intl. Awakening Press—R
Kregel—R
Libros Liguori
Liturgical Press
Living Books for All
Loizeaux
Longwood—R
Lutterworth Press

Magnus Press—R
Master Design—R
McDougal Publishing—R
Novalis—R
Oregon Catholic Press—R
Our Sunday Visitor—R
P & R Publishing
Paulist Press
Pickwick Publications—R
Pilgrim Press
Promise Publishing
Quintessential Books—R
Read 'N Run —R
Review and Herald
St. Anthony Messenger—R
Shaw Pub., Harold—R
Sheed & Ward—R
Southern Baptist Press—R
Still Waters Revival—R
Tekna Books
Trinity Foundation—R
Troista Books
Tyler Press—R
Univ Press of America—R
Westminster John Knox
Zondervan

DRAMA

Art Can Drama—R
Baker Books—R
Baker's Plays
Black Forest—R
Brentwood—R
Canon Press—R
Christian Media—R
Conari Press—R
Contemporary Drama Service
CSS Publishing
Eden Publishing
Eldridge Pub.
Electric Works—R
Fairway Press—R
Goetz
Grace House Press—R
Greenwood Publishing
GROUP Publishing—R
Guardian Books—R
Kregel—R
Lillenas
Longwood—R
Lowenbrown Publishing
Meriwether—R
New Hope—R (missions)
Read 'N Run—R
Southern Baptist Press—R
Spiritual Theater
Standard

Tyler Press—R
United Church Pub.
West Coast Paradise—R
Western Front—R
Zondervan

E-BOOKS*

Alban Institute
Broadman & Holman
Canon Press (soon)
ChristianPublishers.com
College Press
Compradore
Dry Bones Press
Electric Works
Everybook
Faith Fiction
Found/Religious Freedom
Henry Holt
InterVarsity Press
James Russell Publishing
Jireh Publishing
Legacy Press
Longwood
MountainView
Master Design
New World Library
Pelican Publishing
Read 'N Run
Rising Star Press
Scarecrow Press
Sharman Farms
Smyth & Helwys

ECONOMICS

Black Forest—R
Brentwood—R
Christopher Publishing
Cross Cultural—R
Dimension Books—R
Dry Bones Press—R
Eerdmans Publishing—R
Encounter Books—R
Essence Publishing—R
Greenwood Publishing
Guardian Books—R
Haworth Press—R
Huntington House—R
Lowenbrown Publishing
Lutterworth Press
Northfield
Oregon Catholic Press—R
Oxford University
Paragon House—R
Paulist Press
Pilgrim Press

Read 'N Run—R
Regnery—R
Summit Pub. Group—R
Trinity Foundation—R
Tyler Press—R
Univ/Ottawa Press
Vital Issues Press—R

ENVIRONMENTAL ISSUES

Baker Books—R
Black Forest—R
Blue Dolphin
Chalice Press
Christian Univ Press—R
Christopher Publishing
Conari Press—R
Cross Cultural—R
CSS Publishing
Eerdmans Publishing—R
Essence Publishing—R
Facts on File
Grace House Press—R
Greenwood Publishing
Guardian Books—R
Haworth Press—R
Hay House
Hearth Publishing—R
Holy Cross—R
Huntington House—R
Judson Press—R
Liturgy Training
Longwood—R
Lowenbrown Publishing
Lutterworth Press
Monument Press
New World Library
Novalis—R
Oxford University
Paragon House—R
Paulist Press
Promise Publishing
Read 'N Run—R
Southern Baptist Press—R
Tekna Books
Tyler Press—R
United Church Press
United Church Pub.
Vital Issues Press—R
West Coast Paradise—R
Zondervan

ESCHATOLOGY

Alba House—R
Ambassador-Emerald—R
Bridge-Logos
Canon Press—R

Concordia
Editores Betania-Caribe
Guardian Books—R
Kregel—R
Liguori Publications
Longwood—R
Lutterworth Press
Master Design—R
Novalis—R
Oregon Catholic Press—R
OSL Publications—R
Paragon House—R
Pickwick Publications—R
Promise Publishing
Review and Herald
Rising Star Press
Starburst Publishers
Westminster John Knox
WinePress—R

ETHICS

Abingdon Press—R
ACU Press
Alba House—R
Baker Books—R
Baptist Pub. House
Baylor University Press
Bethany House
Black Forest—R
Brentwood—R
Canon Press—R
Chalice Press
Christian Publications
Christian Univ Press—R
Christopher Publishing
Conari Press—R
Conciliar Press—R
Cornell Univ. Press—R
Creation House
Cross Cultural—R
Crossroad Publishing—R
Crossway Books
CSS Publishing
Doubleday
Eerdmans Publishing—R
Electric Works—R
Encounter Books—R
Essence Publishing—R
Forward Movement
Frederick Fell—R
Geneva Press
Gospel Publishing—R
Grace House Press—R
Greenwood Publishing
Guardian Books—R
Haworth Press—R
Hay House

Hearth Publishing—R
Holy Cross—R
Howard Publishing
Huntington House—R
Inkling Books—R
InterVarsity Press
Judson Press—R
Kregel—R
Life Cycle Books—R
Liguori Publications
Lillenas
Logion Press
Longwood—R
Lowenbrown Publishing
Lutterworth Press
McDougal Publishing—R
Multnomah
New Leaf Press—R
Novalis—R
Open Court—R
Oregon Catholic Press—R
Oxford University
P & R Publishing
Paragon House—R
Paulist Press
Perigee Books
Pickwick Publications—R
Pilgrim Press
Promise Publishing
Quintessential Books—R
Read 'N Run—R
Regnery—R
Resource Publications
Review and Herald
Rising Star Press
St. Anthony Messenger—R
Sheed & Ward—R
Smyth & Helwys
Spence Publishing
Still Waters Revival—R
Tekna Books
Trinity Foundation—R
Trinity Press Intl.—R
Troista Books
Tyler Press—R
United Church Press
United Church Pub.
Univ/Ottawa Press
Univ Press of America—R
Vital Issues Press—R
Wadsworth—R
Westminster John Knox
Yale Univ Press—R
Zondervan

ETHNIC/CULTURAL

Abingdon Press—R

ACU Press
Alfred Ali Literary—R
Baker Books—R
Beacon Hill Press
Black Forest—R
Broadman & Holman
Canon Press—R
Carey Library, William
Chalice Press
Christian Univ Press—R
Christopher Publishing
College Press—R
Conari Press—R
Concordia
Cross Cultural—R
Doubleday
Editores Betania-Caribe
Encounter Books—R
Facts on File
Friends United Press—R
Gospel Publishing—R
Grace House Press—R
Greenwood Publishing
Guardian Books—R
Guernica Editions—R
Haworth Press—R
Hay House
Hearth Publishing—R
Hensley Publishing
Holy Cross —R
Huntington House—R
InterVarsity Press
Judson Press—R
Kaleidoscope Press—R
Kregel—R
Libros Liguori
Liguori Publications
Lillenas
Living Books for All
Longwood—R
Lowenbrown Publishing
Lutterworth Press
Master Design—R
Messianic Jewish—R
Monument Press
Moody Press
National Baptist—R
New World Library
Oakwood Publications
Oregon Catholic Press—R
Palisades
Pelican Publishing—R
Pilgrim Press
Read 'N Run—R
Review and Herald
Rising Star Press
St. Anthony Messenger—R
Shaw Pub., Harold—R

Standard (few)
Tekna Books
Thirteen Colonies
United Church Press
United Church Pub.
Univ/Ottawa Press
Upper Room Books
VESTA—R
Westminster John Knox
World Bible—R
Zondervan

EVANGELISM/ WITNESSING

ACU Press
Albury Publishing—R
Ambassador-Emerald—R
Baker Books—R
Baptist Pub. House
Bethany House
Brentwood—R
Bridge-Logos
Bristol House—R
Broadman & Holman
Canon Press—R
Chariot Victor
Chosen Books
Christian Publications
Christopher Publishing
Church Growth Inst.
City Bible Publishing
Concordia
Crossway Books
CSS Publishing
DCTS Publishing—R
Doubleday
Eden Publishing
Eerdmans Publishing—R
Essence Publishing—R
Fairway Press—R
Faith One
Forward Movement
Friends United Press—R
Gospel Publishing—R
Group's FaithWeaver
Guardian Books—R
HarperSanFrancisco
Hendrickson—R
Horizon House—R
Hunt Publishing, John
Huntington House—R
Impact Christian Books—R
InterVarsity Press
James Russell
Judson Press—R
Kregel—R
Lillenas

Living Books for All
Longwood—R
Lowenbrown Publishing
Lutterworth Press
Master Design—R
Messianic Jewish—R
Moody Press
Multnomah
New Hope—R
New Leaf Press—R
Omega House—R
Openbook—R
P & R Publishing
Providence House—R
Ragged Edge—R
Rainbow/Legacy Press—R
Read 'N Run—R
Review and Herald
Rising Star Press
Rose Publishing
Shaw Pub., Harold—R
Son-Rise
Southern Baptist Press—R
Still Waters Revival—R
TEACH Services—R
Tekna Books
Toccoa Falls
Tyler Press—R
United Church Press
Vital Issues Press—R
West Coast Paradise—R
Zondervan

EXEGESIS

AMG Publishers—R
Bridge-Logos
Concordia
Doubleday
Eerdmans Publishing—R
Essence Publishing—R
Guardian Books—R
HarperSanFrancisco
Hendrickson—R
Holy Cross—R
Kregel—R
Longwood—R
Lutterworth Press
Master Design—R
McDougal Publishing—R
Monument Press
Oregon Catholic Press—R
Pickwick Publications—R
Read 'N Run —R
Review and Herald
Tekna Books
Westminster John Knox
Wood Lake Books—R

EXPOSÉS

Brentwood—R
Christian Publications
Encounter Books—R
Frederick Fell—R
Guardian Books—R
Huntington House—R
Kregel—R
Longwood—R
Open Court—R
Promise Publishing
Read 'N Run —R
Southern Baptist Press—R
Trinity Foundation—R
Tyler Press—R
Vital Issues Press—R

FAITH

ACTA Publications
Alba House—R
Ambassador-Emerald—R
Bridge-Logos
City Bible Publishing
Conari Press—R
Daybreak Books
Editores Betania-Caribe
Electric Works—R
Essence Publishing—R
Faith One
Forward Movement
Grace House Press—R
Greenwood Publishing
Guardian Books—R
Hensley Publishing—R
James Russell
Jireh Publishing
Kregel—R
Lillenas
Longwood—R
Loyola Press
Lutterworth Press
Master Design—R
McDougal Publishing—R
Novalis—R
Oregon Catholic Press—R
Paragon House—R
Promise Publishing
Providence House—R
Quintessential Books—R
Read 'N Run —R
Review and Herald
TEACH Services—R
Trinity Foundation—R
Upper Room Books
West Coast Paradise—R
Westminster John Knox

WhiteStone Circle
WinePress—R

FAMILY LIFE

ACTA Publications
ACU Press
Albury Publishing—R
Ambassador-Emerald—R
Baker Books—R
Baptist Pub. House
Beacon Hill Press
Bethany House
Black Forest—R
Blue Dolphin
Brentwood—R
Bridge-Logos
Broadman & Holman
Canon Press—R
Chalice Press
Chariot Victor
Christian Publications
Christopher Publishing
City Bible Publishing
College Press—R
Compradore
Conari Press—R
Concordia
Crossroad Publishing—R
Crossway Books
CSS Publishing
Daybreak Books
DCTS Publishing—R
Dimensions for Living—R
Eden Publishing
Eerdmans Publishing—R
Electric Works—R
Essence Publishing—R
Fairway Press—R
Focus Publishing
Gospel Publishing—R
Grace House Press—R
Guardian Books—R
Haworth Press—R
Hay House
Hensley Publishing—R
Holiday House
Honor Books
Howard Publishing
Huntington House—R
InterVarsity Press
Judson Press—R
Kregel—R
Libros Liguori
Life Cycle Books—R
Lightwave Publishing
Liguori Publications
Living Books for All

Longwood—R
Lowenbrown Publishing
Loyola Press
Lutterworth Press
McDougal Publishing—R
Moody Press
Multnomah
New City Press—R
New Hope—R
New Leaf Press—R
New World Library
Openbook—R
Our Sunday Visitor—R
P & R Publishing
Paragon House—R
Pauline Books
Pelican Publishing—R
Perigee Books
Peter Pauper Press
Promise Publishing
Providence House—R
Quintessential Books—R
Ragged Edge—R
Rainbow/Legacy Press—R
RBC Publishing
Read 'N Run—R
Recovery Communications
Revell
Review and Herald
Shaw Pub., Harold—R
Son-Rise
Southern Baptist Press—R
Sower's Press
Spence Publishing
Starburst Publishers
Still Waters Revival—R
Tekna Books
Tyler Press—R
Upper Room Books
Vital Issues Press—R
Wellness
West Coast Paradise—R
Windflower—R
Wood Lake Books—R
Zondervan

FICTION: ADULT/ RELIGIOUS

Ambassador Books
Ambassador House
America House
AMG Publishers—R
Baker Books—R
Barbour Publishing
Bethany House
Black Forest—R
Blue Dolphin

Bookwrights Press
Bridge Resources
Broadman & Holman
Canon Press—R
CERDIC Publications
Christopher Publishing
Cladach Publishing
Compradore
Creation House
Cross Cultural—R
Crossway Books
CSS Publishing
Doubleday
Dry Bones Press—R
Eerdmans Publishing—R
Electric Works—R
Essence Publishing—R
Frederick Fell—R
Friends United Press—R
Genesis Publishing
Guardian Books—R
Guernica Editions—R
Hay House
HeartQuest
Hearth Publishing—R
Heartsong Presents
Horizon House—R
Huntington House—R
James Russell
Kregel—R
Legacy Press—R
Lowenbrown Publishing
Master Design—R
McDougal Publishing—R
Messianic Jewish—R
Morrow & Company, Wm.
MountainView
Mt. Olive College Press
Multnomah
Noveledit
Pacific Press
Palisades
Pelican Publishing—R
PREP Publishing—R
Promise Press
Read 'N Run—R
Recovery Communications
Revell
Review and Herald
Seniors Market
Shaw Pub., Harold—R
Sligo Press
Starburst Publishers
Troista Books
West Coast Paradise—R
Western Front—R
Windflower—R
WinePress—R

Wood Lake Books—R
Zondervan

FICTION: ADVENTURE

Ambassador House
America House
Barbour Publishing
Bethany House
BJU Press—R
Black Forest—R
Books in Motion
Boyds Mills Press—R
Brentwood—R
Broadman & Holman
Canon Press—R
Christian Ed Pub.
Christopher Publishing
Compradore
Crossway Books
Dry Bones Press—R
Electric Works—R
Essence Publishing—R
Fairway Press—R
Forward Movement
Frederick Fell—R
Guardian Books—R
GROUP Publishing—R
  (juv/teen)
Hearth Publishing—R
HeartQuest
Henry Holt
Huntington House—R
Kaleidoscope Press—R
  (juv)
Legacy Press—R
Lowenbrown Publishing
Lutterworth Press
Master Design—R
Morrow & Co., Wm. (juv)
MountainView
Noveledit
Palisades
PREP Publishing—R
Reader's Digest Children's
Read 'N Run—R
Revell
Seniors Market
Shaw Pub., Harold—R
Southern Baptist Press—R
Toccoa Falls
West Coast Paradise—R
Windflower—R
WinePress—R

FICTION: ALLEGORY

Ambassador House

America House
Black Forest—R
Canon Press—R
Creation House
CSS Publishing
Dry Bones Press—R
Eerdmans Publishing—R
Essence Publishing—R
Fairway Press—R
GROUP Publishing—R
Guardian Books—R
Huntington House—R
Legacy Press—R
Lowenbrown Publishing
Lutterworth Press
Master Design—R
McDougal Publishing—R
Palisades
Reader's Digest Children's
Read 'N Run—R
Wilshire Book—R
WinePress—R
Zondervan

FICTION: BIBLICAL

Ambassador House
AMG Publishers—R
Barbour Publishing
Black Forest—R
Brentwood—R
Canon Press—R
Christopher Publishing
College Press—R
Compradore
Creation House
CSS Publishing
Dry Bones Press—R
Eerdmans/Young Readers
Fairway Press—R
Friends United Press—R
GROUP Publishing—R
Guardian Books—R
HeartQuest
Kregel—R
Legacy Press—R
Lowenbrown Publishing
Lutterworth Press
Master Design—R
McDougal Publishing—R
Messianic Jewish—R
Mt. Olive College Press
Palisades
Pacific Press
PREP Publishing—R
Quintessential Books—R
Ragged Edge—R (juv)
Reader's Digest Children's

Read 'N Run—R
Revell
Review and Herald
Southern Baptist Press—R
Toccoa Falls
Western Front—R
Windflower—R
WinePress—R
Zondervan

FICTION: CONTEMPORARY

America House
Baker Books—R
Barbour Publishing
Bethany House
Black Forest—R
Boyds Mills Press—R
Brentwood—R
Broadman & Holman
Christian Ed Pub.
Christopher Publishing
Creation House
Crossway Books
Dry Bones Press—R
Eerdmans Publishing—R
Essence Publishing—R
Fairway Press—R
Guardian Books—R
HarperSanFrancisco
HeartQuest
Heartsong Presents
Henry Holt
Kindred Productions
Legacy Press—R
Lowenbrown Publishing
Lutterworth Press
MountainView
Mt. Olive College Press
Multnomah
National Baptist—R
Noveledit
One World
Palisades
Pleasant Co.
Promise Press
Quintessential Books—R
Reader's Digest Children's
Read 'N Run—R
Revell
Seniors Market
Shaw Pub., Harold—R
Southern Baptist Press—R
Starburst Publishers
Toccoa Falls
West Coast Paradise—R
Western Front—R

Windflower—R
WinePress—R
Zondervan

FICTION: ETHNIC

Baker Books—R
BJU Press—R
Black Forest—R
Blue Dolphin
CSS Publishing
Eerdmans Publishing—R
Essence Publishing—R
Guardian Books—R
Guernica Editions—R
Henry Holt
Kaleidoscope Press—R (juv)
Legacy Press—R
Living Books for All
Lowenbrown Publishing
Lutterworth Press
Master Design—R
Messianic Jewish—R
One World
Palisades
Pelican Publishing—R
Shaw Pub., Harold—R
WinePress—R

FICTION: FANTASY

Books in Motion
Dry Bones Press—R
Eerdmans Publishing—R
Electric Works—R
Fairway Press—R
Forward Movement
Guardian Books—R
Henry Holt
Legacy Press—R
Lutterworth Press
Master Design—R
Noveledit
Palisades
Read 'N Run —R
Seniors Market
Shaw Pub., Harold—R
WinePress—R
Zondervan

FICTION: FRONTIER

Barbour Publishing
Bethany House
BJU Press—R
Black Forest—R
Books in Motion

Brentwood—R
Christopher Publishing
Dry Bones Press—R
Fairway Press—R
Guardian Books—R
Hearth Publishing—R
James Russell
Kaleidoscope Press—R (juv)
Legacy Press—R
Multnomah
Noveledit
Palisades
Read 'N Run—R
Reconciliation Press (juv)
Revell
Seniors Market, The
Southern Baptist Press—R
Windflower—R
WinePress—R

FICTION: FRONTIER/ROMANCE

Barbour Publishing
Bethany House
Books in Motion
Brentwood—R
Christopher Publishing
Compradore
Dry Bones Press—R
Fairway Press—R
Guardian Books—R
HeartQuest
Heartsong Presents
Hearth Publishing—R
Legacy Press—R
MountainView
Multnomah
Noveledit
Palisades
Proclaim Publishing
Read 'N Run —R
Revell
Seniors Market
Southern Baptist Press—R
Troista Books
WinePress—R
Zondervan

FICTION: HISTORICAL

America House
AMG Publishers—R
Barbour Publishing
Bethany House
BJU Press—R
Black Forest—R

Books in Motion
Boyds Mills Press—R
Brentwood—R
Broadman & Holman
Canon Press—R
Christopher Publishing
Compradore
Crossroad Publishing—R
Crossway Books
Dry Bones Press—R
Eden Publishing
Eerdmans Publishing—R
Eerdmans/Young Readers
Electric Works—R
Essence Publishing—R
Fairway Press—R
Frederick Fell—R
Friends United Press—R
Guardian Books—R
HarperSanFrancisco
Hearth Publishing—R
HeartQuest
Henry Holt
Holiday House
Horizon House—R
James Russell
Kregel—R
Legacy Press—R
Lowenbrown Publishing
Lutterworth Press
Master Design—R
Misty Hill Press
Moody Press
Morrow & Company, Wm.
MountainView
Multnomah
Noveledit
Palisades
Penguin Putnam (juv)
Pleasant Co.
Quintessential Books—R
Ragged Edge—R (juv)
RBC Publishing
Reader's Digest Children's
Read 'N Run—R
Reconciliation Press (juv)
Revell
Seniors Market
Son-Rise
Southern Baptist Press—R
Troista Books
West Coast Paradise—R
Western Front—R
Windflower—R
WinePress—R
YWAM Publishing—R
Zondervan

FICTION: HISTORICAL/ROMANCE

America House
Barbour Publishing
Bethany House
Books in Motion
Brentwood—R
Broadman & Holman
Christopher Publishing
Compradore
Creation House
Crossway Books
Dry Bones Press—R
Fairway Press—R
Guardian Books—R
HeartQuest
Heartsong Presents
Hearth Publishing—R
Horizon House—R
Kregel—R
Legacy Press—R
MountainView
Multnomah
Noveledit
Palisades
Read 'N Run —R
Revell
Seniors Market
Southern Baptist Press—R
Troista Books
WinePress—R
Zondervan

FICTION: HUMOR

Ambassador House
Barbour Publishing
BJU Press—R
Black Forest—R
Boyds Mills Press—R
Canon Press—R
Christopher Publishing
CSS Publishing
Dry Bones Press—R
Essence Publishing—R
Fairway Press—R
Guardian Books—R
Hearth Publishing—R
Henry Holt
Holiday House
Kaleidoscope Press—R (juv)
Legacy Press—R
Lowenbrown Publishing
Lutterworth Press
Noveledit
Palisades
Penguin Putnam (juv)
RBC Publishing

Reader's Digest Children's
Read 'N Run —R
Revell
Seniors Market
Shaw Pub., Harold—R
West Coast Paradise—R

FICTION: JUVENILE (Ages 8-12)

Ambassador Books
America House
Canon Press—R
Bethany House
BJU Press—R
Black Forest—R
Boyds Mills Press—R
Chariot Books
Compradore
CSS Publishing
Eerdmans/Young Readers
Electric Works—R
Essence Publishing—R
Fairway Press—R
Focus Publishing
Forward Movement
Friends United Press—R
GROUP Publishing—R
Guardian Books—R
Hearth Publishing—R
Henry Holt
HOHM Press
Holiday House
Horizon House—R
Huntington House—R
Kaleidoscope Press—R
Kindred Productions
Lightwave Publishing
Liguori Publications
Lutterworth Press
McDougal Publishing—R
Messianic Jewish—R
Misty Hill Press
Moody Press
Pacific Press
Pelican Publishing—R
Penguin Putnam
RBC Publishing
Reader's Digest Children's
Read 'N Run —R
Reconciliation Press
Toccoa Falls
Waldman House
Windflower—R
WinePress—R
YWAM Publishing—R
Zondervan

FICTION: LITERARY

Ambassador Books
America House
Baker Books—R
Black Forest—R
Broadman & Holman
Boyds Mills Press—R
Canon Press—R
Crane Hill—R
Dry Bones Press—R
Eerdmans Publishing—R
Eerdmans/Young Readers
Guardian Books—R
Guernica Editions—R
James Russell
Legacy Press—R
Lutterworth Press
Morrow & Company, Wm.
Mt. Olive College Press
Multnomah
Noveledit
Palisades
Quintessential Books—R
Read 'N Run —R
Seniors Market
Shaw Pub., Harold—R
Troista Books
West Coast Paradise—R
WinePress—R

FICTION: MYSTERY/ROMANCE

America House
Barbour Publishing
Bethany House
Black Forest—R
Books in Motion
Brentwood—R
Compradore
Dry Bones Press—R
Electric Works—R
Fairway Press—R
Guardian Books—R
HeartQuest
Heartsong Presents
Legacy Press—R
Love Inspired
MountainView
Noveledit
Palisades
Read 'N Run—R
Revell
Seniors Market
Southern Baptist Press—R
WinePress—R
Zondervan

FICTION: MYSTERY/SUSPENSE

America House
Baker Books—R
Barbour Publishing
Bethany House
BJU Press—R
Black Forest—R
Books in Motion
Christian Ed Pub.
Dry Bones Press—R
Eerdmans Publishing—R
Electric Works—R
Essence Publishing—R
Guardian Books—R
Henry Holt
Legacy Press—R
Lowenbrown Publishing
Lutterworth Press
Moody Press
Morrow & Company, Wm.
MountainView
Mt. Olive College Press
Multnomah
Noveledit
Palisades
Platinum Press (reprints)
Promise Press
Quintessential Books—R
RBC Publishing
Read 'N Run—R
Revell
Seniors Market
Shaw Pub., Harold—R
Toccoa Falls
Western Front—R
WinePress—R
Zondervan

FICTION: NOVELLAS

Barbour Publishing
Guardian Books—R
HeartQuest
James Russell
Legacy Press—R
Lutterworth Press
Moody Press
MountainView
Noveledit
Read 'N Run —R
Seniors Market
Tyndale House—R

FICTION: PLAYS

Baker's Plays

Brentwood—R
Bridge Resources
Canon Press—R
CSS Publishing
Eldridge Pub. (& musicals)
Essence Publishing—R
Fairway Press—R
Guardian Books—R
Lillenas
Lowenbrown Publishing
Meriwether—R
Mt. Olive College Press
National Baptist—R
Players Press
Read 'N Run —R
Resource Publications
Southern Baptist Press—R

FICTION: ROMANCE

America House
Barbour Publishing
Bethany House
Compradore
Dry Bones Press—R
Electric Works—R
Fairway Press—R
Guardian Books—R
Hearth Publishing—R
HeartQuest
Heartsong Presents
Legacy Press—R
Love Inspired
Lowenbrown Publishing
Morrow & Company, Wm.
MountainView
Multnomah
Palisades
PREP Publishing—R
Read 'N Run —R
Revell
Seniors Market
WinePress—R

FICTION: SCIENCE FICTION

Black Forest—R
Books in Motion
Dry Bones Press—R
Electric Works—R
Forward Movement
GROUP Publishing—R
Guardian Books—R
Huntington House—R
Legacy Press—R
Lutterworth Press
Master Design—R

Morrow & Company, Wm.
Read 'N Run —R
Seniors Market
Skysong Press
WinePress—R

FICTION: SHORT STORY COLLECTION

Barbour Publishing
Black Forest—R
Canon Press—R
Christopher Publishing
Electric Works—R
Essence Publishing—R
Fairway Press—R
GROUP Publishing—R
Guardian Books—R
Hearth Publishing—R
Kaleidoscope Press—R (juv)
Legacy Press—R
Lowenbrown Publishing
Lutterworth Press
MountainView
Mt. Olive College Press
National Baptist—R
RBC Publishing
Read 'N Run —R
Review and Herald
West Coast Paradise—R

FICTION: TEEN/YOUNG ADULT

Ambassador Books
Bethany House
BJU Press—R
Black Forest—R
Boyds Mills Press—R
Canon Press—R
Compradore
Eerdmans/Young Readers
Electric Works—R
Essence Publishing—R
Fairway Press—R
Focus Publishing
Forward Movement
Friends United Press—R
GROUP Publishing—R
Guardian Books—R
Hearth Publishing—R
Henry Holt
Horizon House—R
Huntington House—R
Legacy Press—R
Lowenbrown Publishing
McDougal Publishing—R
Messianic Jewish—R

MountainView
New Canaan
Noveledit
Palisades
Ragged Edge—R
RBC Publishing
Read 'N Run —R
Reconciliation Press
Review and Herald
Saint Mary's Press—R
Seniors Market
Toccoa Falls
Windflower—R
WinePress—R
YWAM Publishing—R
Zondervan

GAMES/CRAFTS

Concordia
Contemporary Drama Service
Eden Publishing
Educational Ministries
Essence Publishing—R
Gospel Publishing—R
GROUP Publishing—R
Group's FaithWeaver
Guardian Books—R
Harcourt Religion
Hunt Publishing, John
Judson Press—R
Kaleidoscope Press—R
Lightwave Publishing (games)
Longwood—R
Lowenbrown Publishing
Lutterworth Press
Meriwether—R
Messianic Jewish—R
Our Sunday Visitor—R
Perigee Books
Pleasant Co.
Rainbow/Rainbow Books—R
Review and Herald
Shining Star
Standard
Tekna Books
Tyler Press—R
Wood Lake Books—R
Zondervan

GIFT BOOKS

ACTA Publications
Albury Publishing—R
Ambassador Books
Ambassador-Emerald—R
America House
Baker Books—R

Barbour Publishing
Black Forest—R
Blue Mountain Arts
Bridge-Logos
Broadman & Holman
Calligraphy Collection
Chariot Victor
Christian Publications
Conari Press—R
Concordia
Contemporary Drama Service
Countryman, J.
Crane Hill—R
Creation House
Daybreak Books
Dimensions for Living—R
Doubleday
Eden Publishing
Eerdmans Publishing—R (art)
Elim Books
Essence Publishing—R
Grace House Press—R
Garborg's
Genesis
Jenkins Group
Guardian Books—R
Hay House
Hearth Publishing—R
Hensley Publishing—R
Honor Books
Howard Publishing
Hunt Publishing, John
Huntington House—R
Image Craft
Judson Press—R
Kaleidoscope Press—R
Kregel—R
Langmarc
Liguori Publications
Longwood—R
Lowenbrown Publishing
Manhattan Greeting Card
Marlene Moore Studio
Mt. Olive College Press
Multnomah
New Leaf Press—R
Our Sunday Visitor—R
Painted Hearts & Friends
Palisades (romantic)
Peter Pauper Press
Promise Publishing
Providence House—R
RBC Publishing
Shaw Pub., Harold—R
Starburst Publishers
Upper Room Books
Western Front—R
WinePress—R

Zondervan

GROUP STUDY BOOKS

AMG Publishers—R
Baker Books—R
Brentwood—R
Bridge Resources
Chariot Victor
College Press—R
CSS Publishing
Essence Publishing—R
Fairway Press—R
Guardian Books—R
HarperSanFrancisco
Hendrickson—R
Hensley Publishing—R
Innisfree Press
Judson Press—R
Kregel—R
Liguori Publications
Longwood—R
Lutterworth Press
Master Design—R
New Hope—R
New Leaf Press—R
Oregon Catholic Press—R
P & R Publishing
Paradise Research—R
Providence House—R
Ragged Edge—R
Resource Publications
St. Anthony Messenger—R
Sheed & Ward—R
Smyth & Helwys
Southern Baptist Press—R
Standard
Tekna Books
Tyler Press—R
Wood Lake Books—R
Zondervan

HEALING

Alba House—R
Albury Publishing—R
America House
Baker Books—R
Bethany House
Black Forest—R
Blue Dolphin
Brentwood—R
Bridge-Logos
Chosen Books
Christian Publications
Christopher Publishing
City Bible Publishing
Conari Press—R

Crossroad Publishing—R
CSS Publishing
Daybreak Books
Dry Bones Press—R
Eerdmans Publishing—R
Elder Books—R
Essence Publishing—R
Fairway Press—R
Faith One
Forward Movement
Frederick Fell—R
Gilgal
Good Book—R
Gospel Publishing—R
Grace House Press—R
Guardian Books—R
HarperSanFrancisco
Haworth Press—R
Hay House
Hensley Publishing—R
Hunt Publishing, John
Impact Christian Books—R
InterVarsity Press
James Russell
Jireh Publishing
Libros Liguori
Liguori Publications
Living Books for All
Lowenbrown Publishing
Loyola Press
Lutterworth Press
McDougal Publishing—R
Northstone—R
Omega House—R
Oregon Catholic Press—R
OSL Publications—R
Paradise Research—R
Perigee Books
Promise Publishing
Providence House—R
Read 'N Run—R
Recovery Communications
Resource Publications
Rising Star Press
Saint Mary's Press—R
Son-Rise
Southern Baptist Press—R
TEACH Services—R
Tekna Books
Tyler Press—R
United Church Press
United Church Pub.
Upper Room Books
Wood Lake Books—R
Zondervan

HEALTH

Accent Books
Albury Publishing—R
Baker Books—R
Bethany House
Black Forest—R
Blue Dolphin
Brentwood—R
Bridge-Logos
Broadman & Holman
Christopher Publishing
Cladach Publishing
Crossroad Publishing—R
Daybreak Books
Doubleday
Dry Bones Press—R
Eerdmans Publishing—R
Elder Books—R
Essence Publishing—R
Facts on File
Fairway Press—R
Faith One
Forward Movement
Frederick Fell—R
Good Book—R
Greenwood Publishing
Guardian Books—R
HarperSanFrancisco
Haworth Press—R
Hay House
HOHM Press
Hunt Publishing, John
Huntington House—R
Kaleidoscope Press—R
Life Cycle Books—R
Liguori Publications
Longwood—R
Loyola Press
Lutterworth Press
McDougal Publishing—R
New World Library
Northstone—R
Pacific Press
Paradise Research—R
Perigee Books
Promise Publishing
Read 'N Run—R
Recovery Communications
Regnery—R
Review and Herald
Rising Star Press
Rodmell Press
Shaw Pub., Harold—R
Son-Rise
Southern Baptist Press—R
Starburst Publishers
TEACH Services—R

Tekna Books
Tyler Press—R
Univ/Ottawa Press
Upper Room Books
VESTA—R
Vital Issues Press—R
Wellness
West Coast Paradise—R
Yes Intl.
Zondervan

HISTORICAL

Albury Publishing—R
Ambassador Books
Ambassador-Emerald—R
America House
Baylor University Press
Bethany House
Black Forest—R
Brentwood—R
Canon Press—R
Canticle Books—R
Christian Publications
Christian Univ Press—R
Christopher Publishing
Conciliar Press—R
Cornell Univ. Press—R
Crane Hill—R
Cross Cultural—R
Crossroad Publishing—R
Custom Communications
Dimension Books—R
Doubleday
Eerdmans Publishing—R
Electric Works—R
Encounter Books—R
Essence Publishing—R
Facts on File
Friends United Press—R
Geneva Press
Gesher—R
Good Book—R
Greenwood Publishing
Guardian Books—R
Hearth Publishing—R
Holiday House
Holy Cross—R
Hunt Publishing, John
Huntington House—R
Impact Christian Books—R
Inkling Books—R
Intl. Awakening Press—R
Judson Press—R
Kregel—R
Liguori Publications
Longwood—R
Lutterworth Press

Magnus Press—R
Master Design—R
Mercer University Press
Monument Press
Morrow & Company, Wm.
Novalis—R
Oregon Catholic Press—R
Our Sunday Visitor—R
Oxford University
Paradise Research—R
Paragon House—R
Pelican Publishing—R
Pickwick Publications—R
Promise Publishing
Providence House—R
Quintessential Books—R
Quixote Publications
Ragged Edge—R
RBC Publishing
Read 'N Run —R
Regnery—R
St. Anthony Messenger—R
St. Augustine's Press—R
Son-Rise
Southern Baptist Press—R
Still Waters Revival—R
Tekna Books
Thirteen Colonies
Trinity Foundation—R
Tyler Press—R
United Church Pub.
Univ/Ottawa Press
Univ Press of America—R
VESTA—R
Vital Issues Press—R
West Coast Paradise—R
WhiteStone Circle
Windflower—R
World Bible—R

HOMILETICS

Abingdon Press—R
Alba House—R
AMG Publishers—R
Black Forest—R
Bridge-Logos
Chalice Press
Concordia
CSS Publishing
DCTS Publishing—R
Eerdmans Publishing—R
Forward Movement
GROUP Publishing—R
Guardian Books—R
Holy Cross—R
Judson Press—R
Kregel—R

Longwood—R
Lutterworth Press
Master Design—R
Novalis—R
Oregon Catholic Press—R
OSL Publications—R
Our Sunday Visitor—R
Pickwick Publications—R
Tekna Books
Thomas More—R
Univ Press of America—R
Westminster John Knox

HOW-TO

Accent Books
Albury Publishing—R
America House
Baker Books—R
Bethany House
Black Forest—R
Blue Dolphin
Brentwood—R
Bridge-Logos
Broadman & Holman
Christian Publications
Christopher Publishing
Church Growth Inst.
Compradore
Conari Press—R
Daybreak Books
Elder Books—R
Encounter Books—R
Essence Publishing—R
Facts on File
Fairway Press—R
Frederick Fell—R
Gesher—R
Gilgal
Grace House Press—R
Guardian Books—R
Harcourt Religion
Hay House
Hearth Publishing—R
Howard Publishing
Hunt Publishing, John
Huntington House—R
Inkling Books—R
InterVarsity Press
James Russell
Judson Press—R
Kaleidoscope Press—R
Lillenas
Longwood—R
Lowenbrown Publishing
Lutterworth Press
Master Design—R
Meriwether—R

Morrow & Company, Wm.
Mt. Olive College Press
Multnomah
New City Press—R
New Leaf Press—R
O'Connor House
Openbook—R
Oregon Catholic Press—R
Pacific Press
Pauline Books
Perigee Books
Players Press
PREP Publishing—R
Read 'N Run—R
Recovery Communications
Resource Publications
Shaw Pub., Harold—R
Sheed & Ward—R
Son-Rise
Southern Baptist Press—R
Standard
Starburst Publishers
Still Waters Revival—R
Tekna Books
Tyler Press—R
Vital Issues Press—R
West Coast Paradise—R

HUMOR

Albury Publishing—R
Barbour Publishing
Black Forest—R
Blue Dolphin
Brentwood—R
Bridge-Logos
Broadman & Holman
Canon Press—R
Christian Publications
Christopher Publishing
Conari Press—R
CSS Publishing
Dimension Books—R
Eden Publishing
Essence Publishing—R
Fairway Press—R
Forward Movement
Friends United Press—R
Grace House Press—R
Guardian Books—R
Hearth Publishing—R
Hendrickson—R
Holiday House
Honor Books
Howard Publishing
Hunt Publishing, John
InterVarsity Press
James Russell

Judson Press—R
Kaleidoscope Press—R
Langmarc
Liguori Publications
Lillenas
Longwood—R
Lowenbrown Publishing
Loyola Press
Lutterworth Press
Moody Press
New Leaf Press—R
Omega House—R
PREP Publishing—R
RBC Publishing
Read 'N Run —R
Regnery—R
Rising Star Press
Shaw Pub., Harold—R
Southern Baptist Press—R
Tekna Books
Tyler Press—R
Vital Issues Press—R
Zondervan

INSPIRATIONAL

Accent Books
ACU Press
Alba House—R
Albury Publishing—R
Alfred Ali Literary—R
America House
AMG Publishers—R
Baker Books—R
Baptist Pub. House
Barbour Publishing
Beacon Hill Press
Bethany House
Black Forest—R
Blue Dolphin
Brentwood—R
Bridge-Logos
Broadman & Holman
Canticle Books—R
Catholic Book Publishing
Chariot Victor
Christian Publications
Christopher Publishing
Cladach Publishing
Compradore
Conari Press—R
Concordia
Countryman, J.
Crane Hill—R
Cross Cultural—R
Crossroad Publishing—R
CSS Publishing
Daybreak Books

DCTS Publishing—R
Dimensions for Living—R
Doubleday
Elder Books—R
Electric Works—R
Elim Books
Essence Publishing—R
Fairway Press—R
Forward Movement
Frederick Fell—R
Friends United Press—R
Gesher—R
Gilgal
Good Book—R
Gospel Publishing—R
Grace House Press—R
Guardian Books—R
HarperSanFrancisco
Hay House
Hearth Publishing—R
Hendrickson—R
Hensley Publishing—R
Holy Cross—R
Honor Books
Howard Publishing
Hunt Publishing, John
Huntington House—R
ICS Publications—R
Impact Christian Books—R
James Russell
Jireh Publishing
Judson Press—R
Kaleidoscope Press—R
Kindred Productions
Langmarc
Libros Liguori
Liguori Publications
Living Books for All
Longwood—R
Lowenbrown Publishing
Lutterworth Press
Magnus Press—R
Master Design—R
McDougal Publishing—R
Mt. Olive College Press
Multnomah
New Leaf Press—R
New World Library
Novalis—R
Pelican Publishing—R
Perigee Books
Peter Pauper Press
PREP Publishing—R
Promise Publishing
Providence House—R
Ragged Edge—R
Rainbow/Legacy Press—R
RBC Publishing

Read 'N Run—R
Review and Herald
Rising Star Press
St. Anthony Messenger—R
Saint Mary's Press—R
Shaw Pub., Harold—R
Sheed & Ward—R
Smyth & Helwys
Son-Rise
Southern Baptist Press—R
Starburst Publishers
TEACH Services—R
Tekna Books
Thomas More—R
Toccoa Falls
Troista Books
Tyler Press—R
United Church Press
United Church Pub.
Upper Room Books
Vital Issues Press—R
Wellness
Wesleyan Publishing House
West Coast Paradise—R
Westminster John Knox
WhiteStone Circle
Zondervan

LEADERSHIP

Abingdon Press—R
ACU Press
Alban Institute
Albury Publishing—R
Baker Books—R
Baptist Pub. House
Beacon Hill Press
Black Forest—R
Bridge-Logos
Broadman & Holman
Chalice Press
Christian Publications
Christopher Publishing
Church Growth Inst.
City Bible Publishing
Compradore
Concordia
Creation House
Cross Cultural—R
Crossway Books
CSS Publishing
Daybreak Books
DCTS Publishing—R
Electric Works—R
Encounter Books—R
Essence Publishing—R
Frederick Fell—R
Gesher—R

Gospel Publishing—R
Greenwood Publishing
GROUP Publishing—R
Guardian Books—R
Hendrickson—R
Honor Books
Huntington House—R
InterVarsity Press
Judson Press—R
Kregel—R
Liguori Publications
Living Books for All
Logos Productions
Longwood—R
Lowenbrown Publishing
Lutterworth Press
Master Design—R
McDougal Publishing—R
Moody Press
Multnomah
Neibauer Press—R
New Leaf Press—R
Openbook—R
Oregon Catholic Press—R
Paulist Press
Perigee Books
Promise Publishing
Providence House—R
Quintessential Books—R
Rainbow/Legacy Press—R
RBC Publishing
Read 'N Run—R
Standard
Starburst Publishers
Tekna Books
Thomas More—R
Tyler Press—R
United Church Press
Upper Room Books
Vital Issues Press—R
Zondervan

LITURGICAL STUDIES

American Cath. Press—R
Blue Dolphin
Brentwood—R
Canon Press—R
Catholic Book Publishing
Chalice Press
Christian Univ Press—R
Christopher Publishing
Cistercian Publications
Conciliar Press—R
Concordia
Cornell Univ. Press—R
Cross Cultural—R
CSS Publishing

Dry Bones Press—R
Eerdmans Publishing—R
Electric Works—R
Fairway Press—R
Forward Movement
Greenwood Publishing
Guardian Books—R
HarperSanFrancisco
Holy Cross—R
InterVarsity Press
Judson Press—R
Liturgy Training
Lutterworth Press
McDougal Publishing—R
Morehouse—R
Novalis—R
Oregon Catholic Press—R
OSL Publications—R
Oxford University
P & R Publishing
Paulist Press
Pelican Publishing—R
Pickwick Publications—R
Ragged Edge—R
Read 'N Run—R
Resource Publications
Sheed & Ward—R
Southern Baptist Press—R
Tekna Books
Trinity Press Intl.—R
Troista Books
Tyler Press—R
United Church Press
United Church Pub.
Univ Press of America—R
Westminster John Knox
Wood Lake Books—R

MARRIAGE

Alba House—R
Albury Publishing—R
America House
Baker Books—R
Baptist Pub. House
Barbour Publishing
Beacon Hill Press
Bethany House
Black Forest—R
Brentwood—R
Bridge-Logos
Broadman & Holman
Canon Press—R
Chalice Press
Chariot Victor
Conari Press—R
Concordia
Countryman, J.

Crossroad Publishing—R
Crossway Books
CSS Publishing
Dimensions for Living—R
Doubleday
Eden Publishing
Eerdmans Publishing—R
Electric Works—R
Essence Publishing—R
Fairway Press—R
Focus on the Family
Focus Publishing
Forward Movement
Frederick Fell—R
Grace House Press—R
Greenwood Publishing
Guardian Books—R
Haworth Press—R
Hay House
Hensley Publishing—R
Holy Cross—R
Honor Books
Howard Publishing
Huntington House—R
InterVarsity Press
Jireh Publishing
Judson Press—R
Kregel—R
Libros Liguori
Liguori Publications
Lillenas
Living Books for All
Logion Press
Longwood—R
Lowenbrown Publishing
Loyola Press
Lutterworth Press
Master Design—R
McDougal Publishing—R
Meriwether—R
Messianic Jewish—R
Multnomah
New Leaf Press—R
Northfield
Novalis—R
Omega House—R
Openbook—R
Oregon Catholic Press—R
P & R Publishing
Pauline Books
Pelican Publishing—R
Perigee Books
PREP Publishing—R
Promise Publishing
Quintessential Books—R
Ragged Edge—R
Read 'N Run—R
Resource Publications

Revell
Review and Herald
Rising Star Press
St. Anthony Messenger—R
Shaw Pub., Harold—R
Sheed & Ward—R
Southern Baptist Press—R
Sower's Press
Spence Publishing
Standard
Starburst Publishers
Still Waters Revival—R
TEACH Services—R
Tekna Books
Tyler Press—R
Upper Room Books
Vital Issues Press—R
Wood Lake Books—R
Zondervan

MEN'S BOOKS

Albury Publishing—R
Baker Books—R
Baptist Pub. House
Barbour Publishing
Beacon Hill Press
Bethany House
Black Forest—R
Blue Dolphin
Bridge-Logos
Broadman & Holman
Canon Press—R
Chalice Press
Christian Publications
Cladach Publishing
Conari Press—R
Concordia
Crossway Books
CSS Publishing
Daybreak Books
DCTS Publishing—R
Dimensions for Living—R
Essence Publishing—R
Focus on the Family
Gospel Publishing—R
Grace House Press—R
Greenwood Publishing
Guardian Books—R
Hay House
Hendrickson—R
Hensley Publishing—R
Honor Books
Huntington House—R
Inkling Books—R
Judson Press—R
Kregel—R
Liguori Publications

Longwood—R
Lowenbrown Publishing
Loyola Press
Lutterworth Press
Master Design—R
McDougal Publishing—R
Multnomah
New Leaf Press—R
Oregon Catholic Press—R
P & R Publishing
Perigee Books
Pilgrim Press
Promise Publishing
Quintessential Books—R
RBC Publishing
Read 'N Run—R
Resource Publications
Rising Star Press
St. Anthony Messenger—R
Son-Rise
Starburst Publishers
Tekna Books
Thomas More—R
Tyler Press—R
United Church Press
Upper Room Books
Vital Issues Press—R
WhiteStone Circle
Zondervan

MIRACLES

Albury Publishing—R
Ambassador-Emerald—R
America House
Baker Books—R
Barbour Publishing
Black Forest—R
Brentwood—R
Bridge-Logos
Chosen Books
Christian Publications
City Bible Publishing
Conari Press—R
CSS Publishing
Essence Publishing—R
Fairway Press—R
Friends United Press—R
Gospel Publishing—R
Grace House Press—R
HarperSanFrancisco
Hay House
Honor Books
Impact Christian Books—R
James Russell
Living Books for All
Longwood—R
Lowenbrown Publishing

Loyola Press
Lutterworth Press
McDougal Publishing—R
Omega House—R
Our Sunday Visitor—R
Pacific Press
Promise Publishing
Read 'N Run—R
Shaw Pub., Harold—R
Southern Baptist Press—R
Troista Books
Tyler Press—R
United Church Press
Zondervan

MISSIONARY

ACU Press
Albury Publishing—R
Ambassador-Emerald—R
Bethany House
BJU Press—R
Black Forest—R
Brentwood—R
Canon Press—R
Carey Library, William
Christian Publications
Christian Univ Press—R
Christopher Publishing
City Bible Publishing
Cladach Publishing
CSS Publishing
Eden Publishing
Eerdmans Publishing—R
Essence Publishing—R
Fairway Press—R
Friends United Press—R
Gospel Publishing—R
Greenwood Publishing
Guardian Books—R
Horizon House—R
Judson Press—R
Lillenas
Living Books for All
Longwood—R
Lowenbrown Publishing
Lutterworth Press
Master Design—R
McDougal Publishing—R
Messianic Jewish—R
New Hope—R
Novalis—R
Omega House—R
Promise Publishing
Read 'N Run—R
Southern Baptist Press—R
TEACH Services—R
Tekna Books

Troista Books
Tyler Press—R
Vital Issues Press—R
YWAM Publishing—R

MONEY MANAGEMENT

Baker Books—R
Bethany House
Black Forest—R
Blue Dolphin
Brentwood—R
Bridge-Logos
Broadman & Holman
Christopher Publishing
Daybreak Books
Doubleday
Essence Publishing—R
Facts on File
Fairway Press—R
Frederick Fell—R
Gesher—R
Guardian Books—R
Hay House
Hensley Publishing—R
Howard Publishing
Kregel—R
Longwood—R
Lowenbrown Publishing
New Leaf Press—R
Northfield
Perigee Books
Providence House—R
Read 'N Run—R
Regnery—R
Southern Baptist Press—R
Starburst Publishers
Summit Pub. Group—R
Tyler Press—R
Zondervan

MUSIC-RELATED BOOKS

ACU Press
Albury Publishing—R
Ambassador-Emerald—R
American Cath. Press—R
Canon Press—R
Christian Media—R
Christopher Publishing
City Bible Publishing
Contemporary Drama Service
Cornell Univ. Press—R
Dimension Books—R
Essence Publishing—R
Frederick Fell—R
Greenwood Publishing
Guardian Books—R

Hay House
Judson Press—R
Kregel—R
Lillenas
Liturgy Training
Longwood—R
Lowenbrown Publishing
Lutterworth Press
Novalis—R
Oregon Catholic Press—R
OSL Publications—R
Ragged Edge—R
Read 'N Run—R
Standard
Tyler Press—R
United Church Pub.
West Coast Paradise—R
Zondervan

PAMPHLETS

Concordia
Cross Way Pub.
Essence Publishing
Forward Movement
Found/Religious Freedom
Fruit-Bearer Pub.
Good Book
Guardian Books
Huntington House
Intl. Awakening Press
Kindred Productions
Libros Liguori
Liguori Publications
Living Books for All
Longwood
Lowenbrown Publishing
Our Sunday Visitor
Paradise Research
Partnership Book
Read 'N Run
Rose Publishing
St. Anthony Messenger
West Coast Paradise
Word For Word Publishing

PARENTING

ACU Press
Albury Publishing—R
America House
Baker Books—R
Baptist Pub. House
Barbour Publishing
Beacon Hill Press
Bethany House
Black Forest—R
Boys Town Press

Brentwood—R
Bridge-Logos
Broadman & Holman
Canon Press—R
Chalice Press
Chariot Victor
Christian Publications
Christopher Publishing
Cladach Publishing
College Press—R
Conari Press—R
Conciliar Press—R
Concordia
Crossroad Publishing—R
Crossway Books
CSS Publishing
Daybreak Books
Dimensions for Living—R
Eerdmans Publishing—R
Electric Works—R
Elim Books
Encounter Books—R
Essence Publishing—R
Facts on File
Fairway Press—R
Focus on the Family
Focus Publishing
Grace House Press—R
Guardian Books—R
HarperSanFrancisco
Hay House
Hensley Publishing—R
Horizon House—R
Howard Publishing
Huntington House—R
InterVarsity Press
Judson Press—R
Kaleidoscope Press—R
Kregel—R
Lightwave Publishing
Liguori Publications
Living Books for All
Longwood—R
Lutterworth Press
Master Design—R
McDougal Publishing—R
Morehouse—R
Multnomah
New Leaf Press—R
Northfield
Northstone—R
Openbook—R
Our Sunday Visitor—R
P & R Publishing
Pauline Books
Perigee Books
Providence House—R
Quintessential Books—R

Ragged Edge—R
Read 'N Run—R
Revell
Review and Herald
St. Anthony Messenger—R
Shaw Pub., Harold—R
Sheed & Ward—R
Standard
Starburst Publishers
Still Waters Revival—R
Tekna Books
Thomas More—R
Tyler Press—R
United Church Press
Vital Issues Press—R
Zondervan

PASTORS' HELPS

Abingdon Press—R
Alba House—R
Alban Institute
Albury Publishing—R
Ambassador-Emerald—R
AMG Publishers—R
Baker Books—R
Beacon Hill Press
Bethany House
BJU Press—R
Boyd, R.H.
Brentwood—R
Bristol House—R
Broadman & Holman
Canon Press—R
Christian Publications
Christopher Publishing
Church Growth Inst.
City Bible Publishing
Concordia
CSS Publishing
DCTS Publishing—R
Eerdmans Publishing—R
Essence Publishing—R
Fairway Press—R
Geneva Press
Gesher—R
Gospel Publishing—R
GROUP Publishing—R
Guardian Books—R
Harcourt Religion
Haworth Press—R
Hendrickson—R
InterVarsity Press
Judson Press—R
Kregel—R
Living Books for All
Logos Productions
Loizeaux

Longwood—R
Master Design—R
Neibauer Press—R
New Leaf Press—R
Oregon Catholic Press—R
Our Sunday Visitor—R
P & R Publishing
Pastor's Choice
Paulist Press
Providence House—R
Read 'N Run —R
Southern Baptist Press—R
Standard
Starburst Publishers
Tekna Books
Tyler Press—R
United Church Press
Vital Issues Press—R
Wellness
Westminster John Knox
Wood Lake Books—R
Zondervan

PERSONAL EXPERIENCE

America House
Barbour Publishing
Black Forest—R
Brentwood—R
Chicken Soup Books
Cladach Publishing
Conari Press—R
Daybreak Books
Dry Bones Press—R
Eden Publishing
Eerdmans Publishing—R
Essence Publishing—R
Fairway Press—R
Forward Movement
Friends United Press—R
Gesher—R
Gilgal
Grace House Press—R
Guardian Books—R
Hay House
Hensley Publishing—R
Honor Books
Huntington House—R
Innisfree Press
Libros Liguori
Living Books for All
Longwood—R
Lowenbrown Publishing
Master Design—R
McDougal Publishing—R
Omega House—R
Openbook—R
Perigee Books

Promise Publishing
Providence House—R
RBC Publishing
Read 'N Run—R
Rising Star Press
Shaw Pub., Harold—R
Son-Rise
Southern Baptist Press—R
Starburst Publishers
TEACH Services—R
Tekna Books
Thomas More—R
Tyler Press—R
United Church Press
VESTA—R
Vital Issues Press—R
West Coast Paradise—R
Zondervan

PERSONAL GROWTH

Alfred Ali Literary—R
Ambassador-Emerald—R
America House
Barbour Publishing
Broadman & Holman
Canticle Books—R
Chariot Victor
City Bible Publishing
Conari Press—R
Countryman, J.
Creative Bound
CSS Publishing
Daybreak Books
DCTS Publishing—R
Eden Publishing
Eerdmans Publishing—R
Essence Publishing—R
Forward Movement
Gesher—R
Grace House Press—R
Guardian Books—R
HarperSanFrancisco
Hay House
Hensley Publishing—R
Holy Cross—R
Innisfree Press
InterVarsity Press
James Russell
Judson Press—R
Liguori Publications
Living Books for All
Longwood—R
Magnus Press—R
Master Design—R
McDougal Publishing—R
Multnomah
Northstone—R

OSL Publications—R
Paragon House—R
Pelican Publishing—R
Perigee Books
Providence House—R
RBC Publishing
Read 'N Run —R
Review and Herald
Rising Star Press
Shaw Pub., Harold—R
Starburst Publishers
Tekna Books
Thomas More—R
Troista Books
United Church Pub.
Wilshire Book—R

PERSONAL RENEWAL

Alfred Ali Literary—R
America House
Baker Books—R
Bethany House
Black Forest—R
Blue Dolphin
Chosen Books
Christian Publications
Christopher Publishing
Countryman, J.
Creation House
CSS Publishing
Daybreak Books
Eerdmans Publishing—R
Essence Publishing—R
Forward Movement
Friends United Press—R
Gesher—R
Guardian Books—R
Haworth Press—R
Hay House
Impact Christian Books—R
Intl. Awakening Press—R
James Russell
Judson Press—R
Libros Liguori
Liguori Publications
Living Books for All
Longwood—R
Master Design—R
McDougal Publishing—R
Multnomah
Omega House—R
OSL Publications—R
Perigee Books
Promise Publishing
Providence House—R
Read 'N Run—R
Review and Herald

Rising Star Press
Shaw Pub., Harold—R
Tekna Books
Thomas More—R
Troista Books
Tyler Press—R
United Church Pub.
Zondervan

PHILOSOPHY

ACU Press
America House
Black Forest—R
Brentwood—R
Canon Press—R
Christopher Publishing
Conari Press—R
Cornell Univ. Press—R
Cross Cultural—R
Crossroad Publishing—R
CSS Publishing
Doubleday
Eerdmans Publishing—R
Essence Publishing—R
Fairway Press—R
Found/Religious Freedom
Friends United Press—R
Genesis Publishing
Gesher—R
Grace House Press—R
Greenwood Publishing
Guardian Books—R
Hay House
Hendrickson—R
Huntington House—R
Inkling Books—R
Longwood—R
Lutterworth Press
Master Design—R
Mercer University Press
Mt. Olive College Press
Novalis—R
Open Court—R
Oxford University
Paragon House—R
Paulist Press
Promise Publishing
Quintessential Books—R
Read 'N Run—R
Regnery—R
Rising Star Press
St. Augustine's Press—R
Still Waters Revival—R
Tekna Books
Trinity Foundation—R
Univ/Ottawa Press
Univ Press of America—R

VESTA—R
Vital Issues Press—R
Wadsworth—R
Yale Univ Press—R
Zondervan

PHOTOGRAPHS (FOR COVERS)

Black Forest
Bridge-Logos
Canadian Institute
Carey Library, William
Christian Ed. Publishers
Church Growth Inst.
Cistercian Publications
City Bible Publishing
Conari Press
Conciliar Press
Daybreak Books
Encounter Books
Essence Publishing
Grace House Press
Guardian Books
Guernica Editions
Harcourt Religion
Innisfree Press
Jireh Publishing
Longwood
Master Design
McDougal Publishing
Neibauer Press
Omega House
Pelican Publishing
Players Press
Quintessential Books
Read 'N Run
Review and Herald
Rising Star Press
St. Anthony Messenger
TEACH Services
Touch Publications
Trinity Foundation
Troista Books
West Coast Paradise
WhiteStone Circle
Wilshire Book
Windflower

POETRY

Black Forest—R
Bookwrights Press
Boyds Mills Press—R
Brentwood—R
Canon Press—R
Christopher Publishing
Cladach Publishing

Compradore
Cross Cultural—R
Cross Way Pub.
CSS Publishing
Dry Bones Press—R
Electric Works—R
Essence Publishing—R
Fairway Press—R
Focus Publishing
Greenwood Publishing
Guardian Books—R
Guernica Editions—R
Image Books—R
Jireh Publishing
Longwood—R
Lowenbrown Publishing
Lutterworth Press
Morrow & Company, Wm.
Mt. Olive College Press
Poets Cove Press
Providence House—R
RBC Publishing
Read 'N Run—R
Southern Baptist Press—R
Tyler Press—R
VESTA—R
Vital Issues Press—R
West Coast Paradise—R
WhiteStone Circle
Windflower—R

POLITICAL

Ambassador House
Baylor University Press
Black Forest—R
Brentwood—R
Canadian Institute—R
Canon Press—R
Christopher Publishing
Cross Cultural—R
Electric Works—R
Encounter Books—R
Essence Publishing—R
Greenwood Publishing
Guardian Books—R
Huntington House—R
Inkling Books—R
Judson Press—R
Longwood—R
Lowenbrown Publishing
Lutterworth Press
Mercer University Press
Monument Press
Open Court—R
Pilgrim Press
Promise Publishing
Quintessential Books—R

RBC Publishing
Read 'N Run—R
Regnery—R
Rising Star Press
Sligo Press
Spence Publishing
Still Waters Revival—R
Trinity Foundation—R
Tyler Press—R
United Church Pub.
Univ Press of America—R
Vital Issues Press—R
Zondervan

PRAYER

ACU Press
Alba House—R
Albury Publishing—R
Ambassador-Emerald—R
American Cath. Press—R
Baker Books—R
Barbour Publishing
Beacon Hill Press
Bethany House
Black Forest—R
Brentwood—R
Bridge-Logos
Bristol House—R
Broadman & Holman
Catholic Book Publishing
Chariot Victor
Chosen Books
Christian Publications
City Bible Publishing
Cladach Publishing
Concordia
Countryman, J.
Creation House
Crossroad Publishing—R
CSS Publishing
Daybreak Books
Doubleday
Eden Publishing
Eerdmans Publishing—R
Essence Publishing—R
Fairway Press—R
Faith One
Forward Movement
Friends United Press—R
Gesher—R
Good Book—R
Gospel Publishing—R
Guardian Books—R
Harcourt Religion
HarperSanFrancisco
Hay House
Hendrickson—R

Hensley Publishing—R
Holy Cross—R
Howard Publishing
ICS Publications—R
Impact Christian Books—R
InterVarsity Press
Jireh Publishing
Judson Press—R
Kregel—R
Libros Liguori
Lightwave Publishing
Liguori Publications
Lillenas
Liturgy Training
Living Books for All
Longwood—R
Lowenbrown Publishing
Lutterworth Press
Master Design—R
McDougal Publishing—R
Moody Press
Morehouse—R
Multnomah
New Hope—R
New Leaf Press—R
Northstone—R
Novalis—R
Omega House—R
OSL Publications—R
Our Sunday Visitor—R
P & R Publishing
Paraclete Press—R
Pauline Books
Promise Publishing
Rainbow/Legacy Press—R
Read 'N Run—R
Resource Publications
Revell
Review and Herald
Rose Publishing
St. Anthony Messenger—R
Saint Mary's Press—R
Shaw Pub., Harold—R
Sheed & Ward—R
Smyth & Helwys
Southern Baptist Press—R
Standard
Starburst Publishers
Still Waters Revival—R
TEACH Services—R
Tekna Books
Toccoa Falls
Troista Books
Tyler Press—R
United Church Press
United Church Pub.
Upper Room Books
Vital Issues Press—R

Wesleyan Publishing
  House
WhiteStone Circle
Wood Lake Books—R
World Bible—R
Zondervan

PROPHECY

Albury Publishing—R
Ambassador-Emerald—R
Ambassador House
Black Forest—R
Blue Dolphin
Brentwood—R
Bridge-Logos
City Bible Publishing
Creation House
CSS Publishing
Essence Publishing—R
Fairway Press—R
Gospel Publishing—R
Greenwood Publishing
Guardian Books—R
HarperSanFrancisco
Kregel—R
Living Books for All
Longwood—R
Lutterworth Press
Master Design—R
Messianic Jewish—R
Multnomah
New Leaf Press—R
Omega House—R
Read 'N Run —R
Review and Herald
Rose Publishing
Small Helm Press
Southern Baptist Press—R
Starburst Publishers
Still Waters Revival—R
Troista Books
Tyler Press—R
Vital Issues Press—R
Western Front—R
Zondervan

PSYCHOLOGY

Alba House—R
America House
Baker Books—R
Bethany House
Black Forest—R
Blue Dolphin
Boys Town Press
Brentwood—R
Christopher Publishing

Circulus Publishing
Conari Press—R
Crossroad Publishing—R
Daybreak Books
Dimension Books—R
Eerdmans Publishing—R
Elder Books—R
Essence Publishing—R
Fairway Press—R
Gesher—R
Grace House Press—R
Greenwood Publishing
Guardian Books—R
HarperSanFrancisco
Haworth Press—R
Hay House
Huntington House—R
Innisfree Press
InterVarsity Press
Judson Press—R
Liguori Publications
Longwood—R
Lowenbrown Publishing
Lutterworth Press
McDougal Publishing—R
Open Court—R
Oxford University
Paragon House—R
Perigee Books
PREP Publishing—R
Quintessential Books—R
Read 'N Run—R
Recovery Communications
Religious Education
Revell
Shaw Pub., Harold—R
Southern Baptist Press—R
Starburst Publishers
Thomas More—R
Troista Books
Tyler Press—R
Univ/Ottawa Press
Univ Press of America—R
Vital Issues Press—R
Wilshire Book—R
Yale Univ Press—R
Zondervan

RECOVERY BOOKS

America House
Baker Books—R
Black Forest—R
Christopher Publishing
Creative Bound
Crossroad Publishing—R
CSS Publishing
Eden Publishing

Elder Books—R
Essence Publishing—R
Gilgal Publications
Good Book—R
Guardian Books—R
Haworth Press—R
Huntington House—R
Jireh Publishing
Judson Press—R
Libros Liguori
Liguori Publications
Longwood—R
Lowenbrown Publishing
McDougal Publishing—R
Openbook—R
Our Sunday Visitor—R
Perigee Books
PREP Publishing—R
Read 'N Run —R
Recovery Communications
Resource Publications
Rose Publishing
RPI Publishing
Tekna Books
Troista Books
Tyler Press—R
Upper Room Books
Wilshire Book—R
Zondervan

REFERENCE BOOKS

Abingdon Press—R
Ambassador-Emerald—R
AMG Publishers—R
Baker Books—R
Baylor University Press
Bethany House
Brentwood—R
Bridge-Logos
Christian Univ Press—R
Cross Cultural—R
Crossroad Publishing—R
CSS Publishing
Dry Bones Press—R
Eerdmans Publishing—R
Fairway Press—R
Frederick Fell—R
Good Book—R
Greenwood Publishing
Guardian Books—R
Hendrickson—R
Hunt Publishing, John
Impact Christian Books—R
Intl. Awakening Press—R
Judson Press—R
Kaleidoscope Press—R
Kregel—R

Lightwave Publishing
Liguori Publications
Living Books for All
Loizeaux
Longwood—R
Lowenbrown Publishing
Lutterworth Press
Master Design—R
McDougal Publishing—R
Novalis—R
Oregon Catholic Press—R
Oxford University
P & R Publishing
Pelican Publishing—R
Paragon House—R
Perigee Books
Ragged Edge—R
Read 'N Run —R
Religious Education
Scarecrow Press
Southern Baptist Press—R
Still Waters Revival—R
Tekna Books
Troista Books
Tyler Press—R
Univ/Ottawa Press
VESTA—R
World Bible—R
Zondervan

RELIGION

Abingdon Press—R
ACTA Publications
ACU Press
Alba House—R
Alfred Ali Literary—R
Amato Publications, Frank
Ambassador Books
Ambassador-Emerald—R
America House
Baker Books—R
Bethany House
BIBAL Press
Black Forest—R
Blue Dolphin
Bookwrights Press
Boys Town Press
Brentwood—R
Canon Press—R
CERDIC Publications
Chariot Victor
Christian Publications
Christopher Publishing
Circulus Publishing
Conari Press—R
Concordia
Cornell Univ. Press—R

Cross Cultural—R
Crossroad Publishing—R
Crossway Books
CSS Publishing
Dimension Books—R
Doubleday
Eerdmans Publishing—R
Eerdmans/Young Readers
Electric Works—R
Encounter Books—R
Essence Publishing—R
Facts on File
Fairway Press—R
Focus Publishing
Forward Movement
Freestar Press
Friends United Press—R
Genesis Publishing
Good Book—R
Grace House Press—R
Greenwood Publishing
Guardian Books—R
HarperSanFrancisco
Hay House
Hendrickson—R
HOHM Press
Holy Cross—R
Honor Books
Hunt Publishing, John
Huntington House—R
Impact Christian Books—R
James Russell
Jenkins Group
Judson Press—R
Kregel—R
Liguori Publications
Lillenas
Liturgy Training
Longwood—R
Lowenbrown Publishing
Lutterworth Press
Master Design—R
McDougal Publishing—R
Mercer University Press
More Press, Thomas
Morrow & Co, Wm.
Mt. Olive College Press
New Hope—R
Northstone—R
Novalis—R
Oakwood Publications
O'Connor House
Open Court—R
Oregon Catholic Press—R
OSL Publications—R
Our Sunday Visitor—R
Oxford University
P & R Publishing

Paraclete Press—R
Paragon House—R
Paulist Press
Pelican Publishing—R
Pilgrim Press
Providence House—R
Quixote Publications
Ragged Edge—R
Read 'N Run —R
Reflection Publishing
Regnery—R
Religious Education
Review and Herald
Rising Star Press
Rodmell Press
Rose Publishing
RPI Publishing
St. Augustine's Press—R
Saint Mary's Press—R
Scarecrow Press
Sheed & Ward—R
Sligo Press
Smyth & Helwys
Southern Baptist Press—R
Spence Publishing
Still Waters Revival—R
Success Systems
Tekna Books
Thirteen Colonies
Thomas More—R
Trinity Press Intl.—R
Troista Books
Tyler Press—R
United Church Press
United Church Pub.
Univ/Ottawa Press
Univ Press of America—R
Upper Room Books
VESTA—R
Vital Issues Press—R
Wadsworth Publishing
Wesleyan Publishing House
Westminster John Knox
Wood Lake Books—R
Yale Univ Press—R
Yes Intl.
Zondervan

RETIREMENT

Baker Books—R
Bethany House
Black Forest—R
Broadman & Holman
Chalice Press
Christian Publications
College Press—R
Eden Publishing

Elder Books—R
Essence Publishing—R
Fairway Press—R
Greenwood Publishing
Guardian Books—R
Judson Press—R
Liguori Publications
Longwood—R
Northstone—R
Read 'N Run —R
Regnery—R
Southern Baptist Press—R
Starburst Publishers
Tekna Books
Tyler Press—R
United Church Pub.
Zondervan

SCHOLARLY

Baker Books—R
Baylor University Press
Black Forest—R
Canon Press—R
Cistercian Publications
Concordia
Cross Cultural—R
Crossroad Publishing—R
Crossway Books
Doubleday
Dry Bones Press—R
Eerdmans Publishing—R
Encounter Books—R
Essence Publishing—R
Greenwood Publishing
Guardian Books—R
Haworth Press—R
Holy Cross—R
Huntington House—R
Impact Christian Books—R
Inkling Books—R
Intl. Awakening Press—R
Kregel—R
Logion Press
Longwood—R
Lutterworth Press
Master Design—R
Mercer University Press
Messianic Jewish—R
Monument Press
Novalis—R
Oregon Catholic Press—R
OSL Publications—R
Our Sunday Visitor—R
Oxford University
P & R Publishing
Paragon House—R
Paulist Press

Pickwick Publications—R
Pilgrim Press
Ragged Edge—R
Read 'N Run—R
Religious Education
Scarecrow Press
Shaw Pub., Harold—R
Smyth & Helwys
Tekna Books
Toccoa Falls
Trinity Foundation—R
Trinity Press Intl.—R
Troista Books
Tyler Press—R
Univ/Ottawa Press
Univ Press of America—R
VESTA—R
Vital Issues Press—R
Zondervan

SCIENCE

Black Forest—R
Boyds Mills Press—R
Christopher Publishing
Cornell Univ. Press—R
Cross Cultural—R
Crossroad Publishing—R
Eerdmans Publishing—R
Electric Works—R
Facts on File
Freestar Press
Guardian Books—R
Huntington House—R
Inkling Books—R
Kaleidoscope Press—R
Longwood—R
Lutterworth Press
Master Books
Northstone—R
Open Court—R
Oxford University
Promise Publishing
Read 'N Run—R
Regnery—R
Summit Pub. Group—R
Tekna Books
Trinity Foundation—R
Troista Books
Tyler Press—R
Univ/Ottawa Press
Vital Issues Press—R
Zondervan

SELF-HELP

Accent Books
Albury Publishing—R

Alfred Ali Literary—R
Ambassador Books
America House
Black Forest—R
Blue Dolphin
Bridge-Logos
Christian Publications
Christopher Publishing
Compradore
Conari Press—R
Creative Bound
Crossroad Publishing—R
Daybreak Books
DCTS Publishing—R
Dimensions for Living—R
Doubleday
Eden Publishing
Elim Books
Encounter Books—R
Essence Publishing—R
Facts on File
Fairway Press—R
Gesher—R
Good Book—R
Grace House Press—R
Guardian Books—R
HarperSanFrancisco
Hay House
Howard Publishing
Huntington House—R
Innisfree Press
James Russell
Jireh Publishing
Judson Press—R
Libros Liguori
Liguori Publications
Longwood—R
Lowenbrown Publishing
McDougal Publishing—R
Mt. Olive College Press
New World Library
Novalis—R
O'Connor House
Openbook—R
Pacific Press
Paradise Research—R
Perigee Books
Peter Pauper Press
Quixote Publications
Ragged Edge—R
Read 'N Run—R
Revell
RPI Publishing
Shaw Pub., Harold—R
Sheed & Ward—R
Starburst Publishers
Summit Pub. Group—R
Tekna Books

Thomas More—R
Troista Books
United Church Pub.
Wilshire Book—R
Zondervan

SENIOR ADULT CONCERNS

Baker Books—R
Bethany House
Black Forest—R
Broadman & Holman
Chalice Press
Christian Publications
Christopher Publishing
Concordia
Eden Publishing
Essence Publishing—R
Facts on File
Fairway Press—R
Forward Movement
Gospel Publishing—R
Guardian Books—R
Haworth Press—R
Horizon House—R
Howard Publishing
Huntington House—R
Judson Press—R
Liguori Publications
Longwood—R
Lowenbrown Publishing
Lutterworth Press
New Leaf Press—R
Oregon Catholic Press—R
Perigee Books
Promise Publishing
Providence House—R
Read 'N Run—R
Shaw Pub., Harold—R
Southern Baptist Press—R
Tekna Books
Tyler Press—R
United Church Pub.
Windflower—R
Zondervan

SERMONS

Alba House—R
Albury Publishing—R
Ambassador-Emerald—R
AMG Publishers—R
Brentwood—R
Church Growth Inst.
CSS Publishing
DCTS Publishing—R
Doubleday
Eerdmans Publishing—R

Fairway Press—R
GROUP Publishing—R
Guardian Books—R
Hendrickson—R
James Russell
Judson Press—R
Kregel—R
Liturgical Press
Longwood—R
Lutterworth Press
Master Design—R
Novalis—R
Oregon Catholic Press—R
Pastor's Choice
Proclaim Publishing
Read 'N Run —R
Southern Baptist Press—R
Still Waters Revival—R
Tekna Books
Troista Books
Tyler Press—R
United Church Press
United Church Pub.
Vital Issues Press—R
Westminster John Knox
Wood Lake Books—R

SINGLES ISSUES

Abingdon Press—R
Albury Publishing—R
America House
Baker Books—R
Barbour Publishing
Bethany House
Brentwood—R
Bridge-Logos
Broadman & Holman
Christian Publications
Daybreak Books
Essence Publishing—R
Gospel Publishing—R
Guardian Books—R
Horizon House—R
Huntington House—R
InterVarsity Press
Judson Press—R
Kregel—R
Liguori Publications
Lillenas
Longwood—R
Lowenbrown Publishing
McDougal Publishing—R
New Leaf Press—R
Oregon Catholic Press—R
Perigee Books
Rainbow/Legacy Press—R
Read 'N Run—R

Review and Herald
Rising Star Press
Tekna Books
Tyler Press—R
Vital Issues Press—R
Zondervan

SOCIAL JUSTICE ISSUES

Baker Books—R
Bethany House
Black Forest—R
Brentwood—R
Canon Press—R
Chalice Press
Cross Cultural—R
CSS Publishing
DCTS Publishing—R
Eden Publishing
Eerdmans Publishing—R
Electric Works—R
Encounter Books—R
Essence Publishing—R
Found/Religious Freedom
Frederick Fell—R
Greenwood Publishing
Guardian Books—R
Haworth Press—R
Huntington House—R
Inkling Books—R
Innisfree Press
Judson Press—R
Libros Liguori
Life Cycle Books—R
Liturgy Training
Longwood—R
Lowenbrown Publishing
Lutterworth Press
New World Library
Northstone—R
Novalis—R
Openbook—R
Oregon Catholic Press—R
Oxford University
Paulist Press
Pilgrim Press
Quintessential Books—R
Ragged Edge—R
Read 'N Run—R
Regnery—R
Rising Star Press
Shaw Pub., Harold—R
Sheed & Ward—R
Still Waters Revival—R
Tekna Books
Troista Books
Tyler Press—R
United Church Press

United Church Pub.
Univ/Ottawa Press
Univ Press of America—R
Vital Issues Press—R
Wood Lake Books—R
Zondervan

SOCIOLOGY

Baker Books—R
Bethany House
Black Forest—R
Brentwood—R
Christopher Publishing
Cross Cultural—R
Electric Works—R
Encounter Books—R
Essence Publishing—R
Greenwood Publishing
Guardian Books—R
Haworth Press—R
Hay House
Huntington House—R
InterVarsity Press
Judson Press—R
Longwood—R
Lowenbrown Publishing
Lutterworth Press
Oxford University
Paragon House—R
Paulist Press
Pelican Publishing—R
RBC Publishing
Read 'N Run—R
Rising Star Press
Still Waters Revival—R
Tekna Books
Troista Books
Univ/Ottawa Press
Univ Press of America—R
Vital Issues Press—R

SPIRITUAL GIFTS

ACTA Publications
Bridge-Logos
City Bible Publishing
Daybreak Books
Editores Betania-Caribe
Essence Publishing—R
Faith One
Forward Movement
Guardian Books—R
Hensley Publishing—R
Kregel—R
Living Books for All
Longwood—R
Lutterworth Press

Master Design—R
McDougal Publishing—R
Omega House—R
Oregon Catholic Press—R
Promise Publishing
Read 'N Run —R
Review and Herald
Rising Star Press
TEACH Services—R
Troista Books
Upper Room Books
WinePress—R

SPIRITUALITY

Abingdon Press—R
ACTA Publications
ACU Press
Alba House—R
Alfred Ali Literary—R
Amato Publications, Frank
Ambassador Books
Ambassador-Emerald—R
America House
Baker Books—R
Bethany House
Black Forest—R
Blue Dolphin
Bookwrights Press
Boys Town Press
Brentwood—R
Broadman & Holman
Canticle Books—R
Chalice Press
Chosen Books
Christian Publications
Christopher Publishing
Circulus Publishing
Conari Press—R
Countryman, J.
Cross Cultural—R
Crossroad Publishing—R
Crossway Books
CSS Publishing
Daybreak Books
DCTS Publishing—R
Dimension Books—R
Doubleday
Dry Bones Press—R
Eerdmans Publishing—R
Elder Books—R
Electric Works—R
Essence Publishing—R
Fairway Press—R
Forward Movement
Found/Religious Freedom
Freestar Press
Friends United Press—R

Gesher—R
Good Book—R
Grace House Press—R
Greenwood Publishing
Guardian Books—R
HarperSanFrancisco
Hay House
Hendrickson—R
HOHM Press
Holy Cross—R
Honor Books
Huntington House—R
Impact Christian Books—R
Innisfree Press
InterVarsity Press
Jenkins Group
Judson Press—R
Kregel—R
Libros Liguori
Liguori Publications
Lillenas
Living Books for All
Longwood—R
Lowenbrown Publishing
Loyola Press
Lutterworth Press
Magnus Press—R
Master Design—R
McDougal Publishing—R
More Press, Thomas
Morehouse—R
Multnomah
New World Library
Northstone—R
Novalis—R
Oakwood Publications
O'Connor House
Omega House—R
Oregon Catholic Press—R
OSL Publications—R
Our Sunday Visitor—R
Oxford University
Paraclete Press—R
Paragon House—R
Pauline Books
Pelican Publishing—R
Perigee Books
Peter Pauper Press
Pilgrim Press
PREP Publishing—R
Promise Publishing
Quintessential Books—R
Quixote Publications
Ragged Edge—R
Rainbow/Legacy Press—R
Read 'N Run—R
Reflection Publishing
Regnery—R

Rising Star Press
Rodmell Press
RPI Publishing
St. Anthony Messenger—R
Saint Mary's Press—R
Shaw Pub., Harold—R
Sheed & Ward—R
Sligo Press
Smyth & Helwys
Southern Baptist Press—R
Success Systems
Tekna Books
Thirteen Colonies
Thomas More—R
Toccoa Falls
Troista Books
Tyler Press—R
United Church Press
United Church Pub.
Vital Issues Press—R
Waldman House
West Coast Paradise—R
Yes Intl.
Westminster John Knox
WhiteStone Circle
Zondervan

SPIRITUAL WARFARE

Albury Publishing—R
Ambassador-Emerald—R
Black Forest—R
Bridge-Logos
Chosen Books
Christian Publications
City Bible Publishing
Creation House
CSS Publishing
Daybreak Books
Eden Publishing
Editores Betania-Caribe
Essence Publishing—R
Gesher—R
Gospel Publishing—R
Guardian Books—R
Hendrickson—R
Huntington House—R
Impact Christian Books—R
InterVarsity Press
Jireh Publishing
Kregel—R
Living Books for All
Longwood—R
Lowenbrown Publishing
Lutterworth Press
Master Design—R
McDougal Publishing—R
Multnomah

Omega House—R
Read 'N Run —R
Rising Star Press
Shaw Pub., Harold—R
Zondervan

SPORTS/RECREATION

Amato Publications, Frank
Ambassador Books
Bridge-Logos
Canon Press—R
Christopher Publishing
Daybreak Books
Essence Publishing—R
Facts on File
Frederick Fell—R
Guardian Books—R
James Russell
Longwood—R
Lutterworth Press
New Leaf Press—R
Openbook—R
Providence House—R
Read 'N Run—R
Rodmell Press
Starburst Publishers
Tekna Books
Tyler Press—R
Zondervan

STEWARDSHIP

Alban Institute
Albury Publishing—R
Baker Books—R
Baptist Pub. House
Black Forest—R
Chalice Press
Christian Publications
Conari Press—R
Creation House
CSS Publishing
Eerdmans Publishing—R
Essence Publishing—R
Gesher—R
Gospel Publishing—R
Grace House Press—R
Guardian Books—R
Hensley Publishing—R
Huntington House—R
Judson Press—R
Kregel—R
Lightwave Publishing
Liguori Publications
Lillenas
Longwood—R
Lowenbrown Publishing

Master Design—R
McDougal Publishing—R
Messianic Jewish—R
Multnomah
Neibauer Press—R
Oregon Catholic Press—R
P & R Publishing
Rainbow/Legacy Press—R
Read 'N Run—R
Review and Herald
Rising Star Press
Shaw Pub., Harold—R
Tekna Books
Tyler Press—R
United Church Pub.
Vital Issues Press—R
Westminster John Knox
Wood Lake Books—R
Zondervan

THEOLOGY

Abingdon Press—R
ACU Press
Alba House—R
Ambassador-Emerald—R
America House
American Cath. Press—R
AMG Publishers—R
Baker Books—R
Bethany House
Black Forest—R
Blue Dolphin
Brentwood—R
Bridge-Logos
Broadman & Holman
Canon Press—R
Canticle Books—R
CERDIC Publications
Chalice Press
Christian Publications
Christian Univ Press—R
Christopher Publishing
City Bible Publishing
Conciliar Press—R
Concordia
Cross Cultural—R
Crossroad Publishing—R
Crossway Books
CSS Publishing
Dimension Books—R
Doubleday
Dry Bones Press—R
Eerdmans Publishing—R
Encounter Books—R
Essence Publishing—R
Fairway Press—R
Forward Movement

Friends United Press—R
Geneva Press
Greenwood Publishing
Guardian Books—R
HarperSanFrancisco
Hay House
Hendrickson—R
Holy Cross—R
Huntington House—R
Impact Christian Books—R
Inkling Books—R
Intl. Awakening Press—R
InterVarsity Press
Judson Press—R
Kregel—R
Liguori Publications
Liturgical Press
Liturgy Training
Loizeaux
Longwood—R
Lutterworth Press
Magnus Press—R
Master Design—R
McDougal Publishing—R
Mercer University Press
Messianic Jewish—R
Morehouse—R
Multnomah
New City Press—R
New Leaf Press—R
Novalis—R
Open Court—R
Oregon Catholic Press—R
OSL Publications—R
Our Sunday Visitor—R
Oxford University
P & R Publishing
Paragon House—R
Paulist Press
Pickwick Publications—R
Pilgrim Press
Promise Publishing
Quintessential Books—R
Ragged Edge—R
Read 'N Run—R
Religious Education
Review and Herald
Rising Star Press
St. Anthony Messenger—R
St. Augustine's Press—R
Shaw Pub., Harold—R (lay)
Sheed & Ward—R
Smyth & Helwys
Southern Baptist Press—R
Still Waters Revival—R
Tekna Books
Trinity Foundation—R
Trinity Press Intl.—R

Troista Books
Tyler Press—R
United Church Press
Univ Press of America—R
Vital Issues Press—R
Westminster John Knox
Wood Lake Books—R
Zondervan

TIME MANAGEMENT

America House
Barbour Publishing
Black Forest—R
Broadman & Holman
Creative Bound
Elim Books
Essence Publishing—R
Forward Movement
Gesher—R
Guardian Books—R
Hensley Publishing—R
Kregel—R
Longwood—R
McDougal Publishing—R
Read 'N Run—R
Shaw Pub., Harold—R
Summit Pub. Group—R
Tekna Books

TRACTS

Essence Publishing
Forward Movement
Fruit-Bearer Pub.
Good News Publishers
Gospel Tract Society
Guardian Books
Intl. Awakening Press
Liguori Publications
Lowenbrown Publishing
Partnership Book
Read 'N Run
Review and Herald
Trinity Foundation
West Coast Paradise
Word For Word Publishing

TRAVEL

Accent Books
Amato Publications, Frank
Black Forest—R
Brentwood—R
Bridge-Logos
Christopher Publishing
Conari Press—R
Eerdmans Publishing—R

Essence Publishing—R
Grace House Press—R
Guardian Books—R
Image Books—R
Liguori Publications
Longwood—R
Lutterworth Press
Mt. Olive College Press
Read 'N Run —R
Tekna Books
United Church Pub.

WOMEN'S ISSUES

Albury Publishing—R
AMG Publishers—R
Baker Books—R
Barbour Publishing
Baylor University Press
Beacon Hill Press
Bethany House
Black Forest—R
Blue Dolphin
Bridge-Logos
Broadman & Holman
Canon Press—R
Chalice Press
Chariot Victor
Christian Publications
Christopher Publishing
Circulus Publishing
City Bible Publishing
Cladach Publishing
Conari Press—R
Cornell Univ. Press—R
Countryman, J.
Creation House
Cross Cultural—R
Crossway Books
Daybreak Books
DCTS Publishing—R
Eerdmans Publishing—R
Elder Books—R
Essence Publishing—R
Facts on File
Fairway Press—R
Focus Publishing
Forward Movement
Gospel Publishing—R
Grace House Press—R
Greenwood Publishing
Guardian Books—R
Guernica Editions—R
HarperSanFrancisco
Haworth Press—R
Hay House
Hearth Publishing—R
Hensley Publishing—R

Holy Cross—R
Honor Books
Horizon House—R
Howard Publishing
Huntington House—R
Inkling Books—R
Innisfree Press
InterVarsity Press
Judson Press—R
Kregel—R
Life Cycle Books—R
Liguori Publications
Lillenas
Longwood—R
Lowenbrown Publishing
Loyola Press
Master Design—R
McDougal Publishing—R
Monument Press
Moody Press
Morehouse—R
Multnomah
New Hope—R
New Leaf Press—R
New World Library
Northstone—R
Openbook—R
Oregon Catholic Press—R
Pacific Press
Paragon House—R
Pelican Publishing—R
Perigee Books
Pilgrim Press
PREP Publishing—R
Promise Publishing
Rainbow/Legacy Press—R
RBC Publishing
Read 'N Run—R
Revell
Rising Star Press
St. Anthony Messenger—R
Shaw Pub., Harold—R
Sheed & Ward—R
Son-Rise
Southern Baptist Press—R
Starburst Publishers
Still Waters Revival—R
Summit Pub. Group—R
Tekna Books
Thomas More—R
Tyler Press—R
United Church Press
Univ/Ottawa Press
Upper Room Books
Vital Issues Press—R
Wood Lake Books—R
Zondervan

WORLD ISSUES

Baker Books—R
Bethany House
Black Forest—R
Blue Dolphin
Bridge-Logos
Carey Library, William
Chalice Press
Christopher Publishing
Cladach Publishing
Conari Press—R
Cross Cultural—R
Encounter Books—R
Essence Publishing—R
Forward Movement
Grace House Press—R
Greenwood Publishing
Guardian Books—R
Guernica Editions—R
Hendrickson—R
Huntington House—R
InterVarsity Press
Kregel—R
Longwood—R
Lowenbrown Publishing
Lutterworth Press
McDougal Publishing—R
Monument Press
New Leaf Press—R
Paragon House—R
Pilgrim Press
Read 'N Run—R
Regnery—R
Shaw Pub., Harold—R
Still Waters Revival—R
Tekna Books
Troista Books
Tyler Press—R
United Church Pub.
VESTA—R
Vital Issues Press—R
Wood Lake Books—R
Zondervan

WORSHIP RESOURCES

Abingdon Press—R
American Cath. Press—R
Art Can Drama—R
Baker Books—R
Bethany House
Catholic Book Publishing
Chalice Press
Christian Publications
City Bible Publishing
Eden Publishing

Educational Ministries
Eerdmans Publishing—R
Essence Publishing—R
Fairway Press—R
Geneva Press
Guardian Books—R
InterVarsity Press
Judson Press—R
Kregel—R
Lillenas
Liturgical Press
Liturgy Training
Logos Productions
Longwood—R
Lowenbrown Publishing
Lutterworth Press
Master Design—R
McDougal Publishing—R
Novalis—R
Oregon Catholic Press—R
OSL Publications—R
Rainbow/Legacy Press—R
Read 'N Run—R
St. Anthony Messenger—R
Sheed & Ward—R
Smyth & Helwys
Standard
Tekna Books
Thomas More—R
Tyler Press—R
United Church Press
United Church Pub.
Vital Issues Press—R
Wood Lake Books—R
Zondervan

WRITING HOW-TO

Black Forest—R
Bridge-Logos
Essence Publishing—R
Fairway Press—R
Guardian Books—R
Lowenbrown Publishing
Perigee Books
Promise Publishing
Shaw Pub., Harold—R
Sheed & Ward—R
Tekna Books
Troista Books
West Coast Paradise—R
Write Now—R

YOUTH BOOKS
(Nonfiction)

Note: Listing denotes books

for 8- to 12-year-olds, junior highs or senior highs. If all three, it will say "all."

Albury Publishing—R (all)
Ambassador-Emerald—R (8-12)
America House (all)
Art Can Drama—R (all)
Baker Books—R (all)
Bethany House (all)
BJU Press—R (8-12/Jr High)
Black Forest—R (all)
Boyds Mills Press—R (8-12/Jr High)
Broadman & Holman (all)
Canon Press—R (all)
Christian Ed Pub. (8-12)
Christian Publications (Jr/Sr High)
Concordia (all)
Contemporary Drama Service
Creation House (Sr High)
CSS Publishing (all)
DCTS Publishing—R (Jr/Sr High)
Eerdmans/Young Readers (all)
Electric Works—R (all)
Essence Publishing—R
Facts on File (all)
Fairway Press—R (all)
Family Hope Services (Jr/Sr High)
Friends United Press—R (Jr High)

Gospel Publishing—R
Guardian Books—R (all)
Health Communications (Sr High)
Horizon House—R (Jr/Sr High)
Huntington House—R (8-12)
Judson Press—R
Kaleidoscope Press—R (8-12)
Langmarc (8-12/Jr High)
Libros Liguori (all)
Lightwave Publishing (8-12)
Longwood—R (all)
Lowenbrown Publishing (Jr/Sr High)
Lutterworth Press (all)
Moody Press (all)
New Canaan (all)
New Hope—R (8-12)
Oregon Catholic Press—R (Jr/Sr High)
Pauline Books—R (all)
Ragged Edge—R (8-12)
Rainbow/Legacy Press—R (8-12)
RBC Publishing (8-12)
Reader's Digest Children's (all)
Read 'N Run (all)
St. Anthony Messenger—R (all)
Shining Star (8-12)
Son-Rise (all)
So. Baptist Press—R (all)
Still Waters Revival—R (all)

TEACH Services—R (8-12/Jr High)
Tekna Books (all)
Tyler Press—R (all)
Vital Issues Press—R
Windflower—R (8-12/Jr High)
World Bible—R (all)
YWAM Publishing—R (all)
Zondervan (all)

YOUTH PROGRAMS

Baker Books—R
Church Growth Inst.
Concordia
Contemporary Drama Service
CSS Publishing
Educational Ministries
Fairway Press—R
Family Hope Services
GROUP Publishing—R
Group's FaithWeaver
Guardian Books—R
Hensley Publishing—R
Judson Press—R
Langmarc
Liguori Publications
Lutterworth Press
Read 'N Run—R
St. Anthony Messenger—R
Standard
Vital Issues Press—R
Wood Lake Books—R
Youth Specialties
Zondervan

ALPHABETICAL LISTINGS OF BOOK PUBLISHERS

(*) An asterisk before a listing indicates unconfirmed or no information update.

(#) A number symbol before a listing indicates it was updated from their guidelines or other current sources.

(+) A plus sign before a listing indicates it is a new listing this year and was not included last year.

If you do not find the publisher you are looking for, look in the General Index. See the introduction of that index for the codes used to identify the current status of each unlisted publisher. If you do not understand all the terms or abreviations used in these listings, read the "How to Use This Book" section.

+A-1 CHRISTIAN EVANGELISTIC PRESS, PO Box 022132, Brooklyn NY 11202. (718)855-3008. Mar Yaqira, ed. Not included in topical listings. No questionnaire returned.

*ABIDE PUBLISHING, 515 E. Harrison, Wheaton IL 60187. Renae Ideboen, ed/pub. New publisher. Open to freelance. Did not return questionnaire; send for guidelines.

#ABINGDON PRESS, 201 8th Ave. S, PO Box 801, Nashville TN 37202. (615)749-6000. Fax (615)749-6512. E-mail: (first initial and last name) @umpublishing.org. Website: www.abingdon.org. United Methodist Publishing House. Editors: Robert Ratcliff, sr. ed; Joseph A. Crowe, gen. interest ed; Peg Augustine (children's books). Books and church supplies directed primarily to a religious market. Publishes 120 titles/yr. Receives 3,000 submissions annually. 5% of books from first-time authors. Reprints books. Prefers 144 pgs. Royalty 7½% on retail; no advance. Average first printing 3,000. Publication within 2 yrs. No simultaneous submissions. Requires disk. Responds in 8 wks. Prefers NRSV. Guidelines; free catalog.

    Nonfiction: Proposal/2 chapters; no phone/fax/e-query.

    Ethnic Books: African-American, Hispanic, Native-American, Korean.

    Tips: "Looking for general-interest books: mainline, social issues, marriage/family, self-help, exceptional people."

ACCENT BOOKS & VIDEOS, PO Box 700, Bloomington IL 61702. (309)378-2961. Fax (309)378-4420. E-mail: acntlvng@aol.com. Website: www.accentonliving.com. Cheever Publishing. Betty Garee, ed. Information for the mobility impaired. Publishes 1-2 titles/yr (mostly how-to books). Receives 15-20 submissions annually. 85% of books from first-time authors. No mss through agents. Prefers 64 pgs (max). Outright purchases. Average first printing 300. Publication within 6 mos. Considers simultaneous submissions. Responds in 2 wks. Accepts disk. Guidelines; catalog $3.50.

    Nonfiction: Query only first; phone/fax/e-query OK.

Also Does: A magazine and some booklets (not religious).

ACTA PUBLICATIONS, 4848 N. Clark St., Chicago IL 60640-4711. (773)271-1030. Fax (773)271-7399. E-mail: acta@one.org. Catholic. Gregory F. Augustine Pierce and Thomas R. Artz, co-pubs. Resources for the "end-user" of the Christian faith. Imprints: Buckley Publications; National Center for the Laity. Publishes 10 titles/yr. Receives 65 submissions annually. 50% of books from first-time authors. Prefers 150-200 pgs. Royalty 10-12½% of net; no advance. Average first printing 3,000. Publication within 1 yr. Disk accepted. Responds in 2 mos. Prefers NRSV. Guidelines; catalog for 9x12 SAE/2 stamps.

> **Nonfiction:** Query or proposal/1 chapter; no phone/fax/e-query.
>
> **Tips:** "Most open to books that are useful to a large number of average Christians. Read our catalog and one of our books first."

ACU PRESS, 1648 Campus Ct., Abilene TX 79601. (915)674-2720. Fax (915)674-6471. E-mail: LEMMONST@acuprs.acu.edu. Website: www.acu.edu/acupress. Church of Christ/Abilene Christian University. Thom Lemmons, ed.; Charme Robarts, asst. ed. Guidance in the religious life for members and leaders of the denomination. Publishes 10 titles/yr. Receives 100 submissions annually. 10% of books from first-time authors. Royalty 10%. Average first printing 5,000. Publication within 3 mos. Considers simultaneous submissions. Responds in 1 mo. Catalog.

> **Nonfiction:** Proposal/3 chapters.

ALBA HOUSE, 2187 Victory Blvd., Staten Island NY 10314-6603. (718)761-0047. Fax (718)761-0057. E-mail: Edmund_Lane@juno.com. Website: www.albahouse.org. Catholic/Society of St. Paul. Edmund C. Lane SSP, ed; Father Victor Viberti, SSP, acq ed. Imprint: St. Pauls. Publishes 24 titles/yr. Receives 450 submissions annually. 20% of books from first-time authors. No mss through agents. Reprints books. Prefers 124 pgs. Royalty 7-10% on retail; no advance. Publication within 9 mos. Prefers disk. Responds in 1-2 mos. Free guidelines/catalog.

> **Nonfiction:** Query.

THE ALBAN INSTITUTE, INC., 7315 Wisconsin Ave., Ste. 1250 W, Bethesda MD 20814-3211. (301)718-4407. Fax (301)718-1958. E-mail: manedit @alban.org. Website: www.alban.org. Episcopal Church. David Lott, mng ed (faith & health; multicultural/diversity); Beth Gaede, acq. ed. (faith, money & lifestyle; women's issues; congregational size issues). Addresses congregational leadership issues from an action-research approach. Publishes 12 titles/yr. Receives 100 submissions annually. No mss through agents. Prefers over 100 pgs. Royalty 8-12% of net; outright purchases for $50-100 for 450-2,000 wd articles on congregational life; advance $500. Average first printing 2,500. Publication within 1 yr. Requires disk. Responds in 4 mos. Prefers NRSV. Guidelines (also by e-mail/Website); free catalog.

> **Nonfiction:** Query first; phone/fax/e-query OK. Books for clergy and laity.
>
> **Also Does:** E-books through Net Library.
>
> **Tips:** "Books on congregational leadership and issues; problems and opportunities in congregational life; the clergy role and career; the

ministry of the laity in church and world." Intelligent/liberal audience.

ALBURY PUBLISHING, PO Box 470406, Tulsa OK 74147. (800)811-3921 or (918)523-5650. Fax (918)496-7702. Website: www.alburypublishing.com. ECI Communications, Inc. Elizabeth Sherman, ed. mng.; Rick Killion, mng. ed.; LaDonna Flagg, project ed. Charismatic Christian lifestyle and doctrinal issues. Publishes 20 titles/yr. Receives 600 submissions annually. 1% of books from first-time authors. Accepts mss through agents. Subsidy publishes 3%. Reprints books. Prefers 208 pgs. Royalty or outright purchase; advance. Average first printing 10,000. Publication within 20 mos. No guidelines or catalog.

> **Nonfiction:** Reviews submissions only through The Writer's Edge or First Edition. "Want well-written and compelling content, whether the topic has to do with personal or corporate Christian experience."
>
> **Fiction:** "We prefer historical or allegorical; no romance."
>
> ****Note:** This publisher serviced by The Writer's Edge and First Edition.

+FRANK AMATO PUBLICATIONS, INC., Box 82112, Portland OR 97282. (503)653-8108. Fax (503)653-2766. Frank Amato, pub. Does sports, travel, and religious/spiritual books. Incomplete topical listings. No questionnaire returned.

+AMBASSADOR BOOKS, 71 Elm St., Worchester MA 01609. (508)756-2893. Fax (508)757-7055.Website: www.ambassador books.com. Kathryn Conlan, acq. ed. Books of intellectual and spiritual excellence. Publishes 7 titles/yr. Receives 75 submissions annually. 50% of books from first-time authors. Accepts mss through agents. Royalty 8-12% of retail; advance. Publication within 10 mos. Considers simultaneous submissions. Responds in 3 mos. Free catalog (or on Website).

> **Nonfiction:** Query or complete ms.
>
> **Fiction:** Query or complete ms. Juvenile, young adult and adult; picture books.

+AMBASSADOR-EMERALD, INTL., 427 Wade Hampton Blvd., Greenville SC 29609. (864)235-2434. Fax (864)235-2491. E-mail: info@emeraldhouse. com. Website: www.emeraldhouse.com. European office: Ambassador Productions, Providence House, Ardenlee, Belfast BT6 82J, N. Ireland. Telephone: 011 441 232 450 010. Fax: 011 442 890 739 659. Emerald House Group, Inc. Tomm Knutson, ed. Dedicated to spreading the Gospel of Christ and empowering Christians through the written word. Publishes 55 titles/yr. Receives 400 submissions annually. 15% of books from first-time authors. Accepts mss through agents. **SUBSIDY PUBLISHES 1%.** Reprints books. Prefers 150-200 pgs. Royalty 5-15% of net; advance $1,000. Average first printing 5,000. Publication within 1 yr. Considers simultaneous submissions. Responds in 3 mos. Prefers KJV. Guidelines (also by e-mail); free catalog.

> **Nonfiction:** Query only; e-query OK.

AMERICA HOUSE (formerly Erica House), PO Box 1109, Frederick MD 21702. (301)631-0747. Fax (301)631-0747. E-mail: writers@publishamerica.com. Website: www.PublishAmerica.com. Christen Beckmann, sr. ed. Applauds those who have turned their stumbling blocks into stepping stones. Publishes 300 titles/yr. Receives 5,000 submissions annually. 75% of books from first-time authors. Variable royalty; advance. Publication within 1 yr. Considers simultaneous submissions. No disk or e-mail. Responds in 1-2 mos. Guidelines (also by e-mail/Website)/catalog on Website.

Nonfiction: Query or complete ms; e-query preferred. "Always looking for works about/for people who overcome steep challenges in life."

Fiction: Query or complete ms. For all ages.

Tips: "We encourage new talent to contact us."

AMERICAN CATHOLIC PRESS, 16565 State St., South Holland IL 60473-2025. (708)331-5485. Fax (708)331-5484. E-mail: acp@acpress.org. Website: www.acpress.org, or www.leafletmissal.com. Catholic worship resources. Father Michael Gilligan, ed dir. Publishes 4 titles/yr. Reprints books. Pays $25-100 for outright purchases only. Average first printing 3,000. Publication within 1 yr. Considers simultaneous submissions. Responds in 2 mos. Prefers NAS. No guidelines; catalog for SASE.

Nonfiction: Query first; no phone/fax/e-query.

Tips: "We publish only materials on the Roman Catholic liturgy. Especially interested in new music for church services."

#AMERICAN COUNSELING ASSOCIATION, 5999 Stevenson Ave., Alexandria VA 22304-3300. (703)823-9800. Carolyn C. Baker, dir of publications. Scholarly books. Publishes 10-15 titles/yr. Receives 325 submissions annually. 5% of books from first-time authors. Royalty 10-15% of net. Publication within 7 mos. Considers simultaneous submissions. Responds in 2-4 mos. Guidelines. Not included in topical listings.

Nonfiction: Proposal/2 chapters. Religion.

AMG PUBLISHERS, PO Box 22000, Chattanooga TN 37422. (423)894-6060. Fax (423)894-9511. E-mail: info@amgpublishers.com. Website: http://www.amgpublishers.com. AMG International. Dr. Warren Baker, mng ed. Primarily supports parent organization with remaining profits. Publishes 15 titles/yr. Receives 75 submissions annually. 10% of books from first-time authors. Reprints books. Prefers 175 pgs. Royalty 5-8% of net; no advance. Average first printing 5,000. Publication within 8 mos. Responds in 6 wks. Accepts disk. Prefers KJV, NASB, NIV, or NKJV. Guidelines (also on Website); free catalog.

Nonfiction: Proposal/2 chapters; see guidelines. "Looking for inspirational, Christian living, and group study books."

Fiction: Proposal/2 chapters. For adults; biblical & historical only.

Also Does: CD Roms.

Tips: "Most open to Bible studies. No poetry, short-story collections, social issues books and those with an acutely controversial flare."

*ANCHOR PUBLISHING, 1111 Baldwin Ln., Waxhaw NC 28173. (704)814-0618. E-mail: info@bibleprophecy.com. Website: www.bibleprophecy.com. Not included in topical listings. Did not return questionnaire.

*ART CAN DRAMA RESOURCES, Promise Productions, Inc., PO Box 927, Glen Rose TX 76043. (800)687-2661. Fax (254)897-3388. E-mail: drama@thepromise.org. Ted Oliver, ed. Supplies Christian schools, churches, and home schools with drama study materials. Publishes 2-3 titles/yr. Receives 50-100 submissions annually. 10% of books from first-time authors. Reprints books. Prefers 150-250 pgs. Royalty 5-10% on retail; $250-500 advance. Average first printing 500-1,000. Publication within 3-6 mos. No simultaneous submissions. Responds in 1-3 mos. Requires disk. Free guidelines/catalog.

Nonfiction: Proposal/1 chapter. Fax query OK.

Special Needs: Stage or radio playscripts. Youth plays (contemporary comedies); children's plays (short sketches), creation dramatics (how-to).

Tips: "Most open to books on the arts in a Christian context; playscripts which have been produced, won awards, and explore the Christian experience."

AUGSBURG BOOKS, 100 S. 5th St., Suite 700 (55402), Box 1209, Minneapolis MN 55440-1209. (612)330-3300. Fax (612)330-3215. Website: www. augsburgfortress.org. Accepting few freelance submissions.

**Note: This publisher is serviced by The Writer's Edge.

BAKER BOOKS, Box 6287, Grand Rapids MI 49516-6287. (616)676-9185. Fax (616)676-9573. Website: www.bakerbooks.com. Evangelical. Submit to Rebecca Cooper, asst. ed. Imprint: New Kids Media. Publishes 120 titles/yr. 10% of books from first-time authors. Reprints books. Prefers 150-300 pgs. Royalty 14% of net; some advances. Average first printing 5,000. Publication within 1 yr. Considers simultaneous submissions. Responds in 3 mos. No disk. Guidelines (on Website); catalog for 9x12 SAE/6 stamps.

Nonfiction: Proposal/3 chapters; no e-query. "Request our brochure on how to prepare a proposal."

Fiction: Proposal/3 chapters. "We are interested in contemporary women's fiction from a Christian world view without being preachy. Our fiction is more literary than popular. Request summary of contemporary women's fiction."

Ethnic Books: Would be interested in publishing specifically for the African-American market; also multicultural fiction.

Tips: "Please prepare a complete, well-organized proposal. Request our guidelines for guidance."

**Note: This publisher serviced by The Writer's Edge.

#BAKER'S PLAYS, PO Box 699222, Quincy MA 02269. (617)745-0805. Fax (617)745-9891. E-mail: info@bakersplays.com. Website: www.bakersplays. com. Ray Pape, assoc. ed. Publishes 1-6 titles/yr. Receives 600 submissions annually. 40% of plays from first-time authors. Production royalty varies; no advance. Average first printing 1,000. Publication within 6-9 mos. Considers simultaneous submissions. Accepts disk. Responds in 2-6 mos. Free guidelines (also on Website); no catalog.

Plays: Complete ms.

Tips: "We currently publish full-length plays, one-act plays for young audiences, theater texts and musicals, plays written by high schoolers, with a separate division which publishes plays for religious institutions. The ideal time to submit work is from September to April." If your play has been produced, send copies of press clippings.

#BALLANTINE BOOKS, 1540 Broadway, New York NY 10036. (212)782-9000. Website: www.randomhouse.com/BB. A Division of Random House. Joanne Wyckoff, religion ed. General publisher that does a few religious books. No guidelines or catalog. Not in topical listings.

> **Nonfiction & Fiction:** Proposal/100 pages of manuscript. From agents only.

BANTAM BOOKS—See Doubleday.

BAPTIST PUBLISHING HOUSE, PO Box 7270, Texarkana TX 75505-7270. (870)773-0054. Fax (870)772-5451. E-mail: info@bph.org. Website: www.bph.org. Baptist Missionary Assn. of America. Jerome Cooper, production dir. Focuses on Bible study, discipleship, and training material, providing resources for Evangelical congregations and personal spiritual development. Imprint: Mirror Press. Publishes 2-4 titles/yr. Receives 10-12 submissions annually. 90% of books from first-time authors. Accepts mss through agents. No reprints. **SUBSIDY PUBLISHES 25%.** Prefers 150-300 pgs. Royalty 10-15% of retail; no advance. Publication within 1 yr. Considers simultaneous submissions. Requires disk. Responds in 2 mos. Prefers KJV. No guidelines; free catalog.

> **Nonfiction:** Query or proposal/1 chapter; e-query OK.
>
> **Photos:** Accepts freelance photos for book covers.

BARBOUR PUBLISHING, INC., 1810 Barbour Dr., PO Box 719, Uhrichsville OH 44683. (740)922-6045. Fax (740)922-5948. E-mail: info@barbour books.com. Website: www.barbourbooks.com. Paul Muckley, ed. dir. Distributes Christian books at bargain prices. Imprints: Barbour Books (nonfiction), Promise Press (original nonfiction and gift books—see separate listing); and Heartsong Presents (fiction—see separate listing); Inspirational Library. Publishes 100 titles/yr. Receives 1,150 submissions annually. 50% of books from first-time authors. No mss through agents. Prefers 50,000 wds (novels & nonfiction); novellas 20,000 wds; juvenile 16,000 wds. Royalty to 12% of net; outright purchases $500-5,000; advance $500. Average first printing 15,000-20,000. Publication within 2 yrs. Considers simultaneous submissions. Responds in 1-3 mos. No disk; prefers e-mail (with prior arrangement). Prefers NIV or KJV. Guidelines (also by e-mail/Website); catalog $2.

> **Nonfiction:** Proposal/3 chapters; no phone/fax/e-query. Children's books for 8-12 year olds.
>
> **Fiction:** Proposal/2 chapters to Rebecca Germany, fiction ed. Novellas 20,000 wds. "We are interested in a mystery/romance series." See separate listing for Heartsong Presents.
>
> **Tips:** "Looking for books for women, fiction (short stories; suspense/drama for men and women readers), and humor. We seek solid, evangelical books with the greatest mass appeal. A good gift book for mothers will go much farther with Barbour than will a commentary on Jude. Do your homework before sending us a manuscript; send material that will work well within our publishing philosophy."

BARCLAY PRESS, 110 S. Elliott Rd., Newberg OR 97132-2144. (503)538-7345. Fax (503)538-7033. E-mail: info@barclaypress.com. Website: www.

barclaypress.com. Friends/Quaker. Dan McCracken, general manager. No unsolicited manuscripts.

Note: This publisher serviced by The Writer's Edge.

BAYLOR UNIVERSITY PRESS, PO Box 97363, Waco TX 76798-7363. (254)710-3164. Fax (254)710-3440. E-mail: david_holcomb@baylor.edu. Website: www.baylor.edu/~BUPress. Baptist. David Holcomb, acq. ed. Imprint: Markham Press Fund. Academic press producing scholarly books on religion and social sciences; church-state studies. Publishes 4 titles/yr. Receives 120 submissions annually. 10% of books from first-time authors. Reprints books. Prefers 250 pgs. Royalty 10% of net; no advance. Average first printing 1,000. Publication within 1 yr. Responds in 2 mos. No guidelines; free catalog.

Nonfiction: Query/outline; no phone query, e-mail query OK.

BEACON HILL PRESS OF KANSAS CITY, PO Box 419527, Kansas City MO 64141. (816)931-1900. Fax (816)753-4071. E-mail: bjp@bhillkc.com. Website: www.bhillkc.com. Nazarene Publishing House/Church of the Nazarene. Kelly Gallagher, acq ed. A Christ-centered publisher that provides authentically Christian resources that are faithful to God's Word and relevant to life. Imprint: Beacon Hill Books. Publishes 30 titles/yr. Receives 1,000 submissions annually. 10% of books from first-time authors. No mss through agents. Prefers 30,000-60,000 wds or 250 pgs. Royalty 12-14% of net; advance; some outright purchases. Average first printing 5,000. Publication within 1 yr. Considers simultaneous submissions. Responds in 3 mos or longer. Free guidelines/catalog.

Nonfiction: Query or proposal/2-3 chapters; no phone/fax query. "Looking for applied Christianity, spiritual formation, and leadership resources."

Ethnic Books: Spanish division—Casa Nazarena De Publicaciones. Publishes in several languages.

Tips: "Nearly all our titles come through acquisitions, and the number of freelance submissions has declined dramatically. If you wish to submit, follow guidelines above. You are always welcome to submit after sending for guidelines."

BETHANY HOUSE PUBLISHERS, 11400 Hampshire Ave. S, Minneapolis MN 55438. (952)829-2500. Fax (952)829-2768. Website: www.bethanyhouse. com. A ministry of Bethany Fellowship, Inc. Submit to Sharon Madison, ms review ed. Steve Laube, sr ed, nonfiction books; David Horton, sr ed, adult fiction; Barbara Lilland, sr ed, adult fiction; Rochelle Gloege, sr ed, children and youth. To publish information that communicates biblical truth and assists people in both spiritual and practical areas of life. Children's Imprint: Bethany Backyard (for 6-12 yrs). Publishes 120+ titles/yr. Receives 3,000 submissions annually. 2% of books from first-time authors. Negotiable royalty on net and advance. Publication within 1 yr. Considers simultaneous submissions. Responds in 3 mos. Guidelines for fiction/nonfiction/juvenile (also on Website); catalog for 9x12 SAE/5 stamps.

Nonfiction: Cover letter, synopsis, 3 chapters; no phone/fax/e-query. "Seeking well-planned and developed books in the following categories: personal growth, devotional, contemporary issues, marriage and family, reference, applied theology and inspirational."

Fiction: Cover letter/synopsis/3 chapters. "We publish adult historical and contemporary fiction, teen/young adult fiction, children's fiction series (8-12 yrs). Send SASE for guidelines."

Tips: "Seeking high quality fiction and nonfiction that will inspire and challenge our readers."

+BEYOND WORDS PUBLISHING, 20827 NW Cornell Rd., Ste. 500, Hillsboro OR 97124. Submit to adult acq. ed or children's acq. ed. Books on personal growth, women, and spiritual issues. Royalty. Not included in topical listings. No questionnaire returned.

Nonfiction: Outline & sample chapters. Adult nonfiction, 150-250 pgs.

Fiction: Complete ms. Children's picture books, 32, 48, 60, or 80 pgs.

BIBAL PRESS/D&F SCOTT PUBLISHING, INC., PO Box 821653, North Richland Hills TX 76182. (817)788-2280. Fax (817)788-9232. E-mail: info@dfscott.com. Website: www.dfscott.com. Dr. William R. Scott, ed/pres. To encourage the study of biblical archaeology and literature. Publishes 20 titles/yr. Receives 65 submissions annually. 10% of books from first-time authors. No mss through agents. Royalty 10-20% of net; no advance. Publication within 6 mos. Considers simultaneous submissions. Responds in 3 mos. Free guidelines/catalog. Incomplete topical listings.

Nonfiction: Proposal/2 chapters. Religion and biblical archaeology.

+BJU PRESS, Trade Division, 1700 Wade Hampton Blvd., Greenville SC 29614. (864)370-1800x4350. Fax (864)298-0268 x4324. E-mail: jb@bju.edu. Website: www.bjup.com. Bob Jones University Press. Susan Young, mng. ed.; Nancy Lohr, youth ed.; Suzette Jordan, Christian Resource ed. Our goal is to publish excellent, trustworthy books for children and adults. Publishes 16-20 titles/yr. Receives 500 submissions annually. 30% of books from first-time authors. Accepts mss through agents. Reprints books. Royalty on net; outright purchases of $1,000 (for first-time authors); advance $1,000. Average first printing 5,000. Publication within 12-18 months. Considers simultaneous submissions. Accepts disks. Responds in 6-8 wks. Prefers KJV. Guidelines (also by e-mail/Website); catalog for 6x9 SAE/3 stamps.

Nonfiction: Proposal/5 chapters or complete ms; no phone/fax/e-query.

Fiction: Proposal/5 chapters or complete ms. "We prefer overtly Christian or Christian worldview."

Tips: "Please review guidelines carefully before submitting."

+BLESSING OUR WORLD, INC., 509 S. Magnolia St., Palestine TX 75801. (903)729-1129. Fax (903)729-0443. E-mail: info@BlessWorld.com. Website: www.BlessWorld.com. Deanna Luke, ed; submit to Jennifer Noland, acq. ed. Christians operating an evangelical outreach to children and parents through their witness, not religion. Publishes children's books.

Nonfiction & Fiction: Query only; no phone/fax/e-query. Children's picture books, easy-readers, and juvenile novels.

Tips: "Looking for wholesome content that teaches godly values and principles without religion. We're engaged in marketing to a secular audience that will develop a trust in our content and want to know more about who we are."

#BLUE DOLPHIN PUBLISHING, INC., PO Box 8, Nevada City CA 95959. (916)265-6925. Fax (916)265-0787. E-mail: Bdolphin@netshel.net. Website: www.bluedolphinpublishing.com. Paul M. Clemens, pub. Imprint: Pelican Pond. Books that help people grow in their social and spiritual awareness. Publishes 12-15 titles/yr. Receives 4,000 submissions annually. 90% of books from first-time authors. Prefers about 60,000 wds or 200-300 pgs. Royalty 10-15% of net; no advance. Average first printing 3,000-5,000. Publication within 10 mos. Considers simultaneous submissions. No disk until contract. Responds in 1-3 mos. Guidelines (also on Website); catalog for 6x9 SAE/2 stamps.

Nonfiction: Proposal/1 chapter; e-query OK. "Looking for books on interspecies and relationships."

Fiction: Query/2-pg synopsis.

Tips: "We look for topics that would appeal to the general market, are interesting, different and that will aid in the growth and development of humanity."

Note: This publisher also publishes books on a range of topics, not necessarily Christian.

BOOKS IN MOTION, 9922 E. Montgomery Dr., Ste. 31, Spokane WA 99206. (509)922-1646. Website: www.booksinmotion.com. Classic Venture Ltd. Cameron Beierle, acq. ed. Secular, audio-book fiction publisher that does some religious books. Publishes unabridged audio books. Publishes 10-20 titles/yr. 10-15% of books from first-time authors. Prefers mss through agents. Reprints books. Royalty 10% of net; no advance. Average first printing 400. Publication within 8-10 mos. Guidelines.

Fiction: Adult fiction; especially needs westerns, fantasy, sci-fi and mystery-suspense. Query or proposal/3 chapters; no phone/fax/e-query. "We need manuscripts well-suited to audio, generally with lots of action, a few well-developed characters, simple plot/storylines, and easy to follow narration."

+BOOKWRIGHTS PRESS, 2255 Westover Dr., Ste. 108, Charlottesville VA 22901. Phone/fax (804)823-8223. E-mail: editor@bookwrights.com. Website: www.mindspring.com/~bookwrights. Mayapriya Long, ed. Does autobiography, biography, fiction, poetry, regional, and religious/spiritual books. Publishes 1-4 titles/yr. Incomplete topical listings. No questionnaire returned.

+R. H. BOYD PUBLISHING CORP., PO Box 91145, Nashville TN 37209-1145. (800)672-6272. Fax (800)615-1815. Website: www.rhboydpublishing. com. National Baptist Publishing Board. Bible studies, commentaries, devotionals, pastors' helps, VBS curriculum, Christian education resources. Incomplete topical listings.

BOYDS MILLS PRESS, 815 Church St., Honesdale PA 18431-1895. (570)253-1164. Website: www.boydsmillspress.com. Highlights for Children. Beth Troop, ms coord. Publishes a wide range of literary children's titles, for preschool through young adult; very few religious. Publishes 50 titles/yr. Receives 10,000 submissions annually. 20% of books from first-time authors. Reprints books. Royalty and advance vary. Considers simultaneous submissions. Responds in 30 days. Free guidelines; catalog for 9x12 SAE/7 stamps.

Nonfiction: Query letter only; no phone query. "No self-help books."

Fiction: Query only for novels; complete ms for picture books. "We are always interested in multicultural settings."

Tips: "Looking for picture books for pre-readers that contain simple, focused, and fun concepts for children ages 3-5, and concept books. We are primarily a general trade book publisher. For us, if stories include religious themes, the stories should still have a wide enough appeal for a general audience."

+BOYS' TOWN PRESS, 14100 Crawford St., Boys Town NE 68010. (402)498-1331. Fax (402)498-1310. E-mail: PeltoL@Boystown.org. Website: www.parenting.org. Lisa Pelto, ed. Does education, parenting, psychology, and religious/spiritual books. Incomplete topical listings. No questionnaire returned.

+BRAZOS PRESS, PO Box 6287, Grand Rapids MI 49516-6287. Division of Baker Book House. Rodney Clapp, ed. dir. Focuses on theology, cultural criticism, and Christian spirituality. Prefers 50,000 wds and up. Royalty. Guidelines. Not included in topical listings. No questionnaire returned.

Nonfiction: Query.

BRIDGE-LOGOS, PO Box 141630, Gainesville FL 32614. (352)472-7900. E-mail: mgraves@bridgelogos.com. Website: www.bridgelogos.com. Harold J. Chadwick, sr. ed. Purpose is to clearly define God's changeless Word to a changing world. Imprints: Logos, Bridge, Selah. Publishes 25 titles/yr. Receives 370 submissions annually. 20% of books from first-time authors. **SUBSIDY PUBLISHES 12%.** Prefers 180 pgs. Royalty 6-25% of net; some advances, $1,000-10,000. Average first printing 5,000. Publication within 6 mos. Considers simultaneous submissions. Responds in 6 wks. No disk. Guidelines (also by e-mail/Website); no catalog.

Nonfiction: Query only. "Most open to evangelism, spiritual growth, self-help and education."

Special Needs: Reference, biography, current issues, controversial issues, church renewal, women's issues and Bible commentary.

Photos: Accepts freelance photos for book covers.

Tips: "Have a great message, a well-written manuscript, and a specific plan and willingness to market your book. Looking for previously published authors with an active ministry who are experts on their subject."

BRIDGE RESOURCES, 100 Witherspoon St., Louisville KY 40202. Website: www.bridgeresources.org. Imprint of Presbyterian Church USA. Does Bible studies, resources for children and youth, study guides, fiction, plays, etc. Incomplete topical listings. See Witherspoon Press.

*BRISTOL HOUSE, LTD., PO Box 4020, Anderson IN 46013-0020. (765)644-0856. Fax (765)622-1045. Sara Anderson, sr ed. Imprint: Bristol Books. Publishes 4 titles/yr. Receives 35-55 submissions annually. Few books from first-time authors. Reprints books. **SOME SUBSIDY**. Prefers 160-240 pgs. Royalty 14% of net; no advance. Average first printing 1,000. Publication within 6-9 mos. Responds in 4 mos. Requires disk, no e-mail. Catalog for 9x12 SAE/2 stamps.

Nonfiction: Proposal/2 chapters; fax/e-query OK. "Looking for books on renewal. Most of our books are Methodist/Wesleyan in emphasis."

BROADMAN & HOLMAN PUBLISHERS, 127 9th Ave. N, Nashville TN 37234-0115. (615)251-3638. Fax (615)251-3752. E-mail: Koverca@lifeway.com. Website: www.broadmanholman.com. Book and Bible division of Lifeway Christian Resources. Leonard Goss, sr. acq. ed. Publishes books in the conservative, evangelical tradition by and for the larger Christian world. Publishes 75 titles/yr. Receives 2,500 submissions annually. 10% of books from first-time authors. Prefers 60,000-80,000 wds. Variable royalty on net; advance. Average first printing 5,000. Publication within 12-18 mos. Considers simultaneous submissions. Responds in 2 mos. Requires disk. Prefers Holman Christian Standard Bible, NIV, or NASB. Guidelines (2 stamps or by e-mail); no catalog.

Nonfiction: Proposal only first; no phone/fax query.

Fiction: Prefers adult contemporary. Full synopsis/2 chapters.

Ethnic: Spanish translations.

Also Does: Rocket E-books.

Tips: "Follow guidelines when submitting. Be informed about the market in general and specifically related to the book you want to write." Expanding into fiction, gift books, and children's books.

**Note: This publisher serviced by The Writer's Edge.

+CAMBRIDGE UNIVERSITY PRESS, 40 W. 20th St., New York NY 10011-4211. Fax (212)924-3900. Website: www.cup.org. University of Cambridge. Books on philosophy and religion. Not included in topical listings. No questionnaire returned.

+CANADIAN INSTITUTE FOR LAW, THEOLOGY & PUBLIC POLICY, INC., 7203—90 Ave., Edmonton AB T6B 0P5 Canada. (780)465-4581. Fax (780) 465-4581. E-mail: ciltpp@cs.com. Will Moore, ed. Integrating Christianity with the study of law and political science. Publishes 2-4 titles/yr. Receives 4-5 submissions annually. 1% of books from first-time authors. Accepts mss through agents. Reprints books. Royalty 7% of retail; no advance. Average first printing 1,000. Publication within 12-24 mos. No simultaneous submissions. Responds in 6-12 mos. Prefers NIV. Free guidelines/catalog.

Nonfiction: Proposal/1 chapter. "Looking for books integrating Christianity with law & political science."

Photos: Accepts freelance photos for book covers.

#CANDY CANE PRESS, 535 Metroplex Dr., Ste. 250, Nashville TN 37211. (615)333-0478, or (800)586-2572. Ideal Publications. Patricia Pingry, pub.; submit to Copy Editor. Christian stories for 3-8 year olds. Publishes 5-10 titles/yr. Royalty; variable advance. Responds in 2 mos. Send for guidelines/catalog.

Fiction: Complete ms. Includes picture books.

+CANON PRESS, PO Box 8729, Moscow ID 83843. (208)882-1456. Fax (208)882-1568. E-mail: canorder@moscow.com. Website: www.canon

press.org. Christ Church (Reformed; Presbyterian). Doug Jones, ed. Aims to expand "medieval Protestantism" in terms of truth, beauty and goodness. Publishes 10-15 titles/yr. Receives 30 submissions annually. 10% of books from first-time authors. Accepts mss through agents. Reprints books. Prefers 100-300 pgs. Royalty on retail; no advance. Average first printing 3,000. Publication within 1 yr. Considers simultaneous submissions. Responds in 4 mos. Prefers KJV, NKJV. Guidelines (also by e-mail/Website); free catalog.

Nonfiction: Proposal/3 chapters; fax/e-query OK.

Fiction: Complete ms. "We want literary fiction, but not genre."

Also Does: Booklets and e-books (soon).

Tips: "Avoid the typical, modern, sentimental evangelical thinking, as well as intellectualistic Presbyterianism. We delight in beauty and humor, creation and the reformed tradition."

+CANTICLE BOOKS, PO Box 2666, Carlsbad CA 92018. (760)806-3743. Fax (760)806-3689. E-mail: magnuspres@aol.com. Imprint of Magnus Press. Warren Angel, ed dir. To publish biblical studies by Catholic authors which are written for the average person and which minister life to Christ's Church. Publishes 6 titles/yr. Receives 60 submissions annually. 50% of books from first-time authors. Reprints books. Prefers 125-375 pgs. Graduated royalty on retail; no advance. Average first printing 5,000. Publication within 1 yr. Considers simultaneous submissions. Accepts disk. Responds in 1 mo. Guidelines (also by e-mail); free catalog.

Nonfiction: Query or proposal/2-3 chapters; fax query OK. "Looking for spirituality, thematic biblical studies, unique inspirational/devotional books."

Tips: "Our writers need solid knowledge of the Bible, and a mature spirituality which reflects a profound relationship with Jesus Christ. Most open to a well-researched, popularly written biblical study, or a unique inspirational or devotional book, e.g. Canine Parables."

*WILLIAM CAREY LIBRARY, 1705 N. Sierra Bonita Ave., Pasadena CA 91104. (626)798-4067. Fax (626)794-0477. Darrell Dorr, gen mgr. Publishes 10-15 titles/yr.

Nonfiction: Query only. "As a specialized publisher, we do only books and studies of church growth, missions, world issues, and ethnic/cultural issues."

Photos: Accepts freelance photos for book covers.

*CATHOLIC BOOK PUBLISHING CORP., 77 West End Rd., Totowa NJ 07512. (973)890-2400. Fax (973)890-2410. E-mail: cbpcl@bellatlantic. net. Website: www.catholicbkpub.com. Catholic. Anthony Buono, mng ed. Inspirational books for Catholic Christians. Acquired Resurrection Press. Publishes 15-20 titles/yr. Receives 75 submissions annually. 30% of books from first-time authors. No mss through agents. Variable royalty or outright purchases; no advance. Average first printing 3,000. Publication within 12-15 mos. No simultaneous submissions. Responds in 2-3 mos. Catalog for 9x12 SAE/5 stamps.

Nonfiction: Query letter only; no phone/fax query.

Tips: "We publish mainly Liturgical books, Bibles, Missals, and prayer books. Most of the books are composed in-house or by direct commission with particular guidelines. We strongly prefer query letters in place of full manuscripts."

CERDIC PUBLICATIONS, PJR-RIC, 11, Rue Jean Sturm, 67520 Nordheim, France. Phone (03)88.87.71.07. Fax (03)88.87.71.25. E-mail: cerdic@ vanadoo.fr. Marie Zimmerman, dir. Publishes 3-5 titles/yr. 50+% of books from first-time authors. Prefers 230 pgs. The first print run in the field of law in religion does not make money; no payment. Average first printing 2,200. Publication within 3 mos (varies). Considers simultaneous submissions. Responds in 4 wks. No guidelines; free catalog.

> **Nonfiction:** Complete ms; phone/fax query OK. "Looking for books on law and religion. All topics checked in topical listings must relate to the law."

> **Tips:** "We publish original studies in law of religion (any) with preference for young, beginning authors; in French only."

#CHALICE PRESS, Box 179, St. Louis MO 63166-0179. (314)231-8500. Fax (314)231-8524. E-mail: chalice@cbp21.com. Website: www.chalicepress. com. Christian Church (Disciples of Christ). Dr. David P. Polk, ed-in-chief; Dr. Jon L. Berquist, academic ed. Books for a thinking, caring church; in Bible, theology, ethics, homiletics, pastoral care, congregational studies, Christian living, and spiritual growth. Publishes 50 titles/yr. Receives 500 submissions annually. 15% of books from first-time authors. No mss through agents. Prefers 144-160 pgs for general books, 160-300 pgs for academic books. Royalty 14-18% of net; advances $500. Average first printing 2,500-3,000. Publication within 1 yr. Accepts simultaneous submissions. Disk required on acceptance. Responds in 1-3 mos. Guidelines on Website; catalog for 9x12 SAE/2 stamps.

> **Nonfiction:** Proposal/2 chapters; fax/e-query OK. "Looking for books that treat current issues perceptively, especially from a moderate-to-liberal perspective."

> **Ethnic Books:** African-American and Hispanic.

> **Photos:** Accepts freelance photos for book covers.

CHARIOT BOOKS—See Cook Communications Ministries

CHARIOT VICTOR PUBLISHING—See Cook Communications Ministries.

CHICKEN SOUP BOOKS—See listings in Periodical section.

CHOSEN BOOKS, Division of Baker Book House, 3985 Bradwater St., Fairfax VA 22031-3702. (703)764-8250. Fax (703)764-3995. E-mail: JECampbell @aol.com. Website: www.bakerbooks.com. Charismatic. Jane Campbell, ed. dir. Books that recognize the gifts and ministry of the Holy Spirit and help the reader live a more empowered and effective life for Christ. Publishes 12 titles/yr. Receives 300 submissions annually. 10% of books from first-time authors. Prefers 60,000 wds or 200 pgs. Royalty on net; modest advance. Average first printing 5,000-7,500. Publication within 18 mos. Considers simultaneous submissions. Responds in 3 mos. Guidelines (also on Website); no catalog.

> **Nonfiction:** Query or proposal/2 chapters (summary, outline, author résumé); e-query OK (no e-proposal). "Looking for books that help the reader live a more empowered and effective life for Jesus Christ."

Tips: "State your theme clearly in your cover letter, along with your qualifications for writing on that subject, and be sure to enclose an SASE if you want a response or your material back."
**Note: This publisher serviced by The Writer's Edge.
CHRISTIAN ED. PUBLISHERS, Box 26639, San Diego CA 92196. (858)578-4700. Fax (858)578-2431 (for queries only). E-mail: Editor@cepub.com or Lackelson@aol.com. Website: www.ChristianEdWarehouse.com. Dr. Lon Ackelson, sr ed. An evangelical publisher of Bible Club materials for ages two through high school; church special-event programs, and Bible-teaching craft kits. Publishes 80 titles/yr. Receives 150 submissions annually. 10% of books from first-time authors. No mss through agents. Outright purchases for .03/wd; no advance. Publication within 1 yr. No simultaneous submissions. Responds in 3-5 mos. Prefers NIV or KJV. Guidelines (also by e-mail); catalog for 9x12 SAE/4 stamps.
　　Nonfiction: Query; phone/fax/e-query OK. Bible studies, curriculum and take-home papers.
　　Fiction: Query first. Juvenile fiction for take-home papers. "Each story is about 900 wds. Write for an application."
　　Photos: Accepts freelance photos for book covers.
　　Tips: "All writing done on assignment. Request our guidelines, then complete a writer application before submitting. Need Bible-teaching ideas for preschool through sixth grade. Also publishes Bible stories for primary take-home papers, 200 wds."
+CHRISTIAN FOCUS PUBLICATIONS, LTD., Geanies House, Fearn, Tain, Ross-shire IV20 1TW Scotland UK. Website: www.christianfocus.com. Malcolm Maclean, mng. ed. Not included in topical listings. No questionnaire returned.
CHRISTIAN MEDIA, Box 448, Jacksonville OR 97530. (541)899-8888. Fax on request. E-mail: James@ChristianMediaNetwork.com. Website: www.ChristianMediaNetwork.com. James Lloyd, ed/pub. Publishes 5 titles/yr. Receives 12 submissions annually. Most books from first-time authors. Would consider reprints. Prefers 200 pgs. Royalty on net; no advance. Considers simultaneous submissions. Responds in 3 wks. Catalog for 9x12 SAE/2 stamps.
　　Nonfiction: Query; phone query OK. Works dealing with the internal workings of the media industry; publishing, broadcasting, records, etc.
　　Tips: "Produces manuals, instructional or otherwise. Exposés; also books of prophetic interpretation, end times, eschatology, interpolations of political events, etc."
CHRISTIAN PUBLICATIONS, 3825 Hartzdale Dr., Camp Hill PA 17011. (717)761-7044. Fax (717)761-7273. E-mail: editors@cpi-horizon.com. Website: www.christianpublications.com. Christian and Missionary Alliance. David E. Fessenden, mng ed.; submit to George McPeek, ed. dir. Publishes books which emphasize Christ as Savior, Sanctifier, Healer, and Coming King. Imprint: Horizon Books. Publishes 35 titles/yr. Receives 2,000 submissions annually. 50% of books from first-time authors. Prefers 35,000-50,000 wds or 150-300 pgs. Royalty 5% of retail on wholesale sales, 10% of retail on retail sales; outright purchases $100-400

(booklets); variable advance. Average first printing 3,000-5,000. Publication within 18 mos. Considers simultaneous submissions on full proposals. Prefers disk. Responds in 1-2 mos. Guidelines (also by e-mail); catalog for 9x12 SAE/5 stamps.

Nonfiction: Query/proposal/2 chapters (include 1st); one-page fax/e-query (copied into message) OK. "Looking for books on applying the power of the Spirit to practical, daily life."

Also Does: Booklets, 10-32 pages.

Tips: "Have a compelling idea that you are passionate about, combined with a thorough grounding in Scripture."

**Note: This publisher serviced by The Writer's Edge.

+CHRISTIAN PUBLISHER.COM, 1506 Pennylane SE, Decatur AL 35601. Fax (256)309-5936. E-mail: submissions@christianpublisher.com. Website: www.christianpublisher.com. E-mail all submissions to e-mail address (as an attachment only); or send on disk or CD-ROM. E-book publisher. Requires 5,000 wds or more. Royalty. Publication within 4-6 wks. Responds in 1 wk. Guidelines on Website. Not included in topical listings.

Nonfiction: Cover letter with synopsis.

CHRISTIAN UNIVERSITIES PRESS, 4720 Boston Way, Lanham MD 20706. (301)459-3366. Fax (301)459-1705. E-mail: info@interscholars.com. Website: www.interscholars.com. An imprint of International Scholar's Publications. Lois Raimond, mng ed. The best obtainable projects in evangelical/Christian research. Publishes 120 titles/yr. Receives 250+ submissions annually. 80% of books from first-time authors. No mss through agents. Reprints books. Prefers up to 264 pgs. Royalty 8-12% of net; no advance. Average first printing 500+. Publication within 8 mos. Considers simultaneous submissions. Responds in 1-2 mos. No disk. Guidelines; free catalog.

Nonfiction: Proposal/2 chapters; fax/e-query OK. "Looking for history and theology."

Ethnic Books: Hispanic (Latin America) or (West) African.

Tips: "Most open to scholarly monograph/dissertation, non-fiction research; New Testament."

*THE CHRISTOPHER PUBLISHING HOUSE, 24 Rockland St., Hanover MA 02339. (781)826-7474. Fax (781)826-5556. E-mail: cph@atigroupinc.com. Member of the ATI Group. Nancy A. Kopp, mng ed. Produces fine quality books for the public's reading enjoyment. Publishes 6-8 titles/yr. Receives 200+ submissions annually. 90% of books from first-time authors. **SUBSIDY PUBLISHES 8-10%.** Prefers 100+ pgs. Royalty 5-30% of net; no advance. Average first printing 2,000. Publication within 12-14 mos. Considers simultaneous submissions. Responds in 6-8 wks. Accepts e-mail submissions. Guidelines (also by e-mail/Website); catalog for #10 SAE/2 stamps.

Nonfiction: Complete ms. Most topics; no juvenile material.

Fiction: Complete ms. Adult only. About 100 pgs.

CHURCH & SYNAGOGUE LIBRARY ASSN. INC., PO Box 19357, Portland OR 97280-0357. (503)244-6919. Fax (503)977-3734. E-mail: csla@world accessnet.com. Website: www.worldaccessnet.com/~csla. Karen Bota, ed. An interfaith group set up to help librarians set up and organize/reorganize their religious libraries. Publishes 6 titles/yr. No mss through agents. No royalty. Average first printing 750. Catalog.

CHURCH GROWTH INSTITUTE, PO Box 7000, Forest VA 24551. (804)525-0022. Fax (804)525-0608. E-mail: cgimail@churchgrowth.org. Website: www.churchgrowth.org. Ephesians Four Ministries. Cindy G. Spear, ed. Providing practical tools for leadership, evangelism, and church growth. Publishes 4-6 titles/yr. Receives 52 submissions annually. 7% of books from first-time authors. No mss through agents. Prefers 64-160 pgs. Royalty 5% on retail or outright purchase; no advance. Average first printing 500. Publication within 1 yr. Considers simultaneous submissions. Responds in 3 mos. Requires disk. Guidelines; catalog for 9x12 SAE/3 stamps.

> **Nonfiction:** Proposal/1 chapter; no phone/fax/e-query. "We prefer our writers to be experienced in what they write about, to be experts in the field."

> **Special Needs:** Topics that help churches grow spiritually and numerically; leadership training; attendance and stewardship programs; new or unique ministries (how-to).

> **Photos:** Accepts freelance photos for book covers.

> **Tips:** "Most open to a practical manual or complete resource packet for the pastor or other church leaders—something unique with a special niche. Must be practical and different from anything else on the same subject—or must be a topic/slant few others have published."

+CIRCULUS PUBLISHING GROUP, 2716 Ninth St., Berkeley CA 94710. (510)848-3600. Fax (510)848-1326. E-mail: Circulus@aol.com. Tamara Traeder, ed. Does religious/spiritual, women's issues, and psychology. Incomplete topical listings. No questionnaire returned.

#CISTERCIAN PUBLICATIONS, INC., Wallwood Hall, WMU Station, Kalamazoo MI 49008. (616)387-8920. Fax (616)387-8921. E-mail: cistpub@wmich.edu. Website: www.wmich.edu/cistern. St. Joseph's Abbey/Catholic/Order of Cistercians of the Strict Observance. Dr. E. Rozanne Elder, ed dir. Publishes 8-14 titles/yr. Receives 30 submissions annually. 50% of books from first-time authors. No mss through agents. Prefers 204-286 pgs. Variable payment. Average first printing 1,500. Publication within 2-10 yrs. Free style sheet/catalog.

> **Nonfiction:** Proposal/1 chapter. History, spirituality and theology.

> **Photos:** Accepts freelance photos for book covers.

> **Tips:** "We publish only on the Christian Monastic Tradition. Most open to scholarly books."

CITY BIBLE PUBLISHING, 9200 NE Fremont, Portland OR 97220. (800)777-6057. Fax (503)257-2228. E-mail: equip@citybiblepublishing. com. Website: www.citybiblepublishing.com. City Bible Church. Mark Daniels, ed. Exalt the Lord, equip the Saints, extend the Kingdom. Publishes 3 titles/yr. Receives 20 submissions annually. 0% of books from first-time authors. Prefers 250-350 pgs. Royalty on retail; no advance. Average first printing 2,000. Publication within 8 mos. No simultaneous submissions. Prefers disk. Responds in 2 wks. Prefers NKJV. No guidelines; free catalog.

> **Nonfiction:** Proposal/outline; phone/fax/e-query OK. "Looking for leadership material; college texts."

Photos: Accepts freelance photos for book covers.

Tips: "Have logical outline and direction."

+CLADACH PUBLISHING, PO Box 355, Fulton CA 95439. (707)528-3128. E-mail: staff@cladach.com. Website: www.cladach.com. Independent Christian publisher. Catherine Lawton, pub/ed. Publishes 1-2 titles/yr. Receives 20 submissions annually. 80% of books from first-time authors. No mss through agents. No reprints. Prefers 50,000-90,000 wds. Royalty on net; no advance. Average first printing 1,500. Publication within 1 yr. Considers simultaneous submissions. Responds in 3 mos. Guidelines; catalog on Website.

Nonfiction: Query.

Fiction: Does little.

COLLEGE PRESS PUBLISHING CO., INC., 223 W. Third St. (64801), Box 1132, Joplin MO 64802. (417)623-6280. Fax (417)623-8250. E-mail: collegepress@collegepress.com. Website: www.collegepress.com. Christian Church/Church of Christ. John M. Hunter, ed. Imprint: Forerunner Books. Christian materials that will help fulfill the Great Commission and promote unity on the basis of biblical truth and intent. Publishes 30 titles/yr. Receives 400+ submissions annually. 1-5% of books from first-time authors. Reprints books. Prefers 250-300 pgs (paperback) or 300-600 pgs (hardback). Royalty 5-15% of net; no advance. Average first printing 2,000. Publication within 6 mos. Considers simultaneous submissions. Requires disk; no e-mail submissions. Responds in 2-3 mos. Prefers NIV, NASB, or NASU. Guidelines (also by e-mail/Website); catalog for 9x12 SAE/5 stamps.

Nonfiction: Query only, then proposal/2-3 chapters; no phone/fax/e-query. "Looking for Bible study, reference, divorced leaders, blended families, and leadership."

Ethnic Books: Reprints their own books in Spanish.

Also Does: E-books.

Tips: "Most open to conservative, biblical exposition with an 'Arminian' view and/or 'amillennial' slant. Most open to commentary or Bible study."

COMPRADORE, 7613 Lynes Ct., Savannah GA 31406. (912)353-9210. Fax (253) 276-8846. E-mail: editor@compradore.com. Website: www.compradore. com. Sharon Outlaw, ed. To bring the family together through well-written literature. Also produces online & audio books. Publishes 7 titles/yr. Pays a sliding scale royalty of 25-30% on quarterly sales. Considers simultaneous submissions. Accepts disk. Responds in 2-3 mos. Prefers NIV. Guidelines (also on Website).

Nonfiction: Query; fax/e-query OK.

Fiction: Query. For all ages, includes children's picture books.

Tips: "Looking for books for juveniles/young adults-ages 10-18. Write a good story! We are looking for new writers with quality manuscripts. We will not read material containing homosexuality, vulgarity or overt sexuality." No longer charges extra fees.

CONARI PRESS, 2550 9th St., Ste. 101, Berkeley CA 94710-2551. (510)649-7175 or (800)685-9595. Fax (510)649-7190. E-mail: conaripub@aol.com, or conari@conari.com. Website: www.conari.com. Leslie Berriman, exec ed; Heather McCarthur, mng ed.; Julie Kessler, acq. ed. Focus is on the human experience. Imprint: Grace House. Publishes 30 titles/yr. Receives 1,000 submissions annually. 50% of books from first-time authors. Reprints bks. Royalty 12-16% of net; variable advance. Average first printing 20,000. Publication within 1-3 yrs. Considers simultaneous submissions. Accepts disk. Responds in 3 mos. Guidelines; catalog for 6x9 SAE/3 stamps.

Nonfiction: Proposal/3 chapters; no phone/fax query; e-query OK.

Photos: Accepts freelance photos for book covers.

Tips: "Most open to spirituality, collections of stories, inspiration. We are the publishers of the Random Acts of Kindness series."

CONCILIAR PRESS, PO Box 76, Ben Lomand CA 95005. (831)336-5118. Fax (831)336-8882. E-mail: marketing@conciliarpress.com. Website: www. conciliarpress.com. Antiochian Orthodox Christian Archdiocese of N.A. Deacon Thomas Zell, ed. Publishes 5-10 titles/yr. Receives 50 submissions annually. 20% of books from first-time authors. Accepts mss through agents. **SUBSIDY PUBLISHES 10%.** Reprints books. Royalty; no advance. Average first printing 5,000. Prefers e-mail submission. Prefers NKJV. Guidelines (also by e-mail); catalog for 9x12 SAE/5 stamps.

Nonfiction: Query only; phone/fax/e-query OK.

Photos: Accepts freelance photos for book covers.

+CONCORDIA ACADEMIC PRESS, 3558 S. Jefferson Ave., St. Louis MO 63118-3968. (314)268-1000. Fax (314)268-1329. Website: www.cph.org. Lutheran Church/Missouri Synod. Imprint of Concordia Publishing House. Scholarly and professional books in biblical studies, 16th-century studies, historical theology, and theology and culture. Publication within 18 mos. Responds in 8-12 wks. Guidelines on Website.

CONCORDIA PUBLISHING HOUSE, 3558 S. Jefferson Ave., St. Louis MO 63118-3968. (314)268-1000. Fax (314)268-1329. Website: www.cph.org. Lutheran Church/Missouri Synod. Dawn Weinstock: adult & youth nonfiction, adult & youth devotionals, youth fiction; Jane Wilke: children's resources, children's & family devotions, teaching resources; Ken Wagener: pastoral, theological resources; Brandy Simmons: guidelines for adults, children's resources. Publishes 130 titles/yr. Receives 3,000 submissions annually. 10% of books from first-time authors. Royalty 2-14% on retail; some outright purchases; some advances $500-1,500. Average first printing 8,000-10,000. Publication within 2 yrs. Considers simultaneous submissions. Responds in 4 mos. Prefers disk. Prefers NIV. Guidelines (also by e-mail/Website); catalog for 9x12 SAE/4 stamps.

Nonfiction: Proposal/2 chapters; no phone/fax query. No poetry, personal experience or biography. "Looking for youth nonfiction on contemporary issues and skill building; focused discussions of family skills (communication, support, etc.); and banner patterns/construction/how-to books (at least 30 designs)."

Fiction: Proposal/2 chapters. No adult fiction. Children's categories: beginning reader, chapter, juvenile, youth. Must have strong Christian message. "We are full in picture books and fiction for the immediate future."

Ethnic Books: Hispanic; Asian-American.

Also Does: Pamphlets & booklets.

Tips: "Most open to family, inspirational/devotional, and teaching resources. Any proposal should be Christ-centered, Bible-based, and life-directed. It must be creative in its presentation of solid scriptural truths."

**Note: This publisher serviced by The Writer's Edge.

+**CONEXUS PRESS**, 6264 Grand River Dr. NE, Ada MI 49301. (616)682-9022. Fax (616)682-9023. E-mail: conexus@iserv.net. Website: www.conexus press.com. Does philosophy and textbooks. Joel Beversluis, ed. Publishes and distributes books and other materials that enhance inter-religious understanding, wisdom and cooperation. Not included in topical listings. No questionnaire returned.

CONTEMPORARY DRAMA SERVICE—See Meriwether Publishing, Ltd.

COOK COMMUNICATIONS MINISTRIES, 4050 Lee Vance View, Colorado Springs CO 80918. (719)536-0100. Fax (719)536-3269. Website: www. cookministries.org. Submit to Editorial Assistant. Brands: Victor (personal spiritual growth); Faithful Woman (women's spiritual growth issues); Faith Marriage (deepening marital intimacy); Faith Parenting (creating "teachable moments"); Faith Kids (equipping kids for life). Publishes 150 titles/yr. 10% of books from first-time authors. Average first printing 10,000. Publication within 1-2 yrs. Considers simultaneous submissions. Responds in 1-3 mos. Prefers NIV. Guidelines; catalog for 9x12 SAE/2 stamps.

Nonfiction: Proposal (2-3 pgs)/2 chapters; no phone/fax/e-query. For picture books send complete ms.

Tips: "Now accepting proposals only from agents or published authors (indicate that on the outside of envelope)."

**Note: This publisher serviced by The Writer's Edge.

DAVID C. COOK PUBLISHING CO.—See Cook Communications Ministries.

CORNELL UNIVERSITY PRESS, Sage House, 510 E. State St., Ithaca NY 14850. (607)277-2338. Website: www.cornellpress.cornell.edu. Nondenominational. Frances Benson, ed-in-chief. Publishes 6-8 titles/yr. Receives 20 submissions annually. 50% of books from first-time authors. Reprints books. Prefers 60,000-120,000 wds. Royalty to 15%; advance to $5,000. Average first printing 1,250. Publication within 1 yr. May consider simultaneous submission. Responds in 3 mos. Free guidelines (also on Website)/catalog.

Nonfiction: Query first/outline. "Looking for historical (especially American, medieval and early modern) and philosophical books."

J. COUNTRYMAN, PO Box 141000, Nashville TN 37214-1000. (615)902-3134. Fax (615)902-3200. Website: www.jcountryman.com. Thomas Nelson Publishers. Jack Countryman, pub/exec VP; Terri Gibbs, exec ed. Giftbook imprint; presenting strong, Bible-based messages in beautifully designed books. Publishes 15-20 titles/yr. Receives 100+ submissions annually. Prefers 128 pgs. Royalty; advance. Average first printing 40,000. Publication within 1 yr. Considers simultaneous submissions. Responds in 2-3 wks. Prefers NKJV. No guidelines; free catalog.

Nonfiction: Query; no phone/fax/e-query. "We will look at other material, but will not guarantee its return."

Tips: "We need books for strong gift-buying times—Christmas, Mother's/Father's Day, wedding, Valentine's Day, new baby, and graduation."

+**CRANE HILL PUBLISHERS**, 3608 Clairmont Ave., Birmingham AL 35222. (205)714-3007. Fax (205)714-3008. E-mail: cranies@aol.com. Website: www.cranehill.com. Shelley DeLuca, ed. Publishes a few religious titles. Receives 500 submissions annually. 50% of books from first-time authors. Accepts mss through agents. Reprints books. Length varies. Royalty. Publication within 1-2 yrs. Considers simultaneous submissions. Responds in 2-6 mos. Free catalog.

Nonfiction: Query only; no phone query.

Fiction: Query only. Literary fiction only.

CREATION HOUSE, 600 Rinehart Rd., Lake Mary FL 32746-4872. (407)333-3132. Fax (407)333-7100. E-mail: creationhouse@strang.com. Website: www.creationhouse.com. Strang Communications. Connie Gamb, submissions; Dave Welday, product dev; Jerry Lenz, curriculum. To provide the charismatic market with books on Spirit-led living. Publishes 40-50 titles/yr. Receives 700 submissions annually. 2% of books from first-time authors. Prefers 40,000 wds or 200 pgs. Royalty 4-18% on retail; advance $1,500-5,000. Average first printing 5,000. Publication within 9 mos. Considers simultaneous submissions. Responds in 2-3 mos. No disk. Free guidelines; no catalog.

Nonfiction: Proposal/3 chapters; fax query OK. "Looking for books of Spirit-filled interest, devotional life, practical Christian living, and Bible study/foundational." Note: Accepting no freelance at this time.

**Note: This publisher serviced by The Writer's Edge.

CREATIVE BOUND INC., Box 424, 151 Tansley Dr., Carp ON K0A 1L0 Canada. (613)831-3641. Fax (613)831-3643. E-mail: info@creativebound. com. Website: www.creativebound.com. Gail Baird, pres.; submit to Barb Clarke, acq. ed. Books that inspire, help and heal. Publishes 1 title/yr. Receives 20 submissions annually. 50% of books from first-time authors. No mss through agents. No reprints. Royalty 11-15% of net; no advance. Average first printing 3,000. Publication within 3 mos. No simultaneous submissions. Responds in 1 mo. Prefers e-mail submissions. Guidelines (also by e-mail); free catalog.

Nonfiction: Query only; fax/e-query OK.

CROSS CULTURAL PUBLICATIONS, INC., PO Box 506, Notre Dame IN 46556. (800)561-6526 or (219)273-6526. Fax (219)273-5973. E-mail: crosscult@aol.com. Website: www.crossculturalpub.com. Catholic. Cyriac K. Pullapilly, gen ed. Promotes intercultural and interfaith understanding. Imprint: CrossRoads Books. Publishes 20 titles/yr. Receives 5,000-7,000 submissions annually. 10% of books from first-time authors. Accepts mss through agents. Reprints books. Prefers 250 pgs. Royalty 10% on net; no advance. Average first printing 1,000-5,000. Publication within 6 mos. Considers simultaneous submissions. Requires disk. Responds in 3-4 mos. No guidelines; free catalog.

Nonfiction: Prefers complete ms; will accept a proposal; no phone/fax/e-query.

Fiction: Prefers complete ms. For adults only.

Ethnic Books: Seeks to serve the cross cultural, intercultural, and multicultural aspects of religious traditions.

Tips: "Most open to solidly researched, well-written books on serious issues. Do a thorough job of writing/editing, etc. Have something constructive, noble and worthwhile to say."

THE CROSSROAD PUBLISHING CO., 481—8th Ave., #1550, New York NY 10001-1820. (212)868-1801. Fax (212)868-2171. Gwendolin Herder, pub.; Alyson Donohue, mng. ed. Books on religion, spirituality, and personal growth that speak to the diversity of backgrounds and beliefs; books that inform, enlighten, and heal. Imprints: Herder & Herder (academic), and Eighth Avenue (general). Publishes 50 titles/yr. Receives 1,200 submissions annually. 10% of books from first-time authors. Rarely subsidy publishes (5%). Reprints books. Prefers 50,000-60,000 wds or 160 pgs. Royalty 8-10-12% of net; small advance (more for established authors). Average first printing 5,000. Publication within 6-8 mos. Considers simultaneous submissions. Responds in 3-4 mos. Accepts disk. Free catalog.

Nonfiction: Proposal/2 chapters or complete ms; fax query OK.

Fiction: Proposal/2 chapters or complete ms. Prefers historical fiction that focuses on important figures or periods in the history of Christianity.

CROSSWAY BOOKS, 1300 Crescent St., Wheaton IL 60187. (630)682-4300. Fax (630)682-4785. Website under construction. A division of Good News Publishers. Marvin Padgett, VP editorial; submit to Jill Carter, ed admin. Publishes books that combine the Truth of God's Word with a passion to live it out, with unique and compelling Christian content. Publishes 90 titles/yr. Receives 2,500 submissions annually. 2% of books from first-time authors. Prefers 25,000 wds & up. Royalty 10-21% of net; advance varies. Average first printing 5,000-10,000. Publication within 18 mos. Considers simultaneous submissions. Requires disk (compatible with Microsoft Word). Responds in 6-8 wks. Any version. Guidelines; catalog for 9x12 SAE/7 stamps.

Nonfiction: Query only, then proposal/2 chapters; fax query OK; no e-query.

Fiction: Proposal/2 chapters (no complete mss). Adult.

Also Does: Tracts. See Good News Publishers.

Tips: "Most open to books that are consistent with what the Bible teaches and stand within the stream of historic Christian truth—books that give a clear sense that the author is a genuine Christian seeking to live a consistent Christian life. Be clear and concise in your synopsis."

**Note: This publisher serviced by The Writer's Edge.

C.S.S. PUBLISHING CO., PO Box 4503, 517 S. Main St., Lima OH 45802-4503. (419)227-1818. Fax (419)228-9184. E-mail: Tom@csspub.com. Website: www.csspub.com. Terry Rhoads, ed; Tom Lentz, acq. ed. A clearing house for the promotion and exchange of creative ideas used in ministry. Publishes 200 titles/yr. Receives 1,200-1,500 submissions annually.

50% of books from first-time authors. **SUBSIDY PUBLISHES** 40% through Fairway Press. Prefers 100-125 pgs. Royalty 3-7% or outright purchases for $25-400. Average first printing 1,000. Publication within 6-10 mos. Considers simultaneous submissions. Responds in 3-4 mos. Accepts disk. Prefers NRSV. Free guidelines (also on Website)/catalog.

> **Nonfiction:** Complete ms; fax/e-query OK. "Looking for pastoral resources for ministry."

> **Fiction:** Complete ms. For all ages. Inspirational; plays (Advent/Christmas); short story collections. Children's books, 6-12 years, series or single books.

> **Tips:** "Suggest what you can do to help promote the book."

*CUSTOM COMMUNICATIONS SERVICES, INC./SHEPHERD PRESS/CUSTOM BOOK, 77 Main St., Tappan NJ 10983. (914)365-0414. Fax (914)365-0864. E-mail: customusa@aol.com. Norman Shaifer, pres. Publishes 50-75 titles/yr. 50% of books from first-time authors. No mss through agents. Royalty on net; some outright purchases for specific assignments. Publication within 6 mos. Responds in 1 month. Guidelines.

> **Nonfiction:** Query/proposal/chapters. "Histories of individual congregations, denominations, or districts."

> **Tips:** "Find stories of larger congregations (750 or more households) who have played a role in the historic growth and development of the community or region."

DAYBREAK BOOKS/RODALE, 400 S. 10th St., Emmaus PA 18098. (610)967-5171. Fax (610)967-8691. Website: www.rodalepress.com. Neil Wertheimer, ed. Offers a fresh, unique approach to fulfilling a primary spiritual need or solving a tough spiritual issue. Publishes books that empower and enlighten. Publishes 6-9 inspirational titles/yr. Receives 200+ submissions annually. 50% of books from first-time authors. Prefers agented mss. Prefers 35,000-50,000 wds. Royalty 6-15% on retail; some outright purchases; advance $10,000 & up. Average first printing 12,000. Publication within 12-18 mos. Considers simultaneous submissions. Responds in 4-6 wks. Requires disk for accepted ms. Free guidelines/catalog.

> **Nonfiction:** Query or proposal 2 chapters; fax/e-query OK. "Looking for motivation, inspiration, self-help, and spiritual topics."

> **Photos:** Accepts freelance photos for book covers.

> **Tips:** "An expert writing in their area, or a professional with some credentials in the area they are writing about, has the best chance of succeeding. Book fulfilling primary spiritual need, such as love, faith, a sense of purpose or meaning; or solving a tough spiritual issue, such as grieving, building closer families, or achieving serenity."

+DEVOTED TO YOU BOOKS, PO Box 300, Sartell MN 56377. (320)202-5961. E-mail: info@devotedtoyoubooks.com. Website: www.devotedtoyoubooks.com. Nondenominational. Tracy Ryks, pub. Seeks to teach children that God is present in their lives today; children's picture books for ages 1-8. Publishes 2 titles/yr. No reprints. Royalty; no advance. Publication within 18 mos. Considers simultaneous submissions. Responds in 8 wks. Prefers NIV. Guidelines on Website; free catalog.

> **Nonfiction:** Complete ms.

Fiction: Complete ms (dummy of book); e-queries OK. Contemporary children's picture books. "Books that portray God working in children's lives, prayer, or those that teach children how to develop a personal relationship with Jesus."

Special Needs: "We are looking for contemporary Christian picture books that show God in children's lives. Also parenting books—could be in devotional form—that inspire parents. Not how-to tips on parenting; we prefer books that make parents better parents by reminding them of their blessings, something heartwarming and inspirational."

Photos: Accepts freelance photos for book covers.

Tips: "Most open to contemporary books for today, children's picture books, and inspirational parenting. Creative, innovative books that meet the needs of a changing society without compromising or changing our core Christian beliefs."

*DIMENSION BOOKS, INC., PO Box 9, Starrucca PA 18462. (570)727-2486. Fax (570)727-2813. Catholic. Thomas P. Coffey, ed. Publishes 12 titles/yr. Receives 800 submissions annually. 2% of books from first-time authors. Reprints books. Prefers 200 pgs. Royalty 10-15% on retail; advance. Average first printing 6,000-20,000. Publication within 6 mos. Considers simultaneous submissions. Responds in 2-5 wks. Catalog for #10 SAE/1 stamp.

   Nonfiction: Query first. Christian spirituality, music, biography and psychology.

*DIMENSIONS FOR LIVING, 201 8th Ave. S, Nashville TN 37203. (615)749-6000. E-mail: jcrowe@umpublishing.org. Website: www.abingdon.org. United Methodist Publishing House. Joseph A. Crowe, ed. Books for the general Christian reader. Publishes 120 titles/yr. Receives 1,000 submissions annually. 5% of books from first-time authors. Reprints books. Prefers 144 pgs. Royalty 7½% on retail; some outright purchases; no advance. Average first printing 3,000. Publication within 2 yrs. No simultaneous submissions. Requires disk. Responds in 6-8 wks. Guidelines; free catalog.

   Nonfiction: Proposal/2 chapters; no phone query.

   Ethnic Books: African-American, Hispanic, Native-American, Korean.

   Special Needs: Inspiration/devotion, self-help, home/family, special occasion gift books.

DISCOVERY PUBLISHING HOUSE, Box 3566, Grand Rapids MI 49501. (616) 942-0218. Fax (616) 957-5741. E-mail: dph@rbc.net. Website: www.rbc.org. Radio Bible Class. Robert DeVries, pub.; submit to Carol Holquist, assoc pub. Guidelines. Not in topical listings.

   **Note: This publisher serviced by The Writer's Edge.

DOUBLEDAY RELIGION, 1540 Broadway, New York NY 10036. (212)354-6500. Fax (212)782-8911. Website: www.randomhouse.com. Random House, Inc. Eric Major, VP of Religion; submit to Trace Murphy, sr ed. Imprints: Image, Galilee, Doubleday Hardcover, Anchor Bible Commentaries. Publishes 45-50 titles/yr. Receives 1,500 submissions annually. 10%

of books from first-time authors. Royalty 7½-15% on retail; advance. Average first printing varies. Publication within 1 yr. Considers simultaneous submissions. Responds in 3 mos. No disk. No guidelines; catalog for 9x12 SAE/3 stamps.

Nonfiction: Agented submissions only. Proposal/3 chapters; no phone query.

Fiction: Agented submissions only. Proposal/3 chapters. For adults.

Ethnic Books: African-American.

Tips: "Most open to a book that has a big and well-defined audience. Have a clear proposal, lucid thesis and specified audience."

#DOVER PUBLICATIONS, INC., 31 E. 2nd St., Mineola NY 11501. (516)294-7000. Fax (516)873-1401. E-mail: dover@inch.com. Paul Negri, ed-in-chief. Publishes some religious titles/yr. Makes outright purchases. Query. Free catalog. Not included in topical listings.

Nonfiction: Query. Religion topics.

DRY BONES PRESS, PO Box 1437, Roseville CA 95678. Phone/fax (415)707-2129. E-mail: drybones@drybones.com. Website: www.drybones.com. Jim Rankin, ed/pub. Nursing and specialty books. Publishes 2-10 titles/yr. Receives 100 submissions annually. 90% of books from first-time authors. Acepts mss through agents. Reprints books. Prefers 108 or 250 pgs (unless poetry, special topic or tract). Royalty 6-10% on retail or as per arrangement; no advance. Does on-demand printing mostly. Publication within 1 yr. Considers simultaneous submissions. Requires disk or e-mail submissions. Responds in 1-2 mos (sometimes longer). Prefers NKJV. Guidelines (also on Website); no catalog (see Website).

Nonfiction: Proposal/1-2 chapters; fax/e-query OK. "Looking for books written by patients about their experience of illness."

Fiction: Proposal/1-2 chapters. Adults. "Looking for good quality, slice-of-life, local color, and controversy. We will accept sci-fi and fantasy."

Also Does: Some e-books.

Tips: "Most open to liturgical books, e.g. psalter; poetry, if not overly trite or sentimental; patient experiences, if well-told and suitable to examination along with professional literature."

+EDEN PUBLISHING, PO Box 20176, Keizer OR 97307-0176. Phone/fax (503)390-9013. E-mail: barbgdan@yahoo.com. Website: www.edenpublishing.com. Barbara Griffin, ed. Inspirational books that foster personal growth. Restarting publication. Receives 400-500 submissions annually. 50% of books from first-time authors. No mss through agents. No reprints. Length varies. Royalty 10%; no advance. Average first printing 1,000-1,500. Publication within 4-6 mos. Considers simultaneous submissions. No disk or e-mail submissions. Responds in 2 wks. Prefers NIV. No guidelines; catalog for #10 SAE/1 stamp.

Nonfiction: Query only first; no phone/fax/e-query. "Would consider home-school materials and will consider helping self-published Christian authors with distribution; willing to share website space on the right books."

Fiction: "We consider only self-published fiction."

Tips: "We seek books that will provide educational, inspirational help to others. Counseling, self-help, how-to, and appropriate gift books will be seriously considered."

*EDITORES BETANIA-CARIBE, PO Box 141000, Nashville TN 37214-1000. (615)902-2370. E-mail: sam@editorialcaribe.com. Website: www.caribe betania.com. Subsidiary of Thomas Nelson. Sam Rodriguez, ed. Targets the needs and wants of the Hispanic community. Imprints: Betania and Caribe. Publishes 45 titles/yr. Receives 50 submissions annually. 90% of books from first-time authors. No mss through agents. Prefers 192 pgs. Royalty on net; advance $500. Average first printing 4,000. Publication within 15 mos. Accepts e-mail submissions. No guidelines; free catalog.

Nonfiction: Query letter only; no phone/fax/e-query. "We currently have a backlog of 18 months."

Ethnic Books: Hispanic imprint.

Also Does: Computer games.

Tips: "Most open to Christian books based on the Bible."

*EDITORIAL PORTAVOZ, PO Box 2607, Grand Rapids MI 49333. (616)451-4775. (800)733-2607. Fax (616)451-9330. Website: www.portavoz.com. Spanish Division of Kregel Publishing.

EERDMANS BOOKS FOR YOUNG READERS, 255 Jefferson SE, Grand Rapids MI 49503. (616)459-4591. Fax (616)459-6540. E-mail: jzylstra@eerdmans. com. Website: www.eerdmans.com/youngreaders. Wm. B. Eerdmans Publishing. Judy Zylstra, ed. Books that nurture children's faith in God and help children and young people understand and explore life in God's world. Publishes 12-15 titles/yr. Receives 3,000 submissions annually. 5% of books from first-time authors. Age-appropriate length. Royalty 5-7½% of retail; advance to previously published authors. Average first printing 10,000 (picture books) and 5,000-6,000 (chapter books/novels). Publication within 1-3 yrs. Considers simultaneous submissions. Responds in 2 mos. Guidelines (also by e-mail/Website); catalog for 9x12 SAE/4 stamps.

Nonfiction: Proposal/3 chapters for book-length; complete ms for picture books; no phone/fax/e-query. For children and teens.

Fiction: Proposal/3 chapters for book-length; complete ms for picture books. For children and teens.

Tips: "Please do not send illustrations with picture book manuscripts unless you are a professional illustrator. When submitting artwork, send color copies, not originals."

WM B. EERDMANS PUBLISHING CO., 255 Jefferson Ave. SE, Grand Rapids MI 49503. (616)459-4591. Fax (616)459-6540. E-mail: sales@eerdmans. com. Website: www.eerdmans.com. Protestant/Academic/Theological. Jon Pott, ed-in-chief. Publishes 12-130 titles/yr. Receives 4,000 submissions annually. 10% of books from first-time authors. Reprints books. Royalty. Average first printing 4,000. Publication within 1 yr. Considers simultaneous submissions. Responds in 3-4 wks. Guidelines; free catalog.

Nonfiction: Proposal/2-3 chapters; no fax/e-query. "Looking for religious approaches to contemporary issues; spiritual growth; scholarly works; biography for middle readers through young adults; children's picture books expressing positive family values."

Fiction: Query letter only. Children/teen/adult. "We are looking for adult novels with high literary merit. For our children's program we look for manuscripts that help a child explore life in God's world, and foster a child's exploration of her or his faith."

Tips: "Most open to material with general appeal, but well researched, cutting-edge material that bridges the gap between evangelical and mainline worlds."

**Note: This publisher serviced by The Writer's Edge.

ELDER BOOKS, PO Box 490, Forest Knolls CA 94933. (415)488-9002. Fax (415)488-4720. E-mail: info@ElderBooks.com. Website: www.ElderBooks.com. Carmel Sheridan, dir. Publishes 6-10 titles/yr. Receives 250 submissions annually. 50% of books from first-time authors. Reprints books. Prefers 130 pgs. Royalty 7% of retail; no advance. Average first printing 3,000. Publication within 9 months. No disk. Responds in 3 mos.

Nonfiction: Proposal/2 chapters. "Most open to parenting, health, women's or seniors' issues."

ELDRIDGE PUBLISHING CO., INC., PO Box 1595, Venice FL 34284. (800)95-CHURCH. Fax (800)453-5179. E-mail: info@95church.com. Website: www.95church.com. Independent Christian drama publisher. Dottie Dunham, ed. To provide superior religious drama to enhance preaching and teaching, whatever your Christian denomination. Publishes 35 plays/yr. Receives 350-400 plays annually. 75% of plays from first-time authors. One-act to full-length plays. Outright purchases of $100-1,000; no advance. Publication within 1 yr. Considers simultaneous submissions. Responds in 1-3 mos. Requires disk or e-mail submission. Free guidelines (also by e-mail or Website)/catalog.

Plays: Complete ms; e-query OK. For children, teens and adults.

Special Needs: Always looking for high quality Christmas and Easter plays but open to other holiday and "anytime" Christian plays too. Can be biblical or current day, for performance by all ages, children through adult.

Tips: "Have play produced at your church and others prior to submission, to get out the bugs. At least try a stage reading."

ELECTRIC WORKS PUBLISHING, 605 Ave. C. East, Bismarck ND 58501. (701)255-0356. E-mail: editors@electricpublishing.com. Website: www.electricpublishing.com. James R. Bohe, ed-in-chief. Digital books. Publishes 30 titles/yr. Receives 280 submissions annually. 80% of books from first-time authors. Reprints books. Prefers up to 40,000 wds. Royalty 36-40% of net; no advance. Publication within 2 mos. Considers simultaneous submissions. Responds in 2 mos. Prefers e-mail submissions. Guidelines & catalog on Website.

Nonfiction: Complete ms; e-query OK.

Fiction: For all ages. Submit complete manuscript electronically. "Must be socially responsible."

Special Needs: Poetry books. Send complete manuscript.

Also Does: E-books.

Tips: "Looking for children's books."

+ELIJAH PRESS, Meadow House Communications, Inc., PO Box 317628,

Cincinnati OH 45231-7628. (513)521-7362. Fax (513)521-7364. E-mail: info@meadowhouse.com. Website: www.elijahpress.com. Published religious/spiritual titles. S.R. Davis, ed. Not included in topical listings. No questionnaire returned.

+ELIM BOOKS, PO Box 704, Hampden MA 01036. (413)566-0282. Fax (413)566-2173. E-mail: editor@elimbooks.com. Website: www.elimbooks. com. Kimberley Converse, ed. Publishes 2 titles/yr. Receives 20 submissions annually. 90% of books from first-time authors. Prefers NIV. No catalog.

Nonfiction: Books & booklets.

ENCOUNTER BOOKS, 116 New Montgomery St., Ste. 206, San Francisco CA 94105. (415)538-1460. Fax (415)538-1461. E-mail: read@encounterbooks. com. Website: www.encounterbooks.com. Peter Collier, pub. Focus is scholarly/educational. Publishes 2-4 titles/yr. Receives 1,000 submissions annually. 5% of books from first-time authors. Reprints books. Prefers 300 pgs. Royalty 7-10% of retail; advance $5,000-25,000. Average first printing 2,500 (hardcopy), 5,000 (paperback). Publication within 18 mos. Considers simultaneous submissions. Requires disk. Responds in 3 mos. Any version. Guidelines; free catalog.

Nonfiction: Proposal/1-2 chapters; fax/e-query OK. "Looking for anything for aging baby boomers."

Photos: Accepts freelance photos for book covers.

Tips: "No adventure stories, even true ones. Looking for home schooling, theology and scholarly books."

ETC PUBLICATIONS, 700 E. Vereda del Sur, Palm Springs CA 92262. (760)325-5352. Fax (760)325-8841. E-mail: etcbooks@earthlink.net. LeeOna S. Hostrop, sr. ed. Publishes textbooks for the Christian and secular markets at all levels of education. Publishes 1 textbook/yr. Royalty 5-15% of net; no advance. Average first printing 1,500. Publication within 9 mos. No simultaneous submissions. Requires disk (or camera-ready). Responds in 1 mo. No guidelines (use *Chicago Manual of Style*); catalog for #10 SAE/1 stamp.

Nonfiction: Query only; fax query OK. "We are interested in Christian-oriented state history textbooks only."

Photos: Accepts freelance photos for book covers.

Tips: "Open only to state histories that are required at a specific grade level and are Christian oriented, with illustrations."

+EVERYBOOK, INC., 2300 Vartan Way, 2nd Floor, Harrisburg PA 17110. (717)703-1010. Fax (717)703-1007. E-book publisher. Not included in topical listings. No questionnaire returned.

#FACTS ON FILE, 11 Penn Plaza, New York NY 10001. (212)967-8800. Fax (212)967-9196. E-mail: llikoff@factsonfile.com. Website: factsonfile.com. Infobase Holdings. Laurie Likoff, ed. School and library reference and trade books tied to curriculum and areas of cross-cultural studies, including religion. Publishes 3-5 religious titles/yr. Receives 10-20 submissions annually. 2% of books from first-time authors. Prefers 224-480 pgs. Royalty 10-15% on retail; outright purchases of $2,000-10,000; advance $10,000. Some work-for-hire. Average first printing 5,000. Publication within 9-12 mos. Considers simultaneous submissions. Responds in 2 mos. Requires disk. Free guidelines/catalog.

Nonfiction: Query or proposal/2 chapters; fax/e-query OK.

+FAITH FICTION, PO Box 62, Bradleyville MO 65614. (417)796-2842. E-mail: submissions@faithfiction.faithweb.com. Website: www.faithfiction. faithweb.com. Jeanene Sutton, pub. Publishes full-length works of Christian fiction. New electronic publisher. Word count flexible. Royalty 50% of retail; paid monthly. Responds in 30 days. E-mail questions to: information@faithfiction.faithweb.com. Guidelines and copy of contract on their Website.

Fiction: Prefers e-mail submissions (as attached file in MS Word.doc format).

Tips: "Must have strong focus on the Spirt-filled and faith-filled life, and demonstrate the power of God."

*FAITH ONE PUBLISHING, 7901 S. Vermont Ave., Los Angeles CA 90044. (323)758-3777. Fax (323)778-5545. E-mail: swilliford@faithdome.org. Website: www.faithdome.org. Crenshaw Christian Center. Stanley O. Williford, ed. Primary focus is to publish works by the pastors and ministers of the Crenshaw Christian Center. Publishes 5-8 titles/yr. Receives 10-25 submissions annually. 15% of books from first-time authors. No mss through agents. No guidelines or catalog.

Nonfiction: Query only.

Tips: "We have not yet begun to pay for manuscripts."

FAMILY HOPE SERVICES, 3315 Fernbrook Ln. N., Plymouth MN 55447. (763)557-8670. Fax (763)557-8673. E-mail: teenhope@familyhopeservices .org. Website: www.familyhopeservices.org. Nondenominational. Sue Thomas, curriculum coord. Promotes hope and life transformation for at-risk teens. Not accepting unsolicited mss at this time.

Tips: "We write curriculum and books for at-risk youth and their families. Writers are contracted on a work-for-hire basis. All proceeds from the sale of curriculum and books are used to support the ministry and outreach of the organization."

+FINDHORN PRESS, PO Box 13939, Tallahassee FL 32317-3939. (850)893-2920. Toll-free (877)390-4425. Fax (850)893-3442. E-mail: findhorn @macguys.com.Website: findhornpress.com. Not included in topical listings. Did not return questionnaire.

Nonfiction: E-mail a short synopsis; no complete ms.

FOCUS ON THE FAMILY PUBLISHERS, 8605 Explorer Dr., Colorado Springs CO 80920-1051. (719)531-3496. Fax (719)531-3484. E-mail: maddoxmh@aol.com. Website: www.family.org. Submit to Mark Maddox, acq. ed. Dedicated to the preservation of marriage and the family. Publishes 10-15 titles/yr. Receives 1,000 submissions annually. Prefers 200 pgs. Average first printing 25,000. Publication within 2 yrs. Considers simultaneous submissions. Responds in 6-8 wks. Free guidelines.

Nonfiction: Submit ONLY a 1-pg query letter.

Tips: "Need highly practical books—tell how to do something and don't make it too complicated. Also looking for writers who are verbal and can do a good, lively interview." Looking for writers to write on assignment.

**Note: This publisher serviced by The Writer's Edge.

FOCUS PUBLISHING, PO Box 665, Bemidji MN 56619. (218)759-9817. Fax (218)751-7210. E-mail: focus@paulbunyan.net. Jan Haley, pres. Does Christian Bible study books and publications geared toward children and homeschooling families. Publishes 4-6 titles/yr. Receives 350 submissions annually. 90% of books from first-time authors. Royalty 7-10% on retail; no advance. Publication within 1 yr. Responds in 2 mos. Free catalog.

> **Nonfiction:** Proposal. Adult Bible study books. Also hopes to build their children's dept.
>
> **Fiction:** No adult fiction at this time.
>
> **Tips:** "Include your target market with proposals, and send SASE."

FORTRESS PRESS, 100 S. 5th St., Suite 700 (55402), Box 1209, Minneapolis MN 55440-1209. (612)330-3300. Fax (612)330-3215. Website: www.augsburgfortress.org. No longer accepting freelance submissions.

FORWARD MOVEMENT PUBLICATIONS, 412 Sycamore St., Cincinnati OH 45202. (513)721-6659. Fax (513)721-0729. E-mail: forwardmovement @msn.com. Website: www.forwardmovement.org. Episcopal. Edward S. Gleason, ed/dir. To help rejuvenate the life of the church. Publishes 12 titles/yr. Receives 50 submissions annually. 50% of books from first-time authors. No mss through agents. Rarely reprints books. Prefers 150 pgs. One-time honorarium; no advance. Average first printing 5,000. Publication within 9 mos. Considers simultaneous submissions. Prefers disk. Responds in 1-2 mos. Prefers NRSV. Guidelines; free catalog.

> **Nonfiction:** Query for book, complete ms if short; fax/e-query OK.
>
> **Fiction:** Query. For children and teens. "We are beginning to publish fiction for middle-school readers." Send for guidelines.
>
> **Ethnic Books:** Hispanic pamphlets.
>
> **Also Does:** Booklets, 4-32 pgs; pamphlets 4-8 pgs; tracts.
>
> **Tips:** "We sell primarily to a mainline Protestant audience. Most open to books that deal with the central doctrines of the Christian faith."

+FOUNDATION FOR RELIGIOUS FREEDOM, 1680 N. Vine St., #415, Los Angeles CA 90028. (323)468-0567. Fax (323)468-0562. E-mail: nancyo @telcocom.com. Nancy O'Meara, assoc. dir. An interfaith group publishing books about overcoming religious prejudice or hatred. Publishes 1-2 titles/yr. New publisher. Accepts mss through agents.

> **Nonfiction:** Query first; phone/fax/e-query OK.
>
> **Fiction:** Query first. For all ages. "We publish books on religious tolerance, and are interested in fiction (or nonfiction) about religious people working together to make the world a better place for all."
>
> **Also Does:** Booklets, pamphlets, e-books.

FREDERICK FELL PUBLISHERS, INC. (formerly Lifetime Books), 2131 Hollywood Blvd., Ste. 305, Hollywood FL 33073. (954)925-5242. Fax (954) 925-5244. E-mail: fellpub@aol.com. Website: www.fellpub.com. Barbara Newman, sr ed. General publisher that publishes 2-4 religious titles/yr. Receives 100 submissions annually. 95% of books from first-time authors. Reprints books. Prefers 60,000 wds or 200-300 pgs. Royalty 6-15% on retail; advance of $500-10,000. Average first printing 7,500. Publication within 1 yr. Considers simultaneous submissions. Responds in 1-2 mos. Free guidelines (on Website)/catalog.

Nonfiction: Proposal/2 chapters; fax query OK. Looking for self-help and how-to books. Include a clear marketing and promotional strategy.

Fiction: Proposal/2 chapters. For adults; adventure and historical. Looking for great story lines, with potential movie prospects."

Tips: "Spirituality, optimism, and a positive attitude have international appeal. Steer clear of doom and gloom; less sadness and more gladness benefits all." Also publishes New Age books.

+FREESTAR PRESS, PO Box 54552, Cincinnati OH 45254-0552. Phone/fax (800)441-6077. Does religious/spiritual and science books. Incomplete topical listings. No questionnaire returned.

FRIENDS UNITED PRESS, 101 Quaker Hill Dr., Richmond IN 47374. (765)962-7573. Fax (765)966-1293. E-mail: friendspress@fum.org. Website: www.fum.org. Friends United Meeting (Quaker). Barbara Bennett Mays, ed. To gather persons into a fellowship where Jesus Christ is known as Lord and Teacher. Publishes 5 titles/yr. Receives 180 submissions annually. 50% of books from first-time authors. No mss through agents. Rarely does subsidy, 5%. Reprints books. Prefers 200 pgs. Royalty 7½% of net; no advance. Average first printing 1,000-1,500. Publication within 1 yr. Considers simultaneous submissions. Responds in 3 mos. Prefers disk or e-mail submissions. Guidelines (also on Website); free catalog.

Nonfiction: Proposal/2 chapters; fax/e-query OK.

Fiction: Proposal/2 chapters. For all ages. Very limited. "Quaker faith must be a significant part of the story or the characters."

Ethnic Books: Howard Thurman Books (African American).

Tips: "Most open to Quaker authors. Looking for Quaker-related spirituality, or current faith issues/practice addressed from a Quaker experience or practice."

+GENEVA PRESS, 100 Witherspoon St., Louisville KY 40202-1396. (502)569-5043. Fax (502)569-5113. E-mail: Kkaye@ctr.pcusa.org. Website: www. pcusa.org/ppc. Presbyterian Church (USA). David Dobson & Martha Gilliss, eds. Imprint of Westminster John Knox Press. Publishes in three categories: (1) heritage, history, doctrine, polity and institutions of the denomination; (2) theological, social, and ethical issues confronting the church; and (3) congregational mission (books for Christian educators, pastors, lay leaders, and laity). Incomplete topical listings.

GILGAL PUBLICATIONS, Box 3399, Sunriver OR 97707. (541)593-8418. Fax (541)593-5604. E-mail: judyo@gilgal.com. Website: www.gilgal.com. Judy Osgood, exec. ed. Focuses on collections of meditations on specific themes. Publishes 1 title/yr. Receives 100+ submissions annually. 25-30% of submissions from first-time authors. No mss through agents. Pays $25/meditation on acceptance, plus 2 copies of the book. Average first printing 3,000. Publication time varies. Responds in 1-2 mos. No disk. Guidelines (required).

Nonfiction: Complete ms (after reading guidelines); fax query OK. "Our books are all anthologies on coping with stress and resolving grief. Not interested in other book mss. Currently interested in meditations on bereavement of various kinds."

Tips: "For the foreseeable future, we will only be continuing our Gilgal Meditation Series and will not be buying book manuscripts."

B. J. GOETZ PUBLISHING CO., 3055 W. John Beers Rd., Stevensville MI 49127. (616)429-6442. Fax (616)429-5353. E-mail: BJGOETZ@market place29ad.com. Website: www.marketplace29ad.com. B. J. Goetz, pub. Specializes in materials to enhance Christian education programs; experiential/environmental concepts. Publishes 1 title/yr. Receives 12 submissions annually. 100% of books from first-time authors. Variable payment for outright purchase. Average first printing 1,000. Responds in 1-3 mos. Any version. No guidelines; catalog.

Nonfiction: Proposal or complete ms. "We need an interdenominational approach in Christian education programs or Bible studies for children 5-12. Also Jewish holidays with a Christian approach; angels and children."

Tips: "Most open to experiential and environmental learning concepts; and dramas."

GOLD 'N' HONEY BOOKS. Bought by Zondervan; no longer a separate imprint.

GOOD BOOK PUBLISHING COMPANY, PO Box 837, Kihei HI 96753-0837. Phone/fax (808)874-4876. E-mail: dickb@dickb.com. Website: www. dickb.com/index.shtml. Christian/Protestant/Bible Fellowship. Ken Burns, pres. Researches and publishes books on the biblical/Christian roots of Alcoholics Anonymous. Publishes 1 title/yr. Receives 8 submissions annually. 80% of books from first-time authors. No mss through agents. Reprints books. Prefers 250 pgs. Royalty 10%; no advance. Average first printing 3,000. Publication within 2 mos. Considers simultaneous submission. Responds in 1 wk. No disk. Prefers KJV. No guidelines; free catalog.

Nonfiction: Proposal; no phone/fax/e-query. Books on the spiritual history and success of A.A.; 12-step spiritual roots.

Also Does: Pamphlets and booklets.

GOOD NEWS PUBLISHERS, 1300 Crescent St., Wheaton IL 60187. (630) 682-4300x308. Fax (630)682-4785. E-mail: gdennis@goodnews-crossway. org. Geoffrey L. Dennis, dir. Tracts only; publishing the gospel message in an attractive and relevant format. Publishes 30 tracts/yr. Receives 500 submissions annually. 2% of tracts from first-time authors. Prefers 650-800 wds. Pays about $150 or a quantity of tracts. Average first printing 250,000. Publication within 8 mos. Considers simultaneous submissions. Responds in 6 wks. Guidelines; free tract catalog.

Tracts: Complete ms.

Also Does: Booklets.

GOSPEL PUBLISHING HOUSE, 1445 Boonville Ave., Springfield MO 65802. (417)862-2781. Website: www.ag.org. Glen Ellard, sr. book ed. Supports the pastors and churches of the Assemblies of God. Publishes 3-5 nondepartmental and 7-9 departmental titles/yr. Receives 260 submissions annually. 33-50% of books from first-time authors. Reprints books. Prefers 50,000 wds or 160 pgs. Royalty on net; no advance. Average first printing 5,000. Publication within 12-18 mos. Considers simultaneous submissions. Responds in 4-6 wks. Requires disk (if accepted). Prefers NIV. Guidelines.

Nonfiction: Query only; no phone/fax/e-query.

Special Needs: Books on Pentecostal and pastoral leadership; Holy Spirit; deaf culture ministries.

Ethnic Books: Hispanic.

Also Does: Booklets.

Tips: "Any books related to departmental ministries would require the interest and support of the corresponding department (such as Christian education or youth)."

*GOSPEL TRACT SOCIETY, INC., PO Box 1118, Independence MO 64051. (816)461-6086. Fax (816)461-4305. Gospel Tract Society, Inc. David Buttram, ed. "We always need good, Bible-based articles that will fit a tract format. We also use poems in tract form."

GRACE HOUSE PRESS, 2550 9th St., Ste. 101, Berkeley CA 94710-2551. (510)649-7175. Fax (510)649-7190. E-mail: conaripub@aol.com, or conari @conari.com. Website: www.conari.com. Mary Jane Ryan, exec ed; Annette Madden, mng ed. Focus is on Christian Acts of Kindness. Imprint of Conari Press. Publishes 2-4 titles/yr. Receives 1,000 submissions annually. 50% of books from first-time authors. Reprints bks. Royalty 12-16% of net; variable advance. Average first printing 20,000. Publication within 1-3 yrs. Considers simultaneous submissions. Accepts disk. Responds in 3 mos. Guidelines; catalog for 6x9 SAE/3 stamps.

Nonfiction: Proposal/3 chapters; no phone/fax query; e-query OK.

Photos: Accepts freelance photos for book covers.

Tips: "Most open to spirituality, collections of stories, inspiration. We are the publishers of the Random Acts of Kindness series."

GREENWOOD PUBLISHING GROUP, 88 Post Road West, Westport CT 06881. (203)226-3571. Fax (203)226-6009. Website: www.Greenwood. com. Reed Elsevier Co. Suzanne Staszak-Silva, ed. Imprints: Greenwood and Praeger. Publishes 0-20 titles/yr. Prefers 70,000-100,000 wds. Royalty on net; some advances. Average first printing 400. Publication within 1 yr. Considers simultaneous submissions. Prefers disk. Responds in 1-3 mos. Guidelines (by e-mail or Website); free catalog.

Nonfiction: Book proposal/1 chapter or all chapters available; phone/e-query OK.

Special Needs: Religious studies (scholarly); criminology (scholarly); sociology (scholarly).

Ethnic Books: Black studies (scholarly).

Tips: "Most open to scholarly/academic books."

GROUP PUBLISHING, INC., 1515 Cascade Ave., Loveland CO 80539-0481. (970)669-3836. Fax (970)679-4370. Website: www.grouppublishing.com. Non-denominational. Dave Thornton, dir. of prod. dev. (Dthornton@

grouppublishing.com); Linda Anderson, children's ed; Kelli Trujillo, youth ed. Imprints: Group Books and Vital Ministry. Helping church leaders change lives with resources that are R.E.A.L. (Relational, Experiential, Applicable, Learner-based). Publishes 50 titles/yr. Receives 1,000+ submissions annually. 5% of books from first-time authors. Prefers mss through agents. Some subsidy. No reprints. Prefers 128-250 pgs. Outright purchases of $25-3,000 or royalty of 6-10% of net; advance $1,500. Average first printing 5,000. Publication within 12-18 mos. Considers simultaneous submissions. Responds in 3 mos. Requires disk. Guidelines; no catalog.

> **Nonfiction:** Query or proposal/1-3 chapters; e-query OK. "Looking for practical ministry tools for pastors, youth workers, C.E. directors, and teachers with an emphasis on active learning. Read *Why Nobody Learns Much of Anything at Church: And How to Fix It* and *The Dirt on Learning* by Thom & Joani Schultz."

> **Tips:** "Most open to practical, active learning manuscripts for church/Sunday school leaders. Be sure to read the writers guidelines. Do not send in materials we do not have a market for, i.e., fiction, children's picture books."

GROUP'S FAITHWEAVER BIBLE CURRICULUM, 1515 Cascade Ave., Loveland CO 80539. (970)679-3836. Fax (970)669-4370. E-mail: kloesche @grouppublishing.com. Website: www.faithweaver.com. Privately held; non-denominational. Kerri Loesche, ed asst. To promote Christian growth in children, youth and adults. Publishes 24 titles/yr. Receives 200 submissions annually. 40% of books from first-time authors. No mss through agents. Outright purchase; work-for-hire; advance. Average first printing 5,000. Publication within 12-18 mos. Accepts simultaneous submissions. Responds in 3-6 mos. Accepts disk. Prefers NIV. Trial assignment guidelines (also by e-mail)/catalog for 9x12 SAE/2 stamps.

> **Nonfiction:** Query requesting a trial assignment for children or youth; phone/fax/e-query OK. Produces curriculum for all age levels from infants to adults. Submissions received are only kept on file for 30 days.

GUERNICA EDITIONS, PO Box 117, Stn. P, Toronto ON M5S 2S6 Canada. (616)658-9888. Fax (616)657-8885. E-mail: antoniodalfonso@cs.com. Website: www.guernicaeditions.com. Antonio D'Alfonso, ed. Interested in the next generation of writers. Publishes 1 religious title/yr. Receives 100 submissions annually. 5% of books from first-time authors. No mss through agents. Reprints books. Prefers 100 pgs. Royalty 10% of net or retail; no advance. Average first printing 1,500. Publication within 18 mos. Responds in 1 mo. Requires disk; no e-mail. No guidelines (read one of our books to see what we like); for catalog send money order for stamps or IRCs (if from US).

> **Nonfiction:** Query first; no phone/fax/e-query. "Looking for books on world issues."

> **Fiction:** Query first. Looking for short and profound literary works.

> **Ethnic Books:** Concentration on other cultures. "We are involved in translations and ethnic issues."

Photos: Accepts freelance photos for book covers.

Tips: "Know what we publish. We're interested in books that bridge time and space; works that fit our editorial literary policies."

HARCOURT RELIGION PUBLISHERS, 1665 Embassy West Dr., Ste. 200, Dubuque IA 52002-2259. (800)922-7696. Fax (319) 557-3720. E-mail: mkrawczuk@harcourtbrace.com. Website: www.harcourtreligion.com. Catholic. Marge Krawczuk, mng ed. Publishes 50-100 titles/yr. Receives 100-300 submissions annually. Variable royalty or outright purchase; rarely pays advance. Average first printing 1,000-3,000. Publication within 1 yr. Considers simultaneous submissions. Responds in 2 mos. Free catalog.

Nonfiction: Complete ms. "Looking primarily for school and parish text books."

Photos: Accepts freelance photos for book covers. Submit to Lynn Molony, production mgr.

HARPER SAN FRANCISCO, 353 Sacramento St., #500, San Francisco CA 94111-3653. (415)477-4400. Fax (415)477-4444. E-mail: hcsanfrancisco @harpercollins.com. Website: www.harpercollins.com. Religious division of HarperCollins. John Loudon, exec. ed. Dedicated to publishing books of highest quality that illuminate diverse religious traditions and spiritual journeys and offer paths toward personal growth and holistic well-being. Publishes 75 titles/yr. Receives 10,000 submissions annually. 5% of books from first-time authors. Prefers 160-256 ms pgs. Royalty 10-15% on cloth, 7½% on paperback, on retail; advance $5,000 and up. Average first printing 7,500-50,000. Publication within 18 mos. Considers simultaneous submissions. Responds in 3-4 mos. Requires disk. No guidelines/catalog.

Nonfiction: Query only; fax query OK.

Tips: "Agented proposals only."

HARRISON HOUSE PUBLISHERS, Box 35035, Tulsa OK 74153. (918)494-5944. Website: www.harrisonhouse.com. Evangelical/Charismatic. This company is booked up for the next 2-3 years.

HARVEST HOUSE PUBLISHERS, 1075 Arrowsmith, Eugene OR 97402. (541)343-0123. Evangelical. Books and products that affirm biblical values and help people grow spiritually strong. Publishes 100 titles/yr. No longer accepting unsolicited submissions, proposals, queries, etc.

**Note: This publisher serviced by The Writer's Edge and ECPA First Edition Website.

#THE HAWORTH PASTORAL PRESS, an imprint of The Haworth Press, 10 Alice St., Binghamton NY 13904-1580. (607)722-5857. Fax (607)722-8465. Website: www.haworthpressinc.com. Bill Palmer, mng ed. Publishes 10 titles/yr. Receives 100 submissions annually. 50% of books from first-time authors. Reprints books. Prefers up to 250 pgs. Royalty 7½-15% of net; advance $500-1,000. Average first printing 1,500. Publication within 1 yr. Requires disk. Responds in 2 mos. Guidelines; free catalog.

Nonfiction: Proposal/3 chapters; no phone/fax query. "Looking for books on psychology/social work, etc., with a pastoral perspective."

HAY HOUSE, INC., PO Box 5100, Carlsbad CA 92018-5100. (760)431-7695. Fax (760)431-6948. E-mail: edit@hayhouse.com. Website: www. hayhouse.

com. Jill Kramer, ed dir. Books to help heal the planet. Publishes 4 religious titles/yr. Receives 200 religious submissions annually. 60% of books from first-time authors. Prefers 70,000 wds or 250 pgs. Royalty; advance. Average first printing 5,000. Publication within 14 mos. Considers simultaneous submissions. Responds in 1 mo. Guidelines (also by e-mail); free catalog for SASE.

   Nonfiction: Proposal/3 chapters; fax/e-query OK. "Looking for self-help/spiritual with a unique angle."

   Fiction: Query only. Rarely publishes fiction. "Only accept spiritual, adult fiction, if by a well-known author."

   Also Does: Some gift books.

   Tips: "We are looking for books with a unique slant, ecumenical, but not overly religious." Includes a broad range of religious titles, including New Age.

HEALTH COMMUNICATIONS, INC., 3201 SW 15th St., Deerfield Beach FL 33442. (954)360-0909. Fax (954)472-7288. E-mail: editorial@hcibooks. com. Website: www.hci-online.com, or www.hcibooks.com. Christine Belleris, ed. Nonfiction that emphasizes self-improvement, personal motivation, psychological health and overall wellness; recovery/addiction, self-help/psychology, health/wellness, soul/spirituality, inspiration, women's issues, relationships and family. Publishes 40 titles/yr. 20% of books from first-time authors. Prefers 250 pgs. Royalty 15% of net. Publication within 9 mos. Considers simultaneous submissions. Responds in 1-3 mos. Must get and follow guidelines for submission. Guidelines (also on Website); catalog for 9x12 SASE. Not in topical listings.

   Nonfiction: Query/outline and 2 chapters; no phone/fax/e-query. Needs books for Christian teens.

+HEALTHY EXCHANGES, 110 Industrial Dr., PO Box 124, DeWitt IA 52742-0124. (319)659-8234. Fax (319)659-2126. E-mail: healthyexchanges@ revealed.net. Website: www.neta.com/~healthy. JoAnna Lund, ed. Does cookbooks, health, lifestyle, religious/spiritual, and self-help books. Not included in topical listings. No questionnaire returned.

*HEART ARBOR BOOKS, 5061 Forest Rd., Mentor Road OH 44060. Karla Whitsitt, pub. No response to questionnaire; send SASE for guidelines.

*HEARTH PUBLISHING, 212 N. Ash, Hillsboro KS 67063. (316)947-3966. Fax (316)947-3392. Stan Thiessen, ed/dir. Wholesome literature of a classic nature, not necessarily religious. Publishes 4-6 titles/yr. Receives 600 submissions annually. 80+% of books from first-time authors. No mss through agents. Reprints books. Prefers 96-224 pgs (poetry 96 pgs). Negotiable royalty and advance. Average first printing 1,500-20,000. Publication within 8+ mos. Considers simultaneous submissions. Responds in 1-3 mos. Requires disk. Guidelines; no catalog.

   Nonfiction: Proposal/3-4 chapters; no phone/fax query. "Any topic, including genealogy and cookbooks."

   Fiction: Proposal/3-4 chapters. "Looking for juvenile and young adult (7-12) series or single books, classic adventure, fun to read; should fit secular markets as well as religious. Call about ongoing anthologies."

   Also Does: Booklets and chapbooks.

Tips: "Most open to books espousing Christian ethics but not necessarily religious. Good, wholesome adventure of any kind. Specialty cookbooks."

#HEART QUEST/TYNDALE HOUSE PUBLISHERS, PO Box 80, Wheaton IL 60189-0080. (630)668-8300. Fax (630)668-6885. Website: www.tyndale. com. Catherine Palmer, consulting ed; Rebekah Nesbitt, acq ed. Romance imprint. To encourage and challenge readers in their faith journey and/or Christian walk. Responds in 3 mos. Guidelines.

Fiction: One-page query/synopsis/3 chapters. "Must incorporate three plot lines—action, emotional, and faith (see guidelines for details). None set in Civil War period." Also considering novellas for anthologies (Victorian and Prairie).

Tips: "We want only historical romances (set in 1600-1945), contemporary romances, novellas and series (no stand-alone romances)."

HEARTSONG PRESENTS, Imprint of Barbour Publishing, Inc., PO Box 719, 1810 Barbour Dr., Uhrichsville, OH 44683. (740)922-6045. Fax (740)922-5948. E-mail: rgermany@barbourbooks.com, or info@heartsongpresents. com. Website: www.heartsongpresents.com. Rebecca Germany, ed; Tracie Peterson, acq ed. Produces affordable, wholesome entertainment through a book club that also helps to enhance and spread the Gospel. Publishes 52 titles/yr. Receives 700+ submissions annually. 15-20% of books from first-time authors. Prefers 50,000-55,000 wds. Outright purchases $2,000-2,500 (work-for-hire contract); no advance. Average first printing 20,000. Publication within 6-9 months. Considers simultaneous submissions. Responds in 6-9 wks. Requires disk. Prefers KJV for historicals; NIV for contemporary. Guidelines (also by e-mail/Website); no catalog.

Fiction: Proposal/3-4 chapters; fax/e-query OK. "We publish 2 contemporary and 2 historical romances every 4 weeks. We cover all topics and settings. Specific guidelines available."

Tips: "Most open to romance with a strong conservative-Christian theme. Read our books and study our style before submitting."

HENDRICKSON PUBLISHERS, 140 Summit St., PO Box 3473, Peabody MA 01961. (978)532-6546. Fax (978)573-8248. E-mail: DPenwell@hendrickson. com. Dan Penwell, mngr of trade products. To provide biblically oriented books for reference, learning and personal growth. Publishes 30-40 titles/yr. Receives 100-150 submissions annually. 25% of books from first-time authors. Reprints books. Prefers 200-500 pgs. Royalty 10-14% of net; some advances. Average first printing 3,000. Publication within 9-12 mos. Considers simultaneous submissions. Responds in 1-2 mos. Prefers e-mail submissions. Follow *Chicago Manual of Style*. Prefers NIV. Guidelines (also by e-mail); catalog for 9x12 SAE/6 stamps.

Nonfiction: Query/summary or sample chapters; fax/e-query OK. "We're looking for apologetics this year." Also publishes academic books through their Academic Book Division.

Special Needs: Books that help the reader's confrontation and interaction with Scripture, leading to a positive change in thought and action; books that give a hunger to studying, understanding and applying

Scripture; books that encourage and facilitate personal growth in such areas as personal devotions and a skillful use of the Bible.

Tips: "Well-written and edited books that are on the cutting edge of current trends."

**Note: This publisher serviced by The Writer's Edge.

HENSLEY PUBLISHING, 6116 E. 32nd St., Tulsa OK 74135. (918)664-8520. Fax (918)664-8562. E-mail: terri@hensleypublishing.com. Website: www. hensleypublishing.com. Terri Kalfas, ed dir. To edify and challenge the readers to a higher level of spiritual maturity in their Christian walk. Publishes 5-10 titles/yr. Receives 800 submissions annually. 50% of books from first-time authors. Reprints books. Prefers up to 250 pgs. Royalty on net; some outright purchases; no advance. Average first printing 5,000. Publication within 18 mos. Considers simultaneous submissions. Disk required in MAC format; no e-mail submissions. Responds in 2 mos. Guidelines (also on Website); catalog for 9x12 SAE/2 stamps.

Nonfiction: Query or proposal/3 consecutive chapters, or complete ms; no phone/fax/e-query. "Looking for short, inspirational books—study, adaptable to our new format, for use by small or large groups or individuals."

Ethnic Books: Will have a limited number of titles available this year.

Tips: "Most open to full-length topical Bible studies with personal application—workbook format."

+HILLCREST PUBLISHING, 1648 Campus Ct., Abilene TX 79601. (915)674-6950, or toll-free: (877)816-4455. Fax (915)674-6471. E-mail: Lemmonst @acuprs.acu.edu. Website: www.hillcrestpublishing.com. Not included in topical listings. No questionnaire returned.

+HIS IMAGE PUBLISHERS, 35220 Paseo Padre Pkwy, Freemont CA 94536-1211. J. Benjamin Young Sr., ed. Not included in topical listings. No questionnaire returned.

+HOHM PRESS, PO Box 2501, Prescott AZ 86302. (520)717-9189. Fax (520)717-1771. Regina Ryan, ed. Does health, religious/spiritual, and children's books. Incomplete topical listings. No questionnaire returned.

+HOLLIS BOOKS, LLC, 5904 Mt. Eagle Dr., #1009, Alexandria VA 22303. E-mail: hollisbooks@aol.com. Website: www.hollisbooks.com. Highly marketable books in any genre. Publishes 42-50 titles/yr. Guidelines on Website. Not included in topical listings. No questionnaire returned.

Nonfiction: Send synopsis by e-mail. "Preview the copy of our contract on our Website before submitting."

Fiction: Send synopsis by e-mail.

Tips: "Please note that while we are not a vanity or subsidy press (we pay for all printing, distribution and marketing), we ask the author to pay the printer's $399 prepress fee, which allows us to do more books."

HENRY HOLT & COMPANY BOOKS FOR YOUNG READERS, 115 W. 18th St., New York NY 10011. (212)886-9200. Henry Holt & Co., Inc. Submit to BYR Submissions. Cutting-edge fiction and nonfiction for the very young through young adults; some religious. Publishes 70 titles/yr. 5% of books from first-time authors. Royalty on retail; advance $3,000 & up.

Publication within 18 mos. Responds in 4 mos. Guidelines; catalog for 9x12 SAE/5 stamps.

Nonfiction: Complete ms. Juvenile illustrated books.

Fiction: Complete ms. Picture books, chapter books, novels.

Also Does: E-books.

HOLY CROSS ORTHODOX PRESS, 50 Goddard Ave., Brookline MA 02445. (617)731-3500. Fax (617)850-1460. Greek Orthodox. Anton C. Vrame, mng ed. Academic and general works of interest to Orthodox Christians in church history, worship, spirituality and life. Publishes 8-10 titles/yr. Receives 15-20 submissions annually. 50% of books from first-time authors. No mss through agents. Reprints bks. Prefers 200-300 pgs. Royalty 8-12% on retail; no advance. Average first printing 750-1,000. Publication within 12-18 mos. Considers simultaneous submissions. Requires disk (MAC). Responds in 3-4 mos. Prefers RSV. No guidelines; free catalog.

Nonfiction: Complete ms. Also open to saints and iconography. "Most open to a book on historic Orthodox Christianity with a sound theological basis; and spirituality based upon liturgical experience."

Ethnic Books: Greek (orthodox).

Tips: "Most open to work with a general interest based upon sound Orthodox Christian theology."

HONOR BOOKS, PO Box 55388, Tulsa OK 74155. (918)496-9007. Fax (918) 496-3588. E-mail: info@honorbooks.com. Website: www.HonorBooks. com. Inspirational/devotional. Submit to Acquisitions Editor. To inspire, encourage, and motivate readers to draw nearer to God, to experience His love and grace. New Imprint: RiverOak Publishing. Publishes 60 titles/yr. Receives 2,000 submissions annually. 2% of books from first-time authors. Royalty on net, outright purchase or work-for-hire assignments; negotiable advance. Publication within 14 mos. Considers simultaneous submissions. Responds in 1-4 mos. Guidelines.

Nonfiction: Proposal/2 chapters. Send photocopies.

Special Needs: Seasonal gift books; third-person stories reflecting God's wisdom applied to everyday life in a devotional format.

Tips: "Our books are for busy, achievement-oriented people who are looking for balance between reaching their goals and knowing that God loves them unconditionally. Our books should challenge spiritual growth, victorious living, and an intimate knowledge of God. Write about what you are for, not what you are against. We look for manuscripts that are biblically correct and that edify the reader."

HOWARD PUBLISHING CO., INC., 3117 N. 7th St., West Monroe LA 71291. (318)396-3122 Fax (318)397-1882. E-mail: dennyb@howardpublishing. com. Website: www.howardpublishing.com. John Howard, pres.; Denny Boultinghouse, exec. ed; submit to Manuscript Review Committee. Christian publisher. Publishes 20-24 titles/yr. Receives 450 submissions annually. 20% of books from first-time authors. Prefers 200-250 pgs. Negotiable royalty & advance. Average first printing 10,000. Publication within 2 yrs. Considers simultaneous submissions. Responds in 6-8 wks. No disk. Prefers NIV. Free guidelines (also on Website)/catalog.

Nonfiction: Proposal/2-3 chapters; no phone query.

Tips: "Our authors must first be Christ-centered in their lives and writing, then qualified to write on the subject of choice. Public name recognition is a plus. Authors who are also public speakers usually have a ready-made audience."

JOHN HUNT PUBLISHING, LTD., 46A West St., New Alresford, Hants, UK S024 9AU. (01) 962 735320. Fax (44) 1962 736881. E-mail: office @johnhuntpub.demon.co.uk. Website: www.johnhunt-publishing. com. John Hunt, ed. Imprints: Hunt & Thorpe; Arthur James Ltd. Color Christian books for the international market, particularly for children. Publishes 40 titles/yr. Receives 300 submissions annually. 2% of books from first-time authors. Royalty 2-10% of net; outright purchases of $100-1,000; advance $250. Average first printing 10,000. Publication within 18 mos. No simultaneous submissions. Responds in 1 wk. No disk. No guidelines; free catalog.

Nonfiction: Proposal/1 chapter; no phone query.

HUNTINGTON HOUSE, PO Box 53788, Lafayette LA 70505. (337)237-7049. Fax (318)237-7060. E-mail: ladawn@eatel.net. Website: www.huntington housebooks.com. Mark Anthony, ed. Focus is on educating readers on current events and the culture war. Publishes 25-30 titles/yr. Receives 1,500 submissions annually. 25% of books from first-time authors. Reprints books. Prefers 50,000-60,000 wds or 208-224 pgs. Royalty 10% of net on first book, graduated royalty on second; negotiable advance. Average first printing 5,000-10,000. Publication within 1 yr. Considers simultaneous submissions. Responds in 4 mos. Call for guidelines (also on Website); free catalog.

Nonfiction: Proposal; phone/fax/e-query OK. "Looking for political, social, current events, One World Government exposés, and anti-New Age."

Fiction: Query. No children's books at this time.

Also Does: Pamphlets and booklets.

Tips: "Authors must be available to perform interviews at our expense."

ICS PUBLICATIONS, 2131 Lincoln Rd. NE, Washington DC 20002. (202)832-8489. Fax (202)832-8967. Website: www.icspublications.org. Catholic/Institute of Carmelite Studies. Submit to Acq. Ed. For those interested in the Carmelite tradition with focus on prayer and spirituality. Publishes 6 titles/yr. Receives 30 submissions annually. 10% of books from first-time authors. Reprints books. Prefers 200 pgs. Royalty 2-6% on retail; some outright purchases; advance $500. Average first printing 3,000-7,000. Publication within 2 yrs. Considers simultaneous submissions. Accepts disk. Responds in 2 mos. No guidelines; catalog for 7x10 SAE/2 stamps.

Nonfiction: Query or outline/1 chapter; phone/fax/e-query OK. "Most open to translation of Carmelite classics; popular introductions to Carmelite themes which show a solid grasp of the tradition."

IN CELEBRATION, 3195 Wilson Dr. NW, Grand Rapids MI 49544. (616)802-3072. Fax (616)802-3007. E-mail: akieda@tribune.com. Website: www. instructionalfair.com. Instructional Fair Group. Alyson Kieda, dir/product dev. Producer of books, and Sunday school, Christian school, and home-schooling aids. 90% freelance. Query or outright submission. Pays standard amount on acceptance for all rts. Rarely pays royalties. Average first printing 5,000. Publication within 1 yr. Considers simultaneous submissions. Responds in 6-8 wks. Open to ideas for children's craft and activity books, parent/teacher resources, and workbooks for home, Sunday school, and Christian schools; and children and youth ministry resources. Guidelines; free catalog.

> **Tips:** "Open to new book ideas. Looking for authors/artists to produce books to match our ideas. We do devotional books for children."

+INKLING BOOKS, 11537—34th Ave. NE, Seattle WA 98125-5613. (206)365-1624. Fax (206)838-1542. E-mail: Inkling@foxinternet.net. Website: www.InklingBooks.com. Michael W. Perry, pub. Publishes 4 titles/yr. Accepts books through agents. Reprints books. Prefers 150-400 pgs. No advance. Prints on demand. Publication within 2 mos. No guidelines or catalog. Not currently accepting submissions.

INNISFREE PRESS, 136 Roumfort Rd., Philadelphia PA 19119-1632. (215) 247-4085. Fax (215)247-2343. E-mail: InnisfreeP@aol.com. Website: www.innisfreepress.com. Marcia Broucek, ed-in-chief. Specializes in books that go beyond traditional boundaries to investigate all aspects of spirituality. Publishes 8 titles/yr. Receives 500 submissions annually. 60% of books from first-time authors. Prefers 40,000-60,000 wds. Royalty 10% of net. Average first printing 5,000. Publication within 1 yr. Considers simultaneous submissions. Responds in 6 wks. Requires disk. Free guidelines (also on Website)/catalog.

> **Nonfiction:** Proposal/2 chapters; no phone/fax/e-query. "Looking for books with a spiritual perspective on everyday living in the workplace, in relationships, in personal growth."
>
> **Photos:** Accepts freelance photos for book covers.
>
> **Tips:** "Looking for books that demonstrate original thinking, not a rehash of what is already available in other forms." Books with personal experience and women's perspective are of special interest.

INTERNATIONAL AWAKENING PRESS, 139 N. Washington, PO Box 232, Wheaton IL 60189. Phone/fax (630)653-8616. E-mail: international awakening@juno.com. Website: www.intl-awaken.com. Intl. Awakening Ministries, Inc. Richard Owen Roberts, pres. Scholarly books on religious awakenings or revivals. Publishes 4 titles/yr. Receives 12 submissions annually. Reprints books. Royalty 10% on retail; no advance. Average first printing 3,000. Publication within 6 mos. Responds in 3 mos. Requires disk. Any translation; no paraphrases. No guidelines; free catalog.

> **Nonfiction:** Query only; no phone/fax query. "Looking for scholarly theology, especially Bible commentaries, church history, and revival-related material."
>
> **Also Does:** Booklets, pamphlets, tracts.
>
> **Photos:** Accepts freelance photos for book covers.

INTERVARSITY PRESS, Box 1400, Downers Grove IL 60515. Receptionist: (630)734-4000. Fax (630)734-4200. E-mail: mail@ivpress.com. Website:

www.ivpress.com. InterVarsity Christian Fellowship. Andrew T. LePeau, ed dir.; submit to Dave Zimmerman, acq. ed. To communicate the Lordship of Christ in all of life through a serious-minded approach to Scripture, the church and the world. Imprint: LifeGuide Bible Studies. Publishes 70-80 titles/yr. Receives 2,500 submissions annually. 15% of books from first-time authors. Prefers 50,000 wds or 200 pgs. Negotiable royalty on retail or outright purchase; negotiable advance. Average first printing 5,500. Publication within 2 yrs. Considers simultaneous submissions. Requires disk; no e-mail submissions. Responds in 3 mos. Guidelines (also on Website: www.gospelcom.net/ivpress); catalog for 9x12 SAE/5 stamps.

> **Nonfiction:** No unsolicited mss (from people they have had no previous contact with); no fax or e-queries. New authors should use The Writer's Edge (see their listing under Editorial Services—IL); fax/e-query OK. "Looking for academic and reference books."
>
> **Ethnic Books:** Looking for ethnic writers: Black, Hispanic, Asian.
>
> **Also Does:** Booklets, 5,000 wds; and e-books.
>
> **Tips:** "We look for a thoughtful approach. We shy away from simple answers. Writers who are nuanced, subtle, discerning and perceptive will get farther at IVP. We're interested in books that fill niches in the basic areas of discipline: prayer, evangelism, apologetics, and spiritual growth."
>
> ****Note:** This publisher serviced by The Writer's Edge.

+ISAIAH'S PUBLISHING COMPANY, PO Box 331064, Houston TX 77233-1064. (713)734-4320. Rev. Samuel J. Blunson, pub. Music publisher, including Country Gospel Music. Not in topical listings. Did not return questionnaire.

JAMES RUSSELL PUBLISHING, 780 Diogenes Dr., Reno NV 89512. (775) 348-8711. Fax (775)348-8711. E-mail: scrnplay@powernet.net. Website: www.powernet.net/~scrnplay. James Russell, ed/pub. Powerful books for powerful minds. New publisher. Receives 25 submissions annually. 95% of books from first-time authors. Accepts mss through agents. No reprints. Prefers 215 pgs. Quarterly royalty 10-15% of net; no advance. Average first printing 1,000-5,000. Publication within 4 mos. Considers simultaneous queries. Accepts disk. Responds in 2 mos. Prefers contemporary version. Guidelines (also by e-mail/Website); catalog for #10 SASE/1 stamp.

> **Nonfiction:** Query only; e-query OK. "Looking for inspirational books."
>
> **Fiction:** Query only. For adults. "We like books with strong educational content for readers."
>
> **Also Does:** E-books.
>
> **Tips:** "How-to book has the best chance. Tell us why your book is better."

+JENKINS GROUP, INC., 121 E. Front St., 4th Fl., Traverse City MI 49684. (616)933-0445. Fax (616)933-0448. E-mail: jenkins.group@bookpublishing.com. Website: www.bookpublishing.com. Jerrold R. Jenkins, pub. Does business, career, gift books, religious/spiritual, and technical books. Incomplete topical listings. No questionnaire returned.

JIREH PUBLISHING, PO Box 4263, San Leandro CA 94579-0263. (800)200-1386. Fax (501)423-2929. E-mail: jammingson@juno.com. Website: www. jirehpublishing.com. Janice Holman, ed. To spread the Gospel and teach the Word of God throughout the world. Publishes 4-6 titles/yr. Receives 20 submissions annually. 95% of books from first-time authors. **SUBSIDY PUBLISHES 8%.** Prefers 96+ pgs. Royalty 10-12% of net; no advance. Average first printing 1,000-3,000. Publication within 18 mos. No simultaneous submissions. Responds in 2-3 wks. Requires disk. Guidelines (also on Website); no catalog.

    Nonfiction: Proposal/3 chapters; phone/fax/e-query OK. "Looking for manuscript which helps teach believers how to walk by faith and receive all the blessings which God has for them."

    Also Does: Booklets and e-books.

    Photos: Accepts freelance photos for book covers.

    Tips: "We're currently looking for books on teaching the Word of God to new believers, i.e., workbooks. We welcome new writers."

JOSSEY-BASS INC., PUBLISHERS/RELIGION IN PRACTICE, 350 Sansome St., San Francisco CA 94104. (415)433-1740. Fax (415)433-0499. Website: www.josseybass.com. John Wiley & Sons, Inc. Sarah Polster, ed. 25% of books from first-time authors. Royalty 10-15%. Publication within 1 yr. Considers simultaneous submissions. Responds in 1-2 mos. No e-mail submissions.

    Nonfiction: Query or proposal. "Our editorial mission is (1) to enrich people's understanding of the life and possibilities of congregations and other religious organizations, and (2) to aid in the education and development of those who serve in them, both as religious leaders and as committed, active laity. We also explore the role of religious institutions in their communities and in society as a whole."

JUDSON PRESS, Box 851, Valley Forge PA 19482-0851. (610)768-2128. Fax (610)768-2441. Website: www.judsonpress.com. American Baptist Churches USA. Randy Frame, acq ed. Publishes 20-30 titles/yr. Receives 750 submissions annually. 50% of books from first-time authors. Reprints books. Prefers 120-140 pgs, or 30,000-89,000 wds. Royalty 8-10% on retail; some work-for-hire agreements; advance $300. Average first printing 3,000. Publication within 10 mos. Considers simultaneous submissions. Responds in 3 mos. Free guidelines/catalog.

    Nonfiction: Proposal/2 chapters; phone query OK.

    Ethnic Books: African-American.

    Tips: "Authors should avoid books based primarily on their own experiences and personal reflections. Writing style must be engaging and the writer should be well qualified to address the topic. We want books that are unusually well written."

    **Note: This publisher serviced by The Writer's Edge.

KALEIDOSCOPE PRESS, 2507 94th Ave. E., Edgewood WA 98371. Phone/fax (253)848-1116. Penny Lent, ed/pub. Overstocked; no freelance this year.

KINDRED PRODUCTIONS, 169 Riverton Ave., Winnipeg MB R2L 2E5 Canada. (204)669-6575. Fax (204)654-1865. E-mail: kindred@mbconf.ca.

Website: www.mbconf.org/kindred.htm. Mennonite Brethren. Marilyn Hudson, mgr. To resource the churches within the denomination (Anabaptist perspective) for Christ-like living and ministry. Publishes 3-4 titles/yr. Receives 60 submissions annually. 90% of books from first-time authors. No mss through agents. **SUBSIDY PUBLISHES 5%.** No reprints. Prefers 200-250 pgs. Royalty 10-15% on net; no advance. Average first printing 1,000-2,000. Publication within 9-12 mos. Considers simultaneous submissions. Responds within 4-5 mos. Requires disk or e-mail submission. Prefers NIV. Free guidelines (also by e-mail)/catalog.

> **Nonfiction:** Proposal/2 chapters; fax/e-query OK. "Looking for books that help people meet God in a nonthreatening way. Only accepting unsolicited manuscripts for inspirational reading books. A crossover potential preferred, but not mandatory."

> **Also Does:** Pamphlets & booklets.

> **Tips:** "Most open to inspirational books; maintain the human element in your writing. Stories, thoughts, and people need to be real."

+KINGDOM PUBLISHING, 719 Lance Creek Rd., PO Box 506, Mansfield PA 16933. (570)662-7515. Michael Orendia, pub. Not in topical listings. Did not return questionnaire.

KREGEL PUBLICATIONS, PO Box 2607, Grand Rapids MI 49501. (616)451-4775. Fax (616)451-9330. E-mail: Editorial@kregel.com. Website: www.kregel.com. Evangelical/Conservative. Dennis R. Hillman, pub. To provide tools for ministry and Christian growth from a conservative, evangelical perspective. Publishes 60 titles/yr. Receives 250+ submissions annually. 20% of books from first-time authors. Reprints books. Royalty 8-16% of net; some outright purchases. Average first printing 5,000. Publication within 16 mos. Considers simultaneous submissions. Requires disk. Responds in 1-2 mos. Guidelines (also by e-mail/Website); catalog for 9x12 SAE/3 stamps.

> **Nonfiction:** Query only; fax/e-query OK.

> **Fiction:** Query only. Looking for high-quality contemporary fiction with strong Christian themes and characters.

> **Ethnic Books:** Spanish division: Editorial Portavoz.

> **Tips:** "Most open to biblically based books of practical Christian teaching or books of interest to the vocational Christian worker. Take the time to study our line of books and tell us how your book meets our needs."

> ****Note:** This publisher serviced by The Writer's Edge.

LANGMARC PUBLISHING, PO Box 33817, San Antonio TX 78265. (210)822-2521. Fax (210)822-5014. E-mail: langmarc@flash.net. Website: www.booksails.com. Lutheran. Lois Qualben, pub. Focuses on spiritual growth of readers. Publishes 4 titles/yr. Receives 200 submissions annually. 50% of books from first-time authors. No mss through agents. No reprints. Prefers 150-300 pgs. Royalty 8-10% on retail; no advance. Average first printing 1,500. Publication usually within 1 yr. Considers simultaneous submissions. Responds in 2-4 mos. Requires disk. Prefers NIV. Guidelines; catalog for #10 SAE/1 stamp.

Nonfiction: Proposal/3 chapters; no phone query. "Most open to inspirational, or materials for teens."

Fiction: Does some.

+LEGACY PRESS, PO Box 7814, Colorado Springs CO 80933. (719)963-6821. Fax (719)637-1606. E-mail: admin@1chapter.com. Website: www.1chapter.com. Nondenominational. Amy Highland, ed. E-book publisher for Christian authors. Publishes 40 titles/yr. Receives 100 submissions annually. 90% of books from first-time authors. Reprints books. Prefers 120 pgs & up. Royalty on retail; no advance. Print on demand. Publication within 24 hrs. Requires disk or e-mail.

   Nonfiction: Complete ms; e-query OK; no phone/fax query.

   Fiction: All categories. Complete ms; e-query OK; no phone/fax query.

   Tips: "We promote new authors as well as established author's works. We charge a small fee for authors to publish their works on our Website."

LIBROS LIGUORI, PO Box 260485, Tampa FL 33685-0485. Phone/fax (877)499-8021. E-mail: ssanchez@liguori.org. Website: www.Liguori.org. Spanish division of Liguori Publications. Sylvia L. Sanchez, ed. To spread the gospel in the Hispanic community by means of low-cost publications. Publishes 15 titles/yr. Receives 6-8 submissions annually. 5% of books from first-time authors. Prefers up to 30,000 wds. Royalty 4-12% of net or outright purchases of $400 (book and booklet authors get royalties; pamphlet authors get $400 on acceptance); advance. Average first printing 3,500-5,000. Publication within 18 mos. No simultaneous submissions. Requires disk. Responds in 4-8 wks. Free guidelines/catalog.

   Nonfiction: Query first; fax/e-query OK. "Looking for issues families face today—substance abuse, unwanted pregnancies, etc.; family relations; religion's role in immigrant's experiences."

   Ethnic Books: Focuses on Spanish-language products.

   Also Does: Pamphlets and booklets; PC software and clip art.

   Tips: "Needs books on the Hispanic experience in the U.S. Keep it concise; avoid academic/theological jargon; and stick to the tenets of the Catholic faith—avoid abstract arguments."

*LIFE CYCLE BOOKS, Box 420, Lewiston NY 14092. (416) 690-8532. Fax (416)690-5860. E-mail: pbroughton@lcbooks.com. Website: www.life cyclebooks.com. Paul Broughton, gen mgr. Specializes in Pro-Life material. Publishes 1-3 titles/yr. Receives 50 submissions annually. 50% of books from first-time authors. Reprints books. Royalty 8% of net; outright purchase of brochure material, $250+; advance $100-300. **SUBSIDY PUBLISHES 10%.** Publication within 10 mos. Responds in 6 wks. Free catalog.

   Nonfiction: Query or complete ms. "Our emphasis is on pro-life and pro-family titles."

   Tips: "We are most involved in publishing leaflets of about 1,500 wds and welcome submissions of mss of this length."

+LIFESONG PUBLISHERS, PO Box 183, Somis CA 93066. (805)655-5644.

E-mail: mailbox@lifesongpublishers.com. Website: www.lifesong publishers. com. Laurie Donahue, pub. Provides Christian families with tools that will aid in growing family members in all areas. Publishes 1-3 titles/yr. New publisher. No mss through agents. No reprints. Royalty 5-10% of net; small advance. Publication within 6 mos. Considers simultaneous submissions. Responds in 2-4 wks. Prefers NIV. No guidelines; catalog for 9x12 SAE/2 stamps. Not included in topical listings.

Nonfiction: Proposal/3 chapters; e-query OK.

Tips: "We are looking for a puzzle/activity book that correlates with our children and teen baptism curriculum (or other creative venue)."

+LIFT EVERY VOICE, 820 N. LaSalle Blvd., Chicago IL 60610. (312)329-2101. Fax (312)329-2144. E-mail: pressinfo@moody.edu. Website: www. moodypress.org. African-American imprint of Moody Press. Moody Bible Institute & Institute for Black Family Development. Submit to Acquisitions Coordinator. To advance the cause of Christ through publishing African-American Christians who educate, edify, and disciple Christians. Not included in topical listings.

LIGHTWAVE PUBLISHING, INC., 26275 98th Ave, Maple Ridge BC V2W 1K3 Canada. (604)462-7890. Fax (604)462-8208. E-mail: christie@lightwave publishing.com. Website: www.lightwavepublishing.com. Interdenominational. Christie Bowler, ed. To help children understand the basics of the Christian faith, and to help parents pass these values on to their children. Publishes 24 titles/yr. Receives 110 submissions annually. No mss through agents. Outright purchases or work-for-hire (pays an hourly or per-project rate, amount depends on project size; wages up front, on delivery of manuscript). Publication within 4-8 mos. No simultaneous submissions. Responds in 2 mos (if requested). Guidelines; catalog on Website.

Nonfiction: Query only to inquire about work-for-hire and send résumé; fax/e-query OK.

Fiction: Query only. "We are moving into the fiction area. We do fiction that teaches children about their Christian faith and imparts biblical values in an exciting way."

Special Needs: Writers with solid biblical foundation and understanding who will work for hire. They buy all rights to the work.

Also Does: Some booklets.

Tips: "We come up with a book idea, then hire a writer/researcher, with expertise in that particular field, to write it."

**Note: This publisher serviced by The Writer's Edge.

LIGUORI PUBLICATIONS, 1 Liguori Dr., Liguori MO 63057. (636)464-2500. Fax (636)464-8449. E-mail: jbauer@liguori.org. Website: www.liguori. org. Catholic/Redemptorists. Judy Bauer, acq ed. Spreading the Gospel of Jesus Christ, primarily through the print and electronic media. Publishes 50 titles/yr. Prefers 100-300 pgs for books; 40-100 pgs for booklets; pamphlets 16-18 pgs. Variable royalty; outright purchase of pamphlets for $400; advance varies. Average first printing 3,500-5,000 on books & booklets, 10,000 on pamphlets. Publication within 2 yrs. Accepts disks. Responds in 9-13 wks. Prefers NRSV. Guidelines (also by e-mail/Website); catalog for 9x12 SASE.

Nonfiction: Proposal/2 chapters (complete ms for pamphlets); phone/fax/e-query OK. "Looking for spirituality, classics, saints, prayer, travel, parenting, and family life."

Fiction: Complete ms. "Generally we don't do fiction, but will consider children's picture books, allegory or biblical books for children, with strong Catholic appeal."

Ethnic Books: Publishes books in Spanish. See separate listing for Libros Liguori.

Also Does: Booklets, pamphlets and tracts; computer games and screen savers. Electronic publishing division does 4 books/yr.

Tips: "Manuscripts accepted by us must have strong, middle-of-the-road, practical spirituality."

LILLENAS PUBLISHING CO., Program Builder Series and Other Drama Resources, Box 419527, Kansas City MO 64141-6527. (816)931-1900. Fax (816)412-8390. E-mail: drama@lillenas.com. Website: www.lillenas.com/drama. Kimberly R. Messer, ed. Imprint: Lillenas Drama Resources. Publishes 10-12 titles/yr. Royalty 10% for drama resources; outright purchase of program builder material; no advance. No simultaneous submissions. Responds in 3 mos. Guidelines; catalog.

Drama Resources: Query or complete ms; phone/fax/e-query OK. Accepts readings, one-act and full-length plays, puppet scripts, program and service features, monologues, and sketch collections.

Special Needs: Youth sketch collections and plays; full-length and one-act plays for adults.

Tips: "Most open to biblically-based sketches and plays that have small- to medium-sized casts and are easy to stage."

LION PUBLISHING, 4050 Lee Vance View, Colorado Springs CO 80918-7102. (719)536-3271. Cook Communications. Accepts no freelance submissions.

THE LITURGICAL PRESS, PO Box 7500, St. John's Abbey, Collegeville MN 56321. (320)363-2213. Fax (800)445-5899. E-mail: mtwomey@osb.org. Website: www.litpress.org/edit.html. St. John's Abbey (a Benedictine group). Imprints: Liturgical Press Books, Michael Glazier Books and Pueblo Books. Mark Twomey, mng ed. Academic manuscripts to Linda Maloney (lmmaloney@osb.org). Publishes 70 titles/yr. Prefers 100-300 pgs. Royalty 10% of net; some outright purchases; no advance. Responds in 3 mos. Guidelines (also on Website); free catalog.

Nonfiction: Query/proposal. Adult only.

Tips: "We publish liturgical, scriptural, and pastoral resources."

#LITURGY TRAINING PUBLICATIONS, Office of Divine Worship, 1800 N. Hermitage Ave., Chicago IL 60622-1101. (773)486-8970. Fax (773)486-7094. E-mail: editors@LTP.org. Website: www.LTP.org. Catholic/Archdiocese of Chicago. Victoria Tufano, sr acq ed. Resources for liturgy in Christian life. Publishes 25 titles/yr. Receives 150 submissions annually. 50% of books from first-time authors. Variable royalty. Average first printing 2,000-5,000. Publication within 1 yr. Considers simultaneous submissions. Responds in 2-10 wks. Requires disk. Catalog.

Nonfiction: Proposal/1 chapter; phone/fax/e-query OK.

LIVING BOOKS FOR ALL, PO Box 98425 (TST), Kowloon, Hong Kong. Phone 852-2723-1525. Fax 852-2366-6519. E-mail: clchk@hkstar.com. Website: www.hkstar.com/~clchk/lbaguide.html. Christian Literature Crusade (CLC) Hong Kong. Mrs. Mare Allison, ed. Prefers books of interest to Asians or Western readers interested in Asia. Imprint: Bellman House (Chinese). Publishes 1-5 titles/yr. Receives 12 submissions annually. Considers Chinese translations of English books. Prefers up to 300 pgs. Royalty 5% on retail or payment in copies of book; no advance. Average first printing 3,000. Publication within 9 mos. Considers simultaneous submissions. Prefers disk or e-mail submission. Responds in 1-3 mos. Guidelines (by e-mail or Website); free catalog.

> **Nonfiction:** Query; proposal with 3 chapters (up to 30 pages), or complete ms; e-query OK.
>
> **Fiction:** "Fiction for adults in an Asian context."
>
> **Ethnic Books:** For Asian market.
>
> **Also Does:** Pamphlets & booklets.
>
> **Tips:** "Write in direct, personal, inclusive style; then simplify. No dissertations. We are looking for Chinese manuscripts." Prefers American spelling to English spelling. Accepts manuscripts in English or Chinese.

LIVING THE GOOD NEWS, 600 Grant St., Ste. 400, Denver CO 80203. Fax (303)832-4971. Division of the Morehouse Group. Not currently accepting submissions.

LOGION PRESS, 1445 Boonville Ave., Springfield MO 65802. (417)862-2781x1475. Fax (417)862-6059. E-mail: shorton@ag.org. Assemblies of God. Dr. Stanley Horton, ed. Academic Line of Gospel Publishing House; primarily college textbooks. Publishes 2 titles/yr. Receives 5 submissions annually. 20% of books from first-time authors. No mss through agents. Prefers up to 185,000 words. Royalty on retail; no advance. Average first printing 3,500. Publication within 1 yr. No simultaneous submissions. Responds in 3 mos. Requires disk. Free guidelines/catalog.

> **Nonfiction:** Proposal/1-2 chapters.
>
> **Tips:** "Books must not contradict our statement of Fundamental Truths that all our ministers must sign annually. Most open to religion/biblical textbooks."

+LOGOS PRODUCTIONS, INC., 6160 Carmen Ave., Inver Grove Hts MN 55076. (612)451-9945. Fax (612)457-4617. Website: www.osiem.org/ospre/enhanced/logosproductions.htm. Pete Velander, ed. Provides biblically centered, culturally aware resources that equip and inspire lay and clergy for ministry in the church and beyond. Not included in topical listings. No questionnaire returned.

#LOIZEAUX, PO Box 277, Neptune NJ 07754-0277. (732)918-2626. Fax (732) 922-9487. Website: www.biblecompanion.org. Evangelical. Marjorie Carlson, mng ed. Publishes 10-15 titles/yr. Receives 50 submissions annually. 2% of books from first-time authors. No mss through agents. Negotiable royalty on net; no advance. Average first printing 4,000. Publication within 24 mos. No simultaneous submissions. No e-mail submissions. Responds in 2-3 wks. Guidelines; free catalog.

Nonfiction: Query only; no phone/fax query. Looking for Bible commentaries.

LOVE INSPIRED/STEEPLE HILL, 300 E. 42nd St., New York NY 10017. (212)682-6080. Fax (212)682-4539. Website: www.romance.net. Harlequin Enterprises. Christian romance imprint. Tara Gavin, ed dir.; Tracy Farrell, sr ed; Shannon Degan, ed. asst. Publishes 36 titles/yr. 10% of books from first-time authors. Rarely reprints books. Prefers 70,000-75,000 wds or 300-320 pgs. Royalty on net; advance. Publication within 12-24 mos. Responds in 4-6 wks. No disk. Guidelines.

Fiction: Query letter or 3 chapters and up to 5-page synopsis; no phone/fax query. Contemporary romance. "Portray Christian characters learning an important lesson about the powers of truth and faith. Include humor, drama, and the many challenges of life and faith. Want strong romance."

#LOWENBROWN PUBLISHING, 3489 Newberry Trail, Decatur GA 30034. (770)478-2700. Lowenbrown Communications. Dr. Pamela M. Brown, ed. Focuses on ethnic issues and sound spiritual instructions. Publishes 6-12 religious titles/yr. Receives 165 submissions annually. 60% of books from first-time authors. **SUBSIDY PUBLISHES 30%.** Negotiable royalty & advance. Considers simultaneous submissions. Responds in 2-3 mos. Guidelines; no catalog.

Nonfiction: Query only; phone query OK.

Fiction: Query only. For teens and adults.

Special Needs: Ethnic products. Also board games, gifts, novelty items, and ceramic products.

Ethnic Books: Black, Hispanic, Asian.

Also Does: Pamphlets, booklets, tracts.

Photos: Accepts freelance photos for book covers.

Tips: "Follow through."

#LOYAL PUBLISHING, PO Box 1892, Sisters OR 97759. (541)549-8890. Matthew L. Jacobson, pres/pub. To draw the heart of mankind to God, to remain faithful to His precepts, and to walk in His ways. Estab. 1999. Not included in topical listings. No questionnaire completed.

Nonfiction: Books, children's books and educational materials.

LOYOLA PRESS, 3441 N. Ashland Ave., Chicago IL 60657. (773)281-1818. Fax (773)281-0152. E-mail: editorial@loyolapress.com. Website: www. loyolapress.org. Catholic. Jim Manney, acq dir. Serving faith formation in the Jesuit tradition. Publishes 20-30 titles/yr. Receives 500 submissions annually. 10% of books from first-time authors. Rarely reprints books. Prefers 60,000-80,000 wds or 200-400 pgs. Variable royalty on net; small advance. Average first printing 5,000-7,500. Publication within 1-2 yrs. Considers simultaneous submissions. Responds in 3 mos. Accepts e-mail submissions. Prefers NRSV (Catholic Edition). Guidelines (also by e-mail); free catalog.

Nonfiction: Proposal/2 chapters; fax/e-query OK. "Looking for family, faith, and social/spiritual issues."

THE LUTTERWORTH PRESS/JAMES CLARKE & CO., PO Box 60, Cambridge CB1 2NT England. (+44)1223 350865. Fax (+44)1223 366951. E-mail:

publishing@lutterworth.com. Website: www.lutterworth.com. Adrian Brink, ed. Imprints: The Lutterworth Press (general); James Clarke & Co. (academic/reference). Publishes 10 titles/yr. Receives 100 submissions annually. 90% of books from first-time authors. **SUBSIDY PUBLISHES 2%.** Royalty on retail; some advances. Publication within 18 mos. No simultaneous submissions. Responds in 3 mos. Requires disk. No guidelines; free catalog.

Nonfiction: Proposal/2 chapters.

Fiction: Query letter only. For children.

MAGNUS PRESS, PO Box 2666, Carlsbad CA 92018. (760)806-3743. Fax (760)806-3689. E-mail: magnuspres@aol.com. Warren Angel, ed dir. To publish biblical studies which are written for the average person and which minister life to Christ's Church. Publishes 6 titles/yr. Receives 60 submissions annually. 50% of books from first-time authors. Reprints books. Prefers 125-375 pgs. Graduated royalty on retail; no advance. Average first printing 5,000. Publication within 1 yr. Considers simultaneous submissions. Accepts disk. Responds in 1 mo. Guidelines (also by e-mail); free catalog.

Nonfiction: Query or proposal/2-3 chapters; fax query OK. "Looking for spirituality, thematic biblical studies, unique inspirational/devotional books. "

Tips: "Our writers need solid knowledge of the Bible, and a mature spirituality which reflects a profound relationship with Jesus Christ. Most open to a well-researched, popularly written biblical study; or a unique inspirational or devotional book, e.g. Canine Parables."

MARLTON PUBLISHERS, INC., PO Box 223, Severn MD 21144. (800)859-0173. No freelance.

MASTER BOOKS, PO Box 727, Green Forest AR 72638. Fax (870)438-5120. E-mail: mbnlp@cswnet.com. Website: www.masterbooks.net. Imprint of New Leaf Press. Roger Howerton, acq. ed. Publishes 12-15 titles/yr. Receives 1,200 submissions annually. 10% of books from first-time authors. Royalty 10% of net; no advance. Average first printing 5,000. Considers simultaneous submissions. Responds in 3-4 wks. Free catalog.

Nonfiction: Query. "Looking for biblical creationism; biblical science; creation/evolution debate material."

Special Needs: Children's books and homeschool science books.

MERCER UNIVERSITY PRESS, 6316 Peake Rd., Macon GA 31210. (478)301-2880. Fax (478)301-2264. E-mail: jolley_m4@mercer.edu. Website: www.mupress.org. Baptist. Marc Jolley, mng ed. Publishes 15 titles/yr. Receives 200 submissions annually. 75% of books from first-time authors. Accepts mss through agents. Some reprints. Royalty on net; no advance. Average first printing 800-1,200. Publication within 15 mos. Prefers disk (no e-mail submissions).

Nonfiction: Proposal/2 chapters; fax/e-query OK. "We are looking for books on history, philosophy, theology and religion, including history of religion, philosophy of religion, Bible studies and ethics."

MERIWETHER PUBLISHING LTD./CONTEMPORARY DRAMA SERVICE, 885 Elkton Dr., Colorado Springs CO 80918. (719)594-4422. Fax (719)

594-9916. E-mail: MerPCDS@aol.com. Website: www.meriwether publishing.com. Arthur L. Zapel, ed; submit to Rhonda Wray. Publishes 2-3 titles/yr.; 25-30 plays/yr. Primarily a publisher of plays for Christian and secular; must be acceptable for use in a wide variety of Christian denominations. Imprint: Contemporary Drama Service. Publishes 3 bks/25 plays/yr. Receives 800 submissions annually (mostly plays). 50% of books from first-time authors. Reprints books. Prefers 200 pgs. Royalty 10% of net or retail, or fee arrangement; no advance. Average first printing of books 2,500, plays 500. Publication within 1 yr. Considers simultaneous submissions. Responds in 4-6 wks. Prefers disk; no e-mail submission. Guidelines (also on Website); catalog $2.

> **Nonfiction:** Query only for books; fax/e-query OK. "Looking for creative worship books, i.e., drama, using the arts in worship, how-to books with ideas for Christian education." Submit books to Meriwether.
>
> **Fiction:** Plays only, for all ages. Always looking for Christmas and Easter plays. Send complete manuscript. Submit plays to Contemporary Drama.
>
> **Special Needs:** Drama, theater, how-to in relation to theater, drama ministry, and Christian education.
>
> **Tips:** "Our books are on drama or any creative, artistic area that can be a part of worship. Writers should familiarize themselves with our catalog before submitting to ensure that their manuscript fits with the list we've already published." Contemporary Drama Service wants easy-to-stage comedies, skits, one-act plays, large-cast musicals, and full-length comedies for schools (junior high through college) and churches (including chancel dramas for Christmas and Easter).

MESSIANIC JEWISH PUBLISHERS, 6204 Park Heights Ave., Baltimore MD 21215. (410)358-6471x261. Fax (410)764-1376. E-mail: editor@messianic jewish.net. Website: www.MessianicJewish.net. Lederer/Messianic Jewish Communications. Janet Chaiet, ed. Books that build up the Messianic Jewish community, witness to unbelieving Jewish people or help Christians understand their Jewish roots. Imprint: Remnant Books (for subsidy books only). Publishes 10-12 titles/yr. Receives 100+ submissions annually. 50% of books from first-time authors. No mss through agents. **SUBSIDY PUBLISHES 50%.** Reprints books. Prefers 50,000-88,000 wds. Royalty 7-15% of net; variable advance. Average first printing 3,000 (subsidy), 5,000 (royalty). Publication within 12-24 mos. No simultaneous submissions. Responds in 3-6 mos. Requires disk. Guidelines; free catalog.

> **Nonfiction:** Query only first; no phone/fax/e-query. Jewish evangelism or Jewish roots of Christian faith.
>
> **Fiction:** Query only; for adults. "Must have Messianic Jewish theme and demonstrate familiarity with Jewish culture and thought."
>
> **Ethnic Books:** Jewish.
>
> **Tips:** "Must request guidelines before submitting. Looking for Messianic Jewish commentaries. Books must address one of the following: Jewish evangelism, Jewish roots of Christianity, or helping Christians understand their Jewish roots."

*MISTY HILL PRESS, 5024 Turner Rd., Sebastopol CA 95472. (707)823-7437. Small press that does some religious titles. Sally C. Karste, ed. Publishes 1 title/yr. Negotiable royalty. Responds in 1 week. Guidelines; catalog for 9x12 SAE/2 stamps.

Fiction: Query first. Historical fiction for children.

Note: Not accepting manuscripts at this time.

*MONUMENT PRESS, 22497 Swordfish Dr., Boca Raton FL 33428-4609. Website: www.publishers-associates.com/monument. Member of the consortium Publishers Associates (8 publishers). Belinda Buxjom, sr ed; submit to Mary Markal. Publishes only scholarly books. Other imprints: Ide House and Tangelwuld. Publishes 20 titles/yr. Receives 1,200 submissions annually. 100% of books from first-time authors. No mss through agents. Any length. Royalty 2-8% on retail; no advance. Average first printing 3,000. Publication within 4 mos. No simultaneous submissions. Prefers disk. Responds in 4 mos (goes to all houses in the consortium). Guidelines; catalog for 4 stamps.

Nonfiction: Query only; no phone/fax query.

Ethnic: Publishes for all ethnic groups.

Tips: "Most open to liberation theology. Scholarly works only. "

MOODY PRESS, 820 N. LaSalle Blvd., Chicago IL 60610. (312)329-2101. Fax (312)329-2144. E-mail: pressinfo@moody.edu. Website: www.moody press.org. Imprint: Northfield Publishing, and Lift Every Voice (African-American). Moody Bible Institute. Submit to Acquisitions Coordinator. To provide books that evangelize, edify the believer, and educate concerning the Christian life. Publishes 65-70 titles/yr. Receives 3,500 submissions annually. 1% of books from first-time authors. Royalty on net; advance $500-50,000. Average first printing 10,000. Publication within 6-9 mos. Considers simultaneous submissions (reluctantly). Prefers e-mail submissions. Responds in 2 mos. Prefers NAS, NLT, NIV. Guidelines (also on Website); catalog for 9x12 SASE.

Nonfiction: Proposal/3 chapters; prefers no phone query; fax/e-query OK. Looking for books for women; female authors.

Fiction: Complete ms; for teens and adults. "We consider fiction with reservations—it has to be amazingly written. Needs strong characterization, a gripping plot with change in the protagonist, and life-changing impact."

Ethnic Books: African-American.

Tips: "Most open to books where the writer is a recognized expert and already has a platform to promote the book."

**Note: This publisher serviced by The Writer's Edge.

+MOONDRAWN BOOKS, 718 S 28th St., Lafayette IN 47904. (765)447-1018. Fax (765)449-0552. E-mail: unthank@att.net. Scottie Patterson, ed. Does psychology, recovery, religious/spiritual, and women's issues. Not included in topical listings. No questionnaire returned.

THOMAS MORE/An RCL Company, 200 E. Bethany Dr., Allen TX 75002. (972)390-6923. Fax (972)390-6620. E-mail: dhampton@rcl-enterprises. com. Website: www.thomasmore.com. Catholic/Resources for Christian Living. Debra Hampton, dir. of product development. Dedicated to providing the highest quality books, video and interactive media that contribute to the dialogue on religion, ethics, social policy, lifestyle and spirituality shaping our future. Publishes 25 titles/yr. Receives 100 submissions annually. 30% of books from first-time authors. Reprints books. Prefers 200 pgs. Royalty 7-15% on retail; advance $5,000. Average first printing 10,000. Publication within 6 mos. Considers simultaneous submissions. Requires disk (Macintosh). Responds in 6-9 wks. Prefers NRS. No guidelines; free catalog.

Nonfiction: Proposal/1 chapter or complete ms; fax/e-query OK. "Looking for books on family, psychology/spiritual growth, scripture (meditation, prayer), spirituality (men's, women's, general), religion (saints), and resources for religion teachers. "

Tips: "Looking for books on theology, commentary, reflection, spirituality and reference—for the serious, but non-scholarly reader (written in popular style)."

MOREHOUSE PUBLISHING CO., 4775 Linglestown Rd., Harrisburg PA 17112. (717)541-8130. Fax (717)541-8136. E-mail: morehouse@more house. com. Website: www.morehousegroup.com. Episcopal/ecumenical. Mark Fretz, ed; artists submit illustration packages to Managing Editor. Academic, devotional, reference, and Bible study materials for Christians of all denominations. Publishes 30 titles/yr; 4-5 picture books/yr. Receives 500 submissions annually. 40% of books from first-time authors. Accepts mss through agents. Reprints books. Prefers 160-224 pgs. Royalty 10% of net; advance $500–$1,000. Average first printing 2,500-3,500. Publication within 12 mos. Considers simultaneous submissions. Requires disk. Responds in 2 mos. Guidelines; for free catalog call (800)877-0012.

Nonfiction: Proposal/1 chapter; no phone/fax query; e-query OK.

Tips: "Stories should contain rich theological concepts in terms children can understand. Seeking manuscripts that are unique, that either approach a topic from a fresh angle, or explore a subject not covered in currently available children's material. Books should appeal to children and adults alike, be theologically sound, as well as fun and entertaining for all."

#WILLIAM MORROW AND CO., 10 E. 53rd St., New York NY 10022. (212)207-7000. Fax (212)207-7145. Website: www.harpercollins.com. The Hearst Corp. Kim Lewis, mng ed. General trade publisher that does a few religious titles. Publishes 5 religious titles/yr. Receives 1,000 submissions annually. 30% of books from first-time authors. Only accepts mss through agents. Prefers 50,000-100,000 wds. Standard royalty on retail; advance varies. Publication within 2 yrs. Considers simultaneous submissions. Responds in 3 mos.

Nonfiction & Fiction: Query only; mss and proposals accepted only through an agent.

Note: Morrow Junior Books accepts no unsolicited manuscripts.

MOUNTAINVIEW PUBLISHING COMPANY, 1022 NE O'Leary St., Oak Harbor WA 98277. E-mail: junebug@whidbey.net. Website: www.whidbey. com/mountainview. Susan Johnson, ed/pub. On-line Christian publisher specializing in romance novels. Receives 300 submissions annually. 13%

of books from first-time authors. Prefers 50,000-80,000 wds. Royalty 20-30% of retail; no advance. Books are published electronically, available on disk or downloaded into buyer's computer. Publication within 6 mos. Considers simultaneous submissions. Responds in 3-4 mos. Guidelines (also by e-mail, Website); catalog.

Fiction: Mailed proposal/3 chapters or e-query/short synopsis. Historical romances, 80,000-100,000 wds; contemporary romances, 65,000-80,000 wds; novellas 20,000-30,000 wds preferred (considers 35,000-50,000). "Seeking high-quality manuscripts that evoke emotion in the reader; cutting-edge books that challenge readers' minds, as well as the tried-and-true old-fashioned romance that readers love so much."

Tips: "Christian romances should contain a faith element. Challenge the reader to think, to look at things through different eyes. Avoid head-hopping and clichés; avoid heavy-handed preaching. No sci-fi or fantasy or dark angel stories. Send consecutive chapters, not random."

*MOUNT OLIVE COLLEGE PRESS, 634 Henderson St., Mount Olive NC 28365. (919)658-2502. Dr. Pepper Worthington, ed. Publishes 5 titles/yr. Receives 1,000 submissions annually. 70% of books from first-time authors. Prefers 220 pgs. Negotiated royalty. Average first printing 500. Publication within 1-3 yrs. No simultaneous submissions. Responds in 6-12 mos. No disk. Free guidelines/catalog.

Nonfiction: Proposal/3 chapters; no phone query. Religion. For poetry submit 6 sample poems.

Fiction: Proposal/3 chapters. Religious.

MULTNOMAH PUBLISHERS, Box 1720, 204 W. Adams St., Sisters OR 97759. (541)549-1144. Fax (541)549-0260. E-mail: editorial@multnomahbooks. com. Website: www.multnomahbooks.com. Imprint information listed below. Publishes 100 titles/yr. Multnomah is currently not accepting unsolicited manuscripts, proposals, or queries. Queries will be accepted through agents and at writers' conferences at which a Multnomah representative is present.

Multnomah Books: Christian living and popular theology books.

Multnomah Fiction: Well-crafted fiction that uses truth to change lives.

Multnomah Gift Books: Substantive topics with beautiful, lyrical writing.

**Note: This publisher serviced by The Writer's Edge.

#NATIONAL BAPTIST PUBLISHING BOARD, 6717 Centennial Blvd., Nashville TN 37209. (615)350-8000. Fax (615)350-9018. E-mail: nbpb@nbpb. org. Website: www.nbpb.org/index.html. National Missionary Baptist Convention of America. Rev. Willie N. Paul, dir of publications. To provide quality Christian education resources to be used by African-American churches. Receives 200 submissions annually. 30% of books from first-time authors. Reprints books. Prefers 130 pgs. Outright purchases; advance. Average first printing 20,000. Publication within 1 yr.

Nonfiction: Complete ms; phone query OK.

Fiction: Complete ms. "We need biblically based fiction for children."

Ethnic Books: African-American publisher.

Tips: "Most open to religious books that can be used for Christian education."

NAVPRESS/PIÑON PRESS, Box 35001, Colorado Springs CO 80935. (719) 548-9222. Website: www.navpress.org or www.gospelcom.net/navs/NP. "We are no longer accepting any unsolicited submissions, proposals, queries, etc."

**Note: This publisher serviced by The Writer's Edge.

NAZARENE PUBLISHING HOUSE—See Beacon Hill Press of Kansas City.

NEIBAUER PRESS, 20 Industrial Dr., Warminster PA 18974. (215)322-6200. Fax (215)322-2495. E-mail: Nathan@neibauer.com. Website: www. ChurchGrowthCenter.com. Nathan Neibauer, ed. For Evangelical/Protestant clergy and church leaders. Publishes 8 titles/yr. Receives 100 submissions annually. 5% of books from first-time authors. No mss through agents. Reprints books. Prefers 200 pgs. Royalty on net; some outright purchases; no advance. Average first printing 1,500. Publication within 6 mos. Considers simultaneous submissions. Responds in 4 wks. Prefers e-mail submissions. Prefers NIV. No guidelines/catalog.

Nonfiction: Query or proposal/2 chapters; fax query OK.

Also Does: Pamphlets and tracts.

Photos: Accepts freelance photos for book covers.

Tips: "Publishes only religious books on stewardship and church enrollment, stewardship and tithing, and church enrollment tracts."

THOMAS NELSON PUBLISHERS, 501 Nelson Pl., Nashville TN 37214. Website: www.thomasnelsonpublishers.com. Accepts no freelance submissions.

**Note: This publisher serviced by The Writer's Edge.

TOMMY NELSON, a division of Thomas Nelson, Inc., 501 Nelson Pl., Nashville TN 37214. (615)889-9000. Children's books and products. Accepting no freelance submissions for now.

**Note: This publisher serviced by The Writer's Edge.

NEW CANAAN PUBLISHING CO., INC., PO Box 752, New Canaan CT 06840. Phone/fax (203)966-3408. E-mail: newcan@sprynet.com. Website: newcanaan publishing.com. Kathy Mittelstadt, ed. Children's books with strong educational and moral content; for grades 1-9. Publishes 1-2 titles/yr. Receives 500 submissions annually. 85% of books from first-time authors. Prefers 20,000-40,000 wds or 140 pgs. Royalty 8-12% of net; no advance. Average first printing 500-5,000. Publication within 8-12 mos. Accepts simultaneous submissions. Responds in 3-4 mos. Requires disk; no e-mail submissions. Guidelines (also on Website); free catalog/SASE.

Nonfiction: Query letter; proposal/2-3 chapters or complete ms; no e-query.

Fiction: Complete ms. For children and teens, 6-14 yrs. "We want children's books with strong educational and moral content; 10,000-20,000 wds." Now accepts picture books.

Special Needs: Middle-school-level educational books.

Photos: Accepts freelance photos for book covers.

Tips: Looking for teen/youth fiction and religious instructional materials for teens/youth.

NEW CITY PRESS, 202 Cardinal Rd., Hyde Park NY 12538. (845)229-0335. Fax (845)229-0351. Website: www.newcitypress.com. Catholic. Gary Bramoll, ed. Focus is on Christian living and unity. Publishes 12 titles/yr. Receives 60 submissions annually. 5% of books from first-time authors. Reprints books. Prefers 56,000 wds. Royalty 10% of net; no advance. Average first printing 5,000. Publication within 16 mos. Considers simultaneous submissions. Responds in 3 mos. Requires disk. Prefers NAB. No guidelines; free catalog.

> **Nonfiction:** Query only; fax/e-query OK. "Looking for how-to and family topics."

#NEW HOPE, Box 12065, Birmingham AL 35202-2065. (205)991-8100. Fax (205)991-4015. E-mail: new_hope@wmu.org. Website: www.newhope publ.com. Imprint of Woman's Missionary Union; Auxiliary to Southern Baptist Convention. Jennifer Law, ed. Publishes 18-24 titles/yr. Receives 350 submissions annually. 25% of books from first-time authors. Reprints books occasionally. Prefers 150-250 pgs. Royalty 7-10% on retail or outright purchases; no advance. Average first printing 5,000-10,000. Publication within 2 yrs. Considers simultaneous submissions. Responds in 6 mos. Requires disk. Guidelines; catalog for 9x12 SAE/3 stamps.

> **Nonfiction:** Complete ms or proposal/3 chapters; no phone/fax/e-query. "All that we publish must have a missions/ministry emphasis, preferably for women or children."

> **Tips:** "Most open to books which focus on spiritual growth that turns faith outward into action; books that equip women and children to share Christ with others; books that lead to involvement in missions; books that teach appreciation for other cultures and people groups. Follow guidelines."

NEW LEAF PRESS, PO Box 726, Green Forest AR 72638-0726. Fax (870)438-5120. E-mail: nlp@newleafpress.net. Website: www.newleafpress.net. Roger Howerton, acq. ed. Imprint: Master Books. Publishes 15-20 titles/yr. Receives 500 submissions annually. 15% of books from first-time authors. Reprints books. Prefers 100-400 pgs. Royalty 10% of net; no advance. Average first printing 10,000. Publication within 10 mos. Considers simultaneous submissions. Responds in 3 mos. Guidelines; catalog for 9x12 SAE/5 stamps.

> **Nonfiction:** Complete ms; phone/fax query OK. "Looking for devotional, gift books and Christian living."

> **Tips:** "Tell us why this book is marketable and why it will be a blessing and fulfill the needs of others."

NEW WORLD LIBRARY, 14 Pamaron Way, Novato CA 94949. (415)884-2100. Fax (415)884-2199. E-mail: escort@nwlib.com. Website: www.nwlib. com. Nondenominational. Submit to Submissions Editor. Dedicated to awakening individual and global potential; inspirational and practical books. Publishes 35 titles/yr. Receives 2,000 submissions annually. 10% of books from first-time authors. Royalty 12-16% of net; advance $3,000-5,000. Average first printing 5,000-7,500. Publication within 12-18 mos. Considers simultaneous submissions. Prefers disk. Responds in 3 mos. Any version. Guidelines (on Website); free catalog.

Nonfiction: Proposal/at least 3 chapters; fax/e-query OK.

Also does: E-books.

#NORTHFIELD PUBLISHING CO., 215 W. Locust St., Chicago IL 60610. (800)678-8001. Fax (312)329-2019. Imprint of Moody Press. Submit to Acquisitions Coordinator. Books for non-Christians or those exploring the faith. Publishes 5-10 titles/yr. 1% of books from first-time authors. Royalty of net; advance $500-50,000. Publication within 1 yr. Reluctantly considers simultaneous submissions. Responds in 2 mos. Guidelines; catalog for 9x12 SAE/2 stamps. Incomplete topical listings.

Nonfiction: Proposal/2-3 chapters.

NORTHSTONE PUBLISHING, 9025 Jim Bailey Rd., Kelowna BC V1Y 9G8 Canada. (250)766-2778. Fax (250)766-2736. E-mail: info@woodlake. com. Website: www.joinhands.com. Wood Lake Books, Inc. Michael Schwartzentruber, ed. To provide high quality products promoting positive social and spiritual values. Publishes 6 titles/yr. Receives 900 submissions annually. 30% of books from first-time authors. Prefers 192-256 pgs. Royalty 7-10% on retail; some advances $1,000. Average first printing 4,000. Publication within 18 mos. Considers simultaneous submissions. Responds in 3 mos. Prefers disk or e-mail. Guidelines; catalog $2.

Nonfiction: Proposal/2 chapters; phone/fax/e-query OK.

Tips: "Although we publish from a Christian perspective, we seek to attract a general audience. Our target audience is interested in spirituality and values, but may not even attend church (nor do we assume that they should)."

NOVALIS, Saint Paul University, 23 Main St., Ottawa ON K1S 1C4 Canada. (613)751-4040. Fax (613)751-4020. E-mail: kburns@ustpaul.uottawa.ca. Website: www.novalis.ca. Unimedia. Kevin Burns, ed. Produces creative and affordable resources that help people explore their religious heritage, live their faith, and deepen their relationship with Christ. Publishes 40 titles/yr. Receives 200 submissions annually. 15% of books from first-time authors. Accepts mss through agents. Reprints books. Variable royalty on retail; variable advance. Average first printing 1,500. Publication within 12 mos. Considers simultaneous submissions. Responds in 4-6 wks. Accepts disk or e-mail submissions. Prefers NRSV. No guidelines; free catalog.

Nonfiction: Query, proposal/2-3 chapters, or complete ms; fax/e-query OK. "Looking for books with broad ecumenical appeal."

+NOVELEDIT, 652 Treece Gulch, Stevensville MT 59870. (406)777-5191. E-mail: cotton@novel.to. Website: www.novel.to. James L. Cotton, ed/pub. Western novels and young adult are of special interest, plus any religious fiction that is not fundamentalist. Imprints: Collaborations, Cottonwood. Publishes 1 religious title/yr. Receives 300 submissions annually. Most books from first-time authors. Accepts books through agents. Any length. Royalty 30-35% of retail; advance to $1,000. Print on demand. Publication within 2 mos. Considers simultaneous submissions. Responds in 1 wk. Any version. Guidelines for SASE/2 stamps; no catalog.

Fiction: For teens and adults. Complete ms preferred; will accept query letter/synopsis or proposal/5-6 chapters; e-query OK.

Tips: "We prefer mss be professionally critiqued. Send for guidelines first and be aware that we print on demand; charge reading fees for sample chapters; and prefer complete manuscripts."

+OAKWOOD PUBLICATIONS, 3827 Bluff St., Torrance CA 90505. Phone/fax (310)378-9245. E-mail: icon@oakwoodpub.com. Phil Tamoush, ed. Does multicultural and religious/spiritual books. Incomplete topical listings. No questionnaire returned.

+O'CONNOR HOUSE, PO Box 90128, Santa Barbara CA 93190. (805)964-9660. Fax (805)964-1395. E-mail: fx@worldnet.att.net. Helene A. O'Connor, pub. Does animal, how-to, self-help, religious/spiritual, and writer's books. Incomplete topical listings. No questionnaire returned.

ONE WORLD/BALLANTINE BOOKS, 1540 Broadway, New York NY 10036. (212)782-8378. Fax (212)782-8442. E-mail: adiggs@randomhouse.com. Website: www.randomhouse.com. Imprint of Ballantine Books. Anita D. Diggs, ed. Novels that are written by and focus on African-Americans; but from an American perspective. Publishes 2 titles/yr. Receives 10-20 submissions annually. 10-20% of books from first-time authors. Submissions from agents only. No reprints. Prefers 80,000 wds. Royalty 10-15% on retail; variable advance. Average first printing 10,000. Publication within 1 yr. Considers simultaneous submissions. Responds in 2 mos. No disk or e-mail. No guidelines/catalog .

Fiction: Proposal/3 chapters; no phone/fax/e-query. "Contemporary/ethnic novels only; for African-American women."

Ethnic Books: All are ethnic books.

Tips: "You must understand African-American culture and avoid time-worn stereotypes."

OPENBOOK PUBLISHERS, Box 1368, GPO, Adelaide, Australia 5001. (618) 8223 5468. Fax (618)8223 4552. Website: www.openbook.com.au. Lutheran. John Pfitzner, ed; submit to Christopher Pfeiffer. Australian resources for Christians of all denominations. Publishes 20 titles/yr. Receives 100+ submissions annually. 60% of books from first-time authors. Reprints books. Prefers 160 pgs. Royalty 10-15% of net; no advance. Average first printing 1,000-2,000. Publication within 6 mos. Considers simultaneous submissions. Prefers e-mail submissions. Responds in 1 mo. No guidelines/catalog.

Nonfiction: Complete ms; phone/fax/e-query OK.

Tips: "Most open to resources for use in congregations and homes."

*OPEN COURT PUBLISHING CO., 332 S. Michigan Ave., Ste. 1100, Chicago IL 60604-9968. Carus Publishing Co. David Ramsay Steele, ed dir. Publishes 4 religious titles/yr. Receives 600 submissions annually. 20% of books from first-time authors. Reprints books. Prefers 250-300 pgs. Royalty 5-12% of net; advance $1,000. Average first printing 500 (cloth), 1,500 (paperback). Publication within 1-3 yrs. Considers simultaneous submissions. Responds in 6 mos. Free catalog.

Nonfiction: Proposal/2 chapters/résumé/vita. "We're looking for works of high intellectual quality for a scholarly or general readership on comparative religion, philosophy of religion, and religious issues."

*OREGON CATHOLIC PRESS, 5536 NE Hassalo, Portland OR 97213.

(800)LITURGY. James Wilde, ed; submit to Melissa Phong. To enhance the worship in the Catholic Church in the United States. Imprint: Pastoral Press. Publishes 10 titles/yr. Receives 72 submissions annually. 5% of books from first-time authors. No mss through agents. Reprints books. Royalty 5-12% of net; no advance. Average first printing 500. Publication within 6 mos. Considers simultaneous submissions. Prefers disk; no e-mail submissions. Responds in 3-6 mos. Free catalog.

Nonfiction: Proposal/1 chapter; no phone/fax/e-query. "Looking for pastoral and liturgical books."

Ethnic Books: Hispanic/Spanish language.

Photos: Accepts freelance photos for book covers.

Tips: "Most open to Catholic liturgical works."

#ORIGINAL WORD PUBLISHERS, PO Box 799, Roswell GA 30077. (800)235-9673 or (770)552-8879. E-mail: charles@originalword.com. Website: www.originalword.com. Dr. Charles Goodwin, ed. A trans-denominational, nonprofit teaching ministry devoted to biblical studies.

*OSL PUBLICATIONS, PO Box 22279, Akron OH 44302-0079. (330)535-8656 Fax (330)535-8656. E-mail: books@Saint-Luke.org. Website: www. Saint-Luke.org. Order of St. Luke. T.J. Crouch, dir. of pub. Publishes 3 titles/yr. Receives 10 submissions annually. 40% of books from first-time authors. No mss through agents. Reprints books. Prefers to 200 pgs. Royalty 5-10%; no advance. Average first printing 1,000. Publication within 9 mos. Considers simultaneous submissions. Free guidelines/catalog.

Nonfiction: Query only.

Tips: "Our primary focus is centered around publishing materials which aid in discovering a sacramental spirituality and providing practical liturgical resources."

OUR SUNDAY VISITOR, INC., 200 Noll Plaza, Huntington IN 46750-4303. (219)356-8400. Fax (219)359-9117. E-mail: booksed@osv.com. Website: www.osv.com. Catholic. Greg Erlandson, ed-in-chief; submit to Acquisitions Editor. To assist Catholics to be more aware and secure in their faith and capable of relating their faith to others. Publishes 30+ titles/yr. Receives 1,000 submissions annually. 10% of books from first-time authors. Reprints books. Royalty 10-12% of net; advance varies. Average first printing 5,000. Publication within 1 yr. Considers simultaneous submissions. Responds in 2-3 mos. Requires disk. Free guidelines (also by e-mail); catalog for 9x12 SASE.

Nonfiction: Proposal/2 chapters; e-query OK. "Most open to devotional books (not first person), church histories, heritage and saints, the parish, prayer and family."

Also Does: Pamphlets and booklets.

Tips: "All books published must relate to the Catholic Church; unique books aimed at our audience. Give as much background information as possible on why the topic was chosen. Follow our guidelines."

OXFORD UNIVERSITY PRESS, 198 Madison Ave., New York NY 10016-4314. (212)726-6000. Fax (212)726-6440. E-mail: car@oup-usa.org. Website: www.oup-usa.org. Academic press. Cynthia Read, exec ed. Service to academic community. Publishes 60+ titles/yr. Receives hundreds of submissions annually. 20% of books from first-time authors. Prefers 250 pgs. Royalty & advance negotiable. Average first printing 900. Publication within 1 yr. Considers simultaneous submissions. Requires disk. Responds in 3 mos. Free catalog.

Nonfiction: Proposal/2 chapters. "Most open to academic books."

#P & R PUBLISHING CO., PO Box 817, Phillipsburg NJ 08865. (908)454-0505. Fax (908)859-2390. Not a denominational house. Allan Fisher, publications dir.; Barbara Lerch, acq. ed. All books must be consistent with the Westminster Confession of Faith. Imprints: Craig Press; Evangelical Press. Publishes 8-10 titles/yr. Receives 200 submissions annually. 20% of books from first-time authors. Prefers 140-240 pgs. Royalty 5-14% of net; no advance. Average first printing 3,000. Publication within 8-10 mos. Considers simultaneous submissions. Disk required. Responds in 1-3 mos. Free guidelines/catalog.

Nonfiction: Proposal/3 chapters; fax query OK.

Tips: "Clear, engaging, and insightful applications of reformed theology to life. Offer us fully developed proposals and polished sample chapters."

PACIFIC PRESS PUBLISHING ASSN., Box 5353, Nampa ID 83653-5353. (208)465-2500. Fax (208)465-2531. E-mail: editor.book@pacificpress. com. Website: www.pacificpress.com. Seventh-Day Adventist. Jerry Thomas, book ed; submit to Tim Lale, acq ed. Books of interest and importance to Seventh-Day Adventists and other Christians of all ages. Publishes 30 titles/yr. Receives 900 submissions annually. 20% of books from first-time authors. Prefers 40,000-70,000 wds or 128-256 pgs. Royalty 12-15% of net; advance $1,500. Average first printing 6,000. Publication within 10 mos. Considers simultaneous submissions. Responds in 3 mos. Requires disk/accepts e-mail submissions. Guidelines (also on Website).

Nonfiction: Query only; e-query OK.

Fiction: Proposal/3 chapters. Adults and children (7-12 years old), series or single books. "Must be true-to-life, focus on some important truth, and have a strong spiritual message. No talking animals."

Ethnic Books: Occasionally publishes for ethnic market.

Tips: "Our Website has the most up-to-date information, including samples of recent publications. Do not send full manuscript unless we request it after reviewing your proposal."

PALISADES/MULTNOMAH. Pure romance novels. See Multnomah Publishers.

PARACLETE PRESS, PO Box 1568, Orleans MA 02653. (508)255-4685. Fax (508)255-5705. E-mail: mail@paraclete-press.com. Website: www. paracletepress.com. Ecumenical. Lillian Miao, sr ed. Publishes 16 titles/yr. Receives 160 submissions annually. Few books from first-time authors. Reprints few books. Prefers 170-300 pgs. Royalty 10-12% on retail or net; no advance. Average first printing 3,000-5,000. Publication within 12-18 mos. Considers simultaneous submissions. Responds in 4-6 wks. Requires hard copy. Prefers NIV, KJV, NKJV, RSV, NRSV. Guidelines (also by e-mail); catalog for 9x12 SAE/3 stamps.

Nonfiction: Proposal/2 chapters; no phone/fax/e-query. "Looking for books on deeper spirituality that appeal to all denominations."

Tips: Vision statement: "In all times, in different branches of the Christian family, there are people who have written, sung, or spoken things that encouraged us to give our lives to God and to listen to His voice. We gather and share these treasures."

PARADISE RESEARCH PUBLICATIONS, INC., PO Box 837, Kihei HI 96753-0837. Phone/fax (808)874-4876. E-mail: dickb@dickb.com. Website: www.dickb.com/index.shtml. Ken Burns, ed. Imprint: Tincture of Time Press. Publishes 5 titles/yr. Receives 8 submissions annually. 80% of books from first-time authors. No mss through agents. Reprints books. Prefers 250 pgs. Royalty 10% on retail; no advance. Average first printing 5,000. Publication within 2 mos. Considers simultaneous submission. Responds in 1 wk. No disk. Prefers KJV. No guidelines; free catalog.

Nonfiction: Query only; no phone/fax/e-query. Books on the biblical/Christian history of early Alcoholics Anonymous.

Also Does: Pamphlets and booklets.

PARAGON HOUSE, 2700 University Ave. W., Ste. 200, St. Paul MN 55114-1016. (651)644-3087. Fax (651)644-0997. E-mail: paragon@paragonhouse.com. Website: www.paragonhouse.com. Intercultural Foundation. Laureen Enright, acq. ed. Serious nonfiction and texts with an emphasis on religion and philosophy. Imprints: New Era Books, Athena, Omega. Publishes 12-15 titles/yr. Receives 500 submissions annually. 7% of books from first-time authors. No reprints. Prefers 256+ pgs. Royalty 7-15% of net; advance $500-1,500. Average first printing 2,000-3,000. Publication within 1 yr. Considers few simultaneous submissions. Prefers disk. Responds in 3 mos. Guidelines (by e-mail/Website); catalog available online.

Nonfiction: Query; proposal/2-3 chapters, or complete ms; fax/e-query OK. "Looking for scholarly overviews of religious teachers and movements; text books in philosophy; and reference books."

*PARTNERSHIP PRESS, PO Box 419527, Kansas City MO 64141. A partnership of authors, pastors and theologians in 22 Holiness and Wesleyan denominations. Publishes 1 title/yr.

Nonfiction: Spiritual formation.

PASTORAL PRESS—See Oregon Catholic Press.

PAULINE BOOKS & MEDIA, 50 St. Paul's Ave., Boston MA 02130-3491. (617)522-8911. Fax (617)541-9805. E-mail: editorial@pauline.org. Website: www.pauline.org. Catholic. Sr. Mary Mark Wickenhiser, F.S.P., acq ed. To help clarify Catholic belief and practice for the average reader. Publishes 25-35 titles/yr. Receives 1,300 submissions annually. 75% of books from first-time authors. No ms through agents. Royalty 8-12% of net; advance $300-500. Average first printing 3,000. Publication within 2 yrs. Responds in 3 mos. Requires disk. Prefers NRSV. Guidelines (also by e-mail/Website); free catalog.

Nonfiction: Proposal/2-3 chapters, fax/e-query OK. "Looking for books on faith and moral values, spiritual growth and development, and Christian formation for families."

Tips: "Open to religion teacher's resources and adult catechetics. No biographical or autobiographical material."

PAULIST PRESS, 997 Macarthur Blvd., Mahwah NJ 07430. (201)825-7300. Fax (201)825-8345. E-mail: info@paulistpress.com. Website: www.paulist press.com. Catholic. Maria Maggi, mng ed; Susan O'Keefe, children's book ed. Imprints: Newman Press; Stimulus Books. Publishes 90-100 titles/yr. Receives 500 submissions annually. 5-8% of books from first-time authors. Prefers 100-400 pgs. Royalty 10% on net; some outright purchases; advance $1,000. Average first printing 3,500. Publication within 10 mos. Responds in 2 mos. Guidelines.

 Nonfiction: Proposal/2 chapters. "Looking for theology (Catholic and ecumenical Christian), popular spirituality, liturgy, and religious education texts." Children's books for 5-7 years or 8-10 years; complete ms.

 Tips: "Most open to progressive, world-affirming, theologically sophisticated, growth-oriented, well-written books. Have strong convictions but don't be pious. Stay well read. Pay attention to contemporary social needs."

PELICAN PUBLISHING CO., INC., PO Box 3110, Gretna LA 70054-3110. (504)368-1175. Fax (504)368-1195. E-mail: editorial@pelicanpub.com. Website: www.pelicanpub.com. Nina Kooij, ed. To publish books of quality and permanence that enrich the lives of those who read them. Imprints: Firebird Press. Publishes 6 titles/yr. Receives 250 submissions annually. 65% of books from first-time authors. Accepts mss through agents. Reprints books. Prefers 200+ pgs. Royalty; some advances. Publication within 9-18 mos. No simultaneous submissions. Responds in 1 mo. Disk on request. Prefers KJV. Guidelines (also on Website); catalog for 9x12 SAE/7 stamps.

 Nonfiction: Proposal/2 chapters; no phone/fax/e-query. Children's picture books to 1,100 wds; middle readers (ages 8 & up) at least 25,000 wds; cookbooks at least 200 recipes.

 Fiction: Complete ms. For ages 5-8 only.

 Also Does: E-books.

 Tips: "On inspirational titles we need a high-profile author who already has an established speaking circuit so books can be sold at these appearances."

#PERIGEE BOOKS, 375 Hudson St., New York NY 10014. (212)366-2000. Fax (212)366-2365. Website: www.penguinputnam.com. Penguin Putnam, Inc. Submit to Book Editor. Publishes 12-15 titles/yr. Receives 200 submissions annually. 30% of books from first-time authors. Prefers mss through agents (but accepts freelance). Prefers 60,000-80,000 wds. Royalty 7 1/2-15%; advance $5,000-150,00. Average first printing varies. Publication within 18 mos. Considers simultaneous submissions. Responds in 2 mos. Guidelines on acceptance; free catalog

 Nonfiction: Query only; no phone query. Looking for spiritual, prescriptive, self-help, and women's issues.

#PETER PAUPER PRESS, 202 Mamaroneck Ave., White Plains NY 10601-5376. (914)681-0144. Fax (914)681-0389. E-mail: pauperp@aol.com.

Lynn Rosen, ed dir. Does small-format illustrated gift books. Imprint: In-spire Books (evangelical imprint). Publishes 40-50 titles/yr. Receives 1,000 submissions annually. No mss through agents. Prefers 800-2,000 wds. Outright purchase only, $250-1,000. Average first printing 10,000. Publication within 1 yr. Considers simultaneous submissions. Requires disk. Responds in 1 mo. Guidelines (also by e-mail); no catalog.

Nonfiction: Query only; no phone/fax/e-query. General inspirational themes.

Tips: "We want original aphorisms, 67-75 to a book. Title should be focused on a holiday or special occasion, family such as mother, sister, graduation, new baby, wedding, etc. "

PICKWICK PUBLICATIONS, 215 Incline Way, San Jose CA 95139-1526. (408)224-6777. Fax (408)224-6683. E-mail: DYH1@aol.com. Website: www.pickwickpublications.com. Dikan Y. Hadidian, ed. Publishes 2-4 titles/yr. Receives several dozen submissions annually. 60% of books from first-time authors. No mss through agents. Reprints books. Royalty of net; no advance. Publication within 12 mos. No simultaneous submissions. No e-mail submissions. Responds in 3 mos. Guidelines; catalog for 9x12 SAE/5 stamps.

Nonfiction: Phone/fax/e-query OK.

THE PILGRIM PRESS, 700 Prospect Ave. E., Cleveland OH 44115-1100. (216)736-3704. Fax (216)736-3703. E-mail: sadlerk@ucc.org. Website: www. pilgrimpress.com. United Church of Christ/Local Church Ministries. Kim Sadler, ed. dir. Church and educational resources. Publishes 12-15 titles/yr. Receives 150+ submissions annually. 50% of books from first-time authors. Royalty 8% of net; or work-for-hire, one-time fee; negotiable advance. Publication within 9-12 mos. No simultaneous submissions. Disk required. Responds in 6-8 wks. Free guidelines/catalog.

Nonfiction: Proposal/2 chapters; e-query OK.

Special Needs: Children's sermons, worship resources, youth materials, and religious materials for ethnic groups.

Ethnic Books: African-American, Native-American, Asisan-American, Pacific Islanders, and Hispanic.

Tips: "Most open to well-written manuscripts that are United Church of Christ specific and/or religious topics that cross denominations. Use inclusive language and follow the *Chicago Manual of Style.*"

PLATINUM PRESS INC., 311 Crossway Parks Dr., Woodbury NY 11797. (516) 364-1800. Fax (516)364-1899. Herbert Cohen, acq. ed. Reprints 100 titles/yr. 25% of books from first-time authors. Royalty 5-10% on retail; advance $500-750. Only buys book-club rights to previously published mysteries.

Nonfiction: Query. Religion subjects.

PLAYERS PRESS, INC., PO Box 1132, Studio City CA 91614-0132. (818)789-4980. Robert W. Gordon, ed. Publishes only dramatic works. Publishes 1-2 titles/yr. Receives 20-25 submissions annually. 25% of books from first-time authors. Reprints few books. Variable royalty; advance. Average first printing 5,000-10,000. Publication within 9-12 mos. No simultaneous submissions. Responds in 1-2 wks on query; 3-12 mos on manuscript. Requires disk. Guidelines; catalog for $2 postage.

Nonfiction/Plays: Query only; no phone query. "Theatrical musicals; theater/film/television how-tos; plays and theater crafts."

Special Needs: Theatre education.

Photos: Accepts freelance photos for book covers.

Tips: "Most open to plays and books on theater, film and television; also how-to."

PLEASANT COMPANY PUBLICATIONS, 8400 Fairway Pl., Middleton WI 53562. Fax (608)836-1999. Website: www.americangirl.com. Material of interest to girls 8-13. Erin Falligant, sub. ed. Imprints: American Girls Collection (historical fiction, 40,000-60,000 wds); American Girls Library (contemporary nonfiction); also adding a contemporary fiction imprint (40,000-60,000 words). Publishes 25-30 titles/yr. Receives 800 submissions annually. Prefers 100-200 pgs; 20,000-50,000 wds. Royalty or flat fee; negotiable advance. Considers simultaneous submissions. Responds in 3-4 mos. Guidelines (also on Website).

Nonfiction: Complete ms, or outline & sample chapters. "We need advice and activity books and nonfiction specifically targeted to girls."

Fiction: Complete ms. "All fiction for historical imprint—History Mysteries—must feature an American girl, age 8-12, from a historical period. Include a 1,000 word essay on the historical period of events featured in the story. We are also open to contemporary fiction for new imprint called AG Fiction; stories must capture the spirit of contemporary American girls (ages 10-12)."

Tips: "If your idea would work for both boys and girls, it probably isn't for us." Does not use inexperienced writers.

*PRAYER POINT PRESS, 10 Coralberry Rd., The Woodlands TX 77381. (281)292-1220. Fax (281)419-6084. E-mail: lponder@swbell.net. Lynn Ponder, ed/pub. Open to freelance. Did not return questionnaire.

PREP PUBLISHING, 1110½ Hay St., Fayetteville NC 28305. (910)483-6611. Fax (910)483-2439. E-mail: PREPPub@aol.com. Website: www.prep-pub. com. PREP, Inc. Anne McKinney, mng ed. Books to enrich people's lives and help them find joy in human experience. Publishes 10 titles/yr. Receives 1,500+ submissions annually. 85% of books from first-time authors. Reprints books. Prefers 250 pgs. Royalty 6-10% on retail; advance. Average first printing 3,000-5,000. Publication within 18 mos. Considers simultaneous submissions. Responds in 1 mo. Guidelines (also on Website) & catalog for #10 SAE/2 stamps.

Nonfiction: Query only; no phone query.

Fiction: Query only. All ages. "We are attempting to grow our Judeo-Christian fiction imprint in 2001."

Tips: "Rewrite, rewrite, rewrite with your reader clearly in focus."

PRESBYTERIAN AND REFORMED PUBLISHING CO.—See P & R Publishing.

PROMISE PRESS/BARBOUR PUBLISHING, INC., 1810 Barbour Dr., PO Box 719, Uhrichsville OH 44683. (740)922-6045. Fax (740)922-5948. E-mail:

info@barbourbooks.com. Website: www.barbourbooks.com. Susan Schlabach, sr ed. Imprint of Barbour Publishing. Publishes 30 titles/yr. Receives 1,500 submissions annually. 25% of books from first-time authors. Accepts mss through agents. Royalty 10-16% of net; advance $1,000-5,000. Average first printing 15,000-25,000. Publication within 1 yr. Considers simultaneous submissions. No disk or e-mail submissions. Responds in 4-6 wks. Prefers KJV or NIV. Guidelines (also by e-mail); catalog for 9x12 SASE.

> **Nonfiction:** Proposal/2-3 chapters; fax/e-query OK. "Looking for humor, prayer, women's devotionals, and short stories."
>
> **Fiction:** Proposal/2-3 chapters. For adults; mystery, suspense, action, drama.
>
> **Tips:** "Most open to a unique idea that can be developed into a series. Know your market and know the publisher before sending your material."
>
> ****Note:** This publisher serviced by The Writer's Edge.

+PROVIDENCE HOUSE PUBLISHERS, 238 Seaboard Ln., Franklin TN 37067. (615)771-2020. Fax (615)771-2002. E-mail: books@providence house.com. Website: www.providencehouse.com. Providence Publishing Corp. Submit to Book Editor. Publishes 50+ titles/yr. 75% of books from first-time authors. Accepts mss through agents. **SUBSIDY PUBLISHES SOME BOOKS.** Reprints books. Considers simultaneous submissions. Prefers disk. Prefers NIV or NKJV. Guidelines (also on Website); free catalog.

> **Nonfiction:** Phone/fax/e-query OK.

G. P. PUTNAM'S SONS, a division of Penguin Putnam/Books for Young Readers (formerly listed as Penguin Putnam), 345 Hudson St., New York NY 10014. (212)366-2000. Fax (212)951-8694. Website: www.penguin putnam.com. Pearson. Nancy Paulsen, pres/pub.; submit to Children's Editorial. Imprint: G.P. Putnam's Sons. Publishes 60-70 titles/yr. Variable royalty on retail; variable advance. Publication within 6 mos. Considers simultaneous submissions. No disk or e-mail submissions. Responds in 3 mos. Guidelines; catalog for 9x12 SAE/3 stamps.

> **Nonfiction:** Query only; fax query OK. "We publish some religious/inspirational books and books for ages 2-18."
>
> **Fiction:** Complete ms for picture books; proposal/3 chapters for novels. Primarily picture books or middle-grade novels.

QUESTAR PUBLISHERS—See Multnomah Publishers.

QUINTESSENTIAL BOOKS, Box 2566, Shawnee Mission KS 66201. (913) 752-5739. Fax (913)671-7728. Maryl Janson, acq. ed. Books that will challenge people to think deeply and live passionately in accordance with sound principles. Publishes 3-4 titles/yr. Receives 75-100 submissions annually. 10% of books from first-time authors. Reprints books. Prefers 60-70,000 wds or 224 pgs. Royalty of net; advance. Average first printing varies. Publication within 18 mos. Considers simultaneous submissions. Responds in 3-4 mos. Accepts disk. Prefers NIV. Guidelines (also by e-mail).

> **Nonfiction:** Query only; no phone/fax query. "Looking for family/parenting, personal responsibility, and leadership."
>
> **Fiction:** Query only. For adults.
>
> **Photos:** Accepts freelance photos for book covers.

Tips: "Most open to something that is cutting-edge/iconoclastic, but kind/generous at the same time."

+QUIXOTE PUBLICATIONS, 490 Merrimak Dr., Berea OH 44017. (440)234-4244. Fax (440)234-1141. E-mail: Patmote@aol.com. Pat M. Mote, ed. Does autobiography, biography, history, religious/spiritual, and self-help books. Willing to work with first-time authors. Incomplete topical listings. No questionnaire returned.

RAGGED EDGE, PO Box 152, Shippenburg PA 17257. (717)532-2237. Fax (717)532-6110. E-mail: marketing@whitemane.com. Website under construction. White Mane Publishing Co., Inc. Harold E. Collier, acq ed. Christian, social science and self-help books; to make a difference in people's lives. Publishes 10-15 titles/yr. Receives 50-75 submissions annually. 50% of books from first-time authors. **SUBSIDY PUBLISHES 20%.** Reprints books. Prefers 200 pgs. Variable royalty of net; advance. Average first printing 3,000. Publication within 1 yr. Considers simultaneous submissions. Responds in 60 days. Free guidelines/catalog.

Nonfiction: Query only; fax/e-query OK.

Fiction: Query only. Historical fiction for middle grades.

Tips: "Most open to a Protestant book in the middle of the spectrum."

RAINBOW PUBLISHERS/LEGACY PRESS, PO Box 261129, San Diego CA 92196. (858)271-7600. E-mail: rainbowed@earthlink.net. Website: www.rainbowpublishers.com. Christy Allen, ed. Publishes nondenominational, nonfiction for children in the evangelical Christian market. Publishes 15 titles/yr. Receives 250 submissions annually. 50% of books from first-time authors. Reprints books. Prefers 150 pgs & up. Royalty 8% and up on net; advance $500+. Average first printing 5,000. Publication within 2 yrs. Considers simultaneous submissions. Responds in 3 mos. Prefers NIV. Guidelines (also by e-mail); catalog for 9x12 SAE/2 stamps.

Nonfiction: Proposal/3-5 chapters; no e-queries. "Looking for nonfiction for girls and boys ages 2-12."

Special Needs: Nonfiction for ages 10-12, particularly Christian twists on current favorites, such as cooking, jewelry-making, games, etc.

Tips: "We are interested in expanding our line for girls called The Criss-Cross Collection. All books must offer solid Bible teaching."

RAINBOW PUBLISHERS/RAINBOW BOOKS, Box 261129, San Diego CA 92196. (858)271-7600. E-mail: rainbowed@earthlink.net. Website: www.rainbowpublishers.com. Christy Allen, ed. Publishes Bible-teaching, reproducible books for children's teachers. Publishes 20 titles/yr. Receives 250 submissions annually. 50% of books from first-time authors. Reprints books. Prefers 96 pgs. Outright purchases $640. Average first printing 2,500. Publication within 2 yrs. Considers simultaneous submissions. Responds in 3 mos. No disk or e-mail submissions. Prefers NIV. Guidelines (also by e-mail); catalog for 9x12 SAE/2 stamps.

Nonfiction: Proposal/3-5 chapters; no phone/e-query. "Looking for fun and easy ways to teach Bible concepts to kids, ages 2-12."

Special Needs: Creative puzzles and unique games.

Tips: "Request a catalog or visit your Christian bookstore to see what we have already published. You can either send a unique proposal or propose an addition to one of our existing series."

+**RAPHA PUBLISHING**, PO Box 1817, Upper Marlboro MD 20773. E-mail: LTLewisRobinson@netscape.net. Lisa Lewis-Robinson, owner. First project, spring 2001. Not included in topical listings. No questionnaire returned.

+**RBC PUBLISHING COMPANY**, 9107 Voos Ct., PO Box 1330, Elk Grove CA 95759. (916)685-5578. Fax 916)685-5958. E-mail: scituate@cwo.com. Website: www.rbcpublishingco.com. Melybar Publishing Co. A.C. Parks, V.P. Inspirational books about ordinary people who have done unique things in life. Publishes 4 titles/yr. Receives 8-10 submissions annually. 60% of books from first-time authors. No reprints. Prefers 240 pgs. Royalty 10-15% on retail; no advance. Average first printing 2,500-5,000. Publication within 6 mos. Considers simultaneous submissions. Responds in 1 mo. No guidelines/catalog.

    Nonfiction: Proposal/3 chapters.

    Fiction: Query only. For children and teens; children's picture books. "Story must have a thread for children that will help them understand the better side of life."

    Tips: "Most open to religious autobiographies, biographies and memoirs."

***READERS DIGEST CHILDREN'S PUBLISHING**, Readers Digest Rd., Pleasantville NY 10570. Anglican/Evangelical. Beverly Larson, ed. To create unique novelty-type books that bring the stories and truth of the Bible to life for young children. Imprint: Reader's Digest Young Families. Publishes 60 titles/yr. Receives 200 submissions annually. 5% of books from first-time authors. Makes outright purchases. Average first printing 25,000. Publication within 9 mos. Considers simultaneous submissions. Responds in 2-3 mos. No guidelines/catalog.

    Nonfiction: Proposal/1 chapter.

    Fiction: Proposal/1 chapter. Children's picture books.

    Special Needs: Produces board games and all kinds of novelty books for children.

    Tips: "We are looking for writers who are excellent at rhyming and can write for preschoolers particularly. We commission authors to write books that we have come up with. Authors should send samples of their best work, rather than sending a specific proposal."

READ 'N RUN BOOKS, PO Box 294, Rhododendron OR 97049. (503)622-4798. Fax (503)658-6233. Crumb Elbow Publishing. Michael P. Jones, pub. Books of lasting interest. Publishes 2 titles/yr. Receives 150 submissions annually. 90% of books from first-time authors. Reprints books. Royalty 30-50% of net; no advance; **SOME COOPERATIVE PUBLISHING**. Average first printing 500-1,000. Publication within 1 yr. Considers simultaneous submissions. Responds in 2 wks. No disk. Responds in 1 mo. Guidelines; catalog $3.

    Nonfiction: Complete ms; no phone/fax query. "Looking for books on cults/occult, history and prophecy."

Fiction: Complete ms. Any type; any age. Looking for historical fiction of the Northwest, Oregon, or the West.

Ethnic Books: Open to.

Also Does: Booklets, pamphlets, tracts, e-books, postcards, note cards, posters.

Photos: Accepts freelance photos for book covers.

Contest: Poetry contest. Send SASE for information.

Tips: "Nature and history are two areas we are seriously looking at, but also interested in poetry and short-story collections."

+REFLECTION PUBLISHING CO., 1 Hendrick Dr., Abilene TX 79602. (915) 692-9651. Fax (915)690-1875. E-mail: info@reflectionpublishing.com. Website: www.reflectionpublishing.com. Lake P. Monhollon, ed. Does religious/spiritual books. Incomplete topical listings. No questionnaire returned.

REGAL BOOKS, 2300 Knoll Dr., Ventura CA 93003. Does not accept unsolicited manuscripts.

#REGNERY PUBLISHING, 1 Massachusetts Ave. NW, Washington DC 20001. (202)216-0600. Fax (202)546-8759. Website: www.regnery.com. Eagle Publishing. Harry Crocker, exec ed; submit to Submissions Editor. Trade publisher that does scholarly Catholic books and evangelical Protestant books. Imprint: Gateway Editions. Publishes 2-4 religious titles/yr. Receives 30-50 submissions annually. Few books from first-time authors. Reprints books. Prefers 250-500 pgs. Royalty 8-15% on retail; advances to $50,000. Average first printing 5,000. Publication within 1 yr. Considers simultaneous submissions. Responds in 6 mos. Free catalog.

Nonfiction: Accepts manuscripts through agents only. Proposal/1-3 chapters or query; no fax query. Looking for history, popular biography and popular history.

Tips: "Religious books should relate to politics, history, current affairs, biography, and public policy. Most open to a book that deals with a topical issue from a conservative point of view—something that points out a need for spiritual renewal; or a how-to book on finding spiritual renewal."

RELIGION AND SPIRITUALITY—See HarperSanFrancisco.

RELIGIOUS EDUCATION PRESS, 5316 Meadow Brook Rd., Birmingham AL 34242. (205)991-1000. Fax (205)991-9669. E-mail: releduc@ix.netcom. com. Website: www.bham.net/releduc. Unaffiliated. James Michael Lee, ed. Mission is specifically directed toward helping fulfill, in an interfaith and ecumenical way, the Great Commission. Publishes 5-6 titles/yr. Receives 500 submissions annually. 40% of books from first-time authors. Prefers 200-500 pgs. Royalty 5% of net; advance. Average first printing 2,000. Publication within 9 mos. Responds in 1 mo. Requires disk. Guidelines; free catalog.

Tips: "We are not accepting manuscripts for the foreseeable future."

RESOURCE PUBLICATIONS, INC., Ste. 290, 160 E. Virginia St., San Jose CA 95112-5876. (408)286-8505. Fax (408)287-8748. E-mail: editor@rpinet. com, or orders@rpinet.com. Website: www.rpinet.com/ml/ml.html. Nick Wagner, ed dir. Publishes 20 titles/yr. Receives 450 submissions annually.

30% of books from first-time authors. Prefers 50,000 wds. Royalty 8% of net: rare advance. Average first printing 3,000. Publication within 1 yr. Responds in 10 wks. Prefers disk. Guidelines; catalog for 9x12 SAE/10 stamps.

Nonfiction: Proposal/1 chapter; phone/fax/e-query OK.

Fiction: Query. Adult/teen/children. Only read-aloud stories for storytellers. "Must be useful in ministerial, counseling, or educational settings."

Also Does: Computer programs; aids to ministry or education.

Tips: "Know our market. We cater to ministers in Catholic and mainstream Protestant settings. We are not an evangelical house or general interest publisher."

FLEMING H. REVELL CO., Box 6287, Grand Rapids MI 49516. (616)676-9185. Fax (616)676-2315. E-mail: lhdupont@bakerbooks.com. Website: www.bakerbooks.com. Subsidiary of Baker Book House. Imprints: Revell, Chosen, Spire. Lonnie Hull Dupont, ed. dir.; submit to Sheila Ingram. Publishes 60 titles/yr. Receives 1,750 submissions annually. 1% of books from first-time authors. Prefers 60,000 wds. Royalty 14-18% of net; advance. Average first printing 5,000. Publication within 1 yr. Considers simultaneous submissions. Responds in 3 mos. Requires disk. Free guidelines (also on Website)/catalog.

Nonfiction: Query or proposal/2 chapters; no phone/fax/e-query. Looking for humor, prayer or spirituality, exceptional devotionals and gift books.

Fiction: Proposal/3 chapters; no phone/fax/e-query. Mostly adult. Looking for contemporary or historical women's fiction.

Tips: "Research the market for what's needed; maintain excellence; address a felt need; use good clarity and focus on topic."

Note: This publisher serviced by The Writer's Edge.

REVIEW AND HERALD PUBLISHING ASSN., 55 W. Oak Ridge Dr., Hagerstown MD 21740-7390. (301)393-3000. Fax (301)393-4055. E-mail: editorial @rhpa.org. Website: www.rhpa.org. Seventh-Day Adventist. Richard Coffen, VP/editorial; Jeannette Johnson, acq ed. Proclaims and upholds to the world the character of a loving Creator God and nurtures a growing relationship with God by providing products that teach and enrich people spiritually, mentally, physically, and socially. Publishes 40-50 titles/yr. Receives 300-400 submissions annually. 50% of books from first-time authors. Accepts mss through agents. No reprints. Prefers 128-256 pgs. Royalty 5-16% of net; advance $500-1,000. Average first printing 3,500-4,500. Publication within 2 yrs. Considers simultaneous submissions. Requires disk. Responds in 1 mo. Any version. Guidelines; free catalog.

Nonfiction: Query, proposal/3 chapters or complete ms; phone/fax/e-query OK. "Looking for Christian living and spiritual growth books."

Fiction: Proposal/3 chapters or complete ms. All ages. Does occasionally.

Also Does: Pamphlets, booklets, tracts.

Photos: Accepts freelance photos for book covers.

Tips: "Looking for books that are practical, how-to, crisp and relevant."

RISING STAR PRESS, PO Box BB, Los Altos CA 94023. (650)966-8920. Fax (650)968-2658. E-mail: editor@risingstarpress.com. Website: www.Rising StarPress.com. Submit to Acquisitions Editor. Quality books that inform and inspire. Publishes 1-2 titles/yr. Receives 200 submissions annually. 50% of books from first-time authors. Length open. Royalty 15% of net; advance $1,000. Average first printing 2,000. Publication within 10 mos. Considers simultaneous submissions. Requires disk. Responds in 6-8 wks. Guidelines & catalog on Website.

> **Nonfiction:** Query or proposal/2-3 chapters; fax/e-query OK."
>
> **Photos:** Accepts freelance photos for book covers.
>
> **Also Does:** E-books.
>
> **Tips:** "Most open to a book that the writer is qualified to write and that will be meaningful to a wide spectrum of readers."

+RODMELL PRESS, 2550 Shattuck Ave., #18, Berkeley CA 94704. (510)841-3123. Fax (510)841-3191. E-mail: RodmellPrs@aol.com. Donald Moyer & Linda Cogozzo, eds. Does health, religious/spiritual, and sports books. Incomplete topical listings. No questionnaire returned.

#ROSE PUBLISHING, 4455 Torrance Blvd., #259, Torrance CA 90503. (310) 370-8962. Fax (310)370-7492. E-mail: rosepubl@aol.com (make subject Carol). Website: www.rosepublishing.net. Nondenominational. Carol Witte, mng ed. Publishes only large Sunday school charts and teaching materials. Publishes 5-10 titles/yr. 5% of books from first-time authors. No mss through agents. Royalty or outright purchases. Publication within 18 mos. Considers simultaneous submissions. Responds in 2-3 mos. Free catalog.

> **Special Needs:** Query with sketch of proposed chart (non-returnable); fax query OK; e-query OK if less than 100 wds (copied into message). Large teaching charts for Sunday schools; church history time lines; charts for children and youth. Also books on the Trinity, creation vs. evolution, Christian history, how we got the Bible, Ten Commandments, and the Lord's Prayer.
>
> **Tips:** "Now accepting more freelance submissions. Material for children, youth, Bible study charts and study guides, pamphlets, maps, timelines."

+RPI PUBLISHING, INC., PO Box 44, Curtis WA 98538. (800)873-8384. Fax (360)245-3757. E-mail: pam@rpipublishing.com. Website: www.rpi publishing.com. The 12-step people. Ron Halvorson, ed. Does recovery, self-help, and religious/spiritual books. Incomplete topical listings. No questionnaire returned.

ST. ANTHONY MESSENGER PRESS, 1615 Republic St., Cincinnati OH 45210-1298. (513)241-5615x123. (800)488-0488. Fax (513)241-0399 or 241-1197. E-mail: StAnthony@AmericanCatholic.org. Website: www. AmericanCatholic.org. Catholic. Lisa Biedenbach, mng ed (lisab@American Catholic.org). Seeks to publish affordable resources for living a Catholic-Christian lifestyle. Imprint: Franciscan Communications and Ikonographics (videos). Publishes 18-20 titles/yr. Receives 240 submissions annually. 5% of books from first-time authors. No mss through agent. Reprints books. Prefers 25,000-50,000 wds or 150-300 pgs. Royalty 10-12% of net; advance

$1,000. Average first printing 5,000. Publication within 12-18 mos. Accepts disk. Responds in 2 mos. Prefers NAB or NRSV. Guidelines (also by e-mail); catalog for 9x12 SAE/4 stamps.

Nonfiction: Query only/500-wd summary; fax/e-query OK. "Looking for family-based catechetical programs; living the Catholic-Christian life at home and in workplace; and Franciscan topics."

Special Needs: Materials that help parents pass on Catholic faith; Catholic identity; Saints and Christian heroes.

Ethnic Books: Hispanic, occasionally.

Also Does: Pamphlets and booklets.

Photos: Accepts freelance photos for book covers.

Tips: "Most open to books with sound Catholic doctrine that includes personal experiences or anecdotes applicable to today's culture. Our books are decidedly Catholic."

+ST. AUGUSTINE'S PRESS, PO Box 2285, South Bend IN 46680. (219)291-3500. Fax (219)291-3700. E-mail: bruce@staugustine.net. Website: www.staugustine.net. A conservative, nondenominational (although mostly Catholic) publisher of academic titles, mainly in philosophy, theology, and cultural history. Bruce Fingerhut, pres. Publishes 2-5 titles/yr. Receives 20-30 submissions annually. 5% of books from first-time authors. Accepts mss through agents. Reprints books. Royalty 6-15% on net; advance $1,000. Average first printing 1,000. Publication within 1 yr. Considers simultaneous submissions. Responds in 3 mos. No guidelines; free catalog.

Nonfiction: Query or proposal/chapters. "Most of our titles are philosophy."

SAINT MARY'S PRESS, 702 Terrace Heights, Winona MN 55987-1320. (507)457-7900. (800)533-8095. Fax (507)457-7990. E-mail: snagel@smp.org. Website: www.smp.org. Catholic. Stephan Nagel, ed-in-chief. Fiction for teens, ages 10-19. Publishes 20-25 titles/yr. Prefers up to 40,000 wds. Royalty; advance. Average first printing 5,000. Publication within 18 mos. Accepts simultaneous submissions. Guidelines (also by e-mail); free catalog.

Fiction: Query/outline & 1 chapter; e-query OK.

Tips: "Books that give insight into the struggle of teens to become healthy, hopeful adults and also shed light on Catholic experience, history or cultures."

SCARECROW PRESS, 4720 Boston Way., Lanham MD 20706. (301)459-3366. Fax (301)459-2118. E-mail: kregen@scarecrowpress.com. Website: www.scarecrowpress.com. Rowman & Littlefield Publishing Group. Shirley Lambert, ed dir; submit to Katie Regen, asst ed. Provides reference and professional materials for librarians. Publishes 5-15 titles/yr. Receives 600-700 submissions annually. 70% of books from first-time authors. Prefers 250-350 pgs. Royalty 8-10% of net; no advance. Average first printing 525. Publication within 18 mos. Considers simultaneous submissions. Responds in 2 mos. Requires disk. Free guidelines (also by e-mail/Website)/catalog.

Nonfiction: Proposal/2-3 chapters or complete ms; phone/fax/e-query OK. "Looking for reference, religion and scholarly books." New: educational administration.

Special Needs: A reference guide to Christian fiction for children and one for young adults.

Also Does: E-books.

SCRIPTURE PRESS—See Cook Communications Ministries.

+SHARMAN FARMS CHRISTIAN EBOOKS, Australia. E-mail: manions@tassie.net.au. Website: www.tassie.net.au/~c_ebook. Monicque Sharman, pub. Author receives half of all profits. Payment made as soon as balance due reaches $25 US. Visit Website for submission details. Fiction and nonfiction accepted. Not included in topical listings. No questionnaire returned.

HAROLD SHAW PUBLISHERS, 2375 Telstar Dr., Ste. 160, Colorado Springs CO 80920. (719)590-4999. Fax (719)590-8977. Website: www.waterbrook press.com. Imprint of WaterBrook Press/Random House. Don Pape, pub. dir. Publishes books specifically focused on health and wellness, family and education, creative nonfiction, Bible study resources. Publishes 20-25 titles/yr. 10-20% of books from first-time authors. Reprints books. Royalty on net or retail; outright purchases $375-2,000 (for Bible study guides and compilations); advance. No unsolicited mss. Queries accepted (attn: Editorial) but not unsolicited mss.

>   **Tips:** "We are looking for unique manuscripts on the above topics that add a fresh voice to the subject."

>   ****Note:** This publisher serviced by The Writer's Edge.

SHEED & WARD, 7373 S. Lovers Lane Rd., Franklin WI 53132. (414)529-6400. Fax (414)529-6419. E-mail: jereditor@aol.com. Website: www.sheedandward.com. Priests of the Sacred Heart. Jeremy Langford, ed-in-chief (773-404-7449). Publishes books of contemporary impact and enduring merit in Catholic-Christian thought and action. Publishes 30 titles/yr. Receives 200 submissions annually. 10% of books from first-time authors. **SUBSIDY PUBLISHES 2%.** Reprints books. Prefers 35,000-55,000 wds. Royalty 6/8/10% on retail; some work-for-hire; flexible advance. Average first printing 3,000. Publication within 6 mos. Responds in 3 mos. Requires disk. Prefers NAB or NRSV (Catholic editions). Guidelines (also on Website); catalog for 7x11 SAE/2 stamps.

>   **Nonfiction:** Complete ms; phone/fax/e-query OK. "Looking for parish ministry (health care, spirituality, leadership, general trade books for mass audiences, sacraments, small group or priestless parish facilitating books)."

>   **Tips:** "Looking for general trade titles and academic titles in areas of spirituality, parish ministry, leadership, sacraments, prayer, faith formation, Church history, and scripture."

*SHINING STAR PUBLICATIONS, 23740 Hawthorne Blvd., Torrance CA 90505. (800)609-1735. E-mail: FSPinfo@aol.com. Website: www.frank schaffer.com. Division of Frank Schaffer Publications. Mina McCullen, ed. Publishes Bible activity books for teachers and parents to teach God's truth to children, preschool-elementary. Publishes 20 titles/yr. Receives 30-40 submissions annually. 25% of books from first-time authors. No mss through agents. Prefers 48-96 pgs. Outright purchases $20/pg.; no advance. Average first printing 3,000. Publication within 12 mos. No simultaneous submissions. Responds in 2 mos. Guidelines; free catalog.

Nonfiction: Query first; phone/fax query OK. "We need reproducible workbooks to teach Scriptures and Christian values; Bible activities; Bible story crafts; skits and songs with a Christian emphasis."

Tips: "We publish only Bible activity books with reproducible pages for teachers and parents to use in home or church teaching situations; no picture books or children's novels."

SKYSONG PRESS, 35 Peter St. S., Orillia ON L3V 5A8 Canada. E-mail: skysong @bconnex.net. Website: www.bconnex.net/~skysong. Steve Stanton, ed. Guidelines on Website.

Fiction: Christian science fiction only. "New authors should not submit novel manuscripts. Send us something for Dreams & Visions (see periodical section) first."

+SLIGO PRESS, 45535 Pueblo Rd., Indian Wells CA 92210. (760)340-6640. Fax (760)722-1539. E-mail: RicSligo@aol.com. Website: www.sligopress. com. Ric Bollinger, ed. Does fiction, political, and religious/spiritual books. Incomplete topical listings. No questionnaire returned.

SMALL HELM PRESS, 622 Baker St., Petaluma CA 94952-2525. (707)763-5757. E-mail: smllhelm@sonic.net. Website: www.sonic.net/~smll helm. Alice Pearl Evans, pub. Interprets direction in contemporary life. Publishes 1 title/yr. Receives few submissions. Reprints books. Prefers 96-224 printed pgs. Outright purchase, negotiable. Average first printing 1,000-2,000. Publication within 9 mos. Considers simultaneous submissions. Responds in 2-4 wks. Prefers NKJV or NIV. Guidelines (also on Website); catalog for 9x12 SAE/3 stamps.

Nonfiction: Query, proposal or complete ms; prefers e-mail query.

Tips: "Most open to nonfiction of interest to general public and based on cultural or philosophical issues with a Christian worldview. Write with conviction and credibility."

SMYTH & HELWYS PUBLISHING, INC., 6316 Peake Rd., Macon GA 31210-3960. (478)301-2117. Fax (478)301-2264. E-mail: shelwys@mindspring. com. Website: www.helwys.com. Theresa Peterlein, VP Book Marketing. Quality resources for the church and individual Christians that are nurtured by faith and informed by scholarship. Publishes 35-40 titles/yr. Receives 600 submissions annually. 40% of books from first-time authors. Prefers 144 pgs. Royalty 7%. Considers simultaneous submissions. Responds in 3 mos. Free guidelines/catalog.

Nonfiction: Query only; fax/e-query OK. "Manuscripts requested for topics appropriate for mainline church and seminary/university textbook market."

Also Does: E-books. Copies of print books, or books in electronic format only. Go to: www.nextsunday.com.

Tips: "Most open to books with a strong secondary or special market. Niche titles and short-run options available for specialty subjects."

*SOWER'S PRESS, PO Box 666306, Marietta GA 30066. (770)977-3784. Jamey Wood, ed. Books to further establish the ministries of speakers and teachers. Publishes 2-3 titles/yr. Responds in 1 mo.

Nonfiction: Proposal/chapters. Marriage and family books.

#SPENCE PUBLISHING COMPANY, 111 Cole St, Dallas TX 75207-7101. (214)939-1700 or (888)773-6782. Fax (214)939-1800. E-mail: muncy @spencepublishing.com. Website: www.spencepublishing.com. Thomas Spence, pub.; Mitchell Muncy, ed-in-chief. Commentary on social and cultural issues related to education, ethics, religion and public life, politics, law, marriage, family and the arts. Publishes 8-10 titles/yr. Royalty 12% of net; no advance. Considers simultaneous submissions. Responds in 1-2 mos. Guidelines; free catalog (also on Website). Incomplete topical listings.

> **Nonfiction:** Query or proposal/1 chapter. Religion.

+SPIRITUAL THEATER INTERNATIONAL, PO Box 538, Littleton CO 80160. (202)662-2132. Website: www.spiritual theater.com/release.htm. Submit to: New Plays Submissions. Seeks plays for purchase or production. Buys all rts. Guidelines & submission form on Website.

> **Special Needs:** Each year they feature their best works at a Spiritual Theater Festival, where a panel of judges selects one new play for full production. To be considered for the Festival, submit plays by February 1.

STANDARD PUBLISHING, 8121 Hamilton Ave., Cincinnati OH 45231. (513)931-4050. Fax (513)931-0950. E-mail: customerservice@standard pub.com. Website: www.standardpub.com. Standex Intl. Corp. Diane Stortz, dir. of Bean Sprouts children's books; Ruth Frederick, dir. of church resources; Dale Reeves (youth products); Jim Eichenberger (adult resources). An evangelical Christian publisher of curriculum, classroom resources, teen resources, children's books, and drama. Publishes 150 titles/yr. Receives 1,500 submissions annually. 25% of books from first-time authors. Royalty & work for hire; advance. Average first printing 10,000 (depends on product). Publication within 18 mos. Considers simultaneous submissions. Responds in 3 mos. Prefers disk. Prefers NIV, ICB. Guidelines (also by e-mail/Website); catalog $2.

> **Nonfiction:** Query to Christian Education Team, Children's Editor, Teen Editor, Drama Team, or Adult Editor; no phone/fax/e-query. Well-presented, clearly stated cover letters are very useful.

> ****Note:** This publisher serviced by The Writer's Edge.

STARBURST PUBLISHERS, PO Box 4123, Lancaster PA 17604. (717)293-0939. Fax (717)293-1945. E-mail: starburst@starburstpublishers.com, or editorial@starburstpublishers.com. Website: www.starburstpublishers.com. Evangelical. David A. Robie, ed. Publishes books that will reach the Christian and general market. Publishes 15 titles/yr. Receives 1,000 submissions annually. 50% of books from first-time authors. Prefers 200-300 pgs. Royalty 6-15% of net; some advances. Average first printing 5,000-10,000. Publication within 12-18 mos. Considers simultaneous submissions. No disks or e-mail submissions. Responds in 2-4 wks. Guidelines (also on Website); catalog for 9x12 SAE/4 stamps.

> **Nonfiction:** Query only first; no phone/fax/e-query. "Looking for gift, health, inspiration, self-help, and Bible study/reference."

Fiction: Query only first. Contemporary adult fiction. "We are looking for good, wholesome fiction."

Tips: "Most open to nonfiction that can be sold in both Christian and general markets. Be fresh!"

STILL WATERS REVIVAL BOOKS, 4710—37A Ave., Edmonton AB T6L 3T5 Canada. (708)450-3730. E-mail: swrb@swrb.com. Website: www.swrb. com. Covenanter Church. Reg Barrow, pres. Publishes 100 titles/yr. Receives few submissions. Very few books from first-time authors. Reprints books. Prefers 128-160 pgs. Negotiated royalty or outright purchase. Considers simultaneous submissions. Catalog for 9x12 SAE/2 stamps.

Nonfiction: Proposal/2 chapters.

Tips: "Only open to books defending the Covenanted Reformation, nothing else."

+**SUCCESS SYSTEMS AT WORK**, 2828 W. Lincoln Ave., Ste. 158, Anaheim CA 92801-6214. (714)828-9377. Henry B. Ambrose, ed. Does religious/spiritual, education, and textbooks. Incomplete topical listings. No questionnaire returned.

THE SUMMIT PUBLISHING GROUP, 3649 Conflans Rd., #103, Irving TX 75061. (972)399-8856. Fax (972)313-9060. E-mail: jbertolet@tapestry pressinc.com. Website: www.tapestrypressinc.com. Tapestry Press, Inc. Jill Bertolet, pub. Secular publisher of contemporary nonfiction books, including some religious; custom publishing or partnership between author and publisher. Publishes 1 title/yr. Receives 50-100 submissions annually. 50% of books from first-time authors. Accepts mss through agents. Reprints books. Royalty on net; no advance. Publication within 6-12 mos. Considers simultaneous submissions. Responds in 3-6 mos. Guidelines on Website; no catalog.

Nonfiction: Query only; fax/e-query OK. Looking for gardening, cooking and business.

Tips: "Books need national distribution appeal. Author's media experience, contacts and exposure are a strong plus."

*****JEREMY P. TARCHER**, 375 Hudson St., New York NY 10014. (212)366-2000. Website: www.penguinputnam.com. Penguin Putnam, Inc. Mitch Horowitz & Wendy Hubbert, sr. eds. Publishes ideas and works about human consciousness that are large enough to include matters of spirit and religion. Publishes 30-40 titles/yr. Receives 1,000 submissions annually. 10% of books from first-time authors. Royalty 5-8% of retail; advance. Considers simultaneous submissions. Free catalog. Not included in topical listings.

Nonfiction: Query. Religion.

TEKNA BOOKS, PO Box 5234, Titusville FL 32783-5234. E-mail: submissions @teknabooks.com. Website: www.teknabooks.com. Ecumenical. Submit to Acquisitions Editor. Seeks to pass the torch of faith to future generations. Publishes 2-5 titles/yr. Receives 100 submissions annually. **SUBSIDY PUBLISHES SOME BOOKS.** No length preference. Royalty 4-12% of retail; no advance. Average first printing 1,000. Publication within 11 mos. Considers simultaneous submissions. Accepts e-mail submissions (in rich text format). Responds in 1-2 mos. Guidelines (also by e-mail or on Website); catalog on Website. For guidelines, e-mail: guide@tekna books.com.

Nonfiction: Proposal/chapters or complete ms; e-query OK.

Tips: "We are currently overstocked and unable to accept submissions through 2001."

+THIRTEEN COLONIES PRESS, 710 S. Henry St., Williamsburg VA 23185-4113. (804)229-1775. John F. Millar, ed. Does history, religious/spiritual, and multicultural books. Incomplete topical listings. No questionnaire returned.

THROUGH THE BIBLE PUBLISHING, 1133 Riverside Ave., Fort Collins CO 80524. (970)484-8483. Fax (970)495-6700. E-mail: info@ThroughtheBible. com. Website: www.ThroughtheBible.com. Mark Steiner, sr ed., Disciple-Land curriculum. Mission is to assist the church in fulfilling the Great Commission. Publishes curriculum only. Guidelines (also by e-mail/ Website).

Tips: "We are seeking freelance writers of curriculum for elementary-level children who are willing to generate alternative activities and questions, along with rewriting and fine-tuning existing text. If qualified, submit a résumé along with samples of your material written for children."

TIME FOR LAUGHTER/WATERBROOK PRESS, Random House Inc., 5446 N. Academy Dr., Ste. 200, Colorado Springs CO 80918. Accepts no freelance.

TOCCOA FALLS COLLEGE PRESS, Toccoa Falls College, PO Box 800067, Toccoa Falls GA 30598. (706)886-6831. Fax (706)282-6014. Marcille P. Jordan, ed. Publishes quality Christian material for the church and academic community. Publishes 4 titles/yr. Receives 100 submissions annually. 75% of books from first-time authors. Very limited subsidy. Prefers 150-250 pgs. Royalty 10% of retail; no advance. Average first printing 1,500-3,000. Publication within 6 mos. Considers simultaneous submissions. Responds ASAP. Guidelines.

Nonfiction: Query, proposal or complete ms; phone/fax query OK. Looking for academic/scholarly books.

Fiction: Query, proposal, or complete ms. For children or teens.

Tips: "We are looking for scholarly, academic material."

TOUCH PUBLICATIONS, PO Box 19888, Houston TX 77224-9888. (281)497-7901. Fax (281)497-0904. E-mail: sboren@touchusa.org. Website: www. touchusa.org. Touch Outreach Ministries. Scott Boren, dir of publishing. To empower pastors, group leaders and members to transform their lives, churches and the world through basic Christian communities called cells. Publishes 8 titles/yr. Receives 25 submissions annually. 40% of books from first-time authors. Reprints books. Prefers 75-200 pgs. Royalty 10-15% of net; no advance. Average first printing 2,000. Not in topical listings.

Nonfiction: Query only. "Must relate to cell church life."

Photos: Accepts freelance photos for book covers.

Tips: "Our market is extremely focused. We publish books, resources and discipleship tools for churches, using a cell group strategy."

THE TRINITY FOUNDATION, PO Box 68, Unicoi TN 37692. (423)743-0199. Fax (423)743-2005. E-mail: jrob1517@aol.com. Website: www.trinity

foundation.org. John W. Robbins, pres. To promote the logical system of truth found in the Bible. Publishes 6 titles/yr. Receives 3 submissions annually. No books from first-time authors. No mss through agents. Reprints books. Prefers 200 pgs. Outright purchase; free books; no advance. Average first printing 3,000. Publication within 9 mos. No simultaneous submissions. Requires disk. Responds in 2 mos. No guidelines: catalog for #10 SAE/1 stamp.

Nonfiction: Query letter only. Most open to Calvinist/Clarkian books, Christian philosophy, economics, and politics.

Also Does: Booklets and tracts.

Photos: Accepts freelance photos for book covers.

Tips: "Most open to nonfiction, biblical, and well-reasoned books."

TRINITY PRESS INTERNATIONAL, PO Box 1321, Harrisburg PA 17105. (717)541-8130. Fax (717)541-8136. E-mail: hcarriga@morehousegroup. com. Website: www.trinitypressintl.com. The Morehouse Group. Henry L. Carrigan Jr., dir. A nondenominational, academic religious publisher. Publishes 40 titles/yr. Receives 150-200 submissions annually. 3% of books from first-time authors. Reprints books. Royalty 10% of net; advance $500 & up. Average first printing 2,000. Publication within 9 mos. Considers simultaneous submissions. Responds in 3-6 mos. Prefers RSV & NRSV. Guidelines (also by e-mail); free catalog.

Nonfiction: Proposal/1 chapter, or complete ms; fax/e-query OK. "Religious material only in the area of Bible studies, theology, ethics, etc." No dissertations or essays.

Special Needs: Religion and film; American religious history; and religion and science.

Tips: "Most open to a book that is academic, to be used in undergraduate biblical studies, theology or religious studies programs."

TROITSA BOOKS, 227 Main St., #100, Huntington NY 11743-6907. (631) 424-6682. Fax (631)424-4666. E-mail: NovaScience@earthlink.net. Nova Science Publishers, Inc. Frank Columbus, ed. Publishes 10-20 titles/yr. Receives 50-100 submissions annually. No mss through agents. Various lengths. Royalty; no advance. Publication within 6 mos. Considers simultaneous submissions. Accepts disk or e-mail submissions. Responds in 1 mo. Free guidelines/catalog.

Nonfiction: Proposal/2 chapters; fax/e-query OK.

Fiction: Proposal/2 chapters. For adults.

Photos: Accepts freelance photos for book covers.

#TYNDALE HOUSE PUBLISHERS, 351 Executive Dr., Box 80, Wheaton IL 60189-0080. (630)668-8300. Fax (630)668-3245. Website: www.tyndale. com. Submit to Manuscript Review Committee. Imprints: Heart Quest (see separate listing). Publishes 100 titles/yr. 5-10% of books from first-time authors. Reprints books. Royalty; outright purchase of some children's books; advance negotiable. Average first printing 5,000-10,000. Publication within 18 mos. Responds in 2 mos. No unsolicited mss. Guidelines (also on Website); catalog for 9x12 SAE/9 stamps.

Nonfiction: Query from agents or published authors only; no phone/ fax query.

Fiction: "We accept queries only from agents, Tyndale authors, authors known to us from other publishers, or other people in the publishing industry. Novellas, 25,000 words. All must have a distinct Christian message."

**Note: This publisher serviced by The Writer's Edge.

+UMI PUBLISHING, 1551 Regency Ct., Calumet City IL 60409. (708)868-7100. Fax (708)868-6759. Website: www.urbanministries.com. Urban Ministries, Inc. Carl Jeffrey Wright, pub. Adult line of black Christian fiction. Not included in topical listings. No questionnaire returned.

Fiction: Adult, for black audience.

#UNITED CHURCH PRESS, 700 Prospect Ave. E., Cleveland OH 44115-1100. (216)736-3715. Fax (216)736-3703. E-mail: sadlerk@ucc.org, or stavet@ucc.org. Website: www.pilgrimpress.com. United Church of Christ/Local Church Ministries. Kim M. Sadler, ed. Publishes 12-15 titles/yr. Receives 150+ submissions annually. 30% of books from first-time authors. Royalty 8% of net; work-for-hire, one-time fee; advance negotiable. Average first printing 3,000. Publication within 18 mos. Considers simultaneous submissions. Responds in 3 mos. Requires disk. Free guidelines/catalog.

Nonfiction: Proposal/2 chapters or complete ms; e-query OK.

Special Needs: Children's sermons, worship resources, youth materials, religious materials for ethnic groups.

Ethnic Books: African-American, Native-American, Asian-American, Pacific Islanders, and Hispanic.

Tips: "Most open to well-written mss that are United Church of Christ specific and/or religious topics that cross denominations. Use inclusive language and follow the *Chicago Manual of Style*."

UNITED CHURCH PUBLISHING HOUSE, 3250 Bloor St. W., 4th floor, Toronto ON M8X 2Y4 Canada. (416)231-5931. Fax (416)232-6004. E-mail: rchevali@uccan.org, or bookpub@uccan.org. Website: www.uccan.org/ucph. The United Church of Canada. Rebekah Chevalier, acting exec. ed. Publishes socially important books that raise awareness of timely issues. Publishes 10 titles/yr. Publication of new books is currently on hold until the end of 2001. Not accepting manuscripts this year.

UNITED METHODIST PUBLISHING HOUSE, PO Box 801, Nashville TN 37202. (615)749-6000. Website: www.abingdon.org. Imprints: Abingdon Press, Dimensions for Living. Publishes 175 titles/yr. Reprints books. Free catalog. Not in topical listings.

Nonfiction & Fiction: For adults.

Photos: Accepts freelance photos for book covers.

UNIVERSITY OF OTTAWA PRESS, 542 King Edward Ave., Ottawa ON K1N 6N5 Canada. (613)562-5246. Fax (613)562-5247. E-mail: press@uottawa.ca. Website: www.uopress.uottawa.ca/en/welcome.html. Dr. V. Bennett, ed-in-chief. Promotes scholarly, academic publications. Publishes 20-25 titles/yr. Receives 300 submissions annually. No mss through agents. Prefers 250-300 pgs. Royalty 8-10% of net; no advance. Average first printing 800. Publication within 10-12 mos. Accepts simultaneous submissions. Responds in 2 wks. Requires disk; e-mail submissions, abstracts only. Free guidelines/catalog.

Nonfiction: Query only first; fax/e-query OK. Scholarly/academic books only (peer reviewed). Social scientific study of religion. No devotionals or memoirs.

Tips: "Do not send SASE with U.S. stamps."

UNIVERSITY PRESS OF AMERICA, 4720 Boston Way, Lanham MD 20706. (301)731-9540. Fax (301)459-2118. E-mail: submitupa@univpress.com. Website: www.univpress.com. Rowman & Littlefield Publishing Group/academic. Submit to acq ed. Publishes scholarly works in the social sciences and humanities; established by academics for academics. Publishes 50 religious titles/yr. Receives 100 submissions annually. 75% of books from first-time authors. Reprints books. Prefers 200 pgs. Royalty 12% of net; no advance. Average first printing 500. Publication within 6 mos. Considers simultaneous submissions. Responds in 1-2 mos. Requires disk. Guidelines (also on Website); free catalog.

    Nonfiction: Complete ms/résumé; phone/fax/e-query OK. "Looking for scholarly manuscripts."

    Ethnic Books: African studies; Black studies.

    Tips: "We publish academic and scholarly books only. Authors are typically affiliated with a college, university or seminary."

UPPER ROOM BOOKS, 1908 Grand Ave., Box 189, Nashville TN 37212. (615)340-7256. Fax (615)340-7266. E-mail: urbooks@bbs.upperroom.org. Website: www.upperroom.org. General Board of Discipleship of the United Methodist Church. Stephen D. Breyant, ed; Karen A. Watts, asst. Publishes 12-15 titles/yr. Receives hundreds of submissions annually. Few books from first-time authors. Royalty 10% of net; advance $1,000-1,500. Average first printing under 10,000. Publication within 10 mos. Considers simultaneous submissions. Responds in 3+ mos. Guidelines (also by e-mail/Website); catalog for 9x12 SAE/2 stamps.

    Nonfiction: Proposal/2-3 chapters; e-query OK.

    Ethnic Books: Black and Hispanic.

*VERBINUM, ul. Ostrobramska 98, 04-118 Warszawa, Poland. (+48 22) 610 78 70. Fax (+48 22) 610 77 75. E-mail: verbinum@wa.onet.pl. Catholic. Fr. George Skrabania SVD, dir. Concentrates mainly on Bible Apostolate, science of religion and mission, cultural anthropology, ecumenism, and children's books. Not in topical listings. Did not return questionnaire.

VICTOR BOOKS—See Cook Communications Ministries.

*VICTORY HOUSE, INC., Box 700238, Tulsa OK 74170. (918)747-5009. Fax (918)747-1970. E-mail: vhigw@aol.com. Lloyd B. Hildebrand, mng ed. To edify the body of Christ. Publishes 4-5 titles/yr. Not accepting unsolicited mss at this time. No mss through agents. No guidelines; catalog for #10 SAE/1 stamp.

+VIRGINIA PINES PRESS, 7092 Jewell-North, Kinsman OH 44428. (330) 876-3504. Website: virginiapines.hypermart.net. Helen C. Caplan, pub. Publishes 12 titles/yr. Publication within 9 mos.

    Nonfiction: Complete ms by mail or e-mail. "Looking for creative nonfiction works which help to document twentieth-century America."

    Fiction: Complete ms by mail or e-mail.

VITAL ISSUES PRESS, Box 53788, Lafayette LA 70505-3788. (337)237-7049.

Fax (337)237-7060. E-mail: ladawn@eatel.net. Website: www.huntington housebooks.com. Imprint of Huntington House Publishers. Mark Anthony, pub. Serves as a positive force in our culture by publishing, marketing, and distributing books that focus on critical issues of today. Publishes 25-30 titles/yr. Receives 1,500 submissions annually. 25% of books from first-time authors. Reprints books. Prefers 50,000-60,000 wds or 208-224 pgs. Royalty 10% of net on first book, graduated royalty on second book; negotiable advance. Average first printing 5,000-10,000. Publication within 1 yr. Considers simultaneous submissions. No disk or e-mail submissions. Responds in 4 mos. Call for free guidelines (also on Website)/catalog.

Nonfiction: Query/outline; phone/fax/e-query OK.

Also does: Booklets.

WADSWORTH PUBLISHING COMPANY, 10 Davis Dr., Belmont CA 94002. (650)595-2350. Fax (650)637-7544. E-mail: peter.adams@wadsworth.com. Website: www.thomson.com/wadsworth.html. Division of Thomson Learning; secular publisher of higher education textbooks. Peter Adams, religion ed. Publishes 5-10 higher education religious textbooks/yr. Receives 200 submissions annually. 35% of books from first-time authors. No mss through agents. Reprints books. Royalty 5-15% of net; few advances. Average first printing 5,000. Publication within 1-3 yrs depending on development time. Considers simultaneous submissions. Responds in 1 mo. Free guidelines (also on Website)/catalog (by subject area).

Nonfiction: Query or proposal/chapters; fax/e-query OK. "Looking for college textbooks, especially on world religions; anthologies."

+WALDMAN HOUSE PRESS, 525 N. 3rd St., Minneapolis MN 55401. (612)341-4044. Fax (612)341-3626. Ned Waldman, ed. Does children's and religious/spiritual books. Incomplete topical listings. No questionnaire returned.

*WARNER PRESS, PO Box 2499, 1200 E. 5th St., Anderson IN 46018. (765)644-7721. Fax (765)640-8005. E-mail: jennieb@warnerpress.org. Church of God/Anderson IN. Jennie Bishop, ed. Christian education titles. This publisher is again publishing books, but did not return a questionnaire. Send for guidelines.

WATERBROOK PRESS, Random House Inc., 2375 Telstar Dr., Ste. 160, Colorado Springs CO 80920. (719)590-4999. Fax (719)590-8977. Website: www.waterbrookpress.com. Imprint: Harold Shaw Publishers. Laura Barker, mng. ed. Accepts no freelance.

**Note: This publisher serviced by The Writer's Edge.

WESLEYAN PUBLISHING HOUSE, Box 50434, Indianapolis IN 46250. (317)570-5300. Fax (317)570-5370. E-mail: publisher@wesleyan.org. Website: www.wesleyan.org. The Wesleyan Church. Donald Cady, pub. Holiness publisher that provides quality resources to help pastors and laypersons reach the lost and disciple believers. Does full royalty publishing, printing, and helps authors with self-publishing. Royalty. Requires disk or e-mail. Responds in 90 days. Guidelines (also by e-mail/Website); free catalog.

Nonfiction: Proposal/1 chapter; fax, e-query OK.

Tips: "We provide Christian curriculum and ministry resources, Bible study materials and books of general interest to Wesleyans. While membership in the Wesleyan Church is not required of our writers, we carefully examine manuscripts for such things as doctrinal compatibility and biblical interpretation."

#WESTERN FRONT, LTD., 11 Ourider Rd., Rolling Hills Estates CA 90274-5200. (800)764-0012. Fax (888)378-8917. E-mail: prezwfl@earthlink.net. Website: www.westernfront.com. Cliff B. Ford, pres. Publishes 4 titles/yr. Receives 30 submissions annually. 10% of books from first-time authors. No mss through agents. Reprints books. Prefers 320 pgs. Royalty 13-18% of net; no advance. Average first printing 15,000. Publication within 1 yr. No simultaneous submissions. Prefers e-mail submissions. Responds in 2-3 mos. No guidelines/catalog.

   Nonfiction: Query only; phone/e-query OK.

   Fiction: Query only. For adults.

WESTMINSTER JOHN KNOX PRESS, 100 Witherspoon St., Louisville KY 40202-1396. (502)569-5043. Fax (502)569-5113. E-mail: ajackson@ctr. pcusa.org. Website: www.pcusa.org/ppc, or www.wjk.org. Presbyterian Church (USA). Dr. Richard E. Brown, dir.; Stephanie Egnotovich, exec ed; G. Nick Street, Dr. Carey Newman, Dr. Donald McKim, eds. Imprint: Geneva Press. Addresses the needs of the Christian community by fostering religious and cultural dialogue by contributing to the intellectual, moral, and spiritual nurture of the church and broader human family. Publishes 80-100 titles/yr. Prefers 200 pgs. Royalty 7-10%; negotiable advance. Average first printing 3,000-4,000. Publication within 1 yr. Responds in 2-3 mos. Requires disk. Prefers NKJV. Guidelines (also by e-mail/Website); free catalog.

   Nonfiction: Proposal/chapters; fax/e-query OK. Looking for Bible studies, ethics, spirituality, and theology.

   Tips: "Most open to religious/theological scholarship."

WHITESTONE CIRCLE PRESS, PO Box 4546, Tubac AZ 85646. (877)424-7253. E-mail: wscpress@hotmail.com. Independent. Wayne A. Ewing, Ph.D., ed. To provide fresh, high-quality, inspirational material on caregiving. Publishes 1-3 titles/yr. 100% of books from first-time authors. No mss through agents. No reprints. Prefers 120-180 pgs. Will contract on individual basis; no advance. Average first printing 3,000. Publication within 18 mos. Considers simultaneous submissions. Prefers disk. Responds in 2-3 mos. Guidelines (also by e-mail); no catalog.

   Nonfiction: Query only; e-query OK.

   Photos: Accepts freelance photos for book covers.

   Tips: "Most open to absolutely startling; creative; useful in the practicalities of caregiving; hopeful, helpful and healing books; devotional and inspirational books; poetry."

WILSHIRE BOOK COMPANY, 12015 Sherman Rd., North Hollywood CA 91605-3781. (818)765-8579. Fax (818)765-2922. E-mail: mpowers@ mpowers. com. Website: www.mpowers.com. A secular publisher of motivational books. Melvin Powers, pres; Marcia Grad, ed. Books that help you become who you choose to be tomorrow. Publishes 6 titles/yr. 90%

of books from first-time authors. Reprints books. Prefers 35,000 wds or 128-160 pgs. Royalty 5% on retail; variable advance. Average first printing 5,000. Publication within 6 mos. Considers simultaneous submissions. No disk or e-mail submissions. Responds in 2 mos. Guidelines (also by e-mail/Website)/catalog for SAE/2 stamps.

Nonfiction: Complete ms; e-query OK. Fables for adults that teach principles of psychological/spiritual growth.

Fiction: Complete ms. Allegory only. "Read two of our best-sellers: *The Knight in Rusty Armor,* by Robert Fisher, and *The Princess Who Believed in Fairy Tales,* by Marcia Grad."

Photos: Accepts freelance photos for book covers.

Tips: "We are looking for adult allegories such as *Illusions,* by Richard Bach, *The Little Prince,* by Antoine de Saint Exupery, and *The Greatest Salesman in the World,* by Og Mandino. Analyze each one to discover what elements make it a winner. Duplicate those elements in your own style, using a creative, new approach and fresh material. We need 35,000-70,000 words."

WITHERSPOON PRESS, 100 Witherspoon St., Louisville KY 40202. (888) 728-7228. Website: horeb.pcusa.org/witherspoon. Presbyterian Church USA. Maureen O'Connor, ed. Estab. 1997. Does church resources in specialized areas. Guidelines on Website. Not in topical listings.

Nonfiction: Proposal/sample chapters.

WOOD LAKE BOOKS, INC., 9025 Jim Bailey Rd., Kelowna BC V4V 1R2 Canada. (250)766-2778. Fax (250)766-2736. E-mail: info@woodlake.com. Website: www.joinhands.com. Ecumenical/mainline; Wood Lake Books, Inc. Michael Schwartzentruber, series ed. Publishes quality resources that respond to the needs of the ecumenical church and promote spiritual growth and commitment to God. Publishes 3 titles/yr. Receives 300 submissions annually. 25% of books from first-time authors. Reprints books. Prefers 200-250 pgs. Royalty of net; compiler's fee (for compilations) $1,000-3,000; some advances $1,000. Average first printing 3,000-4,000. Publication within 18-24 mos. Considers simultaneous submissions. Prefers disk. Responds in 6-12 wks. Guidelines; catalog $2.

Nonfiction: Query or proposal/2 chapters; fax/e-query OK. "Books with inclusive language and mainline, Protestant interest."

Tips: "We publish books, curriculum and resources for the mainline church. All queries and submissions should reflect this in their theological approach and use of inclusive language for God."

WORD PUBLISHING, 545 Marriott Dr., Ste 750, Nashville TN 37214. (615)902-3400. Fax (615)902-3200. E-mail: WRDPUB@aol.com. Website: www.wordpublishing.com. Thomas Nelson, Inc. David Moberg, pub.; Joey Paul, sr VP; submit to Mark Sweeney, assoc pub. Query/outline and sample chapters. Does not accept unsolicited manuscripts. Prefers 65,000-95,000 wds. Royalty. No guidelines; free catalog.

Nonfiction: Proposal/3 chapters; no unsolicited ms. "Nonfiction dealing with the relationship and/or application of biblical principles to everyday life; 65,000-95,000 words."

Fiction: Complete ms. Adult.

**Note: This publisher serviced by The Writer's Edge.

+WORDSMITHS, 1355 Ferry Rd., Grants Pass OR 97526. (541)476-3080. Fax (541)474-9756. E-mail: frode@jsgrammar.com. Website: www.jsgrammar.com. Frode Jensen, ed. To supply quality materials for homeschools and Christian schools. Receives 2-3 submissions annually. No mss through agents. No reprints. Prefers 100-300 pgs. Royalty on wholesale; no advance. Average first printing 2,000-5,000. Publication time varies.

> **Nonfiction:** Proposal/outline; no phone/fax query; e-query OK. "We're most open to educational materials. All our books so far are on language."

> **Tips:** "I am open to books that are educational in nature, primarily text books. Most of my existing market is for junior high and high school, but books for lower grades would be acceptable."

WORLD BIBLE PUBLISHERS, PO Box 370, Iowa Falls IA 50126-0370. Riverside World, Inc. Shari TeSlaa, ed.; submit to Carol A. Ochs, pub asst. Publishes Bibles and Bible-related products. Imprints: World and World Audio. Publishes 5-10 bks/yr; 15-20 Bibles. Receives 200-300 submissions annually. 1% of books from first-time authors. Reprints books. Prefers 200-375 pgs. Royalty 5-12% of net; advance $1,000. Average first printing 5,000-10,000. Publication within 18 mos. Considers simultaneous submissions. Responds in 3 mos. Prefers disk. Guidelines; catalog for 9x12 SAE/5 stamps.

> **Nonfiction:** Proposal/1-2 chapters; no phone/fax/e-query. "Looking for well-written devotional/inspirational books with a unique approach."

> **Ethnic Books:** African-American.

> **Tips:** "Most open to books that are Bible-based; non-technical reference; devotional; books that can incorporate God's Word translation."

+WRITE NOW PUBLICATIONS, 5501 N. 7th Ave., PMB 502, Phoenix AZ 85013. (602)336-8910. Fax (602)532-7123. E-mail: editor@acwpress.com. Website: www.write4him.com. Steven R. Laube, exec ed. To train and develop quality Christian writers; books on writing and speaking for writers and speakers. Royalty division of ACW Press. Est. 1999. Publishes 2-4 titles/yr. Receives 6 submissions annually. 0% from first-time authors. Accepts mss through agents. Reprints books. Royalty 10% of net. Average first printing 3,000. Publication within 12 mos. Considers simultaneous submissions. Requires disk. No guidelines/catalog.

> **Nonfiction:** Writing how-to only. Query letter only; e-query OK.

> ****Note:** This publisher serviced by The Writer's Edge.

#YALE UNIVERSITY PRESS, 302 Temple St., PO Box 209040, New Haven CT 06520. (203)432-0960. Fax (203)432-0948. Website: http//www.yale.edu/yup. Charles Grench, ed-in-chief/religion. Publishes 10 religious titles/yr. Receives 200 submissions annually. 15% of books from first-time authors. Reprints books. Prefers up to 100,000 wds or 400 pgs. Royalty 0-15% of net; advance $500-50,000. Average first printing 1,500. Publication within 1 yr. Considers simultaneous submissions. Requires disk; no e-mail submissions. Responds in 1-2 mos. Free guidelines (also on Website under FAQs)/catalog.

Nonfiction: Proposal/1-2 chapters; fax query OK. "Excellent and salable scholarly books."

Contest: Yales Series of Younger Poets competition. Open to poets under 40 who have not had a book of poetry published. Submit manuscripts of 48-64 pages in February. Entry fee $15. Send SASE for guidelines.

+YES INTERNATIONAL PUBLISHERS, 1317 Summit Ave., St. Paul MN 55105-2602. Phone/fax (612)645-6808. Theresa King, ed. Does lifestyle, health, and religious/spiritual books. Incomplete topical listings. No questionnaire returned.

YOUNG READER'S CHRISTIAN LIBRARY, 1810 Barbour Dr., PO Box 719, Uhrichsville OH 44683. (614)922-6045. Fax (614)922-5948. E-mail: info@ barbourbooks.com. Website: www.barbourbooks.com. Susan Schlabach, sr ed. Children's imprint of Barbour Publishing, Inc. 75% of books from first-time authors. No mss through agents. Reprints books. Prefers about 16,000 wds. Makes outright purchases $1,000. Publication within 2 yrs. Considers simultaneous submissions. Responds in 10 wks. Guidelines; catalog for 9x12 SAE/4 stamps.

Nonfiction & Fiction: Proposal/3-4 chapters.

Tips: "We prefer action-oriented, fast-paced style at a sixth-grade reading level. The subject of the manuscript can be contemporary (post-World War II to today), a Bible character, or an historical figure."

+YOUTH SPECIALTIES, 300 S. Pierce St., El Cajon CA 92020. (619)440-2333. Fax (619)440-0582. E-mail: roni@youthspecialties.com. Website: www. youthspecialties.com. Nondenominational. Submit to Book Editor. Christian resources for youthworkers to use in their youth groups. Receives 60 submissions annually. 25% of books from first-time authors. Accepts mss through agents. Some subsidy. Reprints books. Royalty 10-25%; advance $2,000. Average first printing 2,500-5,000. Publication within 8 mos.

Nonfiction: Proposal/1 chapter; no phone/fax/e-query.

*YWAM PUBLISHING, PO Box 55787, Seattle WA 98155. (425)771-1153. Fax (425)775-2383. E-mail: 75701.2772@compuserve.com. Website: www.ywam. org. Youth With a Mission. James Drake, sr ed. Provides missions-based materials to assist the Body of Christ worldwide in fulfilling the Great Commission. Publishes 15 titles/yr. Receives 100 submissions annually. 20% of books from first-time authors. Reprints books. Prefers 190 pgs. Royalty of net; advance. Average first printing 10,000. Publication within 5 mos. Considers simultaneous submissions. Responds in 3 mos. Accepts disk, no e-mail submissions. Guidelines; catalog for 9x12 SAE/3 stamps.

Nonfiction: Query only; e-query OK. "Needs nonfiction missionary stories from different countries."

Fiction: Query only. For children and teens. "Especially historical mission stories with evangelism themes."

Also Does: Personal prayer diary—daily planner.

ZONDERKIDZ, 5300 Patterson SE, Grand Rapids MI 49530-0002. (616)698-3400. Fax (616)698-3454. E-mail: zpub@zph.com. Website: www.zonder kidz.com. HarperCollins/Zondervan Publishing House. Gary Richardson, children's pub.; Gwen Ellis, acq ed. Children's book lines of Zondervan

Publishing House. Publishes 50 titles/yr. Picture books 24-40 pgs. Royalty on net or flat fee; advance. Average first printing 15,000. Publication within 2 yrs. Accepts simultaneous submissions. Responds in 2-3 wks on queries. Prefers NIrV (revised) for kids 1-10 yrs; NIV for 10-12 yr olds.

Nonfiction: Query required (get guidelines first). Children's picture books and easy readers for children 12 & under.

Also Does: Some specialty products; usually packaged.

Tips: "Most open to a creative, fresh, thoroughly biblical book." Note: Gold 'N' Honey is no longer a separate imprint.

ZONDERVAN PUBLISHING HOUSE, General Trade Books; Academic and Professional Books, 5300 Patterson SE, Grand Rapids MI 49530-0002. (616)698-6900. Fax (616)698-3454. E-mail: zprod@zph.com. Website: www. zondervan.com. HarperCollins. Scott Bolinder, sr VP; Gwen Ellis, gift books; Paul Engle, sr. acq. ed; submit to Manuscript Review Editor. Seeks to meet the needs of people with resources that glorify Jesus Christ and promote biblical principles. Publishes 120 trade titles/yr. Receives about 3,000 submissions annually. 20% of books from first-time authors. Prefers 50,000 wds. Royalty 14% (12% on mass-market paperbacks) of net; variable advance. Publication within 1 yr. Considers simultaneous submissions. Responds in 3 mos. Prefers NIV. Prefers disk. Free guidelines (also on Website at www.zondervan.com/subguide.htm) and catalog.

Nonfiction: Proposal/2 chapters; no phone/fax/e-query.

Fiction: Proposal/2 chapters. Publishes 4 each, contemporary and historical, per year.

Children's Lines: ZonderKidz (see listing above).

Ethnic Books: Vida Publishers division: Spanish, Portuguese, and French.

Tips: "Absolutely stellar prose that meets demonstrated needs of our market always receives a fair and sympathetic hearing."

**Note: This publisher serviced by The Writer's Edge.

SUBSIDY PUBLISHERS

WHAT YOU NEED TO KNOW ABOUT SUBSIDY PUBLISHERS

In this section you will find any publishers who do 50% or more subsidy publishing. For our purposes, I am defining a subsidy publisher as any publisher that requires the author to pay for any part of the publishing costs. They may call themselves by a variety of names, such as a book packager, a cooperative publisher, self-publisher, or simply someone who helps authors get their books published. Note that some of these also do at least some royalty publishing.

As technology makes book publishing more accessible, and with the refinement of desktop publishing, more subsidy publishers have sprung up, and there has been an increase in confusion over who or what type of subsidy publishing is legitimate, and what publishers fall in with what we call "vanity publishers." As many of the legitimate publishers (and even some questionable ones) try to distance themselves from the reputation of the vanity publisher, they have come up with a variety of names to try to form definite lines of distinction. Unfortunately, it has only served to confuse the authors who might use their services. It is my hope in offering this separate listing that I can help you understand what this side of publishing entails, what to look for in a subsidy publisher, as well as what to look out for. To my knowledge the following publishers are legitimate subsidy publishers and are not vanity publishers. It is important that as a writer you understand that any time you are asked to send money for any part of the production of your book, you are entering into a non-traditional relationship with a publisher. In this constantly changing field it becomes a matter of buyer beware.

Realize, too, that some of these publishers will publish any book, as long as the author can afford to pay for it. Others are as selective about what they publish as a royalty publisher would be, or they publish only certain types of books. Many will do only nonfiction—no novels or children's books. These distinctions will be important as you seek the right publisher for your project.

Because there is so much confusion about subsidy publishing, with many authors going into agreements with these publishers having little or no knowledge of what to expect or even what is typical in this situation, many have come away unhappy or disillusioned. For that reason I frequently get complaints from authors who feel they have been cheated or taken advantage of. (Of course, I often get similar complaints about the royalty publishers listed in this book.) Each complaint brings with it an expectation that I should drop that publisher from this book. Although I am sensitive to their complaints, I also have come to the realization that I am not in a position to pass judgment on which publishers should be dropped. It has been my experience in publishing that for every complaint I get on a publisher, I can usually find several other authors who will sing the praises of the same publisher. For that reason, I feel I can serve the needs of authors better by giving them some insight into what to expect from a subsidy publisher and what kinds of terms should send up a red flag.

Because I am not an expert in this field, and because of space limitations, I will keep this brief. Let me clarify first that unless you know your book has a limited audience or you have your own method of distribution (such as being a speaker who can sell your own books when you speak), I recommend that you try all the appropriate royalty publishers first. If you are unsuccessful with the royalty publishers, but feel strongly about seeing your book published and have the financial resources to do so (or have your own distribution), one of the following publishers may be able to help you.

You can go to a local printer and take your book through all the necessary steps yourself, but a legitimate subsidy publisher has the contacts, know-how and resources to make the task easier and often less expensive. It is always good to get more than one bid to determine whether the terms you are being offered are fair and competitive with other such publishers.

There is not currently any kind of watchdog organization for subsidy publishers, but one is in the works. Until that group is in place, and since I do not have direct knowledge about all of the publishers listed below, I would recommend that no matter who makes you a first offer, you get a second one from ACW Press, WinePress Publishing, Essence Publishing or Longwood Communications (ones I can personally recommend).

As with any contract, have someone review it before signing anything. I do such reviews, as do a number of others listed in the Editorial Services section of this book. Be sure that any terms agreed upon are IN WRITING. Verbal agreements won't be binding. A legitimate subsidy publisher will be happy to provide you with a list of former clients as references (if they aren't, watch out). Don't just ask for that list; follow through and contact more than one of those references. Get a catalog of their books or a list of books they have published and try to find them or ask them to send you a review copy of one or two books they have published. Use those to check the quality of their work, the bindings, etc. Get answers to all your questions before you commit yourself to anything.

Keep in mind that the more copies of a book that are printed, the lower the cost per copy, but never let a publisher talk you into publishing more (or fewer) copies than you think is reasonable. Also, find out up front, and have included in the contract, whether and how much promotion the publisher is going to do. Some will do as much as a royalty publisher; others do none at all. If they are not doing promotion, and you don't have any means of distribution yourself, it may not be a good idea to pursue publication. You don't want to end up with a garage full of books you can't sell. At the end of this section I am including the names and addresses of some of the main Christian book distributors. I don't know which ones will consider distributing a subsidy published book, so you will want to contact them to find out before you sign a contract. For more help on self-publishing, go to: www.bookmarket.com/index.html.

Replica Books and Xlibris Corp. are collaborating to provide services to self-publishing authors. Xlibris, which specializes in on-demand book publishing, will provide personalized electronic book design and format services for authors. Replica Books will bond, print, and distribute the books to retail outlets and libraries. For details, go to: www.replicabooks.com, or www. xlibris.com. Also check out www.GlobalDig.com.

Note: For help from an independent source in deciding if subsidy publishing is an appropriate choice for your book project, contact the following: **INDEPENDENT PUBLISHERS FOR CHRIST**, PO Box 280349, Lakewood CO 80228. (303)456-9166. Fax (303)793-0838. This is not a publisher but a group that sponsors seminars on self-publishing. They can help you make a choice with no vested interest in the choice you make. Contact: Cecile Higgins, executive director

LISTING OF SUBSIDY PUBLISHERS

Below is a listing of any publishers that do 50% or more subsidy publishing (author pays some or all of the production costs). Before entering into dealings with any of these publishers, be sure to read the preceding section on what you need to know.

(*) An asterisk before a listing indicates no or unconfirmed information update.
(#) A number symbol before a listing indicates it was updated from their guidelines or other current sources.
(+) A plus sign before a listing indicates it is a new listing this year or was not included last year.

ACW PRESS, 5501 N. 7th Ave., PMB 502, Phoenix AZ 85013. (877)868-9673. Fax (602)532-7123. E-mail: editor@acwpress.com. Website: www.write4 him.com. Steven R. Laube, exec ed; Chuck Dean, dir. of sales. A self-publishing book packager. Imprint: Write Now Publications. Publishes 40 titles/yr. Reprints books. **SUBSIDY PUBLISHES 95%.** Average first printing 1,000 minimum. Publication within 4-5 mos. Prefers e-mail submissions. Responds in 1 wk. Guideline booklet (also on Website). Not in topical listings; will consider any topic.

   Tips: "We offer a high quality publishing alternative to help Christian authors get their material into print. High standards, high quality. If an author has a built-in audience, they have the best chance to make self-publishing a success."

+ALFRED ALI LITERARY WORKS, INC., PO Box 27206, Detroit MI 48227. (313)861-3118. Fax (313)861-3015. E-mail: AALiterary@aol.com. Website: www.smallbusiness.com/ali.htm, and www.booksonblack.com. San Serif, ed. Spreading the word on how the Word of God can change and improve lives. Publishes 1 title/yr. Receives 5 submissions annually. 80% of books from first-time authors. Accepts mss through agents. Reprints books. **SUBSIDY PUBLISHES 70%.** Prefers 210 pgs. Royalty 25% of retail; no advance. Average first printing 1,000-5,000. Publication within 9 mos. Accepts e-mail submissions. No guidelines; catalog $3.

   Nonfiction: Query only; fax query OK.

Ethnic Books: African-American.

Photos: Accepts freelance photos for book covers.

Tips: "Most open to books that are based on inspiration that leads to self-awareness."

*AMBASSADOR HOUSE, 8005 Cattle Dr., Austin TX 78749-3288. E-mail: ambhouse@hotmail.com. Non-denominational. Sandra Myers, pub. Publishes 2-6 titles/yr. Receives 10+ submissions annually. 90% of books from first-time authors. No mss through agents. **SUBSIDY PUBLISHES 95%.** Royalty 35-95%; no advance. Average first printing 1,000. Publication within 2 mos. Considers simultaneous submissions. No disk or e-mail submissions. Responds in 1 mo. Guidelines (also by e-mail); free catalog.

Nonfiction: Query or proposal/3 chapters; phone/fax/e-query OK. "Especially want political, prophecy, end-times."

Fiction: Query or proposal/3 chapters. "Purposeful advancement of situational, historical, prophetic, political and end-times education."

Tips: "Our goal is to help individuals with important messages self-publish their books and get the marketing, public relations and distribution they need. We will strive to insure that bookstores, and ultimately bookstore customers, know that these crucial books exist."

ASSOCIATED COMMUNITY SERVICES—See WinePress Publishing.

BLACK FOREST PRESS, PO Box 6342, Chula Vista CA 91909-6342. (800)451-9404. (800)451-9404 or (619)656-8048. Fax (619)482-8704. E-mail: bfp@ blackforestpress.com. Website: www.blackforestpress.com. Sue Van Gundy, acq ed. A self-publishing company. Imprints: Kinder Books (children's); Dichter Books (black and Hispanic); Abenteuer Books; Sonnenschein Books; Segen Books (inspirational). Publishes 25 titles/yr. Receives 2,000 submissions annually. 75% of books from first-time authors. Accepts mss through agents. **SUBSIDY PUBLISHES 50%** (helps people get published). Reprints books. Prefers 75-350 pgs. Royalty 100% to authors; 68% to authors for Website purchases; promotional contracts vary; no advance. Average first printing 2,000-3,000. Publication within 5-6 months. Considers simultaneous submissions. Requires disk. Responds in 2-3 wks. Prefers Living or Modern. Free guidelines/catalog (also on Website).

Nonfiction: Query/phone number; phone/fax/e-query OK. "Looking for true testimonials and books on angels."

Fiction: Query. "Looking for war novels and prophecy novels; 150-350 pages."

Ethnic Books: Publishes for Black and Hispanic markets.

Photos: Accepts freelance photos for book covers.

Tips: "Looking for books on vital Christian issues; books with literary merit and significant lessons for life."

BRENTWOOD CHRISTIAN PRESS, 4000 Beallwood Ave., Columbus GA 31904. (404)576-5787. (800) 334-8861. Fax (706)317-5808. E-mail: Brentwood@aol.com. Website: www.publishmybook.com. Mainline. Jerry L. Luquire, exec ed. Publishes 267 titles/yr. Receives 2,000 submissions annually. Reprints books. **SUBSIDY PUBLISHES 95%.** Average first printing 500. Publication within 1 mo. Considers simultaneous submissions. Responds in 2 days. Guidelines.

Nonfiction: Complete ms. "Collection of sermons on family topics; poetry; relation of Bible to current day."

Fiction: Complete ms. "Stories that show how faith helps overcome small, day-to-day problems. Prefer under 200 pgs."

Tips: "Keep it short; support facts with reference." This publisher specializes in small print runs of 300-1,000. Can best serve the writer who has a completed manuscript.

CROSS WAY PUBLICATIONS, 1351 Morgan Ave., Williamsport PA 17701-2849. (570)323-3921. E-mail: crosspub@mail.microserve.net. Website: www.ChristianPoetry.org. Jerry Hoffman, ed. Produces poetry books which proclaim Christ as King. Publishes 2 titles/yr. Receives 15 submissions annually. 100% of books from first-time authors. No mss through agents. Prefers 75-100 pgs. No royalty/advance. Does all pre- and post-press preparation at no cost. Printing is done out of house. All copies are shipped to author. Also does Web advertising for free. Average first printing 1,000. Publication within 6 mos. No simultaneous submissions. Responds in 2 wks. Requires disk (.txt format desired). No guidelines/catalog.

Nonfiction: Complete ms; e-query OK. "We accept only Christian poetry. Although we accept all forms, ideas must be clearly stated and openly point to Christ. Not interested in vague ideas which leave the reader wondering."

Also Does: Pamphlets; booklets.

+DCTS PUBLISHING, PO Box 40216, Santa Barbara CA 93140. (805)685-8774. Fax (805)562-9903. E-mail: dennis@dctspub.com. Website: www.dctspub.com. Dennis Hamilton, ed. Books are designed to enrich the mind, encourage the heart and empower the spirit. Publishes 5 titles/yr. Receives 25 submissions annually. 35% of books from first-time authors. No mss through agents. **SUBSIDY PUBLISHES 70%.** Reprints books. Prefers 300 pgs. Royalty 17% on retail; no advance. Average first printing 3,500. Publication within 6-8 mos. No simultaneous submissions. Prefers KJV. No guidelines; catalog for #10 SAE/1 stamp.

Nonfiction: Query or proposal/3 chapters. "We consider most anything but fiction or picture books."

ERICA HOUSE—See AmErica House.

ESSENCE PUBLISHING CO., INC., 44 Moira St. W., Belleville ON K8P 1S3 Canada. (613)962-3294 or (800)238-6376. Fax (613)962-3055. E-mail: info@essencegroup.com. Website: www.essencegroup.com. Essence, Inc. Willow Bouma, sr. ed.; Rikki-Anne McNaught, acq. ed. Provides affordable, short-run book publishing to the Christian community. Imprints: Guardian Books (see separate listing), Epic Press (secular). Publishes 40-50 titles/yr. Receives 250+ submissions annually. 75% of books from first-time authors. **SUBSIDY PUBLISHES 90%.** Reprints books. Any length. Average first printing 500-1,000. Publication within 3-5 mos. Considers simultaneous submissions. Responds in 3-4 wks. Prefers disk. Guidelines (also by e-mail/Website); free catalog.

Nonfiction: Complete ms; phone/fax/e-query OK. Accepts all topics.

Fiction: Complete ms. All genres for all ages. Also picture books.

Also Does: Pamphlets, booklets and tracts.

Photos: Accepts freelance photos for book covers.

FAIRWAY PRESS, Subsidy Division for C.S.S. Publishing Company, 517 S. Main St., Box 4503, Lima OH 45802-4503. (419)227-1818. Fax (419)228-9184. E-mail: csspub@csspub.com. Website: www.csspub.com. Teresa Rhoads, ed; submit to Thomas Lentz. Publishes 100 titles/yr. Receives 200-300 submissions annually. 80% of books from first-time authors. Reprints books. **SUBSIDY PUBLISHES 100%.** Royalty to 50%; no advance. Average first printing 500-1,000. Publication within 6-9 mos. Considers simultaneous submissions. Responds in up to 1 month. Prefers disk. Prefers NRSV. Free guidelines (also on Website)/catalog for 9x12 SAE.

> **Nonfiction:** Complete ms; phone/fax/e-query OK. "Looking for mss with a Christian theme, and seasonal material."

> **Fiction:** Complete ms. For adults, teens, or children; all types.

+FRUIT-BEARER PUBLISHING, PO Box 777, Georgetown DE 19947. (302)856-6649. Fax (302)856-7742. E-mail: dabbott@dmv.com. Branch of Candy's Creations. Candy Abbott, pres. Offers printing services for self-publishers. Publishes 5-10 titles/yr. Receives 10-20 submissions annually. 90% of books from first-time authors. **SUBSIDY PUBLISHES 100%.** No reprints. Prefers up to 200 pgs. Average first printing 30-1,000 (specializes in small print runs). Publication within 1-6 mos. Responds in 1 mo. Brochure for #10 SAE/1 stamp. Not included in topical listings (see Tips).

> **Nonfiction:** Proposal/2chapters; phone/fax/e-query OK.

> **Fiction:** Proposal/2 chapters.

> **Also Does:** Pamphlets, booklets, tracts.

> **Photos:** Accepts freelance photos for book covers.

> **Tips:** "Open to short works with redeeming value. Most receptive to inspirational or wholesome works that strengthen the Body of Christ or reach the unbeliever."

GESHER, PO Box 33373, Philadelphia PA 19142-3373. (215)365-3350. Fax (215)365-3325. E-mail: info@gesher.org. Website: www.gesher.org. Helping people walk in all that God intends for them. Robert Winer, pres. Publishes 4 titles/yr. **SUBSIDY PUBLISHES 90%.** Reprints books. Prefers 150-250 pgs. Royalty 3-10% on retail; advance $250-500. Average first printing 3,000-5,000. Publication within 6-8 mos. Considers simultaneous submissions. Requires disk (Word, WordPerfect, or RTF format). Responds in 1-2 mos. Prefers NKJV. Guidelines (also by e-mail); no catalog.

> **Nonfiction:** Proposal with 2-3 chapters; e-query OK. "Books on deeper spirituality to help people mature in the Lord."

> **Special Needs:** Messianic Jewish in addition to general Christianity.

> **Tips:** "Most open to books that fulfill our mission statement."

GUARDIAN BOOKS., 44 Moira St. W., Belleville ON K8P 1S3 Canada. (613) 962-3294 or (800)238-6376. Fax (613)962-3055. E-mail: info@essence group.com. Website: www.essencegroup.com. Essence, Inc. Deborah Visser, asst ed; submit to Willow Bouma, asst. ed. Provides affordable, short-run book publishing to the Christian community. Imprints: Guardian Books, Epic Press (secular). Publishes 40-50 titles/yr. Receives 250+ submissions annually. 75% of books from first-time authors. **SUBSIDY PUBLISHES**

90%. Reprints books. Any length. Average first printing 500-1,000. Publication within 3-5 mos. Considers simultaneous submissions. Responds in 3-4 wks. Prefers disk. Guidelines (also by e-mail/Website); free catalog.

    Nonfiction: Complete ms; phone/fax/e-query OK. Accepts all topics.

    Fiction: Complete ms. All genres for all ages. Also picture books.

    Also Does: Pamphlets, booklets and tracts.

    Photos: Accepts freelance photos for book covers.

IMPACT CHRISTIAN BOOKS, INC., 332 Leffingwell Ave., Ste. 101, Kirkwood MO 63122. (314)822-3309. Fax (314)822-3325. Website: www.impact christianbooks.com. William D. Banks, pres. Books of healing, miraculous deliverance, and spiritual warfare; drawing individuals into a deeper walk with God. Publishes 20+ titles/yr. Receives 20-50 submissions annually. 50-70% of books from first-time authors. No mss through agents. **SUBSIDY PUBLISHES 50-70%.** Reprints books. Average first printing 5,000. Publication within 2 mos. Considers simultaneous submissions. Responds by prior arrangement in 30 days. Requires disk. Guidelines; catalog for 9x12 SAE/5 stamps. Not in topical listings.

    Nonfiction: Query only; phone/fax query OK. Outstanding personal testimonies, and Christ-centered books.

*INHERITANCE PUBLICATIONS, Box 154, Neerlandia AB T0G 1R0 Canada. Phone/fax (780)674-3949. Roelof Janssen, ed. E-mail: inhpub@telusplanet. net. Reprints books. **SUBSIDY PUBLISHER.**

    Tips: "A book must be very good for us to publish it. We do mostly old books."

LONGWOOD COMMUNICATIONS, 397 Kingslake Dr., DeBary FL 32713. (904)774-1991. Fax (904)774-2144. E-mail: longwood@totcon.com. Murray Fisher, VP. A service for authors who cannot get their books accepted by a traditional house. Publishes 8-12 titles/yr. Receives 80 submissions annually. 85% of books from first-time authors. No mss through agents. **100% SUBSIDY.** Reprints books. Average first printing 5,000. Publication within 3-5 mos. Considers simultaneous submissions. Responds in 1-2 wks. Requires disk. No guidelines; catalog for 2 stamps.

    Nonfiction: Complete ms; phone query OK. Any topic as long as it's Christian and builds up the Body of Christ. Not in topical listings.

    Fiction: Complete ms. For all ages. Any genre.

    Also Does: Pamphlets and booklets; e-books.

    Photos: Accepts freelance photos for book covers.

    Tips: "Looking for well-written, basic Christian books."

THE MASTER DESIGN, PO Box 17865, Memphis TN 38187-0865. (901)309-9655. Fax (520)223-1266. E-mail: info@masterdesign.org. Website: www.masterdesign.org. S. Faithe Finley, submissions ed. To help publish books that make a difference. Publishes 15+ titles/yr. Receives 100 submissions annually. 85% of books from first-time authors. No mss through agents. **90% SUBSIDY.** Reprints books. Prefers 50-300 pgs. Author pays all costs. Average first printing 1,000 & up. Publication within 5 mos. Considers simultaneous submissions. Responds in 2-3 wks. Accepts disk or e-mail (preferred). Guidelines (also by e-mail); catalog on Website.

Nonfiction: Proposal/3 chapters; fax/e-query OK.

Fiction: Proposal/3 chapters. For any age.

Also Does: E-books.

Photos: Accepts freelance photos for book covers.

Tips: "Fiction books containing Scripture woven into the story have a better chance. Nonfiction books expounding truth from God's Word is our top priority."

MCDOUGAL PUBLISHING, PO Box 3595, 727 N. Mulberry St., Hagerstown MD 21740. (301)797-6637. Fax (301)733-2767. E-mail: publishing@ mcdougal.org. Website: www.mcdougal.org. Charismatic, non-denominational. Harold McDougal, pres; Robert Vande Brake, acq. ed. Publishes books for the Body of Christ. Imprints: McDougal and Fairmont. Publishes 30 titles/yr. Receives 250 submissions annually. 70% of books from first-time authors. No mss through agents. **SUBSIDY PUBLISHES 80%.** Reprints books. Prefers 112-250 pgs. Royalty 10%; no advance. Average first printing 3,000-5,000. Publication within 6 mos. Considers simultaneous submissions. Responds in 3 mos. Free guidelines (also by e-mail/Website)/catalog.

    Nonfiction: Complete ms; phone/fax/e-query OK. Looking for renewal and revival titles.

    Fiction: Complete ms.

    Photos: Accepts freelance photos for book covers.

    Tips: "Most open to worship and revival."

OMEGA HOUSE PUBLISHING, PO Box 68, Three Rivers MI 49093. (616) 273-7070. Non-denominational. Zendra Manley, ed. To distribute and increase knowledge in the body of Christ (Hosea 4:6). Publishes 5 titles/yr. Receives 60 submissions annually. 95% of books from first-time authors. No mss through agents. **90% SUBSIDY.** Reprints books. Prefers 80-500 pgs. Royalty 8-10% of net; no advance. Average first printing 2,000-5,000. Publication within 6 mos. Considers simultaneous submissions. Responds in 2 wks. No disk. Guidelines; no catalog.

    Nonfiction: Proposal/3 chapters; no phone/fax query.

    Special Needs: Renewal, inspirational, healing.

    Photos: Accepts freelance photos for book covers.

    Tips: "Develop a proposal that will grab our interest. Manuscripts are turned down that do not bring glory to God, and that are less than marketable. Most open to scripturally referenced manuscripts that are anointed to transform lives; no personal experiences."

*PARTNERSHIP BOOK SERVICES, 212 N. Ash, Hillsboro KS 67063. (316) 947-3966. Fax (316)947-3392. Hearth Publishing, Inc. Stan Thiessen, ed. Publishes 12 religious titles/yr (70 total). Receives 1,500 submissions annually. 85% of books from first-time authors. No mss through agents. **100% SUBSIDY.** Reprints books. Prefers 20,000-150,000 wds or 96-352 pgs. Average first printing 100-20,000. Publication within 6 mos. Considers simultaneous submissions. Responds in 2 wks-3 mos. No disk. Guidelines; no catalog. Not included in topical listings; considers any topic.

Nonfiction/Fiction: Proposal/3-4 chapters; no phone/fax query. Send $35/SASE for manuscript evaluation. "Response includes suggestions for improvement."

Also Does: Booklets, pamphlets, tracts and chapbooks.

Tips: "PBS services include evaluation, editing, cover design, formatting, disk to film, printing, promotions and marketing."

PASTOR'S CHOICE PRESS, 4000 Beallwood Ave., Columbus GA 31904. (404/706)576-5787. Fax (706)317-5808. E-mail: Brentwood@aol.com. Website: www. publishmybook.com. Subsidiary of Brentwood Publishers Group. Jerry Luquire, exec dir. **SUBSIDY OR CUSTOM PUBLISHES 100%.** Focus is on sermon notes, outlines, illustrations, plus news that pastors would find interesting. Publishes 300-500 copies. Cost of about $3-4/book. Publication in 45 days. Same day response.

POET'S COVE PRESS, 4000 Beallwood Ave., Columbus GA 31904. (404/706)576-5787. (800) 334-8861. E-mail: Brentwood@aol.com. Website: www.publishmybook.com. Subsidiary of Brentwood Publishers Group. Jerry Luquire, exec dir. Publishes 125 titles/yr. **SUBSIDY OR CUSTOM PUBLISHES 100%.** Specializes in self-publishing books of religious or inspirational poetry, in small press runs of under 500 copies. Publication in 45 days. Same day response.

Tips: "Type one poem per page; include short bio and photo with first submission."

PROMISE PUBLISHING, PO Box 10759, Santa Ana CA 92711-0759. (714)997-8450. Toll-free (877)599-8450. Fax (714)997-5545. E-mail: edmary@ix.netcom.com. Listed on Barbes & Noble Website. M.B. Steele, V.P. Publishes 6 titles/yr. 50% of books from first-time authors. **100% CO-OPERATIVE PUBLISHING** in support of ministry organizations. Royalty 10% of net (negotiable); no advance. Average first printing 5,000. Publication within 6 mos. Considers simultaneous submissions. Pre-acceptance talks determine acceptance. No guidelines; free catalog.

Nonfiction: Proposal/3 chapters; phone/fax/e-query OK. "We are interested in missionary books or Bible studies."

Special Needs: "We are interested in a topic if it is not contradictory to the Bible."

Tips: "Most open to established ministries that will use the books for their constituency."

RECONCILIATION PRESS, PO Box 209, Manassas VA 20108. (703)330-3262. E-mail: publisher@reconciliation.com. Website: www.reconciliation.com. John Jenkins, ed. Historical fiction with a purpose. Publishes 4 titles/yr. Receives 20 submissions annually. 80% of books from first-time authors. Prefers 60-160 pgs. Royalty 8-15% of net; no advance. Average first printing 2,000. Publication within 6 mos. Considers simultaneous submissions. Requires disk or e-mail submission. Responds in 2 mos. Guidelines on Website; catalog online only.

Fiction: Query; e-query OK.

Tips: "Most open to historical fiction that makes history relevant to young people, with a biblical, but non-religious tone/focus. Guidelines for our historical fiction line, Century War Chronicles are at: www.reconciliation.com/guidelines.htm."

RECOVERY COMMUNICATIONS, INC., PO Box 19910, Baltimore MD 21211. Fax (410)243-8558. Toby R. Drews, ed. Publishes 4-6 titles/yr. No mss through agents. **SUBSIDY PUBLISHER.** Prefers 110 pgs. Co-op projects; no royalty or advance. Average first printing 5,000. Publication within 11 mos. Excellent nationwide distribution and marketing in bookstores.

    Nonfiction or Fiction: Query only.

SHEER JOY! PRESS/PROMOTIONS, 5502 Murphy Rd., Pink Hill NC 28572. (252)568-6101. Fax (530)509-6874. E-mail: sheerjoy@eastlink.net. Protestant. Dr. James R. Adams, pres.; submit to Patricia Adams, ed. Publishes 1-2 titles/yr. Receives 5-10 submissions annually. No mss through agents. **SUBSIDY PUBLISHES 85%.** Prefers 20,000-30,000 wds (200 pgs). Royalty on retail; no advance. Average first printing 1,000. Publication within 6 mos. Considers simultaneous submissions. Responds in 3-4 wks.

SON-RISE PUBLICATIONS, 143 Greenfield Rd., New Wilmington PA 16142. (800)358-0777. Fax (724)946-9057. Florence W. Biros, acq ed. Publishes 5-6 titles/yr. Receives 20 submissions annually. 50% of books from first-time authors. **SUBSIDY PUBLISHES 50%.** Prefers 25,000-40,000 wds or 90-196 pgs. Royalty 7½-10% on retail; no advance. Average first printing 3,000. Publication within 8-9 mos. Responds ASAP.

    Nonfiction: Query. "Most open to Christian teaching and testimony combined."

    Fiction: Query only; overstocked.

    Tips: "We are overstocked with royalty manuscripts. The only ones I can consider for now are subsidy manuscripts."

SOUTHERN BAPTIST PRESS, 4000 Beallwood, Columbus GA 31904. (404)576-5787. (800) 334-8861. E-mail: Brentwood@aol.com. Website: www.publishmybook.com. Jerry L. Luquire, exec ed. Publishes 42 books/yr. Receives 600 submissions annually. Reprints books. **SUBSIDY OR CUSTOM PUBLISHES 95%.** Average first printing 500. Publication within 2 mos. Considers simultaneous submissions. Responds in 1 week. Guidelines.

    Nonfiction: Complete ms. "Collections of sermons on family topics; poetry; relation of Bible to current day."

    Fiction: Complete ms. "Stories that show how faith helps overcome small, day-to-day problems."

    Tips: "Keep it short; support facts with reference."

TEACH SERVICES, INC., 254 Donovan Rd., Brushton NY 12916. (518)358-2125. Fax (518)358-3028. E-mail: acquisions@LNFBooks.com. Website: www.teachservicesinc.com. Timothy Hullquist, pres.; submit to Wayne Reid, acq ed. To publish uplifting books for the lowest price. Publishes 40-50 titles/yr. Receives 100 submissions annually. 35% of books from first-time authors. No mss through agents. **SUBSIDY PUBLISHES 75%** (author has to pay for first printing, then publisher keeps it in print). Reprints books. Prefers 45,000 wds or 96 pgs. Royalty 10% on retail; no advance. Average first printing 2,000. Publication within 4 mos. Disk required. Responds in 2 wks. Prefers KJV. Guidelines (also by e-mail/Website)/catalog for #10 SAE/2 stamps.

Nonfiction: Query only; no phone/fax query. "Looking for books on nutrition."

Special Needs: Vegetarian cookbooks.

Photos: Accepts freelance photos for book covers.

TYLER PRESS, 1221 W.S.W. Loop 323, Tyler TX 75701. (903)581-2255. Fax (903)581-7841. E-mail: tylerpress@electro-image.com. J. A. Johnson, sr ed. A self-publisher's service bureau that will lend its imprint to selected titles. Publishes 20 titles/yr. Receives 250+ submissions annually. 60% of books from first-time authors. **SUBSIDY PUBLISHES 100%.** Reprints books. Prefers 120 pgs & up. Provides full editing and design services, if needed. Average first printing 500-5,000. Publication within 2 mos. No guidelines.

Nonfiction: Query; fax query OK. "We enthusiastically promote self-help/how-to, historical, creation science, current social and political issues, biographies, autobiographies, marriage and family, and women's issues."

Fiction: Query. No children's books.

Also Does: Booklets. Specializes in photo restoration.

*VESTA PUBLICATIONS, LTD., Box 1641, Cornwall ON K6H 5V6 Canada. (613)932-2135. Fax (613)932-7735. E-mail: sg@ican.ca. General trade publisher that does a few religious titles; focus is on world peace. Stephen Gill, ed. Publishes 4 titles/yr. Receives 20-60 submissions annually. 95% of books from first-time authors. No mss through agents. **SUBSIDY PUBLISHES 90%** (author pays about 50% of cost). Reprints books. Any length. Royalty 15% of net; no advance. Average first printing 1,500. Publication within 3 mos. No simultaneous submissions. Responds in 4-7 wks. Requires disk. Catalog for SAE/IRCs.

Nonfiction: Proposal/1 chapter; phone query OK.

Tips: "Most open to scholarly/religious books."

WELLNESS PUBLICATIONS, Box 2397, Holland MI 49423. (616)335-5553 or (800)543-0815. E-mail: dfranken@intraworldcom.net. Website: www.LifeskillsTraining.org. Darrell Franken, pres. Specializes in health and faith books. Publishes 3 titles/yr. Receives 200 submissions annually. All books from first-time authors. **100% SUBSIDY.** Prefers 250 pgs. Royalty 10% on retail; no advance; minimum subsidy $3,000. Average first printing 2,000. Publication within 6 mos. Considers simultaneous submissions. Responds in 2-4 wks. No guidelines; free catalog.

Nonfiction: Complete ms.

Tips: "Most open to health/healing, stress management and psychological concerns."

WEST COAST PARADISE PUBLISHING, Sardis Stn. Main, PO Box 2093, Sardis BC V2R 1A5 Canada. (604)824-9528. Fax (604)824-9541. E-mail: WCPP@telus.net. Website: www.wcpar.com. Robert G. Anstey, pres. Publishes 4 titles/yr. Receives 20 submissions annually. 80% of books from first-time authors. **50% SUBSIDY.** Reprints books. Prefers 200 pgs. Average first printing 100. Publication within 3 mos. Considers simultaneous submissions. Prefers disk. Responds in 1 wk. Prefers disk. Prefers KJV. Guidelines (also by e-mail/Website); free catalog.

Nonfiction: Query only; phone/fax query OK. "Looking for poetry books."

Fiction: Query only. For children and adults.

Also Does: Pamphlets, booklets, and tracts.

Photos: Accepts freelance photos for book covers.

WINDFLOWER COMMUNICATIONS, 67 Flett Ave., Winnipeg MB R2K 3N3 Canada. (204)668-7475. Fax (204)661-8530. E-mail: windflower@brandt family.com. Website: www.mennonitebooks.com. Brandt Family Enterprises. Gilbert Brandt, pres. Publishes quality, wholesome literature for family reading, pleasure and learning. Publishes 2-4 titles/yr. Receives 100 submissions annually. 90% of books from first-time authors. **SUBSIDY PUBLISHES 95%.** Reprints books. Prefers 200 pgs. Royalty 10-20% of net; no advance. Average first printing 2,000. Publication within 14 mos. Considers simultaneous submissions. Responds in 6 mos. Prefers disk/hard copy. Guidelines; free catalog.

Nonfiction: Query only; fax/e-query OK.

Fiction: Query only. All ages. Looking for fiction for junior high age and fiction that deals with current issues.

Photos: Accepts freelance photos for book covers.

Tips: "We are currently focusing on historical fiction."

WINEPRESS PUBLISHING, PO Box 428, 1730 Railroad St., Enumclaw WA 98022. (360)802-9758, (800)326-4674. Fax (360)802-9992. E-mail: info@ winepresspub.com or adean@winepresspub.com. Website: www. winepresspub.com. Ailen Dean, pub.; Athena Dean, acq. ed. Books that challenge readers to think about their Christianity and the need for holy lives. Publishes 100+ titles/yr. Receives 1,000+ submissions annually. 70% of books from first-time authors. No mss through agents. **BOOK PACKAGERS 85%.** Reprints books. Lengths range from 48-1,300 pgs. Author pays production costs, keeps all income from sales. Average first printing 3,000 (1,000 min.). Publication in 4-5 mos. Considers simultaneous submissions. Responds in 48-72 hrs. Accepts disk. Prefers NIV. Free guidelines (also on Website)/catalog. Not included in topical listings because they consider any topic or genre.

Nonfiction: Complete ms; phone/fax/e-query OK. Publishes any topic as long as it's biblical or glorifies God.

Fiction: Complete ms. All ages and all genres.

Also Does: Booklets, gift books, Bibles, full-color children's books.

Photos: Accepts freelance photos for book covers.

Tips: "We offer professional book packaging for Christian writers. We not only offer a full line of editorial, design, layout, and printing services, but cutting-edge marketing, publicity, promotion, order fulfillment, warehousing, and distribution as well. Our in-house team of professionals is committed to serving our authors with excellent customer service and honest advice. We don't purchase rights to books, but we still turn down manuscripts that don't glorify God or have a reasonably good chance of selling at least 1,000 copies."

WORD FOR WORD PUBLISHING CO., 14 MetroTech Center, #217, Brooklyn NY 11201. (718)222-9673. Fax (718)222-1949. E-mail: Word4wrd@aol. com. Website: www.Word-4-Word.com. Michelle A. Edwards, ed. Specializes in religious publications. Receives 200+ submissions annually. 90% of books from first-time authors. **SUBSIDY PUBLISHES 90%.** All profits belong to author; flexible payment plan. No minimum length. Average first printing 1,000. Publication within 6 mos. Responds in 1-2 wks. Free guidelines, catalog, and book samples/$3.20 postage. Will consider most Christian topics.

   Nonfiction & Fiction: "Looking for books that enlighten, empower, and glorify God."

   Also Does: Pamphlets, booklets, and tracts.

   Contest: Annual Writing Contest for Young Christian Writers.

   Tips: "'Write the vision and make it plain, that he may run that readeth it' (Hab. 2:2). Then, actively promote your books. We go as you pay." Will transcribe from tapes.

LISTING OF CHRISTIAN BOOK/MUSIC DISTRIBUTORS

ACCESS PUBLISHERS NETWORK, 6893 Sullivan Rd., Grawn MI 49637. (231)276-5196. Fax (231)276-5197. E-mail: mas49637@aol.com. Contact: Margaret Anne Slawson, Acquisitions Director. Works with 170 small presses and selected self-publishers in distribution to the US bookstore and library trade.

+AMAZON ADVANTAGE PROGRAM. www.amazon.com/exec/obidos/subt/partners/direct/advantage-rules-terms.html/002-2857657-4714424. Site to contact if you want amazon to distribute your book.

*APPALACHIAN, INC., PO Box 1573, 506 Princeton Rd., Johnson City TN 37601. (800)289-2772. Fax (800)759-2779.

*BAY TO BAY DISTRIBUTION, INC., 453 Ravendale Dr., Ste. A, Mountain View CA 94043. (800)647-5749.

BLESSINGWAY BOOKS, PO Box 31280, Santa Fe NM 87594. (800)716-2953 or (505)438-3700. Fax (505)438-3704. E-mail: blessingway@blessingway books.com. Website: www.blessingway.com. Co-op distributor for self-published books. Authors pay $1,500 in two installments and then make 100% profit after that. Request a prospectus by phone or fax, or download from their Website.

*B. BROUGHTON CO., LTD., 2105 Danforth Ave., Toronto ON M4C 1K1 Canada. Canadian distributor.

+CHRISTIAN BOOK DISTRIBUTORS., Website: www.christianbooks.com.

+CHRISTIAN BOOK DISTRIBUTORS OF AUSTRALIA., c/o Turnaround Ministry, 44 Collier Ave., Stirling North SA 5710. Phone/fax (08) 8634 6186. Contact: Larry Norman.

+CHRISTIAN PUBLISHER.COM., www.christianpublisher.com. Distributes original Christian music CDs and tapes. See information on Website.

COOK COMMUNICATIONS CANADA, 55 Woodslee Ave., Box 98, Paris ON N3L 3E5 Canada. (800)263-2664. Fax (800)461-8575. E-mail: cuserv @cook.ca. Website: www.cook.ca. Can distribute only in Canada.

DICKSONS, PO Box 368, Seymour IN 47274. (800)457-9885. Fax (812)522-1319. E-mail: marketing@dicksongifts.com. Website: www.dicksongifts. com.

+FOUNDATION DISTRIBUTING INC., (905)983-1188. Canadian distributor.

*INGRAM BOOK COMPANY, 1125 Heil Quaker Rd., Nashville TN 37217. (615)793-5000. (800)937-8000.

MIDNIGHT CALL, PO Box 280008, Columbia SC 29228. (800)845-2420. Fax (803)755-6002. E-mail: info@midnightcall.com. Website: www. midnightcall.com. Imprint: The Olive Press.

R.G. MITCHELL, 565 Gordon Baker Rd., Willowdale ON M2H 2W2, Canada. (416)499-4615. Fax (416)499-6340. Website: www.rgm.ca.

#NEW DAY CHRISTIAN DISTRIBUTORS, 126 Shivel Dr., Hendersonville TN 37075. (800)251-3633 or (615)822-3633. Fax (800)361-2533.

*NOAH'S ARK DISTRIBUTION, 560-C Industrial Way, Fallbrook CA 92028. (760)723-3101. Fax (760)723-1443. Toll free (800)562-8093.

THE PARABLE GROUP, 3563 Empleo St., San Luis Obispo CA 93401. (800)366-6031, ext. 525. Fax (800)543-2136. Website: www.parable.com. A marketing program for Christian bookstores.

QUALITY BOOKS, 1003 W. Pines Rd., Oregon IL 61061. (815)832-4450. Fax (815)732-4499. E-mail: carolyn.olson@quality-books.com Contact: Carolyn Olson. Distributes small press books, videos, audios and CD-ROMS to secular libraries. Requires 55% discount. Payment 90 days after sales. Asks for 1 copy of the book, plus 30 covers.

#RIVERSIDE DISTRIBUTORS, PO Box 370, Iowa Falls IA 50126-0370. (515)648-4271. (800)922-9777. Fax (800)822-4271. Website: www. firstnetchristian.com.

SLEEPER, DICK, DISTRIBUTION, 18680-B Langensand Rd., Sandy OR 97055-6426. (503)668-3454. Fax (503)668-5314. E-mail: sleepydick@ bigfoot.com. Represents small press authors.

SPRING ARBOR DISTRIBUTORS, PO Box 3006, One Ingram Blvd., Mailstop 684, Lavergne TN 37086. (615)213-5192 or (800)395-4340. Fax (612)213-5192 or (800)395-2682. Website: www.springarbor.com. Contact: Karen K. Bishop, Director of Sales.

*STREAMWOOD DISTRIBUTION, PO Box 91011, Mobile AL 36691. (888)670-7463.

#WARNER CHRISTIAN DISTRIBUTION, 20 Music Square East, Nashville TN 37203-4344. (615)248-3300. Distributes records.

WHITAKER HOUSE DISTRIBUTORS (formerly Anchor Distributors), 30 Hunt Valley Cir., New Kensington PA 15068. (724)334-7000. (800)444-4484. Fax (800)765-1960 or (724)334-1200. E-mail: marketing@ whitakerhouse.com.

MARKET ANALYSIS

ALL PUBLISHERS IN ORDER OF MOST BOOKS PUBLISHED PER YEAR

America House 300
CSS Publishing 200
United Methodist 175
Barbour Publishing 150
Cook Communications 150
Standard Publishing 150
Zondervan 150
Concordia 130
Eerdmans 120-130
Bethany House 120+
Baker Books 120
Christian Univ Press 100
Harvest House 100
Multnomah 100
Starburst Publishers 100
Tyndale House 100
Paulist Press 90-100
Crossway 90
Westmin. John Knox 80-100
Christian Ed Publishers 80
InterVarsity Press 80
Broadman & Holman 75
HarperSanFrancico 75
Henry Holt 70
Liturgical Press 70
Moody Press 65-70
Tommy Nelson 65
G.P. Putnam's Sons 60-70
Honor Books 60+
Kregel 60
Joshua Morris 60
Oxford University 60
Revell 60
Ambassador-Emerald 55
Heartsong Presents 52
Harcourt Religion 50-100
Custom Commun. 50-75
Providence House 50+
Boyds Mills Press 50
Chalice Press 50
Crossroad Publishing 50
GROUP Publishing 50
Liguori Publications 50
Univ Press of America 50
ZonderKidz 50
Doubleday Religion 45-50
Editores Batania-Caribe 45
Creation House 40-50
Peter Pauper Press 40-50

Review and Herald 40-50
Shaw Books 40-45
Christian Publications 40
Health Communications 40
John Hunt Publishing 40
Legacy Press 40
Novalis 40
Love Inspired 36
Smyth & Helwys 35-40
Eldridge 35 (plays)
Morehouse Publishing 35
New World Library 35
Trinity Press Intl. 35
Hendrickson 30-40
Jeremy P. Tarcher 30-40
Our Sunday Visitor 30+
Beacon Hill Press 30
College Press 30
Conari Press 30
Electric Works 30
Good News Publishers 30
  (tracts)
Judson Press 30
Pacific Press 30
Platinum Press 30
Promise Press/Barbour 30
Sheed & Ward 30
Pauline Books 25-35
Huntington House 25-30
Vital Issues Press 25-30
Bridge-Logos 25
Liturgy Training 25
Meriwether 25 (plays)
Thomas More 25
Alba House 24
Lightwave Publishing 24
J Countryman 20-40
Loyola Press 20-30
Saint Mary's Press 20-25
Univ. of Ottawa Press 20-25
Albury Publishing 20
BIBAL Press 20
Cross Cultural 20
Gold 'N' Honey 20
Monument Press 20
Openbook Publishers 20
Rainbow Pub/Rainbow Books
  20
Resource Publications 20

Shining Star 20
Sovereign/Appaloosa 20
New Hope 18-24
St. Anthony Mess. Press 18-20
BJU Press 16-20
Paraclete Press 16
Catholic Book Publishing 15-
  20
New Leaf Press 15-20
AMG Publishers 15
Libros Liguori 15
Mercer University 15
Rainbow Pub/Legacy Press 15
Still Waters 15
YWAM Publishing 15
Palisades 14
Howard Publishing 12-18
Blue Dolphin 12-15
Master Books 12-15
Paragon House 12-15
Perigee Books 12-15
Pilgrim Press 12-15
United Church Press 12-15
Upper Room Books 12-15
Chosen Books 12
Dimension Books 12
Forward Movement 12
New City Press 12
Books in Motion 10-20
Troitsa Books 10-20
American Counseling 10-15
Canon Press 10-15
Carey Library, Wm. 10-15
Focus on the Family 10-15
Loizeaux 10-15
Ragged Edge 10-15
Gospel Publishing House 10-14
Eerdmans/Young Readers 10-
  12
Lillenas 10-12
Messianic Jewish Publishers
  10-12
ACTA Publications 10
ACU Press 10
Alban Institute 10
Haworth Press 10
Lutterworth Press 10
Oregon Catholic Press 10
PREP Publishing 10

United Church Publishing 10
Yale University Press 10
Cistercian Publications 8-14
Holy Cross Orthodox 8-10
P & R Publishing 8-10
Spence Publishing 8-10
Innisfree Press 8
Neibauer Press 8
Touch Publications 8
Ambassador Books 7
Compradore 7
Kaleidoscope Press 7
Lowenbrown Publishing 6-12
Elder Books 6-10
Daybreak Books/Rodale 6-9
Christopher Pub Hs 6-8
Cornell University Press 6-8
Canticle Books 6
Church & Synagogue Libraries 6
ICS Publications 6
Magnus Press 6
Northstone Publishing 6
Pelican Publishing 6
Trinity Foundation 6
Wilshire Book Co. 6
Scarecrow Press 5-15
Conciliar Press 5-10
Hensley Publishing 5-10
Northfield Publishing 5-10
Rose Publishing 5-10
Wadsworth Publishing 5-10
World Bible 5-10
Faith One Publishing 5-8
Religious Education Press 5-6
Christian Media 5
Morrow 5
Mt. Olive College Press 5
Paradise Research 5
Church Growth Institute 4-6
Focus Publishing 4-6
Friends United Press 4-6
Hearth Publishing 4-6
Jireh Publishing 4-6
Pickwick Publications 4-5
Victory House 4-5
American Catholic Press 4
Baylor Univ. Press 4

Bristol House 4
Hay House 4
Inkling Books 4
Intl. Awakening Press 4
Langmarc Publishing 4
Open Court 4
RBC Publishing 4
Reconciliation Press 4
Toccoa Falls College Press 4
Western Front 4
Cerdic Publications 3-5
Facts on File 3-5
Kindred Productions 3-4
Quintessential Books 3-4
City Bible Publishing 3
Meriwether 3
OSL Publications 3
Wood Lake Books 3
Dry Bones Press 2-10
Art Can Drama 2-5
St. Augustine's Press 2-5
Tekna Books 2-5
Baptist Publishing House 2-4
Canadian Institute for Law 2-4
Encounter Books 2-4
Frederick Fell 2-4
Grace House Press 2-4
Regnery Publishing 2-4
Write Now 2-4
Sower's Press 2-3
Devoted to You 2
Elim Books 2
Logion Press 2
One World 2
Read 'N Run Books 2
Baker's Plays 1-6
Barclay Press 1-5
Bookwrights Press 1-4
Life Cycle Books 1-3
LifeSong Publishers 1-3
WhiteStone Circle 1-3
Accent Books & Video 1-2
Cladach Publishing 1-2
New Canaan 1-2
Found/Religious Freedom 1-2
Players Press 1-2
Rising Star Press 1-2
Creative Bound 1

ETC Publications 1
Gilgal Publications 1
Goetz 1
Good Book 1
Guernica Editions 1
Misty Hill Press 1
Noveledit 1
Small Helm Press 1
Summit Pub. Group 1
Living Books for All 1-5
Greenwood Publishing 0-20

SUBSIDY PUBLISHERS

Brentwood 267
Poet's Cove 125
Fairway Press 100
WinePress 100
Southern Baptist Press 42
Essence Publishing 40-50
Guardian Books 40-50
TEACH Services 40-50
ACW Press 40
McDougal Publishing 30
Black Forest Press 25
Impact Books 20
Tyler Press 20
Master Design 15+
Partnership Book Services 12
Longwood Communications 8-12
Promise Publishing 6
Son-Rise 5-6
DCTS Publishing 5
Omega House 5
Recovery Communications 4-6
Gesher 4
Reconciliation Press 4
VESTA Publications 4
West Coast Paradise 4
Wellness Publications 3
Ambassador House 2-6
Windflower Communications 2-4
Cross Way Publications 2
Sheer Joy! 1-2
Alfred Ali Literary 1

BOOK PUBLISHERS WITH THE MOST BOOKS ON THE BESTSELLER LIST FOR THE LAST YEAR

Note: This tally is based on actual sales in Christian bookstores for December 1999-September 2000 (most recent information available). Note that this list is based on only 10 months because of a change in the deadline for this book. The list is broken down by types of books, i.e., children's, teen, fiction, nonfiction in paperback and cloth, mass-market paperbacks, and gift books. Numbers behind the names indicate the number of titles each publisher had on that bestseller list during the year. The combined list indicates the total number a particular publisher had on all the lists combined. If a particular publisher has more than one imprint listed, they are sometimes combined for these totals. It is interesting to note that each year the number of publishers appearing on the list has increased—26 publishers in 1993; 35 publishers in 1994; 43 in 1995, and 60 in 1996, until 1997 and 1998 when it dropped back to 48; 1999 moved up to 52, and this year we drop back to 47. It is interesting to note that there are very dominant leaders in each category.

FICTION BOOKS

1. Tyndale House 15
2. Bethany House 11
3. Barbour 8
4. Harvest House 8
5. Multnomah 8
6. Zondervan 7
7. Chariot Victor 2
8. Thomas Nelson 2
9. Penguin Putnam 2
10. Word 2
11. Crossway 1
12. Honor Books 1
13. Kregel 1
14. Revell 1
15. Viking 1
16. WaterBrook 1

NONFICTION—CLOTH

1. Thomas Nelson 13
2. Zondervan 10
3. Word 8
4. Broadman & Holman 6
5. Multnomah 4
6. Harrison House 2
7. Tyndale House 2
8. Chariot Victor 1
9. Discovery House 1
10. Doubleday 1
11. Putnam 1
12. Regal 1

NONFICTION— PAPERBACK

1. Multnomah 14
2. Zondervan 7
3. Thomas Nelson 5
4. Word 5
5. Harvest House 4
6. Destiny Image 3
7. Regal 3
8. Moody Press 2
9. Waterbrook 2
10. Whitaker House 2
11. Albury 1
12. Broadman & Holman 1
13. Frontier Research 1
14. Harrison House 1
15. Loyal Publishing 1
16. Western Front Ltd. 1

MASS-MARKET PAPERBACKS

1. Barbour Books 17
2. J. Countryman/Word 9
3. Broadman & Holman 5
4. Tyndale House 5
5. Zondervan 4
6. AMG Publishers 1
7. Fortress Press 1
8. Garborg's 1
9. Harrison House 1
10. InterVarsity Press 1
11. NavPress 1
12. Revell 1
13. Victory House 1
14. Whitaker House 1
15. World Publishers 1

CHILDREN'S BOOKS

1. ZonderKidz 32
2. Tommy Nelson 21
3. Standard Publishing 10
4. Crossway 3
5. Legacy Press 3
6. Concordia 2
7. Howard 2
8. Bethany House 1
9. Chariot Victor 1
10. Destiny Image 1
11. Golden Books 1
12. Promise Press 1
13. Rainbow Publishing 1
14. Tyndale House 1
15. Word 1

YOUTH/TEEN BOOKS

1. Tyndale House 12
2. Chariot Victor 1
3. Honor Books 1
4. Multnomah 1
5. Servant 1
6. Zondervan 1

GIFT BOOKS

1. J. Countryman 27
2. Honor Books 12
3. Howard 9
4. Barbour Books 4
5. ZondervanGifts 4
6. Broadman & Holman 3
7. Tommy Nelson 3
8. Thomas Nelson 3
9. Harvest House 2
10. Multnomah 2
11. Word 2
12. Garborg's 1
13. Kregel 1
14. Tyndale House 1
15. WaterBrook 1

COMBINED BESTSELLER LISTS (Combination of seven lists above)

1. J. Countryman/Word 36
2. Tyndale House 36
3. ZonderKidz 32
4. Barbour 29
5. Multnomah 29
6. Zondervan 29
7. Tommy Nelson 24
8. Thomas Nelson 23
9. Word 18
10. Broadman & Holman 15
11. Harvest House 14
12. Honor Books 14
13. Bethany House 12
14. Howard 11
15. Standard 10
16. Chariot Victor 5
17. Crossway 4
18. Destiny Image 4
19. Harrison House 4
20. Regal 4
21. WaterBrook 4
22. ZondervanGifts 4
23. Legacy Press 3
24. Putnam 3
25. Whitaker House 3
26. Concordia 2
27. Garborg's 2
28. Kregel 2
29. Moody Press 2
30. Revell 2
31. Albury 1
32. AMG Publishers 1
33. Discovery House 1
34. Doubleday 1

35. Fortress Press 1
36. Frontier Research 1
37. Golden Books 1
38. InterVarsity 1
39. Loyal Publishing 1

40. NavPress 1
41. Promise Press 1
42. Rainbow Publishing 1
43. Servant 1
44. Victory House 1

45. Viking 1
46. Western Front 1
47. World Publishers 1

BOOK TOPICS MOST POPULAR WITH PUBLISHERS

Note: The numbers following the topics indicate how many publishers said they were interested in seeing a book on that topic. To find the list of publishers interested in each topic, go to the Topical Listings for books (see Table of Contents).

Photographs for Covers 39
Canadian/Foreign Publishers 24
1. Religion 131
2. Spirituality 128
3. Inspirational 117
4. Bible/Biblical Studies 114
5. Christian Living 110
6. Prayer 105
7. Theological 102
8. Women's Issues 101
9. Family Life 99
10. Marriage 97
11. Devotional Books 96
12. Ethics 92
13. Historical 85
14. Parenting 84
15. Current/Social Issues 83
16. Biography 81
17. Discipleship 81
18. Evangelism/Witnessing 76
19. Christian Education 73
20. How-to 71
21. Church Life 70
22. Ethnic/Cultural 70
23. Fiction: Adult/Religious 69
24. Healing 69
25. Leadership 69
26. Doctrinal 67
27. Health 67
28. Church Renewal 65
29. Gift Books 65
30. Men's Books 65
31. Self-Help 65
32. Apologetics 63
33. Fiction: Historical 63
34. Pastor's Helps 61
35. Youth Books 61
36. Death/Dying 58
37. Controversial Issues 57
38. Scholarly 57
39. Psychology 56
40. Reference Books 55
41. Social Justice Issues 55
42. Personal Growth 53

43. Philosophy 53
44. Humor 51
45. Liturgical Studies 51
46. Personal Experience 51
47. Fiction: Contemporary 48
48. Fiction: Juvenile 48
49. Fiction: Adventure 47
50. Personal Renewal 47
51. Autobiography 46
52. Missionary 45
53. Worship Resources 45
54. Children's Picture Books 44
55. Christian Home Schooling 44
56. Stewardship 44
57. Counseling Aids 42
58. World Issues 42
59. Environmental Issues 41
60. Fiction: Biblical 41
61. Faith 40
62. Fiction: Teen/Young Adult 40
63. Miracles 40
64. Booklets 38
65. Political 38
66. Church Traditions 37
67. Group Study Books 37
68. Poetry 37
69. Prophecy 37
70. Recovery Books 37
71. Senior-Adult Concerns 37
72. Bible Commentary 36
73. Divorce 36
74. Fiction: Mystery/Suspense 36
75. Sermons 36
76. Singles Issues 35
77. Archaeology 34
78. Drama 34
79. Cookbooks 33
80. Money Management 33
81. Music-Related Books 33
82. Spiritual Warfare 33
83. Sociology 32

84. Cults/Occult 31
85. Curriculum 31
86. Science 31
87. Fiction: Historical/Romance 30
88. Games/Crafts 30
89. Fiction: Humor 29
90. Economics 28
91. Fiction: Literary 28
92. Homiletics 28
93. *E-books 26
94. Spiritual Gifts 26
95. Children's Easy-Readers 25
96. Fiction: Frontier/Romance 25
97. Retirement 25
98. Christian School Books 24
99. Fiction: Allegory 24
100. Fiction: Frontier 24
101. Fiction: Mystery/Romance 24
102. Pamphlets 24
103. Creation Science 23
104. Eschatology 23
105. Exegesis 23
106. Fiction: Romance 23
107. Youth Programs 23
108. Fiction: Ethnic 22
109. Sports/Recreation 22
110. Fiction: Short Story Collection 21
111. Travel 19
112. Fiction: Fantasy 18
113. Fiction: Plays 18
114. Time Management 18
115. Celebrity Profile 17
116. Fiction: Science Fiction 16
117. Exposes 15
118. Tracts 15
119. Writing How-to 14
120. Fiction: Novellas 12

Comments:

If you are a fiction writer, you are more likely to sell adult fiction (69 possible publishers—4 more than last year) than you are juvenile fiction (48 publishers—2 more than last year) or teen fiction (40 publishers—6 more than last year). These figures indicate that the fiction market is improving for all age groups, especially teen.

The most popular fiction genres with publishers are (1) Historical Fiction, 63 markets, (2) Contemporary Fiction, 48 markets, (3) Adventure Fiction, 47 markets, (4) Biblical Fiction, 41 markets, (5) Mystery/Suspense, 36 markets, and (6) Historical/Romance, 30 markets (the same order as last year, except Historical /Romance beat humorous fiction by one, after tying last year). All the numbers above show an increase in actual markets for each genre, after all showing a decrease the previous year.

This year the book market for poetry moved up from 32 to 37—an encouraging increase. That compares to only 16 in 1994, almost a 57% increase in the last seven years. Even though the market is improving, many will still want to consider self-publishing (look for subsidy publishers listed in another section of this book), or sell to periodicals. Go to the periodical topical listings in this book to find 218 markets for poetry (a few less than last year).

Compared to last year, the same topics are in the top 10, except for Family Life, which moved up into it, and Devotional books which dropped out of it. The rest of the 10 have nearly all changed positions on the list, except Religion, which remains in first place. Spirituality moved up from 5th to 2nd, and Prayer dropped from 3rd to 6th. Among the next 10 topics, most were the same, except Family Life moved up to the top 10, Christian Education moved back into it (22nd to 19th), and Healing dropped out (20th to 24th). Biography moved up from 19th to 16th this year.

In a general comparison to last year, there were not a lot of significant changes. In order from most to least, these topics increased in interest: Children's Picture Books, Christian Home Schooling, Worship Resources, Adventure Fiction, Autobiography, Self-help, and Apologetics. Those dropping the most in interest are Celebrity Profiles, Psychology, World Issues, Environmental Issues and Writing How-to. None of these changes reflects a continuing increase or decrease from last year.

SUMMARY OF INFORMATION ON CHRISTIAN BOOK PUBLISHERS FOUND IN THE ALPHABETICAL LISTINGS

Note: The following numbers are based on the maximum total estimate for each company. For example, if a company gave a range of 5-10, the averages were based on the higher number, 10. This information will be valuable in determining if the contract offered by your publisher is in line with other publishers in some of these areas. For further help, check the section on editorial services to find those who offer contract evaluations, which are most valuable.

TOTAL MANUSCRIPTS RECEIVED:

Two hundred thirty-four publishers indicated they received a combined total of about 149,141 manuscripts during the year. That is an average of 638 manuscripts per editor, per year, a decrease of 3% from last year. It is easy to see why many publishers are refusing to review unsolicited manuscripts. The actual number of manuscripts received ranged from 3 to 10,000 per editor.

NUMBER OF BOOKS PUBLISHED:

Two hundred eighty-one publishers reported that they will publish a combined total of 8,192 titles during the coming year. That is an average of over 29 books per publisher (one less per publisher than last year). The actual number per publisher ranges from 1 to 300. If each publisher actually publishes his maximum estimate of books for the year, about 5.5% of the manuscripts submitted will be published (up 1/2 % from last year).

AVERAGE FIRST PRINT RUN:

Based on 205 book publishers who indicated their average first print run, the average first printing of a book for a new author is about 6,400 books. That's an increase of 16% over last year. Actual print runs ranged from 100 to 250,000 copies.

ROYALTIES:

Of the 232 publishers who indicated that they paid royalties, 64 (28%) pay on the retail price; 115 (50%) pay on the wholesale price or net; and the remaining 53 (22%) did not say which. Not all gave specific percentages for their royalties, but of those who did, the average royalty based on the retail price of the book was 8.65% to 12.29% (compared to 7.9% to 12.1% last year). Actual royalties on retail varied from 2% to 50%. The average royalty based on net varied from 9.5% to 13.98% (compared to 9% to 13.6% last year). Both types of royalties continue to increase from year to year. Actual royalties on net also varied from 2% to 50%. The recommended royalty based on net is 18%, but only 10.5% of the Christian publishers counted here are paying up to 18% or higher (that is down 1.5% from last year).

ADVANCES:

Two hundred and seven publishers responded to the question about whether or not they paid advances. Of those, 117 paid advances and 90 did not—which means those who do are still ahead of those who don't. Of those who pay advances, only 22.7% (47 publishers) gave a specific amount. The average advance for those 47 was $1,550-$10,677 (an 18% drop at the low end, and a 23% increase at the top end, compared to last year). The steady improvement and increase in advances during the last few years is encouraging, but at the same time, more and more publishers are reluctant to give specific amounts anymore. The actual range is still from $100 to $50,000, so ask for the amount that you need or deserve based on past publishing history. Most publishers pay more for established authors or potentially best-selling books. It is not unusual for a first-time author to get no advance or a small one. Once you have one or more books published, feel free to ask for an advance, and raise the amount for each book. Don't be afraid to ask for an advance, even on a first book, if you need the money to support you while you finish the manuscript. Although some publishers are saying they don't give an advance or are reluctant to name an amount, the truth is many of those publishers do give advances when warranted.

REPORTING TIME:

Waiting for a response from an editor is often the hardest part of the writing business. Of the 256 editors who indicated how long you should have to wait for a response from them, the average time was about 10 1/2 weeks (1/2 week less than last year). However, since the times they actually gave ranged from 2 days to 52 weeks, be sure to check the listing for the publisher you are interested in. Give them a 2- to 4-week grace period; then feel free to write a polite letter asking about the current status of your manuscript. Give them another month to respond, and if you don't hear anything, you can call as a last resort.

E-MAIL AND WEBSITES:

As expected, the number of publishers with e-mail and Websites continues to grow. This year, out of 371 book publishers listed, 257 have e-mail (20% over last year), and 271 have Websites (almost 18% more than last year). To connect to any of their Websites, visit my Website at www.stuartmarket.com.

PREFERRED BIBLE VERSION:

For the first time this year, we asked the book publishers to list their preferred Bible version. Of the 78 who responded, 38% wanted NIV, 20% KJV, 17% NRSV, and 13% NKJV. The remaining named only 3 or 4 other versions. Each publisher's preference is indicated in the regular listings.

TOPICAL LISTINGS OF PERIODICALS

As soon as you have an article or story idea, look up that topic in the following topical listings (see Table of Contents for a full list of topics). Study the appropriate periodicals in the primary/alphabetical listings (as well as their writers' guidelines and sample copies) and select those that are most likely targets for the piece you are writing.

Note that most ideas can be written for more than one periodical if you slant them to the needs of different audiences, for example, current events for teens, or pastors, or women. Have a target periodical and audience in mind before you start writing. Each topic is divided by age group/audience, so you can pick appropriate markets for your particular slant.

If the magazine prefers or requires a query letter, be sure to write that letter first and then follow any guidelines or suggestions they make if they give you a go-ahead.

R—Takes reprints
(*)—Indicates new topic this year

BIBLE STUDIES

ADULT/GENERAL
AGAIN—R
America
Arlington Catholic
Banner
Bible Advocate—R
Breakthrough Intercessor—R
CGA World—R
Christian Computing (MO)—R
Christian Motorsports
Christian Ranchman
Christian Standard—R
Christianity Today—R
Church Herald/Holiness—R
Company—R
Connecting Point—R
Creation Care—R
Culture Wars—R
Evangelical Advocate—R
Faith & Friends—R
Fellowship Link—R
First Things
Foursquare World—R
Gem—R
God's Revivalist
Healing Inn—R
Heartlight Internet—R
Hidden Manna—R
Highway News—R

Hunted News
Indian Life—R
Inspirer—R
John Milton—R
Life Gate—R
Lookout—R
Lutheran—R
Lutheran Journal—R
Lutheran Witness
Mennonite—R
Messenger/St. Anthony
Methodist History
Ncubator.com—R
New Freeman—R
North American Voice
Our Family—R
Our Sunday Visitor
Perspectives
Pourastan—R
PrayerWorks—R
Presbyterian Outlook
Presbyterians Today—R
St. Anthony Messenger
St. Willibrord Journal
Seeds
Silver Wings—R
Sojourners
Spiritual Life
Star of Zion
Testimony—R

thegoodsteward.com—R
Times of Refreshing
Today's Christian Senior—R
Touchstone—R
Trumpeter—R
U.S. Catholic
Way of St. Francis—R
Wesleyan Advocate—R

CHILDREN
Celebrate
Discovery (NY)—R

CHRISTIAN EDUCATION/LIBRARY
Children's Ministry
Christian School
Church & Synagogue Lib.
Church Educator—R
GROUP
Leader/Church School Today—R
Preschool Playhouse
Religion Teacher's Journal
Shining Star
Teacher's Interaction

MISSIONS
Catholic Near East
Women of the Harvest

PASTORS/LEADERS
Catholic Servant
Celebration
Cross Currents—R
Emmanuel
Evangelicals Today—R
Five Stones—R
Growing Churches
Journal/Christian Healing—R
Ministries Today
Pastoral Life—R
Priest
PROCLAIM—R
Pulpit Helps—R
Quarterly Review
Reaching Children at Risk
Resource—R
Sewanee Theological Review
Sharing the Practice—R
Single Adult Ministries
Word & World

TEEN/YOUNG ADULT
Conqueror—R
Cross Walk
Devo'Zine—R
Passageway.org—R
Student Leadership—R
Teens on Target—R
YOU!—R
Young Adult Today
Young Salvationist—R
Youth Challenge—R
Youthwalk
WITH—R

WOMEN
Horizons—R
True Woman
Woman's Touch—R
Women Who Minister—R

BOOK EXCERPTS

ADULT/GENERAL
AGAIN—R
Bible Advocate—R
Bridge—R
Charisma/Christian Life
Chicken Soup/Mother—R
Chicken Soup/Woman—R
Christian Motorsports
Christian Observer
Christian Renewal—R
Christianity Online—R
Culture Wars—R
Door

Evangelical Advocate—R
Fellowship Link—R
Good News Journal (TX)
Hidden Manna—R
Homeschooling Today—R
Home Times—R
Hunted News
Living Light News—R
Mennonite—R
MESSAGE/Open Bible—R
Metro Voice—R
Michigan Christian
New Covenant
New Heart—R
NRB Magazine—R
On Mission
Parent Paper—R
Perspectives
Plain Truth—R
Plus—R
Power for Living—R
Presbyterian Outlook
Prism—R
Re:generation
SCP Journal—R
Short Stories Bimonthly
Sojourners
Star of Zion
Sursum Corda!—R
TEAK Roundup—R
thegoodsteward.com—R
Trumpeter—R
United Church Observer—R
Upscale Magazine
U.S. Catholic

CHILDREN
GUIDE—R

CHRISTIAN EDUCATION/ LIBRARY
Christian School Signal—R

MISSIONS
Areopagus—R
East-West Church
Intl. Journal/Frontier—R

PASTORS/LEADERS
Christian Century
Clergy Journal—R
Growing Churches
Five Stones—R
Ivy Jungle Report—R
Ministries Today
Ministry & Liturgy—R

Priest
Sharing the Practice—R
Worldwide Challenge
Youthworker

TEEN/YOUNG ADULTS
Boundless Webzine—R
Breakaway—R
Passageway.org—R
Teens on Target—R
YOU!—R
Youth Challenge—R

WOMEN
Conscience—R
Godly Business Woman
Grace—R
Handmaiden—R
Hearts at Home—R
Link & Visitor—R
Woman's Touch—R
Women Who Minister—R

BOOK REVIEWS

ADULT/GENERAL
About Such Things—R
AGAIN—R
American Wasteland
And He Will Give
Anglican Journal—R
Arkansas Catholic
Arlington Catholic
Bridge—R
Cathedral Age
Catholic Insight
Catholic New Times—R
CBA Marketplace
Charisma/Christian Life
Christian Century
Christian Computing—R
Christian Courier (CAN)—R
Christian Crafter—R
Christian Media—R
Christian Motorsports
Christian Observer
Christian Ranchman
Christian Research
Christianity/Arts
Christianity Today—R
Commonweal
Connecting Point—R
Connection Mag.—R
Cornerstone—R
Creation Care—R
Creation Ex Nihilo
Cresset
Culture Wars—R

Dovetail—R
Dunamis Life—R
Expression Christian
Facts for Faith
Fellowship Link—R
First Things
Good News Journal (MO)
Good News Journal (TX)
Hidden Manna—R
Homeschooling Today—R
Home Times—R
Hunted News
Indian Life—R
Inland NW Christian
Interim—R
John Milton—R
Joyful Noise
Life@Work
Life Gate—R
LifeWise
Light and Life
Liguorian
Mature Years—R
Mennonite Historian—R
Messenger/St. Anthony
Methodist History
Michigan Christian
MovieGuide
National Catholic
Ncubator.com—R
New Moon—R
New Song
No-Debt Living—R
On Mission
Parabola—R
Parenting Our Parents—R
Parent Paper—R
Peoples Magazine—R
Perspectives
Plain Truth—R
Pourastan—R
Prairie Messenger—R
Presbyterian Layman
Presbyterian Outlook
Presbyterian Record—R
Presbyterians Today—R
Prism—R
Re:generation
Sacred Journey—R
SCP Journal—R
Short Stories Bimonthly
Social Justice
Sojourners
Spiritual Life
Star of Zion
Studio—R
TEAK Roundup—R
thegoodsteward.com—R

Trumpeter—R
Upscale Magazine
Upsouth—R
Way of St. Francis—R
Winsome Wit—R

CHILDREN
J.A.M.—R

CHRISTIAN EDUCATION/LIBRARY
Caravan
Catholic Library World
CE Connection—R
Christian Librarian—R
Christian Library Jour.—R
Christian School
Church & Synagogue Lib.
Church Libraries—R
Journal/Adventist Educ.—R
Journal/Christian Education
Journal/Research on C.E.
Religion Teacher's Journal
Vision—R

MISSIONS
Areopagus—R
East-West Church
Evangelical Missions—R
Hope for Children—R
World Christian—R

MUSIC
CCM Magazine
Contemporary Songwriter—R

PASTORS/LEADERS—R
African American Pulpit
Angelos—R
Catechumenate
Christian Century—R
Christian Management—R
Clergy Journal—R
Cross Currents—R
Diocesan Dialogue—R
Enrichment—R
Evangelical Baptist—R
Evangelicals Today—R
Growing Churches
Five Stones—R
Horizons—R
Ivy Jungle Report—R
Journal/Christian Healing—R
Jour/Amer Soc/Chur Growth—
   R
Lutheran Partners—R
Ministries Today
Priest
Pulpit Helps—R

Reaching Children at Risk
Resource—R
Sermon Notes
Sharing the Practice—R
Single Adult Ministries
Theology Today (rarely)
WCA News—R
Word & World
Worship Leader

TEEN/YOUNG ADULT
Boundless Webzine—R
J.A.M.—R
Real Time—R
YOU!—R

WOMEN
Anna's Journal—R
Christian Bride
Conscience—R
Godly Business Woman
Hearts at Home—R
Helping Hand—R
Horizons—R
Lutheran Woman Today—R
True Woman
Wesleyan Woman—R
Woman's Touch—R
Women Who Minister—R

WRITERS
Advanced Chris. Writer—R
Areopagus (UK)
Canadian Writer's Jour—R
Christian Writer—R
Cochran's Corner—R
Contemporary Songwriter—R
Cross & Quill—R
Fellowscript—R
Gotta Write
WE!—R
WIN-Informer
Writer Online—R
Writer's Ink—R
Writer's Potpourri—R
Tickled by Thunder

CANADIAN/FOREIGN MARKETS

ADULT/GENERAL
Anglican Arts
Anglican Journal
Annals of St. Anne
BC Catholic
Bread of Life
Canada Lutheran
Catholic Insight

Catholic New Times
Christian Courier
Christianweek
Companion
Creation Ex Nihilo
Crossway/Newsline
Dreams & Visions
Earthkeeping Ontario
Faith & Friends
Faith Today
Fellowship Link
Friend
Impact
Indian Life
Interim
Living Light News
Mennonite Brethren Herald
Mennonite Historian
Messenger of the Sacred
    Heart
Messenger of St. Anthony
Ncubator.com—R
New Freeman
Our Family
Peoples Magazine
Plowman
Pourastan
Prairie Messenger
Presbyterian Record
Shantyman
TEAK Roundup
Testimony
Time for Rhyme
Times of Refreshing
United Church Observer—R

*CHRISTIAN EDUCATION/
LIBRARY*
Caravan
Christian Educators
    Journal

DAILY DEVOTIONALS
Words of Life

MISSIONS
Areopagus

PASTORS/LEADERS
Evangelical Baptist
Evangelicals Today
Horizons
Reaching Children at Risk
Resource
Technologies for Worship

TEEN/YOUNG ADULT
HYPE

WOMEN
Catherine
Christian Women Today
Esprit
Greater Things
Link & Visitor
Woman Alive
Women Today

WRITERS
Areopagus (UK)
Canadian Writer's Journal
Exchange
Fellowscript
Tickled by Thunder
Writer's Billboard
Writer's Lifeline

CELEBRITY PIECES

ADULT/GENERAL
American Tract Soc.—R
Angels on Earth
Arlington Catholic
Breakthrough Intercessor—R
Catholic Digest—R
Catholic Faith & Family
CBA Frontline
Celebrate Life—R
CGA World—R
Charisma/Christian Life
Chicken Soup/Mother—R
Chicken Soup/Woman—R
Christian Motorsports
Christian Ranchman
Christian Reader—R
Christian Times
Companion
Connection Mag.—R
Door
Episcopal Life—R
Expression Christian
Faith & Friends—R
Fellowship Link—R
Focus on the Family
Good News, Etc—R
Good News Journal (MO)—R
Good News Journal (TX)
Gospel Today
Guideposts
Heartlight Internet—R
Home Times—R
Indian Life—R
Inside Journal—R
Life Gate—R
Lifeglow—R
Light and Life
Living Light News—R

Mature Years—R
Messenger/St. Anthony
Metro Voice—R
Michigan Christian
Minnesota Christian—R
New Freeman—R
New Writing—R
NRB Magazine—R
Our Sunday Visitor
Plus—R
Power for Living—R
PrayerWorks—R
Presbyterian Record—R
Prism—R
Sacred Journey—R
Single-Parent Family
Sports Spectrum
Standard, The—R
Testimony—R
Trumpeter—R
Vibrant Life—R
War Cry—R

CHILDREN
American Girl
GUIDE—R
Guideposts for Kids
Touch—R
Winner—R

*CHRISTIAN EDUCATION/
LIBRARY*
Christian Library Jour.—R
Signal—R

MISSIONS
Latin America Evangelist
So All May Hear—R
Teachers in Focus—R
Worldwide Challenge

MUSIC
Contemporary Songwriter—R
Cooperative Christian—R
Songwriting—R
Gospel Industry Today
Tradition

PASTORS/LEADERS
Catholic Servant
Christian Camp—R
Pastoral Life—R

TEEN/YOUNG ADULT
Boundless Webzine—R
Breakaway—R
Brio
Encounter—R

Essential Connection—R
Listen—R
Passageway.org—R
Sharing the VICTORY (sports) —R
YOU!—R
Young Salvationist—R

WOMEN
Godly Business Woman
Woman Alive

WRITERS
Christian Communicator—R
Contemporary Songwriter—R
Gotta Write
WIN-Informer

CHRISTIAN BUSINESS

ADULT/GENERAL
Angels on Earth
Banner
Breakthrough Intercessor—R
Catholic Sentinel—R
CBA Marketplace
CGA World—R
Christian Businessman
Christian Courier (CAN)—R
Christian Crafter—R
Christian Designer—R
Christian Leader—R
Christian Living—R
Christian News NW—R
Christian Motorsports
Christian Ranchman
Connection Mag.—R
Disciple's Journal—R
Discovery (FL)—R
Dunamis Life—R
Evangel—R
Expression Christian
Faith Today
Gem—R
Good News Journal (MO)—R
Good News Journal (TX)
Gospel Today
Guideposts
Heartlight Internet—R
Indian Life—R
Life@Work
Life Gate—R
Light and Life
Living—R
Living Light News—R
Lutheran Journal—R
Marketplace
Mennonite—R

MESSAGE
Messenger/St. Anthony
Metro Voice
Michigan Christian
Minnesota Christian—R
Nashville Christian—R
Ncubator.com—R
New Covenant
New Freeman—R
NRB Magazine—R
Parent Paper—R
Peoples Magazine—R
Power for Living—R
PrayerWorks—R
Presbyterian Record—R
Prism—R
Reflections
Re:generation
Resource
Social Justice
Standard, The—R
Star of Zion
Stepping Out
Testimony—R
Today's Christian Senior—R
Together—R
Trumpeter—R
2-Soar
War Cry—R

CHRISTIAN EDUCATION/LIBRARY
Christian School Admin.

MISSIONS
Worldwide Challenge

PASTORS/LEADERS
African American Pulpit
Catholic Servant
Christian Camp—R
Christian Management—R
Evangelicals Today—R
Pastoral Life—R
Reaching Children at Risk
Sharing the Practice—R
Today's Parish
Your Church—R

WOMEN
Canticle
Christian Women Today—R
Godly Business Woman
Proverbs 31 Woman—R
Women Today—R
Women Who Minister—R

CHRISTIAN EDUCATION

ADULT/GENERAL
America
Anglican Journal—R
Arkansas Catholic
Arlington Catholic
Banner
B.C. Catholic—R
Bible Advocate—R
Breakthrough Intercessor—R
Canada Lutheran—R
Catholic Digest—R
Catholic New Times—R
Catholic Parent
Catholic Sentinel—R
CGA World—R
Christian C.L. RECORD—R
Christian Courier (CAN)—R
Christian Crafter—R
Christian Home & School
Christian Leader—R
Christian Motorsports
Christian Observer
Christian Parenting—R
Christian Ranchman
Christian Renewal—R
Church Herald/Holiness—R
Church of God EVANGEL
Covenant Companion—R
Culture Wars—R
Evangel—R
Evangelical Advocate—R
Expression Christian
Faith Today
Focus on the Family
Foursquare World—R
Gem—R
God's Revivalist
Good News, Etc.—R
Good News Journal (TX)
Gospel Today
Heartlight Internet—R
Homeschooling Today—R
Home Times—R
Indian Life—R
Inland NW Christian
Interchange
John Milton—R
Joyful Noise
Life Gate—R
Light and Life
Living Church
Lutheran Digest—R
Lutheran Journal—R
Messenger/St. Anthony
Messenger of the Sacred Heart

Methodist History
Metro Voice—R
Michigan Christian
Minnesota Christian—R
Montana Catholic—R
Ncubator.com—R
New Covenant
New Freeman—R
North American Voice
Our Family—R
Our Sunday Visitor
Parent Paper—R
Peoples Magazine—R
Perspectives
Pourastan—R
PrayerWorks—R
Presbyterian Layman
Presbyterian Outlook
Presbyterian Record—R
Preserving Christian Homes—
   R
Prism—R
SCP Journal—R
Social Justice
Star of Zion
Stepping Out
thegoodsteward.com—R
Together—R
Tomorrow's Christian
   Graduate
U.S. Catholic
War Cry—R
Way of St. Francis—R

CHILDREN
Discovery (NY)—R
My Friend
Together Time—R

CHRISTIAN EDUCATION/LIBRARY
(See alphabetical listings)

MISSIONS
East-West Church
So All May Hear—R

MUSIC
Songwriting—R

PASTORS/LEADERS
African American Pulpit
Catholic Servant
Christian Camp—R
Christian Ministry
Church Administration
Clergy Journal—R
Enrichment—R
Eucharistic Minister—R

Evangelical Baptist—R
Evangelicals Today—R
Five Stones—R
Lutheran Partners—R
Ministries Today
Ministry & Liturgy—R
Pastoral Life—R
Pulpit Helps—R
Quarterly Review
Reaching Children at Risk
Resource—R
Rev.
Sabbath School Leadership
Sharing the Practice—R
Theology Today
Today's Christian Preacher—R
Today's Parish
Word & World
Youthworker

TEEN/YOUNG ADULT
Christian College Focus
Cross Walk
Today's Christian Teen—R
YOU!—R

WOMEN
Esprit—R
Godly Business Woman
Horizons—R
Just Between Us—R
Women Who Minister—R

CHRISTIAN LIVING

ADULT/GENERAL
AGAIN—R
Alive!—R
alive now!
And He Will Give
America
American Tract Soc.—R
American Wasteland
Angels on Earth
Annals of St. Anne
Arkansas Catholic
Arlington Catholic
Banner
B.C. Catholic—R
Beacon—R
Bible Advocate—R
Bread of Life—R
Breakthrough Intercessor—R
Bridal Guides—R
Canada Lutheran—R
Catholic Forester—R
Catholic New Times—R
Catholic New York

Catholic Parent
Catholic Sentinel—R
CGA World—R
Charisma/Christian Life
Christian Century
Christian Courier (WI)—R
Christian Crafter—R
Christian Designer—R
Christian Home & School
Christian Leader—R
Christian Living—R
Christian Motorsports
Christian Observer
Christian Parenting—R
Christian Ranchman
Christian Social Action—R
Christian Standard—R
Christianity Online—R
Christianity Today—R
Church Advocate—R
Church Herald/Holiness—R
Church of God EVANGEL
Commonweal
Companion
Companions—R
Connecting Point—R
Conquest
Covenant Companion—R
Crossway/Newsline—R
Culture Wars—R
Decision
Discipleship Journal
Dunamis Life—R
Evangel—R
Evangelical Advocate—R
Faith Today
Family Digest
Fellowship Focus—R
Fellowship Link—R
Focus on the Family
Forefront—R
Foursquare World—R
Gem—R
God Allows U-Turns—R
God's Revivalist
Good News—R
Good News, Etc.—R
Good News Journal (MO)—R
Good News Journal (TX)
Good Shepherd
Gospel Today
Gospel Tract—R
Grit
Guideposts
Heartlight Internet—R
Highway News—R
HomeLife—R
Home Times—R

Hunted News
Impact Magazine—R
Indian Life—R
Inland NW Christian
Inspirer—R
Jewel Among Jewels—R
John Milton—R
Jour/Christian Nursing—R
Keys to Living—R
Leaves—R
Legions of Light—R
Life Gate—R
Lifeglow—R
LifeWise
Light and Life
Liguorian
Live—R
Living—R
Living Church
Living Light News—R
Lookout—R
Lutheran—R
Lutheran Digest—R
Lutheran Journal—R
Lutheran Witness
Marian Helpers—R
Marriage Partnership
Mature Years—R
Mennonite—R
Mennonite Brethren—R
Men of Integrity—R
MESSAGE
MESSAGE/Open Bible—R
Messenger/St. Anthony
Messenger of the Sacred Heart
Methodist History
Metro Voice—R
Michigan Christian
Montana Catholic—R
Moody—R
Nashville Christian—R
Ncubator.com—R
New Covenant
New Freeman—R
New Heart—R
North American Voice
Northwestern Lutheran—R
Now What?—R
NRB Magazine—R
Oblates
On Mission
Our Family—R
Our Sunday Visitor
Parent Paper—R
Pentecostal Evangel
Peoples Magazine—R
Physician—R
Plain Truth—R

Plus—R
Pourastan—R
Power for Living—R
PrayerWorks—R
Presbyterian Layman
Presbyterian Record—R
Presbyterians Today—R
Progress—R
Psychology for Living—R
Purpose—R
SCP Journal—R
Seek—R
Signs of the Times—R
Single-Parent Family
Smart Families
Social Justice
Spirit—R
Spiritual Life
Sports Spectrum
Standard—R
Standard, The—R
Stepping Out
TEAK Roundup—R
Testimony—R
thegoodsteward.com—R
Time of Singing—R
Times of Refreshing
Today's Christian Senior—R
Together—R
Tomorrow's Christian
   Graduate
Touchstone—R
Trumpeter—R
United Church Observer—R
U.S. Catholic
Upsouth—R
Vibrant Life—R
Vision, The—R
War Cry—R
Way of St. Francis—R
Wesleyan Advocate—R

CHILDREN
BREAD/God's Children—R
Club Connection—R
Courage
Discoveries—R
Discovery (NY)—R
Discovery Trails—R
High Adventure—R
J.A.M.—R
My Friend
Partners—R
Pockets—R
Touch—R
Wonder Time

CHRISTIAN EDUCATION/
LIBRARY
Brigade Leader—R
Children's Ministry
Church & Synagogue Lib.
Church Educator—R
GROUP
Leader/Church School
   Today—R
Preschool Playhouse
Religion Teacher's Journal
Resource—R
Shining Star
Signal—R
Teacher's Interaction

MISSIONS
American Horizon—R
Latin America Evangelist
Worldwide Challenge

PASTORS/LEADERS
African American Pulpit
Angelos—R
Catholic Servant
Cell Group—R
Christian Camp—R
Christian Management—R
Emmanuel
Eucharistic Minister—R
Evangelical Baptist—R
Evangelicals Today—R
Five Stones—R
Growing Churches
Journal/Christian Healing—R
Let's Worship
Lutheran Partners—R
Minister's Family
Pastoral Life—R
Preacher's Illus. Service—R
Pulpit Helps—R
Quarterly Review
Reaching Children at Risk
Resource—R
Review for Religious
Sharing the Practice—R
Today's Christian Preacher—
   R
Word & World

TEEN/YOUNG ADULT
Boundless Webzine—R
Certainty
Challenge
Conqueror—R
Devo'Zine—R
Encounter—R
Essential Connection—R

J.A.M.—R
Passageway.org—R
Real Time—R
Student Leadership—R
Teens on Target—R
Today's Christian Teen—R
WITH—R
YOU!—R
Young Adult Today
Young Salvationist—R
Youth Challenge—R

WOMEN

Christian Bride
Connection
Esprit—R
Excellence
Godly Business Woman
Handmaiden—R
Hearts at Home—R
Helping Hand—R
Journey—R
Joyful Woman—R
Just Between Us—R
Link & Visitor—R
Lutheran Woman Today
Lutheran Woman's Quar.
Proverbs 31 Woman—R
SpiritLed Woman
True Woman
Wesleyan Woman—R
Woman's Touch—R
Women of Spirit—R
Women Who Minister—R

WRITERS

Areopagus (UK)

CHURCH GROWTH

ADULT/GENERAL

AGAIN—R
Banner
Bible Advocate—R
Breakthrough Intercessor—R
CGA World—R
Charisma/Christian Life
Christian Leader—R
Christian Motorsports
Christianity Today—R
Church Herald/Holiness—R
Church of God EVANGEL
Connection Mag.—R
Covenant Companion—R
Culture Wars—R
Evangel—R
Evangelical Advocate—R
Faith Today

Fellowship Focus—R
Fellowship Link—R
Gem—R
Good News (KY)—R
Good News, Etc.—R
Gospel Today
Indian Life—R
Inside Journal—R
Interchange
John Milton—R
LifeWise
Liguorian
Living Church
Lutheran Journal—R
Mennonite—R
Messenger/St. Anthony
Messenger of the Sacred Heart
Michigan Christian
Montana Catholic—R
Ncubator.com—R
New Freeman—R
On Mission
Peoples Magazine—R
Presbyterian Layman
Presbyterian Outlook
Presbyterian Record—R
Preserving Christian Homes—
   R
Reflections
Re:generation
Star of Zion
Trumpeter—R
Upsouth—R

*CHRISTIAN EDUCATION/
LIBRARY*

Children's Ministry
Church & Synagogue Lib.
Leader/Church School
   Today—R
Resource—R

MISSIONS

Latin America Evangelist
Missiology
P.I.M.E. World
World Christian—R
World Pulse—R
Worldwide Challenge
Youth & CE Leadership—R

PASTORS/LEADERS

African American Pulpit
Catholic Servant
Church Growth Network—R
Clergy Journal—R
Creator—R
Emmanuel

Enrichment—R
Eucharistic Minister—R
Evangelical Baptist—R
Evangelicals Today—R
Five Stones—R
Growing Churches
Horizons—R
Jour/Amer Soc/Chur
   Growth —R
Let's Worship
Lutheran Forum—R
Lutheran Partners—R
Ministries Today
Ministry
Ministry & Liturgy—R
Pastoral Life—R
Pulpit Helps—R
Resource—R
Rev.
Sermon Notes
Sharing the Practice—R
Technologies/Worship—R
Theology Today
WCA News—R
Worship Leader
Your Church—R

TEEN/YOUNG ADULT

Essential Connection—R

WOMEN

Connection
Esprit—R
Just Between Us—R
Wesleyan Woman—R
Women Who Minister—R

WRITERS

Areopagus (UK)

CHURCH LIFE

ADULT/GENERAL

AGAIN—R
Arkansas Catholic
Banner
Bible Advocate—R
Breakthrough Intercessor—R
CGA World—R
Christian Designer—R
Christian Leader—R
Christian Living—R
Christian Motorsports
Christian News NW—R
Christian Reader—R
Church Herald/Holiness—R
Church of God EVANGEL
Columbia

Companion
Company—R
Conquest
Covenant Companion—R
Decision
Discipleship Journal
Dunamis Life—R
Evangel—R
Evangelical Advocate—R
Faith Today
Family Digest
Fellowship Focus—R
Gem—R
Good News (KY)—R
Good News, Etc.—R
Gospel Today
John Milton—R
Leaves—R
LifeWise
Liguorian
Living Church
Lookout—R
Lutheran Journal—R
Mennonite—R
Messenger/St. Anthony
Michigan Christian
Montana Catholic—R
Moody—R
Ncubator.com—R
New Freeman—R
New Writing—R
North American Voice
On Mission
Our Family—R
Peoples Magazine—R
Presbyterian Outlook
Presbyterian Record—R
Reflections
Re:generation
St. Willibrord Journal
Signs of the Times—R
Star of Zion
Storyteller—R
Times of Refreshing
Today's Christian Senior—R
Upsouth—R
Vision—R
Way of St. Francis—R

CHILDREN

Discovery (NY)—R

CHRISTIAN EDUCATION/
LIBRARY
Children's Ministry
Church Educator—R
GROUP
Youth & CE Leadership—R

MISSIONS
Catholic Near East
Latin America Evangelist

PASTORS/LEADERS
African American Pulpit
Angelos—R
Catholic Servant
Cell Group—R
Christian Ministry
Clergy Journal—R
Enrichment—R
Eucharistic Minister—R
Evangelical Baptist—R
Evangelicals Today—R
Five Stones—R
Growing Churches
Horizons—R
Leadership—R
Let's Worship
Lutheran Partners—R
Minister's Family
Ministry
Ministry & Liturgy—R
Pastoral Life—R
Pulpit Helps—R
Quarterly Review
Resource—R
Rev.
Review for Religious
Sabbath School Leadership
Sharing the Practice—R
Technologies/Worship—R
Theology Today
WCA News—R
Worship Leader

TEEN/YOUNG ADULT
Conqueror—R
Encounter—R
YOU!—R

WOMEN
Esprit—R
Horizons—R
Lutheran Woman Today
SpiritLed Woman
Wesleyan Woman—R
Women Who Minister—R

WRITERS
Areopagus (UK)

CHURCH MANAGEMENT

ADULT/GENERAL
Banner
Biblical Reflections—R

Breakthrough Intercessor—R
CGA World—R
Christian Computing (MO)—R
Christian Crafter—R
Christian Designer—R
Christian Leader—R
Christian News NW—R
Church Herald/Holiness—R
Church of God EVANGEL
Covenant Companion—R
Culture Wars—R
Disciple's Journal—R
Evangelical Advocate—R
Expression Christian
Faith Today
Fellowship Focus—R
Gem—R
Good News, Etc—R
Gospel Today
Joyful Noise
Living Church
Lutheran Digest—R
Lutheran Journal—R
Metro Voice—R
Michigan Christian
Ncubator.com—R
New Freeman—R
Our Sunday Visitor
Presbyterian Layman
Presbyterian Outlook
Presbyterian Record—R
Reflections
Signs of the Times—R
Star of Zion
thegoodsteward.com—R
Trumpeter—R
U.S. Catholic
Wesleyan Advocate—R

CHRISTIAN EDUCATION/
LIBRARY
Children's Ministry
Church Educator—R
Resource—R

PASTORS/LEADERS
African American Pulpit
Catholic Servant
Celebration
Christian Management—R
Christian Ministry
Church Growth Network—R
Clergy Journal—R
Enrichment—R
Evangelical Baptist—R
Evangelicals Today—R
Five Stones—R
Horizons—R

Jour/Amer Soc/Chur Growth—R
Leadership—R
Lutheran Forum—R
Lutheran Partners—R
Ministries Today
Ministry
Pastoral Life—R
Priest
Pulpit Helps—R
Quarterly Review
Resource—R
Rev.
Sharing the Practice—R
Technologies/Worship—R
Theology Today
WCA News—R
Word & World
Worship Leader
Your Church—R
Youthworker

WOMEN
Just Between Us—R
Women Who Minister—R

CHURCH OUTREACH

ADULT/GENERAL
AGAIN—R
Alive!—R
America
And He Will Give
Arkansas Catholic
Banner
Beacon—R
Bible Advocate—R
Breakthrough Intercessor—R
Cathedral Age
Catholic Digest—R
Catholic Forester—R
Catholic Sentinel—R
CGA World—R
Charisma/Christian Life
Christian Leader—R
Christian Motorsports
Christian Reader—R
Church Herald/Holiness—R
Church of God EVANGEL
Columbia
Companion
Companions—R
Company—R
Conquest
Connection Mag.—R
Covenant Companion—R
Culture Wars—R
Decision

Dunamis Life—R
Episcopal Life—R
Evangel—R
Evangelical Advocate—R
Faith Today
Fellowship Focus—R
Gem—R
God's Revivalist
Good News (KY)—R
Good News, Etc.—R
Inspirer—R
John Milton—R
LifeWise
Liguorian
Living Church
Lookout—R
Lutheran—R
Lutheran Digest—R
Lutheran Journal—R
Lutheran Witness
Mennonite—R
Metro Voice—R
Michigan Christian
Moody—R
Nashville Christian—R
Ncubator.com—R
New Covenant
North American Voice
Northwestern Lutheran—R
On Mission
Our Family—R
Our Sunday Visitor
Peoples Magazine—R
Plain Truth—R
Presbyterian Layman
Presbyterian Outlook
Presbyterian Record—R
Presbyterians Today—R
Prism—R
Purpose—R
Reflections
Re:generation
St. Joseph's Messenger—R
SCP Journal—R
Social Justice
U.S. Catholic
Vision—R
Wesleyan Advocate—R

CHILDREN
Discovery (NY)—R
Focus/Clubhouse
J.A.M.—R
Kids' Ministry Ideas—R
Live Wire—R

CHRISTIAN EDUCATION/LIBRARY
Caravan

CE Counselor—R
Children's Ministry
Church Educator—R
GROUP
Journal/Adventist Educ.—R
Leader/Church School
   Today—R
Perspective—R
Religion Teacher's Journal
Resource—R
Signal—R
Youth & CE Leadership—R

MISSIONS
American Horizon—R
East-West Church
Evangelical Missions—R
Latin America Evangelist
World Christian—R
World Pulse—R
Worldwide Challenge

PASTORS/LEADERS
African American Pulpit
Angelos—R
Catholic Servant
Cell Group—R
Christian Management—R
Christian Ministry
Church Administration
Church Growth Network—R
Clergy Journal—R
Enrichment—R
Eucharistic Minister—R
Evangelical Baptist—R
Evangelicals Today—R
Five Stones—R
Growing Churches
Horizons—R
Jour/Amer Soc/Chur Growth—R
Leadership—R
Let's Worship
Lutheran Forum—R
Lutheran Partners—R
Ministries Today
Ministry
Ministry & Liturgy—R
Pastoral Life—R
Priest
Pulpit Helps—R
Quarterly Review
Resource—R
Rev.
Sharing the Practice—R
Technologies/Worship—R
Theology Today
Today's Parish
WCA News—R

Word & World
Worship Leader
Your Church—R

TEEN/YOUNG ADULT
Conqueror—R
J.A.M.—R
WITH—R
Young Adult Today

WOMEN
ChurchWoman
Connection
Esprit—R
Just Between Us—R
SpiritLed Woman
Wesleyan Woman—R
Women Who Minister—R

CHURCH TRADITIONS

ADULT/GENERAL
AGAIN—R
Breakthrough Intercessor—
    R
Bridal Guides—R
Canada Lutheran—R
Catholic Forester—R
Christian Courier (CAN)—
    R
Christian Crafter—R
Christian Designer—R
Christian Leader—R
Christian Renewal—R
Christian Research
Columbia
Company—R
Covenant Companion—R
Decision
Evangelical Advocate—R
Faith Today
Family Digest
Forefront—R
Gem—R
Indian Life—R
John Milton—R
Legions of Light—R
Light and Life
Lifeglow—R
Liguorian
Living Church
Mennonite—R
Messenger/St. Anthony
Montana Catholic—R
Nashville Christian—R
New Freeman—R
Parabola—R
Presbyterian Outlook

Presbyterian Record—R
Sacred Journey—R
St. Willibrord Journal
Seeds
Stepping Out
Storyteller—R
Testimony—R
Together—R
Way of St. Francis—R

CHILDREN
Celebrate
Discovery (NY)—R

MISSIONS
Latin America Evangelist

MUSIC
Tradition

PASTORS/LEADERS
African American Pulpit
Eucharistic Minister—R
Evangelical Baptist—R
Evangelicals Today—R
Five Stones—R
Journal/Christian Healing—R
Lutheran Partners—R
Pastoral Life—R
Priest
Quarterly Review
Resource—R
Sharing the Practice—R

TEEN/YOUNG ADULT
Conqueror—R
YOU!—R
Young & Alive—R

WOMEN
Esprit—R
Handmaiden—R
Lutheran Woman Today
SpiritLed Woman

WRITERS
Areopagus (UK)

CONTROVERSIAL ISSUES

ADULT/GENERAL
Accent on Living—R
AGAIN—R
American Tract Soc.—R
American Wasteland
Bible Advocate—R
Bridal Guides—R
Bridge—R

Catholic Insight
Catholic New Times—R
CGA World—R
Charisma/Christian Life
Christian Century
Christian Courier (CAN)—R
Christian Living—R
Christian Media—R
Christian Motorsports
Christian Parenting—R
Christian Reader—R
Christian Renewal—R
Christian Research
Christian Response—R
Christian Social Action—R
Christian Times
Christianity Online—R
Christianity Today—R
Church Advocate—R
Church of God EVANGEL
Colorado Christian—R
Commonweal
Connection Mag.—R
Cornerstone—R
Covenant Companion—R
Creation Ex Nihilo
Cresset
Culture Wars—R
Discipleship Journal
Discovery (FL)—R
Door
Dovetail—R
Evangelical Advocate—R
Expression Christian
Faith Today
God Allows U-Turns—R
Good News (KY)—R
Good News, Etc.—R
Good News Journal (MO)—
    R
Highway News—R
Home Times—R
Hunted News
Interim—R
John Milton—R
Jour/Christian Nursing—R
Joyful Noise
Legions of Light—R
Life@Work
Light and Life
Living Church
Lutheran—R
MESSAGE (limited)
Messenger/St. Anthony
Metro Voice—R
Michigan Christian
Minnesota Christian—R
Moody—R

MovieGuide
Nashville Christian—R
New Freeman—R
Newsline—R
New Writing—R
Now What?—R
NRB Magazine—R
Our Family—R
Perspectives
Plain Truth—R
Prairie Messenger—R
Presbyterian Layman
Presbyterian Outlook
Presbyterian Record—R
Presbyterians Today—R
Prism—R
Psychology for Living—R
Re:generation
Sacred Journey—R
SCP Journal—R
Seek—R
Social Justice
Standard, The—R
TEAK Roundup—R
Testimony—R
Upsouth—R
U.S. Catholic
War Cry—R
Wesleyan Advocate—R
Winsome Wit—R

CHILDREN
Discovery (NY)—R
Guideposts for Kids
J.A.M.—R

CHRISTIAN EDUCATION/LIBRARY
CE Counselor—R
Children's Ministry
Church Educator—R
Signal—R
Today's Catholic Teacher—R

MISSIONS
American Horizon—R
Intl. Journal/Frontier—R
Latin America Evangelist
So All May Hear—R
Worldwide Challenge

PASTORS/LEADERS
Angelos—R
Christian Century
Christian Ministry
Eucharistic Minister—R
Journal/Pastoral Care
Lutheran Forum—R
Lutheran Partners—R

Ministries Today
Ministry & Liturgy—R
Pulpit Helps—R
Reaching Children at Risk
Resource—R
Rev.
Single Adult Ministries
Word & World
Worship Leader
Youthworker

TEEN/YOUNG ADULT
Boundless Webzine—R
Brio
Essential Connection—R
Insight—R
J.A.M.—R
Passageway.org—R
Student Leadership—R
WITH—R
YOU!—R
Young Adult Today
Young Salvationist—R

WOMEN
Canticle
ChurchWoman
Conscience—R
Esprit—R
Godly Business Woman
Horizons—R
SpiritLed Woman
Today's Christian Woman
Women of Spirit—R

WRITERS
Areopagus (UK)
WIN-Informer

CREATION SCIENCE

ADULT/GENERAL
Banner
Bible Advocate—R
Christian Observer
Christian Research
Christian Renewal—R
Christian Social Action—R
Chrysalis Reader
Colorado Christian—R
Companions—R
Conquest
Cornerstone—R
Creation Ex Nihilo
Discovery (FL)—R
Evangelical Advocate—R
Faith Today
Good News Journal (TX)

Gospel Today
Homeschooling Today—R
Legions of Light—R
Lifeglow—R
Live—R
Living—R
Lutheran Witness
MovieGuide
Ncubator.com—R
Plain Truth—R
PrayerWorks—R
Standard—R
Upsouth—R
War Cry—R

CHILDREN
Courage
Focus/Clubhouse
J.A.M.—R
Nature Friend—R
Partners—R
Primary Pal (IL)

CHRISTIAN EDUCATION/LIBRARY
Journal/Adventist Educ.—R
Vision—R

PASTORS/LEADERS
Christian Camp—R
Cross Currents—R
Pulpit Helps—R

TEEN/YOUNG ADULT
Boundless Webzine—R
Certainty
Challenge
Conqueror—R
Encounter—R
Essential Connection—R
J.A.M.—R
Teens on Target—R
YOU!—R
Young & Alive—R
Youth Challenge—R

WOMEN
Godly Business Woman

CULTS/OCCULT

ADULT/GENERAL
America
American Tract Soc.—R
Banner
Bible Advocate—R
Charisma/Christian Life
Christian Parenting—R
Christian Ranchman

Christian Renewal—R
Christian Research
Church Advocate—R
Church of God EVANGEL
Colorado Christian—R
Companions—R
Conquest
Cornerstone—R
Culture Wars—R
Discovery (FL)—R
Evangelical Advocate—R
God's Revivalist
Good News, Etc—R
Healing Inn—R
Hunted News
Jour/Christian Nursing—R
Latin America Evangelist
Legions of Light—R
Light and Life
Lutheran Witness
Metro Voice—R
Michigan Christian
Minnesota Christian—R
New Heart—R
New Writing—R
Now What?—R
Our Sunday Visitor
Plain Truth—R
SCP Journal—R
Social Justice
Standard, The—R

CHRISTIAN EDUCATION/
LIBRARY
Children's Ministry
Team—R

MISSIONS
American Horizon—R
Areopagus—R
East-West Church
Intl. Journal/Frontier—R
World Christian—R
World Pulse—R

PASTORS/LEADERS
Journal/Christian Healing—
    R
Journal/Pastoral Care
Ministries Today
Word & World

TEEN/YOUNG ADULT
Brio
Certainty
Encounter—R
Essential Connection—R
J.A.M.—R

Teenage Christian—R
Teens on Target—R
YOU!—R
Young Adult Today
Youth Challenge—R

WOMEN
SpiritLed Woman

CURRENT/SOCIAL ISSUES

ADULT/GENERAL
About Such Things—R
Accent on Living—R
Alive!—R
America
American Tract Soc.—R
American Wasteland
Anglican Journal—R
Arlington Catholic
Banner
B.C. Catholic—R
Bible Advocate—R
Bridge—R
Catholic Faith & Family
Catholic Insight
Catholic New Times—R
Catholic New York
Catholic Sentinel—R
Celebrate Life—R
CGA World—R
Charisma/Christian Life
Christian Courier (WI)—R
Christian Courier (CAN)—R
Christian Home & School
Christian Leader—R
Christian Living—R
Christian Motorsports
Christian News NW—R
Christian Observer
Christian Parenting—R
Christian Ranchman
Christian Reader—R
Christian Renewal—R
Christian Social Action—R
Christian Standard—R
Christianity Online—R
Christianity Today—R
Chrysalis Reader
Church Advocate—R
Church & State—R
Church of God EVANGEL
Colorado Christian—R
Columbia
Commonweal
Company—R
Compleat Nurse—R
Connection Mag.—R

Cornerstone—R
Covenant Companion—R
Creation Ex Nihilo
Cresset
Culture Wars—R
Discipleship Journal
Discovery(FL)—R
Door
Dovetail—R
Evangel—R
Evangelical Advocate—R
Faith Today
Fellowship Link—R
First Things
Focus on the Family
Foursquare World—R
Gem—R
God Allows U-Turns—R
Good News (KY)—R
Good News, Etc.—R
Good News Journal (MO)—R
Good News Journal (TX)
Grit
Heartlight Internet—R
Hidden Manna—R
Highway News—R
HomeLife—R
Homeschooling Today—R
Home Times—R
Hunted News
Impact Magazine—R
Indian Life—R
Inland NW Christian
Interim—R
Jewel Among Jewels—R
John Milton—R
Journal of Church & State
Legions of Light—R
Liberty—R
Life Gate—R
Light and Life
Living—R
Lookout—R
Lutheran—R
Lutheran Journal—R
Lutheran Witness
Marian Helpers Bulletin
Mennonite—R
Mennonite Brethren—R
MESSAGE
MESSAGE/Open Bible—R
Messenger/St. Anthony
Metro Voice—R
Michigan Christian
Minnesota Christian—R
Moody—R
Nashville Christian—R
Ncubator.com—R

New Covenant
New Heart—R
New Writing—R
North American Voice
Northwestern Lutheran—R
Now What?—R
NRB Magazine—R
Our Family—R
Our Sunday Visitor
Parent Paper—R
Pentecostal Evangel
Peoples Magazine—R
Perspectives
Plain Truth—R
PrayerWorks—R
Presbyterian Layman
Presbyterian Outlook
Presbyterian Record—R
Presbyterians Today—R
Prism—R
Psychology for Living—R
Purpose—R
Quest
Quiet Revolution—R
Re:generation
St. Joseph's Messenger—R
SCP Journal—R
Seeds
Signs of the Times—R
Social Justice
Sojourners
Standard, The—R
Stepping Out
Testimony—R
Together—R
2-Soar
Upsouth—R
War Cry—R
Way of St. Francis—R
Wesleyan Advocate—R
Winsome Wit—R

CHILDREN
American Girl
Club Connection—R
Discovery Trails—R
God's World News—R
Guideposts for Kids
J.A.M.—R
Skipping Stones
Winner—R

CHRISTIAN EDUCATION/
LIBRARY
Brigade Leader—R
Catechist
Children's Ministry
Christian Classroom

Christian School Admin.
Church Educator—R
Signal—R
Team—R
Today's Catholic Teacher—R

MISSIONS
American Horizon—R
Areopagus—R
East-West Church
Hope for Children—R
Latin America Evangelist
New World Outlook
Women of the Harvest
World Christian—R
Worldwide Challenge

MUSIC
CCM Magazine

PASTORS/LEADERS
African American Pulpit
Catholic Servant
Christian Camp—R
Christian Century
Christian Ministry
Cross Currents—R
Eucharistic Minister—R
Evangelical Baptist—R
Evangelicals Today—R
Growing Churches
Ivy Jungle Report—R
Journal/Christian Healing—R
Journal/Pastoral Care
Lutheran Forum—R
Lutheran Partners—R
Ministries Today
Pastoral Life—R
Priest
Quarterly Review
Reaching Children at Risk
Resource—R
Rev.
Sharing the Practice—R
Single Adult Ministries
WCA News—R
Word & World
Youthworker

TEEN/YOUNG ADULT
Boundless Webzine—R
Brio
Conqueror—R
Devo'Zine—R
Encounter—R
Essential Connection—R
J.A.M.—R
Passageway.org—R

Real Time—R
Teenage Christian—R
Teens on Target—R
Today's Christian Teen—R
WITH—R
YOU!—R
Young Adult Today
Young Salvationist—R
Youth Challenge—R

WOMEN
Canticle
ChurchWoman
Conscience—R
Esprit—R
Excellence
Godly Business Woman
Helping Hand—R
Horizons—R
Jour/Women's Ministries
Journey—R
Link & Visitor—R
Lutheran Woman Today
SpiritLed Woman
Today's Christian Woman
Woman Alive
Woman's Touch—R
Women of Spirit—R

WRITERS
Areopagus (UK)
Writer

DEATH/DYING

ADULT/GENERAL
AGAIN—R
Alive!—R
American Tract Soc.—R
American Wasteland
Arlington Catholic
Banner
Bible Advocate—R
Biblical Reflections—R
Breakthrough Intercessor—
R
Bridge—R
Catholic New Times—R
Celebrate Life—R
CGA World—R
Christian Courier (CAN)—R
Christian Leader—R
Christian Living—R
Christian Parenting—R
Christian Social Action—R
Christianity Today—R
Church Herald/Holiness—R
Colorado Christian—R

Columbia
Companions—R
Compleat Nurse—R
Cornerstone—R
Covenant Companion—R
Creation Ex Nihilo
Discipleship Journal
Evangel—R
Evangelical Advocate—R
Family Digest
Fellowship Link—R
Gem—R
God Allows U-Turns—R
Guideposts
Healing Inn—R
Heartlight Internet—R
HomeLife—R
Interim—R
John Milton—R
Jour/Christian Nursing—R
Legions of Light—R
LifeWise
Liguorian
Lutheran Journal—R
Lutheran Witness
Mature Living
Mature Years—R
Mennonite—R
MESSAGE
Messenger/St. Anthony
Messenger of the Sacred
   Heart
Michigan Christian
Montana Catholic—R
Ncubator.com—R
New Heart—R
New Writing—R
Now What?—R
Pentecostal Evangel
Peoples Magazine—R
Physician—R
Plain Truth—R
Presbyterian Outlook
Presbyterian Record—R
Prism—R
Psychology for Living—R
Re:generation
Sacred Journey—R
Signs of the Times—R
Social Justice
Spirit—R
Star of Zion
Stepping Out
Testimony—R
Today's Christian Senior—R
Upsouth—R
War Cry—R
Way of St. Francis—R

CHILDREN
J.A.M.—R
Skipping Stones

CHRISTIAN EDUCATION/LIBRARY
Church Educator—R
Leader/Church School
   Today—R

PASTORS/LEADERS
Catholic Servant
Celebration
Christian Ministry
Eucharistic Minister—R
Journal/Christian Healing—R
Journal/Pastoral Care
Lutheran Partners—R
Pastoral Life—R
Priest
Pulpit Helps—R
Sharing the Practice—R
Today's Christian Preacher—R

TEEN/YOUNG ADULT
Devo'Zine—R
Encounter—R
Essential Connection—R
J.A.M.—R
WITH—R
YOU!—R
Young Salvationist—R

WOMEN
Esprit—R
Godly Business Woman
Helping Hand—R
Horizons—R
Lutheran Woman Today
Reflections (FL)
Women of Spirit—R

WRITERS
Cochran's Corner—R

DEVOTIONALS/ MEDITATIONS

ADULT/GENERAL
alive now!
And He Will Give
Annals of St. Anne
Arlington Catholic
Banner
Breakthrough Intercessor—R
Bridal Guides—R
Charisma/Christian Life
Christian Century
Christian Motorsports

Christian Reader—R
Christianity Today—R
Church Herald/Holiness—R
Companion
Companions—R
Company—R
Conquest (meditations)
Covenant Companion—R
Creation Care—R
Decision
Dunamis Life—R
Eternal Ink—R
Evangel—R
Evangelical Advocate—R
Fellowship Link—R
Foursquare World—R
Gem—R
God's Revivalist
Good News (KY)—R
Good News Journal (MO)—R
Good News Journal (TX)
Gospel Tract—R
Grit
Healing Inn—R
Heartlight Internet—R
Highway News—R
Ideals—R
Inspirer—R
Jewel Among Jewels—R
John Milton—R
Karitos Review—R
Keys to Living—R
Leaves—R
Legions of Light—R
Life Gate—R
Liguorian
Living Church
Lutheran Journal—R
Lutheran Witness
Mature Years—R
Mennonite Brethren—R
Men of Integrity—R
MESSAGE/Open Bible—R
Messenger/Sacred Heart
Messenger/St. Anthony
Metro Voice—R
New Covenant
New Heart—R
North American Voice
Northwestern Lutheran—R
Our Sunday Visitor
Parenting Our Parents—R
Pentecostal Evangel
Peoples Magazine—R
Perspectives
Plowman—R
Pourastan—R
PrayerWorks—R

Presbyterian Outlook
Presbyterian Record—R
Presbyterians Today—R
Preserving Christian Homes—R
Prism—R
Progress—R (meditations)
Sacred Journey—R
St. Willibrord Journal
Seeds
Selah!Kids
Signs of the Times—R
Silver Wings—R
Sojourners
Spirit—R
Standard—R
Star of Zion
Stepping Out
Testimony—R
Today's Christian Senior—R
Together—R
Upsouth—R
U.S. Catholic
Vision—R
War Cry—R
Way of St. Francis—R

CHILDREN
Club Connection—R
Courage
Discovery (NY)—R
High Adventure—R
Keys for Kids—R
Partners—R
Pockets—R
Primary Pal (IL)

CHRISTIAN EDUCATION/ LIBRARY
Children's Ministry
Church & Synagogue Lib.
Church Educator—R
GROUP
Leader/Church School Today—R
Religion Teacher's Journal
Shining Star
Teacher's Interaction
Today's Catholic Teacher—R

DAILY DEVOTIONAL
(See alphabetical list)

MISSIONS
Areopagus—R
So All May Hear—R
Women of the Harvest

PASTORS/LEADERS
Catholic Servant
Christian Century
Church Worship
Emmanuel
Evangelical Baptist—R
Evangelicals Today—R
Five Stones—R
Growing Churches
Journal/Pastoral Care
Let's Worship
Minister's Family
Pastoral Life—R
Priest
Pulpit Helps—R
Reaching Children at Risk
Sharing the Practice—R

TEEN/YOUNG ADULT
Breakaway—R
Brio
Certainty
Challenge
Conqueror—R
Cross Walk
Devo'Zine—R
Passageway.org—R
Teens on Target—R
Today's Christian Teen—R
WITH—R
Young Adult Today
Young Salvationist—R
Youth Challenge—R

WOMEN
Christian Bride
Connection
Godly Business Woman
Helping Hand—R
Horizons—R
Jour/Women's Ministries
Joyful Woman—R
Lutheran Woman Today
Woman's Touch—R
Women of Spirit—R
Women Who Minister—R

WRITERS
Areopagus (UK)
Cross & Quill—R
Fellowscript—R

DISCIPLESHIP

ADULT/GENERAL
Arlington Catholic
Banner
Bible Advocate—R

Bread of Life—R
Breakthrough Intercessor—R
Canada Lutheran—R
Charisma/Christian Life
Christian Century
Christian Leader—R
Christian Living—R
Christian Motorsports
Christian Parenting—R
Christian Ranchman
Christian Reader—R
Christianity Today—R
Church Herald/Holiness—R
Church of God EVANGEL
Columbia
Companion
Conquest
Covenant Companion—R
Creation Care—R
Cresset
Decision
Discipleship Journal
Dunamis Life—R
Evangel—R
Evangelical Advocate—R
Faith Today
Fellowship Focus—R
Focus on the Family
Gem—R
God Allows U-Turns—R
Good News (KY)—R
Good News, Etc.—R
Good News Journal (MO)—R
Good News Journal (TX)
Heartlight Internet—R
Highway News—R
Indian Life—R
Inland NW Christian
Inspirer—R
John Milton—R
Life Gate—R
LifeWise
Light and Life
Liguorian
Lookout—R
Lutheran Journal—R
Lutheran Witness
Mennonite—R
Men of Integrity—R
Messenger/St. Anthony
Metro Voice—R
Michigan Christian
Moody—R
Ncubator.com—R
New Covenant
North American Voice
Our Family—R
Peoples Magazine—R

Plain Truth—R
PrayerWorks—R
Presbyterian Layman
Presbyterian Outlook
Presbyterian Record—R
Prism—R
Purpose—R
Re:generation
Reflections
St. Joseph's Messenger—R
Signs of the Times—R
Silver Wings—R
Sojourners
Standard, The—R
Stepping Out
Testimony—R
thegoodsteward.com—R
Times of Refreshing
Together—R
Tomorrow's Christian
   Graduate
Touchstone—R
Trumpeter—R
Upsouth—R
U.S. Catholic
War Cry—R
Way of St. Francis—R
Wesleyan Advocate—R

CHILDREN
BREAD/God's Children—R
Club Connection—R
Courage
Evangelizing Today's Child—
   R.
J.A.M.—R

CHRISTIAN EDUCATION/LIBRARY
Brigade Leader—R
Caravan
CE Counselor—R
Children's Ministry
Christian School
Christian School Admin.
Church Educator—R
Evangelizing Today's Child—
   R
GROUP
Leader/Church School
   Today—R
Signal—R
Teacher's Interaction
Team—R
Youth & CE Leadership—R

MISSIONS
American Horizon—R
Latin America Evangelist

Worldwide Challenge

PASTORS/LEADERS
Angelos—R
Catholic Servant
Cell Group—R
Christian Camp—R
Christian Century
Christian Management—R
Christian Ministry
Emmanuel
Eucharistic Minister—R
Evangelical Baptist—R
Evangelicals Today—R
Five Stones—R
Growing Churches
Horizons—R
Ivy Jungle Report—R
Journal/Christian Healing—R
Jour/Amer Soc/Chur Growth—
   R
Let's Worship
Lutheran Forum—R
Lutheran Partners—R
Ministries Today
Ministry
Ministry & Liturgy—R
Pastoral Life—R
Priest
PROCLAIM—R
Pulpit Helps—R
Quarterly Review
Reaching Children at Risk
Rev.
Review for Religious
Sharing the Practice—R
Today's Christian Preacher—R
Word & World
Youthworker

TEEN/YOUNG ADULT
Boundless Webzine—R
Certainty
Challenge
Conqueror—R
Encounter—R
Essential Connection—R
J.A.M.—R
Passageway.org—R
Real Time—R
Student Leadership—R
Teenage Christian—R
Teens on Target—R
Touch—R
WITH—R
YOU!—R
Young Salvationist—R
Youth Challenge—R

WOMEN
Christian Women Today—R
Connection
Esprit—R
Godly Business Woman
Helping Hand—R
Journey—R
Joyful Woman—R
Just Between Us—R
Link & Visitor—R
Lutheran Woman Today
Proverbs 31 Woman—R
SpiritLed Woman
Woman's Touch—R
Women of Spirit—R
Women Today—R
Women Who Minister—R

DIVORCE

ADULT/GENERAL
America
American Wasteland
Angels on Earth
Arlington Catholic
Banner
Bible Advocate—R
Breakthrough Intercessor—R
Catholic Digest—R
Charisma/Christian Life
Chicken Soup/Mother—R
Christian Courier (CAN)—R
Christian Home & School
Christian Living—R
Christian Motorsports
Christian Parenting—R
Christian Ranchman
Christian Social Action—R
Church of God EVANGEL
Colorado Christian—R
Creation Ex Nihilo
Culture Wars—R
Decision
Dovetail—R
Evangel—R
Evangelical Advocate—R
Expression Christian
Faith Today
Focus on the Family
Gem—R
God Allows U-Turns—R
Good News, Etc.—R
Good News Journal (MO)—R
Guideposts
Highway News—R
HomeLife—R
Home Times—R
Impact Magazine—R

Indian Life—R
Interim—R
LifeWise
Life Gate—R
Liguorian
Living—R
Living Church
Lutheran Journal—R
Mature Living
MESSAGE
Metro Voice—R
Michigan Christian
Minnesota Christian—R
Ncubator.com—R
New Covenant
New Heart—R
New Writing—R
Now What?—R
On Mission
Our Family—R
Parent Paper—R
Peoples Magazine—R
Physician—R
PrayerWorks—R
Presbyterian Outlook
Presbyterian Record—R
Presbyterians Today—R
Prism—R
Psychology for Living—R
Purpose—R
Single-Parent Family
Smart Families
Social Justice
Standard, The—R
Star of Zion
Stepping Out
Trumpeter—R
Upsouth—R
U.S. Catholic
War Cry—R

CHILDREN
American Girl
Discovery Trails—R
Guideposts for Kids

*CHRISTIAN EDUCATION/
LIBRARY*
Christian School Admin.
Leader/Church School
    Today—R

MISSIONS
Worldwide Challenge

PASTORS/LEADERS
Journal/Pastoral Care
Lutheran Partners—R

Ministries Today
Ministry
Pastoral Life—R
Priest
PROCLAIM—R
Pulpit Helps—R
Rev.
Sharing the Practice—R
Single Adult Ministries
Word & World

TEEN/YOUNG ADULT
Conqueror—R
Encounter—R
Essential Connection—R
Teenage Christian—R
Young Adult Today

WOMEN
Esprit—R
Godly Business Woman
Helping Hand—R
Journey—R
Joyful Woman—R
Reflections (FL)
SpiritLed Woman
Today's Christian Woman
Woman's Touch—R
Women of Spirit—R

WRITERS
Cochran's Corner—R

DOCTRINAL

ADULT/GENERAL
AGAIN—R
America
American Wasteland
Anglican Journal—R
Banner
B.C. Catholic—R
Bible Advocate—R
Breakthrough Intercessor—
    R
Catholic Insight
CGA World—R
Charisma/Christian Life
Christian Century
Christian Media—R
Christian Motorsports
Christian Research
Christianity Today—R
Church Herald/Holiness—R
Church of God EVANGEL
Columbia
Companions—R
Conquest

Cresset
Culture Wars—R
Evangelical Advocate—R
Fellowship Link—R
Gospel Today
John Milton—R
Light and Life
Liguorian
Mennonite—R
MESSAGE
Messenger/St. Anthony
Metro Voice—R
Montana Catholic—R
Ncubator.com—R
New Writing—R
North American Voice
Our Family—R
Our Sunday Visitor
Peoples Magazine—R
Perspectives
Plain Truth—R
PrayerWorks—R
Presbyterian Layman
Presbyterian Outlook
Presbyterian Record—R
Presbyterians Today—R
Queen of All Hearts
Re:generation
St. Anthony Messenger
St. Willibrord Journal
SCP Journal—R
Silver Wings—R
Social Justice
Star of Zion
Stepping Out
Testimony—R
This Rock
U.S. Catholic
Upsouth—R

CHILDREN
Discovery Trails—R

*CHRISTIAN EDUCATION/
LIBRARY*
Catechist
Shining Star
Teacher's Interaction

MISSION
Intl Jour/Frontier—R
Latin America Evangelist
Worldwide Challenge

PASTORS/LEADERS
Catholic Servant
Christian Century
Cross Currents—R

Emmanuel
Eucharistic Minister—R
Growing Churches
Horizons—R
Lutheran Partners—R
Ministries Today
Ministry
Pastoral Life—R
PROCLAIM—R
Pulpit Helps—R
Quarterly Review
Reaching Children at Risk
Resource—R
Sewanee Theological Review
Theology Today
Word & World
Worship Leader

TEEN/YOUNG ADULT
Certainty
Essential Connection—R
Student Leadership—R
Teenage Christian—R
YOU!—R
Young Adult Today

WOMEN
SpiritLed Woman

ECONOMICS

ADULT/GENERAL
America
American Wasteland
Banner
Catholic Faith & Family
Catholic New Times—R
CBA Marketplace
CGA World—R
Christian Century
Christian C.L. RECORD—R
Christian Courier (CAN)—R
Christian Motorsports
Christian Ranchman
Christian Renewal—R
Christianity Today—R
Compleat Nurse—R
Covenant Companion—R
Cresset
Culture Wars—R
Evangelical Advocate—R
Faith Today
First Things
Good News, Etc.—R
Home Times—R
Life@Work
Life Gate—R
LifeWise

Light and Life
Mennonite—R
Messenger/St. Anthony
Metro Voice—R
Michigan Christian
Minnesota Christian—R
MovieGuide
Nashville Christian—R
No-Debt Living—R
Our Sunday Visitor
Parent Paper—R
Perspectives
Prairie Messenger—R
Presbyterian Layman
Prism—R
Quiet Revolution—R
Re:generation
SCP Journal—R
Single-Parent Family
Social Justice
Sojourners
thegoodsteward.com—R
Today's Christian Senior—R
2-Soar
U.S. Catholic

*CHRISTIAN EDUCATION
/LIBRARY*
Christian School Admin.

PASTORS/LEADERS
Christian Century
Lutheran Partners—R
Pastoral Life—R
Reaching Children at Risk
Rev.
Technologies/Worship—R
Today's Christian Preacher—R
Today's Parish
Word & World
Your Church—R

TEEN/YOUNG ADULT
Young Adult Today

WOMEN
Esprit—R
Godly Business Woman
Helping Hand—R

ENVIRONMENTAL ISSUES

ADULT/GENERAL
American Wasteland
Anglican Journal—R
Banner
Bible Advocate—R
Catholic Faith & Family

Catholic Forester—R
Catholic New Times—R
Catholic Sentinel—R
CGA World—R
Christian Century
Christian Courier (CAN)—R
Christian Living—R
Christian Motorsports
Christian Social Action—R
Christianity Today—R
Chrysalis Reader
Commonweal
Companion
Covenant Companion—R
Creation Care—R
Cresset
Evangelical Advocate—R
Faith Today
Fellowship Link—R
Forefront—R
Grit
Home Times—R
Indian Life—R
John Milton—R
Keys to Living—R
Legions of Light—R
Light and Life
Liguorian
Living—R
Living Church
Lutheran—R
Lutheran Witness
Mennonite—R
Messenger/St. Anthony
Metro Voice—R
Michigan Christian
Minnesota Christian—R
Nashville Christian—R
New Freeman—R
Now What?—R
Our Family—R
Our Sunday Visitor
Parent Paper—R
Perspectives
Plain Truth—R
PrayerWorks—R
Presbyterian Layman
Presbyterian Outlook
Presbyterian Record—R
Presbyterians Today—R
Prism—R
Purpose—R
Reflections
Re:generation
SCP Journal—R
Seeds
Sojourners
Star of Zion

Stepping Out
thegoodsteward.com—R
Time of Singing—R
Total Health
Touchstone—R
Trumpeter—R
Upsouth—R
War Cry—R
Way of St. Francis—R

CHILDREN
Discovery (NY)—R
Guideposts for Kids
My Friend
On the Line—R
Pockets—R
Skipping Stones
Touch—R
Winner—R

CHRISTIAN EDUCATION/LIBRARY
Christian School
Leader/Church School
   Today—R

PASTORS/LEADERS
Christian Camp—R
Christian Century
Christian Ministry
Eucharistic Minister—R
Journal/Christian Education
Lutheran Partners—R
Pastoral Life—R
Reaching Children at Risk
Word & World

TEEN/YOUNG ADULT
Devo'Zine—R
Real Time—R
Student Leadership—R
WITH—R
YOU!—R
Young Adult Today

WOMEN
Esprit—R
Godly Business Woman
Helping Hand—R
Horizons—R
Reflections (FL)

WRITERS
Areopagus (UK)

ESSAYS

ADULT/GENERAL
About Such Things—R

American Wasteland
Annals of St. Anne
Arlington Catholic
Banner
Breakthrough Intercessor—R
Bridge—R
Catholic Answer
Catholic Faith & Family
Catholic Insight
Catholic New Times—R
Catholic Parent
Christian Century
Christian Motorsports
Christian Parenting—R
Christian Renewal—R
Christianity/Arts
Chrysalis Reader
Church Advocate—R
Church & State—R
Commonweal
Company—R
Cornerstone—R
Covenant Companion—R
Creation Care—R
Cresset
Culture Wars—R
Door—R
Dovetail—R
Evangelical Advocate—R
Faith Today
First Things
Gem—R
Good News Journal (TX)
Hidden Manna—R
Home Times—R
Hunted News
Inspirer—R
Interim—R
John Milton—R
Karitos Review—R
Legions of Light—R
Life@Work
Light and Life
Live—R
Living—R
Messenger/St. Anthony
Metro Voice—R
Michigan Christian
National Catholic
New Moon—R
New Song
New Writing—R
Over the Back Fence—R
Parabola—R
Parenting Our Parents—R
Parent Paper—R
Pegasus Review—R
Perspectives

Plain Truth—R
PrayerWorks—R
Presbyterian Outlook
Presbyterians Today—R
Prism—R
Re:generation
SCP Journal—R
Selah!Kids
Short Stories Bimonthly
Sojourners
Spiritual Life
Stepping Out
Storyteller—R
TEAK Roundup—R
Upsouth—R
War Cry—R

CHILDREN
Discovery (NY)—R
Nature Friend—R
Skipping Stones

MISSIONS
Areopagus—R
PFI World Report—R

MUSIC
Contemporary Songwriter—
   R
Creator—R

PASTORS/LEADERS
African American Pulpit
Catholic Servant
Christian Century
Christian Ministry
Cross Currents—R
Growing Churches
Journal/Christian Healing—R
Journal/Pastoral Care
Pastoral Life—R
Reaching Children at Risk
Sharing the Practice—R
Word & World
Youthworker

TEEN/YOUNG ADULT
Boundless Webzine—R
YOU!—R
Young Adult Today

WOMEN
Anna's Journal—R
Esprit—R
Godly Business Woman
Grace—R
Helping Hand—R
SpiritLed Woman

WRITERS

Areopagus (UK)
Byline
Canadian Writer's Jour—R
Once Upon a Time—R
WIN-Informer
Writer's Digest—R
Writer's Ink—R

ETHICS

ADULT/GENERAL

AGAIN—R
American Wasteland
Angels on Earth
Banner
Bible Advocate—R
Biblical Reflections—R
Breakthrough Intercessor—
    R
Bridge—R
Canada Lutheran—R
Catholic Faith & Family
Catholic Insight
Catholic New Times—R
Catholic Parent
CGA World—R
Christian Century
Christian Courier (CAN)—R
Christian Media—R
Christian Motorsports
Christian Observer
Christian Parenting—R
Christian Renewal—R
Christian Research
Christian Social Action—R
Christianity Today—R
Chrysalis Reader
Church Herald/Holiness—R
Church of God EVANGEL
Colorado Christian—R
Commonweal
Companions—R
Compleat Nurse—R
Conquest
Cornerstone—R
Covenant Companion—R
Creation Ex Nihilo
Culture Wars—R
Dovetail—R
Evangelical Advocate—R
Faith Today
Fellowship Link—R
First Things
Good News, Etc.—R
Good News Journal (TX)
Grit
Homeschooling Today—R

Home Times—R
Hunted News
Impact Magazine—R
Indian Life—R
Interim—R
John Milton—R
Jour/Christian Nursing—R
Journal of Church & State
Life@Work
Light and Life
Liguorian
Living—R
Living Church
Lutheran Journal—R
Mennonite Brethren—R
Men of Integrity—R
Metro Voice—R
Michigan Christian
Minnesota Christian—R
Moody—R
Nashville Christian—R
New Covenant
New Freeman—R
Now What?—R
NRB Magazine—R
Our Family—R
Our Sunday Visitor
Pegasus Review—R
Perspectives
Physician—R
Plain Truth—R
Pourastan—R
Prairie Messenger—R
PrayerWorks—R
Presbyterian Layman
Presbyterian Outlook
Presbyterian Record—R
Prism—R
Purpose—R
Reflections
Re:generation
St. Anthony Messenger
St. Willibrord Journal
Seeds
Social Justice
Sojourners
Testimony—R
2-Soar
Upsouth—R
War Cry—R

CHILDREN

Discovery (NY)—R
Guideposts for Kids
High Adventure—R
J.A.M.—R
Skipping Stones
Wonder Time

CHRISTIAN EDUCATION/ LIBRARY

Christian Librarian—R
Journal/Christian Education
Vision—R

MISSIONS

Areopagus—R
East-West Church
Teacher's Interaction
Worldwide Challenge

PASTORS/LEADERS

Christian Century
Christian Management—R
Christian Ministry
Cross Currents—R
Growing Churches
Horizons—R
Ivy Jungle Report—R
Journal/Christian Healing—
    R
Journal/Pastoral Care
Lutheran Partners—R
Pastoral Life—R
Priest
PROCLAIM—R
Quarterly Review
Reaching Children at Risk
Sewanee Theological Review
Sharing the Practice—R
Theology Today
Today's Christian Preacher—
    R
Word & World
Youthworker

TEEN/YOUNG ADULT

Certainty
J.A.M.—R
Teenage Christian—R
Today's Christian Teen—R
WITH—R
YOU!—R
Young Salvationist—R

WOMEN

Canticle
Conscience—R
Esprit—R
Godly Business Woman
Helping Hand—R
Horizons—R

WRITERS

Areopagus (UK)
Canadian Writer's Jour—R

ETHNIC/CULTURAL PIECES

ADULT/GENERAL
About Such Things—R
AGAIN—R
American Tract Soc.—R
American Wasteland
Arlington Catholic
Banner
Beacon—R
Bible Advocate—R
Breakthrough Intercessor—R
Bridal Guides—R
Bridge—R
Catholic Faith & Family
Catholic Insight
Catholic New Times—R
CBA Marketplace
CGA World—R
Christian Century
Christian Courier (CAN)—R
Christian Living—R
Christian Motorsports
Christian News NW—R
Christian Ranchman
Christian Social Action—R
Christianity Online—R
Christianity Today—R
Church of God EVANGEL
Columbia
Company—R
Compleat Nurse—R
Cornerstone—R
Covenant Companion—R
Creation Care—R
Creation Ex Nihilo
Dovetail—R
Episcopal Life—R
Evangelical Advocate—R
Faith Today
Fellowship Link—R
First Things
Foursquare World—R
Gem—R
God Allows U-Turns—R
Good News (KY)—R
Good News, Etc.—R
Gospel Today
Grit
Homeschooling Today—R
Home Times—R
Impact Magazine—R
Indian Life—R
John Milton—R
Jour/Christian Nursing—R
Journal of Church & State
Joyfull Noise

Legions of Light—R
LifeWise
Light and Life
Liguorian
Living—R
Lookout—R
Lutheran Witness
Joyful Noise
Men of Integrity—R
MESSAGE
Messenger/St. Anthony
Michigan Christian
Moody—R
Nashville Christian—R
New Writing—R
Now What?—R
NRB Magazine—R
On Mission
Pentecostal Evangel
Perspectives
Plain Truth—R
PrayerWorks—R
Presbyterian Outlook
Presbyterian Record—R
Prism—R
Purpose—R
Re:generation
Sacred Journey—R
Seeds
Single-Parent Family
Sojourners
Standard, The—R
Trumpeter—R
Upscale Magazine
Upsouth—R
War Cry—R

CHILDREN
Discovery(NY)—R
J.A.M.—R
On the Line—R
Pockets—R
Skipping Stones
Story Friends—R
Winner—R

CHRISTIAN EDUCATION/ LIBRARY
Catechist
Leader/Church School Today—R
Preschool Playhouse

MISSIONS
Hope for Children—R
Latin America Evangelist
Missiology
World Christian—R

PASTORS/LEADERS
African American Pulpit
Christian Ministry
Cross Currents—R
Eucharistic Minister—R
Evangelical Baptist—R
Five Stones—R
Growing Churches
Horizons—R
Journal/Christian Healing— R
Journal/Pastoral Care—R
Lutheran Partners—R
Ministries Today
Pastoral Life—R
Reaching Children at Risk
Rev.
Sharing the Practice—R
Worship Leader

TEEN/YOUNG ADULT
Boundless Webzine—R
Certainty
Conqueror—R
Devo'Zine—R
Essential Connection—R
J.A.M.—R
Student Leadership—R
WITH—R
YOU!—R
Young Adult Today
Young Salvationist—R

WOMEN
Esprit—R
Godly Business Woman
Horizons—R
Link & Visitor—R
Reflections (FL)
SpiritLed Woman
Today's Christian Woman
Women of Spirit—R

EVANGELISM/WITNESSING

ADULT/GENERAL
Alive!—R
American Tract Soc.—R
Anglican Journal—R
Annals of St. Anne
Banner
Beacon—R
Bible Advocate—R
Bread of Life—R
Breakthrough Intercessor—R
Canadian Lutheran—R
Catholic Faith & Family
Catholic Insight

Charisma/Christian Life
Christian Century
Christian Courier (WI)—R
Christian Leader—R
Christian Motorsports
Christian Parenting—R
Christian Ranchman
Christian Reader—R
Christian Research
Christianity Online—R
Christianity Today—R
Church of God EVANGEL
Companion
Companions—R
Connection Mag.—R
Conquest
Cornerstone—R
Covenant Companion—R
Creation Care—R
Creation Ex Nihilo
Crossway/Newsline—R
Decision
Discipleship Journal
Episcopal Life—R
Evangel—R
Evangelical Advocate—R
Faith Today
Fellowship Link—R
First Priority
Gem—R
God Allows U-Turns—R
God's Revivalist
Good News (KY)—R
Good News!
Good News, Etc.—R
Good News Journal (MO)—R
Good News Journal (TX)
Gospel Today
Gospel Tract—R
Highway News—R
Indian Life—R
Inland NW Christian
Inspirer—R
John Milton—R
Journal/Christian Nursing—R
Leaves—R
Legions of Light—R
Life@Work
Life Gate—R
LifeWise
Light and Life
Living Church
Lookout—R
Lutheran—R
Lutheran Digest—R
Lutheran Journal—R
Lutheran Witness
Men of Integrity—R

Mennonite Brethren—R
MESSAGE/Open Bible—R
Messenger/St. Anthony
Metro Voice—R
Michigan Christian
Moody—R
Ncubator.com—R
New Covenant
New Freeman—R
New Heart—R
New Writing—R
Northwestern Lutheran—R
Oblates
On Mission
Our Family—R
Pentecostal Evangel
Peoples Magazine—R
Plain Truth—R
Power for Living—R
PrayerWorks—R
Presbyterian Layman
Presbyterian Record—R
Presbyterians Today—R
Prism—R
Purpose—R
Queen of All Hearts
Reflections
Re:generation
St. Anthony Messenger
SCP Journal—R
Shantyman—R
Sharing—R
Signs of the Times—R
Silver Wings—R
Single-Parent Family
Sojourners
Standard—R
Standard, The—R
Stepping Out
Testimony—R
This Rock
Trumpeter—R
Upsouth—R
U.S. Catholic
War Cry—R
Way of St. Francis—R
Wesleyan Advocate—R

CHILDREN

BREAD/God's Children—R
Club Connection—R
Courage
Discovery (NY)—R
Focus/Clubhouse
J.A.M.—R
Kids' Ministry Ideas—R
Live Wire—R
Primary Pal (IL)

Touch—R

CHRISTIAN EDUCATION/LIBRARY

Brigade Leader—R
Children's Ministry
Church Educator—R
Church Media Journal—R
Evangelizing Today's Child—
   R
GROUP
Leader/Church School
   Today—R
Preschool Playhouse
Resource—R
Shining Star—R
Signal—R
Teacher's Interaction

MISSIONS

American Horizon—R
Evangelical Missions—R
Intl Jour/Frontier—R
Latin America Evangelist
Leaders for Today
Missiology
So All May Hear—R
World Christian—R
World Pulse—R
Worldwide Challenge

MUSIC

Cooperative Christian—R
Quest—R
Songwriting—R

PASTORS/LEADERS

Angelos—R
Cell Group—R
Christian Camp—R
Church Administration
Church Growth Network—R
Emmanuel
Eucharistic Minister—R
Evangelical Baptist—R
Evangelicals Today—R
Five Stones—R
Growing Churches
Horizons—R
Jour/Amer Soc/Chur Growth—
   R
Journal/Christian Healing—R
Let's Worship
Lutheran Forum—R
Lutheran Partners—R
Ministries Today
Pastoral Life—R
PROCLAIM—R
Pulpit Helps—R

Quarterly Review
Reaching Children at Risk
Resource—R
Rev.
Review for Religious
Sermon Notes
Sharing the Practice—R
Today's Christian Preacher—R
WCA News—R
Youthworker

TEEN/YOUNG ADULT
Certainty
Challenge
Conqueror—R
Devo'Zine—R
Encounter—R
Essential Connection—R
J.A.M.—R
Passageway.org—R
Real Time—R
Student Leadership—R
Teenage Christian—R
Teens on Target—R
Today's Christian Teen—R
WITH—R
YOU!—R
Young Adult Today
Young Salvationist—R
Youth Challenge—R

WOMEN
Connection
Esprit—R
Godly Business Woman
Helping Hand—R
Horizons—R
Joyful Woman—R
Just Between Us—R
Lutheran Woman Today
Proverbs 31 Woman—R
SpiritLed Woman
Wesleyan Woman—R
Woman's Touch—R
Women of Spirit—R
Women Who Minister—R

WRITERS
Areopagus (UK)

EXEGESIS

ADULT/GENERAL
Bible Advocate—R
Cornerstone—R
Evangelical Advocate—R
Hidden Manna—R
John Milton—R

Living Church
Ncubator.com—R
Presbyterian Outlook
St. Willibrord Journal
Testimony—R

CHRISTIAN EDUCATION/ LIBRARY
Shining Star

PASTORS/LEADERS
Angelos—R
Enrichment—R
Growing Churches
Pastoral Life—R
Pulpit Helps—R
Reaching Children at Risk
Sharing the Practice—R

WOMEN
Esprit—R
Lutheran Woman Today
SpiritLed Woman

FAITH

ADULT/GENERAL
alive now!
And He Will Give
Bible Advocate—R
Bread of Life—R
Bridal Guides—R
Catholic New Times—R
Christian Courier (CAN)—R
Christian Leader—R
Christian Parenting—R
Christian Reader—R
Christian Social Action—R
Church Herald/Holiness—R
Church of God EVANGEL
Companions—R
Connection Mag.—R
Covenant Companion—R
Disciple's Journal—R
Dovetail—R
Dunamis Life—R
Evangelical Advocate—R
Gem—R
God Allows U-Turns—R
Gospel Tract—R
Grit
Hidden Manna—R
HomeLife—R
Home Times—R
Hunted News
Jewel Among Jewels—R
John Milton—R
Jour/Christian Nursing—R

LifeWise
Liguorian
Live—R
Lutheran Witness
Mature Years—R
Mennonite—R
Men of Integrity—R
MESSAGE/Open Bible—R
Messenger/St. Anthony
Ncubator.com—R
New Freeman—R
New Heart—R
Now What?—R
Peoples Magazine—R
Plain Truth—R
On Mission
Prairie Messenger—R
Presbyterian Record—R
Psychology for Living—R
Purpose—R
Stepping Out
United Church Observer—R
Way of St. Francis—R
Winsome Wit—R

CHILDREN
BREAD/God's Children—R
Discovery (NY)—R
Guideposts for Kids
J.A.M.—R
Live Wire—R
Our Little Friend—R
Primary Treasure—R
Touch—R

CHRISTIAN EDUCATION/ LIBRARY
GROUP
Religion Teacher's Journal

MISSIONS
Catholic Near East
Latin America Evangelist

MUSIC
Cooperative Christian—R

PASTORS/LEADERS
Cross Currents—R
Eucharistic Minister—R
Evangelical Baptist—R
Evangelicals Today—R
Growing Churches
Journal/Christian Healing—R
Pastoral Life—R
Pulpit Helps—R
Quarterly Review

Review for Religious
Sharing the Practice—R
Worship Leader

TEEN/YOUNG ADULT
Boundless Webzine—R
J.A.M.—R
Passageway.org—R
Student Leadership—R
Teens on Target—R
Today's Christian Teen—R
WITH—R
YOU!—R
Young Salvationist—R
Youth Challenge—R

WOMEN
Esprit—R
Godly Business Woman
Horizons—R
Just Between Us—R
Lutheran Woman Today
Reflections (FL)
Women Who Minister—R

WRITERS
Areopagus (UK)

FAMILY LIFE

ADULT/GENERAL
Accent on Living—R
And He Will Give
AGAIN—R
Alive!—R
America
Angels on Earth
Annals of St. Anne
Arlington Catholic
Banner
B.C. Catholic—R
Beacon—R
Bible Advocate—R
Bread of Life—R
Breakthrough Intercessor—R
Bridal Guides—R
Canada Lutheran—R
Catholic Digest—R
Catholic Faith & Family
Catholic Forester—R
Catholic Insight
Catholic New Times—R
Catholic Parent
Celebrate Life—R
CGA World—R
Charisma/Christian Life
Chicken Soup/Mother—R
Chicken Soup/Woman—R

Christian C.L. RECORD—R
Christian Courier (WI)—R
Christian Courier (CAN)—R
Christian Crafter—R
Christian Designer—R
Christian Home & School
Christian Leader—R
Christian Living—R
Christian Motorsports
Christian Parenting—R
Christian Ranchman
Christian Reader—R
Christian Renewal—R
Christian Social Action—R
Christianity Online—R
Church Advocate—R
Church Herald/Holiness—R
Church of God EVANGEL
Columbia
Companion
Connecting Point—R
Conquest
Covenant Companion—R
Creation Ex Nihilo
Culture Wars—R
Disciple's Journal—R
Decision
Dovetail—R
Evangel—R
Evangelical Advocate—R
Expression Christian
Family Digest
Fellowship Focus—R
Fellowship Link—R
Focus on the Family
Foursquare World—R
Gem—R
God Allows U-Turns—R
God's Revivalist
Good News, Etc.—R
Good News Journal (MO)—R
Good News Journal (TX)
Grit
Guideposts
Heartlight Internet—R
Highway News—R
HomeLife—R
Homeschooling Today—R
Home Times—R
Ideals—R
Impact Magazine—R
Indian Life—R
Inland NW Christian
Interim—R
Jewel Among Jewels—R
John Milton—R
Joyfull Noise
Keys to Living—R

LA Catholic Agitator
Legions of Light—R
Life@Work
Life Gate—R
LifeWise
Light and Life
Liguorian
Live—R
Living—R
Living Church
Living Light News—R
Lookout—R
Lutheran—R
Lutheran Digest—R
Lutheran Journal—R
Lutheran Witness
Mennonite—R
Men of Integrity—R
MESSAGE
MESSAGE/Open Bible—R
Messenger
Messenger/St. Anthony
Metro Voice—R
Michigan Christian
Minnesota Christian—R
Moody—R
Nashville Christian—R
Ncubator.com—R
New Freeman—R
North American Voice
Now What?—R
Oblates
On Mission
Our Family—R
Our Sunday Visitor
Over the Back Fence—R
Parenting Our Parents—R
Parent Paper—R
Pegasus Review—R
Pentecostal Evangel
Peoples Magazine—R
Physician—R
Plain Truth—R
Plus—R
Pourastan—R
Power for Living—R
Prairie Messenger—R
PrayerWorks—R
Presbyterian Layman
Presbyterian Record—R
Presbyterians Today—R
Preserving Christian Homes—
R
Progress—R
Psychology for Living—R
Purpose—R
Re:generation
Sacred Journey—R

Say Amen—R
Signs of the Times—R
Single-Parent Family
Smart Families
Social Justice
Sojourners
Spirit—R
Standard—R
Standard, The—R
Star of Zion
Stepping Out
Storyteller—R
Testimony—R
Time of Singing—R
Today's Christian Senior—R
    (grandparenting)
Together—R
Tomorrow's Christian
    Graduate
United Church Observer—
    R
Upsouth—R
U.S. Catholic
Vibrant Life—R
Vision—R
War Cry—R
Way of St. Francis—R
Wesleyan Advocate—R
Winsome Wit—R

CHILDREN
American Girl
BREAD/God's Children—R
Celebrate
Club Connection—R
Courage
Discoveries—R
Discovery (NY)—R
Discovery Trails—R
High Adventure—R
J.A.M.—R
Live Wire—R
My Friend
Nature Friend—R
Pockets—R
Preschool Playhouse
Skipping Stones
Touch—R
Winner—R
Wonder Time

CHRISTIAN EDUCATION/
LIBRARY
Caravan
CE Connection—R
CE Counselor—R
Children's Ministry
Church Educator—R

Leader/Church School
    Today—R
Preschool Playhouse
Shining Star
Signal—R
Teacher's Interaction

MISSIONS
American Horizon—R
Latin America Evangelist
Worldwide Challenge

PASTORS/LEADERS
African American Pulpit
Catholic Servant
Christian Camp—R
Evangelical Baptist—R
Evangelicals Today—R
Growing Churches
Journal/Pastoral Care
Lutheran Partners—R
Minister's Family
Ministries Today
Pastoral Life—R
Preacher's Illus. Service—R
Priest
PROCLAIM—R
Pulpit Helps—R
Reaching Children at Risk
Rev.
Sharing the Practice—R
Today's Christian Preacher—
    R
Today's Parish
Word & World
Youthworker

TEEN/YOUNG ADULT
Breakaway—R
Certainty
Challenge
Devo'Zine—R
Encounter—R
Essential Connection—R
J.A.M.—R
Teens on Target—R
WITH—R
YOU!—R
Young Adult Today
Youth Challenge—R

WOMEN
Canticle
Esprit—R
Excellence
Godly Business Woman
Handmaiden—R
Hearts at Home—R

Helping Hand—R
Horizons—R
Journey—R
Joyful Woman—R
Just Between Us—R
Lutheran Woman's Quar.
Lutheran Woman Today
Proverbs 31 Woman—R
Reflections (FL)
SpiritLed Woman
Today's Christian Woman
Welcome Home
Wesleyan Woman—R
Woman's Touch—R
Women of Spirit—R
Women Who Minister—R

WRITERS
Cochran's Corner—R

FILLERS: ANECDOTES

ADULT/GENERAL
Alive!—R
Angels on Earth
Bridal Guides—R
Catholic Digest—R
Chicken Soup/Mother—R
Chicken Soup/Woman—R
Christian Courier (WI)—R
Christian Crafter—R
Christian Designer—R
Christian Motorsports
Christian Parenting—R
Christian Ranchman
Christian Reader—R
Christian Response—R
Church Herald/Holiness—R
Church of God EVANGEL
Companion
Companions—R
Compleat Nurse—R
Conquest
Decision
Disciple's Journal—R
Family Digest
Forefront—R
Foursquare World—R
Gem—R
God Allows U-Turns—R
Good News Journal (TX)
Grit
Guideposts
Healing Inn—R
Heartlight Internet—R
Home Times—R
Impact Magazine—R
Inspirer—R

Jewel Among Jewels—R
John Milton—R
Joyfull Noise
Legions of Light—R
Life@Work
Life Gate—R
Liguorian
Live—R
Living—R
Lutheran Digest—R
Lutheran Journal—R
Mature Living
Mennonite—R
Messenger/St. Anthony
Metro Voice—R
MovieGuide
Nashville Christian—R
New Heart—R
Now What?—R
Our Family—R
Peoples Magazine—R
Pourastan—R
Presbyterian Record—R
Presbyterians Today—R
Purpose—R
Single-Parent Family
Spirit—R
Stepping Out
Storyteller—R
TEAK Roundup—R
War Cry—R
Way of St. Francis—R

CHILDREN
Club Connection—R
Discovery (NY)—R
Guideposts for Kids
High Adventure—R
J.A.M.—R
Skipping Stones

CHRISTIAN EDUCATION/
LIBRARY
Christian Classroom
Christian Librarian—R
Christian School
Christian School Admin.
Religion Teacher's Journal
Shining Star
Teachers in Focus—R
Women of the Harvest

MUSIC
Church Musician
Church Pianist, etc.
Contemporary Songwriter—
    R
Creator—R

PASTORS/LEADERS
Christian Management—R
Christian Ministry
Eucharistic Minister—R
Five Stones—R
Growing Churches
Ivy Jungle Report—R
Journal/Christian Healing—R
Pastoral Life—R
Pulpit Helps—R
Resource—R
Sharing the Practice—R

TEEN/YOUNG ADULT
Guideposts for Teens—R
J.A.M.—R
Young Salvationist—R

WOMEN
Anna's Journal—R
Grace—R
Hearts at Home—R
Just Between Us—R
Today's Christian Woman
Wesleyan Woman—R
Woman's Touch—R

WRITERS
Areopagus (UK)
Byline
Canadian Writer's Jour—R
Cochran's Corner—R
Cross & Quill—R
Fellowscript—R
Once Upon a Time—R
Tickled by Thunder
WE!—R
Writers' Journal—R
Write Touch—R

FILLERS: CARTOONS

ADULT/GENERAL
Alive!—R
alive now!
Angels on Earth
Banner
Bridal Guides—R
Bridge—R
Catholic Digest—R
Catholic Forester—R
CBA Frontline
CBA Marketplace
Chicken Soup/Mother—R
Chicken Soup/Woman—R
Christian Computing (MO)—R
Christian Crafter—R
Christian Designer—R

Christian Motorsports
Christian Ranchman
Church Herald/Holiness—R
Commonweal
Companion
Compleat Nurse—R
Connecting Point—R
Connection Mag.—R
Cornerstone—R
Covenant Companion—R
Creation Care—R
Culture Wars—R
Disciple's Journal—R
Discovery (FL)—R
Door
Evangel—R
Faith & Friends—R
Foursquare World—R
Gem—R
Good News Journal (MO)—R
Good News Journal (TX)
Grit
Healing Inn—R
Heartlight Internet—R
Home Times—R
Impact Magazine—R
Inside Journal
Inspirer—R
Jewel Among Jewels—R
John Milton—R
Legions of Light—R
Life@Work
LifeWise
Light and Life
Lookout—R
Lutheran—R
Lutheran Digest—R
Lutheran Journal—R
Mature Living
Mature Years—R
Mennonite—R
MESSAGE/Open Bible—R
Messenger/St. Anthony
Metro Voice—R
Michigan Christian
MovieGuide
Nashville Christian—R
New Heart—R
Our Family—R
Pegasus Review—R
Peoples Magazine—R
Physician—R
Power for Living—R
Presbyterian Record—R
Presbyterians Today—R
Purpose—R
Reflections
Single-Parent Family

Sojourners
Spirit—R
Storyteller—R
TEAK Roundup—R
thegoodsteward.com—R
Today's Christian Senior—R
Touchstone—R
Trumpeter—R
United Church Observer—R
Way of St. Francis—R
Wireless Age—R

CHILDREN

Club Connection—R
Discoveries—R
Focus/Clubhouse Jr.
High Adventure—R
J.A.M.—R
My Friend
On the Line—R
Skipping Stones
Story Friends—R

*CHRISTIAN EDUCATION/
LIBRARY*

CE Connection—R
CE Counselor—R
Children's Ministry
Christian Classroom
Christian Librarian—R
Christian School Admin.
GROUP
Journal/Adventist Educ.—R
Team—R
Today's Catholic Teacher—R
Vision—R

MISSIONS

Hope for Children—R
Mission Frontiers

MUSIC

Church Musician
Church Pianist, etc.
Contemporary Songwriter—R
Cooperative Christian—R
Creator—R
Songwriting—R
Senior Musician—R
Tradition

PASTORS/LEADERS

Catholic Servant
Christian Century
Christian Management—R
Christian Ministry
Clergy Journal—R
Diocesan Dialogue—R

Eucharistic Minister—R
Five Stones—R
Growing Churches
Horizons—R
Ivy Jungle Report—R
Leadership—R
Lutheran Partners—R
Preaching
Priest
Pulpit Helps—R
Reformed Worship
Resource—R
Rev.
Sermon Notes
Sharing the Practice—R
Small Group Network
WCA News—R
Your Church—R

TEEN/YOUNG ADULT

Breakaway—R
Brio
Guideposts for Teens—R
J.A.M.—R
Listen—R
Live Wire—R
Real Time—R
WITH—R
YOU!—R
Young Salvationist—R

WOMEN

Hearts at Home—R
Horizons—R
Joyful Woman—R
Just Between Us—R
Today's Christian Woman
Wesleyan Woman—R
Women Alive!—R

WRITERS

Byline
Cochran's Corner—R
Cross & Quill—R
Fellowscript—R
Heaven—R
Once Upon a Time—R
WE!—R
Writers' Journal—R

FILLERS: FACTS

ADULT/GENERAL

Alive!—R
Angels on Earth
Bible Advocate—R
Bread of Life—R
Bridal Guides—R

Catholic Digest—R
CBA Marketplace
Christian Courier (WI)—R
Christian Crafter—R
Christian Designer—R
Christian Motorsports
Christian Ranchman
Christian Reader—R
Christian Response—R
Compleat Nurse—R
Disciple's Journal—R
Forefront—R
Gem—R
God Allows U-Turns—R
God's Revivalist
Good News Journal (TX)
Healing Inn—R
Inspirer—R
Jewel Among Jewels—R
John Milton—R
Legions of Light—R
Life@Work
Life Gate—R
Lutheran Digest—R
Lutheran Journal—R
Mature Living
Mennonite—R
MESSAGE/Open Bible—R
Messenger/St. Anthony
MovieGuide
Now What?—R
Peoples Magazine—R
PrayerWorks—R
Presbyterian Record—R
Reflections
Single-Parent Family
Stepping Out
Storyteller—R
Vibrant Life—R
Way of St. Francis—R

CHILDREN

Club Connection—R
Discoveries—R
Discovery Trails—R
Focus/Clubhouse
Guideposts for Kids
High Adventure—R
J.A.M.—R
Live Wire—R
On the Line—R

*CHRISTIAN EDUCATION/
LIBRARY*

CE Connection—R
Christian Classroom
Christian School Admin.
Shining Star

Today's Catholic Teacher—R
Vision—R

MISSIONS
Hope for Children—R
So All May Hear—R

MUSIC
Contemporary Songwriter—
   R

PASTORS/LEADERS
Christian Ministry
Church Management—R
Growing Churches
Ivy Jungle Report—R
Journal/Christian Healing—
   R
Pastoral Life—R
Single Adult Ministries

TEEN/YOUNG ADULT
Breakaway—R
Brio
Certainty
Guideposts for Teens—R
J.A.M.—R
Student Leadership—R
Young Salvationist—R

WOMEN
Anna's Journal—R
Connection
Excellence
Grace—R
Hearts at Home—R

WRITERS
Areopagus (UK)
Cochran's Corner—R
Fellowscript—R
We!—R
Writers' Journal—R
Write Touch—R

FILLERS: GAMES

ADULT/GENERAL
Alive!—R
Angels on Earth
Bridal Guides—R
Catholic Digest—R
CGA World—R
Christian Crafter—R
Christian Designer—R
Christian Motorsports
Christian Ranchman
Connecting Point—R

Disciple's Journal—R
Faith & Friends—R
Gem—R
Good News Journal (MO)—R
Good News Journal (TX)
Heartlight Internet—R
Inspirer—R
Joyfull Noise
Keys to Living—R
Lutheran Journal—R
Mature Living
MovieGuide
Peoples Magazine—R

CHILDREN
Celebrate
Club Connection—R
Courage
Discoveries—R
Discovery (NY)—R
Focus/Clubhouse Jr.
GUIDE—R
Guideposts for Kids
High Adventure—R
J.A.M.—R
Live Wire—R
On the Line—R
Pockets—R
Primary Pal (IL)
Together Time—R
Touch—R

*CHRISTIAN EDUCATION/
LIBRARY*
Christian Classroom
Christian School Admin.
GROUP
Leader/Church School
   Today—R
Perspective—R
Religion Teacher's Journal
Shining Star

MUSIC
Contemporary Songwriter—R

PASTORS/LEADERS
Rev.

TEEN/YOUNG ADULT
Challenge
Conqueror—R
J.A.M.—R
Listen—R
Minister's Family
Student Leadership—R
YOU!—R
Young Salvationist—R

WRITERS
Areopagus (UK)

FILLERS: IDEAS

ADULT/GENERAL
Angels on Earth
Bridal Guides—R
Catholic Parent
CBA Marketplace
CGA World—R
Christian Crafter—R
Christian Designer—R
Christian Home & School
Christian Motorsports
Christian Parenting—R
Christian Ranchman
Church of God EVANGEL
Compleat Nurse—R
Conquest
Disciple's Journal—R
Gem—R
God Allows U-Turns—R
God's Revivalist
Good News Journal (TX)
Healing Inn—R
Heartlight Internet—R
Inspirer—R
Jewel Among Jewels—R
John Milton—R
Joyfull Noise
Legions of Light—R
Messenger/St. Anthony
Metro Voice—R
MovieGuide
Pourastan—R
Presbyterian Record—R
Reflections
St. Joseph's Messenger—R
Seek—R
Stepping Out
TEAK Roundup—R

CHILDREN
Celebrate
Club Connection—R
Discovery (NY)—R
Guideposts for Kids
High Adventure—R
J.A.M.—R
Live Wire—R
Pockets—R
Together Time—R

*CHRISTIAN EDUCATION/
LIBRARY*
CE Connection—R
Christian Classroom

Christian School Admin.
GROUP
Leader/Church School
    Today—R
Parish Teacher
Religion Teacher's Journal
Shining Star
Teacher's Interaction
Team—R

MISSIONS
Hope for Children—R

MUSIC
Contemporary Songwriter—
    R
Creator—R
Senior Musician—R
Songwriting—R

PASTORS/LEADERS
Church Worship
Enrichment—R
Five Stones—R
Growing Churches
Journal/Christian Healing—
    R
Lutheran Partners—R
Pastoral Life—R
Pray!—R
Preacher's Illus. Service—R
Rev.
Single Adult Ministries
Small Group Network
WCA News—R

TEEN/YOUNG ADULT
Brio
Campus Life—R
Certainty
J.A.M.—R

WOMEN
Hearts at Home—R
Wesleyan Woman—R
Woman's Touch—R

WRITERS
Areopagus (UK)
Canadian Writer's Jour—R
Dedicated Author
Fellowscript—R
Just Between Us—R
Tickled by Thunder
WE!—R
Writer's Ink—R
Writers' Journal—R
Write Touch—R

FILLERS: JOKES

ADULT/GENERAL
Angels on Earth
Catholic Digest—R
Christian Crafter—R
Christian Designer—R
Christian Motorsports
Christian Ranchman
Compleat Nurse—R
Connection Mag.—R
Disciple's Journal—R
Faith & Friends—R
Gem—R
Good News Journal (MO)—
    R
Good News Journal (TX)
Grit
Healing Inn—R
Heartlight Internet—R
Home Times—R
Impact Magazine—R
Inspirer—R
Joyfull Noise
Legions of Light—R
Liguorian
Lutheran—R
Lutheran Digest—R
Mature Years—R
MovieGuide
Nashville Christian—R
New Heart—R
Our Family—R
PrayerWorks—R
Seek—R
Spirit—R
thegoodsteward.com—R
Today's Christian Senior—R

CHILDREN
Club Connection—R
Discovery (NY)—R
Guideposts for Kids
High Adventure—R
J.A.M.—R
Live Wire—R
My Friend
On the Line—R
Pockets—R (& riddles)

*CHRISTIAN EDUCATION/
LIBRARY*
CE Connection—R
Christian Classroom
Christian School Admin.

MUSIC
Creator—R

PASTORS/LEADERS
Five Stones—R
Ivy Jungle Report—R
Journal/Christian Healing—R
Pastoral Life—R
Preacher's Illus. Service—R
Sharing the Practice—R

TEEN/YOUNG ADULT
Guideposts for Teens—R
J.A.M.—R
Real Time—R
YOU!—R

WOMEN
Joyful Woman—R

WRITERS
Areopagus (UK)
WE!—R
Writers' Journal—R

FILLERS: NEWSBREAKS

ADULT/GENERAL
Angels on Earth
Anglican Journal—R
Arkansas Catholic
B.C. Catholic—R
Bridal Guides—R
Canada Lutheran—R
Catholic New Times—R
Catholic Telegraph
CBA Marketplace
Celebrate Life—R
Christian Courier (WI)—R
Christian Crafter—R
Christian Designer—R
Christian Motorsports
Christian Ranchman
Christian Renewal—R
Compleat Nurse—R
Disciple's Journal—R
Eternal Ink—R
Gem—R
God Allows U-Turns—R
Good News Journal (TX)
Heartlight Internet—R
Home Times—R
Indian Life—R
Inspirer—R
Jewel Among Jewels—R
Legions of Light—R
Living Light News—R
Metro Voice—R
MovieGuide
NRB Magazine—R
Reflections

TEAK Roundup—R

CHILDREN
Club Connection—R

*CHRISTIAN EDUCATION/
LIBRARY*
Christian Librarian—R

MISSIONS
Hope for Children—R
So All May Hear—R

MUSIC
Contemporary Songwriter—R

PASTORS/LEADERS
Christian Ministry
Ivy Jungle Report—R
Journal/Christian Healing—R
Preacher's Illus. Service—R
Single Adult Ministries

TEEN/YOUNG ADULT
Certainty

WOMEN
Anna's Journal—R
Connection
Conscience—R
Grace—R
Joyful Woman—R

WRITERS
Areopagus (UK)
Cochran's Corner—R
WE!—R
Writer's Ink—R

FILLERS: PARTY IDEAS

ADULT/GENERAL
Bridal Guides—R
Christian Crafter—R
Christian Designer—R
Christian Ranchman
Disciple's Journal—R
Good News Journal (TX)
Joyfull Noise
MovieGuide
TEAK Roundup—R

CHILDREN
Club Connection—R
Guideposts for Kids
J.A.M.—R
Live Wire—R
On the Line—R

*CHRISTIAN EDUCATION/
LIBRARY*
Pastoral Life—R
Perspective—R
Team—R

MUSIC
Creator—R
Senior Musician—R

TEEN/YOUNG ADULT
Conqueror—R
J.A.M.—R
Student Leadership—R

WOMEN
Hearts at Home—R
Proverbs 31 Woman—R
Wesleyan Woman—R

WRITERS
Areopagus (UK)

FILLERS: PRAYERS

ADULT/GENERAL
alive now!
Angels on Earth
Bridal Guides—R
CGA World—R
Christian Crafter—R
Christian Designer—R
Christian Motorsports
Christian Ranchman
Church Herald/Holiness—R
Compleat Nurse—R
Cornerstone—R
Creation Care—R
Disciple's Journal—R
Eternal Ink—R
Forefront—R
Gem—R
God Allows U-Turns—R
Good News Journal (TX)
Gospel Tract—R
Healing Inn—R
Heartlight Internet—R
Inspirer—R
Jewel Among Jewels—R
John Milton—R
Legions of Light—R
Liguorian
Mature Years—R
MovieGuide
Our Family—R
Plowman—R
Pourastan—R
PrayerWorks—R

Presbyterian Record—R
Way of St. Francis—R

CHILDREN
J.A.M.—R
Pockets—R
Primary Pal (IL)
Touch—R

*CHRISTIAN EDUCATION/
LIBRARY*
Christian Classroom
Christian School Admin.
Religion Teacher's Journal
Teacher's Interaction

PASTORS/LEADERS
Angleos—R
Church Management—R
Clergy Journal—R
Growing Churches
Pastoral Life—R
Reformed Worship

TEEN/YOUNG ADULT
J.A.M.—R
YOU!—R
Young Salvationist—R

WOMEN
Anna's Journal—R
Horizons—R
Journey—R
Joyful Woman—R
Just Between Us—R

WRITERS
Areopagus (UK)
Cochran's Corner—R
Cross & Quill—R
WIN-Informer

FILLERS: PROSE

ADULT/GENERAL
Angels on Earth
Bible Advocate—R
Bread of Life—R
Christian Crafter—R
Christian Designer—R
Christian Motorsports
Christian Parenting—R
Christian Ranchman
Church Herald/Holiness—R
Companions—R
Conquest
Decision
Disciple's Journal—R

Discovery (FL)—R
Forefront—R
Gem—R
God Allows U-Turns—R
God's Revivalist
Good News Journal (TX)
Grit
Healing Inn—R
Heartlight Internet—R
Inspirer—R
Jewel Among Jewels—R
John Milton—R
Legions of Light—R
Live—R
Lutheran Journal—R
MovieGuide
Now What?—R
Pegasus Review—R
Pentecostal Evangel
Plowman—R
Presbyterian Record—R
Presbyterians Today—R
TEAK Roundup—R
Way of St. Francis—R
Wesleyan Advocate—R
Wireless Age—R

CHILDREN
Courage
Guideposts for Kids
J.A.M.—R

*CHRISTIAN EDUCATION/
LIBRARY*
CE Connection—R
Christian Classroom
Christian School Admin.

PASTORS/LEADERS
Growing Churches
Pastoral Life—R
Preacher's Illus. Service—R
Pulpit Helps—R

TEEN/YOUNG ADULT
Brio
Certainty
Conqueror—R
Guideposts for Teens—R
J.A.M.—R
Real Time—R

WOMEN
Anna's Journal—R
Excellence
Today's Christian Woman

WRITERS
Areopagus (UK)
Cochran's Corner—R
Once Upon a Time—R
WE!—R
The Writer
Write Touch—R

FILLERS: QUIZZES

ADULT/GENERAL
Alive!—R
Angels on Earth
Bridal Guides—R
Catholic Digest—R
Christian Crafter—R
Christian Designer—R
Christian Motorsports
Christian Parenting—R
Christian Ranchman
Disciple's Journal—R
Door
Faith & Friends—R
Gem—R
Good News Journal (MO)—
   R
Good News Journal (TX)
Home Times—R
Impact Magazine—R
Inspirer—R
Jewel Among Jewels—R
Joyfull Noise
Keys to Living—R
Liguorian
Lutheran Journal—R
Mature Living
MovieGuide
Peoples Magazine—R
St. Willibrord Journal
thegoodsteward.com—R
Today's Christian Senior—R
Vibrant Life—R

CHILDREN
Club Connection—R
Crusader—R
Discoveries—R
Discovery (NY)—R
Focus/Clubhouse
GUIDE—R
Guideposts for Kids
J.A.M.—R
Nature Friend—R
On the Line—R
Partners—R
Skipping Stones
Story Mates—R
Touch—R

*CHRISTIAN EDUCATION/
LIBRARY*
Christian Classroom
Christian School Admin.

MUSIC
Senior Musician—R

PASTORS/LEADERS
Ivy Jungle Report—R

TEEN/YOUNG ADULT
Breakaway—R
Brio
Certainty
Conqueror—R
Guideposts for Teens—R
J.A.M.—R
Listen—R
Real Time—R
Student Leadership—R
Teens on Target—R
YOU!—R
Young Salvationist—R
Youth Challenge—R

WOMEN
Anna's Journal—R

WRITERS
Areopagus (UK)
Fellowscript—R
Once Upon a Time—R
WIN-Informer
Writer's Ink—R

FILLERS: QUOTES

ADULT/GENERAL
Angels on Earth
Bible Advocate—R
Bread of Life—R
Bridal Guides—R
Catholic Digest—R
Christian Crafter—R
Christian Designer—R
Christian Motorsports
Christian Ranchman
Christian Response—R
Companion
Compleat Nurse—R
Connection Mag.—R
Culture Wars—R
Disciple's Journal—R
Faith & Friends—R
Forefront—R
Gem—R
God Allows U-Turns—R

Good News Journal (TX)
Grit
Guideposts
Healing Inn—R
Heartlight Internet—R
Home Times—R
Inspirer—R
Jewel Among Jewels—R
John Milton—R
Legions of Light—R
Life@Work
Liguorian
Lutheran Journal—R
MESSAGE/Open Bible—R
Messenger/St. Anthony
Metro Voice—R
MovieGuide
Nashville Christian—R
Now What?—R
Our Family—R
Pegasus Review—R
Pourastan—R
PrayerWorks—R
Seek—R
Storyteller—R

CHILDREN
Discovery (NY)—R
J.A.M.—R
Live Wire—R
Skipping Stones

*CHRISTIAN EDUCATION/
LIBRARY*
Christian School Admin.
Shining Star

MUSIC
Contemporary Songwriter—
    R

PASTORS/LEADERS
Christian Management—R
Growing Churches
Ivy Jungle Report—R
Journal/Christian Healing—R
Pulpit Helps—R
Single Adult Ministries

TEENS/YOUNG ADULTS
J.A.M.—R
YOU!—R

WOMEN
Anna's Journal—R
Excellence
Joyful Woman—R
Just Between Us—R

Wesleyan Woman—R

WRITERS
Areopagus (UK)
Cochran's Corner—R
WE!—R
WIN-Informer
Writer's Ink—R

FILLERS: SHORT HUMOR

ADULT/GENERAL
Alive!—R
Angels on Earth
Bridal Guides—R
Catholic Digest—R
Chicken Soup/Mother—R
Chicken Soup/Woman—R
Christian Crafter—R
Christian Designer—R
Christian Motorsports
Christian Parenting—R
Christian Ranchman
Christian Reader—R
Church Herald/Holiness—R
Companion
Compleat Nurse—R
Connection Mag.—R
Covenant Companion—R
Creation Care—R
Disciple's Journal—R
Door
Eternal Ink—R
Evangel—R
Gem
God Allows U-Turns—R
God's Revivalist
Good News Journal (TX)
Gospel Tract—R
Grit
Guideposts
Healing Inn—R
Heartlight Internet—R
Home Times—R
Impact Magazine—R
Inspirer—R
Jewel Among Jewels—R
John Milton—R
Joyfull Noise
Legions of Light—R
Life@Work
Living—R
Living Light News—R
Lutheran—R
Lutheran Digest—R
Lutheran Journal—R
Mature Living
MESSAGE/Open Bible—R

Metro Voice—R
MovieGuide
Nashville Christian—R
New Heart—R
Our Family—R
Peoples Magazine—R
Pourastan—R
PrayerWorks—R
Presbyterian Record—R
Presbyterians Today—R
Purpose—R
St. Willibrord Journal
Seek—R
Selah!Kids
Spirit—R
Star of Zion
Storyteller—R
TEAK Roundup—R
Winsome Wit—R

CHILDREN
Club Connection—R
Discovery (NY)—R
Discovery Trails—R
Guideposts for Kids
J.A.M.—R
Touch—R

*CHRISTIAN EDUCATION/
LIBRARY*
CE Connection—R
Christian Classroom
Christian Librarian—R
Christian School Admin.
Teachers in Focus
Team—R

MISSIONS
Women of the Harvest

MUSIC
Contemporary Songwriter—
    R
Creator—R
Senior Musician—R

PASTORS/LEADERS
Catholic Servant
Christian Management—R
Enrichment—R
Eucharistic Minister—R
Five Stones—R
Ivy Jungle Report—R
Journal/Christian Healing—
    R
Leadership—R
Pastoral Life—R
Preacher's Illus. Service—R

Pulpit Helps—R
Resource—R
Sermon Notes
Sharing the Practice—R

TEEN/YOUNG ADULT
Brio
Certainty
Guideposts for Teens—R
J.A.M.—R
Real Time—R
Young Salvationist—R

WOMEN
Grace—R
Hearts at Home—R
Journey—R
Joyful Woman—R
Just Between Us—R
Wesleyan Woman—R

WRITERS
Areopagus (UK)
Byline
Cochran's Corner—R
Once Upon a Time—R
Tickled by Thunder
WE!—R
Writers' Journal—R
Write Touch—R

FILLERS: WORD PUZZLES

ADULT/GENERAL
Alive!—R
Bridal Guides—R
CGA World—R
Christian Crafter—R
Christian Designer—R
Christian Ranchman
Companion
Connecting Point—R
Conquest
Disciple's Journal—R
Faith & Friends—R
Gem—R
Good News Journal (TX)
Heartlight Internet—R
Impact Magazine—R
Inspirer—R
Jewel Among Jewels—R
Joyfull Noise
Mature Living
Mature Years—R
Michigan Christian
MovieGuide
Power for Living—R
Standard—R

Today's Christian Senior—
R

CHILDREN
Club Connection—R
Courage
Crusader—R
Discoveries—R
Discovery (NY)—R
Focus/Clubhouse
Focus/Clubhouse Jr.
GUIDE—R
Guideposts for Kids
J.A.M.—R
Nature Friend—R
On the Line—R
Our Little Friend—R
Partners—R
Pockets—R
Primary Pal (IL)
Skipping Stones
Story Friends—R
Story Mates—R

*CHRISTIAN EDUCATION/
LIBRARY*
Christian Classroom
Leader/Church School
Today—R
Parish Teacher
Shining Star

PASTORS/LEADERS
Pulpit Helps—R

TEEN/YOUNG ADULT
Certainty
Challenge
Conqueror—R
J.A.M.—R
Listen—R
Live Wire—R
Real Time—R
Teens on Target—R
YOU!—R
Young Salvationist—R
Youth Challenge—R

WRITERS
Heaven—R

FOOD/RECIPES

ADULT/GENERAL
Bridal Guides—R
Catholic Digest—R
Catholic Forester—R
Catholic Parent

CGA World—R
Christian C.L. RECORD—R
Dovetail—R
Fellowship Link—R
Good News Journal (TX)
Grit
Healing Inn—R
Home Times—R
Ideals—R
John Milton—R
Joyfull Noise
Living—R
Lutheran Digest—R
Lutheran Journal—R
Mature Living
MESSAGE
Over the Back Fence—R
Parent Paper—R
Peoples Magazine—R
Progress—R
Short Stories Bimonthly
Today's Christian Senior—
R
Vibrant Life—R

CHILDREN
Celebrate
Club Connection—R
Discovery (NY)—R
Focus/Clubhouse
Focus/Clubhouse Jr.
Live Wire—R
On the Line—R
Pockets—R (recipes)
Skipping Stones
Together Time—R
Touch—R

PASTORS/LEADERS
Minister's Family

WOMEN
Christian Women Today—R
Godly Business Woman
Hearts at Home—R
Helping Hand—R
Joyful Woman—R
True Woman
Welcome Home
Woman Alive
Women Today—R

HEALING

ADULT/GENERAL
And He Will Give
Angels on Earth
Banner

Bible Advocate—R
Biblical Reflections—R
Bread of Life—R
Breakthrough Intercessor—R
Canada Lutheran—R
Catholic Digest—R
Catholic New Times—R
Celebrate Life—R
CGA World—R
Charisma/Christian Life
Chicken Soup/Mother—R
Chicken Soup/Woman—R
Christian Motorsports
Christian Ranchman
Chrysalis Reader
Compleat Nurse—R
Connecting Point—R
Connection Mag.—R
Evangelical Advocate—R
Foursquare World—R
Gem—R
God Allows U-Turns—R
Good News (KY)—R
Good News!
Good News, Etc.—R
Good News Journal (MO)—R
Guideposts
Healing Inn—R
John Milton—R
Jour/Christian Nursing—R
Legions of Light—R
Life Gate—R
Light and Life
Liguorian
Live—R
Living—R
Mature Years—R
Mennonite—R
Metro Voice—R
Michigan Christian
Ncubator.com—R
New Covenant
New Heart—R
New Writing—R
Now What?—R
Our Family—R
Peoples Magazine—R
Prayer Closet
PrayerWorks—R
Presbyterian Record—R
Presbyterians Today—R
Preserving Christian Homes—R
Purpose—R
Sacred Journey—R
SCP Journal—R
Sharing—R
Sojourners

Spiritual Life
Testimony—R
Total Health
United Church Observer—R
Upsouth—R
Vision—R
Way of St. Francis—R

CHILDREN
BREAD/God's Children—R
Discovery (NY)—R
Discovery Trails—R
High Adventure—R

MISSIONS
American Horizon—R
Areopagus—R

PASTORS/LEADERS
African American Pulpit
Journal/Christian Healing—R
Journal/Pastoral Care
Lutheran Partners—R
Ministries Today
Ministry
Pastoral Life—R
Priest
Sharing the Practice—R
Word & World

TEEN/YOUNG ADULT
Conqueror—R
Devo'Zine—R
Young Adult Today

WOMEN
Godly Business Woman
Helping Hand—R
Woman's Touch—R

WRITERS
Areopagus (UK)

HEALTH

ADULT/GENERAL
Accent on Living—R
Alive!—R
And He Will Give
Angels on Earth
Anglican Journal—R
Banner
B.C. Catholic—R
Bible Advocate—R
Biblical Reflections—R
Breakthrough Intercessor—R
Canada Lutheran—R
Catholic Digest—R

Catholic Forester—R
Catholic New Times—R
Celebrate Life—R
CGA World—R
Charisma/Christian Life
Christian Courier (WI)—R
Christian Courier (CAN)—R
Christian Living—R
Christian Motorsports
Christian Ranchman
Christian Reader—R
Christian Social Action—R
Companion
Compleat Nurse—R
Creation Care—R
Disciple's Journal—R
Discovery (FL)—R
Expression Christian
Faith Today
Fellowship Link—R
Good News Journal (MO)—R
Good News Journal (TX)
Gospel Today
Grit
Guideposts
Home Times—R
Inland NW Christian
Inside Journal—R
John Milton—R
Jour/Christian Nursing—R
Lifeglow—R
LifeWise
Light and Life
Living—R
Living Light News—R
Lutheran Digest—R
Lutheran Journal—R
Lutheran Witness
Marriage Partnership
Mature Years—R
Mennonite—R
MESSAGE
Metro Voice—R
Michigan Christian
Ncubator.com—R
New Heart—R
Parent Paper—R
Peoples Magazine—R
Physician—R
Plus—R
Pourastan—R
PrayerWorks—R
Sacred Journey—R
SCP Journal—R
Short Stories Bimonthly
Single-Parent Family
Smart Families
Standard, The—R

Studio Classroom
TEAK Roundup—R
thegoodsteward.com—R
Today's Christian Senior—R
Total Health
Trumpeter—R
Upscale Magazine
Upsouth—R
Vibrant Life—R
War Cry—R

CHILDREN
BREAD/God's Children—R
Club Connection—R
Focus/Clubhouse Jr.
High Adventure—R
Live Wire—R
On the Line—R
Skipping Stones
Touch—R

*CHRISTIAN EDUCATION/
LIBRARY*
Leader/Church School
   Today—R

MISSIONS
Areopagus—R

PASTORS/LEADERS
Christian Camp—R
Journal/Christian Healing—
   R
Journal/Pastoral Care
Lutheran Partners—R
Minister's Family
Ministries Today
Pastoral Life—R
Reaching Children at Risk
Word & World

TEEN/YOUNG ADULT
Conqueror—R
Essential Connection—R
Today's Christian Teen—R
Young Adult Today
Young & Alive—R

WOMEN
Canticle
Christian Women Today—R
Esprit—R
Excellence
Godly Business Woman
Hearts at Home—R
Helping Hand—R
Horizons—R
Journey—R

Lutheran Woman's Quar.
Shine
Today's Christian Woman
Welcome Home
Woman's Touch—R
Women Today—R

HISTORICAL

ADULT/GENERAL
AGAIN—R
America
Angels on Earth
Arlington Catholic
Banner
Baptist History
Cathedral Age
Catholic Answer
Catholic Digest—R
Catholic Insight
Catholic New Times—R
Catholic Sentinel—R
Celebrate Life—R
Christian C.L. RECORD—R
Christian Courier (CAN)—R
Christian History—R
Christian Motorsports
Christian Observer
Christian Ranchman
Christian Reader—R
Christian Renewal—R
Christianity Today—R
Chrysalis Reader
Church & State—R
Columbia
Companions—R (church)
Company—R (of Jesuits)
Conquest
Covenant Companion—R
Creation Ex Nihilo
Cresset
Dallas/Ft. Worth Heritage
Dovetail—R
Evangelical Advocate—R
Faith Today
Fellowship Link—R
Good News, Etc.—R
Good News Journal (TX)
Gospel Today
Grit
Hidden Manna—R
Homeschooling Today—R
Home Times—R
Hunted News
Indian Life—R
John Milton—R
Jour/Christian Nursing—R
Journal of Church & State

Legions of Light—R
Lifeglow—R
Light and Life
Live—R
Lutheran Journal—R
Lutheran Witness
Mennonite Historian—R
Messenger/St. Anthony
Methodist History
Michigan Christian
Minnesota Christian—R
Nashville Christian—R
Ncubator.com—R
New Moon—R
Our Sunday Visitor
Over the Back Fence—R
Peoples Magazine—R
Presbyterian Layman
Presbyterian Outlook
Presbyterians Today—R
Pourastan—R
Power for Living—R
PrayerWorks—R
Purpose—R
Re:generation
Sacred Journey—R
SCP Journal—R
Sharing—R
Social Justice
Storyteller—R
TEAK Roundup—R
Today's Christian Senior—R
Upscale Magazine
Upsouth—R

CHILDREN
Courage
Discovery(NY)—R
Focus/Clubhouse
Guideposts for Kids
My Friend
Nature Friend—R
On the Line—R
Partners—R

*CHRISTIAN EDUCATION/
LIBRARY*
Vision—R

MISSIONS
American Horizon—R
Areopagus—R
East-West Church
Missiology
So All May Hear—R
Women of the Harvest
World Christian—R
Worldwide Challenge

MUSIC
Church Pianist, etc.
Creator—R

PASTORS/LEADERS
African American Pulpit
Five Stones—R
Journal/Christian Healing—R
Lutheran Partners—R
Ministry
Pastoral Life—R
Reaching Children at Risk
Sewanee Theological Review
   (church)
Sharing the Practice—R
Today's Parish—R
Word & World

TEEN/YOUNG ADULT
Certainty
Challenge
Essential Connection—R
Listen—R
Student Leadership—R
Young Adult Today
Young & Alive—R

WOMEN
Horizons—R
Just Between Us—R

WRITERS
Areopagus (UK)

HOLIDAY/SEASONAL

ADULT/GENERAL
Accent on Living—R
Alive!—R
alive now!
American Tract Soc.—R
Angels on Earth
Annals of St. Anne
Arlington Catholic
Banner
Bread of Life—R
Breakthrough Intercessor—
   R
Bridal Guides—R
Canada Lutheran—R
Cathedral Age
Catholic Digest—R
Catholic Faith & Family
Catholic Forester—R
Catholic New York
Catholic Parent
Catholic Sentinel—R
CGA World—R

Charisma/Christian Life
Chicken Soup/Mother—R
Chicken Soup/Woman—R
Christian Century
Christian C.L. RECORD—R
Christian Courier (WI)—R
Christian Home & School
Christian Living—R
Christian Motorsports
Christian Parenting—R
Christian Ranchman
Christian Reader—R
Christian Renewal—R
Christian Standard—R
Christianity Today—R
Church Herald/Holiness—R
Companions—R
Connecting Point—R
Connection Mag.—R
Conquest
Covenant Companion—R
Decision
Discovery (FL)—R
Dovetail—R
Evangel—R
Evangelical Advocate—R
Expression Christian
Family Digest
Fellowship Focus—R
Fellowship Link—R
Focus on the Family
Forefront—R
Foursquare World—R
Gem—R
God's Revivalist
Good News Journal (TX)
Good News, Etc.—R
Gospel Today
Gospel Tract—R
Grit
Guideposts
Healing Inn—R
Heartlight Internet—R
Homeschooling Today—R
Home Times—R
Ideals—R
Indian Life—R
Inside Journal—R
Inspirer—R
John Milton—R
Jour/Christian Nursing—R
Keys to Living—R
Legions of Light—R
Life Gate—R
Lifeglow—R
Light and Life
Liguorian
Live—R

Living—R
Living Church
Living Light News—R
Lutheran Digest—R
Lutheran Journal—R
Lutheran Witness
Marriage Partnership
Mature Living
Mennonite—R
MESSAGE
Messenger
Messenger/St. Anthony
Michigan Christian
Minnesota Christian—R
Montana Catholic—R
Nashville Christian—R
Ncubator.com—R
North American Voice
NRB Magazine—R
Oblates
On Mission
Our Sunday Visitor
Over the Back Fence—R
Parent Paper—R
Pegasus Review—R
Pentecostal Evangel
Peoples Magazine—R
Plain Truth—R
Plus—R
Power for Living—R
PrayerWorks—R
Presbyterian Outlook
Presbyterian Record—R
Presbyterians Today—R
Preserving Christian Homes—
   R
Progress—R
Psychology for Living—R
Purpose—R
St. Joseph's Messenger—R
Sharing—R
Signs of the Times—R
Smart Families
Sojourners
Standard—R
Standard, The—R
Storyteller—R
TEAK Roundup—R
Testimony—R
Time of Singing—R
Today's Christian Senior—R
Together—R
Trumpeter—R
United Church Observer—R
U.S. Catholic
Vibrant Life—R
War Cry—R
Way of St. Francis—R

Wesleyan Advocate—R

CHILDREN
Club Connection—R
Courage
Discovery (NY)—R
Discovery Trails—R
Focus/Clubhouse
Focus/Clubhouse Jr.
Guideposts for Kids
Live Wire—R
On the Line—R
Partners—R
Pockets—R
Primary Pal (IL)
Skipping Stones
Together Time—R
Touch—R
Wonder Time

CHRISTIAN EDUCATION/
LIBRARY
CE Connection—R
Children's Ministry
Church Educator—R
Evangelizing Today's Child—
R
Leader/Church School
Today—R
Parish Teacher
Shining Star
Teacher's Interaction
Vision—R

MISSIONS
Worldwide Challenge

MUSIC
Church Pianist
Contemporary Songwriter—R
Creator—R
Quest—R

PASTORS/LEADERS
African American Pulpit
Catholic Servant
Celebration
Christian Camp—R
Christian Management—R
Enrichment—R
Five Stones—R
Let's Worship
Lutheran Forum—R
Lutheran Partners—R
Ministry & Liturgy—R
Pastoral Life—R
Proclaim
Pulpit Helps—R

Rev.

TEEN/YOUNG ADULT
Breakaway—R
Certainty
Challenge
Conqueror—R
Cornerstone—R
Devo'Zine—R
Encounter—R
Essential Connection—R
Listen—R
Real Time—R
Teenage Christian—R
YOU!—R
Young & Alive—R
Young Salvationist—R

WOMEN
Anna's Journal—R
Christian Women Today—R
Esprit—R
Hearts at Home—R
Helping Hand—R
Horizons—R
Journey—R
Joyful Woman—R
Lutheran Woman's Quar.
Today's Christian Woman
Woman's Touch—R
Women of Spirit—R
Women Today—R

WRITERS
Areopagus (UK)

HOME SCHOOLING

ADULT/GENERAL
Anglican Journal—R
Arlington Catholic
Banner
Bible Advocate—R
Breakthrough Intercessor—
R
Catholic Faith & Family
Catholic Insight
CBA Marketplace
Charisma/Christian Life
Christian C.L. RECORD—R
Christian Computing—R
Christian Motorsports
Christian Observer
Christian Parenting—R
Christian Ranchman
Creation Care—R
Disciple's Journal—R
Discovery (FL)—R

Expression Christian
Focus on the Family
Good News, Etc.—R
Good News Journal (MO)—
R
Good News Journal (TX)
Homeschooling Today—R
Home Times—R
Inspirer—R
Interim—R
Joyfull Noise
Life Gate—R
Liguorian
Living Light News—R
Lutheran Life—R
MESSAGE/Open Bible—R
Metro Voice—R
Michigan Christian
Minnesota Christian—R
Nashville Christian—R
Ncubator.com—R
Parent Paper—R
Preserving Christian Homes—
R
Psychology for Living—R
Social Justice
Sursum Corda!—R
Trumpeter—R
Wesleyan Advocate—R

CHILDREN
BREAD/God's Children—R
Skipping Stones

CHRISTIAN EDUCATION/
LIBRARY
CE Counselor—R
Christian Educators Jour—R
Christian Library Jour.—R
Christian School
Jour/Ed & Christian Belief—
R

PASTORS/LEADERS
Pastoral Life
Reaching Children at Risk
Today's Christian Preacher—
R

TEEN/YOUNG ADULT
Conqueror—R
YOU!—R

WOMEN
Esprit—R
Hearts at Home—R
Helping Hand—R

HOMILETICS

ADULT/GENERAL
Bible Advocate—R
Church Herald/Holiness—R
Light and Life
Ncubator.com—R
Presbyterian Outlook
St. Willibrord Journal
Testimony—R

PASTORS/LEADERS
African American Pulpit
Angelos—R
Christian Ministry
Clergy Journal—R
Growing Churches
Leadership—R
Lutheran Partners—R
Pastoral Life—R
Preacher's Illus. Service—R
Priest
Pulpit Helps—R
Quarterly Review
Sharing the Practice—R

HOW-TO ACTIVITIES (JUV.)

ADULT/GENERAL
Catholic Forester—R
Christian Crafter—R
Christian Designer—R
Christian Parenting—R
Christian Ranchman
Church Herald/Holiness—R
Compleat Nurse—R
Creation Care—R
Dovetail—R
Good News Journal (MO)—R
Healing Inn—R
Homeschooling Today—R
Indian Life—R
Joyfull Noise
Living—R
Lutheran Life—R
Michigan Christian

CHILDREN
American Girl
BREAD/God's Children—R
Celebrate
Club Connection—R
Courage
Crusader—R
Discovery (NY)—R
Discovery Trails—R
Focus/Clubhouse

Focus/Clubhouse Jr.
God's World News—R
GUIDE—R
Guideposts for Kids
High Adventure—R
Kids' Ministry Ideas—R
Live Wire—R
My Friend
Nature Friend—R
On the Line—R
Partners—R
Pockets—R
Preschool Playhouse
Primary Pal (IL)
Together Time—R
Touch—R
Winner—R
Wonder Time

CHRISTIAN EDUCATION/ LIBRARY
Christian Classroom
Christian School Admin.
Church Educator—R
Early Childhood News
Evangelizing Today's Child—R
GROUP
Junior Teacher—R
Leader/Church School Today—R
Perspective—R
Preschool Playhouse
Shining Star
Signal—R
Today's Catholic Teacher—R

MUSIC
Songwriting—R

PASTORS/LEADERS
Let's Worship
Reaching Children at Risk

TEEN/YOUNG ADULT
Breakaway—R
Real Time—R
Young Salvationist—R

WOMEN
Godly Business Woman
Just Between Us—R
Reflections (FL)

WRITERS
Cochran's Corner—R

HOW-TO

ADULT/GENERAL
Accent on Living—R
Bridal Guides—R
Catholic Faith & Family
Catholic Forester—R
CBA Frontline
CBA Marketplace
Celebrate Life—R
CGA World—R
Charisma/Christian Life
Christian Crafter—R
Christian Designer—R
Christian Home & School
Christian Living—R
Christian Motorsports
Christian Observer
Christian Parenting—R
Christian Ranchman
Christian Reader—R
Christian Standard—R
Christianity Online—R
Church of God EVANGEL
Compleat Nurse—R
Connecting Point—R
Conquest
Covenant Companion—R
Creation Care—R
Discipleship Journal
Discovery (FL)—R
Expression Christian
Family Digest
Fellowship Link—R
Good News, Etc.—R
Gospel Today
Healing Inn—R
HomeLife—R
Homeschooling Today—R
Home Times—R
Inland NW Christian
Jour/Christian Nursing—R
Joyfull Noise
Legions of Light—R
Life@Work
Light and Life
Living—R
Living Church
Living Light News—R
Lutheran Digest—R
Lutheran Witness
Marriage Partnership
Mature Living
MESSAGE
Michigan Christian
New Writing—R
NRB Magazine—R
Our Sunday Visitor

Physician—R
Plus—R
PrayerWorks—R
Preserving Christian Homes—
    R
Quiet Revolution—R
Single-Parent Family
Smart Families
Standard—R
Standard, The—R
TEAK Roundup—R
thegoodsteward.com—R
Total Health
Trumpeter—R
2-Soar
Vibrant Life—R

CHILDREN

Discovery (NY)—R
High Adventure—R
J.A.M.—R
Kids' Ministry Ideas—R

*CHRISTIAN EDUCATION/
LIBRARY*

Brigade Leader—R
Catechist
Catholic Library World
CE Connection
    Communique—R
CE Counselor—R
Christian Classroom
Christian Librarian—R
Children's Ministry
Christian School
Christian School Admin.
Church & Synagogue Lib.—
    R
Church Educator—R
Church Libraries—R
GROUP
Leader/Church School
    Today—R
Lollipops
Perspective—R
Shining Star
Teacher's Interaction
Today's Catholic Teacher—R
Vision—R
Youth & CE Leadership—R

MISSIONS

Hope for Children—R
PFI World Report—R

MUSIC

Contemporary Songwriter—
    R

Songwriting—R
Gospel Industry Today
Tradition

PASTORS/LEADERS

Christian Camp—R
Church Administration
Clergy Journal—R
Evangelicals Today—R
Growing Churches
Ivy Jungle Report—R
Lutheran Partners—R
Ministry & Liturgy—R
Newsletter Newsletter
Reaching Children at Risk
    Rev.
Small Group Network
Worship Leader
Youthworker

TEEN/YOUNG ADULT

Boundless Webzine—R
Breakaway—R
Certainty
Challenge
Encounter—R
Guideposts for Teens—R
J.A.M.—R
Real Time—R
Teens on Target—R
YOU!—R
Youth Challenge—R

WOMEN

Christian Women Today—R
Connection
Esprit—R
Handmaiden—R
Helping Hand—R
Horizons—R
Just Between Us—R
Reflections (FL)
Today's Christian Woman
Women Today—R

WRITERS

Byline
Canadian Writer's Jour—R
Christian Communicator—R
Cochran's Corner—R
Contemporary Songwriter—
    R
Cross & Quill—R
Exchange—R
NW Christian Author
Once Upon a Time
WE!—R
Writer's Digest—R

Writer's Forum (OH)—R
Writer's Ink—R

HUMOR

ADULT/GENERAL

Accent on Living—R
Alive!—R
American Wasteland
Angels on Earth
Catholic Digest—R
Catholic Faith & Family
Catholic Forester—R
Catholic Parent
CBA Frontline
CGA World—R
Charisma/Christian Life
Chicken Soup/Mother—R
Chicken Soup/Woman—R
Christian C.L. RECORD—R
Christian Computing—R
Christian Courier (CAN)—R
Christian Home & School
Christian Living—R
Christian Motorsports
Christian Parenting—R
Christian Ranchman
Christian Reader—R
Christianity Online—R
Church Herald/Holiness—R
Church of God EVANGEL
Companion
Compleat Nurse—R
Connecting Point—R
Connection Mag.—R
Covenant Companion—R
Disciple's Journal—R
Door—R (satire)
Dovetail—R
Evangelical Advocate—R
Faith Today
Family Digest
Fellowship Link—R
Gem—R
Good News, Etc.—R
Good News Journal (MO)—
    R
Good News Journal (TX)
Gospel Today
Gospel Tract—R
Grit
Healing Inn—R
HomeLife—R
Home Times—R
Impact Magazine—R
Indian Life—R
Inland NW Christian
John Milton—R

Joyfull Noise
Karitos Review—R
Legions of Light—R
Life@Work
Life Gate—R
Light and Life
Lifeglow—R
Liguorian
Living—R
Living Church
Living Light News—R
Lookout—R
Lutheran—R
Lutheran Digest—R
Lutheran Journal—R
Lutheran Witness
Marriage Partnership
Mature Living
MESSAGE/Open Bible—R
Messenger/St. Anthony
Michigan Christian
Minnesota Christian—R
Nashville Christian—R
New Freeman—R
New Heart—R
New Moon—R
NRB Magazine—R
Our Family—R
Over the Back Fence—R
Parenting Our Parents—R
Pegasus Review—R
Peoples Magazine—R
Plain Truth—R
PrayerWorks—R
Presbyterian Record—R
Presbyterians Today—R
Preserving Christian Homes—
    R
Psychology for Living—R
Reflections
Seek—R
Selah!Kids
Single-Parent Family
Smart Families
Sojourners
Spirit—R
Standard, The—R
Star of Zion
Stepping Out
Storyteller—R
Testimony—R
thegoodsteward.com—R
Today's Christian Senior—R
Together—R
Trumpeter—R
Upsouth—R
Vision—R
War Cry—R

Winsome Wit—R
Wireless Age—R

CHILDREN
Club Connection—R
Courage
Discovery (NY)—R
Focus/Clubhouse
Focus/Clubhouse Jr.
GUIDE—R
Guideposts for Kids
High Adventure—R
Live Wire—R
My Friend
On the Line—R
Touch—R
Winner—R
Wonder Time

*CHRISTIAN EDUCATION/
LIBRARY*
CE Connection—R
Children's Ministry
Christian Classroom
Christian School
Christian School Admin.
GROUP
Leader/Church School
    Today—R
Signal—R
Teachers in Focus—R
Teacher's Interaction
Team—R

MISSIONS
Areopagus—R
Women of the Harvest
Worldwide Challenge

MUSIC
Church Pianist, etc.
Contemporary Songwriter—
    R
Creator—R
Quest—R

PASTORS/LEADERS
Catholic Servant
Christian Camp—R
Christian Ministry
Clergy Journal—R
Enrichment—R
Eucharistic Minister—R
Evangelical Baptist—R
Evangelicals Today—R
Five Stones—R
Growing Churches
Leadership—R

Let's Worship
Minister's Family
Ministries Today
Ministry & Liturgy—R
Pastoral Life—R
Preacher's Illus. Service—R
Pulpit Helps—R
Rev.
Sermon Notes
Sharing the Practice—R
Small Group Network
Today's Parish
WCA News—R

TEEN/YOUNG ADULT
Boundless Webzine—R
Breakaway—R
Brio
Certainty
Challenge
Conqueror—R
Devo'Zine—R
Encounter—R
Essential Connection—R
Guideposts for Teens—R
Listen—R
Real Time—R
WITH—R
YOU!—R
Young Adult Today
Young & Alive—R
Young Salvationist—R

WOMEN
Esprit—R
Grace—R
Hearts at Home—R
Helping Hand—R
Just Between Us—R
Lutheran Woman's Quar.
Reflections (FL)
SpiritLed Woman
Today's Christian Woman
Wesleyan Woman—R
Woman's Touch—R
Women of Spirit—R

WRITERS
Areopagus (UK)
Byline
Canadian Writer's Jour—R
Cochran's Corner—R
Contemporary Songwriter—
    R
Exchange—R
Once Upon a Time—R
WIN-Informer
Writer's Potpourri—R

INSPIRATIONAL

ADULT/GENERAL

And He Will Give
Angels on Earth
Annals of St. Anne
Arlington Catholic
Banner
Bible Advocate—R
Bread of Life—R
Breakthrough Intercessor—R
Bridal Guides—R
Canada Lutheran—R
Catholic Answer
Catholic Digest—R
Catholic Faith & Family
Catholic Forester—R
Catholic New Times—R
Catholic Parent
CBA Frontline
Celebrate Life—R
CGA World—R
Charisma/Christian Life
Chicken Soup/Mother—R
Chicken Soup/Woman—R
Christian Crafter—R
Christian Designer—R
Christian Living—R
Christian Motorsports
Christian Reader—R
Church Advocate—R
Church Herald/Holiness—R
Church of God EVANGEL
Companions—R
Connecting Point—R
Connection Mag.—R
Covenant Companion—R
Decision
Dunamis Life—R
Eternal Ink—R
Evangel—R
Evangelical Advocate—R
Faith & Friends—R
Family Digest
Fellowship Link—R
Foursquare World—R
Gem—R
God Allows U-Turns—R
God's Revivalist
Good News—R
Good News Journal (MO)—R
Good News Journal (TX)
Gospel Today
Gospel Tract—R
Grit
Guideposts
Healing Inn—R

Heartlight Internet—R
Highway News—R
HomeLife—R
Home Times—R
Ideals—R
Indian Life—R
Inland NW Christian
Inspirer—R
Jewel Among Jewels—R
John Milton—R
Karitos Review—R
Keys to Living—R
Leaves—R
Legions of Light—R
Life Gate—R
Lifeglow—R
LifeWise
Light and Life
Liguorian
Live—R
Living—R
Living Church
Living Light News—R
Lookout—R
Lutheran—R
Lutheran Digest—R
Lutheran Journal—R
Marian Helpers—R
Mature Living
Mature Years—R
Mennonite Brethren—R
MESSAGE
MESSAGE/Open Bible—R
Messenger/Sacred Heart
Messenger/St. Anthony
Michigan Christian
Nashville Christian—R
Ncubator.com—R
New Covenant
New Freeman—R
New Heart—R
New Moon—R
New Writing—R
Northwestern Lutheran—R
Now What?—R
Oblates
On Mission
Our Sunday Visitor
Over the Back Fence—R
Parenting Our Parents—R
Pegasus Review—R
Pentecostal Evangel
Peoples Magazine—R
Plain Truth—R
Plowman—R
Plus—R
Pourastan—R
Power for Living—R

PrayerWorks—R
Presbyterian Record—R
Presbyterians Today—R
Preserving Christian Homes—R
Psychology for Living—R
Purpose—R
Queen of All Hearts
Sacred Journey—R
St. Joseph's Messenger—R
Say Amen—R
Seeds
Seek—R
Shantyman—R
Single-Parent Family
Smart Families
Sojourners
Spirit—R
Standard—R
Stepping Out
Sursum Corda!—R
TEAK Roundup—R
Testimony—R
thegoodsteward.com—R
Time of Singing—R
Today's Christian Senior—R
Together—R
Total Health
2-Soar
United Church Observer—R
Upscale Magazine
Upsouth—R
U.S. Catholic
Vision—R
War Cry—R
Way of St. Francis—R
Wesleyan Advocate—R
Whispers From Heaven—R
Worldwide Challenge

CHILDREN

BREAD/God's Children—R
Club Connection—R
Discovery (NY)—R
GUIDE—R
Guideposts for Kids
High Adventure—R
J.A.M.—R
Partners—R
Touch—R
Wonder Time

*CHRISTIAN EDUCATION/
LIBRARY*

CE Connection—R
CE Counselor—R
Children's Ministry
Christian Classroom

Christian School
Christian School Admin.
Church & Synagogue Lib.
Journal/Adventist Educ.—R
Junior Teacher—R
Leader/Church School
   Today—R
Perspective—R
Shining Star
Signal—R
Teacher's Interaction
Today's Catholic Teacher—
   R
Vision—R

MISSIONS
American Horizon—R
Areopagus—R

MUSIC
Creator—R
Quest—R
Senior Musician—R
Tradition

PASTORS/LEADERS
Catholic Servant
Cell Group—R
Christian Camp—R
Christian Management—R
Evangelical Baptist—R
Evangelicals Today—R
Growing Churches
Journal/Pastoral Care
Leadership—R
Minister's Family
Ministry
Pastoral Life—R
PROCLAIM—R
Pulpit Helps—R
Reaching Children at Risk
Resource—R
Sharing the Practice—R
Today's Christian Preacher—
   R

TEEN/YOUNG ADULT
Breakaway—R
Conqueror—R
Devo'Zine—R
Encounter—R
Guideposts for Teens—R
J.A.M.—R
Real Time—R
Teenage Christian—R
Teens on Target—R
Today's Christian Teen—R
WITH—R

YOU!—R
Young Adult Today
Young & Alive—R
Youth Challenge—R

WOMEN
Christian Women Today—
   R
Connection
Esprit—R
Godly Business Woman
Grace—R
Hearts at Home—R
Helping Hand—R
Horizons—R
Journey—R
Joyful Woman—R
Just Between Us
Lutheran Woman's Quar.
Lutheran Woman Today
Proverbs 31 Woman—R
Reflections (FL)
SpiritLed Woman
Wesleyan Woman—R
Woman's Touch—R
Women Alive!—R
Women of Spirit—R
Women Today—R

WRITERS
Areopagus (UK)
Byline
Canadian Writer's Jour—R
Cochran's Corner—R
Fellowscript—R
Once Upon a Time—R
Writer's Digest—R
Writer's Forum (OH)—R

INTERVIEWS/PROFILES

ADULT/GENERAL
Accent on Living—R
AGAIN—R
Alive!—R
American Tract Soc.—R
Anglican Journal—R
Arkansas Catholic
Arlington Catholic
Breakthrough Intercessor—
   R
Catholic Faith & Family
Catholic New York
Catholic Parent
Catholic Sentinel—R
Celebrate Life—R
Charisma/Christian Life
Christian C.L. RECORD—R

Christian Courier (CAN)—R
Christian Courier (WI)—R
Christian Crafter—R
Christian Designer—R
Christian Motorsports
Christian News NW—R
Christian Observer
Christian Parenting—R
Christian Ranchman
Christian Reader—R
Christian Social Action—R
Christian Times
Christianity Online—R
Christianity Today—R
Church Advocate—R
Church & State—R
Company—R
Compleat Nurse—R
Connection Mag.—R
Cornerstone—R (music)
Creation Care—R
Creation Ex Nihilo
Culture Wars—R
Discipleship Journal
Door
Dovetail—R
Dunamis Life—R
Episcopal Life—R
Eternal Ink—R
Expression Christian
Faith Today
Family Digest
Focus on the Family
Forefront—R
Gem—R
Good News—R
Good News, Etc.—R
Good News Journal (MO)—
   R
Good News Journal (TX)
Gospel Today
Grit
Guideposts
Healing Inn—R
Heartlight Internet—R
Hidden Manna—R
Highway News—R
HomeLife—R
Homeschooling Today—R
Home Times—R
Impact Magazine—R
Indian Life—R
Inside Journal—R
Interim—R
John Milton—R
Jour/Christian Nursing—R
Joyfull Noise
Joyful Noise

Legions of Light—R
Life@Work
Lifeglow—R
LifeWise
Light and Life
Liguorian
Living—R
Living Church
Living Light News—R
Lookout—R
Lutheran—R
Lutheran Journal—R
Mature Years—R
Mennonite—R
Mennonite Historian—R
MESSAGE
Messenger
Messenger/St. Anthony
Metro Voice—R
Michigan Christian
Minnesota Christian—R
Montana Catholic—R
Nashville Christian—R
New Covenant
New Heart—R
New Moon—R
New Writing—R
No-Debt Living—R
NRB Magazine—R
On Mission
Our Sunday Visitor
Over the Back Fence—R
Physician—R
Plain Truth—R
Power for Living—R
Presbyterian Layman
Presbyterian Outlook
Presbyterian Record—R
Presbyterians Today—R
Priority!
Prism—R
Quiet Revolution—R
Re:generation
Sacred Journey—R
St. Anthony Messenger
Say Amen—R
SCP Journal—R
Short Stories Bimonthly
Signs of the Times—R
Single-Parent Family
Sojourners
Standard, The—R
Stewardship
Sursum Corda!—R
thegoodsteward.com—R
Today's Christian Senior—R
Trumpeter—R
United Church Observer—R

Upscale Magazine
Upsouth—R
U.S. Catholic
War Cry—R
Wireless Age—R

CHILDREN
Discovery (NY)—R
Focus/Clubhouse
Guideposts for Kids
J.A.M.—R
Live Wire—R
Pockets—R
Skipping Stones
Touch—R

CHRISTIAN EDUCATION/LIBRARY
Brigade Leader—R
Children's Ministry
CE Counselor—R
Christian Educators Jour—R
Christian Librarian—R
Christian School
Church Libraries—R
Leader/Church School
   Today—R
Perspective—R
Signal—R
Teachers in Focus—R

MISSIONS
American Horizon—R
Catholic Near East
East-West Church
Evangelical Missions—R
Hope for Children—R
Latin America Evangelist
Leaders for Today
PFI World Report—R
So All May Hear—R
Worldwide Challenge

MUSIC
Church Music World
Contemporary Songwriter—R
Gospel Industry Today
Quest—R

PASTORS/LEADERS
Angelos—R
Catholic Servant
Cell Group—R
Christian Camp—R
Christian Management—R
Clergy Journal—R
Evangelicals Today—R
Five Stones—R
Growing Churches

Ivy Jungle Report—R
Journal/Christian Healing—R
Leadership—R
Lutheran Partners—R
Ministries Today
Ministry & Liturgy—R
Pastoral Life—R
PROCLAIM—R
Reaching Children at Risk
Sabbath School Leadership
Sermon Notes
Technologies/Worship—R
Youthworker

TEEN/YOUNG ADULT
Boundless Webzine—R
Breakaway—R
Christian College Focus
Devo'Zine—R
Encounter—R
Essential Connection—R
Guideposts for Teens—R
Insight—R
J.A.M.—R
Passageway.org—R
Real Time—R
Sharing the VICTORY—R
Teenage Christian—R
YOU!—R
Young Adult Today
Young & Alive—R
Young Salvationist—R

WOMEN
Christian Bride
Esprit—R
Excellence
Grace—R
Handmaiden—R
Hearts at Home—R
Horizons—R
Jour/Women's Ministries
Journey—R
Woman Alive
Women Who Minister—R

WRITERS
Advanced Christian Writer—R
Areopagus (UK)
Canadian Writer's Jour—R
Christian Communicator—R
Christian Writer—R
Cochran's Corner—R
Contemporary Songwriter—R
Cross & Quill—R
Exchange—R
Fellowscript—R
NW Christian Author—R

Once Upon a Time—R
WIN-Informer
Writer Online—R
Writer's Info
Writer's Ink—R
Writer's Potpourri—R

LEADERSHIP

ADULT/GENERAL
Angels on Earth
Banner
Bible Advocate—R
Breakthrough Intercessor—R
Catholic Forester—R
CGA World—R
Christian Century
Christian Leader—R
Christian Living—R
Christian Motorsports
Christian Ranchman
Church Advocate—R
Church Herald/Holiness—R
Compleat Nurse—R
Connection Mag.—R
Covenant Companion—R
Culture Wars—R
Decision
Discipleship Journal
Disciple's Journal—R
Dunamis Life—R
Evangel—R
Evangelical Advocate—R
Expression Christian
Faith Today
Fellowship Focus—R
Foursquare World—R
Gem—R
Good News (KY)—R
Good News, Etc.—R
Good News Journal (TX)
Gospel Today
Grit
Heartlight Internet—R
Inland NW Christian
John Milton—R
Jour/Christian Nursing—R
Life@Work
Light and Life
Liguorian
Living Church
Lookout—R
Lutheran Journal—R
MESSAGE/Open Bible—R
Michigan Christian
Nashville Christian—R

Ncubator.com—R
New Freeman—R
NRB Magazine—R
Our Family—R
Our Sunday Visitor
Perspectives
Plain Truth—R
Pourastan—R
Presbyterian Layman
Presbyterian Outlook
Presbyterian Record—R
Prism—R
Purpose—R
Reflections
Re:generation
thegoodsteward.com—R
Trumpeter—R
United Church Observer—R
Way of St. Francis—R
Wireless Age—R

CHILDREN
BREAD/God's Children—R
Club Connection—R
Discovery (NY)—R
Skipping Stones

*CHRISTIAN EDUCATION/
LIBRARY*
Brigade Leader—R
CE Connection
   Communique—R
CE Counselor—R
Children's Ministry
Christian Classroom
Christian Librarian—R
Christian School Admin.
Church Educator—R
GROUP
Journal/Christian Education
Leader/Church School
   Today—R
Perspective—R
Resource—R
Signal—R
Teacher's Interaction
Team—R
Vision—R
Youth & CE Leadership—R

MISSIONS
American Horizon—R
Catholic Near East
East-West Church
Latin America Evangelist
Leaders for Today
Missiology
Worldwide Challenge

PASTORS/LEADERS
Angelos—R
Catholic Servant
Cell Group—R
Christian Camp—R
Christian Century
Christian Management—R
Christian Ministry
Church Growth Network—R
Church Management—R
Church Worship
Clergy Journal—R
Emmanuel
Enrichment—R
Eucharistic Minister—R
Evangelical Baptist—R
Evangelicals Today—R
Five Stones—R
Growing Churches
Horizons—R
Ivy Jungle Report—R
Jour/Amer Soc/Chur Growth—R
Leadership—R
Lutheran Partners—R
Minister's Family
Ministries Today
Ministry
Pastoral Life—R
Pulpit Helps—R
Quarterly Review
Reaching Children at Risk
Resource—R
Rev.
Sabbath School Leadership
Sermon Notes
Sharing the Practice—R
Today's Christian Preacher—R
WCA News—R
Word & World
Worship Leader
Your Church—R
Youthworker

TEEN/YOUNG ADULT
Student Leadership—R
Teenage Christian—R

WOMEN
Esprit—R
Godly Business Woman
Helping Hand—R
Horizons—R
Just Between Us—R
SpiritLed Woman
Woman's Touch—R
Women of Spirit—R

LITURGICAL

ADULT/GENERAL

AGAIN—R
Arkansas Catholic
Arlington Catholic
Banner
Breakthrough Intercessor—R
Catholic Insight
Catholic Parent
CGA World—R
Christian Century
Christian Courier (CAN)—R
Christian Motorsports
Commonweal
Companion
Cresset
Culture Wars—R
Episcopal Life—R
Evangelical Advocate—R
John Milton—R
Living Church
Lutheran Journal—R
Messenger (KY)
Messenger/ Sacred Heart
Messenger/St. Anthony
New Writing—R
North American Voice
Our Family—R
Our Sunday Visitor
Perspectives
Prairie Messenger—R
Presbyterian Record—R
Reflections
St. Anthony Messenger
St. Willibrord Journal
Silver Wings—R
Standard—R
Touchstone—R
U.S. Catholic
Way of St. Francis—R

*CHRISTIAN EDUCATION/
LIBRARY*

Catechist
Church Educator—R
Parish Teacher
Religion Teacher's Journal

MISSIONS

Areopagus—R
Catholic Near East

MUSIC

Church Pianist, etc.
Gospel Industry Today
Hymn

PASTORS/LEADERS

Catechumenate
Catholic Servant
Celebration
Christian Century
Christian Ministry
Church Administration
Church Worship
Diocesan Dialogue—R
Emmanuel
Eucharistic Minister—R
Leadership—R
Let's Worship
Lutheran Forum—R
Lutheran Partners—R
Ministries Today
Ministry & Liturgy—R
Parish Liturgy
Pastoral Life—R
Preacher's Illus. Service—R
Priest
PROCLAIM—R
Quarterly Review
Reformed Worship
Sharing the Practice—R
Theology Today
Today's Parish
Word & World

WOMEN

Esprit—R
Horizons—R
Lutheran Woman Today

MARRIAGE

ADULT/GENERAL

Accent on Living—R
Alive!—R
America
American Tract Soc.—R
American Wasteland
And He Will Give
Angels on Earth
Arkansas Catholic
Arlington Catholic
Banner
Bible Advocate—R
Bread of Life—R
Breakthrough Intercessor—R
Bridal Guides—R
Canada Lutheran—R
Catholic Digest—R
Catholic Faith & Family
Catholic Forester—R
Catholic Parent
Celebrate Life—R
Charisma/Christian Life

Chicken Soup/Mother—R
Chicken Soup/Woman—R
Christian C.L. RECORD—R
Christian Courier (CAN)—R
Christian Crafter—R
Christian Designer—R
Christian Home & School
Christian Leader—R
Christian Living—R
Christian Motorsports
Christian Parenting—R
Christian Ranchman
Christian Reader—R
Christian Social Action—R
Church Advocate—R
Church Herald/Holiness—R
Church of God EVANGEL
Columbia
Companions—R
Connection Mag.—R
Cornerstone—R
Covenant Companion—R
Culture Wars—R
Decision
Discipleship Journal
Disciple's Journal—R
Dovetail—R
Evangel—R
Evangelical Advocate—R
Expression Christian
Faith Today
Family Digest
Fellowship Focus—R
Focus on the Family
Foursquare World—R
Gem—R
God Allows U-Turns—R
Good News, Etc.—R
Good News Journal (MO)—R
Good News Journal (TX)
Gospel Today
Grit
Guideposts
Heartlight Internet—R
Highway News—R
HomeLife—R
Home Times—R
Impact Magazine—R
Indian Life—R
Inside Journal—R
Interim—R
Joyfull Noise
Joyful Noise
Life Gate—R
Lifeglow—R
LifeWise
Light and Life

Living—R
Living Church
Living Light News—R
Lookout—R
Lutheran—R
Lutheran Digest—R
Lutheran Journal—R
Marriage Partnership
Mennonite Brethren—R
Men of Integrity—R
MESSAGE
Messenger/St. Anthony
Metro Voice—R
Michigan Christian
Minnesota Christian—R
Montana Catholic—R
Moody—R
Ncubator.com—R
New Covenant
New Freeman—R
North American Voice
Northwestern Lutheran—R
On Mission
Our Family—R
Our Sunday Visitor
Pegasus Review—R
Pentecostal Evangel
Peoples Magazine—R
Physician—R
Plain Truth—R
Plus—R
Pourastan—R
Prairie Messenger—R
PrayerWorks—R
Presbyterian Layman
Presbyterian Record—R
Presbyterians Today—R
Preserving Christian Homes—
    R
Prism—R
Progress—R
Psychology for Living—R
Purpose—R
Re:generation
St. Anthony Messenger
Say Amen—R
Seek—R
Signs of the Times—R
Social Justice
Standard—R
Standard, The—R
Stepping Out
Testimony—R
Together—R
Upsouth—R
U.S. Catholic
Vibrant Life—R
War Cry—R

Wesleyan Advocate—R

*CHRISTIAN EDUCATION/
LIBRARY*
CE Connection—R
Children's Ministry

MISSIONS
Worldwide Challenge

PASTORS/LEADERS
Angelos—R
Catholic Servant
Cell Group—R
Evangelical Baptist—R
Evangelicals Today—R
Five Stones—R
Growing Churches
Journal/Pastoral Care
Let's Worship
Lutheran Forum—R
Lutheran Partners—R
Minister's Family
Ministries Today
Pastoral Life—R
Preacher's Illus. Service—R
Priest
PROCLAIM—R
Pulpit Helps—R
Rev.
Sharing the Practice—R
Today's Christian Preacher—R
Today's Parish
Word & World

TEEN/YOUNG ADULT
Boundless Webzine—R
YOU!—R
Young Adult Today
Young & Alive—R

WOMEN
Anna's Journal—R
Canticle
Christian Bride
Esprit—R
Godly Business Woman
Handmaiden—R
Hearts at Home—R
Helping Hand—R
Journey—R
Joyful Woman—R
Just Between Us—R
Lutheran Woman's Quar.
Proverbs 31 Woman—R
Reflections (FL)
SpiritLed Woman
Today's Christian Woman

True Woman
Welcome Home
Wesleyan Woman—R
Woman's Touch—R
Women Alive!—R
Women of Spirit—R

MEN'S ISSUES

ADULT/GENERAL
American Tract Soc.—R
American Wasteland
Annals of St. Anne
Arlington Catholic
Banner
Beacon—R
Bible Advocate—R
Bread of Life—R
Breakthrough Intercessor—R
Catholic Digest—R
Catholic Faith & Family
Catholic New Times—R
Catholic Parent
Charisma/Christian Life
Christian Courier (CAN)—R
Christian Designer—R
Christian Leader—R
Christian Living—R
Christian Motorsports
Christian News NW—R
Christian Ranchman
Christian Social Action—R
Chrysalis Reader
Church Herald/Holiness—R
Church of God EVANGEL
Columbia
Companion
Compleat Nurse—R
Decision
Discipleship Journal
Disciple's Journal—R
Dunamis Life—R
Evangel—R
Evangelical Advocate—R
Expression Christian
Focus on the Family
Foursquare World—R
Gem—R
God Allows U-Turns—R
Good News, Etc.—R
Good News Journal (MO)—
    R
Gospel Today
Grit
Heartlight Internet—R
Highway News—R
Home Times—R
Indian Life—R

Inland NW Christian
Inside Journal—R
Interim—R
Joyful Noise
Life Gate—R
LifeWise
Liguorian
Light and Life
Living—R
Living Light News—R
Lookout—R
Marriage Partnership
Men of Integrity—R
Messenger/St. Anthony
Metro Voice—R
Michigan Christian
Moody—R
Nashville Christian—R
Ncubator.com—R
New Freeman—R
Newsline—R
Northwestern Lutheran—R
Our Family—R
Peoples Magazine—R
Physician—R
Plain Truth—R
Plus—R
PrayerWorks—R
Presbyterian Outlook
Presbyterian Record—R
Preserving Christian Homes—
R
Prism—R
Psychology for Living—R
Purpose—R
Re:generation
Smart Families
Standard—R
Testimony—R
Together—R
Touchstone—R
Trumpeter—R
United Church Observer—
R
Upsouth—R
Vibrant Life—R (health)

*CHRISTIAN EDUCATION/
LIBRARY*
Brigade Leader—R

MISSIONS
American Horizon—R
Brigade Leader—R
Worldwide Challenge

MUSIC
Quest—R

PASTORS/LEADERS
Angelos—R
Christian Ministry
Eucharistic Minister—R
Evangelicals Today—R
Journal/Christian Healing—
R
Journal/Pastoral Care
Lutheran Partners—R
Ministries Today
Pastoral Life—R
Pulpit Helps—R
Sharing the Practice—R
Word & World

TEEN/YOUNG ADULT
YOU!—R

WOMEN
Reflections (FL)

MIRACLES

ADULT/GENERAL
America
Angels on Earth
Bible Advocate—R
Bread of Life—R
Breakthrough Intercessor—R
Bridal Guides—R
Catholic Digest—R
CGA World—R
Charisma/Christian Life
Christian Designer—R
Christian Motorsports
Christian Ranchman
Church Advocate—R
Church Herald/Holiness—R
Church of God EVANGEL
Connecting Point—R
Connection Mag.—R
Creation Ex Nihilo
Culture Wars—R
Dunamis Life—R
Evangelical Advocate—R
Gem—R
God Allows U-Turns—R
God's Revivalist
Good News, Etc.—R
Good News Journal (MO)—R
Gospel Today
Grit
Guideposts
Healing Inn—R
Home Times—R
Hunted News
Impact Magazine—R
John Milton—R

Legions of Light—R
Lifeglow—R
Light and Life
Liguorian
Live—R
Lutheran Digest—R
Messenger/St. Anthony
Michigan Christian
Ncubator.com—R
New Freeman—R
New Heart—R
North American Voice
Pegasus Review—R
PrayerWorks—R
Preserving Christian Homes—
R
Priority!
Queen of All Hearts
Spirit—R
Standard, The—R
Stepping Out
Total Health
Upsouth—R
Vision—R

CHILDREN
BREAD/God's Children—R
Discovery (NY)—R
Guideposts for Kids
Leader/Church School
Today—R

MISSIONS
American Horizon—R
Areopagus—R
Latin America Evangelist
So All May Hear—R

PASTORS/LEADERS
Evangelicals Today—R
Lutheran Partners—R
Ministries Today
Pastoral Life—R
Sharing the Practice—R
Word & World

TEEN/YOUNG ADULT
Guideposts for Teens—R
WITH—R
YOU!—R
Young Adult Today
Young & Alive—R

WOMEN
Godly Business Woman
Helping Hand—R
SpiritLed Woman
Woman's Touch—R

MISSIONS

ADULT/GENERAL
AGAIN—R
Alive!—R
Anglican Journal—R
Banner
B.C. Catholic—R
Bible Advocate—R
Breakthrough Intercessor—R
Catholic Digest—R
Charisma/Christian Life
Christian Leader—R
Christian Motorsports
Christian News NW—R
Christian Ranchman
Christian Reader—R
Christianity Today—R
Church Advocate—R
Church Herald/Holiness—R
Church of God EVANGEL
Companions—R
Connecting Point—R
Connection Mag.—R
Conquest
Culture Wars—R
Discipleship Journal
Decision
Episcopal Life—R
Evangelical Advocate—R
Faith Today
Gem—R
Good News—R
Good News, Etc.—R
Good News Journal (MO)—R
Gospel Today
Gospel Tract—R
John Milton—R
Jour/Christian Nursing—R
Legions of Light—R
Life Gate—R
LifeWise
Light and Life
Liguorian
Live—R
Living Church
Lookout—R
Lutheran—R
Lutheran Journal—R
MESSAGE/Open Bible—R
Messenger/St. Anthony
Michigan Christian
Nashville Christian—R
Ncubator.com—R
New Freeman—R
New Heart—R (medical)
North American Voice

On Mission
Our Family—R
Our Sunday Visitor
Peoples Magazine—R
Power for Living—R
PrayerWorks—R
Presbyterian Layman
Presbyterian Outlook
Presbyterians Today—R
Prism—R
Purpose—R
Queen of All Hearts
Re:generation
Seeds
Standard—R
Standard, The—R
Stepping Out
TEAK Roundup—R
Testimony—R
Tomorrow's Christian Graduate
Upsouth—R

CHILDREN
BREAD/God's Children—R
Discovery(NY)—R
J.A.M.—R
Partners—R

CHRISTIAN EDUCATION/ LIBRARY
Brigade Leader—R
Children's Ministry
Christian Librarian—R
Church Educator—R
Courage
Evangelizing Today's Child—R
GROUP
Leader/Church School Today—R
Perspective—R
Shining Star
Signal—R

MISSIONS
(See alphabetical listings)

MUSIC
Quest—R

PASTORS/LEADERS
Christian Management—R
Christian Ministry
Church Administration
Emmanuel
Enrichment—R
Evangelicals Today—R

Growing Churches
Horizons—R
Lutheran Partners—R
Ministries Today
Pastoral Life—R
PROCLAIM—R
Pulpit Helps—R
Rev.
Resource—R
Sharing the Practice—R
Today's Christian Preacher—R
Word & World
Youthworker

TEEN/YOUNG ADULT
Certainty
Challenge
Devo'Zine—R
Essential Connection—R
J.A.M.—R
Passageway.org—R
Real Time—R
Student Leadership—R
Today's Christian Teen—R
WITH—R
YOU!—R
Young Adult Today
Young Salvationist—R

WOMEN
Esprit—R
Godly Business Woman
Horizons—R
Just Between Us—R

MONEY MANAGEMENT

ADULT/GENERAL
Anglican Journal—R
Banner
Bridal Guides—R
Catholic Faith & Family
Catholic Forester—R
Catholic Parent
CBA Marketplace
CGA World—R
Christian C.L. RECORD—R
Christian Courier (CAN)—R
Christian Crafter—R
Christian Designer—R
Christian Living—R
Christian Motorsports
Christian Parenting—R
Christian Ranchman
Church Advocate—R
Church Herald/Holiness—R
Columbia

Connecting Point—R
Conquest
Decision
Disciple's Journal—R
Evangel—R
Evangelical Advocate—R
Expression Christian
Gem—R
Good News Journal (MO)—
   R
Gospel Today
Gospel Tract—R
Heartlight Internet—R
Highway News—R
Home Times—R
Inland NW Christian
Joyfull Noise
Life@Work
Life Gate—R
Lifeglow—R
LifeWise
Light and Life
Living Light News—R
Lookout—R
Lutheran Journal—R
MESSAGE
MESSAGE/Open Bible—R
Michigan Christian
Ncubator.com—R
No-Debt Living—R
NRB Magazine—R
Parent Paper—R
Physician—R
Plain Truth—R
Presbyterian Layman
Preserving Christian Homes—
   R
Signs of the Times—R
Single-Parent Family
Smart Families
Stepping Out
Stewardship
thegoodsteward.com—R
Tomorrow's Christian
   Graduate
Today's Christian Senior—
   R
Trumpeter—R
War Cry—R

CHILDREN
Courage
J.A.M.—R

*CHRISTIAN EDUCATION/
LIBRARY*
Children's Ministry
Christian School

Christian School Admin.
Church Educator—R

PASTORS/LEADERS
Cell Group—R
Christian Ministry
Clergy Journal—R
Enrichment—R
Evangelical Baptist—R
Evangelicals Today—R
Ministries Today
Reaching Children at Risk
Rev.
Sharing the Practice—R
Today's Christian Preacher—
   R
Today's Parish
Your Church—R
Youthworker

TEEN/YOUNG ADULT
Boundless Webzine—R
Certainty
Challenge
Christian College Focus
J.A.M.—R
Today's Christian Teen—R
Young Adult Today

WOMEN
Christian Women Today—R
Excellence
Godly Business Woman
Journey—R
Just Between Us—R
Shine
True Woman
Wesleyan Woman—R
Woman's Touch—R
Women Today—R

MUSIC REVIEWS

ADULT/GENERAL
About Such Things—R
American Wasteland
Arlington Catholic
Banner
Bridge—R
CBA Marketplace
Charisma/Christian Life
Christian Crafter—R
Christian Designer—R
Christian Media—R
Christian Parenting—R
Christian Renewal—R
Christianity/Arts
Commonweal

Connection Mag.—R
Cornerstone—R
Dunamis Life—R
Expression Christian
Good News Journal (MO)—
   R
Heartlight Internet—R
Homeschooling Today—R
Home Times—R
Hunted News
Impact Magazine—R
Indian Life—R
Interim—R
Life Gate—R
Light and Life
Mature Years—R
Michigan Christian
MovieGuide
Ncubator.com—R
On Mission
Plowman—R
Presbyterian Record—R
Prism—R
Re:generation
Sojourners
TEAK Roundup—R
Testimony—R
Trumpeter—R
Upsouth—R
Winsome Wit—R

CHILDREN
Club Connection—R
J.A.M.—R

*CHRISTIAN EDUCATION/
LIBRARY*
CE Counselor—R
Church Libraries—R

MUSIC
CCM Magazine
Cooperative Christian—R
Creator—R
Songwriting—R
Gospel Industry Today
Hymn
Quest—R
Release
Tradition

PASTORS/LEADERS
Horizons—R
Ivy Jungle Report—R
Ministries Today
Technologies/Worship—R
Reformed Worship
Worship Leader

TEEN/YOUNG ADULT

Boundless Webzine—R
Conqueror—R
Devo'Zine—R
Essential Connection—R
J.A.M.—R
Real Time—R
Teenage Christian—R
WITH—R
YOU!—R
Young Salvationist—R

WOMEN

Godly Business Woman

NATURE

ADULT/GENERAL

Alive!—R
Catholic Digest—R
Catholic Forester—R
Catholic New Times—R
Christian Courier (CAN)—R
Christian Renewal—R
Chrysalis Reader
Covenant Companion—R
Creation Care—R
Creation Ex Nihilo
Fellowship Link—R
Gem—R
Grit
Ideals—R
Keys to Living—R
Legions of Light—R
Lifeglow—R
Light and Life
Lutheran Digest—R
Messenger/St. Anthony
Pegasus Review—R
Peoples Magazine—R
Pourastan—R
PrayerWorks—R
Stepping Out
Storyteller—R
thegoodsteward.com—R
Time of Singing—R
Today's Christian Senior—R
Upsouth—R
Vision—R

CHILDREN

Club Connection—R
Courage
Crusader—R
Discovery (NY)—R
Discovery Trails—R
GUIDE—R
Guideposts for Kids

Live Wire—R
My Friend
Nature Friend—R
On the Line
Partners—R
Skipping Stones
Story Friends—R

CHRISTIAN EDUCATION/ LIBRARY

Leader/Church School
  Today—R
Shining Star

PASTORS/LEADERS

Christian Camp—R
Pastoral Life—R
Word & World

TEEN/YOUNG ADULT

Teenage Christian—R
YOU!—R
Young & Alive—R

WOMEN

Esprit—R
Horizons—R
Reflections (FL)

WRITERS

Cochran's Corner—R

NEWSPAPERS

Alabama Baptist
Anglican Journal
Arkansas Catholic
Arlington Catholic
B.C. Catholic
Catholic New Times
Catholic New York
Catholic Peace Voice
Catholic Sentinel
Catholic Telegraph
CE Connection
Christian Courier (CAN)
Christian Courier (WI)
Christian Media
Christian News NW
Christian Observer
Christian Ranchman
Christian Renewal
Christian Times
Christianweek
Church Advocate
Colorado Christian Chronicle
Connection
Dallas/Ft. Worth Heritage

Disciple's Journal
Discovery (FL)
Episcopal Life
Expression Christian
Faro de Luz
GDP Previewer
Good News, Etc.
Good News Journal (MO)
Good News Journal (TX)
Grit
Harvest Press
Home Times
Hunted News
Indian Life
Inland NW Christian
Inside Journal
Interchange
Interim
John Milton
Kentucky Christian
Life Gate
Live Wire
Living
Living Light News
Messenger
Metro Voice
Michigan Christian
Minnesota Christian
Montana Catholic
Nashville Christian
National Catholic Reporter
Network
New Freeman
New Frontier
Our Sunday Visitor
Parent Paper
PrayerWorks
Presbyterian Layman
Presbyterian-Week
Pulpit Helps
Save Our World
Shantyman
Southeast Outlook
Star of Zion
Together

ONLINE MAGAZINES

ADULT/GENERAL

American Wasteland
Books & Culture
Bridge
Cathedral Age
Catholic Digest
Catholic Sentinel
Celebrate Life
Christian Computing
Christian Families Online

Christian Home & School
Christian Online
Christian Reader
Christian Single Online
Christianity & the Arts
Christianity Online
Company
Connection
Cornerstone
Decision
Disaster News Network
Disciple's Journal
Dunamis Life
Eternal Ink
Great Families
Harvest E-Zine
Healing Inn
Heartlight
Heartwarmers
Interim
Living Religion E-zine
Lutheran
National Catholic
Ncubator.com
New Writing
No-Debt Living
Now What?
NRB Magazine
On Mission
Plain Truth
Presbyterians-Week
Quest
Reflections
St. Anthony Messenger
Selah! Kids
Smart Families
Sports Spectrum Online
Studio Classroom
Testimony
thegoodsteward.com
Trumpeter
Visions of Glory
Winsome Wit

CHILDREN
J.A.M.

*CHRISTIAN EDUCATION/
LIBRARY*
CE Connection Communique

DAILY DEVOTIONAL
Forward Day By Day

MISSIONS
Latin America Evangelist
Mission Frontiers
Voices in the Wilderness

MUSIC
CCM Magazine

PASTORS/LEADERS
Angelos
Evangelical Baptist
Issacharfile
Leadership
Preaching
Sermon Notes
Small Group Dynamics
Technologies for Worship
WCA News
Youthworker

TEEN/YOUNG ADULT
Beautiful Christian Teen
Boundless Webzine
HYPE
Passageway.org
Student Leadership
Young Salvationist

WOMEN
Connection
Excellence
True Woman
Women Today
Women Who Minister

WRITERS
Dedicated Author
Fiction Writer Online
Keystrokes
Teachers & Writers
Writer Online

OPINION PIECES

ADULT/GENERAL
About Such Things—R
American Wasteland
Annals of St. Anne
Arlington Catholic
Banner
B.C. Catholic—R
Bible Advocate—R
Bridal Guides—R
Bridge—R
Catholic Faith & Family
Catholic New Times—R
Catholic New York
Charisma/Christian Life
Christian Courier (CAN)—R
Christian Crafter—R
Christian Designer—R
Christian Living—R
Christian Motorsports

Christian News NW—R
Christian Renewal—R
Christian Research
Christian Social Action—R
Christianity Today—R
Colorado Christian—R
Commonweal
Compleat Nurse—R
Cornerstone—R
Culture Wars—R
Door
Dovetail—R
Episcopal Life—R
Evangelical Advocate—R
Faith Today
First Things
Good News, Etc.—R
Good News Journal (MO)—
R
Gospel Today
Home Times—R
Indian Life—R
Inland NW Christian
Interim—R
Jour/Christian Nursing—R
Legions of Light—R
Life@Work
Light and Life
Liguorian
Living Church
Lutheran—R
Mennonite Brethren—R
MESSAGE/Open Bible—R
Messenger
Messenger/St. Anthony
Metro Voice—R
Michigan Christian
Minnesota Christian—R
Nashville Christian—R
Ncubator.com—R
New Freeman—R
New Moon—R
Perspectives
Plain Truth—R
PrayerWorks—R
Presbyterian Outlook
Presbyterian Record—R
Presbyterians Today—R
Quiet Revolution—R
Re:generation
Seeds
Social Justice
Sojourners
Stepping Out
TEAK Roundup—R
thegoodsteward.com—R
Touchstone—R
United Church Observer—R

Upsouth—R
U.S. Catholic
Way of St. Francis—R
Winsome Wit—R

CHILDREN
J.A.M.—R
Skipping Stones

CHRISTIAN EDUCATION/
LIBRARY
Today's Catholic Teacher—R

MISSIONS
American Horizon—R
Areopagus—R
East-West Church
Hope for Children—R
So All May Hear—R
World Christian—R

MUSIC
Contemporary Songwriter—
R

PASTORS/LEADERS
Christian Century
Christian Ministry
Journal/Pastoral Care
Lutheran Forum—R
Lutheran Partners—R
Pastoral Life—R
Pulpit Helps—R
Word & World
Worship Leader

TEEN/YOUNG ADULT
Boundless Webzine—R
J.A.M.—R
YOU!—R
Young Adult Today

WOMEN
Anna's Journal—R
Conscience—R
Reflections (FL)

WRITERS
Advanced Christian Writer—
R
Areopagus (UK)
Canadian Writer's Jour—R
Contemporary Songwriter—
R
Exchange—R
Once Upon a Time—R
WE!—R
WIN-Informer

Writer's Ink—R

PARENTING

ADULT/GENERAL
American Tract Soc.—R
And He Will Give
Angels on Earth
Annals of St. Anne
Arkansas Catholic
Arlington Catholic
Banner
Bible Advocate—R
Bread of Life—R
Breakthrough Intercessor—R
Canada Lutheran—R
Catholic Digest—R
Catholic Faith & Family
Catholic Forester—R
Catholic New Times—R
Catholic Parent
Catholic Sentinel—R
Celebrate Life—R
Charisma/Christian Life
Chicken Soup/Mother—R
Chicken Soup/Woman—R
Christian Courier (CAN)—R
Christian Crafter—R
Christian Designer—R
Christian Home & School
Christian Living—R
Christian Motorsports
Christian Observer
Christian Parenting—R
Christian Ranchman
Christian Renewal—R
Church Advocate—R
Church Herald/Holiness—R
Columbia
Companions—R
Covenant Companion—R
Creation Care—R
Culture Wars—R
Decision
Discipleship Journal
Disciple's Journal—R
Dovetail—R
Evangel—R
Evangelical Advocate—R
Expression Christian
Family Digest
Fellowship Focus—R
Focus on the Family
Foursquare World—R
Gem—R
God Allows U-Turns—R
God's Revivalist
Good News, Etc.—R

Good News Journal (MO)—R
Good News Journal (TX)
Gospel Today
Grit
Heartlight Internet—R
Highway News—R
HomeLife—R
Homeschooling Today—R
Home Times—R
Impact Magazine—R
Indian Life—R
Inside Journal—R
Interim—R
Jewel Among Jewels—R
Joyfull Noise
Life Gate—R
LifeWise
Light and Life
Liguorian
Live—R
Living—R
Living Light News—R
Lookout—R
Lutheran—R
Lutheran Digest—R
Lutheran Journal—R
Lutheran Witness
Marriage Partnership
Mennonite—R
Mennonite Brethren—R
MESSAGE
Messenger/St. Anthony
Metro Voice—R
Michigan Christian
Moody—R
MovieGuide
Nashville Christian—R
Ncubator.com—R
New Covenant
New Freeman—R
New Moon—R
On Mission
Our Family—R
Our Sunday Visitor
Parent Paper—R
Pegasus Review—R
Pentecostal Evangel
Peoples Magazine—R
Plain Truth—R
Plus—R
Pourastan—R
Power for Living—R
PrayerWorks—R
Presbyterian Record—R
Presbyterians Today—R
Preserving Christian Homes—
R
Progress—R

Psychology for Living—R
Purpose—R
Sacred Journey—R
St. Anthony Messenger
St. Joseph's Messenger—R
Seek—R
Single-Parent Family
Smart Families
Social Justice
Sojourners
Standard—R
Standard, The—R
Stepping Out
Together—R
Upsouth—R
U.S. Catholic
Vibrant Life—R
Vision—R
War Cry—R
Way of St. Francis—R
Wesleyan Advocate—R

*CHRISTIAN EDUCATION/
LIBRARY*
CE Counselor—R
Children's Ministry
Christian School
Leader/Church School
   Today—R

MISSIONS
Worldwide Challenge

PASTORS/LEADERS
Catholic Servant
Evangelicals Today—R
Lutheran Partners—R
Minister's Family
Pastoral Life—R
Preacher's Illus. Service—R
Pulpit Helps—R
Reaching Children at Risk
Rev.
Sharing the Practice—R
Single Adult Ministries
Today's Christian Preacher—R
Youthworker

WOMEN
Connection
Esprit—R
Excellence
Godly Business Woman
Handmaiden—R
Hearts at Home—R
Helping Hand—R
Joyful Woman—R
Just Between Us—R

Link & Visitor—R
Lutheran Woman's Quar.
Proverbs 31 Woman—R
Reflections (FL)
Today's Christian Woman
SpiritLed Woman
True Woman
Welcome Home
Wesleyan Woman—R
Woman's Touch—R
Women Alive!—R
Women of Spirit—R

PERSONAL EXPERIENCE

ADULT/GENERAL
AGAIN—R
alive now!
And He Will Give
Angels on Earth
Annals of St. Anne
Banner
B.C. Catholic—R
Bible Advocate—R
Breakthrough Intercessor—R
Bridal Guides—R
Catholic Digest—R
Catholic Faith & Family
Catholic Forester—R
Catholic New Times—R
Catholic New York
Catholic Sentinel—R
Celebrate Life—R
CGA World—R
Chicken Soup/Mother—R
Chicken Soup/Woman—R
Christian Courier (CAN)—R
Christian Crafter—R
Christian Designer—R
Christian Home & School
Christian Motorsports
Christian Observer
Christian Ranchman
Christian Reader—R
Christianity Online—R
Chrysalis Reader
Church Advocate—R
Church Herald/Holiness—R
Church of God EVANGEL
Commonweal
Compleat Nurse—R
Connection Mag.—R
Conquest
Cornerstone—R
Covenant Companion—R
Crossway/Newsline—R
Decision
Door

Dovetail—R
Eternal Ink—R
Evangel—R
Evangelical Advocate—R
Faith & Friends—R
Gem—R
God Allows U-Turns—R
God's Revivalist
Good News, Etc.—R
Good News Journal (MO)—R
Good News Journal (TX)
Gospel Today
Grit
Guideposts
Healing Inn—R
Hidden Manna—R
Highway News—R
HomeLife—R
Home Times—R
Hunted News
Ideals
Impact Magazine—R
Indian Life—R
Inland NW Christian
Inspirer—R
Inside Journal—R
Interim—R
Jewel Among Jewels—R
John Milton—R
Jour/Christian Nursing—R
Joyfull Noise
Keys to Living—R
Leaves—R
Legions of Light—R
LifeWise
Light and Life
Liguorian
Live—R
Living—R
Living Church
Lookout—R
Lutheran—R
Lutheran Digest—R
Lutheran Journal—R
Lutheran Witness
Marian Helpers—R
Marriage Partnership
Mennonite—R
Mennonite Brethren—R
MESSAGE
Messenger/St. Anthony
Michigan Christian
Minnesota Christian—R
Moody—R
MovieGuide
Ncubator.com—R
New Covenant
New Freeman—R

New Heart—R
New Moon—R
Newsline—R
New Writing—R
North American Voice
Now What?—R
NRB Magazine—R
Oblates
Our Family—R
Over the Back Fence—R
Pentecostal Evangel
Plain Truth—R
Plus—R
PrayerWorks—R
Presbyterian Record—R
Presbyterians Today—R
Priority!
Progress—R
Psychology for Living—R
Purpose—R
Quest
Sacred Journey—R
St. Anthony Messenger
SCP Journal—R
Seeds
Seek—R
Shantyman—R
Sharing—R
Single-Parent Family
Sojourners
Spiritual Life
Standard—R
Stepping Out
Stewardship
Sursum Corda!—R
Time of Singing—R
Tomorrow's Christian
   Graduate
Together—R
Upscale Magazine
Upsouth—R
VISION—R
Vision—R
War Cry—R
Way of St. Francis—R
Wesleyan Advocate—R
Whispers From Heaven—R

CHILDREN
Club Connection—R
Courage
Discovery (NY)—R
GUIDE—R
J.A.M.—R
Live Wire—R
Partners—R
Skipping Stones
Touch—R

CHRISTIAN EDUCATION/LIBRARY
CE Counselor—R
Children's Ministry
GROUP
Journal/Adventist Educ.—R
Perspective—R
Religion Teacher's Journal
Today's Catholic Teacher—R
Vision—R

MISSIONS
American Horizon—R
Areopagus—R
Heartbeat—R
Hope for Children—R
Latin America Evangelist
P.I.M.E. World
So All May Hear—R
Worldwide Challenge

MUSIC
Contemporary Songwriter—
   R
Songwriting—R
Tradition

PASTORS/LEADERS
Catholic Servant
Cell Group—R
Christian Camp—R
Christian Century
Christian Ministry
Evangelical Baptist—R
Evangelicals Today—R
Five Stones—R
Journal/Pastoral Care
Minister's Family
Pastoral Life—R
Preacher's Illus. Service—R
Reaching Children at Risk
Sabbath School Leadership
Sharing the Practice—R
Single Adult Ministries
Theology Today (rarely)
Today's Parish
Worship Leader
Youthworker

TEEN/YOUNG ADULT
Boundless Webzine—R
Breakaway—R
Campus Life—R
Certainty
Challenge
Christian College Focus
Conqueror—R
Devo'Zine—R
Encounter—R

Guideposts for Teens—R
J.A.M.—R
Listen—R
Passageway.org—R
Real Time—R
Sharing the VICTORY—R
Teens on Target—R
YOU!—R
Young Adult Today
Young & Alive—R
Youth Challenge—R

WOMEN
Anna's Journal—R
Canticle
Christian Bride
Esprit—R
Godly Business Woman
Grace—R
Handmaiden—R
Hearts at Home—R
Helping Hand—R
Horizons—R
Journey—R
Jour/Women's Ministries
Joyful Woman—R
Just Between Us—R
Lutheran Woman Today
Proverbs 31 Woman—R
Reflections (FL)
SpiritLed Woman
Today's Christian Woman
Welcome Home
Wesleyan Woman—R
Woman's Touch—R
Women Alive!—R
Women of Spirit—R

WRITERS
Areopagus (UK)
Byline
Cochran's Corner—R
Contemporary Songwriter—
   R
Exchange—R
Fellowscript—R
Once Upon a Time—R
Writer's Ink—R
Writer's Potpourri—R

PERSONAL GROWTH

ADULT/GENERAL
alive now!
And He Will Give
Annals of St. Anne
Bible Advocate—R
Breakthrough Intercessor—R

Bridal Guides—R
Catholic Forester—R
Catholic New Times—R
Chicken Soup/Mother—R
Chicken Soup/Woman—R
Christian Crafter—R
Christian Designer—R
Church Herald/Holiness—R
Church of God EVANGEL
Cornerstone—R
Covenant Companion—R
Decision
Discipleship Journal
Dovetail—R
Dunamis Life—R
Evangel—R
Evangelical Advocate—R
Gem—R
God Allows U-Turns—R
Grit
Healing Inn—R
Highway News—R
Home Times—R
Indian Life—R
John Milton—R
Jour/Christian Nursing—R
Leaves—R
Legions of Light—R
Light and Life
Liguorian
Live—R
Living—R
Living Church
Living Light News—R
Lookout—R
Lutheran Witness
Messenger/St. Anthony
Nashville Christian—R
Ncubator.com—R
New Heart—R
Northwestern Lutheran—R
On Mission
Peoples Magazine—R
Presbyterian Record—R
Preserving Christian Homes—
    R
Psychology for Living—R
Reflections
Seek—R
Single-Parent Family
Spirit—R
Stepping Out
Together—R
Tomorrow's Christian
    Graduate
Trumpeter—R
Vision—R
Way of St. Francis—R

CHILDREN
Discovery(NY)—R
GUIDE—R
J.A.M.—R
Skipping Stones

*CHRISTIAN EDUCATION/
LIBRARY*
GROUP
Shining Star

MUSIC
Songwriting—R

PASTORS/LEADERS
Eucharistic Minister—R
Evangelicals Today—R
Growing Churches
Lutheran Partners—R
Pastoral Life—R
Pulpit Helps—R
Reaching Children at Risk
Rev.
Sharing the Practice—R
Today's Christian Preacher—
    R

TEEN/YOUNG ADULT
Christian College Focus
Conqueror—R
Encounter—R
J.A.M.—R
Passageway.org—R
WITH—R
YOU!—R
Young Salvationist—R

WOMEN
Anna's Journal—R
Canticle
Connection
Esprit—R
Excellence
Godly Business Woman
Hearts at Home—R
Joyful Woman—R
Just Between Us—R
Proverbs 31 Woman—R
Reflections (FL)
SpiritLed Woman
Today's Christian Woman
Wesleyan Woman—R
Women of Spirit—R
Women Who Minister—R

WRITERS
Areopagus (UK)
Cochran's Corner—R

PHOTO ESSAYS

ADULT/GENERAL
alive now!
Bridal Guides—R
Catholic Faith & Family
Christian Courier (CAN)—R
Christian Social Action—R
Home Times—R
Impact Magazine—R
Indian Life—R
Mennonite—R
Messenger/St. Anthony
Over the Back Fence—R
Prairie Messenger—R
Say Amen—R

CHILDREN
Guideposts for Kids
On the Line—R
Skipping Stones

MISSIONS
Latin America Evangelist

TEEN/YOUNG ADULT
Passageway.org—R
YOU!—R

WOMEN
Grace—R
Reflections (FL)

PHOTOGRAPHS

Note: "Reprint" indicators (R)
have been deleted from this
section and "B" for black &
white glossy prints or "C" for
color transparencies inserted.
An asterisk (*) before a listing
indicates they buy photos with
articles only.

ADULT/GENERAL
ABS RECORD
*Accent on Living—B/C
Alive!—B
alive now!—B/C
American Tract Soc.
Anglican Journal—B/C
*Annals of St. Anne—B/C
Arlington Catholic—B
Banner
Beacon
Bible Advocate—C
Bridal Guides—B/C
*Bridge—B/C

Calvinist Contact—B/C
Canada Lutheran—B
*Cathedral Age—B
*Catholic Digest—B/C
Catholic Faith & Family
Catholic Forester—B/C
Catholic New Times
Catholic New York—B
Catholic Parent
*Catholic Sentinel—B/C
Catholic Telegraph—B
CBA Frontline—C
CBA Marketplace—C
*Celebrate Life—C
Charisma/Christian Life—C
Christian Century—B
*Christian Courier (CAN)—B
Christian Drama—B/C
*Christian History—B/C
Christian Home & School—C
Christian Leader—B/C
Christian Living—B
*Christian Motorsports—B
Christian Parenting Today—
    B/C
*Christian Reader—B/C
Christian Social Action—B
Christian Standard—B/C
*Christianity Today—C
Church Advocate
Church & State
Church of God EVANGEL—C
*Commonweal—B/C
Companion—B
*Company
Connecting Point—B
Connection Mag.
*Conquest—B/C
Cornerstone—B/C
Covenant Companion—B/C
Culture Wars—B/C
Dovetail—B
Episcopal Life—B
*Evangel—B
Evangelical Advocate—B/C
*Facts for Faith—C
*Faith & Friends—C
Faith Today—B
Fellowship Focus—B
Focus on the Family—B/C
Foursquare World—C
Good News, Etc.—C
*Good News Journal (MO)—B
Good News Journal (TX)
Gospel Tract—C
*Grit—B/C
*Guideposts—B/C
Highway News—B

Homeschooling Today—B/C
*Home Times—B/C
Impact Magazine—C
Indian Life—B/C
Inland NW Christian—B
*Inside Journal—B
Inspirer—B
Interchange—B
*Interim—B/C
*Journal/Christian Nursing—
    B/C
Joyfull Noise
Joyful Noise
Leaves—B/C
Liberty—B/C
*Lifeglow—B/C
Light and Life—B/C
*Liguorian—C
Live—B/C
Living—B/C
Living Church—B/C
*Living Light News—B/C
Lookout—B/C
Lutheran—B
*Lutheran Journal—B/C
*Lutheran Witness—C
Marian Helpers—B/C
Mature Living
*Mature Years—C
Mennonite—B/C
Mennonite Brethren—B
MESSAGE—B/C
Messenger—B
*Messenger/St. Anthony—B/C
Michigan Christian—B
*Minnesota Christian
*Montana Catholic—B
*Nashville Christian—B/C
Nat. Christian Reporter—
    B/C/prints
*New Heart—C
New Moon—B
Northwestern Lutheran
*On Mission—C
Our Family—B/C
Our Sunday Visitor—B/C
Over the Back Fence—C
Pentecostal Evangel—B/C
Parabola—B
*Plain Truth—B/C (few)
*Power for Living—B
*Prairie Messenger—C
*Presbyterian Layman—B
Presbyterian Outlook—B/C
Presbyterian Record—B/C
Presbyterians Today—B/C
*Priority!
Prism—B/C

Progress—C
Psychology for Living—C
*Purpose—B
Quiet Revolution—B
Re:generation
Sacred Journey—B
*St. Anthony Messenger—B/C
*Say Amen—C
SCP Journal—B/C
Short Stories Bimonthly
Signs of the Times—C
Sojourners—B/C
Spiritual Life—B
Sports Spectrum—C
Standard—B
Standard, The
*Star of Zion
*Storyteller—B
*Sursum Corda!—R
*Testimony—B/C
Together—B/C
Total Health—B/C
Twin Cities Christian—B
*United Church Observer—
    B/C
Upscale Magazine
*Vibrant Life—C
VISION—B/C
War Cry—B/C
Way of St. Francis—B
Wesleyan Advocate—C

CHILDREN

American Girl—C
Celebrate—C
*Courage
Crusader
Discovery Trails—C
*Focus/Clubhouse Jr.—C
God's World News—C
Guideposts for Kids—C
Live Wire—C
Nature Friend—B/C
My Friend
On the Line—B/C
*Pockets—B/C
*Primary Pal (IL)
*Skipping Stones—B/C
Story Friends—B
Together Time—C
Touch—C
*Winner—C
Wonder Time—B/C

*CHRISTIAN EDUCATION/
LIBRARY*

Brigade Leader—B
CE Counselor—B/C

Children's Ministry—C
*Christian Classroom—C
Christian Librarian—B
Christian School—C
*Christian School Admin.—C
*Church Educator—B
*Church Libraries—B/C
Early Childhood News—C
Evangelizing Today's Child—
   B/C
Journal/Adventist Education—
   B
Junior Teacher—B/C
*Leader/Church School
   Today—B
Lollipops
Parish Teacher—B
Religion Teacher's Journal—
   B/C
Signal—B
Teachers in Focus—C
*Teachers Interaction—B
Team—B/C
*Today's Catholic Teacher—C
Youth & CE Leadership—B/C

DAILY DEVOTIONALS
Daily Dev. for Deaf—C
Secret Place—B/C
Words of Life—B/C

MISSIONS
American Horizon
Areopagus—B/C
*Catholic Near East—C
Evangelical Missions
Hope for Children—B/C
Missions Frontiers B/C
PFI World Report
*P.I.M.E. World—C
*New World Outlook—C
World Christian—B/C
*World Pulse

MUSIC
Church Musician—B
*Contemporary Songwriter
Cooperative Christian—B
*Creator—B/C
*Tradition

PASTORS/LEADERS
*Angelos—B
Catholic Servant
Christian Camp—B/C
Christian Century—B/C
Christian Ministry—B
Clergy Journal—B

Environment & Art—B/C
Eucharistic Minister—B/C
Evangelical Baptist—B/C
Growing Churches
Horizons—C
Leadership—B
Lutheran Forum—B
*Lutheran Partners—B
   (rarely)
Mennonite Brethren Herald
Ministry—B
Pray!
Resource—B/C
Rev.—C
Today's Parish—B/C
WCA News—C
*Worship Leader—C
*Your Church—B/C

TEEN/YOUNG ADULT
Boundless Webzine
Breakaway—C
Brio—C
Campus Life—C
*Certainty—B
*Challenge
The Conqueror—B/C
Encounter—C
Essential Connection—B/C
*Guideposts for Teens
Lighted Pathway—B/C
*Listen—B/C
*Real Time—B
*Sharing the VICTORY—C
Student Leadership—B/C
WITH—B
Young Adult Today—B
*Young & Alive—B

WOMEN
Anna's Journal—B
Conscience—B
*Esprit—B
*Grace—C
Hearts at Home—B/C
Helping Hand—B
*Horizons—B/C
Jour/Women's Ministries—B
*Journey
Joyful Woman—B/C
*Link & Visitor—B
*Lutheran Woman Today—
   B/C
Wesleyan Woman—B/C
Women Alive!—B

WRITERS
*Byline

Gotta Write—B
Tickled by Thunder
*Writer's Digest—B

POETRY

ADULT/GENERAL
About Such Things—R
alive now!
Banner
Bible Advocate—R
Breakthrough Intercessor—R
Bridal Guides—R
Bridge—R
Christian Century
Christian Courier (CAN)—R
Christian Crafter—R
Christian Designer—R
Christianity/Arts
Christian Living—R
Christian Motorsports
Christian Publisher.com
Christian Ranchman
Church Herald/Holiness—R
Commonweal
Companion
Compleat Nurse—R
Connecting Point—R
Cornerstone—R
Covenant Companion—R
Creation Care—R
Cresset
Culture Wars—R
Decision
Door
Dovetail—R
Eternal Ink—R
Evangel—R
First Things
Forefront—R
Foursquare World—R
Gem—R
Good News Journal (TX)
Gospel Tract—R
Grit
Healing Inn—R
Heartlight Internet—R
Heart Songs
Hidden Manna—R
Home Times—R
Hunted News
Ideals—R
Impact Magazine—R
Inspirer—R
Jewel Among Jewels—R
John Milton—R
Jour/Christian Nursing—R
Karitos Review—R

Leaves—R
Legions of Light—R
Liberty (little)—R
Life Gate—R
Light and Life
Lighthouse Story
Liguorian
Live—R
Living Church
Lutheran Digest—R
Lutheran Journal—R
Mature Living
Mature Years—R
Mennonite—R
Mennonite Brethren—R
Miraculous Medal
New Heart—R
New Song
New Writing—R
North American Voice
Oblates
Our Family—R
Over the Back Fence—R
Parenting Our Parents—R
Parent Paper—R
Pegasus Review—R
Penwood Review
Peoples Magazine—R
Perspectives
Plowman—R
Pourastan—R
Prairie Messenger—R
PrayerWorks—R
Presbyterian Layman
Presbyterian Record—R
Purpose—R
Queen of All Hearts
Re:generation
Sacred Journey—R
St. Anthony Messenger
St. Joseph's Messenger—R
San Diego Co. Christian
Selah!Kids (for kids)
Sharing—R
Short Stories Bimonthly
Silver Wings—R
Sojourners
Spirit—R
Standard—R
Star of Zion
Stepping Out
Storyteller—R
Studio—R
TEAK Roundup—R
Testimony—R
Time for Rhyme
Time of Singing—R
Today's Christian Senior—R

2-Soar
Upsouth—R
U.S. Catholic
Vision—R
War Cry—R
Wesleyan Advocate—R
West Wind Review
Winsome Wit—R

CHILDREN
Celebrate
Club Connection—R
Discovery (NY)—R
Discovery Trails—R
Focus/Clubhouse Jr.
Guideposts for Kids
J.A.M.—R
Mission
On the Line—R
Partners—R
Pockets—R
Skipping Stones
Story Friends—R
Story Mates—R
Together Time—R
Touch—R

CHRISTIAN EDUCATION/
LIBRARY
Christian Educators Jour—R
Christian School
Church Educator—R
Lollipops
Resource—R
Shining Star
Today's Catholic Teacher—
 R
Vision—R

DAILY DEVOTIONALS
Abba's Arms
God's Courtroom
Living Words—R
Secret Place
These Days

MISSIONS
Hope for Children—R
Women of the Harvest

MUSIC
Choir Herald, etc.
Church Pianist, etc.
Quest—R
Senior Musician—R

PASTORS/LEADERS
Angelos—R

Catechumenate
Christian Century
Cross Currents—R
Emmanuel
Growing Churches
Journal/Christian Healing—R
Journal/Pastoral Care
Lutheran Forum—R
Lutheran Partners—R
Pastoral Life—R
Preacher's Illus. Service—R
Pulpit Helps—R
Review for Religious
Sharing the Practice—R
Theology Today

TEEN/YOUNG ADULT
Campus Life
Devo'Zine—R
Encounter—R
Essential Connection—R
 (by teens)
Guideposts for Teens—R
Insight—R
J.A.M.—R
Live Wire—R
Passageway.org—R
Real Time—R (by teens)
Sharing the VICTORY—R
Student Leadership—R
Teenage Christian—R
YOU!—R
Young Adult Today
Young Salvationist—R

WOMEN
Anna's Journal—R
Conscience—R
Esprit—R
Grace—R
Handmaiden—R
Hearts at Home—R
Horizons—R
Jour/Women's Ministries
Joyful Woman—R
Link & Visitor—R
Lutheran Woman Today
Reflections (FL)—R
Welcome Home
Wesleyan Woman—R

WRITERS
Areopagus (UK)
Byline
Canadian Writer's Jour—R
Christian Communicator—
 R
Cochran's Corner—R

Cross & Quill—R
Gotta Write
Heaven—R
My Legacy—R
Omnific—R
Once Upon a Time—R
Poetry Connection
Tickled by Thunder
WE!—R
WIN-Informer
Writer Online—R
Writer's Digest—R
Writer's Ink—R
Writers' Journal—R
Write Touch—R

POLITICAL

ADULT/GENERAL
American Wasteland
Anglican Journal—R
Arkansas Catholic
Arlington Catholic
Banner
Bible Advocate—R
Bridge—R
Catholic Insight
Catholic New Times—R
Christian C.L. RECORD—R
Christian Courier (WI)—R
Christian Courier (CAN)—R
Christianity Today—R
Christian Motorsports
Christian Renewal—R
Christian Social Action—R
Commonweal
Company—R
Connection Mag.—R
Creation Care—R
Cresset
Faith Today
First Things
Good News, Etc.—R
Gospel Today
Home Times—R
Inland NW Christian
Interim—R
Journal of Church & State
Light and Life
Messenger/St. Anthony
Metro Voice—R
Michigan Christian
Minnesota Christian—R
Nashville Christian—R
NRB Magazine—R
Perspectives
Presbyterian Outlook
Presbyterians Today—R

Prism—R
Re:generation
SCP Journal—R
Social Justice
Sojourners
Upsouth—R

CHRISTIAN EDUCATION/
LIBRARY
Today's Catholic Teacher—R

MISSIONS
Areopagus—R
East-West Church

PASTORS/LEADERS
Christian Century
Lutheran Partners—R
Preacher's Illus. Service—R
Word & World

TEEN/YOUNG ADULT
Inteen
WITH—R
YOU!—R
Young Adult Today

WOMEN
Conscience—R

PRAYER

ADULT/GENERAL
AGAIN—R
alive now!
And He Will Give
Angels on Earth
Annals of St. Anne
Banner
Bible Advocate—R
Bread of Life—R
Breakthrough Intercessor—
   R
Bridal Guides—R
Canada Lutheran—R
Catholic Digest—R
Catholic Faith & Family
Catholic New Times—R
Celebrate Life—R
CGA World—R
Charisma/Christian Life
Christian Courier (CAN)—R
Christianity Today—R
Christian Leader—R
Christian Living—R
Christian Motorsports
Christian Ranchman
Christian Reader—R

Church Advocate—R
Church Herald/Holiness—R
Church of God EVANGEL
Columbia
Companions—R
Connecting Point—R
Conquest
Cornerstone—R
Covenant Companion—R
Creation Care—R
Culture Wars—R
Decision
Discipleship Journal
Dunamis Life—R
Episcopal life—R
Evangel—R
Evangelical Advocate—R
Faith Today
Family Digest
Fellowship Link—R
Focus on the Family
Forefront—R
Foursquare World—R
Gem—R
God's Revivalist
Good News —R
Good News, Etc.—R
Good News Journal (MO)—
   R
Good News Journal (TX)
Gospel Today
Gospel Tract—R
Grit
Heartlight Internet—R
Highway News—R
Home Times—R
Hunted News
Inland NW Christian
Inspirer—R
John Milton—R
Jour/Christian Nursing—R
Leaves—R
Legions of Light—R
Life Gate—R
Lifeglow—R
LifeWise
Light and Life
Liguorian
Live—R
Living Church
Lookout—R
Lutheran—R
Lutheran Digest—R
Lutheran Journal—R
Lutheran Witness
Marian Helpers—R
Mature Years—R
Mennonite—R

Mennonite Brethren—R
Men of Integrity—R
MESSAGE
MESSAGE/Open Bible—R
Messenger/St. Anthony
Metro Voice—R
Michigan Christian
Montana Catholic—R
Moody—R
Ncubator.com—R
New Covenant
New Freeman—R
North American Voice
Northwestern Lutheran—R
Now What?—R
On Mission
Our Family—R
Our Sunday Visitor
Pegasus Review—R
Peoples Magazine—R
Plain Truth—R
Plowman—R
Plus—R
Pourastan—R
Prairie Messenger—R
Prayer Closet
PrayerWorks—R
Presbyterian Outlook
Presbyterian Record—R
Presbyterians Today—R
Priority!
Purpose—R
Queen of All Hearts
Re:generation
Sacred Journey—R
St. Anthony Messenger
St. Willibrord Journal
Seeds
Seek—R
Silver Wings—R
Social Justice
Sojourners
Spirit—R
Spiritual Life
Standard—R
Standard, The—R
Stepping Out
Time of Singing—R
Today's Christian Senior—R
Together—R
Trumpeter—R
Upsouth—R
U.S. Catholic
Vision—R
War Cry—R
Way of St. Francis—R
Wesleyan Advocate—R

CHILDREN

BREAD/God's Children—R
Club Connection—R
Courage
Discovery (NY)—R
Guideposts for Kids
High Adventure—R
J.A.M.—R
Touch—R
Wonder Time

CHRISTIAN EDUCATION/ LIBRARY

CE Counselor—R
Children's Ministry
Church Educator—R
Evangelizing Today's Child—R
Leader/Church School Today—R
Religion Teacher's Journal
Shining Star
Teacher's Interaction
Vision—R

MISSIONS

American Horizon—R
Areopagus—R
Intl Jour/Frontier—R
Latin America Evangelist
PFI World Report—R
So All May Hear—R
Worldwide Challenge

MUSIC

Creator—R
Quest—R

PASTORS/LEADERS

Angelos—R
Catholic Servant
Celebration
Christian Ministry
Church Worship
Diocesan Dialogue—R
Emmanuel
Enrichment—R
Eucharistic Minister—R
Evangelical Baptist—R
Evangelicals Today—R
Five Stones—R
Growing Churches
Horizons—R
Journal/Christian Healing—R
Leadership—R
Let's Worship
Lutheran Partners—R
Minister's Family

Ministries Today
Ministry
Ministry & Liturgy—R
Pastoral Life—R
Pray!—R
Preacher's Illus. Service—R
Priest
PROCLAIM—R
Pulpit Helps—R
Reaching Children at Risk
Reformed Worship
Rev.
Sharing the Practice—R
Theology Today
Today's Christian Preacher—R
Today's Parish
Word & World
Worship Leader

TEEN/YOUNG ADULT

Certainty
Challenge
Conqueror—R
Devo'Zine—R
Encounter—R
Essential Connection—R
Inteen
J.A.M.—R
Passageway.org—R
Real Time—R
Student Leadership—R
Teenage Christian—R
Teens on Target—R
Today's Christian Teen—R
Vision—R
WITH—R
YOU!—R
Young Adult Today
Young & Alive—R
Young Salvationist—R
Youth Challenge—R

WOMEN

Connection
Esprit—R
Helping Hand—R
Horizons—R
Journey—R
Joyful Woman—R
Just Between Us—R
Lutheran Woman's Quar.
Lutheran Woman Today
Proverbs 31 Woman—R
Reflections (FL)
SpiritLed Woman
Women Alive!—R
Women of Spirit—R
Women Who Minister—R

WRITERS
Areopagus (UK)
Cochran's Corner—R

PROPHECY

ADULT/GENERAL
Apocalypse Chronicles—R
Banner
Bible Advocate—R
Bread of Life—R
Breakthrough Intercessor—
R
Charisma/Christian Life
Christian Leader—R
Christian Motorsports
Church of God EVANGEL
Connection Mag.—R
Conquest
Creation Ex Nihilo
Evangelical Advocate—R
Fellowship Link—R
Foursquare World—R
God's Revivalist
Good News, Etc.—R
Good News Journal (MO)—
R
Gospel Tract—R
John Milton—R
Legions of Light—R
MESSAGE
Messenger/St. Anthony
Metro Voice—R
Michigan Christian
Ncubator.com—R
New Freeman—R
New Writing—R
Our Family—R
Queen of All Hearts
SCP Journal—R
Signs of the Times—R
Silver Wings—R
Today's Christian Senior—R
Upsouth—R

MUSIC
Tradition

PASTORS/LEADERS
Journal/Christian Healing—
R
Ministries Today
Pastoral Life—R
PROCLAIM—R
Pulpit Helps—R
Sharing the Practice—R
Today's Christian Preacher—
R

Word & World

TEEN/YOUNG ADULT
Certainty
Inteen
Young Adult Today

WOMEN
SpiritLed Woman
Woman's Touch—R

PSYCHOLOGY

ADULT/GENERAL
American Wasteland
Banner
Biblical Reflections—R
Bridal Guides—R
Catholic Faith & Family
Catholic New Times—R
Christian Courier (CAN)—R
Christian Crafter—R
Christian Designer—R
Christian Motorsports
Chrysalis Reader
Church Advocate—R
Compleat Nurse—R
Dovetail—R
Evangelical Advocate—R
Gem—R
Good News, Etc.—R
Good News
   Journal (MO)—R
Healing Inn—R
John Milton—R
Legions of Light—R
Light and Life
Michigan Christian
New Covenant
Our Family—R
Psychology for Living—R
Reflections
SCP Journal—R
Social Justice
Spiritual Life
Total Health
Trumpeter—R
Upsouth—R
Vibrant Life—R

*CHRISTIAN EDUCATION/
LIBRARY*
Catechist
Church Educator—R

MISSIONS
Hope for Children—R

PASTORAL/LEADERS
Cell Group—R
Christian Ministry
Five Stones—R
Journal/Christian Healing—
R
Journal/Pastoral Care
Lutheran Partners—R
Ministries Today
Pastoral Life—R
Reaching Children at Risk
Sharing the Practice—R
Word & World

PUPPET PLAYS

Children's Ministry
Christianity/Arts
Church Street Press
Club Connection—R
Evangelizing Today's
   Child—R
Focus/Clubhouse Jr.
Good News Journal (MO)—
R
Good News Journal (TX)
Kids' Ministry Ideas—R
Leader/Church School
   Today—R
Let's Worship
Lillenas
One Way Street
Preschool Playhouse
Reaching Children at Risk
Reflections
Sharing the Practice—R
Sheer Joy! Press
Shining Star
Touch—R

RELATIONSHIPS

ADULT/GENERAL
Accent on Living—R
And He Will Give
Angels on Earth
Annals of St. Anne
Banner
Bible Advocate—R
Breakthrough Intercessor—
R
Bridal Guides—R
Bridge—R
Canada Lutheran—R
Catholic Digest—R
Catholic Faith & Family
Catholic Forester—R
Celebrate Life—R

Charisma/Christian Life
Chicken Soup/Mother—R
Chicken Soup/Woman—R
Christian Courier (CAN)—R
Christian Crafter—R
Christian Designer—R
Christian Leader—R
Christian Living—R
Christian Motorsports
Christian Parenting—R
Christian Ranchman
Christian Reader—R
Chrysalis Reader
Church Advocate—R
Church Herald/Holiness—R
Church of God EVANGEL
Columbia
Connection Mag.—R
Conquest
Cornerstone—R
Covenant Companion—R
Decision
Discipleship Journal
Dovetail—R
Dunamis Life—R
Evangel—R
Evangelical Advocate—R
Faith Today
Family Digest
Fellowship Link—R
Forefront—R
Foursquare World—R
Gem—R
God Allows U-Turns—R
Good News, Etc.—R
Good News Journal (MO)—R
Good News Journal (TX)
Gospel Today
Grit
Guideposts
Heartlight Internet—R
Highway News—R
HomeLife—R
Home Times—R
Indian Life—R
Inside Journal—R
John Milton—R
Jour/Christian Nursing—R
Joyfull Noise
Legions of Light—R
Life@Work
Life Gate—R
LifeWise
Light and Life
Liguorian
Live—R
Living—R

Living Light News—R
Lookout—R
Lutheran Digest—R
Lutheran Journal—R
Marriage Partnership
MESSAGE
Messenger/St. Anthony
Michigan Christian
Moody—R
Ncubator.com—R
New Heart—R
New Writing—R
Now What?—R
On Mission
Pegasus Review—R
Peoples Magazine—R
Plain Truth—R
Plus—R
Pourastan—R
PrayerWorks—R
Preserving Christian Homes—R
Progress—R
Purpose—R
Reflections
Say Amen—R
Seeds
Seek—B
Silver Wings—R
Single-Parent Family
Standard, The—R
Stepping Out
Testimony—R
thegoodsteward.com—R
Time of Singing—R
Together—R
Trumpeter—R
Upscale Magazine
Upsouth—R
U.S. Catholic
Vibrant Life—R
Vision—R
War Cry—R

CHILDREN
BREAD for God's Children
Club Connection—R
Discovery (NY)—R
Focus/Clubhouse Jr.
High Adventure—R
J.A.M.—R
My Friend
Touch—R
Winner—R

CHRISTIAN EDUCATION/ LIBRARY
Children's Ministry
Leader/Church School Today—R
Perspective—R

MISSIONS
American Horizon—R
Latin America Evangelist
Worldwide Challenge

PASTORS/LEADERS
Cell Group—R
Christian Camp—R
Evangelicals Today—R
Five Stones—R
Growing Churches
Journal/Christian Healing—R
Lutheran Partners—R
Minister's Family
Ministries Today
Ministry
Pastoral Life—R
Reaching Children at Risk
Rev.
Sharing the Practice—R
Single Adult Ministries
Today's Christian Preacher—R
Youthworker
Word & World

TEEN/YOUNG ADULT
Boundless Webzine—R
Certainty
Challenge
Conqueror—R
Devo'Zine—R
Encounter—R
Essential Connection—R
J.A.M.—R
Listen—R
Passageway.org—R
Real Time—R
Student Leadership—R
Teenage Christian—R
Teens on Target—R
Today's Christian Teen—R
WITH—R
YOU!—R
Youth Challenge—R

WOMEN
Christian Bride
Connection
Esprit—R

Excellence
Helping Hand—R
Horizons—R
Journey—R
Joyful Woman—R
Just Between Us—R
Link & Visitor—R
Lutheran Woman's Quar.
Proverbs 31 Woman—R
Reflections (FL)
SpiritLed Woman
Today's Christian Woman
Welcome Home
Wesleyan Woman—R
Woman's Touch—R
Women of Spirit—R
Women Who Minister—R

WRITERS
Cochran's Corner—R

RELIGIOUS FREEDOM

ADULT/GENERAL
America
American Wasteland
Arlington Catholic
Banner
Bible Advocate—R
Bread of Life—R
Breakthrough Intercessor—
  R
Catholic Faith & Family
Catholic New Times—R
Charisma/Christian Life
Christian C.L. RECORD—R
Christian Courier (CAN)—R
Christian Courier (WI)—R
Christian Leader—R
Christian Motorsports
Christian Observer
Christian Ranchman
Christian Response—R
Christian Social Action—R
Christian Times
Christianity Today—R
Church & State—R
Church Herald/Holiness—R
Church of God EVANGEL
Colorado Christian—R
Connecting Point—R
Connection Mag.—R
Cornerstone—R
Cresset
Episcopal Life—R
Evangelical Advocate—R
Faith Today
First Things

Gem—R
God's Revivalist
Good News, Etc.—R
Good News Journal (TX)
Healing Inn—R
Home Times—R
Interim—R
John Milton—R
Journal of Church & State
Legions of Light—R
Liberty—R
Life Gate—R
MESSAGE
MESSAGE/Open Bible—R
Messenger/St. Anthony
Metro Voice—R
Michigan Christian
Minnesota Christian—R
Moody—R
Nashville Christian—R
Ncubator.com—R
New Freeman—R
NRB Magazine—R
On Mission
Our Family—R
Our Sunday Visitor
Pegasus Review—R
Pourastan—R
Presbyterian Layman
Presbyterian Outlook
Presbyterians Today—R
Prism—R
Re:generation
SCP Journal—R
Seeds
Social Justice
Spiritual Life
Standard—R
Star of Zion
Stepping Out
Testimony—R
Together—R
Touchstone—R
Trumpeter—R
U.S. Catholic
Upsouth—R
Winsome Wit—R

CHILDREN
High Adventure—R
Skipping Stones

MISSIONS
Areopagus—R
East-West Church
Evangelical Missions—R
Latin America Evangelist
World Pulse—R

Worldwide Challenge

MUSIC
Quest—R

PASTORS/LEADERS
Catholic Servant
Cell Group—R
Christian Century
Christian Ministry
Church Worship
Cross Currents—R
Five Stones—R
Lutheran Partners—R
Ministry
Pastoral Life—R
Pulpit Helps—R
Sharing the Practice—R
Theology Today
Word & World

TEEN/YOUNG ADULT
Essential Connection—R
Inteen
Young Adult Today

WOMEN
Esprit—R

SALVATION TESTIMONIES

ADULT/GENERAL
American Tract Soc.—R
Banner
Bible Advocate—R
Breakthrough Intercessor—
  R
Christian Motorsports
Christian Ranchman
Christian Reader—R
Church Herald/Holiness—R
Church of God EVANGEL
Companions—R
Connecting Point—R
Connection Mag.—R
Conquest
Crossway/Newsline—R
Decision
Evangel—R
Evangelical Advocate—R
Faith & Friends—R
Fellowship Link—R
Gem—R
God Allows U-Turns—R
God's Revivalist
Good News, Etc.—R
Good News Journal (TX)
Gospel Tract—R

Guideposts
Home Times—R
Indian Life—R
Inside Journal—R
Inspirer—R
Leaves—R
Lutheran Journal—R
Mennonite Brethren—R
Men of Integrity—R
MESSAGE/Open Bible—R
Messenger/St. Anthony
Michigan Christian
Moody—R
Ncubator.com—R
New Covenant
New Freeman—R
New Heart—R
On Mission
Peoples Magazine—R
Power for Living—R
PrayerWorks—R
Quest
SCP Journal—R
Seek—B
Shantyman—R
Silver Wings—R
Spirit—R
Standard, The—R
Stepping Out
Together—R
Upsouth—R
Wesleyan Advocate—R

CHILDREN
BREAD/God's Children—R
Club Connection—R
Courage
Discovery (NY)—R
J.A.M.—R

CHRISTIAN EDUCATION/
LIBRARY
Evangelizing Today's Child—
   R

MISSIONS
American Horizon—R
Latin America Evangelist
So All May Hear—R
Worldwide Challenge

PASTORS/LEADERS
Cell Group—R
Christian Camp—R
Evangelicals Today—R
Ministry
Pastoral Life—R
Pulpit Helps—R

Small Group Network

TEEN/YOUNG ADULT
Challenge
Essential Connection—R
Inteen
J.A.M.—R
Passageway.org—R
Real Time—R
WITH—R (1st person teen)
Young Adult Today

WOMEN
Esprit—R
Godly Business Woman
Helping Hand—R
Journey—R
Joyful Woman—R
SpiritLed Woman
Wesleyan Woman—R
Woman Alive
Woman's Touch—R

WRITERS
Areopagus (UK)

SCIENCE

ADULT/GENERAL
Banner
Biblical Reflections—R
Catholic New Times—R
Christian C.L. RECORD—R
Christian Courier (CAN)—R
Christian Motorsports
Christian Social Action—R
Christianity Today—R
Companions—R
Creation Ex Nihilo
Evangelical Advocate—R
Facts for Faith
Faith Today
First Things
Home Times—R
Legions of Light—R
Lifeglow—R
Light and Life
Messenger/St. Anthony
Metro Voice—R
Michigan Christian
New Freeman—R
PrayerWorks—R
SCP Journal—R
Standard, The—R
Upsouth—R

CHILDREN
Discovery Trails—R

Guideposts for Kids
Live Wire—R
My Friend
Nature Friend—R
Skipping Stones

CHRISTIAN EDUCATION/
LIBRARY
Christian Classroom
Christian School Admin.
Shining Star

PASTORS/LEADERS
Lutheran Partners—R
Technologies/Worship—R
Word & World

TEEN/YOUNG ADULT
Inteen
Young Adult Today

WOMEN
Esprit—R

SELF-HELP

ADULT/GENERAL
And He Will Give
Bridal Guides—R
Catholic Faith & Family
CGA World—R
Chicken Soup/Mother—R
Chicken Soup/Woman—R
Christian Crafter—R
Christian Designer—R
Christian Living—R
Christian Motorsports
Christian Parenting—R
Christian Ranchman
Companion
Compleat Nurse—R
Covenant Companion—R
Disciple's Journal—R
Evangelical Advocate—R
Expression Christian
Fellowship Link—R
God Allows U-Turns—R
Good News Journal (MO)—R
Grit
John Milton—R
Living—R
MESSAGE
Messenger/St. Anthony
Michigan Christian
New Writing—R
Our Family—R
St. Anthony Messenger
Single-Parent Family

Social Justice
Standard—R
Stepping Out
Together—R
Touchstone—R
Trumpeter—R
2-Soar
Vibrant Life—R
Vision—R

CHILDREN
Skipping Stones
Winner—R

PASTORS/LEADERS
Cell Group—R
Evangelicals Today—R
Journal/Christian Healing—R
Pastoral Life—R
Reaching Children at Risk

TEEN/YOUNG ADULT
Encounter—R
Listen—R
Teenage Christian—R

WOMEN
Esprit—R
Journey—R
Reflections (FL)
Wesleyan Woman—R
Women of Spirit—R
Women of the Harvest

WRITERS
Cochran's Corner—R

SENIOR ADULT ISSUES

ADULT/GENERAL
Alive!—R
Angels on Earth
Anglican Journal—R
Annals of St. Anne
Banner
B.C. Catholic—R
Breakthrough Intercessor—R
Canada Lutheran—R
Catholic Digest—R
Catholic Forester—R
Catholic New Times—R
CGA World—R
Christian Courier (CAN)—R
Christian Home & School
Christian Living—R
Christian Motorsports
Christian Social Action—R
Church Advocate—R

Church Herald/Holiness—R
Columbia
Conquest
Covenant Companion—R
Decision
Discovery (FL)—R
Dovetail—R
Evangel—R
Evangelical Advocate—R
Family Digest
Fellowship Link—R
Gem—R
God Allows U-Turns—R
Good News, Etc.—R
Good News Journal (MO)—R
Good News Journal (TX)
Grit
Home Times—R
Indian Life—R
Inspirer—R
John Milton—R
Jour/Christian Nursing—R
Legions of Light—R
Life Gate—R
Lifeglow—R
LifeWise
Liguorian
Live—R
Living—R
Lookout—R
Lutheran—R
Lutheran Digest—R
Mature Living
Mature Years—R
Messenger/St. Anthony
Metro Voice—R
Michigan Christian
Minnesota Christian—R
Moody—R
New Freeman—R
On Mission
Our Family—R
Our Sunday Visitor
Parenting Our Parents—R
Pentecostal Evangel
Plus—R
Power for Living—R
PrayerWorks—R
Presbyterians Today—R
Purpose—R
Reflections
Resource—R
Sacred Journey—R
Sojourners
Standard, The—R
Today's Christian Senior—R
U.S. Catholic
Vision—R

War Cry—R
Wesleyan Advocate—R

*CHRISTIAN EDUCATION/
LIBRARY*
CE Connection—R
CE Counselor—R
Church Educator—R
Youth & CE Leadership—R

MISSIONS
Worldwide Challenge

MUSIC
Senior Musician—R

PASTORS/LEADERS
Christian Ministry
Diocesan Dialogue—R
Eucharistic Minister—R
Evangelical Baptist—R
Evangelicals Today—R
Five Stones—R
Lutheran Partners—R
Pastoral Life—R
Sharing the Practice—R
Word & World

WOMEN
Esprit—R
Horizons—R
Reflections (FL)
Today's Christian Woman
Woman's Touch—R

WRITERS
Canadian Writer's Jour—R

SERMONS

ADULT/GENERAL
Arlington Catholic
Banner
Breakthrough Intercessor—R
Cathedral Age
Christian Motorsports
Christian Social Action—R
Church Herald/Holiness—R
Creation Care—R
Cresset
Evangelical Advocate—R
God's Revivalist
Good News, Etc.—R
Healing Inn—R
Inspirer—R
John Milton—R
Joyful Noise
Messenger/St. Anthony

Presbyterians Today—R
Seeds
Sojourners
Star of Zion
Stepping Out
Trumpeter—R
Upsouth—R
Wireless Age—R

PASTORS/LEADERS
African American Pulpit
Celebration
Christian Ministry
Church Worship
Clergy Journal—R
Enrichment—R
Evangelicals Today—R
Growing Churches
In Season
Pastoral Life—R
Preacher's Illus. Service—R
Preaching
Priest
PROCLAIM—R
Pulpit Helps—R
Sermon Notes
Sharing the Practice—R
Today's Parish

SHORT STORY: ADULT/RELIGIOUS

About Such Things—R
Alive!—R
alive now!
Annals of St. Anne
Anna's Journal—R
Areopagus (UK)
Banner
Bridal Guides—R
Canadian Writer's Jour—R
Catholic Forester—R
CGA World—R
Christian Century
Christian Courier (CAN)—R
Christian Crafter—R
Christian Designer—R
Christian Educators Journal
Christian Living—R
Christian Reader—R
Christian Renewal—R
Christian School
Christianity/Arts
Church & Synagogue Lib.
Cochran's Corner—R
Companion
Companions—R
Compleat Nurse—R
Connecting Point—R

Conquest
Cornerstone—R
Covenant Companion—R
Creation Ex Nihilo
Discovery (FL)—R
Dreams & Visions—R
Esprit—R
Evangel—R
Fellowship Focus—R
Fellowship Link—R
Five Stones—R
Gem—R
Gems of Truth—R
God's Revivalist
Good News Journal (MO)—R
Gospel Tract—R
Grace—R
Grit
Healing Inn—R
Heartlight Internet—R
Heaven
Helping Hand—R
Hidden Manna—R
Highway News—R
Home Times—R
Horizons—R
Hunted News
Impact Magazine—R
Indian Life—R
Inspirer—R
John Milton—R
Journal/Christian Healing—R
Journal/Pastoral Care
Joyful Woman—R
Karitos Review—R
Legions of Light—R
Life@Work (business)
Lighthouse Story
Liguorian
Live—R
Living—R
Living Light News—R
   (Christmas)
Lookout—R
Lutheran Digest
Lutheran Partners—R
Lutheran Witness
Lutheran Woman's Quar.
Lutheran Woman Today
Mature Living
Mature Years—R
Mennonite Brethren—R
Messenger/Sacred Heart
Messenger/St. Anthony
Miraculous Medal
Moody—R

My Legacy—R
Ncubator.com—R
New Writing—R
North American Voice
Pastoral Life—R
Pegasus Review—R
Peoples Magazine—R
Perspectives
Plowman—R
PrayerWorks—R
Presbyterian Record—R
Preserving Christian Homes—R
Queen of All Hearts
Quest—R
St. Anthony Messenger
St. Joseph's Messenger—R
San Diego Co. Christian
Seeds
Seek—R
Short Stories Bimonthly
Standard—R
Star of Zion
Stepping Out
Storyteller—R
Studio—R
Studio Classroom
Sursum Corda!—R
TEAK Roundup—R
Testimony—R
Tickled by Thunder
Today's Christian Senior—R
Today's Christian Woman
Upsouth—R
U.S. Catholic
Vision—R
War Cry—R
West Wind Review
Winsome Wit—R
Women Alive!—R
Writer Online—R
Write Touch—R
YOU!—R

SHORT STORY: ADVENTURE

ADULT
About Such Things—R
Alive!—R
Annals of St. Anne
Areopagus (UK)
Byline
Christian Courier (CAN)—R
Christianity/Arts
Dreams & Visions—R
Gem—R
Grace—R
Grit

North American Voice
Pockets—R
Preacher's Illus. Service—R
Selah!Kids

TEEN/YOUNG ADULT
Annals of St. Anne
Conqueror—R
Discovery (FL)—R
Essential Connection—R
Inteen
J.A.M.—R
John Milton—R
Karitos Review—R
Passageway.org—R
Preacher's Illus. Service—R
Real Time—R
Student Leadership—R
Teenage Christian—R
Teens on Target—R
YOU!—R
Young Adult Today
Youth Challenge—R

SHORT STORY: CONTEMPORARY

ADULT
About Such Things—R
Annals of St. Anne
Areopagus (UK)
Bridge—R
Byline
Canadian Lutheran—R
Christian Century
Christian Living—R
Christian Renewal—R
Christianity/Arts
Companion
Connecting Point—R
Conquest
Cornerstone—R
Covenant Companion—R
Dreams & Visions—R
Esprit—R
Evangel—R
Gem—R
Grit
Heartlight Internet—R
Hidden Manna—R
Horizons—R
Hunted News
Indian Life—R
Inspirer—R
Karitos Review—R
Legions of Light—R
Lighthouse Story
Liguorian
Living Light News—R

Lookout—R
Mature Living
Messenger/St. Anthony
Miraculous Medal
Moody—R
My Legacy—R
New Moon—R
New Writing—R
Pastoral Life—R
Peoples Magazine—R
Perspectives
St. Anthony Messenger
St. Joseph's Messenger—R
Seek—B
Short Stories Bimonthly
Standard—R
Stepping Out
Studio—R
TEAK Roundup—R
Tickled by Thunder
Upsouth—R
U.S. Catholic
War Cry—R
West Wind Review

CHILDREN
American Girl
Annals of St. Anne
BREAD/God's Children—R
Canada Lutheran—R
Celebrate
Discoveries—R
Discovery (NY)—R
Discovery Trails—R
Focus/Clubhouse
Focus/Clubhouse Jr.
Guideposts for Kids
J.A.M.—R
Lighthouse Story
On the Line—R
Partners—R
Pockets—R
Selah!Kids
Story Friends—R
Together Time—R
Touch—R
Winner—R

TEEN/YOUNG ADULT
Annals of St. Anne
BREAD/God's Children—R
Certainty
Challenge
Discovery (FL)—R
Encounter—R
Essential Connection—R
J.A.M.—R
Karitos Review—R

Lighthouse Story
Listen—R
Passageway.org—R
Pastoral Life—R
Real Time—R
Teenage Christian—R

SHORT STORY: ETHNIC

ADULT
About Such Things—R
Bridge—R
Byline
Christian Living—R
Dreams & Visions—R
Fellowship Link—R
Gem—R
Grace—R
Grit
Hidden Manna—R
Indian Life—R
Karitos Review—R
Legions of Light—R
Liguorian
Live—R
Seek—B
Studio—R
Upsouth—R

CHILDREN
Discovery (NY)—R
Discovery Trails—R
J.A.M.—R
Skipping Stones
West Wind Review

TEEN/YOUNG ADULT
Discovery (FL)—R
Encounter—R
Essential Connection—R
J.A.M.—R
Karitos Review—R
Passageway.org—R
Young Salvationist—R

SHORT STORY: FANTASY

ADULT
Areopagus (UK)
Boundless Webzine—R
Byline
Christian Courier (CAN)—R
Christianity/Arts
Connecting Point—R
Dreams & Visions—R
Esprit—R
Gem—R
Good News Journal (MO)—R

Karitos Review—R
Legions of Light—R
Messenger/St. Anthony
My Legacy—R
Presbyterian Record—R
Storyteller—R
Tickled by Thunder

CHILDREN

Cochran's Corner—R
Discovery (NY)—R
Guideposts for Kids
J.A.M.—R
Lollipops (young)
Touch—R
West Wind Review

TEEN/YOUNG ADULT

Discovery (FL)—R
Essential Connection—R
Inteen
J.A.M.—R
Karitos Review—R
WITH—R
Young Adult Today
Young Salvationist—R

SHORT STORY: FRONTIER

ADULT

Byline
Christianity/Arts
Connecting Point—R
Dreams & Visions—R
Gem—R
Grit
Indian Life—R
Inspirer—R
Karitos Review—R
Legions of Light—R
Lighthouse Story
Miraculous Medal
My Legacy—R
Upsouth—R
West Wind Review

CHILDREN

Discovery Trails—R
Focus/Clubhouse
Focus/Clubhouse Jr.
Guideposts for Kids
High Adventure—R
Lighthouse Story
Touch—R

TEEN/YOUNG ADULT

Essential Connection—R
Karitos Review—R

Lighthouse Story

SHORT STORY: FRONTIER/ROMANCE

Bridal Guides—R
Byline
Christianity/Arts
Connecting Point—R
Dreams & Visions—R
Essential Connection—R
Gem—R
Grit
Healing Inn—R
Helping Hand—R
Legions of Light—R
Lighthouse Story
Miraculous Medal
My Legacy—R
Storyteller—R
West Wind Review

SHORT STORY: HISTORICAL

ADULT

About Such Things—R
Alive!—R
Areopagus (UK)
Byline
Christian Classroom
Christian Courier (CAN)—R
Christian Living—R
Christian Renewal—R
Christianity/Arts
Companions—R
Connecting Point—R
Conquest
Dreams & Visions—R
Esprit—R
Fellowship Link—R
Gem—R
Grit
Healing Inn—R
Heartlight Internet—R
Hidden Manna—R
Home Times—R
Indian Life—R
Karitos Review—R
Legions of Light—R
Lighthouse Story
Live—R
Lutheran Witness
Lutheran Woman's Quar.
Messenger/St. Anthony
Miraculous Medal
My Legacy—R
New Writing—R
North American Voice
Pastoral Life—R

Peoples Magazine—R
Perspectives
Presbyterian Record—R
Stepping Out
Storyteller—R
Studio—R
TEAK Roundup—R
Today's Christian Senior—R
Upsouth—R
West Wind Review

CHILDREN

Cochran's Corner—R
Courage
Discovery (NY)—R
Discovery Trails—R
Focus/Clubhouse
Focus/Clubhouse Jr.
Friend
Guideposts for Kids
High Adventure—R
J.A.M.—R
Lighthouse Story
Nature Friend—R
On the Line—R
Touch—R

TEEN/YOUNG ADULT

BREAD/God's Children—R
Challenge
Discovery (FL)—R
Essential Connection—R
Inteen
J.A.M.—R
John Milton—R
Karitos Review—R
Lighthouse Story
Young Adult Today
Youth—R

SHORT STORY: HISTORICAL/ROMANCE

Areopagus (UK)
Bridal Guides—R
Byline
Christianity/Arts
Cochran's Corner—R
Connecting Point—R
Dreams & Visions—R
Essential Connection—R
Gem—R
Grit
J.A.M.—R
Legions of Light—R
Lighthouse Story
Messenger/St. Anthony
Miraculous Medal
My Legacy—R

Storyteller—R
West Wind Review

SHORT STORY: HUMOROUS

ADULT

Alive!—R
Areopagus (UK)
Boundless Webzine—R
Bridge—R
Byline
Canada Lutheran—R
Catholic Forester—R
Christian Courier (CAN)—R
Christianity/Arts
Church & Synagogue Lib.
Companion
Compleat Nurse—R
Connecting Point—R
Conquest
Covenant Companion—R
Dreams & Visions—R
Esprit—R
Five Stones—R
Gem—R
Gospel Tract—R
Grit
Healing Inn—R
Helping Hand—R
Heartlight Internet—R
Hidden Manna—R
Highway News—R
Home Times—R
Horizons—R
Impact—R
Inspirer—R
John Milton—R
Karitos Review—R
Legions of Light—R
Lighthouse Story
Liguorian
Live—R
Living—R
Living Light News—R
Lutheran Witness
Mature Living
Mature Years—R
Messenger/St. Anthony
Miraculous Medal
My Legacy—R
New Writing—R
Pastoral Life—R
Peoples Magazine—R
Preacher's Illus. Service—R
Presbyterian Record—R
Preserving Christian Homes—
  R

St. Joseph's Messenger—R
Seek—R
Storyteller—R
TEAK Roundup—R
Tickled by Thunder
Today's Christian Senior—R
Upsouth—R
West Wind Review
Winsome Wit—R

CHILDREN

American Girl
Cochran's Corner—R
Crusader—R
Discovery (NY)—R
Discovery Trails—R
Focus/Clubhouse
Focus/Clubhouse Jr.
Guideposts for Kids
High Adventure—R
J.A.M.—R
Lighthouse Story
Living—R
My Friend
On the Line—R
Preacher's Illus. Service—R
Reflections
Selah!Kids
Story Friends—R
Touch—R
Winner—R
Wonder Time

TEEN/YOUNG ADULT

Breakaway—R
Brio—R
Campus Life—R
Challenge
Discovery (FL)—R
Encounter—R
Essential Connection—R
Inteen
J.A.M.—R
Karitos Review—R
Lighthouse Story
Listen—R
Preacher's Illus. Service—R
Real Time—R
Reflections
Student Leadership—R
Teenage Christian—R
Teens Today—R
WITH—R
YOU!—R
Young Adult Today
Young Salvationist—R

SHORT STORY: JUVENILE

American Girl
Annals of St. Anne
Areopagus (UK)
Beginner's Friend—R
BREAD/God's Children—R
Bridal Guides—R
Catholic Forester—R
Celebrate (3-4's)
Children's Church—R (6-8)
Christian Home & School
  (few)
Christian Renewal—R
Church Educator—R
Church & Synagogue Lib.
Cochran's Corner—R
Courage
Crusader—R
Discoveries—R
Discovery (NY)—R
Discovery Trails—R
Evangelizing Today's Child—
  R
Focus/Clubhouse
Focus/Clubhouse Jr.
Good News Journal (MO)—
  R
Guideposts for Kids
High Adventure—R
J.A.M.—R
Junior Companion—R
Legions of Light—R
Lighthouse Story
Living—R
Lollipops
Lutheran Woman Today
MESSAGE (5-8 yrs)
Messenger/St. Anthony
My Friend
My Legacy—R
On the Line—R
Parent Paper—R
Partners—R
Peoples Magazine—R
Pockets—R
Presbyterian Record—R
Primary Pal (IL)
Primary Pal (KS)—R
Reflections
Selah!Kids
Skipping Stones
Story Friends—R
Storyteller—R (some)
Today's Catholic Teacher—R
Together Time—R (3-4)
Touch—R
United Church Observer—R

War Cry—R
Winner—R
Wonder Time
Write Touch
Young Salvationist—R

SHORT STORY: LITERARY

ADULT
About Such Things—R
Areopagus (UK)
Bridge—R
Byline
Christian Century
Christian Classroom
Christian Courier (CAN)—R
Christian Living—R
Christianity/Arts
Chrysalis Reader
Conquest
Cornerstone—R
Covenant Companion—R
Dreams & Visions—R
Esprit—R
Gem—R
Healing Inn—R
Hidden Manna—R
Horizons—R
Hunted News
Karitos Review—R
Legions of Light—R
Mennonite Brethren Herald—R
Messenger/St. Anthony
Miraculous Medal
My Legacy—R
New Writing—R
Pastoral Life—R
Perspectives
Seek—R
Short Stories Bimonthly
Standard—R
Storyteller—R
Studio—R
Tickled by Thunder
Upsouth—R
War Cry—R
West Wind Review

CHILDREN
Cochran's Corner—R
Discovery (NY)—R
J.A.M.—R
Reflections (FL)
Story Friends—R

TEEN/YOUNG ADULT
Essential Connection—R

J.A.M.—R
Karitos Review—R
Passageway.org—R
Reflections (FL)
Young Salvationist—R

SHORT STORY: MYSTERY

ADULT
Byline
Christian Courier (CAN)—R
Christianity/Arts
Connecting Point—R
Dreams & Visions—R
Gem—R
Grit
Healing Inn—R
Heartlight Internet—R
Indian Life—R
Karitos Review—R
Legions of Light—R
Lighthouse Story
Messenger/St. Anthony
Miraculous Medal
My Legacy—R
New Writing—R
Quest
Storyteller—R
Tickled by Thunder
West Wind Review

CHILDREN
American Girl
Cochran's Corner—R
Courage
Discovery (NY)—R
Discovery Trails—R
Focus/Clubhouse Jr.
Guideposts for Kids
J.A.M.—R
Lighthouse Story
On the Line—R
Touch—R

TEEN/YOUNG ADULT
Challenge
Discovery (FL)—R
Encounter—R
Essential Connection—R
Inteen
J.A.M.—R
Karitos Review—R
Lighthouse Story
Young Adult Today
Young Salvationist—R

SHORT STORY: MYSTERY/ROMANCE

Bridal Guides—R
Byline
Christianity/Arts
Cochran's Corner—R
Connecting Point—R
Dreams & Visions—R
Essential Connection—R
Gem—R
Grit
J.A.M.—R
Legions of Light—R
Lighthouse Story
Messenger/St. Anthony
Miraculous Medal
Reflections (FL)
Standard—R
Storyteller—R
West Wind Review

SHORT STORY: PARABLES

ADULT
alive now!
America
Annals of St. Anne
Areopagus (UK)
Christian Classroom
Christian Courier (CAN)—R
Christian Living—R
Christianity/Arts
Church Worship
Companion
Covenant Companion—R
Discovery (FL)—R
Dreams & Visions—R
Esprit—R
Fellowship Link—R
Five Stones—R
Gem—R
God's Revivalist
Good News Journal (MO)—R
Healing Inn—R
Heartlight Internet—R
Helping Hand—R
Hidden Manna—R
Highway News—R
Home Times—R
Horizons—R
Impact Magazine—R
Indian Life—R
Inspirer—R
Karitos Review—R
LA Catholic

Legions of Light—R
Liguorian
Lutheran
Mennonite Brethren—R
MESSAGE
Messenger/St. Anthony
Ncubator.com—R
New Writing—R
Pastoral Life—R
Peoples Magazine—R
Perspectives
Preacher's Illus. Service—R
Presbyterian Record—R
Star of Zion
Stepping Out
Testimony—R
Upsouth—R
U.S. Catholic
West Wind Review

CHILDREN
Annals of St. Anne
Church Educator—R
Courage
Discovery (NY)—R
Guideposts for Kids
High Adventure—R
John Milton—R
MESSAGE
Pockets—R
Preacher's Illus. Service—R
Touch—R

TEEN/YOUNG ADULT
Annals of St. Anne
Church Educator—R
Discovery (FL)—R
Essential Connection—R
Inteen
John Milton—R
Karitos Review—R
Preacher's Illus. Service—R
Student Leadership—R
Testimony—R
WITH—R
YOU!—R
Young Adult Today

SHORT STORY: PLAYS

American Girl
Areopagus (UK)
Challenge
Christian Drama
Church Worship
Courage (short short)
Discovery (NY)—R
Esprit—R

Fellowship Link—R
Five Stones—R
Focus/Clubhouse Jr.
Guideposts for Kids
Hidden Manna—R
Horizons—R
Lutheran Digest
Messenger/St. Anthony
National Drama Service
New Writing—R
Shining Star
Touch—R

SHORT STORY: ROMANCE

ADULT
Alive!—R
Bridal Guides—R
Byline
Christianity/Arts
Cochran's Corner—R
Connecting Point—R
Dreams & Visions—R
Gem—R
Grit
Healing Inn—R
Helping Hand—R
Indian Life—R
Legions of Light—R
Lighthouse Story
Mature Living
Messenger/St. Anthony
Miraculous Medal
Preserving Christian Homes—
  R
St. Joseph's Messenger—R
Storyteller—R
West Wind Review

TEEN/YOUNG ADULT
Brio
Discovery (FL)—R
Encounter—R
Essential Connection—R
Healing Inn—R
Lighthouse Story
Reflections (FL)
Teens Today—R
WITH—R
Young Salvationist—R

SHORT STORY: SCIENCE FICTION

ADULT
Boundless Webzine—R
Bridge—R
Byline

Christian Courier (CAN)—
Christianity/Arts
Connecting Point—R
Dreams & Visions—R
Gem—R
Grit
Impact Magazine—R
Karitos Review—R
Legions of Light—R
Tickled by Thunder
West Wind Review

CHILDREN
Focus/Clubhouse Jr.
J.A.M.—R

TEEN/YOUNG ADULT
Breakaway—R
Essential Connection—R
Inteen
J.A.M.—R
Karitos Review—R
WITH—R
Young Adult Today
Young Salvationist—R

SHORT STORY: SKITS

ADULT
Church Worship
Esprit—R
Five Stones—R
Helping Hand—R
Horizons—R
New Writing—R
Peoples Magazine—R
Wesleyan Woman—R

CHILDREN
Discovery (NY)—R
Shining Star
Touch—R

TEEN/YOUNG ADULT
Student Leadership—R
YOU!—R

SHORT STORY: SUSPENSE

ADULT
Gem—R
Grit
Karitos Review—R
Storyteller—R
West Wind Review

CHILDREN
Guideposts for Kids
J.A.M.—R

TEEN/YOUNG ADULT
J.A.M.—R
Passageway.org—R

**SHORT STORY:
TEEN/YOUNG ADULT**
Annals of St. Anne
Beautiful Christian Teen
BREAD/God's Children—R
Breakaway—R
Bridal Guides—R
Brio
Campus Life—R
Canada Lutheran—R
Certainty
Challenge
Christian Crafter—R
Christian Designer—R
Church & Synagogue Lib.
Church Educator—R
Companions—R
Compleat Nurse—R
Conqueror—R
Encounter—R
Essential Connection—R
Evangel—R
Fellowship Focus—R
Five Stones—R
Good News Journal (MO)—R
Grit
High Adventure—R
Inteen
J.A.M.—R
Karitos Review—R
Legions of Light—R
Lighthouse Story
Liguorian
Listen—R
Parent Paper—R
Partners—R
Passageway.org—R
Pastoral Life—R
Peoples Magazine—R
Presbyterian Record—R
Quest—R
Real Time—R
Reflections (FL)
Skipping Stones
Star of Zion
Student Leadership—R
Teenage Christian—R
Teens on Target—R
Testimony—R

Touch—R
War Cry—R
West Wind Review
WITH—R
Write Touch—R
YOU!—R
Young Adult Today
Young Salvationist—R
Youth Challenge—R
Youth Compass—R

SINGLES ISSUES

ADULT/GENERAL
Annals of St. Anne
Banner
Breakthrough Intercessor—R
Bridal Guides—R
Catholic Digest—R
Christian Courier (CAN)—R
Christian Crafter—R
Christian Designer—R
Christian Living—R
Christian Motorsports
Christian Parenting—R
Christian Social Action—R
Church Advocate—R
Church of God EVANGEL
Colorado Christian—R
Columbia
Compleat Nurse—R
Connection Mag.—R
Conquest
Covenant Companion—R
Discipleship Journal
Dovetail—R
Evangel—R
Evangelical Advocate—R
Foursquare World—R
Gem—R
God Allows U-Turns—R
Good News, Etc.—R
Gospel Today
Heartlight Internet—R
Highway News—R
Home Times—R
Indian Life—R
Light and Life
Liguorian
Live—R
Living—R
Living Light News—R
Lookout—R
Lutheran—R
Lutheran Digest—R
Lutheran Witness
MESSAGE
Messenger/St. Anthony

Metro Voice—R
Michigan Christian
Minnesota Christian—R
Moody—R
Ncubator.com—R
Newsline—R
Northwestern Lutheran—R
Now What?—R
On Mission
Pastoral Life—R
Peoples Magazine—R
Power for Living—R
Presbyterian Layman
Presbyterian Record—R
Presbyterians Today—R
Psychology for Living—R
Purpose—R
Seek—R
Signs of the Times—R
Single-Parent Family
Sojourners
Standard, The—R
Stepping Out
Testimony—R
Trumpeter—R
U.S. Catholic
Vibrant Life—R
War Cry—R
Wesleyan Advocate—R

*CHRISTIAN EDUCATION/
LIBRARY*
CE Connection—R
Leader/Church School
   Today—R
Youth & CE Leadership—R

MISSIONS
Women of the Harvest
Worldwide Challenge

MUSIC
Quest—R

PASTORS/LEADERS
Church Administration
Eucharistic Minister—R
Evangelical Baptist—R
Five Stones—R
Lutheran Partners—R
Ministries Today
Pastoral Life
Sharing the Practice—R
Single Adult Ministries
Word & World

TEEN/YOUNG ADULT
Boundless Webzine—R

Conqueror—R
Inteen
Young Adult Today

WOMEN
Anna's Journal—R
Christian Women Today—R
Esprit—R
Excellence
Godly Business Woman
Horizons—R
Joyful Woman—R
Reflections (FL)
SpiritLed Woman
Today's Christian Woman
True Woman
Wesleyan Woman—R
Women of Spirit—R
Women Today —R

SOCIAL JUSTICE

ADULT/GENERAL
American Wasteland
Arkansas Catholic
Arlington Catholic
Banner
Catholic Digest—R
Catholic Insight
Catholic New Times—R
Catholic Sentinel—R
Charisma/Christian Life
Christian Century
Christian Courier (CAN)—R
Christian Leader—R
Christian Living—R
Christian Motorsports
Christian Social Action—R
Christianity Today—R
Church Advocate—R
Church of God EVANGEL
Columbia
Commonweal
Company—R
Compleat Nurse—R
Covenant Companion—R
Cresset
Culture Wars—R
Evangelical Advocate—R
Faith Today
Forefront—R
Foursquare World—R
Gem—R
Good News, Etc.—R
Hidden Manna—R
Home Times—R
Indian Life—R
Inland NW Christian

John Milton—R
Light and Life
Liguorian
Living—R
Mennonite—R
Mennonite Brethren—R
Messenger/St. Anthony
Michigan Christian
Montana Catholic—R
Moody—R
Nashville Christian—R
North American Voice
NRB Magazine—R
Our Family—R
Perspectives
Pourastan—R
Prairie Messenger—R
Presbyterian Layman
Prism—R
Purpose—R
Re:generation
Social Justice
Sojourners
Spiritual Life
United Church Observer—R
Upsouth—R
Way of St. Francis—R

CHILDREN
Skipping Stones

*CHRISTIAN EDUCATION/
LIBRARY*
Church Educator—R
Journal/Adventist Educ.—R
Religion Teacher's Journal

MISSIONS
Catholic Near East
Missiology
P.I.M.E. World
World Christian—R

PASTORS/LEADERS
African American Pulpit
Celebration
Emmanuel
Five Stones—R
Horizons—R
Lutheran Partners—R
Ministries Today
Pastoral Life—R
Quarterly Review
Reaching Children at Risk
Sharing the Practice—R

TEEN/YOUNG ADULT
Boundless Webzine—R

Devo'Zine—R
Teenage Christian—R
YOU!—R
Young Salvationist—R

WOMEN
ChurchWoman
Lutheran Woman Today
SpiritLed Woman
Woman's Touch—R

SOCIOLOGY

ADULT/GENERAL
American Wasteland
Anglican Journal—R
Catholic New Times—R
Christianity Online—R
Commonweal
Compleat Nurse—R
Culture Wars—R
Evangelical Advocate—R
Faith Today
Fellowship Link—R
Gem—R
Good News, Etc.—R
Good News Journal (MO)—
   R
John Milton—R
Journal of Church & State
Light and Life
Michigan Christian
Quiet Revolution—R
Re:generation
SCP Journal—R
Social Justice
Standard, The—R
Upsouth—R

*CHRISTIAN EDUCATION/
LIBRARY*
Catechist
Church Educator—R

MISSIONS
Areopagus—R
Missiology

PASTORS/LEADERS
Eucharistic Minister—R
Five Stones—R
Journal/Christian Healing—R
Jour/Amer Soc/Chur Growth—
   R
Pastoral Life—R
Reaching Children at Risk
Word & World

TEEN/YOUNG ADULT
Inteen
Young Adult Today

WOMEN
Esprit—R

SPIRITUAL GIFTS

ADULT/GENERAL
alive now!
Christian Crafter—R
Christian Designer—R
Christian Leader—R
Christian Reader—R
Church of God EVANGEL
Connection Mag.—R
Covenant Companion—R
Dunamis Life—R
Evangelical Advocate—R
God Allows U-Turns—R
Grit
LifeWise
Liguorian
Ncubator.com—R
New Freeman—R
Peoples Magazine—R
Prairie Messenger—R
Presbyterian Record—R
Reflections
Spirit—R
Stepping Out
thegoodsteward.com—R
Way of St. Francis—R

CHILDREN
Guideposts for Kids
Our Little Friend—R
Primary Treasure—R
Touch—R

PASTORS/LEADERS
Evangelicals Today—R
Horizons—R
Journal/Christian Healing—
    R
Pastoral Life—R
Review for Religious
Sharing the Practice—R
WCA News—R
Worship Leader

TEEN/YOUNG ADULT
Essential Connection—R
Today's Christian Teen—R
WITH—R
YOU!—R

WOMEN
Esprit—R
Godly Business Woman
Horizons—R
Just Between Us—R
SpiritLed Woman
Women Who Minister—R

SPIRITUALITY

ADULT/GENERAL
AGAIN—R
alive now!
American Tract Soc.—R
American Wasteland
Angels on Earth
Annals of St. Anne
Arlington Catholic
Banner
Bible Advocate—R
Bread of Life—R
Breakthrough Intercessor—R
Cathedral Age
Catholic Digest—R
Catholic Insight
Catholic New Times—R
Catholic Parent
CGA World—R
Charisma/Christian Life
Christian Century
Christian Crafter—R
Christian Home & School
Christian Leader—R
Christian Living—R
Christian Motorsports
Christian Parenting—R
Christianity Today—R
Chrysalis Reader
Church Advocate—R
Church of God EVANGEL
Columbia
Commonweal
Companions—R
Company—R
Compleat Nurse—R
Conquest
Covenant Companion—R
Cresset
Chrysalis Reader
Culture Wars—R
Decision
Door
Dovetail—R
Episcopal Life—R
Evangelical Advocate—R
Faith Today
Family Digest
Fellowship Link—R

Forefront—R
Gem—R
God Allows U-Turns—R
God's Revivalist
Good News—R
Good News, Etc.—R
Good News Journal (MO)—
    R
Gospel Today
Grit
Guideposts
Heartlight Internet—R
Hidden Manna—R
HomeLife—R
Inland NW Christian
John Milton—R
Jour/Christian Nursing—R
Leaves—R
Legions of Light—R
Life Gate—R
Lifeglow—R
LifeWise
Light and Life
Liguorian
Living—R
Living Church
Lookout—R
Lutheran—R
Lutheran Journal—R
Mature Years—R
Mennonite—R
Mennonite Brethren—R
Messenger/St. Anthony
Messenger of the Sacred
    Heart
Michigan Christian
Montana Catholic—R
Ncubator.com—R
New Covenant
New Freeman—R
New Heart—R
Newsline—R
New Writing—R
North American Voice
Now What?—R
Oblates
On Mission
Our Family—R
Our Sunday Visitor
Pegasus Review—R
Peoples Magazine—R
Perspectives
Plowman—R
Prairie Messenger—R
Presbyterian Outlook
Presbyterians Today—R
Preserving Christian Homes—
    R

Prism—R
Purpose—R
Queen of All Hearts
Re:generation
Sacred Journey—R
St. Anthony Messenger
SCP Journal—R
Seek—R
Signs of the Times—R
Social Justice
Sojourners
Spiritual Life
Standard—R
Standard, The—R
Stepping Out
Testimony—R
Together—R
Touchstone—R
Upsouth—R
U.S. Catholic
War Cry—R
Way of St. Francis—R
Wesleyan Advocate—R
Wireless Age—R

CHILDREN
BREAD/God's Children—R
Discoveries—R
Discovery (NY)—R
Guideposts for Kids
J.A.M.—R
Pockets—R
Skipping Stones
Wonder Time

*CHRISTIAN EDUCATION/
LIBRARY*
Christian School
Church Educator—R
Journal/Christian Education
Jour/Ed & Christian Belief—
R
Leader/Church School
Today—R
Religion Teacher's Journal
Teacher's Interaction

MISSIONS
Areopagus—R
Catholic Near East
Evangelical Missions—R
Latin America Evangelist
Worldwide Challenge

MUSIC
Quest—R

PASTORS/LEADERS
African American Pulpit
Celebration
Christian Century
Christian Ministry
Church Worship
Clergy Journal—R
Cross Currents—R
Diocesan Dialogue—R
Emmanuel
Eucharistic Minister—R
Evangelical Baptist—R
Evangelicals Today—R
Five Stones—R
Growing Churches
Horizons—R
Journal/Christian Healing—
R
Journal/Pastoral Care
Let's Worship
Lutheran Partners—R
Ministries Today
Ministry
Pastoral Life—R
Preacher's Illus. Service—R
PROCLAIM—R
Pulpit Helps—R
Quarterly Review
Reaching Children at Risk
Reformed Worship
Review for Religious
Sharing the Practice—R
Theology Today
Today's Christian Preacher—
R
Today's Parish
WCA News—R
Word & World
Worship Leader
Youthworker

TEEN/YOUNG ADULT
Devo'Zine—R
Inteen
J.A.M.—R
Teenage Christian—R
WITH—R
YOU!—R
Young Adult Today
Young & Alive—R
Young Salvationist—R

WOMEN
Connection
Esprit—R
Excellence
Godly Business Woman
Grace—R

Handmaiden—R
Horizons—R
Just Between Us—R
Lutheran Woman's Quar.
Lutheran Woman Today
SpiritLed Woman
Today's Christian Woman
Women of Spirit—R
Women Who Minister—R

WRITERS
Areopagus (UK)

SPIRITUAL WARFARE

ADULT/GENERAL
AGAIN—R
Angels on Earth
Banner
Bible Advocate—R
Bread of Life—R
Breakthrough Intercessor—
R
Celebrate Life—R
CGA World—R
Charisma/Christian Life
Christian Leader—R
Christian Motorsports
Christian Ranchman
Christian Research
Church Herald/Holiness—R
Church of God EVANGEL
Connection Mag.—R
Discipleship Journal
Dunamis Life—R
Evangelical Advocate—R
Fellowship Link—R
Gem—R
God Allows U-Turns—R
Good News —R
Good News, Etc.—R
Good News Journal (MO)—
R
Gospel Tract—R
Heartlight Internet—R
John Milton—R
Leaves—R
Legions of Light—R
Life Gate—R
Light and Life
Lutheran Journal—R
Lutheran Witness
Men of Integrity—R
MESSAGE
Ncubator.com—R
New Freeman—R
New Heart—R
Now What?—R

On Mission
Pentecostal Evangel
Peoples Magazine—R
Prayer Closet
PrayerWorks—R
Preserving Christian Homes—
   R
Spirit—R
Stepping Out
Times of Refreshing
Upsouth—R

CHILDREN
BREAD/God's Children—R
Discovery (NY)—R
High Adventure—R
J.A.M.—R
Shining Star

MISSIONS
Latin America Evangelist

PASTORS/LEADERS
Cell Group—R
Christian Camp—R
Cross Currents—R
Evangelicals Today—R
Journal/Christian Healing—
   R
Ministries Today
Pulpit Helps—R
Reaching Children at Risk
Sharing the Practice—R

TEEN/YOUNG ADULT
Essential Connection—R
J.A.M.—R
Real Time—R

WOMEN
Godly Business Woman
Joyful Woman—R
Just Between Us—R
SpiritLed Woman
Women of Spirit—R
Women Who Minister—R

SPORTS/RECREATION

ADULT/GENERAL
Accent on Living—R
American Tract Soc.—R
Angels on Earth
Arlington Catholic
Banner
Catholic Digest—R
Christian Courier (CAN)—R
Christian Courier (WI)—R

Christian Designer—R
Christian Living—R
Christian Motorsports
Christian Parenting—R
Christian Ranchman
Christian Renewal—R
Colorado Christian—R
Connecting Point—R (Special
   Olympics)
Connection Mag.—R
Expression Christian
Gem—R
Good News, Etc.—R
Good News Journal (TX)
Guideposts
Home Times—R
Joyfull Noise
Lifeglow—R
Light and Life
Living Light News—R
Messenger/St. Anthony
Metro Voice—R
Minnesota Christian—R
New Freeman—R
New Writing—R
Over the Back Fence—R
Sports Spectrum
Standard, The—R

CHILDREN
BREAD/God's Children—R
Club Connection—R
Courage
Crusader—R
Discovery (NY)—R
Focus/Clubhouse
Guideposts for Kids
High Adventure—R
J.A.M.—R
Live Wire—R
On the Line—R
Skipping Stones

*CHRISTIAN EDUCATION/
LIBRARY*
Christian Classroom
Christian School
Youth & CE Leadership—R

MISSIONS
Worldwide Challenge

MUSIC
Quest—R

PASTORS/LEADERS
Preacher's Illus. Service—R
Reaching Children at Risk

TEEN/YOUNG ADULT
Boundless Webzine—R
Breakaway—R
Certainty
Challenge
Conqueror—R
Devo'Zine—R
Encounter—R
Inteen
J.A.M.—R
Passageway.org—R
Real Time—R
Sharing the VICTORY—R
Young Adult Today
Young & Alive—R

WOMEN
Esprit—R
Reflections (FL)

STEWARDSHIP

ADULT/GENERAL
Angels on Earth
Banner
Bible Advocate—R
Breakthrough Intercessor—R
Celebrate Life—R
Christian Courier (CAN)—R
Christian Leader—R
Christian Living—R
Christian Motorsports
Christian Parenting—R
Christian Ranchman
Christian Social Action—R
Church Advocate—R
Church of God EVANGEL
Columbia
Companions—R
Covenant Companion—R
Creation Care—R
Decision
Discipleship Journal
Evangel—R
Evangelical Advocate—R
Faith Today
Fellowship Focus—R
Gem—R
Good News, Etc.—R
Gospel Today
Life@Work
Life Gate—R
LifeWise
Liguorian
Live—R
Living Church
Lutheran Digest—R
Lutheran Journal—R

MESSAGE
Michigan Christian
Montana Catholic—R
Moody—R
Nashville Christian—R
Ncubator.com—R
No-Debt Living—R
Northwestern Lutheran—R
NRB Magazine—R
Peoples Magazine—R
Plain Truth—R
Power for Living—R
Presbyterian Layman
Presbyterian Outlook
Presbyterian Record—R
Prism—R
Reflections
Re:generation
Seeds
Spirit—R
Star of Zion
Stepping Out
Stewardship
Testimony—R
thegoodsteward.com—R
Today's Christian Senior—R
Together—R
Trumpeter—R
United Church Observer—R
U.S. Catholic

CHILDREN
BREAD/God's Children—R
J.A.M.—R
Skipping Stones

CHRISTIAN EDUCATION/LIBRARY
Children's Ministry
Christian Classroom
Christian School Admin.
Church Educator—R
Leader/Church School
    Today—R
Preschool Playhouse

MISSIONS
Latin America Evangelist
So All May Hear—R

PASTORS/LEADERS
African American Pulpit
Cell Group—R
Clergy Journal—R
Evangelicals Today—R
Five Stones—R
Horizons—R
Let's Worship
Lutheran Partners—R

Ministries Today
Ministry
Pastoral Life—R
Priest
Pulpit Helps—R
Quarterly Review
Reaching Children at Risk
Resource—R
Sharing the Practice—R
Theology Today
Today's Christian Preacher—R
Your Church—R

TEEN/YOUNG ADULT
J.A.M.—R
Teens on Target—R
Today's Christian Teen—R
WITH—R
Young Salvationist—R
Youth Challenge—R

WOMEN
Connection
Esprit—R
Godly Business Woman
Horizons—R
Just Between Us—R
Lutheran Woman Today
Proverbs 31 Woman—R
SpiritLed Woman

TAKE-HOME PAPERS

ADULT/GENERAL
Companions
Conquest
Evangel
Gems of Truth
Live
Lookout
Power for Living
Purpose
Seek
Standard
Vision

CHILDREN
Beginner's Friend
Courage
Discoveries
Discovery Trails
Junior Companion
Our Little Friend
Partners
Preschool Playhouse
Primary Pal (IL)
Primary Pal (KS)
Primary Treasure

Promise
Seeds
Story Mates
Together Time
Wonder Time

TEEN/YOUNG ADULT
Cross Walk
Encounter
I.D.
Insight
Real Time
Teens on Target
Youth Challenge
Youth Compass (KS)

THEOLOGICAL

ADULT/GENERAL
AGAIN—R
America
American Wasteland
Anglican Journal—R
Annals of St. Anne
Arlington Catholic
Banner
B.C. Catholic—R
Breakthrough Intercessor—R
Catholic Insight
Catholic New Times—R
Charisma/Christian Life
Christian Century
Christian Leader—R
Christian Motorsports
Christian Renewal—R
Christian Research
Christian Social Action—R
Christianity Today—R
Church Herald/Holiness—R
Church of God EVANGEL
Commonweal
Companions—R
Company—R
Compleat Nurse—R
Conquest
Cornerstone—R
Creation Care—R
Creation Ex Nihilo
Cresset
Culture Wars—R
Episcopal Life—R
Evangelical Advocate—R
Facts for Faith
Faith Today
Fellowship Link—R
First Things
Good News —R
Hidden Manna—R

John Milton—R
Journal of Church & State
Legions of Light—R
Light and Life
Liguorian
Living Church
Lutheran—R
Messenger/St. Anthony
Messenger of the Sacred Heart
Michigan Christian
Montana Catholic—R
Ncubator.com—R
New Freeman—R
North American Voice
On Mission
Our Family—R
Our Sunday Visitor
Perspectives
Prairie Messenger—R
Presbyterian Layman
Presbyterian Outlook
Presbyterian Record—R
Presbyterians Today—R
Queen of All Hearts
Re:generation
St. Anthony Messenger
St. Willibrord Journal
SCP Journal—R
Silver Wings—R
Social Justice
Sojourners
Spiritual Life
Stepping Out
Testimony—R
Touchstone—R
United Church Observer—R
U.S. Catholic
Way of St. Francis—R

*CHRISTIAN EDUCATION/
LIBRARY*
Catholic Library World
Church Educator—R
Shining Star
Teacher's Interaction

MISSIONS
Areopagus—R
Catholic Near East
East-West Church
Latin America Evangelist
Missiology
World Christian—R
Worldwide Challenge

PASTORS/LEADERS
African American Pulpit
Catechumenate

Celebration
Christian Camp—R
Christian Century
Christian Ministry
Church Worship
Cross Currents—R
Diocesan Dialogue—R
Emmanuel
Eucharistic Minister—R
Evangelical Baptist—R
Evangelicals Today—R
Five Stones—R
Growing Churches
Horizons—R
Journal/Christian Healing—R
Journal/Pastoral Care
Jour/Amer Soc/Chur Growth—
   R
Let's Worship
Lutheran Forum—R
Lutheran Partners—R
Ministries Today
Ministry
Ministry & Liturgy—R
Pastoral Life—R
Preacher's Illus. Service—R
Priest
PROCLAIM—R
Pulpit Helps—R
Quarterly Review
Reaching Children at Risk
Review for Religious
Sewanee Theological Review
Sharing the Practice—R
Theology Today
Today's Parish
Word & World
Worship Leader
Youthworker

TEEN/YOUNG ADULT
Essential Connection—R
Inteen
Young Adult Today

WOMEN
Conscience—R
Esprit—R
Godly Business Woman
Horizons—R
Jour/Women's Ministries
Lutheran Woman Today
SpiritLed Woman

THINK PIECES

ADULT/GENERAL
Alive!—R

alive now!
American Wasteland
Annals of St. Anne
Banner
Bible Advocate—R
Bridal Guides—R
Bridge—R
Catholic Digest—R
Catholic Forester—R
Catholic New Times—R
CGA World—R
Christian C.L. RECORD—R
Christian Leader—R
Christian Living—R
Christian Social Action—R
Church of God EVANGEL
Commonweal
Conquest
Covenant Companion—R
Creation Care—R
Door
Episcopal Life—R
Expression Christian
First Things
Forefront—R
Gem—R
Good News, Etc.—R
Good News Journal (MO)—R
Good News Journal (TX)
Heartlight Internet—R
Hidden Manna—R
Home Times—R
Inspirer—R
John Milton—R
Legions of Light—R
Life@Work
Living—R
Lutheran—R
Lutheran Journal—R
MESSAGE
Messenger/St. Anthony
Metro Voice—R
Michigan Christian
Minnesota Christian—R
Ncubator.com—R
New Writing—R
Now What?—R
NRB Magazine—R
Pegasus Review—R
Plain Truth—R
PrayerWorks—R
Presbyterian Layman
Presbyterian Outlook
Presbyterians Today—R
Purpose—R
Re:generation
Short Stories Bimonthly
Sojourners

Stepping Out
Testimony—R
Upsouth—R
Way of St. Francis—R
Wesleyan Advocate—R
Winsome Wit—R
Wireless Age—R

CHILDREN
Discovery (NY)—R
J.A.M.—R
Skipping Stones

*CHRISTIAN EDUCATION/
LIBRARY*
Christian School Admin.
Resource—R

MISSIONS
Areopagus—R

MUSIC
Quest—R

PASTORS/LEADERS
Catholic Servant
Celebration
Evangelicals Today—R
Five Stones—R
Growing Churches
Horizons—R
Journal/Pastoral Care
Lutheran Partners—R
Ministries Today
Reaching Children at Risk
Sharing the Practice—R
Single Adult Ministries
Technologies/Worship—R
Word & World

TEEN/YOUNG ADULT
Boundless Webzine—R
Certainty
Conqueror—R
J.A.M.—R
Vision—R

WOMEN
Anna's Journal—R
Esprit—R
Godly Business Woman
Horizons—R
Reflections (FL)
Wesleyan Woman—R

WRITERS
Areopagus (UK)
WE!—R

TIME MANAGEMENT

ADULT/GENERAL
Breakthrough Intercessor—R
Bridal Guides—R
Catholic Forester—R
CBA Marketplace
Christian Courier (CAN)—R
Christian Crafter—R
Christian Designer—R
Decision
Disciple's Journal—R
Discipleship Journal
Evangelical Advocate—R
Gem—R
Good News Journal (TX)
HomeLife—R
Homeschooling Today—R
Home Times—R
Jour/Christian Nursing—R
Joyfull Noise
Life@Work
LifeWise
Living Light News—R
Lutheran Witness
No-Debt Living—R
Standard, The—R
Stepping Out
thegoodsteward.com—R
Together—R
Tomorrow's Christian
  Graduate
Trumpeter—R
Wireless Age—R

CHILDREN
J.A.M.—R

*CHRISTIAN EDUCATION/
LIBRARY*
Christian Classroom
Christian Librarian—R
Christian School Admin.
Vision—R

PASTORS/LEADERS
Christian Ministry
Enrichment—R
Evangelicals Today—R
Five Stones—R
Horizons—R
Lutheran Partners—R
Priest
Reaching Children at Risk
Rev.
Sharing the Practice—R
Today's Christian Preacher—R
Your Church—R

TEEN/YOUNG ADULT
Christian College Focus
Encounter—R
J.A.M.—R
Student Leadership—R
Today's Christian Teen—R

WOMEN
Esprit—R
Godly Business Woman
Joyful Woman—R
Just Between Us—R
Proverbs 31 Woman—R
Reflections (FL)
Today's Christian Woman
Wesleyan Woman—R
Women of Spirit—R
Women Who Minister—R

WRITERS
Canadian Writer's Jour—R
Writer

TRAVEL

ADULT/GENERAL
Accent on Living—R
Alive!—R
Angels on Earth
Arlington Catholic
Bridal Guides—R
Catholic Digest—R
Catholic Faith & Family
Charisma/Christian Life
Christian Courier (CAN)—R
Christian Crafter—R
Christian Parenting—R
Christian Ranchman
Evangelical Advocate—R
Family Digest
Fellowship Link—R
Gem—R
Good News Journal (TX)
Grit
John Milton—R
Joyfull Noise
Joyful Noise
Legions of Light—R
Life@Work
Lutheran Journal—R
Mature Living
Mature Years—R
Mennonite Historian—R
Messenger/St. Anthony
Michigan Christian
MovieGuide
Over the Back Fence—R
Peoples Magazine—R

Stepping Out
Studio Classroom
Time of Singing—R
Today's Christian Senior—R
Upscale Magazine
Upsouth—R

CHILDREN
Discovery (NY)—R
High Adventure—R
Skipping Stones

MISSIONS
Areopagus—R
East-West Church
Latin America Evangelist

MUSIC
Tradition

PASTORS/LEADERS
Preacher's Illus. Service—R

TEEN/YOUNG ADULT
Teenage Christian—R

WOMEN
Esprit—R
Godly Business Woman
Reflections (FL)
Woman Alive

TRUE STORIES

ADULT/GENERAL
Alive!—R
And He Will Give
Angels on Earth
Bible Advocate—R
Breakthrough Intercessor—R
Bridal Guides—R
Catholic Digest—R
Catholic Faith & Family
Catholic New Times—R
CBA Frontline
Chicken Soup/Mother—R
Chicken Soup/Woman—R
Christian Courier (CAN)—R
Christian Crafter—R
Christian Designer—R
Christian Living—R
Christian Motorsports
Christian Observer
Christian Ranchman
Christian Reader—R
Christianity Online—R
Church Advocate—R

Church of God EVANGEL
Colorado Christian—R
Connection Mag.—R
Conquest
Creation Care—R
Crossway/Newsline—R
Culture Wars—R
Evangelical Advocate—R
Faith & Friends—R
Fellowship Link—R
Foursquare World—R
Gem—R
God Allows U-Turns—R
God's Revivalist
Good News, Etc.—R
Good News Journal (MO)
Good News Journal (TX)
Gospel Today
Grit
Guideposts
Healing Inn—R
Heartlight Internet—R
Hidden Manna—R
HomeLife—R
Home Times—R
Hunted News
Impact Magazine—R
Indian Life—R
Inspirer—R
Jewel Among Jewels—R
John Milton—R
Jour/Christian Nursing—R
Keys to Living—R
Life@Work
Lifeglow—R
LifeWise
Live—R
Living—R
Living Light News—R
Lutheran—R
Lutheran Journal—R
Lutheran Witness
Marriage Partnership
Mennonite—R
Messenger/St. Anthony
Metro Voice—R
Michigan Christian
Minnesota Christian—R
Moody—R
New Heart—R
New Writing—R
Now What?—R
NRB Magazine—R
Our Family—R
Pentecostal Evangel
Peoples Magazine—R
Physician—R
Plus—R

Power for Living—R
PrayerWorks—R
Preserving Christian Homes—R
Quiet Revolution—R
SCP Journal—R
Seeds
Short Stories Bimonthly
Signs of the Times—R
Spirit—R
Standard—R
Stepping Out
Storyteller—R
TEAK Roundup—R
Today's Christian Senior—R
Together—R
Vision—R
War Cry—R
Wesleyan Advocate—R

CHILDREN
Celebrate
Club Connection—R
Courage
Discovery (NY)—R
Discovery Trails—R
Focus/Clubhouse
Focus/Clubhouse Jr.
GUIDE—R
High Adventure—R
J.A.M.—R
Live Wire—R
Mission
Nature Friend—R
Our Little Friend—R
Partners—R
Pockets—R
Primary Treasure—R
Skipping Stones
Story Friends—R
Touch—R
Winner—R

CHRISTIAN EDUCATION/LIBRARY
Church Media Journal—R
GROUP
Perspective—R
Vision—R

MISSIONS
American Horizon—R
Areopagus—R
Heartbeat—R
Latin America Evangelist
Leaders for Today
So All May Hear—R
Worldwide Challenge

MUSIC
Quest—R

PASTORS/LEADERS
Cell Group—R
Evangelicals Today—R
Five Stones—R
Growing Churches
Minister's Family
Pastoral Life—R
Preacher's Illus. Service—R
Sharing the Practice—R

TEEN/YOUNG ADULT
Boundless Webzine—R
Certainty
Challenge
Conqueror—R
Encounter—R
Essential Connection—R
Guideposts for Teens—R
Insight—R
J.A.M.—R
Passageway.org—R
Real Time—R
Teens on Target—R
Today's Christian Teen—R
WITH—R
YOU!—R
Young & Alive—R
Young Salvationist—R
Youth Challenge—R

WOMEN
Esprit—R
Godly Business Woman
Handmaiden—R
Hearts at Home—R
Helping Hand—R
Journey—R
Just Between Us—R
Proverbs 31
    Woman—R
Reflections (FL)
Wesleyan Woman—R
Woman's Touch—R
Women of Spirit—R

WRITERS
Areopagus (UK)
Cochran's Corner—R

VIDEO REVIEWS

ADULT/GENERAL
About Such Things—R
American Wasteland
Arlington Catholic

Bridal Guides—R
Bridge—R
CBA Marketplace
Christian Courier (CAN)—R
Christian Crafter—R
Christian Designer—R
Christian Renewal—R
Christianity/Arts
Connection Mag.—R
Expression Christian
Forefront—R
Good News Journal (MO)—R
Hidden Manna—R
Homeschooling Today—R
Hunted News
Indian Life—R
Interim—R
Michigan Christian
MovieGuide
Testimony—R
Trumpeter—R
Upsouth—R
Winsome Wit—R

CHILDREN
Club Connection—R

CHRISTIAN EDUCATION/ LIBRARY
Catholic Library World
Church Libraries—R

MUSIC
Songwriting—R

PASTORS/LEADERS
Evangelicals Today—R
Five Stones—R
Horizons—R
Lutheran Partners—R
Ministries Today
Sharing the Practice—R
Worship Leader

TEEN/YOUNG ADULT
Devo'Zine—R
YOU!—R

WEBSITE REVIEWS*

ADULT/GENERAL
Dunamis Life—R

WOMEN'S ISSUES

ADULT/GENERAL
American Tract Soc.—R
Anglican Journal—R

Annals of St. Anne
Arlington Catholic
Banner
Beacon—R
Bread of Life—R
Breakthrough Intercessor—
    R
Bridal Guides—R
Catholic Digest—R
Catholic Faith & Family
Catholic Forester—R
Catholic Insight
Catholic New Times—R
Catholic Parent
CBA Marketplace
Celebrate Life—R
CGA World—R
Charisma/Christian Life
Chicken Soup/Mother—R
Christian C.L. RECORD—R
Christian Courier (CAN)—R
Christian Designer—R
Christian Leader—R
Christian Living—R
Christian News NW—R
Christian Parenting—R
Christian Ranchman
Christian Social Action—R
Chrysalis Reader
Church Advocate—R
Church of God EVANGEL
Columbia
Compleat Nurse—R
Decision
Discipleship Journal
Disciple's Journal—R
Episcopal Life—R
Evangel—R
Evangelical Advocate—R
Expression Christian
Faith Today
Focus on the Family
Foursquare World—R
Gem—R
God Allows U-Turns—R
Good News, Etc.—R
Good News Journal (MO)—
    R
Good News Journal (TX)
Grit
Heartlight Internet—R
HomeLife—R
Homeschooling Today—R
Home Times—R
Indian Life—R
Interim—R
John Milton—R
Joyful Noise

Keys to Living—R
Legions of Light—R
Life@Work
Life Gate—R
LifeWise
Light and Life
Liguorian
Living—R
Living Light News—R
Lookout—R
Lutheran—R
Lutheran Witness
Mennonite Brethren—R
MESSAGE
Metro Voice—R
Michigan Christian
Minnesota Christian—R
Moody—R
Ncubator.com—R
New Freeman—R
New Moon—R
Newsline—R
New Writing—R
On Mission
Our Sunday Visitor
Pentecostal Evangel
Peoples Magazine—R
Perspectives
Plain Truth—R
Plus—R
Presbyterian Layman
Presbyterian Outlook
Presbyterian Record—R
Presbyterians Today—R
Psychology for Living—R
Purpose—R
Reflections
St. Joseph's Messenger—R
Signs of the Times—R
Sojourners
Standard, The—R
Stepping Out
Together—R
Total Health
Touchstone—R
Trumpeter—R
United Church Observer—R
Vibrant Life—R
Vision—R
War Cry—R

*CHRISTIAN EDUCATION/
LIBRARY*
Resource—R

MISSIONS
American Horizon—R
East-West Church

Women of the Harvest
Worldwide Challenge

PASTORS/LEADERS
Cell Group—R
Christian Century
Christian Ministry (feminist)
Enrichment—R
Eucharistic Minister—R
Evangelical Baptist—R
Evangelicals Today—R
Horizons—R
Journal/Christian Healing—R
Lutheran Partners—R
Ministries Today
Ministry
Pastoral Life—R
Reaching Children at Risk
Sharing the Practice—R
Youthworker
Word & World

TEEN/YOUNG ADULT
Boundless Webzine—R
Brio
Vision—R
YOU!—R

WOMEN
(See alphabetical listing)

WORLD ISSUES

ADULT/GENERAL
AGAIN—R
Alive!
America
American Wasteland
Annals of St. Anne
Arlington Catholic
Banner
Bible Advocate—R
Breakthrough Intercessor—R
Bridal Guides—R
Bridge—R
CGA World—R
Charisma/Christian Life
Christian Century
Christian Leader—R
Christian Living—R
Christian Motorsports
Christian Observer
Christian Ranchman
Christian Renewal—R
Christian Social Action—R
Church of God EVANGEL
Columbia
Commonweal

Covenant Companion—R
Creation Care—R
Creation Ex Nihilo
Culture Wars—R
Decision
Discipleship Journal
Evangel—R
Evangelical Advocate—R
Expression Christian
Faith Today
First Things
Gem—R
God Allows U-Turns—R
God's Revivalist
Good News, Etc.—R
Good News Journal (MO)—
   R
Good News Journal (TX)
Gotta Write
Heartlight Internet—R
Home Times—R
Inland NW Christian
Interchange
Interim—R
John Milton—R
Journal of Church & State
Legions of Light—R
Liberty—R
Light and Life
Liguorian
Living Church
Lookout—R
Lutheran—R
Lutheran Journal—R
MESSAGE
Messenger
Messenger/St. Anthony
Metro Voice—R
Michigan Christian
Minnesota Christian—R
Moody—R
New Freeman—R
Now What?—R
NRB Magazine—R
Our Sunday Visitor
Plain Truth—R
Presbyterian Layman
Presbyterian Outlook
Presbyterians Today—R
Quiet Revolution—R
Reflections
Re:generation
SCP Journal—R
Seeds
Sojourners
Stepping Out
TEAK Roundup—R
Testimony—R

Trumpeter—R
United Church Observer—R
War Cry—R
Wireless Age—R

CHILDREN
Discovery (NY)—R
God's World News—R
J.A.M.—R
Skipping Stones

*CHRISTIAN EDUCATION/
LIBRARY*
Christian School Admin.

MISSIONS
Areopagus—R
Catholic Near East
East-West Church
Hope for Children—R
Latin America Evangelist
Missiology
New World Outlook
P.I.M.E. World
So All May Hear—R
World Christian—R
World Pulse—R
Worldwide Challenge

PASTORS/LEADERS
Cell Group—R
Christian Century
Evangelicals Today—R
Lutheran Partners—R
Ministries Today
Pastoral Life—R
Preacher's Illus. Service—R
Quarterly Review
Reaching Children at Risk
Rev.
Sharing the Practice—R
Word & World
Youthworker

TEEN/YOUNG ADULT
Boundless Webzine—R
J.A.M.—R
Teenage Christian—R
Young Salvationist—R

WOMEN
Esprit—R
Helping Hand—R
Horizons—R
SpiritLed Woman

WRITERS
Areopagus (UK)

WORSHIP

ADULT/GENERAL
AGAIN—R
Angels on Earth
Annals of St. Anne
Arlington Catholic
Bible Advocate—R
Bread of Life—R
Breakthrough Intercessor—
R
Bridge—R
Cathedral Age
Catholic Digest—R
Catholic New Times—R
CGA World—R
Charisma/Christian Life
Christian Century
Christian Courier (CAN)—R
Christian Leader—R
Christian Motorsports
Christianity Today—R
Church Herald/Holiness—R
Church of God EVANGEL
Commonweal
Connection Mag.—R
Conquest
Cornerstone—R
Covenant Companion—R
Creation Care—R
Cresset
Culture Wars—R
Decision
Discipleship Journal
Dovetail—R
Evangel—R
Evangelical Advocate—R
Faith Today
Family Digest
Fellowship Link—R
Foursquare World—R
God Allows U-Turns—R
Good News, Etc.—R
Good News Journal (MO)—
R
Hunted News
Inspirer—R
John Milton—R
Joyful Noise
Legions of Light—R
Life Gate—R
Lifeglow—R
LifeWise
Light and Life
Liguorian
Living Church
Lutheran—R
Lutheran Journal—R

Mennonite—R
Men of Integrity—R
MESSAGE/Open Bible—R
Messenger/St. Anthony
Michigan Christian
Montana Catholic—R
Moody—R
Ncubator.com—R
New Freeman—R
New Heart—R
North American Voice
On Mission
Our Family—R
Our Sunday Visitor
Peoples Magazine—R
Perspectives
Power for Living—R
Prairie Messenger—R
PrayerWorks—R
Presbyterian Outlook
Presbyterian Record—R
Presbyterians Today—R
St. Anthony Messenger
St. Willibrord Journal
Seeds
Silver Wings—R
Spiritual Life
Standard—R
Stepping Out
Testimony—R
Time of Singing—R
Touchstone—R
United Church Observer—
R
U.S. Catholic
War Cry—R
Way of St. Francis—R
Wesleyan Advocate—R
Wireless Age—R

CHILDREN
BREAD/God's Children—R
J.A.M.—R
Wonder Time

*CHRISTIAN EDUCATION/
LIBRARY*
Children's Ministry
Christian Ed Journal—R
Church Educator—R
Church Media Journal—R
Evangelizing Today's Child—
R
GROUP
Leader/Church School
Today—R
Shining Star
Youth & CE Leadership—R

MISSIONS
American Horizon—R
Areopagus—R
Latin America Evangelist
Worldwide Challenge

MUSIC
Church Pianist, etc.
Creator—R
Songwriting—R
Gospel Industry Today
Hymn

PASTORS/LEADERS
African American Pulpit
Celebration
Cell Group—R
Christian Century
Christian Management—R
Church Worship
Clergy Journal—R
Cross Currents—R
Emmanuel
Enrichment—R
Environment & Art
Evangelical Baptist—R
Evangelicals Today—R
Five Stones—R
Growing Churches
Horizons—R
Jour/Amer Soc/Chur
   Growth—R
Leadership—R
Let's Worship
Lutheran Forum—R
Lutheran Partners—R
Ministries Today
Ministry
Ministry & Liturgy—R
Pastoral Life—R
Preacher's Illus. Service—R
Preaching
PROCLAIM—R
Pulpit Helps—R
Reaching Children at Risk
Reformed Worship
Resource—R
Rev.
Sharing the Practice—R
Today's Christian Preacher—
   R
Today's Parish
Word & World
Worship Leader
Youthworker

TEEN/YOUNG ADULT
Encounter—R

Essential Connection—R
J.A.M.—R
Real Time—R
Student Leadership—R
Teenage Christian—R
Teens on Target—R
Today's Christian Teen—R
WITH—R
Youth Challenge—R

WOMEN
Connection
Esprit—R
Godly Business Woman
Horizons—R
Lutheran Woman Today
Proverbs 31 Woman—R

WRITING HOW-TO

ADULT/GENERAL
CBA Marketplace
Christian Observer
Christian Social Action—R
Home Times—R
Michigan Christian
Ncubator.com—R
New Song
New Writing—R
Short Stories Bimonthly
Star of Zion
TEAK Roundup—R

CHILDREN
Discovery (NY)—R
J.A.M.—R
Preschool Playhouse
Winner—R

CHRISTIAN EDUCATION/
LIBRARY
Children's Ministry
Leader/Church School
   Today—R

MUSIC
Songwriting—R

PASTORS/LEADERS
Evangelicals Today—R
Newsletter Newsletter
Reaching Children at Risk
Technologies/Worship—R

TEEN/YOUNG ADULT
J.A.M.—R

WOMEN
Godly Business Woman
Just Between Us—R

WRITERS
Advanced Chris. Writer—R
Areopagus (UK)
Byline
Canadian Writer's Jour—R
Christian Writer—R
Cochran's Corner—R
Contemporary Songwriter—R
Cross & Quill—R
Exchange—R
Fellowscript—R
NW Christian Author—R
Once Upon a Time—R
Teachers & Writers
Tickled by Thunder
WE!—R
Writer
Writer Online—R
Writer's Digest—R
Writer's Forum—R
Writers' Journal—R
Writer's Potpourri—R
Writing World

YOUTH ISSUES

ADULT/GENERAL
American Tract Soc.—R
Annals of St. Anne
Arlington Catholic
Banner
Beacon—R
Breakthrough Intercessor—R
Catholic Faith & Family
Catholic Forester—R
Catholic New Times—R
Charisma/Christian Life
Christian Courier (CAN)—R
Christian Designer—R
Christian Leader—R
Christian Living—R
Christian Motorsports
Christian Parenting—R
Christian Ranchman
Christian Renewal—R
Church Herald/Holiness—R
Church of God EVANGEL
Companions—R
Covenant Companion—R
Culture Wars—R
Decision
Evangel—R
Evangelical Advocate—R
Expression Christian

Faith Today
Foursquare World—R
Good News, Etc.—R
Good News Journal (TX)
Gospel Today
Grit
Homeschooling Today—R
Home Times—R
Jewel Among Jewels—R
John Milton—R
Joyfull Noise
Legions of Light—R
Life Gate—R
Living—R
Living Church
Living Light News—R
Lutheran—R
Lutheran Witness
MESSAGE
Messenger/St. Anthony
Metro Voice—R
Michigan Christian
Ncubator.com—R
New Freeman—R
On Mission
Our Family—R
Peoples Magazine—R
Prairie Messenger—R
Presbyterian Outlook
Presbyterian Record—R
Presbyterians Today—R
Prism—R
Reflections
Seeds
Sojourners
Stepping Out
U.S. Catholic

CHILDREN
American Girl
BREAD/God's Children—R
Children's Ministry
Club Connection—R
Courage
Crusader—R
Discovery (NY)—R
Focus/Clubhouse Jr.
Guideposts for Kids
J.A.M.—R
My Friend
On the Line—R
Skipping Stones
Touch—R

CHRISTIAN EDUCATION/LIBRARY
CE Connection—R
CE Counselor—R
Christian Classroom
Christian School Admin.
Church Educator—R
Enrichment—R
GROUP
Journal/Adventist Educ.—R
Leader/Church School
  Today—R
Parish Teacher
Perspective—R
Preschool Playhouse
Resource—R
Shining Star
Signal—B
Team—R
Vision—R
Youth & CE Leadership—R

MISSIONS
American Horizon—R
Worldwide Challenge

MUSIC
Quest—R

PASTORS/LEADERS
Catholic Servant
Cell Group—R
Christian Camp—R
Eucharistic Minister—R
Evangelical Baptist—R
Evangelicals Today—R
Five Stones—R
Horizons—R
Ivy Jungle Report—R
Lutheran Partners—R
Minister's Family
Ministries Today
Pastoral Life—R
Pulpit Helps—R
Reaching Children at Risk
Sharing the Practice—R
Word & World
Youthworker

TEEN/YOUNG ADULT
(See alphabetical listing)

WOMEN
Godly Business Woman
Horizons—R
Just Between Us—R
Proverbs 31 Woman—R
Reflections (FL)
Wesleyan Woman—R

ALPHABETICAL LISTINGS OF PERIODICALS & E-ZINES

Following are the listings of periodicals. They are arranged alphabetically by type of periodical (see Table of Contents for a list of types). Nonpaying markets are indicated in bold letters within those listings, e.g. **NO PAYMENT**. For the first time this year, paying markets are indicated with a $ in front of the listing.

If a listing is preceded by an asterisk (*), it indicates that publisher did not send updated information. If it is preceded by a number symbol (#) it was updated from current guidelines, their Website, or available sources. If it is preceded by a (+) it is a new listing. It is important that freelance writers request writer's guidelines and a recent sample copy before submitting to any of these publications, but especially to those with the * and # symbols.

If you do not find the publication you are looking for, look in the General Index. See the introduction of that index for the codes used to identify the current status of each unlisted publication.

For a detailed explanation of how to understand and get the most out of these listings, as well as solid marketing tips, see the "How to Use This Book" section at the front of the book. Unfamiliar terms are explained in the Glossary at the back of the book.

(*) An asterisk before a listing indicates no or unconfirmed information update.

(#) A number symbol before a listing means it was updated from the current writer's guidelines, their Websites, or other sources.

(+) A plus sign means it is a new listing.

($) A dollar sign before a listing indicates a paying market.

ADULT/GENERAL MARKETS

#ABOUT SUCH THINGS, Tenth Presbyterian Church, 1701 Delancey St., Philadelphia PA 19103. (215)849-1583. Fax (215)735-3960. E-mail: about such@yahoo.com. Website: world.std.com/~pduggan/ast/astroot.html. Presbyterian Church of America. Laurel W. Garver, mng ed. Readership seeks to interact with culture at large in a thoughtful, morally grounded manner. Biannual mag (deadlines are January 20 and July 20 each year); 28-32 pgs; circ 300. Subscription $7. 100% unsolicited freelance. Complete ms. PAYS 2 COPIES for 1st rts. Not copyrighted. Articles to 2,500 wds (4-6/yr); fiction to 3,000 wds (6-8/yr); reviews to 2,500 wds. Responds in 1 yr. Seasonal January 20 (Easter) and July 20 (Christmas). Accepts simultaneous submissions & reprints (tell when/where appeared). Prefers disk; no e-mail submissions. Open to sidebars. Prefers NIV or NRSV. Guidelines (also on Website); copy $3/9x12 SAE/4 stamps.

> **Poetry:** Accepts 25-40/yr. Avant-garde and free verse; 4-60 lines. Submit max 5 poems.

Special Needs: Looking for more reviews; essays evaluating popular culture issues, events, and trends from a Christian perspective. In fiction, emphasize character development and theme. Characters should be multi-faceted and should change or grow during the course of the story.

Tips: "Most open to poetry. Become familiar with good contemporary poetry with religious themes; no sing-song or greeting-card verse. Don't send overly personal, confessional-style pieces. Short stories and essays must be neat, with proper grammar and spelling. Steer clear of clichés and write with a genuine voice."

$ACCENT ON LIVING, PO Box 700, Bloomington IL 61702-0700. (309)378-2961. Fax (309)378-4420. E-mail: acntlvng@aol.com. Website: www. accentonliving.com. Cheever Publishing. Betty Garee, ed. Provides information on new devices and easier ways to do things, so people with physical disabilities can enjoy a better and more satisfying lifestyle. Quarterly mag (5x7); 96 pgs; circ 20,000. Subscription $12. 75% freelance. Query; phone/fax/e-query OK. Pays .10/wd on publication for one-time rts. Articles 250-1,000 wds (30-40/yr). Responds in 4 wks. Seasonal 6 mos ahead. Accepts simultaneous submissions & reprints (tell when/where appeared). Accepts disk or e-mail submission (copied into message). Some sidebars. Guidelines (also by e-mail); copy $3.50. (Ads)

Fillers: Cartoons; $20.

Tips: "We prefer an informal, rather than academic approach. We want to show individuals with disabilities getting involved in all aspects of life. Accessibility and fitness are two popular subjects."

ADORATION: A Journal of Christian Poetry, PO Box 802954, Santa Clarita CA 91380-2954. E-mail: editor@adorationpress.com. Website: www. adorationpress.com. Adoration Press. Kurt McCullum, ed. Christian poetry. Quarterly mag; 32 pgs; circ. 100. Subscription $12. Estab. 2000. 100% unsolicited freelance. Complete ms; no cover letter; e-query OK. **PAYS 2 COPIES.** Responds in 1-2 wks. Considers simultaneous submissions and reprints. Accepts e-mail submissions (copied into message). No sidebars. Guidelines (also by e-mail/Website); copy $3.50. (No ads)

Poetry: Accepts 100-130/yr. Free verse, traditional; 4-50 lines. Submit max 5 poems.

AGAIN MAGAZINE, PO Box 76, Ben Lomond CA 95005. (831)336-5118. Fax (831)336-8882. E-mail: editor@conciliarpress.com. Website: www. conciliarpress.com. Antiochian Orthodox Archdiocese of North America/Conciliar Press. Deacon R. Thomas Zell, mng ed. Historic Eastern Orthodox Christianity applied to our modern times. Quarterly mag; 32 pgs; circ 5,000. Subscription $14.50. 1% unsolicited freelance; 99% assigned. Query; e-query OK. **USUALLY PAYS IN COPIES.** Articles 1,500-2,500 wds (4/yr); book reviews 800-1,000 wds. Responds in 6-8 wks. Seasonal 4-6 mos ahead. Serials 2 parts. Accepts reprints (tell when/where appeared). Prefers disk or e-mail (copied into message). Some sidebars. Prefers NKJV. Guidelines (also by e-mail); copy for 9x12 SAE/4 stamps. (No ads)

Tips: "We are Orthodox in orientation, and interested in thoughtful, intelligent articles dealing with church history, Protestant/Orthodox dialog, relations between Protestants and Orthodox in foreign countries; also in modern ethical dilemmas—no fluff."

THE ALABAMA BAPTIST, 3310 Independence Dr., Birmingham AL 35209-5602. (205)870-4720. Fax (205)870-8957. E-mail: news@alabapnews.org. The Alabama Baptist, Inc. Dr. Bob Terry, ed. Shares news and information relevant to members of Baptist churches in Alabama. Weekly (50X) newspaper; circ 111,000. Subscription $10.75. Open to freelance. Query. Not in topical listings. (Ads)

**1999 EPA Award of Excellence—Newspaper; 1998 EPA Award of Merit—Newspaper.

$#ALIVE! A MAGAZINE FOR CHRISTIAN SENIOR ADULTS, PO Box 46464, Cincinnati OH 45246-0464. (513)825-3681. Christian Seniors Fellowship. June Lang, office ed. Focuses on activities and opportunities for active Christian senior adults, 55 and older; upbeat rather than nostalgic. Bimonthly mag; 24 pgs; circ 3,000. Subscription/membership $15. 70% unsolicited; 10% assigned. Complete ms/cover letter; no e-query. Pays .04-.06/wd ($18-75) on publication for one-time or reprint rts. Articles 600-1,200 wds (25-50/yr); fiction 600-1,500 wds (12/yr). Responds in 9 wks. Seasonal 4 mos ahead. Accepts reprints (tell when/where appeared). No disk. Some sidebars. Guidelines; copy for 9x12 SAE/3 stamps. (Ads)

> **Poetry:** Rarely use. Free verse, light verse, traditional; $3-10. Submit max 3 poems.
>
> **Fillers:** Buys 15/yr. Anecdotes, cartoons, quizzes, short humor, and word puzzles, 50-500 wds; $2-25.
>
> **Columns/Departments:** Buys 35/yr. Heart Medicine (humor, grandparent/grandchild anecdotes), to 100 wds, $5-10.
>
> **Tips:** "Most open to fresh material of special appeal to Christian senior adults. Avoid nostalgia. Our market is seniors interested in living in the present, not dwelling on the past. We pay little attention to credits/bios; articles stand on their own merit. Stories of seniors in short-term missions or other Christian activities; or active senior groups involved in service—not just social activities."

$ALIVE NOW! PO Box 340004, Nashville TN 37203-0004. (615)340-7218. Fax (615)340-7267. E-mail: alivenow@upperroom.org. Website: www.upperroom.org/alivenow. United Methodist/The Upper Room. Melissa Tidwell, interim ed. Short theme-based writings in attractive graphic setting for reflection and meditation. Bimonthly mag; 64 pgs; circ 65,000. 25% unsolicited freelance; 75% assigned. Complete ms/cover letter. Pays $20-30 or more on publication for newspaper, periodical and electronic rts. Articles 250-500 wds. Responds 13 wks before issue date. Seasonal 6-8 mos ahead. Accepts simultaneous submissions and reprints (tell when/where appeared). Accepts disk. Guidelines/theme list (also by e-mail/Website); copy for 6x9 SAE/4 stamps.

> **Poetry:** Avante-garde, free verse, traditional; to 40 lines or one page; pays $10-25. Submit max 5 poems.
>
> **Fillers:** Prayers.

ALLIANCE LIFE, PO Box 35000, Colorado Springs CO 80935-3500. (719)599-5999. Fax (719)599-8234. E-mail: alife@cmalliance.org. Website:

www.alliancelife.org. The Christian & Missionary Alliance/denominational. Stephen P. Adams, ed. To teach and inspire readers concerning principles of Christian living. Monthly mag; circ 30,000. Subscription $13. Accepts freelance. Prefers query. Not in topical listings. (No ads)
**1998 EPA Award of Merit—Denominational.

$AMERICA, 106 W. 56th St., New York NY 10019-3893. (212)581-4640. Fax (212)399-3596. E-mail: articles@americapress.org. Website: www.america press.org. Catholic. Thomas J. Reese, S.J., ed-in-chief. For thinking Catholics and those who want to know what Catholics are thinking. Weekly mag; 32+ pgs; circ 41,000. Subscription $43. 100% freelance. Complete ms/cover letter; fax/e-query OK. Pays $100-200 on acceptance. Articles 1,500-2,000 wds. Responds in 6 wks. Seasonal 3 mos ahead. No sidebars. Guidelines (also on Website); copy for 9x12 SAE. (Ads)

AMERICAN TRACT SOCIETY, Box 462008, Garland TX 75046. (972)276-9408. Fax (972)272-9642. E-mail: PBatzing@ATSTracts.org. Website: www.ATStracts.org. Peter Batzing, tract ed. Majority of tracts written to win unbelievers. Bimonthly new tract releases; 40 new titles produced annually. 5% unsolicited freelance; 2% assigned. Complete ms/cover letter; e-query OK. **PAYS IN COPIES** on publication for exclusive tract rts. Tracts 600-1,200 wds. Responds in 6-8 wks. Seasonal 1 yr ahead. Accepts simultaneous submissions & reprints (tell when/where appeared). Accepts disk or e-mail submission (attached or copied into message). Prefers NIV or KJV. Guidelines (also by e-mail)/free samples for #10 SAE/1 stamp. (No ads)
   Special Needs: Youth issues, Hispanic, African-American.
   Tips: "Read our current tracts; submit polished writing; relate to people's needs and experiences."

AMERICAN WASTELAND, 11285 McGill Rd., Soddy-Daisy TN 37379. E-mail: submissions@americanwasteland.com. Website: www.americanwasteland. com. Marty Lasley, co-ed. A commentary, for adults, on the spiritual vacuity and degeneracy of American culture. Online journal. Estab. 1999. Open to freelance. Query by e-mail only. **NO PAYMENT** (hopes to pay within 1 yr) for one-time rts. Articles 500-2,000+ wds. Responds in 1 wk. Accepts simultaneous submissions. Requires e-mail submission (attached or copied into message). Prefers NIV. Guidelines on Website. (Ads)
   Tips: "All areas are open. Submissions must have a sharp Christian perspective, yet engage, discuss and interact with secular ideas. Articles need some spunk, verve, and edge. Browse our site to get a feel."

$+ANCIENT PATHS, PMB #223, 2000 Benson Rd. S., #115, Renton WA 98055. E-mail: skylar.burris@gte.net. Website: www.geocities.com/journal ancient/index.html. Christian/nondenominational. Skylar Hamilton Burris, ed. A forum for quality literature on Christian themes. Biannual mag. Subscription $6. Complete ms/cover letter; phone/fax/e-query OK. Pays $2 for prose and $2 for artwork. Articles to 2,500 wds; fiction to 2,500 wds. Accepts e-mail submissions (copied into message). Guidelines (also on Website); copy $3. Not in topical listings. (Ads)
   Poetry: Buys poetry to 60 lines. Traditional and free verse. Submit max 5 poems. Pays $1.

Contest: All accepted manuscripts are entered in a contest. Prize is $10 and an extra copy of the magazine.

Tips: "All forms and styles are considered, but avoid preachy or didactic work. Subtle is better."

AND HE WILL GIVE YOU REST, PO Box 502928, San Diego CA 92150. (888) 751-7378. E-mail: rest@restministries.org. Website: www.restministries. org. Rest Ministries, Inc. Lisa Copen, ed. For people who live with chronic illness or pain; offers encouragement, support and hope dealing with everyday issues. Monthly newsletter. 40% unsolicited freelance; 60% assigned. E-query OK. **PAYS IN COPIES**. Articles. E-mail submissions OK. Guidelines (also on Website); free copy.

Tips: "Avoid articles about physical healing and people who have physically overcome their illness. Write for people who will live with their illness indefinitely, but who are searching for how to live joyfully despite the 'thorn.'"

$ANGELS ON EARTH, 16 E. 34th St., New York NY 10016. (212)251-8100. Fax (212)684-0679. E-mail: angelsedtr@guideposts.org. Website: www. guideposts.org. Guideposts. Colleen Hughes, ed-in-chief; Catherine Scott, depts. ed. for features and fillers. Presents true stories about God's angels and humans who have played angelic roles on earth. Bimonthly mag; circ 800,000. Subscription $16.95. 90% freelance. Complete ms/ cover letter. Pays $25-400 on publication for all rts. Articles 100-2,000 wds (80-100/yr; all stories must be true). Responds in 12 wks. Seasonal 6 mos ahead. Regular sidebars. No disk. Guidelines; copy for 7x10 SAE/4 stamps.

Fillers: Buys many. Anecdotal shorts of similar nature; to 250 wds; $25-100.

Columns/Departments: Accepts 25/yr. Earning Their Wings (good deeds), 150 wds; Only Human? (human or angel?/mystery), 250 wds; $50-100.

Tips: "We are not limited to stories about heavenly angels. We also accept stories about human beings doing heavenly duties."

ANGLICAN ARTS, 14845-6 Yonge St., Ste 158, Aurora ON L4G 6H8 Canada. Fax (905)841-1802. E-mail: angarts@musica-mundana.com. Michael Leach, ed. For those with an above average interest in the artistic and aesthetic aspects of their spiritual lives as practitioners or observers and how the sacred arts help or hinder them. Biannual journal. Estab 1998.

$ANGLICAN JOURNAL, 600 Jarvis St., Toronto ON M4Y 2J6 Canada. (416)924-9192. Fax (416)921-4452. E-mail: editor@national.anglican.ca. Website: www.anglicanjournal.com. Anglican Church of Canada. Vianney (Sam) Carriere, acting ed. Informs Canadian Anglicans about the church at home and overseas. Newspaper (10x/yr); 20 pgs; circ 272,000. 25% freelance. Query only; phone query OK. Pays $50-300 CAN, on acceptance for 1st rts. Articles to 1,000 wds. Responds in 2 wks. Seasonal 2 mos ahead. Accepts reprints. Guidelines.

$THE ANNALS OF SAINT ANNE DE BEAUPRE, PO Box 1000, St. Anne de Beaupre QC G0A 3C0 Canada. (418)827-4538. Fax (418)827-4530. Catholic/Redemptorist Fathers. Father Roch Achard, C.ss.R., ed. Promotes

Catholic family values. Monthly mag; 32 pgs; circ 45,000. Subscription $10 US, $12.50 CAN. 35% unsolicited freelance. Complete ms/cover letter; no phone/fax query. Pays .03-.04/wd on acceptance for 1st N.A. serial rts only. Articles & fiction (250/yr); 500-1,500 wds. Responds in 4 wks. Seasonal 4-5 mos ahead. No disk. No sidebars. Prefers NRSV. Guidelines; copy for 9x12 SAE/IRC. (No ads)

Tips: "Writing must be uplifting and inspirational; clearly written, not filled with long quotations. We tend to stay away from extreme controversy and focus on the family, good family values, devotion and Christianity." No simultaneous submissions or reprints; rights must be clearly stated. Typed manuscripts only.

$THE APOCALYPSE CHRONICLES, Box 448, Jacksonville OR 97530. (541)899-8888. E-mail: James@ChristianMediaNetwork.com. Website: www.ChristianMediaNetwork.com. Christian Media. James Lloyd, ed/pub. Deals with the apocalypse exclusively. Quarterly newsletter; circ 2,000-3,000. Query; prefers phone query. Payment negotiable for reprint rts. Articles. Responds in 3 wks. KJV only. Copy for #10 SAE/2 stamps.

Tips: "It's helpful if you understand your own prophetic position and are aware of its name, i.e., Futurist, Historicist, etc."

$ARKANSAS CATHOLIC, PO Box 7417, Little Rock AR 72217. (501)664-0125. Fax (501)664-9075. E-mail: mhargett@dolr.org. Catholic Diocese of Little Rock. Malea Hargett, ed. Regional newspaper for the local diocese. Weekly tabloid; 16 pgs; circ 7,000. Subscription $16. 1% unsolicited freelance; 10% assigned. Query/clips; e-query OK. Pays on acceptance or publication for 1st rts. Articles 400-800 wds (2/yr). Accepts simultaneous submissions. Accepts disk. Regular sidebars. Prefers Catholic Bible. Guidelines; copy for 7x10 SAE/2 stamps. (Ads)

Columns/Departments: Kathy Neal. Accepts 2/yr. Seeds of Faith (education).

Tips: "Make stories as localized as possible."

$ARLINGTON CATHOLIC HERALD, 200 N. Glebe Rd., Ste. 607, Arlington VA 22203. (703)841-2590. Fax (703)524-2782. E-mail: achflach@aol.com, or editorial@catholicherald.com. Website: catholicherald.com/index.htm. Catholic Diocese of Arlington. Michael Flach, ed. Regional newspaper for the local diocese. Weekly newspaper; 28 pgs; circ 53,000. Subscription $14. 10% freelance. Query; phone/fax/e-query OK. Pays $50-150 on publication for one-time rts. Articles 500-1,500 wds. Responds in 2 wks. Seasonal 3 mos ahead. Accepts simultaneous submissions. Prefers disk. Regular sidebars. Guidelines (also on Website); copy for 11x17 SAE. (Ads)

Columns/Departments: Sports; School News; Local Entertainment; 500 wds.

Tips: "All submissions must be Catholic-related. Avoid controversial issues within the Church."

$+AT THE FENCE, Website: www.atthefence.com. Nora Penia, ed. Articles. Paying market. Did not return questionnaire.

$#THE BANNER, 2850 Kalamazoo Ave. SE, Grand Rapids MI 49560. (616) 224-0732. Fax (616)224-0834. E-mail: editorial@thebanner.org. Website: www.thebanner.org. Christian Reformed Church. John D. Suk, ed; Joyce

Kane, assoc ed. Denominational; to inform, challenge, educate, comfort, and inspire members of the church. Biweekly mag; 39 pgs; circ. 30,000. Subscription $34.95. 5% unsolicited freelance; 95% assigned. Query or complete ms/cover letter; phone/fax/e-query OK. Pays $125-200 on acceptance for all rts. Articles 850 or 1,200-1,800 wds (5/yr); fiction to 2,500 wds; book/music/video reviews, 850 wds, $75. Responds in 8 wks. Seasonal 6-8 mos ahead. Requires disk. Kill fee 50%. Regular sidebars. Prefers NIV. Guidelines/theme list; copy for 9x12 SAE/4 stamps. (Ads)

   Poetry: Buys 10/yr. Any type; 5-50 lines; $40. Submit max 5 poems.

   Fillers: Buys 48/yr. Church-related cartoons; $50.

   Tips: "Members of the Christian Reformed Church have a better chance of being accepted. Writers must know our audience and address topics of interest to members."

   **1997 EPA Award of Merit—Denominational.

$*BAPTIST HISTORY AND HERITAGE, Editor's address: Carson-Newman College, 1646 Russell Ave., Jefferson City TN 37760. (431)471-3200. Fax (423)471-3502. Southern Baptist Historical Society and Carson-Newman College. Mel Hawkins, mng ed. A scholarly journal focusing on Baptist history. Quarterly journal; 64 pgs; circ 2,000. Subscription $25. 20% unsolicited freelance; 80% assigned. Query by e-mail. Pays $150 (for assigned only) for all rts. Articles to 4,000 wds. Responds in 9 wks. Prefers disk. Guidelines. (No ads)

   Tips: "Most open to issues in Baptist history that have not been fully explored: gender, race, African-American Baptists."

$B.C. CATHOLIC, 150 Robson St., Vancouver BC V6B 2A7 Canada. (604)683-0281. Fax (604)683-8117. E-mail: bcc@rcav.bc.ca. Website: www.rcav.bc.ca/bcc. Catholic. Paul Schratz, ed. News, education and inspiration for Canadian Catholics. Weekly (48X) newspaper; 20 pgs; circ 20,000. 20% freelance. Query; phone query OK. Pays .15/wd on publication for 1st rts. Photos $25. Articles 500-1,000 wds. Responds in 6 wks. Seasonal 4 wks ahead. Accepts simultaneous submissions & reprints. Prefers e-mail submission (Word attached file or copied into message). No guidelines; free copy. (Ads)

   Tips: "Items of a Catholic nature are preferred."

$BEACON, 418 Fourth St. NE, Charlottesville VA 22902. (804)961-2500. Fax (804)961-2507. E-mail: DianeMc@journeygroup.com. Website: www.efca.org/beacon.html. Evangelical Free Church of America/Journey Communications. Diane McDougall, ed. Denominational. Bimonthly (7X) mag; 32 pgs; circ 35,000. Subscription $12. 5% unsolicited freelance; 95% assigned. Complete ms/cover letter; fax/e-query OK. Pays .23/wd on acceptance for 1st & subsidiary (free use on EFCA Website or church bulletins) rts. Articles 300-1,200 wds (6/yr). Responds in 6 wks. Seasonal 6 mos ahead. Accepts simultaneous submissions & reprints (tell when/where appeared). Prefers e-mail (attached file) or hard copy. Kill fee 50%. Regular sidebars. Guidelines (also by e-mail); copy $1/10x13 SAE/6 stamps. (Ads)

   Columns/Departments: Buys 6/yr. Home Base (topics affecting women's, men's & youth ministries, as well as families); Cover-theme

Section (variety of topics applicable to church leadership), 550-1,200 wds, pays .23/wd.

Special Needs: Stories of EFCA churches in action.

Tips: "Have a unique story about a Free Church in action. The vast majority of articles are geared to sharing the Free Church at work." **1999 EPA Award of Merit—Denominational.

$BIBLE ADVOCATE, Box 33677, Denver CO 80233. (303)452-7973. Fax (303)452-0657. E-mail: bibleadvocate@cog7.org. Website: www.cog7. org/BA. Church of God (Seventh-Day). Calvin Burrell, ed; Sherri Langton, assoc ed. Adult readers; 50% not members of the denomination. Monthly (10X) mag; 24 pgs; circ 13,500. Subscription free. 100% unsolicited freelance. Complete ms/cover letter; e-query OK. Pays $25-55 on publication for 1st, one-time, reprint, electronic & simultaneous rts. Articles 1,000-1,800 wds (20-25/yr). Responds in 4-8 wks. Seasonal 9 mos ahead. Accepts simultaneous submissions & reprints (tell when/where appeared). Accepts disk or e-mail submission (copied into message). Kill fee up to 50%. Regular sidebars. Prefers NIV, NKJV. Guidelines/theme list (also on Website); copy for 9x12 SAE/3 stamps. (No ads)

Poetry: Buys 6-10/yr. Free verse, traditional; 5-20 lines; $20. Submit max 5 poems.

Fillers: Buys 5-10/yr. Facts, prose, quotes; 100-400 wds; $20.

Columns/Departments: Accepts 5/yr. Viewpoint (social or religious issues), 600-650 wds, pays copies.

Special Needs: Articles centering on themes for 2001 (see theme list).

Tips: "If you write well, all areas are open to freelance, especially personal experiences that tie in with the monthly themes. Fresh writing with keen insight is most readily accepted. Writers may also submit sidebars that fit our theme for each issue."

*** BIBLICAL REFLECTIONS ON MODERN MEDICINE**, PO Box 14488, Augusta GA 30919. (706)736-0161. Fax (706)721-0758. Dr. Ed Payne, ed. For all Christians interested in medical-ethical issues. Bimonthly newsletter; 8 pgs; circ 1,100. Subscription $19. 1% unsolicited freelance. Complete ms/cover letter; e-query OK. **PAYS IN COPIES & SUBSCRIPTION**, for 1st rts. Articles to 1,500 wds (5/yr). Responds in 1-4 wks. Accepts simultaneous submissions & reprints. Accepts e-mail submissions. No sidebars. Prefers NAS. Guidelines/copy for #10 SAE/1 stamp. (No ads)

Tips: "Most open to careful biblical/critical analysis of medicine and medical ethics."

#BOOKS & CULTURE, 465 Gundersen Dr., Carol Stream IL 60188. (630)260-6200. Fax (630)260-0114. E-mail: WilsonBKS@aol.com. Website: www.booksandculture.net. Christianity Today Intl. John Wilson, ed. To edify, sharpen, and nurture the evangelical intellectual community by engaging the world in all its complexity from a distinctly Christian perspective. Bimonthly & online mag; circ 12,000. Subscription $24.95. Open to freelance. Query. Not in topical listings. (Ads)

$THE BREAD OF LIFE, 209 MacNab St. N., Box 395, Hamilton ON L8N 3H8 Canada. (905)529-4496. Fax (905)529-5373. Catholic. Fr. Peter Coughlin, ed. Catholic Charismatic; to encourage spiritual growth in areas of renewal in the Catholic Church today. Bimonthly mag; 32 pgs; circ 3,500. Subscription $30. 5% unsolicited freelance. Complete ms/cover letter; fax query OK. Articles 1,100-1,300 wds; book reviews 250 wds. Responds in 4-6 wks. Seasonal 6 mos ahead. Accepts reprints (tell when/where appeared). No disk. No sidebars. Prefers NAB or NJB. Guidelines; copy for 9x12 SAE/6 stamps. (Ads)

Fillers: Accepts 10-12/yr. Facts, prose, quotes; to 250 wds.

THE BREAKTHROUGH INTERCESSOR, PO Box 121, Lincoln VA 20160. (540)338-5522. Fax (540)338-1934. E-mail: breakthrough@intercessors. org. Website: www.intercessors.org. Nondenominational. Andrea Doudera, ed.; Trudi Schwarting, in-house ed. Preparing and equipping people who pray; encouraging in prayer and faith. Quarterly mag; 32-36 pgs; circ 9,100. Subscription $15. 100% unsolicited freelance. Complete ms/cover letter; phone/fax/e-query OK. **NO PAYMENT.** Articles about 1,000 wds (50/yr). Responds in 6 wks. Seasonal 2 mos ahead. Accepts simultaneous submissions & reprints (tell when/where appeared). Accepts disk or e-mail submission. Regular sidebars. Any version. Guidelines; copy for 6x9 SAE/2 stamps. (No ads)

Poetry: Accepts 5/yr. Traditional.

Special Needs: All articles must have to do with prayer.

Contest: Pays $25 for article with most reader impact.

Tips: "Break in by submitting true articles/stories about prayer and its miraculous results."

$*BRIDAL GUIDES, PO Box 1264, Huntington WV 25714. (304)416-1423. Tellstar Productions/Interdenominational. Shannon Bridget Murphy, ed. A guide for planning Christian weddings, formals, and receptions. Quarterly mag; 80-100 pgs; circ 50,000. Subscription $42. Estab 1998. 75-90% freelance. Complete ms/cover letter. Pays .01/wd on acceptance for 1st or one-time rts. Articles 500+ wds or features 800-2,000 wds (60/yr); fiction 500+ wds (60/yr); book review (exchange for the book or product). Responds in 8 wks. Seasonal 2-3 mos ahead. Accepts Simultaneous submissions & reprints (tell when/where appeared). No disk. Regular sidebars. Guidelines; copy $10. (Ads)

Poetry: Buys many/yr. Any type or length. Pays variable rates. Submit any number.

Fillers: Buys many/yr. Anecdotes, cartoons, facts, games, ideas, newsbreaks, party ideas, prayers, quizzes, quotes, short humor, word puzzles. Pays variable rates.

Special Needs: Picture books for children; cards. Fiction on weddings.

Contest: Send SASE for contest information.

Tips: "Most open to personal experiences of weddings, formals, receptions and planning for events; how-to articles. Functional wedding, formal and reception creations and patterns. Photographs from events."

**This periodical was #31 on the 2000 Top 50 Christian Publishers list.

THE BRIDGE, 170 Huntington Cir., Alpharetta GA 30004. (770)442-9637. Fax (770)442-9637. E-mail: bridgemail@spaceport.com. Website: bridgemag. cjb.net. Sean Taylor, ed. Quarterly online mag. 40% unsolicited freelance; 60% assigned. Submit by e-mail/cover letter. **NO PAYMENT FOR NOW** for 1st rts. Articles 1,500-3,000 wds; fiction to 3,000 wds; reviews 200 wds. Responds in 2 wks. Seasonal 6 mos ahead. Accepts simultaneous submissions & reprints (tell when/where appeared). Prefers e-mail submission (attached file). Regular sidebars. Any version. Guidelines (also by e-mail/Website). (Ads)

  Poetry: Accepts 4-10/yr. Avant-garde, free verse; 10-30 lines. Submit max 2 poems.

  Fillers: Accepts 4-8/yr. Editorial cartoons only.

  Columns/Departments: Accepts 4/yr. What's the World Coming To? (1st person experience as a member in today's culture without being of it.)

  Special Needs: Cutting-edge looks at culture from the standpoint of biblical Christianity. Also publishes satire.

  Tips: "Most open to first-person column, but any writer with solid skills and the right attitude stands a good chance at repeat work with us."

$CANADA LUTHERAN, 302-393 Portage Ave., Winnipeg MB R3B 3H6 Canada. (204)984-9150. Fax (204)984-9185. E-mail: kward@elcic.ca. Website: www.elcic.ca/clweb. Evangelical Lutheran Church in Canada. Kenn Ward, ed. Denominational. Monthly (9X) mag; 56 pgs; circ 17,000. Subscription $23 US. 40% unsolicited freelance; 60% assigned. Query or complete ms/cover letter; fax/e-query OK. Pays $40-110 CAN on publication for one-time rts. Articles 800-1,500 wds (15/yr); fiction 850-1,200 wds (4/yr). Responds in 5 wks. Seasonal 10 mos ahead. Accepts simultaneous submissions & reprints. Prefers e-mail submission (copied into message). Some sidebars. Prefers NRSV. Guidelines (also by e-mail). (Ads)

  Tips: "Canadians/Lutherans receive priority, but not the only consideration. Want material that is clear, concise and fresh. Articles that talk about real life experiences of faith receive our best reader response."

$CATHEDRAL AGE, Mount St. Alban, Massachusetts & Wisconsin Aves NW, Washington DC 20016-5098. (202)537-5681. Fax (202)364-6600. E-mail: Cathedral_Age@cathedral.org. Website: www.cathedral.org/cathedral. Washington National Cathedral (Episcopal). Craig W. Stapert, ed. About what's happening in and to cathedrals and their programs. Quarterly & online mag; 36 pgs; circ 29,000. Subscription $15. 20% freelance. Query/ clips; phone/fax query OK. Pays to $500 on acceptance for all rts. Articles 1,000-1,500 wds (10/yr); book reviews 600 wds, $100. Responds in 4 wks. Seasonal 6 mos ahead. Requires disk or e-mail submission (attached file). Kill fee 50%. Regular sidebars. Prefers NRSV. No guidelines; copy $5/9x12 SAE/5 stamps. (No ads)

  Special Needs: Art, architecture, music.

  Tips: "We assign all articles, so query/clips first. Always write from the viewpoint of an individual first, then move into a more general discussion of the topic. Human interest angle important."

$THE CATHOLIC ANSWER, 200 Noll Plaza, Huntington IN 46750. (800)348-2440. E-mail: tcanswer@osv.com. Website: www.osv.com. Our Sunday Visitor/Catholic. Father Peter Stravinskas, mng ed. Answers to questions of belief for orthodox Catholics. Bimonthly mag; 64 pgs; circ 50,000. 50% freelance. Query/clips. Pays $100 on publication for 1st rts. Articles 800-1,600 wds (50/yr). Seasonal 6 mos ahead. Guidelines; free copy.

$CATHOLIC DIGEST, 2115 Summit Ave., St. Paul MN 55105-1048. (651) 962-6739. Fax (651)962-6758. E-mail: cdigest@stthomas.edu. Website: www.CatholicDigest.org. Catholic/University of St. Thomas. Richard J. Reese, ed; submit to Kathleen Stauffer, mng. ed. Readers have a stake in being Catholic and a wide range of interests: religion, family, health, human relationships, good works, nostalgia, and more. Monthly & online mag; 128 pgs; circ 509,390. Subscription $19.95. 15% unsolicited freelance; 20% assigned. Complete ms (for original material)/cover letter, tear sheets for reprints. Pays $200-400 ($100 for reprints) on acceptance for one-time rts. Online-only articles receive $100, plus half of any traceable revenue. Articles 1,000-5,000 wds (60/yr). Responds in 6-8 wks. Seasonal 5 mos ahead. Accepts reprints (tell when/where appeared). Accepts disk or e-mail submission (copied into message). Regular sidebars. Prefers NAB. Guidelines (also on Website); copy for 7x10 SAE/2 stamps. (Ads)

Fillers: Buys 200/yr. Anecdotes, cartoons, facts, games, jokes, quizzes, quotes, short humor; to 500 wds; $2/published line on publication.

Columns/Departments: Buys 75/yr. Open Door (personal stories of conversion to Catholicism); 200-500 wds; pays $2/published line. See guidelines for full list.

Special Needs: Family and career concerns of Baby Boomers who have a stake in being Catholic.

Contest: See Website for current contest, or send an SASE.

Tips: "We favor the anecdotal approach. Stories must be strongly focused on a definitive topic that is illustrated for the reader with a well-developed series of true-life, interconnected vignettes."

**This periodical was #44 on the 2000 Top 50 Christian Publishers list (#15 in 1999, #9 in 1998, #27 in 1997, #29 in 1996, #30 in 1995, #25 in 1994).

$CATHOLIC FAITH & FAMILY 33 Rossotto Dr., Hamden CT 06514. (203)288-5600. Fax (203)288-5157. E-mail: editor@twincircle.com. Catholic/Circle Media, Inc. Duncan Anderson, ed. dir. Features writing for Catholics and/or Christian families of all ages. Bimonthly magazine; 80 pgs; circ 20,000. Subscription $14.95. 20% unsolicited freelance; 80% assigned. Query/clips or complete ms/cover letter; phone/fax/e-query OK. Pays $75 for opinion pcs; $74, $150, or $300 for features, on publication for 1st rts. Opinion pieces, 600 or 825 wds; features 600, 1,100, or 2,000 wds; reviews 500 wds, $75. Responds in 8 wks. Seasonal 2 mos ahead. Serials 3 parts. Prefers e-mail submission (attached file or copied into message). Kill fee. Regular sidebars. Prefers NAB. Guidelines (also by e-mail); copy for 10x13 SAE/2 stamps. (Ads)

Columns/Departments: Buys 75/yr. Point of View (opinion on various Catholic issues), 450, 650 or 750 wds, $75. Query.

Tips: "Most open to well-written feature articles employing good quotations, anecdotes, and transitions about an interesting aspect of family life."

**This periodical was #67 on the 2000 Top 50 Christian Publishers list.

$CATHOLIC FORESTER, Box 3012, Naperville IL 60566-7012. (630)983-3381. Fax (800)811-2140. E-mail: cofpr@aol.com. Website: www.catholic forester.com. Catholic Order of Foresters. Mary Anne File, ed. For mixed audience, primarily parents and grandparents between the ages of 30 and 80+. Bimonthly mag; 36 pgs; circ 100,000. Free/membership. 10% unsolicited freelance. Complete ms/cover letter; no phone/fax/e-query. Pays .20/wd on acceptance for 1st, one-time, or reprint rts. Articles 1,000-1,500 wds (5/yr); fiction for all ages 500-1,200 wds (5/yr). Responds in 12-16 wks. Seasonal 4-6 mos ahead. Accepts simultaneous submissions & reprints (tell when/where appeared). Accepts disk or e-mail submission. Kill fee 5%. Some sidebars. Prefers Catholic version. Guidelines; copy for 9x12 SAE/4 stamps. (No ads)

Poetry: Buys 5/yr. Light verse, traditional. Pay varies. Submit max 5 poems.

Fillers: Keith Halla, ed. Buys 5/yr. Cartoons. Pay varies.

Tips: "Looking for informational, inspirational articles on finances and parenting. Write for our audience. Writing should be energetic with good style and rhythm."

**This periodical was #62 on the 2000 Top 50 Christian Publishers list (#45 in 1998, #28 in 1997, #50 in 1996).

$CATHOLIC INSIGHT, PO Box 625, Adelaide Sta., 36 Adelaide St. E., Toronto ON M5C 2J8 Canada. (416)204-9601. Fax (416)204-1027. E-mail: catholic@catholicinsight.com. Website: www.catholicinsight.com. Life Ethics Information Center. Alphonse de Valk, ed/pub. News, analysis and commentary on social, ethical, political, and moral issues from a Catholic perspective. Monthly (10X) mag; 32-36 pgs; circ 3,600. Subscription $25 CAN, $28 US. 2% unsolicited freelance; 98% assigned. Query; phone/fax/e-query OK. Pays $200 for 1,500 wds ($250 for 2,000 wds) on publication for all rts. Articles 750-1,500 wds (20-30/yr); book reviews 750 wds, $75. Responds in 6-8 wks. Seasonal 2 mos ahead. Accepts disk or e-mail submissions. Some sidebars. Prefers RSV (Catholic). Copy $4 CAN/9x12 SAE/.90 CAN postage or IRC. (Ads)

Tips: "We are interested in political/social/current affairs—Canadian—from the viewpoint of informed readership and encouraging involvement in the political process as essential to social change."

$+CATHOLIC NEW TIMES, 80 Sackville St., Toronto ON M5A 3E5 Canada. (416)361-0761. Fax (416)361-0796. E-mail: cnt@total.net. Website: www. catholicnewtimes.org. New Catholic Times, Inc. Dr. Maura Hanrahan, ed. An independent journal in the Catholic tradition that focuses on faith and social justice. Biweekly newspaper; 20 pgs; circ 8,000. Subscription $24. 25% unsolicited freelance; 75% assigned. Query; phone/fax/e-query OK.

Pays $75-300 on publication for one-time rts. Articles 500-1,200+ wds (40/yr); book reviews 500-800 wds; music reviews 500 wds; video reviews 500-700 wds; pays $50-100. Guidelines; copy for 9x12 SAE/3 stamps. Not in topical listings. (Ads)

Fillers: Newsbreaks.

Columns/Departments: Buys 40/yr. (assigned). Witness (first-person experience) 1,200 wds; Frontburner (opinion) 500-600 wds; Faith & Spirituality (experiences of faith) to 1,200 wds; Canada (Canadian news/features) 300-1,200+ wds; World (world news) 300-1,200+ wds. Query. Pays $100.

Tips: "Call me with an idea and we can chat about it. Our office is in Toronto, but we want to reflect all parts of the country, so writers in all provinces and terretories are encouraged to get in touch."

$CATHOLIC NEW YORK, 1011 1st Ave., 17th Fl., New York NY 10022. (212)688-2399. Fax (212)688-2642. E-mail: cny@cny.org. Website: www. cny.org. Catholic. Anne Buckley, ed-in-chief. To inform New York Catholics. Weekly newspaper; 44 pgs; circ 130,000. Subscription $20. 10% freelance. Query or complete ms/cover letter. Pays $15-100 on publication for one-time rts. Articles 500-800 wds. Responds in 5 wks. Copy $1.

Columns/Departments: Comment; Catholic New Yorkers (profiles of unique individuals); 325 wds.

Tips: "Most open to articles that show how to integrate Catholic faith into work, hobbies or special interests."

$CATHOLIC PARENT, 200 Noll Plaza, Huntington IN 46750. (800)348-2440 or (219)356-8400. Fax (219)359-9117. E-mail: cparent@osv.com. Website: www.osv.com. Catholic. Woodeene Koenig-Bricker, ed. Practical advice for Catholic parents, with a specifically Catholic slant. Bimonthly mag; 52 pgs; circ 35,000. Subscription $21. 5% unsolicited freelance; 95% assigned. Query/clips or complete ms/cover letter; fax query OK; e-query OK. Pays $100-200 on acceptance for 1st rts. Articles 250-1,000 wds (50/yr). Responds in 12 wks. Seasonal 6 mos ahead. Kill fee. Considers simultaneous submissions. Accepts disk. Regular sidebars. Guidelines; copy $3. (Ads)

Fillers: York Young, ed. Parenting tips, 100-200 wds, $25.

Columns/Departments: This Works! (short parenting tips), 200 wds. Pays $15-25.

Tips: "We need personal, inspirational, spiritual, first-person accounts dealing with family life and parenting."

**This periodical was #68 on the 2000 Top 50 Christian Publishers list (#39 in 1999, #17 in 1998, #20 in 1997, #51 in 1996, #25 in 1995, #26 in 1994).

$CATHOLIC PEACE VOICE, 532 W. 8th, Erie PA 16502-1343. (814)453-4955. Fax (814)452-4784. E-mail: peacevoice@paxchristiusa.org. Website: www. paxchristiusa.org. Dave Robinson, ed. For members of US Catholic Peace Movement. Quarterly newspaper; 20 pgs; circ 20,000. Distributed free. 5% freelance. Query; phone/fax/e-query OK. Pays on publication for one-time rts. Accepts simultaneous submissions & reprints. Prefers disk. Guidelines; copy for 9x12 SAE/2 stamps. Not in topical listings. (Ads)

Tips: "Emphasis is on nonviolence. No sexist language."

$CATHOLIC SENTINEL, PO Box 18030, Portland OR 97218-0030. (503)281-1191. Fax (503)281-1191. E-mail: casentinel@aol.com. Website: www.sentinel.org. Catholic. Robert Pfohman, ed. For Catholics in the Archdiocese of western and eastern Oregon. Weekly tabloid & online version; 16-24 pgs; circ 15,000. Subscription $26. 25% assigned freelance. Query; phone/fax/e-query OK (if timely). Pays $25-150 on publication for one-time rts. Not copyrighted. Articles 800-1,800 wds (15/yr). Responds in 6 wks. Seasonal 1 month ahead. Accepts reprints (on columns, not news or features; specify it's a reprint). Prefers e-mail submissions. Kill fee 100%. Regular sidebars. Copy 50 cents/9x12 SAE/2 stamps. (Ads)

> **Columns/Departments:** Buys about 30/yr. Opinion Page, 600 wds, $10. Query first.
>
> **Tips:** "Find active Catholics living their faith in specific, interesting, upbeat, positive ways."

$CATHOLIC TELEGRAPH, 100 E. 8th St., Cincinnati OH 45202. (513)421-3131. Fax (513)381-2242. E-mail: tctnews@aol.com. Catholic. Dennis O'Connor, ed. Diocese newspaper for Cincinnati area (all articles must have a Cincinnati or Ohio connection). Weekly newspaper; 20 pgs; circ 27,000. 10% freelance. Send résumé and writing samples for assignment. Pays varying rates on publication for all rts. Articles. Responds in 2-3 wks. Kill fee. Guidelines sent on acceptance; free copy.

> **Fillers:** Newsbreaks (local).

CATHOLIC WORLD REPORT, Domus Enterprises, Inc., Box 1608, South Lancaster MA 01561. (978)365-7208. Website: www.ignatius.com/mags/cwr.htm. Catholic. A news magazine that not only reports on important events in the Church, but helps to shape them. Philip Lawler, ed; submit to Ed Corres. Monthly mag. Subscription $39.95. Not in topical listings.

$CBA FRONTLINE, PO Box 62000, Colorado Springs CO 80962-2000. (719)265-9895 or (800)252-1950. Fax (719)272-3510. E-mail: publications @cbaonline.org. Website: www.cbaonline.org. Christian Booksellers Assn. Steve Parolini, ed; Debby Weaver, mng ed. To give product knowledge and inspiration to the frontline staff in Christian retail stores. Monthly trade journal; 36 pgs; circ 7,000. Subscription $8-$15. Estab 1997. 0% unsolicited freelance; 75% assigned. Query/clips; phone/fax/e-query OK. Pays .25-.35/wd. on acceptance for all rts. Articles to 1,500 wds. Responds in 4 wks. Seasonal 4-5 mos ahead. Accepts disk. Kill fee. Regular sidebars. Editorial calendar; copy for $3.20/9x12 SAE. (Ads)

> **Columns/Departments:** Buys many/yr. Humor (true Christian retail-oriented anecdotes & cartoons), 25-100 wds. 1,500 wds. Pays $25.
>
> **Tips:** "Most open basic tips for product merchandising, and features articles that give specific training for Christian retail salespeople. We look for writers with experience in the Christian retail sales field. We rarely accept unsolicited mss, but assign 2-5 articles per month to freelancers based on our agenda. Send cover letter, including experience and areas of interest, plus clips. Request editorial calendar. Also looking for retail and product anecdotes."

$CBA MARKETPLACE, PO Box 62000, Colorado Springs CO 80962-2000. (719)265-9895 or (800)252-1950. Fax (719)272-3510. E-mail: publications

@cbaonline.org. Website: www.cbaonline.org. Christian Booksellers Assn. Debby Weaver, mng. ed. To provide Christian bookstore owners and managers with professional retail skills, product information, and industry news. Monthly trade journal; 110-260 pgs; circ 8,000. Subscription $50. 0% unsolicited freelance; 30% assigned. Query/clips; phone/fax/e-query OK. Pays .25-.35/wd on acceptance for all rts. Articles 800-2,500 wds (30/yr assigned); book reviews 100-150 wds, $30; music/video reviews 100-150 wds, $25. Responds in 8 wks. Seasonal 4-5 mos ahead. Prefers disk. Regular sidebars. Accepts any modern version. Theme list; copy $5/9x12 SAE/6 stamps. (Ads)

> **Fillers:** Buys 12/yr. Cartoons ($100), retail facts, ideas, trends, newsbreaks.
>
> **Columns/Departments:** Buys 10-20/yr. Industry Watch; Music News; Gift News; Video & Software News; Book News; Kids News; Spanish News; all 100-500 wds. Pays .16-.25/wd. Query.
>
> **Special Needs:** Trends in retail, consumer buying habits, market profiles. By assignment only.
>
> **Tips:** "Looking for writers who have been owners/managers/buyers/sales staff in Christian retail stores. All our articles are by assignment and focus on producing and selling Christian products or conducting retail business. Send cover letter, including related experience and areas of interest, plus samples. We also assign reviews of books, music, videos, Spanish products, kids products, and software. Ask for calendar for product news and market-segment features."

$CELEBRATE LIFE, Box 1350, Stafford VA 22555. (540)659-4171. Fax (540) 659-2586. E-mail: clmag@all.org. Website: www.all.org. American Life League. Rich Gelina, ed. A pro-life, pro-family magazine for Christian audience. Bimonthly & online mag; 48 pgs; circ 80,000. Subscription $12.95. 40% unsolicited freelance; 40% assigned. Query/clips or complete ms/cover letter; fax/e-query OK. Pays .05-.10/wd (for unsolicited), .20/wd (for assignments) on publication for 1st or reprint rts. Articles 300-1,050 wds (40/yr). Responds in 2-13 wks. Seasonal 4 mos ahead. Accepts simultaneous submissions & reprints (tell when/where appeared). Prefers e-mail submission. Kill fee 25%. Some sidebars. Guidelines/theme list (also by e-mail); copy for 9x12 SAE/4 stamps. (Ads)

> **Fillers:** Buys 5/yr. Newsbreaks (local or special pro-life news); 75-200 wds; $10.
>
> **Special Needs:** Personal experience about abortion, post-abortion stress/healing, adoption, activism/young people's involvement, death/dying, euthanasia, eugenics, special needs children, personhood, chastity, and large families.
>
> **Tips:** "We are No-Exceptions pro-life. The importance of that philosophy should be emphasized. Photos are preferred."
>
> **This periodical was #66 on the 1994 Top 50 Christian Publishers list.

$*CGA WORLD, PO Box 3658, Scranton PA 18503. (570)342-3294. Fax (570)586-7721. Catholic Golden Age. Barbara Pegula, ed. For Catholics 50+. Quarterly mag; 32 pgs; circ. 100,000. Subscription/membership $8.

Query. Pays .10/wd on publication for 1st, one-time, or reprint rts. Articles & fiction. Responds in 6 wks. Seasonal 6 mos ahead. Accepts reprints (tell when/where appeared). Accepts disk. Guidelines; copy for 9x12 SAE/3 stamps. (Ads)

Fillers: Games, ideas, prayers, word puzzles.

$CHARISMA & CHRISTIAN LIFE, Strang Communications, 600 Rinehart Rd., Lake Mary FL 32746. (407)333-0600. Fax (407)333-7133. E-mail: charisma @strang.com. Website: www.charismamag.com. Strang Communications. Lee Grady, exec ed.; Billy Bruce, news ed; Adrienne Gaines, mng. ed.; Adrienne S. Gaines, book & music review ed. Primarily for the Pentecostal and Charismatic Christian community. Monthly mag; 100+ pgs; circ 250,000. Subscription $24.97. 75% assigned freelance. Query only; e-query OK. Pays $100-800 on publication for 1st rts. Articles 2,500 wds; book/music reviews, 200 wds, $25-35. Responds in 8-12 wks. Seasonal 4 mos ahead. Kill fee $50. Prefers e-mail submissions. Regular sidebars. Guidelines; copy $4. (Ads)

Tips: "Most open to news section, reviews or features. Query (published clips help a lot)." No unsolicited manuscripts.

**1998 EPA Award of Excellence—General.

$+CHICKEN SOUP BOOKS. For a list of current Chicken Soup books open to submissions, as well as related opportunities, go to: www.angelfire. com/de/lagana/psoup.html. If no contact listed, send to: stories@canfield group.com. Timelines vary, so send stories any time as they may fit another project. You may submit the same story to more than one project, but you must send a separate copy to each. Most stories 1,000 wds or less. E-mail submissions preferred. When submitting, indicate which project it is for and whether you want it held for consideration in any of their other books.

$*CHICKEN SOUP FOR THE MOTHER'S SOUL, Dept. CW, PO Box 1262, Fairfield IA 52556. Fax (515)472-3720. Carol Kline, ed. Did not return questionnaire.

$*CHICKEN SOUP FOR THE MOTHER'S SOUL #2, Dept. CW, PO Box 1959, Fairfield IA 52556. (515)472-4047. Fax (515)472-7288. E-mail: chicken soup@lisco.com. Chicken Soup for the Soul. Submit to Editor. 101 stories to open the hearts and rekindle the spirits of mothers. Stories go into a book. Sales of 2 million. Release date: Unknown. 100% freelance. Complete ms/cover letter. Pays $300/story (plus 1 copy of bk) on publication for one-time rts. Articles 200-1,200 wds (101/bk). Responds in 16 wks. Accepts simultaneous submissions & reprints (tell when/where appeared). Accepts e-mail submission (copied into message). Guidelines (also by e-mail/Website); sample stories for #10 SAE/1 stamp.

Fillers: Buys 25/book. Anecdotes, cartoons, short humor; 100-200 wds. Pays $250.

Special Needs: Looks for true stories about motherhood that inspire and touch mothers. The stories are universal and non-denominational.

Tips: "Read some of our Chicken Soup for the Soul Books."

Deadline: This book currently on hold.

$+CHICKEN SOUP FOR THE VOLUNTEER'S SOUL, PO Box 7816, Wilmington

DE 19803-7816. (302)475-4825. E-mail: Lagana@juno.com, or NurseAngel @juno.com. Website: www.angelfire.com/de/lagana/volunteersoul.html. (or llagana.) Tom and Laura Lagana, co-eds. Stories go into a book. Pays $300/story (plus 1 copy of bk) on publication for one-time rts. Articles 300-1,000 wds (101/bk). Submit by e-mail. Guidelines on Website.

$CHICKEN SOUP FOR THE WOMAN'S SOUL #3, Dept. CW, PO Box 2049, Fairfield IA 52556. (800)380-0107. Fax (515)472-7288. E-mail: chicken soup@lisco.com. Chicken Soup for the Soul. Submit to Editor. 101 stories to open the hearts and rekindle the spirits of women. Stories go into a book. Sales of 1 million. Release date: October 2002. 100% freelance. Complete ms/cover letter. Pays $300/story (plus 1 copy of bk) on publication for one-time rts. Articles 200-1,200 wds (101/bk). Responds in 16 wks. Accepts simultaneous submissions & reprints (tell when/where appeared). Accepts e-mail submission (copied into message). Guidelines (also by e-mail); sample stories for #10 SAE/1 stamp.

    Fillers: Buys 25/book. Anecdotes, cartoons, short humor; 100-200 wds. Pays $250.

    Special Needs: Looking for true stories about women that inspire, uplift and touch other women. The stories are universal and non-denominational.

    Tips: "Read some of our Chicken Soup for the Soul Books."

    Deadline: August 31, 2001.

*THE CHRISTIAN BUSINESSMAN, 7001 SW 24th Ave., Gainesville FL 32607-3704. Carlson Communications. Rob Dilbone, ed. To equip and empower working men with the tools they need to become successful spiritually, personally, and financially, while advancing the gospel of Christ. Query only. Incomplete topical listings.

THE CHRISTIAN CIVIC LEAGUE OF MAINE RECORD, Box 5459, Augusta ME 04332. (207)622-7634. Fax (207)621-0035. E-mail: email@cclmaine. org. Website: www.cclmaine.org/ethics5.htm. Cyndee Randall, ed. Focuses on church, public service and political action. Monthly newsletter; 4 pgs; circ 4,600. 10% freelance. Query. **NO PAYMENT** for one-time rts. Articles (10-12/yr). Responds in 4-8 wks. Accepts simultaneous query & reprints. Free copy. Not in topical listings. (No ads)

CHRISTIAN COMPUTING MAGAZINE, PO Box 10, Lee's Summit MO 64083. (816)246-1358. Fax (816)246-1828. E-mail: steve@ccmag.com. Website: www.ccmag.com. Steve Hewitt, ed-in-chief. For Christian/church computer users. Monthly (11X) & online mag; 2 pgs; circ. 30,000. Subscription $14.95. 40% freelance. Query/clips; fax/e-query OK. **NO PAYMENT** for all rts. Articles 1,000-1,800 wds (12/yr). Responds in 4 wks. Seasonal 2 mos ahead. Accepts reprints. Requires disk. Regular sidebars. Guidelines; copy for 9x12 SAE.

    Fillers: Accepts 6 cartoons/yr.

    Columns/Departments: Accepts 12/yr. Telecommunications (computer), 1,500-1,800 wds.

    Special Needs: Articles on Internet, DTP, computing.

THE CHRISTIAN COURIER, 1933 W. Wisconsin Ave., Milwaukee WI 53233. (414)344-7300. Fax (414)344-7375. E-mail: probucolls@juno.com.

ProBuColls Assn. John M. Fisco, Jr., pub.; Rita Bertolas, ed. To propagate the Gospel of Jesus Christ in the Midwest. Monthly newspaper; circ 10,000. 10% freelance. Query; phone/fax/e-query OK. **PAYS IN COPIES**, for one-time rts. Not copyrighted. Articles 300-1,500 wds (6/yr). Responds in 4-8 wks. Seasonal 2 mos ahead. Accepts reprints. Guidelines; free copy. (Ads)

> **Fillers:** Anecdotes, facts, newsbreaks; 10-100 wds.
>
> **Tips:** "We are always in need of seasonal feature/filler type of articles: Christmas, Easter, 4th of July, etc."

$CHRISTIAN COURIER, 4-261 Martindale Rd., St. Catherines ON L2W 1A1 Canada. (US address: Box 110, Lewiston NY 14092-0110.) (905)682-8311. (800)969-4838. Fax (905)682-8313. E-mail: ccmneditor@aol.com. Website under construction. Reformed Faith Witness. Harry DerNederlanden, ed. To present Canadian and international news, both religious and secular, from a Reformed Christian perspective. Biweekly tabloid; 28 pgs; circ 6,000. 10% unsolicited freelance; 90% assigned. Complete ms/cover letter; fax/e-query OK. Pays $15-100 US, up to .10/wd; about 2 wks after publication for one-time rts. Articles 600-1,200 wds (40/yr); fiction to 1,200-1,800 wds (4/yr); book reviews 600 wds. Responds in 6 wks. Seasonal 2 mos ahead. Accepts simultaneous submissions & reprints (tell when/where appeared). Prefers e-mail submissions (attached file). Some sidebars. Prefers NIV. Guidelines/theme list (also by e-mail); copy for 9x12 SAE. (Ads)

> **Poetry:** Buys 20/yr. Avant-garde, free verse, traditional; 10-30 lines; $15-30. Submit max 5 poems.
>
> **Tips:** "Suggest an aspect of the theme which you believe you could cover well, have insight into, could treat humorously, etc. Show that you think clearly, write clearly, and have something to say that we should want to read. Have a strong biblical worldview and avoid moralism and sentimentality."

$*CHRISTIAN CRAFTER, PO Box 1264, Huntington WV 25714. (304)416-1423. Shannon Bridget Murphy, ed. For Christian craftspeople who sell their work and/or organize and produce craft shows. Quarterly mag; 10 pgs; circ 1,000. Subscription $12. Estab. 1999. 95% unsolicited freelance; 5% assigned. Complete ms/cover letter. Pays .01/wd on acceptance for 1st & one-time rts. Articles 500+ wds (32-64/yr); fiction 500+ wds (18-20/yr); reviews 500 wds. Responds in 4 wks. Seasonal 2 mos ahead. Accepts simultaneous submissions & reprints (tell when/where appeared). Regular sidebars. Guidelines; copy $5. (Ads)

> **Poetry:** Buys several/yr. Any type. Send any number.
>
> **Fillers:** Buys several/yr. Any type.
>
> **Special Needs:** Personal experience about organizing craft shows (how-to articles); business articles related to crafting; and experiences from crafters about their art form, examples of their talent.

$*CHRISTIAN DESIGNER, PO Box 1264, Huntington WV 25714. (304)416-1423. Shannon Bridget Murphy, ed. Interior design ideas for churches and homes. Quarterly newsletter; 10 pgs; circ 1,000. Subscription $12. 95% unsolicited freelance; 5% assigned. Complete ms/cover letter. Pays

.01/wd on acceptance for 1st & one-time rts. Articles 500+ wds (60/yr); fiction 500+ wds (60/yr); reviews 500 wds. Responds in 4 wks. Seasonal 2 mos ahead. Accepts simultaneous submissions & reprints (tell when/where appeared). Regular sidebars. Guidelines; copy $5. (Ads)

Poetry: Buys several/yr. Any type. Send any number.

Fillers: Buys several/yr. Any type.

Special Needs: Interior design.

+**CHRISTIAN DRAMA EMAGAZINE,** 1824 Celestia Dr., Walla Walla WA 99362. E-mail: cdm@hiddennook.com. Website: hiddennook.com. Victor R. Phillips, ed/pub. Play scripts and articles related to Christian drama. E-magazine. Distributed free. Open to freelance. Prefers e-mail submissions. **NO PAYMENT FOR NOW.** Articles 300-1,000 wds. Incomplete topical listings.

Fillers: Short articles on what different churches and drama groups are doing and anecdotes of effective results of drama ministries; 300 wds and up.

Special Needs: Articles on script writing, directing, acting, set design, lighting, costumes, performance reviews, script reviews, and news about Christian drama groups.

Tips: "No monologues." Features a Directory of Touring Christian Drama Groups.

$+**CHRISTIAN FAMILIES NEWSLETTER & CHRISTIAN FAMILIES ONLINE.** E-mail: cfnonline@home.com. Website: members.home.net/cfnonline/guidelines.htm. Lisa Beamer, ed. To encourage and support Christian families as they face the challenges of today's world. Monthly e-mail publication. Open to freelance. Query or complete ms by e-mail (copied into message). Pays to $15 on publication for one-time and one-time electronic rts. Articles 300-600 wds; book/video/software reviews (query), 300 wds, $10. No payment for reprints. Prefers NIV. Guidelines on Website. Incomplete topical listings. (Ads)

Poetry: Extremely theme-related poetry to 30 lines; pays .20/line.

Columns/Departments: Thought for Your Family (family-oriented devotional); 400-500 wds.

Special Needs: Features, personal essays, activity features (query), and Web highlights (family-oriented websites—query).

$**CHRISTIAN HISTORY,** 465 Gundersen Dr., Carol Stream IL 60188. (630) 260-6200. Fax (630)260-0114. E-mail: CHeditor@christianhistory.net. Website: www.christianhistory.net. Christianity Today, Intl. Mark Galli, ed; submit to Elesha Coffman, assoc. ed. To teach Christian history to educated readers in an engaging manner. Quarterly mag; 52 pgs; circ 55,000. Subscription $19.95. 2% unsolicited freelance; 98% assigned. Query; fax/e-query only. Pays .10-.20/wd on acceptance for 1st, electronic & some ancillary rts. Articles 1,000-3,000 wds (1/yr). Responds in 2 wks. Accepts reprints (tell when/where appeared). Prefers disk. Kill fee 50%. Some sidebars. Guidelines/theme list (also on Website); copy $5.50. (Ads)

Tips: "Let us know your particular areas of specialization and any books or papers you have written in the area of Christian history.

After learning about our theme, then pitch your idea. We are purely thematic. Themes for 2001 include Dante, the Huguenots, Christianity and science through history."

**2000 & 1998 EPA Award of Merit—General.

$CHRISTIAN HOME & SCHOOL, 3350 East Paris Ave. SE, Grand Rapids MI 49512. (616)957-1070x239. Fax (616)957-5022. E-mail: RogerS@CSIonline. org, or GBordewyk@aol.com. Website: www.csionline.org/chs. Christian Schools Intl. Gordon L. Bordewyk, exec. ed.; Roger Schmurr, sr. ed. Focuses on parenting and Christian education; for parents who send their children to Christian schools. Bimonthly & online mag; 32 pgs; circ 67,000. Subscription $11.95. 95% unsolicited; 5% assigned. Complete ms or e-query. Pays $125-200 on publication for 1st rts. Articles 1,000-2,000 wds (30/yr); fiction 1,000-2,000 wds (5/yr); book reviews $25 (assigned). Responds in 1 wk. Seasonal 5 mos ahead. Accepts simultaneous query. Accepts disk (clean copy they can scan); prefers e-mail submission (attached file). Some sidebars. Prefers NIV. Guidelines/theme list (also on Website); copy for 9x12 SAE/4 stamps. (Ads)

Fillers: Ideas; 75-150 wds. Pays $25-40.

Tips: Most open to feature articles on parenting and education.

**This periodical was #49 on the 2000 Top 50 Christian Publishers list. 1997 EPA Award of Merit—Organizational.

$CHRISTIAN LEADER, PO Box V, Hillsboro KS 67063. (316)947-5543. Fax (316)947-3266. E-mail: chleader@southwind.net. U.S. Conference of Mennonite Brethren. Carmen Andres, ed. Denominational. Monthly mag; 36 pgs; circ. 9,800. Subscription $16. 20% unsolicited freelance; 80% assigned. Complete ms; e-query OK. Pays .06/wd on publication for 1st rts. Articles 1,200 wds (2/yr). Responds in 8 wks. Seasonal 4 mos ahead. Accepts simultaneous submissions & reprints (tell when/where appeared). Prefers disk or e-mail submissions (copied into message). Regular sidebars. Guidelines/theme list (also by e-mail); no copy. (Ads)

Tips: "Most open to features section. Ask for theme list; query specific topic/article."

$CHRISTIAN LIVING, 616 Walnut Ave., Scottdale PA 15683-1999. (724)887-8500. Fax (724)887-3111. E-mail: cl@mph.org. Website: www.mph.org/cl. Herald Press. Sarah Kehrberg, mng ed. Denominational with focus on contemporary stories of faith in action in a variety of contexts. Monthly (8X) mag; 28-36 pgs; circ 4,000. Subscription $24.95. 95% freelance. Complete ms/cover letter; e-query preferred. Pays .03-.05/wd on acceptance for one-time, reprint or simultaneous rts. Articles 1,500 wds (6/yr); fiction 1,500 wds (1-2/yr). Responds in 6-8 wks. Seasonal 4-6 mos ahead. Accepts simultaneous submissions & reprints (tell when/where appeared). Prefers e-mail submissions (attached file or copied into message). Some sidebars. Prefers NRSV. Guidelines/theme list; copy for 9x12 SAE/3 stamps. (Ads)

Poetry: Jean Janzen. Buys 15/yr. Free verse, haiku; 3-25 lines; pays $15-30. Submit max 5 poems.

Ethnic: Targets all ethnic groups involved in the Mennonite religion. Needs articles on issues of race.

Tips: "Looking for good articles on peace issues. A good understanding of issues related to our emphasis and community, family and peace and justice will help the writer."

**This periodical was #36 on the 2000 Top 50 Christian Publishers list (#51 in 1995, #56 in 1994).

CHRISTIAN MEDIA, Box 448, Jacksonville OR 97530. (541)899-8888. E-mail: James@ChristianMediaNetwork.com. Website: www.ChristianMedia Network.com. James Lloyd, ed/pub. For emerging Christian songwriters, artists, and other professionals involved in music, video, film, print, and broadcasting. Bimonthly tabloid; 24 pgs; circ 2,000-6,000. Query; prefers phone query. **NO PAYMENT** for negotiable rts. Articles; book & music reviews, 3 paragraphs. Accepts simultaneous submissions & reprints. Prefers disk. KJV only. Copy for 9x12 SAE/2 stamps.

Special Needs: Particularly interested in stories that expose dirty practices in the industry—royalty rip-offs, misleading ads, financial misconduct, etc. No flowery pieces on celebrities; wants well-documented articles on abuse in the media.

$CHRISTIAN MOTORSPORTS ILLUSTRATED, PO Box 129, Mansfield PA 16933. (570)549-2282. Fax (570)549-3366. E-mail: cpo@epix.net. Website: www.christianmotorsports.com. CPO Publishing. Roland Osborne, pub.; Tom Winfield, ed. Covers Christians involved in motorsports. Bimonthly mag; 64 pgs; circ 40,000. Subscription $19.96. 50% freelance. Complete ms; no phone/fax/e-query. Pays .20/wd on publication for 1st rts. Articles 500-2,000 wds (30/yr). Seasonal 4 mos ahead. Requires disk. Regular sidebars. Free copy. (Ads)

Poetry: Buys 10/yr. Any type. Pays .20/wd. Submit max 10 poems.

Fillers: Buys 100/yr. Anecdotes, cartoons, facts, games, ideas, jokes, newsbreaks, prayers, prose, quizzes, quotes, short humor. Pays .20/wd.

Columns/Departments: Buys 10/yr.

Tips: "Send a story on a Christian involved in motorsports."

CHRISTIAN NEWS NORTHWEST, PO Box 974, Newberg OR 97132. Phone/fax (503)537-9220. E-mail: cnnw@juno.com. Website: www.cnnw.com. John Fortmeyer, ed/pub. News of ministry in the evangelical Christian community in western and central Oregon and southwest Washington; distributed primarily through evangelical churches. Monthly newspaper; 28-36 pgs; circ 28,000. Subscription $15. 10% unsolicited freelance; 5% assigned. Query; phone/fax/e-query OK. **NO PAYMENT.** Not copyrighted. Articles 300-400 wds (100/yr). Responds in 4 wks. Seasonal 3 mos ahead. Accepts reprints (tell when/where appeared). Accepts e-mail submission. Regular sidebars. Guidelines (also by e-mail); copy $1.50. (Ads)

Tips: "We are heavily devoted to ministry news pertaining to the Pacific Northwest, so it would probably be difficult for anyone outside the region to break into our publication."

THE CHRISTIAN OBSERVER, 9400 Fairview Ave., Ste. 200, Manassas VA 22110. (703)335-2844. Fax (703)368-4817. E-mail: Elliott@xc.org. Website: www.LOCLNET.com/co. Christian Observer Foundation; Presbyterian Reformed. Dr. Edwin P. Elliott, ed. To encourage and edify God's people and families; print version of *Presbyterians-Week.* Monthly newspaper; 32 pgs; circ 3,500. Subscription $27. 10% unsolicited freelance; 90% assigned. Query; phone/e-query OK. NO PAYMENT. Accepts e-mail submissions. (Ads)

+**CHRISTIAN ONLINE MAGAZINE**, PO Box 262, Wolford VA 24658. E-mail: darlene@christianmagazine.org. Website: www.zyworld.com/magazine/online.htm. Darlene Osborne, ed. Articles 500-1,000 wds. No poetry for now. Not included in topical listings. Did not return questionnaire.

$**CHRISTIAN PARENTING TODAY**, 465 Gundersen Dr., Carol Stream IL 60188-2498. (630)260-6200. Fax (630)260-0114. E-mail: cpt@christianparenting.net. Website: www.Christianparenting.net. Christianity Today Inc. Submit to acquisitions ed. Practical advice for parents (of kids birth-14), from a Christian perspective, that runs the whole gamut of needs: social, educational, spiritual, medical, etc. Bimonthly mag; 76-96 pgs; circ 90,000. Subscription $17.95. 50% unsolicited freelance; 50% assigned. Query; fax/e-query OK. Pays .15-.25/wd on acceptance for 1st rts. Articles 450-1,500 wds (50/yr); product reviews (games, toys, etc.), 150 wds, $25-35. Responds in 8-12 wks. Seasonal 9 mos ahead. Accepts reprints (tell when/where appeared). Accepts disk or e-mail submissions (copied into message). Kill fee 50%. Regular sidebars. Prefers NIV. Guidelines (also on Website); copy $3.95/9x12 SAE. (Ads)

Fillers: Buys 100/yr. Anecdotes, ideas, prose, quizzes, short humor; 100-400 wds. Pays $25.

Columns/Departments: Buys 50/yr. Growing Up, 500 wds, $150; Ideas That Work (problem-solving ideas), 50 wds, $25; Life in Our House (insightful anecdotes), 50 wds, $25.

Contest: Sponsors several per year; none planned for 2001.

Tips: "Study past issues for tone and style. Cultivate journalism skills. Be selective in sending clips that demonstrate the kind of writing we publish. Demonstrate that you can identify with our readers. Address subjects that readers are dealing with now. Offer solutions that work and tell reader why they work. Use fresh research and real-life anecdotes."

**This periodical was #4 on the 2000 Top 50 Christian Publishers list (#12 in 1999, #1 in 1997, #20 in 1996, #2 in 1995, #27 in 1994). 1999 EPA Award of Merit—Most Improved Publication.

THE CHRISTIAN RANCHMAN, 7022-A Lake County Dr., Fort Worth TX 76179. (817)236-0023. Fax (817)236-0024. E-mail: cowboysforchrist@juno.com. Interdenominational. Ted Pressley, ed. Monthly tabloid; 12 pgs; circ 28,000. No subscription. Open to freelance. Complete ms/cover letter. **NO PAYMENT** for all rts. Articles; book/video reviews (length open). No sidebars.

Poetry: Accepts 40/yr. Free verse. Submit max 3 poems.

Fillers: Accepts all types.

$**CHRISTIAN READER**, 465 Gundersen Dr., Carol Stream IL 60188-2498. (630)260-6200. Fax (630)260-0114. E-mail: creditor@christianreader.net. Website: www.christianreader.net. Christianity Today Intl. Bonne Steffen, ed. A Christian "Reader's Digest" that uses both reprints and original material. Bimonthly & online mag; 96 pgs; circ 185,000. Subscription $17.95.

35% unsolicited freelance; 20% assigned. Complete ms/cover letter; phone/fax/e-query OK. Pays $100-250 (.10/wd) on acceptance for 1st rts. Articles 500-1,500 wds (50/yr). Responds in 3 wks. Seasonal 9 mos ahead. Accepts reprints ($50-100, tell when/where appeared). Accepts e-mail submission (copied into message). Kill fee. Sidebars, 150-300 wds. Prefers NIV. Guidelines/theme list (also on Website); copy for 6x9 SAE/4 stamps. (Ads)

Fillers: Buys 25-35/yr. Anecdotes, facts, short humor (see Lite Fare); 25-400 wds; pays $15-35.

Columns/Departments: Cynthia Thomas. Buys 150/yr. Lite Fare (adult church humor); Kids of the Kingdom (kids say and do funny things); Rolling Down the Aisle (true humor from weddings/rehearsals); all to 250 wds; $25-35.

Contest: Annual contest, March 1 deadline. Prizes $1,000, $500, $250. Send SASE for contest fact sheet.

Tips: "Send us reprints from other publications, and start with our humor columns. Most open to fillers, end-of-article vignettes, annual writing contest, humor anecdotes." Online version uses original material, or reprints with permission.

**This periodical was #14 on the 2000 Top 50 Christian Publishers list (#13 in 1999, #4 in 1998, #29 in 1997, #7 in 1996, #63 in 1995).

$CHRISTIAN RENEWAL, Box 770, Lewiston NY 14092-0770. (905)562-5719. Fax (905)562-7828. E-mail: JVANDYK@aol.com. Reformed (Conservative). John Van Dyk, mng ed. Church-related and world news for members of the Reformed community of churches in North America. Biweekly newspaper; 20 pgs; circ 4,000. Subscription $29. 5% freelance. Query/clips; e-query OK. Pays $25-100 for one-time rts. Articles 500-3,000 wds; fiction 2,000 wds (6/yr); book reviews 50-200 wds. Responds in 9 wks. Seasonal 3 mos ahead. Accepts simultaneous submissions & reprints. Prefers e-mail submission (copied into message). Some sidebars. Prefers NIV or NKJV. No guidelines; copy $1. (Ads)

$CHRISTIAN RESEARCH JOURNAL, PO Box 7000, Rancho Santa Margarita, CA 92688-7000. (949)858-6100. Fax (949)858-6111. E-mail: on Website. Website: www.equip.org. Christian Research Institute. Elliot Miller, ed-in-chief. For those who have been affected by cults and the occult. Quarterly journal; 63 pgs; circ 35,000. Subscription $24. 1% unsolicited freelance. Query or complete ms/cover letter; fax query OK; no e-mail submissions. Pays .15/wd on publication for 1st rts. Articles to 5,000 wds (1/yr); book reviews 1,100-2,500 wds. Responds in 16-20 wks. Accepts simultaneous submissions. Kill fee to 50%. Requires disk. Sidebars assigned. Guidelines (also by e-mail); copy $6. (Ads)

Columns/Departments: Witnessing Tips (evangelism), 1,000 wds; Viewpoint (opinion on cults, ethics, etc.), 875 wds.

Tips: "Be patient; we sometimes review mss only twice a year, but we will get back to you. Most open to features (on cults), book reviews, opinion pieces and witnessing tips."

**1999 EPA Award of Merit—Organizational; 1997 EPA Award of Excellence—Organizational.

$THE CHRISTIAN RESPONSE, PO Box 125, Staples MN 56479-0125. (218) 894-1165. E-mail: hapco@brainerd.net. Website: www.brainerd.net/~hapco. HAPCO Industries. Hap Corbett, ed. Exposes anti-Christian bias in America & encourages readers to write letters against such bias. Bimonthly newsletter; 6 pgs; circ 300. Subscription $13. 10% freelance. Complete ms/cover letter; phone/e-query OK. Pays $5-20 on acceptance for one-time rts. Articles 50-500 wds (4-6/yr). Responds in 2 wks. Seasonal 6 mos ahead. Accepts simultaneous submissions & reprints. No sidebars. Guidelines; copy for $1 or 3 stamps. (Ads—classified only)

   Fillers: Buys 2-4/yr. Anecdotes, facts, quotes; 150 wds; $5-20.

   Special Needs: Articles on anti-Christian bias; tips on writing effective letters to the editor; pieces on outstanding accomplishments of Christians in the secular media.

   Tips: "We are looking for news/articles about anti-Christian bias in the media, and how you, as a writer, responded to such incidents."

$CHRISTIAN RETAILING, 600 Rinehart Rd., Lake Mary FL 32746. (407)333-0600. Fax (407)333-7133. E-mail: retailing@strang.com. Website: www.christianretailing.com. Strang Communications Co. Melissa Bogdany, mng ed. This publisher is now using only assignment writers and has more writers than they can use.

$CHRISTIAN SINGLE, 127 9th Ave. N, Nashville TN 37234-0140. (615)251-2230. Fax (615)251-5008. E-mail: christiansingle@lifeway.com, or christiansingle@bssb.com. Website: www.christiansingle.com. No freelance.

CHRISTIAN SINGLE ONLINE, 127 9th Ave. N, Nashville TN 37234-0140. (615)251-2230. Fax (615)251-5008. E-mail: christiansingle@lifeway.com, christiansingle@bssb.com or wgibson@bssb.com. Website:www.christiansingle.com.

$CHRISTIAN SOCIAL ACTION, 100 Maryland Ave. NE, Washington DC 20002. (202)488-5621. Fax (202)488-1617. E-mail: ealsgaard@umc-gbcs.org. Website: www.umc-gbcs.org. United Methodist. Erik Alsgaard, ed. Information and analysis of critical social issues from the perspective of Christian faith. Bimonthly mag; 40 pgs; circ 2,500. Subscription $15. 10% unsolicited freelance; 15% assigned. Query/clips or complete ms/cover letter; e-query OK. Pays $75-150 on publication for all rts (negotiable). Articles 2,000 wds (12/yr); book reviews 500 wds, $25. Responds in 4 wks. Consider simultaneous submissions & reprints (tell when/where appeared). Prefers disk. Regular sidebars. Prefers RSV. Guidelines; copy for 9x12 SAE/2 stamps. (Ads)

   Columns/Departments: Buys 10/yr. Talking (readers write), 1,000 wds; Media Watch (reviews), 500 wds. Pays $25-50.

   Special Needs: Articles on racism; urban issues, children's issues, environment.

   Tips: "Send a query letter that makes me take notice—well-written, sharp, even funny. Most open to well-written pieces on current, social-justice issues that speak from a Christian perspective, and also answer the 'What do I do with this, why should I care' questions."

$CHRISTIAN STANDARD, 8121 Hamilton Ave., Cincinnati OH 45231.

(513)931-4050. Fax (513)931-0950. E-mail: christianstd@standardpub. com. Standard Publishing/Christian Churches/Churches of Christ. Sam E. Stone, ed. Devoted to the restoration of New Testament Christianity, its doctrines, its ordinances, and its fruits. Weekly mag; 24 pgs; circ 58,000. Subscription $22.50. 50% freelance. Complete ms/cover letter; no phone/fax/e-query. Pays $10-80 on publication for 1st or one-time rts. Articles 400-1,600 wds (200/yr). Responds in 9 wks. Seasonal 8-12 mos ahead. Accepts reprints. Guidelines; copy for 9x12 SAE/3 stamps or $1. (No ads)

$CHRISTIAN TIMES, PO Box 2606, El Cajon CA 92021. (619)660-5500. Fax (619)660-5505. E-mail: info@christiantimes.com. Website: www.christian times.com. iExalt Electronic Publishing. Submit to The Editor. Monthly newspaper; 24-36 pgs; circ 153,000. Subscription $19.95. 10% unsolicited freelance; 1% assigned. Query; e-query OK. Pays .05-.10/wd, on publication. Articles 750-1,200 wds. Prefers e-mail submissions (copied into message). No sidebars. Guidelines; no copy. (Ads)

> **Tips:** "We prefer news stories."

> ****1999 EPA Award of Merit—Newspaper.**

$CHRISTIANITY AND THE ARTS, PO Box 118088, Chicago IL 60611. (312)642-8606. Fax (312)266-7719. E-mail: CHRNARTS@aol.com. Website: www.christianarts.net. Nondenominational. Marci Whitney-Schenck, ed/pub. Celebrates the revelation of God through the arts and encourages excellent Christian artistic expression. Quarterly & online mag; 72 pgs; circ 5,000. Subscription $21. 75% freelance. Query or complete ms/cover letter; phone/fax/e-query OK. Sometimes pays $100 on acceptance or publication for 1st rts. Articles 2,000 wds (20/yr); fiction 2,000 wds (uses little); book, music, video reviews 500 wds. Responds in 3 wks. Seasonal 6 mos ahead. Accepts simultaneous submissions. Accepts disk. Regular sidebars. Theme list; copy $6. (Ads)

> **Poetry:** Robert Klein Engler, 901 S. Plymouth Ct, #1801, Chicago IL 60605. Accepts 12/yr. Avant-garde, free verse, haiku, traditional. No payment.

> **Special Needs:** Visual arts, dance, music, literature, drama.

> **Contest:** Poetry contests with cash prizes. Deadlines vary. Entry fee is discounted subscription to the magazine at $15.

> **Tips:** "Interested in features and interviews that focus on ethnic celebration of Christian arts, social problems and the arts, and Jewish-Christian links. We don't have room for most fiction, but if we find the right short story, we might change our minds."

$#CHRISTIANITY ONLINE, 465 Gundersen Dr., Carol Stream IL 60189-2498. (630)260-6200. Fax (630)260-0114. E-mail: COmagazine@aol.com. Website: ChristianityOnline.com/comag/current. Christianity Today Intl. Mark Moring, mng ed.; Matt Connelly, asst. ed. (comptmatt@aol.com). A guide to the Internet for Christian adults. Quarterly mag; 50 pgs; circ 100,000. Subscription $14.95. Estab. 1999. 15-20% unsolicited freelance; 10-15% assigned. Query; fax/e-query OK. Pays .15-.20/wd on acceptance for 1st & electronic rts. Articles 1,000-2,000 wds (2-4/yr). Responds in 2-4 wks. Seasonal 8-10 mos ahead. Accepts reprints (tell when/where appeared). Accepts e-mail submission (copied into message). Kill fee 50%. Regular sidebars. Prefers NIV. Guidelines (also by e-mail/Website); copy $2/9x12 SAE. (Ads)

> **Tips:** "All topics must relate to the Internet. Most open to feature articles, especially about Net trends and how they affect believers, are needed. Also, human-interest stories—Christians who are using the net for good, or those who have been touched by the Net."
>
> **This periodical was #69 on the 2000 Top 50 Christian Publishers list.

$CHRISTIANITY TODAY, 465 Gundersen Dr., Carol Stream IL 60188-2498. (630)260-6200. Fax (630)260-0114. E-mail: ctedit@aol.com. Website: www.christianitytoday.net. Christianity Today Intl. David Neff, exec. ed. For evangelical Christian thought leaders who seek to integrate their faith commitment with responsible action. Magazine published 14X/yr; 80-120 pgs; circ 155,000. Subscription $24.95. 80% (little unassigned) freelance. Query only; phone/fax/e-query OK. Pays $100-1,000 (.10/wd) on acceptance for 1st rts. Articles 1,000-4,000 wds (60/yr); book reviews 800-1,000 wds, pays per-page rate. Responds in 13 wks. Seasonal 8 mos ahead. Accepts reprints (tell when/where appeared—payment 25% of regular rate). Kill fee 25%. No sidebars. Prefers NIV. Guidelines; copy for 9x12 SAE/3 stamps. (Ads)

> **This periodical was #50 on the 2000 Top 50 Christian Publishers list (#40 in 1999). 1999 EPA Award of Merit—General.

$+CHRISTIANWEEK, PO Box 725, Winnipeg MB R3C 2K3 Canada. (204) 982-2062. Fax (204)947-5632. E-mail: cw@christianweek.org. Website: www.christianweek.org. Trans-denominational. Doug Koop, ed (dkoop @christianweek.org); Kevin Heinrichs, mng. ed. (kheinrichs@christian week.org). Canada's National Christian Newspaper. Biweekly newspaper; circ 5,000. Query. News 300-600 wds. Prefers e-mail submissions. Pays $30-100 on publication. Guidelines. (Ads)

> **Tips:** "Writers are encouraged to submit articles about people or news events in their own community or denomonation that would be of interest to readers in other denominations or in other areas of the country."

$CHRYSALIS READER, Rte. 1, Box 184, Dillwyn VA 23936. (804)983-3021. Fax (804)983-1074. Swedenborg Foundation. Carol S. Lawson & Rob Lawson, co-eds. Focuses on spiritual life and literature. An annual collection of stories, articles and poetry in book form and focusing on a single theme; 208 pgs; circ. 3,000. $13.95/issue. 70% unsolicited freelance; 30% assigned. Query; no e-query. Pays $50-150 (plus 5 copies) on publication for one-time rts. Articles and short stories 2,000-3,500 wds (15-25/yr). Responds in 8 wks. Prefers disk. No sidebars. Guidelines/theme list; copy $10/7x10 SAE/5 stamps. (No ads)

> **Poetry:** Robert Lawson. Buys 15/yr. Avant-garde, free verse, haiku; $25 plus 3 copies. Submit max 6 poems.
>
> **Special Needs:** October 15, 2001 is first-draft deadline for for "Serendipity" theme. See guidelines for details. Also education.
>
> **Tips:** "Each issue is on a theme, so we always need essays on those themes; also literary fiction on the theme."

$#THE CHURCH ADVOCATE, Box 926, 700 E. Melrose Ave., Findlay OH 45839. (419)424-1961. Fax (419)424-3433. E-mail: communications@ cggc.org. Website: www.cggc.org. Churches of God General Conference. Martin Cordell, ed. Denominational. Quarterly tabloid; 16 pgs; circ 16,000. Subscription free to denomination. Little freelance. Complete ms. Pays $10/printed pg. on publication for one-time rts. Articles 750 wds & up (6/yr). Seasonal 6 mos ahead. Accepts simultaneous submissions & reprints. Accepts e-mail submission. Regular sidebars. Prefers NIV. Guidelines; copy for 9x12 SAE. (No ads)

> **Tips:** Uses little freelance. Most open to personal experience.

$CHURCH & STATE, 518 C St. NE, Washington DC 20002. (202)466-3234. Fax (202)466-2587. E-mail: americansunited@au.org. Website: www.au. org. Americans United for Separation of Church and State. Joseph L. Conn, ed. Emphasizes religious liberty and church/state relations matters. Monthly (11X)mag; 24-32 pgs; circ 33,000. Subscription $18. 10% freelance. Query; no phone/fax/e-query. Pays $150-300 on acceptance for all rts. Articles 600-2,600 wds (11/yr), prefers 800-1,600. Responds in 9 wks. Accepts simultaneous query & reprints. Guidelines; copy for 9x12 SAE/3 stamps. (No ads)

> **Tips:** "We are not a religious magazine. You need to see our magazine before you try to write for it."

CHURCH HERALD AND HOLINESS BANNER, 7415 Metcalf, Box 4060, Overland Park KS 66204. (913)432-0331. Fax (913)722-0351. E-mail: HBeditor@juno.com. Website: www.sunflower.org/~kccbslib. Church of God (Holiness)/Herald and Banner Press. Mark D. Avery, ed. Denominational; conservative/Wesleyan/evangelical people. Biweekly mag; 20 pgs; circ 1,700. Subscription $12.50. 25% unsolicited freelance; 50% assigned. Complete ms/cover letter; e-query OK. **NO PAYMENT** for one-time, reprint or simultaneous rts. Not copyrighted. Articles 200-600 wds (40/yr). Responds in 4 wks. Seasonal 3 mos ahead. Accepts simultaneous submissions & reprints (tell when/where appeared). Accepts disk or e-mail submission (copied into message). Some sidebars. Prefers KJV. Guidelines (also by e-mail); copy for 6/9 SAE/2 stamps. (No ads)

> **Poetry:** Buys few. Traditional; 8-24 lines. Submit max 4 poems.
>
> **Fillers:** Anecdotes, facts, prose, quotes; 150-400 wds.
>
> **Tips:** "Most open to devotional articles. Must be concise, well-written, and get one main point across; 200-600 wds."

$CHURCH OF GOD EVANGEL, PO Box 2250, Cleveland TN 37320-2250. (423)476-4512. Fax (423)478-7616. E-mail: bill_george@pathwaypress. org. Website: www.pathwaypress.org. Church of God (Cleveland, TN). Bill George, ed. Denominational. Monthly mag; 40 pgs; circ 51,000. Subscription $15. 10-20% unsolicited freelance; 0% assigned. Complete ms/cover letter only; no e-query. Pays $10-50 on acceptance for 1st, one-time, simultaneous rts. Articles 300-1,200 wds (50/yr). Responds in 6-8 wks. Seasonal 4 mos ahead. Accepts simultaneous submissions. Some sidebars. Prefers KJV, NKVJ, NIV. Free guidelines/copy. (No ads)

> **Fillers:** Anecdotes & ideas.
>
> **Tips:** "We always need short articles (300-500 wds) with a salvation

appeal. Also human interest stories with a spiritual application. Outstanding writing on timely topics will get our attention."

**1999 EPA Award of Merit—Denominational.

$COLORADO CHRISTIAN CHRONICLE, PO Box 62040, Colorado Springs CO 80926. (719)520-0073. Fax (719)520-0063. E-mail: ccchron1@aol.com. Website: www.ColoradoChristianChronicle.com. Beard Communications, Inc. Patton Dodd, ed. Monthly tabloid; 24 pgs; circ 32,000. Subscription $18. Accepts freelance. Complete ms/cover letter. Payment negotiable. Articles 800-2,000 wds. Responds in 4 wks. Seasonal 2 mos ahead. Accepts simultaneous submissions & reprints. Accepts disk or e-mail submission (copied into message). Some sidebars. Guidelines; free copy. (Ads)

   Columns/Departments: Sounding Board (opinion), 800 wds.

$COLUMBIA, PO Box 1670, 1 Columbus Plaza, New Haven CT 06510-3326. (203)772-2130. Fax (203)777-0114. E-mail: thickey@kofc-supreme.com, or info@kofc.org. Website: www.kofc.org. Knights of Columbus (Catholic). Tim S. Hickey, ed. Geared to a general Catholic family audience. Monthly mag; 32 pgs; circ 1.6 million. Subscription $6; foreign $8. 25% unsolicited freelance; 75% assigned. Query; fax/e-query OK. Pays to $250-600 on acceptance for 1st & electronic rts. Articles 1,500 wds (12/yr). Responds in 2 wks. Seasonal 3 mos ahead. Occasional reprint (tell when/where appeared). Prefers e-mail submission (copied into message). Kill fee. Regular sidebars. Free guidelines (also by e-mail)/copy. (No ads)

   Special Needs: Essays on spirituality, personal conversion. Catholic preferred. Query first.

   Tips: "Most open to feature writers who can handle Church issues, social issues from an orthodox Roman Catholic perspective. Must be aggressive, fact-centered writers for these typeset features."

   **This periodical was #18 on the 2000 Top 50 Christian Publishers list (#55 in 1998, #38 in 1997, #25 in 1996, #32 in 1995, #19 in 1994).

$COMMONWEAL, 475 Riverside Dr., Room 405, New York NY 10115-0499. (212)662-4200. Fax (212)662-4183. E-mail: commonweal@msn.com. Website: www.commonwealmagazine.org. Commonweal Foundation/Catholic. Patrick Jordan, mng ed. A review of public affairs, religion, literature and the arts, for an intellectually engaged readership. Biweekly mag; 32 pgs; circ 19,000. Subscription $44. 20% freelance. Query/clips; phone query OK. Pays $50-100 (.03/wd) on acceptance or publication for all rts. Articles 1,000 or 3,000 wds (20/yr). Responds 4 wks. Seasonal 2 mos ahead. Prefers disk or e-mail submission. Kill fee 2%. Some sidebars. Guidelines; copy for 9x12 SAE/4 stamps. (Ads)

   Poetry: Rosemary Deen. Buys 20/yr. Free verse, traditional; to 75 lines; .50-.75/line (on publication). Submit max 5 poems. Submit October-May.

   Columns/Departments: Upfronts (brief, newsy facts and information behind the headlines), 750-1,000 wds; The Last Word (commentary based on insight from personal experience or reflection), 700 wds.

   Tips: "Most open to meaningful articles on social, political, religious and cultural topics; or columns."

$*COMPANION MAGAZINE, 695 Coxwell Ave., Ste 600, Toronto ON M4C 5R6 Canada. (800)461-1619 or (416)690-5611. Fax (416)690-3320. Catholic/Franciscan. Friar Phil Kelly, ed. An adult, Catholic, inspirational, devotional family magazine. Monthly (11X) mag; 32 pgs; circ 5,000. Subscription $16 CAN or $18 US & foreign. 40% unsolicited freelance; 60% assigned. Complete ms/cover letter; phone/fax query OK. Pays .06/wd CAN on publication for 1st rts. Articles 500-1,000 wds (35/yr); fiction 500-1,000 wds (7/yr). Responds in 6 wks. Seasonal 5 mos ahead. Accepts disk (Mac). Guidelines; copy for 7x10 SAE with IRCs. (Ads)
  Poetry: Free verse, light verse, traditional. Pays .60/line CAN.
  Fillers: Anecdotes, cartoons, prayers, quotes, short humor, word puzzles.
  Special Needs: Articles on St. Francis, Franciscan spirituality, and social justice.
  Tips: "Write upbeat, pro-Vatican II, Catholic-oriented material—optimistic, personal, challenging."

$COMPANIONS, PO Box 555, Seymour MO 65746. (516)935-4639. Fax (516)514-1143. Mennonite/Christian Light Publications. Roger L. Berry, ed. Consistent with conservative Mennonite doctrine: believer baptism, nonresistance, and nonconformity. Monthly take-home paper; 4 pgs; circ 9,000. Subscription $9.70. 75% freelance. Complete ms only. Pays .02-.05/wd on acceptance for all, 1st, one-time, simultaneous or reprint rts. Articles 100-750 wds (150/yr); true stories 800-2,000 wds (50/yr). Responds in 6-8 wks. Seasonal 6 mos ahead. Accepts simultaneous submissions & reprints (tell when/where appeared). No disk. No sidebars. KJV only. Guidelines; copy for 9x12 SAE/2 stamps. (No ads)
  Fillers: Buys 20/yr. Anecdotes, prose; 30-100 wds.
  Columns/Departments: Buys 12/yr. Science and Scripture (creationist/Biblicist), 400-700; Archaeology and Scripture (archaeology that supports biblical truths); 400-700 wds.
  Tips: "We are most open to freelancers in our columns, or short inspirational articles and meditations. Pay close attention to our list of dos and don'ts. Because of lifestyle differences, stories are the most difficult for non-Mennonite freelancers to write for us. We are overstocked on poetry."
  ****This periodical was #61 on the 2000 Top 50 Christian Publishers list (#46 in 1999, #49 in 1998, #51 in 1997, #45 in 1996, #14 in 1995, #28 in 1994).

$COMPANY: A Magazine of the American Jesuits, PO Box 60790, Chicago IL 60660. (773)761-9432. E-mail: editor@companysj.com. Website: www.companysj.com. Martin McHugh, ed; Becky Troha, asst ed. For people interested in or involved with Jesuit ministries. Quarterly & online mag; 32 pgs; circ 120,000. Free circulation. 40% unsolicited freelance; 60% assigned. Complete ms/cover letter; e-query OK. Pays $250-450 on publication for one-time rts. Articles 1,500 wds. Responds in 6 wks. Seasonal 3 mos ahead. Accepts simultaneous submissions & reprints (tell when/where appeared). Prefers e-mail submission (attached file). Prefers NRSV, NAB, NJB. Guidelines; copy for 9x12 SAE/4 stamps. (No ads)

Columns/Departments: Books with a Jesuit connection; Minims and Maxims (short items of interest to Jesuit world), 100-150 wds/photo; Letters to the Editor; Obituaries. No payment (usually).

Tips: "We welcome manuscripts as well as outlines of story ideas and indication of willingness to accept freelance assignments (please include résumé and writing samples with the latter two). Articles must be Jesuit-related."

COMPASS DIRECT, PO Box 27250, Santa Ana CA 92799. (949)862-0314. Fax (949)752-6536. E-mail: compassdr@compuserve.com. Website: www.compassdirect.org. Jeff Taylor, ed. To raise awareness of and encourage prayer for Christians worldwide who are persecuted for their faith. Monthly newsletter; circ 500. Subscription $75. Accepts freelance. Prefers query. Not in topical listings. (No ads)

#THE COMPLEAT NURSE, PO Box 597, Roseville CA 95678-0597. E-mail: webmaster@drybones.com. Website: www.drybones.com. Dry Bones Press, Inc. Jim Rankin, ed. Nursing and specialty publications. Monthly newsletter; 4-6 pgs. Query; e-query OK. **PAYS IN COPIES** for one-time rts & anthology reprint rts. Articles (10/yr); fiction; reviews 500 wds. Responds in 4-6 wks. Accepts simultaneous submissions & reprints (tell when/where appeared). Requires disk or e-mail submission (attached file). Some sidebars. Guidelines (also by e-mail/Website); copy for #10 SAE/2 stamps.

   Poetry: Accepts 10/yr. Any type. Submit max 5 poems.

   Fillers: Anecdotes, cartoons, facts, ideas, jokes, newsbreaks, prayers, quotes, short humor.

   Columns/Departments: Accepts 5/yr.

   Special Needs: Humorous fiction on health/health-related issues.

CONNECTING POINT, Box 685, Cocoa FL 32923. (321)773-2691. Fax (321)773-4921. E-mail: ircgathering@juno.com. Linda G. Howard, ed. For and by the mentally challenged (disabled) community; primarily deals with spiritual and self-advocacy issues. Monthly mag; circ 1,000. 75% freelance. Complete ms. **NO PAYMENT** for 1st rts. Articles (24/yr) & fiction (12/yr), 250-750 wds; book reviews 150 wds. Responds in 3-6 wks. Seasonal 3 mos ahead. Accepts simultaneous submissions & reprints. Guidelines; copy for 9x12 SAE/6 stamps.

   Poetry: Accepts 4/yr. Any type; 4-66 lines. Submit max 10 poems.

   Fillers: Accepts 12/yr. Cartoons, games, word puzzles; 50-250 wds.

   Columns/Departments: Accepts 24/yr. Devotion Page, 1,000 wds; Bible Study, 500 wds. Query.

   Special Needs: Record reviews, self-advocacy, integration/normalization, justice system.

   Tips: "All mss need to be in primary vocabulary."

$+CONNECTION MAGAZINE, 11607 Tonsing Dr., Garfield Heights OH 44125. (216)581-5800. Fax (216)581-8161. E-mail: noahstask@iol13.com. Website: www.connectionmagazine.org. Omega Industries. Jon Hanna, ed. Articles on actors, athletes, politicians, and ordinary people who have experienced the power of Jesus Christ in their lives, to reach the world with a message of hope, love, healing and forgiveness. Online & monthly tabloid; 32 pgs; circ 90,000. Subscription free. Estab. 1997. 50% unsolicited freelance; 50% assigned. Complete ms; fax/e-query OK. Pays $30-50 on publication for 1st or reprint rts. Articles 300-2,300 wds (70/yr); book & video reviews 200 wds; music reviews 300-500 wds, $10-20. Responds in 1-2 wks. Seasonal 3-6 mos ahead. Accepts simultaneous submissions & reprints. Accepts disk or e-mail submission (attached). Some sidebars. Prefers NKJV. No guidelines; copy for 9x12 SAE/5 stamps. (Ads)

Fillers: Buys 60/yr. Cartoons, jokes, quotes, short humor; $5-10.

Special Needs: Sports figures or politicans with faith.

Tips: "Send interviews with actors, athletes, politicians, and celebrities who have faith in Jesus."

$CONQUEST, 1300 N Meacham Rd., Schaumburg IL 60173-4888. (847)843-1600. Fax (847)843-3757. Website: www.garbc.org/rbp. Regular Baptist. Joan E. Alexander, ed. For adults associated with fundamental Baptist Churches. Weekly take-home paper. Note: This periodical has been redesigned. Still working on new guidelines.

$#CORNERSTONE, 939 W. Wilson Ave., Chicago IL 60640-5718. (773)561-2450x2080. Fax (773)989-2076. E-mail: info@cornerstonemag.com; fiction@cornerstonemag.com; poetry@cornerstonemag.com; nonfiction @cornerstonemag.com. Website: www.cornerstonemag.com. Cornerstone Communications, Inc. Jon Trott, ed.; submit to Tara Anderson, submissions ed. For young adults, 18-35; to communicate doctrinal truth based on Scripture and to break the "normal Christian" mold with a stance that has cultural relevancy. Quarterly (3-4 issues) & online mag; 64-72 pgs; circ 38,000. Subscription free. 10% unsolicited freelance; 90% assigned. Complete ms by e-mail only. Pays .08-.10/wd after publication for 1st, one-time, reprint & simultaneous rts. Articles to 4,000 wds (20/yr); fiction 250-4,000 wds (1-4/yr); book/music reviews 500-1,000 wds, $24. Responds in 13-26 wks to accepted mss only (discards others; don't send SASE). Seasonal 6 mos ahead. Encourages simultaneous submissions; reprints (tell when/where appeared). Prefers e-mail submission (accepts disk). Regular sidebars. Guidelines (also on Website); copy for 9x12 SAE/5 stamps. (Ads)

Poetry: Poetry Editor. Buys 15-24/yr. Avant-garde, free verse, haiku, light verse; $10-25. Submit any number.

Fillers: Buys 1-4/yr. Cartoons, prayers; 500-1,000 wds. Pays .08-.10/wd.

Columns/Departments: Buys 1-4/yr. News items, 500-1,000 wds; Music Interviews (Christian & secular artists) to 2,700 wds; Music & Book Reviews (Christian & secular).

Tips: "Most open to avant-garde, creative, thought-provoking, original poetry, and fiction with a Christian worldview."

$THE COVENANT COMPANION, 5101 N. Francisco Ave., Chicago IL 60625. (773)784-3000. Fax (773)784-4366. E-mail: companion@covoffice.org. Website: www.covchurch.org. Evangelical Covenant Church. Jane K. Swanson-Nystrom, ed. Informs, stimulates thought, and encourages dialogue on issues that affect the denomination. Monthly mag; 40 pgs; circ 16,000. Subscription $19.95. 5% unsolicited freelance; 35% assigned. Complete ms/cover letter; fax/e-query OK. Pays $35-100 on publication for one-time or simultaneous rts. Articles 800-1,200 wds (15/yr). Prefers e-mail submission. Responds in 4 wks. Seasonal 3 mos ahead. Accepts simultaneous submissions & reprints (tell when/where appeared). Some kill fees. Regular sidebars. Prefers NRSV. Guidelines/theme list (also by e-mail); copy for 9x12 SAE/5 stamps; or $2.50. (Ads)

Fillers: Cartoons, short humor.

$*CREATION CARE, 10 E. Lancaster Ave., Wynnewood PA 19096. (610)645-9390. Fax (610)649-8090. Evangelicals for Social Action. Stan LeQuire, ed. For Christians who care about earth stewardship. Quarterly mag; 20 pgs; circ 5,000. Subscription $25. 90% freelance. Query; fax/e-query OK. Pays to $150 on publication for one-time & electronic rts. Articles 500-1,200 wds (20/yr); book reviews 200 wds (no payment). Responds in 6-8 wks. Seasonal 4 mos ahead. Accepts reprints (tell when/where appeared). Prefers disk. Regular sidebars. Prefers NRSV or NIV. Guidelines; copy for 10x13 SAE/4 stamps. (Ads)

Poetry: All types; 5-30 lines. No payment. Submit max 3 poems.

Fillers: Buys 10-12/yr. Cartoons, newsbreaks, prayers, short humor; 50-250 wds; $10-25.

Tips: "Looking for well-written personal testimony on writer's discovery of Christian/biblical basis for conservation. Other than that, we don't need articles that say 'What a surprise! The Bible says to care for God's creation.'"

CREATION EX NIHILO, PO Box 6302, Acacia Ridge QLD 4110 Australia. Phone: 07 3273 7650. Fax 07 3273 7672. E-mail: admin@answersin genesis.com. Website: www.answersingenesis.org. Answers in Genesis. Carl Weiland, ed. A family, nature, science magazine focusing on creation/evolution issues. Quarterly mag; 56 pgs; circ 50,000. Subscription $25. 50% freelance. Complete ms/cover letter; phone/fax/e-query OK. **NO PAYMENT** for all rts. Articles to 1,500 wds (20/yr); fiction 1,000-1,500 wds (1/yr). Responds in 2-3 wks. Prefers disk or e-mail submission (attached file). Regular sidebars. Prefers KJV. Guidelines; copy $6.95. (No ads)

$CREATION ILLUSTRATED, PO Box 7955, Auburn CA 95604. (530)269-1424. Fax (530)269-1428. E-mail: creation@foothill.net. Website: www.creationillustrated.com. Tom Ish, ed/pub. A Christian nature magazine that is uplifting, Bible-based, and glorifies God; for ages 9-99. Quarterly mag; 68 pgs; circ 13,000. Subscription $19.95. 60% unsolicited freelance; 40% assigned. Query or query/clips; fax/e-query OK. Pays $75-125 on publication for 1st rts. Articles 1,000-2,000 words (25/yr). Responds in 3 weeks. Seasonal 6 mos ahead. Accepts simultaneous submissions & reprints (tell when/where appeared). Prefers e-mail submission (copied into message). Some kill fees. Some sidebars. Prefers NKJV. Guidelines/theme list (also on Website); copy $3/9x12 SAE/$1.75 postage. (No ads)

Poetry: Buys 8/yr. Light verse, traditional; 10-20 lines. Pays $15. Submit max 4 poems.

Fillers: Games, 100-200 wds. Pays variable rates.

Contest: Photography contest in each issue for best nature, animal and creation shots.

Tips: "Most open to an experience with nature/creation that brought you closer to God and will inspire the reader to do the same. Include spiritual lessons and supporting scriptures—at least 3 or 4 of each."

$THE CRESSET, A Review of Arts, Literature & Public Affairs, Huegli Hall #10, Valparaiso IN 46383. (219)464-5274. Fax (219)464-5211. E-mail: cresset@valpo.edu. Website: www.valpo.edu. Valparaiso University/Lutheran. Gail McGrew Eifrig, ed. For college educated, professors, pastors, lay people; serious review essays on religious-cultural affairs. Bimonthly (7X) mag; 36 pgs; circ 4,700. Subscription $8.50. 50% freelance. Complete ms/cover letter; e-query OK. Pays $35 on publication for 1st rts. Articles 2,500-5,000 wds (20-30/yr). Responds in 12 wks. Seasonal 3 mos ahead. Prefers disk. No sidebars. Copy for 9x12 SAE/5 stamps.

> **Poetry:** John Ruff. Buys 15-20/yr. Avant-garde, free verse, traditional; to 40 lines; $15. Submit max 5 poems.

*CROSSWAY/NEWSLINE/FAIRFORD NEWS, PO Box 10, Lightwater, Surrey GU18 SJS England. Phone/fax 012764 72724. Airline Aviation & Aerospace Christian Fellowship. J. Brown, gen. sec. For non-Christians working in aviation. Crossway is an annual magazine; Newsline a quarterly newsletter; 16 pgs. Subscription free. 100% freelance. Complete ms/cover letter. **NO PAYMENT.** Sometimes copyrighted. Articles on aviation to 2,000 wds. Accepts simultaneous submissions & reprints.

$CULTURE WARS, 206 Marquette Ave., South Bend IN 46617. (219)289-9786. Fax (219)289-1461. E-mail: jones@culturewars.com. Website: www.culturewars.com. Ultramontagne Associates, Inc. Dr. E. Michael Jones, ed. Issues relating to Catholic families and issues affecting America that impact all people. Monthly (11X) mag; 35 pgs; circ. 3,500. Subscription $25. 20% freelance. Complete ms/cover letter; fax/e-query OK. Pays $100 & up on publication for all rts. Articles (25/yr); book reviews $50. Responds in 12-24 wks. Query about reprints. Prefers disk. Some sidebars. Developing guidelines; copy for 9x12 SAE/5 stamps.

> **Poetry:** Buys 15/yr. Free verse, light verse, traditional; 10-50 lines; $25. Submit max 2 poems.
> **Fillers:** Buys 15/yr. Cartoons, quotes; 25 wds & up; variable payment.
> **Columns/Departments:** Buys 25/yr. Commentary, 2,500 wds; Feature, 5,000 wds; $100-250.
> **Tips:** "All fairly open except cartoons. Single-spaced preferred; avoid dot matrix; photocopies must be clear."

THE DALLAS/FORT WORTH HERITAGE, 1701 N Hampton Rd, Ste. A, DeSoto TX 75115. (972)298-4211. Fax (972)298-6369. E-mail: lblyon@swbell.net. Website: www.fni.com/heritage/index.html. Today Newspapers, Inc. L.B. Lyon, ed. To help preserve and sustain America's Christian heritage and pass it on to the nation's children. Monthly newspaper; 50-70 pgs; circ 45,000. Subscription $25. Open to freelance. E-mail submissions OK. Query. (Ads)

$DECISION, PO Box 779, Minneapolis MN 55440-0779. (612)338-0500. Fax (612)335-1299. E-mail: submissions@bgea.org. Website: www.decisionmag.org, or www.decisiontoday.org. Billy Graham Evangelistic Assn.

Bob Paulson, assoc ed. Evangelism/Christian nurture. Monthly (11X) & online mag; 44 pgs; circ 1,300,000. Subscription $9. 25% freelance. Complete ms/cover letter (no queries); no phone/fax/e-query. Pays $55-230 on publication for all or 1st rts. Articles 600-1,000 wds (20/yr). Responds 10-12 wks. Seasonal 10-12 mos ahead. Accepts disk; accepts e-mail submission (copied into message). Kill fee. Regular sidebars. Prefers NIV. Guidelines/theme list (also by e-mail/Website); copy for 10x13 SAE/3 stamps. (No ads)

> **Poetry:** Buys 6/yr. Free verse, light verse, traditional; 4-16 lines; Pays .60/wd. Submit max 7 poems.
> **Fillers:** Buys 50/yr. Anecdotes, prose; 300-500 wds; $25-75.
> **Columns/Departments:** Buys 12/yr. Where Are They Now? (people who have become Christians through Billy Graham ministries); 500-600 wds; $85.
> **Tips:** "The best way for a writer to break into our publication is to submit an article with a strong takeaway for the readers. Remember that your specific experience is not the point. The point is what you learned and applied that the readers could apply to their own experience."
> **This periodical was #59 on the 1994 Top 50 Christian Publishers list.

$DISASTER NEWS NETWORK, 7855 Rappahannock Ave., Ste. 20, Jessup MD 20794. (443)755-9999 or (888)203-9119. Fax (443)755-9995. E-mail: info @disasternews.net. Website: www.disasternews.net. Villagelife.org, Inc. Submit to The Editor. Online; an interactive daily news site on the World Wide Web. Query; phone/fax/e-query (preferred) OK. Pays $85-100 after publication for 1st & global electronic rts. Articles; book reviews, $30-40. Accepts few reprints (tell when/where appeared). Requires e-mail submission. Guidelines on the Website. Not in topical listings.

> **Tips:** "Authors are expected to have an e-mail submission address, which will be included in the credits of published articles."

$DISCIPLESHIP JOURNAL, Box 35004, Colorado Springs CO 80935. (719)548-9222. Fax (719)598-7128. E-mail: sue.kline@navpress.com. Website: www.discipleshipjournal.com. The Navigators. Sue Kline, ed. For motivated, maturing Christians desiring to grow spiritually and to help others grow; biblical and practical. Bimonthly mag; 96+ pgs; circ 130,000. Subscription $19.97. 95% freelance. Query; fax/e-query OK. Pays .25/wd (.05/wd for reprints) on acceptance for 1st & electronic rts. Articles 1,500-2,500 wds (60/yr); fiction 1,500-2,500 wds (1-2/yr). Responds in 6-8 wks. Accepts simultaneous submissions. Prefers disk or e-mail submission (attached file). Kill fee 50%. Regular sidebars. Prefers NIV. Guidelines/theme list (also on Website). (Ads)

> **Columns/Departments:** Buys 15+/yr. On the Home Front (Q & A regarding family issues); 1,000 wds; Getting into God's Word (how-to), to 1,000 wds; DJ Plus (ministry how-to on missions, evangelism, serving, discipling, teaching & small groups), to 500 wds, DJ Plus editor: Kimberly Hurst (KJHurst@aol.com). Pays .25/wd.
> **Tips:** "Most open to non-theme articles, departments, DJ Plus and

sidebars. Our articles focus on biblical passages or topics. Articles should derive main principles from a thorough study of Scripture; should illustrate each principle; should show how to put each principle into practice; and should demonstrate with personal illustrations and vulnerability that the author has wrestled with the subject in his or her life."

**This periodical was #1 on the 2000 Top 50 Christian Publishers list (#1 in 1999, #5 in 1998, #10 in 1997, #2 in 1996, #15 in 1995, #8 in 1994). 1998 EPA Award of Merit—General.

DISCIPLE'S JOURNAL, 10 Fiorenza Dr., PO Box 100, Wilmington MA 01887-4421. (978)657-7373. Fax (978)657-5411. E-mail: dddj@disciplesdirectory. com. Website: www.disciplesdirectory.com. Kenneth A. Dorothy, ed. To strengthen, edify, inform and unite the body of Christ. 9X/yr & online newspaper; 24-32 pgs; circ 8,000. Subscription $14.95. 5% freelance. Query; fax/e-query OK. **NO PAYMENT** for one-time rts. Articles 400 wds (24/yr); book/music/video reviews 200 wds. Responds in 2 wks. Seasonal 2 mos ahead. Accepts simultaneous submissions & reprints (tell when/ where appeared). Prefers disk or e-mail submission (attached file). Some sidebars. Prefers NIV. Guidelines/theme list (also by e-mail); copy for 9x12 SAE/$1.70 postage. (Ads)

    Fillers: Accepts 12/yr. All types; 100-400 wds.

    Columns/Departments: Financial; Singles; Men; Women; Business; Parenting; 400 wds.

    Tips: "Most open to men's, women's or singles' issues; missions; or homeschooling. Send sample of articles for review."

*DISCOVERY**, 400 W. Lake Brantley Rd., Altamonte Springs FL 32714-2715. (407)682-9494. Fax (407)682-7005. E-mail: am950wtln@aol.com. Website: www.wtln.com. Radio Stations WTLN & WHIM. Janice Willis, station mgr. For Christian community in Central Florida. Monthly newspaper; 20 pgs; circ 50,000. Subscription free/$12 for home delivery. 20% freelance. Complete ms/cover letter; fax/e-query OK. **NO PAYMENT**. Not copyrighted. News-driven articles under 500 wds. Seasonal 1+ mos ahead. Accepts reprints. Regular sidebars. No disk; e-mail submission OK. No guidelines; free copy. (Ads)

    Fillers: Accepts several/yr. Cartoons and word puzzles.

    Columns/Departments: Local/National News, Local Ministries, Broadcaster's Information, Sports, Christian Living, Seasonal-themed features.

    Tips: "We may submit articles to our other publications in Knoxville and Philadelphia."

$**THE DOOR**, PO Box 1444, Waco TX 76703-1444. (817)752-1468. Fax (254)752-4914. E-mail (submissions): rfd3@flash.net. Website: www. thedoormagazine.com. Trinity Foundation. Robert Darden, ed. Satire of evangelical church plus issue-oriented interviews. Bimonthly mag; 66 pgs; circ 14,000. Subscription $29.95. 90% unsolicited freelance; 10% assigned. Complete ms; e-query OK. Pays $60-200 on publication for 1st rts. Not copyrighted. Articles to 1,500 wds, prefers 750-1,000 wds (30/yr).

Responds in 6 wks. Accepts simultaneous submissions & reprints (if from noncompeting markets). Kill fee $40-50. Regular sidebars. Guidelines (also by e-mail); copy $5 (from PO Box 33, Dallas TX 75221). (Ads)

> **Tips:** "We look for biting satire/humor—*National Lampoon* not *Reader's Digest*. You must understand our satirical slant. Read more than one issue to understand our 'wavelength.' We desperately need genuinely funny articles with a smart, satiric bent. Write funny stuff about religion. Interview interesting people with something to say about faith and/or religion." This is the old Wittenburg Door; only the name has changed.

$DOVETAIL: A Journal by and for Jewish/Christian Families, 775 Simon Greenwell Ln., Boston KY 40107. (502)549-5440. Fax (549)540-3543. E-mail: di-ifr@bardstown.com. Website: www.mich.com/~dovetail. Dovetail Institute for Interfaith Family Resources. Mary Rosenbaum, ed. Offers balanced, nonjudgmental articles for interfaith families and the professionals who serve them. Bimonthly mag; 12-16 pgs; circ 1,500. Subscription $25. 85% unsolicited freelance; 15% assigned. Query; phone/fax/e-query OK. Pays $10-20 on publication for all rts. Articles 800-1,000 wds (18-20/yr); book reviews 500 wds, $10. Responds in 4 wks. Seasonal 4 mos ahead. Accepts simultaneous submissions & reprints (tell when/where appeared). Prefers disk or e-mail submission (copied into message). Some sidebars. Prefers RSV. Guidelines/theme list (also by e-mail); copy for 9x12 SAE/3 stamps. (Ads)

> **Columns/Departments:** Buys 3-6/yr. Food & Family (Jewish & Christian), 500 wds, $20. Complete ms.
> **Special Needs:** Divorce/annulment, or death and dying (from an intermarriage perspective only).
> **Poetry:** Buys 1-2/yr. Traditional; $10. Submit max 4 poems.
> **Tips:** "Demonstrate real, concrete, practical knowledge of the challenges facing Jewish and Christian partners in a marriage. Do not send pieces of Christian interest only. No proselytizing."

$#DREAMS & VISIONS, 35 Peter St. S., Orillia ON L3V 5A8 Canada. Phone/fax (705)329-1770. E-mail: skysong@bconnex.net. Website: www.bconnex.net/~skysong. Skysong Press. Steve Stanton, ed. An international showcase for short literary fiction written from a Christian perspective. Irregular journal; 56 pgs; circ 200. Subscription $12. 100% freelance. Complete ms/cover letter; fax/e-query OK. Pays .005/wd on publication for 1st rts & one non-exclusive reprint. Fiction 2,000-6,000 wds (10/yr). Responds in 6 wks-6 mos. Seasonal 6 mos ahead. Accepts simultaneous submissions & reprints (tell when/where appeared). Accepts disk. Guidelines (also on Website); copy $4.95 (4 back issues to writers $10).

$DUNAMIS LIFE, 1090 B St., Ste. 120, Hayward CA 94541. (510)727-4466. Fax (510)583-9057. E-mail: editor@dunamislife.com. Website: www.DunamisLife.com. Dunamis Life Publications/nondenominational. Dale Tafoya, ed/pub.; Pat Baldwin, mng ed. About victorius Christian living; primarily for the Pentecostal and Charismatic Christian community. Bimonthly mag & e-zine; 40 pgs; circ 15,000. Subscription $10.95. Estab. 1998. 70% unsolicited freelance. Query/clips; e-query OK. Pays .15/wd to

$250 on publication for all rts. Articles 1,500 wds (25/yr). Responds in 4-6 wks. No seasonal. Accepts simultaneous submissions & reprints. Prefers e-mail submissions (copied into message). Some sidebars. Prefers NIV. Guidelines (also by e-mail); copy for 9x12 SAE/5 stamps. (Ads)

Columns/Departments: Buys 15/yr. Youth Explosion (radical for Christ), Singled Out (dealing with victorious singles), Minister's Edge (today's effective minister); all 500 wds, $50.

Special Needs: Book & Website reviews.

Tips: "Looking for victorious Christian living articles and writers with interviewing and bio skills. Our publication is dedicated to the Christian who dares to dream."

$+EARTHKEEPING ONTARIO, 2nd Floor, 115 Woolwich St., Guelph ON N1H 3V1 Canada. (519)837-1620. Fax (519)824-1835. E-mail: ek-ont@ christianfarmers.org. Website: www.christianfarmers.org. Christian Farmers Federation of Ontario (CFFO). Nellie van Donkersgoed, mng. ed.; Elbert van Donkersgoed, ed. (elbert@christianfarmers.org). A Christian perspective on farm life and rural/agricultural issues. Quarterly mag; 16 pgs; circ 6,000. Subscription $25 CAN; $30 US. Open to freelance. Query; prefers e-query. Pays .15-.20/wd for 1st rts. Articles 200-500 wds. Guidelines.

Columns/Departments: Unsolicited columns, 200-500 wds; pays $30-80.

Special Needs: Stories about our members; essays on issues of interest to farmers; feature articles (a series is possible); thought pieces; personal faith reflections; poetry; rural life/cultural stories.

Tips: "Your Christian faith should be obvious in your material, but don't preach to the reader about theirs. Use stories, examples, and anecdotes to make your point."

$EPISCOPAL LIFE, 815 2nd Ave., New York NY 10017. (212)716-6108. Fax (212)949-8059. E-mail: episcopal.life@ecunet.org. Website: www.dfms. org/episcopal-life. Episcopal Church. Jerrold F. Hames, ed; Edward P. Stannard, mng ed. Denominational. Monthly newspaper; 32 pgs; circ 248,000. Subscription $7. 0% unsolicited freelance; 10% assigned. Query/ clips or complete ms/cover letter; phone query on breaking news only; e-query OK. Pays $50-300 on publication for 1st, one-time or simultaneous rts. Articles 250-1,200 wds (12/yr); assigned book reviews 400 wds ($35). Responds in 5 wks. Seasonal 4 mos ahead. Accepts simultaneous submissions & reprints. Accepts e-mail submission. Kill fee 50%. Guidelines (by e-mail); free copy. (Ads)

Columns/Departments: Nan Cobbey (ncobbey@dfms.org). Buys 36/yr. Commentary on political/religious topics; 300-600 wds; $35-75. Query.

Tips: "All articles must have Episcopal Church slant or specifics. We need topical/issues, not devotional stuff. Most open to feature stories about Episcopalians—clergy, lay, churches, involvement in local efforts, movements, ministries."

+ETERNAL INK, 25 Powers Rd., Lawrenceburg TN 38464. (931)762-2974. E-mail: davidh@usit.net. Website: associate.com/eternal_ink. Non-denominational. David Davis, ed.; Carl Phillips, articles ed. (CarlPhil10@

aol.com). Offers spiritual refreshment. Online e-zine (every other Friday); circ 620. Subscription free. Estab. 1999. 67% unsolicited freelance; 33% assigned. Complete ms; e-query OK. **NO PAYMENT** for one-time and electronic rts. Articles 200-750 wds (52/yr). Responds in 1-2 wks. Seasonal 2 mos ahead. Accepts reprints (tell when/where appeared). Requires e-mail submissions (copied into message). Prefers KJV. Guidelines/theme list by e-mail/Website; copy by e-mail only. (Ad swaps only)

Poetry: David Davis. Accepts 26/yr. Free verse, light verse, traditional; 10-20 lines. Submit max 2 poems.

Fillers: Michael Powers (thunder27@aol.com). Accepts 104/yr. Newsbreaks, prayers, short humor, 150-200 wds.

Columns/Departments: Mary Ellen Grisham (fantasy@apci.net). Accepts 52/yr. Devotions (inspirational), to 250 wds.

Special Needs: Spotlight articles on local ministries making an impact for the better; or teens making a difference for the positive.

Tips: "All departments, sections are open to freelancers. Construct a well-written article that adheres to guidelines for your type of article. We offer an excellent opportunity for freelancers to break into print."

$EVANGEL, Box 535002, Indianapolis IN 46253-5002. (317)244-3660. Fax (317)244-1247. Free Methodist/Light and Life Communications. Julie Innes, ed. For young to middle-aged adults; encourages spiritual growth. Weekly take-home paper; 8 pgs; circ 19,000-20,000. Subscription $7.40. 100% unsolicited freelance. Query; no e-query. Pays .04/wd on publication for one-time rts. Articles to 1,200 wds (100/yr); fiction to 1,200 wds (100/yr). Responds in 6-8 wks. Seasonal 9-12 mos ahead. Accepts simultaneous submissions & reprints (tell when/where appeared). Accepts disk. Some sidebars. Prefers NIV. Guidelines; copy for #10 SAE/1 stamp. (No ads)

Poetry: Buys 30/yr. Free verse, light verse; 3-16 lines; $10. Submit max 5 poems. Rhyming poetry not usually taken too seriously.

Fillers: Buys 20/yr. Cartoons, short humor; to 100 wds; humor $10, cartoons $20.

Tips: "Be sure to submit material appropriate for the market and audience. Don't ramble; stick to one thesis or theme. A returned manuscript isn't always because of poor writing. Don't give up—keep writing and submitting."

THE EVANGEL, PO Box 348, Marlow OK 73055. (580)658-5631. Fax (580)658-2867. E-mail: umi@umi.org. Website: www.umi.org. UMI Ministries. Dennis A. Wright, pres. A Christian Apologetics ministry that exposes Mormonism and explains its views of doctrine, history and current events. Monthly mag; circ 3,000. Subscription $15, 6-month subscription free to new subscribers. Open to freelance. Complete ms. Not in topical listings. (Ads)

THE EVANGELICAL ADVOCATE, Box 30, 1426 Lancaster Pike, Circleville OH 43113. (740)474-8856. Fax (740)477-7766. E-mail: cccudoc@bright.net. Website: www.bright.net/~cccudoc. Churches of Christ in Christian Union. Ralph Hux, dir. of communications. Provides news, information and features which emphasize current events and world-view, appealing to the needs of our constituency, emphasizing fundamental evangelical holiness. Monthly mag; 24-28 pgs; circ 4,000. Subscription $12. 15% unsolicited freelance; 15% assigned. Complete ms/cover letter; fax/e-query OK. **NO PAYMENT** for one-time rts. Articles 500-1,000 wds (15-20/yr). Responds in 2 wks. Seasonal 2 1/2 mos ahead. Accepts simultaneous submissions & reprints (tell when/where appeared). Prefers e-mail submissions (attached file). Regular sidebars. Prefers KJV & NIV. Theme list (no guidelines); copy for 9x12 SAE. (No ads)

Special Needs: Spiritual formation and devotional life enhancement.

$EXPRESSION CHRISTIAN NEWSPAPER, PO Box 44148, Pittsburgh PA 15205-0348. (412)920-5547. Fax (412)920-5549. E-mail: expressionnews @home.com. The Sonshine Foundation Intl., Inc. Cathy Hickling, ed. Geared toward bringing unity among the churches in the Pittsburgh and west PA area. Monthly newspaper; 24-32 pgs; circ 15,000. Subscription $20. 10% freelance. Query; e-query OK. Pays $25-100 on publication for one-time rts. Not copyrighted. Articles 300-500 or 750-1,000 wds; book/music/video reviews 300 wds. Responds in 3-4 wks. Seasonal 2 mos ahead. Accepts simultaneous submissions. Regular sidebars. Accepts disk. Guidelines/theme list; copy for 9x12 SAE/3 stamps. (Ads)

Fillers: Buys 4-6/yr. Cartoons; $10-25.

Tips: "Send local/state stories, for example: Interview with local guy, Mel Blount (ex-Steeler), who has a half-way house for boys. Most open to editorials, PA stories of interest."

$+FACTS FOR FAITH, 731 E. Arrow Hwy., Glendora CA 91740. (626)335-1480. Fax (626)963-2493. E-mail: reasons@reasons.org. Website: www. reasons.org. Reasons to Believe. Joe Aquirre, mng. ed. For an educated Christian laity that is interested in science, theology, and apologetics. Quarterly mag; 68 pgs; circ 5,300. Subscription $24. Estab. 2000. 100% assigned. Query; phone/e-query OK. Pays negotiable rates on publication. Articles 2,400-3,600 wds. Prefers disk. Some sidebars. Prefers NIV. Guidelines/theme list; copy for 9x12 SAE/3 stamps. (Ads)

Columns/Departments: Well-Equipped Apologist (conservative/evangelical), 600 wds. Pay to be determined.

Special Needs: Apologetics and philosophy.

Tips: "Submissions must be evangelical/conservative in theological orientation (Reformed welcome); must have educational credentials for either science or theology articles; and must reflect careful scholarship which offers the reader compelling evidence for Christian faith."

$FAITH & FRIENDS, 2 Overlea Blvd., Toronto ON M4H 1P4 Canada. (416)425-2111. Fax (416)422-6120. E-mail: faithandfriends@sallynet.org. Website: faithandfriends.salvationarmy.ca. The Salvation Army. Geoff Moulton, sr ed. Monthly mag; 16 pgs; circ 60,000. Subscription $15 CAN. Estab. 1998. 90% assigned. Query/clips; e-query OK. Pays up to $200 CAN on publication for 1st rts. Articles 650-1,500 wds. Responds in 2 wks. Seasonal 6 mos ahead. Accepts simultaneous submissions & reprints (tell when/where appeared). Prefers e-mail submissions (attached file). Some sidebars. Prefers NIV. Guidelines (also on Website); free copy. (No ads)

Fillers: Buys 10/yr. Cartoons, games, jokes, quizzes, quotes, word puzzles, recipes; 50 wds. Pays $25.

Columns/Departments: God in My Life (how Christians in the workplace find faith relevant), 600 wds; Words to Live By (simple Bible studies/discussions of faith), 600 wds; Faith Builders; Someone Cares.

$FAITH IN ACTION, PO Box 1, Yakima WA 98907. (509)575-1965. Fax (509)575-4732. E-mail: kengaub@aol.com. Website: www.kengaub.com. Ken Gaub Worldwide Ministry/radio ministry. Ken Gaub, pres. Quarterly mag; 12-16 pgs; circ 10,000. Subscription free. Buys all rts. Articles. Not in topical listings. (No ads)

$FAITH TODAY, M.I.P. Box 3745, Markham ON L3R 0Y4 Canada. (905)479-5885. Fax (905)479-4742. E-mail: ft@efc-canada.com. Website: www.efc-canada.com. Evangelical Fellowship of Canada. Gail Reid, mng ed; Bill Fledderus, news/features ed. Informing Canadian evangelicals on thoughts, trends, issues and events. Bimonthly mag; 56-80 pgs; circ 18,000. Subscription $25.68 CAN; $28.68 US. 20% unsolicited freelance; 80% assigned. Query; fax/e-query OK. Pays $50-800 on publication for 1st rts. Articles 400-3,000 wds (90/yr); news stories 400 wds; profiles 900 wds. Responds in 2 wks. Prefers e-mail submission. Kill fee 30-50%. Regular sidebars. Any version. Guidelines/theme list (also by e-mail, eventually on Website); copy for 9x12 SAE/$2.05 in Canadian funds. (Ads)

Columns/Departments: Buys 6/yr. Other Voices Guest Column (current social/political/religious issues of concern to Canadian church); 600 wds; $90.

Special Needs: "Canadian news. All topics to be approached in a journalistic—not personal viewpoint—style (except for 'Other Voices')."

Contest: The Annual God Uses Ink Writer's Contest is open to work published in 2000, until February 7, 2001. Contest guidelines and entry forms available from *Faith Today.*

Tips: "Feature/Cover section is most open to freelancers. Be sure to submit analytical journalistic articles on a Canadian event, trend or issue of current interest. Keep cover and feature articles 1,200-5,000 words." All unsolicited manuscripts will not be returned.

**This periodical was #54 on the 2000 Top 50 Christian Publishers List (#42 in 1998, #4 in 1997, #65 in 1996, #43 in 1994).

$THE FAMILY DIGEST, PO Box 40137, Fort Wayne IN 46804. Catholic. Corine B. Erlandson, ed. Dedicated to the joy and fulfillment of Catholic family life and its relationship to the Catholic parish. Bimonthly journal/booklet; 48 pgs; circ 150,000. Distributed through parishes. 90% freelance. Complete ms/cover letter; no phone/fax/e-query. Pays $40-60, 4-8 wks after acceptance, for 1st rts. Articles 700-1,200 wds (60/yr). Responds in 4-8 wks. Seasonal 7 mos ahead. Occasionally buys reprints. No disk. No sidebars. Prefers NAB. Guidelines & copy for 6x9 SAE/2 stamps. (Ads—Call 952-929-6765)

Fillers: Buys 24/yr. Anecdotes drawn from experience, 20-100 wds, $25.

Tips: "Prospective freelance writers should be familiar with the types

of articles we accept and publish. We are looking for upbeat articles which affirm the simple ways in which the Catholic faith is expressed in daily life. Articles on family life, parish life, seasonal articles, how-to pieces, inspirational, prayer, spiritual life and Church traditions will be gladly reviewed for possible acceptance and publication."
**This periodical was #52 on the 1995 Top 50 Christian Publishers list (#57 in 1994).

#FARO DE LUZ, PO Box 4116, Gainesville FL 32613. (352)378-0078. Fax (352)378-0042. E-mail: CCLfarodeluz@cs.com. Jose Flores, ed. Monthly newspaper; circ 9,500. For the whole family; promoting the unity of the family, the church and the body of Christ in general. Subscription $17. Accepts freelance. Complete ms. Not in topical listings. (Ads)

$FELLOWSHIP FOCUS (formerly Gospel Tidings), 5800 S. 14th St., Omaha NE 68107-3584. (402)731-4780. Fax (402)731-1173. E-mail: febcoma@ aol.com. Fellowship of Evangelical Bible Churches. Robert L. Frey, ed. To inform, educate and edify members of affiliate churches. Bimonthly mag; 20 pgs; circ 2,300. Subscription $8. 5% freelance. Query or complete ms/cover letter; fax/e-query OK. Pays $15-35 on publication for all rts. Articles (2/yr) & fiction (1/yr); 1,500/2,500 wds. Responds ASAP. Seasonal 3 mos ahead. Accepts simultaneous submissions & reprints (tell when/ where appeared). Accepts disk or e-mail submission (copied into message). Some sidebars. Prefers NIV. Guidelines (also by e-mail); copy for 9x12 SAE/3 stamps. (No ads)

*THE FELLOWSHIP LINK, 679 Southgate Dr., Guelph ON N1G 4S2 Canada. (519)821-4830. Fax (519)821-9829. Fellowship of Evangelical Baptist Churches in Canada. Dr. T. Starr, ed. To edify and strengthen people 55+ through the various stages of aging. Quarterly mag; 24 pgs; circ. 2,000. Subscription $12. 90% freelance. Query w/wo clips. **NO PAYMENT** for all rts. Not copyrighted. Articles 300-350 wds (12/yr); fiction 300-350 wds (12/yr); book reviews 100 wds. Responds in 2 weeks. Seasonal 3 mos ahead. Accepts simultaneous submissions & reprints (tell when/where appeared). Guidelines; copy for 9x12 SAE/.90 postage or IRCs. (Ads)

> **Poetry:** Accepts 3/yr. Traditional; short. Submit max 2 poems.
>
> **Fillers:** Accepts 6/yr. Anecdotes, cartoons, games, ideas, jokes, quizzes, short humor; to 250 wds.
>
> **Tips:** "Most open to devotional articles or short stories, true or fictional."

+FIRST PRIORITY, PO Box 1173, Portland OR 97207. (503)614-1500. Fax (503)614-1599. E-mail: firstpriority@palau.org. Website: www.iChristian. com/firstpriority. Luis Palau Evangelistic Assn. Mike Umlandt, ed. Encourages Christians to make evangelism a greater priority in their lives and churches. Quarterly mag. Subscription free. Accepts freelance. Prefers query. Not in topical listings. Did not return questionnaire. (No ads)

$FIRST THINGS: A Monthly Journal of Religion and Public Life, 156 Fifth Ave., Ste. 400, New York NY 10010. (212)627-1985. Fax (212)627-2184. E-mail: ft@firstthings.com. Website: www.firstthings.com. Institute on Religion & Public Life. James Nuechterlein, ed. Shows relation of religion and religious insights to contemporary issues of public life. Monthly (10X) mag; 64-84 pgs; circ 32,000. Subscription $29. 60% freelance. Complete ms/cover letter. Pays $300-800 on publication for all rts. Articles 4,000-6,000 wds, opinion 1,500 wds (50-60/yr); book reviews, 1,500 wds, $300. Responds in 2-3 wks. Seasonal 4-5 mos ahead. Prefers disk or e-mail submission (attached file) after acceptance. Kill fee. No sidebars. Any version. Guidelines; copy for 9x12 SAE/9 stamps. (Ads)

Poetry: Poetry Editor (poety@firstthings.com). Buys 30/yr. Traditional; to 40 lines; $50.

Columns/Departments: Opinion, 1,800 wds.

Tips: "Most open to opinion and articles."

$FOCUS ON THE FAMILY MAGAZINE, 8605 Explorer Dr., Colorado Springs CO 80920. (719)548-5881. Fax (719)531-3499. Website: www.family.org. Focus on the Family. Tom Neven, ed. To help families utilize Christian principles to strengthen their marriages, to improve their child-rearing and to help in the problems of everyday life. Monthly mag; 24 pgs; circ 2,700,000. Free to donors. 10% freelance. Query/clips; no phone/fax query. Pays $100-500 on publication for 1st rts. Articles 500-1,000 wds (20/yr). Responds in 4-6 wks. Seasonal 6 mos ahead. Accepts disk. Kill fee 25%. Regular sidebars. Prefers NIV. Guidelines; copy for 9x12 SAE/2 stamps. (No ads)

Tips: "This magazine is 90% generated from within our ministry. It's very hard to break in. Must be a unique look at a subject or very interesting topic not usually seen in our magazine, but still fitting the audience."

**This periodical was #51 on the 1998 Top 50 Christian Publishers list (#11 in 1997, #54 in 1994).

*FOREFRONT: The Desert and the City, Box 219, Crestone CO 81131. (719)256-4778. E-mail: 4front@fone.net. Website: www.spirituallife institute.org. Spiritual Life Institute/Catholic. Submit to The Editor. Practical spirituality and contemplative prayer; inter-religious dialogue and culture. Quarterly mag; 32 pgs; circ 2,000. Subscription $16. 15% unsolicited freelance; 10% assigned. Complete ms/cover letter; no phone/fax/e-query. PAYS 3 COPIES for 1st rts. Articles 1,000-2,500 wds (4/yr). Responds in 15 wks. Seasonal 8 mos ahead. Accepts reprints (tell when/where appeared). No disk or e-mail submissions. Some sidebars. No guidelines; copy $2.50/10x13 SAE. (No ads)

Poetry: Accepts 3/yr. Free verse, haiku, traditional; to 25 lines. Submit max 2 poems.

Fillers: Accepts 5/yr. Anecdotes, facts, prayers, prose, quotes; 50-250 wds.

Special Needs: Inter-religious dialogue, arts and culture.

Tips: "Avoid personal reflection/anecdotal pieces. Prefer articles that are informative, well-researched, accessible to a busy, educated readership of inter-denominational background. Avoid moralisms and preachy tone."

$FOURSQUARE WORLD ADVANCE, 1910 W. Sunset Blvd., Ste. 200, Los Angeles CA 90026-0176. (213)989-4220. Fax (213)989-4590. E-mail:

comm@foursquare.org. Website: www.foursquare.org/advmag. International Church of the Foursquare Gospel. Dr. Ronald Williams, ed. Denominational. Bimonthly magazine; 23 pgs; circ 102,000. Subscription free. .001% unsolicited freelance; 99.9% assigned. Complete ms/cover letter; phone/fax/e-query OK. Pays $75 on publication for 1st, one-time, simultaneous, or reprint rts. Not copyrighted. Articles 1,000-1,200 wds (2-3/yr); fiction. Responds in 2 wks. Seasonal 6 mos ahead. Accepts simultaneous submissions & reprints. Accepts e-mail submission (attached file). Regular sidebars. Free guidelines/theme list (also on Website)/copy. (Ads)

Poetry: Buys 1-2/yr. Pays $50.

Fillers: Buys 1-2/yr. Anecdotes, cartoons; 250-300 wds; $50.

+THE FRIEND, 33844 King Rd., Abbotsford BC V2S 7M8 Canada. (604)853-7441 x4319. University College of the Fraser Valley. Ron Dart, pub. A platform for the humanist Christian tradition. Quarterly mag; 24 pgs. Not in topical listings.

GDP PREVIEWER, PO Box 1483, Champaign IL 61824-1483. (217)359-1483. Fax (217)359-1492. E-mail: wyper@soltec.net. Website: www.gdpPreViewer.com. Sharon Wyper, ed. To provide a forum for discussion and enjoyment in the context of traditional family values and our Judeo-Christian heritage; and to serve the community. Monthly newspaper; circ 10,000. Subscription free. Accepts freelance. Prefers query. Not in topical listings. (Ads)

$#THE GEM, 700 E. Melrose Ave., Box 926, Findlay OH 45839-0926. (419) 424-1961. Fax (419)424-3433. E-mail: communications@cggc.org. Website: www.cggc.org. Churches of God, General Conference. Martin Cordell, ed. Monthly (13X) take-home paper for adults; 8 pgs; circ 7,100. Subscription $9.20. 80% unsolicited freelance; 20% assigned. Complete ms/cover letter; phone/fax/e-query OK. Pays $15 after publication for one-time rts. Articles 300-1,600 wds (125/yr); fiction 2,000 wds (125/yr); book/music reviews, 750 wds, $10. Responds in 12 wks. Seasonal 3 mos ahead. Accepts simultaneous submissions & reprints (tell when/where appeared). Accepts disk; no e-mail submission. Some sidebars. Prefers NIV. Guidelines (also by e-mail)/copy for #10 SAE/2 stamps. (No ads)

Poetry: Buys 100/yr. Any type, 3-40 lines. Pays $5-15. Submit max 3 poems.

Fillers: Buys 100/yr. All types, except party ideas; 25-100 wds. Pays $5-15.

Special Needs: Missions and true stories. Be sure that fiction has a clearly religious/Christian theme.

Tips: "Most open to real-life experiences where you have clearly been led by God. Make the story interesting and Christian."

$*GEMS OF TRUTH, PO Box 4060, Overland Park KS 66204. (913)432-0331. Fax (913)722-0351. Church of God (Holiness)/Herald & Banner Press. Arlene McGehee, Sunday school ed. Denominational. Weekly adult take-home paper; 8 pgs; circ 14,000. Subscription $1.90. Complete ms/cover letter; phone/fax query OK. Pays .005/wd on publication for 1st rts.

Fiction 1,000-2,000 wds. Seasonal 6-8 mos ahead. Accepts simultaneous submissions & reprints (tell when/where appeared). Prefers KJV. Guidelines/theme list; copy. Not in topical listings. (No ads)

$+GOD ALLOWS U-TURNS, A Child Shall Lead Them, The God Allows U-Turns Project, P.O. Box 717, Faribault, MN 55021-0717. Fax (507) 334-6464. E-mail: editor@godallowsuturns.com. Website: www.godallows uturns.com. Submit to Editor. Include volume subtitle in submission. Christian inspirational book series. Each book in the series will contain over one hundred uplifting, encouraging and inspirational true short stories written by contributors from all over the world. This volume is specifically about children of all ages. Stories go into a book (100+/bk). Multiple volumes are planned. Release date: Unknown. 100% freelance. Pays $50-$100/story upon publication (plus 1 copy of book). Byline and short bio. Articles 500-2,000 wds. Send complete ms/cover letter. One-time rights, reprint rights, editorial rights, no returns. Responds in 16+ wks. Accepts simultaneous submissions & reprints (tell when/where appeared). Prefers submission via Website. Accepts e-mail submission (copied into message, NO attachments). Guidelines and sample story appear on Website, or by sending #10 SAE/1 stamp.

    Fillers: Buys 25-50/book. Anecdotes, facts, ideas, newsbreaks, prayers, prose, quotes, short humor. Pays $25-$50 on publication.

    Special Needs: This volume celebrates children and childhood. Stories written by, for and/or about children. Open to well-written, personal inspirational pieces showing how faith in God can inspire, encourage and heal. Hope should prevail. Human-interest stories with a spiritual application, affirming ways in which faith is expressed in daily life. These true stories MUST touch the emotions. Our contributors are a diverse group with no limits on age or denomination.

    Tips: "See the Website for a sample story. Keep it real. Ordinary people doing extraordinary things with God's help. Focus on timeless, universal themes like love, forgiveness, salvation, healing, hope, faith, etc. Be able to tell a good story with drama, description and dialogue. Avoid moralisms and preachy tone. The point of the story should be some practical spiritual help the reader receives from what the author learned through his experience."

    Deadline: Deadline for volume one is December 30, 2001. Continue to send stories after this deadline for future volumes. Ongoing book series. Check Website for frequent series updates.

$+GOD ALLOWS U-TURNS, Faithful Stories for Hopeful Hearts, The God Allows U-Turns Project, P.O. Box 717, Faribault, MN 55021-0717. Fax (507) 334-6464. E-mail: editor@godallowsuturns.com. Website: www.godallows uturns.com. Submit to Editor. Include volume subtitle in submission. Christian inspirational book series. Each book in the series will contain over one hundred uplifting, encouraging and inspirational true short stories written by contributors from all over the world. This volume is specifically for the General Market. Stories go into a book (100+/bk). Multiple volumes are planned. Release date: Unknown. 100% freelance. Pays $50-$100/story upon publication (plus 1 copy of book). Byline and short bio.

Articles 500-2,000 wds. Send complete ms/cover letter. One-time rights, reprint rights, editorial rights, no returns. Responds in 16+ wks. Accepts simultaneous submissions & reprints (tell when/where appeared). Prefers submission via Website. Accepts e-mail submission (copied into message, NO attachments). Guidelines and sample story appear on Website, or by sending #10 SAE/1 stamp.

Fillers: Buys 25-50/book. Anecdotes, facts, ideas, newsbreaks, prayers, prose, quotes, short humor. Pays $25-$50 on publication.

Special Needs: Open to well-written, personal inspirational pieces showing how faith in God can inspire, encourage and heal. Hope should prevail. Human-interest stories with a spiritual application, affirming ways in which faith is expressed in daily life. These true stories MUST touch the emotions. Our contributors are a diverse group with no limits on age or denomination.

Tips: "See the Website for a sample story. Keep it real. Ordinary people doing extraordinary things with God's help. Focus on timeless, universal themes like love, forgiveness, salvation, healing, hope, faith, etc. Be able to tell a good story with drama, description and dialogue. Avoid moralisms and preachy tone. The point of the story should be some practical spiritual help the reader receives from what the author learned through his experience."

Deadline: Deadline for volume one is June 30, 2001. Continue to send stories after this deadline for future volumes. Ongoing book series. Check Website for frequent series updates.

$+GOD ALLOWS U-TURNS, Golden Memories, The God Allows U-Turns Project, P.O. Box 717, Faribault, MN 55021-0717. Fax (507) 334-6464. E-mail: editor@godallowsuturns.com. Website: www.godallowsuturns.com. Submit to Editor. Include volume subtitle in submission. Christian inspirational book series. Each book in the series will contain over one hundred uplifting, encouraging and inspirational true short stories written by contributors from all over the world. This volume is specifically for and about senior citizens. Stories go into a book (100+/bk). Multiple volumes are planned. Release date: unknown. 100% freelance. Pays $50-$100/story on publication (plus 1 copy of book). Byline and short bio. Articles 500-2,000 wds. Send complete ms/cover letter. One time rights, reprint rights, editorial rights, no returns. Responds in 16+ wks. Accepts simultaneous submissions & reprints (tell when/where appeared). Prefers submission via Website. Accepts e-mail submission (copied into message, NO attachments). Guidelines and sample story appear on Website, or by sending #10 SAE/1 stamp.

Fillers: Buys 25-50/book. Anecdotes, facts, ideas, newsbreaks, prayers, prose, quotes, short humor. Pays $25-$50 on publication.

Special Needs: This special volume is by, for and about senior citizens and their special life stories. Open to well-written, personal inspirational pieces showing how faith in God can inspire, encourage and heal. Hope should prevail. Human-interest stories with a spiritual application, affirming ways in which faith is expressed in daily life.

These true stories MUST touch the emotions. Our contributors are a diverse group with no limits on age or denomination.

Tips: "See the Website for a sample story. Keep it real. Ordinary people doing extraordinary things with God's help. Focus on timeless, universal themes like love, forgiveness, salvation, healing, hope, faith, etc. Be able to tell a good story with drama, description and dialogue. Avoid moralisms and preachy tone. The point of the story should be some practical spiritual help the reader receives from what the author learned through his experience."

Deadline: Deadline for volume one is December 30, 2001. Continue to send stories after this deadline for future volumes. Ongoing book series. Check Website for frequent series updates.

$+GOD ALLOWS U-TURNS, Medical Miracles, The God Allows U-Turns Project, P.O. Box 717, Faribault, MN 55021-0717. Fax (507) 334-6464. E-mail: editor@godallowsuturns.com. Website: www.godallowsuturns.com. Submit to Editor. Include volume subtitle in submission. Christian inspirational book series. Each book in the series will contain over one hundred uplifting, encouraging and inspirational true short stories written by contributors from all over the world. This volume is specifically about Medical Miracles. Stories go into a book (100+/bk). Multiple volumes are planned. Release date: Unknown. 100% freelance. Pays $50-$100/story on publication (plus 1 copy of book). Byline and short bio. Articles 500-2,000 words. Send complete ms/cover letter. One-time rights, reprint rights, editorial rights, no returns. Responds in 16+ wks. Accepts simultaneous submissions & reprints (tell when/where appeared). Prefers submission via Website. Accepts e-mail submission (copied into message, NO attachments). Guidelines and sample story appear on Website, or by sending #10 SAE/1 stamp.

Fillers: Buys 25-50/book. Anecdotes, facts, ideas, newsbreaks, prayers, prose, quotes, short humor. Pays $25-$50 on publication.

Special Needs: This volume is about medical miracles, from birth to death. Open to well-written, personal inspirational pieces showing how faith in God can inspire, encourage and heal. Hope should prevail. Human-interest stories with a spiritual application, affirming ways in which faith is expressed in daily life. These true stories MUST touch the emotions. Our contributors are a diverse group with no limits on age or denomination.

Tips: "See the Website for a sample story. Keep it real. Ordinary people doing extraordinary things with God's help. Focus on timeless, universal themes like love, forgiveness, salvation, healing, hope, faith, etc. Be able to tell a good story with drama, description and dialogue. Avoid moralisms and preachy tone. The point of the story should be some practical spiritual help the reader receives from what the author learned through his experience."

Deadline: Deadline for volume one is December 30, 2001. Continue to send stories after this deadline for future volumes. Ongoing book series. Check Website for frequent series updates.

*GOD'S REVIVALIST, 1810 Young St., Cincinnati OH 45210. (513)721-7944 x296. Fax (513)721-3971. Larry Smith, ed. Salvation theme; Wesleyan persuasion. Monthly mag; 24 pgs; circ 20,000. Subscription $8. Occasional freelance. Complete ms/cover letter. **NO PAYMENT** for one-time rts. Articles 600-1,400 wds (3/yr). Responds in 9 wks. Seasonal 2 mos ahead. Accepts simultaneous submissions. Guidelines; copy $1/9x12 SAE.

Poetry: Accepts 5/yr. Free verse, light verse, traditional; 8-20 lines. Submit max 10 poems.

Fillers: Accepts 5/yr. Facts, ideas, prose, short humor; 50-90 wds.

Tips: "We need some information about the author."

$GOOD NEWS, PO Box 150, Wilmore KY 40390. (606)858-4661. Fax (606) 858-4972. E-mail: steve@goodnewsmag.org. Website: www.goodnewsmag.org. United Methodist/Forum for Scriptural Christianity, Inc. Steve Beard, ed; submit to Moriah Davis, ed asst. Focus is evangelical renewal within the denomination. Bimonthly mag; 44 pgs; circ 100,000. Subscription free. 20% freelance. Query; no phone/fax/e-query. Pays $100-150 on publication for one-time rts. Articles 1,500-1,850 wds (25/yr). Responds in 24 wks. Seasonal 4-6 mos ahead. Accepts simultaneous submissions & reprints (tell when/where appeared). Accepts disk. Kill fee. Regular sidebars. Prefers NIV. Guidelines (also on Website); copy $2.75/9x12 SAE. (Ads)

Tips: "Most open to features."

$GOOD NEWS, ETC., PO Box 2660, Vista CA 92085. (760)724-3075. Fax (760)724-8311. E-mail: rmonroe@goodnewsetc.com. Website: www.goodnewsetc.com. Good News Publishers, Inc. of California. Rick Monroe, ed. Feature stories and local news of interest to Christians in San Diego County. Monthly tabloid; 24-32 pgs; circ 42,000. Subscription $15. 5% unsolicited freelance; 5% assigned. Query; e-query OK. Pays $20 on publication for all, 1st, one-time or reprint rts. Articles 500-700 wds (15/yr). Responds in 2 wks. Seasonal 2 mos ahead. Accepts simultaneous submissions & reprints (tell when/where appeared). Prefers disk. Regular sidebars. Prefers NIV. Guidelines; copy for 9x12 SAE/4 stamps. (Ads)

Tips: "Most open to local, personality-type articles."

**1993 EPA Award of Merit—Newspaper.

#*GOOD NEWS JOURNAL (MO), Box 1882, Columbia MO 65205. (573)875-8755. Fax (573)874-4964. Good News Publishers. Teresa Parker, ed. Christian newspaper for mid-Missouri area. Monthly tabloid; 12-16 pgs; circ 25,000-50,000. Subscription $20. 10% freelance. Query; complete ms for fiction. **NO PAYMENT** for one-time rts. Articles 500 wds (2/yr); fiction 750 wds (5/yr); book/music/video reviews, 50 wds. Responds in 6-8 wks. Seasonal 3 mos ahead. Accepts simultaneous submissions & reprints (tell when/where appeared). Accepts disk. Some sidebars. Prefers NIV. Copy $1/9x12 SAE. (Ads)

Fillers: Accepts 1-6/yr. Cartoons, games, jokes, quizzes, no pay.

Columns/Departments: Accepts 12/yr. Good News Kids (fiction for kids up to 12 yrs), 500-750 wds; Golden Digest (testimonies or devotionals for those over 55), 1,000 wds.

Special Needs: Testimonies of healing with verification of physician.

Tips: "Interested in testimonies and personal experience stories that illustrate Christian growth or Christian principles."

GOOD NEWS JOURNAL (TX), 1901 S. Hwy 183, Leander TX 78641. (512)260-1800. Fax (512)259-0892. E-mail:goodnews98@aol.com. Website: www.goodnewsjournal.com. Evelyn W. Davison, pub. Christian paper for national circulation by subscription and Central Texas by free distribution. Monthly newspaper; 16-20 pgs; circ 60,000. Subscription $29.95. Estab 1997. 40% unsolicited freelance; 60% assigned. Query; fax/e-query OK. NO PAYMENT for one-time rts. Articles 200-600 wds. Accepts reprints. Prefers e-mail submissions. Guidelines (also by e-mail/Website); copy for 9x12SAE/2 stamps. (Ads)
> **Poetry:** Accepts 4-6/yr. Traditional.
> **Fillers:** Accepts many. All types; 10-50 wds.
> **Tips:** "All areas are open."

*****THE GOOD SHEPHERD**, 171 White Plains Rd., Bronxville NY 10708. (914)337-5172. Fax (914)779-5274. E-mail: shepherd@concordia-ny.edu. The Good Shepherd Press. Deborah Cook, mngr. For Christian families and family-life professionals, including pastors and teachers. Quarterly mag; 32 pgs; circ 20,000. Subscription $15. 0% unsolicited freelance; 100% assigned. Query by e-mail. (Ads).

$*GOSPEL TODAY MAGAZINE, 761 Old Hickory Blvd., Ste. 205, Brentwood TN 37027. (615)376-5656. Fax (615)376-0882. E-mail: gospel@usit.net. Websites: www.gospeltoday.com, and www.gospeltodaymag.com. Horizon Concepts, Inc. Teresa Harris, pub. Ministry and Christian/gospel music; Christian lifestyles directed toward African Americans. Bimonthly (8X) mag; 60 pgs; circ 50,000. Subscription $20. 50% freelance. Query; fax query OK. Pays $150-250 on publication for all, one-time or simultaneous rts. Articles 1,000-3,500 wds (4/yr); book reviews 1,000-1,500 wds. Responds in 4 wks. Seasonal 4 mos ahead. Requires disk. Kill fee 15%. Regular sidebars. Prefers KJV. Guidelines/theme list; copy for 10x13 SAE/8 stamps. (Ads)
> **Columns/Departments:** Precious Memories (historic overview of renowned personality), 1,500-2,000 wds; From the Pulpit (issue-oriented observation from clergy), 2,500-3,000 wds; Life & Style (travel, health, beauty, fashion tip, etc.), 1,500-2,500 wds. Pays $50-75.
> **Tips:** "Looking for more human-interest pieces—ordinary people doing extraordinary things."

#GOSPEL TRACT HARVESTER, 1105 S. Fuller St., Independence MO 64050. (816)461-6086. Fax (816)461-4305. Gospel Tract Society, Inc. David Buttram, ed. For Christians of all ages (few unchurched readers). Monthly mag; 16 pgs; circ 70,000. Subscription free (donations). 20% unsolicited freelance. Query; no phone/fax query. PAYS UP TO 20 COPIES for all rts. Not copyrighted. Articles 1,000 wds (10/yr); fiction 1,000 wds. Responds in 4-6 wks. Seasonal 4 mos ahead. Accepts reprints (tell when/where appeared). Some sidebars. Prefers KJV. Guidelines; copy for 9x12 SAE/2 stamps. (No ads)
> **Poetry:** Accepts 8-12/yr. Light verse, traditional; 6-20 lines. Submit max 5 poems.
> **Fillers:** Accepts 8-12/yr. Anecdotes, facts, games, quotes, short humor, word puzzles, 100-500 wds.

Special Needs: Good, fresh, well-written tracts.

Tips: "Most open to personal testimonies if well-written and documented; children's games (cross-word puzzles, etc.). Have a message to share and a sincere desire to share the message of salvation. Be concise. Be correct in grammar and references."

$GREAT FAMILIES, PO Box 500050, San Diego CA 92150-0050. (858)513-7150. Fax (858)513-7142. E-mail: asb@familyuniversity.com. Family University. Paul Lewis, ed. Helpful, how-to advice and humorous "slice-of-life" anecdotes on matters concerning the family. Online version. 20% unsolicited freelance. E-query OK. Pays $50-300 for one-time and electronic rts. Articles 200-1,000 wds. Responds in 1-3 wks. Accepts reprints. Not in topical listings. (No ads)

$GRIT, 1503 SW 42nd St., Topeka KS 66609. (785)274-4300. Fax (785)274-4305. E-mail: grit@cjnetworks.com. Website: www.grit.com. Ogden Publications. Donna Doyle, ed-in-chief. For 50+ year olds in small towns; features with positive messages. Biweekly tabloid; 40-48 pgs; circ 170,000. Subscription $27.98. 90% unsolicited freelance. Query by mail only. Pays .15-.22/wd for nonfiction, .10-.22/wd for fiction; on publication for 1st or one-time rts. Articles 1,200-1,500 wds (300/yr); fiction 1,500-2,000 wds, serials 3,500-10,000 wds (30/yr). Response time varies. Seasonal 6 mos ahead. No simultaneous submissions or reprints. Prefers disk (Mac). Regular sidebars. Guidelines/theme list; copy $4/9x12 SAE. (Ads)

Poetry: Attn: Poetry Editor. Buys 100+/yr. Free verse, light verse, traditional. Pays $2/line ($30 minimum). Submit max 5 poems.

Fillers: Attn: Fillers Dept. Buys 200/yr. Anecdotes, cartoons, jokes, prose, original quotes, short humor, 10-50 wds. Pays $5-15.

Columns/Departments: Buys 100-200/yr. Looking Back (nostalgia with a message), 500 wds; Cook of the Month (unique people with storyteller recipes), 1,000 wds; Braggin Wagon (our children & grandchildren), 100-200 wds; Pet Tales (unusual tales and tails), 200-1,200 wds; Coping (survivors with a positive message), 1,200 wds. Payment varies.

Special Needs: True inspirational stories, true nostalgia, senior lifestyles, how love endures, humor, your favorite gardens. Always needs seasonal stories and photos (Christmas, Thanksgiving, Easter, Mother's Day, Father's Day, Memorial Day, etc.). Also accepts historical, mystery, western, adventure and romance serials of 3,500-15,000 words, in 1,000 word installments with cliff hangers. Submit to "Fiction Dept."

Contest: Sponsors various contests throughout the year: Christmas photo contest, pet photo contest, seasonal essays, TrueGrit Awards—annually in November issue (unsung heroes).

Tips: "Our publication is all original material either written by our readers/freelancers or occasionally by our staff. Every department, every article is open. Break in by reading at least 6 months of issues to know our special audience." Submissions are not acknowledged or status reports given.

$GUIDEPOSTS, 16 E 34th St., New York NY 10016-4397. (212)251-8100.

Website: www.guideposts.org. Interfaith. Mary Ann O'Roark, exec. ed. Personal faith stories showing how faith in God helps each person cope with life in some particular way. Monthly mag; 52 pgs; circ 3 million. Subscription $13.94. 30% unsolicited freelance; 20% assigned. Complete ms/cover letter, by mail only. Pays $100-500 on acceptance for all rts. Articles 750-1,500 wds (40-60/yr). Responds 9 wks. Seasonal 6 mos ahead. Accepts simultaneous submissions and reprints. Kill fee 20%. Some sidebars. Free guidelines/copy. (No ads)

> **Fillers:** Catherine Scott (cscott@guideposts.org). Buys 15-20/yr. Anecdotes; quotes, short humor; 10-200 wds; $25-100.
>
> **Columns/Departments:** Catherine Scott. Buys 24/yr. His Mysterious Ways (divine intervention), 250 wds; What Prayer Can Do, 250 wds; Angels Among Us, 400 wds; Divine Touch (tangible evidence of God's help), 400 wds ("This is our most open area. Write in 3rd person."); $100.
>
> **Contest:** Writers Workshop Contest held on even years with a late June deadline. Winners attend a week-long seminar (all expenses paid) on how to write for Guideposts. Also Young Writers Contest; $36,000 in college scholarships; best stories to 1,200 wds; deadline November 29.
>
> **Tips:** "Be able to tell a good story, with drama, suspense, description and dialogue. The point of the story should be some practical spiritual help the reader receives from what the author learned through his experience." First person only.
>
> **This periodical was #22 on the 1998 Top 50 Christian Publishers list (#47 in 1996, #54 in 1995, #44 in 1994).

*HARVEST PRESS, PO Box 2876, Newport News VA 23609. (757)886-0713. Fax (757)886-1295. Tyrone Campbell, ed. To proclaim the gospel of Jesus Christ, to reach the unreached and promote unity within the body of Christ. Monthly newspaper; circ 20,000. Subscription $25. Open to freelance. Query. Not in topical listings. (Ads)

THE HEALING INN, PO Box 36395, Las Vegas NV 89133. Phone/fax (702)259-9579. E-mail: Jshafhid@juno.com. Website: www.healinginn.org. June Shafhid, ed. Offers healing for Christians wounded by a church or religious cult. Quarterly online mag. Free online. 100% freelance. Complete ms by e-mail; fax query OK. **NO PAYMENT** for 1st or reprint rts. Articles 500-2,500 wds; fiction 500-3,000 wds. Responds in 4 wks. Seasonal 4 mos ahead. Accepts simultaneous submissions & reprints (tell when/where appeared). No disk; e-mail only (attached or copied into message). Some sidebars. Prefers KJV. Guidelines/theme list (on Website). (Ads)

> **Poetry:** All types; open length. Accepts many. Submit max 10 poems.
>
> **Fillers:** Accepts many. Anecdotes, cartoons, facts, ideas, jokes, prose, prayers, quotes, short humor.
>
> **Tips:** "Most open to a good fiction story that touches the heart and a good testimony that encourages the soul."

HEARTLIGHT INTERNET MAGAZINE, 8332 Mesa Dr., Austin TX 78759. (514)345-6386. Fax (512)345-6634. E-mail: phil@heartlight.org. Website: www.heartlight.org. Westover Hills Church of Christ. Phil Ware & Paul

Lee, co-eds. Offers positive Christian resources for living in today's world. Weekly online mag (see Website above); 20+ pgs; circ 70,000+. Subscription free. 20% freelance. E-query. **NO PAYMENT** for electronic rts. Articles 300-450 wds (25-35/yr); fiction 500-700 wds (12-15/yr). Responds in 3 wks. Seasonal 2 mos ahead. Accepts simultaneous submissions & reprints (tell when/where appeared). Prefers e-mail submission. Regular sidebars. Prefers NIV. Copy available on the Internet.

> **Poetry:** Accepts 10/yr. Free verse, light verse, traditional. Submit max 10 poems.

> **Fillers:** Accepts 12/yr. Anecdotes, cartoons, games, ideas, jokes, newsbreaks, prayers, prose, quotes, short humor, word puzzles; to 350 wds.

> **Tips:** "Most open to feature articles, Just for Men or Just for Women, or Heartlight for Children."

$+HEART SONGS, 1351 Morgan Ave., Williamsport PA 17701-2849. (570) 323-3921. E-mail: crosspub@mail.microserve.net. Website: www. ChristianPoetry.org. Cross Way Publications. Jerry Hoffman, ed. Quarterly mag. Copy $5 (also on Website).

> **Poetry:** Buys 80/yr. Pays $5/poem.

+HEARTWARMERS4U. Submit to: moderator@heartwarmers4u.com. Website: www.heartwarmers4u.com. Personal, heartwarming experiences. Online mag. Stories to 700 wds. **NO PAYMENT** for one-time rts, but they will link your story to your Website or e-mail. Requires e-mail submissions (copied into message only). Does not respond to submissions. Guidelines on Website.

> **Poetry:** Short.

> **Tips:** "We like stories with a humorous or surprise twist."

#HIDDEN MANNA, 17914 Valley Knoll, Houston TX 77084. E-mail: hidden manna@triquetra.org. Website: www.triquetra.org. Triquetra Publishing. Daniel C. Massey, ed. For thoughtful Christians who believe that faith nurtured by story is a faith that endures. Quarterly journal; 40 pgs; circ 500. Subscription $15. Estab 1998. 90% unsolicited freelance; 10% assigned. Complete ms/cover letter; e-query OK. PAYS IN COPIES & SUBSCRIPTION for 1st or reprint rts. Articles 500-2,000 wds (6/yr); fiction 500-3,000 wds (6/yr), Flash Fiction to 500 wds; Analysis of Fiction 500-2,000 wds; Faith Journeys 500-2,000 wds; book/video reviews 500 wds. Responds in 6 mos. Accepts simultaneous submissions & reprints (tell when/where appeared). Requires disk. No sidebars. Any version. Guidelines (also on Website); copy $4 (check to Triquetra Publishing)/ 6x9 SAE. (No ads)

> **Poetry:** Accepts 6-20/yr. Avant-garde, free verse, traditional, literary; to 40 lines (few longer). Submit max 3 poems.

> **Columns/Departments:** Accepts 12/yr. Dialogues (interviews with everyday Christians with great stories) 1,500-2,500 wds; Essays (creative, scholarly essays on narrative theology, with emphasis on biblical narrative; also analysis of fiction) 500-2,000 wds.

> **Special Needs:** Unconventional Christian fiction with a literary bent; fiction with an uncommon Christian voice.

Tips: "All submissions must celebrate paradox, leave more questions than answers. Write fiction with mature Christian themes from everyday life, and tell the story on several levels. Don't interview famous people, but the lonely, the outcast, the quiet forgotten ones with great untold stories. Send essays that show how narrative points to a complex incarnate God." Does not return manuscripts.

HIGHWAY NEWS AND GOOD NEWS, PO Box 303, Denver PA 17517-0303. (717)721-9800. Fax (717)721-9351. E-mail: tfcdenver@juno.com. Website: www.layover.com. Transport for Christ. Lisa Graham, ed. For truck drivers and their families; evangelistic, with articles for Christian growth. Monthly mag; 16 pgs; circ 35,000. Subscription $25 or donation. 30% freelance. Query or complete ms/cover letter; phone query OK; no e-query. **PAYS IN COPIES** for rights offered. Articles 600 or 1,200 wds and fiction 1,200-1,400 wds. Seasonal 4 mos ahead. Accepts simultaneous submissions & reprints (tell when/where appeared). Accepts disk. Some sidebars. Prefers NIV. Guidelines/theme list; free copy for 9x12 SAE. (No ads)

Fillers: Short humor, 100 wds.

Tips: "All articles/stories must relate to truckers; need pieces on marriage, parenting, and fatherhood. Most open to features."

$HOLINESS TODAY, 6401 The Paseo, Kansas City MO 64131. (816)333-7000 x2302. Fax (816)333-1748. Church of the Nazarene. Gay L. Leonard, exec ed. No freelance.

$HOMELIFE, 127 Ninth Ave. N, Nashville TN 37234-0140. (615)251-2271. Fax (615)251-5008. E-mail: homelife@lifeway.com, or jwalke@lifeway. com. Website: www.lifeway.com. Lifeway Christian Resources of the Southern Baptist Convention. Jon Walker, ed; Susan Garland, copy ed. To celebrate and serve the Christian family. Monthly mag; 68 pgs; circ 475,000. Subscription $19.95. 100% assigned. Query (see tips). Pays on acceptance for all, 1st, reprint, and electronic rts. Articles. Responds in 12-16 wks. Seasonal 9 mos ahead. Accepts reprints (tell when/where appeared). Prefers e-mail submission (attached file). Kill fee. Regular sidebars. Prefers NIV. Copy for 9x12 SAE/4 stamps. (No ads)

Tips: If you'd like to be considered for an assignment, send your résumé and clippings (if available). Include a list of topics you feel qualified to address. They provide guidelines for each assigned article (no fiction or poetry).

$HOMESCHOOLING TODAY, PO Box 1608, Fort Collins CO 80522-1608. (970)493-3793. Fax (970)493-8781. E-mail: publisher@homeschooltoday. com. Website: www.homeschooltoday.com. S. Squared Productions. Maureen McCaffrey, ed-in-chief. Practical articles and lessons for homeschoolers. Bimonthly mag; 68 pgs; circ 25,000. Subscription $19.99. 90% freelance. Query/clips; fax/e-query OK. Pays .08/wd on publication for 1st rts. Articles 500-2,000 wds (20/yr). Responds in 6 wks. Accepts simultaneous submissions & reprints (tell when/where appeared). Requires disk, no e-mail submission. Regular sidebars. Any version. Guidelines; copy for 9x12 SAE. (Ads)

Columns/Departments: Buys 10-12/yr. Parents Speak Out, 500-700 wds. (See guidelines for other departments.) Query. Pays .08/wd.

Tips: "We use fewer and fewer unsolicited pieces. We have a regular stable of freelancers."

$HOME TIMES, 3676 Collins Dr., #16, West Palm Beach FL 33406. (561)439-3509. Fax (561)968-1758. E-mail: hometimes2@aol.com. Website: www. hometimes.org. Neighbor News, Inc. Dennis Lombard, ed/pub. Conservative, pro-Christian community newspaper. Monthly tabloid; 24 pgs; circ 5,200. Subscription $16. 20% unsolicited freelance; 30% assigned. Complete ms only/cover letter; no phone/fax/e-query. Pays $5-35 ($5-25 for fiction) on publication for one-time rts. Articles to 800 wds (25/yr); fiction to 800 wds (6/yr); book reviews 300 wds, $5-15. Responds in 2-3 wks. Seasonal 2 mos ahead. Accepts simultaneous submissions & reprints (tell when/where appeared). No disk or e-mail submission (unless requested). Some sidebars. Prefers NIV. Guidelines; 3 copies $3. (Ads)

Poetry: Buys 12/yr. Free verse, light verse, traditional; 4-28 lines; $5. Submit max 3 poems.

Fillers: Accepts 30-40/yr. Anecdotes, cartoons, jokes, newsbreaks, quizzes, quotes, short humor; to 100 wds; pays 3-6 copies.

Columns/Departments: Buys 15/yr. See guidelines for departments, to 600 wds; $5-15.

Special Needs: Good short stories (true, creative nonfiction, or fiction). More faith, miracles, and personal experiences.

Contest: Planning a contest for local, wannabe journalists within the next year.

Tips: "Very open to new writers, but study guidelines and sample first; we are different. Published by Christians, but not religious. Looking for more positive articles and stories."

THE HUNTED NEWS, PO Box 9101, Warwick RI 02889. (401)826-7307. The Suburban Press. Mike Wood, ed. Good writers dealing honestly with faith. Semiannual tabloid; 40 pgs; circ 1,000. Subscription free. 100% unsolicited freelance. Complete ms/cover letter; query for fiction. **PAYS IN COPIES** for one-time rts. Not copyrighted. Articles 700 wds (1/yr); fiction 700 wds (5/yr); reviews 700 wds. Responds in 3 wks. No seasonal. Accepts simultaneous submissions. No disk or e-mail submissions. No sidebars. Prefers KJV. Guidelines; copy for #10 SAE/2 stamps. (No ads)

Poetry: Accepts 10-15/yr. Avant-garde, free verse, haiku, traditional; any length. Submit max 10 poems.

Tips: "A writer can break into my publication by being a good writer, i.e., care about craft and style. No dogma or homilies."

$IDEALS MAGAZINE, Ideals Publishing, Inc., 535 Metroplex Dr., Ste. 250, Nashville TN 37211. (615)333-0478. Website: www.idealspublications. com. Michelle Prater Burke, ed. Seasonal, inspirational, nostalgic magazine for mature men and women of traditional values. Bimonthly mag.; 88 pgs; circ 180,000. Subscription $19.95. 95% freelance. Complete ms/cover letter; no phone query. Pays .10/wd on publication for one-time rts. Articles 800-1,000 wds (20/yr). Responds in 9 wks. Seasonal 8 mos ahead. Accepts simultaneous submissions & reprints (tell when/where appeared). No disk. No sidebars. Prefers KJV. Guidelines; copy $4.

Poetry: Buys 100+/yr. Free verse, light verse, traditional; 12-50 lines; $10. Submit max 5 poems.

Tips: "Most open to optimistic poetry oriented around a season or theme."

*IMMACULATE HEART MESSENGER, 240 5th St. W., Alexandria SD 57311-0158. Catholic/Fatima Family Apostate. Fr. Robert J. Fox, ed. Bimonthly mag; circ. 10,000. Subscription $13. 50% freelance. **NO PAYMENT** for one-time rts. Articles 5 double-spaced pgs. Seasonal 6 mos ahead. Not in topical listings.

$IMPACT MAGAZINE, 301 Geyland Centre, #03-04 Geyland Rd., Singapore 389 344. Phone 65-748-1244. Fax 65-748-3744. E-mail: impact@pacific. net.sg. Website: www.impact.com.sg. Impact Christian Comm., Ltd. Andrew Goh, ed. To help young working adults apply Christian principles to contemporary issues. Bimonthly mag; 56 pgs; circ 6,000. Subscription $16. 10-15% freelance. Query or complete ms/cover letter; phone/fax/e-query OK. Ranges from no payment up to $20/pg, for all rts. Articles (12/yr) & fiction (6/yr); 1,000-2,000 wds. Seasonal 2 mos ahead. Accepts reprints. Accepts e-mail submission (attached file). Some sidebars. Prefers NIV. Guidelines (also by e-mail); copy for $3 & $1.70 postage (surface mail). (Ads)

Poetry: Accepts 2-3 poems/yr. Free verse, 20-40 lines. Submit max 3 poems.

Fillers: Accepts 6/yr. Anecdotes, cartoons, jokes, quizzes, short humor, and word puzzles.

Columns/Departments: Closing Thoughts (current social issues), 600-800 wds; Testimony (personal experience), 1,500-2,000 wds; Parenting (Asian context), 1,000-1,500 wds; Faith Seeks Understanding (answers to tough questions of faith/Scripture), 80-1,000 wds.

Tips: "We're most open to fillers."

**1997 EPA Award of Merit—Missionary.

$INDIAN LIFE, PO Box 3765, RPO Redwood Centre, Winnipeg MB R2W 3R6 Canada. US address: Box 32, Pembina ND 58271. (204)661-9333. Fax (204)661-3982. E-mail: jim.editor@indianlife.org. Website: www.indian life.org. Indian Life Ministries. Jim Uttley, ed; Viola Fehr, asst ed. An evangelistic publication for English-speaking aboriginal people in North America. Bimonthly newspaper; 16 pgs; circ 32,000. Subscription $10. 10% unsolicited freelance; 25% assigned. Query; e-query OK. Pays $10-150 on acceptance for 1st and Internet rts. Articles 300-1,500 wds (20/yr); fiction 300-1,200 wds (4/yr); reviews, 500 wds, $40. Responds in 4 wks. Seasonal 4 mos ahead. Accepts simultaneous submissions & reprints. Accepts disk. Some sidebars. Prefers NLV or NIV. Guidelines; copy $2. (Ads)

Special Needs: Celebrity pieces must be aboriginal only.

Tips: "Most open to first-person accounts, interviews with First Nations people, and stories of salvation. Native authors preferred, but some others are published. Aim at a 10th-grade reading level; short paragraphs; avoid multisyllable words and long sentences."

**1987 & 1998 EPA Award of Excellence—Newspaper.

$INLAND NORTHWEST CHRISTIAN NEWS, 222 W. Mission, #132, Spokane

WA 99201. (509)328-0820. Fax (509)326-4921. E-mail: inldnwchrist@ spocom.net. John McKelvey, ed. To inform, motivate and encourage evangelical Christians in Spokane and the Inland Northwest. Newspaper published 18X/yr; 12 pgs; circ 7,500. Subscription $17.95. 30% freelance. Query; phone query OK. Pays $1/column inch on publication for 1st rts. Articles 400 wds. Responds in 9 wks. (Ads)

$INSIDE JOURNAL, PO Box 17429, Washington DC 20041-0429. (703)478-0100x560. Fax (703)318-0235. E-mail: 74171.511@compuserve.com, or Jeff_Peck@pfm.org. Website: www.pfm.org. Prison Fellowship Ministries. Terry White, ed; submit to Jeff Peck, mng ed. To proclaim the gospel to non-Christian prisoners within the context of a prison newspaper. Bimonthly (8X) tabloid; 8 pgs; circ 380,000. Subscription $10. 5% unsolicited freelance; 10% assigned. Query; phone/fax/e-query OK. Modest payment, depending on situation, on acceptance for one-time rts. Articles to 1,200 wds (25/yr). Responds in 4 wks. Seasonal 4 mos ahead. Accepts disk or e-mail submission. Regular sidebars. Guidelines (also by e-mail); free copy. (No ads)

> **Columns/Departments:** Buys 15-20/yr. Shortimer (those preparing for release within 6 wks), 500 wds; Especially for Women (issues for incarcerated women), 600-800 wds. Variable payment.
>
> **Tips:** "Always need seasonal material for Christmas, Easter and Thanksgiving. Also celebrity stories that demonstrate triumph over adversity. Address our prison audience with authenticity. Preachy church talk doesn't work. Be practical. Inspire or equip prisoner to serve his/her sentence or live a new life when released."
>
> **1994 EPA Award of Merit—Newspaper.

THE INSPIRER, 737 Kimsey Ln., #620, Henderson KY 42420-4917. (502) 826-5720. Billy Edwards, ed. Overstocked; no freelance for now.

$INTERCHANGE, 412 Sycamore St., Cincinnati OH 45202. (513)421-0311. Fax (513)421-0315. E-mail: ken_ericson@episcopal-dso.org. Website: www.episcopal-dso.org. Episcopal. Rev. Canon John E. Lawrence, ed. Regional paper for the Episcopal and Anglican Church in southern Ohio. Bimonthly tabloid; 28 pgs; circ 12,600. Free. 5% freelance. Query or complete ms/cover letter. Pays $35-50 on publication for all rts. Articles 500-2,000 wds (1-2/yr). Responds in 9 wks. Accepts simultaneous submissions. Prefers disk (Mac compatible). Regular sidebars. Copy for 9x12 SASE.

> **Tips:** "Most open to features, especially with a local angle."

$*THE INTERIM, (416)368-0250. Fax (416)368-8575. E-mail: interim@ globalserve.net. Website: www.lifesite.net. The Interim Publishing Co. Ltd. David Curtin, ed-in-chief. Abortion, euthanasia, pornography, feminism and religion from a pro-life perspective; Catholic and evangelical Protestant audience. Monthly & online newspaper; 24 pgs; circ 30,000. Subscription $25 CAN or US. 60% freelance. Query; phone/fax/e-query OK. Pays $50-150 CAN, on publication. Articles 400-750 wds; book, music, video reviews, 500 wds ($50-75 CAN). Responds in 2 wks. Seasonal 2 mos ahead. Accepts simultaneous submissions & reprints (tell when/where appeared). Prefers e-mail submission (copied into message).

Kill fee. Some sidebars. Prefers RSV & others. No guidelines; catalog. (Ads)

Tips: "We are most interested in articles relating to issues of human life and the family."

*JEWEL AMONG JEWELS ADOPTION NEWS, PO Box 502065, Indianapolis IN 46256. Phone/fax (317)849-5651. Nondenominational. Sherrie Eldridge, ed. To celebrate God's sovereignty through the act of adoption, to educate about the realities of relinquishment and to empower all those touched by adoption to enter into a relationship with Jesus Christ and become a jewel among jewels. Quarterly newsletter; 8 pgs; circ. 1,500. Subscription free in US. 75% unsolicited freelance; 25% assigned. Complete ms/cover letter; fax/e-query OK. **NO PAYMENT**. Articles 750 wds. Responds in 2 wks. Seasonal 3 mos ahead. Accepts simultaneous submissions & reprints. Prefers disk or e-mail submission (attached file). Regular sidebars. Prefers NIV. Guidelines/theme list (also on Website); copy for 1 stamp. (No ads)

Poetry: Free verse, traditional. Submit any number.

Fillers: Accepts 10/yr. Anecdotes, cartoons, facts, ideas, newsbreaks, prose, quizzes, prayers, quotes, short humor, word puzzles; 100-150 wds.

Columns/Departments: Common Threads, Passages of Adoption, The Great Awakening, Trigger Points, Reframing the Loss, The Blessings of Adoption; all 250 wds. See guidelines for descriptions.

Special Needs: Adoptive parenting, adoption, grief & loss, identity in Christ, bonding & attachment perspectives, 12-step writing about adoption, how to find therapist who understands adoption issues, adoption and mental health professionals.

Tips: "Tell how you have been touched by adoption and how God has worked in and through your experience. Birth mother stories are most sought after."

JOHN MILTON MAGAZINE, 475 Riverside Dr., Rm. 455, New York NY 10115. (212)870-3335. Fax (212)870-3229. E-mail: order@jmsblind.org. Website: www.jmsblind.org. John Milton Society for the Blind/nonsectarian. Darcy Quigley, exec dir. Reprints material from over 60 religious periodicals in a large-type digest for the visually impaired. Quarterly tabloid; 24 pgs; circ 5,000. Free to visually impaired. 1% freelance. Complete ms/cover letter; fax query OK. **NO PAYMENT** for reprint rts. Not copyrighted. Articles 750-1,500 (1/yr); fiction 750-1,500 (1/yr). Responds in 6 wks. Seasonal 9-12 mos ahead. Accepts simultaneous submissions & reprints (tell when/where appeared). Accepts disk. No sidebars. Any version. Guidelines (also on Website); copy for 9x12 SAE/3 stamps. (No ads)

Poetry: Accepts 4/yr. Any type; 5-30 lines. Submit max 3 poems. Seasonal/holiday.

Fillers: Accepts 1/yr. Anecdotes, cartoons, facts, games, prayers, prose, quotes, short humor; 10-150 wds.

Tips: "Most open to poems, prayers and personal inspirational pieces about more timeless themes: Christian holidays, overcoming challenges like visual impairment, love, forgiveness, etc. If writing about blindness, don't be patronizing. Send complete manuscripts requiring little or no editing. Look at the magazines we typically reprint from (see guidelines)."

$JOURNAL OF CHRISTIAN NURSING, PO Box 1650, Downers Grove IL 60515-1650. (630)734-4030. Fax (630)734-4200. E-mail: jcn@ivpress.com. Website: www.ncf-jcn.org. Nurses Christian Fellowship of InterVarsity Christian Fellowship. Melodee Yohe, mng ed. Personal, professional, practical articles to help nurses view nursing through the eyes of faith. Quarterly mag; 48 pgs; circ 9,000. Subscription $19.95. 25% unsolicited freelance; 10% assigned. Query or complete ms/cover letter; phone/fax/e-query OK. Pays $25-80 on publication for all (rarely), one-time or reprint rts (few). Not copyrighted. Articles 6-12 pgs (20/yr). Responds in 4-6 wks. Seasonal 1 yr ahead. Accepts some reprints (tell when/where appeared). Accepts disk. Kill fee 50%. Regular sidebars. Prefers NRSV. Guidelines/theme list (also on Website); copy $4.50/9x12 SAE/6 stamps. (Ads)

Columns/Departments: Pulse Beats (this and that).

Special Needs: Healing prayer, missions/cross-cultural nursing, standards in nursing/advanced practice, and feeding our faith.

Contests: Sponsors an occasional contest. None planned for now.

Tips: "All topics must relate to Christian nurses, or contain illustrations using nurses. Freelancers can interview and write about Christian nurses involved in creative ministry (include pictures)."

**1999 & 1995 EPA Award of Merit—Christian Ministries.

JOURNAL OF CHURCH AND STATE, Baylor University, PO Box 97308, Waco TX 76798-7308. (254)710-1510. Fax (254)710-1571. E-mail: Derek_Davis @Baylor.edu. Website: www.baylor.edu/~church_state. Baylor University/Interdenominational. Dr. Derek H. Davis, dir. Provides a forum for the critical examination of the interaction of religion and government worldwide. Quarterly journal; 225 pgs; circ 1,700. Subscription $20. 75% unsolicited freelance; 25% assigned. Complete ms (3 copies)/cover letter; phone/fax query OK; no e-query. **NO PAYMENT** for all rights. Articles 25-30 pgs/footnotes (24/yr). Responds in 2-4 mos. Prefers disk, no e-mail submission. No sidebars. Prefers KJV. Guidelines (also by e-mail); copy $8 + $1.50 postage. (Ads)

Special Needs: Church-state issues.

Tips: "Most open to articles. Send three copies of manuscript and cover letter. Follow writer's guidelines."

+JOYFULL NOISE, PO Box 60, Sartell MN 56377. E-mail: editor@joyfullnoise. com. Website: www.joyfullnoise.com. Paul Dunham, ed-in-chief. For families with 4 or more children. Magazine. Open to freelance. Query first. **NO PAYMENT/3 COPIES.** Articles 850-3,000 wds. Responds in 4-6 wks. Accepts simultaneous submissions. Incomplete topical listings.

Columns/Departments: Finding the Floor (household organization); Seen and Herd (humor); Kitchen Clamor (recipes); Downshift (family time together); Stealing Away (strengthening marital relations); Noisemakers' Page (kid's page).

Special Needs: To celebrate and encourage large families by offering practical solutions and stories drawn from real-life adventures of other large families; practical topics. Cooking for a small army, traveling with lots of children, household organization, home education, home improvement projects, etc.

Tips: They do spell Joyfull with two Ls.

$*JOYFUL NOISE, 4259 Elkcam Blvd. SE, St. Petersburg FL 33705-4216. Nondenominational. William W. Maxwell, ed. Deals with African-American life and religious culture. Bimonthly mag. Complete ms/cover letter or query/clips. Pays $50-250 on acceptance for 1st rts. Articles 700-3,000 wds. Guidelines.

+KAIROS JOURNAL, PO Box 450, Clarence NY 14031. (716)759-1058. Fax (716)759-0731. E-mail: kairos@eagleswings.to. Website: www.eagleswings. to. Eagles'Wings. David Trementozzi, ed. Proclaims timely and relevant words and themes for the church today. Quarterly mag; circ 10,000. Subscription $12.95. Accepts freelance. Query or complete ms. Not in topical listings. Did not return questionnaire. (Ads)

THE KARITOS REVIEW, 35689 N. Helendale Rd., Ingleside IL 60041. (847)587-9111. E-mail: robuserid@prodigy.net. Website: www.karitos. com. Karitos Christian Arts Festival (Chicago). Gina Merritt (fiction) and Karen Beattie (nonfiction), eds. Distributed by the Karitos Christian Arts Festival in June; gives precedence to writers planning to attend the festival, but will look at anyone's work. Annual journal; 40 pgs; circ. varies. Subscription $3/copy, plus postage. Estab. 1999. 50% unsolicited freelance; 50% assigned. Complete ms; phone/e-query OK. **PAYS IN COPIES** for one-time & reprint rts. Articles to 1,500 wds (2/yr); fiction to 2,500 wds (4/yr). Responds in June. Accepts simultaneous submissions & reprints (tell when/where appeared). No sidebars. Any version. Guidelines: Send two copies of your submission with SASE. Copy $2/6x9 SAE/4 stamps. (No ads)

Poetry: Accepts 10/yr. Any type; to 2 pgs. Submit max 2 poems. "Don't decorate your poetry."

Special Needs: "Theme for 2001 is '2001-A Praise Odyssey.' Fiction can be any type as long as it's high quality. No romance; romance can be an element but we don't want anything that's mainly romance. I'm looking for more realistic, contemporary fiction."

Tips: "The work must have some literary merit. It doesn't necessarily have to be on the theme, and it doesn't necessarily have to be religious. We are looking for quality material written from a Christian world-view. We have a strong multicultural commitment and would like to encourage more submissions by minority authors."

KEYS TO LIVING, PO Box 154, Washingtonville PA 17884. (717)437-2891. E-mail: owcam@sunlink.net. Connie Mertz, ed/pub. Educates and encourages readers through inspirational writings while presenting an appreciation for God's natural world. Quarterly newsletter; 10 pgs; circ 200. Subscription $7. 20% freelance. Complete ms/cover letter; no phone query. **PAYS 2 COPIES** for one-time or reprint rts. Articles 350-500 wds. Responds in 4 wks. Seasonal 2-4 mos ahead. Accepts reprints. No disk; e-mail submission OK (copied into message). Prefers NIV. Guidelines/theme list; copy for 7x10 SAE/2 stamps. (No ads)

Fillers: Games, quizzes, nature, Bible activities for children; to 100 wds.

Tips: "We need devotional material on themes only. Send for theme list, which is included with writer's guidelines. We are a ministry—not publishing for profit."

+LEAVES, PO Box 87, Dearborn MI 48121-0087. (313)561-2330. Fax (313) 561-9486. E-mail: leaves-mag@juno.com. Website: www.rc.net/detroit/marianhill/leaves.htm. Catholic/Marianhill Mission Society. Jacquelyn M. Lindsey, ed. For all Catholics, it promotes devotion to God and His saints and publishes readers' spiritual experiences, petitions, and thanksgivings. Bimonthly mag; 24 pgs; circ 75,000. Subscription free. 50% unsolicited freelance. Complete ms/cover letter; phone/fax/e-query OK. **NO PAYMENT** for 1st or reprint rts. Not copyrighted. Articles 500 wds (6-12/yr). Responds in 4 wks. Seasonal 4 mos ahead. Accepts reprints. Accepts e-mail submissions (copied into message). No sidebars. Prefers NAB or RSV (Catholic edition). No guidelines or copy. (No ads)

Poetry: Accepts 6-12/yr. Traditional; 8-20 lines. Submit max 4 poems.

Special Needs: Testimonies of conversion or reversion to Catholicism.

Tips: "Besides being interestingly and attractively written, an article should be confidently and reverently grounded in traditional orthodox Catholic doctrine and spirituality. The purpose of our magazine is to edify our readers."

$#THE LEGIONS OF LIGHT, Box 874, Margaretville NY 12455. Phone/fax (914)586-2759. E-mail: dancing_hawk@yahoo.com. Website: www.stepahead.net/~lol/legions.htm. Art By Beth. Elizabeth Mami, ed. A literary magazine for readers of all ages. Bimonthly mag; length varies; circ 2,000. Subscription $15. 100% unsolicited freelance. Query or complete ms/cover letter; phone/e-query OK. Pays $5-10 on publication for one-time rts. Not copyrighted. Articles 500-1,500 wds (10-20/yr); fiction 1,500 wds (20-30/yr). Responds in 6 wks. Seasonal 6 mos ahead. Accepts simultaneous submissions & reprints (tell when/where appeared). Prefers e-mail submission (copied into message). Some sidebars. Guidelines (also by e-mail/Website); copy $3.

Poetry: Buys 15-30/yr. All types; any length. Pays $5-10.

Fillers: Buys 5-10/yr. Anecdotes, cartoons, facts, ideas, jokes, newsbreaks, prayers, prose, quotes, short humor. Pays $5-10.

Tips: "We are especially open to unpublished writers, particularly children. Be open and honest in your writing. We accept about 90% of submissions."

$*LIBERTY, Religious Liberty Dept., 12501 Old Columbia Pike, Silver Springs MD 20904. Fax (301)680-6695. Seventh-Day Adventist. Clifford R. Goldstein, ed. Deals with religious liberty issues for government officials, civic leaders, and laymen. Bimonthly mag; 32 pgs; circ 250,000. 90% freelance. Query; phone/fax/e-query OK. Pays .06-.08/wd on acceptance for 1st rts. Articles & essays to 2,500 wds. Responds in 4 wks. Requires disk. Guidelines.

$LIFE@WORK JOURNAL, PO Box 1928, Fayetteville AR 72702. (501)444-0664. Fax (501)443-4125. E-mail: scaldwell@lifeatwork.com. Website: www.lifeatwork.com. Submissions to: submissions@lifeatwork.com. The Life@Work Co. Stephen Caldwell, exec. ed. Features Christian professionals addressing such issues as faith in the workplace, skill development, and implementing biblical values at work. Bimonthly journal; circ 20,000. Subscription $14.95. 2% unsolicited freelance; 56% assigned. Query/clips; no phone query; e-query OK. Pays .30/wd on acceptance for all rts. Articles 200-3,000 wds. Responds in 4 wks. Regular sidebars. Prefers NIV. Guidelines (also by e-mail/Website). (Ads)

> **Fillers:** Buys some. Anecdotes, cartoons, facts, quotes, short humor, to 200 wds. Pays $25.50.
>
> **Special Needs:** Book reviews, think pieces, commentaries, news features, and profiles of leaders and companies that successfully apply biblical wisdom for business excellence. Also business-related fiction.
>
> **Tips:** "Help business leaders link their faith and their work. Be precise with the idea, especially if it relates to the theme. We especially need articles from or about successful Christian women."
>
> **1999 EPA Award of Excellence—General.

#LIFE GATE, 2017 Colorado Ave., Portsmouth VA 23701-2917. E-mail: Lifegate @richmond.hofi.net. By His Design, Inc. Submit to The Editor. Positive news for Protestant Christians. Monthly tabloid; circ. 23,000. 40% freelance. Query; fax/e-query OK. **NO PAYMENT.** Articles 250-500 wds (12/yr); book/music reviews 350 wds. Seasonal 4 mos ahead. Accepts simultaneous submissions & reprints. Prefers disk. Prefers NIV. Copy $1.50.

> **Poetry:** Accepts 8-10/yr. Avant-garde, free verse, light verse, traditional; 100-500 wds. Submit max 5 poems.
>
> **Fillers:** Anecdotes, facts.

$LIFEGLOW, Box 6097, Lincoln NE 68506. (402)448-0981. Fax (402)488-7582. E-mail: crsnet@compuserve.net. Website: www.crs.org. Christian Record Services. Gaylena Gibson, ed. For sight-impaired adults over 25; interdenominational Christian audience; inspirational/devotional articles. Quarterly mag; 65-70 pgs (lg. print); circ 30,000. Free to sight-impaired. 95% freelance. Complete ms; no phone/e-query. Pays .04-.05/wd on acceptance for one-time rts. Articles & true stories 750-1,400 wds. Responds in 12 wks. Seasonal anytime. Accepts simultaneous submissions & reprints. Accepts disk. No sidebars. Guidelines; copy for 7x10 SAE/5 stamps.

> **Special Needs:** Handicapped experiences. Overstocked on relationships.
>
> **Tips:** "Remember the readers are sight impaired or physically handicapped. Would the topics be relevant to them? Follow guidelines and write quality work."

$LIFEWISE, 8605 Explorer Dr., Colorado Springs CO 80920. (719)548-5885. Fax (719)531-3499. E-mail: lifewise@macmail.fotf.org. Website: www. family.org or www.lifewise.com. Focus on the Family. Bonnie Shepherd, ed. Encourages and empowers Christians 50 and older, and helps them grow in faith, serve their families and communities, and make an impact on their world. Estab. 1999. Bimonthly mag; 48 pgs; circ 70,000. Subscription $16.50. 20% unsolicited freelance; 30% assigned. Query or complete ms/cover letter; fax/e-query OK. Pays $75-400 or .12-.175/wd on acceptance for 1st rts. Articles 400-1,200 wds; book reviews 400 wds, $75-100. Responds in 4-6 wks. Seasonal 9 mos ahead. Accepts e-mail submissions (attached file). Some sidebars. Prefers NIV. Guidelines; copy for 9x12 SAE/5 stamps. (Ads)

> **Fillers:** Cartoons, $50.

> **Tips:** "Submit a thought-provoking, well-written article."

LIGHT, 901 Commerce St., Ste. 550, Nashville TN 37203. (615)244-2495. Fax (615)242-0065. E-mail: kdhastings@erlc.com. Website: www.erlc.com. Ethics & Religious Liberty Commission; Southern Baptist. Dwayne Hastings, ed. To equip and encourage evangelical Christians to address the moral, ethical, and public policy issues of our day using scriptural precepts. Bimonthly mag; circ 91,000. Subscription for donation. Accepts freelance. Prefers query. Not in topical listings. (No ads)

$LIGHT AND LIFE, Box 535002, Indianapolis IN 46253-5002. (317)244-3660. Fax (317)248-9055. E-mail: LLMEditor@fmcna.org. Free Methodist Church of North America. Doug Newton, ed. Christian growth, ministry to saved and unsaved, denominational news; thought-provoking Wesleyan-Arminian perspective. Bimonthly mag; 72 pgs; circ 21,000. Subscription $16. 40% freelance. Query; fax/e-query OK. Pays .04-.05/wd on publication for 1st or one-time rts. Articles 500-600 or 800-1,800 wds (30/yr). Responds in 6-8 wks. Seasonal 8 mos ahead. Accepts simultaneous submissions. Prefers disk or e-mail submission (attached file) after acceptance. Kill fee 50%. Some sidebars. Prefers NIV. Guidelines; copy $4. (Ads)

> **Poetry:** Buys 2-3/yr. Uses as sidebars to articles.

> **Fillers:** Cartoons.

> **Tips:** "Best to write a query letter. We are emphasizing contemporary issues articles, well researched. Ask the question, 'What topics are not receiving adequate coverage in the church and Christian periodicals?'"
> **1999 EPA Award of Excellence—Denominational; 1998 EPA Award of Merit—Denominational.

$*LIGHTHOUSE STORY COLLECTION (formerly Lighthouse Fiction Collection), PO Box 43114, Watauga TX 76148-0114. Joyce Parchman and Doris Best, eds. Timeless fiction for the whole family. Quarterly mag; 56 pgs; circ 300. Subscription $7.95 for 6/$14.95 for 12. 100% freelance. Complete ms/cover letter. Pays $5-50 on publication for 1st or one-time rts. Fiction for all ages 250-5,000 wds (40-50/yr). Responds in 6-18 wks. Seasonal anytime. Guidelines; copy $3.

> **Poetry:** Buys 12-20/yr. Free-verse, light verse, traditional; 6-80 lines; $1-5. Submit max 5 poems.

> **Tips:** "Read and follow guidelines. Basic need is for good stories and poems—well-written, interesting, new plot."

$LIGUORIAN, One Liguori Dr., Liguori MO 63057-9999. (800)464-2555 or 636-464-2500. Fax (800)325-9526. E-mail: aweinert@liguori.org. Website: www.liguori.org. Catholic/Liguori Publications. Allan Weinert, CSSR, ed-in-chief. To help readers lead a fuller Christian life through the sharing of experiences, scriptural knowledge, and a better understanding of the church. Monthly (10X) mag; 40 pgs; circ 227,000. Subscription $20. 20-30% unsolicited freelance; 70-80% assigned. Query/clips; phone/fax/e-query OK. Pays $150-225 (.13-.15/wd) on acceptance for all & electronic rts. Articles to 1,700 wds (30-50/yr); fiction to 1,700 wds (10/yr); book reviews 250 wds. Responds in 8 wks. Seasonal by July 15th. Prefers disk or e-mail submission (attached or copied into message). Kill fee 50%. Regular sidebars. Prefers NAS (St. Joseph edition). Guidelines (also by e-mail/Website); copy for 9x12 SAE/3 stamps. (Ads)

Fillers: Buys 100/yr. Anecdotes, jokes, prayers, quizzes, quotes, short humor, word puzzles; 250-500 wds; $50-100.

Tips: "Most open to fiction and personal testimony. Polish your own manuscript."

$LIVE, 1445 Boonville Ave., Springfield MO 65802-1894. (417)862-2781. Fax (417)862-6059. E-mail: rl-live@gph.org. Website: www.radiantlife.org. Assemblies of God/Gospel Publishing House. Paul W. Smith, adult ed. Inspiration and encouragement for adults. Weekly take-home paper; 8 pgs; circ 115,000. Subscription $9.60. 100% unsolicited freelance. Complete ms/cover letter; no phone/fax query. Pays .10/wd (.07/wd for reprints) on acceptance for 1st, one-time, simultaneous or reprint rts. Articles 500-1,500 wds (80-90/yr); fiction 500-1,500 wds (20/yr). Responds in 4-6 wks. Seasonal 12-18 mos ahead. Accepts simultaneous submissions & reprints (tell when/where appeared). Accepts e-mail submissions (copied into message). Few sidebars. Prefers NIV or KJV. Guidelines (also by e-mail/Website); copy for #10 SAE/1 stamp. (No ads)

Poetry: Buys 15/yr. Any type; 12-25 lines; pays $60 ($35 for reprints) when scheduled. Submit max 3 poems.

Fillers: Buys 6-8/yr. Anecdotes, prose; 200-700 wds; pays .10/wd (.07/wd for reprints).

Tips: "We are already scheduled into the first quarter of 2003. Follow our guidelines. Most open to well-written personal experience with biblical application. Send no more than two articles in the same envelope and send an SASE. We always need holiday articles, other than Christmas."

**This periodical was #13 on the 2000 Top 50 Christian Publishers list (#24 in 1999, #23 in 1998, #31 in 1997, #26 in 1996, #16 in 1995, #20 in 1994).

$LIVING, 13241 Port Republic Rd., Grottoes VA 24441. (540)249-3900. Fax (540)249-3177. E-mail: Tgether@aol.com. Website: www.churchoutreach.com. Shalom Foundation, Inc. Melodie Davis, ed. A positive, practical and uplifting publication for the whole family; mass distribution. Quarterly tabloid; 32 pgs; circ 40,000. Subscription free. 95% unsolicited freelance. Query or complete ms/cover letter; e-query OK. Pays $35-50 on publication for one-time rts. Articles 500-1,000 wds (40-50/yr); fiction (4/yr). Responds in 12-16 wks. Seasonal 4 mos ahead. Accepts simultaneous submissions & reprints (tell when/where appeared). Accepts disk or e-mail submission (copied into message). Some sidebars. Prefers NIV. Guidelines/theme list (also by e-mail); copy for 9x12 SAE/4 stamps. (Ads)

Fillers: Buys 4-8/yr. Anecdotes, short humor; 100-200 wds; $20-25.

Tips: "We are directed toward the general public, many of whom have no Christian interests, and we're trying to publish high-quality writing on family issues/concerns from a Christian perspective. That means religious language must be low key. Too much of what we receive is directed toward a Christian reader. We use fiction for adults or children, 6-14 (has to be emotionally moving/involving). We get far more than we can use, so something really has to stand out. Please carefully consider before sending."

**This periodical was #56 on the 2000 Top 50 Christian Publishers list.

$THE LIVING CHURCH, PO Box 514036, Milwaukee WI 53203-3436. (414)276-5420. Fax (414)276-7483. E-mail: tlc@livingchurch.org. Website: www.livingchurch.org. Episcopal/The Living Church Foundation, Inc. John Schuessler, mng ed. Independent news coverage of the Episcopal Church for clergy and lay leaders. Weekly mag; 24+ pgs; circ 9,000. Subscription $39.50. 85% unsolicited freelance; 15% assigned. Query; phone/fax/e-query OK. Pays $25-100 (for solicited articles, nothing for unsolicited) for one-time rts. Articles 1,000 wds (10/yr). Responds in 2-4 wks. Seasonal 2 mos ahead. Prefers disk or e-mail submission (attached or copied into message). Some sidebars. Guidelines (by e-mail); free copy. (Ads)

Poetry: Accepts 5-10/yr. Light verse, traditional; 4-15 lines. Submit max 3 poems.

Columns/Departments: Accepts 5/yr. Benediction (devotional/inspirational), 200 wds. Complete ms. No payment.

Tips: "Most open to features, as long as they have something to do with the Episcopal Church."

$LIVING LIGHT NEWS, #200, 5306-89 St., Edmonton AB T6E 5P9 Canada. (780)468-6397. Fax (780)468-6872. E-mail: shine@livinglightnews.org. Website: www.livinglightnews.org. Living Light Ministries. Jeff Caporale, ed. To motivate and encourage Christians; witnessing tool to the lost. Bimonthly (7X) tabloid; 40 pgs; circ 20,000. Subscription $19.95 US. 40% unsolicited freelance; 60% assigned. Query; fax/e-query OK. Pays $20-125 (.05-.10/wd) on publication for all, 1st, one-time, simultaneous or reprint rts. Articles 350-700 wds (75/yr); fiction 500-1,200 wds (3/yr for Christmas only). Responds in 4 wks. Seasonal 3-4 mos ahead. Accepts simultaneous submissions & reprints (tell when/where appeared). Accepts disk or e-mail submissions (attached file in rich text format). Regular sidebars. Prefers NIV. Guidelines/theme list (also by e-mail/Website); copy for 9x12 SAE/$2.50 CAN postage or IRCs. (Ads)

Fillers: Newsbreaks, short humor; 200-400 wds. Pays $10-30.

Columns/Departments: Buys 20/yr., 450-600 wds, $10-30. Parenting; Relationships. Query.

Special Needs: Celebrity interviews/testimonials of well-known personalities; interesting fiction and nonfiction stories related to Christmas; unique ministries.

Tips: "Most open to a timely article about someone who is well known in North America, say in sports, entertainment, or politics. They may or may not be Christian, but the article focuses on a Christian perspective."

**2000 & 1998 EPA Award of Merit—Newspaper.

+**LIVING RELIGION E-ZINE**, 1506 Pennylane SE, Decatur AL 35601. E-mail: submissions@christianpublisher.com. Website: www.christianpublisher. com/LivingReligion.html. Submit to The Editor. Goal is to bring exposure to writers and share information and entertainment. E-zine. Subscription free. Complete ms. **NO PAYMENT** for use in the e-zine, but published pieces will eventually be included in an eBook collection, and royalties will be paid to all contributors at that time. Submitting material grants publisher full electronic rights for as long as piece appears online (then rights revert to author unless contract is issued for inclusion in an eBook). Articles; fiction; commentaries. Requires submissions by e-mail (attached file), disk, or CD-ROM. Guidelines on Website. Incomplete topical listings.

    Poetry: Accepts.

    Tips: "All our agreements are done online."

$**LIVING WITH TEENAGERS**, 127 Ninth Ave. N, Nashville TN 37234-0140. (615)251-2229. Fax (615)251-5008. E-mail: lwt@bssb.com. Website: www.lifeway.com, or www.bssb.com. LifeWay Press. No freelance at this time.

$**THE LOOKOUT**, 8121 Hamilton Ave., Cincinnati OH 45231-9981. (513)931-4050. Fax (513)931-0950. E-mail: lookout@standardpub.com. Website: www.standardpub.com. Standard Publishing. David Faust, ed; Patricia McCarty, asst ed. For adults in Sunday school who are interested in learning more about applying the gospel to their lives. Weekly take-home paper; 16 pgs; circ 102,000. Subscription $21. 40-50% freelance. Pays .05-.15/wd on acceptance for 1st, one-time, simultaneous or reprint rts. Articles 400-1,800 wds or 400-700 wds (50/yr). Responds in 18 wks. Seasonal 6 mos ahead. Accepts simultaneous submissions & reprints (tell when/where appeared). Accepts disk, no e-mail submission. Kill fee 33%. Regular sidebars. Prefers NIV. Guidelines/theme list; copy for .75. (No ads)

    Fillers: Cartoons, $50.

    Columns/Departments: Buys 24/yr. The Outlook (personal opinion), 500-900 wds; Salt & Light (innovative ways to reach out into the community), 500-900 wds. Pays .05-.07/wd.

    Tips: "Get a copy of our theme list and query (by letter) about a theme-related article at least six months in advance to see if issue is filled. Columns best way to break in. Send samples of published material."

    **This periodical was #39 on the 2000 Top 50 Christian Publishers list (#32 in 1999, #37 in 1998, #40 in 1997, #1 in 1996, #3 in 1993 & 1995). 1999 & 1998 EPA Award of Excellence—Sunday School Take-Home.

$THE LUTHERAN, 8765 W. Higgins Rd., Chicago IL 60631-4183. (773)380-2540. Fax (773)380-2751. E-mail: lutheran@elca.org. Website: www.the lutheran.org. Evangelical Lutheran Church in America. David L. Miller, ed. Addresses broad constituency of the church. Monthly & online mag; 68 pgs; circ 620,000. 15% freelance. Query/clips; fax/e-query OK. Pays $400-700 (assigned), $100-500 (unsolicited) on acceptance for 1st rts. Articles 400-1,500 wds (40/yr). Responds in 6 wks. Seasonal 4 mos ahead. Accepts reprints. Disk or e-mail submission OK. Kill fee 50%. Guidelines/theme list; free copy.

> **Fillers:** Julie Sevig, ed. Buys 50/yr. Cartoons, jokes, short humor. Uses only true anecdotes from ELCA congregations; 25-100 wds; $10.
>
> **Tips:** "Most open to feature articles."
>
> **This periodical was #7 on the 2000 Top 50 Christian Publishers list (#5 in 1999, #2 in 1998, #12 in 1997, #31 in 1996, #7 in 1995, #9 in 1994).

$THE LUTHERAN DIGEST, Box 4250, Hopkins MN 55343. (612)933-2820. Fax (612)933-5708. E-mail: lutherandigest@inetmail.att.net. Website: www.lutherandigest.com. Lutheran. David L. Tank, ed. Blend of secular and light theological material used to win non-believers to the Lutheran faith. Quarterly mag 64-72 pgs; circ 115,000. Subscription $14. 100% unsolicited freelance. Query/clips or complete ms/cover letter; no phone/fax query. Pays $25-50 on acceptance for one-time rts. Articles to 1,000 wds (25-30/yr). Responds in 4-9 wks. Seasonal 6-9 mos ahead. Accepts reprints (70% is reprints). No disk. Some sidebars. Guidelines; copy $3/6x9 SAE/3 stamps. (Ads)

> **Poetry:** Accepts 45-50/yr. Light verse, traditional; any length; no payment. Submit max 3 poems.
>
> **Fillers:** Anecdotes, cartoons, facts, jokes, short humor; to 100 wds; no payment.
>
> **Tips:** "Compose well-written, short pieces that would be of interest to middle-age and senior Christians—and also acceptable to Lutheran church pastors. To catch our attention, the topic has to be catchy and the writing good. (The word *hope* is frequently associated with our publication.)"
>
> **This periodical was #50 on the 1994 Top 50 Christian Publishers list.

$THE LUTHERAN JOURNAL, 7317 Cahill Rd., Ste. 201, Minneapolis MN 55439-2081. (952)562-1234. Fax (952)941-3010. Macalester Park Publishing. Rev. Armin Deye, ed; submit to Jessica Person, ed asst. Family magazine for church members, middle-aged and older. Triannual mag; 32 pgs; circ 130,000. Subscription $6. 60% freelance. Complete ms/cover letter; fax query OK. Pays about .01-.04/wd on publication for one-time rts only. Articles 400-1,500 wds (25-30/yr); book reviews, 150 wds, $5. Responds in 4 mos. Seasonal 4-5 mos ahead. Accepts simultaneous submissions & reprints. Regular sidebars. Prefers NIV, NAS or KJV. Accepts disk. Guidelines; copy for 9x12 SAE/3 stamps. (Ads)

> **Poetry:** Buys 6-9/yr. Free verse, haiku, light verse, traditional; to 2 pgs. Pays $5-30. Submit max 5 poems.

Fillers: Buys 5/yr. Anecdotes, cartoons, facts, games, prose, quizzes, quotes, short humor; to 100 wds; $5-30.

Columns/Departments: Buys 40/yr. Apron Strings (short recipes); About Books (reviews), 50-150 wds. Pays $5-25.

Tips: "Most open to Lutheran lifestyles or Lutherans in action."

$LUTHERAN WITNESS, 1333 S. Kirkwood Rd., St. Louis MO 63122-7295. (314)965-9000. Fax (314)996-1126. E-mail: david.mahsman@lcms.org, or don.folkemer@lcms.org. Lutheran Church-Missouri Synod. Don Folkemer, mng ed. Denominational. Monthly mag; 36 pgs; circ 270,000. Subscription $18. 40% unsolicited freelance; 40% assigned. Complete ms/cover letter. Pays $100-350 on acceptance for all or 1st rts. Articles 500-1,500 wds (40/yr); fiction 500-1,500 wds (8/yr). Responds in 8 wks. Seasonal 6 mos ahead. Considers simultaneous submissions. Prefer disk or e-mail submission (attached file). Some sidebars. Prefers NIV. Free guidelines (also by e-mail)/copy for 9x12 SAE. (Ads)

**This periodical was #65 on the 2000 Top 50 Christian Publishers list (#21 in 1999).

$MARIAN HELPERS BULLETIN, Marian Helpers Center, Eden Hill, Stockbridge MA 01263. (413)298-3691. Fax (413)298-1320. E-mail: kane@marian.org. Website: www.marian.org. Catholic. Dave Kane, ed. Quarterly mag; circ 500,000. 20% freelance. Query/clips or complete ms/cover letter. Pays .10/wd on acceptance for all, 1st, or reprint rts. Articles 500-900 wds; book reviews. Responds in 3 wks. Seasonal 6 mos ahead. Accepts reprints. Kill fee 30%. Free guidelines/copy.

Tips: "Also needs articles on mercy in action or devotion to Blessed Virgin Mary."

MARKETPLACE, 12900 Preston Rd., Ste. 1215, Dallas TX 75230. (972)385-7657. Fax (972)385-7307. E-mail: mmimedia@marketplaceministries. com. Website: www.marketministries.com. Marketplace Ministries. Art Stricklin, ed. Focus is on working in the corporate workplace. Semi-annual mag; 12 pgs; circ 13,000. Subscription free. 10% assigned. Query or complete ms; e-query OK. **NO PAYMENT** for all rts. Articles. Prefers e-mail submission. No copy. Incomplete topical listings. (Ads)

Tips: "We are attempting to cut back on freelance and use only assigned stories."

$MARRIAGE PARTNERSHIP, 465 Gundersen Dr., Carol Stream IL 60188. (630)260-6200. Fax (630)260-0114. E-mail: mp@marriagepartnership. com. Website: www.marriagepartnership.com. Christianity Today Inc. Caryn D. Rivadeneira, mng ed. To promote and strengthen Christian marriages. Quarterly mag; 74 pgs; circ 55,000. Subscription $19.95. 5% unsolicited freelance; 95% assigned. Query only; fax/e-query OK. Pays .15-.30/wd on acceptance for 1st rts. Articles 800-2,000 wds. Responds in 8-10 wks. Seasonal 9 mos ahead. Prefers e-mail submissions (copied into message). Kill fee 50%. Regular sidebars. Prefers NIV. Guidelines (also on Website); copy $5/9x12 SAE. (Ads)

Columns/Departments: Work it Out (working out a marriage problem). Most open to this column; query with ideas. Pays $150.

$MATURE LIVING, 127 Ninth Ave. N., Nashville TN 37234-0140. (615)251-

2274. Fax (615)251-5008. E-mail: matureliving@lifeway.com. Website: www.lifeway.com. LifeWay Press/Southern Baptist. Judy Pregel, ed. Christian leisure reading for senior adults (50+) characterized by human interest and Christian warmth. Monthly mag; 52 pgs; circ 350,000. Subscription $17.95. 70% freelance. Complete ms. Pays .055/wd ($75 min.) on acceptance for all (preferred) or one-time rts. Articles 600-1,200 (100/yr); fiction 900-1,200 wds (12/yr). Responds in 3 mos. Seasonal 1 yr ahead. Serials. Some sidebars. Prefers KJV or NIV. Guidelines; copy for 9x12 SAE/4 stamps. (No ads)

Poetry: Buys 30/yr. Light verse, traditional; senior adult themes; any length; $13-25. Submit max 5 poems.

Fillers: Buys 120/yr. Anecdotes, facts, games, short humor; to 50 wds; $15.

Columns/Departments: Cracker Barrel (brief humor), $15; Grandparent's Brag Board, $15-25.

Tips: "Looking for crafts and Christian fiction."

**This periodical was #66 on the 2000 Top 50 Christian Publishers list (#43 in 1999, #52 in 1998, #53 in 1997).

$MATURE YEARS, Box 801, Nashville TN 37202. (615)749-6292. Fax (615)749-6512. E-mail: matureyears@umpublishing.org. United Methodist. Marvin W. Cropsey, ed. Inspiration, information, and leisure reading for persons of retirement age. Quarterly mag; 112 pgs; circ 70,000. Subscription $16. 60% unsolicited freelance; 40% assigned. Complete ms/cover letter; fax/e-query OK. Pays .05/wd on acceptance for one-time rts. Articles 900-2,000 wds (60/yr); fiction 1,200-2,000 wds (4/yr). Responds in 2 mos. Seasonal 14 mos ahead. Accepts reprints. Regular sidebars. Prefers NRSV or NIV. Guidelines (also by e-mail); copy $5. (No ads)

Poetry: Buys 24/yr. Free verse, haiku, light verse, traditional; 4-16 lines; pays $.50-$1/line. Submit max 6 poems.

Fillers: Buys 20/yr. Anecdotes (to 300 wds), cartoons, jokes, prayers, word puzzles (religious only); to 30 wds; $5-25.

Columns/Departments: Buys 20/yr. Health Hints, 900-1,200 wds; Modern Revelations (inspirational), 900-1,100 wds; Fragments of Life (true-life inspirational), 250-600 wds; Going Places (travel), 1,000-1,500 wds; Money Matters, 1,200-1,800 wds.

Special Needs: Articles on crafts and pets. Fiction on older adult situation.

**This periodical was #33 on the 2000 Top 50 Christian Publishers list (#56 in 1998, #63 in 1997, #56 in 1996, #65 in 1995, #51 in 1994).

$THE MENNONITE, Box 347, Newton KS 67114. (316)283-5100. Fax (316) 283-0454. E-mail: TheMennonite@gcmc.org. Website: www.mph.org/themennonite. General conference Mennonite Church. Gordon Houser, assoc ed (gordonh@gcmc.org). Practical articles on aspects of Christian living. Weekly mag; 16 pgs. Estab 1998. 75% unsolicited freelance; 25% assigned. Complete ms/cover letter; e-query OK. Pays .07/wd on publication for one-time rts. Articles 1,200-1,500 wds (10/yr). Responds in 1-2 wks. Seasonal 3 mos ahead. Accepts simultaneous submissions & reprints. Prefers e-mail submission (attached or copied into message). Kill fee 1%. Regular sidebars. Prefers NRSV. Guidelines (also by e-mail/Website); copy for 9x12 SAE/4 stamps. (Ads)

Poetry: Buys 10/yr. Avant-garde, free verse; $30-75. Submit max 3 poems.

Fillers: Buys 3/yr. Anecdotes, cartoons; 100-400 wds; $10-30.

Columns/Departments: Buys 8/yr. Speaking Out (opinion, usually related to issues in Mennonite church), 700 wds. Pays .07/wd to $50.

Tips: "Most of our writers are Mennonite. Our freelance material is primarily features. Tell a good story without moralizing. Let a person's actions speak for themselves."

$MENNONITE BRETHREN HERALD, 3-169 Riverton Ave., Winnipeg MB R2L 2E5 Canada. (204)669-6575. Fax (204)654-1865. E-mail: mbherald@mbconf.ca. Website: www.mbherald.com. Canadian Conference of Mennonite Brethren Churches. Susan Brandt, mng ed.; Jim Coggins, ed. (mbheraldjc@bcmb.org). Denominational; for information, communication and spiritual enrichment. Biweekly mag; 32 pgs; circ 16,000. Subscription $30. 75% unsolicited freelance; 25% assigned. Query or complete ms/cover letter; phone/e-query OK. Pays .07/wd on publication for 1st rts. Articles 1,200 wds (40/yr); fiction 1,000-2,000 wds (10/yr). Responds in 20 wks. Seasonal 5 mos ahead. Accepts reprints (tell when/where appeared). Prefers disk or e-mail submission. Regular sidebars. Prefers NIV. Guidelines/theme list; copy for 9x12 SAE/$1 Canadian postage. (Ads)

Poetry: Buys 15/yr. Avant-garde, free verse, traditional; any length; pays to $10.

Tips: "Most open to feature articles on relevant topics, but not with an American bias."

MENNONITE HISTORIAN, 600 Shaftesbury Blvd., Winnipeg MB R3P 0M4 Canada. (204)888-6781. Fax (204)831-5675. E-mail: aredekopp@mennonitehurch.ca. Website: www.mbnet.mb.ca/mhc. Conference of Mennonites in Canada. Alf Redekopp, dir. Gathers and shares historical material related to Mennonites; focus on North America, but also beyond. Quarterly newsletter; 8 pgs; circ. 2,600. Subscription $9. 60% freelance. Complete ms/cover letter; phone/fax query OK. **NO PAYMENT EXCEPT BY SPECIAL ARRANGEMENT** for 1st rts. Articles 250-1,000 wds (6/yr). Responds in 3 wks. Seasonal 3 mos ahead. Accepts simultaneous submissions & reprints (depending on where published). Prefers disk or e-mail submission (attached file). Guidelines (also by e-mail); copy $1/9x12 SAE. (Ads)

Tips: "Must be Mennonite related. Most open to lead articles. Write with your ideas. Also genealogical articles."

$MEN OF INTEGRITY, 465 Gundersen Dr., Carol Stream IL 60188. (630) 260-6200. Fax (630)260-0114. E-mail: pkmenmag@aol.com. Website: www.Promisekeepers.org (or AOL keyword: Men of Integrity). Christianity Today, Inc. Harry Genet, mng ed. Uses narrative to apply biblical truth to specific gritty issues men face. Bimonthly pocket-sized mag; 64 pgs;

circ 60,000. Subscription $19.95. Estab. 1998. Accepts freelance. Complete ms. Pays $50 ($75 for full-length interview, 300 wds) on acceptance for one-time and electronic rts. Articles 200 wds (15/yr). Responds in 3 wks. Accepts simultaneous submissions & reprints (tell when/where appeared). Accepts disk or e-mail submission (attached file or copied into message). No sidebars. Prefers NIV. Guidelines/theme list (also by e-mail); copy $4/#10 SAE. (No ads)

$MESSAGE, Review and Herald Pub. Assn., 55 W. Oak Ridge Dr., Hagerstown MD 21740. (301)791-7000. Fax (301)393-4099. E-mail: message@RHPA. org, or Desmond@rhpa.org. Website: www.Messagemagazine.org. Review & Herald/Seventh-Day Adventist. Dwain N. Esmond, assoc. ed. Blacks and other minorities who have an interest in current issues and are seeking a better lifestyle. Bimonthly mag; 32 pgs; circ 80,000. Subscription $12.95. Most articles assigned. Query or complete ms/cover letter; fax/e-query OK. Pays $50-300 ($50-75 for fiction) on acceptance for 1st rts. Articles 700-1,200 wds (50/yr); parables; fiction (6/yr) for children (ages 5-8), 500 wds. Responds in 6-10 wks. Seasonal 6 mos ahead. Prefers disk, no e-mail submission. Regular sidebars. Prefers NIV. Guidelines; copy for 9x12 SAE/2 stamps. (No ads)

> **Columns/Departments:** Buys 12/yr. Healthspan (health issues), 700 wds; MESSAGE Jr. (biblical stories or stories with clear-cut moral for ages 5-8), 500 wds. Pays $75-150.
>
> **Tips:** "As with any publication, writers should have a working knowledge of *Message*. They should have some knowledge of our style and our readers."
>
> **This periodical was #47 on the 1999 Top 50 Christian Publishers list (#24 in 1998, #18 in 1997, #28 in 1995). Also 1995 EPA Award of Merit—Missionary.

MESSAGE OF THE OPEN BIBLE, 2020 Bell Ave., Des Moines IA 50315-1096. (515)288-6761. Fax (515)288-2510. E-mail: message@openbible.org. Website: www.openbible.org. Open Bible Standard Churches. Andrea Johnson, ed. To inspire, inform and educate the Open Bible family. Bimonthly mag; 16 pgs; circ 4,100. Subscription $9.75. 3% unsolicited freelance; 3% assigned. Query or complete ms/cover letter; e-query OK. **PAYS 5 COPIES**. Not copyrighted. Articles 750 wds (2/yr). Responds in 4 wks. Seasonal 4 mos ahead. Accepts simultaneous submissions & reprints (tell when/where appeared). Accepts disk or e-mail submission. Regular sidebars. Prefers NIV. Guidelines/theme list; copy for 9x12 SAE/2 stamps. (No ads)

> **Fillers:** Accepts 6/yr. Cartoons, facts, quotes, short humor; 50 wds.
>
> **Tips:** "Most open to articles on stepping out in faith; inspiration or evangelistic pieces. A writer can best break in by giving us something valuable for an upcoming theme or something that would inspire or uplift the average church member, specifically as they relate to Open Bible."
>
> **1995 EPA Award of Merit—Denominational.**

$*MESSENGER, Box 18068, Covington KY 41018-0068. (606)283-6226. Fax (606)283-6226. Catholic. Diane Reder, news ed. Diocese paper of

Covington KY. Weekly (45X) newspaper; 24 pgs; circ 16,000. Subscription $18. 40% freelance. Query/clips. Pays $1.25/column inch on publication for 1st rts. Articles 500-800 wds. Responds in 1 wk. Seasonal 1 mo ahead. Accepts simultaneous submissions. Guidelines; free copy. (Ads)

$MESSENGER OF THE SACRED HEART, 661 Greenwood Ave., Toronto ON M4J 4B3 Canada. (416)466-1195. Catholic/Apostleship of Prayer. Rev. F.J. Power, S.J., ed. Help for daily living on a spiritual level. Monthly mag; 32 pgs; circ 13,000. Subscription $14. 20% freelance. Complete ms; no phone query. Pays .06/wd on acceptance for 1st rts. Articles 800-1,500 wds (30/yr); fiction 800-1,500 wds (12/yr). Responds in 5 wks. Seasonal 5 mos ahead. No disk. No sidebars. Guidelines; copy $1/9x12 SAE.

> **Tips:** "Most open to inspirational stories and articles."

$THE MESSENGER OF ST. ANTHONY, Via Orto Botanico 11, 35123 Padova, Italy (US address: Anthonian Assn., 101 St. Anthony Dr., Mt. Saint Francis IN 47146). (812)923-6356. Fax (812)923-3200. E-mail: m.conte@mess-s-antonio.it. Website: www.mess-s-antonio.it. Catholic/Provincia Padovana F.M.C. Edward D. Pruett, asst ed. For middle-age and older Catholics in English-speaking world; articles that address current issues. Monthly mag; 50 pgs; circ 25,000. Subscription $29 US. 35-40% unsolicited freelance; 20-25% assigned. Query (complete ms for fiction); phone/fax/e-query OK. Pays .08-.10/wd on publication for one-time rts. Articles 600-2,400 wds (40/yr); fiction 900-1,200 wds (11/yr); book reviews 600 wds, $60. Responds in 8-10 wks. Seasonal 3 mos ahead. Accepts simultaneous submissions. Prefers e-mail submission (attached file). Regular sidebars. Prefers NEB (Oxford Study Edition). Guidelines (also by e-mail); free copy. (No ads)

> **Fillers:** Buys 11/yr. Anecdotes, cartoons, facts, ideas, quotes; 600-800 wds. Pays $55.
>
> **Columns/Departments:** Buys 50-60/yr. Documentary (issues), 600-2,000 wds; Spirituality, 600-2,000 wds; Church Life, 600-2,000 wds; Saint Anthony (devotional), 600-1,400 wds; Living Today (family life), 600-1,400 wds. Pays $55-200. Complete ms.
>
> **Special Needs:** New feature: human rights.
>
> **Tips:** "Most open to particular general-interest stories; politics from a human rights perspective; Saint Anthony, and devotional articles/parishes named after Saint Anthony."

METHODIST HISTORY, PO Box 127, Madison NJ 07940. (973)408-3189. Fax (973)408-3909. E-mail: cyrigoyen@gcah.org. Website: www.gcah.org. United Methodist. Charles Yrigoyen Jr., ed. History of the United Methodism and Methodist/Wesleyan churches. Quarterly journal; 64 pgs; circ 800. Subscription $20. 100% unsolicited freelance. Query; phone/fax/e-query OK. **PAYS IN COPIES** for all rts. Historical articles to 5,000 wds (15/yr); book reviews 500 wds. Responds in 8 wks. Requires disk. No sidebars. Guidelines; copy $5. (Ads)

*METRO VOICE, 108 SE 3rd St., Lee's Summit MO 64063. (816)524-4522. Fax (816)525-4423. Non-denominational. Dwight & Anita Widaman, pubs; Melanie Miles, ed. To promote Christian business, ministries and organizations; provide thought-provoking commentary for edification of the body of Christ. Monthly newspaper; circ 35,000. Subscription $14. 50% freelance. Complete ms/cover letter; short phone query OK. **PAYS IN COPIES** or limited amount for well-researched pieces, for one-time or reprint rts. Not copyrighted. Articles to 1,200 wds (100/yr). Responds in 6 wks. Seasonal 6 mos ahead. Accepts reprints. Guidelines; copy for 9x12 SAE/$1 postage.

Fillers: Accepts 12/yr. Anecdotes, cartoons, ideas, newsbreaks, quotes, short humor; to 500 wds.

Tips: "We look for up-to-date information. Willing to work with new writers who want to learn."

$MICHIGAN CHRISTIAN ADVOCATE, 316 Springbrook Ave., Adrian MI 49221. (517)265-2075. Fax (517)263-7422. E-mail: MIAdvocate@aol.com. United Methodist. Rev. Ann Whiting, ed. For Michigan United Methodists. Biweekly tabloid; 16 pgs; circ 12,000. Subscription $12. 75% freelance. Complete ms/cover letter; fax query OK. Pays $30-50 on publication for one-time rts. Articles 400-550 wds; book/music/video reviews, 200 wds, $15. Responds in 4 wks. Seasonal 3 mos ahead. Accepts simultaneous submissions. Accepts disk. Regular sidebars. Prefers NRSV. Copy available. (Ads)

Fillers: Buys 30-35/yr. Cartoons, word puzzles. Pay varies.

Columns/Departments: Buys 20-26/yr. My Experience (true), 450-550 wds; In My Opinion (church topics), 400-500 wds. Pays $30.

Special Needs: Easter, My Experience columns, 350-450 wds.

Tips: "Always looking for touching true experience columns—be brief, not sappy. Always looking for good cartoonists—pay $25-50 depending on artist. Young cartoonists please apply."

$MINNESOTA CHRISTIAN CHRONICLE, 7317 Cahill Rd., #201, Minneapolis MN 55439. (952)562-1234. Fax (952)941-3010. E-mail: susan@ mcchronicle.com. Website: www.mcchronicle.com. Beard Communications. Doug Trouten, sr. ed.; Susan Detlefsen, asst. ed. Local news and features of interest to the Christian community. Biweekly newspaper; 28 pgs; circ 20,000. Subscription $19.95 (some free distribution). 5% unsolicited freelance; 5% assigned. Query; phone/fax/e-query OK. Accepts e-mail submissions (attached or copied into message). Pays $50-200 on publication for one-time rts. Articles 500-1,500 wds (25/yr). Responds in 13 wks. Seasonal 2 mos ahead. Accepts simultaneous query & reprints (tell when/where appeared). Regular sidebars. Guidelines; copy $2. (Ads)

Tips: "Not interested in anything without a Minnesota 'hook.' Tell us about people and ministries we're not aware of." Loves e-queries.

****1996 EPA Award of Merit—Newspaper. (1995 EPA Award of Excellence—Newspaper.)

$THE MIRACULOUS MEDAL, 475 E. Chelten Ave., Philadelphia PA 19144-5785. (215)848-1010. Fax (215)848-1010. Website: www.cmphila.org/camm. Catholic. Rev. William J. O'Brien C.M., ed. Fiction & poetry for Catholic adults, mostly women. Quarterly mag; 36 pgs; circ 340,000. 40% unsolicited freelance. Query by mail only. Pays .02/wd & up, on acceptance for 1st rts. Religious fiction 1,600-2,000 wds; some 1,000-1,200 wds

(6/yr). Responds in 3 mos. Seasonal anytime. Accepts simultaneous submissions. Guidelines; copy for 6x9 SAE/2 stamps. (No ads)

Poetry: Buys 6/yr. Free verse, traditional; to 20 lines; .50 & up/line. Send any number. "Must have religious theme, preferably about the Blessed Virgin Mary."

$*THE MONTANA CATHOLIC, PO Box 1729, Helena MT 59624-1729. (406)442-5820. Fax (406)442-5191. Catholic. Alex Lobdell, ed. News and features for the Catholic community of western Montana. Monthly tabloid; 20-24 pgs; circ 9,200. Subscription $12 (in state), $16 (out of state). 5% freelance. Complete ms/cover letter or query; e-query OK. Pays .05-.10/wd on acceptance for 1st, one-time, simultaneous or reprint rts. Articles 200-950 wds (5/yr). Responds in 5 wks. Seasonal 2 mos ahead. Accepts simultaneous submissions & reprints (tell when/where appeared). Accepts disk, no e-mail submission. Kill fee 25%. Regular sidebars. Prefers NAS or RSV. Guidelines; copy $2. (Ads)

Tips: "Our greatest need is for freelance writers who reside in western Montana, have an understanding of the Catholic Church, and are willing to take on news and feature writing assignments of local interest. Photographic ability helpful. On rare occasions we use feature articles by other freelancers, particularly when geared toward seasons and days of the liturgical year or our semi-annual special sections on religious vocations."

$MOODY MAGAZINE, 820 N. LaSalle Blvd., Chicago IL 60610. (312)329-2164. Fax (312)329-2149. E-mail: MoodyLtrs@aol.com. Website: www.moody.edu/MOODYMAG. Moody Bible Institute. Andrew Scheer, mng ed.; Elizabeth Cody Newenhuyse, sr. ed. To encourage and equip evangelical Christians to think and live biblically. Bimonthly mag; 84-96 pgs; circ 115,000. Subscription $24. 40% unsolicited freelance; 60% assigned. Query only; no phone/fax/e-query. Pays $210-500 (.15-.20/wd) on acceptance for 1st & non-exclusive electronic rts. Articles 1,200-2,200 wds (55/yr); fiction 1,200-2,000 wds (1-3/yr). Responds in 9 wks. Seasonal 9 mos ahead. Accepts reprints (tell when/where appeared). Kill fee 50%. Requires disk. Regular sidebars. Prefers NIV. Guidelines (also by e-mail); copy for 9x12 SASE/8 stamps. (Ads)

Columns/Departments: Buys 6/yr. Salvation testimonies—may be as-told-to, 800-900 wds; $150-225.

Special Needs: Seeking 1,200- to 1,400-word narratives relating a "breakthrough exeperience" in evangelism or apologetics by an ordinary Christian. For example, "How I finally saw my need to present the gospel to my brother-in-law, whom I never thought would be interested in spiritual things," or "How I was able to keep from arguing when I talked about what the Bible says with a co-worker who is an active member of a cult." Needs strong takeaway.

Tips: "We want feature articles from freelancers for the second (non-cover) section of each issue. We're always looking for tight, dynamic narratives chronicling one's process of spiritual growth in a specific area—and the difference it is making." Continues to look for a few 1,500-word parenting pieces.

**This periodical was #26 on the 2000 Top 50 Christian Publishers list (#25 in 1999, #12 in 1998, #13 in 1997, #9 in 1996, #4 in 1995 & 1994). 1999 EPA Award of Merit—General.

MOVIEGUIDE, 2510-G Los Posas Rd., #502, Camarillo CA 93010. (805)383-2000. Fax (805)383-4089. E-mail: office@movieguide.org. Website: movieguide.org. Good News Communications/Christian Film & TV Commission. Dr. Theodore Baehr, pub. Family guide to media entertainment from a biblical perspective. Biweekly mag; 23+ pgs.; circ 3,000. Subscription $40. 40% freelance. Query/clips. **NO PAYMENT** for all rts. Articles 1,200 wds (100/yr); book/music/video/movie reviews, 1,200 wds. Responds in 6 wks. Seasonal 6 mos ahead. Accepts disk. Regular sidebars. Guidelines/theme list; copy for SAE/4 stamps. (Ads)

   Fillers: Accepts 1,000/yr; all types; 20-50 wds.

   Columns/Departments: MovieGuide; TravelGuide; VideoGuide; CDGuide, etc.; 1,200 wds.

+**NASHVILLE CHRISTIAN BANNER**, 141 Spencer Creek Rd., Franklin TN 37069. (615)599-0989. Fax (615)599-0993. E-mail: WmLeeM3@aol.com. Website: www.Cbanner.cc.com. Banner Publications of Nashville. William Lee Matheny, ed. To report news relevant to Christians and supply special interest stories, articles, book/movie reviews from a Christian perspective. Monthly newspaper; 16-24 pgs; circ 20,000. Subscription $15. Estab. 1999. 10% unsolicited freelance; 90% assigned. Query/clips or complete ms; phone/fax/e-query OK. **NO PAYMENT.** Articles (15/yr). Responds in 2 wks. Seasonal 2 mos ahead. Accepts simultaneous submissions and reprints (tell when/where appeared). Requires disk or e-mail submissions (copied into message). Some sidebars. Guidelines (also by e-mail); copy $1. (Ads)

   Fillers: Short only. Anecdotes, cartoons, jokes, quotes, short humor.

   Columns/Departments: Accepts 12/yr. Gospel Feet (stories/reports on missionaries), 600 wds; Feature Articles (issues, ministries, informative), 1,200 wds.

   Tips: "Contact the editor or submit your manuscript."

$**NATIONAL CATHOLIC REPORTER**, 115 E. Armour Blvd., Kansas City MO 64111. (816)531-0538. Fax (816)968-2268. E-mail: ncr_editor@natcath. com. Website: www.natcath.com. Catholic. Thomas Fox, pub; Michael Farrell, ed. Independent. Weekly (44X) & online newspaper; 44-48 pgs; circ 48,000. Query/clips. Pays varying rates on publication. Articles any length. Responds in 9 wks. Accepts simultaneous submissions.

   Columns/Departments: Query with ideas for columns.

+**NCUBATOR.COM**, 111 Parkdale Cr., Kingsville ON N9Y 1Y9 Canada. (519) 733-9883. E-mail: editor@ncubator.com. Website: www.ncubator.com. Ncubator Internet Resources. Jody Smith, sr. mng. ed. To edify, build up, and teach Christians; fundamental with a touch of Charismatic. Online e-zine (4 times monthly); 700 pgs; 65,000 views/mo. Estab. 1997. 90% unsolicited freelance; 10% assigned. Query; e-query OK. **NO PAYMENT** for one-time rts. Not copyrighted. Articles 500-900 wds; fiction; reviews 400 wds. Responds in 1 wk. Seasonal 2 mos ahead. Some reprints (tell when/where appeared). Requires e-mail submissions (copied into message). Some sidebars. Guidelines on Website. (Ads)

Columns/Departments: Accepts 300-400/yr. See site for categories.
*NETWORK, PO Box 131165, Birmingham AL 35213-6165. (205)328-7112. Fax (205)250-0101. E-mail: nwnews@bellsouth.net. Interdenominational. Dolores Milazzo Hicks, ed/pub. To encourage and nurture dialog, understanding and unity in Jewish and Christian communities. Monthly tabloid; 12-16 pgs; circ 15,000. 50% freelance. **NO PAYMENT**. Not copyrighted. Accepts simultaneous submissions. Articles and news.
$NEW COVENANT, 200 Noll Plaza, Huntington IN 46750. (219)356-8400. Fax (219)356-8472. E-mail: newcov@osv.com. Website: www.osv.com. Catholic/Our Sunday Visitor. Mike Aquilina, ed. Serves readers interested in orthodox Catholic spirituality. Monthly mag; 36 pgs; circ 20,000. Subscription $18. 85% freelance. Query only; fax/e-query OK. Pays $100-200 on acceptance for 1st or one-time rts. Articles 1,000-1,200 wds (40/yr). Responds in 5 wks. Seasonal 5 mos ahead. Prefers disk. Guidelines; copy for 9x12 SAE/5 stamps. (Ads)

> **Tips:** "Most open to practical, useful approaches to deepening one's spiritual life and relationship with Christ. Be familiar with New Covenant's style so you can speak to our audience."
> **This periodical was #67 on the 1997 Top 50 Christian Publishers list (#33 in 1996, #48 in 1995, #46 in 1994).

$*THE NEW FREEMAN, One Bayard Dr., St. John NB E2L 3L5. (506)653-6806. Fax (506)653-6818. E-mail: tnf@nbnet.nb.ca. Roman Catholic Diocese of St. John. Bill Donovan, mng. ed. Weekly tabloid; 12 pgs; circ 7,000. Subscription $18.69 CAN, $30 US. 70% unsolicited freelance; 30% assigned. Query/clips; phone/fax/e-query OK. Pays variable rates on publication. Not copyrighted. Articles about 200 wds. Seasonal 2 mos ahead. Accepts simultaneous submissions & reprints (tell when/where appeared). Accepts disk or e-mail submissions (attached/.txt format or copied into message). Kill fee. Some sidebars. No guidelines/copy. (Ads)

> **Tips:** "We are very open to all sorts of freelance possibilities."

NEW FRONTIER, 180 E. Ocean Blvd., 4th Fl., Long Beach CA 90802. (310) 544-6423. Fax (310)265-6545. E-mail: safrontier@aol.com. Website: www. salvationarmy.usawest.org/newfrontier. Salvation Army—Western Territory. Robert Docter, ed. To share the good news of the gospel and the work of The Salvation Army in the western territory with salvationists and friends. Biweekly newspaper; circ 25,500. Subscription $8. Accepts freelance. Prefers query. Not in topical listings. (Ads)

> **1997 EPA Award of Merit—Newspaper.

A NEW HEART, Box 4004, San Clemente CA 92674-4004. (949)496-7655. Fax (949)496-8465. E-mail: HCFUSA@juno.com. Website: www.HCFUSA. com. Aubrey Beauchamp, ed. For Christian healthcare-givers; information regarding medical/Christian issues. Quarterly mag; 16 pgs; circ 5,000. Subscription $25. 20% unsolicited freelance; 10% assigned. Complete ms/cover letter; phone/fax/e-query OK. **PAYS 2 COPIES** for one-time rts. Not copyrighted. Articles 600-1,800 wds (20-25/yr). Responds in 2-3 wks. Accepts simultaneous submissions & reprints. Accepts e-mail submission. No sidebars. Guidelines (also by fax); copy for 9x12 SAE/3 stamps. (Ads)

> **Poetry:** Accepts 1-2/yr. Submit max 1-3 poems.

Fillers: Accepts 3-4/yr. Anecdotes, cartoons, facts, jokes, short humor; 100-120 wds.

Columns/Departments: Accepts 20-25/yr. Chaplain's Corner, 200-250 wds; Physician's Corner, 200-250 wds.

Tips: "Most open to real-life situations which may benefit and encourage healthcare givers and patients. True stories with medical and evangelical emphasis."

$NEW MOON NETWORK: For Adults Who Care about Girls, PO Box 3620, Duluth MN 55803. (612)929-8942. Fax (218)728-0314. E-mail: newmoon @newmoon.org. Website: www.newmoon.org. New Moon Publishing, Inc. Lynette Lamb, ed. For adults (teachers, parents, etc.) who work with girls 8-14. Bimonthly newsletter; 16 pgs; circ 3,500. Subscription $25. 10% unsolicited freelance; 60% assigned. Query; e-query OK. Pays $20-50 on publication for all or 1st rts. Articles 750-1,400 wds (6/yr); book reviews 900 wds. Responds in 8 wks. Accepts simultaneous submissions. Prefers e-mail submission (attached file). Some sidebars. Guidelines (also on Website); copy $6.50. (Ads)

Columns/Departments: Buys 3/yr. Mothering (personal experience), 900 wds; Fathering, 900 wds; Current Research (girl related), 900-1,800 wds. Query.

Tips: "Study our guidelines carefully, follow our themes, and understand our goals." Has a diverse readership and does not accept material that focuses specifically on Christian themes.

$A NEW SONG, PO Box 629 W.B.B., Dayton OH 45409-0629. (937)294-4552. E-mail: NSongPress@aol.com. New Song Press. Susan Jelus, ed. Contemporary poetry that addresses all aspects of life in faith; some articles. Semi-annual journal; 35-60 pgs; circ 300. Subscription $12.95. 100% freelance. Pays $25-60 for articles, in copies for poetry, on acceptance for 1st rts. Articles 500-2,000 wds (2-3/yr); book reviews 500-1,500 wds. Responds in 12 wks. Seasonal 6-8 mos ahead. Accepts disk or e-mail submission (attached in RTF or Doc format or copied into message). No sidebars. Any Bible version. Guidelines (also by e-mail); copy $3. (Ads)

Poetry: Accepts 100/yr. Avant-garde & free verse; any length. No payment. Submit max 5 poems. Poetry should emphasize 'real life' spirituality—the way faith is applied to contemporary life—rather than standard religious doctrine, rehashed . We like poems about people, beauty, nature, and experiences of God. No rhyming poetry.

Contest: Annual poetry chapbook contest. Deadline: July 1. Cash prize, plus publication and copies.

Tips: "Looking for articles on the aging process, the earth, and the depth of spiritual experience. Also seeking short reviews of new books of poetry by spiritually-grounded authors, and black and white illustrations for covers."

*NEW WRITING MAGAZINE, Box 1812, Amherst NY 14226-7812. (716)834-1067. E-mail: info@newwriting.com. Website: www.newwriting.com. New Writing Agency. Richard Lynch, co-ed. The best of new writing by beginning and established writers. Annual online mag. Free on the Internet. 95% freelance. Complete ms/cover letter; e-query OK. **NO PAYMENT** for

1st rts. Not copyrighted. Articles (5/yr); fiction (20/yr). Responds in 6-8 wks. Seasonal 6 mos ahead. Accepts simultaneous submissions & reprints (tell when/where appeared). Guidelines. (Ads)

Poetry: Buys 20/yr. Avant-garde, free verse, traditional; any length. Submit max 5 poems.

Contest: "We run a writing contest and literary agency. Visit Website: members.aol.com/newwriting.contest.html."

$NO-DEBT LIVING: Financial Management with a Christian Perspective, PO Box 282, Veradale WA 99037-0282. Phone/fax (509)922-8733. E-mail: rfrank@nodebtnews.com. Website: www.nodebtnews.com. Robert E. Frank, ed. Financial and home-management information from a Christian perspective. Online newsletter; 400-1,000 visitors/day. 25% assigned freelance. Brief query or complete ms; e-query OK. Pays $15-30 (for vignettes) and $30-50 (for features) on publication for print & electronic rts. Feature articles 700-1,200 wds (40/yr); 300-600 wds (vignettes) (33-40/yr); book reviews 300-500 wds. Responds in 2 wks. Seasonal 2 mos ahead. Accepts reprints (tell when/where appeared). Prefers e-mail submission in ASCII format (copied into message or attached). Some sidebars. Prefers NAS. Guidelines/theme list on Website; copy for 6x9 SAE/3 stamps.

Special Needs: Consumer-related news, time-management, money-saving strategies, and taxes. Book reviews on financial or time-management topics.

Tips: "Follow AP style. Use original quotes from at least two well-known professionals (preferably Christians). Link story to a current news trend or issue. Most open to money-management (if writer has experience and/or professional expertise) and time-management topics."

$THE NORTH AMERICAN VOICE OF FATIMA, 1023 Swan Rd., Youngstown NY 14174. (716)754-7489. Fax (716)754-9130. E-mail: FatimaShr@aol.com. Barnabite Fathers, Inc./Catholic. Seeking new editor. A Marian publication with emphasis on apparitions of Our Lady of Fatima. Bimonthly mag; 20 pgs; circ 3,000. Subscription $4.50. 50% freelance. Complete ms/cover letter. Pays .04/wd on publication for 1st rts. Not copyrighted. Articles & fiction 1,000 wds. Responds in 6 wks. Seasonal 4 mos ahead. Accepts simultaneous submissions & reprints. No disk. Regular sidebars. Guidelines/copy for #10 SAE.

Poetry: Buys 20/yr. Free verse, traditional. Pays $10.

$NORTHWESTERN LUTHERAN, 2929 N Mayfair Rd., Milwaukee WI 53222-4398. (414)256-3888. Fax (414)256-3899. E-mail: fic@sab.wels.net. Wisconsin Evangelical Lutheran Synod. Gary P. Baumler, ed. Denominational. Monthly mag; 36 pgs; circ 55,000. Subscription $10. 5% unsolicited freelance; 95% assigned. Complete ms/cover letter; no phone/fax query; e-query OK. Pays $50/pg on publication for one-time rts. Articles 500-1,000 wds (50/yr). Responds in 4-6 wks. Seasonal 4 mos ahead. Accepts reprints (tell when/where appeared). Accepts disk or e-mail submission (copied into message). Regular sidebars. Prefers NIV. Guidelines (also by e-mail); copy for 9x12 SAE/2 stamps. (No ads)

Tips: "Most of our writers belong to the denomination and write about our members, organizations or institutions. Most open to strong personal witness; strong inspirational example of Christian living." Note: This publication is now temporarily called *Forward/ Northwestern Lutheran* as part of their 150th anniversary celebration.

$NOTRE DAME MAGAZINE, 538 Grace Hall, Notre Dame IN 46556. E-mail: ndmag.1@nd.edu. Website: www.nd.edu/~ndmag. University of Notre Dame. Kerry Temple, ed. (temple.1@nd.edu). Reports on alumni activities; covers institutional events, people, and trends; and examines a broad spectrum of cultural issues. Quarterly mag; circ. 142,000. 75% freelance. Query/clips; complete ms OK for Perspectives section. Pays $250-1,500 on acceptance for 1st and electronic rts. Articles 750-3,000 wds & up (35/yr). Responds in 5 wks. Rarely uses reprints. Requires disk; e-mail submissions on assigned articles OK. Kill fee. Guidelines on Website; copy on Website or by e-mail. Not in topical listings.

Columns/Departments: Campus News; Alumni Notes.

Special Needs: "Perspectives" section contains 3-4 essays per issue; often in first person, 750-1,500 wds; and deals with a wide array of issues—some topical, some personal, some serious, some light.

Tips: "Main part of magazines is feature stories, 3,000 words and up, addressing a variety of issues appealing to college-educated readers who take an active interest in the contemporary world. Usually assigned."

$NOW WHAT? (formerly Bible Advocate Online), Box 33677, Denver CO 80233. (303)452-7973. Fax (303)452-0657. E-mail: bibleadvocate@cog7.org. Website: nowwhat.cog7.org. Church of God (Seventh-Day). Calvin Burrell, ed; Sherri Langton, assoc ed. Articles on salvation, Jesus, social issues, life problems that are seeker-sensitive. Monthly online mag; available only online. 75% unsolicited freelance. Complete ms/cover letter; phone/e-query OK. Pays $25-55 on publication for first, one-time, electronic, simultaneous & reprint rts. Articles 1,200-1,500 wds (20/yr). Responds in 4-8 wks. Seasonal 6 mos ahead. Accepts simultaneous submissions & reprints (tell when/where appeared). Accepts disk or e-mail submission (copied into message). Regular sidebars. Prefers NIV. Guidelines (also on Website); copy of online article for #10 SAE/1 stamp. (No ads)

Fillers: Buys 5-10/yr. Anecdotes, facts, prose, quotes; 50-100 wds. Pays $20.

Special Needs: "Personal experiences must still show a person's struggle that either brought him/her to Christ or deepened faith in God. What has changed is that the entire Now What? Site is built around a personal experience each month. We draw points out of the story that prompts readers' interaction and introspection. We have many personal experiences, but need more objective articles that relate to the story's topic."

Tips: "It's a real plus for writers submitting a personal experience to also submit an objective article related to their story. Or they can contact Sherri Langton for upcoming personal experiences that need related articles."

$NRB MAGAZINE, National Religious Broadcasters, 7839 Ashton Ave., Manassas VA 22109. (703)330-7000x515. Fax (703)530-7621. E-mail: cpryor@nrb.com. Website: www.nrb.com. Christine L. Pryor, mng. ed. Topics relate to Christian radio, television, satellite and Internet; promoting access and excellence in religious broadcasting. Monthly (10X) mag, with online version; 52 pgs; circ 9,100. Subscription $24. 70% freelance. Complete ms/cover letter; fax/e-query OK. **PAYS 6 COPIES** ($100-200 for assigned) on publication for 1st or reprint rts. Articles 1,000-2,000 wds (30/yr). Responds in 6 wks. Seasonal 6 mos ahead. Accepts simultaneous submissions & reprints (tell when/where appeared). Prefers e-mail submissions. Regular sidebars. Prefers NASB. Free guidelines/theme list/copy. (Ads)

> **Columns/Departments:** Accepts 10/yr. Trade Talk (summary paragraphs of news items/events in religious broadcasting), 50 wds; Opinion (social issues), 750 wds.
>
> **Special Needs:** Electronic media; education. All articles must relate in some way to broadcasting: radio, TV, programs on radio/TV.
>
> **Tips:** "Most open to feature articles relevant to Christian communicators. Become acquainted with broadcasters in your area and note their struggles, concerns, and victories. Find out what they would like to know, research the topic, then write about it."
>
> **1999 EPA Award of Merit—Most Improved Publication.

$OBLATES, 9480 N. De Mazenod Dr., Belleville IL 62223-1160. (618)398-4848. Fax (618)398-8788. Website: www.snows.org. Catholic/Missionary Assn. of Missionary Oblates of Mary Immaculate. Mary Mohrman, mss ed. To inspire, comfort, uplift, and motivate a Catholic/Christian audience. Bimonthly mag; 24 pgs; circ 500,000. Free to members. 15% freelance. Complete ms only/cover letter; no phone/fax query. Pays $150 on acceptance for 1st rts. Articles 500-600 wds. Responds in 9 wks. Seasonal 6 mos ahead. Considers simultaneous submissions. No disk. No sidebars. Prefers NAB. Guidelines; copy for 6x9 SAE/2 stamps. (No ads)

> **Poetry:** Free verse, traditional; to 12 lines; $50. Submit max 2 poems.
>
> **Tips:** "Need personal, inspirational articles with a strong spiritual theme firmly grounded to a particular incident and poetry. No Christmas issue."

$ON MISSION, 4200 North Point Pkwy, Alpharetta GA 30022-4176. (770)410-6284. Fax (770)410-6105. E-mail: onmission@namb.net, or ccurtis@namb.net. Website: www.onmission.com. North American Mission Board, Southern Baptist. Carolyn Curtis, ed. Helping readers share Christ in the real world. Bimonthly & online mag; 56 pgs; circ 100,000. Subscription $14.95. 1-5% unsolicited freelance; 50-60% assigned. Query/clips for assignments; e-query OK. Pays .25-.50/wd on acceptance for all, 1st, one-time, reprint and electronic rts. Articles 250-2,000 wds, most 750-1,200 wds (6/yr). Responds in 2-4 mos. Seasonal 8 mos ahead. Accepts e-mail submission (copied into message). Kill fee. Regular sidebars. Prefers NIV. Guidelines on Website. (Ads)

Special Needs: Needs 700-1,000 word, principle-based articles with practical applications for how to live a lifestyle of personal evangelism.

Tips: "Write a solid, 750-word, how-to article geared to 20- to 40-year-old men and women who want fresh ideas and insight into sharing Christ in the real world in which they live, work, and play. Send a résumé, along with your best writing samples. We are an on-assignment magazine."

**1999 EPA Award of Excellence—Missionary.

$OUR FAMILY, Box 249, Battleford SK S0M 0E0 Canada. (306)937-7771. Fax (306)937-7644. E-mail: editor@ourfamilymagazine.com. Website: www. ourfamilymagazine.com. Catholic/Missionary Oblates of St. Mary's Province. Marie-Louise Ternier-Gommers, ed. All aspects of family life in the light of Christian faith. Monthly (11X) mag; 40 pgs; circ 8,000. Subscription $17.98 CAN. 60% unsolicited freelance; 15% assigned. Complete ms; phone/e-query OK. Pays .05/wd US on acceptance for 1st & electronic rts. Articles 700-1,700 wds (80-100/yr). Responds in 5-6 wks. Seasonal 5-6 mos ahead. Accepts simultaneous submissions & reprints (tell when/where appeared). Accepts e-mail submissions (copied into message). Kill fee 100%. Some sidebars. Prefers NRSV. Guidelines/theme list (also on Website); copy $3/9x12 SASE/Canadian postage or IRCs. (No ads)

Poetry: Buys 35-50/yr. Free verse, haiku, light verse, traditional, inspirational; 2-30 lines; .75-$1/line; .45 US/line.

Fillers: Buys 40-60/yr. Anecdotes, cartoons, jokes, short humor; to 100 wds. Pays .05 US/wd.

Tips: "Your SASE must have Canadian postage. We aim at the average reader. Looking for articles which deal with specific Catholic issues; articles that are rooted in social justice, service to others, ecumenism, and the Sunday liturgy. Articles need an experiential point of view with practical guidelines." Emphasis is on using Canadian authors.

**This periodical was #9 on the 2000 Top 50 Christian Publishers list (#3 in 1999, #30 in 1998, #47 in 1997, #39 in 1996 & 1995, #29 in 1994).

$OUR SUNDAY VISITOR, 200 Noll Plaza, Huntington IN 46750. (219)356-8400 or (800)348-2440. Fax (219)359-9117. E-mail: oursunvis@osv.com. Website: www.osv.com. Catholic. Gerald Korson, interim ed. Vital news, spirituality for today's Catholic. Weekly newspaper; 24 pgs; circ 75,000. Subscription $36. 3% freelance. Query; phone/fax/e-query OK. Pays $100-300 on acceptance for 1st rts. Articles to 1,100 wds (25/yr). Responds in 6 wks. Seasonal 2 mos ahead. Kill fee. Guidelines; copy for #10 SASE.

Columns/Departments: Buys 35/yr. Viewpoint (editorial/op-ed), 750 wds, $100.

Tips: "Need familiarity with Catholic Church issues and with Catholic Press—newspapers and magazines."

**This publication was #1 on the 1994 Top 50 Christian Publishers list.

$OVER THE BACK FENCE/NORTHERN OHIO, 5311 Meadow Lane Ct., Ste. 3, Elyria OH 44035. (440)934-1812. Fax (440)934-1816. E-mail: kbsagert @aol.com. Website: www.backfence.com. Back Fence Publishing, Inc.

Kelly Boyer Sagert, mng ed. Positive news about Northern Ohio. Quarterly mag; 64 pgs; circ 15,000. Subscription $9.97. 20% unsolicited freelance; 80% assigned. Query/clips; fax/e-query OK. Pays .10-.20/wd on publication for one-time rts. Articles 1,000 wds (28/yr). Responds in 4 wks. Seasonal 6-12 mos ahead. Accepts simultaneous submissions & reprints (tell when/where appeared). Requires disk or e-mail submission (copied into message). Regular sidebars. Guidelines (also by e-mail/Website); copy $4/9x12 SAE. (Ads)

Poetry: Buys 4-8/yr. Free verse, light verse, traditional; 1 pg. Pays $25. Submit max 5 poems.

Columns/Departments: Buys 12-20/yr. Profiles From the Past (interesting history that never made the headlines), 800-1,000 wds; Heartstrings (touching essays), 800 wds; Shorts (humorous essays), 800 wds. Complete ms. Pays $80-120.

Special Needs: Think upbeat and positive. Articles on nature, history, travel, nostalgia and family.

Tips: "Write about one of our 11 counties and include information about specific events happening in a specific season. To break into the magazine, think seasonally and focus tightly on our specific area of Ohio."

$OVER THE BACK FENCE/SOUTHERN OHIO, 14 S. Paint St., Ste. 69, PO Box 756, Chillicothe OH 45601. (740)772-2165. Fax (740)773-7626. E-mail: backfenc@bright.net. Website: www.backfence.com. Back Fence Publishing, Inc. Sarah Williamson, mng ed. Positive news about Southern Ohio. Quarterly mag; 64 pgs; circ 15,000. Subscription $9.97. 100% freelance. Query/clips; fax/e-query OK. Pays .12-.20/wd on publication for one-time rts. Articles 1,000 wds (28/yr). Responds in 4 wks. Seasonal 6-12 mos ahead. Accepts simultaneous submissions & reprints (tell when/where appeared). Requires disk or e-mail submission (copied into message). Regular sidebars. Guidelines (also by e-mail/Website); copy $4/9x12 SAE. (Ads)

Poetry: Buys 4-8/yr. Free verse, light verse, traditional; 1 pg. Pays $25. Submit max 5 poems.

Columns/Departments: Buys 10-20/yr. Profiles From the Past (interesting history that never made the headlines), 800-1,000 wds; Heartstrings (touching essays), 800 wds; Shorts (humorous essays), 800 wds. Complete ms. Pays $80-120.

Special Needs: Think upbeat and positive. Articles on nature, history, travel, nostalgia and family.

Tips: "Following tips on our Tip Sheet will help a writer break in. We work with writers to get their articles into publishable form."

$PARABOLA: Myth, Tradition, and the Search for Meaning, 656 Broadway, New York NY 10012. (212)505-6200x315. Fax (212)979-7325. E-mail: parabola@panix.com. Website: www.parabola.org. The Society for the Study of Myth and Tradition. Natalie Baan, mng. ed. Devoted to the exploration of the search for meaning as expressed in the myths, symbols, rituals, and art of the world's religious traditions. Quarterly journal; 144 pgs; circ 40,000. Subscription $24. 60% unsolicited freelance; 40% assigned. Query; fax/e-query OK. Pays $150-400 on publication for 1st, one-time and reprint rts. Articles 1,000-3,000 wds (40/yr); book/video reviews 500-700 wds, $75. Responds in 12 wks. Accepts simultaneous submissions & reprints (tell when/where appeared). Accepts e-mail submissions (attached file or copied into message). Kill fee $100. Some sidebars. Prefers KJV. Guidelines/theme list (also by e-mail/Website); copy $6.95. (Ads)

   Columns/Departments: Buys 40/yr. Reviews (books, audios, videos, software), to 700 wds; Epicycles (retellings of traditional stories), to 1,500 wds; pays $75-150.

   Tips: "All submissions must relate to themes. We look for well-researched, well-written, and authentic material that strikes a balance between the personal and the objective. No journalistic or self-improvement articles, evangelism, or profiles of specific persons or organizations."

$PARENTING OUR PARENTS, 55 Binks Hill Rd., Plymouth NH 03264. Fax (603)536-4851. E-mail: me.allen@juno.com. Website: www.homepage. fcgnetworks.net/jetent/mea. Mary Emma Allen, ed. Quarterly newsletter; 4-6 pgs; circ 100. Subscription $8. Estab. 1999. Open to freelance. Complete ms/cover letter; e-query OK. Pays $5-10 on acceptance for one-time rts. Short articles (4-6/yr); book reviews 250 wds, $5. Responds in 4-6 wks. Seasonal 6 mos ahead. Accepts simultaneous submissions & reprints (tell when/where appeared). Prefers e-mail submission (copied into message). Guidelines (also by e-mail); copy $1/#10 SAE/1stamp. (No ads)

   Poetry: Buys 4/yr. Free verse, traditional; 8-20 lines. Pays $2.50-5. Submit max 4 poems.

   Special Needs: All articles must relate to caregiving.

   Tips: "You almost need to be a caregiver of an elder person to provide self-help and inspirational articles here."

PARENTLIFE, 127 Ninth Ave. N., Nashville TN 37234-0140. (615)251-2229. Fax (615)251-5008. E-mail: parentlife@bssb.com. Website: www.bssb. com/kidtrek/prntlife.htm#top. No freelance at this time.

*THE PARENT PAPER, PO Box 1313, Manchester TN 37349. (931)728-8309. Fax (931)723-1902. E-mail: rhurst@edge.net. Rebekah Hurst, pub. A Christian perspective on topics that benefit the family. Monthly newspaper; 12-20 pgs; circ. 5,000. Subscription $15. 20% unsolicited freelance. Complete ms; e-query OK. **PAYS 3 COPIES** for 1st or reprint rts. Articles; fiction for children or teens (400-600 words). Seasonal 6 mos ahead. Accepts simultaneous submissions & reprints. Accepts e-mail submission (attached file). Some sidebars. Prefers NIV. Guidelines; copy for 9x12 SAE/4 stamps. (Ads)

   Poetry: Accepts 6/yr; to 32 lines.

   Tips: "Any area is open to freelancers. Freelancers can best break in by writing about issues that affect the family."

THE PEGASUS REVIEW, PO Box 88, Henderson MD 21640-0088. (410)482-6736. E-mail: bounds@dmv.com. Art Bounds, ed. Theme-oriented poetry, short fiction & essays; not necessarily religious; in calligraphy format. Bimonthly mag; 6-10 pgs; circ 120. Subscription $12. 100% unsolicited freelance. Complete ms/cover letter. **PAYS 2 COPIES** for one-time rts. Fiction $2\frac{1}{2}$ pgs max., single-spaced (6-10/yr); also one-page essays. Responds in 4 wks. Accepts simultaneous submissions & reprints (tell when/where appeared). No disk or e-mail submissions. No sidebars. Prefers KJV. Guidelines/theme list; copy $2.50. (No ads)

Poetry: Accepts 20-30/yr. Any type; 4-12 lines (shorter the better). Theme oriented. Submit max 3 poems.

Fillers: Accepts 10-20/yr. Prayers, prose, essays.

Special Needs: 2001 themes: Jan/Feb—Months; Mar/Apr—Teachers & Teaching; May/Jun—Courtship; Jul/Aug—Imagination; Sep/Oct—Age and youth; and Nov/Dec—Forgiveness.

Tips: "Believe in your craft and persevere. Become active in a local writer's group, especially one that does critiquing. Follow the theme, submit 3 poems or one story, and heed editor's suggestions."

PENTECOSTAL EVANGEL, 1445 Boonville, Springfield MO 65802-1894. (417)862-2781. Fax (417)862-0416. E-mail: pe@ag.org. Website: www.ag. org. Assemblies of God. Hal Donaldson, ed. Denominational; Pentecostal. Weekly mag (some articles online); 32 pgs; circ 264,000. Subscription $24.99. 5% unsolicited freelance; 95% assigned. Query or complete ms/cover letter; fax/e-query OK. Pays .06-.08/wd (.03/wd for reprints) on acceptance for 1st and electronic rts. Articles 800-1,000 wds. Responds in 6-8 wks. Seasonal 6-8 mos ahead. Kill fee 100%. Prefers e-mail submission (attached file). Regular sidebars. Prefers NIV or KJV. Guidelines on Website; no copy. (Ads)

Fillers: Practical, how-to pieces on family life, devotions, evangelism, seasonal, current issues, Christian living; 50-200 wds. Pays $20.

Tips: Needs general inspirational articles with a strong focus; feature articles targeted to the unsaved; seasonal articles (major holidays). A large percentage of articles are now assigned. Send samples of previous things published and indicate you are open for assignments.

**This periodical was #61 on the 1998 Top 50 Christian Publishers list (#28 in 1996, #11 in 1995, #23 in 1994).

+THE PENWOOD REVIEW, PO Box 862, Los Alamitos CA 90720-0862. E-mail: bcame39696@aol.com. Website: members.aol.com/bcame39696/penwood.htm. Lori Cameron, ed. Poetry, plus thought-provoking essays on poetry, literature and the role of spirituality and religion in the literary arts. Biannual journal; 40+ pgs; circ 50-100. Subscription $12. Estab. 1997. 99% unsolicited freelance; 1% assigned. Complete ms (February 25 & August 25 deadlines); no e-query. **NO PAYMENT** ($2 off subscription & 1 free copy), for one-time and electronic rts. Responds in 9-12 wks. Accepts disk or e-mail submissions (copied into message). Guidelines (also by e-mail/Website); copy $6.

Poetry: Accepts 70-80/yr. Avant-garde, free verse, traditional; to 2 pgs. Submit max 5 poems.

Tips: "We publish poetry almost exclusively, and are looking for well-crafted, disciplined poetry, not doggerel or greeting-card-style poetry. Visit our Website or buy a copy for an idea of what we publish."

THE PEOPLES MAGAZINE, 374 Sheppard Ave. E., Willowdale ON L4G 6M1 Canada. (416)222-3341x142. Fax (416)222-3344. E-mail: timothy@

peoplesministries.org. The Peoples Church/Toronto Canada. Dr. T. Starr, mng ed. Quarterly mag; 24 pgs; circ 7,800. Subscription free/donation. 15% unsolicited freelance; 85% assigned. Complete ms/cover letter. NO PAYMENT. Articles 500-800 wds (20/yr); fiction 350-500 wds; book/video reviews 150 wds. Responds in 2 wks. Seasonal 3 mos ahead. Accepts simultaneous submissions & reprints (tell when/where appeared). Accepts disk. Regular sidebars. Any version. Guidelines; copy for 9x12 SAE/$1.15 CAN postage. (Ads)

> **Poetry:** Accepts 1-2/yr. No payment.
>
> **Fillers:** Accepts 1-5/yr; 50 wds. Anecdotes, cartoons, facts, games, quizzes, short humor, 25-40 wds.
>
> **Columns/Departments:** Accepts 20/yr. Complete ms. No payment.

PERSPECTIVES: A Journal of Reformed Thought, PO Box 1196, Holland MI 49422-1196. (616)957-6528. Fax (616)957-8508. E-mail: boogaart@ macatawa.org. Reformed Church Press. Dr. Leanne Van Dyk, Dr. David Timmer, and Dr. Roy Anken, eds. To express the Reformed faith theologically; to engage issues that Reformed Christians meet in personal, ecclesiastical, and societal life. Monthly (10X) mag; 24 pgs; circ. 3,000. Subscription $24.95. 70% unsolicited freelance; 30% assigned. Query or complete ms/cover letter; fax/e-query OK. **PAYS IN COPIES** for all rts (usually). Articles (10/yr) and fiction (3/yr), 2,000-2,500 wds; book & movie reviews 500-1,500 wds. Responds in 4-6 wks. Seasonal 4 mos ahead. Prefers disk. Sidebars rare. Prefers NRSV. Guidelines by e-mail; copy for 9x12 SAE/$1.50 postage. (Ads)

> **Poetry:** Francis Fike. Free verse, traditional. Accepts 5-7/yr. Submit max 2 poems.
>
> **Columns/Departments:** Accepts 20-24/yr. As We See It (editorial/ opinion) 750-1,500 wds; Inside Out (biblical exegesis) 750 wds. Complete ms.
>
> **Tips:** "I would say that a reading of past issues and a desire to join in a contemporary conversation of the Christian faith would help you break in here."

$PHYSICIAN, 8605 Explorer Dr., Colorado Springs CO 80920. (719)548-5891. Fax (719)531-3499. E-mail: physician@macmail.fotf.org. Website: www.family.org. Focus on the Family. Susan Stevens, ed. To encourage physicians and their families. Bimonthly mag; 24 pgs; circ 81,700. Free to medical profession/donors. 20% freelance. Query or complete ms/cover letter; phone/fax/e-query OK. Pays $100-500 on acceptance for 1st rts. Articles 900-2,400 wds (20-30/yr). Responds in 9 wks. Accepts reprints. Kill fee. Regular sidebars. Prefers NIV. Copy available. (No ads)

> **Fillers:** Cartoons; $50.
>
> **1997 EPA Award of Merit, 1996 EPA Award of Excellence—Christian Ministry.

$THE PLAIN TRUTH, 300 W. Green St., Pasadena CA 91129. (626)304-6181. Fax (626)304-8172. E-mail: phyllis_duke@ptm.org, or marlene_reed@ ptm.org. Website: www.ptm.org. Plain Truth Ministries. Greg Albrecht, ed; submit to Phyllis Duke, asst. ed. Proclaims the Gospel of Jesus Christ, emphasizing the central teachings of Christianity and making teachings plain and clear. Bimonthly & online mag; 68 pgs; circ 110,000. Subscription $12.95. 50% unsolicited freelance; 50% assigned. Query/clips or complete ms/cover letter; fax/e-query OK. Pays .25/wd (.15/wd for reprints) on publication for 1st, one-time, reprint, and world (all languages) rts. Articles 750-2,500 wds (48-50/yr); book/music/video reviews 100 wds, $25. Responds in 4-6 wks. Seasonal 6 mos ahead. Accepts simultaneous submissions & reprints (tell when/where appeared). Requires disk or e-mail submission. Kill fee $50. Regular sidebars. Prefers NIV. Guidelines (also by e-mail/Website); copy for 9x12 SAE/5 stamps. (Ads)

> **Columns/Departments:** Buys 18/yr. Family (family issues), 1,500 wds; Commentary (hot topic editorials), 550-650 wds; Christian People (testimonial/interviews), 1,500 wds. Query or complete ms. Pays .15-.25/wd.
>
> **Tips:** "Best to send tear sheets of previously published articles and submit detailed query for standard articles."
>
> **This periodical was #30 on the 2000 Top 50 Christian Publishers list (#48 in 1999).

THE PLOWMAN, Box 414, Whitby ON L1N 5S4 Canada. (905)668-7803. The Plowman Ministries/Christian. Tony Scavetta, ed/pub. Poetry and prose of social commentary; any topics. Semiannual newsletter; 20 pgs; circ 5,000. Subscription $10 US. 90% freelance. Query; phone query OK. **NO PAYMENT.** Articles (10/yr) & fiction (50/yr), 1,000 wds. Responds in 2-4 wks. Accepts simultaneous submissions & reprints. No disk. No sidebars. Free guidelines/copy for 9x12 SAE. (Ads)

> **Poetry:** Accepts 100/yr. All types; to 38 lines (55 characters across max). Submit max 4 poems.
>
> **Fillers:** Accepts 25/yr. Cartoons, prayers, short humor; 25-30 wds.
>
> **Special Needs:** Also publishes chapbooks; 20% royalties.
>
> **Contest:** Sponsors monthly poetry contests; $2/poem entry fee.
>
> **Tips:** "All sections open, especially poetry and short stories."

$*PLUS, 16 E. 34th St., New York NY 10016. (212)251-8100. Website: www.guideposts.org. Guideposts. Submit to The Editor. Spiritually oriented, based on positive thinking and faith. Monthly (10X) mag; 36 pgs; circ 600,000. Subscription $10. 30% freelance. Complete ms/cover letter; phone/fax query OK. Pays $25/pg on publication for 1st or one-time rts. Articles 500-2,500 wds (8/yr). Responds in 3-4 wks. Seasonal 6 mos ahead. Accepts reprints. Some sidebars. Guidelines; copy for #10 SAE/1 stamp.

> **Tips:** "Have a deep, living knowledge of Christianity. Our audience is 65-70% female, average age is 55."
>
> **This periodical was #31 on the 1995 Top 50 Christian Publishers list.

POETS' PAPER, PO Box 85, Easton PA 18044-0085. (610)559-9287. Not publishing for now; not sure when publication will resume.

POURASTAN, 615 Stuart Ave., Outremont QB H2V 3H2 Canada. (514)279-3066. Fax (514)276-9960. E-mail: sourpkrikor@qc.aibn.com. St. Gregory the Illuminator Armenian Cathedral. Very Rev. Fr. Ararat Kaltakjian, chief ed. Denominational; religious, social and community oriented. Bimonthly mag; 36 pgs; circ 1,250. Free for donations. 100% unsolicited freelance. Complete ms/cover letter; phone/fax/e-query OK. **NO PAYMENT.** Not copyrighted. Articles 250-1,500 wds (10/yr); book reviews, 300 wds. Seasonal 1 mo ahead. Accepts simultaneous submissions & reprints. No sidebars. Accepts disk. No guidelines; copy for 9x12 SAE/90 cents. (Ads)

Poetry: Accepts 10/yr. Traditional, 4-40 lines. Submit max 2 poems.

Fillers: Anecdotes, ideas, prayers, quotes, short humor, 10-50 wds.

Tips: "Most open to social issues in general, but particularly related to the Armenian community."

Note: This publication is published in Armenian with occasional English and French.

$POWER FOR LIVING, Box 36640, Colorado Springs CO 80936. (719)536-0100. Fax (719)536-3243. Cook Communications/Scripture Press Publications. Don Alban Jr., ed. To expressly demonstrate the relevance of specific biblical teachings to everyday life via reader-captivating profiles of exceptional Christians. Weekly take-home paper; 8 pgs; circ 250,000. Subscription $10. 15% unsolicited freelance; 85% assigned. Complete ms; no phone/fax/e-query. Pays up to .15/wd (reprints up to .10/wd) on acceptance for 1st or one-time rts. Articles 700-1,500 wds (20/yr); vignettes 450-1,500 wds. Responds in 4 wks. Seasonal 1 yr ahead. Accepts simultaneous submissions & reprints (tell when/where appeared). Accepts disk only on request. Kill fee. Some sidebars. Prefers KJV. Guidelines (also by e-mail: WritersGuide@SPpublications.org)/copy for #10 SAE/1 stamp. (No ads)

Special Needs: Third-person profiles of truly out-of-the-ordinary Christians who express their faith uniquely. We use very little of anything else.

Tips: "Most open to vignettes, 450-1,500 wds, of prominent Christians with solid testimonies or profiles from church history. Focus on the unusual. Signed releases required."

**This periodical was #11 on the 1996 Top 50 Christian Publishers list (#9 in 1995, #21 in 1994).

$PRAIRIE MESSENGER: Catholic Journal, PO Box 190, Muenster SK S0K 2Y0 Canada. (306)682-1772. Fax (306)682-5285. E-mail: pm.editor@ stpeters.sk.ca. Website: www.stpeters.sk.ca/prairie_messenger. Catholic/ Benedictine Monks of St. Peter's Abbey. Maureen Weber, assoc ed. For Catholics in Saskatchewan & Manitoba, and Christians in other faith communities. Weekly tabloid; 20 pgs; circ 7,300. Subscription $26 CAN. 10% freelance. Complete ms/cover letter; phone/fax/e-query OK. Pays $40-60 ($2/column inch for news items) on publication for 1st, one-time, simultaneous & reprint rts. Not copyrighted. Articles 800-900 or 2,500 wds (15/yr). Responds in 9 wks. Seasonal 3 mos ahead. Accepts simultaneous submissions & reprints. Regular sidebars. Guidelines (also by e-mail/ Website); copy for 9x12 SAE/$1 CAN/$1.24 US. (Ads)

Poetry: Accepts 46/yr. Free verse; 6-25 lines.

Special Needs: Ecumenism; social justice; native concerns.

Tips: "Comment/feature section is most open. Send topic of concern or interest to Prairie readership. It's difficult to break into our publication."

**This periodical was selected #1 for general excellence by the Canadian Church Press (10 times during the last 16 years).

+**THE PRAYER CLOSET**, 595 Stratton Road, Decatur, MS 39327. (601) 635-2180. Fax (601) 635-4025. E-mail: prayercloset_1998@yahoo.com. Website: www.prayerclosetministries.org. Dr. Kevin Meador, editor. Challenges and equips believers in the area of prayer, fasting, spiritual warfare, journaling, and healing. Monthly newsletter; circ. 3,000. Free subscription. **PAYS IN COPIES**. Prefers NKJV. Guidelines.

> **Tips:** "We are looking for sound, biblically based articles concerning the above-listed topics."

PRAYERWORKS, PO Box 301363, Portland OR 97294. (503)761-2072. Fax (503)760-1184. E-mail: 76753.3202@compuserve.com. Website under construction. V. Ann Mandeville, ed. For prayer warriors in retirement centers; focuses on prayer. Weekly newspaper; 4 pgs; circ 1,000. Subscription free. 100% unsolicited freelance. Complete ms; phone/fax query OK. **PAYS IN COPIES/SUBSCRIPTION** for one-time rts. Not copyrighted. Articles (30-40/yr) & fiction (30/yr); 300-500 wds. Responds in 3 wks. Seasonal 2 mos ahead. Accepts simultaneous submissions & reprints. No sidebars. Guidelines; copy for #10 SAE/1 stamp. (No ads)

> **Poetry:** Accepts 20-30/yr. Free verse, haiku, light verse, traditional. Submit max 10 poems.

> **Fillers:** Accepts up to 50/yr. Facts, jokes, prayers, quotes, short humor; to 50 wds.

> **Tips:** "Write tight. Half our audience is over 70, but 30% is young families. Subject matter isn't important as long as it is scriptural and designed to help people pray. Have a strong, catchy takeaway."

$#**THE PRESBYTERIAN LAYMAN**, 136 Tremont Park, PO Box 2210, Lenoir NC 28645. (828)758-8716. Fax (828)758-0920. E-mail: art@abts.net. Website: www.layman.org. Presbyterian Lay Committee. Parker T. Williamson, exec ed. For the conservative/evangelical members of the Presbyterian Church (USA). Bimonthly newspaper; 24 pgs; circ. 575,000. No subscriptions. 10% freelance. Query. Pays negotiable rates on publication for 1st rts. Articles 800-1,200 wds (12/yr). Responds in 2 wks. Seasonal 2 mos ahead. Prefers disk. Regular sidebars. Copy for 9x12 SAE/3 stamps. (No ads)

> **Poetry:** Traditional; pay negotiable. Submit max 1 poem.

THE PRESBYTERIAN OUTLOOK, Box 85623, Richmond VA 23285-5623. (804)359-8442. Fax (804)353-6369. E-mail: outlook@pcusa.org. Website: www.pres-outlook.com. Presbyterian Church (USA)/Independent. Robert H. Bullock Jr., ed. For ministers, members and staff of the denomination. Weekly (43X) mag; 16-40 pgs; circ 12,734. Subscription $31.50. 5% unsolicited freelance; 95% assigned. Query; phone/fax/e-query OK. **NO PAYMENT** for all rts. Not copyrighted. Articles to 1,000 wds; book reviews $1\frac{1}{2}$ pgs. Responds in 1-2 wks. Seasonal 2 mos ahead. Requires disk; accepts e-mail submission (copied into message); save as ASCII or plain text. Some sidebars. Prefers NRSV. Guidelines; free copy. (Ads)

Tips: "Correspond (mail or e-mail) with editor regarding current needs; most open to features. Most material is commissioned; anything submitted should be of interest to Presbyterians."

$PRESBYTERIAN RECORD, 50 Wynford Dr., Toronto ON M3C 1J7 Canada. (416)444-1111. Fax (416)441-2825. E-mail: pcrecord@presbyterian.ca. Website: www.presbyterian.ca. The Presbyterian Church in Canada. Rev. John Congram, ed. Denominational. Monthly (11X) mag; 52 pgs; circ 51,000. Subscription $15 CAN; $20 US & foreign. 30% unsolicited freelance; 70% assigned. Query (preferred) or complete ms/cover letter; fax/e-query OK. Pays $50 CAN on publication for 1st, one-time, reprint or simultaneous rts. Articles 1,000-1,500 wds (15-20/yr); book/music reviews, to 400 wds/no pay. Responds in 9-13 wks. Seasonal 3 mos ahead. Accepts simultaneous submissions & reprints. Accepts e-mail submission (attached file). Regular sidebars. Prefers NRSV. Guidelines (also by e-mail); copy for 9x12 SAE/$1 Canadian postage or IRCs from US writers. (Ads)

> **Poetry:** Thomas Dickey. Buys 8-15/yr. Free verse, haiku, light verse, traditional; 10-30 lines preferred; $35. Send any number.
>
> **Fillers:** Buys 6/yr. Anecdotes, cartoons, facts, ideas, prose, prayers, short humor; to 200 wds; $15-25.
>
> **Columns/Departments:** Buys 12/yr. Vox Populi (controversial issues), 750 wds; $35-50.
>
> **Tips:** "It helps if submissions have some connection to Canada and/or the Presbyterian Church."

$PRESBYTERIANS TODAY, 100 Witherspoon St., Louisville KY 40202-1396. (502)569-5637. Fax (502)569-8632. E-mail: today@pcusa.org. Website: www.pcusa.org/pcusa/today. Presbyterian Church (USA). Catherine Cottingham, mng ed.; submit to Eva Stimson, ed. Denominational; not as conservative or evangelical as some. Monthly (10X) mag; 44 pgs; circ 82,000. Subscription $12.95. 65% freelance. Complete ms/cover letter; phone/fax/e-query OK. Pays $75-200 on acceptance for 1st rts. Articles 1,000-1,800 wds (20/yr). Responds in 1 mo. Seasonal 3 mos ahead. Some reprints. Kill fee 50%. Guidelines; free copy. (Ads)

> **Fillers:** Cartoons, $25, short humor to 100 wds, no payment.
>
> **Tips:** "Most open to feature articles or news articles about Presbyterian people and programs (600-800 wds, $75). Do not often use inspirational or testimony-type articles."

**This periodical was #21 on the 2000 Top 50 Christian Publishers list (#47 in 1998, #48 in 1997, #64 in 1996, #41 in 1995).

*PRESBYTERIANS-WEEK, 9400 Fairview Ave., Ste. 200, Manassas VA 22110. (703)335-2844. Fax (703)368-4817. Christian Observer Foundation; Presbyterian Reformed. Edwin P. Elliott, ed. To encourage and edify God's people and families. Free online electronic weekly newspaper. Limited freelance. Query only; phone/fax/e-query OK. NO PAYMENT. Not in topical listings. (Ads)

$PRESERVING CHRISTIAN HOMES, 8855 Dunn Rd., Hazelwood MO 63042-2299. (314)837-7300. Fax (314)837-4503. E-mail: youth@upci.org. Website: www.upci.org. United Pentecostal Church. Todd Gaddy, ed. Addresses relevant topics for the Christian family. Bimonthly mag; 16 pgs;

circ 4,500. Subscription $9. 40% freelance. Complete ms/cover letter; phone/fax/e-query OK. Pays $30-40 on publication for one-time or simultaneous rts. Articles 500-1,500 wds (15/yr); fiction 500-1,500 wds (6/yr). Responds in 2-9 wks. Seasonal 6 mos ahead. Accepts simultaneous submissions & reprints (tell when/where appeared). No disk; accepts e-mail submission. Some sidebars. Prefers KJV. Guidelines; copy for 10x13 SAE/2 stamps. (No ads)

> **Poetry:** Buys 3/yr. Light verse, traditional; 10-40 lines. Pays $20-25. Submit max 5 poems.
>
> **Fillers:** Buys 2/yr. Cartoons, games, quizzes, word puzzles; 50-200 wds. Pays $10-20.
>
> **Tips:** "Most open to fiction and relationships. Be relevant and practical."

$PRIORITY! A Magazine About People in USA East, 440 W. Nyack Rd., West Nyack NY 10994. (845)620-7450. Fax (845)620-7753. E-mail: priority @salvationarmy.org, or ljohnson@usn.salvationarmy.org. The Salvation Army. Linda Johnson, ed. Quarterly mag; 48 pgs; circ 40,000. Subscription $6.95. Estab. 1999. 20% assigned. Query/clips; e-query OK. Pays .25/wd or $150 & up on acceptance for all rts. Articles 750-1,500 wds (5-10/yr). All articles assigned. Seasonal 4 mos ahead. Prefers e-mail submissions (copied into message). Kill fee 25%. Regular sidebars. Prefers NIV. No guidelines; copy $1/9x12 SAE. (Ads from non-profits only)

> **Columns/Departments:** Buys 20/yr. Prayer Power (stories about answered prayer, or harnessing prayer power), 200-300 wds, $100-200.
>
> **Special Needs:** All articles must have a connection to The Salvation Army.
>
> **Tips:** "Most open to features on people. The more a writer knows about The Salvation Army, the better. We are interested in finding a group of freelancers we can assign to specific features. We cover Maine to Kentucky and west to Ohio."

$#PRISM, PO Box 4287, Wheaton IL 60189. E-mail: prism@esa-online.org. Website: www.esa-online.org. Evangelicals for Social Action. Rodney Clapp, ed. For Christians who are interested in the social and political dimensions of the gospel. Bimonthly mag; 44 pgs; circ 9,000. Subscription $25. 25% freelance. Query/clips; fax/e-query OK. Pays to $200 ($100 for fiction) 6 wks after publication for 1st or reprint rts. Articles 500-2,800 wds (10-12/yr); fiction, 700-1,600 wds (1/yr); book/video reviews, 500 wds, $0-100. Responds in 2-9 wks. Seasonal 6 mos ahead. Accepts reprints (tell when/where appeared). Prefers disk. Regular sidebars. Prefers NRSV. Guidelines; copy $3. (Ads)

> **Tips:** "Looking for analysis on religious right; social justice fiction. Understand progressive evangelicals and E.S.A. Read Tony Campolo, Ron Sider and Richard Foster. Most open to features."
>
> **1997 EPA Award of Merit—Organizational.

PROGRESS, Box 9609, Kansas City MO 64134-0609. (816)763-7800. Fax (816)765-2522. E-mail: progress@stonecroft.org. Website: www.stonecroft. org. Stonecroft Ministries. Susan Collard, mng ed. For women and their families who are involved in some aspect of Stonecroft Ministries. Bi-monthly mag; 64 pgs; circ 30,000. Subscription $8.50. 15% freelance. Complete ms/cover letter; phone/fax query OK. **PAYS IN COPIES** for 1st rts. Not copyrighted. Articles 300-600 wds (15/yr). Responds in 2 wks. Seasonal 6 mos ahead. Accepts reprints (tell when/where appeared). Accepts disk. Some sidebars. Prefers NIV. Guidelines; copy for 6x9 SAE/4 stamps.

>**Columns/Departments:** Buys 12/yr. Coping Series (how God helped through crisis or stress—prefers other than illness); Family Builders (help for families); 1,000-1,200 wds. These columns most open to freelance.

>**Tips:** "We do not include controversial or doctrinal issues about which Christians disagree. Material should be Christ-centered and biblically based."

+**PSYCHOLOGY FOR LIVING**, 250 W. Colorado Blvd., Ste. 200, Arcadia CA 91007. (626)821-8400.Fax (626)821-8409. E-mail: dick@ncfliving.org. Website: www.gospelcom.net/narramore. Narramore Christian Foundation. Dick Innes, ed. Addresses issues of everyday life from a Christian and psycological viewpoint. Bimonthly mag; 25 pgs; circ. 9,000. Subscription for a $20 donation. Open to freelance. Complete ms/cover letter; fax/e-query OK. Pays to $200, plus a subscription, on publication for 1st, one-time or reprint rts. Articles 1,000-1,700 wds. Responds in 1-2 wks. Seasonal 4 mos ahead. Accepts reprints (tell when/where appeared). Prefers e-mail submissions (copied into message). Some sidebars. Prefers NIV. Guidelines (also by e-mail); free copy. (No ads)

>**Tips:** "We're looking for good writers. Write a 1,000-1,700 word article that is psychologically and biblically sound."

$**PURPOSE**, 616 Walnut Ave., Scottdale PA 15683-1999. (724)887-8500. Fax (724)887-3111. E-mail: Horsch@mph.org. Website: www.mph.org. Mennonite Church. James E. Horsch, ed. Denominational, for older youth and adults. Monthly take-home paper; 8 pgs; circ 11,600. Subscription $18. 95% unsolicited freelance; 5% assigned. Complete ms (only)/cover letter; phone/e-query OK. Pays .05/wd on acceptance for one-time rts. Articles & fiction, to 750 wds (130/yr). Responds in 13 wks. Seasonal 6 mos ahead. Accepts simultaneous submissions & reprints (tell when/where appeared). Regular sidebars. Guidelines (also by e-mail); copy for 6x9 SAE/2 stamps. (No ads)

>**Poetry:** Buys 130/yr. Free verse, light verse, traditional; 3-12 lines; up to $2/line ($7.50-20). Submit max 10 poems.

>**Fillers:** Buys 15/yr. Anecdotes, cartoons, short humor; 200-500 wds; .04/wd.

>**Tips:** "Articles must carry a strong story line. First person is preferred. Don't exceed maximum word length."

>**This periodical was #10 on the 2000 Top 50 Christian Publishers list (#44 in 1999, #39 in 1998, #49 in 1997, #48 in 1996, #20 in 1995, #22 in 1994).

$**QUEEN OF ALL HEARTS**, 26 S. Saxon Ave., Bay Shore NY 11706-8993. (631)665-0726. Fax (631)665-4349. E-mail: pretre@worldnet.att.net. Website: www.montfortmissionaries.com. Catholic/Montfort Missionaries. Rev.

Roger M. Charest, SMM, mng ed. Focus is Mary, the Mother of Jesus. Bi-monthly mag; 48 pgs; circ 2,600. Subscription $20. 80% freelance. Complete ms/cover letter; phone/fax query OK. Pays variable rates on publication for 1st rts. Not copyrighted. Articles (40/yr) and fiction (6/yr) 1,500-2,000 wds; book reviews 100 wds. Responds in 3 wks. Seasonal 4 mos ahead. No disk. Some sidebars. Prefers NRSV. Guidelines; copy for $3.50/9x12 SAE. (No ads)

> **Poetry:** Buys 12/yr. Free verse; to 25 lines; Marian themes only. Pays 2 year subscription and 6 copies. Submit max 2 poems.

#QUEST, Santa Ynez Presbyterian Church, 1825 Alamo Pintado Rd., Solvang CA 93463. E-mail: quest@syv.com. Website: QUEST.syv.com. Webpage with articles dealing with many life crises. Online magazine. **NO PAYMENT** for one-time or reprint rts. Articles about 500 wds (2 screens). Accepts simultaneous submissions & reprints. Prefers disk or e-mail submission (attached file, saved as text only). Guidelines (syvpc.syv.com, under Evangelism); copy for 9x12 SAE/3 stamps. Incomplete topical listings.

THE QUIET REVOLUTION, 1655 St. Charles St., Jackson MS 39209. (601) 353-1635. Fax (601)944-0403. E-mail: VOCM@go.com. Website: www. voiceofcalvary.com. Voice of Calvary Ministries. Meredith McGee, ed. Interracial ministry to the poor; conservative/evangelical. Quarterly mag; 7 pgs; circ 3,000. 10% freelance. Query or complete ms/cover letter. **NO PAYMENT** for one-time rts. Articles 3-4 pgs. Responds in 5 wks. Accepts reprints. Free copy.

> **Tips:** "Most open to articles about the history of Christianity."

REFLECTIONS, 48028 Andover Dr., Novi MI 48374. (734)261-2001. Fax (734)261-3282. E-mail: lucy@qix.net. Website: www.epc-reflections.org. Evangelical Presbyterian Church (EPC). Lucy McGuire, ed. To encourage people in their devotion to Christ and His Kingdom and to foster an awareness and appreciation of what God is doing in the ECP family. Triannual & online mag; 32 pgs; circ 29,000. Subscription free. 60% unsolicited freelance; 40% assigned. Query or complete ms/cover letter; fax/e-query OK. **PAYS IN COPIES** for one-time print & electronic rts. Articles 300-1,500 wds; technology articles, 250-700 wds (6/yr). Responds in 4 wks. Seasonal 6 mos ahead. Accepts simultaneous submissions. Accepts e-mail submissions (copied into message). Regular sidebars. Any version. Guidelines (also by e-mail/Website); copy for 9x12 SAE/4 stamps. (Ads)

> **Fillers:** Cartoons, facts, ideas, newsbreaks.
>
> **Columns/Departments:** Accepts 12/yr. Creative Ministries (church problem solving or unusual EPC ministries), 50-750 wds; National Outreach (EPC church stories), 350-1,500 wds; World Outreach (EPC efforts worldwide), 350-1,500 wds; News (from EPC churches or members of community), 50-200 wds; Technology.
>
> **Tips:** "Your chances are best if reporting on EPC church news or activities and/or EPC members. Deadlines for three issues are: December 31, April 14, and August 30."
>
> **1999 EPA Most Improved Publication.

$RE:GENERATION QUARTERLY, PO Box 381042, Cambridge MA 02238-1042. (617)868-3659. Fax (617)249-0270. E-mail: editor@regenerator.

com. Website: www.regenerator.com. The Regeneration Forum, Inc. Andrew Crouch, ed. Christians seeking to integrate faith and culture. Quarterly mag; 48 pgs; circ 3,000. Subscription $19.95. 40% unsolicited freelance; 60% assigned. Complete ms/cover letter; phone/fax/e-query OK. Pays $50-500 on publication for 1st, reprint and electronic rts. Articles 500-3,000 words (60/yr); book/music/video reviews 800 words, pays up to $100. Responds in 12-16 wks. Requires disk. Some sidebars. Prefers NRSV. Guidelines (also by e-mail/Website); sample for 9x12 SAE/$1.75 postage. (Ads)

> **Poetry:** Buys 4/yr. Avant-garde, free verse; 4-30 lines. Pays up to $200. Submit max 4 poems.
>
> **Tips:** "We're looking for manuscripts that relate Christianity to modern culture, or interpret culture through the lens of Christianity. Articles that emphasize the role of/need for Christian community are particularly desirable. Urban issues, sociology, cultural trends, ecumenicisms, new perspectives/fresh ideas all welcome."
>
> **This periodical was #15 on the 2000 Top 50 Christian Publishers list (#34 in 1999).

$+RELATE MAGAZINE, 2013 Barbara Dr., Slidell LA 70458. E-mail: editor@relatemagazine.org. Website: www.RelateMagazine.org. Inspirational stories and testimonies for the disabled. David Hudson, ed. Monthly mag. Launched 11/00. Complete ms (pasted into e-mail). Pays $40/article on publication for 1st, one-time or reprint rts. Articles to 800 wds. Seasonal 2 mos ahead. Accepts reprints. Guidelines on Website. Not in topical listings.

> **Tips:** "For each issue we need 3 pieces from disabled individuals and 2 from caregivers, family or friends. Include a 1-paragraph bio (plus e-mail or Website) with submissions."

#THE RESOURCE, PO Box 49, Jacksonville FL 32210. (904)387-2266. Fax (904)387-9212. E-mail: wzvara@wlz.com. Website: www.wlz.com. Christian Professional's Resource, Inc. William L. Zvara, ed. To proclaim the Gospel of Jesus Christ to professional, business and working people, and to provide Christian fellowship and instruction. Quarterly newsletter; circ 4,500. Subscription free. Accepts freelance. Complete ms. Incomplete topical listings. (Ads)

SACRED JOURNEY: The Journal of Fellowship in Prayer, 291 Witherspoon St., Princeton NJ 08542. (609)924-6863. Fax (609)924-6910. E-mail: editorial@sacredjourney.org. Website: www.sacredjourney.org. Fellowship In Prayer, Inc. Rebecca Laird, ed. An interfaith spirituality journal. Bimonthly journal; 48 pgs; circ 10,000. Subscription $16. 100% unsolicited freelance. Complete ms/cover letter; fax/e-query OK. **PAYS IN COPIES & SUBSCRIPTION** for one-time & electronic rts. Articles to 1,500 wds (40/yr); book reviews 400 wds. Responds in 8 wks. Seasonal 4 mos ahead. Accepts simultaneous submissions & reprints (tell when/where appeared). Requires disk or e-mail submission. No sidebars. Guidelines (also by e-mail); copy for 6x9 SAE/3 stamps. (No ads)

> **Poetry:** Accepts 6-8/yr. Free verse, haiku, light verse, traditional; 10-35 lines. Submit max 3 poems.

Columns/Departments: Buys 30/yr. A Transforming Experience (personal experience of spiritual significance); Pilgrimage (journey taken for spiritual growth or service); Spirituality and the Family; Spirituality and Aging; to 750 wds.

Special Needs: Meditation and service to others.

Tips: "Write well about your own spiritual experience and we'll consider it. Most open to a transforming experience feature."

$ST. ANTHONY MESSENGER, 1615 Republic St., Cincinnati OH 45210-1298. (513)241-5615. Fax (513)241-0399. E-mail: StAnthony@American Catholic.org. Website: www.AmericanCatholic.org. Jack Wintz, O.F.M., ed. For Catholic adults and families. Monthly & online mag; 60 pgs; circ 345,000. Subscription $22. 40% freelance. Query; fax/e-query OK. Pays .16/wd on acceptance for 1st, reprint (right to reprint), & electronic rts. Articles 1,500-2,500 wds (45-50/yr); fiction 1,500-2,500 wds (12/yr); book reviews 500 wds, $25. Responds in 8 wks. Seasonal 6+ mos ahead. Kill fee. Some sidebars. Prefers NAB. Guidelines; copy for 9x12 SAE. (Ads)

Poetry: Susan Hines-Brigger. Buys 20/yr. Free verse, haiku, traditional; 3-25 lines; $2/line ($10 min.) Submit max 2 poems.

Fillers: Cartoons.

Tips: "Most open to articles, fiction, profiles, interviews of Catholic personalities, personal experiences and prayer. Writing must be professional, use Catholic terminology and vocabulary. Writing must be faithful to Catholic belief and teaching, life and experience."

**This periodical was #35 on the 2000 Top 50 Christian Publishers list (#45 in 1999, #55 in 1997, #40 in 1994).

$ST. JOSEPH'S MESSENGER AND ADVOCATE OF THE BLIND, PO Box 288, Jersey City NJ 07303-0288. (201)798-4141. Catholic/Sisters of St. Joseph of Peace. Sister Mary Kuiken, CSJP, ed. For older Catholics interested in supporting ministry to the aged, young, blind, and needy. Triannual mag; 16 pgs; circ 15,500. Subscription $5. 30% freelance. Complete ms. Pays $35-50 on acceptance for 1st rts. Articles 800-1,200 wds (24/yr); fiction 800-1,200 wds (30/yr). Responds in 5 wks. Seasonal 3 mos ahead. Accepts simultaneous submissions & reprints (tell when/where appeared). No sidebars. Guidelines; copy for 9x12 SAE/2 stamps. (No ads)

Poetry: Buys 25/yr. Light verse, traditional; 4-16 lines; $10-25 on publication. Submit max 5 poems.

Fillers: Buys 20/yr. Ideas, 50-100 wds; $5-10.

Tips: "Most open to contemporary fiction. No Christmas issue."

*ST. WILLIBRORD JOURNAL**, Box 271751, Houston TX 77277-1751. (713) 515-8206. Fax (713)622-5311. Christ Catholic Church. Rev. Monsignor Charles E. Harrison, ed. Strictly Catholic; concentrating on the unchurched. Quarterly journal; 40 pgs; circ 500. Subscription $8. 5% unsolicited freelance. Complete ms/cover letter; no phone/e-query. **NO PAYMENT** for one-time rts. Not copyrighted. Articles to 1,000 wds. Responds in 9 wks. Seasonal 6 mos ahead. Some sidebars. Any version. No guidelines; copy $2. (No ads)

Columns/Departments: Question Box; Q & A column on doctrinal and biblical questions.

Tips: "We will read anything if it is sincere and orthodox. Most open to what's happening in the Christian church: doctrinal changes, attitude adjustments, moral attitudes. Especially want essays. Keep it short. Spare us your personal opinions; and remember the virtue of the simple, declarative sentence."

$+SAY AMEN MAGAZINE: The Magazine for Living in Christian Authority, PO Box 360658, Decatur GA 30036-0658. (770)808-4595. Fax (770) 808-0046. E-mail: vconwell@sayamen.com. Website: www.sayamen.com. Word Communications. Vikki Conwell, ed-in-chief. Focus is Christian lifestyles. Quarterly mag; circ 50,000. 80-90% freelance. Query/clips; fax/e-query OK. Pays $50-250 (assigned) or $50-150 (unsolicited) on publication for 1st rts. Articles 500-2,000 wds (16-20/yr). Responds in 4-9 wks. Seasonal 4 mos ahead. Accepts reprints. Free guidelines/copy. Incomplete topical listings.

Columns/Departments: Our Community (issues and concerns), 1,000 wds; Doing Good (profile of a positive ministry, organization, or activity), 1,000 wds; Relationships (family, friends, couples), 1,500 wds; Wealthwise (financial/business), 1,000 wds; $50-250.

Tips: "We cover basic lifestyle concerns in a lighthearted but thought-provoking way."

$#SCP JOURNAL & NEWSLETTER (Spiritual Counterfeits Project), PO Box 4308, Berkeley CA 94704-4308. (510)540-0300. Fax (510)540-1107. E-mail: scp@dnai.com. Website: www.scp-inc.org. Tal Brooke, ed. Christian apologetics for the college educated. Quarterly journal 55 pgs & newsletter; circ 15,000. Subscription $25. 5-10% freelance. Query/clips; phone query encouraged; e-query from Website. Pays $20-35/typeset pg on publication for negotiable rts. Articles 2,500-3,500 wds (5/yr); book reviews 1,500 wds. Responds in 13 wks. Accepts simultaneous query & reprints. Requires disk or e-mail submission (attached file). Some sidebars. Guidelines (also by e-mail); copy $8.75. (No ads)

Tips: "Must be an extremely good writer who is aware of the issues. Most of our writers come from the top 20 universities."

SEEDS MAGAZINE, 602 James Ave., Waco TX 76706-1476. (254)755-7745. Fax (254)753-1909. E-mail: SeedsHope@aol.com. Website: www.seeds publishers.org. Seeds of Hope Publishers. Katie Cook, ed. Committed to the healing of hunger and poverty in our world. Quarterly worship packet; 20 pgs. Subscription $120. E-query OK. **NO PAYMENT.**

$SEEK, 8121 Hamilton Ave., Cincinnati OH 45231. (513)931-4050x365. Fax (513)931-0950. E-mail: ewilmoth@standardpub.com. Website: www. Standardpub.com. Standard Publishing. Eileen H. Wilmoth, ed. Light, inspirational, take-home reading for young and middle-aged adults. Weekly take-home paper; 8 pgs; circ 45,000. No subscriptions. 98% freelance. Complete ms/cover letter. Pays .05/wd on acceptance for 1st or one-time rts, .025/wd for reprints. Articles 400-1,200 wds (150-200/yr); fiction 400-1,200 wds. No disk. Some sidebars. Responds in 13 wks. Seasonal 1 yr ahead. Accepts reprints (tell when/where appeared). Guidelines; copy for 6x9 SAE/2 stamps. (No ads)

Fillers: Buys 50/yr. Ideas, jokes, short humor. Pays $15.

**This periodical was #47 on the 2000 Top 50 Christian Publishers list (#54 in 1998, #56 in 1997, #49 in 1996, #57 in 1995, #36 in 1994).

$+SELAH!KIDS. E-mail: alessia@writefullyyoursfreelance.com. Website: www. writefullyyoursfreelance.com/selah!kids.htm. Alessia Cowee, ed/pub. Dedicated to the biblical ministry of parenting. Monthly print newsletter and e-zine. Subscription $12. Pays $3-6 on publication for 1st, electronic and archival rts. Responds in 4 wks. Accepts reprints. Prefers e-mail submissions. Guidelines by e-mail or Website. Incomplete topical listings.

Columns/Departments: SpiritLed (activities and ministries in which children are involved); Mini-Features by age group (infants, toddlers, preschoolers, elementary, jr. high, high-school, college-age and grown); and a special pull-out section for kids (includes fiction, poetry, activities, and coloring pages).

Special Needs: Feature articles, devotionals for parents and families, humor, essays. Each issue also included original essays, stories and artwork by children.

$THE SHANTYMAN, 2476 Argentia Rd., Ste. 213, Mississauga ON L5N 6M1 Canada. (905)821-6310. Fax (905)821-6311. E-mail: shanty@pathcom. com. Shantymen's Christian Assn. Phil Hood, mng ed. Distributed by their missionaries in remote areas of Canada and northern US as an evangelism tool. Bimonthly mini-tabloid; 16 pgs; circ 17,000. Subscription $12. 90% freelance. Complete ms/cover letter; no phone/fax query. Pays $20-50 CAN, on publication for one-time or reprint rts. Articles 800-1,600 wds (30/yr). Responds in 4-6 wks. Seasonal 6 mos ahead. Accepts reprints (tell when/where appeared). No disk. Some sidebars. Prefers NAS. Guidelines; copy for #10 SAE/2 stamps or IRCs.

Columns/Departments: Accepts 6/yr. Way of Salvation (fresh look at gospel message), 300-400 wds.

Tips: "We always have a need for salvation testimonies, first person (preferred) or as-told-to. We always have too many inspirational stories."

SHARING: A Journal of Christian Healing, 6807 Forest Haven St., San Antonio TX 78240-3343. (888)824-5387 or (210)681-5146. Fax (210)681-5146. E-mail: Marjorie_George@ecunet.org. Order of St. Luke the Physician. Marjorie George, ed. For Christians interested in spiritual and physical healing. Monthly journal; 32 pgs; circ 9,000. Subscription $12. 100% freelance. Complete ms/cover letter. **NO PAYMENT** for one-time or reprint rts. Articles 750-900 wds (50/yr). Responds in 3 wks. Seasonal 2 mos ahead. Accepts simultaneous submissions & reprints (tell when/where appeared). Prefers disk. Some kill fees. Some sidebars. Prefers RSV. Guidelines; copy for 8x10 SAE/2 stamps.

Poetry: Accepts 10-12/yr. Free verse, traditional; 6-14 lines.

Tips: "The entire magazine is open. We're looking for crisp, clear, well-written articles on the theology of healing and personal witness of healing. We do not return mss or poems, nor do we reply to inquiries regarding manuscript status."

SHORT STORIES BIMONTHLY, 5713 Larchmont Dr., Erie PA 16509. Phone/

fax (814)866-2543. E-mail: 75562.670@compuserve.com. Website: www. thepoetryforum.com. Poetry Forum. Gunvor Skogsholm, ed. Poetry and prose that takes an honest look at the human condition. Bimonthly mag; 24 pgs; circ 500. Subscription $26. 90% unsolicited freelance; 10% assigned. Query or complete ms/cover letter; fax/e-query OK. **NO PAYMENT** for one-time & electronic rts (buys only from subscribers). Not copyrighted. Articles 200 wds (5/yr); fiction 2,500 wds (50/yr); book reviews 200 wds. Responds in 4 wks. Seasonal 3 mos ahead. Accepts simultaneous submissions. Prefers disk or e-mail submission (copied into message). Some sidebars. Guidelines (also by e-mail/Website); copy $4. (Ads)

> **Poetry:** Accepts 200/yr. Any type; to 50 lines. Submit max 7 poems.
> **Fillers:** Accepts 3/yr. Prose, 20-50 wds.
> **Contest:** Chapbook contest, $12 entry fee. Prize: publication and 20 copies. Send SASE for information. December 15 deadline (may vary).
> **Tips:** "Our main strength is trying not to slant the magazine in order to let the authors speak. Buy a sample and find out what we use."

$SIGNS OF THE TIMES, Box 5353, Nampa ID 83653-5353. (208)465-2579. Fax (208)465-2531. E-mail: signs@pacificpress.com or mmoore@pacificpress. com. Website: www. pacificpress.com/signs. Seventh-Day Adventist. Marvin Moore, ed. Biblical principles relevant to all of life; for general public. Monthly mag; 32 pgs; circ 225,000. Subscription $18.95. 40% unsolicited freelance; 60% assigned. Complete ms/no cover letter. Pays $100-400 (.10-.20/wd) on acceptance for 1st rts. Articles 500-2,000 wds (75/yr). Responds in 4-9 wks. Seasonal 1 yr ahead. Accepts reprints (tell when/where appeared). Prefers disk/hard copy. Kill fee 50%. Some sidebars. Guidelines (also on Website); copy for 9x12 SAE/3 stamps. (No ads)

> **This periodical was #57 on the 2000 Top 50 Christian Publishers list (#44 in 1998, #33 in 1997, #34 in 1996, #42 in 1995, #33 in 1994).

SILVER WINGS MAYFLOWER PULPIT, PO Box 1000, Pearblossom CA 93553-1000. (661)264-3726. E-mail: poetwing@yahoo.com. Poetry on Wings. Jackson Wilcox, ed. Christian understanding and uplift through poetry. Bimonthly mag; 12-16 pgs; circ 200. Subscription $10. 100% unsolicited freelance. Complete ms; no phone/fax/e-query. **PAYS 1 COPY** for 1st rts. Not copyrighted. Poetry only. Responds in 3 wks. Seasonal 5 mos ahead. Accepts reprints. No disk or e-mail submissions. No sidebars. Prefers KJV. Guidelines; copy $2/6x9 SAE. (No ads)

> **Poetry:** Accepts 100/yr. Free verse, haiku, light verse, traditional; 2-20 lines. Submit max 5 poems. No payment.
> **Contest:** Annual poetry contest (December 31 deadline); send SASE for details.
> **Tips:** "Our publication seeks to be evangelical—for some a first opportunity to be published."

$SINGLE-PARENT FAMILY, 8605 Explorer Dr., Colorado Springs CO 80920. (719)531-3400. Fax (719)531-3499. E-mail: spfmag@macmail.fotf.org. Website: www.family.org. Focus on the Family. Susan Goodwin Graham, ed. To encourage and equip single parents to do the best job they can at creating stable, godly homes for themselves and their children. Monthly mag; 8 pgs; circ. 70,000. Subscription $15. 15% unsolicited freelance; 50% assigned. Complete ms/cover letter; fax query OK. Pays .10-.15/wd, on receipt of signed contract, for 1st, electronic & foreign rts. Articles 500-1,650 wds. Responds in 4 wks. Seasonal 5-6 mos ahead. Accepts e-mail submissions (attached file or copied into message). Kill fee 50%. Some sidebars. Prefers NIV. Guidelines (also by e-mail/Website); catalog for 9x12 SAE/3 stamps. (Ads—Briargate Media, Attn: Becky Blair 719-531-3400)

> **Fillers:** Buys 84/yr. Anecdotes, cartoons, facts; 50-100 wds; $25-75.

> **Columns/Departments:** Brad Cope, assoc. ed. Buys 36/yr. Money Talk (cutting expenses); For Fathers (single fathers); Focus on Counseling (special needs of single parents); all to 1,000 wds; $150-225.

> **Tips:** "Query showing a single-parent focus and why you are qualified to speak to the issues. We still take unsolicited manuscripts in the areas of adult, emotional, financial, parenting, and lifeskill issues. We want new ways to convey timeless messages using quotes and statistics and personal stories where possible."

$*SMART FAMILIES, PO Box 500050, San Diego CA 92150-0050. (858)513-7150. Fax (858)513-7142. E-mail: info@familyuniversity.com. Website: www.familyuniversity.com. Submit to editor. Christian parenting, with strong crossover to secular families. Quarterly & online newsletter; 16 pgs; circ 140,000. Subscription $24 (includes 2 tapes). 20% unsolicited freelance. Complete ms preferred; fax/e-query OK. Pays $50-250 on publication for 1st rts. Articles 200-1,000 wds. Responds in 1-3 wks. Seasonal 4 mos ahead. Accepts simultaneous submissions & reprints. Prefers disk; accepts e-mail submission (attached file). Some sidebars. Prefers NIV. Guidelines (also by e-mail); copy for 10x13 SAE/4 stamps. (No ads)

> **Fillers:** Games, ideas, quotes.

> **Tips:** "We are not a magazine and have tight length requirements. Because of crossover audience, we do not regularly print Scripture references or use traditional God-word language."

$SOCIAL JUSTICE REVIEW, 3835 Westminster Pl., St. Louis MO 63108-3472. (314)371-1653. E-mail: centbur@juno.com. Website: www.socialjustice review.org. Catholic Central Union of America. Rev. John H. Miller, C.S.C., ed. For those interested in the social teaching of the Catholic Church. Bimonthly journal; 32 pgs; circ 4,950. Subscription $20. 90% freelance. Query or complete ms/cover letter. Pays .02/wd on publication for one-time rts. Not copyrighted. Articles to 3,000 wds (80/yr); book reviews 500 wds (**no pay**). Responds in 1 wk. Seasonal 3 mos ahead. Accepts reprints (tell when/where appeared). No disk or e-mail submission. No sidebars. Guidelines; copy for 9x12 SAE/3 stamps. (No ads)

> **Columns/Departments:** Virtue; Economic Justice; variable length. Query.

> **Tips:** "Fidelity to papal teaching and clarity and simplicity of style; thoughtful and thought-provoking writing."

$SOJOURNERS, 2401 15th St. NW, Washington DC 20009. (202)328-8842. Fax (202)328-8757. E-mail: sojourners@sojourners.com. Website: www.

sojourners.com. Jim Rice, mng ed. For those who seek to turn their lives toward the biblical vision of justice and peace. Bimonthly mag; 68 pgs; circ. 24,000. Subscription $30. 5% unsolicited freelance; 25% assigned. Query; e-query OK. Pays $75-200 on publication for all rts. Articles 600-3,600 wds (10/yr); book/music reviews, 650-1,300 wds, $50-100 (to Molly Marsh, asst ed). Responds in 6 wks. Seasonal 6 mos ahead. Kill fee. Prefers NRSV. Regular sidebars. Guidelines (also by e-mail/Website); copy for 9x12 SAE. (Ads)

Poetry: Rose Marie Berger. Accepts 6-10/yr. Free verse, haiku; $50.

Fillers: Accepts 6 cartoons/yr; also other unsolicited artwork and photographs.

Columns/Departments: Buys 15/yr. Culture Watch (reviews), 650-1,300 wds; Commentary (editorials), 650 wds; $75.

Tips: "Looking for cartoons this year. Most open to features, Culture Watch reviews, and short pieces on groups working successfully in their communities to empower the poor, create jobs, and promote peace and reconciliation."

**1996 EPA Award of Merit—General; 1999 ACP Award: Best in Class.

#THE SOUTHEAST LOOKOUT, 300 Envoy Cir, Ste 300, Louisville KY 40299. (502)499-0185. Fax (502)499-6968. E-mail: outlookgm@christianliving. net, or rmcintire@secc.org. Rick McIntire, ed. To reach the lost, edify the saved, and hold up a biblical standard of truth. Weekly newspaper; circ 18,200. Subscription for donation. Accepts freelance. Prefers complete ms. Not in topical listings. (Ads)

$SPIRIT, PO Box 850, 4901 Pennsylvania, Joplin MO 64802. (417)624-7050. Fax (417)624-7102. E-mail: aaronw@pcg.org. Website: www.PCG.org. Pentecostal Church of God. Aaron M. Wilson, ed. Sharing testimonies, life experiences, and spiritual insight related to the work of the Holy Spirit in today's world. Monthly mag; 32 pgs; circ 14,000. Subscription $8.50. Complete ms; e-query OK. Pays .02/wd on publication for 1st, one-time or reprint rts. Articles 400-1,200 wds (100/yr). Responds in 2 wks (by e-mail immediately). Seasonal 3 mos ahead. Accepts simultaneous submissions & reprints (tell when/where appeared). Accepts disk or e-mail submissions (attached or copied into message). Some sidebars. Prefers KJV. Guidelines/theme list (also by e-mail); copy for 6x9 SAE/2 stamps. (Ads)

Poetry: Buys 10-12/yr. Free verse, traditional; 16-20 lines. Pays $2-8.

Fillers: Buys 20/yr. Anecdotes, cartoons, jokes, short humor; 250-300 wds. Pays .02/wd.

Tips: "Any writer who can effectively share answered-prayer stories, etc., can make it here. We help new writers if material is worthy."

$SPIRITUAL LIFE, 2131 Lincoln Rd. NE, Washington DC 20002-1199. (202) 832-8489. Fax (202)832-8967. E-mail: edodonnell@aol.com. Website: www.Spiritual-Life.org. Catholic. Edward O'Donnell, O.C.D., ed. For college-educated Christians interested in spirituality. Quarterly mag; 64 pgs; circ 12,000. Subscription $15. 80% freelance. Complete ms/cover letter; phone/fax query OK. Pays $50-250 ($10/ms pg) on acceptance for 1st rts. Articles/essays 3,000-5,000 wds (20/yr); book reviews 1,500 wds, $15. Responds in 9 wks. Seasonal 9 mos ahead. Accepts simultaneous submissions. Requires disk. No sidebars. Prefers NAB. Guidelines; copy for 7x10 SAE/5 stamps.

Tips: "No stories of personal healing, conversion, miracles, etc."

$SPORTS SPECTRUM and SPORTS SPECTRUM ONLINE, 3000 Kraft SE, PO Box 3566, Grand Rapids MI 49512. (616)974-2711. Fax (616)957-5741. E-mail: ssmag@sport.org. Website: www.sport.org. Discovery House Publishers. Dave Branon, mng ed. A high-quality national sports magazine that features Christian athletes. Bimonthly & online mag; 32 pgs; circ 45,000. Subscription $17.97. 65% assigned. Query/clips; fax/e-query OK. Pays .21/wd on acceptance for all rts. Not copyrighted. Articles 250-2,200 wds (40/yr). Responds in 3-4 wks. Accepts disk or e-mail submission. Kill fee 30-50%. Regular sidebars. Prefers NIV. Guidelines (also by e-mail); copy for 9x12 SAE/4 stamps. (Ads)

> **Columns/Departments:** Buys 15/yr. Legends (past/retired Christian athletes), 250 wds; Champions (lesser-known athletes), 800 wds. Pays .21/wd. Query.
>
> **Tips:** "The best thing a writer can do is to be aware of the special niche *Sports Spectrum* has developed in sports ministry. Then, find athletes who fit that niche and who haven't been covered in the magazine."
>
> **This periodical was #69 on the 1994 Top 50 Christian Publishers list. 1998 EPA Award of Merit—General.

+SR: A JOURNAL FOR LUTHERAN REFORMATION, E-mail: jglange@ allwest.net. Website: members.aol.com/SemperRef. Semper Reformada. Rev. Jonathan G. Lange, ed. Publishes reformation theses only. Complete ms by e-mail. Open to original articles and reprints of essays from old theological journals. No mention of payment. Guidelines on Website.

$STANDARD, 6401 The Paseo, Kansas City MO 64131. (816)333-7000. Fax (816)333-4439. Website: www.nazarene.org. Nazarene. Rev. Everett Leadingham, ed. Examples of Christianity in everyday life for adults, college-age through retirement. Weekly take-home paper; 8 pgs; circ 160,000. Subscription $8.95. 100% freelance. Complete ms. Pays .035/wd (.02/wd for reprints) on acceptance for one-time or reprint rts. Articles (20/yr) or fiction (200/yr) 500-1,500 wds. Responds in 10 wks. Seasonal 6 mos ahead. Accepts simultaneous submissions & reprints (tell when/ where appeared). No disk. Kill fee. No sidebars. Prefers NIV. Guidelines/ copy for #10 SAE/2 stamps.

> **Poetry:** Buys 50/yr. Free verse, haiku, traditional; to 50 lines; pay .25/line. Submit max 5 poems.
>
> **Fillers:** Buys 50/yr. Word puzzles; $20.
>
> **Tips:** "Fiction or true-experience stories must demonstrate Christianity in action. Show us, don't tell us. Action in stories must conform to Wesleyan-Arminian theology and practices." Themes follow the Christian year, not celebrating national holidays.
>
> **This periodical was #22 on the 2000 Top 50 Christian Publishers list (#18 in 1999, #15 in 1998, #68 in 1997, #41 in 1996, #12 in 1995, #2 in 1994).

THE STANDARD, 2002 S. Arlington Hts. Rd., Arlington Hts. IL 60005.

(847)228-0200. Fax (847)228-5376. E-mail: jhanning@baptistgeneral.org. Website: www.bgc.bethel.edu. Baptist General Conference. Jodi Hanning, mng ed. Denominational. Monthly (10X) mag; 32 pgs; circ. 9,000. Subscription $15.75. 60-70% freelance. Query or complete ms/no cover letter; e-query OK. Pays $15-200+ on publication for 1st & electronic rts. Articles 500-1,200 wds (20-30/yr). Responds in 6-8 wks. Seasonal 3 mos ahead. Accepts simultaneous submissions & reprints (tell when/where appeared). Prefers disk or e-mail submission (copied into message). Kill fee 50%. Regular sidebars ($20). Prefers NIV. Guidelines/theme list (also by e-mail); copy for 9x12 SAE/4 stamps. (Ads)

> **Special Needs:** Looking for reporters willing to work with editor on assignments about the Baptist General Conference. Open to denominational news, 30-150 words.
>
> **Tips:** "When we use a general article, it has to be tailor-made to fit our themes."
>
> **1997 EPA Award of Merit—Denominational.

*THE STAR OF ZION, 401 E. 2nd St., Charlotte NC 28231. (704)377-4329. Fax (704)377-2809. E-mail: starozion@juno.com. African Methodist Episcopal Zion Church. Dr. Marie P. Tann, assoc ed. Ethnic publication; moderate; conservative. Biweekly tabloid; 16-20 pgs; circ 8,000. Subscription $33. 90% unsolicited freelance. Query; phone/fax/e-query OK. **PAYS 5 COPIES.** Articles & fiction to 600 wds. Responds in 9 wks. Seasonal 2 mos ahead. Accepts simultaneous submissions. No sidebars. Copy $1/10x14 SAE/2 stamps. (Ads)

> **Poetry:** African-American themes.
>
> **Fillers:** Short humor.

STEPPING OUT OF THE DARKNESS, PO Box 712, Hingham MA 02043. (781)878-5531 (no calls). E-mail: ThePuritanLight@aol.com. Website: members.tripod.com/puritan55. Puritan emphasis. Sharon White, ed. Designed to draw heart and soul close to God. Monthly newsletter; 10-17 pgs; circ 60, plus free distribution in Boston. Subscription $15. Estab. 1998. 25% unsolicited freelance; 5% assigned. Complete ms/cover letter. **NO PAYMENT.** Articles 100-1,600 wds (24/yr); family fiction 100-700 wds (12/yr). Responds in 2-4 wks. Seasonal 2 mos ahead. No disk. No sidebars. KJV only. Guidelines; copy $3/#10 SAE/2 stamps. (No ads)

> **Poetry:** Rachel White. Accepts 12-24/yr. Any type; 4-40 lines. Submit max 4 poems.
>
> **Fillers:** Accepts 12/yr. Anecdotes, facts, ideas; 25-100 wds.
>
> **Special Needs:** Personal accounts of Puritan missionary work in America. Letters of testimony from teens who have overcome the darkness of the world.
>
> **Contest:** Puritan History Day Contest. Deadline January 15, 2001. Fiction and articles on Puritan living in the present (see guidelines for specifics). Open to subscribers only. Contact for information on future contests.
>
> **Tips:** "Be familiar with Puritan life in the 1600's. Find a way to bring history alive for us now and show how we can live fully dedicated lives to God. Do not seek to entertain our readers; strive to transform

them. You must read our publication and understand our focus. We are becoming more selective but are always open to new writers. (We offer a free critique on request.) If you are willing to forsake the world with all its distractions, focus your heart on God, and pray for guidance from the Holy Spirit, we want to see your work."

$STEWARDSHIP, 200 E. Big Beaver Rd., Troy MI 48083. (248)680-4600. Fax (248)680-4601. Parish Publications, Inc. Richard Meurer, ed. To help church members understand stewardship. Monthly newsletter; 4 pgs. 50% freelance. Query or complete ms/cover letter; fax query OK. Pays $25-100 on acceptance for all rts. Articles 160 or 200 words exactly. Responds in 2 wks. Prefers hard copy. Some sidebars. Free copy. (No ads)

Tips: "Write articles that zero in on stewardship—general, time, talent, or treasure—as it relates to the local church."

THE STORYTELLER, 2442 Washington Rd., Maynard AR 72444. (870)647-2137. Fax (870)647-2137. E-mail: storyteller1@cox-internet.com. Fossil Creek Publishing. Regina Cook Williams, ed/pub. Family audience; geared to (but not limited to) new writers. Quarterly mag; 64 pgs; circ 350. Subscription $20. 100% unsolicited freelance. Complete ms/cover letter; no phone/fax/e-query. **NO PAYMENT** for 1st rts. Articles 1,500 wds (50/yr); fiction 1,500 wds. Responds in 3-4 wks. Seasonal 3 mos ahead. Accepts simultaneous submissions & reprints (tell when/where appeared). No disk. No sidebars. Guidelines; copy $6/9x12 SAE/$1.13 postage. (Ads)

Poetry: Accepts 100/yr. Free verse, haiku, light verse, traditional; 3-40 lines. Submit max 3 poems.

Fillers: Accepts 10/yr. Anecdotes, cartoons, facts, quotes, short humor; 25-35 wds. Writing related only.

Contest: Each quarter the magazine has a contest and the published works of that quarter are automatically entered. Winners in fiction, nonfiction, essays and poetry receive a free copy of the magazine.

Tips: "Since the magazine is geared to new writers, we are very open to their work. Well-written stories are all that are accepted. Follow guidelines. Stories will be rejected without being read if they are too long, wrong subjects, and/or handwritten."

STUDIO: A Journal of Christians Writing, 727 Peel St., Albury NSW 2640 Australia. Phone/fax (+61)2 6021 1135. E-mail: pgrover@bigpond.com. Submit to Studio Editor. Quarterly journal; 36 pgs; circ 300. Subscription $48 AUD. 90% unsolicited freelance; 10% assigned. Query. **PAYS IN COPIES** for one-time rts. Articles 3,000 wds (15/yr); fiction 3,000 wds (50/yr); book reviews 300 wds. Responds in 3 wks. Accepts simultaneous submissions & reprints (tell when/where appeared). No disks or e-mail submissions. No sidebars. Guidelines (send IRC); copy for $8 AUD. Incomplete topical listings. (Ads)

Poetry: Accepts 200/yr. Any type; 4-100 lines. Submit max 3 poems.

Contest: See copy of journal for details.

$STUDIO CLASSROOM, 51 Wrangler Dr., Bozeman MT 59718. Fax (406) 586-1571. E-mail: ruth@imt.net. Website: www.ortv.tw. Overseas Radio & Television (a Christian ministry). Ruth Seamans Devlin, exec ed. Used to teach English to the Chinese in Taiwan. Print and online version. 50% unsolicited freelance. Query or complete ms; fax/e-query OK. Pays .25/wd on acceptance. Articles 600-800 wds. (Ads)

Fillers: Anecdotes, cartoons, quizzes, short humor, and word puzzles.

Special Needs: Short stories, travel articles, health or business tips.

Tips: "Most readers are not Christians, so articles shouldn't be religious (except material for the Christmas and Easter issues). Our magazine content is similar to *Reader's Digest*."

+SUNFLOWER PRESS MAGAZINES, 914 S. Henderson St., Galesburg IL 61401-5747. E-mail: moellersunflower@yahoo.com. Website: members. xoom.com/Sunflowersun/SUNFLOWER.htm. Produces several magazines & 1 e-zine. Mary Moeller, ed/pub. Quarterly and bimonthly mags and annuals. Subscriptions $10-15. Not in topical listings. (Ads)

Poetry: Accepts any length or type.

Contest: Entry fee for poetry, $1 for 2 poems; $5 for 2 short stories (3,000 wds); $1 for 1 essay/article. Prizes $5-$40.

$*SURSUM CORDA! The Catholic Revival, PO Box 993, Ridgefield CT 06877. Fax (203)438-1305. Foundation for Catholic Reform. Roger McCaffrey, ed; submit to Tom Woods, mng ed. Covers the good things that happen in the Catholic Church; includes a 16-page homeschooling section. Quarterly mag; circ 16,000. Complete ms; fax query OK. Pays $150-500 on publication for one-time or reprint rts. Articles 2,000-5,000 wds (2/yr); religious fiction. Responds in 5-9 wks. Accepts simultaneous submissions & reprints. Free copy.

Tips: "Keep in mind that the theme of our magazine is the orthodox Catholic Revival. We are conservative."

TEAK ROUNDUP, Sardis Stn. Main, PO Box 2093, Sardis BC V2R 1A5 Canada. (604)824-9528. Fax (604)824-9541. E-mail: wcpp@telus.net. Website: www.wcpar.com. West Coast Paradise Publishing. Robert G. Anstey, ed. General, family-oriented poetry and prose. Quarterly mag; 52 pgs; circ. 200. Subscription $13 US, $17 CAN. Query; phone/fax query OK. **NO PAYMENT** for 1st rts. Articles to 1,500 wds (30/yr) & fiction to 1,500 wds; book reviews to 1,000 wds. Responds in 1 wk. Seasonal 2 mos ahead. Accepts simultaneous submissions & reprints. Accepts disk. Some sidebars. Prefers KJV. Guidelines; copy $4 US/$5 CAN/6x9 SAE/$1 CAN postage or $1.21 US. (Ads)

Poetry: Accepts 200/yr. Any type; to 40 lines. Submit max 5 poems.

Fillers: Anecdotes, cartoons, ideas, newsbreaks, party ideas, prose, short humor. Also accepts line-art drawings.

Columns/Departments: Accepts 40/yr. Markets (listing of other magazines), short; Writing (how-to), short. Query.

Contest: For subscribers only.

Tips: Most open to prose and poetry. Subscribers only are eligible for publication.

$TESTIMONY (formerly The Pentecostal Testimony), 2450 Milltower Ct., Mississauga ON L5N 5Z6 Canada. (905)542-7400. Fax (905)542-7313. E-mail: testimony@paoc.org. Website: www.paoc.org. The Pentecostal Assemblies of Canada. Rick Hiebert, ed. Focus is inspirational and Christian living; Pentecostal holiness slant. Monthly & online mag; 24 pgs; circ 21,500. Subscription $24 US/$17 CAN. 10% freelance. Query; fax/e-query OK. Pays $20-75 on publication for 1st or reprint rts. Articles 800-1,000 wds. Responds in 6-8 wks. Seasonal 4 mos ahead. Accepts reprints (tell when/where appeared). Prefers e-mail submission (copied into message). Regular sidebars. Prefers NIV. Guidelines; copy $2/9x12 SAE. (Ads)

> **Special Needs:** Prayer; reaching postmoderns.
>
> **Tips:** "Our readership is 98% Canadian. We prefer Canadian writers or at least writers who understand that Canadians are not Americans in long underwear."

THEGOODSTEWARD.COM, 2518 Plantation Dr., Matthews NC 28105. (704)841-7828. Fax (704)321-0185. E-mail: info@wallwatchers.org. Website: www.thegoodsteward.com. Wall Watchers. Michael Barrick, ed. To increase the level of giving to Christian ministries and provide a central source of information on those ministries. Weekly e-zine. 2% unsolicited freelance; 10% assigned. Query; e-query OK. **USUALLY NO PAYMENT**, except for providing a link to your e-mail or Website on publication. Articles 500-750 wds; book reviews 500 wds. Responds in 2 wks. Seasonal 2 mos ahead. Accepts simultaneous submissions and reprints. Requires e-mail submissions (attached file). No sidebars. Guidelines on Website. (No ads)

> **Special Needs:** Looking for information/articles that match well with the site's themes—biblical stewardship, life stewardship, environmental stewardship, and responsible giving. Books reviewed must be published within last 90 days.
>
> **Tips:** "Subject areas include: Biblical Principles (general precepts of biblical stewardship); Life Stewardship (physical health, fitness and well being, spiritual gifts, talents, use of time, and relationships); Financial Matters (saving, budgeting, investing, tax strategy, insurance and estate planning); Giving Wisely (tithing and responsible giving); and Environment (ecology, recycling, environmental management, and conservation)."

$*THIS ROCK, 2020 Gillespie Way, El Cajon CA 92020, or PO Box 19000, San Diego CA 92159-9000. (619)387-7200. Fax (619)387-0042. E-mail: editor@catholic.com. Website: www.catholic.com. Catholic. Tim Ryland, ed. Deals with doctrine, evangelization and apologetics. Monthly (10X) mag; 48 pgs; circ 15,000. Subscription $39.95. 70% freelance. Query. Pays up to $300 on publication for 1st rts. Articles 1,500-3,500 wds. Responds in 4-6 wks. Guidelines (also by e-mail).

TIME FOR RHYME, PO Box 1055, Battleford SK S0M 0E0 Canada. (306)445-5172. Family Books. Richard W. Unger, ed. Poetry only; not strictly Christian (but editor is). Quarterly mag; 32 pgs; circ about 100. Subscription $12, US or CAN. 80% unsolicited freelance; 0% assigned. Complete ms/cover letter; phone query OK. **PAYS IN COPIES** for 1st rts. Responds as soon as possible. Seasonal 1 yr ahead. Accepts reprints (tell when/where appeared). Prefers KJV. Guidelines; copy $3.25 US or CAN. (Classified ads)

> **Poetry:** Buys 50/yr; light verse or traditional; 2-32 lines. Rhyming only; light or serious. Submit max 5 poems.

Tips: "Write poetry honest to the heart. Truly see, smell, etc., the experience first—focus—then write. Don't hold readers at arm's length; let them experience it with you (show, don't tell)." US authors can send a $1 US bill to cover return postage—no US stamps.

TIME OF SINGING: A Magazine of Christian Poetry, PO Box 149, Conneaut Lake PA 16316. E-mail: timesing@toolcity.net. Website: www.timeofsinging.bizland.com. Lora Zill, ed. We try to appeal to all poets and lovers of poetry. Quarterly booklet; 44 pgs; circ 250. Subscription $15. 95% unsolicited freelance; 5% assigned. Complete ms/cover letter; e-query OK. **PAYS IN COPIES** for 1st, one-time or reprint rts. Poetry only. Responds in 6-8 wks. Seasonal 6-8 mos ahead. Accepts simultaneous submissions & reprints (tell when/where appeared). Accepts e-mail submission. Guidelines/theme list (also by e-mail); copy $4.

> **Poetry:** Accepts 150-200/yr. Free verse, haiku, light verse, traditional forms; 3-50 lines. Submit max 5 poems. Always need form poems (sonnets, villanelles, triolets) with Christian themes.
> **Contest:** Sponsors 1-2 annual poetry contests on specific themes or forms ($2 entry fee/poem) with cash prizes (send SASE for rules).
> **Tips:** "Study poetry, read widely—both Christian and non-Christian. Work at the craft. Be open to suggestions and critique, and take it seriously. If I have taken time to comment on your work, it is close to publication. If you don't agree, submit elsewhere."

*TIMES OF REFRESHING, Box 6855, Fort St. John BC V1J 4J3 Canada. (250)785-7215. Daniel Yordy, ed. A deeper expression of the gospel for mature Christians. Monthly newsletter; 8 pgs; circ 60. Subscription $20 CAN, $18 US. Open to freelance. Complete ms. **PAYS A SUBSCRIPTION** for one-time rts. Articles 1,500-2,000 wds (3-4/yr). Prefers NKJV. Guidelines; copy for #10 SAE/1 stamp. (No ads)

> **Tips:** "We look for a fresh word from God for his church. Interested in pieces that point to a closer walk with God, based on the Scriptures."

$#TODAY'S CHRISTIAN SENIOR, 128 Pleasant Dr., Schaumburg IL 60194-3535. E-mail: BryanBice@aol.com. Scepter Publication. Bryan Bice, ed. Geared to senior citizens in the areas of health, finances, ministry and travel. Quarterly mag; 16 pgs; circ 50,000. Subscription free. 15% freelance. Complete ms/cover letter; e-query OK. Pays $150 on publication for 1st, one-time or simultaneous rts. Articles & fiction 900-1,000 wds. Responds in 4 wks. Seasonal 9 mos ahead. Accepts reprints (tell when/where appeared). Prefers disk. Regular sidebars. Prefers KJV. Guidelines/theme list; copy for 9x12 SAE/3stamps. (Ads)

> **Poetry:** Light verse, traditional. Pays $25. Submit max 3 poems.
> **Fillers:** Cartoons, jokes; $10.

$TOGETHER, 13241 Port Republic Rd., Grottoes VA 24441. (540)249-3900. Fax (540)249-3177. E-mail: Tgether@aol.com. Website: www.churchoutreach.com. Shalom Foundation, Inc. Melodie Davis, ed. An outreach magazine distributed by churches to attract the general public to Christian faith & life. Quarterly tabloid; 8 pgs; circ 150,000. Free. 95% unsolicited freelance. Complete ms/cover letter; e-query OK. Pays $30-50 on publication for one-time rts. Articles 500-1,200 wds (16/yr). Responds in 12-16 wks. Seasonal 4 mos ahead. Accepts simultaneous submissions & reprints. Accepts disk or e-mail submission (copied into message). Some sidebars. Prefers NIV. Guidelines/theme list (also by e-mail); copy for 9x12 SAE/4 stamps. (No ads)

> **Tips:** "Always looking for contemporary stories. We need a variety of salvation testimonies from all racial/ethnic groups, with excellent photos available (don't submit photos until requested)."

$TOMORROW'S CHRISTIAN GRADUATE, PO Box 1357, Oak Park, IL 60304. (708)524-5070. Fax: (708) 524-5174. E-mail: WINPress7@aol. com. Website: www.christiangraduate.com. Kipland Publishing House/WINPress. Phillip Huber, mng.ed. Planning guide for adults pursuing a seminary or Christian graduate education. Annual mag; 32+ pgs; circ 150,000. Free to prospective seminary or Christian graduate school students. 0% unsolicited freelance; 85% assigned. Prefers 1-page query; fax/e-query OK. Payment .06-.15/wd on publication for all rts (usually). Articles 800-1,200 wds. Prefers e-mail submissions (attached file). Kill fee. Regular sidebars. Prefers NIV. Guidelines/theme list (also by e-mail); copy $3. (Ads)

> **Special Needs:** First-person and how-to features that express the value of a seminary or Christian graduate education and focus on all topics of interest to adults pursuing graduate studies, including paying for graduate school, earning a degree at home, financial aid and scholarships, study tips, entrance requirements, Christian education for marketplace careers, spending time with God, selecting a school, interdisciplinary studies, applying for admission, time management, training for missions.

> **Tips:** "We are open to working with new/unpublished authors, especially current graduate students, graduates, professors, admissions personnel, career counselors and financial aid officers. Visit our Website to view articles we've previously published."

$*TOTAL HEALTH, 165 N. 100 E. Ste 2, St. George UT 84770-2505. Submit to Arpi Coliglow, asst ed. A family health magazine. Bimonthly mag; 70 pgs; circ 90,000. Subscription $16. 75% freelance. Query or complete ms/cover letter. Pays $50-75 on publication for all and reprint rts. Articles 1,400-1,800 wds (48/yr). Responds in 4 wks. Seasonal 4 mos ahead. Accepts simultaneous submissions. Regular sidebars. Requires disk (Mac). Guidelines; copy $1/9x12 SAE/5 stamps.

> **Columns/Departments:** Contemporary Herbal, 1,000 wds, $50.

> **Tips:** "Most open to self-help and prevention articles."

$TOUCHSTONE: A Journal of Mere Christianity, PO Box 410788, Chicago IL 60641. (773)481-1090. Fax (773)481-1095. E-mail: touchstone@fsj. org. Website: www.fsj.org. Fellowship of St. James. James Kushiner, ed. News and opinion devoted to a thoughtful appreciation of orthodox Christian faith. Monthly (10x) mag; 48 pgs; circ 4,200. 20% unsolicited freelance; 80% assigned. Complete ms; fax/e-query OK. Pay $100/typeset pg on publication for one-time & electronic rts. Articles 3,000-6,000 wds (6/yr); book/video reviews 2,000-3,000 wds. Responds in 4 wks. Seasonal 4 mos ahead. Accepts simultaneous submissions & reprints (tell when/where appeared). Prefers disk or e-mail submission (attached file). Regular sidebars. Prefers RSV or NIV. Guidelines; copy for 10x13 SAE/7 stamps. (Ads)

Fillers: Cartoons.

THE TRUMPETER, 6767 Sunset Dr., Ste. 200, South Miami FL 33143-4823. (305)668-6462. Fax (305)668-3596. E-mail: info@thetrumpeter.com. Website: www.thetrumpeter.com. Non-denominational. Martiele Swanko, ed-in-chief. Unites all South Florida Christian denominations, ethnic groups, and cultures. Bimonthly & online mag; 60 pgs; circ 50,000. 100% freelance. Complete ms/cover letter; e-submission OK. Features & sports, 900-1,000 wds; articles 500-1,700 wds; book reviews, 150 wds; music reviews, 125 wds; video reviews, 100 wds. **NO PAYMENT**. Accepts reprints (tell when/where appeared). Requires disk or e-mail submission. Regular sidebars. Prefers NIV. Guidelines/theme list (also by e-mail or Website). (Ads)

Fillers: Cartoons.

Columns/Departments: Around Town (local talk), 100-125 wds; Arts & Entertainment, 400 wds; Legal, 450 wds; Political/Viewpoint, 100-125 wds.

Tips: "Be a good writer. Know how to affectively write a paragraph by the rules and use active verbs instead of adjectives."

*2-SOAR, 222 S. Falcon, South Bend IN 46619. (219)289-8760. Church of God in Christ (Pentecost). Izola Bird, pub. Denominational. Quarterly newsletter; 8 pgs; circ 7,000. Subscription $15. 95% freelance. Complete ms/cover letter; no phone query. **PAYS IN COPIES** for all rts. Articles 1 pg. Responds in 4 wks. No disk. No sidebars. No guidelines; copy $3.75. (Ads)

Poetry: Accepts 4-10/yr. Free verse, light verse, traditional, love, spiritual, inspirational; to 20 lines. Submit max 4 poems.

Contest: Spring poetry contest; entry fee $10. Send SASE for details.

Tips: "All areas open to freelancers. We want to hear from African-American writers."

$THE UNITED CHURCH OBSERVER, 478 Huron St., Toronto ON M5R 2R3 Canada. (416)960-8500. Fax (416)960-8477. E-mail: general@ucobserver.org. Website: www.ucobserver.org. United Church of Canada. Muriel Duncan, ed. No freelance for 2001.

$UPSCALE MAGAZINE: Exposure to the World's Finest, 600 Bronner Brothers Way SW, Atlanta GA 30310. (404)758-7467. Fax (404)755-9892. E-mail: upscale8@mindspring.com. Website: www.upscalemagazine.com. Upscale Communications, Inc. Sheila Bronner, ed-in-chief; submit to Sylviette McGill, mng ed. To inspire, inform, and entertain African-Americans. Monthly mag; circ 242,000. 75-80% freelance. Query; fax/e-query OK. Pays $100 & up for all rts. Articles (135/yr); novel excerpts. Seasonal 6 mos ahead. Accepts simultaneous submissions. Kill fee 25%. Guidelines; copy $2.

Columns/Departments: Kim Hamilton. Buys 25/yr. Positively You, Viewpoint, Perspective (personal inspiration/perspective). Query. Pays $75. These columns most open to freelance.

Tips: "We are open to queries for exciting and informative nonfiction." Uses inspirational and religious articles.

UPSOUTH, 323 Bellevue Ave., Bowling Green KY 42101-5001. (502)843-8018. E-mail: galen@ky.net. Website: www.expage.com/page/upsouth. Christian. Galen Smith, ed. By freelance poets and writers interested in spiritual and Southern life and issues. Quarterly newsletter; 12-16 pgs; circ 75. Subscription $8. 98% unsolicited freelance; 2% assigned. Query; e-query OK. **PAYS FREE COPY** for one-time rts. Articles & fiction to 500 wds; book/music/video reviews to 500 wds. Responds in 2-8 wks. Accepts simultaneous submissions & reprints. No disk or e-mail submission. No sidebars. Guidelines; copy $2/#10 SAE/1 stamp. (Ads-classifieds only)

Poetry: Any type, to 25 lines. Submit max 3 poems.

Tips: "Prefer short, concise pieces that are crisp, interesting and uplifting. Writing about the South should be culture-centered. Most open to good poetry—spiritual, inspirational and uplifting poems that can move a reader."

$U.S. CATHOLIC, 205 W. Monroe St., Chicago IL 60606. (312)236-7782. Fax (312)236-8207. E-mail: editors@uscatholic.org. Website: www.uscatholic.org. The Claretians. Tom McGrath, exec ed.; Meinrad Schrer-Emunds, mng ed. Devoted to starting and continuing a dialogue with Catholics of diverse lifestyles and opinions about the way they live their faith. Monthly mag; 52 pgs; circ 40,000. Subscription $22. 95% freelance. Complete ms/cover letter; phone/fax/e-query OK. Pays $250-600 (fiction $300-400) on acceptance for all rts. Articles 2,500-4,000 wds; fiction 2,500-3,500 wds. Responds in 5 wks. Seasonal 6 mos ahead. Accepts disk or e-mail submission. Regular sidebars. Guidelines; copy for 10x13 SASE. (Ads: Dianne Wade, 312-236-7782x474)

Poetry: Maureen Abood, (312)236-7782x515. Buys poetry. Pays $100.

Columns/Departments: (See guidelines first.) Sounding Board, 1,100-1,300 wds, $250; Gray Matter and A Modest Proposal, 1,100-1,800 wds, $250; Practicing Catholic, 750 wds, $150.

Tips: "All articles (except for fiction or poetry) should have an explicit religious dimension that enables readers to see the interaction between their faith and the issue at hand. Fiction should be well-written, creative, with solid character development."

$VIBRANT LIFE, 55 W. Oak Ridge Dr., Hagerstown MD 21740-7390. (301)393-4019. Fax (301)393-4055. E-mail: vibrantlife@rhpa.org. Website: www.vibrantlife.com. Seventh-Day Adventist/Review & Herald. Larry Becker, ed. Total health publication (physical, mental and spiritual); plus articles on family and marriage improvement; ages 35-55. Bimonthly mag; 32 pgs; circ 50,000. Subscription $15.95. 50% unsolicited freelance; 30% assigned. Query/clips; fax/e-query OK. Pays $75-300 on acceptance for 1st, one-time, reprint, simultaneous or electronic rts. Not copyrighted. Articles 500-1,500 wds (50-60/yr). Responds in 9 wks. Seasonal 9 mos ahead. Accepts simultaneous submissions & reprints (tell when/where appeared). Accepts disk. Kill fee 50%. Regular sidebars. Prefers NIV. Guidelines (also on Website); copy $1/9x12 SAE. (Ads)

Fillers: Buys 6-8/yr. Facts, quizzes, 50-500 wds. Pays $25-100.

Columns/Departments: Buys 12-18/yr. Fit People (people whose lives are changed for the better when applying timeless health principles/before & after photos), 500-650 wds; $75-175.

Tips: "Articles need to be very helpful, practical, and well-documented. Don't be preachy. Sidebars help a lot."

**This periodical was #16 on the 2000 Top 50 Christian Publishers List (#29 in 1999, #48 in 1998, #57 in 1997, #22 in 1996).

$THE VISION, 8855 Dunn Rd., Hazelwood MO 63042-2299. (314)837-7300. Fax (314)837-4503. E-mail: WAP@upci.org. Website: www.upci.org. United Pentecostal Church. Richard M. Davis, ed; submit to Lisa Henson, ed. designer. Denominational. Weekly take-home paper; 4 pgs; circ 10,000. Subscription $4.40. 95% unsolicited freelance. Complete ms/cover letter; no e-query. Pays $18-25 on publication for 1st rts. Articles 1,200-1,600 wds (to 120/yr); fiction 1,200-1,600 wds (to 120/yr). Seasonal 9 months ahead. Accepts simultaneous submissions & reprints. Guidelines (also by e-mail); free copy. (No ads)

Poetry: Buys 30/yr. Pays $3-12.

Tips: "Most open to fiction short stories, real-life experiences, and short poems. Stay within word count. Be sure manuscript has a pertinent spiritual application." Accepts material primarily from members of the denomination.

VISIONS OF GLORY. E-mail: editor@vog.org. Website: www.visionsofglory. org/guide.htm. Online mag. Submit by e-mail. Complete ms. **NO PAYMENT.** Articles 300-500 wds or less. Guidelines on Website. Not included in topical listings.

Tips: "Try to keep the focus of the article on one small moment or event in your life, or the life of someone close to you, which revealed part of the glorious nature of our Lord; His faithfulness, His mercy, His grace, His provision, etc."

$WAR CRY, 615 Slaters Ln., Alexandria VA 22313. (703)684-5500. Fax (703)684-5539. E-mail: Warcry@USN.salvationarmy.org. Website: publications.salvationarmyusa.org. The Salvation Army. Lt. Col. Marlene Chase, ed-in-chief; Jeff McDonald, mng ed. Pluralistic readership reaching all socioeconomic strata and including distribution in institutions. Biweekly mag; 24 pgs; circ 500,000. Subscription $7.50. 20% freelance. Complete ms/brief cover letter; no phone/fax/e-query. Pays .15-.20/wd (.12-.15/wd for reprints) on acceptance for one-time or reprint rts. Articles & fiction 1,200-1,500 wds (58/yr). Responds in 4 wks. Seasonal 1 yr ahead. Accepts simultaneous submissions & reprints (tell when/where appeared). Regular sidebars. Prefers NIV. Guidelines/theme list (also on Website); copy for 9x12 SAE/3 stamps. (No ads)

Poetry: Buys 10-20/yr. Free verse, traditional; to 16 lines. Inspirational only. Pays by the word. Submit max 5 poems.

Fillers: Buys 10-20/yr. Anecdotes (inspirational), 200-500 wds. Pays .15-.20/wd.

Tips: "We are soliciting more short fiction, inspirational articles and poetry, interviews with Christian athletes, evangelical leaders and celebrities, and theme-focused articles. Always looking for theologically sound coverage of essential Christian doctrine and how it applies to daily living. Also short contemporary articles (400 wds) with an evangelical message."

**This periodical was #17 on the 2000 Top 50 Christian Publishers list (#36 in 1999, #19 in 1998, #25 in 1997, #6 in 1996, #70 in 1994).

$THE WAY OF ST. FRANCIS, 1500 34th Ave., Oakland CA 94601-3092. (916)443-5717. Fax (916)443-2019. E-mail: ofmcaway@att.net. Website: www.sbfranciscans.org. Franciscan Friars of California/Catholic. Camille Franicevich, ed. For those interested in the message of St. Francis of Assisi as lived out by contemporary people. Bimonthly mag; 48 pgs; circ 5,000. Subscription $12. 10% unsolicited freelance; 20% assigned. Complete ms/cover letter; no phone/fax query; e-query OK. Pays $25-100 on publication for 1st rts. Articles 500-1,500 wds (4-6/yr). Responds in 6 wks. Seasonal 6 mos ahead. Accepts simultaneous submissions & reprints (tell when/where appeared). Prefers disk or e-mail submission. Regular sidebars. Any version. Guidelines/theme list (also by e-mail); copy for 6x9 SAE/6 stamps. (No ads)

> **Fillers:** Anecdotes, cartoons, facts, prayers, prose; to 100 wds. Pays $25-50.

> **Columns/Departments:** Buys 12/yr. First Person (opinion/issue), to 900 wds; Portrait (interview or personality), to 1,200 wds; Inspirations (spiritual), to 1,200 wds. Pays $25-50.

> **Tips:** "Most open to columns. Make direct connection to St. Francis, St. Clare, or a recognizable aspect of their life and vision."

$WESLEYAN ADVOCATE, Box 50434, Indianapolis IN 46250-0434. (317) 576-8156. Fax (317)842-1649. E-mail: communications@wesleyan.org. Website: www.wesleyan.org. The Wesleyan Church Corp. Jerry Brecheisen, mng ed. A full salvation family mag; denominational. Monthly mag; 36 pgs; circ 20,000. Subscription $15. 50% freelance. Complete ms/cover letter; phone query OK. Pays $10-40 for assigned, $5-25 for unsolicited, .01-.02/wd for reprints on publication for 1st or simultaneous rts. Not copyrighted. Articles 500-700 wds (50/yr). Responds in 2 wks. Seasonal 6 mos ahead. Accepts simultaneous submissions & reprints (tell when/where appeared). Guidelines; copy $2. (Ads)

> **Poetry:** Buys 30/yr. Free verse or traditional; 10-15 lines; $5-10. Send max 6 poems.

> **Fillers:** Prose, 100-300 wds. Pays $2-6.

> **Columns/Departments:** Personal Experiences, 700 wds; Ministry Tips, 600 wds; $10.

+WEST WIND REVIEW, 1250 Siskiyou Blvd., Ashland OR 97520. (541)552-6518. E-mail: WestWing@students.sou.edu. Southern Oregon University. Submit to Fiction/Poetry Ed. Strives to bring well-written, insightful stories and poems to the public. Annual jour; 200 pgs; circ 500. Open to freelance. Complete ms/cover letter; phone/e-query OK. **NO PAYMENT** for 1st rts. Not copyrighted. Fiction (all types). Responds in 5-10 wks. No simultaneous submissions or reprints. Accepts e-mail submissions (attached or copied into message). No sidebars. Guidelines (also by e-mail); no copy.

Poetry: Accepts any type.

$WHISPERS FROM HEAVEN, 7373 N. Cicero, Lincolnwood IL 60646. (847) 329-5656. Fax (847)329-5387. E-mail: tgavin@pubint.com. Publications International, Ltd. Julie Greene, ed; submit to Theresa Gavin, assoc. acq. ed. Inspirational human interest; not overtly religious. Bimonthly mag; 80 pgs; circ. 120,000. 100% freelance. Query with or without clips; phone/fax/e-query OK. Pays $100-300 for assigned, $100-225 for unsolicited, on acceptance for all rts. Articles 1,000-1,500 wds (150/yr). Seasonal 5 mos ahead. Accepts simultaneous submissions & reprints. Kill fee 25%. Free guidelines. Incomplete topical listings.

Tips: "Looking for real-life experiences that lift the human spirit. Be inspiring."

+WHITE WING MESSENGER, PO Box 3000, Cleveland TN 37320. (423)559-5413. Fax (423)559-5444. E-mail: jenny@wingnet.net. Denominational. Virginia Chatham, ed. Denominational news. Monthly mag; circ 8,000. Subscription $12. Accepts freelance. Prefers query. Not in topical listings. Did not return questionnaire. (No ads)

+WINSOME WIT, 12971 Fieldstone Rd., Milaca MN 56353. (320)983-5910. E-mail: jbeuoy@winsomewit.com. Website: www.winsomewit.com. Non-denominational. Jay Beuoy, ed. We write to persuade the unbeliever through the use of satire, from a Christian worldview. Online e-zine. Estab. 2000. 75% unsolicited freelance. Complete ms; e-query OK. **NO PAYMENT FOR NOW** for one-time & electronic rts. Not copyrighted. Articles & short stories 500-2,000 wds; reviews 500-700 wds. Responds in 1 wk. No seasonal. Accepts simultaneous submissions & reprints (tell when/where appeared). Prefers e-mail submissions (attached as word.doc or copied into message). Guidelines & copy on Website. (Ads)

Poetry: Open to poetry if it fits their style; any type; to 100 lines. Submit max 10 poems.

Fillers: Short humor.

Special Needs: "Writers with a good sense of humor. We want satire, but keep it friendly."

Contest: Details on Website.

Tips: "Check our Website. We encourage you to submit if you can write from a Christian perspective; use satire, parody and the like; and be creative. We hope to launch a hard copy newsletter by mid-2001."

$WIRELESS AGE, 5350 N. Academy Blvd., Ste. 200, Colorado Springs CO 80918. (719)536-9000. Fax (719)598-7461. E-mail: wirelessage@westarmediagroup.com. Website: www.westarmediagroup.com. Westar Media Group. Michelle Moy DeVilbiss, assoc. ed. For Christian media professionals working in the industry—especially those in radio. Bimonthly (5X) mag; 48 pgs; circ 4,700. Subscription $24.95. Estab 1997. 15% unsolicited freelance; 85% assigned. Query; fax/e-query OK. Pays variable rates for 1st rts. Articles 300-2,500 wds; book reviews 150-250 wds. Responds in 2 wks. Accepts simultaneous submissions & reprints (tell when/where appeared). Prefers e-mail submissions (attached or copied into message). Regular sidebars. Prefers NIV. Guidelines (also by e-mail); copy for 10x13 SAE/$2.10 postage. (Ads)

Fillers: Buys 3/yr. Cartoons, prose, 50-300 wds; pay varies.

Columns/Departments: Buys 48-55/yr. TV/Film (Christian TV/film issues/concerns); Radio (Christian broadcasting issues/concerns); Internet (using the Internet effectively); Programming/Production (radio program and production development); Music (profiles, reviews, news); Publishing (publishing concerns/issues); Technology (reviews, technology issues); Ministry (highlights, development of); plus others; all 800 wds, payment varies.

Special Needs: Technology pieces: affecting the way Christians communicate the Gospel.

CHILDREN'S MARKETS

$AMERICAN GIRL, 8400 Fairway Pl., Middleton WI 53562. (608)836-4848. Fax (608)831-7089. E-mail: im_agmag_editor@pleasantco.com. Website: www.americangirl.com. Pleasant Company Publications. Kristi Thom, ed; Barbara Stretchberry, mng. ed. Secular; for girls ages 8 and older to recognize and celebrate girls' achievements yesterday and today, inspire their creativity, and nurture their hopes and dreams. Bimonthly mag; 50 pgs; circ 750,000. Subscription $19.95. 5% unsolicited freelance; 10% assigned. Query (complete ms for fiction). Pays $1/wd on acceptance for all rts. Articles 150-800 wds (10/yr); fiction to 3,000 wds (1/yr). Responds in 6 mos. Seasonal 6 mos ahead. Accepts simultaneous submissions. Kill fee 50%. Some sidebars. Guidelines; copy $3.95 (check)/9x12 SAE/8 stamps. (No ads)

> **Poetry:** All poetry is by children.
>
> **Columns/Departments:** Buys 10/yr. Girls Express (short profiles on girls), to 175 wds (query); Giggle Gang (visual puzzles, mazes, word games, math puzzles, seasonal games/puzzles), send complete ms. Pays $50-200.
>
> **Contest:** Contests vary from issue to issue.
>
> **Tips:** "Girls Express offers the most opportunities for freelancers. We're looking for short profiles of girls who are doing great and interesting things. A key: A girl must be the 'star' and the story written from her point of view. Be sure to include the ages of the girls you are pitching to us. Write for 8-12 year olds—not teenagers."

$*BEGINNER'S FRIEND, PO Box 4060, Overland Park KS 66204. (913)432-0331. Fax (913)722-0351. E-mail: Hbpress@juno.com. Church of God (holiness)/Herald and Banner Press. Arlene McGehee, Sunday school ed. Denominational; for young children. Weekly take-home paper; 4 pgs; circ 2,700. Subscription $1.30. Complete ms/cover letter; phone/fax query OK. Pays .005/wd on publication for 1st rts. Fiction 500-800 wds. Seasonal 6-8 mos ahead. Accepts simultaneous submissions & reprints (tell when/where appeared). Prefers KJV. Guidelines/theme list; copy. Not in topical listings.

$BREAD FOR GOD'S CHILDREN, Box 1017, Arcadia FL 34265-1017. (863)494-6214. Fax (863)993-0154. E-mail: BREAD@sunline.net. Bread Ministries, Inc. Judith M. Gibbs, ed. A family magazine for serious Christians who are concerned about their children or grandchildren (ages 6-18). Monthly (8X) mag; 32 pgs; circ 10,000. Subscription free. 20-25% unsolicited freelance. Complete ms; no e-query. Pays $20-30 ($30-50 for fiction) on publication for 1st or one-time rts. Not copyrighted. Articles 600-800 wds (6/yr); fiction & true stories 600-900 wds for 4-10 yrs, 900-1,500 wds for teens (15/yr). Responds in 8-12 wks (may hold longer). Some simultaneous submissions & reprints (tell when/where appeared). Some sidebars. Prefers KJV. Guidelines (also by e-mail or Website); 3 copies for 9x12 SAE/5 stamps; 1 copy 3 stamps. (No ads)

> **Columns/Departments:** Buys 5-8/yr. Let's Chat (discussion issues facing children), 500-800 wds; Teen Page (teen issues), 600-900 wds; and Idea Page (object lessons or crafts for children), 300-800 wds. Pays $10-30.

> **Tips:** "Most open to fiction or real-life stories of overcoming through faith in Jesus Christ and/or guidance from godly principles. No tag endings or adult solutions coming from children. Create realistic characters and situations. No 'sudden inspiration' solutions. Open to any areas of family life related from a godly perspective."

$CELEBRATE (formerly Listen), Box 419527, Kansas City MO 64141. (816) 931-1900. Fax (816)753-4071. E-mail: psmits@nazarene.org. Website: www.nazarene.org. Nazarene/Wesleyan/WordAction. Pamela Smits, ed. Weekly activity/story paper for 4-6 yr olds; 6 pgs; circ 20,000+. Bulk mailing $9.50. 50% unsolicited freelance; 50% assigned. Complete ms/cover letter; no e-query. Pays $25/story, $5-15/activity, on publication for all rts. Not copyrighted. Parent ideas and articles 100 wds. Responds in 6-8 wks. Seasonal 10-12 mos ahead. No disk or e-mail submission. No sidebars. Prefers NIV. Guidelines/theme list/copy for #10 SAE/1 stamp. (No ads)

> **Poetry:** Buys 35/yr. Light verse, traditional; 8-10 lines; $2 or .25/line. Submit max 10 poems.

> **Fillers:** Buys 15/yr. Games, ideas/activities (age-appropriate), prayers; $5-15.

> **Special Needs:** Exciting, age-appropriate activities for back page; adventure stories; poetry. Looking for parental helps, educational development quick ideas and spiritual family growth.

> **Tips:** "Not currently sending out guidelines or accepting submissions because of pending changes in curriculum. We're also deciding whether we'll accept freelance submissions in the future. If interested in writing for us, send your name and address and we'll put your name on file and send guidelines when available."

$CLUB CONNECTION, 1445 Boonville Ave., Springfield MO 65802-1894. (417)862-2781. Fax (417)862-0503. E-mail: clubconnection@ag.org. Website: www.missionettes.ag.org. Gospel Publishing House. Seeking new editor. For girls grades 4-8 (with leader edition for Missionettes leaders). Estab. 1997. Quarterly mag; 32 pgs; circ 14,700. Subscription $6.50 (leader's $7.50). 30-40% freelance. Complete ms/cover letter. Pays $10-50 on publication for 1st or one-time rts. Articles 500 wds (4-6/yr). Responds in 10 wks. Seasonal 10-12 mos ahead. Accepts simultaneous submissions & reprints (tell when/where appeared). Accepts disk. Kill fee. Regular sidebars. Prefers NIV. Guidelines/theme list; copy for 9x12 SAE/3 stamps. (No ads)

Poetry: Buys 1-2 /yr. Light verse; 4-20 lines; $5-10. Submit max 2 poems.

Fillers: Buys 6-8/yr. Anecdotes, cartoons, facts, games, ideas, jokes, newsbreaks, party ideas, quizzes, short humor, word puzzles; 20-50 or 100 wds; $5-20.

Columns/Departments: Buys 4-6/yr. Pays $10-50.

Tips: *"Fruit of the Spirit* theme for this year. Articles with a Christian slant of interest to girls."

+**CLUB TRAIN.** E-mail: ClubTrain@aol.com Larry Ellicott, ed. (lwe500@ juno.com). Inspirational Children's Fiction Club for children 6-10 yrs. Short stories or short story collection (related) 1,500-3,000 wds. E-mail cover letter and 1-pg synopsis to ClubTrain@aol.com. **NO PAYMENT FOR NOW.**

Tips: "Impart spiritual principles in a way that elementary-age children can apply them to their lives, but avoid preachiness and lectures. Avoid excessive school settings; many of our readers are home schooled."

$**COUNSELOR**, 4050 Lee Vance View, Colorado Springs CO 80918. (719) 536-0100. Fax (719)533-3045. E-mail: Counseloreditor@sppublications. org. Cook Communications Ministries, Scripture Press Division. Janice K. Burton, ed. No freelance this year.

**This periodical was #25 on the 2000 Top 50 Christian Publishers List (#65 in 1998, #61 in 1996, #67 in 1994). 1994 EPA Award of Merit & 1984 EPA Award of Excellence—Sunday School Take-Home.

***COURAGE**, 1300 N. Meacham Rd., Schaumburg IL 60173-4888. (847)843-1600. Fax (847)843-3757. Website: www.garbc.org/rbp. Regular Baptist Press. Joan Alexander, ed. For children, 9-12, in Sunday school. Weekly take-home paper. Subscription $1.59/quarter. Send for new guidelines before submitting.

$**CRUSADER**, 1333 Alger SE, PO Box 7259 (49510), Grand Rapids MI 49507. (616)241-5616. Fax (616)241-5558. Website: www.gospelcom.net/Cadets. Calvinist Cadet Corp. G. Richard Broene, ed. To show boys ages 9-14 how God is at work in their lives and in the world around them. Mag published 7X/yr; 24 pgs; circ 11,400. Subscription $10.50. 35% unsolicited freelance. Complete ms/cover letter. Pays .04-.06/wd on acceptance for 1st, one-time, or reprint rts. Articles 500-1,000 wds (7/yr); fiction 900-1,500 wds (14/yr). Responds in 4 wks. Accepts simultaneous submissions & reprints (tell when/where appeared). No disk. Regular sidebars. Prefers NIV. Guidelines/theme list; copy for 9x12 SAE/4 stamps. (Ads)

Fillers: Buys 12-18/yr. Cartoons, quizzes, word puzzles; 20-200 wds; $5 & up.

Tips: "Most open to fiction or fillers tied to themes; request new theme list in January of each year. Also looking for simple projects/ crafts, and puzzles (word, logic)."

**1994 EPA Award of Merit—Youth.

$**DISCOVERIES**, 6401 The Paseo, Kansas City MO 64131. (816)333-7000. Fax (816)333-4439. E-mail: vfolsom@nazarene.org. Website: www.nazarene.

org. Nazarene/Word Action Publishing. Virginia Folsom, ed.; Emily Tummons, ed asst. For 8-10 yr olds, emphasizing Christian values and holy living; follows theme of Sunday school curriculum. Weekly take-home paper; 4 pgs; circ 30,000. 75% unsolicited freelance; 25% assigned. Complete ms/cover letter; fax query OK. Pays .05/wd on publication for multi-use rts. Fiction (30/yr), to 500 wds. Responds in 6 wks. Seasonal 1 yr ahead. Accepts simultaneous submissions & reprints (tell when/where appeared). No disk; accepts e-mail submission. Regular sidebars. Prefers NIV. Guidelines/theme list/copy for #10 SAE/2 stamps. (No ads)

Fillers: Buys 60/yr. Cartoons, facts, word puzzles, 75-200 wds. Pays $10-15.

Columns/Departments: Buys 30/yr. Complete ms. Pays $10-15.

Tips: "Follow guidelines and theme list. Most open to nonfiction and fiction."

DISCOVERY, 475 Riverside Dr., Rm. 455, New York NY 10115. (212)870-3335. Fax (212)870-3229. E-mail: order@jmsblind.org. Website: www.jmsblind.org. The John Milton Society for the Blind. Ingrid Peck, asst ed. For blind children ages 8-18, in Braille; reprints articles from Christian and other magazines for youth. Quarterly mag; 44 pgs; circ 1,100. Subscription free. 5% unsolicited freelance; 0% assigned. Complete ms/cover letter; phone query OK. **NO PAYMENT** for reprint rts. Not copyrighted. Articles 500-1,500 wds (1/yr); fiction 500-1,500 wds (1/yr). Responds in 6 wks. Seasonal 9-12 mos ahead. Accepts simultaneous submissions & reprints (tell when/where appeared). Accepts disk. No sidebars. Guidelines (also on Website); free copy in Braille only.

Poetry: Accepts 1/yr. Any type; 5-30 lines.

Fillers: Anecdotes, games, ideas, jokes, quizzes, prayers, quotes, short humor, word puzzles; 10-150 wds.

Tips: "Most open to poems, prayers and personal inspirational pieces about more timeless themes: Christian holidays, overcoming challenges like visual impairment, prejudice, love, forgiveness, etc. If writing about blindness, don't be patronizing. Send complete manuscripts requiring little or no editing. Look at the magazines we typically reprint from (see guidelines)."

$DISCOVERY TRAILS, 1445 Boonville Ave., Springfield MO 65802-1894. (417)862-2781. Fax (417)862-6059. E-mail: rl-discoverytrails@gph.org. Website: www.home.ag.org/sscl. Assemblies of God. Sinda S. Zinn, ed. Teaching of Christian principles through fiction stories about children (10-12 yrs). Weekly take-home paper; 4 pgs; circ 35,000. Subscription $10. 90% unsolicited freelance. Complete ms/no cover letter; no e-query. Pays .07-.10/wd on acceptance for one-time rts. Articles 200-400 wds (50/yr); fiction 700-1,000 wds (50/yr). Responds in 2-4 wks. Seasonal 12-24 mos ahead. Accepts simultaneous submissions & reprints. No disk; accepts e-mail submission (copied into message). No sidebars. Prefers NIV. Guidelines/theme list (also by e-mail); copy for #10 SAE/1 stamp.

Poetry: Buys 6-8/yr. Free verse, haiku, light verse, traditional; $5 & up. Submit max 3 poems.

Fillers: Buys 8-10/yr. Facts, short humor; 200-300 wds; .07-.10/wd.

Tips: "Most open to fiction stories, especially mystery with a spiritual emphasis. Write interesting stories for the age level—less narrative, more action and dialogue. We are featuring short, punchy items of interest to 9-12 year olds. Including a spiritual emphasis in them is a plus."
**This periodical was #6 on the 2000 Top 50 Christian Publishers list (#8 in 1999, #33 in 1998, #36 in 1997, #17 in 1996, #23 in 1995).

$FOCUS ON THE FAMILY CLUBHOUSE, 8605 Explorer Dr., Colorado Springs CO 80920. (719)548-4595. Fax (719)531-3499. Website: www.clubhousemagazine.org. Focus on the Family. Jesse Florea, ed. For children 8-12 yrs in Christian homes. Monthly mag; 24 pgs; circ 123,300. Subscription $15. 15% unsolicited freelance; 25% assigned. Complete ms/cover letter; fax query OK. Pays $25-250 (.10-.25/wd) for articles, $200 & up for fiction on acceptance for 1st rts. Articles 600-800 wds (5/yr); fiction 1,200-1,600 wds (30/yr). Responds in 4-6 wks. Seasonal 6 mos ahead. No disk. Kill fee. Regular sidebars. Prefers NIV. Guidelines; copy for $1/9x12 SAE. (No ads)

Fillers: Buys 10/yr. Games, party ideas, quizzes, word puzzles; 150-500 wds; $35-150.

Tips: "Biggest need is for biblical fiction stories (less than 1,000 wds) that stay true to the Bible, but bring text to life; also historical, other cultures or frontier; or how-to with a theme (doing stuff for dad, making neighborhood beautiful, Christmas crafts, etc.). Send mss with list of credentials. Read past issues."
**This periodical was #63 on the 2000 Top 50 Christian Publishers list (#21 in 1998, #2 in 1997, #62 in 1996, #38 in 1995, #15 in 1994). Also 1997 & 1994 EPA Award of Merit—Youth.

$FOCUS ON THE FAMILY CLUBHOUSE JR., 8605 Explorer Dr., Colorado Springs CO 80920. (719)548-5740. Fax (719)531-3499. Website: www.family.org. Focus on the Family. Annette Bourland, ed. For ages 4-8 yrs. Monthly mag; 16 pgs; circ 96,000. Subscription $15. 25% unsolicited freelance; 10% assigned. Complete ms/cover letter; no phone/fax/e-query. Pays $75-200 on acceptance for one-time rts. Articles 100-500 wds (1-2/yr); fiction 250-1,000 wds (10/yr); Bible stories 250-800 wds; one-page rebus stories to 200 wds. Responds in 4-6 wks. Seasonal 5-6 mos ahead. Kill fee. No sidebars. Guidelines; copy $1.25/9x12 SAE. (No ads)

Poetry: Buys 3/yr. Free verse, light verse, traditional; 10-25 lines (to 250 wds); $25-100.

Fillers: Buys 1-2/yr. Cartoons, games, word puzzles; $15-30.

Special Needs: Bible stories.

Tips: "Most open to short, non-preachy fiction, beginning reader stories, and read-to-me. Be knowledgeable of our style and try it out on kids first."
**This periodical was #51 on the 2000 Top 50 Christian Publishers list (#60 in 1998, #52 in 1997, #53 in 1996 & 1995, #15 in 1994). 1996 EPA Award of Excellence—Youth.

$GOD'S WORLD NEWS, PO Box 2330, Asheville NC 28802. (828)253-8063. Fax (828)253-1556. E-mail: nbomer@gwpub.com. God's World Publications. Norman W. Bomer, sr ed. Current events, published in 4 editions, for kindergarten through jr. high students, mostly in Christian and home schools. Weekly mag (during school yr); 8 pgs; circ 320,000. Subscription $24.95. 16% freelance. Complete ms/cover letter. Pays $100 on acceptance for one-time rts. Articles 700-900 wds. Responds in 9 wks. Accepts reprints (tell when/where appeared). Accepts disk or e-mail submission (attached file). Some sidebars. Guidelines; free copy. (No ads)

    Tips: "Keep vocabulary simple. Must present a distinctly Christian world view without being moralistic."

$GUIDE, 55 W. Oak Ridge Dr., Hagerstown MD 21740. (301)393-4038. Fax (301)393-4055. E-mail: Guide@rhpa.org. Website: www.guidemagazine. org. Seventh-Day Adventist/Review and Herald Publishing. Randy Fishell, ed; Helen Lee, asst ed. A Christian journal for 10-14 yr olds, presenting true stories relevant to their needs. Weekly magazine; 32 pgs; circ 33,000. Subscription $41.95/yr. 100% unsolicited freelance. Complete ms/cover letter; fax/e-query OK. Pays .08-.12/wd on acceptance for 1st, one-time, reprint, or electronic rts. Not copyrighted. True stories 500-1,200 wds (200/yr). Responds in 4-6 wks. Seasonal 6 mos ahead. Accepts reprints (tell when/where appeared; pays 50% of standard rate). Accepts disk or e-mail submission (attached file). Some sidebars. Prefers NIV. Guidelines/theme list (also by e-mail); copy for 6x9 SAE/2 stamps.

    Fillers: Buys 100/yr. Games, quizzes, word puzzles on a spiritual theme; 20-50 wds; $20-50.

    Special Needs: "Most open to true action/adventure and Christian humor. Kids want that—put it together with dialogue and a spiritual slant, and you're on the 'write' track for our readers. School life."

    Tips: "We use true or based-on-truth short stories, including school situations, humorous circumstances, adventure, short historical and biographical stories, and almost any situation relevant to 10-14 year olds. Stories must have a spiritual point or implication."

    **This periodical was #12 on the 2000 Top 50 Christian Publishers list (#14 in 1999, #27 in 1998, #22 in 1995, #38 in 1994).

$GUIDEPOSTS FOR KIDS, PO Box 638, Chesterton IN 46304. (219)929-4429. Fax (219)926-3839. E-mail: gp4k@guideposts.org. Website: www. gp4k.com. Guideposts, Inc. Mary Lou Carney, ed; Rosanne Tolin, mng ed; Allison Payne, asst. ed. For kids 7-12 yrs (emphasis at upper level). Bimonthly mag; 32 pgs; circ 200,000. Subscription $15.95. 50% unsolicited freelance; 50% assigned. Query/clips (complete ms for fiction); no phone/fax/e-query. Pays $100-400 ($300-500 for fiction) on acceptance for all & electronic rts. Articles 300-1,200 wds (24/yr); fiction 500-1,400 wds (6/yr). Responds in 4-6 wks. Seasonal 6 mos ahead. No disk or e-mail submission. Kill fee. Regular sidebars. Prefers NIV. Guidelines; copy $3.25/10x13 SAE. (Ads)

    Poetry: Allison Payne. Buys 4-6/yr. Any type; 3-20 lines; $15-50. Submit max 5 poems.

    Fillers: Buys 15-20/yr. Anecdotes, cartoons, facts, games, ideas, jokes, party ideas, prose, quizzes, short humor, word puzzles; to 300 wds; $20-75.

Columns/Departments: Buys 20/yr. The Buzz (true, interesting kid profiles, paired with sidebars on a particular topic), 300-600 wds; Tips from the Top (Christian celebrities/sports figures), 500-700 wds; $250-450.

Tips: "Send something for The Buzz—our topical department that focuses on a particular subject, like BMX biking. A kid profile is the peg to introduce the subject, with sidebars following."

**This periodical was #32 on the 2000 Top 50 Christian Publishers list (#31 in 1999, #28 in 1998, #30 in 1997, #54 in 1996, #55 in 1995).

$HIGH ADVENTURE, 1445 Boonville Ave., Springfield MO 65802-1894. (417)862-2781x4177. Fax (417)831-8230. E-mail: RoyalRangers@ag.org. Website: www.rangers.ag.org. Assemblies of God. Jerry Parks, ed-in-chief. For the Royal Rangers (boys), 5-17 yrs; slanted toward teens. Quarterly mag; 16 pgs; circ 86,000. 25% unsolicited freelance; 60% assigned. Complete ms/cover letter; e-query OK. Pays .04-.06/wd on acceptance for 1st, one-time, simultaneous or reprint rts. Articles 500-900 wds (30/yr); fiction 500-900 wds (15/yr). Responds in 4-5 wks. Seasonal 7 mos ahead. Accepts simultaneous submissions & reprints (tell when/where appeared). Regular sidebars. Prefers NIV. Guidelines/theme list (also by e-mail); copy for 9x12 SAE/3 stamps. (No ads)

Fillers: Buys 30/yr. Cartoons, jokes, short humor; 50 wds, $25-30; quizzes, word puzzles, $12-15.

**This periodical was #55 on the 2000 Top 50 Christian Publishers list (#14 in 1997).

J.A.M. (JUNIOR APOSTLES MAGAZINE), PMB 366, 3402 Edgement Ave., Brookhaven PA 19015. (610)485-3512. E-mail: chuckjoy@bellatlantic.net. Website: www.jamag.org. Nondenominational. Joy Kieffer, ed; Devon Sitaris, articles ed; Brandon Hopkins, fiction ed. Written by young people, 8-18 yrs. Bimonthly print & online mag; 24 pgs; circ 7,000. Subscription $12. Estab 1997. 60% unsolicited freelance; 40% assigned. Complete ms; e-query OK. **PAYS IN COPIES/SUBSCRIPTION** for one-time rts. Articles 500-700 wds; fiction 40-2,500 wds; book reviews to 200 wds. Responds in 4 wks. Seasonal 3 mos ahead. Accepts reprints (tell when/where appeared). Accepts e-mail submissions (attached in .txt or copied into message). Guidelines (also by e-mail/Website); copy for 9x12 SAE/$2 postage. (Ads)

Poetry: Margarita Glabets. Accepts 12+/yr. Free verse, haiku, light verse, traditional; 4-30 lines. Submit max 7 poems.

Fillers: Accepts 36/yr. Anecdotes, cartoons, facts, games, ideas, jokes, party ideas, prayers, prose, quizzes, quotes, short humor, word puzzles.

Special Needs: Writers must be between 8 and 18 years of age, with the exception of articles by writers or artists on their craft, and how it is influenced by their faith. From kids need articles on peer pressure, use of talents, gifts.

Contest: Sponsors several; see magazine or Website.

Tips: "Most open to fiction, articles about youth issues, current issues, life stories (testimonies) and inspirational."

$*JUNIOR COMPANION, PO Box 4060, Overland Park KS 66204. (913)432-0331. Fax (913)722-0351. Church of God (holiness)/Herald and Banner Press. Arlene McGehee, Sunday school ed. Denominational; for 4th-6th graders. Weekly take-home paper; 4 pgs; circ 3,500. Subscription $1.30. Complete ms/cover letter; phone/fax query OK. Pays .005/wd on publication for 1st rts. Fiction 500-1,200 wds. Seasonal 6-8 mos ahead. Accepts simultaneous submissions & reprints (tell when/where appeared). Prefers KJV. Guidelines/theme list; copy. Not in topical listings.

$KEYS FOR KIDS, Box 1, Grand Rapids MI 49501. (616)451-2009. E-mail: kfk@cbhonline.com. Website: www.cbhministries.org. CBH Ministries. Hazel Marett, ed. A daily devotional booklet for children (8-14) or for family devotions. Bimonthly booklet; 80 pgs; circ 60,000. Subscription free. 100% unsolicited freelance. Complete ms. Pays $20-25 on acceptance for 1st or simultaneous rts. Not copyrighted. Devotionals (includes short fiction story) 375-425 wds (60-70/yr). Responds in 2-4 wks. Seasonal 4-5 mos ahead. Accepts simultaneous submissions & reprints. Prefers KJV or NIV. Guidelines; copy for 6x9 SAE/4 stamps. (No ads)

    Tips: "If you are rejected, go back to the sample and study it some more."

$LIVE WIRE, 8121 Hamilton Ave., Cincinnati OH 45231. (513)931-4050. Fax (513)931-0950. E-mail: mredford@standardpub.com. Website: www.StandardPub.com. Margie Redford, ed. Geared to 10-12 year olds who want to connect to Christ. Weekly newspaper; 4 pgs; circ 40,000. Subscription $12. 25% unsolicited freelance; 25% assigned. Complete ms; e-query OK. Pays .06-.08/wd on acceptance for all, 1st, & reprint rts. Articles 250-350 wds (most 100-250). Responds in 9-13 wks. Seasonal 9-12 mos ahead. Accepts simultaneous submissions & reprints (tell when/where appeared). Accepts disk. Regular sidebars. Prefers NIV. Guidelines/theme list; copy for #10 SAE/2 stamps. (No ads)

    Poetry & Fiction: From preteens only.

    Fillers: Cartoons ($15-20), Bible facts, games, ideas, jokes, party ideas, quotes ($15-17.50).

    Special Needs: Mission stories with facts of interest to preteens; spotlights on church youth group projects/activities.

    Tips: "We want real articles about real preteens you know who have done something interesting or significant for their church or community. Submit articles closely related to themes; articles must be interesting 'news briefs.'"

    **This periodical was #37 on the 2000 Top 50 Christian Publishers list (#42 in 1999, #29 in 1998).

$MY FRIEND: The Catholic Magazine for Kids, 50 St. Paul's Ave., Boston MA 02130-3495. (617)522-8911. Fax (617)541-9805. E-mail: myfriend@pauline.org. Website: www.pauline.org (click on Kidstuff). Pauline Books & Media. Sr. Kathryn James, ed. Christian values and basic Catholic doctrines for children, ages 6-12. Monthly (10X) mag; 32 pgs; circ 12,000. Subscription $18. 30% unsolicited freelance; 70% assigned. Complete ms/cover letter; fax/e-query OK. Pays $85-150 after acceptance for all or 1st rts. Articles 150-1,100 wds (20/yr) & fiction 500-1,100 wds (8/yr).

Responds in 9 wks. Seasonal 6 mos ahead. Accepts e-mail submission (attached file). Kill fee. Regular sidebars. Guidelines; copy $2.95.

Fillers: Cartoons, jokes; $7-15.

Tips: "True stories or stories on issues are most open to freelancers. Good research combined with tight, exciting writing is the best way to break in. In fiction, include physically challenged, and universality or ethnic inclusion. Send fun fiction with values; polished fiction with original slant."

**This periodical was #66 on the 1997 Top 50 Christian Publishers list (#32 in 1996, #34 in 1995, #39 in 1994).

$NATURE FRIEND, 2727 Township Rd. 421, Sugarcreek OH 44681-9465. (330)852-1900. Fax (330)852-3285 or (800)852-4482. Carlisle Press. Marvin Wengerd, ed. For children (ages 4-14); about God's wonderful world of nature and wildlife. Monthly mag; 36 pgs; circ 9,000. Subscription $22. 10% unsolicited freelance; 40% assigned. Complete ms/cover letter; no phone/fax query. Pays .05/wd on publication for 1st or one-time rts. Articles 250-1,200 wds (50/yr); or fiction 500-1200 wds (40/yr). Responds in 4-13 wks. Seasonal 2 mos ahead. Accepts simultaneous submissions & reprints (tell when/where appeared). No disk. Some sidebars. KJV only. Guidelines $4; copy $2.50/7x10 SAE/3 stamps. (No ads)

Fillers: Buys 12/yr. Quizzes, word puzzles; 100-500 wds. Pays $10-25.

Tips: "Don't bother submitting to us unless you have seen our guidelines and a sample copy. We are very conservative in our approach. Everything must be nature-related. Write on a children's level, stories, facts, puzzles about animals and nature subjects. No evolution."

$ON THE LINE, 616 Walnut Ave., Scottdale PA 15683-1999. (724)887-8500. Fax (724)887-3111. E-mail: otl@mph.org. Website: www.mph.org. Mennonite/Herald Press. Mary Clemens Meyer, ed. Reinforces Christian values in 9-14 yr olds. Monthly mag; 28 pgs; circ 6,000. Subscription $26.50. 90% unsolicited freelance; 10% assigned. Complete ms; fax/e-query OK. Pays .03-.05/wd on acceptance for one-time or reprint rts. Articles 300-500 wds (25-30/yr); fiction 1,000-1,800 wds (45-50/yr). Responds in 4 wks. Seasonal 6 mos ahead. Accepts simultaneous submissions & reprints (tell when/where appeared). No e-mail submission. Regular sidebars. Prefers NIV or NRSV. Guidelines (also by e-mail or Website); copy for 7x10 SAE/2 stamps. (No ads)

Poetry: Buys 10-15/yr. Free verse, haiku, light verse, traditional; 3-24 lines; $10-25.

Fillers: Buys 25-30/yr. Cartoons, facts, games, jokes, party ideas, quizzes, word puzzles; to 350 wds; $10-25.

Tips: "Watch kids 9-14. Listen to them talk. Write stories that sound natural—not moralizing, preachy, with adults quoting Scripture. Our readers like puzzles, especially theme crosswords. Most sections of our magazine rely on freelancers for material; especially need fiction and puzzles."

**This periodical was #29 on the 2000 Top 50 Christian Publishers list. (#28 in 1999, #50 in 1998, #59 in 1997, #38 in 1996, #44 in 1995, #52 in 1994)

$OUR LITTLE FRIEND, Box 5353, Nampa ID 83653-5353. (208)465-2580. Fax (208)465-2531. E-mail: ailsox@pacificpress.com. Website: www.pacificpress.com. Seventh-Day Adventist. Aileen Andres Sox, ed. For theme and comments, see **Primary Treasure**. Weekly take-home paper for 1-5 yr olds (through 1st grade); 8 pgs; circ 45,000-50,000. 10% unsolicited freelance, 40% assigned. Complete ms; fax/e-query OK (e-mail preferred). Pays $25-50 on acceptance for one-time or reprint rts. True stories to 650 wds (52/yr). Responds in 13 wks. Seasonal 7 mos ahead. Accepts simultaneous submissions & reprints. No disk, e-mail submission OK. Guidelines (also on Website)/theme list; copy for 9x12 SAE/2 stamps. (No ads)

    Tips: "Stories need to be crafted for this age reader in plot and vocabulary."

$PARTNERS, Christian Light Publications, Inc., Box 1212, Harrisonburg VA 22801-1212. (540)434-0768. Fax (540)433-8896. E-mail: donplank@juno.com. Mennonite. Norma Plank, ed. For 9-14 yr olds. Weekly take-home paper; 4 pgs; circ 5,975. Subscription $9.20. 99% unsolicited freelance; 1% assigned. Complete ms. Pays up to .03/wd on acceptance for all, 1st, or reprint rts. Articles 200-1,000 wds (50/yr); fiction & true stories 1,000-1,600 wds (50-75/yr); serial stories up to 1,600/installment; short-short stories to 400 wds. Responds in 6 wks. Seasonal 6 mos ahead. Accepts simultaneous submissions (treated as reprints) & reprints (tell when/where appeared); serials 2-13 parts (2-4 parts preferred). Requires KJV. Guidelines/theme list/copy for 9x12 SAE/3 stamps. (No ads)

    Poetry: Buys 25/yr. Traditional, story poems; 4-24 lines; .50/line. Submit max 6 poems.

    Fillers: Buys 50-75/yr. Quizzes, word puzzles (Bible related). Payment varies, about $5.

    Columns/Departments: Character Corner; Cultures & Customs; Historical Highlights; Maker's Masterpiece; Missionary Mail; Torches of Truth; or Nature Nooks; all 200-800 or 1,000 wds.

    Tips: "Someone who has experienced a genuine spiritual 'rebirth' and follows our writer's guidelines carefully has a much better chance of receiving an acceptance. Write in a lively way and on a child's level of understanding (ages 9-14). We do not require that you be Mennonite, but we do send a questionnaire for you to fill out."

    **This periodical was #34 on the 2000 Top 50 Christian Publishers list (#33 in 1999, #43 in 1998, #44 in 1997, #63 in 1996, #66 in 1995).

$POCKETS, PO Box 340004, Nashville TN 37203-0004. (615)340-7333. Fax (615)340-7267. E-mail: pockets@upperroom.org. Website: www.upperroom.org/pockets. United Methodist. Janet Knight, ed; submit to Lynn W. Gilliam, assoc ed. Devotional magazine for children (6-11 yrs). Monthly (11X) mag; 48 pgs; circ 93,000. Subscription $16.95. 75% unsolicited freelance. Complete ms/brief cover letter; no phone/fax/e-query. Pays .14/wd on acceptance for 1st rts. Articles 400-800 wds (20/yr) & fiction 500-1,500 wds (55/yr). Responds in 4 wks. Seasonal 1 yr ahead. Accepts reprints (tell when/where appeared). Kill fee 33%. No e-mail submission.

Some sidebars. Prefers NRSV. Guidelines/theme list (also by e-mail/ Website); copy for 7x9 SAE/3 stamps. (No ads)

Poetry: Buys 30/yr. Free verse, haiku, light verse, traditional; 4-20 lines; $25-50 or $2/line. Submit max 7 poems.

Fillers: Buys 44/yr. Games, ideas, jokes, prayers, riddles, word puzzles; $25.

Columns/Departments: Buys 40/yr. Kids Cook; Pocketsful of Love (ways to show love), 200-300 wds; Peacemakers at Work (children involved in environmental, community and peace/justice issues; include action photos if possible, with name of photographer), to 600 wds; Pocketsful of Prayer, 400-600 wds.

Special Needs: "Two-page stories for ages 5-8, 600 words max. Need role model stories and retold Bible stories. Stories about someone you'd like to know."

Contest: Fiction-writing contest; submit between 3/1 & 8/15 every yr. Prize $1,000. Length 1,000-1,500 wds. Must be unpublished and not historical fiction. Previous winners not eligible. Send to Pockets Fiction Contest at above address, and include an SASE for return of manuscript and response.

Tips: "Get our theme list first. All areas open to freelance. Nonfiction probably easiest to sell and Peacemakers at Work. Read, read, read and study—be attentive to guidelines, themes, and past issues."

**This periodical was #27 on the 2000 Top 50 Christian Publishers list (#9 in 1999, #38 in 1998, #22 in 1997, #10 in 1996, #8 in 1995, #18 in 1994).

$POWER AND LIGHT, 6401 The Paseo, Kansas City MO 64131. (816)333-7000x2243. Fax (816)333-4439. E-mail: mprice@nazarene.org. Website: www.nazarene.org. No freelance until 2004-05.

$POWER STATION, 4050 Lee Vance View, Colorado Springs CO 80918. (719)536-0100. Fax (719)533-3045. E-mail: powerstationeditor@ SPPublications.org. Cook Communication Ministries, Scripture Press Division. Janice K. Burton, ed. No freelance for 2001.

**This periodical was #20 on the 2000 Top 50 Christian Publishers list (#17 in 1999).

$PRESCHOOL PLAYHOUSE, 1551 Regency Ct., Calumet City IL 60409. (708)868-7100. Fax (708)868-6759. Website: www.urbanministries. com. Urban Ministries, Inc. K. Steward, ed. Sunday school magazine with activities for 2-5 year olds with accompanying teacher's manual. Quarterly magazine for teachers; take-home paper for students; 96 pgs. Subscription $4.59 (teacher) and $2.45 (student). 80% assigned. Query/clips; fax/e-query OK. Pays $150, 120 days after acceptance, for all rts. Articles 9,100 characters for teacher, 2,900 characters for student (4/yr). Responds in 4 wks. Seasonal 6 mos ahead. Accepts simultaneous submissions. Requires disk. Prefers NIV. Guidelines; copy $2.25/#10 SASE. (No ads)

Tips: "Send query with a writing sample, or attend our annual conference on the first weekend in November each year. Manuscripts are evaluated at the conference."

$*PRIMARY PAL (IL), 1300 N. Meacham Rd., Schaumburg IL 60173-4888. (847)843-1600. Fax (847)843-3757. Website: www.garbc.org/rbp. Regular Baptist Press. Joan Alexander, ed. For ages 6-8; fundamental, conservative. Weekly take-home paper. Note: This periodical has been redesigned. Still working on new guidelines.

$*PRIMARY PAL (KS), PO Box 4060, Overland Park KS 66204. (913)432-0331. Fax (913)722-0351. Church of God (holiness)/Herald and Banner Press. Arlene McGehee, Sunday school ed. Denominational; for 1st-3rd graders. Weekly take-home paper; 4 pgs; circ 2,900. Subscription $1.30. Complete ms/cover letter; phone/fax query OK. Pays .005/wd on publication for 1st rts. Fiction 500-1,000 wds. Seasonal 6-8 mos ahead. Accepts simultaneous submissions & reprints (tell when/where appeared). Prefers KJV. Guidelines/theme list; copy. Not in topical listings.

$PRIMARY TREASURE, Box 5353, Nampa ID 83653-5353. (208)465-2500. Fax (208)465-2531. E-mail: ailsox@pacificpress.com. Website: www.pacific press.com. Seventh-Day Adventist. Aileen Andres Sox, ed. To teach children Christian belief, values, and practice. God's loving us and our loving him makes a difference in every facet of life, from how we think and act to how we feel. Weekly take-home paper for 6-9 yr olds (2nd-4th grades); 16 pgs; circ 35,000. 50% freelance (assigned), 50% reprints or unsolicited. Complete ms; fax/e-query OK (e-mail preferred). Pays $25-50 on acceptance for one-time or reprint rts. True stories 900-1,000 wds (52/yr); articles used rarely (query). Responds in 13 wks. Seasonal 7 mos ahead. Accepts simultaneous submissions; serials to 10 parts (query). E-mail submissions (attached file). Guidelines (also on Website); copy for 9x12 SAE/2 stamps. (No ads)
   Tips: "We need positive, lively stories about children facing modern problems and making good choices. We always need strong stories about boys. We need a spiritual element that frequently is missing from submissions. We're changing; refer to guidelines."

$*PROMISE, 330 Progress Rd., Dayton OH 45449. (937)847-5900. Fax (937)847-5910. E-mail: pliservice@aol.com. Website: www.pflaum.com. Catholic. Joan Mitchell CSJ, ed. For Kindergarten & Grade 1; encourages them to participate in parish worship. Weekly (32X) take-home paper. Not in topical listings.

$*SEEDS, 330 Progress Rd., Dayton OH 45449. (937)847-5900. Fax (937)847-5910. E-mail: pliservice@aol.com. Website: www.pflaum.com. Catholic. Joan Mitchell CSJ, ed. Prepares children to learn about God; for preschoolers. Weekly (32X) take-home paper; 4 pgs. Not in topical listings.

SKIPPING STONES: A Multicultural Magazine, PO Box 3939, Eugene OR 97403. Phone/fax (541)342-4956. E-mail: skipping@efn.org. Website: www.efn.org/~skipping. Not specifically Christian. Arun N. Toké, ed. A multicultural awareness and nature appreciation magazine for young people 7-17, worldwide. Bimonthly mag; 36 pgs; circ 2,500. Subscription $25. 85% unsolicited freelance; 15% assigned. Query or complete ms/cover letter; no phone query; e-query/submission OK. **PAYS IN COPIES** for 1st, electronic or reprint rts. Articles (15-25/yr) 500-750 wds; fiction for teens, 750-1,000 wds. Responds in 4-8 wks. Seasonal 2-4 months ahead. Accepts simultaneous submissions. Accepts disk. Regular sidebars.

Guidelines/theme list (also by e-mail/Website); copy $5 and 4 stamps. (No ads)

Poetry: Only from kids under 18. Accepts 100/yr. Any type; 3-30 lines. Submit max 4-5 poems.

Fillers: Accepts 10-20/yr. Anecdotes, cartoons, games, quizzes, short humor, word puzzles; to 250 wds.

Columns/Departments: Accepts 10/yr. Noteworthy News (multicultural/nature/international/social, appropriate for youth), 200 wds.

Special Needs: Challenging disability; living in other cultures/countries; cross-cultural communications; outstanding moments in life; your inspirations and role models; Hawaiian culture.

Contest: Annual Book Awards for published books and authors; Annual Youth Honor Awards for students 7-17. Send SASE for guidelines. June 20 deadline.

Tips: "We're seeking submissions by minority, multicultural, international, and/or youth writers. Do not be judgmental or preachy; be open or receptive to diverse opinions."

$STORY FRIENDS, 616 Walnut St., Scottdale PA 15683. (724)887-8500. Fax (724)887-3111. E-mail: rstutz@mph.org. Website: www.mph.org. Herald Press/Mennonite. Rose Mary Stutzman, ed. For children 4-9 yrs; reinforces Christian values in a non-moralistic manner. Monthly mag; 20 pgs; circ 7,000. Subscription $18. 75% freelance. Complete ms/cover letter. Pays .03-.05/wd on acceptance for one-time rts. Articles (5-10/yr) & fiction (30/yr), 300-800 wds. Responds in 8 wks. Seasonal 6 mos ahead. Accepts simultaneous submissions & reprints (tell when/where appeared). Prefers NIV. Guidelines; copy for 9x12 SAE/2 stamps.

Poetry: Buys 12/yr. Traditional; 4-12 lines; $10. Submit max 3 poems.

Fillers: Buys 2-3/yr. Cartoons, word puzzles.

Ethnic: Targets all ethnic groups involved in the Mennonite church.

Tips: "Send stories that show rather than tell. Realistic fiction (no fantasy). Send good literary quality with a touch of humor that will appeal to children. Cover letter should give your experience with children."

$STORY MATES, Christian Light Publications, Inc., Box 1212, Harrisonburg VA 22803-1212. (540) 434-0768. Fax (540)433-8896. E-mail: crystals@clp.org. Mennonite. Crystal Shank, ed. For 4-8 yr olds. Weekly take-home paper; 4 pgs; circ 5,850. Subscription $9.20. 90% freelance. Complete ms. Pays up to .03/wd on acceptance for 1st rts (.04-.05/wd for all rts). Realistic or true stories to 800-900 wds (50-75/yr); picture stories 120-150 wds. Responds in 6 wks. Seasonal 6 mos ahead. Accepts simultaneous submissions & reprints (tell when/where appeared). No disk. Requires KJV. Guidelines/theme list/copy for 9x12 SAE/3 stamps. Will send questionnaire to fill out. (No ads)

Poetry: Buys 25/yr. Traditional, any length. Likes story poems. Pays up to .50/line.

Fillers: Quizzes, word puzzles, craft ideas. "Need fillers that correlate with theme list; Bible related." Pays about $5-6.

Tips: "We would welcome more puzzles for this age group. Carefully read our guidelines and understand our conservative Mennonite applications of Bible principles." Very conservative.
**This periodical was #58 on the 2000 Top 50 Christian Publishers list (#50 in 1999, #64 in 1998).

$TOGETHER TIME, 6401 The Paseo, Kansas City MO 64131. (816)333-7000x2359. Fax (816)333-4439. E-mail: kjohnson@nazarene.org. Website: www.nazarene.org. WordAction Publishing Co./Church of the Nazarene. Kathleen Johnson, assoc. ed. For 3-4 yr olds and parents. Weekly take-home paper; 2 pgs; circ 19,000. Subscription $9.95. 75% unsolicited freelance; 25% assigned. Complete ms/cover letter; fax/e-query OK. Pays .05/wd or $15 on publication for multi-use rts. Articles 150 wds (0/yr). Responds in 4 wks. Seasonal 12 mos ahead. Accepts simultaneous submissions and reprints (tell when/where appeared). Kill fee 5%. Prefers e-mail submission (attached file or copied into message). No sidebars. Prefers NIV. Guidelines/theme list; copy for #10 SAE/1 stamp. (No ads)
  Poetry: Buys 20/yr. Free verse, traditional; 4-8 lines; $2-4. Submit max 5 poems.
  Fillers: Games, ideas, activities; 150 wds. Pays $15 for crafts & ideas, finger plays, recipes.
  Tips: "Open to poetry or fillers. Know the age level of 3-4 year olds. Integrate Christian education throughout; don't tack it on the end."

$TOUCH, Box 7259, Grand Rapids MI 49510. (616)241-5616. Fax (616)241-5558. E-mail: sara@gemsgc.org, or servicecenter@gemsgc.org. Website: www.gospelcom.net/gems. GEMS Girls Clubs (Christian Reformed, Reformed, and Presbyterian). Jan Boone, ed; Sara Lynn Hilton, mng ed. To show girls, ages 9-14, that God is at work in their lives and the world around them. Monthly (10X) mag; 24 pgs; circ 15,000. Subscription $12.50. 80% unsolicited freelance; 20% assigned. Complete ms; e-query OK. Pays $5-20 ($15-50 for fiction) or .03/wd on publication for 1st, reprint or simultaneous rts. Articles 200-400 wds (10/yr); fiction 400-1,000 wds (30/yr). Responds in 3 wks. Seasonal 10 mos ahead. Accepts simultaneous submissions & reprints. Accepts disk. Regular sidebars. Prefers NIV. Guidelines/theme list (also by e-mail/Website); copy $1/9x12 SAE/3 stamps. (No ads)
  Poetry: Buys 3/yr. Haiku, light verse, traditional; 4-12 lines; $5-10. Poetry fits themes.
  Fillers: Buys 10/yr. Games, party ideas, prayers, quizzes, short humor; 50-200 wds; $5-15.
  Special Needs: Annual theme is "The Perfect 9" so all articles and stories should be on the 9 Fruits of the Spirit. See Update for ideas.
  Tips: "Be realistic—we get a lot of fluffy stories with Pollyanna endings. We are looking for real-life-type stories that girls relate to. We mostly publish short stories, are open to short reflective articles, use puzzles and quizzes a lot. The readers seem to like the quiz that builds on itself. One answer leads to the next question or a final question is answered by doing the questions before it. Know what girls face today and how they cope in their daily lives. We need angles

from home life and friendships, peer pressure and the normal growing-up challenges girls deal with."

**This periodical was #42 on the 1996 Top 50 Christian Publishers list (#45 in 1995).

$THE WINNER, 55 W. Oak Ridge Dr., Hagerstown MD 21740. (301)393-4010. Fax (301)393-4055. E-mail: winner@healthconnection.org. Larry Becker, ed; submit to Anita Jacobs, asst ed. For elementary school children, grades 4-6. Monthly (during school year) mag; 16 pgs; circ 15,000. Subscription $17.95. 40% unsolicited freelance; 60% assigned. Query by e-mail. Pays $40-80 on acceptance for 1st rts. Articles 500-600 wds (25-30/yr); fiction 500-600 wds. Responds in 8-10 wks. Seasonal 9 mos ahead. Accepts simultaneous submissions & reprints (tell when/where appeared). Prefers e-mail (attached file). Some sidebars. Guidelines; copy $1/9x12 SAE/2 stamps.

    Tips: "Most open to positive, true stories or true-to-life stories of children making a difference in their school, neighborhood, etc."

$WONDER TIME, 6401 The Paseo, Kansas City MO 64131-1213. (816)333-7000. Fax (816)333-4439. E-mail: dfillmore@nazarene.org, or pcraft@nazarene.org. Website: www.nazarene.org. Church of the Nazarene. Patty Craft, assoc ed. For 6-8 yr olds (1st & 2nd graders); emphasis on principles, character-building, and brotherhood. Weekly take-home paper; 4 pgs; circ 40,000. 75% unsolicited freelance. Complete ms/with cover letter; fax/e-query OK. Pays $25 on publication for all rts. Fiction 250-350 wds (40/yr). Responds in 9 wks. Seasonal 1 yr ahead. Accepts disk or e-mail submission (copied into message). Kill fee $15. No sidebars. Prefers NIV. Guidelines/theme list; copy for 9x12 SAE/2 stamps. (No ads)

    Tips: "We accept freelance stories that follow our theme list. Stories should be contemporary, life-related, at a 1st-2nd grade readability, and directly correlate with our Sunday school curriculum. Avoid trite situations." New theme list available February 2001.

CHRISTIAN EDUCATION/LIBRARY MARKETS

$BRIGADE LEADER, Box 150, Wheaton IL 60189. (630)582-0630. Fax (630)582-0623. E-mail: dchristensen@csbministries.org. Website: www.csbministries.org. Christian Service Brigade. Deborah Christensen, ed. For men leading boy's clubs; emphasis on Brigade leadership. Quarterly mag; 16 pgs; circ 6,500. Subscription $6. No unsolicited freelance; 25% assigned. Query (most articles assigned); no phone/fax/e-query. Pays .05-.10/wd on publication for 1st or reprint rts. Articles 500-1,500 wds (2-3/yr). Responds in 4 wks. Accepts reprints (tell when/where appeared). Accepts e-mail submissions (copied into message). Kill fee $35. Regular sidebars. Prefers NIV. Guidelines; copy $1.50/9x12 SAE/5 stamps. (No ads)

    Special Needs: Articles on discipling boys.

    Tips: "We're especially looking for men who are familiar with Christian Service Brigade and how to disciple boys—the dynamics of 'building men to serve Christ.'"

$CARAVAN: A Resource for Adult Religious Educators, 90 Parent Ave., Ottawa ON K1N 7B1 Canada. (613)241-9461. Fax (613)241-8117. E-mail:

jchafe@cccb.ca. Canadian conference of Catholic Bishops. Joanne Chafe, ed. A resources for adult educators who work in church settings. Quarterly mag; 16 pgs; circ 1,500. Subscription $26.75 CAN; $27 US. 10% unsolicited freelance; 90% assigned. Complete ms/cover letter. Pays variable rate on acceptance or publication. Copyrighted; rights released on request. Articles (30-40/yr). Responds in 4-6 wks. Seasonal 3 mos ahead. Accepts simultaneous submissions. Regular sidebars. Guidelines/copy.

> **Columns/Departments:** Adult religious education: New Initiatives, New Releases, Creative program ideas.
>
> **Special Needs:** Workshop models.
>
> **Tips:** "Send suggested annotated outline of material. Request guidelines and sample copy."

$CATECHIST, 330 Progress Rd., Dayton OH 45449. (937)847-5900. Fax (937)847-5910. E-mail: raffio@aol.com. Website: www.catechist.com. Catholic. Patricia Fischer, ed. For Catholic school teachers and parish volunteer catechists. Mag. published 7X/yr; 52 pgs; circ 50,000. 30% unsolicited freelance; 70% assigned. Query (preferred) or complete ms. Pays $25-150 on publication for all rts. Articles 1,200-1,500 wds. Responds in 9-18 wks. Guidelines (also on Website); copy $2.50.

CATHOLIC LIBRARY WORLD, 291 Springfield St., Chicopee MA 01013-2839. (413)594-2761. Fax (413)594-7418. E-mail: gallagherm@elms.edu. Website: www.cathla.org. Catholic Library Assn. Sr. Mary E. Gallagher, editorial chair. For libraries at all levels—preschool to post-secondary to academic, parish, public and private. Quarterly journal; 80 pgs; circ 1,000. Subscription $60/$70 foreign. Query; phone/fax/e-query OK. PAYS 1 COPY. Articles; book/video reviews, 300-500 wds. Accepts disk. Some sidebars. No guidelines; copy for 9x12 SAE. Not in topical listings. (Ads)

> **Special Needs:** Topics of interest to academic libraries, high school and children's libraries, parish and community libraries, archives, and library education. Reviewers cover areas such as theology, spirituality, pastoral, professional, juvenile books and material, and media.
>
> **Tips:** "Review section considers taking on new reviewers who are experts in field of librarianship, theology, and professional studies. No payment except a free copy of the book or materials reviewed."

C.E. CONNECTION, Box 12609, Oklahoma City OK 73157. (405)787-7110. Fax (405)789-3957. E-mail: kristy@iphc.org. Website: www.iphc.org. General Christian Education Dept./International Pentecostal Holiness Church. Kristy Cofer, coordinating ed. Targets pastors and local Christian education workers/leaders for training/how-to. Quarterly tabloid; 12 pgs; circ 6,600. Free. 100% freelance. Complete ms/cover letter; e-query OK. **NO PAYMENT.** Not copyrighted. Articles (10/yr) & fiction to 450 wds. Responds in 2-3 wks. Seasonal 6 mos ahead. Accepts simultaneous submissions & reprints (tell when/where appeared). Prefers e-mail submission (attached file or copied into message). Regular sidebars. Guidelines/theme list (also by e-mail), free copy 9x12 SAE. (No ads)

> **Fillers:** Cartoons, facts, ideas, jokes, prose, short humor. Pays $20-25.

Tips: "All sections are open. We use freelance material when our regular writers miss deadlines."

$CE CONNECTION COMMUNIQUE, PO Box 12624, Roanoke VA 24027. Phone/fax (540)342-7511. E-mail: ccmbbr@juno.com. Website: www. EquippingForMinistry.org. Betty Robertson, ed. Virginia Christian Education Assn. Monthly e-newsletter; circ 2,750. 25% unsolicited freelance; 75% assigned. Query; no phone/fax query; e-query OK. Pays $5-10 on acceptance for 1st, one-time, simultaneous rts. Not copyrighted. Articles 100-600 wds. Responds in 6 wks. Seasonal 6 mos ahead. Accepts simultaneous submissions & reprints. Guidelines (by e-mail).

$CHILDREN'S MINISTRY, PO Box 481, Loveland CO 80539. (970)669-3836. Fax (970)679-4392. E-mail: ajones@grouppublishing.com, or info@grouppublishing.com. Website: www.grouppublishing.com. Group Publishing. Christine Yount, ed; Amy Jones, asst ed. For Christians who work with kids from birth to 6th grade. Bimonthly mag; 85 pgs; circ 65,000. Subscription $24.95. 73% unsolicited freelance; 20% assigned. Query with or without clips; fax/e-query OK. Pays $40-175 on acceptance for all rts. Articles 50-1,200 wds (40/yr). Responds in 9 wks. Seasonal 5 mos ahead. Accepts disk. Regular sidebars. Guidelines (also on Website); copy $2/9x12 SASE or on Website. (Ads)

Fillers: Buys 5-10/yr. Cartoons, kid quotes; $15-35.

Columns/Departments: Buys 50/yr. For Parents Only (practical parenting tips); Preschool Page (hints, songs, Bible activities); Nursery Notes; Group Games; Seasonal Specials (parties, service projects, worship celebrations); Quick Devotions; 50-150 wds; $25-35. Complete mss.

Special Needs: Crafts, seasonal ideas, children's trends; tried and true ideas that work.

Tips: "Through experience in children's ministry, offer new and refreshing insights or ideas that can be easily incorporated into children's ministry programs."

$THE CHRISTIAN CLASSROOM, 2026 Exeter Rd., Ste. 2, Germantown TN 38138. (901)624-5911. Fax (901)624-5910. E-mail: tcc@grtriver.com. Website: www.grtriver.com. Great River Publishing Co. Sherry Campbell, ed. Ideas and information for teachers in Christian schools. Quarterly mag; 32-48 pgs; circ 22,000. Subscription $19.95. Estab 1997. 33% freelance. Complete ms/cover letter; phone/fax/e-query OK. Pays $50-200 on publication for all rts. Articles 1,000-1,500 wds (6/yr). Responds in 3 wks. Seasonal 6 mos ahead. Accepts simultaneous submissions. Accepts e-mail submissions (copied into message). Kill fee 10%. Some sidebars. Any version. Guidelines/theme list; copy for 9x12 SAE/3 stamps. (Ads)

Fillers: Buys 1-4/yr. Anecdotes, cartoons, facts, games, ideas, jokes, prayers, prose, quizzes, short humor, word puzzles; 25-500 wds. Pays $75.

Tips: "Provide information to help Christian school teachers do their jobs better and easier."

$CHRISTIAN EDUCATION COUNSELOR, 1445 Boonville Ave., Springfield MO 65802-1894. (417)862-2781. Fax (417)862-0503. E-mail: ceeditor@

ag.org. Website: www.we-build-people.org/cec. Assemblies of God. Sylvia Lee, ed. Presents teaching and administrative helps to lay leaders in local churches. Bimonthly mag; 32 pgs; circ 10,800. Subscription $12. 5% freelance. Complete ms/cover letter. Pays .08-.12/wd on acceptance for 1st, simultaneous & reprint rts. Articles 300-800 wds (50/yr); book reviews, 400-500 wds, $35. Responds in 4 wks. Seasonal 6 mos ahead. Accepts simultaneous submissions & reprints. Accepts disk. Regular sidebars. Guidelines; copy for 9x12 SAE/2 stamps. (No ads)

   Fillers: Buys cartoons, games, ideas, quizzes; $35-85.

   Tips: "We need short articles, 300 words or less, on an idea that works. We want practical helps for our readers and first-hand experience is best."

   **This periodical was #52 on the 1996 Top 50 Christian Publishers list (#62 in 1995, #64 in 1994).

CHRISTIAN EDUCATION JOURNAL, 2065 Half Day Rd., Deerfield IL 60015. (847)317-8048. Fax (847)317-8128. E-mail: CEJ@tiu.edu. Trinity Evangelical Divinity School. Dr. Perry G. Downs, ed. Complete ms (disk & hard copy)/cover letter; phone/fax/e-query OK. Articles 10-25 pgs, on Christian education topics. Accepts e-mail submissions. No guidelines. Not in topical listings. (Ads)

   Special Needs: Writers must send academically sound and well-researched articles for consideration. CEJ is primarily a journal for academics and well-studied practitioners. Open to all areas related to Christian education, including church ministry and leadership; educational articles related to organizational development and leadership.

CHRISTIAN EDUCATION LEADERSHIP—See Youth and Christian Education Leadership.

$CHRISTIAN EDUCATORS JOURNAL, 73 Highland Ave., St. Catherines ON L2R 4H9 Canada. Phone/fax (905)684-3991. E-mail: bert.witvoet@ sympatico.ca. Christian Educators Journal Assn. Bert Witvoet, mng ed. For educators in Christian day schools at the elementary, secondary, and college levels. Quarterly journal; 36 pgs; circ 4,200. Subscription $7.50 (c/o Peter C. Boogaart, 1828 Mayfiar Dr. NE, Grand Rapids MI 49503). 50% unsolicited freelance; 50% assigned. Query; phone/e-query OK. Pays $30 on publication for one-time rts. Articles 750-1,500 wds (20/yr); fiction 750-1,500 wds. Responds in 5 wks. Seasonal 4 mos ahead. Accepts simultaneous submissions & reprints. Guidelines/theme list; copy $1.50 or 9x12 SAE/4 stamps. (Limited ads)

   Poetry: Buys 6/yr. On teaching day school; 4-30 lines; $10. Submit max 5 poems.

   Tips: "No articles on Sunday school, only Christian day school. Most open to theme topics and features."

THE CHRISTIAN LIBRARIAN, Ryan Library, PLNU 3600 Lomaland Dr., San Diego CA 92106. (619)849-2208. Fax (619)849-7024. E-mail: apowell@ ptloma.edu. Website: www.acl.org. Assn. of Christian Librarians. Anne-Elizabeth Powell, ed-in-chief. Geared toward academic librarians of the Christian faith. Quarterly (3X) journal; 40 pgs; circ 500. Subscription $25.

50% unsolicited freelance; 50% assigned. E-mail; fax/e-query OK. **NO PAYMENT** for one-time rts. Not copyrighted. Articles 1,000-3,000 words; research articles to 5,000 wds (6/yr); reviews 150-300 wds. Responds in 5 wks. Accepts simultaneous submissions & reprints (tell when/where appeared). Prefers e-mail submissions (attached file). Some sidebars. Guidelines; copy $5. (Ads)

   Fillers: Anecdotes, ideas, short humor; 25-300 wds.

   Special Needs: Articles on censorship and international librarianship.

CHRISTIAN LIBRARY JOURNAL, 1240—34th Pl., Florence OR 97439-8936. E-mail: heschclj@harborside.com. Website: www.christianlibraryj.org. Christian Library Services. Nancy Hesch, ed/pub; Andrew Seddon, articles ed. Provides reviews of library materials and articles about books, authors, and libraries for the Christian librarian. Quarterly mag; 88 pgs; circ. 1,000. Subscription $45. 10% unsolicited freelance; 90% assigned. Query; fax/e-query OK. **PAYS A SUBSCRIPTION** for 1st or reprint rts. Articles (10/yr) 1,500 wds; book /video reviews, 200-300 wds (ask Nancy Hesch to be a reviewer), book or other item plus subscription in payment. Responds in 10-12 wks. Accepts reprints (tell when/where appeared). Prefers e-mail submissions (attached file or copied into message). Guidelines/theme list (also by e-mail/Website); copy for 9x12 SAE/$1.58 postage. (Ads)

   Special Needs: Library how-tos, Websites, author profiles, and annotated bibliographies.

   Tips: "Most open to articles, book reviews, especially written by librarians and teachers."

*****CHRISTIAN SCHOOL**, 2025-A N. Main St., Wheaton IL 60187-9136. (630)653-4588. Phil Landrum, pub. A publication for Christian-school educators and parents. Quarterly mag; 48 pgs; circ 3,000 schools. 2% freelance. Query; phone query OK. **NO PAYMENT.** Articles 500-1,500 wds (1/yr); fiction 1,000-1,500 (1/yr). Responds in 2-4 wks. Free guidelines/copy.

   Poetry: Accepts 1/yr. Traditional. Submit max 5 poems.

   Fillers: Accepts 1/yr. Anecdotes.

   Special Needs: Education how-to; youth trends; training techniques; children's books.

$THE CHRISTIAN SCHOOL ADMINISTRATOR, 2026 Exeter Rd., Ste. 2, Germantown TN 38138. (901)624-5911. Fax (901)624-5910. E-mail: csa@grtriver.com. Website: www.grtriver.com. Great River Publishing Co. Sherry Campbell, ed. The information source for Christian school operations. Bimonthly mag; 32-64 pgs; circ 16,000. Subscription $15. 25% freelance. Complete ms/cover letter; phone/fax/e-query OK. Pays $50-200 on publication for all rts. Articles 1,000-1,500 wds (6/yr). Responds in 3 wks. Seasonal 6 mos ahead. Accepts simultaneous submissions. Accepts e-mail submissions (copied into message). Some sidebars. Any version. Guidelines/theme list; copy for 9x12 SAE/3 stamps. (Ads)

   Fillers: Buys 1-4/yr. Anecdotes, cartoons, facts, games, ideas, jokes, prayers, prose, quizzes,quotes, short humor; 25-500 wds. Pays $25-75.

Tips: "Provide how-to information on some aspect of operating a private Christian school."

CHURCH & SYNAGOGUE LIBRARIES, PO Box 19357, Portland OR 97280-0357. (503)244-6919. Fax (503)977-3734. E-mail: csla@worldaccessnet. com. Website: www.worldaccessnet.com/~csla. Church and Synagogue Library Assn. Judith Janzen, exec dir. To help librarians run congregational libraries. Bimonthly; 20 pgs.; circ. 3,000. Subscription $25, $35 CAN, $45 foreign. Query; no e-mail query. **NO PAYMENT.** Requires disk. Articles. Book & video reviews 1-2 paragraphs. No guidelines; copy available. (Ads)

> **Fillers:** Ideas.

$CHURCH EDUCATOR, 165 Plaza Dr., Prescott AZ 86303. (520)771-8601. Fax (520)771-8621. E-mail: edmin2@aol.com. Educational Ministries, Inc. Linda Davidson, ed. For mainline Protestant Christian educators. Monthly journal; 32 pgs; circ 4,000. Subscription $28, CAN $34, foreign $36. 95% freelance. Complete ms/cover letter; phone/fax/e-query OK. Pays .03/wd, 60 days after publication, for 1st rts. Articles 500-2,000 wds (200/yr); fiction 500-1,500 wds (10/yr). Responds in 2-17 wks. Seasonal 7 mos ahead. Accepts simultaneous submissions & reprints (tell when/ where appeared). Regular sidebars. Guidelines/theme list; copy for 9x12 SAE/4 stamps.

> **Fillers:** Bible games and Bible puzzles.

> **Tips:** "Talk to the educator at your church. What would they find useful? Most open to seasonal articles dealing with the liturgical year. Write up church programs with specific how-tos of putting the program together."

$CHURCH LIBRARIES, 9731 N. Fox Glen Dr., #6F, Niles IL 60714-4222. (847)296-3964. Fax (847)296-0754. E-mail: linjohnson@compuserve.com. Website: members.aol.com/EChurchLibrary/home.htm. Evangelical Church Library Assn. Lin Johnson, managing ed. To assist church librarians in setting up, maintaining, and promoting church libraries and media centers. Quarterly mag; 40 pgs; circ 500. Subscription $25. 100% unsolicited freelance. Complete ms; fax/e-query OK. Pays .04/wd on acceptance for 1st, one-time, or reprint rts. Articles 500-1,000 wds (24-30/yr); book/music/video/cassette reviews by assignment, 75-150 wds, free product. Responds in 6-8 wks. Seasonal 6 mos ahead. Accepts reprints (tell when/where appeared). Requires e-mail submission. Regular sidebars. Prefers NIV. Guidelines (also by e-mail/ Website); copy for 9x12 SAE/6 stamps. (Ads)

> **Tips:** "Talk to church librarians or get involved in library or reading programs. Most open to articles, and promotional ideas; profiles of church libraries; round-ups on best books in a category (query on topic first). Need for reviewers fluctuates; if interested send SASE for questionnaire."

> **This periodical was #45 on the 2000 Top 50 Christian Publishers list.

$CHURCH MEDIA JOURNAL (formerly Church Media Library Magazine), 127 9th Ave. N, Nashville TN 37234-0140. (615)251-2752. Fax (615)251-5607. E-mail: mezell@lifeway.com. Website: www.lifeway.com. LifeWay/

Southern Baptist. Judi Hayes, design ed.; submit to Mancil Ezell, submissions ed. Supports the establishment and development of church media libraries; provides how-to articles and articles of inspiration and encouragement to media library workers. Quarterly mag; 52 pgs; circ 30,000. Query. Pays .055/wd on publication for all, 1st, or reprint rts. Articles 600-1,500 wds (10-15/yr). Responds in 5 wks. Seasonal 14 mos ahead. Free guidelines/copy.

$*EARLY CHILDHOOD NEWS, 330 Progress Rd., Dayton OH 45449. (937) 847-5900x142. Fax (937)847-5910. E-mail: ecneditor@aol.com. Website: www.earlychildhoodnews.com. Catholic. Megan Shaw, ed. Dedicated to serving the professional development needs of early childhood educators. Bimonthly mag; circ 23,000. Open to freelance. Complete ms on disk (will not be acknowledged or returned). Pays $75-200 for all rts. Articles 1,500-3,000 wds. No reprints. Requires disk. Guidelines/theme list (also on Website). Incomplete topical listings.

> **Tips:** "Feel free to call editor about the status of your manuscript."

$EVANGELIZING TODAY'S CHILD, Box 348, Warrenton MO 63383-0348. (636)456-4321. Fax (636)456-2078. E-mail: ETCeditor@cefinc.org. Website: www.cefinc.org/etcmag. Child Evangelism Fellowship. Elsie C. Lippy, ed. To equip Christians to win the world's children (4-11) to Christ and disciple them. Bimonthly mag; 64 pgs; circ 17,000. Subscription $20. 25% unsolicited freelance; 75% assigned. Complete ms; no phone/fax query; e-query OK. Pays .12-.14/wd (.08/wd for fiction) within 60 days of acceptance for one-time rts. Articles 1,200 wds (24/yr); fiction 700-800 wds (12/yr). Responds in 4-6 wks. Seasonal 1 yr ahead. Accepts few reprints (tell when/where appeared). No disk; e-mail submission OK. Kill fee 30%. Regular sidebars. Prefers NIV. Guidelines; copy $2/9x12 SAE/6 stamps. (Ads)

> **Resource Center:** Buys 40-60/yr. Complete ms, 200-300 wds. Pays $25 for teaching hints, bulletin board ideas, object lessons, missions incentives, seasonal ideas with spiritual focus.
>
> **Special Needs:** Reproducible activity pages on Christian growth that child can do with the family. Can be seasonal. Pays $35-50.
>
> **Tips:** "Most open to Resource Center which includes short ideas ($10); 200-300 word ideas ($25), or reproducible pages ($35-50). Submit ideas you've used in your teaching ministry. We want something 'fresh' that both new/old teachers can incorporate into their teaching ministry."
>
> **This periodical was #62 on the 1997 Top 50 Christian Publishers list (#64 in 1995, #49 in 1994).

$GROUP MAGAZINE, Box 481, Loveland CO 80538. (970)669-3836. Fax (970)679-4392. E-mail: rlawrence@grouppublishing.com, or kdieterich@grouppublishing.com. Website: www.grouppublishing.com, or www.groupmag.com. Rick Lawrence, ed; Kathleen Dieterich, asst ed. For leaders of Christian youth groups; to supply ideas, practical help, inspiration and training for youth leaders. Bimonthly mag; 85 pgs; circ 55,000. Subscription $29.95. 65% unsolicited freelance; 25% assigned. Query; e-query OK. Pays $40-225 on acceptance for all rts. Articles 500-1,800 wds

(150/yr). Responds in 8 wks. Seasonal 5 mos ahead. No simultaneous submissions or reprints. Accepts e-mail submissions (copied into message). No kill fee. Some sidebars. Any version. Guidelines (also on Website); copy $2/9x12 SAE/4 stamps. (Ads)

Fillers: Buys 5-10/yr. Cartoons, games, ideas; $15-35.

Columns/Departments: Buys 30-40/yr. Try This One (youth group activities), to 300 wds; Strange But True (strange youth-ministry stories), to 500 wds; Hands-on Help (tips for leaders), to 175 wds; Good News About Kids (positive news about teens), 150 wds; $40. Complete ms.

Special Needs: Articles geared toward working with teens; programming ideas; youth ministry issues.

Tips: "We're always looking for effective youth ministry ideas—especially those tested by youth leaders in the field. Most open to Hands-On-Help column (use real-life examples, personal experiences, practical tips, scripture, and self-quizzes or checklists)."

$THE JOURNAL OF ADVENTIST EDUCATION, 12501 Old Columbia Pike, Silver Springs MD 20904-6600. (301)680-5075. Fax (301)622-9627. E-mail: 74617.1231@compuserve.com. Seventh-Day Adventist. Beverly J. Rumble, ed. For Seventh-Day teachers teaching in the church's school system, K-University. Bimonthly (5X) journal; 48 pgs; circ 8,500. Subscription $17.25 (add $1 outside US). 10% freelance. Query or complete ms; phone/fax/e-query OK. Pays $25-200 on publication for 1st & translation rts. Articles to 1,000-1,500 wds (2-20/yr). Responds in 6 wks. Seasonal 6 mos ahead. Accepts reprints (tell when/where appeared). Accepts disk. Kill fee to 25%. Regular sidebars. Guidelines; copy for 9x12 SAE/$2 postage.

Fillers: Cartoons only, no pay.

Special Needs: "All articles in the context of parochial schools (*not Sunday school tips*); professional enrichment and teaching tips for Christian teachers. Need feature articles."

+JOURNAL OF CHRISTIAN EDUCATION, PO Box 139, Lidcombe NSW 1825 Australia. Phone 61 2 9764 2084. Fax 61 2 9746 2710. E-mail: ahukins@bigpond.com, submit to: harkness@ttc.edu.sg. Website: jce. acfe.org.au. Australian Christian Forum on Education, Inc. Dr. Allan G. Harkness, ed. To consider the implications of the Christian faith for the entire field of education. Triannual jour.; 64 pgs; circ 500. Subscription $35 AUS, $32 US. 40% unsolicited freelance; 60% assigned. Complete ms/cover letter; phone/fax/e-query OK. **NO PAYMENT** for one-time rts. Articles 3,000-5,000 wds (6/yr). Responds in 4 wks. Seasonal 6 mos ahead. Accepts disk or e-mail (attached file). No sidebars. Free guidelines (also on Website) & copy. (No ads)

Tips: "Send for a sample copy, study guidelines, and submit manuscript."

+JOURNAL OF EDUCATION & CHRISTIAN BELIEF, The Stapleford Centre, the Old Lace Mill, Frederick Road, Stapleford, Nottingham NG9 8FN, United Kingdom. (0115)939 6270. Fax (0115)9392076. E-mail: jecb@ stapleford-centre.org. Website: www.stapleford-centre.org. Association of

Christian Teachers. Dr. John Shortt, ed. Semiannual journal; 80 pgs; circ 400. Subscription 20-80 pounds. Estab. 1997. 80% unsolicited freelance; 20% assigned. Complete ms/cover letter; e-query OK. **NO PAYMENT** for 1st rts. Articles 5,000 wds (12/yr). Responds in 4-8 wks. Accepts reprints (tell when/where appeared). Prefers disk or e-mail submissions (attached file). No sidebars. Guidelines by e-mail; no copy. (No ads)

JOURNAL OF RESEARCH ON CHRISTIAN EDUCATION, Andrews University, Information Services Bldg., Ste. 211, Berrien Springs MI 49104. (616)471-6080. Fax (616)471-6224. E-mail: jrce@andrews.edu. Website: www.jrce.org. Andrews University. Dr. Lyndon G. Furst, ed. Research related to Christian schooling (all levels) within the Protestant tradition. Semi-annual journal; 150+ pgs; circ 400. Subscription $21 (individual) or $30 (institution). 100% unsolicited freelance. Complete ms/cover letter; phone/fax/e-query OK. **NO PAYMENT**. Articles 13-26, double-spaced pgs (12-18/yr); book reviews, 2-5 pgs. Responds in 1 wk; decision within 6 mos (goes through review board). Requires disk. No sidebars. Guidelines (also by e-mail). (No ads)

> **Tips:** "This is a research journal. All manuscripts should conform to standards of scholarly inquiry. Manuscripts are submitted to a panel of 3 experts for their review. Publication decision is based on recommendation of reviewers. Authors should submit manuscripts written in scholarly style and focused on Christian schooling."

$KIDS' MINISTRY IDEAS, 55 W. Oak Ridge Dr., Hagerstown MD 21740. (301)393-4115. Fax (301)393-4055. E-mail: KidsMin@rhpa.org. Seventh-Day Adventist. Patricia Fritz, ed; Tamara Michalenko Terry, mng ed. For adults leading children (birth-8th grade) to Christ. Quarterly mag; 32-40 pgs; circ. 5,000. Subscription $17.50. 25% unsolicited freelance; 75% assigned. Query; fax/e-query OK. Pays $25-120 on acceptance for one-time or reprint rts. Articles 500-1,300 wds (10/yr). Responds in 6-8 wks. Seasonal 9 mos ahead. Accepts simultaneous submissions & reprints (tell when/where appeared). Accepts e-mail submission. Regular sidebars. Prefers NIV. Guidelines (also by e-mail); copy for 9x12 SAE/4 stamps. (Ads, call [410]799-1955)

> **Columns/Departments:** Buys 20-30/yr. Try This (short ideas that have worked in teaching kids), 2-3 paragraphs. Pays free book.

> **Special Needs:** Leading children to Christ, reaching unchurched children, ministering to live-wire kids, dealing with children in transition, help for small churches, involving kids in church service, nurturing volunteers, building kids' faith, encouraging family involvement, helping children of divorce, finding quality volunteers, teaching the concept of grace, children's church, multi-age classes, bulletin boards, innovative crafts, active learning, quizzes/puzzles/games, fidget & boredom busters, attendance/memory verse/study lesson devices, free or inexpensive decorating/props, and junior/youth programs.

> **Tips:** "Looking for program ideas, outreach ideas, something that has worked to draw kids closer to Jesus. This is a how-to oriented magazine. I'd be interested in active teaching ideas on general themes, such as faith, trust, prayer and grace."

**This periodical was #64 on the 2000 Top 50 Christian Publishers list.

$LEADER IN THE CHURCH SCHOOL TODAY, 201 Eighth Ave. S., Nashville TN 37203. (615)749-6488. Fax (615)749-6512. E-mail: smcgee@umpublishing.org. United Methodist. Jill S. Reddig, ed. For pastors and Christian education leaders in the church. Quarterly mag; 64 pgs; circ 4,500. Subscription $16. 30% unsolicited freelance; 70% assigned. Complete ms/cover letter; phone/fax/e-query OK. Pays $25-125 (.05/wd) on publication for all, 1st, one-time or reprint rts. Articles 650-1,300 wds (98/yr); book reviews 150 wds. Responds in 6-8 wks. Seasonal 6-12 mos ahead. Accepts reprints (tell when/where appeared). Prefers disk or e-mail submission. Some sidebars. Prefers NRSV (never Living Bible). Guidelines/theme list; copy $4.75/9x12 SAE. (No ads)

> **Fillers:** Buys 25-30/yr. Games, ideas, word puzzles; 50-250 wds. Pays $15-50.

> **Columns/Departments:** Buys 30/yr. Idea Exchange (what worked for us; for children/youth/adult classes), 50-150 wds; Teacher/leader Development (teacher training), 700-2,500 wds; Days & Seasons (seasonal Christian ed.), 700-2,500 wds.

> **Tips:** "Most open to columns. Send a sample of your writing."
> **This periodical was #46 on the 1998 Top 50 Christian Publishers List (#45 in 1997, #66 in 1996).

$*LOLLIPOPS: The Magazine for Early Childhood Educators, Good Apple, Inc., Box 2649, Columbus OH 43216-2649. Donna Borst, ed. Easy-to-use, hands-on, practical teaching ideas and suggestions for early childhood educators. Magazine published 5X/yr; circ 20,000. 20% freelance. Query or complete ms. Pays $10-100 on publication for all rts. Articles 200-1,000 wds; fiction (for young children) 500-1,200 wds. Seasonal 6 mos ahead. Guidelines (2 stamps); copy for 9x12 SAE/3 stamps.

> **Poetry:** Light verse.

> **Tips:** "Looking for something new and different for teachers of young children; seasonal material."

$MOMENTUM, 1077 30th St. NW, Ste. 100, Washington DC 20007-3852. (202)337-6232. Fax (202)333-6706. E-mail: momentum@ncea.org. Website: www.ncea.org. National Catholic Educational Assn. Margaret Anderson, ed. Features outstanding programs, issues, and research in education. Quarterly jour; circ 28,000. 50% freelance. Query or complete ms. Pays $25-75 on publication for 1st rts. Articles 500-1,500 wds (25-30/yr); book reviews. Query. No simultaneous submissions. Guidelines; copy $5/9x12 SAE/8 stamps. Not in topical listings.

$PARISH TEACHER, Box 1209, Minneapolis MN 55440-1209. (612)330-3449. Fax (612)330-3215. E-mail: goplinv@augsburgfortress.org. Website: www.augsburgfortress.org. ELCA/Augsburg Fortress Publishers. Vicky Goplin, ed. Articles and ideas for Lutheran and mainline Christian volunteers who are leaders in Christian education programs. Monthly (9X, Sept-May) mag; 16 pgs; circ 50,000. Subscription $9.95. 12.5% unsolicited freelance; 87.5% assigned. Complete ms/cover letter. Pays $60 on publication for all rts (preferred). Articles 550-650 wds (15/yr); plays

400-800 wds (1-2/yr). Responds in 12-16 wks. Seasonal 4-6 mos ahead. Requires disk. No sidebars. Prefers NRSV. Guidelines; copy for 9x12 SAE/4 stamps.

Fillers: Buys 70+ ideas/yr.; 100-200 wds; $20.

Tips: "Most open to ideas or feature articles that are practical and inspirational in Christian education settings. Focus on how teachers/leaders can help learners discover faith in their everyday lives."

$PERSPECTIVE, PO Box 788, Wheaton IL 60189-0788. (630)293-1600. Fax (630)293-3053. E-mail: pcbecky@enteract.com. Website: www.pioneer clubs.org. Pioneer Clubs. Rebecca Powell Parat, ed. To help and encourage Pioneer Clubs leaders (for children ages 2-18). Triannual mag; 32 pgs; circ 24,500. Subscription $6. 30% freelance. Query/clips (preferred); phone/fax/e-query OK. Pays .06-.10/wd ($60-130) on acceptance for all or 1st rts. Articles 1,000-1,500 wds (2-3/yr). Responds in 9 wks. Seasonal 9 mos ahead. Accepts simultaneous query & reprints (tell when/where appeared). Prefers disk or accepts e-mail submission (copied into message). Regular sidebars. Prefers NIV. Guidelines; copy $1.75/9x12 SAE/6 stamps. (No ads)

Columns/Departments: Buys 2-3/yr. Storehouse (ideas for crafts, games, service projects, tips for leaders, etc.); 150-250 wds; $8-15. Complete ms.

Tips: "Most articles done on assignment. We'd like to hear from freelancers who have experience with, or access to, a Pioneer Clubs program or Camp Cherith. They should send samples of their work along with a letter introducing themselves."

$PRESCHOOL PLAYHOUSE, 1551 Regency Ct., Calumet City IL 60409. (708) 868-7100. Fax (708)868-6759. Website: www.urbanministries.com. Urban Ministries, Inc. K. Steward, ed. Sunday school magazine with activities for 2-5 year olds with accompanying teacher's manual. Quarterly magazine for teachers; take-home paper for students; 96 pgs. Subscription $4.59 (teacher) and $2.45 (student). 80% assigned. Query/clips; fax/e-query OK. Pays $150, 120 days after acceptance, for all rts. Articles 9,100 characters for teacher, 2,900 characters for student (4/yr). Responds in 4 wks. Seasonal 6 mos ahead. Accepts simultaneous submissions. Requires disk. Prefers NIV. Guidelines; copy $2.25/#10 SASE. (No ads)

Tips: "Send a query with writing samples, or attend our annual conference on the first weekend in November each year. Manuscripts are evaluated at the conference."

$RELIGION TEACHER'S JOURNAL, Box 180, Mystic CT 06355. (860)536-2611. Fax (860)572-0788. E-mail: ttpubsedit@aol.com. Twenty-Third Publications/Catholic. Alison Berger, ed dir. For volunteer religion teachers who need practical, hands-on information as well as theological background for teaching religion to K through high school. 7X yearly mag; 40 pgs; circ 40,000. Subscription $19.95. 20% unsolicited freelance; 80% assigned. Query; fax/e-query OK. Pays to $100 on acceptance for 1st rts. Not copyrighted. Articles to 6 pgs (50/yr). Responds in 2-4 wks. Seasonal 2 mos ahead. Prefers disk. Regular sidebars. Guidelines/theme list; copy for 9x12 SAE/4 stamps. (Ads)

Fillers: Buys 20-30/yr. Anecdotes (about teaching), games, ideas, prayers, successful class activities; to 1 pg; $5-25.

Tips: "Know our audience and address their needs. Most open to feature articles about teaching skills, spirituality, successful class activities or projects."

$#RESOURCE, 6401 The Paseo, Kansas City MO 64131. (816)333-7000 x2224. Fax (816)363-7092. E-mail: dfelter@nazarene.org. Website: www. nazarene.org. Church of the Nazarene. David Felter, ed. To provide information, training, and inspiration to those who are involved in ministering within the Christian Life and Sunday school departments of the local church. Quarterly journal; 34 pgs; circ 9,000. Subscription $6.25. 50-65% freelance. Query; fax/e-query OK. Query for electronic submissions. Pays .04/wd on acceptance for all, 1st, one-time, or reprint rts. Articles 1,000-4,000 wds (150/yr); book reviews 300 wds. Responds in 2 wks. Seasonal 6 mos ahead. Accepts reprints. Accepts disk. Regular sidebars. Prefers NIV or NRSV. Guidelines/theme list; copy for 9x12 SAE/2 stamps. (Ads)

Poetry: Buys 4/yr. Seasonal or on outreach/Sunday school; to 30 lines; .25/line, $5 minimum. Submit max 1 poem.

Fillers: Buys 4 cartoons/yr; $10-25.

Tips: "Looking for succinct pieces that instruct, train, motivate, etc."
**This periodical was #46 on the 2000 Top 50 Christian Publishers list (#58 in 1998, #50 in 1997, #18 in 1996, #10 in 1995).

$#SHINING STAR MAGAZINE, 13720 Clayton Rd., Chesterfield MO 63017. Frank Schaeffer Publications. Mina McMullen, ed. Reproducible Bible activities for Sunday school, VBS & Christian schools; pre-K-6th grades. Quarterly mag; 80 pgs; circ 11,000. Subscription $16.95. 90% freelance. Query; phone query OK. Pays $15-40 on publication for all rts. Articles 1-2 pages (uses mostly activities—200/yr); little fiction (6-10/yr). Responds in 4-6 wks. Seasonal 9 mos ahead. Accepts simultaneous submissions. Hard copy only. No sidebars. Prefers NIV. Guidelines/theme list; copy $4.95/9x12 SAE. (No ads)

Poetry: Buys 10-12/yr. Light verse, traditional; 8-30 lines; $10-30. Submit max 5 poems.

Fillers: Buys 30/yr. Anecdotes, facts, games, ideas, quizzes, quotes, word puzzles; 100-300 wds; $10-40.

Special Needs: Puzzles, games, crafts for kids. Always needs more activities/ideas for preschoolers.

Tips: "Be familiar with what our mission/purpose is. Find a new, different, fun way to teach God's Word to children. Try out material on children before you consider it ready to submit."

$SIGNAL, One E. Bode Rd., Streamwood IL 60107-6658. (630)213-2000. Fax (630)213-5986. E-mail:donh@awana.org, or jimj@awana.org. Website: www.awana.org. Awana Clubs International. Don Hampton, mng. ed. Seeks to provide motivation, inspiration, and information for Awana leaders. Quarterly mag; 24 pgs; circ 130,000. Subscription $7.95. 10% unsolicited freelance; 10% assigned. Complete ms/cover letter. Pays $75-250 on publication for 1st rts. Articles 500-1,500 wds (3/yr). Responds in 1-2 wks. Seasonal 6 mos ahead. Accepts reprints (tell when/where appeared).

Prefers e-mail submissions (attached file). Kill fee. Regular sidebars. Prefers KJV. Guidelines (also by e-mail); copy for 9x12 SAE/3 stamps. (No ads)

Columns/Departments: Buys 4/yr. Council Time (tips for teaching time), 400-500 wds, $50-100.

Special Needs: Articles reflecting the impact Awana has had on a famous person.

$TEACHERS IN FOCUS, 8605 Explorer Dr., Colorado Springs CO 80920. (719)548-5855. Fax (719)548-5860. E-mail: tifeditor@fotf.org. Website: www.family.org/cforum/teachersmag. Focus on the Family. Mark Hartwig, ed; submit to Heather Koerner, assoc ed. To encourage, inform and support Christian teachers in public and private education (K-12). Monthly (9X) mag; 24 pgs; circ 26,400. Subscription $20. 80% freelance. Query; fax/e-query OK. Pays $200 & up on acceptance for 1st rts. Articles 1,500 wds; book reviews (educational resources), $25-50. Responds in 12 wks. Accepts reprints (tell when/where appeared). Accepts disk or e-mail submission (copied into message). Kill fee varies. Regular sidebars. Prefers NIV. Guidelines (also on Website); copy for 9x12 SAE/4 stamps. (Ads)

Fillers: Buys 50/yr. Humorous classroom anecdotes; 50-150 wds; $25.

Columns/Departments: Teammates (profiles on support staff), 500 wds; Guest Speaker (misc. education and religious topics), 500 wds. Pays $100.

Tips: "Emphasis is on practical application. Uses articles of interest to teachers trying to cope in the classroom situation. Education issues. Avoid educational and religious jargon."

**This periodical was #11 on the 2000 Top 50 Christian Publishers list (#11 in 1999, #40 in 1998, #23 in 1997, #12 in 1996, #29 in 1995, #55 in 1994). 1998 & 1997 EPA Award of Merit—Christian Ministry (1994 EPA Award of Excellence—Christian Ministry).

$TEACHERS INTERACTION, 3558 S. Jefferson Ave., St. Louis MO 63118-3968. (314)268-1083. Fax (314)268-1329. E-mail: tom.nummela@cph.org. Concordia Publishing House/Lutheran Church-Missouri Synod. Tom Nummela, ed. A magazine teachers of the faith grow by. Quarterly mag; 32 pgs; circ. 10,000. Subscription $10.25. 50% freelance. Complete ms/cover letter; fax/e-query OK. Pays $55-110 on publication for all rts. How-tos to 100 wds, articles 1,200 wds (6/yr). Responds in 13 wks. Seasonal 1 yr ahead. Prefers disk. Some sidebars. Prefers NIV. Guidelines/theme list; copy $2.75. (No ads)

Songs: Buys occasionally. First rts. $50.

Fillers: Buys 48/yr. Teacher tips/ideas, 50 wds. Pays $25.

Columns/Departments: Departments for early childhood teachers, lower elementary grade teachers, middle school teachers, The Adaptive Teacher, Internet Connections, Law and Gospel, Outreach/Evangelism, and support staff (pastors, directors of CE and superintendents); 550 wds, $55.

Special Needs: Practical, how-to articles that will help the volunteer church worker.

Tips: "We need feature articles in four areas—inspiration, theology, practical and informational—in the area of volunteer Christian education. Theology must be compatible with Lutheranism."

$TEAM, Box 7259, Grand Rapids MI 49510. (616)241-5616. Fax (616)241-5558. E-mail: silbrink@youthunlimited.org. Youth Unlimited. Shari Ilbrink, ed. Geared to leadership in Christian-based ministries for grades 7-12, not Sunday school. Triannual mag; circ 2,000. 10% freelance. Complete ms (prefers not to return them). Pays $30 on publication for 1st, simultaneous or reprint rts. Articles 700-2,000 wds (6/yr). Responds in 5 wks. Seasonal 6 mos ahead. Kill fee 50%. Accepts simultaneous submissions & reprints. Guidelines; copy $1/9x12 SAE/2 stamps.

Fillers: Jr/Sr High Christ-centered youth meetings, cartoons, ideas, games/mixer ideas, short humor.

Columns/Departments: Street Beat (issues in urban youth ministry).

$TODAY'S CATHOLIC TEACHER, 330 Progress Rd., Dayton OH 45449-2386. (937)847-5900. Fax (937)847-5910. E-mail: mnoschang@peterli.com. Website: www.catholicteacher.com. Catholic/Peter Li Education Group. Mary C. Noschang, ed. Directed to personal and professional concerns of teachers and administrators in K-12 Catholic schools. Monthly mag (6X during school yr); 60 pgs; circ 50,000. Subscription $14.95. 30% unsolicited freelance; 30% assigned. Query; phone/fax/e-query OK. Pays $65-250 after publication for all rts. Articles 600-800, 1,000-1,200 or 1,200-1,500 wds (40-50/yr). Responds in 18 wks. Seasonal 3 mos ahead. Accepts simultaneous submissions & reprints (tell when/where appeared). Prefers disk or e-mail submission (copied into message). Guidelines/theme list (also on Website); copy $3. (Ads)

Special Needs: Activity pages teachers can copy and pass out to students to work on. Try to provide classroom-ready material teachers can use to supplement curriculum.

Tips: "Looking for material teachers in grades 3-9 can use to supplement curriculum material. Most open to articles or lesson plans."

$VISION MAGAZINE/CEAI NEWSLETTER, Box 41300, Pasadena CA 91114. (626)798-1124. Fax (626)798-2346. E-mail: info@ceai.org. Website: www.ceai.org. Christian Educators Assn., Intl. Denise Jones, ed. To encourage, equip and empower Christian educators in serving in public and private schools. CEAI Newsletter is published 9x/yr in a special edition of Teachers in Focus magazine; 4 pgs. Vision is quarterly newsletter; 16 pgs; circ 8,000. Subscription $25. 50-60% unsolicited freelance; 40-50% assigned. Query; phone/fax/e-query OK. Pays $20-40 on publication for 1st & reprint rts. Articles 50-1,500 wds (12-15/yr); fiction (1-2/yr); book reviews 50 wds, pays copies. Responds in 4-6 wks. Seasonal 4 mos ahead. Accepts simultaneous submissions & reprints (tell when/where appeared). Accepts disk or e-mail submission (attached or copied into message). Regular sidebars. Any version. Guidelines/theme list; copy for 9x12 SAE/6 stamps. (Ads)

Poetry: Accepts 2-3/yr. Free verse, haiku, light verse, traditional; 4-16 lines; no payment. Submit max 3 poems.

Fillers: Accepts 6/yr. Cartoons, facts; 20-100 wds; no payment. Educational only.

Special Needs: Legal and other issues in public education.

Tips: "Know public education, write from a positive perspective as our readers are involved in public education by calling and choice. Most open to tips for teachers for living out their faith in the classroom in legally appropriate ways. All topics covered must be public-education related."

$YOUTH AND CHRISTIAN EDUCATION LEADERSHIP, 1080 Montgomery Ave., Cleveland TN 37311. (423)478-7599. Fax (423)478-7616. E-mail: ycessce@extremegen.org. Website: www.pathwaypress.org. Church of God/Pathway Press. Tony P. Lane, ed. For Christian education teachers and leaders. Quarterly mag; 32 pgs; circ 9,800. Subscription $8. 35% unsolicited freelance; 45% assigned. Complete ms/cover letter; e-query OK. Pays $25-55 on acceptance for one-time, simultaneous or reprint rts. Articles 500-1,200 wds (12/yr). Responds in 4 wks. Seasonal 4 mos ahead. Accepts simultaneous submissions & reprints (tell when/where appeared). Accepts disk. Regular sidebars. Prefers NKJV or NIV. No guidelines; copy for 9x12 SAE/4 stamps. (Ads)

Columns/Departments: Sunday School; Teen Ministry; Outreach; The Pastor and C.E.; Kids Church; 400-800 wds; $25-50.

Special Needs: Local church ministry stories; articles on youth ministry, children's ministry, Christian education and Sunday school.

DAILY DEVOTIONAL MARKETS

Due to the nature of the daily devotional market, the following market listings may include only the name, address, phone number (if available) and editor's name. Because most of these markets assign all material, they do not wish to be listed in the usual way, if at all.

If you are interested in writing daily devotionals, send to the following markets for guidelines and sample copies, write up sample devotionals to fit each one's particular format, and send to the editor with a request for an assignment. **DO NOT** submit any other type of material to these markets unless indicated.

ABBA'S ARMS, 745 Hickory St., Ste. 247, Akron OH 44303-2213. (330)434-1544. Fax (330)535-6452. E-mail: mhsobah@mindspring.com. Website: www. fovgc.org. Mary H. Sobah, publications supervisor. Read guidelines, then send a couple of samples and request an assignment. Written for adolescents; some are juvenile offenders. **NO PAYMENT.** Accepts poetry. Guidelines/copy for 9x6 SAE/2stamps.

DAILY DEVOTIONS FOR THE DEAF, 21199 Greenview Rd., Council Bluffs IA 51503-4190. (712)322-5493. Fax (712)322-7792. E-mail: DeafMissions @deafmissions.com. Website: www.deafmissions.com. Jo Krueger, ed. Quarterly. Circ. 26,000. Prefers to see completed devotionals; 225 wds. **NO PAYMENT.**

#THE DAILY WALK, 4201 N. Peachtree Rd., Atlanta GA 30341. (770)458-9300. Fax (770)454-9313. E-mail: pkirk@walkthru.org. Website: www.

walkthru.org. Walk Thru the Bible Ministries, Inc. Paula A. Kirk, ed. To encourage people to read and study God's word on a daily basis. Monthly mag; circ 50,000. Subscription $18. Accepts freelance. Query or complete ms. (Ads)

DEVOTIONS, 8121 Hamilton Ave., Cincinnati OH 45231. (513)931-4050. Eileen Wilmoth, ed. No devotions or poetry. Buys photos only.

FORWARD DAY BY DAY, 412 Sycamore St., Cincinnati OH 45202-4195. (800)543-1813 or (513)721-6659. Fax (513)721-0729. E-mail: esgleason@ forwarddaybyday.com. Website: www.forwardmovement.org. Edward S. Gleason, ed. Also online version. Send a couple of sample devotions to fit our format and request an assignment. **NO PAYMENT.** (No ads)

FRUIT OF THE VINE, Barclay Press, 110 S. Elliott St., Newberg OR 97132-2144. (503)538-7345. Fax (503)538-7033. E-mail: info@barclaypress. com. Website: www.barclaypress.com. Editorial team: Harlow Ankeny, Susan Fawver, Sherry Macy, Paula Hampton. Send samples and request assignment. Prefers 250-290 wds. **PAYS FREE SUBSCRIPTION.** Guidelines.

$GOD'S COURTROOM, 745 Hickory St., Ste. 247, Akron OH 44303-2213. (330)434-1544. Fax (330)535-6452. E-mail: wjsprinkle@mindspring.com. Website: www.fovgc.org. Intl. Tai Gazette. Dr. Wanda J. Sprinkle, sr ed. Read guidelines, then send completed devotionals or send a couple of samples and request an assignment (4-7 devotions). Written specifically for inmates in jail, prisons, and residents of halfway house facilities (male and female). Pays $5 on acceptance for all rts. Responds in 4 wks. Also accepts poetry. Guidelines (also on Website)/copy for 9x6 SAE/2stamps.

THE HOME ALTAR, Box 1209, Minneapolis MN 55440-1209. (612)330-3419. E-mail: biddlecc@augsburg-fortress.org. Cynthia Biddlecomb, ed. No freelance this year (2001). Sample writing and inquiries are welcome.

$*PATHWAYS TO GOD, PO Box 2499, Anderson IN 46018-2499. (800)741-7721. Fax (765)622-9511. Warner Press. William A. White, ed. Query.

$THE QUIET HOUR, 4050 Lee Vance View, Colorado Springs CO 80919. (719)536-0100. Fax (407)359-2850. E-mail: gwilde@mac.com. Cook Communications Ministries. Gary Wilde, ed. 100% freelance. Pays $15-35/devotional on acceptance. Send résumé and list of credits, rather than a sample.

$*REJOICE! 1218 Franklin St. NW, Salem OR 97304-3902. (503)585-4458. Mennonite. Philip Wiebe, ed. Quarterly. Pays $110 for 7-day assigned meditations, 300 wds. Doesn't send samples or guidelines to unsolicited writers. Prefers that you send a couple of sample devotions and inquire about assignment procedures. Don't apply for assignment unless you are familiar with the publication and Anabaptist theology.

$THE SECRET PLACE, Box 851, Valley Forge PA 19482-0851. (610)768-2240. Fax (610)768-2441. E-mail: fran.marlin@abc-usa.org. Kathleen Hayes, sr ed. Prefers to see completed devotionals, 200 wds (use unfamiliar Scripture passages). Uses poetry and photos. 64 pgs. Pays $15 for 1st rts. Accepts poetry and buys photos. Guidelines.

$THESE DAYS, 100 Witherspoon St., Louisville KY 40202-1396. No phone calls. Fax (502)569-5113. Presbyterian Publishing Corp. Kay Snodgrass, ed. Send for issue themes and Scripture references; then query/samples. 95% freelance. Pays $15/page for 1st and nonexclusive reprint rts (makes work-for-hire assignments); 200 wds. Uses poetry (2-6/yr), pays $15. Wants short, contemporary poetry on church holidays and seasons of the year—overtly religious (15 lines, 33-character/line maximum).

$THE UPPER ROOM, PO Box 340004, Nashville TN 37203-0004. (615)340-7252 (no "cold" calls; get guidelines first). Fax (615)340-7267. E-mail: TheUpperRoomMagazine@upperroom.org. Website: www.upperroom. org. Mary Lou Redding, mng. ed. 95% freelance. Pays $25/devotional on publication. 72 pgs. Note: This publication wants freelance submissions and does not make assignments. Phone/fax/e-query OK. Send devotionals of 250-300 wds. Buys one-time use of art work (transparencies/slides requested). No disk. Guidelines (also on Website); copy for 5x7 SAE/2 stamps.(No ads)

> **Tips:** "We do not return submissions. Accepted submissions will be notified in 6-9 wks. Follow guidelines."

$THE WORD IN SEASON, PO Box 1209, Minneapolis MN 55440-1209. (414)771-1408. Fax (612)330-3215. E-mail: rymhwe@execpc.com. Website: www.augsburgfortress.org. Rochelle Melander, ed. 96 pgs. Devotions 200 wds. Pays $18/devotion. Guidelines for #10 SAE/2 stamps.

> **Tips:** "We prefer that you write for guidelines. We will send instructions for preparing sample devotions. We accept new writers based on the sample devotions we request and make assignments after acceptance."

$WORDS OF LIFE: Daily Reflections for Your Spirit. St. Paul University, 223 Main St., Ottawa ON K1S 1C4 Canada. (613)782-3036. Fax (613)782-3004. E-mail: cgreen@ustpaul.uottawa.ca. Caryl Green, ed. Send samples and request an assignment. Prefers 125 wds. Pays $40 CAN. Buys photos.

MISSIONS MARKETS

#AIM INTERNATIONAL, PO Box 178, Pearl River NY 10965. (914)735-4014. Fax (914)735-1814. Website: www.aim-us.org. Africa Inland Mission. Andy Hornberger, ed. To inform readers about how AIM is working to plant maturing churches through evangelization and preparing church leaders. Quarterly mag; circ 24,000. Subscription free. Accepts freelance. Prefers query. Not in topical listings. (Ads)

$AMERICAN BAPTISTS IN MISSION, PO Box 851, Valley Forge PA 19482-0851. (610)768-2077. Fax (610)768-2320. E-mail: richard.schramm@abc-usa.org. Website: www.abc-usa.org. Richard W. Schramm, ed. Denominational. Bimonthly mag; 24-32 pgs; circ 39,000. Subscription free. 10% unsolicited freelance; 90% assigned. Query; fax/e-query OK. Pays negotiable rates on publication. Articles 750-1,000 wds (few/yr). Prefers e-mail submission (attached file). Some sidebars. Prefers NRSV. Guidelines (also by e-mail); copy. Not in topical listings but will accept any article of substantial interest to American Baptists. (Ads)

$#AMERICAN HORIZON, 1445 Boonville Ave., Springfield MO 65802-1894. (417)862-2781x3264. Fax (417)863-7276. E-mail: dhm@ag.org. Website:

www.ag.org. Assemblies of God. Dan Van Veen, ed. Denominational magazine of home missions, mostly on assignment. Bimonthly mag; 20 pgs; circ 45,000. Free to contributors. 25% freelance. Query or complete ms/cover letter; phone/e-query OK. Pay $25/1 pg; $40/2 pg; $15/photo; on publication for 1st rts. Articles 600-1,100 wds (17/yr). Responds in 6 wks. Seasonal 5 mos ahead. Accepts simultaneous submissions & reprints. Free guidelines/copy. (No ads)

   Tips: "Make sure your story is specific to Assemblies of God Home Missions. Stories must be about our home missionaries and how God is working though them and their ministries."

$*AREOPAGUS MAGAZINE, PO Box 33, Shatin, New Territories, Hong Kong. (852)691-1904. Fax (852)265-9885. Tao Fong Shan Christian Centre. John G. LeMond, ed. Provides a forum for dialogue between the good news of Jesus Christ and people of faith both in major world religions and new religious movements. Quarterly mag; 50 pgs; circ 1,000. Subscription $24. 75% freelance. Complete ms; e-mail submission OK. Pays $100-300 on publication for 1st rts. Articles 1,000-5,000 wds (40/yr); book reviews, 500-750 wds, $100. Responds in 6-13 wks. Seasonal 6 mos ahead. Accepts simultaneous submissions & reprints. Prefers disk. Kill fee 50%. Guidelines; copy $4.

   Columns/Departments: Buys 10/yr. Complete ms. Pays $50-100.
   Special Needs: Interfaith dialogue.
   Tips: "We look for compassionate, direct, and unself-conscious prose that reflects a writer who is firmly rooted in his/her own tradition but is unafraid to encounter other religions."

+BIBLES FOR THE WORLD REPORT, PO Box 470, Colorado Springs CO 80901. (719)630-7733. Fax (719)630-1449. E-mail: BFTW@ccnmail.com. Bibles for the World. John L. Pudaite, ed. To inform, challenge, and encourage believers in the task of giving God's Word to the world. Quarterly; circ 50,000. Subscription free. Accepts freelance. Prefers query. Not in topical listings. Did not return questionnaire. (No ads)

$CATHOLIC NEAR EAST, 1011 First Ave., New York NY 10022-4195. (212)826-1480. Fax (212)826-8979. Website: www.cnewa.org. Catholic Near East Welfare Assn. Michael La Civita, exec. ed; submit to Helen C. Packard, asst. ed. Interest in cultural, religious, human rights development in Middle East, NE Africa, India and Eastern Europe. Bimonthly mag; 32 pgs; circ 100,000. Subscription $12. 20% unsolicited freelance; 30% assigned. Query/clips; fax query OK. Pays .20/edited wd ($200) on publication for all rts. Articles 1,200-1,800 wds (15/yr). Responds in 9 wks. Accepts disk. Kill fee $200. Regular sidebars. Prefers NAS. Guidelines; copy for 7x10 SAE/2 stamps.

   Tips: "We strive to educate our readers about the culture, faith, history, issues and people who form the Eastern Christian churches. Material should not be academic."

+COMMISSIONED, Box 386001, Minneapolis MN 55438-6001. (952)996-1385. Fax (952)996-1386. E-mail: STEMmin@aol.com. Website: www.stemmin.com. STEM Ministries. Roger P. Peterson, ed. To follow-up on STEM's short-term missionaries, and to mobilize Christians in fulfilling

424 MISSIONS MARKETS/Periodical Publishers

the Great Commission. Quarterly mag; circ 4,400. Subscription $10/donation. Accepts freelance. Prefers query. Not in topical listings. Did not return questionnaire. (Ads)

EAST-WEST CHURCH & MINISTRY REPORT, The Global Ctr./Beeson Divinity School, Samford University, Birmingham AL 35229-2268. (205)726-2170. Fax (205)726-2271. E-mail: ewcmreport@samford.edu. Website: www.samford.edu/groups/global/ewcmreport. The Global Center/Samford University. Dr. Mark Elliott, ed. Encourages Western Christian ministry in Central and Eastern Europe and the former Soviet Union that is effective, culturally sensitive and cooperative. Quarterly newsletter; 16 pgs; circ 430. Subscription $44.95. 75% freelance. Query; e-query OK. **NO PAYMENT** for all rts. Articles 1,500 wds (3/yr); book reviews, 100 wds. Responds in 4 wks. Prefers disk or e-mail submission. Regular sidebars. Any version. Guidelines (also by e-mail/Website); copy $11.95. (No ads)

> **Tips:** "All submissions must relate to Central and Eastern Europe, the former Soviet Union or evangelical missions."
>
> **2000 & 1998 EPA Award of Merit—Newsletter.

$EVANGELICAL MISSIONS QUARTERLY, PO Box 794, Wheaton IL 60189. (630)752-7158. Fax (630)752-7155. E-mail: emqjournal@aol.com. Website: www.wheaton.edu/bgc/emis. Evangelical Missions Information Service. Gary Corwin, ed. For missionaries and others interested in missions trends, strategies, issues, problems, and resources. Quarterly journal; 128 pgs; circ 7,000. Subscription $21.95. 65% unsolicited; 35% assigned. Query; fax/e-query OK. Pays $100 on publication for all rts. Articles 2,500 wds (30/yr); book reviews 400 wds (query), $25. Responds in 4 wks. Accepts few reprints (tell when/where appeared). Prefers disk or e-mail submission (copied into message). Some sidebars. Prefers NIV. Free guidelines (also by e-mail)/copy. (Ads)

> **Columns/Departments:** Buys 4/yr. In the Workshop (tips to increase missionary effectiveness), 1,500-2,000 wds. Pays $100.
>
> **Tips:** "Present an article idea and why you are qualified to write it. All articles must target evangelical, cross-cultural missionaries. 'In the Workshop' is most open to freelancers. Most authors have a credible connection to and experience in missions."

+THE GOSPEL MESSAGE, 10000 N. Oak Trafficway, Kansas City MO 64155. (816)734-8500. Fax (816)734-4601. E-mail: mphillip@gmu.org. Gospel Missionary Union. Michele Phillips, ed. To increase knowledge of what is happening around the world, and stimulate involvement in world missions. Quarterly mag; circ 65,000. Subscription free. Accepts freelance. Prefers query. Not in topical listings. Did not return questionnaire. (No ads)

$HEARTBEAT, PO Box 5002, Antioch TN 37011-5002. (615)731-6812. Fax (615)731-5345. E-mail: heartbeat@nafwb.org. Website: www.nafwb.org. Free Will Baptist Foreign Missions. Don Robirds, ed. To inform and challenge church members with mission needs. Bimonthly mag; 8 pgs; circ 20,000. Subscription free. 1% freelance. Complete ms/cover letter; fax/e-query OK. Pays .04/wd on publication for one-time rts. Articles 800 wds

(2/yr). Responds in 6 wks. Seasonal 4 mos ahead. Accepts reprints (tell when/where appeared). Prefers disk or e-mail submission (copied into message). No sidebars. Prefers KJV. Guidelines; copy for #10 SAE. (No ads)

+HOPE FOR CHILDREN IN CRISIS, PO Box 101, Fort Mill SC 29716. (803)548-2811. Fax (803)548-5839. E-mail: ROHTS@aol.com. Website: www.wec-int.org/rainbows. Rainbows of Hope. Thirza Schoots, ed. To equip and train those involved with children in crisis, and to improve awareness of the problem among Christians. Quarterly mag; 16 pgs; circ 3,000. Subscription $15. Estab. 1999. 5% unsolicited freelance; 50% assigned. Query; fax/e-query OK. **PAYS 3 COPIES** for all rts. Articles 1,000-1,500 wds (8/yr); book reviews 30 wds. Responds in 2 wks. Seasonal 5 mos ahead. Accepts reprints (tell when/where appeared). Accepts disk, prefers e-mail submission (copied into message). Some sidebars. Prefers NIV. Guidelines (also by e-mail); copy $4/9x12 SAE/3 stamps. (No ads)

> **Poetry:** Accepts 4/yr. All types; 20-50 lines. Submit any number.
>
> **Fillers:** Accepts several/yr. Cartoons, facts, ideas, newsbreaks, 50-200 wds.
>
> **Special Needs:** One-on-one articles with children; teaching articles on children in crisis issues; day-in-the-life-of articles on needy children; first-person articles of children in crisis.
>
> **Tips:** "We are looking for qualified freelancers who are experts in a certain field of ministry to children in crisis and who can teach on their subject of expertise."

INTERNATIONAL JOURNAL OF FRONTIER MISSIONS, 7665 Wenda Way, El Paso TX 79915. (915)775-2464. Fax (915)775-8588. E-mail: 103121.2610@ compuserve.com. Hans Weerstra, ed. Dedicated to frontier missions in people groups that have no viable Christian church. Quarterly journal; 56 pgs; circ 600. Subscription $15. 100% unsolicited freelance. Complete ms/cover letter; phone/fax/e-query OK. **NO PAYMENT** for one-time rts. Articles 3-7 pgs. Seasonal 3 mos ahead. Accepts simultaneous submissions & reprints. Accepts e-mail submission. No sidebars. Prefers NKJV or NIV. Guidelines/theme list (also by e-mail); copy $2/10x13 SAE. (Ads)

> **Special Needs:** Contextualization, church in missions, training for missions, mission trends and paradigms, de-westernization of the gospel, worldview development, biblical mission theology, Anamism, Islam, Buddhism, Hinduism, non-literate peoples, tentmaking, mission care, etc.
>
> **Tips:** "Writers on specific issues we cover are always welcome. Although the circulation is small, the print run is 3,000 and used for promotional purposes. Highly recommended for mission schools, libraries, and mission executives."

$#LATIN AMERICA EVANGELIST, Box 52-7900, Miami FL 33152-7900. (305)884-8400. Fax (305)885-8649. E-mail: INFO@lam.org. Website: www.lam.org. Latin America Mission. Susan G. Loobie, ed (sgloobie@ lam.org). To present God's work through the churches and missionaries in Latin America. Quarterly & online mag; 24 pgs; circ 17,000. Subscription $10. 5% unsolicited freelance; 15% assigned. Query/clips first;

phone/fax/e-query OK. Pays $125 on publication for 1st rts. Articles 1,000 wds. Reporting time varies. Accepts simultaneous submissions. Accepts e-mail submission. Regular sidebars. Prefers NIV. Guidelines (also by e-mail); free copy. (No ads)

Tips: "Looking for news and analysis of the religious climate and social conditions in Latin America."

$LEADERS FOR TODAY, Box 13, Atlanta GA 30370. (770)449-8869. Fax (770)449-8457. E-mail: hiatlanta@haggai-institute.com. Website: www.haggai-institute.com. Haggai Institute. Scott Schreffler, ed. (scotts@haggai-institute.com). Primarily for donors to ministry; focus is alumni success stories. Quarterly mag; 16 pgs; circ 7,500. Subscription free. 100% assigned to date. Query; fax query OK. Pays .10-.25/wd on acceptance for all rts. Articles 1,000-2,000 wds. Responds in 2-3 wks. Requires disk or e-mail submissions (attached file). Kill fee 100%. Regular sidebars. Prefers NIV. Guidelines/theme list; copy for 9x12 SAE/4 stamps. (No ads)

Tips: "All articles are pre-assigned. Query first."

**1999 EPA Award of Merit—Missionary; 1998 EPA Award of Excellence—Missionary.

MISSIOLOGY: An International Review, Asbury Theological Seminary, 204 N. Lexington Ave., Wilmore KY 40390. (859)858-2215. Fax (859)858-2375. E-mail: Darrell_Whiteman@asburyseminary.edu. Website: www.asmweb.org. American Society of Missiology. Darrell L. Whiteman, ed. A professional organization for mission studies. Quarterly journal; 128 pgs; circ 2,000. Subscription $28. 70% unsolicited freelance; 30% assigned. Complete ms/cover letter; phone/fax/e-query OK. PAYS 20 COPIES for all rts. Articles 5,000 wds (20/yr); book reviews, 200-300 wds. Responds in 2 mos. Requires disk, no e-mail submission. No sidebars. Any version. Guidelines (also by e-mail); free copy. (Ads)

Tips: "Whole journal is open to freelancers as long as they write from a missiological perspective and have adequate documentation."

MISSION FRONTIERS, 1605 Elizabeth St., Pasadena CA 91104. (626)398-2121. Fax: (626)398-2263. E-mail: mission.frontiers@uscwm.org. Website: www.missionfrontiers.org. U.S. Center for World Mission. Rick Wood, mng. ed. To stimulate a movement to establish indigenous churches where still needed around the world. Bimonthly & online mag; 40 pgs; circ 120,000. Subscription $8. 10% unsolicited freelance; 90% assigned. Query. NO PAYMENT. Articles. Rarely responds. Accepts disk or e-mail submissions (copied into message). Regular sidebars. No guidelines; free copy. Not in topical listings. (Ads)

Fillers: Cartoons.

Tips: "Be a published missionary or former missionary. Be on the cutting edge of strategic breakthrough or methods of reaching an unreached ethnic group." Looking for true-life, short sidebars of Muslims accepting Jesus, or impact of prayer in missions.

**1999 EPA Award of Merit—Most Improved Publication.

$#NEW WORLD OUTLOOK, 475 Riverside Dr., Room 1476, New York NY 10115-1476. (212)870-3765. Fax (212)870-3940. E-mail: nwo@gbgm-umc.org. Website: gbgm-umc.org/nwo. United Methodist. Alma Graham, ed. Denominational missions. Bimonthly mag; 48 pgs; circ 22,000. Subscription $15. 20% freelance. Query; fax/e-query OK. Pays $50-300 on publication for all & electronic rts. Articles 500-2,000 wds (24/yr); book reviews 200-500 wds (assigned). No guaranteed response time. Seasonal 4 mos ahead. Kill fee 50% or $100. Prefers e-mail submission (WordPerfect 6.1 or 8.1 in attached file). Regular sidebars. Prefers NRSV. Guidelines; copy $3. (Ads)

Tips: "Ask for a list of United Methodist mission workers and projects in your area. Investigate them, propose a story, and consult with the editors before writing. Most open to articles and/or color photos of US or foreign mission sites visited as a stringer, after consultation with the editor."

$#PFI WORLD REPORT, Box 17434, Washington DC 20041. (703)481-0000. Fax (703)481-0003. E-mail: chris@pfi.org. Prison Fellowship, Intl. Christopher P. Nicholson, ed. Targets issues and needs of prisoners, ex-prisoners, justice officials, victims, families and PFI staff, and volunteers in 75 countries. Bimonthly newsletter; 4-8 pgs; circ 4,750. Subscription free. 10% freelance. Query; fax/e-query OK. Pays $100-350 on acceptance for all rts. Articles 500-750 wds (4/yr). Responds in 2 wks. Seasonal 4 mos ahead. Accepts simultaneous submissions & reprints (tell when/where appeared). Accepts disk. Kill fee. Regular sidebars. Guidelines (also on Website); copy for #10 SAE/1 stamp. (No ads)

Special Needs: Prison issues, justice issues, anything that relates to international prison ministry.

Tips: "Looking for personal profiles of people active in prison ministry (preferably PFI officials); ex-prisoner success stories; how-to articles about various aspects of prison ministry. Avoid American slant."

$P.I.M.E. WORLD, 17330 Quincy St., Detroit MI 48221-2765. (313)342-4066. Fax (313)342-6816. E-mail: pimeworld@pimeusa.org. Website: www.pimeusa.org. Pontifical Inst. for Foreign Missions/Catholic. Christian Busque, mng. ed. For those interested in and supportive of foreign missions. Monthly (10X) mag; 20-24 pgs; circ 26,000. Subscription $15. 10% unsolicited freelance. Complete ms/cover letter; e-query OK. Pays .10/wd on publication for all rts. Photos $10. Not copyrighted. Articles 800-1,200 wds. Responds in 4 wks. Seasonal 2 mos ahead. Accepts simultaneous submissions & reprints (tell when/where appeared). Prefers disk or e-mail submission. Regular sidebars. Prefers NAB. Guidelines (also by e-mail/Website); copy for 2 stamps. (No ads)

Tips: "Issues like hunger, human rights, women's rights, peace and justice as they are dealt with in developing countries by missionaries and locals alike; stories of missionary service."

*THE RAILROAD EVANGELIST, PO Box 5026, Vancouver WA 98668-5026. (360)699-7208. Fax (360)750-5618. E-mail: rejoe@integrityonline.com. Joe Spooner, ed. For railroad and transportation employees and their families. Quarterly mag; 16 pgs; circ 2,500. Subscription $8. 100% freelance. Complete ms/no cover letter; phone query OK. NO PAYMENT.

Articles 100-700 wds (10-15/yr). Seasonal 4 months ahead. Accepts simultaneous submissions & reprints. Accepts e-mail submission. No sidebars. Guidelines; copy for 9x12 SAE/2 stamps. (No ads)

Poetry: Accepts 4-8/yr. Traditional, any length. Send any number.

Fillers: Accepts many. Anecdotes, cartoons, quotes; to 100 wds.

Tips: "We need 400- to 700-word railroad-related salvation testimonies; or railroad-related human-interest stories."

#SAVE OUR WORLD, 2490 Keith St. NW, PO Box 8016, Cleveland TN 37320-8016. (423)478-7190. Fax (423)478-7155. E-mail: info@cogwm.org. Website: www.cogwm.org. Church of God (Cleveland TN). Robert D. McCall, ed. Denominational publication for missions awareness. Quarterly tabloid; 16 pgs; circ. 97,000. Free. 10% unsolicited freelance. Query/clips; phone/fax query OK. **NO PAYMENT** (pays $50 for some) for one-time rts. Articles 400-650 wds. Responds in 4 wks. Accepts reprints. Prefers disk. Regular sidebars. Prefers KJV. No guidelines; copy $3/9x12 SAE. (No ads)

Fillers: Accepts 4/yr. Facts, newsbreaks; 50-100 wds.

Tips: "Most open to mission trips made to foreign fields, missions experiences, material promoting missions giving and its rewards, missions-related stories, etc."

#VOICES IN THE WILDERNESS, PO Box 5303, Charlottesville VA 22905. (804)823-7777. Fax (804)823-7776. E-mail: anm@adnamis.org. Website: www.adnamis.org. Advancing Native Missions. Virginia Tobias, ed. To communicate the story/message/needs of indigenous missionaries to North American Christians. Annual & online mag; circ 9,000. Subscription free. Query; phone/fax/e-query OK. Not in topical listings. (No ads)

WOMEN OF THE HARVEST, PO Box 151297, Lakewood CO 80215-9297. (303)985-2148. Fax (303)989-4239. E-mail: harvestmag@aol.com. Website: www.womenoftheharvest.com. Women of the Harvest Ministries Intl., Inc. Stephanie Nelson, ed; Cary C. Griffith, submissions ed. To support and encourage women serving in cross-cultural missions. Bimonthly mag; 20 pgs; circ 2,500. Subscription $24. 90% unsolicited freelance; 10% assigned. Complete ms; e-query OK. NO PAYMENT for one-time rts. Articles 350-650 wds. Seasonal 3 mos ahead. Prefers e-mail submission or disk. Guidelines (also by e-mail); copy for SASE. (No ads)

Poetry: Free verse, traditional, haiku; variable length. Submit max 5 poems.

Fillers: Accepts. Anecdotes, short humor. 100 wds.

Tips: "This is a magazine designed especially for women serving cross-culturally. We need articles, humor, and anecdotes related to this topic."

$WORLD CHRISTIAN MAGAZINE, PO Box 1357, Oak Park, IL 60304. (708)524-5070. Fax: (708) 524-5174. E-mail: WINPress7@aol.com. WIN Press, a division of World In Need, USA. Phillip Huber, mng ed. To inform, encourage, provoke and mobilize this generation in obedience to the Great Commission. Quarterly mag; 40 pgs; circ 30,000. Subscription $14.95. Estab. 1999. 10% unsolicited freelance; 85% assigned. Query; e-query OK. Pays $55 or .10/wd. on publication, for all, 1st or electronic rts.

Articles 1,200-2,000 wds (20-25/yr); book reviews 750 wds, $85. Responds in 4 wks. Seasonal 4 mos ahead. Accepts reprints (tell when/where appeared). Prefers e-mail submissions (attached file). Kill fee 25%. Regular sidebars. Prefers NIV. Guidelines/theme list (also by e-mail); sample copy $3/9x12 SAE/4 stamps. (Ads)

> **Columns/Departments:** Buys 30/yr. Speak Out (mission-related opinion/commentary), 750-800 wds; In Action (profile of active world Christian), 750-800 wds; Notebook (Website reviews, profiles of unreached people groups), 400-500 wds; World Scene (missions-related news/updates), 750-800 wds. Pays $55-85. Query.

> **Tips:** "Looking for profiles of people, churches, and agencies, and how they are reaching cities and nations for Christ. Best way to break in is in our columns. Submit queries or manuscripts that show originality and creativity in reaching world with the Gospel. Articles should show evidence of multiple and multidenominational sources with a global rather than a Western-dominated mind-set."

$WORLD PULSE, PO Box 794, Wheaton IL 60189. (630)752-7158. Fax (630)752-7155. E-mail: pulsenews@aol.com. Website: www.wheaton.edu/bgc/emis. Evangelism & Missions Information Service (EMIS). Stan Guthrie, ed. Articles and news items from around the world, related to missions and Christians. Bimonthly newsletter; 8 pgs; circ 4,000. Subscription $29.95. 20% unsolicited; 80% assigned. Query; fax/e-query OK. Pays $100 on publication for all rts. Articles 800-900 wds. Responds in 2 wks. Accepts reprints (tell when/where appeared). Prefers disk or e-mail submission (copied into message). Kill fee 60%. No sidebars. Prefers NIV. Free guidelines (also by e-mail)/copy for #10 SAE. (No ads)

> **Tips:** "Send specific ideas on what missions and national churches are actually doing and tell why you are qualified to write it."

$WORLDWIDE CHALLENGE, 100 Lake Hart Dr., Orlando FL 32832-0100. (407)826-2390. Fax (407)826-2374. E-mail: WChallenge@ccci.org. Website: www.wwcmagazine.org. Campus Crusade for Christ. Mark Winz, ed. For financial supporters of Campus Crusade. Bimonthly mag; 48 pgs; circ 90,000. Subscription $12.95. 5% freelance. Query only/clips; no e-query. Pays .10/wd + a flat fee of $100-200 (depending on research) on acceptance for 1st rts (all rts for assigned articles). Articles 800-1,600 wds (6/yr). Responds in 6-8 wks. Seasonal 6-8 mos ahead. Accepts simultaneous submissions. Prefers disk. Kill fee 50%. Regular sidebars. Prefers NAS. Guidelines; copy for 9x12 SAE/5 stamps. (Ads)

> **Columns/Departments:** Buys 6/yr. Insight (personal experience/commentary); 400-800 wds; query or complete ms; Lisa Master, ed.

> **Tips:** "Give the human face behind a topic or story. Show how the topic relates to evangelism and/or discipleship. Wants articles about Campus Crusade staff. Most open to column."

> **This periodical was #43 on the 1996 Top 50 Christian Publishers List (#35 in 1994). 1999 EPA Award of Excellence—Organizational; 1995 EPA Award of Merit—Organizational.

MUSIC MARKETS

$#CCM MAGAZINE,104 Woodmont Blvd., 3rd Fl., Nashville TN 37205-2245. (615)386-3011. Fax (615)385-4112. E-mail: feedback@ccmcom.com, or ahefner@ccmmagazine.com. Website: www.ccmmagazine.com. CCM Communications. April Hefner, mng ed. Encourages spiritual growth through contemporary music; provides news and information about the Christian music market. Monthly & online mag; 80 pgs; circ 70,000. Subscription $19.95. 75% freelance. Query/clips; phone/fax query OK. Pays .20/wd for short pieces, or $100/published page for features, on publication for all rts. Articles 500-2,500 wds; music reviews 250-350 wds. Responds slowly. Seasonal 3 mos ahead. Kill fee 50%. Prefers disk or e-mail submission (copied into message). Regular sidebars. Guidelines; copy for 9x12 SAE/$4. (Ads)

    **1995 EPA Award of Merit—Youth.

$CHURCH MUSICIAN TODAY, 127 9th Ave. N., Nashville TN 37234-0140. (615)251-2913. Fax (615)251-2869. E-mail: churchmusician@lifeway.com. Southern Baptist. Jere V. Adams, design ed. A ministry resource for music and worship leaders. Monthly mag; 34 pgs; circ 10,000. Subscription $3. 10% unsolicited freelance; 90% assigned. Complete ms/cover letter; e-query OK. Pays .07/wd on disk or by e-mail submission on acceptance for all rts. Articles 1,200 wds (12-15/yr); book reviews 300 wds. Responds in 12 wks. Seasonal 1 yr ahead. Accepts few reprints (pays 50%—tell when/where appeared). Accepts disk or e-mail submission. Some sidebars. Guidelines; copy for 10x13 SAE/3 stamps. (Ads)

    Fillers: Short humor (with a musical slant); 15-25 wds; $5-15.

    Special Needs: Articles on choral techniques, instrumental groups, worship planning, music administration, directing choirs (all ages), rehearsal planning, music equipment, new technology, drama/pageants and related subjects, hymn studies, book reviews, and music-related fillers.

    Tips: "Material must be relevant and practical to trained, practicing ministers of music, pastors, and other worship leaders."

$*CHURCH PIANIST/SAB CHOIR/THE CHOIR HERALD, Box 268, Alcoa TN 37701. Now a division of The Lorenz Corp. Hugh S. Livingston Jr., ed. Each of these music magazines has one page devoted to articles that deal with problems/solutions of choirs and accompanists. Bimonthly mag; 36-52 pgs; circ 25,000. 45% freelance. Complete ms/cover letter. Pay $15-150 on publication for all rts. Articles 250-1,250 wds (10-20/yr). Seasonal 1 yr ahead. Responds in 3-6 wks. Guidelines; copy for 9x12 SAE/3 stamps.

    Poetry: Accepts 25/yr. Free verse, light verse, traditional, or poetry suitable for song lyrics; $10. Submit max 5 poems.

    Fillers: Accepts 5-10/yr. Anecdotes, cartoons.

    Special Needs: Choir experiences; pianist/organist articles.

    Tips: "Best approach is from direct experience in music with the small church."

$CONTEMPORARY SONGWRITER MAGAZINE, PO Box 25879, Colorado Springs CO 80936-5879. (719)232-4489. Fax (303)223-1638. E-mail:

contemposong@yahoo.com. Website: www.contemporarysongwriter.com. Roberta Redford, ed. For songwriters, from beginning to professional. Bimonthly mag; 36 pgs; circ 3,000. Estab 1998. 50% unsolicited freelance; 50% assigned. Query/clips or complete ms/cover letter; no phone query; e-query OK. Pays .05/wd on publication for one-time rts. Articles 1,000-3,000 wds (150/yr); book reviews, 250-1,000 wds, $50. Responds in 2-3 wks. Seasonal 4 mos ahead. Accepts reprints (tell when/where appeared). Prefers disk. Kill fee. Regular sidebars. Guidelines (also by e-mail/Website); copy $3. (Ads)

> **Fillers:** Buys 50/yr. Anecdotes, cartoons, facts, games, ideas, newsbreaks, quotes, short humor, 50-250 wds. Pays $5-20.

> **Columns/Departments:** Buys 100-120/yr. Grace Notes (songwriters making a difference), 1,500 wds; Ad Lib (song writer's personal experiences), 1,200-1,500 wds; Open Mike (advice), 1,000-1,500 wds; Ledger Lines (short items on songwriting), 50-250 wds. Pays $50 for columns.

> **Contest:** Monthly lyric contest, plus a major songwriting contest each year.

> **Tips:** "Any area open to writers who are willing to do their homework. Songwriters can write about their own experiences for Ad Lib and Open Mike (columns). Always looking for good interviews with songwriters. The Story Behind the Song section tells how a hit song came to be. Just remember that the focus is on songwriters, not musicians or performers."

> **This periodical was #35 on the 1999 Top 50 Christian Publishers list.

$COOPERATIVE CHRISTIAN RADIO BULLETIN (CCRB), 7057 Bluffwood Ct., Brownsburg IN 46112. (317)892-5031. Fax (317)892-5034. E-mail: info@ccrb.org. Website: www.ccrb.org. Joyful Sounds. Les Roberts, ed. Trade paper for Christian country and inspirational radio formats. Biweekly trade paper; 10-12 pgs; circ 300-1,200. Subscription $36 (paper) or $24 (if delivered by e-mail). 25% unsolicited freelance; 75% assigned. Query or complete ms/cover letter; phone/fax/e-query OK. Negotiable payment & rights. Articles 600-2,000 wds; music reviews, 100-300 wds. Responds in 2 wks. Seasonal 2 mos ahead. Accepts reprints. Requires disk (DOS-ASCII), prefers e-mail submission. Guidelines (also by e-mail); copy for 9x12 SAE/2 stamps. (Ads)

> **Fillers:** Cartoons, short humor (particularly radio or music related).

> **Columns/Departments:** Insider (artist interview); Programming 101 (radio technique); retail, inspirational, especially for musicians and radio people; 600-2,000 wds.

> **Special Needs:** Songwriting and performance.

> **Tips:** "Most open to artist interviews. Must be familiar with Christian country music, Inspirational music, or today's Praise & Worship music."

$CREATOR MAGAZINE, 451 Hudson, Healdsburg CA 95448. (707)473-9836. Website: www.creatormagazine.com. Rod Ellis, ed. For interdenominational music ministry; promoting quality, diverse music programs in the church. Bimonthly mag; 48-56 pgs; circ 6,000. Subscription $32.95. 35% freelance. Query or complete ms/cover letter; fax/e-query OK. Pays $30-75 for assigned, $30-60 for unsolicited, on publication for 1st or one-time rts. Articles 1,000-10,000 wds (20/yr); book reviews $20. Responds in 4-12 wks. Seasonal 4 mos ahead. Accepts simultaneous submissions & reprints (tell when/where appeared). Prefers disk. Regular sidebars. Prefers NRSV. Guidelines/theme list; copy for 9x12 SAE/5 stamps. (Ads)

> **Fillers:** Buys 20/yr. Anecdotes, cartoons, ideas, jokes, party ideas, short humor; 10-75 wds; $5-25.

> **Special Needs:** Articles on worship; staff relationships.

$*GOSPEL INDUSTRY TODAY, 761 Old Hickory Blvd., Ste. 205, Brentwood TN 37027-4513. E-mail: gospel@usit.net. Horizon Concepts, Inc. Teresa Harris, pub. About the Christian and Gospel music industry. Monthly (10X) mag; 20 pgs; circ 3,500. Subscription $24. 50% freelance. Query; fax/e-query OK. Pays $75-250 on publication for 1st rts. Articles 1,500-3,000 wds. Responds in 5-9 wks. Seasonal 3 mos ahead. Prefers disk. Kill fee 10%. Regular sidebars. Prefers KJV. Guidelines/theme list; copy for 10x13 SAE/8 stamps. (Ads)

THE HYMN: A Journal of Congregational Song, School of Theology, Boston University, 745 Commonwealth Ave., Boston MA 02215-1401. (800) THEHYMN. E-mail: hymneditor@att.net. Website: www.bu.edu/sth/hymn/ www.hymnsociety.org. Hymn Society in the US & Canada. Carol A. Pemberton, ed, Box 46485, Eden Prairie MN 55344. For church musicians, hymnologists, scholars; articles related to the congregational song. Quarterly journal; 60 pgs; circ 3,000. Subscription $55. 85% unsolicited freelance; 15% assigned. Query; phone/e-query OK. **NO PAYMENT** for all rts. Articles any length (12/yr); book & music reviews any length. Responds in 4 wks. Seasonal 4 mos ahead. Prefers disk, no e-mail submission. Regular sidebars. Any version. Guidelines; free copy. (Ads)

> **Special Needs:** Articles on history of hymns or practical ways to teach or use hymns. Contact editor.

> **Contest:** Hymn text and tune contests for special occasions or themes.

$*MUSIC MAKERS, 127 9th Ave. N., Nashville TN 37234-0140. (615)251-2000. Southern Baptist. Darrell Billingsley, ed. For children ages 6-11. Quarterly mag; circ 105,000. Pays .06/wd on acceptance for all rts. Articles & fiction 250-500 wds. Responds in 4 wks. Guidelines/copy. Not in topical listings.

$*MUSIC TIME, 127 9th Ave. N., Nashville TN 37234-0140. (615)251-2000. Southern Baptist. Darrell Billingsley, literary design ed. For 4 & 5 yr olds; directly related to unit material found in The Music Leader. Quarterly mag; circ 60,000. Complete ms. Pays .05/wd for stories. Pays $9-12 on acceptance for all rts. Stories for 4 & 5 yr olds. Responds in 2-5 wks. Not in topical listings. Guidelines; free copy.

> **Poetry:** 1-7 lines; $5-9.

$#PROFILE MAGAZINE, 3670 Central Pike, Ste. J, Hermitage TN 37076. (615) 872-8080. Fax (615)872-9786. E-mail: profile@profilemagazine.com. Website: www.profilemagazine.com. VoxCorp, Inc. Chris Well, ed-in-chief.

Covers music, books and media for the retail shopper. Bimonthly mag; 100 pgs; circ 80,000. Subscription $15.95. 70% freelance. E-query OK. Pays .06-.10/wd, 45 days after publication. Articles 500-2,500 wds (20-30/yr). Prefers e-mail submission (copied into message). No guidelines. Not in topical listings. (Ads)

> **Columns/Departments:** K.I.D.Z. column (Selena Carlton, ed); need information on kids' products, videos, books, music, etc.
>
> **Tips:** "Send us clips and demonstrate that you have knowledge of the products and personalities we cover."

*QUEST, PO Box 14804, Columbus OH 43214. Rick Welke, ed. Geared to 16-30 yr olds and radio personnel. Monthly newsletter. Query; fax query OK. **PAYS A SUBSCRIPTION.** Articles 100-500 wds (4/yr); fiction, 150-750 wds (4/yr); book/music reviews, 30-75 wds. Seasonal 3 mos ahead. Accepts simultaneous submissions & reprints. Theme list; copy for #10 SAE/2 stamps.

> **Poetry:** Accepts 12/yr. Any type, 4-24 lines. Submit max 4 poems.
>
> **Fillers:** Accepts 36/yr. Cartoons, facts, jokes, quizzes, quotes, short humor, word puzzles.
>
> **Columns/Departments:** Artist Action (any specific artist information).
>
> **Special Needs:** Organizational pieces; new music releases/photos; artist's concert schedules; radio station playlists.
>
> **Tips:** "Submit between the 10th and 20th of each month for best review."

$RELEASE, 3670 Central Pike, Ste. J, Hermitage TN 37076. (615)872-8080. Fax (615)872-9786. E-mail: editorial@voxcorp.com, or release@release magazine.com. Website: www.releasemagazine.com. Vox Corp Inc. Chris Well, ed-in-chief. Bimonthly mag; 50 pgs; circ 110,000. Subscription $19.95. 100% assigned. Query/clips; e-query OK. Pays .06-.10/wd, 30 days after publication, for 1st & electronic rts. Articles 500-2,500 wds (45/yr); music reviews. Accepts e-mail submission (copied into message). Seasonal 4 mos ahead. Kill fee. Some sidebars. Guidelines; copy $5. (Ads)

> **Tips:** "Show us you know the music and give us an idea of the styles you're most comfortable with."

$THE SENIOR MUSICIAN, 127 9th Ave. N., Nashville TN 37234-0160. (615)251-2913. Fax (615)251-2869. E-mail: youthadult@lifeway.com. Southern Baptist. Jere V. Adams, ed. Easy choir music for senior adult choirs to use in worship, ministry, and recreation; for music directors, pastors, organists, pianists, and choir coordinators. Quarterly mag; 26 pgs; circ 32,000. 90% unsolicited freelance; 10% assigned. Complete ms. Pays .07/wd on publication for 1st rts. Articles 500-900 wds (6-7/yr). Responds in 2-4 wks. Seasonal 1 yr ahead. Some simultaneous submissions; reprints. Guidelines; free copy. (No ads for now)

> **Poetry:** Buys 2-3/yr. Traditional.
>
> **Fillers:** Buys 3-4/yr. Cartoons, ideas, party ideas, musical quizzes, short humor.
>
> **Special Needs:** Leisure reading, music training, fellowship suggestions, and choir projects for personal growth.
>
> **Tips:** "All topics must relate to senior adult musicians and senior

choirs—anything else will be returned. Our publication includes 8 pages of literary and 24 pages of music."

$7BALL, 3670 Central Pike, Ste. J, Hermitage TN 37076. (615)872-8080. Fax (615)872-9786. E-mail: 7ball@7ball.com. Website: www.7ball.com. Vox-Corp, Inc. Chris Well, ed-in-chief; submit to Cameron Strang, mng ed. Covers modern and alternative Christian rock. Bimonthly mag; circ 60,000. Subscription $19.95. 70% freelance. Query/clips; e-query OK. Pays .06-.10/wd, 30 days after publication for 1st and electronic rts. Articles 500-2,500 wds (20/yr). Prefers e-mail submission (copied into message). Seasonal 4 mos ahead. No guidelines; copy $5 or on Website. Not in topical listings. (Ads)

$SONGWRITING: The Journal (formerly Elements of Songwriting), PO Box 40935, Mesa AZ 85274-0935. (480)964-0710. E-mail: songwriting@crosshome. com. Christian Songwriters Resource. George Martinez, ed. Written to, for and about the serious songwriter. Bimonthly jour.; 20 pgs; circ 4,000. Subscription $15. 50% unsolicited freelance; 50% assigned. Query; e-query OK. Pays $15-25 on publication for all rts. Articles 100-500 wds; music/video reviews 200 wds, $10. Responds in 4-8 wks. Seasonal 4 mos ahead. Accepts simultaneous submissions & reprints (tell when/where appeared). Accepts e-mail submissions (copied into message). Some sidebars. Prefers NIV. Guidelines (also by e-mail); copy for 6x9 SAE/2 stamps. (Ads)

Fillers: Buys 6/yr. Cartoons, ideas. Pays $5-10.

Special Needs: Songwriting; and songwriters who want to write articles about their ministry.

Tips: "Most open to how-to columns, especially from songwriters; personal experiences in songwriting; and how-to. Write directly to our readers, naturally, not mechanically. Write to educate, encourage or inform."

*TRADITION MAGAZINE, PO Box 492, Anita IA 50020. (712)762-4363. Fax (712)762-4363. National Traditional Country Music Assn., Inc. Bob Everhart, pres/ed. Bimonthly mag; 56 pgs; circ 2,500. Subscription $20. 30% unsolicited freelance; 70% assigned. Query. **PAYS IN COPIES** for one-time rts. Articles 1,000-2,000 wds (4/yr). Responds in 6-8 wks. Some sidebars. Prefers KJV. Guidelines; copy for 9x12 SAE/2 stamps. (Ads)

Fillers: Cartoons.

Columns/Departments: Accepts 4-6/yr. Query.

Tips: "Most articles need to deal with traditional music."

PASTOR/LEADERSHIP MARKETS

$THE AFRICAN AMERICAN PULPIT, PO Box 851, Valley Forge PA 19482-0851. (610)768-2128. Fax (610)768-2441. E-mail: Victoria.McGoey@abc-usa.org. Website: www.judsonpress.com. Judson Press/American Baptist Churches. Submit to: The African American Pulpit, Judson Press Editorial Dept. The only journal focused exclusively on the art of black preaching. Quarterly journal; 96 pgs; circ 2,000. Subscription $29.95 (may change). 50% unsolicited freelance; 50% assigned. Complete ms/cover letter; phone/e-query OK. Pays on publication for 1st rts. Articles/sermons to

2,500 wds. Responds in 13-26 wks. Seasonal 6-9 mos ahead. Requires disk or e-mail submission. No sidebars. Any version. Guidelines (also by e-mail/Website); copy. (Ads)

Special Needs: Any type of sermon by African American preachers, and related articles or essays.

Tips: "The entire journal is open to freelancers. We strongly encourage freelancers to submit to us (as many pieces as you can), and freelancers can call anytime with questions. We are always looking for how-to articles, sermon helps, and practical pieces."

+ANGELOS, PO Box 757800, Memphis TN 38175-7800. (901)757-7977. Fax (901)757-1372. E-mail: OMI@olford.org. Website: www.olford.org. Olford Ministries Intl. Mark N. Boorman, Dir of Communications. Bimonthly & online mag; 20-24 pgs; circ 4,500. Subscription $10 (voluntary). 5% unsolicited; 95% assigned. Query; phone/e-query OK. **NO PAYMENT** for one-time rts. Articles (1-3/yr) 500 wds; book/video reviews 250 wds. Responds in 2-3 wks. Seasonal 3-4 mos ahead. Might accept reprints (tell when/where appeared). Prefers disk or e-mail submission (attached file). Regular sidebars. Prefers NKJV. Copy for 9x12 SAE/4 stamps. (No ads)

Poetry: Accepts 1-2 /yr. Traditional; 4-20 lines. Submit max 2 poems.

Fillers: Accepts 4-6/yr. Prayers, 100-200 wds.

Tips: "Call and ask if we need article complementary to theme of upcoming issue."

$*CATECHUMENATE: A Journal of Christian Initiation, 1800 N. Hermitage Ave., Chicago IL 60622-1101. (773)486-8970. Fax (800)933-7094. E-mail: editors@ltp.org. Catholic. Victoria M. Tufano, ed. For clergy and laity who work with those who are planning to become Catholic. Bimonthly journal; 48 pgs; circ 5,600. Subscription $20. Complete ms/cover letter; phone/fax/e-query OK. Pays $100-250 on publication for all rts (poetry, one-time rts). Articles 1,500-3,000 wds (10/yr). Responds in 2-6 wks. Accepts simultaneous submissions. Prefers disk. Kill fee. No sidebars. Guidelines; copy for 6x9 SAE/4 stamps.

Poetry: Buys 6/yr. Free verse, traditional; 5-20 lines; $75. Submit max 5 poems.

Columns/Departments: Buys 12/yr. Sunday Word (Scripture reflection on Sunday readings, aimed at catechumers); 450 wds; $200-250. Query for assignment.

Special Needs: Christian initiation; reconciliation.

Tips: "It helps if the writer has experience working with Christian initiation. Approach is that this is something we are all learning together through experience and scholarship."

$THE CATHOLIC SERVANT, PO Box 24142, Minneapolis MN 55424. (612) 729-7321. Fax (612)724-8695.Website: www.catholicservant.org. Catholic. John Sondag, ed/pub. For Catholic evangelization, catechesis, and apologetics. Monthly mag; 12 pgs; circ 33,000. Query/clips; fax query OK. Pays $50-60 on publication. Articles 750-1,000 wds (12/yr). Responds in 4 wks. Seasonal 3 mos ahead. Prefers disk; no e-mail submissions. Some sidebars. (Ads)

Fillers: Cartoons & short humor.

Columns/Departments: Opinion column, 500-750 wds.

Tips: "We buy features or column only."

$*CELEBRATION, 207 Hillsboro Dr., Silver Spring MD 20902-3125. William J. Freburger, ed. National Catholic Reporter Publishing House. Monthly mag; 48 pgs; circ 9,000. Subscription $64.95. 15% freelance. Complete ms/cover letter. Pays $100-200 on acceptance for one-time rts. Articles 1,000-2,500 wds (15-20/yr). Responds in 2 wks. Seasonal 7 mos ahead. Prefers disk. No sidebars. Copy for 10x13 SAE/4 stamps. (Ads)

   Contest: Monthly contest on different themes, usually worship ideas for specific occasions (New Year, Easter, etc.).

   Tips: "I am always looking for descriptions of worship services (texts), ideas for worship occasions (seasonal, special), unsentimental and non-obvious stories as teaching/preaching aids, etc."

CELL GROUP JOURNAL (formerly Cell Church Magazine), PO Box 19888, Houston TX 77224. (281)497-7901. Fax (281)497-0904. E-mail: randall@ touchusa.org. Website: www.touchusa.org. Touch Outreach Ministries. Randall Neighbour, ed dir. For Cell Church pastors, leaders and consultants working to impact the world for Christ through the church. Quarterly mag; 32 pgs; circ 12,000. Subscription $14. 70-80% freelance. Query/clips; fax/e-query OK. **PAYS 10 COPIES.** Articles 1,000-1,500 wds (20-30/yr). Responds in 2 wks. Seasonal 3 mos ahead. Accepts simultaneous submissions & reprints (tell when/where appeared). Prefers disk. Some sidebars. Prefers NIV. Guidelines/theme list; copy $3.50/9x12 SAE/3 stamps. (Ads)

   Columns/Departments: Accepts 20-25/yr. Youth, Children's Ministry, Transitioning (to Cell Church), Global Input, Pastor's Pilgrimage (pastor's testimonial about Cell Church), ToolKit (500-wd testimonies about cell life, tips from cell leaders/interns, icebreakers), and Heart to Heart (heartfelt testimony about cell life); all 1,000-1,500 wds.

   Special Needs: Global issues; practical tips and ideas relevant to Cell Church concept. Needs youth Cell Church writers.

$CHRISTIAN CAMP & CONFERENCE JOURNAL, 405 W. Rockrimmon Blvd., PO Box 62189 (80962-2189), Colorado Springs CO 80919. (719)260-9400. Fax (719)260-6398. E-mail: nroth@cciusa.org. Website: www. cciusa.org. Christian Camping Intl./USA. Natalee Roth, ed. To inform, inspire, and motivate all who serve in Christian camping. Bimonthly mag; 36 pgs; circ 7,500. Subscription $26.95. 20% unsolicited freelance; 80% assigned. Query; fax/e-query OK. Pays .16/wd on publication for 1st & electronic rts. Articles 800-2,000 wds (12/yr). Responds in 4-6 wks. Seasonal 4 mos ahead. Accepts simultaneous submissions & reprints (tell when/where appeared). Prefers e-mail submission (attached file) with fax backup. Kill fee. Regular sidebars. Prefers NIV. Guidelines (also by e-mail); copy $2.25/9x12 SAE/5 stamps. (Ads)

   Special Needs: Outdoor setting; purpose and objectives; administration and organization; personnel development; camper/guest needs; programming; health and safety; food service; site/facilities maintenance; business/operations; marketing and PR; and fund-raising.

Tips: "Get guidelines first. Don't send general camping-related articles. We print stories specifically related to Christian camp and conference facilities; changed lives or innovative programs; how a Christian camp or conference experience affected a present-day leader."

$CHRISTIAN CENTURY, 104 S. Michigan Ave., Ste. 700, Chicago IL 60603-5905. (312)263-7510. Fax (312)263-7540. E-mail: main@christiancentury. org. Website: www.christiancentury.org. Christian Century Foundation. Submit to Attention Manuscripts. For ministers, educators and church leaders interested in events and theological issues of concern to the ecumenical church. Weekly magazine; 32 pgs; circ 30,000. Subscription $42. 20% unsolicited freelance; 80% assigned. Query (complete ms for fiction); phone/fax query OK. Pays $75-200 ($75-150 for unsolicited) on publication for all rts. Articles 1,000-3,000 wds (150/yr); fiction 1,000-3,000 wds (3/yr); book reviews, 800-1,500 wds; music or video reviews 1,000 wds; pays $0-75. Responds in 1-9 wks. Seasonal 4 mos ahead. Accepts simultaneous submissions. No kill fee. Regular sidebars. Prefers NRSV. Guidelines/theme list; copy $3. (Ads)

Poetry: Buys 50/yr. Any type (religious but not sentimental); to 20 lines; $50. Submit max 10 poems.

Special Needs: Film, popular culture commentary; news topics and analysis.

Tips: "Keep in mind our audience of sophisticated readers, eager for analysis and critical perspective that goes beyond the obvious. We are open to all topics if written with appropriate style for our readers."

CHRISTIAN MANAGEMENT REPORT, PO Box 4090, San Clemente CA 92674-4090. (949)487-0900. Fax (949)487-0927. E-mail: DeWayne@CMAonline. org. Website: www.CMAonline.org. Christian Management Association. DeWayne Herbrandson, ed. Management resources and leadership training for Christian non-profit organizations and larger churches. Bimonthly journal; 48 pgs; circ 3,500. Subscription $39.95. 1% unsolicited freelance; 99% assigned. Complete ms; e-query encouraged. NO PAYMENT for all rts. Articles 700 wds/bio; book reviews 100-200 wds. Responds in 6 wks. Seasonal 6 mos ahead. Accepts simultaneous submissions & reprints. CMA members first choice. Guidelines; free copy. (Ads)

Fillers: Anecdotes, cartoons, quotes, short humor; 20-50 wds.

Columns/Departments: Board Governance, CEO/Leadership, Human Resources, Communications/Public Relations, Fund Development/Marketing, Financial Management, Church Management, Tax & Legal Trends; 650 wds. Query.

Special Needs: Evangelical Calendar of Events, Ministry Profiles/Case Studies; hot ministry news, and trends.

$CHURCH ADMINISTRATION, MSN 157, 127 9th Ave. N., Nashville TN 37234-0157. (615)251-2062. Fax (615)251-3866. E-mail: cjohnson@lifeway. com. Website: www.lifeway.com. Southern Baptist. Chris Johnson, ed. Practical pastoral ministry/church administration ideas for pastors and staff. Quarterly mag; 50 pgs; circ 12,000. 15% freelance. Query. Pays .065/wd on acceptance for all rts. Articles 1,600-2,000 wds (60/yr). Responds in 8 wks. Guidelines/copy for #10 SAE/2 stamps.

Columns/Departments: Buys 60/yr. Weekday Dialogue; Minister's Mate; Secretary's File; all 2,000 wds.

Tips: "Manuscripts must be typed and have return postage."

$CHURCH GROWTH NETWORK, PO Box 892589, Temecula CA 92589-2589. Phone/fax (909)506-3086. E-mail: gary_mcintosh@peter.biola.edu. Website: www.mcintoshcgn.com. Dr. Gary L. McIntosh, ed. For pastors and church leaders interested in church growth. Monthly newsletter; 2 pgs; circ 8,000. Subscription $16. 10% unsolicited freelance; 90% assigned. Query; fax/e-query OK. Pays $25 for one-time rts. Not copyrighted. Articles 1,000-2,000 wds (2/yr). Responds in 4 wks. Accepts simultaneous submissions & reprints. Accepts disk. No sidebars. Copy for #10 SAE/1 stamp. (No ads)

> **Tips:** "Write articles that are short (1,200 words), crisp, clear, with very practical ideas that church leaders can put to use immediately. All articles must have a church-growth slant, be very practical, how-to material; very tightly written with bullets, etc."

$CHURCH WORSHIP, 165 Plaza Dr., Prescott AZ 86303. (520)771-8601. Fax (520)771-8621. E-mail: edmin2@aol.com. Educational Ministries. Robert Davidson, ed. Supplementary resources for church worship leaders. Monthly journal; 24 pgs; circ 1,500. Subscription $24. 100% unsolicited freelance. Complete ms/cover letter; phone/fax/e-query OK. Pays .03/wd, 60 days after publication, for 1st rts. Articles 500-1,500 wds; fiction 100-1,500 wds. Responds in 3-18 wks. Seasonal 6 mos ahead. Guidelines/theme list; copy for 9x12 SAE/4 stamps. (No ads)

> **Special Needs:** Complete worship services; seasonal sermons.
> **Tips:** "Most open to creative worship services using music, drama or art."

$THE CLERGY JOURNAL, 6160 Carmen Ave. E, Inver Grove Heights MN 55076-4422. (651)451-9945. Fax (651)457-4617. Website: www.join hands.com. Logos Productions, Inc. Sharilyn Figueroa, mng ed. Directed mainly to clergy—a practical guide to church leadership and personal growth. Monthly (10X) mag; 56 pgs; circ. 8,000. Subscription $34.95. 5% unsolicited freelance; 95% assigned. Complete ms/cover letter. Pays $50-125 on publication for 1st rts. Articles 1,000-1,500 wds. Responds in 2-3 wks. Seasonal 6 mos ahead. Accepts reprints (tell when/where appeared). Prefers disk or e-mail submission (attached). Some sidebars. Prefers NRSV. Guidelines/theme list (also by e-mail); copy for 9x12 SAE/4 stamps. (Ads)

> **Fillers:** Cartoons, $25.
> **Columns/Departments:** Ministry Issues; Preaching & Worship; Personal Issues.
> **Special Needs:** Humorous fiction for pastors and children's sermons.
> **Tips:** "On the religious spectrum from very conservative to very liberal, our audience is in the middle to left. We are interested in meeting the personal and professional needs of clergy in areas like worship planning, church and personal finances, and self-care—spiritual, physical and emotional."

CROSS CURRENTS, College of New Rochelle, 29 Castle Pl., New Rochelle NY 10805-2339. (914)235-1439. Fax (914)235-1584. E-mail: aril@ecunet.org.

Website: www.crosscurrent.org. Association for Religion and Intellectual Life. Kenneth Arnold, ed. For thoughtful activists for social justice and church reform. Quarterly journal; 144 pgs; circ 5,000. Subscription $30. 25% unsolicited; 75% assigned. Mostly written by academics. Complete ms/cover letter; phone/fax query OK/no e-query. **PAYS IN COPIES** for all rts. Articles 3,000-5,000 wds; book reviews 1,000 wds (James Giles). Responds in 6-8 wks. Seasonal 6 mos ahead. Accepts simultaneous submissions & reprints. Requires disk. No sidebars. Guidelines; copy for 6x9 SAE/4 stamps. (Ads)

> **Poetry:** Beverly Coyle. Accepts 12/yr. Any type or length; no payment. Submit max 5 poems.
>
> **Tips:** "Send 2 double-spaced copies; SASE; use *Chicago Manual of Style;* and non-sexist language."

$DIOCESAN DIALOGUE, 16565 S. State St., South Holland IL 60473. (708)331-5485. Fax (708)331-5484. E-mail: acp@acpress.org. Website: www.acpress.org. A Mexican Catholic Press. Fr. Michael Gilligan, editorial dir. Targets Latin-Rite dioceses in the US that sponsor a mass broadcast on TV or radio. Annual newsletter; 8 pgs; circ. 750. Free. 20% freelance. Complete ms/cover letter; no phone/fax/e-query. Pays on publication for all rts. Responds in 10 wks. Accepts simultaneous submissions & reprints. Some sidebars. Prefers NAB (Confraternity). No guidelines; copy $3/9x12 SAE/2 stamps. (No ads)

> **Fillers:** Cartoons, 2/yr.
>
> **Tips:** "Writers should be familiar with TV production of the Mass and/or the needs of senior citizens, especially shut-ins."

$*EMMANUEL, 5384 Wilson Mills Rd., Cleveland OH 44143-3092. (440)449-2103. Fax (440)449-3862. Catholic. Rev. Anthony Schueller, ed; book reviews to Dr. Patrick Riley. Eucharistic spirituality for priests and others in church ministry. Monthly (10X) mag; 60 pgs; circ 4,000+. Subscription $19.95. 75% freelance. Query or complete ms/cover letter; fax query OK. Pays $75-150 for articles, $50 for meditations, on publication for all rts. Articles 2,000-2,750 wds; meditations 1,000-1,250 wds; book reviews 500-750 wds. Responds in 2 wks. Seasonal 4 mos ahead. Accepts disk. Prefers RNAB. Guidelines/theme list. (Ads)

> **Poetry:** Buys 15/yr. Free verse; 25-100 lines. Pays $35-50. Submit max 2-3 poems.

$ENRICHMENT: A Journal for Pentecostal Ministry, 1445 Boonville Ave., Springfield MO 65802. (417)862-2781. Fax (417)862-0416. E-mail: enrichment@ag.org. Website: www.enrichmentjournal.ag.org. Assemblies of God. Gary R. Allen, exec. ed.; Rick Knoth, mng ed. Directed to part- or full-time ministers and church leaders. Quarterly journal; 128-144 pgs; circ 32,500. Subscription $22, $38/2 yrs; foreign add $6. 5-10% freelance. Complete ms/cover letter. Pays .03-.10/wd ($75-175) on publication for one-time rts. Articles 1,200-2,500 wds (25/yr); book reviews, 250 wds, $25. Responds in 8-12 wks. Seasonal 1 yr ahead. Accepts simultaneous submissions & reprints (tell when/where appeared). Requires disk or e-mail submission (copied into message). Kill fee 50%. Regular sidebars. Prefers NIV. Guidelines/theme list; copy for $3/10x13 SAE. (Ads)

Fillers: Cartoons. Pays $50-75.

Columns/Departments: Buys many/yr. For Women in Ministry (leadership ideas), Associate Ministers (related issues), Managing Your Ministry (how-to), Financial Concepts (church stewardship issues), Family Matters (minister's family), View from the Pew (layperson's perspective on ministry); all 1,200-1,500 wds. Pays $125-150.

Tips: "Most open to sermon outlines, how-to articles (fillers), sermon illustrations, practical ideas on ministry-related topics."
**1999 EPA Award of Merit—Denoninational; 1997 EPA Award of Excellence—Denominational; EPA Most Improved Publication 1997.

$*ENVIRONMENT & ART LETTER, 1800 N. Hermitage Ave., Chicago IL 60622-1101. (773)486-8970. Fax (773)486-7094. Catholic. David Philippart, ed. For artists, architects, building professionals, pastors, parish committees interested in church architecture, art and decoration. Monthly newsletter; 12 pgs; circ 2,500. Subscription $20. 80% freelance. Query/clips; phone/fax query OK. Pays $25/ms page on publication for all rts. Responds in 18 wks. Seasonal 2 mos ahead. Accepts simultaneous submissions. Theme list; copy for 9x12 SAE/3 stamps.

Tips: "Need a thorough knowledge of the liturgical documents pertaining to architecture and art, especially environment and art for Catholic worship."

$EUCHARISTIC MINISTER, 115 E. Armour Blvd., Box 419493, Kansas City MO 64111. (816)531-0538. Fax (816)968-2268. E-mail: celpubs3@aol. com. Website: www.ncrpub.com. Catholic. Joan A. Wingert, ed. For Eucharistic ministers. Monthly newsletter; 8 pgs; circ 50,000. 20% unsolicited freelance; 80% assigned. Complete ms/cover letter. Pays $50-125 on publication for one-time rts. Articles 500-1,250 wds (12/yr). Responds in 1-2 wks. Seasonal 6 mos ahead. Accepts reprints (tell when/where appeared). Prefers e-mail submissions (attached or copied into message). No sidebars. Guidelines (also by e-mail); copy for 10x13w SAE/2 stamps. (Ads—e-mail for specifications).

Fillers: Buys 10-12/yr. Anecdotes, cartoons, short humor.

Columns/Departments: Buys 12/yr. Living My Ministry (reflections on minister's experiences, anecdotes, inspirational personal experiences), 500 wds, $50. Complete ms.

Tips: "We want articles to be practical, inspirational, or motivational. They need to be simple and direct enough for the average person to read easily—no heavy theology, pious inspiration, or excess verbiage."

$THE EVANGELICAL BAPTIST, 679 Southgate Dr., Guelph ON N1G 4S2 Canada. (519)821-4830. Fax (519)821-9829. E-mail: eb@fellowship.ca. Website: www.fellowship.ca. Fellowship of Evangelical Baptist Churches in Canada. Ginette Cotnoir, mng ed, 18 Louvigny, Lorraine QC J6Z 1T7 Canada. To enhance the life and ministry of pastors and denominational leaders in local churches. Bimonthly (5X) mag (soon to be online); 32 pgs; circ 3,000. Subscription $12. 5-10% unsolicited freelance; 20% assigned. Complete ms/cover letter; e-query OK. Pays $25-75 on publication for one-time rts. Articles 800-2,400 wds. Responds in 6-8 wks.

Accepts simultaneous submissions & reprints (tell when/where appeared). Prefers e-mail submission. Some sidebars. Guidelines (also by e-mail); copy for 9x12 SAE/.90 Canadian postage. (Ads)

Columns/Departments: Buys 5/yr. Joy in the Journey (inspiration in everyday life), 600-800 wds; View From the Pew (humorous, first-person essay with a twist), 600-800 wds. Pays $25-50. Complete ms.

Special Needs: Church Life department looking for practical church ministry ideas; how to enhance Sunday school, small groups, worship, youth ministry, women's ministries, etc.; 600-800 wds

Tips: "This magazine is for church leaders—pastors, elders, deacons, and anyone involved in a church ministry. Most articles are assigned. Most open to columns. Preference given to writers from Fellowship Baptist Churches in Canada."

$EVANGELICALS TODAY, 62 Molave St., Project 3, Quezon City 1102, Philippines. (632)433-1546 to 1549. Fax (632)913-1675. E-mail: pcec@amanet.net. Philippine Council of Evangelical Churches. Bishop Efraim M. Tendero, exec. ed. To equip pastors, Christian leaders/workers and the rest of Christ's Body in the various areas of Christian life and ministry by providing inspiring and enriching articles and relevant news reports. Bimonthly mag; 36 pgs; circ 3,000. Subscription $6.25 (local) or $50 (foreign). 5% unsolicited freelance; 95% assigned. Complete ms by e-mail. Pays $12.50/article on publication. Articles 1,000-1,500 wds. Responds in 2 wks. Seasonal 2 mos ahead. Accepts simultaneous submissions & reprints (tell when/where appeared). Prefers disk or e-mail submissions (attached file or copied into message). Prefers NIV. No guidelines. (Ads)

$THE FIVE STONES, 69 Weymouth St., Providence RI 02906-2335. Phone/fax (401)861-9405. E-mail: pappas@tabcom.org. Website: www. tabcom.org. American Baptist. Anthony G. Pappas, ed. Primarily to small church pastors and laity, denominational staff, and seminaries; to equip for service. Quarterly journal; 24 pgs; circ 1,200. Subscription $8-12. 100% freelance. Complete ms/cover letter. Pays $5 on publication for one-time rights. Not copyrighted. Articles (20/yr) & fiction (4/yr), 500-2,000 wds; book reviews 500 wds, $5. Responds in 10-12 wks. Seasonal 10 mos ahead. Accepts simultaneous submissions & reprints. Accepts disk or e-mail submission. Some sidebars. Any version. Guidelines/theme list; copy for 9x12 SAE/4 stamps. (No ads)

Fillers: Buys 12/yr. Anecdotes, cartoons, ideas, jokes, short humor; 20-200 wds; $5.

Tips: "Always looking for everything related to small church life (nature and dynamics of small churches); fresh programming. Good place for unpublished to break in. Use first-person. Best to call and talk."

+FORMINISTRY.COM. Website: www.forministry.com. American Bible Society. James Watkins (watkins@fwi.com), ed. for Church Leaders; Cynthia L. Freeman (Cynthia.L.Freeman.93@Alum.Dartmouth.org), ed. for Community Outreach and Evangelism; Jan L. Johnson (JanJohnson@compuserve.com), ed. for Discipleship and Christian Education; Andy Sloan (AndrewS@ratedg.com), ed. for Lay Development, Men's Ministries,

Small Group Ministries; Marlee Alex (Marleebooks@aol.com), ed. for Women's Ministries, Ministry to Your Culture, Missions & Evangelism; David Kennedy (iansfolks@earthlink.net), ed. for Worship & Music; Faith McDonald (Fsmcdonald@aol.com), ed. for Ministry to Your Children, Ministry to Your Community, Ministry to Your Spouse. (Submit to proper editor.) Strives to serve Christians of all backgrounds—Catholic, Orthodox, and Protestant—who come together to obtain and exchange information on ministry. E-magazine. Short articles, essays, stories and intervies; to 900 wds. Open to freelance. Send by e-mail. **NO PAYMENT FOR NOW** (but provides a link to your organization, church or personal site). Guidelines (by e-mail or on Website: www2.fwi.com/~watkins/forministry.htm). Incomplete topical listings.

Special Needs: News briefs, data on events, seminars, conferences, and tips on books appropriate for reviews.

Tips: "Use ecumenical and inclusive language."

$#GROWING CHURCHES, 127 Ninth Ave. N., Nashville TN 37234-0157. (615)251-3837. Fax (615)251-3609. E-mail: Rhodge@lifeway.com. Website: www.lifeway.com. Lifeway Christian Resources of the Southern Baptist Convention. Dr. Ralph Hodge, design ed. To provide pastors and church leaders with the latest resources for growing healthy churches. Quarterly mag; 50 pgs; circ 81,000. Subscription $12.80. 20% unsolicited freelance; 80% assigned. Query or complete ms/cover letter; phone/fax/e-query OK. Pays .065/wd (to $200) on acceptance for all rts. Articles 1,500-3,500 wds; reviews 300 wds, pays $50. Responds in 2 wks. Prefers disk or e-mail submissions (attached file). Some sidebars. Guidelines (also by e-mail); copy for 10x13 SAE. (No ads)

Poetry: Buys 5/yr. Avante-garde, traditional; pays $50-200. Submit max 10 poems.

Fillers: Anecdotes, cartoons, facts, ideas, prayers, prose, quotes. Pays $20-50.

Columns/Departments: Send complete ms.

Tips: "Query by e-mail with an idea as response to specific need expressed by editor. E-mail is best communication method."

$HORIZONS, 2 Overlea Blvd., Toronto ON M4H 1P4 Canada. (416)425-2111. Fax (416)422-6120. E-mail: horizons@sallynet.org. Website: horizons.salvationarmy.ca. The Salvation Army. Geoff Moulton, sr ed. For officers and lay leaders of The Salvation Army, focusing on leadership, discipleship, theology, social issues and Christian ministry. Bimonthly mag; 24 pgs; circ 4,600. Subscription $12.84 CAN. 100% assigned. Query/clips; fax/e-query OK. Pay negotiated for 1st rts. Articles 1,500 wds (30/yr); reviews 250 wds. Responds in 2 wks. Accepts simultaneous submissions & reprints (tell when/where appeared). Prefers e-mail submission (attached file). Some sidebars. Prefers NIV. Guidelines (also on Website); free copy. (No ads)

Fillers: Cartoons.

Columns/Departments: Accepts 20/yr. Future Frontiers (what's new in church ministry), 850 wds; Practical Ministry (practical helps), 850 wds; Strategic Advance (church leadership/growth issues), 1,500 wds;

Reaching Out (evangelism), 1,500 wds; Bookmarks (reviews), 250-300 wds; Creed & Deed (theology), 850 wds. No payment.

ISSACHARFILE, PO Box 12609, Oklahoma City OK 73157. (405)787-7110. Fax (405)789-3957. E-mail: Shirley@iphc.org. Website: www.LifeSprings. net. Intl. Pentecostal Holiness Church. Shirley G. Spencer, ed. Denominational; keeping church leaders in touch with the times. Monthly & online mag; circ 3,000. Subscription $11.95. 10% unsolicited freelance; 90% assigned. Query; fax/e-query OK. Not in topical listings. (No ads)

THE IVY JUNGLE REPORT, 400 Park Ln., Lake Bluff IL 60044-2323. E-mail: ivyjungle@aol.com. Website: www.ivyjungle.org. Woodruff Resources. Mike Woodruff, pub. For people who minister to collegians. Quarterly mag; 16 pgs; circ 800. Subscription $20. 20% freelance. Query; fax/e-query OK. **NO PAYMENT** for one-time rts. Not copyrighted. Articles 500-1,500 wds (16/yr); book/music reviews, 500 wds. Responds in 2 wks. Accepts simultaneous submissions & reprints. Prefers e-mail submission (attached file). Regular sidebars. Copy for 2 stamps. (Ads)

> **Fillers:** Accepts 10+/yr. Anecdotes, cartoons, facts, jokes, news breaks, quizzes, quotes, short humor; 15-100 wds.
>
> **Columns/Departments:** Out of the Classroom (student missions), 750-1,000 wds (4/yr). Query.
>
> **Tips:** "We are looking for writers who understand the unique demands and challenges of college ministry, both church and parachurch."

*JOURNAL OF CHRISTIAN HEALING, 6728 Old McLean Village Dr., McLean VA 22101. (703)556-9222. Fax (703)556-8729. E-mail: Nov45@aol.com, or Act@Healthy.net. Assoc of Christian Therapists. Father Louis Lussier, OSCAS, ed. Focuses on the healing power and presence of Jesus Christ, for health and mental health professionals and healing ministries. Quarterly journal; 40 pgs; circ 1,200. 100% freelance. Complete ms/cover letter; phone/e-query OK. **PAYS IN COPIES** for all rts. Articles 10-20 pgs (12/yr); fiction 2-5 pgs; book reviews, 2-5 pgs. Accepts reprints. Responds in 8 wks. Guidelines; copy $8. (Ads)

> **Poetry:** Charles Zeiders. Accepts 12/yr. Free verse, haiku, light verse or traditional; to 40 lines. Submit max 10 poems.
>
> **Fillers:** Accepts 10/yr. Various; to 250 wds.
>
> **Columns/Departments:** Accepts 12/yr. Resources, Medical Practices, Nursing, Pastoral Ministry, Psychiatry, Prayer Ministry, Sexuality, Dreams; 2-5 pgs.
>
> **Tips:** "All articles or short stories must relate to healing or Christian witness."

THE JOURNAL OF PASTORAL CARE, 1068 Harbor Dr. SW, Calabash NC 28467. Phone/fax (910)579-5084. E-mail: OrloS@aol.com. Website: www.jpcp.org. Orlo Strunk, Jr., mng ed. For chaplains/pastors/professionals involved with pastoral care and counseling in other than a church setting. Quarterly journal; 116 pgs; circ. 10,000. Subscription $22.50. 80% freelance. Query; phone/fax/e-query OK. **PAYS IN COPIES** for 1st rts. Articles 5,000 wds or 20 pgs (30/yr); book reviews 5 pgs. Responds in 8 wks. Accepts disk. No sidebars. Guidelines (on Website); no copy. (Ads)

> **Poetry:** Accepts 16/yr. Free verse; 5-16 lines. Submit max 3 poems.

Tips: "Readers are highly trained clinically, holding professional degrees in religion/theology. Writers need to be professionals on topics covered."

JOURNAL OF THE AMERICAN SOCIETY FOR CHURCH GROWTH, c/o Dr. Gary L. McIntosh, ed, Talbot School of Theology, 13800 Biola Ave., LaMirada CA 90639. (562)944-0351. Fax (562)906-4502. E-mail: gary_mcintosh@peter.biola.edu. American Society for Church Growth. Dr. Gary L. McIntosh, ed. Targets professors, pastors, denominational executives and seminary students interested in church growth and evangelism. Quarterly journal (3X—fall, winter, spring); 100 pgs; circ 400. Subscription $24. 66% unsolicited freelance; 33% assigned. Complete ms/cover letter; phone/fax/e-query OK. **PAYS IN COPIES** for one-time rts. Not copyrighted. Articles 15 pgs or 4,000-5,000 wds (10/yr); book reviews 750-2,000 wds. Responds in 8-12 wks. Accepts simultaneous submissions & reprints (tell when/where appeared). Prefers disk or e-mail submission (copied into message). No sidebars. Any version. Guidelines (also in journal)/theme list; copy $10.

Tips: "All articles must have a church-growth slant. We're open to new writers at this time."

$LEADERSHIP, 465 Gundersen Dr., Carol Stream IL 60188. (630)260-6200. Fax (630)260-0114. E-mail: LJEditor@LeadershipJournal.net. Website: www.leadershipjournal.net. Christianity Today Intl. Marshall Shelley, ed. Practical help for pastors/church leaders. Quarterly journal; 130 pgs; circ 65,000. Also online edition. Subscription $24.95. 20% unsolicited; 80% assigned. Query or complete ms; fax/e-query OK. Pays $75-375 (.15/wd) on acceptance for 1st rts, rt to reprint & electronic rts. Articles 500-3,000 wds (50/yr). Responds in 3-5 wks. Seasonal 6 mos ahead. Accepts reprints (tell when/where appeared). Accepts disk or e-mail submission (copied into message). Kill fee 50%. Regular sidebars. Prefers NIV or NLT. Guidelines/theme list (also on Website); copy $3. (Ads)

Fillers: Buys 80/yr. Cartoons, short humor; to 150 wds. Pays $25-50.

Columns/Departments: Buys 80/yr. Ideas That Work, 150 wds; To Illustrate (sermon illustrations), 150 wds. Complete ms. Pays $25-50.

Special Needs: Material on prayer-driven churches and ministries to broken people.

Tips: "Tell the story of a real-life experience in church involving pain/redemption and lasting benefit."

**This periodical was #19 on the 2000 Top 50 Christian Publishers list (#16 in 1999, #14 in 1998, #14 in 1996, #27 in 1995, #16 in 1994). 1999 EPA Award of Excellence—Christian Ministries; 1998 EPA Award of Merit—General.

$LET'S WORSHIP, MSN 157, 127 9th Ave. N., Nashville TN 37234. (615)251-2496. Fax (615)251-3609. E-mail: info@lifeway.com. Website: www.lifeway.com. Southern Baptist/LifeWay Christian Resources. Submit to The Editor. Resources for worship leaders: music, drama, litanies, prayers, children's sermons, orders of worship and family worship. Quarterly mag; 100 pgs; circ 7,000. Subscription $62.25. 40% freelance. Complete ms/cover letter; e-query OK. Pays $200 (.055/wd) on acceptance for all or

1st rts. Articles 1,500 wds (50/yr). Responds in 6 wks. Seasonal 1 yr ahead. Accepts reprints rarely (tell when/where appeared). Prefers disk or e-mail submission (attached file). Some sidebars. Prefers NIV. Free guidelines/ theme list/copy.

Tips: "Most open to short dramas, dramatic readings, dramatic monologues/dialogues."

LUTHERAN FORUM, PO Box 327, Delhi NY 13753-0327. (607)746-7511. Fax (607)829-2158. E-mail: dkra/pb@aol.com. American Lutheran Publicity Bureau. Ronald Bagnall, ed. For church leadership—clerical and laity. Quarterly journal; 64 pgs; circ 3,200. 100% freelance. Complete ms/cover letter. **NO PAYMENT.** Articles 1,000-3,000 wds. Responds in 26-32 wks. Accepts simultaneous submissions & reprints. Requires disk. Guidelines; copy for 9x12 SAE/6 stamps. (Ads)

$LUTHERAN PARTNERS, 8765 W. Higgins Rd., Chicago IL 60631-4195. (800)638-3522x2875 or 2884. (773)380-2875. Fax (773)380-2829. E-mail: lpartmag@elca.org or LUTHERAN_PARTNERS@ecunet.org. Website: www. elca.org/dm/lp. Evangelical Lutheran Church in America. Carl E. Linder, ed. To encourage and challenge rostered leaders in the ELCA, including pastors and lay ministers. Bimonthly mag; 48+ pgs; circ 20,000. Subscription $12.50 (free to leaders), $18.75 outside North America. 10-15% unsolicited freelance; 85-90% assigned. Query; phone/fax/e-query OK. Pays $120-170 on publication for one-time rts. Articles 500-2,000 wds (12-15/yr). Responds in 12-16 wks. Seasonal 9 mos ahead. Accepts simultaneous submissions & reprints (tell when/where appeared). Kill fee (rare). Prefers disk or e-mail submission (copied into message). Regular sidebars. Prefers NRSV. Guidelines/theme list (also by e-mail/Website); copy $2/9x12 SAE/5 stamps. (Ads)

Poetry: Buys 6-10/yr. Free verse, traditional: $50-75. Keep concise. Submit max 6-10 poems.

Fillers: Buys 4-5/yr. Cartoons; ideas for parish ministry (called Jottings); to 500 wds; $25.

Special Needs: Book reviews. Query Thelma Megill-Cobbler, Valparaiso University, Dept. of Theology, Valparaiso IN 46383. Uses books predominately from mainline denominational and some evangelical publishers. Payment is copy of book. Youth and family issues, rural and urban ministry issues, men's issues. More articles from women and ethnic authors (especially if ordained or are in official lay ministry leadership roles).

Tips: "Query us with solid idea. Understand Lutheran Christian theology and ELCA congregational life. Be able to see life from a pastor/lay leader's point of view; think leadership. What are parish leaders, both ordained and lay, grappling with now?"

$THE MINISTER'S FAMILY, MSN 166, 127 9th Ave. N., Nashville TN 37234-0166. (615)251-2598. Fax (615)251-5618. E-mail:. ministersfamily@lifeway. com. Southern Baptist. Debbie Whisenant, ed; Dean Richardson, ms asst. A leisure-reading magazine designed to encourage, inspire, inform, and enrich the lives of ministers and their families. Quarterly mag; 50 pgs. Subscription $18.28. 10% freelance. Complete ms/cover letter; no phone/

fax query. Pays per word on acceptance for all rts. Articles 1,600-2,000 wds. Responds in 6-8 wks. Seasonal 6-12 mos ahead. Accepts simultaneous submissions. Prefers disk or e-mail submissions. Regular sidebars. Prefers NIV. Guidelines; copy for 9x12 SAE.

Tips: "Most open to experience-based humor."

$#MINISTRIES TODAY, 600 Rinehart Rd., Lake Mary FL 32746. (407)333-0600. Fax (407)333-7133. E-mail: lkeefauv@strang.com. Website: www.ministriestoday.com. Strang Communications. Larry Keefauver, ed; Bill Shepson, mng. ed.; Adrienne Gaines, review ed. Helps for pastors and church leaders primarily in Pentecostal/charismatic churches. Bimonthly mag; 90 pgs; circ 30,000. Subscription $24.95. 60-80% freelance. Query; fax/e-query OK. Pays $50 or $500-800 on publication for all rts. Articles 2,000-2,500 wds (25/yr); book/music/video reviews, 300 wds, $25. Responds in 4 wks. Prefers disk. Kill fee. Regular sidebars. Prefers NIV. Guidelines; copy $4/9x12 SAE. (Ads)

Columns/Departments: Buys 36/yr.

Tips: "Most open to columns. Write for guidelines and study the magazine."

MINISTRY & LITURGY, 160 E. Virginia St., #290, San Jose CA 95112. (408)286-8505. Fax (408)287-8748. E-mail: mleditor@rpinet.com. Website: www.rpinet.com/ml. Resource Publications, Inc. Nick Wagner, ed dir. To help liturgists and ministers make the imaginative connection between liturgy and life. Monthly (10X) mag; 50 pgs; circ 20,000. Subscription $45. Query only; fax/e-query OK. **PAYS IN COPIES & SUBSCRIPTION** on publication for 1st rts. Articles 1,000 wds (30/yr). Responds in 4 wks. Seasonal 6 mos ahead. Accepts reprints (tell when/where appeared). Requires disk. Regular sidebars. Guidelines/theme list; copy $4/11x14 SAE/2stamps. (Ads)

Contest: Visual Arts Awards.

$MINISTRY MAGAZINE: International Journal for Pastors, 12501 Old Columbia Pike, Silver Spring MD 20904. (301)680-6510. Fax (301)680-6502. E-mail: norcott@gc.adventist.org. Website: www.ministerialassociation.com. Seventh-Day Adventist. Willmore D. Eva, ed; Julia W. Norcott, asst ed. For Pastors. Monthly journal; 32 pgs.; circ 20,000. Subscription $29.95. 90% freelance. Query; fax/e-query OK. Pays $50-150 on acceptance for all rts. Articles 1,000-1,500 wds; book reviews 100-150 wds ($25). Responds in 2-3 wks. Prefers disk. Some sidebars. Guidelines/theme list; copy for 9x12 SAE/5 stamps. (Ads)

$*NATIONAL DRAMA SERVICE, MSN 170, 127 Ninth Ave. N., MSN 158, Nashville TN 37234. (615)251-5045. Fax (615)251-2614. E-mail: Christy_M_Haines@compuserve.com, or churchdrama@earthlink.net. Website: www.lifeway.com. Southern Baptist. Christy Haines, ed. Conservative, evangelical dramas for stage, street and sanctuary. Drama, puppets, clowns, mime, movement, comedy, seeker-oriented, dramatic worship service plans. Quarterly script collections; 48 pages; 5,000 subscription base. 100% freelance. Complete ms/cover letter. Pays about $25/published page. Scripts 5-7 minutes in length. No one-acts, full length or musicals. Responds in 10 wks. Seasonal 9 mos ahead. Accepts simultaneous submissions. Guidelines.

$THE NEWSLETTER NEWSLETTER, 4150 Belden Village St. 4th Floor, Canton OH 44718. (330)493-7880. Fax (330)493-7897. E-mail: jburns@comresources. com. Communication Resources. John Burns, ed. To help church secretaries and church newsletter editors prepare their newsletter. Monthly newsletter; 14 pgs. Subscription $44.95. 30% freelance. Complete ms. Pays $50-150 on acceptance for all rts. Articles 800-1,000 wds (8/yr). Responds in 4 wks. Seasonal 8 mos ahead. Accepts simultaneous submissions. Requires disk; accepts e-mail submission. Kill fee. Regular sidebars. Copy for 9x12 SAE/3 stamps.

$PARISH LITURGY, 16565 S. State St., South Holland IL 60473. (708)331-5485. Fax (708)331-5484. E-mail: acp@acpress.org. Website: www.acpress. org. Catholic. Father Michael Gilligan, ed dir. A planning tool for Sunday and Holyday liturgy. Quarterly mag; 32 pgs; circ 22,000. Subscription $24. 10% freelance. Query; no phone/e-query. All rts. Articles 400 wds. Responds in 4 wks. Seasonal 4 mos ahead. Accepts simultaneous submissions & reprints (tell when/where appeared). Some sidebars. Prefers NAB. No guidelines; copy available. (No ads)

$PASTORAL LIFE, PO Box 595, Canfield OH 44406-0595. (330)533-5503. Fax (330)533-1076. E-mail: paultheapostle@msn.com. Website: www. albahouse.org. Catholic. Rev. Matthew Roehig, ed.; submit to Bro. Joshua Seidl, SSP. Focuses on the current problems, needs, issues and all important activities related to all phases of pastoral work and life. Monthly (11X) mag; 64 pgs; circ 2,000. Subscription $17. 75% unsolicited freelance; 25% assigned. Query; e-query OK. Pays .04/wd on publication for 1st rts. Not copyrighted. Articles to 3,500 wds (150/yr); fiction 3,500 wds (2/yr). Responds in 4 wks. Seasonal 3-4 mos ahead. Accepts reprints (tell when/where appeared). Prefers e-mail submissions (attached file). No kill fee. Some sidebars. Prefers NAB. Guidelines/theme list (also by e-mail); free copy. (Ads)

  Poetry: Buys up to 15/yr. Any type. Pays .04/word or no payment. Submit max 4 poems.

  Fillers: Buys up to 24/yr. Anecdotes, facts, ideas, jokes, party ideas, prayers, prose, and short humor, to 30 wds. No payment.

  Special Needs: Inculuration and minority issues; articles and reflections. Fiction for ages 13 and up.

  Tips: "Research your work, check our guidelines, and be of use to pastors. We feature pastoral homilies for Sundays and Holydays. Articles should be eminently pastoral in approach and content."

+THE PASTOR'S FRIEND. E-mail: editor@pastors.com. Rick Warren and Jon Walker, eds. A free e-mail newsletter for pastors. Circ. 40,000+. E-query OK. No payment.

  Special Needs: Time management, conflict resolution, facilitating change, communication and preaching, stewardship, worship, lay ministry, temptation, spiritual vitality, family matters, finances, creative ideas for ministry, vision, power, and authority.

PLUGGED IN, 8605 Explorer Dr., Colorado Springs CO 80920. (719)531-3400. Fax (719)531-3347. E-mail: waliszrs@fotf.org. Website: www.family.

org/pluggedin. Focus on the Family. Bob Smithouser, ed; Steven Isaac, assoc ed. Helping parents and youth leaders guide teens through the world of popular youth culture. Monthly newsletter; 12 pgs; circ 53,300. Subscription $20. Freelance OK. Query. **NO PAYMENT**. No guidelines. Not in topical listings. (No ads)

> **1999 EPA Award of Merit—Newsletter; 1998 EPA Award of Excellence—Newsletter.

$PRAY! PO Box 35004, Colorado Springs CO 80935-3504. (719)548-9222. Fax (719)598-7128. E-mail: pray.mag@navpress.com. Website: www.praymag.com. Jonathan L. Graf, ed.; submit to Sandie Higley, ed. asst. A magazine entirely about prayer, geared toward intercessors and prayer mobilizers (pastors and leaders who encourage prayer). Bimonthly mag; 40-48 pgs; circ 35,000. Subscription $19.97. 75% unsolicited freelance; 25% assigned. Query or complete ms/cover letter; fax/e-query OK. Pays .10/wd (.05/wd for reprints) on acceptance for 1st, reprint & electronic rts. Articles 600-1,500 wds (30/yr). Responds in 12-16 wks. Accepts simultaneous submissions & reprints (tell when/where appeared). Accepts disk or e-mail submission (copied into message). Kill fee 50%. Regular sidebars. Prefers NIV. Guidelines (also by e-mail/Website); copy for 9x12 SAE/6 stamps. (Ads)

> **Fillers:** Ideas on prayer; 75-500 wds. Pays $20.

> **Special Needs:** Starting an 8-page section just for pastors, so needs articles for pastors, written by pastors. Also needs non-theme feature articles on various aspects of prayer. New: *PrayKids!* insert.

> **Tips:** "We most frequently purchase short material for our Ideas section. If you submit a general article it better be unique. Most of our theme articles are assigned."

> **This periodical was #28 on the 2000 Top 50 Christian Publishers list (#22 in 1999, #31 in 1998).

$PREACHER'S ILLUSTRATION SERVICE, Box 3102, Margate NJ 08402. (609)822-9401. Fax (609)822-1638. E-mail: sermons@voicings.com. Website: www.voicings.com. Voicings Duplications. James Colaianni, pub. Sermon illustration resource for professional clergy. Bimonthly loose-leaf booklet, 16 pgs. Subscription $37.50. 5% unsolicited freelance; 0% assigned. Complete ms; e-query OK. Pays .15/wd on publication for any rts. Illustrations/anecdotes 50-250 wds. Responds in 6 wks. Seasonal 4 mos ahead. Accepts reprints. Prefers disk or e-mail submissions. Guidelines/topical index (also by e-mail); copy for 9x12 SAE. (Ads)

> **Poetry:** Light verse, traditional; 50-250 lines; .15/wd. Submit max 3 poems.

> **Fillers:** Various; sermon illustrations; 50-250 wds; .15/wd.

> **Tips:** "All sections open."

$PREACHING, PO Box 369, Jackson TN 38302-0369. (901)668-9948. Fax (901)668-9633. E-mail: preaching@compuserve.com. Website: www.preaching.com. Preaching Resources, Inc. Dr. Michael Duduit, ed; submit to Jonathan Kever, mng ed. Professional magazine for evangelical preachers; focus is on preaching and worship leadership. Bimonthly & online mag; 64 pgs; circ 9,200. Subscription $29.95. 40% unsolicited freelance; 60% assigned. Query or complete ms/cover letter; fax/e-query OK. Pays $35-50 on publication for 1st rts. Articles 1,000-2,000 wds (8-24/yr). Responds in 18 wks. Seasonal 1 yr ahead. Prefers disk. Regular sidebars. Prefers NIV. Some sidebars. Guidelines; copy $3.50. (Ads)

Fillers: Buys 10-15/yr. Cartoons only; $25.

Tips: "Need how-to articles about specific areas of preaching and worship leadership. We only accept articles from pastors or seminary/college faculty."

$THE PRIEST, 200 Noll Plaza, Huntington IN 46750-4304. (219)356-8400. Fax (219)359-0029. E-mail: tpriest@osv.com. Website: www.osv.com. Catholic/Our Sunday Visitor, Inc. Msgr. Owen F. Campion, ed. For Catholic priests, deacons and seminarians; to help in all aspects of ministry. Monthly jour.; 48 pgs; circ 8,000. Subscription $39.95. 80% unsolicited freelance. Query or complete ms/cover letter; phone/fax/e-query OK. Pays $175-250 on acceptance for 1st rts. Articles to 1,500-5,000 wds (96/yr); some 2-parts. Responds in 10-12 wks. Seasonal 6 mos ahead. Some sidebars. Prefers e-mail submissions (attached file). Prefers NAB. Free guidelines; copy for 9x12 SASE. (Ads)

Fillers: Murray Hubley. Cartoons; $35.

Columns/Departments: Buys 36/yr. Viewpoint (about priests or the church), under 1,000 wds, $50. Complete ms.

Tips: "Write to the point, with interest. Most open to nuts and bolts issues for priests, or features. Keep the audience in mind; need articles or topics important to priests and parish life. Include Social Security number."

**This periodical was #43 on the 2000 Top 50 Christian Publishers list (#49 in 1999, #57 in 1998, #62 in 1994).

$#PROCLAIM, 127 Ninth Ave. N., Nashville TN 37234-0157. (615)251-3837. Fax (615)251-3609. E-mail: Rhodge@lifeway.com.Website: www.lifeway.com. Lifeway Christian Resources of the Southern Baptist Convention. Dr. Ralph Hodge, design ed. Strives to provide quality sermons and preaching resources for biblical preachers. Quarterly mag; 50 pgs; circ 16,000. Subscription $12.80. 20% unsolicited freelance; 80% assigned. Complete ms/cover letter; phone/fax/e-query OK. Pays .065/wd (to $200) on acceptance for all rts. Articles 1,500-3,500 wds; reviews 300 wds, pays $50. Responds in 2 wks. Prefers disk or e-mail submissions (attached file). Some sidebars. Guidelines (also by e-mail); copy for 10x13 SAE. (No ads)

Poetry: Buys 5/yr. Avante-garde, traditional; pays $50-200. Submit max 10 poems.

Fillers: Anecdotes, cartoons, facts, ideas, prayers, prose, quotes. Pays $20-50.

Columns/Departments: Send complete ms.

Special Needs: Sermons, sermon outlines, and sermon series ideas.

Tips: "Query by e-mail with an idea as response to specific need expressed by editor. E-mail is best communication method."

**This periodical was #68 on the 1994 Top 50 Christian Publishers list.

PULPIT HELPS, 6815 Shallowford Rd, Chattanooga TN 37421. (800)251-7206. (423)894-6060. Fax (423)570-8074. E-mail: publisher@pulpithelps.

com. Website: www.pulpithelps.com. AMG International. Bob Dasal, ed-in-chief. To help evangelical preachers and serious students of the Bible. Monthly tabloid; 36 pgs; circ 75,000. Subscription $19.99. 25% unsolicited freelance; 75% assigned. Query; e-query OK. **NO PAYMENT.** Articles to 700-900 wds (60-80/yr); book reviews 400 wds. Responds in 4 wks. Seasonal 4 mos ahead. Accepts simultaneous submissions & reprints (tell when/where appeared). Accepts e-mail submission (attached or copied into message). Some sidebars. Prefers KJV. Guidelines/theme list (also by e-mail); copy for 9x12 SAE/2 stamps. (Ads)

   Poetry: Accepts 10-12/yr. Traditional; short. Submit max 3 poems.

   Fillers: Ted Kyle, mng ed. Accepts 10-20/yr. Anecdotes, cartoons, prose; quotes, short humor, word puzzles; 300-500 wds.

   Columns/Departments: Ted Kyle, mng ed. Family Helps, 100-1,000 wds; Illustrations (for sermons), 50-100 wds; Sermon Starters (brief).

   Tips: "Most open to Illustrations & Sermon Starters—short, pointed anecdotes/articles preachers can use as illustrations."

QUARTERLY REVIEW: A Journal of Theological Resources for Ministry, 1001 19th Ave. S., PO Box 340007, Nashville TN 37203-0007. (615)340-7334. Fax (615) 340-7048. E-mail: hpieterse@gbhem.org. Website: www.quarterlyreview.org. United Methodist. Dr. Hendrik R. Pieterse, ed. A theological approach to subjects of interest to clergy—Scripture study, ethics, and practice of ministry in Wesleyan tradition. Quarterly journal; 112 pgs; circ 1,100. Subscription $24. 20% unsolicited; 80% assigned. Complete ms/cover letter; phone/fax/e-query OK. **PAYS IN COPIES** for 1st rts. Articles to 5,000 wds (20/yr); book reviews to 1,000 wds. Responds in 6-8 wks. Seasonal 8 mos ahead. Prefers disk, no e-mail submission. No sidebars. Prefers NRSV. Guidelines/theme list (also by e-mail); copy for 9x12 SAE/$2 postage. (No ads)

   Tips: "A section called 'Outside the Theme' is reserved for articles of high quality unrelated to the theme of the issue. I often consider unsolicited manuscripts for this section. We look for writers who have strong academic/theological training and whose work addresses concerns and interests of those in ministry. Awareness of current scholarly literature, a well-developed argument, and clear expository prose are essential."

REACHING CHILDREN AT RISK, PO Box 633, Oxford OX2 OXZ, United Kingdom. Phone + 44 1865 450 800. Fax + 44 1865 203 567. E-mail: RCAR@viva.org. Website: www.viva.org. The Viva Network. Sarah O'Connor, ed. God-centered, child-focused, relational development for those working with children in especially difficult circumstances or at high social risk. Triannual journal; 32 pgs; circ 2,000 in 40 nations. Subscription $3.75/copy. 95% freelance. Query; phone/e-query OK. **PAYS IN COPIES.** Articles 500-1,000 wds. Accepts disk or e-mail submission. Regular sidebars. Prefers NIV. Guidelines/theme list (also by e-mail); copy $3.75. (Ads)

   Special Needs: This is a specialist publication with an ethos of Christian values and principles tailored to the unique challenges which children's workers face today. It serves to promote a common excellence in child care, and to provide skills training, practical models, creative solutions and access to a spectrum of resources.

Tips: "New writers welcome. Submissions negotiated in advance with the editor, according to theme of issue and requirements. Quality with simplicity needed, sensitive to the international and multicultural readership. All items must be in keeping with our aims and ethos."

$REFORMED WORSHIP, 2850 Kalamazoo SE, Grand Rapids MI 49560-0001. (616)224-0785. Fax (616)224-0834. E-mail: info@reformedworship.org. Website: www.reformedworship.org. Christian Reformed Church in North America. Dr. Emily R. Brink, ed. To provide liturgical and musical resources for pastors, church musicians, and other worship leaders. Quarterly mag; 48 pgs; circ 4,500. Subscription $23.95. 10% unsolicited freelance; 70% assigned. Query or complete ms/cover letter; e-query OK. Pays .05/wd on publication for all rts (negotiable). Articles 2,000 wds; book reviews 250 wds, $25. Responds in 4 wks. Seasonal 6 mos ahead. Rarely accepts reprints (tell when/where appeared). Kill fee 50%. Prefers e-mail submission (copied into message). Regular sidebars. Prefers NIV or NRSV. Guidelines/theme list (also by e-mail); copy for 9x12 SAE/$2 postage. (No ads)

Fillers: Buys 4-5/yr. Cartoons, prayers; $20-50.

Columns/Departments: View From the Pew (humorous or reflective vignettes on worship experiences), 1,000-1,500 wds.

Tips: "You need to understand the Reformed tradition of worship."
**1997 EPA Award of Excellence—Christian Ministries.

$RESOURCE: The National Leadership Magazine, 2450 Milltower Ct., Mississauga ON L5N 5Z6 Canada. (905)542-7400. Fax (905)542-7313. E-mail: resource@paoc.org. Website: www.paoc.org. Pentecostal Assemblies of Canada. Michael Horban, ed. For church leadership; practical how-tos on leadership issues. Quarterly mag; 32 pgs; circ 8,000. Subscription $20. 80% unsolicited freelance; 20% assigned. Query only; fax/e-query OK. Pays $30-50 on publication for all rts. Articles 500-1,200 wds (8-10/yr); book reviews 250 wds, $20. Responds in 4-6 wks. Seasonal 3 mos ahead. Accepts reprints. Prefers disk or e-mail submission (copied into message). Regular sidebars. Prefers NIV. Guidelines/theme list; copy $2/9x12 SAE. (Ads)

Fillers: Buys 4-8/yr. Anecdotes, cartoons, short humor; 200-300 wds; $20-30.

Tips: "Say something positive to leaders that stretches and enriches them. We prefer e-mail queries."

$REV., 1515 Cascade Ave., Loveland CO 80538. (970)669-3836. Fax (970) 6679-9392. E-mail: Rector@Rev-magazine.com. Website: www.onlinerev. com. Group Publishing, Inc. Paul Allen, ed. For pastors; practical. Bimonthly mag; 104 pgs; circ 25,000. 60% unsolicited freelance; 40% assigned. Query or complete ms/cover letter; fax/e-query OK. Pays $300-400 on acceptance for all rts. Articles 1,500-2,000 wds. Responds in 4-8 wks. Seasonal 5 mos ahead. Prefers disk or e-mail submission (attached file). Regular sidebars. Guidelines (also on Website); copy $2/9x12 SAE/5 stamps. (Ads)

Fillers: Buys 5-10/yr. Cartoons, ideas, sermon illustrations. Pays $30-50.

Columns/Departments: Family Ministry, Effective Outreach, Worship Experience, Preaching & Teaching, Practical Discipleship, Team Work (staff & lay leaders), Church Biz (leadership & administration), Personal Growth, Home Front (pastor's family issues), all 250-350 wds. Pays $35-50.

Tips: "We are most open to short (250 word) practical articles for our departments."

$REVIEW FOR RELIGIOUS, 3601 Lindell Blvd., Rm. 428, St. Louis MO 63108-3393. (314)977-7363. Fax (314)977-7362. E-mail: foppema@slu. edu. Website: www.reviewforreligious.org. Catholic/Jesuits of Missouri Province. Rev. David L. Fleming, S.J., ed. A forum for shared reflection on the lives and experience of all who find that the church's rich heritages of spirituality support their personal and apostolic Christian lives. Bimonthly mag; 112 pgs; circ 8,000. Subscription $24. 100% unsolicited freelance. Complete ms/cover letter; no phone/fax/e-query. Pays $6/pg on publication for 1st rts. Articles 1,500-5,000 wds (50/yr). Responds in 9 wks. Seasonal 8 mos ahead. Accepts disk. No sidebars. Prefers RSV or NAB. Guidelines; copy for 10x13 SAE/5 stamps. (No ads)

Poetry: Buys 10/yr. Light verse, traditional; 3-12 lines; $6. Submit max 4 poems.

Tips: "Be familiar with at least three past issues. Submit an article based on our guidelines."

$SABBATH SCHOOL LEADERSHIP, 55 W. Oak Ridge Dr., Hagerstown MD 21740. (301)393-4095. Fax (301)393-4055. E-mail: fcrumbly@rhpa.org. Website: www.Sabbathschoolleadership.com. Faith Crumbly, ed. Denominational; nurtures, educates and supports adult Sabbath school leaders by providing program helps, resources, instructional material, and networking opportunities. 5% unsolicited freelance; 25% assigned. Complete ms; e-query OK. Pays on publication (on acceptance for solicited material) for 1st rts. Articles 70-800 wds. Responds in 6-8 wks. Seasonal 4-6 mos ahead. Requires disk. Guidelines/theme list; copy. (For ads, contact: Genia Blumenberg at gblumenberg@rhpa.org)

$SERMON NOTES (formerly Ministry Now), 1420 Osborne St., Ste. 10, Humboldt TN 38343. (901)784-9239. Fax (901)784-7469. E-mail: stevemay@sermonnotes.com. Website: www.sermonnotes.com. Alderson Press. Stephen May, ed. Sermon helps for ministers. Quarterly & online mag; 96 pgs; circ 5,000. Subscription $39. 25% freelance. Complete ms/cover letter; fax/e-query OK. Pays $35-50 for articles & sermons ($5 for illustrations) on publication for one-time rts. Sermons & articles (8/yr) 1,500 wds; illustrations 80-100 wds; book reviews 500 wds ($20). Responds in 5 wks. Seasonal 4 mos ahead. Accepts reprints (tell when/where appeared). Prefers disk. Regular sidebars. Prefers NIV. Guidelines/theme list; copy $2/6x9 SAE. (Ads)

Fillers: Buys 12/yr. Cartoons, short humor or church newsletter ideas. Pays $15.

Columns/Departments: Buys 6/yr. Q & A (interview with Christian leader), 1,000-1,500 wds; Pastor's Library (book or product review), 500 wds. Pays $35-50.

Tips: "We are always interested in sermons. Right now we have an even greater interest in articles about church growth, preaching, or about a particular minister who is pastoring a growing church of any size." Also publishes on diskette.

+SEWANEE THEOLOGICAL REVIEW, University of the South, 335 Tennessee Ave., Sewanee TN 37383-0001. (931)598-1475. E-mail: jjones@ sewanee.edu. Website: www.sewanee.edu/Theology/str. Anglican/Episcopal. Rev. Christopher Bryan, ed. For Anglican/Episcopal clergy. Quarterly jour.; 120 pgs. Subscription $19. Accepts freelance. Complete ms/cover letter; e-query OK. **NO PAYMENT** for all rts. Articles (20/yr). Responds in 2-6 mos. Seasonal 24 mos ahead. No simultaneous submissions or reprints. Prefers disk or e-mail submissions (attached file). Prefers NRSV. No guidelines; copy $2. Incomplete topical listings.

Special Needs: Anglican and Episcopal history/doctrine/ethics.

SHARING THE PRACTICE, 8919 Clemsonville Rd., Union Bridge MD 21791-7413. (301)694-6338. E-mail: darryl.zoller@juno.com Website: www. apclergy.org. Academy of Parish Clergy/Ecumenical/Interfaith. Rev. Darryl Zoller, ed-in-chief. Growth toward excellence through sharing the practice of parish ministry. Quarterly international journal; 32 pages; circ 350 (includes 100 seminary libraries). Subscription $25/yr. (send to: APC, 1295 Thicket Ct., Columbus IN 47201-9713). 100% unsolicited freelance. Complete ms/cover letter; phone/e-query OK. PAYS IN COPIES for 1st, reprint, simultaneous or electronic rts. Articles 500-2500 words (25/yr); reviews 200 wds. Responds in 2 wks. Seasonal 6 mos ahead. Accepts simultaneous submissions & reprints (tell when/where appeared). Prefers e-mail submissions (copied into message). Some sidebars. Prefers NRSV or NIV. Guidelines/theme list (also by e-mail); copy/9X12 SAE/4 stamps. (Ads)

Poetry: Accepts 12/yr. Any type; 25-35 lines. Submit max 2 poems.

Fillers: Accepts 6/yr. Anecdotes, cartoons, jokes, short humor; 50-100 wds.

Contest: Book of the Year Award ($100+), Top Ten Books of the Year list, Parish Pastor of the Year award ($200+). Inquire by e-mail to: DIELPADRE@aol.com.

Tips: "We desire articles and poetry by practicing clergy of all kinds who wish to share their practice of ministry. For 2001, we especially desire articles on healthy churches and healthy pastors."

#SINGLE ADULT MINISTRIES JOURNAL, PO Box 2739, El Granada CA 94018-2739. Cook Communications Ministries. Terry Fisher, ed. For pastors and lay leaders involved in ministry with single adults. Bimonthly journal; 32 pgs; circ 3,000. Subscription $24. 10% freelance. Query; fax/e-query OK. **USUALLY NO PAYMENT** for 1st rts. Articles 200-2,500 wds (2/yr); book reviews 50-300 wds/$15-75. Responds in 4 wks. Seasonal 1 yr ahead. Accepts simultaneous submissions & reprints (tell when/where appeared). Prefers e-mail submission (copied into message). Regular sidebars. Prefers NIV. Theme list; copy for 9x12 SAE/4 stamps. (Ads)

Fillers: Buys 0-5/yr. Facts, newsbreaks, quotes; 25-200 wds; $10-50.

Tips: "Write to the pastor or leader, not to singles themselves. Interview singles or the leaders who work with them. Want very practical, how-to or 600-word essay on a controversial topic of interest to single adult leaders."

$SMALL GROUP DYNAMICS, PO Box 621, Zionville IN 46077. (317)733-0945. E-mail: dlentz@smallgroups.com. Website: smallgroups.com. Small Group Network. Dan Lentz, owner. How-to for small groups. Online newsletter. Query; e-query OK. Pays $20-50 for one-time rts. Articles 500-1,000 wds. Seasonal 2-3 mos ahead. Prefers disk or e-mail submission (attached file). Accepts reprints. Prefers NIV. Guidelines/theme list. Incomplete topical listings. (Ads)

Fillers: Small group cartoons.

Special Needs: Brief testimonies of how God has worked in your group; humor in groups; ice-breaker ideas, etc.

Tips: "Follow our themes. We use mostly practical, how-to oriented articles."

$SUNDAY SERMONS, PO Box 3102, Margate NJ 08402. (609)822-9401. Fax (609)822-1638. E-mail: sermons@voicings.com. Website: www.voicings.com. Voicings Duplications/Ecumenical. J. Colaianni, ed-in-chief. Full-text sermon resource for clergy. Bimonthly bound workbook; 54-60 pgs. 5% freelance. Pays on publication for all rts. Responds in 6 wks. Seasonal 6 mos ahead. Accepts reprints. Prefers disk. Guidelines/theme list; copy for 9x12 SAE. Not in topical listings.

Tips: "Sermons must include several relevant illustrations."

$+TEAM NYI MAGAZINE, 6401 The Paseo, Kansas City MO 64131. E-mail: TeamNYI@nazarene.org. Standard Publishing. Edie MacPhearson, ed. To train, equip and encourage professional and lay Christian youth workers. Quarterly mag. Open to freelance. Prefers e-query. Pays $75-100. Articles 1,000-1,500 wds.

Fillers: Prose fillers to 300 wds. Pays $25-35.

TECHNOLOGIES FOR WORSHIP, PO Box 35, Aurora ON L4G 3H1 Canada. (905)830-4300. Fax (905)853-5096. E-mail: amip@inforamp.net. Website: www.tfwm.com. TWM Media. Kevin Rogers Cobus, ed. Bimonthly & on-line mag; 68-72 pgs; circ 20,000. Subscription $29.95. 100% unsolicited freelance. Query; phone/fax/e-query OK. **NO PAYMENT** for one-time rts. Articles 700-1,200 wds. Responds in 2 wks. Seasonal 2 mos ahead. Accepts simultaneous submissions & reprints (tell when/where appeared). Prefers e-mail submissions (attached or copied into message). Some sidebars. Free guidelines/theme list (also on Website)/copy. (Ads)

Special Needs: Website streaming resources for churches and ministries; technologies: audio, video, music, computers, broadcast, lighting, and drama; 750-2,500 wds.

Tips: Call/fax/e-mail the editor to discuss idea for article or column. Should know a lot about today's technologies and be willing to contribute an educational editorial.

$THEOLOGY TODAY, PO Box 29, Princeton NJ 08542. (609)497-7714. Fax (609)497-7870. E-mail: theology.today@ptsem.edu. Submit to The Editor.

Explores key issues, current thoughts and trends in the fields of religion and theology. Quarterly journal; 144-160 pgs; circ 14,000. Subscription $24. Little unsolicited accepted. Complete ms/cover letter and disk; phone query OK. Pays to $250 on publication for all rts. Articles 13-17 manuscript pgs; book reviews 500-750 wds. Responds in several wks. Seasonal 1 yr ahead. No disk. Regular sidebars. Guidelines; free copy. (Display ads)

Poetry: Buys 12/yr. Free verse, traditional; $50. Submit max 5 poems.

Tips: "We rarely accept unsolicited material, but do look for new talent. The best route to acceptance is strong familiarity with the journal and types of articles we publish. We expect inclusive language."

$TODAY'S CHRISTIAN PREACHER, 3 Park Plaza, Wyomissing PA 19610-1399. (610)913-0796. Fax (610)913-0797. E-mail: tcpubs@mkpt.com. Marketing Partners. Jerry Thacker, ed. To provide material on current topics to help preachers in their personal lives. Quarterly mag; 20 pgs; circ 25,000. Subscription free. 20% unsolicited freelance; 80% assigned. Complete ms/cover letter; fax/e-query OK. Pays $150 on publication for one-time or simultaneous rts. Articles 800-1,000 wds (10-15/yr). Responds in 6-8 wks. Seasonal 1 yr ahead. Accepts simultaneous submissions & reprints (tell when/where appeared). Prefers disk. Regular sidebars. Requires KJV. Guidelines (also by e-mail); copy for 9x12 SAE/3 stamps. (Ads)

$*TODAY'S PARISH, Box 180, Mystic CT 06355. (860)536-2611. Fax (860) 572-0788. E-mail: ttpubsedit@aol.com. Catholic. Daniel Connors, ed. Practical ideas and issues relating to parish life, management and ministry. Mag published 7X/yr; 40 pgs; circ 14,800. Subscription $22.95. 25% freelance. Query or complete ms. Pays $75-100 on publication for 1st rts. Articles 800-1,800 wds (15/yr). Responds 13 wks. Seasonal 6 mos ahead. Guidelines; copy for 9x12 SASE.

$WCA NEWS, PO Box 3188, Barrington IL 60011-5046. (847)765-0070. Fax (847)765-5046. E-mail: BraoudaP@willowcreek.org. Website: www.willowcreek.com. Willow Creek Assn. Paul Braoudakis, mng ed. For church leaders who are willing to take risks for the sake of the gospel. Bimonthly & online newsletter; 16-20 pgs; circ 10,000. Subscription $39. 10% unsolicited; 90% assigned. Query/clips; phone/fax/e-query OK. Pays $25 on publication for all rts. Articles 500-1,000 wds; book/music reviews 500 wds, video reviews 300 wds. Responds in 2 wks. Seasonal 2 mos ahead. Accepts simultaneous submissions & reprints (tell when/where appeared). Requires disk or e-mail submission (attached file). Some sidebars. Prefers NIV. Guidelines (also by e-mail/Website); free copy. (No ads)

Fillers: Accepts many. Cartoons, ideas, short humor; 50-75 wds. Pays $10.

Columns/Departments: News From the Frontlines (creative ministries within the church), 50-100 wds; Strategic Trends (trends from growing churches), 200-250 wds. Pays $10-25. Complete ms.

Tips: "Submit articles that will help other churches do what they do better. Any articles that pertain to doing a seeker-sensitive type of ministry will be considered. Also leadership issues in the church, outreach ideas, and effective evangelism."

$*WORD & WORLD: Theology for Christian Ministry, 2481 Como Ave., St. Paul MN 55108. (651)641-3482. Fax (651)641-3354. E.L.C.A./Luther Northwestern Theological Seminary. Frederick J. Gaiser, ed. Addresses ecclesiastical and secular issues from a theological perspective and addresses pastors and church leaders with the best fruits of theological research. Quarterly journal; 104 pgs; circ 3,100. Subscription $18. 10% freelance. Complete ms/cover letter; phone query OK. Pays $50 on publication for all rts. Articles 5,000-6,000 wds. Responds in 2-8 wks. Guidelines/theme list; copy $5.

> **Tips:** "Most open to general articles. We look for serious theology addressed clearly and interestingly to people in the practice of ministry. Creativity and usefulness in ministry are highly valued."

$WORSHIP LEADER, 104 Woodmont Blvd, 3rd Fl., Nashville TN 37205. (615)386-3011. Fax (615)385-4112. E-mail: ddisabatino@ccmcom.com. Website: www.worshipleader.org. CCM Communications. David Di Sabatino, mng ed. A planning resource for all those involved in church worship. Bimonthly mag; 48-64 pgs; circ 43,000. Subscription $19.95. 40% unsolicited freelance; 60% assigned. Query or complete ms/cover letter; phone/fax/e-query OK. Pays .25/wd ($400-500) on publication for all rts. Articles 2,000 wds (20/yr); reviews 300 wds. Responds in 6-8 wks. Seasonal 6-8 mos ahead. Kill fee 25%. Accepts e-mail submissions (attached file—MS Word). Kill fee 25%. Some sidebars. Prefers NIV. Guidelines/theme list (also by e-mail). (Ads)

> **Columns/Departments:** Managing Change (how worship leader has dealt with change or conflict), 800 wds.

> **Tips:** "Read our magazine. Become familiar with our themes. Submit a detailed and well-thought-out idea that fits our vision."

$YOUR CHURCH, 465 Gundersen Dr., Carol Stream IL 60188. (630)260-6200. Fax (630)260-0114. E-mail: YCEditor@aol.com. Website: www. christianity.net/yc. Christianity Today Intl. Phyllis Ten Elshof, ed. Focuses on church business/administration, purchasing and facilities management. Bimonthly mag; 80+ pgs; circ 150,000. Subscription free to church administrators. 10% unsolicited freelance; 90% assigned. Query or complete ms/cover letter; fax/e-query OK. Query for electronic submissions. Pays $100 & up on acceptance for 1st rts. Articles 1,000-1,500 wds (60/yr). Responds in 2-4 wks. Seasonal 6 mos ahead. Accepts reprints (tell when/where appeared). Prefers e-mail submission (copied into message). Kill fee 50%. Regular sidebars. Prefers NIV. Guidelines/theme list; copy for $1 postage. (Ads)

> **Fillers:** Cartoons, $125.

> **Columns/Departments:** Query. Pays $100.

> **Special Needs:** Church management articles; audio/visual equipment; books/curriculum resources; music equipment; church products; furnishings; office equipment; computers/software.

Tips: "Almost all articles are assigned to writers with expertise in a certain area. Write and ask for an assignment; tell your strengths, interests and background."

**This periodical was #48 on the 2000 Top 50 Christian Publishers list (#37 in 1999, #25 in 1998, #42 in 1997).

\$YOUTHWORKER: The Contemporary Journal for Youth Ministry, 104 Woodmont Blvd. 3rd Fl., Nashville TN 37205. (615)386-3011. Fax (615) 385-4112. E-mail: Will@YouthSpecialties.com, or YS@YouthSpecialties. com. Website: www.Youthworker.com. Salem Communications. Will Penner, ed. For youth workers/church and parachurch. Bimonthly & online journal; 72 pgs; circ 20,000. Subscription \$39.95. 80% freelance. Query or complete ms (only if already written); e-query preferred. Pays \$200-300 on acceptance for 1st rts. Articles 2,000-3,500 wds (30/yr). Responds in 8 wks. Seasonal 10 mos ahead. No reprints. Kill fee \$50. Guidelines/theme list (also by e-mail: Roni@YouthSpecialties.com); copy \$3/ 10x13 SAE. (Ads)

> **Columns/Departments:** Buys 10/yr. Parachurch Perspective; Junior High Ministry; Family Ministry; On Volunteers; What's On My Mind; 1,500 wds; pays \$200.
>
> **Tips:** "Read *Youthworker;* imbibe its tone (professional, though not academic; conversational, though not chatty). Query me with specific, focused ideas that conform to our editorial style. It helps if the writer is a youth minister, but it's not required. Check *Youthworker* Website for additional info, upcoming themes, etc."
>
> **This periodical was #60 on the 2000 Top 50 Christian Publishers list (#38 in 1999, #59 in 1998, #60 in 1997, #46 in 1995, #53 in 1994). 1998 & 1999 EPA Award of Merit—Christian Ministries.

TEEN/YOUNG ADULT MARKETS

BEAUTIFUL CHRISTIAN TEEN, #7 Bergoo Rd., Webster Springs WV 26288. (304)847-7537. Fax (304)847-7552. E-mail: kimwolfe@access.mountain. net. Website: www.beautifulchristianteen.com. Kimberly Short Wolfe, ed. Conservative publication for Christian teen girls; evangelistic. Bimonthly webzine. 25% freelance. Prefers e-mail submissions. **NO PAYMENT.** Columns & fiction.

\$BOUNDLESS WEBZINE, 8605 Explorer Dr., Colorado Springs CO 80920. (719)531-3430. Fax (719)548-5860. E-mail: wattercz@macmail.fotf.org. Website: www.boundless.org. Focus on the Family. Candice Watters, ed. For college students exploring love, faith, and imagination in the context of a Christian world-view. Online Web magazine. 30,000 visitors/wk. Estab. 1998. 15% unsolicited freelance; 85% assigned. E-query. Pays .15-.40/wd on publication for one-time rts. Articles 1,000-1,500 wds (5/yr); fiction 1,000-1,500 wds; reviews 500-1,500 wds, \$150-250. Responds in 3 wks. Seasonal 1-2 mos ahead. Accepts simultaneous submissions & reprints (tell when/where appeared). Requires e-mail submission (attached and copied into message). Regular sidebars. Prefers NIV. Guidelines (by e-mail/Website); copy online. (Ads)

Columns/Departments: Page (book reviews/excerpt); @Play (entertainment/culture); Beyond Buddies (relationships); Campus Culture (college life/issues); Head and Heart (spirituality); Finding Your Place (career/future planning); Isms & Ologies (worldview); The Podium (speeches); all 1,000-2,000 wds, pays .20-.40/wd.

Tips: "Develop an understanding of web journalism and a voice that will compel college students."

**This periodical was #23 on the 2000 Top 50 Christian Publishers list.

$#**BREAKAWAY**, 8605 Explorer Dr., Colorado Springs CO 80920. (719)548-4576. Fax (719)531-3499. E-mail: breakaway@macmail.fotf.org. Website: www.family.org/teenguys/breakmag. Focus on the Family. Michael Ross, ed. The 14-year-old, unchurched teen (boy) in the public school is our target; boys 11-18 yrs. Monthly mag; 24-32 pgs; circ 105,800. Subscription $15. 60-70% freelance. Complete ms/cover letter; phone query OK. Pays .12-.15/wd on acceptance for all, 1st, one-time & reprint rts. Articles 400-1,800 wds (40/yr); fiction 1,200-2,200 wds (15/yr); music reviews, 300 wds, $30-40. Responds in 5 wks. Seasonal 8 mos ahead. Accepts simultaneous submissions & reprints. Kill fee 33-50%. Guidelines/theme list; copy for 9x12 SAE/3 stamps. (Ads)

Fillers: Buys 50/yr. Cartoons ($75), facts, quizzes; 200-600 wds; .20-.25/wd.

Columns/Departments: Buys 12/yr. Plugged In (devotional); 700-900 wds.

Tips: "Need strong lead. Brevity and levity a must. Have a teen guy or two read it. Make sure the language is up-to-date, but not overly hip." Needs drama-in-life stories involving boys.

**This periodical was #8 on the 2000 Top 50 Christian Publishers list (#7 in 1999, #3 in 1998, #9 in 1997, #3 in 1996, #6 in 1995, #5 in 1994). 1999 EPA Award of Merit—Youth.

$#**BRIO**, 8605 Explorer Dr., Colorado Springs CO 80920. (719)548-4577. Fax (719)531-3499. E-mail: brio@macmail.fotf.org. Website: www.family.org/girls/briomag. Focus on the Family. Susie Shellenberger, ed. For teen girls, 12-16 yrs. Monthly mag; 32 pgs; circ 206,500. Subscription $15. 60% freelance. Complete ms/cover letter; phone query OK. Pays .08-.15/wd on acceptance for 1st rts. Articles 800-1,000 wds (10/yr); fiction 1,200-2,000 wds (10/yr). Responds in 4-9 wks. Seasonal 5 mos ahead. Kill fee $100. Guidelines; copy $1.50. (Ads)

Fillers: Buys 15/yr. Cartoons, facts, ideas, quizzes, short humor; 50-200 wds. Pays $75-100.

Special Needs: All topics of interest to female teens are welcome: boys, makeup, dating, weight, ordinary girls who have extraordinary experiences, female adjustments to puberty, etc. Also teen-related female fiction.

Tips: "Study at least 3 issues of *Brio* before submitting. We're looking for a certain, fresh, hip-hop conversational style. Most open to fiction, articles and quizzes."

**This periodical was #63 on the 1998 Top 50 Christian Publishers list (#58 in 1997, #60 in 1996, #61 in 1995, #37 in 1994). Also 1995 EPA Award of Merit—Youth.

$CAMPUS LIFE, 465 Gundersen Dr., Carol Stream IL 60188. (630)260-6200. Fax (630)260-0114. E-mail: clmag@campuslife.net. Website: www.campuslife.net. Christianity Today Intl. Christopher Lutes, ed. Seeks to help teenagers navigate adolescence with their Christian faith intact. Bimonthly (plus 3 special Christian College issues) mag; 68-94 pgs; circ 100,000. Subscription $19.95. 20% assigned. Query only/clips; fax/e-query OK. Pays .15-.25/wd on acceptance for 1st or one-time rts. Articles 750-1,200 wds (5-10/yr); fiction 1,000-2,000 wds (1-5/yr). Responds in 5-9 wks. Seasonal 5 mos ahead. Accepts simultaneous submissions & reprints (tell when/where appeared). Accepts disk. Kill fee 50%. Regular sidebars. Guidelines (also on Website); copy $3/9x12 SAE/3 stamps. (Ads)

> **Poetry:** Buys 1-5/yr. Free verse; 5-20 lines; $25-50. Submit max 2 poems. Rarely purchase.

> **Tips:** "Most open to as-told-to stories. Interview students and get their stories."

> **This periodical was #41 on the 2000 Top 50 Christian Publishers list (#30 in 1999, #35 in 1998, #37 in 1996, #49 in 1995, #63 in 1994). 1998 & 1999 EPA Award of Excellence—Youth.

$CHRISTIAN COLLEGE FOCUS, PO Box 1357, Oak Park, IL 60304. (708) 524-5070. Fax: (708)524-5174. E-mail: WinPress7@aol.com. Website: www.collegefocus.com. Kipland Publishing House. Phillip Huber, mng. ed. College planning guide for high school juniors and seniors. Annual mag; 40+ pgs; circ 200,000. Free to college-bound high schoolers. 85% assigned. Prefers 1-page query; fax/e-query OK. Pays .08/wd and up, on publication, for all rts (usually). Articles 800-1,600 wds (6/yr). Some sidebars. Prefers NIV. Guidelines/theme list (also by e-mail); copy $3. (Ads)

> **Special Needs:** First-person and how-to features that express the value of a Christian college or university education and focus on all topics of interest to high schoolers planning for college, including: the college application process, paying for college, choosing a major, selecting a school, financial aid and scholarships, spending time with God, campus life, time management, short-term missions.

> **Tips:** "We are open to working with new/unpublished authors, especially college graduates, current college students, college professors, admissions personnel, career counselors and financial aid officers. Visit our Website to view articles previously published."

$THE CONQUEROR, 8855 Dunn Rd., Hazelwood MO 63042. (314)837-7300. Fax (314)837-4503. E-mail: youth@upci.org. Website: www.upci.org/youth. United Pentecostal Church, Intl. Travis Miller, ed. For teenagers in the denomination. Bimonthly mag; 16 pgs; circ 6,000. Subscription $9. 75% unsolicited freelance; 25% assigned. Complete ms; e-query OK. Pays $20-50 on publication for various rts. Articles & fiction (many/yr) 600-800 wds. Responds in 10 wks. Seasonal 4 mos ahead. Accepts simultaneous submissions & reprints. Prefers KJV. Guidelines (also by e-mail); copy for 11x14 SAE/2 stamps. (No ads)

Fillers: Various.

Tips: "Articles should be written with the idea of conservative morals, standards and ethics in mind." Cutting down on their backlog of submissions.

$CROSS WALK, 6401 The Paseo, Kansas City MO 64131. (816)333-7000 x2211. Fax (816)333-4315. E-mail: crosswalk@nazarene.org. Website: www.nazarene.org. Holiness denominations. Matt Price, ed. Written by teens (and youth leaders) for teens. Weekly take-home paper; 8 pgs; circ 30,000. Subscription $9.20. 100% assigned. Query or complete ms; e-query OK. Pays on acceptance for all rts. Responds in 2 wks. Kill fee 50%. No sidebars. Guidelines; copy for 9x12 SAE/2 stamps. (No ads)

> **Tips:** "Open only to a youth worker (professional or volunteer) and five teens from his/her youth group. The youth leader will write devotionals for Saturday and Sunday, and the five teens will write devotionals for Monday-Friday." Writers must be subscribers.

$DEVO'ZINE, PO Box 340004, Nashville TN 37203-0004. (615)340-7247. Fax (615)340-7267. E-mail: devozine@upperroom.org. Website: www. upperroom.org/devozine/default.html. The Upper Room. Robin Pippin, ed. Devotional; to help teens (12-18) develop and maintain their connection with God and other Christians. Bimonthly mag; 64 pgs; circ 92,000. Subscription $16.95. 85% unsolicited freelance; 15% assigned. Query; phone/fax/e-query OK. Pays $25 for meditations, $100 for feature articles (assigned) on acceptance for these one-time rts: newspaper, periodical, electronic and software-driven rts and the right to use in future anthologies. Meditations 150-250 wds (350/yr), articles 350-500 wds; book/music/video reviews, 350-500 wds, $100. Responds in 16 wks. Seasonal 6-8 mos ahead. Accepts reprints (tell when/where appeared). Accepts disk or e-mail submission. Regular sidebars. Prefers NRSV, NIV, CEV. Guidelines/theme list; copy/7x10 SAE. (No ads)

> **Poetry:** Buys 25-30/yr. Free verse, light verse, haiku, traditional; to 150 wds or 10-20 lines. Pays $25. Submit max 1 poem/theme, 9 themes/issue.
>
> **Tips:** "Call with ideas for weekend features related to specific themes."
>
> **This periodical was #3 on the 2000 Top 50 Christian Publishers list (#4 in 1999, #10 in 1998, #6 in 1997).

$ENCOUNTER, 8121 Hamilton Ave., Cincinnati OH 45231. (513)931-4050. Fax (513)931-0950. E-mail: kcarr@standardpub.com. Standard Publishing. Kelly Carr, ed. For Christian teens (12-19 yrs). Weekly take-home magazine; 8 pgs; circ 30,000. Subscription price not available. 50% unsolicted freelance; 50% assigned. Complete ms/cover letter; no phone/fax/e-query. Pays .08/wd (.06/wd for one-time or reprint rts) on acceptance for 1st, one-time, or reprint rts. Articles 400-1,100 wds (52+/yr); fiction to 1,100 wds (52/yr). Responds in 8-12 wks. Seasonal 9-12 mos ahead. Accepts simultaneous submissions & reprints. Accepts disk. Some sidebars. Prefers NIV. Guidelines/theme list; copy for #10 SAE/2 stamps. (No ads)

> **Poetry:** Free verse, light verse, traditional; from teens only; $15. Submit max 5 poems.

Columns/Departments: Teen Profiles (teens making a difference), 400-500 wds.

Tips: "Looking for articles pertaining to self-esteem, sports, friendships, all from a Christian viewpoint. Spend time around teens; find out current issues, language, thoughts and trends of today's teens in order to reach them. We're looking for teen writers too."

**This periodical was #42 on the 2000 Top 50 Christian Publishers list (#6 in 1999, #8 in 1998, #17 in 1997, #13 in 1996, #5 in 1995, #17 in 1994).

$ESSENTIAL CONNECTION, 127 Ninth Ave. N., MSN 174, Nashville TN 37234-0170. (615)251-2008. Fax (615)251-2795. E-mail: bbunn@lifeway. com. Website: www.youthscape.com. LifeWay Christian Resources of the Southern Baptist Convention. Bob Bunn, ed. Christian leisure reading and devotional guide for 7th-12th graders. Monthly mag; 60 pgs; circ 120,000. Subscription $3.84 (3 issues per quarter). 15% unsolicited freelance; 85% assigned. Complete ms/cover letter; e-query OK. Pays $80-120 on publication for all (preferred), 1st, one-time, simultaneous or reprint rts. Articles 750-800 wds (2-3/yr); fiction 1,100-1,200 wds (10-12/yr). Responds in 10 wks. Seasonal 8-9 mos ahead. Accepts simultaneous submissions & reprints (tell when/where appeared). Accepts disk or e-mail submission (attached file). Kill fee. Some sidebars. Prefers NIV. Guidelines; free copy. (No ads)

Poetry: Accepts 36/yr. All types. From teens only.

Special Needs: Always in search of Christian humor; sports profiles. Most open to fiction (send complete ms).

+GO!, 916 N. Wahsatch Ave., Colorado Springs CO 80903-2915. (719)520-0830. E-mail: jjjones1@mindspring.com. Jana Jones, ed. Mag. Not included in topical listings. Did not return questionnaire.

$GUIDEPOSTS FOR TEENS, PO Box 638, Chesterton IN 46304. (219)929-4429. Fax (219)926-3839. E-mail: gp4t@guideposts.org. Website: www. guideposts.org. Guideposts, Inc. Mary Lou Carney, ed-in-chief; Betsy Kohn, mng ed.; Allison Payne, asst. ed. For teens, 13-21; features teens who show courage, strength, and positive attitudes through faith in God. Bimonthly mag; 48 pgs. Subscription $19.95. 95% freelance. Query/clips; e-query OK. Pays $300-500 for true stories, $100-300 for shorter pieces on acceptance for all, 1st, one-time or reprint rts. Articles 750-2,000 wds. Responds in 4-6 wks. Seasonal 6+ mos ahead. Accepts reprints (tell when/where appeared). Accepts disk or e-mail submission. Kill fee 25%. Some sidebars OK. Prefers NIV. Guidelines (also by e-mail); copy $4.50. (Ads)

Poetry: Buys 3-6/yr. Avant-garde, free verse, traditional; 8-16 lines. Pays $25-100. Submit max 3 poems.

Fillers: Buys 25-100/yr. Anecdotes, cartoons, facts, jokes, prose, quizzes, short humor, 50-250 wds. Pays $25-100.

Columns/Departments: Buys 30-40/yr. Send complete ms. My Most Embarrassing Moment, 200-300 wds; Are You Laughing at Me? (humor, true or fictional), 500-1,000 wds; Seen and Heard (fun clips of weird news items), 100 wds; Who's in Charge? (teens initiating volunteer activities), 200-300 wds. Pays $25-300.

Special Needs: Need 1st-person (ghost-written) true stories of teens with a spiritual point (7-8/issue); see guidelines.

Contest: Laws of Life essay contest for teens, 13-18. Prizes of $5,000, $3,000 and $2,000. Send SASE for guidelines.

Tips: "Most open to how-to features, humor/embarrassing moment; Who's in Charge? (column). Want true stories of teens in the Guideposts tradition; teens in dangerous, inspiring, miraculous situations. Study guidelines."

**This periodical was #2 on the 2000 Top 50 Christian Publishers list (#2 in 1999).

HYPE: Hyper Young People Evangelizing, 76 Bella Vista Dr., Baulkman Hills, Sydney NSW 2153. E-mail: ranita@ihug.com.au. Website: www. hypezine.com. Ranita Row, sr ed. Online magazine run entirely by teenagers who submit freelance work over the Internet. Estab 1997. 40% unsolicited freelance; 60% assigned. NO PAYMENT. Not in topical listings. (No ads)

Tips: "Our staff is involved in all facets of Web publication, and this is a great way for teens to break into the writing world, by working with a team of dedicated and fun Christian teens from all over the world. Get involved—and help us reach the world and the WWW for God."

$#I.D., 4050 Lee Vance View, Colorado Springs CO 80918. (719)536-0100. Fax (719)536-3296. Website: www.cookministries.com. Cook Communications Ministries. Frieda Nossamon, ed. Articles and stories relating Christianity to a teen's daily life. Weekly take-home paper; circ 75,000. Subscription free. Accepts freelance. Query or complete ms. Not in topical listings. (No ads)

**1996 EPA Award of Excellence, Sunday School Take-home paper.

$INSIGHT, 55 W. Oak Ridge Dr., Hagerstown MD 21740-7301. (301)393-4037. Fax (301)393-4055. E-mail: insight@rhpa.org. Website: www. insightmagazine.org. Review and Herald/Seventh-Day Adventist. Lori Peckham, ed. A magazine of positive Christian living for Seventh-Day Adventist teenagers, 14-18 years. Weekly take-home mag; 16 pgs; circ 16,600. Subscription $41.95. 60% unsolicited freelance. Complete ms/cover letter; e-query OK. Pays $25-125 on acceptance for one-time rts. Not copyrighted. Articles 500-1,500 wds (100/yr). Responds in 4 wks. Seasonal 6 mos ahead. Accepts reprints (tell when/where appeared). Prefers e-mail submission (attached file). Regular sidebars. Prefers NIV. Guidelines (also by e-mail/Website); copy $2/9x12 SAE/2 stamps. (No ads)

Poetry: Buys to 36/yr. All types; to 1 pg. By teens only. Pays $10.

Columns/Departments: Buys 50/yr. On the Edge (drama in real life), 800-1,500 wds, $50-100; It Happened To Me (personal experience in first-person), 600-900 wds, $50-75; Big Deal (big topics, such as prayer, premarital sex, knowing God's will, etc.) with sidebar, 1,200-1,700 wds, $75 + $25 for sidebar; So I Said (first-person opinion), 300-500 wds, $25-100.

Contest: Sponsors a nonfiction & poetry contest; includes a category for students under 21. Prizes to $250. May or June deadline (may vary). Send SASE for rules.

Tips: "We are desperately in need of true, dramatic stories involving Christian teens. Also need stories by male authors, particularly some humor. Also profiles of Seventh-Day Adventist teenagers who are making a notable difference."

**This periodical was #52 on the 2000 Top 50 Christian Publishers list (#41 in 1999, #6 in 1998, #5 in 1997, #8 in 1996, #18 in 1995, #6 in 1994). 1998 EPA Award of Merit—Youth.

$INTEEN, 1551 Regency Ct., Calumet City IL 60409. (708)868-7100x239. Fax (708)868-6759. E-mail: umi1551@aol.com. Website: www.urbanministries. com. Urban Ministries, Inc. Katara Washington, ed. Teen curriculum for ages 14-17 (student and teacher manuals). Quarterly booklet; 32 pgs; circ 20,000. Subscription $11.25. 1% unsolicited freelance; 99% assigned. Query/clips; phone query OK; no e-query. Pays $75-150 on acceptance for all rts. Articles & fiction 1,200 wds. Responds in 4 wks. Seasonal 9 mos ahead. Accepts some reprints (tell when/where appeared). Accepts disk or e-mail submission (copied into message). Prefers NIV. Free guidelines/theme list/copy for 10x13 SAE. (No ads)

Poetry: Buys 4/yr. Free verse; variable length. Pays $25-60.

Tips: "Write in with sample writings and be willing and ready to complete an assignment. Most open to Bible study guides."

$LISTEN, 55 W. Oak Ridge Dr., Hagerstown MD 21740. (301)393-4010. Fax (301)393-4055. E-mail: Listen@HealthConnection.org. Website: www. rhpa.org. Review and Herald/Seventh-Day Adventist. Larry Becker, ed. To educate teens against alcohol/drugs in a uniquely positive way; emphasizes moral values in a secular tone. Monthly mag (September-May); 32 pgs; circ 40,000. Subscription $24.95. 50% unsolicited freelance; 50% assigned. Query; phone/fax/e-query OK. Pays .06-.10/wd ($50-250) on acceptance for 1st or reprint rts. Articles 1,200-1,500 wds (30-50/yr); fiction 1,200 wds (15/yr). Responds in 9 wks. Seasonal 1 yr ahead. Accepts simultaneous submissions & reprints (tell when/where appeared). Accepts disk. Regular sidebars. Guidelines; copy $1/9x12 SAE/2 stamps. (No ads)

Fillers: Buys 12/yr. Quizzes, word puzzles, 150-300 wds. Pays $15.

Tips: "Need good activity articles. Address a specific lifestyle topic (i.e., alcohol, tobacco, marijuana, etc.). Make it believable and interesting to teen readers."

**This periodical was #36 on the 1998 Top 50 Christian Publishers List (#21 in 1997, #15 in 1996).

$*LIVING MY FAITH (replaces *Challenge*), 1300 N. Meacham Rd., Schaumburg IL 60173-4888. (847)843-1600. Fax (847)843-3757. Website: www.garbc.org/rbp. Regular Baptist Press. Mel Walker, youth ed. For junior high youth (12-14); conservative/fundamental. Devotional booklet. Send for guidelines before submitting, or check this Website: www. rbpstudentministries.org/contribute.

$PASSAGEWAY.ORG (formerly Passageway), 1300 Harmon Pl., Minneapolis MN 55403-1988. E-mail: ed@passageway.org. Website: www.passageway. org. Billy Graham Evangelistic Assn. Steve Knight, content ed. Online publication for teens. Weekly e-zine. Open to freelance submissions. E-query OK. No information on payment, for all, electronic or reprint rts. Articles 700-1,000 wds ; fiction 700-1,000 wds. Accepts simultaneous submissions & reprints (tell when/where appeared). Requires e-mail submission (attached or copied into message). Some sidebars. Prefers NIV. Guidelines by e-mail; copy online. (No ads)

Poetry: Avant-garde, free verse.

Columns/Departments: ETC. section and Pop Culture.

Tips: "Most open to columns/department."

$*REAL FAITH IN LIFE (replaces *Certainty*), 1300 N. Meacham Rd., Schaumburg IL 60173-4888. (847)843-1600. Fax (847)843-3757. Website: www.garbc.org/rbp. Regular Baptist Press. Mel Walker, youth ed. For senior high youth (15-18); conservative/fundamental. Devotional magazine. Send for new guidelines before submitting, or check this Website: www.rbpstudentministries.org/contribute.

$*REAL TIME, PO Box 36640, Colorado Springs CO 80936. (719)533-3044. Fax (719)533-3045. Cook Communications/Scripture Press. Chris Lyon, ed. To help young teens (11-15 yrs) explore ways Jesus relates to them in everyday life. Weekly take-home paper; 8 pgs, circ 30,000. Subscription $11.50. 90% freelance. Complete ms/no cover letter; no phone/fax query. Pays $50-100 on acceptance for one-time or pick-up (reprint) rts. Articles 600-1,200 wds (10/yr); fiction & true stories 800-1,200 wds (20/yr). Responds in 9-13 wks. Seasonal 1 yr ahead. Accepts simultaneous submissions & reprints. Prefers disk or e-mail only on request. Regular sidebars. Any version. Guidelines (also by e-mail: WritersGuide@SPpublications.org)/theme list (after March 1)/copy for #10 SAE/1 stamp. (No ads)

Poetry: From teens only. Free verse, light verse, traditional.

Fillers: Buys 10/yr. Cartoons, jokes, prose, quizzes, word puzzles; $15.

Tips: "Looking for remarkable Christian teens doing remarkable things, and how their Christianity affects that. Also looking for humor that teaches biblical truth." Send Social Security number. Theme lists are created in late spring each year.

**This periodical was #40 on the 2000 Top 50 Christian Publishers list (#23 in 1999, #34 in 1997, #21 in 1996 & 1995, #41 in 1994).

$SHARING THE VICTORY, 8701 Leeds Rd., Kansas City MO 64129-1680. (816)921-0909. Fax (816)921-8755. E-mail: stv@fca.org, or apalmeri@fca.org. Website: www.fca.org. Fellowship of Christian Athletes (Protestant and Catholic). Allen Palmeri, ed. Equipping and encouraging athletes and coaches to take their faith seriously, in and out of competition. Monthly (9X-double issues in Jan., Jun. & Aug.) mag; 48 pgs; circ 80,000. Subscription $18. 50% freelance. Query only/clips; e-query OK. Pays $25-200 on publication for one-time rts. Articles 500-1,500 wds (20/yr). Responds in 10-15 wks. Seasonal 6 mos ahead. Accepts reprints, pays 50% (tell when/where appeared). Accepts disk or e-mail submission (attached or copied into message). Kill fee .05%. Some sidebars. Prefers NIV. Guidelines (also by e-mail); copy $1/9x12 SAE. (No ads)

Poetry: Buys 9/yr. Traditional; 5-30 lines; $25. Submit max 6 poems.

Special Needs: Articles on FCA camp experiences. All articles must have an athletic angle.

Tips: "FCA angle important; pro & college athletes and coaches giving solid Christian testimony; we run stories according to athletic season; need articles/poetry on female athletes."

**1996 EPA Award of Merit—Organizational.

SPIRIT: Lectionary-based Weekly for Catholic Teens, 1884 Randolph Ave., St. Paul MN 55105-1700. No freelance.

$STUDENT LEADERSHIP JOURNAL, Box 7895, Madison WI 53707-7895. (608)274-9001x425. Fax (608)274-7882. E-mail: slj@ivcf.org. Website: www.ivcf.org/slj. InterVarsity Christian Fellowship. Jeff Yourison, ed. Undergraduate college student Christian leaders, single, ages 18-26. Triannual & online journal; 32 pgs; circ 8,500. Subscription $12. 2% unsolicited; 20% assigned. Query/clips; no e-query. Pays $35-125 on acceptance for 1st or one-time rts. Articles to 2,000 wds (1/yr); book reviews 150-400 wds, $25-50. Responds in 16 wks. Seasonal 8 mos ahead. Accepts reprints. No e-mail submission. Regular sidebars. Guidelines/theme list; copy $4/9x12 SAE/4 stamps. (No ads)

> **Poetry:** Buys 4-6/yr. Avant-garde, free verse; to 15 lines; $25-50. Submit max 5 poems.

> **Fillers:** Buys 0-5/yr. Facts, games, party ideas, quizzes; to 200 wds; $10-50.

> **Columns/Departments:** Buys 6-10/yr. Collegiate Trends, 20-100 wds; Student Leadership Network, 500-800 wds; Chapter Strategy (how-to planning strategy for campus groups), 500-800; $10-75. Query.

> **Special Needs:** Campus issues/trends/ministry/spiritual growth/leadership; Kingdom values; multi-ethnic reconciliation.

> **Tips:** "Most open to main features targeted to college-age students. Be upbeat, interesting and fresh. Writers who were involved in campus fellowship as students have the 'write' perspective and experience."

**1997 & 1995 EPA Award of Merit—Christian Ministry.

$#TEENAGE CHRISTIAN, 105 Shelter Cove, Hendersonville TN 37075. (800)637-2613. Church of Christ/Christian Publishing Inc. Shana Curtis, ed. Spiritual answers to tough questions for Christian teens (13-19 yrs). Bimonthly mag; 32 pgs; circ 10,500. Subscription $14.95. 50% freelance. Complete ms/cover letter. Pays $35 on publication for one-time & reprint rts. Articles 600-1,200 wds (20/yr); fiction 600-1,500 wds (9/yr). Responds in 3-4 wks. Accepts disk. Seasonal 6 mos ahead. Accepts simultaneous submissions & reprints (tell when/where appeared). Rarely uses sidebars. Prefers NIV. Copy for 9x12 SAE/$2.50. (Ads)

> **Poetry:** Buys 3-4/yr. Free verse; 10-25 lines; $15-25. Submit max 5 poems.

> **Fillers:** Buys 5-10/yr. Cartoons, quizzes, prayers, word puzzles; 150-350 wds; $15-25.

> **Tips:** "Most open to practical nonfiction. Fiction should be excellent, realistic, and up to date."

$#TEENS ON TARGET, 8855 Dunn Rd., Hazelwood MO 63042. (314)837-7300.

Fax (314)837-4503. E-mail: wapeditor@aol.com. Website: www. upci.org. Word Aflame Publications. P. Daniel Buford, assoc ed. For teens 12-14 years. Weekly take-home paper; 4 pgs; circ 7,000. Subscription $4.40. 75% freelance. Complete ms/cover letter; no e-query. Pays .01-.02/wd on publication for 1st or simultaneous rts. Articles 1,200-1,400 wds; fiction 1,200-1,400 wds (40/yr). Seasonal 1 yr ahead. Accepts simultaneous submissions & reprints. Some sidebars. Prefers KJV. Guidelines; copy for 6x9 SAE/2 stamps. (No ads)

Fillers: Buys 2-3/yr. Quizzes, word puzzles; $5-12.

Tips: "Articles should be human interest with practical application of Christian principles for 12- to 14-year-olds."

$TODAY'S CHRISTIAN TEEN, PO Box 100, Morgantown PA 19543. (610)913-0796. Fax (610)913-0797. E-mail: tcpubs@mkpt.com, or Jerry@ netmpi.clrs.com. Marketing Partners. Jerry Thacker, ed. To help today's Christian teens by presenting material which applies the Bible to contemporary issues; conservative. Triannual mag; 24 pgs; circ 100,000. Subscription free. 80% unsolicited freelance; 20% assigned. Complete ms/cover letter; fax/e-query OK. Pays $150 on publication for first, one-time or reprint rts. Articles 800-1,000 wds (3/yr). Responds in 6 wks. Seasonal 6 mos ahead. Accepts reprints (tell when/where appeared). Prefers disk. Regular sidebars. Requires KJV. Guidelines (also by e-mail); copy for 9x12 SAE/4 stamps. (No ads)

Tips: "Send well-written articles that use biblical principles and application. Make a good solid point using KJV quotes."

VISIONS: Lectionary-based Weekly for Catholic Junior Highs, 1884 Randolph St., St. Paul MN 55105. No freelance.

$WITH: The Magazine for Radical Christian Youth, Box 347, Newton KS 67114-0347. (316)283-5100. Fax (316)283-0454. E-mail: deliag@gcmc. org. Faith & Life Press/Mennonite, Brethren & Mennonite Brethren. Carol Duerksen, ed. For high-school teens (15-18 yrs), Christian and non-Christian. Bimonthly mag; 32 pgs; circ 6,200. Subscription $23.50. 20% unsolicited freelance; 80% assigned. Query (on first-person and how-to articles); complete ms on others/cover letter; no phone/fax/e-query. Pays .06/wd (.03/wd for reprints) on acceptance for 1st, one-time, simultaneous or reprint rts. Articles 500-1,800 wds (15/yr); fiction 1,000-2,000 wds (15/yr); music reviews, 500 wds, .05/wd (query for assignment). Responds in 4 wks. Seasonal 6 mos ahead. Accepts simultaneous submissions & reprints (tell when/where appeared). No disk. Kill fee 25-50%. Regular sidebars. Prefers NRSV. Guidelines/theme list; copy for 9x12 SAE/4 stamps. Separate guidelines for 1st-person and how-to articles sent only when requested. (No ads)

Fillers: Buys 20 cartoons/yr; $35-40.

Tips: "We need good Christmas stories; true, powerful stories or fiction that reads as well as truth. Send for theme list and write for the theme. Humor—both cartoons and short articles—are hard to find. Our readers expect high-quality humor."

**This periodical was #59 on the 2000 Top 50 Christian Publishers list (#41 in 1998, #35 in 1997, #23 in 1996, #17 in 1995, #12 in 1994). 1999 & 1998 EPA Award of Merit—Youth.

*YOU! MAGAZINE: Youth for the Next Millennium, 29963 Mulholland Hwy., Agoura Hills CA 91301-3009. (818)991-1813. Fax (818)991-2024. E-mail: youmag@earthlink.net. Website: www.youmagazine.com. Catholic. Submissions Editor. An alternative teen magazine (13-23 yrs) aimed at bridging the gap between religion and pop culture. Monthly (10X) mag; 35 pgs; circ 35,000. (Youthbeat, a newspaper insert, also available.) Subscription $19.95. 20% unsolicited freelance; 80% assigned. Query; fax/e-query OK. **PAYS IN COPIES** for all rts. Articles 200-1,000 wds (130/yr); fiction 900 wds (15/yr); book reviews 200 wds; music reviews 150 wds; video reviews 100 wds. Responds in 2 wks. Seasonal 3 mos ahead. Accepts simultaneous query & reprints (tell when/where appeared). Accepts disk. Regular sidebars. Prefers NAB. Guidelines/theme list; copy $2/9x12 SAE/4 stamps. (Ads)

> **Poetry:** Accepts 24/yr. Free verse, light verse, traditional, 5-30 lines. Submit max 3 poems.
>
> **Fillers:** Cartoons, games, jokes, prayers, quizzes, quotes, and word puzzles; to 300 wds.
>
> **Columns/Departments:** Patrick Lorenz. Watch It/Hear It (positive movie & music reviews), 50-150 wds.
>
> **Special Needs:** Teen issues, sports, back-to-school, pro-life issues, religious vocations, and alternative Christian music.
>
> **Tips:** "All sections of the magazine are open to freelancers. There is a particular interest in issue features. The best way to 'break in' is to send articles for editorial perusal. Be sure to include SASE and e-mail address, if available."

$YOUNG ADULT TODAY, 1551 Regency Ct., Calumet City IL 60409. (708) 868-7100x239. Fax (708)868-6759. E-mail: umi1551@aol.com. Website: www. urbanministries.com. Urban Ministries, Inc. Katara Washington, ed. Young adult curriculum for ages 18-24 (student and teacher manuals). Quarterly booklet; 80 pgs; circ 10,000. Subscription $14.75. 99% assigned. Query/clips; phone query OK; no e-query. Pays $75-150 on acceptance for all rts. Articles (24/yr) & fiction (12/yr); under 1,000 wds. Responds in 4 wks. Seasonal 9 mos ahead. Accepts some reprints (tell when/where appeared). Accepts disk or e-mail submission (copied into message). Prefers KJV. Free guidelines/theme list/copy for 10x13 SAE. (No ads)

> **Poetry:** Buys 4/yr. Free verse; variable length. Pays $25-60.
>
> **Tips:** "We assign articles based on the Uniform Lesson Series for Sunday schools. Writers should send samples of their writing to be considered for an assignment. We very rarely publish unassigned submissions."

$YOUNG AND ALIVE, Box 6097, Lincoln NE 68506. (402)488-0981. Website: www.crs.org. Christian Record Services. Gaylena Gibson, ed. For sight-impaired young adults, 16-25 yrs; for interdenominational Christian audience. Quarterly mag; 65-70 pgs; circ 25,000. 95% freelance. Complete ms; no phone query. Pays .04-.05/wd on acceptance for one-time rts. Articles & true stories 200-1,400 wds (40/yr). Responds in 5 wks. Seasonal anytime. Accepts simultaneous submissions & reprints. Accepts disk. No sidebars. Guidelines; copy for 7x10 SAE/5 stamps. (No ads)

Special Needs: Adventure and careers for the handicapped.

Tips: "Although many blind and visually impaired young adults have the same interests as their sighted counterparts, the material should meet their needs specifically." Follow guidelines.

$YOUNG SALVATIONIST, PO Box 269, Alexandria VA 22313-0269. (703) 684-5500. Fax (703)684-5539. E-mail: ys@usn.salvationarmy.org. Website: publications.salvationarmyusa.org. The Salvation Army. Tim Clark, mng ed. For teens & young adults in the Salvation Army. Monthly (10X) & online mag; 20 pgs; circ 48,000. Subscription $4. 80% unsolicited freelance; 20% assigned. Complete ms; e-query OK. Pays .15/wd (.10 for reprints) on acceptance for 1st, one-time or reprint rts. Articles (60/yr) & fiction (10/yr); 500-1,200 wds. Responds in 9 wks. Seasonal 6 mos ahead. Accepts reprints (tell when/where appeared). Accepts disk or e-mail submission. Some sidebars. Prefers NIV. Guidelines/theme list (also on Website); copy for 9x12 SAE/3 stamps. (No ads)

Contest: Sponsors a contest for fiction, nonfiction, poetry, original art and photography. Send SASE for details.

Tips: "Our greatest need is for nonfiction pieces that are relevant to the readers and offer clear application to daily life. We are most interested in topical pieces on contemporary issues that affect a teen's daily life, and pieces that work with the day-to-day challenges of faith. Although we use fiction and poetry, they are a small percentage of the total content of each issue."

**This periodical was #5 on the 2000 Top 50 Christian Publishers list (#10 in 1999, #16 in 1998, #24 in 1997, #36 in 1996, #43 in 1995, #14 in 1994).

$*YOUTH CHALLENGE, 8855 Dunn Rd., Hazelwood MO 63042. (314)837-7300. Fax (314)837-4503. E-mail: wapeditor@aol.com. Website: www.upci.org. Word Aflame Publications. P. Daniel Buford, assoc ed. For teens in 10th-12th grades. Weekly take-home paper; circ 5,500. Subscription $4.40. 75% freelance. Complete ms/cover letter; no e-query. Pays .01-.02/wd on publication for 1st or simultaneous rts. Articles 1,200-1,400 wds; fiction 1,200-1,400 wds (40/yr). Seasonal 1 yr ahead. Accepts simultaneous submissions & reprints. Some sidebars. Prefers KJV. Guidelines; copy for 6x9 SAE/2 stamps. (No ads)

Fillers: Buys 2-3/yr. Quizzes, word puzzles; $5-12.

Tips: "Articles should be human interest with practical application of Christian principles for 15-17-year-olds."

$*YOUTH COMPASS, PO Box 4060, Overland Park KS 66204. (913)432-0331. Fax (913)722-0351. Church of God (holiness)/Herald and Banner Press. Arlene McGehee, Sunday school ed. Denominational; for teens. Weekly take-home paper; 4 pgs; circ 4,800. Subscription $1.30. Complete ms/cover letter; phone/fax query OK. Pays .005/wd on publication for 1st rts. Fiction 800-1,500 wds. Seasonal 6-8 mos ahead. Accepts simultaneous submissions & reprints (tell when/where appeared). Prefers KJV. Guidelines/theme list; copy. Not in topical listings.

+YOUTHWALK, 4201 N. Peachtree Rd., Atlanta GA 30341. (770)458-9300. Fax (770)454-9313. E-mail: twalker@walkthru.org. Website: www. youthwalk.org. Walk Thru the Bible Ministries. Tim Walker, ed. To encourage teenagers to invest time daily getting to know God and His Word. Monthly mag; circ 36,000. Subscription $18. Accepts freelance. Query or complete ms. Not in topical listings. Did not return questionnaire. (Ads)

WOMEN'S MARKETS

ANNA'S JOURNAL, PO Box 341, Ellijay GA 30540. Phone/fax (706)276-2309. E-mail: annas@ellijay.com. Website: www.annasjournal.com. Catherine Ward-Long, ed. Spiritual support for childless couples who for the most part have decided to stay that way. 80% unsolicited freelance; 20% assigned. Complete ms/cover letter; fax/e-query OK. 1st, simultaneous or reprint rts. Not copyrighted. Articles 500-2,000 wds (8-12/yr); fiction 1,000-2,000 wds (1-3/yr). Seasonal 3 months ahead. Accepts simultaneous submissions & reprints (tell when/where appeared). No disk; e-mail OK (copied into message). No sidebars. Prefers KJV. No guidelines or copy. (No ads) Note from publisher: "Thank you for your patience and support of Anna's Journal. I am in the process of forming an e-zine on the WWW, so business correspondence will require more time. This project will be completed during 2001."

> **Poetry:** Accepts 4-10/yr. Any type. Submit max 3 poems.
> **Fillers:** Accepts 3-4/yr. Anecdotes, facts, newsbreaks, prose, prayers, quizzes, quotes, letters; 50-250 wds.
> **Special Needs:** Articles from married, childless men; articles discussing the meaning of childless, childfree and childless by choice.
> **Tips:** "Looking for innovative ways to improve the child-free lifestyle and self-esteem. It helps if writer is childless."

$CANTICLE: The Voice of Today's Catholic Woman, 517 Middle Rd., East Greenwich RI 02818-2326. E-mail: canticle@mindspring.com. Catholic. Genevieve S. Kineke, ed. Covers issues of faith and femininity for Catholic women. Bimonthly mag. 50% unsolicited freelance; 50% assigned. Complete ms; fax/e-query OK. Pays on publication for one-time rts. Articles to 2,000 wds. Prefers e-mail submissions. Guidelines (also by e-mail); copy $3. Incomplete topical listings. (Ads)

> **Tips:** "Practicality and orthodoxy are key. Positive themes." Interested writers' list receives updated themes via e-mail.

$+CATHERINE MAGAZINE, 2 Overlea Blvd., Toronto ON M4H 1P4 Canada. Fax (416)422-6120. E-mail: catherine@sallynet.org. Major Linda Bradberry, ed. For Salvation Army women in Canada. Accepts freelance. Pays $50 for one-time or reprint rts. Articles 1,000 wds. Accepts simultaneous submissions & reprints (tell when/where appeared).

$#CHRISTIAN BRIDE, PO Box 148548, Nashville TN 37214. (615)872-8080. Fax (615)872-9786. Website: www.christianbride.com. Vox Publishing. Gina Cohen, assoc pub. For women planning to get married. Quarterly mag; 200 pgs; circ 3,000. Estab. 1999. 100% assigned. Query; e-query OK. Pays

.06-.10/wd on publication for one-time rts. Articles 1,000-2,000 wds (20/yr). Responds in 6 wks. Seasonal 6-8 mos ahead. Accepts simultaneous submissions. Accepts e-mail submissions (copied into message). Kill fee. Some sidebars. Prefers NIV. Guidelines; copy for 7x10 SAE. (Ads)

> **Columns/Departments:** Chris Well. Query. Pays $.06-.08/wd.
>
> **Tips:** "A good wedding story or new slant is helpful."

$CHRISTIAN WOMEN TODAY, Box 300, Vancouver BC V6C 2X3, Canada. (604) 514-2000. Fax (604)514-2002. E-mail: katherine@mkehler.com. Website: www.christianwomentoday.com. Campus Crusade for Christ, Canada. Katherine Kehler, exec ed. For Christian woman, 20-40 years. Monthly. 30% freelance. Query; fax query OK. Pays $25-100 on publication. Articles 100-700 wds. Seasonal 4 mos ahead. Accepts reprints (tell when/where appeared). Prefers e-mail submission. Regular sidebars. Guidelines. (Ads)

> **Columns/Departments:** Life Stories (inspiration, how God helped), 250 wds; Feature (Christ-centered or practical), 1,200 wds; Potpourri (women's interests), 100 wds.
>
> **Tips:** "The writer needs to have a global perspective, and have a heart to build women in their faith, and help develop them to win others to Christ."

CHURCHWOMAN (formerly The Church Woman), 475 Riverside Dr., Ste. 500, New York NY 10115. (212)870-2347. Fax (212)870-2338. E-mail: cwu@churchwomen.org. Website: www.churchwomen.org. Church Women United. Elizabeth Young, mng ed; Mary Stamp, ed. Shares stories of women acting on their faith and engaging in peace and justice issues. Quarterly mag; 24 pgs; circ 10,000. Subscription $10. Uses little freelance. Query. **PAYS IN COPIES.** Articles to 3 pgs. Prefers e-mail submissions (copied into message). Guidelines; copy $1.

> **Special Needs:** Priority is to strengthen families worldwide in the 21st century, related to issues of racism, diversity, health care, violence, economic justice, media, technology, and education.

$CLARITY, 16 E. 34th St., New York NY 10016. Guideposts, Inc. Janice Wright, ed-in-chief. No freelance for now.

CONNECTION, 40000 Six Mile Rd., Northville MI 48167. Fax (248)349-9773. E-mail: lucy@qix.net. Website: www.wardepc.org/connection. Ward Presbyterian Church. Lucy McGuire, ed-in-chief. For women; seeks to communicate and reflect Christ's love in action. Quarterly & online newsletter; 12 pgs; circ 3,000. 75% unsolicited freelance; 25% assigned. Complete ms/cover letter; submit by e-query. **PAYS IN COPIES** for 1st rts. Articles 250-300 wds. Responds in 6 wks. Seasonal 4 mos ahead. Accepts simultaneous submissions. Accepts e-mail submissions (copied into message). Some sidebars. Any version. Guidelines/theme list (also by e-mail/Website). (No ads)

> **Fillers:** Accepts 30/yr. Facts, newsbreaks, 10-20, to 200 wds.
>
> **Columns/Departments:** Working (using faith to balance work and home); Homemaking; Seasonal themes; Networking (outreach).
>
> **Special Needs:** Articles for working women.
>
> **Tips:** "Most open to women-specific news, well documented."

$CONSCIENCE: A Newsjournal of Prochoice Catholic Opinion, 1436 U St NW, Ste. 301, Washington DC 20009-3997. (202)986-6093. E-mail: conscience @catholicsforchoice.org. Website: www.catholicsforchoice.org. Catholic. Submit to The Editor. For lay people, theologians, policy makers, and clergy. Quarterly newsjournal; 48 pgs; circ 12,000. Subscription $10. 80% freelance. Query/clips or complete ms/cover letter; e-query OK. Pays $25-150 on publication for 1st rts, or work-for-hire. Articles 1,000-4,000 wds (8-12/yr); book reviews 500-800 wds, $25-150. Responds in 12 wks. Seasonal 6 mos ahead. Accepts simultaneous submissions & reprints (tell when/where appeared). Kill fee. Guidelines; copy for 9x12 SAE/4 stamps.

   Poetry: Andrew Merton. Buys 16/yr. Any type, on subject, to 50 lines; $10. Submit max 5 poems.

   Fillers: Buys 6-8/yr. Newsbreaks; 100-300 wds; $25-35.

   Tips: "Focus on issues of reproductive choice. Raise serious ethical questions within a generally prochoice framework. Most open to feature articles and book reviews."

$ESPRIT, Evangelical Lutheran Women, 302-393 Portage Ave., Winnipeg MB R3B 3H6 Canada. (204)984-9160. Fax (204)984-9162. E-mail: esprit@ elcic.ca. Website: www.elw.ca. Evangelical Lutheran Church in Canada. Gayle Johannesson, ed. For denominational women. Quarterly mag; 56 pgs; circ 6,500. Subscription $15.50 CAN, $25 US. 50% unsolicited freelance; 50% assigned. Complete ms/cover letter; phone/fax/e-query OK. Pays $12.50-15/pg CAN on publication for 1st, one-time or reprint rts. Articles (34/yr) and fiction (4/yr) 325-1,400 wds; book reviews 150 wds ($6.25 CAN). Responds in 2-4 wks. Seasonal 4 mos ahead. Accepts simultaneous submissions & reprints (tell when/where appeared). Accepts disk (Macintosh) or e-mail submission (copied into message). Regular sidebars. Prefers NRSV. Guidelines/theme list (also by e-mail); copy for 6x9 SAE/.90 CAN postage or $1 US. (No ads)

   Poetry: Buys 4-8/yr. Free verse, light verse, traditional; 8-100 lines; $10-20. Submit max 2 poems.

   Columns/Departments: Buys 4/yr, 325 wds. Pays $12.50-15/pg.

   Tips: "Articles must be in accordance with Lutheran theology. Preference is given to Canadian Lutheran women writers. Use inclusive language (no male pronoun references to God), focus on women and spiritual/faith issues. Check our theme calendar; almost all articles and poems are theme related."

EXCELLENCE: The Lifestyle for Victorious Christian Women, PO Box 90051, Harrisburg PA 17109. (800)773-6011. Fax (717)541-5343. E-mail: vcw@ezonline.com. Website: www.vcwministries.com. VCW Ministries. Audree L. Ashe, pub. This publication is on hold until further notice.

THE GODLY BUSINESS WOMAN, PO Box 181004, Casselberry FL 32718-1004. (407)696-2805 or (800)560-1090. Fax (407)695-8033. E-mail: godlybwmn@aol.com. Website: www.godlybusinesswoman.com. Kathleen B. Jackson, pub; Tracey Davison, mng ed. Our goal is to educate, inspire and encourage women to be all they can be through Jesus Christ; to be a resource that will shed light on God's view of the responsibilites they have been given. Mag; 48 pgs; circ. 25,000. Subscription $20.65. Estab.

1999. 30% unsolicited freelance; 70% assigned. Query; prefers e-queries. Regular sidebars. Guidelines. (Ads)

Columns/Departments: Gifts from the Heart; Missions Hall of Fame; Body, Mind, Spirit; and others. Query. No payment.

Tips: "Our goal is to encourage educated decision making and harmony in women's lives whether they are in or out of the workplace."

$+GRACE, A Companion for Women on Their Spiritual Journey, 301 S. Bedford St., #213, Madison WI 53703-3695. (608)294-9008. Fax (608) 294-9010. E-mail: gracemag1@aol.com. Grace Press, Inc. Norine Conroy, ed/pub. Celebrates and honors the lives and voices of women on their spiritual journey. Bimonthly mag; circ 1,000. 70% freelance. Query; phone/fax/e-query OK. Pays $50 & up on publication for 1st rts. Articles 1,500-3,000 wds (10/yr); fiction 1,500-3,000 wds (15/yr). Responds in 4-9 wks. Accepts simultaneous submissions & reprints. Kill fee 50%. Free guidelines/theme list/copy. Incomplete topical listings.

Poetry: Buys 5/yr. Avant-garde, free verse, haiku, light verse, traditional. Pays $50 & up. Submit max 5 poems.

Fillers: Buys 5/yr. Anecdotes, facts, newsbreaks, short humor; 50-300 wds. Pays $50 & up.

Special Needs: Upcoming themes: Love, Bodies, Abundance, Forgiveness, and Truth. No evangelical or witnessing pieces.

Tips: "Write to our themes. For us, spirituality honors all religious traditions."

***GREATER THINGS**, PO Box 645, St. Maarten, Netherlands Antilles. Phone 599-5-95730. Fax 599-5-25393. E-mail: ccwc@sintmaarten.com.Greater Works Foundation. Patricia Varlack, ed. Quarterly mag. One-page articles. Submit by mail/fax/e-mail. Not in topical listings.

Special Needs: The four quarterly theme deadlines are: January 1, 2001; March 1, 2001; July 1, 2001; and October 1, 2001.

Tips: "Include your résumé/testimony with submission."

THE HANDMAIDEN, PO Box 76, Ben Lomond CA 95005. (831)336-5118. Fax (831)336-8882. E-mail: bobnmarya@aol.com, or vhnieuwsma@prodigy. net. Website: www.conciliarpress.com. Antiochian Orthodox Archdiocese of North America. Mary Armstrong & Virginia Nieuwsma, co-eds. For women serving God within the Eastern Orthodox tradition. Quarterly journal; 64 pgs; circ 3,000. Subscription $15. 5% unsolicited freelance; 95% assigned. Query; e-query OK. **PAYS IN COPIES/SUBSCRIPTION.** Articles 1,000-2,000 wds (8/yr). Responds in 6-8 wks. Seasonal 6 mos ahead. Accepts reprints (tell when/where appeared). Prefers hard copy or e-mail submissions (copied into message). Some sidebars. Prefers NKJV. Guidelines/theme list; copy for 7x10 SAE/4 stamps. To request the theme list, or guidelines for writers, poets or artists, send an SASE to: Mary Armstrong, 8018—38th Dr. NE, Marysville WA 98270. (No ads)

Poetry: Donna Farley, ed. Accepts 4-8/yr. Free verse, light verse, traditional. Submit max 3 poems.

Columns/Departments: Heroines of the Faith (lives of women saints within Orthodox tradition), 1,000-2,000 wds.

Tips: "Most open to theme features, sidebars, and poetry."

+**HEARTS AT HOME**, 900 W. College Ave., Normal IL 61761. (309)888-6667. Fax (309)888-4525. E-mail: hearts@dave-world.com. Website: www. hearts-at-home.org. Connected to annual conferences by the same name (held in Bloomington IL, Lansing MI, Minnapolis MN, and Tulsa OK). Marilyn Snook, co-ed; Rachel Kitson, ed. for columns, poetry and fillers. To encourage and educate mothers at home. Monthly mag; 16 pgs; circ. 2,000. Subscription 15. Estab. 1997. 30-40% unsolicited freelance; 60-70% assigned. Complete ms by mail or e-mail; e-query OK. **PAYS 5 COPIES** for one-time rts. Articles to 1,000 wds (40-50/yr); devotionals to 750 wds; book reviews 500 wds. Responds in 2 wks. Seasonal 3 mos ahead. Accepts reprints (tell when/where appeared). Prefers e-mail submissions (attached Word file or copied into message). No kill fee. Some sidebars. Any version. Guidelines/theme list (also by e-mail/Website); copy $2/6x9 SAE/2 stamps. (No ads)

> **Poetry:** Accepts 5-8/yr. Light verse, traditional; 10-25 lines. Submit max 3 poems.
>
> **Fillers:** Accepts 100/yr. Anecdotes, cartoons, facts, ideas, party ideas, short humor; 25-100 wds.
>
> **Columns/Departments:** Accepts 15-20/yr., Motherhood; Parenting; Marriage; Personal Growth; Spiritual Growth; Family Management; to 1,000 wds.
>
> **Special Needs:** Articles that challenge mothers in their growth as a parent; uplift spouses in relationship with each other and children; encourage spiritual growth; educate mothers on networking, finding time for themselves, or overcoming personal challenges; tips on saving time and money; and using personal experiences to better parent kids. Looking for more articles by, for and about moms at home with older children (pre-teen and older).
>
> **Tips:** "Submit a well-written, balanced, positive article which will encourage, educate and/or entertain our audience. Personal stories of the triumphs and trials of being an at-home mom are preferred. This publication is designed to be by moms and for moms. Please include a short biography to go with your article."

$**THE HELPING HAND**, Box 12609, Oklahoma City OK 73157-2609. (405) 787-7110. Fax (405)789-3957. E-mail: MBJohnson@IPHC.org. Website: www.iphc.org. Pentecostal Holiness Church/Women's Ministries. Mary Belle Johnson, ed. Denominational; for women. Bimonthly mag; 16 pgs; circ 4,000. Subscription $9.95. 5% assigned. Query; no e-query. Pays $20 on publication for one-time or simultaneous rts. Articles 500-800 wds (3/yr); fiction 500-1,300 wds (2/yr). Responds in 8 wks. Seasonal 4 mos ahead. Accepts reprints (tell when/where appeared). Accepts disk or e-mail (copied into message). Some sidebars. Prefers NIV. Guidelines; copy for 9x12 SAE/2 stamps. (No ads)

> **Poetry:** Buys 5/yr. Traditional; $10-20. Submit max 4 poems.
>
> **Tips:** "We now accept material only from women in this denomination."

$**HORIZONS**, 100 Witherspoon St., Louisville KY 40202-1396. (502)569-5379. Fax (502)569-8085. E-mail: LBradley@ctr.pcusa.org. Website: www.

pcusa.org/horizons. Presbyterian Church (USA). Leah Bradley, assoc. ed. Justice issues and spiritual life for Presbyterian women. Bimonthly mag & annual Bible study; 40 pgs; circ 25,500. Subscription $15. 10% unsolicited freelance; 90% assigned. Query; fax/e-query OK. Pays $50-$125/ printed page on acceptance for 1st rts. Articles 1,200 wds (10/yr) & fiction 1,200-1,800 wds (5/yr); book reviews 100 wds, $25. Responds in 4 wks. Seasonal 6 mos ahead. Accepts simultaneous submissions & reprints (tell when/where appeared). Accepts disk or e-mail submission (attached or copied into message). Kill fee. Regular sidebars. Prefers NRSV. Guidelines/theme list (also by e-mail/Website); copy $3. (No ads)

Poetry: Buys 5/yr. All types; $50-100. Submit max 5 poems.

Fillers: Cartoons, church-related graphics; $50.

Tips: "Poetry, features, fiction are open to freelancers. Should be relevant to Presbyterian women and church leadership. Devotionals for the inside front cover are also accepted. Seasonal fiction or nonfiction are most likely to be used."

$*JOURNAL OF WOMEN'S MINISTRIES, 815 Second Ave., New York NY 10017. (Editor's address: 344 S. Maple Ave., Apt 2B, Oak Park IL 60302-3436). (800)334-7626. Fax (708)763-9454. E-mail: wimm@dfms.org. Website: www.dfms.org/women. Episcopal/Women in Missions and Ministries. Marcy Darin, ed. Deals with issues of interest to women from a liberal perspective. Biannual mag; 36 pgs; circ 10,000. Subscriptions (800-374-9510). Query. Pays $50 on publication for 1st rts. Articles 1,200-1,500 wds. Responds in 5 wks. Seasonal 3 mos ahead. Guidelines; copy for 9x12 SAE/3 stamps.

Poetry: Free verse, traditional. Submit max 2 poems.

$#JOURNEY, 127 Ninth Ave. N., Nashville TN 37234. (615)251-5659. Fax (615)251-5008. Website: www.lifeway.com. Southern Baptist. Selma Wilson, ed; Pamela Nixon, mng ed. Devotional magazine for women 30-45 years old. Monthly mag; 44 pgs; circ 150,000. 20% freelance. Subscription $18.95. Query/clips or complete ms/cover letter; no phone/fax/e-query. Pays $25-150 on acceptance for all, 1st, one-time or reprint rts. Articles 350-1,000 wds (10-12/yr). Responds in 8 wks. Seasonal 6-7 mos ahead. Accepts simultaneous submissions & reprints (tell when/where appeared). Regular sidebars. Prefers NIV. Accepts disk. Guidelines; copy for 6x9 SAE/2 stamps.

Fillers: Prayers, short humor; 200-350 wds.

Special Needs: Strong feature articles 90-1,000 words; profiles of Christian women in leadership positions.

Tips: "Would like to see articles for our weekend pages and an occasional 3-page feature article on topics of interest to women 30-45 years old."

**This periodical was #54 on the 1997 Top 50 Christian Publishers list (#55 in 1996).

$JOYFUL WOMAN, PO Box 90028, Chattanooga TN 37412-6028. (706)866-5522. Fax (706)866-2432. E-mail: JoyfulWoman1@cs.com. Website: www. joyfulwoman.org. Joyful Christian Ministries, Inc. Joy Rice Martin, ed. For and about Bible-believing women who want God's best. Bimonthly mag; 32 pgs; circ 6,000. Subscription $19.95. 16% unsolicited freelance; 0% assigned. Query with first page of article; fax/e-query OK. Pays $20-30 (.03-.04/wd) on publication for 1st rts. Articles & fiction 500-1,000 wds (45/yr). Responds in 6 wks. Seasonal 3 mos ahead. Accepts simultaneous submissions & reprints (tell when/where appeared). Accepts disk or e-mail submission (attached file). Kill fee. Some sidebars. KJV only. Guidelines; copy for 9x12 SAE/6 stamps. (Ads)

> **Poetry:** Buys 6/yr. Free verse, light verse, traditional; 15-40 lines; $15-25. Submit max 2 poems.
>
> **Fillers:** Buys few. Cartoons, jokes, newsbreaks, prayers, quotes, short humor; 25-300 wds; $15-20.
>
> **Columns/Departments:** Buys 6/yr. Positively Single, 300 wds. Complete ms. Pays $25.
>
> **Tips:** "Our biggest need is true-life stories and inspirational articles. We prefer 1,000-word-or-less manuscripts, and would like color pictures of author and/or manuscript subject. Please allow 16 weeks before you call about your manuscript."

JUST BETWEEN US, 777 S. Barker Rd., Brookfield WI 53045. (262)786-6478 or (800)260-3342. Fax (262)796-5752. E-mail: jbu@elmbrook.org. Website: www.justbetweenus.org. Elmbrook Church, Inc. Shelly Esser, ed. Ideas, encouragement and resources for wives of evangelical ministers and women in leadership. Quarterly mag; 32 pgs; circ 6,000. Subscription $14.95. 85% unsolicited freelance; 15% assigned. Query; phone/fax/e-query OK. **NO PAYMENT** for one-time rts. Articles 250-500 wds or 800-1,500 wds (50/yr). Responds in 8 wks. Accepts simultaneous submissions & reprints. Regular sidebars. Prefers NIV. Guidelines/theme list (also by e-mail/Website); copy $2/9x12 SAE. (Ads)

> **Fillers:** Buys 15/yr. Anecdotes, cartoons, ideas, prayers, quotes, short humor; 50-250 wds.
>
> **Columns/Departments:** Buys 12/yr. Money Savers; Keeping Your Kids Christian; Women's Ministry (program ideas); all 500-700 wds.
>
> **Tips:** "Most open to feature articles addressing the unique needs of women in leadership (Bible-study leaders, women's ministry directors, pastor's wives, missionary wives, etc.). Some of these needs would include relationship with God, staff, leadership skills, balancing ministry and family, and marriage. The best way to break in is to contact the editor directly. Follow themes."

*LEAH'S SISTERS: A Newsletter for Woman Conquering Rejection and Loss, PO Box 17-1234, Irving TX 75017. Mary Dunham, ed. Bimonthly newsletter. Subscription $12.50.

$THE LINK & VISITOR, 15 Michael Dr., Toronto ON M2H 2A2 Canada. (416)651-7192. Fax (416)651-0438. E-mail: linkvis@idirect.com. Baptist Women's Missionary Society of Ontario and Quebec. Krysia P. Lear, ed. A positive, practical magazine for Canadian Baptist women who want to make a difference in their world. Monthly (9X) mag; 16 pgs; circ 4,300. Subscription $12 CAN, $15 US. 15% unsolicited freelance; 85% assigned. Query/clips or complete ms/cover letter; e-query OK. Pays .05-.08/wd

CAN, on publication for one-time or simultaneous rts; some work-for-hire. Articles 750-2,000 wds (30-35/yr). Responds in 36 wks. Seasonal 3 mos ahead. Accepts simultaneous submissions & reprints (tell when/where appeared). Accepts disk. Some sidebars. Prefers NIV (inclusive language), NRSV, or LB. Guidelines/theme list; copy for 9x12 SAE/.90 Canadian postage. (Ads—limited/Canadian)

Poetry: Buys 6/yr. Free verse; 12-32 lines; $10-25. Submit max 3 poems.

Special Needs: Mentoring, sharing our faith, developing a deeper faith in Christ as adults, and cross-cultural relationships. Also cross cultural photos; seasonal; women in ministry (send JPEG and cost).

Tips: "Canadian perspective, please. Query first."

LUTHERAN WOMAN'S QUARTERLY, 3121 Chelsea Ct., South Bend IN 46614-2207. Phone/fax (219)291-8297. E-mail: donnajs@michiana.org, or lwml@lwml.org. Lutheran Women's Missionary League. Donna Streufert, ed-in-chief. For women of the Lutheran Church—Missouri Synod. Quarterly mag; 44 pgs; circ 200,000. Subscription $4.50. 25% unsolicited freelance; 75% assigned. Complete ms/cover letter. **NO PAYMENT.** Not copyrighted. Articles 750-1,200 wds (4/yr); fiction 750-1,200 wds (4/yr). Responds in 2 wks. Seasonal 5 mos ahead. Regular sidebars. Prefers NIV. Guidelines/theme list; no copy.

Tips: "Most open to articles. Must reflect the Missouri Synod teachings. Most of our writers are from the denomination. We set themes two years ahead. Contact us for themes and guidelines."

$LUTHERAN WOMAN TODAY, 8765 W. Higgins Ave., Chicago IL 60631-4189. (800)638-3522x2743 or (773)380-2743. E-mail: lwt@elca.org. Website: www.elca.org/wo/lwthome.html. Evangelical Lutheran Church in America. Deb Bogaert, mng. ed. For women in the denomination. Monthly (10X) mag: 48 pgs; circ 180,000. 10% unsolicited freelance; 90% assigned. Complete ms/cover letter; e-query or submissions OK. Pays $70-300 on acceptance for 1st rts. Articles 700-1,500 wds (20/yr) & fiction to 1,250 wds (5/yr). Responds in 12 wks. Seasonal 7 mos ahead. Accepts simultaneous submissions & reprints (tell when/where appeared). Prefers submissions on disk or e-mail (attached file). Kill fee. Some sidebars. Prefers NRSV. Guidelines/theme list (also on Website at: www.elca.org/wo/lwt); free copy. (No ads)

Poetry: Buys 6-8/yr. Avante-garde, free verse, light verse; to 60 lines; $15-60. Submit max 3 poems. Poetry must have a spiritual and women's focus.

Columns/Departments: Buys 5/yr. Devotion, 350 wds; Season's Best (reflection on the church year), 350-700 wds; About Women (profiles); Forum (essay); pays $50-250.

Tips: "Looking for articles on prayer and spirituality. Submit a short, well-written article using inclusive language and offering a women's and spiritual focus."

THE PROVERBS 31 WOMAN (formerly The Proverbs 31 Homemaker), PO Box 17155, Charlotte NC 28227-0099. (704)849-2270. Fax (704)849-7267. E-mail: P31home@proverbs31.org. Website: www.proverbs31.org. The Proverbs 31 Ministry. Glynnis Whitwer, ed. To encourage and inspire women in their many roles and responsibilites. Monthly newsletter; 16 pgs; circ 6,000. Subscription $15 donation. 50% unsolicited freelance; 50% assigned. Complete ms; e-query OK. **PAYS IN COPIES** for one-time rts. Not copyrighted. Articles 200-1,000 wds (40/yr); book reviews 200-250 wds. Responds in 4-6 wks. Seasonal 3 mos ahead. Accepts simultaneous submissions & reprints. Prefers e-mail submissions (attached file). No sidebars. Prefers NIV. Guidelines; copy for 9x12 SAE/2 stamps. (No ads)

> **Poetry:** Accepts 6-10/yr. Traditional. Submit max. 2 poems.
>
> **Fillers:** Accepts 12/yr. Ideas, party ideas, prose; to 100 wds.
>
> **Tips:** "Looking for articles that encourage women and offer practical advice as well."

*REFLECTIONS, 5351 NW 11th St., Lauderhill FL 33313-6406. (954)587-0129. Ellen Waldron, pub. Good news and inspiration for all ages. Quarterly newsletter; 20+ pgs. Subscription $15. 90% unsolicited freelance; 10% assigned. Complete ms/cover letter. **PAYS 4 COPIES.** Not copyrighted. Articles 400 wds (6/yr); fiction 1,000 wds (6/yr). Responds in 6-8 wks. Seasonal 2 mos ahead. No disk or e-mail submissions. Some sidebars. Guidelines/theme list; copy for $2/10x13 SAE/$1.50 postage. (Ads)

> **Poetry:** Accepts 10/yr. Free verse, haiku, light verse, traditional; 5-30 lines. Submit max 5 poems.
>
> **Columns/Departments:** Accepts 6/yr. Pen Pals Corner (write service families in armed forces); Helpful Hints (ideas to help others), 400 wds; Joy, Joy, Joy (good news), 400 wds; Chicklette Gazette (children ages 4-12), 200 wds; Teen Corner (sharing ideas for 13-19 year olds, 400 wds; On the Road (travel).
>
> **Tips:** "Have an interest in writing; write from the heart. No foul language or anything offensive. Writers must send a notarized release before we can print their work (under 18 years, parent must sign). Fiction is for children or teens."

SHARE, 10 W. 71st St., New York NY 10023-4201. (212)877-3041. Fax (212) 724-5923. E-mail: cdosanatl@aol.com. Website: www.catholicdaughters. org. Catholic Daughters of the Americas. Peggy Eastman, ed. For Catholic women. Quarterly mag; circ 118,000. Free with membership. Most articles come from membership, but is open. **NO PAYMENT.** Buys color photos and covers. Guidelines/copy. Not in topical listings. (Ads)

*SHINE, 105 Mariah Dr., Weatherford TX 76087. (817)613-0188. Michelle Toholsky, ed/pub. Fashion magazine for Christian women; devoted to connecting a woman's inner, spiritual beauty with her outer, physical beauty. Bimonthly mag; circ 100,000. Estab. 1999. Accepts only poems or articles for the feature called "The Mom Connection." Did not return questionnaire.

> **Columns/Departments:** The Mom Connection (articles or poems dealing with family).
>
> **Tips:** "For all women who strive for excellence in every area of their lives and are devoted to spiritual and social responsibility. Average reader is female, age 43, educated, and married."

$SPIRITLED WOMAN, 600 Rinehart Rd., Lake Mary FL 32746. (407)333-0600. Fax (407)333-7133. E-mail: spiritledwoman@strang.com, or bdavis@strang.com. Website: www.spiritledwoman.com. Strang Communications. Brenda J. Davis, ed. To call women, ages 20-60, into intimate fellowship with God so He can empower them to fulfill His purpose for their lives. Bimonthly mag; 100 pgs; circ. 26,000. Subscription $12. Estab 1998. 1% unsolicited freelance; 99% assigned. Query (limit to 500 wds); fax/e-query OK. Pays on publication for 1st rts and all electronic rts. Articles 1,200-2000 wds. Responds in 4-6 mos. (Ads)

> **Columns/Departments:** Testimonies; Final Fun (funny stories or embarrassing moments, to 200 wds); cartoons; pays $25-50.
>
> **Tips:** "Mainly we want impacting articles that depict a practical and spiritual application of scriptural teachings. Need brief testimonies of 300 words or less. Articles need to deal with the heart issues that hold a woman back."

+SUNDAY/MONDAY WOMAN, Box 1209, Minneapolis MN 55440-1209. (612)330-3300. Fax (612)330-3215. Website: www.augsburgfortress.org. Augsburg/Fortress. For Christian women. Bimonthly mag. Not included in topical listings. Did not return questionnaire.

$TODAY'S CHRISTIAN WOMAN, 465 Gundersen Dr., Carol Stream IL 60188-2498. (630)260-6200. Fax (630)260-0114. E-mail: TCWedit@TodaysChristianWoman.net. Website: www.TodaysChristianWoman.net. Christianity Today Intl. Jane Johnson Struck, mng. ed.; submit to Ginger McFarland, asst. ed. To help Christian women grow in their relationship to God by providing practical, biblical perspectives on marriage, sex, parenting, work, health, friendship, single life, and self. Bimonthly mag; 80-150 pgs; circ 320,000. Subscription $17.95. 25% unsolicited freelance; 75% assigned. Query only; fax/e-query OK. Pays .20/wd on publication (on acceptance for assignments) for 1st rts. Articles 1,500-1,800 wds (6-12/yr); no fiction. Responds in 6-8 wks. Seasonal 6 mos ahead. Accepts reprints (tell when/where appeared); no simultaneous submissions. Accepts e-mail submission (copied into message). Regular sidebars. Prefers NIV. Guidelines; copy $5. (Ads)

> **Columns/Departments:** Jane Struck, mng ed. Buys 6/yr. My Story (dramatic story of overcoming a difficult situation), 1,500 wds, $300, query. Faith@work (how you shared faith in the marketplace), 300 wds, $25. My Favorite Website, 100 wds, $25. Reader's Picks (book or CD review), 200 wds.
>
> **Tips:** "Make sure your writing has a fresh approach to a relational topic and that it has a personal tone and anecdotal approach. Please query first."
>
> **This periodical was #57 on the 1996 Top 50 Christian Publishers list (#34 in 1994). Also 1996 EPA Award of Merit—General.

TRUE WOMAN, PO Box 8732, Columbia SC 29202. E-mail: faithwebbin@yahoo.com. Website: www.gentle.org/TrueWoman. Ty Mitchell, owner. For Christian women. Online mag. Complete ms by e-mail submission. NO PAYMENT. Guidelines on Website.

> **Fillers:** Beauty, health and household tips.

Special Needs: Arts and crafts, mentoring, mothering, any articles of interest to women.

Tips: "If you are the writer, please send information about yourself as well (a short bio and contact e-mail submission address for readers). If you are not the writer, please include proper credits."

WELCOME HOME, 9493-C Silver King Ct., Fairfax VA 22031. (703)827-5903 or (800)783-4MOM. E-mail: mah@mah.org. Website: www.mah.org. Mothers at Home, Inc. Laura M. Jones, ed-in-chief; submit to Manuscript Coordinator. For women who have chosen to stay at home with their children. Monthly journal; 30 pgs; circ. 15,000. Subscription $18. 100% unsolicited freelance. Complete ms/cover letter. **NO (OR LIMITED) PAYMENT** for one-time rts. Articles to 2,400 wds, most 500-1,500 wds (60/yr). Acknowledges receipt in 2-4 wks, decision in 4-6 mos. Seasonal 1 yr ahead. No e-mail submission. Some sidebars. Guidelines (request specific guidelines for departments interested in; also on Website); copy for 7x10 SAE/3 stamps. (No ads)

> **Poetry:** Winnie Peterson Cross. Accepts 48/yr. Free verse, haiku, light verse, traditional.

> **Columns/Departments:** Accepts 36/yr. From a Mother (surprising/sudden insights); Resource Roundup (books/resources); New Dimensions (personal growth/development); Heartwarming (cooking/recipes); Health & Safety (mother's/child's health, family safety); Time to Care (volunteer work); all 700-1,000 wds.

> **Tips:** "This is a publication for all mothers at home, and not for those with any particular religious background. Articles which focus on a religious theme will not be accepted."

$THE WESLEYAN WOMAN, PO Box 50434, Indianapolis IN 46250-0434. (317)570-5164. Fax (317)570-5254. E-mail: wwi@wesleyan.org. Website: www.wesleyan.org. Wesleyan Church. Martha Blackburn, mng ed. Inspiration, education and sharing to meet the needs of Wesleyan women. Quarterly mag; 24 pgs; circ 3,500. Subscription $12.95. 50% unsolicited freelance; 50% assigned. Complete ms/cover letter; phone/fax query OK. Pays .04/wd (.02-.03/wd for reprints) on publication for one-time or reprint rts. Articles 500-700 wds (1-10/yr). Responds in 10-12 wks. Seasonal 6 mos ahead. Accepts simultaneous submissions & reprints (tell when/where appeared). Accepts disk. Regular sidebars. Guidelines/theme list; free copy. (No ads)

> **Poetry:** Accepts 4/yr. Free verse, light verse, traditional. Pays .04/wd, up to $10. Submit max 2 poems.

> **Fillers:** Accepts few. Anecdotes, cartoons, ideas, party ideas, quotes, short humor; 150-350 wds.

> **Tips:** "Most open to personal stories of 'guts' and grace to follow the Lord. Ways you see God at work in your life—personal, not preachy."

$WOMAN ALIVE, Herald House Ltd., 96 Dominion Rd., Worthing, West Sussex BN14 8JP United Kingdom. (44) 1903 821082. Fax (44) 1903 821081. E-mail: womanalive@christianmedia.org.uk. Interdenominational. Liz Trundle, ed. Britain's only Christian women's magazine; discusses issues relevant to active Christians. Open to freelance. Query or complete ms;

e-query OK. Pays 72 pounds (about $100) on publication for 1st UK rts. Articles 750-1,300 wds (interviews 1,300 wds; 1st-person testimonies to 800 wds; contemporary issues 800-1,300 wds; celebrity profiles 800 wds). Responds in 3 wks. Guidelines (also by e-mail). Incomplete topical listings.

Special Needs: Travel, practical advice, crafts, home, garden, and cooking; 750-1,200 wds.

$WOMAN'S TOUCH, 1445 Boonville Ave., Springfield MO 65802-1894. Fax (417)862-0503. E-mail: dknoth@ag.org. Website: www.ag.org/womans touch. Assemblies of God Women's Ministries Dept. Lillian Sparks, ed.; Darla J. Knoth, mng. ed. Inspirational magazine for career-oriented women, self-employed women, homemakers, and retirees. Bimonthly mag; 32 pgs; circ 12,200. Subscription $8. 40% unsolicited freelance; 60% assigned. Complete ms/cover letter; no e-query. Pays $20-35 (.03/wd) on publication for one-time and electronic rts. Articles 500-800 wds (20/yr). Responds in 13 wks. Seasonal 10 mos ahead. Accepts simultaneous submissions & reprints (tell when/where appeared). Accepts disk or e-mail submission. Kill fee. Regular sidebars. Prefers KJV or NIV. Guidelines/ theme list (also by e-mail); copy for 9x12 SAE/3 stamps. (No ads)

Fillers: Buys 10/yr. Anecdotes, ideas; 50-200 wds; $5-15.

Columns/Departments: Buys 30/yr. A Better You (health/fitness), 500 wds; A Final Touch (human interest on home/family/career), 350 wds; A Lighter Touch (true humorous anecdotes), 100 wds; History's Women (great women of faith), 500 wds. Pays $10-40.

Tips: "Writers who beome acquainted with our style and focus are more likely to be published. Read two back issues before submitting." **This periodical was #35 on the 1996 Top 50 Christian Publishers list.

$WOMEN ALIVE! Box 4683, Overland Park KS 66204. Phone/fax (913)649-8583. Website: www.womenalivemagazine.org. Aletha Hinthorn, ed. To encourage women to live holy lives by applying Scripture to their daily lives. Bimonthly mag; 20 pgs; circ 5,000-6,000. Subscription $13.95. 50% unsolicited freelance; 0% assigned. Complete ms/no cover letter; no phone/fax query. Pays $25-50 on publication for 1st or reprint rts. Articles 300-1,800 wds (7/yr). Responds in 4-6 wks. Seasonal 4 mos ahead. Accepts reprints. Some sidebars. No disk. Prefers KJV or NIV. Guidelines/ theme list; copy for 9x12 SAE/4 stamps. (No ads)

Fillers: Buys 0-1/yr. Cartoons, jokes, short humor.

Tips: "We look for articles that draw women into a deeper spiritual life—articles on surrender, prayer, Bible study—yet written with personal illustrations."

$WOMEN OF SPIRIT, 55 W. Oak Ridge Dr., Hagerstown MD 21740-7390. (301)393-4125. Fax (301)393-4055. E-mail: WomenofSpirit@rhpa.org. Website: www.womenofspirit.com. Review and Herald/Seventh-Day Adventist. Penny Estes Wheeler, ed. To inspire, nurture and challenge Christian women. Bimonthly mag; 32 pgs; circ 15,000. Subscription $17.95. Complete ms/cover letter; fax/e-query OK. Pays on acceptance. Articles 500-1,000 wds. Responds in 12 wks. Seasonal 6 mos ahead. Accepts reprints (tell when/where appeared). Accepts disk, prefers e-mail submission (attached file). Regular sidebars. Prefers NIV. Guidelines (also by e-mail); copy for 9x12 SAE/2 stamps. (Ads)

$WOMEN TODAY MAGAZINE, Box 300, Vancouver BC V6C 2X3, Canada. (604) 514-2000. Fax (604)514-2002. E-mail: katherine@mkehler.com. Website: www.womentodaymagazine.com. Campus Crusade for Christ, Canada. Katherine Kehler, exec ed. For the professional, non-Christian woman, 20-40 years. Monthly mag. Estab 1997. 30% freelance. Query; e-query OK. Pays $25-100 on publication. Articles 100-500 wds. Seasonal 4 mos ahead. Accepts reprints (tell when/where appeared). Prefers e-mail submission. Regular sidebars. Guidelines. (Ads)

> **Columns/Departments:** Life Stories (testimony of adult conversion), 250 wds; Feature (Christ-centered, but not religious), 700 wds; Potpourri (women's interests), 100 wds.
> **Tips:** "The writer needs to have global perspective, and have a heart to reach women with the gospel."

+WOMEN WHO MINISTER TO WOMEN (WWM2W) EZINE, 2217 Lake Park Dr., Longmont CO 80503. (303)772-2035. Fax (303)678-0260. E-mail: RightToTheHeart@aol.com. Website: www.righttotheheart.org. Straight From the Heart. Amy Unger, ed. For Christian women in leadership and ministry (women's directors, authors, speakers, Bible teachers, etc.). Quarterly online e-zine; 15 pgs; circ 1,500-5,000. Subscription free. 10% unsolicited freelance; 90% assigned. Query; e-query OK. **NO PAYMENT** for one-time rts & right to post on Web. Articles 50-200 wds (10/yr); book reviews 100 wds. Responds in 5 wks. Seasonal 2 mos ahead. Accepts simultaneous submissions & reprints. Requires e-mail (copied into message). No kill fee. Some sidebars. No guidelines; copy on Website. (No ads for now)

> **Columns/Departments:** Accepts 10/yr. Women Bible Teachers; Profiles of Women in Ministry; Women's Ministry Tips; Author's and Speaker's Tips; 100 wds. Query.
> **Special Needs:** Book reviews must be in first person, by the author.
> **Contest:** Send 150 word nominations for Woman's Minister of the Year, and Women's Ministry of the Year.
> **Tips:** "For free subscription, write *Subscribe* in subject line and send to RightToTheHeart@aol.com. Read to determine what we accept."

WRITER'S MARKETS

$ADVANCED CHRISTIAN WRITER, 9731 N. Fox Glen Dr., #6F, Niles IL 60714-4222. (847)296-3964. Fax (847)296-0754. E-mail: linjohnson@compuserve.com. Website: www.ECPA.org/ACW. American Christian Writers/Reg Forder, Box 110390, Nashville TN 37222, (800)21-WRITE, regaforder@aol.com. Lin Johnson, mng ed. A professional newsletter for published writers. Bimonthly newsletter; 8 pgs; circ 500. Subscription $19. 60% unsolicited freelance; 0% assigned. Query and correspondence by e-mail only. Pays $20 on publication for 1st or reprint rts. Articles 500-1,000 wds (18/yr). Responds in 6-8 wks. Seasonal 6 mos ahead. Accepts reprints (tell when/where appeared). Regular sidebars. Requires e-mail submission. Prefers NIV. Guidelines (also by e-mail); copy for #10 SAE/1 stamp (order from ACW, PO Box 110390, Nashville TN 37222). (Ads)

Special Needs: Behind the scenes look at a publishing house (how it started, how editorial operates, current needs, submission procedures).

Tips: "We accept articles only from professional, well-published writers. We need manuscripts about all aspects of being a published freelance writer and how to increase sales and professionalism; on the advanced level; looking for depth beyond the basics."

$AREOPAGUS MAGAZINE (UK), Mrs. P. Lindsay, 107 Coopers Green, Bicester OXON OX6 9US, United Kingdom. E-mail for UK: areo@bigfoot.com. E-mail for US: AreopagUSA@aol.com. Website: www.churchnet.org.uk/areopagus/index.html. Areopagus Publications. Julian Barritt, ed. For amateur and semi-professional Christian writers, producing both secular and Christian writing. Quarterly mag; 32 pgs; circ 140. Subscription $17 (now on sale in US). 80% unsolicited freelance; 20% assigned. Complete ms/cover letter (if subscriber); e-query OK. Pays 2-5 pounds (or equivelent in dollars) when funds allow, on publication for 1st & electronic rts. Articles 1,200 wds (40/yr); fiction 1,200 wds (15/yr); book reviews 250 wds. Responds in 2 wks. Seasonal 4 mos ahead. Accepts e-mail submissions (attached or copied into message). No sidebars. Any version. Guidelines; copy (also on Website) for 9x12 SAE/equivalent of 31 pence for postage. (Ads)

Poetry: Accepts 40/yr. Any type; to 41 lines. Pays 2 pounds when funds allow. Submit max 1 poem.

Fillers: Accepts 12/yr. Anecdotes, facts, games, ideas, jokes, newsbreaks, party ideas, prayers, prose, quizzes, quotes, short humor, to 200 wds. No payment.

Contest: Sponsors a quarterly, subscribers-only, writing competition (fiction, nonfiction or poetry theme) with a prize of 10 pounds.

Tips: "Items are selected by merit from subscribers only. If not accepted, a recommendation for re-submission is given if there is potential."

$BYLINE, Box 130596, Edmond OK 73013-0001. Phone/fax (405)348-5591. E-mail: Mpreston@bylinemag.com. Website: www.ByLineMag.com. Secular. Marcia Preston, ed; Carolyn Wall, fiction ed. Offers practical tips, motivation and encouragement to freelance writers and poets. Monthly (11X) mag; 32 pgs; circ 3,000+. Subscription $22. 80% freelance. Query or complete ms; no phone/fax query; e-query OK. Pays $75 for features; $100 for fiction; less for shorts, on acceptance for 1st rts. Articles 1,500-1,800 wds; personal essays 700 wds; fiction 2,000-4,000 wds (10/yr). Responds in 6 wks. Seasonal 6 mos ahead. Accepts simultaneous submissions. No e-mail submissions. Encourages sidebars. Guidelines (also on Website); copy $4. (Ads)

Poetry: Sandra Soli. Buys 50-100/yr. Any type; to 30 lines; $10. Writing themes only. Submit max 3 poems.

Fillers: Anecdotes, prose, short humor for humor page, 100-400 wds, pays $15-25. Must pertain to writing.

Columns/Departments: Buys 50-60/yr. End Piece (personal essay on writing theme), 700 wds, $35; First Sale accounts, 200-400 wds, $20; Only When I Laugh (writing humor), short, $15-25. Complete ms.

Contests: Sponsors many year round; details included in magazine.

Special Needs: Accepts articles only about writing and selling; likes mainsteam fiction.

Tips: "Most open to First Sale account; be upbeat about writing. Need articles, essays and poetry on writing topics; general interest short stories (no religious). Keep trying."

$CANADIAN WRITER'S JOURNAL, White Mountain Publications, Box 5180, New Liskeard ON P0J 1P0 Canada. (705)647-5424. Canada-wide toll-free (800)258-5451. Fax (705)647-8366. E-mail: cwj@ntl.sympatico.ca. Website: www.net/~cwj/index.htm. Deborah Ranchuk, ed/pub. How-to articles for writers. Bimonthly mag; 64 pgs; circ 350. Subscription $22.50. 85% unsolicited freelance; 15% assigned. Complete ms/cover letter; phone/fax/e-query OK. Pays $5 CAN/published pg on publication for one-time rts. Articles 500-2,000 wds (150/yr); book reviews to 500 wds/$5. Responds in 9-10 wks. Seasonal 3 mos ahead. Accepts simultaneous submissions & reprints (tell when/where appeared). Prefers e-mail submission (copied into message). Some sidebars. Prefers KJV. Guidelines (also by e-mail/Website); copy $5. (Ads)

Poetry: Buys 40-60/yr. All types; to 50 lines. Pays $2-5. Submit max. 10 poems.

Fillers: Buys 15-20/yr. Ideas, quotes; 20-200 wds. Pays $3-5.

Contest: Sponsors semi-annual short fiction contest (March 31 and September 30 deadlines); to 1,200 wds. Entry fee $5. Prizes $100, $50, $25. All fiction needs are filled by this contest.

Tips: "Send clear, complete, consise how-to-write articles with a sense of humor and usefulness. Read the guidelines and follow them, please."

$THE CHRISTIAN COMMUNICATOR, 9731 N Fox Glen Dr., #6F, Niles, IL 60714-4222. (847)296-3964. Fax (847)296-0754. E-mail: linjohnson@ compuserve.com. Website: www.ecpa.org/acw. American Christian Writers/ Reg Forder, Box 110390, Nashville TN 37222, (800)21-WRITE (for advertising or subscriptions), fax (615)834-0450; regaforder@aol.com. Lin Johnson, mng ed. For Christian writers/speakers who want to improve their writing craft and speaking ability, stay informed about writing markets, and be encouraged in their ministries. Monthly (11X) mag; 20 pgs; circ 3,000. Subscription $25. 70% unsolicited freelance; 30% assigned. Complete ms/queries by e-mail only. Pays $5-10 on publication for 1st, one-time or reprint rts. Articles 350-1,000 wds (80/yr). Responds in 8-10 wks. Seasonal 6 mos ahead. Accepts reprints (tell when/where appeared). Requires e-mail submission. Guidelines by e-mail; copy for 9x12 SAE/3 stamps. (Ads)

Poetry: Accepts 12/yr. Poems on writing; $5. Send to Gretchen Sousa, gretloriat@earthlink.net.

Columns/Departments: Buys 22/yr. Interviews (published authors or editors), 650-1,000 wds; Speaker's Corner (techniques for speakers), 600-1,000 wds.

$CHRISTIAN WRITER, PO Box 22416, Denver CO 80222-0416. E-mail: Suwriter@aol.com. Sue Wright, ed. Focuses on Christians who are writing for both the Christian and general market. Quarterly mag. Subscription $25. Query; e-query OK. Pays $25-75 on acceptance for 1st rts. Articles 800-2,300 wds. Some reprints. Guidelines (also by e-mail); copy $6.

>   **Special Needs:** We are looking for several types of articles: inspirational aspect of writing (must include Scripture and quotes from historical/literary figues); how-to or encouragement for writers; interviews with editors, agents, or well-established writers; industry trends on specific needs of editors or on trends in the industry; and book reviews of recently published writing books.

>   **Tips:** "We publish writing articles to encourage and support Christians who write."

COCHRAN'S CORNER, 1003 Tyler Ct., Waldorf MD 20602-2964. (361)876-1664. Jeannie Saunders, exec ed. To encourage a greater interest in writing for art's sake and provide a publication where aspiring and young writers can be published. Quarterly mag; 32 pgs. Circ 500. Subscription $20. 100% unsolicited freelance. Complete ms/cover letter. **PAYS IN COPIES** for one-time rts. Articles 1,000 wds (25/yr); fiction 1,000 wds (25/yr). Responds in 6 wks. Seasonal 3 mos ahead. Accepts reprints. No disk. No sidebars. Prefers KJV. Guidelines; copy $5/9x12 SAE. (Ads)

>   **Poetry:** Accepts 70/yr. All types; 4-20 lines. Submit max 5 poems.

>   **Fillers:** Accepts 25/yr. Anecdotes, cartoons, facts, newsbreaks, prayers, prose, quotes, and short humor, to 150 wds.

>   **Columns/Departments:** Accepts 5/yr. Gardening (how to grow something, for adults, but simple enough a child could do it), 1,000 wds.

>   **Contest:** Sponsors a short-story contest quarterly.

>   **Tips:** "A well-crafted story without violence, pornography or blue language has the best chance with us."

$CONTEMPORARY SONGWRITER MAGAZINE, Box 25879, Colorado Springs CO 80936-5879. (719)232-4489. Fax (303)223-1638. E-mail: contemporarysong@yahoo.com. Website: www.angelfire.com/co2/contempo, or www.contemporary.bigstep.com. Secular. Roberta C. Redford, pub/ed. Helps readers learn about the craft and business of songwriting. Estab 1998. Monthly mag; circ 5,000. 100% freelance. Query with/without clips; e-query OK. Pays .05/wd on acceptance for 1st rts. Articles 200-2,500 wds (80/yr). Kill fee 20%. Responds in 3-4 wks. Seasonal 8 mos ahead. Guidelines; copy $3.

>   **Columns/Departments:** Looking for columnists.

>   **Special Needs:** Interviews with songwriters, how-to pieces on writing lyrics and melodies, how-to pieces on promotion and marketing of songs.

>   **Tips:** "Write in a way that is both informational and personal." Very open to unpublished writers.

>   **This periodical was #24 on the 2000 Top 50 Christian Publishers list.

$CROSS & QUILL, 1624 Jefferson Davis Rd., Clinton SC 29325-6401. (864)697-6035. E-mail: cwfi@cwfi-online.org. Website: www.cwfi-online. org. Christian Writers Fellowship Intl. Sandy Brooks, ed/pub. For Christian writers, editors, agents, conference directors. Bimonthly newsletter; 16 pgs; circ 1,000+. Subscription $20; CWFI membership $40. 75% unsolicited freelance; 25% assigned. Complete ms; no e-query; query for electronic submissions. Pays honorarium for feature articles on publication for 1st or reprint rts. Articles 800-1,000 wds (24/yr); book reviews 100 wds (pays copies). Responds in 2 wks. Seasonal 6 mos ahead. Accepts reprints (tell when/where appeared). Regular sidebars. Accepts disk, no e-mail submission. Guidelines; copy $2/9x12 SAE/2 stamps. (Ads)

> **Poetry:** Accepts 12/yr. Any type; to 12 lines. Submit max 3 poems. Must pertain to writing/publishing. Currently overstocked.
>
> **Fillers:** Accepts 12/yr. Anecdotes, cartoons, prayers; to 100 wds. Pays in copies.
>
> **Columns/Departments:** Accepts 36/yr. Writing Rainbows! (devotional), 600 wds; Writer to Writer (how-to), 900 wds; Editor's Roundtable (interview with editor), 200-800 wds; Tots, Teens & In-Betweens (juvenile market), 200-800 wds; BusinessWise (business side of writing), 200-800 wds; Connecting Points (how-to on critique group), 200-800 wds.
>
> **Special Needs:** Good "meaty" informational articles on children's writing; writing for teens; how-tos on organizing and operating writers' groups; and how to organize and run a writer's workshop, conference or seminar.
>
> **Tips:** "Most open to informational articles that explain how to improve writing skills, how to keep records, how to organize and run a writers' group. Keep in mind our audience is primarily writers and others associated with Christian publishing."

$+DEDICATED AUTHOR, (all contacts made by e-mail). E-mail: dedicated author@hotmail.com. S. Seifert, ed. Focuses on Christians who are professional writers, editors, teachers, agents, and conference leaders. Biweekly e-zine. Starting January 2001. Subscription free. Open to freelance. Query or complete ms, by e-mail. Pays $5 on acceptance for 1st electronic rts. Fillers 30-150 wds.

> **Special Needs:** Although authors, publishers and conference leaders write most of our tips on how to teach and speak about writing to promote their conference or books, we accept a small amount of filler that demonstrates an awesome writing technique or exercise, and short anecdotes that speakers can use in their talks about writing.
>
> **Tips:** "We publish concise tips and job opportunities for busy professional writers, to help them move further into all that God has called them to be."

$EXCHANGE, 1275 Markham Rd., #305, Toronto ON M1H 3A2 Canada. (416)439-4320. Fax (416)439-5089. E-mail: exchange@ica.net. Audrey Dorsch, ed. A forum for Christian writers to share information and ideas. Quarterly newsletter; 8 pgs; circ 185. Subscription $19.26 CAN, $15 US.

65% unsolicited freelance; 10% assigned. Complete ms/cover letter; fax/e-query OK. Pays .10 CAN & .07 US on publication for one-time rts. Not copyrighted. Articles 400-600 wds (20/yr). Responds in 4-6 wks. Accepts reprints (tell when/where appeared). Accepts disk, prefers e-mail submission (attached file). No sidebars. Prefers NIV. Guidelines (also by e-mail)/copy for #10 SAE/2 Canadian stamps (.55). (Ads—classified)

Special Needs: Material geared to experienced, professional writers.

Tips: "Take a very deliberate approach to the 'how' of good writing. I get too much for the novice writer. If you submit something an experienced writer will learn from, you face much less competition."

$FELLOWSCRIPT, 121 Morin Maze, Edmonton AB T6K 1V1 Canada. Fax (403)461-1809. E-mail: nharms@oanet.com. Website: www.inscribe.org. Inscribe Christian Writers' Fellowship. Nathan Harms, ed. To provide encouragement, instruction and news to Christians who write. Quarterly (5X) newsletter; 24 pgs; circ 250. Subscription $30 (includes membership). 100% freelance. Complete ms/cover letter; e-query OK. Pays $30-50 for assigned, $15-30 for unsolicited, on publication for one-time, reprint or simultaneous rts. Not copyrighted. Articles 350-1,000 wds (15-25/yr); book reviews, 300-350 wds, $5. Responds in 12 wks. Seasonal 4 mos ahead. Accepts simultaneous submissions & reprints (tell when/where appeared). Accepts disk. Kill fee 50%. Regular sidebars. Prefers KJV. Guidelines; copy $1. (Ads)

Fillers: Anecdotes, cartoons, facts, ideas, quotes, market updates; to 140 wds. Buys 8-25/yr. Pays $2-7.

Columns/Departments: Open to ideas for columns.

Special Needs: Articles of practical help to writers; how to put together a promotional package for the writer.

Contest: Sponsors two a year, one in March for members, one in August that is open. Send #10 SAE/$1 to "Contest Info."

Tips: "Most open to writer's tips, market information, and instructional articles on very specific topics (no general, how-to-write-better items). We are less interested in articles intended to 'inspire' other writers. We appreciate e-mail submissions."

$+FICTION FIX NEWSLETTER, The Nuts and Bolts of Crafting Better Fiction. E-mail: ffeditor@coffeehouse4writers.com. Website: www.coffee houseforwriters.com/news.html. Karen Hertzberg, mng. ed. For writers and aspiring writers of short stories and novels. Monthly; circ. 2,200. To subscribe, send blank e-mail to: FictionFix-subscribe@topica.com. Query. Responds in 2-3 wks. Pays $10-20 on publication. How-to articles 800-1,000 wds. Did not return questionnaire.

Columns/Departments: This Writer's Opinion (reviews of writing books); The Writing Life (personal writing stories). No payment.

$+FICTION WRITER ONLINE LITERARY MAGAZINE. E-mail: submissions @thefictionwriter.com. Website: www.thefictionwriter.com. Secular. Joyce Siedler, mng ed. Online mag. Open to freelance. Complete ms. Pays $50 for features, $35 for short stories, essays or nonfiction on publication for exclusive rts to publish article on site for 1 yr, and non-exclusive rts to fiction. Articles 1,000-3,500 wds; fiction 1,500-5,000 wds. Requires e-mail submission (copied into message only). Guidelines on Website. Incomplete topical listings.

Fillers: Buys short-short humorous pieces to 10 lines, $5.

Special Needs: Some acceptable genres are romance, sci-fi, speculative, mysteries, and historical fiction.

Contest: Sponsors a short fiction contest. Details on Website. May not be done every year.

Tips: "For nonfiction, please substantiate your claims with concrete examples, names, and quotes from editors, Website URLs and snail mail addresses where writers can find related information. You must have experts and facts to back up your point. Don't wander or generalize."

$GOTTA WRITE NETWORK LITMAG, 515 E. Thacker St., Hoffman Estates IL 60194-1957. E-mail: netera@aol.com. Secular/Maren Publications. Denise Fleischer, ed. A support system for writers, beginner to well established. Semiannual mag; circ 300. Subscription $15. 80% freelance. Query or complete ms/cover letter; e-query OK. Pays $5 for articles ($10 for fiction) after publication for 1st rts. Articles 3-5 pgs (25/yr); fiction 5-10 pgs (10+/yr) on writing techniques; book reviews 2 pgs. Responds in 3 mos. Seasonal 6 mos ahead. Guidelines; copy $6.

Poetry: Accepts 75+/yr. Avant-garde, free verse, haiku, experimental; 4 lines to 1 pg. Submit max 5 poems.

Tips: "Most open to articles on writing techniques. Give me something different and in-depth. No I-love-writing, how-I-did-it." No religious material. Seeking GWN state representatives.

HEAVEN, HCR-13 Box 21AA, Artemas PA 17211. (814)458-3102. E-mail: weems@hereintown.net. Kay Weems, ed. Published for Easter. $5/copy. Every other year booklet. 100% freelance. **NO PAYMENT.** Short stories to 2,500 wds. Responds in 4-12 wks. Accepts simultaneous submissions & reprints.

Poetry: All types of poetry on heaven, to 36 lines. Submit max 10 poems.

Tips: "Does different themes throughout the year."

$+KEYSTROKES. E-mail: editor@writelinks.com. Website: www.writelinks. com. General. Submit to The Editor. To assist published and new writers to improve their writing skills and find paying markets. Free, monthly online mag. Open to freelance. Complete ms; e-query OK. Pays $25 on publication. Articles to 5,000 wds. Requires e-mail submissions in ASCII (copied into messsage). Guidelines on Website.

Special Needs: Articles and essays on writing, book reviews, and interviews with people in the writing business.

Tips: "Let us know if you want us to list your e-mail address with your published piece." Material must reach the editor by the 15th of the month to be included in the following month's edition.

$MERLYN'S PEN: Fiction, Essays, and Poems by America's Teens, Box 1058, East Greenwich RI 02818. (401)885-5175. Fax (401)885-5222. E-mail: merlynspen@aol.com. Website: www.merlynspen.com. Secular. R. James Stahl, ed; submit to Naomi Mead-Ward, ms. coord. Written by students in grades 6-12 only. Annual mag; circ. 5,000. 100% unsolicited freelance (from teens). Complete ms. Articles 100-5,000 wds (10/yr); fiction to 5,000 wds (40/yr); reviews and travel pieces to 1,000 wds. Pays $25-200, plus copies; on publication; for all rts. Responds in 13 wks. Not in topical listings. Guidelines and sample articles on Website. (Ads—educational/literature related).

Poetry: Buys 25/yr. Any type; 3-250 lines. Pays $25-250. Submit max 3 poems.

MY LEGACY, HCR-13 Box 21AA, Artemas PA 17211. (814)458-3102. E-mail: weems@hereintown.net. Kay Weems, ed. For young adults and up. Quarterly booklet; 70-80 pgs; circ 200+. Subscription $16. 100% freelance. **NO PAYMENT.** No articles; fiction to 2,500 wds (100/yr). Responds in 14-16 wks. Accepts simultaneous submissions & reprints. Guidelines; copy for 6x9 SAE/4 stamps & $4.50.

Poetry: Accepts 200+/yr. Any type; to 36 lines.

NORTHWEST CHRISTIAN AUTHOR, 10663 NE 133rd Pl., Kirkland WA 98034-2030. (425)821-6647. Fax (206)823-8590. E-mail: the.newtons@verizon.net. Website: www.seanet.com/~nwca. Northwest Christian Writers Assn. Lorinda Newton, ed. To encourage Christian authors to share the gospel through the written word and to promote excellence in writing. Bimonthly newsletter; 8 pgs; circ. 80. Subscription $10. 100% unsolicited freelance. Complete ms/cover letter; e-query OK. **PAYS 3 COPIES** for 1st, one-time, reprint or simultaneous rts. Not copyrighted. Articles 500-1,000 wds (18/yr). Responds in 8 wks. Accepts simultaneous submissions & reprints (tell when/where appeared). Prefers e-mail submission (attached file). Regular sidebars. Guidelines/theme list (also by e-mail/Website); copy for 6x9 SAE/2 stamps. (No ads)

Special Needs: How-tos on fiction and a piece about print on demand.

Tips: "Most open to articles on writing techniques, particularly for specific genres. We've had too many how-to-submit articles. Stay within word count. E-queries should have 'NW Christian Author' in subject line. Include 1-2 sentence author bio with article."

OMNIFIC, HCR-13 Box 21AA, Artemas PA 17211. (814)458-3102. E-mail: weems@hereintown.net. Kay Weems, ed. Family-type publication for writers/adults. Quarterly booklet; 100+ pgs; circ 300+. Subscription $20. 100% freelance. **SMALL AWARDS GIVEN.** Accepts simultaneous submissions & reprints. No articles; poetry only. Guidelines; copy for 6x9 SAE/4 stamps & $5.

Poetry: Any type; to 36 lines. Submit max 4-8 poems.

ONCE UPON A TIME . . ., 553 Winston Ct., St. Paul MN 55118. (651)457-6223. Fax (651)457-9565. E-mail: AUDREYOUAT@aol.com. Website: members.aol.com/ouatmag. Audrey B. Baird, ed/pub. A support publication for children's writers and illustrators. Quarterly mag; 32 pgs; circ 1,000. Subscription $24.25. 50% unsolicited freelance. Complete ms/cover letter. **PAYS IN COPIES** for one-time rts. Articles to 800 wds (80-100/yr). Responds in 4-5 wks. Seasonal 6 mos ahead. Accepts simultaneous submissions & reprints (tell when/where appeared). Some sidebars. Guidelines (also on Website); copy $5. (Ads)

Poetry: Buys 35/yr. Free verse, haiku, light verse, traditional; any length. Writing/illustrating related. Submit max 6 poems.

Fillers: Buys 50/yr. Anecdotes, cartoons, prose, quizzes, short humor (all writing/illustrating related); to 100 wds.

Special Needs: How-to articles on writing & illustrating up to 800 wds; short pieces on writing & illustrating, 100-400 wds.

Tips: "Send a good, tight article on the writing life—any aspect—that is either educational, informative, entertaining, humorous, or inspiring. About rhyming poetry: Pay attention to rhythm—it's not enough to rhyme—rhyming poetry must have rhythm (and near rhyme is not enough). I'm willing to help and to edit and to suggest, but do your part first with revision until the piece is as good as you can get it."

THE POETRY CONNECTION/MAGIC CIRCLE, 13455 SW 16th Ct., #F-405/CWM, Pembroke Pines FL 33027. (954)431-3016. Fax (509)351-7401. E-mail: poetryconnect@webtv.net. Sylvia Shichman, ed/pub. Information for poets, writers and song writers; also greeting card markets. Monthly newsletter; flyer format; circ 200. Subscription $20. Query; phone/fax/e-query OK. **PAYS A SUBSCRIPTION.** Not copyrighted. Responds immediately. Accepts simultaneous submissions. Guidelines; copy $7; minisample $3/10x13 SAE. (Ads)

Poetry: All forms, any length. Magic Circle membership required.

Contests: Lists contests in newsletter; also sells *The Avisson Book of Contests & Prize Competitions for Poets.*

Note: Offers membership in the Magic Circle, a poetry reading network service for poetry. Membership $30 (50 copies) or $60 (100 copies). Make check to Sylvia Shichman. Your bio and one poem sent directly to publishers. In addition, rents a mailing list that includes poets.

TEACHERS & WRITERS, 5 Union Square W, New York NY 10003. (212)691-6590. Fax (212)675-0171. E-mail: info@twc.org. Website: www.twc.org. Ron Padgett & Chris Edgar, eds. On teaching creative and imaginative writing for children. Mag published 5X/yr & online mag; circ 1,500-2,000. Query. **PAYS IN COPIES.** Articles 3,000-6,000 wds. Copy $2.50.

$TICKLED BY THUNDER, 14076 86A Ave., Surrey BC V3W 0V9 Canada. Phone/fax (604)591-6095. E-mail: thunder@istar.ca. Website: home.istar.ca/thunder. Larry Lindner, ed. For writers wanting to better themselves. Quarterly chapbook (3-4X); 24 pgs; circ 1,000. Subscription $12 (or $10 US). 90% unsolicited freelance; 10% assigned. Complete ms/cover letter; e-query OK. Pays $2-5 (in Canadian or US stamps) on publication for one-time rts. Articles 2,000 wds (5/yr); fiction 2,000 wds (20/yr); book/music/video reviews 1,000 wds. Responds in 16 wks. Seasonal 6 mos ahead. Accepts simultaneous submissions. Prefers disk, no e-mail submission. Some sidebars. Guidelines (also by e-mail/ Website); copy $2.50/9x12 SAE. (Ads)

Poetry: Accepts 20-40/yr. Any type; to 40 lines. Submit max 7 poems.

Contest: For fiction (February 15 annual deadline) and poetry (February 15, May 15, August 15, and October 15 annual deadlines). Article contests for subscribers only (February 15, May 15, August 15, and October 15 deadlines). Send SASE for guidelines.

Tips: "Write a 300-word article describing how you feel about your successes/failures as a writer. Be specific, and focus—don't be at all general or vague."

WE! (formerly Writer's Exchange), 129 Thurman Ln., Clinton TN 37716-6611. E-mail: Eboone@aol.com. Website: members.aol.com/WriterNet. R.S.V.P. Press. Eugene Boone, ed. Features writings and small press markets for writers and poets at all levels. Quarterly mag; 40 pgs; circ 350. Subscription $12. 100% freelance. Complete ms/cover letter. **PAYS IN COPIES** for one-time rts. Articles 350-5,000 wds (20-30/yr); book reviews 500 wds. Responds in 2-4 wks. Seasonal 6-12 mos ahead. Accepts reprints (tell when/where appeared). Accepts disk. Regular sidebars. Guidelines; copy $2. (Ads)

Poetry: Accepts 100-150/yr. Any type; 3-35 lines. Submit max 8 poems.

Fillers: Accepts 300/yr. Various; 10-750 wds.

Special Needs: Poetry how-to; writing techniques; personal experiences with writing groups, conferences, writing courses, using computers, etc. What worked and what didn't.

Contest: Quarterly poetry contest; send SASE for rules.

$WIN-INFORMER, PO Box 11337, Bainbridge Island WA 98110. (206)842-9103. Fax (206)842-0536. E-mail: writersinfonetwork@juno.com. Website: www.bluejaypub.com/win or www.ecpa.org/win. Writers Information Network. Elaine Wright Colvin, ed. Industry news and trends to keep professionals in touch with the changing marketplace. Bimonthly (5X) mag; 24-44 pgs. Subscription $35 ($40 Canada/foreign). 30% unsolicited; 20% assigned. Complete ms/cover letter; phone/fax/e-query OK. Pays $10-50 (copies or subscription) on publication for 1st rts. Articles 100-800 wds (30/yr); book reviews, 300 wds. Accepts e-mail submission. Some sidebars. Guidelines (also by e-mail/Website); copy $5/9x12 SAE/$1.70 postage. (Members and writing-related ads)

Poetry: Any type; writing related.

Fillers: Anecdotes, facts, ideas, newsbreaks, quizzes, quotes, prayers, short humor; 50-300 wds; $10-20.

Columns/Departments: Buys 42/yr. Industry News, Bulletin Board, Computer Corner, Speakers' Microphone, Prayer Requests, Poetry News, Agency News, Changes in the Industry, Watch on the World, Look Over My Shoulder, and Readers Q & A; $10-50.

Special Needs: Tips for new book authors on promoting yourself and your work.

Tips: "Pick a topic we all want to know about and do a round-up report with lots of quotes from editors, agents, and professional writers/speakers. Put your best investigative reporting skills to work. Attend a Christian writers' conference and give us an eye-witness report on what the editors and professionals are telling you about the market place. Hot news press releases really get our attention."

$WRITER ONLINE, 40 Royal Oak Dr., Rochester NY 14624. E-mail: creosote1@hotmail.com. Website: www.novalearn.com/wol.WriteRead.com. T.M. Wright, ed. For writers seeking timely, professional advice on the art, craft, and marketing of writing. Biweekly online newsletter; circ 34,000. Subscription free. Estab 1998. 60% freelance. Prefers hard-copy queries, but does accept e-mail submissions. Query by e-mail with "Writer" in the body of e-mail submission. Pays .05-.10/wd on publication for one-time and archival rts. Articles 800-1,800 wds (60-80/yr); Flash Fiction to 99 wds; fiction 300-1,200 wds; book reviews, 800-1,800 wds, $50 ($20 for reprint). Responds in 2-4 wks. Seasonal 2-3 mos ahead. Accepts simultaneous submissions & reprints (tell when/where appeared). Requires e-mail submission (attached file). Kill fee 50% or $25. Some sidebars. Guidelines (also by e-mail/Website); copy on Website. (Ads)

> **Poetry:** All types, to 40 lines. Pays $1/line
>
> **Columns/Departments:** Buys 10-20/yr. Creative Nonfiction; International Writer; Children's Writer; Writer's Advocate (legal); Technical Writer; Public Relations Writer; Interview; Book Reviews; M.O.: Mystery and Mayhem; Guest (various topics), 800-1,200 wds, $20-50. Query.
>
> **Tips:** "Most open to Guest columns on writing how-tos: markets, craft, technique. Also interviews with famous or well-published writers."

$#THE WRITER, 21027 Crossroads Cir., Waukesha WI 53189. E-mail: writer@user1.channel1.com. Website: www.channel1.com/the writer. Secular. Gerald Boettcher, ed/pub. How-to for writers; lists religious markets in December. Monthly mag; 52 pgs; circ 50,000. Subscription $29. 75% freelance. Query; no phone/fax query; e-query OK. Pays $100 (varies) on acceptance for 1st rts. Articles to 2,000 wds (60/yr). Responds in 3 wks. No e-mail submissions. No sidebars. Copy $4. (Ads)

> **Poetry:** Accepts poetry for critiques in "Poet to Poet" column; to 30 lines; no payment. No religious poetry. Submit max 3 poems.
>
> **Fillers:** Prose.
>
> **Columns/Departments:** Buys 24+/yr. Rostrum (shorter pieces on the craft of writing), 1,000 wds; Off the Cuff (somewhat more personal tone), 1,000-1,200 wds; $75.
>
> **Special Needs:** How-to on the craft of writing only.
>
> **Tips:** "Material must be practical, targeted to beginning writers, and include plenty of how-to, advice, and tips on techniques."

*THE WRITER'S BILLBOARD, PO Box 645, St. Maarten, Netherlands Antilles. Phone 599-5-95730. Fax 599-5-25393. E-mail: ccwc@sintmaarten.com. Greater Works Foundation. Patricia Varlack, ed. Biannual mag (May & October). One-page articles. Submit by mail/fax/e-mail. Not in topical listings.

> **Tips:** "Deadlines are March and August. Include your résumé with submission."

+WRITER'S CHRONICLE, The Magazine for Serious Writers, George Mason University, Associated Writing Programs, Tallwood House, MSN 1E3, 4400 University Dr., Fairfax VA 22030-9736. (703)993-4304. Fax (703)

993-4302. E-mail: awp@gmu.edu. Website: www.awpwriter.org. D.W. Fenza, ed-in-chief. Bimonthly mag. Subscription $20.

Special Needs: Author interviews, essays, trends and literary controversies.

$WRITER'S DIGEST, 1507 Dana Ave., Cincinnati OH 45207. (513)531-2222. Fax (513)531-1843. E-mail: writersdig@fwpubs.com. Website: www. writersdigest.com. Secular/F & W Publications. Melanie Rigney, ed; submit to Katie Dumont, assoc ed. To inform, instruct or inspire the freelancer. Monthly mag; 76 pgs; circ 180,000. Subscription $27. 20% unsolicited; 80% assigned. Query/clips (preferred); e-query OK. Pays .25-.50/wd on acceptance for 1st rts. Articles 800-1,500 wds (60/yr). Responds in 4-6 wks. Seasonal 6-8 mos ahead. Requires disk or e-mail submission (attached or copied into message). Kill fee 20%. Regular sidebars. Guidelines (also on Website); copy $5.25 (plus sales tax in OH). (Ads)

> **Columns/Departments:** Buys 12/yr (unsolicited). The Writing Life (anecdotes about writing life & short profiles), 50-200 wds; Tip Sheet (short solutions to writer/business-related problems), 50-300 wds.
>
> **Contests:** Sponsors annual contest for articles, short stories, poetry and scripts. Also The National Self-Publishing Book Awards. Send SASE for rules.
>
> **Tips:** "This magazine underwent a major redesign in January 2000; review the magazine and send for updated guidelines."

$WRITER'S FORUM, Writer's Digest School, 1507 Dana Ave., Cincinnati OH 45207. (513)531-2690. Fax (513)531-0798. E-mail: WritersDig@fwpubs. com. Secular/F&W Publications. Joe Squance, ed. Writing techniques, marketing and inspiration for *Writer's Digest* correspondence school students. Triannual newsletter; 16 pgs; circ 13,000. Subscription $10. 100% unsolicited freelance. Complete ms/cover letter. Pays $10-25 on acceptance for reprint rts. Articles 500-1,000 wds (20/yr). Responds in 6 wks. Seasonal 4 mos ahead. Accepts reprints (tell when/where appeared). Accepts e-mail submissions. Free guidelines (also by e-mail)/copy for #10 SAE/3 stamps. (Ads)

> **Tips:** "A great market for reprints. How-to pieces geared toward beginning writers always stand a good chance. Looking for articles that help others improve their writing, and marketing tips that work. Approach the field of how-to articles with freshness and originality."

*WRITER'S INK, PO Box 93156, Henderson NV 89009-3156. (800)974-8465. Panabaker Publications. Darla R. Panabaker, ed. Supplies writers with information on writing and selling. Monthly newsletter; 12 pgs; circ. 100. Subscription $24. 90-95% freelance. Query or complete ms. **PAYS IN COPIES** for 1st, one-time or simultaneous rts. Articles 50-1,000 wds (200/yr); book reviews, 500 wds. Responds in 4 wks. Seasonal 3-6 mos ahead. Accepts simultaneous submissions & reprints. Regular sidebars. Guidelines; copy for 9x12 SAE/2 stamps.

> **Poetry:** All types; on writing topics; to 50 lines. Send any number.
>
> **Fillers:** Ideas, newsbreaks, quizzes, quotes; to 50 wds.
>
> **Columns/Departments:** Looking for freelancers to write columns. Topics and subject matter open. Please inquire.

Contest: 2001 Poetry Competition. $100 grand prize. Deadline November 15. Send SASE for rules.

Tips: "Send article with letter describing your previous experience. All areas open. We use a different writer for each cover article."

$WRITER'S JOURNAL, PO Box 394, Perham MN 56573-0394. (218)346-7921. Fax (218)346-7924. E-mail: writersjournal@wadena.net. Website: www. writersjournal.com. Val-Tech Media/Secular. Leon Ogroske, ed. For current, aspiring, amateur, and professional writers. Bimonthly mag; 64 pgs; circ 33,000. 90% unsolicited freelance; 10% assigned. Complete ms/cover letter; fax/e-query OK. Pays subscription and up to $25 on publication for one-time rts. Articles to 2,000 wds (30-40/yr); book reviews 200 wds, $5. Responds in 12 wks. Accepts simultaneous submissions & reprints (tell when/where appeared). Accepts disk or e-mail submission (copied into message). Some sidebars. Guidelines; copy $5/9x12 SAE. (Ads)

Poetry: Esther M. Leiper. Buys 40/yr. All types; to 25 lines; pays $5/ poem. Submit as contest entries only.

Fillers: Anecdotes, cartoons, facts, ideas, jokes, short humor, 50 wds. Pay varies.

Contest: Runs several contests each year. Prizes $300. Categories are short story, horror/ghost, romance, travel writing, and fiction; 3 poetry; photo. Send an SASE requesting guidelines.

Tips: "We need good articles on the skills of writing; good how-to articles on story composition."

WRITER'S LIFELINE, Box 1641, Cornwall ON K6H 5V6 Canada. (613)932-2135. Fax (613)932-7735. E-mail: stefgill@hotmail.com. Stephen Gill, mng ed. For professional freelancers and beginning writers. Bimonthly mag; 16-35 pgs; circ 1,500. Needs articles of interest to writers, news items of national and international interest, letters to the editor, poetry, interviews. Needs book reviewers; **PAYS IN BOOK REVIEWED & COPIES.** Not in topical listings.

$WRITER'S POTPOURRI, 55 Binks Hill Rd., Plymouth NH 03264. Fax (603)536-4851. E-mail: me.allen@juno.com. Website: homepage. fcgnetworks.net/jetent/mea. MEA Productions. Mary Emma Allen, ed. Tips and information of interest to writers. Quarterly newsletter; 6 pgs; circ 100. Subscription $8. 25% freelance. E-query OK. Pays $5, plus 2 copies, on acceptance for one-time, reprint or simultaneous rts. Articles 250-500 wds max (4-6/yr); book reviews 250 wds, $5. Responds in 4 wks. Accepts simultaneous submissions & reprints (tell when/where appeared). Prefers e-mail submission (copied into message). Guidelines (also by e-mail); copy $1/#10 SAE/1 stamp. (No ads)

Special Needs: Market trends for writers, self-publishing information and Internet information for writers and publishers (usually from other writers).

Tips: "Most open to helpful tips for writers. Stay within word allowance; no long articles, poetry or fiction. We also use some announcements about writer's acomplishments; keep brief (no pay for these)."

+WRITES OF PASSAGE, PO Box 11805, Kansas City MO 64138-0305. (816)765-7406. E-mail: StackEdits@aol.com. Kansas City Christian

494 WRITER'S MARKETS/Periodical Publishers

Writers' Network. Debi Stack, ed. Newsletter. Open to assigning 400-word articles to freelancers. Query. **NO PAYMENT.** Articles 400 wds. Guidelines. Incomplete topical listings.

*THE WRITE TOUCH, PO Box 695, Selah WA 98942. (509)966-3524. Tim Anderson, ed. For writers trying to get published. Monthly newsletter; 12 pgs; circ 40. Subscription $15/yr. 100% freelance. Complete ms/cover letter. **PAYS 3 COPIES,** for one-time rts. Essays on various subjects (120/yr) & fiction for all ages (120/yr), 100-500 wds. Responds in 2-4 wks. Seasonal 2 mos ahead. Discourages simultaneous submissions & reprints. Accepts disk. Guidelines; copy $1.

Poetry: Any type; 4-30 lines. Submit maximum 3 poems.

Fillers: Anecdotes, facts, ideas, prose, short humor; 15-50 wds.

*WRITING WORLD, 44 Tarleton Rd., Newton MA 02159. Submit to The Editor. Bimonthly newsletter; 8 pgs. Subscription $39. Little freelance. Copy for $5/#10 SAE. Not in topical listings.

Contest: Occasionally; see sample issues.

Tips: "Look at back issues and send a fantastic query that shows you've read us."

MARKET ANALYSIS

PERIODICALS IN ORDER BY CIRCULATION

ADULT/GENERAL

Guideposts 3,000,000
Focus on the Family 2,700,000
Columbia 1,600,000
Decision 1,300,000
Angels on Earth 800,000
The Lutheran 620,000
Plus 600,000
Catholic Digest 509,390
Marion Helpers 500,000
Oblates 500,000
HomeLife 475,000
Mature Living 350,000
St. Anthony Messenger
    345,000
Miraculous Medal 340,000
War Cry 300,000
Anglican Journal 272,000
Lutheran Witness 270,000
Pentecostal Evangel 264,000
Charisma & Christian Life
    250,000
Liberty 250,000
Power for Living 250,000
Episcopal Life 248,000
Upscale Magazine 242,000
Liguorian 227,000
Signs of the Times 225,000
Christian Reader 185,000
Ideals 180,000
Grit 170,000
Christianity Today 155,000
Christian Times 153,000
The Family Digest 150,000
Standard 150,000
Tomorrow's Christian
    Graduate 150,000
Smart Families 140,000
Discipleship Journal 130,000
Lutheran Journal 130,000
Company 120,000
Whispers From Heaven
    120,000
Live 115,000
Lutheran Digest 115,000
Moody 115,000
The Plain Truth 110,000
Presbyterian Survey 105,000

The Lookout 102,000
Foursquare World Advance
    102,000
Catholic Forester 100,000
CGA World 100,000
Christianity Online 100,000
Good News (KY) 100,000
On Mission 100,000
United Church Observer
    100,000
Light 91,000
Connection Magazine 90,000
Living (tabloid) 90,000
Total Health 90,000
Physician 81,700
Celebrate Life 80,000
Message 80,000
Leaves 75,000
Our Sunday Visitor 75,000
Heartlight Internet 70,000
Lifewise 70,000
Mature Years 70,000
Single-Parent Family 70,000
Christian Home & School
    67,000
alive now! 65,000
Faith & Friends 60,000
Good News Journal 60,000
Men of Integrity 60,000
Christian Standard 58,000
Christian History 55,000
Conquest 55,000
Northwestern Lutheran
    55,000
Presbyterian Record 55,000
Marriage Partnership 53,000
Church of God Evangel 51,000
Bridal Guides 50,000
Catholic Answer 50,000
Creation Ex Nihilo 50,000
Daily Walk 50,000
Gospel Today 50,000
Say Amen 50,000
Today's Christian Senior
    50,000
The Trumpeter 50,000
Vibrant Life 50,000
Annals of St. Anne 45,000
Seek 45,000

Sports Spectrum 45,000
America 41,000
Christian Motorsports 40,000
Parabola 40,000
A Positive Approach 40,000
Priority! 40,000
U.S. Catholic 40,000
Cornerstone 38,000
Good News Journal 35,000-
    50,000
Beacon 35,000
Catholic Parent 35,000
Christian Research Journal
    35,000
Gospel Tract 35,000
Highway News 35,000
Church & State 33,000
Colorado Christian Chronicle
    32,000
First Things 32,000
Alliance Life 30,000
The Banner 30,000
Catholic Twin Circle 30,000
Christian Computing 30,000
Lifeglow 30,000
Progress 30,000
Cathedral Age 29,000
Reflections 29,000
New Frontier 25,500
Homeschooling Today 25,000
Interim 25,000
Messenger of St. Anthony
    25,000
Sojourners 24,000
Testimony 21,500
God's Revivalist 20,000
Good Shepherd 20,000
Life@Work 20,000
Light and Life 20,000
New Covenant 20,000
Wesleyan Advocate 20,000
Evangel 19,000-20,000
Commonweal 19,000
Southeast Lookout 18,200
Accent on Living 18,000
Faith Today 18,000
Canada Lutheran 17,000
Nashville Christian Banner
    17,000

Covenant Companion 16,000
The Door 16,000
Mennonite Brethren Herald 16,000
St. Joseph's Messenger 15,500
Dunamis Life 15,000
Over the Back Fence/NW 15,000
Over the Back Fence/SW 15,000
SCP Journal 15,000
This Rock 15,000
Gems of Truth 14,000
Spirit (MO) 14,000
Bible Advocate 13,500
Creation Illustrated 13,000
Marketplace 13,000
Messenger/Sacred Heart 13,000
Presbyterian Outlook 12,734
Purpose 11,600
Spiritual Life 11,000
Review for Religious 10,200
Disciple's Journal 10,000
Immaculate Heart Messenger 10,000
Kairos Journal 10,000
Sacred Journey 10,000
The Vision 10,000
Christian Leader 9,800
Faro de Luz 9,500
Montana Catholic 9,300
Breakthrough Intercessor 9,100
NRB Magazine 9,100
Celebration (Catholic) 9,000
Companions 9,000
Journal of Christian Nursing 9,000
Living Church 9,000
Prism 9,000
Psychology for Living 9,000
Sharing 9,000
The Standard 9,000
Catholic New Times 8,000
CBA Marketplace 8,000
Our Family 8,000
White Wing Messenger 8,000
Peoples Magazine 7,800
Prairie Messenger 7,300
The Gem 7,100
CBA Frontline 7,000
MN Christian Chronicle 7,000
New Freeman 7,000
2 Soar 7,000
Christian Courier (CAN) 6,000
Impact 6,000
Facts for Faith 5,300

AGAIN 5,000
Christianity & the Arts 5,000
Companion 5,000
Creation Care 5,000
A New Heart 5,000
The Plowman 5,000
Way of St. Francis 5,000
Social Justice Review 4,950
Cresset 4,700
Wireless Age 4,700
Christian Civic League/ME 4,600
The Resource 4,500
Touchstone 4,200
Message/Open Bible 4,100
Christian Living 4,000
Christian Renewal 4,000
The Evangelical Advocate 4,000
Preserving Christian Homes 4,000
The Witness 4,000
Catholic Insight 3,600
Bread of Life 3,500
Cross Currents 3,500
Culture Wars 3,500
New Moon 3,500
Servant Life 3,500
Perspectives on Science 3,300
Alive! 3,000
Chrysalis Reader 3,000
The Evangel 3,000
Evangelical Baptist 3,000
Legions of Light 3,000
MovieGuide 3,000
North American Voice 3,000
Perspectives 3,000
Prayer Closet 3,000
Quiet Revolution 3,000
Re:generation 3,000
Mennonite Historian 2,600
Queen of All Hearts 2,600
Christian Social Action 2,500
The Messenger (NC) 2,500
Railroad Evangelist 2,500
Fellowship Focus 2,300
Apocalypse Chronicles 2-3,000
Baptist History & Heritage 2,000
Fellowship Link 2,000
Forefront 2,000
Church Herald/Holiness Banner 1,700
Journal/Church & State 1,700
Dovetail 1,500
Jewel Among Jewels 1,500
Pourastan 1,250
Christian Crafter 1,000

Christian Designer 1,000
Connecting Point 1,000
Head to Head 1,000
The Hunted News 1,000
Methodist History 800
The Storyteller 750
Eternal Ink 620
Hidden Manna 500
St. Willibrord Journal 500
Short Stories 500
West Wind Review 500
Christian Response 400
About Such Things 300
Lighthouse Story 300
A New Song 300
Studio 300
Time of Singing 250
Dreams & Visions 200
Keys to Living 200
Silver Wings 200
TEAK Roundup 200
Pegasus Review 120
Parenting Our Parents 100
Time for Rhyme 100
Upsouth 75
Stepping Out/Darkness 60+
Times of Refreshing 60
Penwood Review 50-100

CHILDREN

American Girl 750,000
God's World News 320,000
Guideposts for Kids 200,000+
FOF Clubhouse 123,300
FOF Clubhouse Jr. 96,000
Pockets 93,000
High Adventure 86,000
Keys for Kids 65,000
Our Little Friend 45-50,000
Courage 40,000
Live Wire 40,000
Wonder Time 40,000
Discovery Trails 35,000
Primary Treasure 35,000
GUIDE 33,000
Celebrate 20,000
Together Time 19,000
Venture 18,000
Touch 15,000
The Winner 15,000
Club Connection 14,700
My Friend 12,000
Crusader (MI) 11,400
BREAD for God's Children 10,000
Nature Friend 9,000
J.A.M. 7,000

Story Friends 7,000
On the Line 6,000
Partners 5,975
Story Mates 5,850
Junior Companion 3,500
Primary Pal 2,900
Beginner's Friend 2,700
Skipping Stones 2,500
Discovery 1,100

CHRISTIAN EDUCATION/LIBRARY

Signal 130,000
Children's Ministry 65,000
GROUP 55,000
Catechist 50,000
Parish Teacher 50,000
Today's Catholic Teacher 50,000
Religion Teacher's Journal 40,000
Church Media Library 30,000
Momentum 28,000
Teachers in Focus 26,400
Perspective 24,500
Christian Classroom 22,000
Lollipops 20,000
Evangelizing Today's Child 17,000
Christian School Administrator 16,000
Shining Star 11,000
CE Counselor 10,800
Teachers Interaction 10,000
Youth & CE Leadership 9,800
Resource 9,000
Journal/Adventist Ed 8,500
Vision (CA) 8,000
CE Connection 6,600
Kids' Ministry Ideas 5,000
Leader/Church School Today 4,500
Christian Educator's Journal 4,200
Church Educator 4,000
Church & Synagogue Libraries 3,000
CE Connection Communique 2,750
Team 2,000
Caravan 1,500
Catholic Library World 1,000
Christian Library Journal 1,000
Christian Librarian 500
Church Libraries 500

Journal/Christian Education 500
Jour/Ed & Christian Belief 400
Jour/Research on C.E. 400

MISSIONS

Mission Frontiers 120,000
Catholic Near East 100,000
Worldwide Challenge 90,000
Gospel Message 65,000
Bible for the World 50,000
American Horizon 45,000
American Baptist in Mission 39,000
World Christian 30,000
P.I.M.E. World 26,000
AIM International 24,000
New World Outlook 22,000
Heartbeat 20,000
Latin America Evangelist 17,000
Faith in Action 10,000
Voices in the Wilderness 9,000
Leaders for Today 7,500
Evangelical Missions 7,000
PFI World Report 4,750
World Pulse 4,000
Hope for Children in Crisis 3,000
Women of the Harvest 2,500
Missiology 2,000
Areopagus 1,000
Intl. Journal/Frontier 600
East-West Church 430

MUSIC

Release 110,000
Music Makers 105,000
Profile 80,000
CCM Magazine 70,000
Music Time 60,000
7ball 60,000
Church Pianist 35,000
Senior Musician 32,000
Church Musician 10,000
Creator 6,000
Contemporary Songwriter 5,000
Songwriting 4,000
Gospel Industry Today 3,500
The Hymn 3,000
Tradition 2,500

Cooperative Chr. Radio 300-1,200

NEWSPAPERS

Presbyterian Layman 575,000
Inside Journal 380,000
Anglican Journal 272,000
Episcopal Life 170,000
Together 150,000
Catholic New York 130,000
Our Sunday Visitor 125,000
Alabama Baptist 111,000
So All May Hear 97,000
Pulpit Helps 75,000
Arlington Catholic Herald 53,000
Discovery 50,000
Good News Journal (MO) 50,000
National Catholic Reporter 48,000
Dallas/Ft Worth Heritage 45,000
Good News Etc. 42,000
Live Wire 40,000
Living 40,000
Metro Voice 35,000
You! 35,000
Catholic Servant 33,000
Indian Life 32,000
The Interim 30,000
Christian News NW 28,000
Christian Ranchman 28,000
Catholic Telegraph 27,000
Life Gate 23,000
B.C. Catholic 20,000
Catholic Faith & Family 20,000
Catholic Peace Voice 20,000
Harvest Press 20,000
Living Light News 20,000
Minnesota Chr. Chronicle 20,000
Nashville Christian 20,000
Shantyman 17,000
Church Advocate 16,000
Catholic Sentinel 15,000
Expression Christian 15,000
Messenger 15,000
Network 15,000
Interchange 12,600
Michigan Christian 12,000
Christian Courier (WI) 10,000
Disciple's Journal 10,000
Montana Catholic 8,300
Star of Zion 8,000
Inland NW Christian 7,500

Arkansas Catholic 7,000
Home Times 5,200
Christian Courier (Canada)
   5,000
John Milton 5,000
The Parent Paper 5,000
Christian Renewal 4,500
Christian Observer 3,500
Christian Media 2-6,000
Christian Edge 1,500
Prayerworks 1,000

PASTORS/LEADERS

Your Church 150,000
Growing Churches 85,000
Pulpit Helps 75,000
Leadership 65,000
Plugged In 53,300
Eucharistic Minister 50,000
Worship Leader 43,000
Pray! 35,000
Enrichment 32,500
Christian Century 30,000
Rev. 25,000
Today's Christian Preacher
   25,000
Parish Liturgy 22,000
Lutheran Partners 20,000
Ministry 20,000
Ministry & Liturgy 20,000
Technologies/Worship 20,000
Youthworker 20,000
PROCLAIM 16,000
Today's Parish 14,800
Theology Today 14,000
Cell Group 12,000
Church Administration 12,000
Jour/Pastoral Care 10,000
WCA News 10,000
Celebration 9,000
Preaching 9,000
Student Leadership Journal
   8,500
Church Growth Network
   8,000
Clergy Journal 8,000
The Priest 8,000
Resource (CAN) 8,000
Review for Religious 8,000
Christian Camp & Conference
   7,500
Let's Worship 7,000
Brigade Leader 6,500
Christian Ministry 6,500
Journal/Christian Camping
   6,000
Catechumenate 5,600

Cross Currents 5,000
National Drama Service 5,000
Angelos 4,500
Reformed Worship 4,500
Emmanuel 4,000+
Christian Management Report
   3,500
Lutheran Forum 3,200
Word & World 3,100
Evangelicals Today 3,000
Issachar File 3,000
Sermon Notes 3,000
Single Adult Min Jour 3,000
Environment & Art 2,500
African American Pulpit 2,000
Pastoral Life 2,000
Reaching Children at Risk
   2,000
Church Worship 1,200
Five Stones 1,200
Jour/Christian Healing 1,200
Quarterly Review 1,100
Ivy Jungle Report 800
Jour/Amer Soc/Chur Growth
   400

TEEN/YOUNG ADULT

Brio 206,500
Christian College Focus
   200,000
Essential Connection 120,000
Breakaway 105,800
Campus Life 100,000
Today's Christian Teen
   100,000
Devo'Zine 92,000
Sharing the Victory 80,000
Young Salvationist 48,000
Youthwalk 36,000
You! 35,000
Cross Walk 30,000
Encounter 30,000
Listen 30,000
Young & Alive 25,000
Inteen 20,000
Real Faith in Life 18,000
Insight 16,600
Living My Faith 16,000
Teenage Christian 10,500
Young Adult Today 10,000
Student Leadership 8,500
Teens on Target 7,000
The Conqueror 6,000
With 6,000
Youth Challenge 5,500
Beautiful Christian Teen 5,000
Youth Compass 4,800

WOMEN

Today's Christian Woman
   320,000
Lutheran Woman's Quarterly
   200,000
Lutheran Woman Today
   180,000
Journey 150,000
SpiritLed Woman 126,000
Share 118,000
Horizons 25,500
Godly Business Women
   25,000
Welcome Home 15,000
Women of Spirit 15,000
Woman's Touch 12,200
Church Woman 10,000
Conscience 10,000
Excellence 10,000
Journal/Women's Ministries
   10,000
Esprit 6,500
Joyful Woman 6,000
Just Between Us 6,000
Proverbs 31 Woman 6,000
Women Alive! 5,000-6,000
Link & Visitor 4,500
Helping Hand 4,000
Wesleyan Woman 3,500
Christian Bride 3,000
Connection 3,000
The Handmaiden 3,000
Hearts at Home 2,000
Women of God's Word 1,700
Women Who Minister 1,500-
   5,000
Grace 1,000

WRITERS

Writer's Digest 180,000
The Writer 50,000
Writer OnLine 34,000
Writers' Journal 33,000
Writer's Forum 13,000
Byline 3,000+
Christian Communicator
   3,000
Fiction Fix Newsletter 2,200
Teachers & Writers 1,500-
   2,000
Writer's Lifeline 1,500
Cross & Quill 1,000+
New Writing 1,000
Once Upon a Time 1,000
Tickled by Thunder 1,000
Advanced Christian Writer 500

Canadian Writer's Journal 385
WE! 350
Omnific 300+
Gotta Write Network 300
FellowScript 250

My Legacy 200+
The Poetry Connection 200
Exchange 185
Areopagus (UK) 140
Adoration 100

Writer's Ink 100
Writer's Potpourri 100
Northwest Christian Author 80
The Write Touch 40

PERIODICAL TOPICS IN ORDER OF POPULARITY

NOTE: Following is a list of topics in order by popularity. To find the list of publishers interested in each of these topics, go to the Topical Listings for periodicals and find the topic you are interested in. The numbers indicate how many periodical editors said they were interested in seeing something of that type or topic. There are 269 photography markets this year. (*—new topic this year)

Non-topics:
   -Photographs 269
   -Newspapers 65
   -Canadian/Foreign 65
   -Online Magazines 81
   -Take-home Papers 33
1. Christian Living 273
2. Family Life 258
3. Personal Experience 248
4. Inspirational 244
5. Prayer 242
6. Current/Social Issues 237
7. Interviews/Profiles 235
8. Evangelism/Witnessing 218
9. Poetry 218
10. Spirituality 211
11. Holiday/Seasonal 208
12. Humor 205
13. Marriage 190
14. Relationships 187
15. Discipleship 179
16. Book Reviews 178
17. Women's Issues 178
18. Christian Education 172
19. True Stories 172
20. Parenting 171
21. Worship 166
22. Fillers: Cartoons 163
23. Youth Issues 162
24. Devotionals/Meditations 157
25. How-to 154
26. Church Outreach 152
27. Controversial Issues 148
28. Leadership 148
29. Ethics 144
30. Theological 144
31. Ethnic/Cultural 140
32. Missions 129
33. Short Story: Adult 125
34. World Issues 125
35. Historical 123

36. Health 119
37. Bible Studies 117
38. Fillers: Anecdotes 117
39. Opinion Pieces 116
40. Fillers: Short Humor 115
41. Divorce 112
42. Essays 112
43. Church Life 109
44. Men's Issues 109
45. Religious Freedom 109
46. Stewardship 109
47. Death/Dying 108
48. Singles Issues 108
49. Personal Growth 106
50. Money Management 103
51. Think Pieces 103
52. Environmental Issues 102
53. Short Story: Humorous 102
54. Senior Adult Issues 100
55. Church Growth 98
56. Faith 97
57. Doctrinal 95
58. Celebrity Pieces 93
59. Salvation Testimonies 93
60. Healing 90
61. Fillers: Ideas 89
62. Short Story: Contemporary 89
63. Social Justice 89
64. Fillers: Facts 88
65. Christian Business 84
66. Miracles 81
67. Book Excerpts 79
68. Church Management 77
69. Liturgical 77
70. Spiritual Warfare 76
71. Short Story: Parables 75
72. Short Story: Biblical 74
73. Music Reviews 73
74. Fillers: Quotes 71
75. Sports/Recreation 70
76. Short Story: Historical 68

77. Fillers: Quizzes 67
78. How-to Activities (juv.) 67
79. Church Traditions 65
80. Economics 65
81. Short Story: Adventure 65
82. Fillers: Prose 64
83. Time Management 64
84. Cults/Occult 61
85. Fillers: Word Puzzles 61
86. Home Schooling 61
87. Fillers: Jokes 60
88. Short Story: Juvenile 60
89. Fillers: Prayers 59
90. Political 58
91. Fillers: Games 57
92. Fillers: Newsbreaks 56
93. Nature 56
94. Self-Help 56
95. Short Story: Teen/YA 56
96. Creation Science 54
97. Travel 51
98. Prophecy 50
99. Short Story: Literary 50
100. Food/Recipes 48
101. Psychology 48
102. Writing How-to 48
103. Spiritual Gifts 46
104. Short Story: Allegory 44
105. Science 43
106. Sermons 43
107. Short Story: Mystery 42
108. Video Reviews 39
109. Sociology 36
110. Short Story: Fantasy 32
111. Short Story: Romance 31
112. Short Story: Ethnic 30
113. Fillers: Party Ideas 25
114. Short Story: Frontier 25
115. Short Story: Science Fiction 24
116. Photo Essays 21

117. Short Story: Plays 21
118. Homiletics 20
119. Puppet Plays 20
120. Exegesis 19

121. Short Story: Historical/Romance 18
122. Short Story: Mystery/Romance 18

123. Short Story: Frontier/Romance 16
124. Short Story: Skits 13
125. Short Story: Suspense 9

COMMENTS:

If you are a short story writer, the biggest market is for adult fiction (125 markets—down 2 from last year). Children's is still in second place with 60 (3 less than last year), followed closely by teen with 56 (6 less than last year). The most popular genres (in order) are Humorous, Contemporary, Parables, Biblical, Historical, Adventure, Literary, Allegory, and Mystery. Compared to last year, they are in the same order, except for Parable, which moved ahead of Biblical, and Allegory which moved ahead of Mystery. The least popular are still the genre romances. Note: Suspense is at the bottom, but is new to the list.

This year poetry dropped to 218 markets, down from 222 last year and 230 the year before. However, it remains the ninth most popular topic, the same as last year, while the total number of poems expected to be bought or accepted by those markets has gone down from 5,160 last year to about 4,850 this year—310 less than last year. The good news is that the book market for poetry went up to 37 (up from 31 last year), but I still recommend that the serious poet pursue the periodical markets and establish a good reputation as a poet before ever attempting to sell a book of poetry.

This year the same topics are in the top 11 again. The first three are in the same order, but Current/Social Issues and Evangelism/Witnessing moved up, while Holiday/Seasonal dropped from 6th to 11th. The tallies for each topic are not as significant as the order this year, since many publishers are sending their updates by fax or e-mail and not including their topical listings.

In looking at the differences in interest in specific topics, those showing the greatest increase in interest are Faith, Discipleship, Time Management, Personal Growth, Singles Issues, and Youth Issues. Those dropping the most in interest are Celebrity Pieces, Biblical Short Stories, Think pieces, and Sports/Recreation.

SUMMARY OF INFORMATION ON CHRISTIAN PERIODICAL PUBLISHERS FOUND IN THE ALPHABETICAL LISTINGS

NOTE: The following numbers are based on the maximum total estimate for each periodical. For example, if they gave a range of 4-6, the average was based on the higher number, 6. These figures were all calculated from those periodicals that reported information in each category.

WANTS QUERY OR COMPLETE MANUSCRIPT:

Of those periodicals that indicated a preference, 46% ask for or will accept a complete manuscript (down 3% from last year), and 39% want or will accept a query (up 1% from last year). Only 2% require a query (same as last year). This year, as last, 13% of all reporting will accept either.

ACCEPTS PHONE QUERY:

This year, 149 periodical publishers are accepting phone queries—one less than last year. Many seem to now prefer fax or e-mail to phone queries. It is suggested that you reserve phone queries for timely material that won't wait for the regular mailed query. If you phone in a query, be sure you have your idea well thought out and can present it succinctly and articulately.

ACCEPTS FAX QUERY:

More and more publishers have fax numbers and a good many are willing (and even prefer) to accept fax queries, but some are also beginning to say no to them. Last year, 34% of all the periodical publishers accepted fax queries. This year, 245 publishers (36%) will accept them. Since a fax query will not have an SASE, it is suggested that you make fax queries only if you have your own fax machine to accept their response.

ACCEPTS E-MAIL QUERY:

This is the sixth year we have asked about e-mail queries, and, as expected, the number of publishers with e-mail addresses continues to grow. Last year 325 publishers were open to receiving messages or submissions by e-mail. This year 572 publications have e-mail, and 281 publishers are open to e-mail queries. In addition, 455 publishers have Websites (up from 388 last year).

SUBMISSIONS ON DISK:

Of the 265 periodicals that responded to the question about whether or not they accepted, preferred, or required accepted submissions on disk, 97 (37%) said they accepted disks, 85 (32%) preferred disks, only 36 (14%) required disks, and 47 (17%) do not want disks.

SUBMISSIONS BY E-MAIL:

This area is beginning to show some significant changes in editor's perception of e-mail submissions. When asked if they would accept submissions by e-mail, of the 273 that answered, 88 (32%) said yes. Of those who would accept them, 29% wanted them copied into the message, 26% wanted them sent an as attached file, and the last 13% would accept them either way.

PAYS ON ACCEPTANCE OR PUBLICATION:

Of the 412 publishers that indicated, 40 percent of the publishers pay on acceptance (down 2% from last year), while 60% pay on publication.

PERCENTAGE OF FREELANCE:

Most of the publishers responded to the question about how much freelance material they use. Last year we made the question more definitive by asking them to specify the percentage unsolicited and the percentage assigned, and this year a greater number of them gave us both figures. Based on the figures we have, for the average publisher, just over 44% of the material purchased is unsolicited freelance (down 9% from last year). Of those publishers who assign, the average one uses 49.5% assigned (down a half a percent from last year).

CIRCULATION:

In dividing the list of periodicals into three groups, according to size of circulation, the list comes out as follows: Publications with a circulation of 100,000 or more (up to 3,000,000), 13.8% (14% last year); publications with circulations between 50,000 and 100,000, 10.7% (10% last year); the remaining 75.5% have circulations of 50,000 or less (76% last year). If we break that last group into three more groups by circulation, we come out with 13% of those from 33,000-50,000 (8% last year); 17% from 17,000-32,000 (up 1% from last year); and the remaining 70% with less than 17,000. That means that 54% of all the periodicals that reported their circulation are at a circulation of 17,000 or less.

RESPONSE TIME:

According to the 350 publishers who indicated response time, the average response time remains about 7 1/2 weeks. Those who are writing and submitting regularly will have no problem believing that most publishers are taking longer than they used to to respond to submissions.

REPRINTS:

More than 56% of the periodicals reporting accept reprints; that's up more than 3% over last year. Although until the last four or five years it was not necessary to tell a publisher where a piece had been published previously, that has changed. Most Christian publishers are now wanting a tear sheet of the original publication and a cover letter telling when and where it appeared originally. Be sure to check the individual listings to see if a publisher wants to know when and where a piece has appeared previously. Many are also paying less for reprints than for original material.

PREFERRED BIBLE VERSION:

Although we are not running the percentages anymore, it is obvious that the most preferred Bible version is the NIV, the preference of more than half the publishers. Other preferred versions are the KJV, the New Revised Standard Version, the New American Bible, New American Standard, Revised Standard Version, and New King James. The NIV seems a good choice for those that didn't indicate a preference, although the more conservative groups seem to favor the KJV.

GREETING CARD/GIFT/SPECIALTY MARKETS

PLEASE NOTE: This listing contains both Christian/religious card publishers and secular publishers who have religious lines or produce some religious or inspirational cards. Keep in mind that the secular companies may produce other lines of cards that are not consistent with your beliefs, and that for a secular company, inspirational cards usually do not include religious imagery.

(*) Indicates that publisher did not return questionnaire
(#) Indicates that listing was updated from guidelines or other sources
(+) Indicates new listing

NOTE: See the end of this listing for specialty product lists.

CARD PUBLISHERS

+AFRICAN AMERICAN GREETINGS, 8120 Berry Ave., Ste. B, Sacramento CA 95828-1608. (916)424-5000. Fax (916)424-5053. E-mail: gregperkins@ black-gifts.com. Website: www.black-gifts.com. Greg Perkins, pres. Christian card publishers and specialty products. Open to freelance; buys 5-10 ideas/yr. Prefers outright submissions. Pays $35 on acceptance. No royalty. Responds in 2 wks. Uses unrhymed poetry. Produces humorous, inspirational, and religious cards. Needs all types. Holiday/seasonal 9 mos ahead. Open to ideas for new card lines; calendars/journals, novelty/gift items, magnets, post cards and stationery. No guidelines; free catalog.

BOB SIEMON DESIGNS INC., 3501 W. Segerstrom Ave., Santa Ana CA 92704-6497. (714)549-0678. Fax (714)979-2627. Website: www.bobsiemon. com. No freelance.

CATHEDRAL ART METAL CO., 25 Manton Ave., Providence RI 02909-3349. (401)273-7200x227. Fax (401)273-6262. E-mail: camco@cathedralart. com. Website: www.cathedralart.com. Fritzi Frey, art dir. Producer of specialty products. Open to freelance; buys 2 ideas/yr. Outright submissions; e-query OK. Pays $50 on acceptance for all rights. Royalties 3-5%. Responds in 1-4 wks. Uses rhymed, unrhymed, traditional, light verse; 2-8 lines (for plaques). Produces plaques and pins with inspirational messages for special occasions: baby, communion, confirmation, graduation, wedding and anniversary. Holiday/seasonal 6 mos ahead. Open to ideas for bookmarks, figurines, plaques, jewelry/pins, wind chimes, frames. Guidelines; catalog for 9x12 SAE/$3.20 postage.

*CELEBRATION GREETINGS (A div. of Leanin' Tree), Box 9500, Boulder CO 80301. (303)530-1442. Fax (303)530-2152. Nancy Trumble Fox, V.P. Product. Christian/religious card publisher and specialty products. 50% freelance. Buys 30 ideas/yr. Query. Pays $100 on publication for all rts. No royalties. Responds in 12 wks. Any type of verse, including humorous;

to 8 lines. Produces conventional, humorous, informal, inspirational, religious. Needs anniversary, birthday, Christmas, Easter, friendship, get well, graduation, keep in touch, love, miss you, Mother's Day, new baby, sympathy, thank you, Valentines, wedding, encouragement, pastor appreciation, baptism, confirmation, and first communion. Christmas ideas 12 mos ahead. Not open to new card lines. Prefers 12-20 ideas. Open to ideas for magnets, mugs, and posters. Guidelines; no catalog.

+CHRISTIAN INSPIRATIONS, 30 E. 33rd St., New York NY 10016. (212) 685-0751. Fax (212)889-6868. Suzanne Kruck, vice pres. Christian card publisher. No unsolicited submissions; request permission in writing to send submissions. Pays on acceptance; no royalty. All types of verse, 4-6 lines. All kinds of cards and greetings, except Halloween and St. Patrick's. Seasonal 12 months ahead. Not open to new card lines or specialty products. No guidelines; catalog.

CREATIVE CHRISTIAN MINISTRIES, PO Box 12624, Roanoke VA 24027. No freelance for now.

CURRENT, INC., PO Box 2559, Colorado Springs CO 80901. (719)594-4100. Fax (719)534-6259. Mar Porter, freelance coordinator. No freelance.

DAYSPRING CARDS, INC., Box 1010, 20984 Oak Ridge Rd., Siloam Springs AR 72761. (501)549-6303. Fax (501)524-8959. E-mail: info@dayspring. com (type "write" in message or subject line). Website: www.dayspring. com. Christian/religious card publisher. Currently only accepting submissions from previously published greeting card authors. Please read guidelines before submitting. Prefer outright submission. Pays $50/idea on acceptance for all rts. No royalty. Responds in 4-8 wks. Uses unrhymed, traditional, light verse, conversational, contemporary; various lengths. Looking for inspirational cards for all occasions, including anniversary, birthday, relative birthday, congratulations, encouragement, friendship, get well, new baby, sympathy, thank you, wedding. Also needs seasonal cards for friends and family members for Christmas, Valentines, Easter, Mother's Day, Father's Day, Thanksgiving, graduation, and Clergy Appreciation Day. Seasonal 13 mos ahead. Send 10 ideas or less. Guidelines by phone or e-mail; no catalog.

> **Tips:** This company now accepts submissions from published card writers only, or by request of an editor. Write "Previously Published" on lower, left corner of envelope. Prefers submissions on 8½ x 11 inch sheets, not 3x5 cards (one idea per sheet).

DESIGNER GREETINGS, 250 Arlington Ave., Staten Island NY 10303. (718)981-7700. Fern Gimbelman, art dir. 50% freelance. Holiday/seasonal 6 mos ahead. Responds in 2 mos. Pays on acceptance for greeting card rts. Free guidelines. Uses rhymed or unrhymed verse. Produces announcements, conventional, humorous, informal, inspirational, invitations, juvenile, sensitivity, soft line, studio.

DIVINE INSPIRATION GREETING CARDS, PO Box 407, Brice OH 43109. (800)364-9450. Lori G. Billingsley, pres. No freelance for now.

GALLANT GREETINGS CORP., 4300 United Pkwy, Schiller Park IL 60176. (847)671-6500. Fax (847)671-5900. E-mail: info@gallantgreetings.com.

Website: gallantgreetings.com. General card publisher with a religious line and several inspirational lines. Chris Allen, VP/Sales & Marketing. 25% freelance. Query. Responds in 12 wks. Pays on publication for worldwide rts. No royalties. Uses rhymed, unrhymed, traditional and light verse. Produces announcements, conventional, humorous, informal, inspirational, invitations, juvenile, religious, sensitivity, softline. Needs all types of greetings, except Halloween. Holiday/seasonal 6 months ahead. Open to new card lines. Prefers 20 ideas/submission. No guidelines/catalog.

GENESIS MARKETING GROUP, 16 Wellington Ave., Greenville SC 29609. (864)233-2651. Fax (864)232-0059. Website: www.genesislink.com. Peter Sullivan, pres. Christian/religious card publisher. 100% freelance. Buys 10 ideas/yr. Outright submission. Royalty 5%. Traditional and light verse. Produces inspirational, religious, sensitivity. Needs anniversary, birthday, Christmas, congratulations, Easter, friendship, get well, graduation, keep in touch, love, miss you, new baby, please write, relatives, sympathy, thank you, Valentines, wedding. Also produces calendars, gift books, magnets, mugs, plaques, posters, T-shirts. No guidelines.

GIBSON GREETINGS, PO Box 371804, Cincinnati OH 45222-1804. E-mail: wcallah@gibsongreetings.com. Website: www.gibsongreetings.com. No freelance.

*THE HERITAGE COLLECTION, 77 W Sheffield Ave., Englewood NJ 07631-4804. Allison Powe, creative dir. General card publisher with a religious line. 20% freelance; buys 50-60 ideas/yr. Outright submission. Pays $35 on publication for domestic rights. No royalties. Responds in 4 wks. Prefers unrhymed; to 3 paragraphs. Produces announcements, inspirational, religious, and sensitivity. Needs anniversary, birthday, congratulations, friendship, get well, keep in touch, love, miss you, new baby, sympathy, thank you, and wedding. Also open to ideas for mugs. Guidelines/needs list; free catalog.

IMAGE CRAFT, INC. and **LAWSON FALLE LTD.**, 1245 Franklin Blvd., Box 814, Cambridge ON N1R 5X9 Canada. (519)622-4310. Fax (519)621-6774. Website: www.lawson-falle.com. Submit to: Editor. Christian/religious card publisher and general card publisher with a religious line. Open to freelance. Query. Pays on acceptance. No royalties. Responds in 4-6 wks. Prefers unrhymed, traditional and humorous, 6-12 lines. Produces announcements, conventional, humorous, informal, inspirational, invitations, juvenile, religious, sensitivity and studio cards. Needs anniversary, birthday, Christmas, congratulations, Easter, friendship, get well, graduation, Halloween, keep in touch, love, miss you, new baby, Mother's Day/Father's Day, relatives, St. Patrick's Day, all occasion, sympathy, Thanksgiving, thank you, Valentines, wedding, confirmation, and First Communion. Seasonal 8 mos ahead. Not open to new card lines. Send 6-8 ideas.

    Tips: "We need good but clean humor."

INSPIRATIONS UNLIMITED, PO Box 9097, Cedar Pines Park CA 92322. (909)338-6758. Fax (909)338-2907. General card publisher that does a few inspirational/religious cards. Open to freelance. Buys 50 ideas/yr.

Prefers outright submission. Pays $25 on acceptance. No royalties. Responds in 4 wks. Prefers unrhymed verse (something that tugs at the heart). Produces conventional, informal, inspirational, religious, sensitivity. All types. Holiday/seasonal 1 yr ahead. Open to ideas for new card lines, plaques, stationery, note cards and gift tags. Send up to 10 ideas. No guidelines or catalog.

J-MAR BY UNIVERSAL DESIGNS, PO Box 23149, Waco TX 76702-3149. (254)751-0100. Fax (254)751-0054. E-mail: amykfbrown@netscape.net. Amy Brown, marketing mgr. Christian/religious publisher that does 2x3 cards, posters and pocket-size cards. 25% freelance; buys 50 ideas/yr. Outright submission. Pays variable rates on acceptance for all rts; no royalties. Responds in 6 wks. Prefers unrhymed (short, focused submissions receive the most attention). Produces humorous, informal, inspirational, novelty. Needs friendship, love, and thank you cards. Open to new card lines. Send 5-10 ideas. Open to ideas for bookmarks, 2x3 inspirational cards, gift/novelty items, posters, pocket-size verse cards, stationery. Guidelines; no catalog.

> **Tips:** "We appreciate writing submissions that are focused on inspirational Christian themes. These themes can include biblical references or verses, poems and/or text."

KATE HARPER DESIGNS, E-mail: kateharp@aol.com. Website: www.hometown.aol.com/katehar/myhomepage/index.html. Submit to: Quote Submissions—Christian. A general card publisher with a religious line. Open to freelance. Buys 100 ideas/yr. Prefers e-mail contact. Send SASE for guidelines first. Pays $25/quote, on acceptance, for nonexclusive rts. No royalties. Responds in 6 wks. Uses less than 20 wds for front of card only. Produces humorous, inspirational, religious, sensitivity, and children's. Needs birthday, love, sympathy and children's (90% are children's). Holiday/seasonal material 10 mos ahead. Not open to ideas for new card lines. Send up to 20 ideas. Guidelines (also by e-mail); no catalog.

> **Tips:** "Looking for children's quotes (under age 12). Send SASE for specific guidelines or e-mail, specifying 'kid's guidelines.'" Also accepts submissions from children.

*LAURA LEIDEN CALLIGRAPHY, INC., PO Box 141, Watkinsville GA 30677. (706)769-6989. Fax (706)769-0628. E-mail: llc@lauraleiden.com. Contact: Jennifer. 99% freelance/45 ideas per yr. Seasonal/holiday 1 yr ahead. Responds in 1-6 mos. Buys all rts on acceptance. Prefers rhymed verse; sentimental/nostalgic; three or more stanzas. Produces inspirational, relatives, traditional. Send 6 ideas.

*LIFE GREETINGS, Box 468, Little Compton RI 02837. (401)635-8535. Kathy Brennan, ed. Christian/religious card publisher. 100% freelance. Outright purchases. Pays $10 on acceptance for all rts. No royalties. Responds in 2 wks. Uses rhymed, unrhymed, traditional; 6-8 lines. Produces announcements, conventional, humorous, inspirational, juvenile, religious, sensitivity. Needs congratulations, friendship, get well, new baby, sympathy, thank you and wedding. Also clergy reassignment, ordination, anniversary of ordination, and pro-life Christmas. Holiday/seasonal 6 mos ahead. Open to new card lines. Prefers 12 ideas/submission. Guidelines; no catalog.

+**LIFESONG PUBLISHERS**, PO Box 183, Somis CA 93066. (805)655-5644. E-mail: mailbox@lifesongpublishers.com. Website: www.lifesongpublishers.com. Laurie Donahue, pub. A Christian publisher interested in introducing a line of baptism cards; also a few specialty items. Open to freelance: buys 1-2 ideas/yr. Outright submissions. Pays on publication for all rts. Responds in 6-8 wks. Need baptism cards for older child or teen; include artwork. Looking for activity book to complement their baptism curriculum. No guidelines; catalog for SAE/2 stamps.

***MANHATTAN GREETING CARD CO.**, 150 E 52 St. c/o Platzer/Fineberg, New York NY 10022. (718)894-7600. Paula Haley, ed. General card publisher/inspirational line. 100% freelance. Pays $5-250. Responds in 3 wks. Produces announcements, conventional, humorous, informal, inspirational, invitations, juvenile, sensitivity, soft line, studio, Christmas (85% of the line). Holiday/seasonal 18 months ahead. Also open to ideas for bumper stickers, calendars, gift books, greeting books, post cards, and promotions. Free guidelines.

***MARLENE MOORE STUDIO**, 300 E. 34th St., New York NY 10016. (212) 481-0124. 100% freelance. Responds in 1 mo. Pays on acceptance. Prefers unrhymed verse. Produces inspirational, sensitivity. Send 6 ideas. Open to ideas for calendars, gift books, greeting books, plaques, posters, and puzzles.

***NOVO CARD PUBLISHERS, INC.**, 3630 W. Pratt Ave., Lincolnwood IL 60645. (847)763-0077. Fax (847)763-0020. Thomas Benjamin/Molly Morawski, art dirs. General card publisher that does a few inspirational and religious cards. 95% freelance; buys 200-500 ideas/yr. Prefers query for writers and outright submissions for art samples. Pays $2/line on publication for greeting card rts. No royalties. Responds in 9 wks. Uses any type verse, variable lengths. Produces all types of cards. Needs birthday, congratulations, friendship, graduation, keep in touch, relatives (all occasions), sympathy, thank you. Seasonal 8 mos ahead. Open to ideas for new card lines. Submit enough ideas to show style. Guidelines/needs list; samples for 9x12 SAE/5 stamps.

   Tips: "Sympathy cards need to be a bit more inspirational than just 'my deepest sympathy.'"

***PACIFIC PAPER GREETINGS, INC.**, Box 2249, Sidney BC V8L 3S8 Canada. (604)656-0504. Louise Rytter, ed. Inspirational cards. 50% freelance; buys 20 ideas/yr. Pays on acceptance for all rts. Responds in 3 wks. Produces conventional, inspirational, romantic, sensitivity, soft line. Holiday/seasonal 12 months ahead. Guidelines for SAE/1 IRC.

PAINTED HEARTS & FRIENDS, 1222 N. Fair Oaks Ave., Pasadena CA 91103-3614. (818)798-3633, Fax (818)798-7385. E-mail: teri@paintedhearts.com. Website: www.paintedhearts.com. Ines Duran, ed. General card publisher that does a few inspirational and religious cards. 20% freelance. Query or outright submission (copies only, no original artwork). Pays $25/message on acceptance. 5% royalty on artwork only. Responds in 1-2 wks. Uses unrhymed, traditional, light verse; 2-3 liners. Produces announcements, inspirational, invitations. Needs most types of greetings (no Please Write), plus graduation and Jewish holidays. Holiday/seasonal

3 mos ahead. See guidelines for submission schedule. Open to ideas for new card lines. Submit 12 art designs max, or 24 messages. Open to ideas for banners, gift books, invitations, postcards, posters and stationery. Guidelines/market list for #10 SASE.

PORTAL PUBLICATIONS, INC., 201 Alameda Del Prado, Novato CA 94949. (415)884-6200. Fax (415)382-3377. Website: www.portalpub.com. Julie Johnson, art dir. A general poster publisher with one or more inspirational lines; posters and calendars. Open to freelance. Does few strictly religious cards; 20-30 inspirational ideas/yr. Prefers outright submissions. Pays royalty (5%) or flat fee for world-wide rights; $50-100/line or $500-800 for posters. Payment within 30 days. Responds in 3-4 weeks (calls for acceptances). Produces conventional, humorous, inspirational, novelty, religious, sensitivity, and studio. Needs anniversary, birthday, Christmas, congratulations, Easter, Father's Day, friendship, get well, graduation, keep in touch, love, Mother's Day, new baby, sympathy, Thanksgiving, thank you, Valentines, wedding, alternative looks and humor, pop-culture look. Open to new ideas for card lines or specialty products. Submit 12-50 ideas. Open to ideas for calendars/journals, gift/novelty ideas, posters, stationery. Guidelines on Website; no catalog (research their cards/products at Michael's, Hobby Lobby, Cost-Plus stores, or on Website).

    Tips: "We are new to publishing faith-oriented cards, posters and calendars—only recently developing a small line in posters and calendars. We are hoping to do cards next. We are mostly interested in poster and calendar concepts or in source writers who specialize in faith inspirational material. Anything submitted for posters will also be shared with the card division."

P. S. GREETINGS, 5730 N. Tripp Ave., Chicago IL 60646-6723. (773)725-9308. Website: www.psg-fpp.com. Jennifer Dodson, art dir. 100% freelance; 200-300 ideas/yr. Holiday/seasonal 6 mos ahead. Responds in 1 mo. Pays flat fee on acceptance. Rhymed or unrhymed verse. Produces conventional, humorous, inspirational, invitations, juvenile, sensitivity, soft line, and studio. Send 10 ideas. Guidelines/market list for #10 SASE.

*RED FARM STUDIO, 1135 Roosevelt Ave., Pawtucket RI 02862-0347. (401)728-9300. Fax (401)728-0350. Submit to Production Coordinator. General card publisher with a religious line. 100% freelance; buys 100 ideas/yr. Outright submission. Pays variable rates (about $4/line) within 1 mo. of acceptance for exclusive rts. No royalties. Responds in 2 mos. Use traditional and light verse; 1-4 lines. Produces announcements, invitations, religious. Needs anniversary, birthday, Christmas, friendship, get well, new baby, sympathy, wedding. Holiday 6 months ahead. Not open to ideas for new card lines. Submit any number of ideas. Guidelines/needs list for SASE.

SPS STUDIOS, INC.(formerly Blue Mountain Arts, Inc.), PO Box 1007, Boulder CO 80306-1007. (303)449-0536. Fax (303)447-0939. E-mail: bma@rmi.net. Web site: www. bluemountainarts.com. Card line: Blue Mountain Arts. Submit to Editorial Department. General card publisher that does a few inspirational cards. Open to freelance; buys 50-100 ideas per year. Prefers outright submissions. Pays $200 for all rts, or $25 for one-time use in a book, on publication. No royalties. Responds in 12-16 wks. Uses unrhymed or traditional poetry; short or long, but no one-liners. Produces inspirational and sensitivity. Needs anniversary, birthday, Christmas, congratulations, Easter, Father's Day, friendship, get well, graduation, keep in touch, love, miss you, Mother's Day, new baby, please write, relatives, sympathy, thank you, Valentines, wedding, reaching for dreams. Holiday/seasonal 3 mos ahead. Open to ideas for new card lines. Send any number of ideas (1 per pg). Open to ideas for bookmarks, calendars, gift books, and mugs. Guidelines; no catalog.

Contest: Sponsors a triannual poetry card contest online. Details on their Website.

Tips: "We are interested in reviewing poetry and writings for greeting cards, and expanding our field of freelance poetry writers."

ADDITIONAL CARD PUBLISHERS

The following greeting card publishers did not complete a questionnaire but are included for reference or to contact on your own. Do not submit to them before you send for guidelines or ascertain their needs. Card publishers who do not accept freelance submissions are now listed in the General Index.

#AMERICAN GREETINGS, 1 American Rd., Cleveland OH 44144-2398. (216)252-7300. Website: www.americangreetings.com. Kathleen McKay, ed. No unsolicited material, except humor. Send for Humorous Writing guidelines.

APPALACHIAN BIBLE CO. INC., 506 Princeton Rd, Johnson City TN 37601.

ART BEATS, 129 Glover Ave., Norwalk CT 06850-1311.

BERG CHRISTIAN ENTERPRISES, 4525 SE 63rd Ave., Portland OR 97206.

BLACK FAMILY GREETING CARDS, 20 Cortlandt Ave., New Rochelle NY 10801. Bill Harte, pres.

CAROLYN BEAN PUBLISHING, 1700 Corporate Cir., Petaluma CA 94954-6924.

CD GREETING CARDS, PO Box 5084, Brentwood TN 37024-5084.

FREDERICK SINGER AND SONS, INC., 2-15 Borden Ave., Long Island City NJ 11101.

FRIENDLY SALES, PO Box 755, Quakertown PA 18951.

FRIENDS OF ISRAEL GOSPEL MINISTRIES, PO Box 908, Bellmawr NJ 08099-9900.

GREENLEAF, INC., 200 Wending Way, Spartanburg SC 29306.

THE HERMITAGE ART COMPANY INC., 5151 N. Ravenswood Ave., Chicago IL 60640.

HIGHER HORIZONS, Box 78399, Los Angeles CA 90016.

KIMBERLY ENTERPRISES INC., 15029 S. Figueroa St., Gardena CA 90248. Inspirational cards.

KRISTEN ELLIOTT, INC., 6 Opportunity Way, Newburyport MA 01950.

THE LORENZ COMPANY, 1208 Cimmaron Dr., Waco TX 76712-8174.

MCBETH CORP., PO Box 400, Chambersburg PA 17201.

MERI MERI, 11 Vista Ave., San Mateo CA 94403-4612.

MORE THAN A CARD, 5010 Baltimore Ave., Bethesda MD 20816.

+NOBLE WORKS, Box 1275, 108 Clinton St., Hoboken NJ 07030. (210)420-0095.

OAKSPRINGS IMPRESSIONS, Box 572, Woodacre CA 94973.

RANDALL WILCOX PUBLISHING, 826 Orange Ave., #544, Coronado CA 92118. (619)437-1321.

SENDJOY GREETING CARDS, Laurel Park, Wappingers Falls NY 12590.

SOUL-SEARCHER GREETING CARDS, 1336 N 6th St., Mankato MN 56001-4216. Inspirational cards.

THESE THREE, INC., 2105 N. Scott St., #79, Arlington VA 22209-1023. Jean Bridgers, ed.

THINGS GRAPHIC & FINE ARTS, 1522 14th St. NW, Washington DC 20005.

T.S. DENISON GREETING CARDS, PO Box 1650, Grand Rapids MI 49501.

WEST GRAPHICS, 1117 California Dr., Burlingame CA 94010-3505. (415) 548-1117. Carol West, ed.

NOTE: Many of the markets listed below for games, gift items and videos have not indicated their interest in receiving freelance submissions. Contact these markets on your own for information on submission procedures before sending them anything.

GAME MARKETS

*BIBLE GAMES CO., 14389 Cassell Rd., PO Box 237, Fredericktown OH 43019. (740)694-8042. Fax (740)694-8072. E-mail: biblegames@juno. com. Website: www.biblegamescompany.com. Kelly Vozar, asst. Produces Bible games. 10% freelance. Buys 1-2 ideas/yr. Query. Pays on publication for all rts (negotiable). Royalties 8%. Responds in 6-8 wks. Open to new ideas. One game per submission. Guidelines; catalog for 9x12 SAE/6 stamps.

> **Tips:** "Send developed and tested game play; target market and audience. Must be totally non-sectarian and fully biblical—no fictionalized scenarios." Board games, CD-ROMs, computer games and video games.

+J.D. BRODIE, INC., PO Box 384, Bensalem PA 19020. Board games.

*DIVINITY RELIGIOUS PRODUCTS, 5115 Avenida Encinas, Ste. B, Carlsbad CA 92008. (760)929-1090. Fax (760)929-0479. E-mail: DivinityRP@aol. com. Website: www.catholicgames.com. Michael J. McKay, VP. Open to ideas for board games, computer games, and CD-ROMs. No guidelines; will send catalog.

*FORJOY CONCEPTS, PO Box 360590, Brooklyn NY 11236. (800)407-0034. Card games.

*GOODE GAMES INTERNATIONAL, PO Box 21231, Columbia SC 29221. (800)257-7767.

*GOOD STEWARD GAME CO., 6412 Sunnyfield Way, Sacramento CA 95823-5781. (916)393-4263. William Parker, ed. Board games.

MARTIN LEVY INC., 615—36th Ave., San Mateo CA 94403-4150. Board games.

*M.J.N. ENTERPRISES, 1624 McMillan, Memphis TN 38106. (901)946-8185. Board games.

TALICOR, 4741 Murietta St., Chino CA 91710-5156. (909)517-0076. Fax (909)517-1962. E-mail: webmaster@Talicor.com. Website: www.Talicor. com. Lew Herndon, pres. Produces board games and puzzles. 100% freelance; buys 10 ideas/yr. Outright submissions. Pays variable rates on publication for all rts. Royalty 4-6%. Responds in 4 wks. Seasonal 6 mos ahead. Open to new ideas. Submit 1-4 ideas. No guidelines; free catalog.

WISDOM TREE, PO Box 8682, Tucson AZ 85738-8682. (520)825-5702. Fax (520)825-5710. E-mail: wisdom@www.christianlink.com. Web site: www. christianlink.com/media/wisdom. Brenda Huff, owner. Produces Bible-based computer games. 30% freelance (Beta versions). Query. Negotiable rights. Pays variable rates on publication. Variable royalties. Responds in 1-6 wks. Seasonal 8 mos ahead. Open to ideas for computer games, computer software or video games. No guidelines; catalog on request.

    Special Needs: "Storybook/puzzles and game engine."

GIFT/SPECIALTY ITEM MARKETS

ARGUS COMMUNICATIONS, 400 W. Bethany Dr., Ste. 110, Allen TX 75013-3706. (972)396-6500. Fax (972)396-6789. Website: www.argus.com. Beth Davis, ed. Produces posters and other message-based products. 90% freelance. Query. Outright purchase. Pays $50-75 on acceptance for all rts. Responds in 6-8 wks. Open to ideas for banners, magnets, post cards, and posters. Guidelines; no catalog.

    Special Needs: "We need messages for teens and adults that are positive, inspirational and motivational. We're looking for direct messages that have an impact and relevance to today's issues."

B & H GIFTS, a division of Broadman & Holman. See book listing.

THE CALLIGRAPHY COLLECTION, 2604 NW 74th Pl., Gainesville FL 32653. (352)375-8530. Fax (352)374-9957.E-mail: ArtistKaty@aol.com. Katy Fischer, owner/ed. General publisher/inspirational line of framed prints. 40% freelance; 20 ideas/yr. Outright submission. Pays $75-200 for framed print idea on publication for all rts; no royalties. Responds in 6 months. Uses rhymed, unrhymed (preferred), traditional, light verse; under 50 words. Produces inspirational (not too specific or overly religious), framed prints for friends, family, teachers, etc. Send 3 ideas/batch. Also open to ideas for gift books, plaques, and musical framed pieces. Guidelines; no catalog.

CARPENTREE, 2724 N. Sheridan, Tulsa OK 74115. (918)582-3600. Fax (918) 587-4329. E-mail: customerservice@carpentree.com. Website: www. carpentree.com. Submit to Design Dept. Produces framed art & verse. Buys several ideas/yr. Prefers outright submission. Rights purchased are negotiable. Pays on publication; negotiable royalty. Responds in 12-15 wks. Uses rhymed, unrhymed, and traditional verse for framed art; 4-16 lines. Open to ideas for new specialty items. Submit max 3-10 ideas. Open to ideas for framed art. Guidelines; catalog $5/10x13 SAE.

THE CHRISTIAN INTERMARKET, PO Box 3000, Cleveland TN 37312 (888)

946-4639. Fax (423)559-5444. E-mail: Info@christianintermarket.com. Website: www.christianintermarket.com. This is an online wholesale Christian gift show designed to connect retail store buyers with suppliers on the Internet. It is a gift product distributor, not a publisher/producer of gift products.

*CITY OF DAVID, INC., 23679 Calabasas Rd., Ste. 250, Calabasas CA 91302. (818)222-0393. Fax (818)222-0306. Christian apparel.

*COLORADO CASUAL (formerly LAS Creations), 5850 Championship View, Ste. E., Colorado Springs CO 80922. (719)570-1999. Fax (719)570-7319. Holly Smethers, V.P. Produces Christian apparel. Open to freelance ideas. Query. Pays royalties. Responds in 4 weeks. Open to ideas for T-shirt and apparel designs; home textiles. Holiday/seasonal 5 mos ahead. Submit 4-6 ideas. No guidelines; free catalog.

DICKSONS, INC., 709 B Ave. East., PO Box 368, Seymour IN 47274. (812) 522-1308. Fax (812)522-1319. E-mail: rdeppen@dicksonsgifts.com. Website: www.dicksonsgifts.com. Rita Deppen, product dev. Produces gift items. Open to freelance (1-2%). Submit cover letter/sample (no originals). Outright purchase; all rts preferred. Pays $50 on acceptance. Variable royalties. Responds in 4-6 wks. Uses rhymed verse. Needs Christmas, Father's Day, friendship, graduation, love, Mother's Day, thank you, and wedding. Holiday/seasonal 1 yr ahead. Send any number of ideas. Uses religious/inspirational verses for bookmarks, Quik Notes, plaques, etc. Open to ideas for bookmarks, gift/novelty items, magnets, mugs, plaques, stationery and T-shirts. Guidelines; no copy.

*FIRST HOUSE PUBLISHING, 2209 Hand Blvd., Orlando FL 32806. (407)895-3547. Posters.

GARBORG'S, 2060 W. 98th St., Bloomington MN 55431. (612)888-5727. Fax (612)888-4775. Barbara Farmer, ed. Producer of specialty products. Imprint: Front Porch Books. 2% freelance, buys 2-3 ideas/yr. Query or outright submission. Pays negotiable rates on publication. Negotiable royalties. Responds in 4-6 wks. No seasonal. Open to ideas for calendars, bookmarks, gift books, journals, or stationery. Submit 1 idea. Guidelines; catalog for 9x12 SAE/5 stamps.

> Tips: "Our main product is a page-a-day perpetual calendar with inspirational thoughts, quotes and Scripture. Looking for material with a relationship emphasis that will inspire a diverse audience, secular as well as Christian. No 'Christianese,' no clichés, just fresh language and gentle inspiration." Open to gift books and journals for Front Porch Book line.

+HERITAGE PUZZLE, INC., 340 Witt St., Winston-Salem NC 27103. (888)348-3717. Website: www.lighthouses.org. Religious jigsaw puzzles.

*KNOW HIM, 11613 Pine Grove Ln., Parker CO 80138. (303)805-5190. (888)256-6944. Fax (303)805-5174. Christian apparel.

NEW LEAF GIFTS, a division of New Leaf Press. See book listing.

*NEW VENTURES, RR 1 Box 2091, Moretown VT 05660-9511. (802)229-1020. Fax (802)229-1020. Action figures.

*PEELE ENTERPRISES SHIRT PRINTS, LTD., 3401 Hwy 25N, Hodges SC 29653. (803)374-7339. Christian T-shirts and sweatshirts.

+REVELATIONS, 610 E. Bell Rd.,Ste. 2-100, Phoenix AZ 85022. (800)886-5420. Website: www.giftwarecompany.com. Variety of gift products.

*SCANDECOR, 430 Pike Rd., Southampton PA 18966. (215)355-2410. Fax (215)364-8737. Lauren Harris Karp, product mgr. A general poster publisher that does a few inspirational posters for children, teens and adults. 40% freelance; buys 50 ideas/yr. Makes outright purchase, for world-wide, exclusive rts. Pays $100 on publication, depends on size of poster. No royalties. Responds in 9 wks. Uses rhymed, unrhymed and light verse; one line up to 20 lines. Produces humorous, inspirational, juvenile, novelty and soft line. No holiday posters. Submit several ideas. Open to ideas for calendars, posters and novelty products/copy. Guidelines; no catalog.

SIERRA GIFT CO., 2448 E. 81st St., Ste. 4900, Tulsa OK 74137-4285. (765) 643-1214. Lana Ginder, mgr. Various gift lines.

#SWANSON INC., 1200 Park Ave., Murfreesboro TN 37129. (615)896-4114. Fax (615)898-1313. E-mail: swanson@hotcom.net. Website: www.hotcom. net/swanson. Jason Crisler, marketing. Produces specialty products. Just opening up to freelancers. Query. Pays on publication. No royalties. Responds in 8-10 wks. Uses rhymed, unrhymed, traditional and light verse; short. Inspirational/Christian. Open to new ideas. Send any number. Open to ideas for coloring books, gift/novelty items, magnets, mugs, post cards, puzzles, T-shirts. No guidelines or catalog.

*WARNER PRESS INC., 1200 E 5th St., PO Box 2499, Anderson IN 46018-9988. (765)644-7721. Fax (765)640-8005. E-mail: jennieb@warnerpress. org. Jennie Bishop, sr ed. Producer of specialty products. 30% freelance; buys 30-50 ideas/yr. Query for guidelines. Pays $30-35 on acceptance (for bulletins); material for bulletins cannot be sold elsewhere for bulletin use, but may be sold in any other medium. No royalties. Responds in 4-6 wks. Uses rhymed, unrhymed, traditional verse and devotionals for bulletins; 16-24 lines. Accepts 10 ideas/submission. Also open to ideas for coloring books, church resource items. Guidelines for bulletins (must send for before submitting); no catalog.

   Tips: "Most of our present purchases are for church bulletins. Writers must apply for Master Writer status according to guidelines before submitting bulletin materials."

*YOUTH LIFE CREATIONS, 2004 Carrolton, Muncie IN 47304. (800)784-0078. Action cards.

SOFTWARE DEVELOPERS

*AGES SOFTWARE, PO Box 1926, Albany OR 97321-0509. (541)926-1370. Fax (541)917-0839. Steve Radda, president. Contact: Mario Aranda.

BAKER BOOK HOUSE. See book listing.

BIBLESOFT, 22014 7th Ave. S., Seattle WA 98198-6235. (206)824-0547. Fax (206)824-1828. Website: www.biblesoft.com.

BROADMAN & HOLMAN. See book listing.

CLOUD TEN PICTURES, PO Box 1440, Niagara Falls NY 14302. Or, One St. Paul St., The Penthouse, St. Catherines ON L2R 7L2 Canada. (905)684-

5561. Fax (905)684-7946. E-mail: JonesB@cloudtenpictures.com. Website: www.cloudtenpictures.com. Sales Manager: Byron Jones. Videos.

ELLIS ENTERPRISES, INC. 4205 McAuley Blvd., #385, Oklahoma City OK 73120. (405)749-0273. Fax (405)751-5168. E-mail: mail@ellisenterprises.com. Website: www.ellisenterprises.com. Contact person: Gene Massey. Produces The Bible Library 4.0 Deluxe, Special, and Basic Editions. A shareware product may also be downloaded from their Website. Check out additional products on their Website.

*EPIPHANY SOFTWARE, 15897 Alta Vista Way, San Jose CA 95127. (408)251-9788.

EXEGESES BIBLES CD ROM—The only Literal Translations and Transliterations—Ever. PO Box 1776, Orange CA 92856. Phone/fax 1 800 9BIBLE9. (714)835-1705. E-mail: exegeses@exegesesbibles.org. Website: www.exegesesbibles.org.

*KIRKBRIDE TECHNOLOGIES, PO Box 606, Indianapolis IN 46206. (317) 633-1900.

LOGOS RESEARCH SYSTEMS, 715 SE Fidalgo Ave., Oak Harbor WA 98277-4049. (360)679-6575. Fax (360)675-8169. E-mail: info@logos.com. Website: www.logos.com.

LOIZEAUX BROTHERS. See book listing.

+MIDISOFT., 1605 NW Sammamish Rd., Ste. 205, Issaqua WA 98027. (800) 989-5118. Fax (425)391-3422. E-mail: dans@midisoft.com. Worship software.

NAVPRESS SOFTWARE, 16002 Pool Canyon Rd., Austin TX 78734. (512) 266-1700.

*PARSONS TECHNOLOGY, 1 Martha's Way, Hiawatha IA 52233-0100. (319) 395-9626.

TOMMY NELSON, PO Box 141000, Nashville TN 37214. (615)902-3301. Fax (615)902-3330. Website: www.tommynelson.com. Video producer; software developer.

ZONDERVAN CORP. See book listing.

VIDEO/CD MARKETS

+ANIMAZING ENTERTAINMENT, 2221 Niagara Falls Blvd., Niagara Falls NY 14304. (800)641-7926. Children's animated videos.

*CHRISTIAN DUPLICATIONS INTL., INC., 1710 Lee Reed Rd., Orlando FL 32810. (800)327-9332. Videos.

DALLAS CHRISTIAN VIDEO, 1878 Firman, Richardson TX 75081. (800)231-0095. Fax (972)644-5926. E-mail: DCV6681@aol.com. Website: www.DallasChristianVideo.com. Contact: Bob Hill.

*EVERLAND ENTERTAINMENT, 3319 West End Ave., Ste. 200, Nashville TN 37203. (800)876-9673.

*HEARTSONG, PO Box 2455, Glenview IL 60025. (800)648-0755. Videos.

+PROPHECY PARTNERS VIDEOS, PO Box 2204, Niagara Falls NY 14302.

*PROPHECY PUBLICATIONS, PO Box 7000, Oklahoma City OK 73153. (800)475-1111. Fax (905)684-7946. E-mail: Jonesb@niagara.com. Religious education videos; fiction videos.

RANDOLF PRODUCTIONS, 18005 Sky Park Cir., Ste. K, Irvine CA 92614-6514. (800)266-7741. Fax (949)794-9117. E-mail: RWRAY@keynote.org. Website: www.goccc.com. Distributor of music and video from Campus Crusade for Christ. Contact: Randy Ray. Videos, CDs, and DVD.

RUSS DOUGHTEN FILMS, INC., 5907 Meredith Dr., Des Moines IA 50322. (515)278-4737. Fax (515)334-0460. E-mail: production@rdfilms.com. Website: www.rdfilms.com. Submit to Production Dept. Produces feature-length Christian movies. Open to ideas. Guidelines; free catalog.

ST. ANTHONY MESSENGER PRESS. See book listing.

SOLDIERS OF LIGHT PRODUCTIONS, 18701 Victory Blvd., Reseda CA 91335-6459. (813)345-3866. Fax (818)345-1162. Videos.

*THIS WEEK IN BIBLE PROPHECY, PO Box 1440, Niagara Falls NY 14302. (905)684-7700. Fax (905)684-7946. Videos.

THOMAS MORE. See book listing.

TOMMY NELSON. See above listing.

+VISUAL ENTERTAINMENT, INC., 55 University Ave. Ste. 1100, Toronto ON M5H 2H7 Canada. Toll-free: (888)387-2200. E-mail: info@visualbible.com. Website: www.visualbible.com. Videos and CDs.

ZONDERVAN. See book listing.

SPECIALTY PRODUCTS TOPICAL LISTINGS

NOTE: Most of the following publishers are greeting card publishers, but some will be found in the book publisher listings.

ACTIVITY/COLORING BOOKS

Chariot (Rainfall)
LifeSong
Rainbow Books
Shining Star
Standard
Swanson
Warner Press

AUDIO TAPES

Eldridge Publishing
Liguori Publications
Success Publishers
Tyndale House
Word
World Publishing
Zondervan

BANNERS

Argus Communications
Painted Hearts & Friends

BOARD GAMES/GAMES

Bethel Publishing

Bible Games Co.
Brodie, Inc, R.J.
Chariot (Rainfall Inc.)
Divinity Religious
ForJoy Concepts
Good Steward Game Co.
Lightwave Publishing
Master Books
Joshua Morris Publishing
M.J.N. Enterprises
Review and Herald
Shining Star
Standard Publishing
Talicor
Tyndale House

BOOKMARKS

Cathedral Art
Dicksons
Garborg's
J-Mar
SPS Studios

CALENDARS/DAILY JOURNALS

Abingdon

African American Greetings
American Tract Society
Argus Communications
Barbour & Co.
Front Porch Books (journals)
Garborg's
Genesis
Group Publishing
Manhattan Greeting Card
Marlene Moore Studio
Neibauer Press
Portal Publications
Read 'N Run Books
Scandecor
SPS Studios
Tyndale House
Women of the Promise

CD-ROMS

Bible Games Co.
Chariot
GROUP Publishing
Image Books/Doubleday
Lydia Press
NavPress
Our Sunday Visitor
Talicor

World Publishing

CHARTS

Rose Publishing

COMIC BOOKS

Kaleidoscope Press
Thomas Nelson

COMPUTER GAMES

Bible Games Co.
Brown-ROA
Chariot Victor
Divinity Religious
Editores Betania-Caribe
NavPress Software
Talicor
Wisdom Tree
Wood Lake Books

COMPUTER SOFTWARE

Ages Software
Baker (BakerBytes)
BibleSoft
Concordia
Epiphany Software
Gospel Light
Kirkbride Technology
Logos Research Systems
Loizeaux Brothers
NavPress Software
Parsons Technology
Resource Publications
Talicor
Wisdom Tree
Zondervan

GIFT BOOKS

(See listing under Book Topics)
Front Porch Books
Garborg's
Genesis
Image Craft
Marlene Moore Studio
Painted Hearts & Friends
Review and Herald
SPS Studios

GIFT/NOVELTY ITEMS

Abingdon
African American Greetings
Cathedral Art

Chariot Victor
Dicksons
Garborg's
J-Mar
Manhattan Greeting Card
New Boundary Designs
Portal Publications
Scandecor
Sierra Gift Co.
Swanson
Zondervan

GREETING BOOKS

Calligraphy Collection
Joshua Morris (novelty books)
Manhattan Greeting Card
Marlene Moore Studio
New Boundary Designs
SPS Studios

MAGNETS

African American Greetings
Argus Communications
Celebration Greetings
Dicksons
Genesis
New Boundary Designs
Swanson

MUGS

Celebration Greetings
Dicksons
Genesis
Heritage Collection
SPS Studios
Swanson

PLAQUES

Calligraphy Collection
Cathedral Art
Dicksons
Genesis
Inspirations Unlimited
Laura Leiden
Marlene Moore Studio
New Boundary Designs

POST CARDS

Abingdon
African American Greetings
Argus Communications
J-Mar (pocket verse cards)
Manhattan Greeting Card

New Boundary Designs
Read 'N Run Books
Swanson
Warner Press
Zondervan

POSTERS

Argus Communications
Celebration Greetings
First House
Genesis
J-Mar
Marlene Moore Studio
Portal Publications
Read 'N Run Books
Scandecor
Standard Publishing

PUZZLES

LifeSong
Marlene Moore Studio
Swanson
Talicor

STATIONERY

African American Greetings
Dicksons
Inspirations Unlimited
J-Mar
Painted Hearts & Friends
Portal Publications

SUNDAY BULLETINS

Logos Productions
    (children's)
Warner Press

T-SHIRTS

Dicksons
Genesis
LAS Creations
Peele Enterprises
Swanson
Women of the Promise

VIDEOS/VIDEO GAMES

Abingdon
Augsburg
Bible Games Co.
Brentwood Music
Broadman & Holman
Brown-ROA

Chariot (Rainfall)
Church Street Press
Destiny Image
Diamante
Russ Doughten Films
Editorial Unilit
Focus on the Family
Gospel Light/Regal
Group Publishing

Howard Publishing
Integrity Music
InterVarsity
Liguori Publications
Master Books
Moody Press
Paraclete Press
Pauline Video
Prophecy Publications

Star Song
Talicor
Tyndale Family Video
Vermont Story Works
Victor Books
Vision Video
Wisdom Tree
Word
Zondervan

CHRISTIAN WRITERS' CONFERENCES AND WORKSHOPS

(*) Indicates information was not verified or updated by the group leader
(+) Indicates a new listing

Note: Visit the following Websites for information on these and other conferences available across the country: www.authorlink.com/con_yr.html, or www.shawguides.com/index.cgi?s=11, or www.writer.org/conflist/conflst1. htm, or www.bluejaypub.com/win/conferences.htm, or www.screenwriter. com/insider/WritersCalendar.html.

ALABAMA

+AMERICAN CHRISTIAN WRITERS BIRMINGHAM CONFERENCE. January 23, 2001. Contact: Reg A. Forder, Box 110390, Nashville TN 37222. 1-800-21-WRITE. Website: www.ECPA.org/ACW. Attendance: 35-50.

+AMERICAN CHRISTIAN WRITERS MOBILE CONFERENCE. November 9-10, 2001. Contact: Reg A. Forder, Box 110390, Nashville TN 37222. 1-800-21-WRITE. Website: www.ECPA.org/ACW. Attendance: 35-50.

*SOUTHERN CHRISTIAN WRITERS CONFERENCE. Birmingham/Samford University, June 2001. Contact: Joanne Sloan, SCWC, PO Box 1106, Northport AL 35476. (205)333-8603. Fax (205)339-4528. E-mail: Visionslo @aol.com. Attendance: 150-200.

ARIZONA

AMERICAN CHRISTIAN WRITERS PHOENIX CONFERENCE. October 26-27, 2001. Contact: Reg A. Forder, Box 110390, Nashville TN 37222. 1-800-21-WRITE. Website: www.ECPA.org/ACW. Attendance: 35-50.

SOUTH-EASTERN ARIZONA CHRISTIAN WRITERS SEMINAR. Benson; November 2001. Contact: Floyd Pierce, HC2 Box 3868, Willcox AZ 85643. (520)384-3064. E-mail: piniq@vtc.net.

*TEMPE WRITERS WORKSHOP/WRITE NOW! February 2001. Sponsored by Creative Copy Ink. Contact: Kitty Bucholtz, PO Box 50993, Phoenix AZ 85076-0993. Phone/fax (480)783-9863. E-mail: jkbuch@primenet.com.

ARKANSAS

*56TH ANNUAL ARKANSAS WRITERS' CONFERENCE. Little Rock; June 2001 (held annually on 1st weekend of June). Contact: Barbara Longstieth-Mulkey, 17 Red Maple Ct., Little Rock AR 72211-3117. (501)312-1747. E-mail: blm@aristotle.net. Attendance: 200.

SILOAM SPRINGS WRITERS' CONFERENCE. Siloam Springs; August of each year. Contact: Margaret Weathers, 716 N. University, Siloam Springs AR 72761-2658. (501)524-6598.

CALIFORNIA

ACT ONE: WRITING FOR HOLLYWOOD. Hollywood, August 1-31, 2001; and New York City, June 1-30, 2001. Speakers: Ken Wales, Michael Warren and Karen Hall. Contact: Barbara R. Nicolosi, 1760 N. Gower St., Hollywood CA 90028. (323)462-1348. Fax (323)462-3199. E-mail: Actone 2000@aol.com. Website: www.ActOneprogram.com. Limited to 30 students. This is a month-long intensive training session for screenwriters. Applications will be accepted starting February 2001. Weekend Adaptation Seminars are available for small groups of published CBA authors looking to adapt their books to film or television. These weekends are held in Los Angeles in October, February and April.

+AMERICAN CHRISTIAN WRITERS ANAHEIM CONFERENCE. October 19-20, 2001. Contact: Reg A. Forder, Box 110390, Nashville TN 37222. 1-800-21-WRITE. Website: www.ECPA.org/ACW. Attendance: 35-50.

AMERICAN CHRISTIAN WRITERS SACRAMENTO CONFERENCE. October 13, 2001. Contact: Reg A. Forder, Box 110390, Nashville TN 37222. 1-800-21-WRITE. Website: www.ECPA.org/ACW. Attendance: 35-50.

CASTRO VALLEY CHRISTIAN WRITERS SEMINAR. Castro Valley, February 23-24, 2001. Speakers: Deborah Hedstrom, Ethel Herr, Lauraine Snelling. Contact: Pastor Jon Drury, 19300 Redwood Rd., Castro Valley CA 94546-3465. (510)886-6300. Fax (510)581-5022. E-mail: jond@redwoodchapel. org. Attendance: 160.

*CEHUC SPANISH CHRISTIAN WRITERS SEMINAR. Los Angeles, San Diego or Tijuana; April 2001. Contact: Magdalena Latorre, 9802 Quail Canyon Rd., El Cajon CA 92021-6000. Phone/fax (619)390-3747.

CHRISTIAN WRITERS FELLOWSHIP OF ORANGE COUNTY WRITERS DAYS. Irvine, April 28 and October 2001. Contact: Beverly Bush Smith or Bonnie Compton Hanson, PO Box 538, Lake Forest CA 92630. (949)458-8981. Fax (949)458-1807. E-mail: bonnieh1@worldnet.att.net or 2smith @pacbell.net. Attendance: 100.

EVANGELICAL PRESS ASSOCIATION CONVENTION. San Diego CA, May 6-9, 2001. (Held in different location each year.) Contact: Ron Wilson, dir, 314 Dover Rd., Charlottesville VA 22901. (804)973-5941. Fax (804)973-2710. E-mail: 74473.272@compuserve.com. Website: www.epassoc.org. Attendance: 300-400. Annual convention; freelance communicators welcome.

+FICTIONARIES. Orange County. Contact: DeMarco Barrett, (949)760-8086. E-mail: fictionaries@aol.com. Professional secular group; requires audition.

*LODI ALL-DAY WRITERS SEMINAR. Stockton, date not set for 2001 (usually July). General writing conference; not just Christian writers. Contact: Dee Porter, PO Box 1863, Lodi CA 95241. Phone/fax (209)334-0603. E-mail: crcomm@lodinet.com. Write and ask to be put on mailing list.

MASTER CLASS. Pine Valley Bible Conference Center, Pine Valley, March

2001. A creative writing workshop co-sponsored by San Diego Co. Christian Writers Guild and AD LIB Christian Arts. Contact: Judith Deem Dupree, PO Box 365, Pine Valley CA 91962. Phone/fax (619)473-8683.

MOUNT HERMON CHRISTIAN WRITERS CONFERENCE. Mount Hermon (near Santa Cruz), April 6-10, 2001, March 22-26, 2002. Speakers include Jerry Jenkins. Advanced track with Sally Stuart and Karen Ball; new Professional Forum with Lauraine Snelling. Contact: David R. Talbott, Box 413, Mount Hermon CA 95041-0413. (831)430-1240. Fax (831)335-9413. E-mail: slist@mhcamps.org. Website: www.mounthermon.org. Attendance: 350.

+NATIONAL CONFERENCE ON WRITING & ILLUSTRATING FOR CHILDREN. Los Angeles; August 2001. Mid-Year Conference; New York City, February 17-18, 2001. Contact: Lin Oliver or Stephen Mooser, 8271 Beverly Blvd., Los Angeles CA 90048. (323)782-1010. Fax (323)782-1892. E-mail: scbwi@scbwi.org. Website: www.scbwi.org. Includes a track for professionals. Attendance: 650.

SAN DIEGO CHRISTIAN WRITERS GUILD FALL CONFERENCE. San Diego, September 2001. Contact: Robert Gillespie, 17041 Palacio Pl., San Diego CA 92127. Phone/fax (858)673-3921. E-mail: riters@adnc. com. Attendance: 150.

SAN DIEGO STATE UNIVERSITY WRITERS CONFERENCE. San Diego/ Doubletree Hotel Mission Valley, January 19-21, 2001. To advanced writers offers a read and critique by editors and agents. Contact: Diane Dunaway, 8465 Jane St., San Diego CA 92129. (858)484-8575. Fax (619)594-8577. E-mail: ddunaway@aol.com. Website: www.writers conferences.com. Attendance: 500.

SANTA BARBARA CHRISTIAN WRITERS CONFERENCE. Westmont College; October 6, 2001. Contact: Rev. Opal Mae Dailey, PO Box 42429, Santa Barbara CA 93140. (805)647-9162.

+STANFORD PROFESSIONAL WRITING COURSE. Stanford; July 2001. An intensive 13-day program for professionals in book and magazine publishing, presented by leaders in publishing and new media. Contact: Stanford Professional Publishing Course, 424 Santa Teresa St., Stanford CA 94305-4005. 650-725-6259. Fax 650-725-9712.

VALLEY BIBLE CHRISTIAN WRITERS CONFERENCE. Hercules; October 19-20, 2001. Contact: Sandy Ormeo, 1477 Bayberry Ave., Hercules CA 94547. (510)779-3171. Fax (510)799-3174. E-mail: Sandywrites@yahoo. com.

WRITERS SYMPOSIUM BY THE SEA. San Diego/Point Loma Nazarene University, February 22-24, 2001; February 2002. Contact: Dean Nelson, Professor, Journalism Dept. PLNU, 3900 Lomaland Dr., San Diego CA 92106. (619)849-2592. Fax (619)849-2566. E-mail: deannelson@ptloma.edu. Attendance: 100-200.

*****THE WRITE TOUCH.** A six-week School of Christian Writing class, teaching the basics of fiction, newspaper pieces, children's books, poetry, personal experience articles and marketing. Taught as requested in your area. For information or to book the school, contact: Glenda Palmer, 1687 Via Elisa

Dr., El Cajon CA 92021-3559. (619)440-3020 or Peggy Leslie at (619)447-6258.

COLORADO

*AD LIB CHRISTIAN ARTS RETREAT. Black Forest/Colorado Springs, September or October 2001. Contact: Judith Deem Dupree, PO Box 365, Pine Valley CA 91962-0365. Phone/fax (619)473-8683. Designed as a forum and format for renewal. Solitude, issues and ideas, critiquing. Attendance: 40+.

+AMERICAN CHRISTIAN WRITERS COLORADO SPRINGS CONFERENCE. September 7-8, 2001. Contact: Reg A. Forder, Box 110390, Nashville TN 37222. 1-800-21-WRITE. Website: www.ECPA.org/ACW. Attendance: 35-50.

COLORADO CHRISTIAN WRITERS CONFERENCE. Estes Park; May 10-12, 2001. Director: Marlene Bagnull, Litt.D, 316 Blanchard Rd., Drexel Hill PA 19026-3507. Phone/fax (610)626-6833. E-mail: mbagnull@aol. com. Website: www.writehisanswer.com. Offers track for advanced writers, and a Teens Write! For 2 1/2 hours on Saturday. Attendance: 250.

COLORADO WRITERS FELLOWSHIP SEMINARS. Denver; (3/yr) April—nonfiction; July—for published writers only; and October—fiction topics. Contact: Su Wright, CWF Executive Director, PO Box 22416, Denver CO 80222-0416. (303)758-6556. Fax (303)758-9272. E-mail: Suwriter@aol. com. Attendance: 50-100 (Christians & non-Christians).

*INDEPENDENT PUBLISHERS FOR CHRIST. Denver. Sponsors semi-annual seminar in the spring and fall focusing on various aspects of self-publishing. Copies of seminar tapes available. Also provides speakers for writing groups. Contact: Cecile Higgins, PO Box 280349, Lakewood CO 80228. (303)456-9166. Fax (303)793-0838.

WESTERN SLOPE CHRISTIAN WRITERS ASSOCIATION SEMINARS. Grand Junction; 3-day conference in Fall 2001. Discount for teens and seniors. Contact: Steve Henderson, 2948 Shelley Dr., Grand Junction CO 81503. (970)245-5084 (Debbie Brockett). Fax (970)245-1997. E-mail: WSCWA@ netscape.net. Offers advanced track. Attendance 120.

CONNECTICUT

WESLEYAN WRITERS CONFERENCE. Wesleyan University/Middletown, late June 2001. Contact: Anne Greene, 279 Court St., Middletown CT 06457. (860)685-3604. Fax (860)685-2441. E-mail: agreene@wesleyan.edu. Website: www.wesleyan.edu/writing/conferen.html. Includes an advanced track. Attendance: 100.

FLORIDA

AMERICAN CHRISTIAN WRITERS ORLANDO CONFERENCE. November 16-17, 2001. Contact: Reg Forder, Box 110390, Nashville TN 37222. 1-800-21-WRITE. Website: www.ECPA.org/ACW. Attendance: 20-50.

FLORIDA CHRISTIAN WRITERS CONFERENCE. Park Avenue Retreat

Center/Titusville; January 25-28, 2001; January 24-27, 2002. Offers advanced track by application only. Contact: Billie Wilson, 2344 Armour Ct., Titusville FL 32780. (321)269-5831. Fax (321)264-0037. E-mail: bwilson@ digital.net. Website: www.kipertek.com/writer. Attendance: 225.

WRITING STRATEGIES FOR THE CHRISTIAN MARKET. Not offered in seminar; only as independent studies, with manual and assignments. Contact instructor: Rosemary J. Upton, 2712 S. Peninsula Dr., Daytona Beach FL 32118-5706. Phone/fax (904)322-1111. E-mail: romy14@juno. com. Write to be put on mailing list.

GEORGIA

+AMERICAN CHRISTIAN WRITERS ATLANTA CONFERENCE. July 6-7, 2001. Contact: Reg Forder, Box 110390, Nashville TN 37222. 1-800-21-WRITE. Website: www.ECPA.org/ACW. Attendance: 35-50.

CBA CONVENTION. (Held in a different location each year.) July 7-12, 2001, Atlanta. July 13-19, 2002, Anaheim CA. Contact: CBA, Box 62000, Colorado Springs CO 80962-2000. (800)252-1950 or (719)265-9895. Entrance badges available through book publishers.

NORTHEAST GEORGIA WRITERS CONFERENCE. Gainesville, October 2002 (biennial/even-numbered years). Contact: Elouise Whitten, 660 Crestview Terrace, Gainesville GA 30501-3110. (770)532-3007. E-mail: E6625Whitt@aol.com. Attendance: 100. Elouise Whitten also holds private writing workshops: Putting Novels into Screenplays; Short Story Workshop; and Novel Workshop. Contact her for dates and location.

#SOUTHEASTERN WRITERS CONFERENCE. St. Simons Island; June 2001. Contact: Patricia S. Laye, Rt. 1 Box 102, Cuthbert GA 31740. (912)679-5445. Website: www.southeasternwriters.com. Attendance: 100 (limited). Awards cash prizes in every genre and free manuscript critiques.

SPAN PUBLISHING COLLEGE & TRADE SHOW 2001. Atlanta; October 19-21, 2001. Sponsored by the Small Publishers Assn. of North America. Speakers: Tom & Marilyn Ross. A marketing-specific, information-packed conference for authors, self-publishers and independent presses. Contact: Marilyn Ross, PO Box 1306, Buena Vista CO 81211-1306. (719)395-4790. Fax (719)395-8374. E-mail: SPAN@SPANnet.org. Website: www. SPANnet.org/2001. Attendance: 200.

IDAHO

+AMERICAN CHRISTIAN WRITERS BOISE CONFERENCE. September 14-15, 2001. Contact: Reg A. Forder, Box 110390, Nashville TN 37222. 1-800-21-WRITE. Website: www.ECPA.org/ACW. Attendance: 35-50.

ILLINOIS

*ASSOCIATED CHURCH PRESS 2001 ANNUAL CONVENTION. Chicago; March/April 2001. Contact: Joe Roos, The Associated Church Press, PO Box 7, Riverdale MD 20738-0007.

*INTERNATIONAL BLACK WRITERS CONFERENCE. Chicago, June 2001. Contact: Mable Terrell, PO Box 1030, Chicago IL 60690-1030. (312)409-2292.

KARITOS CHRISTIAN ARTS FESTIVAL. Homewood; May 31-June 2, 2001. Contact: Bob Hay and Mike Schoder, 1116 State St. PMB 21, Lemont IL 60439. (847)506-9814 or (630)243-8127. E-mail: FMSch757644@aol. com. Website: www.karitos.com. Speakers include Curt Mortimer and Chris Wave. Offers beginner and advanced track. Karitos is a festival conducting classes and showcases in all areas of the arts, including writing. Attendance: 500-600.

*MISSISSIPPI VALLEY WRITERS CONFERENCE. Augustana College/Rock Island, June 2001. Contact: David R. Collins, 3403 45th St., Moline IL 61265-6608. (309)762-8985. E-mail: kimseuss@aol.com. Offers advanced novel track. Welcomes beginners and polished professionals. Attendance: 75.

*THE SALVATION ARMY CHRISTIAN WRITERS' CONFERENCE. Des Plaines, April 2002 (held every other year). Contact: Elizabeth Kinzie, 10 W. Algonquin Rd., Des Plaines IL 60016-6006. (847)294-2050. Attendance: 60. For S.A. officers, laymen, and employee staff.

WRITE-TO-PUBLISH CONFERENCE. Wheaton (Chicago area); June 6-9, 2001. Contact: Lin Johnson, 9731 N. Fox Glen Dr., #6F, Niles IL 60714-4222. (847)296-3964. Fax (847)296-0754. E-mail: linjohnson@compuserve. com. Website: www.writetopublish.com. Offers advanced track (prerequisite 2 published books). Majority of faculty are editors. Attendance: 200.

INDIANA

+AMERICAN CHRISTIAN WRITERS FORT WAYNE CONFERENCE. April 6-7, 2001. Speakers: Dr. Dennis Hensley, Linda Wade, Holly G. Miller, Bob Hostetler. Contact: Reg A. Forder, Box 110390, Nashville TN 37222. 1-800-21-WRITE. Website: www.ECPA.org/ACW. Attendance: 35-50.

AMERICAN CHRISTIAN WRITERS INDIANAPOLIS CONFERENCE. August 11, 2001. Contact: Reg Forder, Box 110390, Nashville TN 37222. 1-800-21-WRITE. Website: www.ECPA.org/ACW. Attendance: 35-50.

*BETHEL COLLEGE CHRISTIAN WRITERS' WORKSHOP. Mishawaka; may not be held every year. Contact: Jeanne Haverstick, 1001 W. McKinley Ave., Mishawaka IN 46545-5509. (219)257-3352. Attendance: 120.

EARLHAM SCHOOL OF RELIGION ANNUAL COLLOQUIUM/THE MINISTRY OF WRITING. Richmond; October 19-20, 2001 (always 3rd weekend). Speaker: Elizabeth Cox. Contact: '01 Writing Colloquium, J. Brent Bill, Earlham School of Religion, 228 College Ave., Richmond IN 47374. (800)432-1377. (765)983-1423. Fax (765)983-1688. E-mail: billbr@earlham. edu. Website: www.earlham.edu/~esr. Attendance: 150.

EARLHAM SCHOOL OF RELIGION/QUAKER HILL CONFERENCE CENTER SATURDAY WRITING SEMINARS. Richmond. Following are scheduled seminars: February 2001, The Writing Life, Alan Garinger; March 2001, Poetry Workshop, Mary Brown; April 15, 2001, The Art of Revision, Barbara Bennett Mays; and May 13, 2001, The Writer as Contemplative, Peter Anderson. Contact: Quaker Hill Conference Center, 10 Quaker Hill

Dr., Richmond IN 47374. (765)962-5741. E-mail: quakrhil@infocom. com. Website: www.infocom.com/~quakrhil.

+FORT WAYNE CHRISTIAN WRITERS WORKSHOP. Shipshewana; March 25-30, 2001. Author in residence: Jim Watkins. Contact: Linda R. Wade, 739 W. Fourth St., Fort Wayne IN 46808-2613. (219)422-2772. E-mail: linda_wade@juno.com. Cost $500; send $100 deposit. Balance due by January 31, 2001. Working conference.

MIDWEST WRITERS WORKSHOP. Muncie, July 26-28, 2001. Contact: Dr. Earl Conn, Dept. of Journalism, Ball State University, Muncie IN 47306-0675. (765)285-5587. Fax (765)285-7997. E-mail: econn@bsu.edu. Attendance: 125.

IOWA

+IOWA SUMMER WRITING FESTIVAL. University of Iowa/Iowa City; June & July 2001. This is a secular writer's conference that comes highly recommended for good, solid instruction. Contact: Iowa Summer Writing Festival, 100 Oakdale Campus, Ste. W310, the University of Iowa, Iowa City IA 52242, 319-335-4160, fax 319-335-4039. For two months, June and July, you can sign up for either one-week workshops or weekend workshops on a wide variety of topics. Write for a catalogue of offerings.

KANSAS

*BOONDOCKS RETREAT. Dodge City; possibly June, date not set. Contact: Linda Fergerson, 2500 Memory Ln., Dodge City KS 67801. (316)225-1126. Attendance: 25-40. Offers a spiritual retreat for writers, rather than a nuts & bolts conference.

*FIFTH LITERARY ARTS FESTIVAL. The Milton Center/Wichita; February 2001. Co-sponsored with Newman University English Department. Theme: Identity (will examine the role personal, ethnic, spiritual, and religious identity plays in literature). Contact: The Milton Center, Newman University, 3100 McCormick, Wichita KS 67213-2097. (316)942-4291. Fax (316) 942-4483. E-mail: milton@newmanu.edu. Website: www.newmanu.edu.

KANSAS CITY CHRISTIAN WRITERS' NETWORK SEMINARS. Kansas City area (KS & MO); held four times a year: January, April, July & October. Contact: Teresa Vining, 1438 N. Lucy Montgomery Way, Olathe KS 66061-6706. Phone/fax (913) 764-4610. E-mail: KCCWN@aol.com. Offers an advanced track. Attendance: 50-100 at each seminar.

PITTSBURG CHRISTIAN WRITERS' WORKSHOP. Gerard; April 14, 2001. Speaker: Aletha Hinthorn. Contact: Carol Russell, Walkertown 894—165th St., Fort Scott KS 66701. (316)547-2472. E-mail: rlrussell@ckt.net. Attendance: 50.

KENTUCKY

5th ANNUAL KENTUCKY CHRISTIAN WRITERS' SEMINAR. Elizabethtown;

June 1-2, 2001. Speaker: Susan Titus Osborn. Contact: Betty Whitworth, 15763 Leitchfield Rd., Leitchfield KY 42754. (270)257-2461. E-mail: blwhit@bbtel.com. Attendance: 50-70.

*WRITERS WORKSHOP AT LOUISVILLE PRESBYTERIAN SEMINARY. Louisville; March 2001. Co-directors/keynote speakers. Contact: Dr. James Andrews, Louisville Presbyterian Seminary, 1044 Alta Vista Rd., Louisville KY 40205. (800)264-1839. Fax (502)895-1096. Attendance: 40.

MAINE

EIGHTH ANNUAL CHRISTIAN WRITERS' CONFERENCE. China Lake Conference Center, August 16-18, 2001. Contact: Dr. Ken Parker, Minister of Conferencing & Camping, China Lake Conference Center, PO Box 149, China ME 04926. (207)968-2101. Fax (207)968-2434. E-mail: kparker@larck.net, or jvschad@larck.net. Sponsors Dorothy Templeton Writer's Contest, and publishes an anthology of writing by conferees. Attendance: 40-50.

*STATE OF MAINE WRITERS' CONFERENCE. Ocean Park; August 2001. Contact: Richard F. Burns, PO Box 7146, Ocean Park ME 04063-7146. (207) 934-9806. Attendance: 25-40. Contest announcement available March 1; brochure available June 1. Half-price tuition for teens.

MARYLAND

*CATHOLIC PRESS ASSOCIATION ANNUAL CONVENTION. Baltimore, May 2001. Contact: Owen McGovern, exec dir, 3555 Veterans Memorial Hwy, Ste. O, Ronkonkoma NY 11779-7636. (631)471-4730. Fax (631)471-4804. E-mail: CathJourn@aol.com. For media professionals. Attendance: 400.

SANDY COVE CHRISTIAN WRITERS CONFERENCE. Sandy Cove/North East, September 30-October 4, 2001; September 29-October 3, 2002; October 5-9, 2003. Offers Advanced Track. Contact: Jim Watkins, Writers' Conference Director, Sandy Cove Ministries, 60 Sandy Cove Rd., North East MD 21901. (800)234-2683. E-mail: info@sandy cove.com. Website: www.noble can.org/watkins/sandycov.htm. Attendance: 150.

MASSACHUSETTS

CAPE COD WRITERS' CONFERENCE. Craigville Conference Center, August 19-24, 2001. Contact: Joseph Ryan or Director, Box 186, West Barnstable MA 02630. (508)375-0516. E-mail: ccwc@capecod.net. Website: www. capecod.net/writers. Attendance: 125. Also offers CAPE LITERARY ARTS WORKSHOPS: 6 simultaneous week-long workshops (poetry, romance novels, juvenile writing, children's book illustrating, and play writing), August 2001. Limited to 10 in each workshop.

MICHIGAN

AMERICAN CHRISTIAN WRITERS ANN ARBOR CONFERENCE. Quality Inn, June 5, 2001. Contact: Reg Forder, Box 110390, Nashville TN 37222. 1-800-21-WRITE. Website: www.ECPA.org/ACW. Attendance: 35-50.

AMERICAN CHRISTIAN WRITERS GRAND RAPIDS CONFERENCE. Holiday Inn, June 1-2, 2001. Contact: Reg Forder, Box 110390, Nashville TN 37222. 1-800-21-WRITE. Website: www.ECPA.org/ACW. Attendance: 35-50.

*****CHRISTIAN WRITERS CONFERENCE.** Almont, April 2001. Contact: Dr. Richard Henderson and Dr. Kate Thoreson, PO Box 1, Novi MI 48376-0001. (248)349-5666. Fax (248)349-2345. Attendance: 40.

*****JOURNEY WRITING WORKSHOPS/LIFELINE: A SPIRITUAL JOURNEY FOR WRITERS.** Leelanau Center for Education. Glen Arbor MI. Held every 6 weeks. Contact: Elizabeth Hawkins, 1049 Floral Dr. SE, East Grand Rapids MI 49506. (616)245-9245. Classes limited to 20.

MARANATHA CHRISTIAN WRITERS SEMINAR. Maranatha Bible & Missionary Conference/Muskegon, August 2001. Contact: Leona Hertel, 4759 Lake Harbor Rd., Muskegon MI 49441-5299. (231)798-2161. Attendance: limited to 50.

*****"SPEAK UP WITH CONFIDENCE" SEMINAR.** Hillsdale; June 2001. Contact: Carol Kent, 1614 Edison Shores Pl., Port Huron MI 48060. (810)982-0898. Fax (810)987-4163. E-mail: Speakupinc@aol.com. Speaker: Carol Kent. Speaking seminar. Offers advanced training. Also offers a seminar on writing for publication. Attendance: 110.

MINNESOTA

AMERICAN CHRISTIAN WRITERS MINNEAPOLIS CONFERENCE. August 3-4, 2001. Contact: Reg Forder, Box 110390, Nashville TN 37222. 1-800-21-WRITE. Website: www.ECPA.org/ACW. Attendance: 35-50.

MINNESOTA CHRISTIAN WRITERS GUILD SPRING SEMINAR. Northwestern College/St. Paul, March 24, 2001. Speaker: Dr. Dennis Hensley. Contact: Sharon M. Knudson, 1596 Beechwood Ave., St. Paul MN 55116. (651)695-0609. E-mail: sharonknudson@hotmail.com. Attendance: 80-100.

THE WRITING ACADEMY SEMINAR. Sponsors year-round correspondence writing program and annual seminar in various locations. 2001 seminar is in Minneapolis, August 2-6, 2001. Contact: Chris Hefte, 21445 Sunny Dr., Fergus Falls MN 56537-9519. (218)736-2032. E-mail: pattyk@wams.org. Website: www.wams.org. Attendance: 30-40.

*****WRITING SEMINAR - NORTH HENNEPIN COMMUNITY COLLEGE.** Minneapolis; September 2001. Instructor: Louise B. Wyly. Topics include fiction, children's writing, personal experiences, memoirs and nonfiction. Contact: Louise Wyly, 6916—65th Ave. N, Minneapolis MN 55428-2515. (612)533-6207. E-mail: lsnowbunny@aol.com. Watch NHCC Bulletin for details, or call (612)424-0880 to inquire.

MISSISSIPPI

+AMERICAN CHRISTIAN WRITERS JACKSON CONFERENCE. January 20, 2001. Contact: Reg A. Forder, Box 110390, Nashville TN 37222. 1-800-21-WRITE. Website: www.ECPA.org/ACW. Attendance: 35-50.

MISSOURI

+AMERICAN CHRISTIAN WRITERS ST. LOUIS CONFERENCE. March 8, 2001. Contact: Reg A. Forder, Box 110390, Nashville TN 37222. 1-800-21-WRITE. Website: www.ECPA.org/ACW. Attendance: 35-50.

AMERICAN CHRISTIAN WRITERS SPRINGFIELD CONFERENCE. July 27-28, 2001. Contact: Reg A. Forder, Box 110390, Nashville TN 37222. 1-800-21-WRITE. Website: www.ECPA.org/ACW. Attendance: 35-50.

*MARK TWAIN WRITERS CONFERENCE. Hannibal, Heartland Lodge, four separate weeks in June, July, August & September, 2001. Contact: Cyndi Allison, 921 Center St., Hannibal MO 63401. (800)747-0738. (573)221-2462. Fax (573)221-6409. Attendance: 25 per conference. Note: This is a general conference under the direction of evangelical Christians.

NEBRASKA

MY THOUGHTS EXACTLY WRITERS RETREAT. St. Benedict Retreat Center/ Schuyler; October 2001. Contact: Cheryl Paden, PO Box 1073, Fremont NE 68026-1073. (402)727-6508. Geared toward the beginning writer. Attendance: Limited to 20.

NEW HAMPSHIRE

+MONADNOCK AREA CHRISTIAN WRITERS' DAYS. Dublin area; May and October. Contact: Elizabeth M. Hoekstra, PO Box 103, Dublin NH 03444. (603)563-9202. Fax (603)563-7739. E-mail: hoekstra@directpath.org. Attendance: 25-40.

THE WRITER & THE INTERNET WORKSHOP. Taught as requested by writer's groups, conferences, and schools. Contact: Mary Emma Allen (instructor), 55 Binks Hill Rd., Plymouth NH 03264. Fax (603)536-4851. E-mail: me.allen@juno.com. Website: homepage.fcgnetworks.net/jetent. mea. Additional classes offered as requested: Workshops for Young Writers (for schools and home parenting groups); Workshops for Teachers and Homeparenting Parents; Writing for Children Workshop; Writing for the Weekly Newspaper Workshop; Writing Newspaper, Magazine, and Online Columns Workshop; and Travel Writing Workshop.

NEW JERSEY

NEW JERSEY SOCIETY OF CHRISTIAN WRITERS FALL SEMINAR. Millville, November 3, 2001; November 2, 2002; November 1, 2003. Speakers:

Marlene Bagnull (2001); Dr. Roger Palms (2002); Gayle Roper (2003). Contact: Dr. Mary Ann Diorio, P.O. Box 405, Millville, NJ 08332-0405. (856)327-1231. Fax (856)327-0291. madiorio@aol.com or daystar405@ aol.com. Website: daystaministries.com/njscw. Attendance: 30-50.

NEW MEXICO

*GHOST RANCH WRITING WORKSHOPS. Abiquiu; October 2001. Contact: Ghost Ranch, HC 77 Box 11, Abiquiu NM 87510-9601.

THE GLEN WORKSHOP. St. John's College/Santa Fe; August 5-12, 2001. Includes fiction, poetry, nonfiction, memoir, on-site landscape painting, figure drawing, pottery making, and several master classes. Contact: Image, 3307 Third Ave. W., Seattle WA 98119. (206)281-2988. Fax (206)281-2335. E-mail: glenworkshop@imagejournal.org. Website: www.image journal.org. Attendance: 100.

GLORIETA CHRISTIAN WRITERS' CONFERENCE. Glorieta (18 mile N. of Santa Fe); October 16-20, 2001. Speakers 2001 include: Barbara Nicolosi. Offers 7 continuing classes (including writing for children, speaking and screenwriting), 42 workshops, editorial appointments, evening critique groups, a writing contest, and paid critiques. Contact: Glorieta Conference Center at (800)797-4222 or Mona Hodgson, PO Box 999, Cottonwood AZ 86326-0999. (505)757-6161. Fax (505)757-6149. E-mail: mona @sedona.net. Attendance: 225.

#IMAGE FESTIVAL OF LITERATURE AND THE ARTS. Location pending; early November 2001. Contact: Gregory Wolfe, Image, 3307 Third Ave. W., Seattle WA 98119. (206)281-2988. Fax (206)281-2335. E-mail: conference@imagejournal.org. Website: www.imagejournal.org.

#SOUTHWEST CHRISTIAN WRITERS ASSN. SEMINAR. Hesperus, September 2001. Contact: Kathy Cordell, PO Box 1008, Flora Vista NM 87415. (505)334-0617. E-mail: acampbell@cyberport.com (Anne Campbell, vice pres). Attendance: 30.

SOUTHWEST WRITERS ANNUAL CONFERENCE. Albuquerque, September 20-23, 2001. Contact: Stephanie Dooley, 8200 Mountain Rd. NE, Ste. 106, Albuquerque NM 87110-7835. (505)265-9485. Fax (505)265-9483. E-mail: SWriters@aol.com. Website: www.southwestwriters.org. Offers advanced classes; Young Writers Contest (for New Mexico teens only). Send SASE/.55 postage for brochure, after May 1, 2001. Attendance: 400-500.

NEW YORK

+AMERICAN CHRISTIAN WRITERS SYRACUSE CONFERENCE. June 8-9, 2001. Contact: Reg Forder, Box 110390, Nashville TN 37222. 1-800-21-WRITE. Website: www.ECPA.org/ACW. Attendance: 35-50.

+16th ANNUAL INTERNATIONAL CONFERENCE ON HUMOR & CREATIVITY. Saratoga Springs; April 2001. Secular. Contact: The HUMOR Project, Inc., 480 Broadway, Ste. 210, Saratoga Springs NY 12866. (518) 587-8770. Fax (800)600-4242.

NORTH CAROLINA

BLUE RIDGE MOUNTAIN CHRISTIAN WRITERS CONFERENCE. Ridgecrest Conference Center; April 1-5, 2001. Contact: Robin Hawkins, PO Box 128, Black Mountain NC 28770. (828)669-3596. Fax (828)669-4843. E-mail: rhawkin@lifeway.com. Attendance: 175-200.

OHIO

AMERICAN CHRISTIAN WRITERS COLUMBUS CONFERENCE. Holiday Inn, May 25-26, 2001. Hosted by Columbus Christian Writers Assn./Pat Zell, (937)593-9207. Contact: Reg Forder, Box 110390, Nashville TN 37222. 1-800-21-WRITE. Website: www.ECPA.org/ACW. Attendance: 35-50.

COLUMBUS CHRISTIAN WRITERS CONFERENCE. Columbus, May 24-26, 2001. Contact: Reg Forder, Box 110390, Nashville TN 37222. 1-800-21-WRITE. Website: www.ECPA.org/ACW.

+MEDINA ALLIANCE/LOGOS CHRISTIAN WRITERS SEMINAR. Medina; May 5, 2001. Speaker: Mark Littleton. Contact: Lisa Wiener, 973 Pheasant Run Dr., Medina OH 44256-3043. (330)722-8820. Fax (413)473-6423. E-mail: lisaw@ohio.net.

NORTHWEST OHIO CHRISTIAN WRITERS SEMINAR. Bowling Green; late September 2001. Contact: Diane Kashmer, 8322 W. Mudcreek Rd., Oak Harbor OH 43449. (419)898-1343. E-mail: kamio@kros.net. Attendance: 50-75.

*SET FORTH CHRISTIAN WRITERS GUILD SEMINAR. North Central OH/Mansfield area; Spring 2001. Contact: Donna Caudill, 836 Delph Ave., Mansfield OH 44906. (419)747-1755.

*WEST-DAYTON CHRISTIAN WRITERS CONFERENCE. Englewood; July 2001. Contact: Tina V. Toles, PO Box 251, Englewood OH 45322-2049. Phone/fax (937)832-0541.

OKLAHOMA

AMERICAN CHRISTIAN WRITERS OKLAHOMA CITY CONFERENCE. LaQuinta Inn, March 2-3, 2001. Contact: Reg Forder, Box 110390, Nashville TN 37222. 1-800-21-WRITE. Website: www.ECPA.org/ACW. Attendance: 35-50.

*WRITING WORKSHOPS. Various locations and dates. Contact: Kathryn Fanning, PO Box 18472, Oklahoma City OK 73154-0472.

OREGON

DRAMA IMPROVEMENT CONFERENCE. Greater Portland Area, October 12-13, 2001. Contact: Judy Straalsund, PO Box 19844, Portland OR 97280-0844. (503)245-6919. Fax (503)244-5421. E-mail: tapestry@teleport.com. Website: www.tapestrytheatre.org. Special track for teen actors. Geared to all Christian dramatists, and features workshops, performances, networking, forums and a book table. Playwrights are encouraged to attend.

HEART TALK. A workshop for women beginning to speak publicly or write for publication. Portland/Western Seminary, March 11, 2001, Sally Stuart (writing track); additional speakers to be announced. Contact: Beverly Hislop, dir., Women's Center for Ministry, Western Seminary, 5511 SE Hawthorne Blvd., Portland OR 97215. (503)233-8561 or (800)547-4546. Fax (503)239-4216. E-mail: bwhislop@westernseminary.edu. Website: www.westernsem inary.edu. Attendance: 150+.

OREGON CHRISTIAN WRITERS COACHING CONFERENCE. Salem/Western Baptist College, June 2001. Contact: Duane Young, PO Box 219103, Portland OR 97225-9103. (503)252-4433. Website: cs.georgefox.edu/rzempel/ocw. Includes about 7 hours of training under a specific coach/topic. Attendance: 150.

PENNSYLVANIA

GREATER PHILADELPHIA CHRISTIAN WRITERS' CONFERENCE. Glenside, August 2-4, 2001. Especially encourages African-American writers. Contact: Marlene Bagnull, Litt.D, 316 Blanchard Rd., Drexel Hill PA 19026-3507. Phone/fax (610)626-6833. E-mail: mbagnull@aol.com. Website: www.writehisanswer.com. Attendance: 200.

***MONTROSE CHRISTIAN WRITERS CONFERENCE.** Montrose, July 2001. Contact: Patti Souder, c/o Montrose Bible Conference, 5 Locust St., Montrose PA 18801-1112. (800)598-5030. (570)278-1001. Fax (570)278-3061. E-mail: info@montrosebible.org. Website: www.montrosebible.org. Includes advanced track. Attendance: 90.

***TENTH ANNUAL ONE-DAY WRITERS' WORKSHOP** (sponsored by St. David's Writers' Conference), Mercer, April 2001. Contact: Evelyn Minshull, 724 Airport Rd., Mercer PA 16137. (724)475-3239 or Lucinda Norman (814)328-2067. E-mail: eminshull@juno.com. Website: www.stdavidswriters. com.

ST. DAVID'S CHRISTIAN WRITERS' CONFERENCE. Geneva College/Beaver Falls, near Pittsburgh, June 17-22, 2001 (44th annual). Offers advanced track and a special teen day. Speakers include: Ethel Herr, Hal Hostetler, and Gayle Roper. Lora Zill, director. Contact: Audrey Stallsmith, registrar, 87 Pines Rd. E., Hadley PA 16130-1019. (724)253-2738. Fax (724)946-3689. E-mail: audstall@nauticom.net. Website: www.stdavidswriters.com. Attendance: 85.

SOUTH CAROLINA

+AMERICAN CHRISTIAN WRITERS CHARLESTON CONFERENCE. March 24, 2001. Contact: Reg A. Forder, Box 110390, Nashville TN 37222. 1-800-21-WRITE. Website: www.ECPA.org/ACW. Attendance: 35- 50.

TENNESSEE

+AMERICAN CHRISTIAN WRITERS CHATTANOOGA CONFERENCE. January 27, 2001. Contact: Reg Forder, Box 110390, Nashville TN 37222. 1-800-21-WRITE. Website: www.ECPA.org/ACW. Attendance: 35-50.

+**AMERICAN CHRISTIAN WRITERS MEMPHIS CONFERENCE.** January 17, 2001. Contact: Reg Forder, Box 110390, Nashville TN 37222. 1-800-21-WRITE. Website: www.ECPA.org/ACW. Attendance: 35-50.

AMERICAN CHRISTIAN WRITERS MENTORING WEEKEND. Nashville, April 20-21, 2001. Contact: Reg Forder, Box 110390, Nashville TN 37222. 1-800-21-WRITE. Website: www.ECPA.org/ACW. Attendance: 35-50.

TEXAS

AMERICAN CHRISTIAN WRITERS AUSTIN CONFERENCE. Chariot Inn, February 16-17, 2001. Contact: Reg Forder, Box 110390, Nashville TN 37222. 1-800-21-WRITE. Website: www.ECPA.org/ACW. Attendance: 35-50.

AMERICAN CHRISTIAN WRITERS DALLAS CONFERENCE. Holiday Inn, February 23-24, 2001. Contact: Reg Forder, Box 110390, Nashville TN 37222. 1-800-21-WRITE. Website: www.ECPA.org/ACW. Attendance: 35-50.

+**AMERICAN CHRISTIAN WRITERS EL PASO CONFERENCE.** October 26-27, 2001. Contact: Reg A. Forder, Box 110390, Nashville TN 37222. 1-800-21-WRITE. Website: www.ECPA.org/ACW. Attendance: 35-50.

AMERICAN CHRISTIAN WRITERS HOUSTON CONFERENCE. Ramada Inn; February 9-10, 2001; February 15-16, 2002. Contact: Reg A. Forder, Box 110390, Nashville TN 37222. 1-800-21-WRITE. Website: www.ECPA.org/ACW. Attendance: 35-50.

*****AUSTIN CHRISTIAN WRITERS' SEMINAR.** February 2001. Contact: Lin Harris, 129 Fox Hollow Cv., Cedar Creek TX 78612-4844. (512)243-2305. Fax (512)243-2317. E-mail: linjer@ix.netcom.com.

*****CHRISTIAN SCHOLARS WRITING TO PUBLISH CONFERENCE.** Dallas; spring 2001. For Christian college and university faculty who want to publish in scholarly journals in their field. Contact: Dr. D. Barry Lumsden, 1900 Westminster, Ste. 105, Denton TX 76205-7875. (940)243-1467. Fax (815)366-3935. E-mail: swi@aol.com. Website under construction. Attendance: 200.

GREENVILLE CHRISTIAN WRITERS' CONFERENCE. Greenville; October 27, 2001. Speakers: Becky Freeman & Reg Grant. Contact: James H. Pence, 1551 Hunt Co. Rd. 4109, Campbell TX 75422-1201. (903)450-4944. E-mail: james@pence.com. Website: www.gcwg.org. Attendance: 50.

*****INSPIRATIONAL WRITERS ALIVE!/AMARILLO SEMINAR.** April 2001. Contact: Helen Luecke, 2921 S. Dallas, Amarillo TX 79103-6713. (806)376-9671.

TEXAS CHRISTIAN WRITERS FORUM. Houston; August 4, 2001. Contact: Martha Rogers, 6038 Greenmont, Houston TX 77092-2332. (713)686-7209. E-mail: mrogers 353@aol.com. Attendance: 45-60.

YWAM HANDS-ON SCHOOL OF WRITING AND WRITERS TRAINING WORKSHOPS. Lindale; various dates, Spring (April) and summer (July) workshops; September 26 - December 12, 2002. Contact: Pamela Warren, PO Box 1380, Lindale TX 75771-1380. (903)882-9663. Fax (903)882-1161. E-mail: info@ywamwoodcrest.com. Website: www.ywamwoodcrest. com. Send SASE for list of workshops. Offers advanced workshops if requested (let them know if you are interested).

VIRGINIA

AMERICAN CHRISTIAN WRITERS RICHMOND CONFERENCE. Holiday Inn; March 30-31, 2001. Contact: Reg A. Forder, Box 110390, Nashville TN 37222. 1-800-21-WRITE. Website: www.ECPA.org/ACW. Attendance: 35-50.
*CAPITAL CHRISTIAN WRITERS ONE-DAY CONFERENCES. Annandale; February, April, and June 2001. Contact: CCW, PO Box 873, Burke VA 20122. Phone/fax (703)803-9447. E-mail: JenniferF@compuserve. com.

WASHINGTON

AMERICAN CHRISTIAN WRITERS SEATTLE CONFERENCE. September 21-22, 2001. Contact: Reg Forder, Box 110390, Nashville TN 37222. 1-800-21-WRITE. Website: www.ECPA.org/ACW. Attendance: 35-50.
*SDA CAMP MEETING WRITING CLASS. Auburn, June 2001. Open to non-Adventists; free. Contact: Marian Forschler, PO Box 58785, Renton WA 98058-1785. (425)235-1435. Fax (425)204-2070. Attendance: 50.
SEATTLE PACIFIC CONFERENCE. May 4-6, 2001. (206)281-2492. E-mail: Lwagner@spu.edu.
WENATCHEE CHRISTIAN WRITERS MINI-SEMINAR. Wenatchee, September 2001 (tentative). Contact: Shirley Pease, 1818 Skyline Dr., #31, Wenatchee WA 98801-2302. (509)662-8392. E-mail: mocrane@aol.com. Attendance: 35-40.
WRITERS HELPING WRITERS. Spokane; March 22-24, 2001. This is not a conference, but a booth offering manuscript evaluation and help to writers during the annual Christian Workers Conference, plus one workshop. Contact: Darrel Bursch, 301 W. Boone, Spokane WA 99201. (509)448-5123. Fax (509)324-8112. Attendance: 20-35.
WRITER'S WEEKEND AT THE BEACH. Ocean Park, February 23-25, 2001. Contact: Birdie Etchison, PO Box 877, Ocean Park WA 98640. (360)665-6576. E-mail: etchison@pacifier.com. Attendance: Limited to 45-50.

WISCONSIN

+AMERICAN CHRISTIAN WRITERS MILWAUKEE CONFERENCE. August 7, 2001. Contact: Reg Forder, Box 110390, Nashville TN 37222. 1-800-21-WRITE. Website: www.ECPA.org/ACW. Attendance: 35-50.
GREEN LAKE CHRISTIAN WRITER'S CONFERENCE. Green Lake, June 30-July 7, 2001. Contact: Program Dept., American Baptist Assembly, W2511 State Hwy 23, Green Lake WI 54941-9300. (800)558-8898 or (920)294-7364. Fax (920)294-3848. E-mail for information: glcc@worldnet.att.net.

Website: www.abc-usa.org. Attendance: 80. Also provides Christian Writer's Weeks when you can stay at the conference center for writing time; January 7-12, March 4-9, November 4-9.

*TIMBER-LEE CHRISTIAN WRITER'S CONFERENCE. Timber-Lee Christian Center/East Troy, February or April 2001. Contact: Mary Kay Meeker, N8705 Scout Rd., East Troy WI 53120. (414)642-7345. Attendance: 30-40.

CANADA/FOREIGN

GOD USES INK WRITERS CONFERENCE/ON. Guelph, Ontario; June 14-16, 2001. Speakers: James C. Schaap & Don Bastian. Contact: Bill Fledderus, c/o Faith Today, M.I.P. Box 3745, Markham ON L3R 3H9 Canada. (905)479-6071x255. Fax (905)479-4742. E-mail: ft@efc-canada.com. Website: www.efc-canada.com. Attendance: 100-120.

*INSCRIBE CHRISTIAN WRITERS' FELLOWSHIP FALL CONFERENCE, 21st Anniversary. Edmonton AB Canada, September 2001. Contact: Elsie Montgomery, pres., 333 Hunter's Run. Edmonton AB T6R 2N9 Canada. (780)988-5622. Fax (780)430-0139. E-mail: emontgom@compusmart.ab. ca. Website under construction.

*WORDPOWER. Clearbrook, schedule for 2001 unknown. Contact: Susan Brandt, MB Herald, 3-169 Riverton Ave., Winnipeg MB R2L 2E5 Canada. (204)669-6575. Fax (204)654-1865. E-mail: mbherald@cdnmbconf.ca. Offers workshops for advanced and young writers. Attendance: 100-150.

*ASSOCIATION OF CHRISTIAN WRITERS SEMINARS. London, England; March 2001. "Hold the Front Page." And October 2001. "Tell Me a Story." Contact: Warren Crawford, 73 Lodge Hill Rd., Farnham, Surrey, UK GU10 3RB. Phone/fax: +44 (0)1252 715746. Fax +44 (0)1252 715746. E-mail: christian-writers@dial.pipex.com. Attendance 80+.

*ASSOCIATION OF CHRISTIAN WRITERS WEEKEND. Hothorpe Hall, Leicestershire, England. Next weekend is July 2001. Contact: Warren Crawford, 73 Lodge Hill Rd., Farnham, Surrey, UK GU10 3RB. Phone/fax: +44 (0)1252 715746. E-mail: christian-writers@dial.pipex.com. Website: dspace.pipex.com/christian-writers. Attendance 90.

CARIBBEAN CHRISTIAN WRITER'S CONFERENCES FOR 2001. St. Maarten, Netherlands Antilles; May 2001; Curacoa, Netherlands Antilles; June 2001; Cost for each conference is $60 US for 1½ days. Contact: Patricia Varlack, PO Box 645, St. Maarten, Netherlands Antilles. Phone (599)5-95730. Fax (599)5-25393. E-mail: pvarlack@sint maarten.net.

*CHRISTIAN COMICS TRAINING COURSES. For information on these conferences held around the world, visit the ROX35 Media, Inc. Website at: www.ROX35Media.org. E-mail: ROX35Media@aol.com.

*LITT-WORLD 2001. Hoddesdon, Hertfordshire, England (near London); October 2001. Contact: John D. Maust, director, Sharyl J. Sieh, registrar, 130 N. Bloomingdale Rd., Ste. 101, Bloomingdale IL 60108-1035. (630)893-1977. Fax (630)893-1141. E-mail: AI_LittWorld@compuserve. com. Website: www.littworld.org. Attendance 140.

*WRITERS' SUMMER SCHOOL. Swanwick, Derbyshire, England; August 2001. Contact: Brenda Courtie, The New Vicarage, Parsons St., Woodford

Halse, Daventry, Northants, NN11 3RE, England, United Kingdom. Phone/fax: +44-7050-630949. E-mail: bcourtie@aol.com. A secular conference attended by many Christians. Attendance: 300-350.

WRITERS' TOUR OF ENGLAND AND IRELAND 2002. England, Ireland and you decide where else; April 2002. For details, send an SASE to: Rowena Hughes, PO Box 514, Troutdale OR 97060-0514. (503)491-8067. E-mail: 101461,2252@compuserve.com. This is a one-of-a-kind, do-it-yourself tour. Input at this point will help each tourist plan the tour by letting the leader know which British and Irish writers most interest them. If very interested, send three .33 stamps (no envelope) for a full planning packet.

CONFERENCES THAT CHANGE LOCATIONS

AMERICAN CHRISTIAN WRITERS CONFERENCES. Various dates and locations (see individual states where held). Also sponsors an annual Caribbean cruise, November 25-December 2, 2001. Contact: Reg A. Forder, Box 110390, Nashville TN 37222. 1-800-21-WRITE. Website: www.ECPA. org/ACW.

*ASSOCIATED CHURCH PRESS 2001 ANNUAL CONVENTION. Chicago; March/April 2001. Contact: Joe Roos, The Associated Church Press, PO Box 7, Riverdale MD 20738-0007.

*CATHOLIC PRESS ASSOCIATION ANNUAL CONVENTION. Baltimore, May 2001. Contact: Owen McGovern, exec dir, 3555 Veterans Memorial Hwy, Ste. O, Ronkonkoma NY 11779-7636. (631)471-4730. Fax (631)471-4804. E-mail: CathJourn@aol.com. For media professionals. Attendance: 400.

CBA CONVENTION. (Held in a different location each year.) July 7-12, 2001, Atlanta GA. July 13-19, 2002, Anaheim CA. Contact: CBA, Box 62000, Colorado Springs CO 80962-2000. (800)252-1950 or (719)265-9895. Entrance badges available through book publishers.

CHRISTIAN LEADERS AND SPEAKERS SEMINARS (The CLASSeminar). Various dates & locations across the country for 2001: February 26-28, Houston TX; May 7-9, 2001, Cedar Lake IN; The CLASS Reunion, July 7-10, 2001, Atlanta GA (limited to first 80 people). Additional seminars to be added in Southern California, Southeast US, and Eastern US. For anyone who wants to improve their communication skills for either the spoken or written word, for professional or personal reasons. Speakers: Florence Littauer and Marita Littauer. Contact: Marita Littauer, PO Box 66810, Albuquerque NM 87193. (800)433-6633. (505)899-4283. Fax (505)899-9283. E-mail: info@classervices.com. Website: www.classervices. com. Attendance: 80-120.

EVANGELICAL PRESS ASSOCIATION CONVENTION. May 6-9, 2001; San Diego CA. (Held in a different location each year.) Contact: Ron Wilson, dir, 314 Dover Rd., Charlottesville VA 22901. (804)973-5941. Fax (804)973-2710. E-mail: 74473.272@compuserve.com. Website: www. epassoc.org. Attendance: 300-400. Annual convention; freelance communicators welcome.

ORTHODOX AUTHOR'S ASSN. ANNUAL CONFERENCE. Indianapolis (tentative), October 2001. Contact: Agafia Prince, 1580 Tyler Creek, Ashland OR 97402. Phone/fax (541)488-7718. E-mail: eugeneoaa@prodigy.net. Website: www.strannik.com/oaa.

+TURNING POINT SEMINARS. Various dates and locations (send SASE for seminar schedule). Contact: Rajendra Pillai, Turning Point, PO Box 255, Clarksburg MD 20871-0255. (301)972-6351.

+WINSUN COMMUNICATIONS WRITING SEMINARS/MARK LITTLETON. Various dates and locations. Available for your conference at your location. Contact: Mark Littleton, WINSUN Communications, 2144 Sycamore Ave., Hanover Park IL 60103. Phone/fax: 630-830-4956. E-mail: MarkLitt@ aol.com.

"WRITE HIS ANSWER" SEMINARS. Various locations around U.S.; dates throughout the year; a choice of focus on periodicals or books (includes self-publishing). Contact: Marlene Bagnull, Litt.D., 316 Blanchard Rd., Drexel Hill PA 19026-3507. Phone/fax (610)626-6833. E-mail: mbagnull@ aol.com. Website: www.writehisanswer.com. Attendance: 30-100. One and two-day seminars by the author of *Write His Answer—A Bible Study for Christian Writers.*

+WRITE THE VISION RETREATS. Various location and dates. For women; by application only. During 2001 will offer Level One and Level Two Retreats, plus a symposium for those who have attended previous retreats or have equivalent writing experience. During 2002 will add Level Three Retreats to the above. Contact: Judith Couchman, Judith & Company, Box 1656, Colorado Springs CO 80901. (719)365-7566. Fax (719)442-0556. E-mail: Visionretreats@aol.com.

THE WRITING ACADEMY SEMINAR. Sponsors year-round correspondence writing program and annual seminar in various locations. August 2-6, 2001. Contact: Nancy James, 301 Brookside Ln., Seven Fields PA 16046. (724)776-7225. Fax (724)776-7228. E-mail: gracie@pathway.net. Website: www.wams.org. Attendance: 30-40.

AREA CHRISTIAN WRITERS' CLUBS, FELLOWSHIP GROUPS, AND CRITIQUE GROUPS

(*) An asterisk before a listing means the information was not verified or updated by the group leader.
(+) A plus sign before a listing indicates a new listing.

ALABAMA

*CHRISTIAN FREELANCERS. Tuscaloosa. Contact: Joanne Sloan, 3230 Mystic Lake Way, Northport AL 35476. (205)333-8603. Fax (205)339-4528. Membership (25) open.

ALASKA

+PUSHKIN LITERARY SOCIETY-CHAPTER OF THE ORTHODOX AUTHORS' ASSN. Kodiak. Contact: Mamas Poussen, St. Innocent's Academy, PO Box 1517, Kodiak AK 99615. (907)486-4376. E-mail: innocent @ptialaska.net.

ARIZONA

FOUNTAIN HILLS CHRISTIAN WRITERS GROUP. Contact: Rosemary Malroy, 10413 N. Demaret Dr., Fountain Hills AZ 85268. (480)837-8494. E-mail: rmalroy@aol.com. Membership (25) open.
*PHOENIX CHRISTIAN WRITERS' FELLOWSHIP. Contact: Victor J. Kelly Sr., 2135 W. Cactus Wren Dr., Phoenix AZ 85021. (602)864-1390. Membership (20) open.
SOUTH-EASTERN CHRISTIAN WRITERS FELLOWSHIP. Benson. Contact: Floyd Pierce, HC2 Box 3868, Willcox AZ 85643. (520)384-3064. E-mail: piniq@vtc.net. Membership (18) open.
*TEMPE CHRISTIAN WRITERS CLUB. Contact: Kitty Bucholtz, PO Box 68114, Phoenix AZ 85082-8114. (602)267-8529. Fax (602)273-1314. E-mail: jkbuch@primenet.com.
*WRITER'S BLOC. Wilcox. Christian and secular writers. Contact: Bea Carlton, HCR 1 Box 153C, Wilcox AZ 85643. (520)384-9232. Membership (9-12) open.

ARKANSAS

+ACW—FAMILY LIFE CHAPTER. Little Rock area. Contact: Mary Larmoyeux, 3900 N. Rodney Parham Rd., Little Rock AR 72212. (501)228-1723. E-mail: mlarmoyeux@familylife.com. Membership open.

NORTHWEST ARKANSAS CHRISTIAN WRITERS CLUB. Fayetteville. Contact: Lois Spoon, 3498 Remington St., Springdale AR 72764-7093. (501) 751-2680. E-mail: LoisSpoon@aol.com. Membership (25) open.

NORTHWEST ARKANSAS CREATIVE WRITERS GUILD. Rogers. Contact: Karin S. Croft, 1911 South P St., Rogers AR 72758-9139. (501)936-7945. Membership (6+) open.

*OZARK MOUNTAIN CHRISTIAN WRITERS GUILD. Kingston area. Contact: Judith Gillis, PO Box 217, Kingston AR 72742. (501)665-2595. Fax (501)665-2578. Membership (8-10) open.

ROGERS AREA CHRISTIAN WRITERS GUILD. Rogers. Contact: Karin Croft, 1911 South P St., Rogers AR 72758-9139. (501)936-7945. Membership (6+) open.

SILOAM SPRINGS WRITERS. Contact: Margaret Weathers, 716 W. University, Siloam Springs AR 72761-2658. (501)524-6598. Membership (25) open. Sponsoring a contest open to non-members and an annual August seminar.

+WHITE RIVER WRITERS FELLOWSHIP. Contact: Brian Stiles, 50 Riverwood Ave., West Fork AR 72774. (501)839-2107. E-mail: edribbler@ hotmail.com. Membership open.

CALIFORNIA

+AMERICAN CHRISTIAN WRITERS INLAND EMPIRE. Corona area. Contact: Guen Ballew, 11353 Siesta Ln., Corona CA 92883-7113. (909)277-0929. E-mail: rejoycNHim@juno.com. Membership (4) open.

+ANNIE BIDWELL CHAPTER OF THE ORTHODOX AUTHORS' ASSN. Chico area. Contact: Nina Barfield, 1934 Honey Run Rd., Chico CA 95928. (530)894-6527. E-mail: valaam@aol.com.

CASTRO VALLEY CHRISTIAN WRITERS GROUP. Contact: Pastor Jon Drury, 19300 Redwood Rd., Castro Valley CA 94546-3465. (510)886-6300. Fax (510)581-5022. E-mail: jond@redwoodchapel.org. Membership (10) open. Sponsoring a Christian Writers Seminar, February 23-24, 2001.

*CEHUC SPANISH CHRISTIAN WRITERS GROUP. El Cajon. Contact: Magdalena Latorre, 9802 Quail Canyon Rd., El Cajon CA 92021-6000. (619)390-3747. Fax (619)561-6172. Membership (34) open. Sponsors a contest open to non-members. Planning a Spanish conference for February 2001 in Tijuana, Mexico.

+CHINO VALLEY WRITERS CRITIQUE GROUP. Chino. Contact: Nancy I. Sanders, 15212 Mariposa Ave., Chino CA 91709. (909)393-8998. E-mail: jndbsand@juno.com. Membership (8-12) open.

*CHRISTIAN WRITERS FELLOWSHIP OF ORANGE COUNTY. Various groups meeting throughout the county. Contact: Bonnie Compton Hanson and Carol Fitzpatrick, PO Box 538, Lake Forest CA 92630. (949)768-3891. Membership (200+) open. Monthly newsletter. Sponsors critique groups throughout Southern California. Sponsors two annual Writers' Days: May 20 and October 2001; and contests open to non-members.

DIABLO VALLEY CHRISTIAN WRITERS GROUP. Danville. Contact: Marcy

Weydemuller, 3623 Corte Segundo, Concord CA 94519. (925)676-6555. E-mail: mcyweyde@hotcoco.infi.net. Membership (8-10) open.

*EVEN FRIDAYS CRITIQUE GROUP. Tustin. Contact: David R. Beaucage, 1581 Garlend Ave., Tustin CA 92780-3932. 714-832-3327. E-mail: Rec. Room@juno.com. Membership (10) open.

HAYWARD AREA WRITERS CRITIQUE GROUP. Castro Valley. Contact: Launa Herrmann, 21555 Eden Canyon Rd., Castro Valley CA 94552-9721. (510)889-7564. Membership (10) open (to experienced writers only).

*HIGH DESERT CHRISTIAN WRITERS GUILD. Lancaster. Contact: Ellen Bergh, 3600 Brabham Ave., Rosamond CA 93560-6891. (661)256-1266. E-mail: mastermedia@hughes.net. Membership (25) open.

LODI WRITERS ASSOCIATION. (General membership, not just Christian.) Contact: Dee Porter, PO Box 1863, Lodi CA 95241. Phone/fax (209)334-0603. E-mail: crcomm@lodinet.com. Membership (70) open. Sponsors one-day workshop, usually in July.

+MARIPOSA CHRISTIAN WRITERS. Contact: Steve Radanovich, 5660 Lillian Ln., Mariposa CA 95338. Phone/fax (209)742-5463. E-mail: yvonne_radanovich@nps.go. Membership (8) open.

NATIONAL WRITER'S ASSN./SOUTHERN CALIFORNIA CHAPTER. Fountain Valley. Liaison: Douglas Shaner, 2470 Antelope Dr., Corona CA 92882-5618. (909)383-6478. Website: www.nationalwriters.com, or www. writepage.com/groups.htm. Membership (142) open. Secular group/ many Christians.

*NORTH BAY CHRISTIAN WRITERS. Fairfield. Contact: Dr. Bill Nesbitt, 2100 Pennsylvania Ave., Fairfield CA 94533. (707)425-3622. (707)425-5471. E-mail: billn@jps.net. Membership (12-15) open.

SACRAMENTO CHRISTIAN WRITERS. Contact: Toni Lawson, 7025 Springmont Dr., Elk Grove CA 95758. (916)691-0526. E-mail: gtlawson@ pacbell.net. Membership (32) open.

*SAN DIEGO COUNTY CHRISTIAN WRITERS' GUILD. Contact: Robert Gillespie, 17041 Palacio Pl., San Diego CA 92027. Phone/fax (858)673-3921. E-mail: riters@adnc.com. Membership (250) open. Sponsors fall seminar (September 2001) and March awards banquet. Contest for members.

+SOUTH VALLEY CHRISTIAN WRITERS. Hanford. Contact: Mary Kirk, 247 E. Cortner St., Hanford CA 93230-1845. (559)582-8442. E-mail: mkirk@ cnetech.com. Membership (6) open.

VALLEY BIBLE CHRISTIAN WRITERS GROUP. Hercules. Contact: Sandy Ormeo, 1477 Bayberry Ave., Hercules CA 94547. (510)779-3171. Fax (510)799-3174. E-mail: Sandywrites@yahoo.com. Membership (10-15) open. Seminar October 19-20, 2001.

COLORADO

*CHRISTIAN WRITERS OF SOUTHERN COLORADO. Colorado Springs. Contact: Sue Sutherland or Sharon McAllister, 4605 Splendid Cir. S., Colorado Springs CO 80917. (719)591-0370. Membership (8) open.

COLORADO WRITERS FELLOWSHIP. Denver. Contact: Su Wright, CWF Executive Director, PO Box 22416, Denver CO 80222-0416. (303)758-6556. Fax (303)758-9272. E-mail: Suwriter@aol.com. Has 8 monthly meetings; 3 seminars; bi-monthly newsletter, Networking; bi-weekly e-zine for published members, Dedicated Author; and quarterly magazine, Christian Writer. Membership (30) open.

WESTERN SLOPE CHRISTIAN WRITERS ASSOCIATION. Grand Junction. Contact: WSCWA, 2948 Shelley Dr., Grand Junction CO 81503. (970)245-5084 (Debbie Brockett). Fax (970)245-1997. E-mail: WSCWA@netscape. net. Membership (50) open.

DELAWARE

DELMARVA CHRISTIAN WRITERS' FELLOWSHIP. Georgetown. Contact: Candy Abbott, PO Box 777, Georgetown DE 19947-0777. (302)856-6649. Fax (302)856-7742. E-mail: dabbott@dmv.com. Membership (24) open.

FLORIDA

*ADVENTURES IN CHRISTIAN WRITING. Orlando. Contact: Mary F. Shaw, 350 E . Jackson St., #811, Orlando FL 32801. (407)841-4866. Membership (20) open.

+CENTRAL FLORIDA CHRISTIAN WRITERS GROUP. Lake Mary. Contact: Carmen Lael, PO Box 952163, Lake Mary FL 32795-2163. (407)328-0981. E-mail: carmen@writerspeaker.com. Membership (10-12) open. Willing to hold extra meeting if needed.

CLEWISTON CHRISTIAN WRITERS GROUP. Contact: Cheryl Abney, PO Box 1178, Clewiston FL 33440. (941)902-1188. E-mail: yenba@gate.net. Membership (10) open. An American Christian Writers chapter.

DAYTONA BEACH CHRISTIAN WRITERS. Contact: Ann Hill, 112—5th St., Holly Hill FL 32114. (904)255.3420. E-mail: hollyhilla@aol.com. Membership (5) open. ACW chapter.

MIAMI AMERICAN CHRISTIAN WRITERS CHAPTER. Contact: Karen Whiting, 10936 SW 156th Pl., Miami FL 33196. (305)388-8656. Fax (305)408-3681. E-mail: whiting@gate.net. Membership (10) open.

SUNCOAST CHRISTIAN WRITERS GROUP. Largo. Contact: Elaine Creasman, 13014—106th Ave. N., Largo FL 34644-5602. (727)595-8963. Fax (727)398-5730. E-mail: emcreasman@aol.com. Membership (20+) open.

TITUSVILLE CHRISTIAN WRITERS' FELLOWSHIP. Contact: TCW, 2600 S. Park Ave.,Titusville FL 32780. Membership (8) not currently open.

+"WRITE-ON" SARASOTA COUNTY. Sarasota/Venice. Contact: Sharon McCampbell, 1530 Fundy Rd., Venice FL 34293-5513. (941)493-0335. E-mail: smm-10@yahoo.com. Membership (5) open.

WRITING STRATEGIES CRITIQUESHOP. Daytona Beach. Meets monthly (10X). Sponsors workshops the 2nd Tuesday of each month (except July & August) for working authors who have completed one course of Writing Strategies (see conference listing). Speakers: Rosemary Upton & Kistler London. Send SASE for brochure. Contact: Rosemary J. Upton,

2712 S. Peninsula Dr., Daytona Beach FL 32118. Phone/fax (904)322-1111. E-mail: romy14@juno.com. Membership (20) open.

GEORGIA

GEORGIA WRITERS, INC./CHRISTIAN WRITERS POD. Contact: Lloyd Blackwell, 2633 Foxglove Dr., Marietta GA 30064. (770)421-1203. Fax (770)943-0325. E-mail: lloydblackwell@worldnet.att.net. Website: www.georgiawriters.org. Membership open.

LAMBLIGHTERS CRITIQUE GROUP. Lilburn. Contact: Cisi Morrow-Smith, 1056 Sawgrass Ct., Lilburn GA 30047-1864. (770)978-9129. E-mail: cmorrows@bellsouth.net. Membership (6-8) open.

NORTHEAST GEORGIA WRITERS. Gainesville. Contact: Elouise Whitten, 660 Crestview Terrace, Gainesville GA 30501-3110. (770)532-3007. E-mail: E6625Whitt@aol.com. Membership (30) open. Sponsors a conference every two years, on even-numbered years (October 2002).

IDAHO

CHRISTIAN WRITERS OF IDAHO. Boise. Contact: Diana James, 393 W. Willowbrook Dr., Meridian ID 83642-1689. (208)288-0983. Fax (208)288-2574. E-mail: DianaJames@aol.com. Website: www.idahochristianwriters.com. Sponsors a contest open to nonmembers. Planning a conference for fall 2002. Membership (35) open. An American Christian Writers chapter.

*INTERNATIONAL NETWORK OF COMMUNICATORS & THE ARTS. Coeur d'Alene. Contact: Sheri Stone, Box 1754, Post Falls ID 83854-1754. Phone/fax (208)667-9730. Membership (25) open. Sponsors a contest.

ILLINOIS

+CHICAGO CHRISTIAN WRITERS' FELLOWSHIP. Chicago, north side. Contact: Michaelle McClowry, 1338 W Thorndale Ave., #1, Chicago IL 60660. Phone: (773)506-9320. E-mail: Aurian39@aol.com. Website: www.egroups.com/group/ChicagoChristianWritersFellowship. Membership (10+) open.

INTERNATIONAL BLACK WRITERS. Chicago. Contact: Mable Terrell, PO Box 1030, Chicago IL 60690-1030. (312)458-9254. Membership (2,000) open. Sponsors a contest open to members. Conference in Chicago, no date set.

*JUVENILE FORUM. Moline. Contact: David R. Collins, 3403 45th St., Moline IL 61265-6608. (309)762-8985. E-mail: kimseuss@aol.com. Membership (12) open to those writing for children or youth.

INDIANA

BLOOMINGTON AREA CHRISTIAN WRITERS. Bloomington/Ellettsville. Contact: Kathi Adams, 9576 W. St. Rd. 48, Bloomington IN 47404-9737. (812)876-8265. E-mail: katadams55@aol.com. Membership (8) open.

EVANSVILLE-AREA CHRISTIAN WRITERS' FELLOWSHIP. Need new contact for this group. Membership (21) open.

FORT WAYNE CHRISTIAN WRITERS CLUB. Fort Wayne. Contact: Linda R. Wade, 739 W. Fourth St., Fort Wayne IN 46808-2613. (219)422-2772. E-mail: linda_wade@juno.com. Membership (30) open. Having a Writer's Worshop in Shipshewana, March 25-30, 2001, and co-sponsoring a writers' conference with Reg Forder/American Christian Writers in Fort Wayne, August 11, 2001.

OPEN DOOR CHRISTIAN WRITERS. Westport. Contact: Janet Teitsort, PO Box 129, Westport IN 47283-0129. Phone/fax (812)591-2210. E-mail: teitsort@hsonline.net. Membership (15) open.

IOWA

CEDAR RAPIDS CHRISTIAN WRITER'S CRITIQUE GROUP. Contact: Susan Fletcher, 513 Knollwood Dr. S.E., Cedar Rapids IA 52403. (319)365-9844. E-mail: skmcfate@msn.com. Membership (12) open. A day and a night group.

*RIVER CITY WRITERS. Council Bluffs. Contact: Dee Barrett, 16 Susan Lane, Council Bluffs IA 51503. (712)322-7692. Fax (712)329-9615. E-mail: barrett@mitec.net. Membership (30) open.

KANSAS

CREATIVE WRITERS FELLOWSHIP. Newton, North Newton & Hesston. Contact: Esther Groves, sec., 500 W. Bluestem, Apt. H4, North Newton KS 67117-8014. (316)283-7224. E-mail: estherbg@southwind.net. Membership (20) open.

KANSAS CITY CHRISTIAN WRITERS' NETWORK. Kansas City Metro area. Contact: Teresa Vining, 1438 N Lucy Montgomery Way, Olathe KS 66061-6706. Phone/fax: (913)764-4610. E-mail: KCCWN@aol.com. Membership (150) open. Sponsors contest, monthly meetings, and one-day seminars four times a year: January, April, July and October. Hold events on both the Kansas and Missouri sides of Kansas City.

PITTSBURG CHRISTIAN WRITERS FELLOWSHIP. Gerard. Contact: Carol Russell, Walkertown 894—165th St., Fort Scott KS 66701. (316)547-2472. E-mail: rlrussell@ckt.net. Membership (15) open. Sponsors a contest, and a seminar on April 14, 2001.

KENTUCKY

JACKSON CHRISTIAN WRITERS' CLUB. Vancleve area homes or library. Contact: Donna J. Woodring, Box 10, Vancleve KY 41385-0010. (606)666-5000. E-mail: donnaw@kmbc.edu. Membership (6) open.

LOUISVILLE CHRISTIAN WRITERS. Contact: Ken Walker, 10213 Blue Lick Rd., Louisville KY 40229-2607. (502)584-1367. E-mail: LanaHJackson@gateway.net. Membership (15) open. An American Christian Writers chapter.

LOUISIANA

+INSPIRATIONAL WRITERS ALIVE! Logan's Port Chapter. Contact: Martha Rogers, 6038 Greenmont, Houston TX 77092-2332. (713)686-7209. E-mail: mrogers353@aol.com. Membership (130) open. Sponsors summer seminar, August 4, 2001, monthly newsletter, and annual contest (November 1-April 1).

SCRIBES OF NEW ORLEANS. Harahan. Contact: Jack Cunningham, PO Box 55601, Metairie LA 70005-5601. (504)837-4397. E-mail: JMCunn2@cs.com. Membership (5) open.

MAINE

MAINE FELLOWSHIP OF CHRISTIAN WRITERS. China Lake Conference Center. Contact: Vicki Schad, RR 1, Box 540, N. Vassalboro ME 04962-9709. (207)923-3956. E-mail: jvschad@larck.net. Membership (25) open. Sponsors contest open to non-members. Conference, August 16-18, 2001.

MARYLAND

ANNAPOLIS FELLOWSHIP OF CHRISTIAN WRITERS. Annapolis. Contact: Jeri Sweany, 3107 Ervin Ct., Annapolis MD 21403-4620. (410)267-0924. Membership (10-12) open.

THIRD SATURDAY CHRISTIAN WRITERS GROUP. Contact: Claire DeBakey, 10732 Faulkner Ridge Circle., Columbia MD 21044. (410)715-4863. E-mail: plsntbay@gateway.net. Membership (6) open.

MASSACHUSETTS

WESTERN MASSACHUSETTS CHRISTIAN WRITERS FELLOWSHIP. Springfield. Contact: Barbara A. Robidoux, 127 Gelinas Dr., Chicopee MA 01020-4813. (413)592-4386. Fax (413)594-8375. E-mail: ebwordpro@aol.com. Membership (50+) open.

MICHIGAN

*MICHIGAN CHRISTIAN WRITERS. Grandville. Contact: Jeanne Russell, 2839 Eastern SE, Grand Rapids MI 49508. (616)241-1180. Fax (616)245-4870. E-mail: Jruss@triton.net. Membership (10) open.

+SOUTHEASTERN MICHIGAN ACW GROUP. Ann Arbor area. Contact: Debbie Mitchell, 2920 Dexter Rd., Ann Arbor MI 48103. E-mail: Mitch266@pilot.msu. Membership open.

WEST MICHIGAN AMERICAN CHRISTIAN WRITERS CHAPTER. Contact: Flavia Crowner, 211 S Maple St., Fennville MI 49408. (616)561-5296. E-mail: flacro@datawise.net. Membership open.

MINNESOTA

*MINNESOTA CHRISTIAN WRITERS GUILD. Minneapolis. Contact: Jane Kise, 5504 Grove St., Edina MN 55436. (612)926-4343. E-mail: jagkise@ aol.com. Membership (125) open. Sponsors a contest (open to non-members) and an annual spring seminar in March (March 17-18, 2001).

MISSISSIPPI

+NORTHEAST MISSISSIPPI ACW GROUP. Belden area. Contact: Karen Battles, 2646 Smokehouse Cir., Belden MS 38826. (662)844-0788.

MISSOURI

+ACW CHRISTIAN WRITERS WORKSHOP. Arnold area. Contact: Ruth Houser, 3148 Arnold Tenbrook Rd., Arnold MO 63010-4732. (636)464-1187.
*CHRISTIAN WRITERS WORKSHOP. St. Louis. Contact: Ruth McDaniel, 15233 Country Ridge Dr., St. Louis MO 63017-7432. (636)532-7584. Membership (20-25) open.
GREATER ST. LOUIS CHRISTIAN WRITERS. This group is no longer meeting, but contact person for writers in the area is Lila Shelburne, 707 Gran Lin Dr., St. Charles MO 63303-6025. (636)441-2131. Fax (636)922-2459. E-mail: lila@anet-stl.com. Consults and tutors aspiring writers and teaches one class annually.
KANSAS CITY CHRISTIAN WRITERS' NETWORK. Kansas City Metro area. Contact: Teresa Vining, 1438 N Lucy Montgomery Way, Olathe KS 66061-6706. Phone/fax: (913)764-4610. E-mail: KCCWN@aol.com. Membership (150) open. Sponsors contest for those who attend seminars, monthly meetings, and one-day seminars four times a year: January, April, July and October. Holds events on both the Kansas and Missouri sides of Kansas City.
*NORTHLAND CHRISTIAN WRITERS. Kansas City. Contact: Margaret Owen, 207 NW 67th St., Gladstone MO 64118. (816)436-5240. E-mail: MadgeO@aol.com. Membership (10) open.
*SPRINGFIELD CHRISTIAN WRITERS CLUB. Contact: Owen Wilkie, 4909 Old Wire Rd., Brookline MO 65619-9655. (417)882-5185. E-mail: owenwilkie@aol.com. Membership (7) open.
WEST COUNTY A/G WRITER'S GROUP. Chesterfield. Contact: Mary Lou Kretschmar, 14 Broadview Farm, St. Louis MO 63141. (314)878-2125. E-mail: tkretschma@aol.com. Membership (10) open. An American Christian Writers chapter.

MONTANA

*MONTANA CHRISTIAN WRITERS. Helena. Contact: Lori Soloman, 659 N. Warren, Helena MT 59601. (406)443-8528. E-mail: Lsolomon_mt@hotmail. com.

WRITERS IN THE SKY. Helena. Contact: Lenore Puhek, 1215 Hudson, Helena MT 59601-1848. (406)443-2552. Membership (10) currently closed.

NEBRASKA

MY THOUGHTS EXACTLY WRITERS GROUP. Fremont. Contact: Cheryl A. Paden, PO Box 1073, Fremont NE 68025. (402)727-6508. Membership (6) open. Periodically sponsors a writers' retreat; next one October 2001.

NEW HAMPSHIRE

+MONADNOCK AREA CHRISTIAN WRITER'S GROUP. Dublin. Contact: Elizabeth M. Hoekstra, PO Box 103, Dublin NH 03444. (623)563-9202. Fax (623)563-7739. E-mail: hoekstra@directpath.org. Membership (12) open. Sponsors two Writer's Days in May and October.

LIVING WORD WRITERS FELLOWSHIP. Lebanon. Contact: James A. Blaine, 80½ Mascoma St., Lebanon NH 03766-2646. (603)448-4609. Membership (15) open.

WORDSMITHS' CHRISTIAN WRITERS' FELLOWSHIP. Nashua. Contact: Cynthia Vlatas, 5 Jeremy Ln., Hudson NH 03051. (603)882-2851. Fax (603)883-7518. E-mail: sasacindy@aol.com. Membership (35) open.

NEW JERSEY

CENTRAL JERSEY CHRISTIAN WRITERS' FELLOWSHIP. Zarephath. Contact: Catherine J. Barrier, 13 Oliver St., Somerset NJ 08873-2142. (732)545-5168. Fax (732)545-0640. Membership (25) open. Morning and evening meetings.

+NORTH JERSEY CHRISTIAN WRITER'S GROUP. Ringwood. Contact: Louise Bergmann DuMont, 24 Welch Rd., Ringwood NJ 07456. (973)962-9267. E-mail: louise_dumont@berlex.com. Membership (12) open.

NEW JERSEY SOCIETY OF CHRISTIAN WRITERS. Millville. Contact: Dr. Mary Ann Diorio, P.O. Box 405, Millville, NJ 08332-0405. (856)327-1231. Fax (856)327-0291. E-mail: madiorio@aol.com. Website: daystaministries. com/njscw. Membership (26) open. Sponsors a Fall Seminar; November 3, 2001.

NEW MEXICO

*SOUTHWEST CHRISTIAN WRITERS ASSOCIATION, Farmington. Contact: Patti Cordell, #74, RD 3535, Flora Vista NM 87415. (505)334-2258. Membership (14) open. Sponsors annual one-day seminar the third Saturday in September in Hesperus CO.

SOUTHWEST WRITERS. Albuquerque. Contact: Suzanne Spletzer, 8200 Mountain Rd NE, Ste 106, Albuquerque NM 87110-7835. (505)265-9485. Fax (505)265-9483. E-mail: SWriters@aol.com.Website: www.southwest writers.org. Membership (950) open. Sponsors a contest (open to non-members) and a conference in Albuquerque, September 20-23, 2001.

NEW YORK

BROOKLYN WRITER'S CLUB. Contact: Ann Dellarocco, PO Box 184, Bath Beach Station, Brooklyn NY 11214-0184. (718)680-4084. Membership (25) open.

*INTERNATIONAL BLACK WRITERS. New York & Chicago. Contact: Mable Terrell, PO Box 1030, Chicago IL 60690-1030. (312)409-2292. Membership (2,000) open. Sponsors a contest open to nonmembers. Conference in Chicago, June 2001.

NEW YORK CHRISTIAN WRITERS GROUP. New York City. Contact: Marilyn Driscoll, 350 First Ave., New York NY 10010, (212)529-6087; or Zoe Blake (718)636-5547. Membership (12) open.

SOUTHERN TIER CHRISTIAN WRITERS' FELLOWSHIP. Binghamton. Contact: Kenneth Cetton, 20 Pine St., Port Crane NY 13833-1512. (607)648-7249. E-mail: KC1933@juno.com. Membership (6) open.

NORTH CAROLINA

*COVENANT WRITERS. Lincolnton. Contact: Janice Stroup, 403 S. Cedar St., Lincolnton NC 28092-3342. (704)735-8851. Membership (10) open.

TRIAD NORTH CAROLINA AMERICAN CHRISTIAN WRITERS CHAPTER. Contact: Marcia Cox, 117 Brandon Ln., Trinity NC 27370-9358. (336)431-8532. E-mail: macoxx@juno.com. Membership open.

+TRIANGLE CHAPTER OF AMERICAN CHRISTIAN WRITERS. Contact: Katherine W. Parrish, 909 Tanglewood Dr., Cary NC 27511-4641. (919) 467-1924. E-mail: jstaley@prodigy.net. Membership (30) open.

OHIO

ASHLAND AREA CHRISTIAN WRITERS GROUP. Contact: April Boyer, 1552 County Rd. 995, Ashland OH 44805. (419)281-1766. E-mail: apple_b45 @yahoo.com. Membership (12) open.

*CHRISTIAN WRITERS GUILD. Youngstown area. Contact: Susan K. Virgalitte, 240 Sawmill Run Dr., Canfield OH 44406. Phone/fax (330)533-5833. E-mail: TOVIR@aol.com. Membership (30) open.

COLUMBUS CHRISTIAN WRITERS ASSN. Contact: Becky Miller, 1324 B Lakeshore Dr., Columbus OH 43204. (614)486-6890. E-mail: personal56 @hotmail.com. Membership (20) open. Co-sponsoring a writers workshop with the American Christian Writers, May 24-26, 2001.

DAYTON CHRISTIAN SCRIBES. Kettering. Contact: Lois Pecce (secretary), Box 41613, Dayton OH 45441-0613. (937)433-6470. E-mail: epecce@ compuserve.com. Membership (30) open.

GREATER CINCINNATI CHRISTIAN WRITERS' FELLOWSHIP. Contact: Wayne Holmes, 5499 Yellowstone Dr., Fairfield OH 45014. Phone/fax (513) 858-6609. E-mail: wwriter@fuse.net. Membership (25) open. Dues $15.

*MEDINA CHRISTIAN WRITERS GROUP. Contact: Lisa Wiener, 973 Pheasant Run Dr., Medina OH 44256-3043. (330)722-8820. Fax (413)473-6423. E-mail: lisaw@ohio.net. Membership (5-7) open.

NORTHWEST OHIO CHRISTIAN WRITERS. Bowling Green. Contact: Judy Gyde, 3072 Muirfield Ave., Toledo OH 43614-3766. (419)382-7582. E-mail: begyde@glasscity.net. Membership (35) open. Sponsors a Saturday seminar, late September 2001.

*****SET FORTH WRITERS GUILD.** North Central OH/Mansfield area. Contact: Donna Caudill, 836 Delph Ave., Mansfield OH 44906. (419)747-1755. Membership (35) open. Planning seminar for July 2001.

WEST CENTRAL OHIO CHRISTIAN WRITERS. West Liberty. Contact: Pat Zell, 545 S. Madriver St., Bellefontaine OH 43311-1833. (937)593-9207. Fax (937)593-9207. E-mail: pzbelle@pocketmail.com. Membership (10-15) open.

*****WEST-DAYTON CHRISTIAN WRITERS GUILD.** Contact: Tina V. Toles, PO Box 251, Englewood OH 45322-2049. Phone/fax (937)832-0541. E-mail: Poet11@ix.netcom.com. Membership (50) open. Sponsoring a July 2001 seminar, and a contest open to non-members.

OKLAHOMA

FELLOWSHIP OF CHRISTIAN WRITERS (formerly Tulsa Christian Writers). Meet in Tulsa. This group starting new groups across the country. Currently has one in Muskogee (contact: Suzie Eller, eller@intellex.com). Contact for additional locations. Contact: JoAnn R. Wray, 812 W. Glenwood St., Broken Arrow OK 74011-6419. (918)451-4017. Fax (918) 451-4417. E-mail: epistle@webzone.net. Free newsletter: Ready Writer Online. (To subscribe to newsletter, put "Subscribe RW Light" in subject line of e-mail above. Indicate HTML or Plain Text in body of message.) Website: www.onelist.com/subscribe/TulsaChristianWriter. Membership (60+) open. Quarterly contests (for members) and workshops. Planning a contest open to members and nonmembers during 2001. Membership $30/yr.

+MUSKOGEE CHRISTIAN WRITERS' GROUP. Contact: Donna Cowan, PO Box 35625, Tulsa OK 74135. (918)665-8844. E-mail: 104676.1742@compuserve.com. Membership open.

WORDWRIGHTS OKLAHOMA CITY CHRISTIAN WRITERS. Contact: Nancy Vineyard, 2720 SW 75th St., Oklahoma City OK 73159. (405)685-7625. Fax (405)232-9659. E-mail: nvwritesok@aol.com. Membership (30+) open. Co-sponsors an annual writers' conference with American Christian Writers, March 2001, in Oklahoma City; send SASE for information.

OREGON

+EUGENE ROSE CHAPTER OF THE ORTHODOX AUTHOR'S ASSN. Contact: Sarah Cowie, 25372 Eldale Dr., Eugene OR 97402. Phone/fax (541)935-6763. E-mail: eugeneoaa@prodigy.net. Website: www.strannik.com/oaa.

OREGON CHRISTIAN WRITER'S CLUB. Portland. Contact: Frances Dixon, 15426 SE Bush St., Portland OR 97236. (503)761-8175. E-mail:

dixon728@yahoo.com. Membership (12+) open. Occasional local workshops; annual conference in Yakima WA, May 2001.

OREGON CHRISTIAN WRITERS. Contact: Debbie Hedstrom, pres., PO Box 219103, Portland OR 97225-9103. (503)370-9153. Fax (503)365-1801. E-mail: dhdstrom@wbc.edu. Website: cs.georgefox.edu/~rzempel/ocw. Attendance: Meets three times annually: February in Salem, May in Eugene, and October in Portland. All-day Saturday conferences. Membership (350) open. Sponsors a contest, and annual conference, June (Salem). Newsletter & critique groups.

OREGON CITY CHRISTIAN WRITERS GROUP. Milwaukie. Contact: Geneva Iijima, 20349 S. Leland Rd., Oregon City OR 97045-9131. (503)656-3632. Serious group; must write regularly. Waiting list available.

PORTLAND CHRISTIAN WRITERS GROUP. Contact: Stan Baldwin, (503)659-2974. Serious group; must write regularly. Waiting list available.

*SALEM I CHRISTIAN WRITERS GROUP. Contact: Marcia Mitchell, 4427 Rodeo Dr. NE, Salem OR 97305. (503)588-0372. Fax (503)375-8406. E-mail: 74747.1161@compuserve.com. Membership (7) open.

*SALEM II CHRISTIAN WRITERS GROUP. Contact: Diane Hopper, (503)378-7974. Membership (6) open.

*SUNNYSIDE CHRISTIAN WRITER'S GROUP. Portland/Clackamas area. Contact: Linda Barr Batdorf, 7018 SE Furnberg, Milwaukie OR 97222. (503)653-9501. E-mail: LINDYBEE@aol.com. Membership open.

+TREASURE VALLEY CHRISTIAN WRITERS: ONTARIO CHAPTER. Contact: Lorena Keck, 615 SE 7th St., Ontario OR 97914-3813. (541)889-2642. Membership open.

WORDSMITHS. Gresham OR/Vancouver WA/Battle Ground WA. Contact: Susan Thogerson Maas, 27526 SE Carl St., Gresham OR 97080-8215. (503)663-7834. E-mail: STM663@aol.com. Membership (6) open. Christian and secular writers.

WRITER'S DOZEN CRITIQUE GROUP. Eugene. Contact: Dorothy A. Grant, PO Box 502, Eugene OR 97440. (541)343-2187. Membership (6-8) open (max. 13).

PENNSYLVANIA

THE FIRST WORD. Sewickley. Contact: Shirley Stevens, 326 B Glaser Ave., Pittsburgh PA 15202-2910. (412)761-2618. E-mail: snevets@stargate.net. Membership (15) open.

GREATER JOHNSTOWN AREA CHRISTIAN WRITERS' GUILD. Contact: Betty Rosian, 108 Deerfield Ln., Johnstown PA 15905-5703. (814)255-4351. Fax (708)810-3087. E-mail: BLRosian@aol.com. Membership (20) open.

GREATER PHILADELPHIA CHRISTIAN WRITERS' FELLOWSHIP. Springfield. Contact: Marlene Bagnull, 316 Blanchard Rd., Drexel Hill PA 19026. Phone/fax (610)626-6833. E-mail: mbagnull@aol.com. Website: www.writehisanswer.com. Membership (40) open. Sponsors annual writers' conference (August 2-4, 2001), and contest (open to registered conferees only). Also offers Monday evening writing classes, and half-day seminars (January 13, February 17, and March 24); full-day seminar April 28.

INDIANA CHRISTIAN WRITERS FELLOWSHIP. Indiana PA. Contact: Jan Woodard, 270 Sunset Dr., Indiana PA 15701. (724)465-5886. Fax (208) 330-6059. E-mail: jwoodard@wpia.net. Membership (12) open.

+INDIAN VALLEY CHRISTIAN WRITERS FELLOWSHIP. Souderton. Contact: Wanda Schwandt, 45 S. Allentown Rd., Telford PA 18969-1305. (215)257-0636. E-mail: daphni@voicenet.com. Website: www.geocities. com/ivcwf/index.html. Membership (22) open.

LANCASTER AREA CHRISTIAN WRITERS FELLOWSHIP. Contact: John Brenneman, 258 Brenneman Rd., Lancaster PA 17603-9623. (717)872-5183. Membership open.

*MONTROSE CHRISTIAN WRITERS FELLOWSHIP. Contact: Patti Souder, PO Box 159, Montrose PA 18801-1059. (717)278-4815. Membership (12) open. Holding a conference July 2001.

PUNXSUTAWNEY AREA CHRISTIAN WRITERS FELLOWSHIP. Contact: Michele T. Huey, 121 Homestead Ln., Glen Campbell PA 15742-8404. Phone/fax (814)845-7683. E-mail: mthuey@penn.com. Membership (10) open.

WEST BRANCH CHRISTIAN WRITERS. Williamsport. Contact: Barbara Sutryn, 2230 Fairview Rd., Montoursville PA 17754. (570)322-1984. E-mail: bars@csrlink.net. Membership (20) open. Sponsors occasional contest and workshop (none for 2001).

SOUTH CAROLINA

GREENVILLE CHRISTIAN WRITERS GROUP. Contact: Nancy Parker, 3 Ben St., Greenville SC 29601. (864)232-1705. E-mail: NKPediting@aol.com. Membership (6) open.

TEXAS

+AMERICAN CHRISTIAN ROMANCE WRITERS. Lynn Coleman, pres. Contact: DiAnn Mills, 14410 Dracaena Ct., Houston TX 77070. (281)320-9995. E-mail: ACRWinfo@acrw.net. Website: www.acrw.net. Online chatroom. Send membership inquiries to address above. Membership (80) open.

*AUSTIN CHRISTIAN WRITERS' GUILD. Contact: Lin Harris, 129 Fox Hollow Cv., Cedar Creek TX 78612-4844. (512)243-2305. Fax (512)243-2317. E-mail: linjer@ix.netcom.com. Membership (100) open. Monthly newsletter (print and electronic). Seminar February 2001.

*GREENVILLE CHRISTIAN WRITERS' GROUP. Greenville. Contact: Jim Pence, 1551 Hunt Co. Rd. 4109, Campbell TX 75422-1201. (903)450-4944. E-mail: james@pence.com. Membership (10) open. Sponsoring an October 2001 seminar.

INSPIRATIONAL WRITERS ALIVE! Groups meet in Houston, Amarillo, Pasadena, Humble, and Jacksonville. Contact: Martha Rogers, 6038 Greenmont,

Houston TX 77092-2332. (713)686-7209. E-mail: mrogeres353@aol.com. Membership (130) open. Sponsors summer seminar, August 4, 2001, monthly newsletter, and annual contest (November 1-April 1).

*INSPIRATIONAL WRITERS ALIVE!/EAST TEXAS CHAPTER. Jacksonville. Contact: Maxine Holder, Rt. 4, Box 81-H, Rusk TX 75785-9410. (903)795-3986. Membership (26) open. Planning a fall conference for October 2001 (in Jacksonville or Tyler). Sponsors a writing contest open to non-members; contact: Martha Rogers, 6038 Greenmont, Houston TX 77092.

+READY WRITERS. Contact: Frank Ball, PO Box 820802, Fort Worth TX 76182. (817)271-8334. Fax (817)589-5900. E-mail: frank.ball@santech.com. Membership (6) open. An ACW chapter.

+SUPER SCRIBES. Contact: Frank Ball, PO Box 820802, Fort Worth TX 76182. (817)271-8334. Fax (817)589-5900. E-mail: frank.ball@santech.com. Membership (4) open. An ACW chapter.

UTAH

UTAH CHRISTIAN WRITERS FELLOWSHIP. Salt Lake City area. Contact: Kimberly Malkogainnis, 117 W. Park St., Bingham Canyon UT 84006-1134. (801)568-7761. Fax (801)565-7447. E-mail: kmalkos@uswest.net. Membership (20+) open.

VIRGINIA

CAPITAL CHRISTIAN WRITERS. Vienna. Leader: Betsy Dill, PO Box 873, Centreville VA 20122. Phone/fax (703)803-9447. E-mail: ccwriters@juno.com. Website: www.ccwriters.org. Sponsors a spring contest. No conference for now. Membership (150) open.

GREATER ROANOKE CHRISTIAN WRITER'S CLUB'S GROUP. Roanoke. Contact: Amanda Davis, 1998 Cahas Mtn. Rd., Boones Mill VA 24065. (540)265-9183. Fax (540)265-9183. E-mail: conservflwrchild@hotmail.com. Membership (5-8) open.

NEW COVENANT WRITER'S GROUP. Hampton. Contact: Mary Tatem, 451 Summer Dr., Newport News VA 23606-2515. Phone/fax (757)930-1700. E-mail: rwtatem@juno.com. Membership (5) open.

+RICHMOND ASSN. OF CHRISTIANS WHO WRITE. Contact: Thomas Lacy, 12114 Walnut Hill Dr., Rockville VA 23146-1854. (804)749-4050. Fax (804)749-4939. E-mail: RevTCL@aol.com. Membership (15) open. Sponsors a contest open to non-members.

S.O.N. WRITERS. Alexandria. Contact: Susan Lyttek, 5940 Telegraph Rd., Alexandria VA 23310. Phone/fax (703)768-5582. E-mail: SusanAJL@usa.net. Membership (5-10) open.

WASHINGTON

*ADVENTIST WRITERS ASSOCIATION OF WESTERN WASHINGTON. Auburn. Contact: Marian Forschler, PO Box 58785, Renton WA 98058-1785.

(425)235-1435. Fax (425)204-2070. Membership (40) open. Newsletter $10/yr. Sponsors annual writers' conference in late June.

*CAPITOL CHRISTIAN WRITERS ASSN. Olympia. Contact: Karen Strand, (360)493-1552. Membership (19) open.

+CHRISTIAN WRITERS FELLOWSHIP OF MOSES LAKE. Contact: Judith Gonzales. (509)765-4829. E-mail: jmg.sp.ink@juno.com. Membership open.

NORTHWEST CHRISTIAN WRITERS ASSN. Bellevue. Contact: Lorinda Newton, 10663 NE 133rd Pl., Kirkland WA 98034-2030. (425)821-6647. Fax (425)823-8590. E-mail: the.newtons@verizon.net. Website: www. seanet.com/~ncwa. Membership (70) open.

*SPOKANE CHRISTIAN WRITERS. Contact: Niki Anderson, 1405 E 54th Ave., Spokane WA 99223-6374. (509)448-6622. Fax (509)448-2277. E-mail: Nander1405@aol.com. Or Christine Tangvald, 6016 E. Willow Springs Rd., Spokane WA 99223-9235. (509)448-0593. Membership (10) open.

*SPOKANE NOVELISTS. Contact: Joan Mochel, 12229 N. Ruby Rd., Spokane WA 99218-1924.(509)466-2938. E-mail: MOCHEL@aol.com. Membership (18) open. Secular group with mostly Christian members.

WALLA WALLA CHRISTIAN WRITERS. Contact: Dolores Walker, 904 Ankeny, Walla Walla WA 99362-3705. (509)529-2974. E-mail: Klinker@ bmi.net. Membership (10) open.

*WALLA WALLA VALLEY CHRISTIAN SCRIBES. Walla Walla. Contact: Helen Heavirland, PO Box 146, College Place WA 99324-0146. Phone/fax (541)938-3838. E-mail: hlh@bmi.net. Newsletter $6/yr. September-May. Membership (6-8) open.

WASHINGTON CHRISTIAN WRITERS. Sponsors 3-4 conferences, workshops and seminars in various locations. Contact: Elaine Wright Colvin, PO Box 11337, Bainbridge Island WA 98110. (206)842-9103. Fax (206)842-0536. E-mail: writersinfonetwork@juno.com. Website: www. bluejaypub.com/win. Check Website for announcements of conferences and news updates.

WENATCHEE CHRISTIAN WRITERS' FELLOWSHIP. Contact: Shirley R. Pease, 1818 Skyline Dr., #31, Wenatchee WA 98801. (509)662-8392. E-mail: mocrane@aol.com. Membership (20) open. Usually holds a one-day seminar in September.

WISCONSIN

WORD & PEN CHRISTIAN WRITERS CLUB. Menasha. Contact: Beth Ziarnik, 1963 Indian Point Rd., Oshkosh WI 54901-1371. (414)235-0664. E-mail: bethz@eliteone.net. Membership (20) open. An American Christian Writers Chapter.

CANADA

FRASER VALLEY CHRISTIAN WRITERS GROUP. Abbotsford BC. Contact: Ingrid Shelton, 2082 Geneva Ct., Clearbrook BC V2T 3Z2 Canada (Box 783, Sumas WA 98295). (604)859-7530. Membership (30+) open.

*INSCRIBE CHRISTIAN WRITERS' FELLOWSHIP (formerly Alberta Christian Fellowship—Canadawide). Calgary & Edmonton. Contact: Elsie Montgomery, pres, 333 Hunter's Run, Edmonton AB T6R 2N9, Canada. (780)988-5622. Fax (780)430-0139. E-mail: emontgom@compusmart.ab. ca. Website under construction. Membership (210) open. Newsletter. Membership fee $30. Sponsors seminars the last weekend of April (in Calgary) & September. See conference listing. Sponsors 2 contests, spring & fall (fall open to non-members).

*MANITOBA CHRISTIAN WRITERS ASSN. Winnipeg. Contact: Edward D. Hughes, 39 Valleyview Dr., Winnipeg MB R2Y 0R5 Canada. (204)889-0460. E-mail: hughes@aecc.escape.ca. Membership (15) open.

*SOUTHERN MANITOBA FELLOWSHIP OF CHRISTIAN WRITERS. Winkler, Roland or Carman. Contact: Ellie Reimer, 173 10th St., Winkler MB R6W 1W8 Canada. (204)325-7701. Membership (4) open.

*SPIRITWOOD SCRIBES. Meets 19X/yr. Contact: Elmer Bowes, Spiritwood SK, S0J 2M0. (306)883-2003. Annual dues $5. Membership open.

*SWAN VALLEY WRITERS GUILD. Swan River, Manitoba. Contact: Julie Bell, Box 2115, Swan River MB R0L 1Z0 Canada. (204)734-7890. Membership (7-8) open. Sponsors a seminar.

FOREIGN

*ASSOCIATION OF CHRISTIAN WRITERS. London + network of area groups in England. Contact: Warren Crawford, 73 Lodge Hill Rd., Farnham, Surrey, UK GU10 3RB. Phone/fax: +44 (0) 1252 715746. Fax +44 (0)1252 715746. E-mail: christian-writers@dial.pipex.com. Membership (750) open. Sponsors a biennial writers weekend. Next one July 2001 (Leicestershire, England).

*CARIBBEAN CHRISTIAN WRITER'S GROUPS. St. Maarten, Netherlands Antillies; biweekly meetings; call Patricia Varlack, 599-5-95730. Curacao, Netherlands Antillies; monthly meetings on western side of island; call Ingrid Jacobus Quarton at 599-9-868-3890. Curacao, Netherlands Antillies; monthly meetings on eastern side of the island; call Lisette Quarton at 599-9-736-6107.

NATIONAL/INTERNATIONAL GROUPS (no state location)

AMERICAN CHRISTIAN WRITERS SEMINARS. Sponsors conferences in various locations around the country (see individual states for dates and places). Call for dates and locations. Contact: Reg Forder, Box 110390, Nashville TN 37222. 1-800-21-WRITE. Website: www.ECPA.org/ACW.

CHRISTIAN WRITERS FELLOWSHIP INTL. (CWFI) Contact: Sandy Brooks, 1624 Jefferson Davis Rd., Clinton SC 29325-6401. (864)697-6035. E-mail: cwfi@cwfi-online.org. To contact Sandy Brooks personally: sandybrooks @cwfi-online.org. Website: www.cwfi-online.org. No meetings, but offers market consultations, critique service, writers books and conference workshop tapes. Connects writers living in the same area, and helps start writers' groups. Membership (1,000+) open.

#FAITH, HOPE & LOVE is the inspirational chapter of Romance Writers of America. Dues for the chapter are $15/yr, but you must also be a member of RWA to join (dues $65/yr). Chapter offers these services: online list service for members, including an annual contest. Contest is open to members who do not have a novel published. To join, contact RWA National Office, 3707 FM 1960 West, Ste. 550, Houston TX 77068. (281)440-6885. Fax (281)440-7510. Website: www.rwanational.com. Or go to FHL Website: www.webpak.net/robinlee/FHL/info.html. New Inspirational Readers Choice Contest; deadline February 14, 2001; no cash prizes. Send SASE for guidelines.

+GEGRAPHA (CWFI). This Christian organization for professional journalists was established in July 1998 with three goals: 1. To build a global fellowship of Christians in Journalism, supporting those already in it and encouraging others to enter it. 2. To model Christian standards of excellence and personal ethics within the profession of journalism. 3. To be channels of God's grace and truth within the profession. Held a conference in August 1999 in England. For more information, contact Diane Bryhn at diane@eppc.org.

*INDEPENDENT PUBLISHERS FOR CHRIST. Contact: Cecile Higgins, PO Box 280349, Lakewood CO 80228. (303)456-9166. Fax (303)793-0838. Quarterly newsletter and semi-annual seminars focusing on self-publishing issues. Provides speakers for writing groups. Annual dues. Membership open.

ORTHODOX AUTHOR'S ASSN. National organization. Contact: Sarah Cowie, 25372 Eldale Dr., Eugene OR 97402. Phone/fax (541)935-6763. E-mail: sarahcowie@aol.com. Membership (70) open. October writer's seminar possibly in Indianapolis IN, October 2001.

PEN-SOULS. Conducted entirely by e-mail. Contact: Janet Collins, 1511—8th St., Alameda CA 94501-3415. (510)522-7681. E-mail: wordlove@jps.net. Membership (8) open.

THE PRESBYTERIAN WRITERS GUILD. No regular meetings. National writers' organization with a quarterly newsletter. Dues $15 per year. Contact: Nancy Regensburger, 615 Wightman St., Vassar MI 48768. Membership (220) open. Sponsors contests for members each year. Sponsors annual conference.

+WRITE ON! A new kind of writer's group. Its 13 members are mostly beginning writers, but they write assignments for editors under the supervision of a professional writer/editor. The leader puts the appropriate writer together with the editor and then makes sure the assignments are written professionally to meet the editor's needs. The leader/editor then takes a commission from the writer's payment. For additional information, contact: Pat Humphrey, PO Box 169, Keene TX 76059-0169. 817-648-0867. Fax 817-645-9408. E-mail: pat@onramp.net.

WRITERS INFORMATION NETWORK. The Professional Association for Christian Writers, PO Box 11337, Bainbridge Island WA 98110. (206)842-9103. Newsletter, seminars, editorial services.

THE WRITING ACADEMY. Contact: Nancy Remmert, (314)524-3718. E-mail: nremm10335@aol.com. Website: www.wams.org. Membership (75) open.

Sponsors year-round correspondence writing program and annual seminar in August (held in various locations).

Note: If your group is not listed here, please send information to Sally Stuart, 1647 SW Pheasant Dr., Aloha OR 97006. September 25 is the deadline for next year's edition.

EDITORIAL SERVICES

The following listing is included because so many writers contact me looking for experienced/qualified editors who can critique or evaluate their manuscripts. These people from all over the country offer this kind of service. I cannot personally guarantee the work of any of those listed, so you may want to ask for references or samples of their work.

The following abbreviations indicate what kinds of work they are qualified to do:

GE—general editing/
   manuscript evaluation,
LC—line editing or copy
   editing

GH—ghostwriting
CA—co-authoring
B—brochures
NL—newsletters

SP—special projects
BC—book contract
   evaluation

The following abbreviations indicate the types of material they evaluate:

A—articles
SS—short stories
P—poetry
F—fillers
N—novels

NB—nonfiction books
BP—book proposals
JN—juvenile novels
PB—picture books
QL—query letter

BS—Bible studies
TM—technical material
E—essays
D—devotionals
S—scripts

Always send a copy they can write on and an SASE for return of your material.

(*) Indicates that editorial service did not return questionnaire.
(#) Indicates updated from guidelines or other sources.
(+) Indicates new listing.

ARIZONA

CARLA'S MANUSCRIPT SERVICE/CARLA BRUCE, 4326 N. 50th Ave., Phoenix AZ 85031-2031. Phone/fax (623)247-0174. E-mail: Carla@ww-web.com. Call/e-mail/write. GE/LC/GH/B/NL/typesetting. Does A/SS/P/F/N/NB/BP/QL/BS/TM/E/D. Charges by the page or gives project estimate after evaluation. Does ghostwriting for pastors & teachers; professional typesetting. Twenty years ghostwriting/editing; 7 years typesetting.

JOY P. GAGE, 2370 S. Rio Verde Dr., Cottonwood AZ 86326-5923. (520)646-6534. E-mail: joypg@juno.com. Send material with 10% deposit. GE. Does A/SS/N/NB/BS/doctrinal books. Charges $2.25/pg. Author of 14 books (fiction, nonfiction, Bible studies) and many articles.

+PROFESSIONAL PROOFREADING/JODI DECKER, 5642 W. Carol Ave.,

Glendale AZ 85302. (623)939-1199. Fax (623)939-0393. E-mail: jdecker1 @access1.net. Website: proofreadingpro.homestead.com. Call/e-mail. GE/LC/GH/CA. Does A/SS/F/N/NB/JN/PB/BS/TM/E/D/S. Charges by the page, hour or project. Has M. Ed. in Education; B.A. in communication; college writing teacher, editor of 3 books.

ARKANSAS

+**HOPE EDITING SERVICE/SARA DESMOND,** 1208 N 9th St, De Queen AR 71832. (870)642-7849. E-mail: sdesmond@ipa.net. Call/write/e-mail. LC. Does A/SS/N/JN/NB/BP/BS. Charges $1/pg.

+**SHARON'S DESKTOP/SHARON THREATT,** 310 Carey, Glenwood AR 71943. (870)356-5119. E-mail: threatt@ipa.net. E-mail. GE/LC/NL. Does A/SS/N/NB/BS. Charges $350-500 for books up to 200 pages; short material $2.25/page. Six to eight years experience as writer and editor.

CALIFORNIA

#**PATRICIA M. BELCHER TRANSCRIPTION SERVICE,** 21909 Tranquil Ln., Anderson CA 96007-8331. Transcribes tapes and the spoken word into the computer.

***CAVANAUGH'S WORD FORGE/ELIZABETH & JACK CAVANAUGH,** 1966 Duke St., Chula Vista CA 91913-2706. (619)421-4129. Fax (619)216-1539. E-mail: wjackc@home.com. Write/e-mail. GE. Does N/BP. Charges $125 for proposal/3chapters; $500 for complete ms. Full report and market recommendations, plus audio instructional tape. Award-winning, best-selling novelist; conference speaker, author of more than a dozen novels.

CHRISTIAN COMMUNICATOR MANUSCRIPT CRITIQUE SERVICE/SUSAN TITUS OSBORN, 3133 Puente St., Fullerton CA 92835-1952. (714) 990-1532. Fax (714) 990-0310. E-mail: Susanosb@aol.com. Website: www. christiancommunicator.com. Call/write. For book, send material with $100 deposit. Staff of 14 editors. GE/LC/GH/CA/SP/BC. Edits all types of material. A/SS/PB. $70. Three chapter-book proposal $100. Additional editing $25/hr.

CORNERSTONE INDEXING/SHIRLEY WARKENTIN, 1862 Tenaya Ave., Clovis CA 93611-0630. (559)322-2145. E-mail: indexer@juno.com. Website: homestead.juno.com/indexer. Call/e-mail. Writes subject and Scripture indexes for nonfiction books from a Christian perspective. Charges $3.00 per page, average. Member, American Society of Indexers; 5 years' experience.

***DIANE FILLMORE PUBLISHING SERVICES,** PO Box 489, La Habra CA 90633-0489. (562)697-1541. E-mail: dibofi@aol.com. E-mail/write. GE/LC/GH/CA/B/NL/SP. Does A/F/QL/BS/TM/E/D/small group or SS curriculum. Charges $20/hr. Member of Assn. of Professional Writing Consultants; book editor, former magazine editor.

***VICKI HESTERMAN, Ph.D./WRITING, EDITING, PHOTOGRAPHY,** PO Box 6788, San Diego CA 92166. (619)849-2260. E-mail: vhesterm@

ptloma.edu. E-mail preferred. Phone consultation/print evaluation: $60/hr. Estimates given for longer projects. Edits/develops nonfiction material, including editorials; works with book and article writers and publishers as co-author, line editor, or in editorial development.

DARLENE HOFFA, 512 Juniper St., Brea CA 92821. (714)990-5980. E-mail: j@jhoffa.com. Call. GE. Does NB/BS/D. Charges $35/article or short piece; $65 for book ms up to 52 pgs, plus $1.25/pg; or $15/hr.

MAIN ENTRY EDITIONS/REBECCA JONES, 1057 Chestnut Dr., Escondido CA 92025. Phone/fax (760)741-3750. E-mail: info@spirit-wars.com. E-mail. GE/GH/SP/basic formatting. Does A/SS/P/JN/BS/D; theological material. Flat rate of $30/hr online. Graduate writing instructor, Westminster Theological Seminary in California.

KIMURA CREATIONS/DENELLA KIMURA, PO Box 785, Benicia CA 94510-0785. Phone/fax (707)746-8421. E-mail: dkimura@juno.com. Call/write/send/$50 deposit. GE/LC. Does poetry/poetry book proposals/chapbooks. Send $50 for 5 poems (for poetry editing and critique). Charges $150 to set up a chapbook for printing (included one set of masters and a sample copy); must be camera-ready (editing extra). Production price depends on how many copies ordered.

LIGHTHOUSE EDITING/DR. LON ACKELSON, 13326 Community Rd., #11, Poway CA 92064-4734. (619)748-9258. Fax (619)748-7134. E-mail: Isaiah68LA@aol.com. E-mail/write. GE/LC/GH/CA. Does A/SS/NB/BP/QL/BS/D. Charges $35 for article/short story critique; $50 for 3-chapter book proposal; $1 faxes or e-mails/day. Send SASE for full list of fees. Editor since 1981; senior editor since 1984; edited over 300 books.

MARY CARPENTER REID, 925 Larchwood Dr., Brea CA 92821. (714)529-3755. E-mail: MARYCREID@aol.com. Call/write. GE. Does A/SS/N/BP/JN/PB. Charges $25/hr. Author of 17 books.

LAURAINE SNELLING/KMB COMMUNICATIONS, INC., 19872 Highline Rd., Tehachapi CA 93561-7796. (805)823-0669. Fax (661)823-9427. E-mail: snelling@inreach.com. Call/write/e-mail. GE. Does N/BP/QL/JN. Charges $50/hr with $100 deposit, or by the project after discussion with client. Author of 37 books (YA & adult fiction, 2 nonfiction).

SHIRL'S EDITING SERVICE/SHIRL THOMAS, 9379 Tanager Ave., Fountain Valley CA 92708-6557. (714)968-5726. E-mail: ShirlTH@aol.com. Call/e-mail/write, and send material with $50 deposit. GE/LC/GH/CA/Rewriting. Does A/SS/P/F/N/NB/BP/QL/TM/E/greeting cards/synopses. Consultation/evaluation, $50/hr; copy editing $45/hr; content editing/rewriting, $55/hr. Teaches two 6-week classes, three times a year, "Stepping Stones to Getting Published," and "Writing for the Greeting Card Market."

+VANTAGE POINT/BRANDILYN COLLINS, 7 Bennett Rd., Redwood City CA 94062. (650)366-7638. Fax (650)366-7639. GE/LC. Does N/NB. Specializes in fiction, from basic story structure to polished manuscript.

COLORADO

ARIEL COMMUNICATIONS & DESIGN/DEBBIE BARKER, 115 Silo Ct., Mead CO 80542. (970)570-535-0499. Fax (970)535-0527. E-mail: dkbarker@

cris.com. Call or e-mail. GE/LC. Does A/SS/N/NB/BP/JN/PB/E/TM. Negotiable rates on a project basis.

*ECLIPSE EDITORIAL SERVICES/TRACI MULLINS, 5110 Golden Hills Ct., Colorado Springs CO 80919. (719)265-5741. Fax (719)265-5752. E-mail: tlmullins@earthlink.net. E-mail/write. GE/LC/CA/SP/book proposal preparation and some agenting. Does NB/BP/QL/BS/D. Charges $45/hr or flat fee by project. B.A. Journalism; 12 years in-house editing; 2 years freelance editing.

STANFORD CREATIVE SERVICES/ERIC STANFORD, 7645 N. Union Blvd. PMB 235, Colorado Springs CO 80920. (719)599-7808. Fax (719)590-7555. E-mail: stanford@pcisys.net. Website: www.stanfordcreative.com. Call. GE/LC/GH/CA. Does A/NB/BS/D. Charges $25/hr and up. An editor for 10 years at David C. Cook.

WILLIAM PENS/WILLIAM D. WATKINS, PO Box 6426, Longmont CO 80501-2078. (303)485-5851. Fax (303)485-5864. E-mail: Wmpens@aol.com. Write/e-mail. GE/BC/consulting, contract negotiations, literary representation, mentoring. Does A/N/NB/BP/QL/JN/PB/BS/E/D (only for clients he mentors, agents, or consults with). Fee sheet available. See listing under Agents.

CONNECTICUT

*KAREN ORFITELLI, 502 Mill Pond Dr., South Windsor CT 06074-3565. (860)645-1100. E-mail: KarenOrf@aol.com. Write. GE/LC/GH. Does A/F/BS/E/D. Charges $25/hr. Estimates given.

FLORIDA

KNUTH EDITORIAL SERVICES/DEBORAH L. KNUTH, 3965 Magnolia Lake Ln., Orlando FL 32810. (407)293-2029. Write; send with $50 deposit. GE/LC/B/NL/SP/BC. Does A/SS/F/N/NB/BP/QL/JN/PB/BS/TM/E/D. Charges $20/hr. Specializes in historical fiction. Has a B.A. in creative writing and 4 years' experience editing.

LESLIE SANTAMARIA, PO Box 780066, Orlando FL 32878-0066. E-mail: santamaria@mpinet.net. E-mail inquiry or send material (1-chapter book proposal, article up to 2,500 words, or poems to 5 pages) with $30 for an initial review. Will give a critique and description of editing services recommended, including cost estimate. GE/LC/GH/CA/SP. Does A/SS/N/NB/BP/QL/JN/BS/TM/E/D. Charges $25 per 2,500 words for initial review; by the page or project for additional editing. Published article and book author; experienced book editor.

WILDE CREATIVE SERVICES/GARY A. WILDE, 382 Raleigh Pl., Oviedo FL 32765. (407)977-3869. Fax (407)359-2850. E-mail: gwilde@mac.com. GE/GH/CA/SP. A publishing support company providing book doctoring, editorial project management, collaborative writing, and copywriting services. Negotiated flat fee based on $50/hr. Former staff editor for major publisher.

GEORGIA

BONNIE C. HARVEY, Ph.D., 309 Carriage Place Ct., Decatur GA 30033-5939. (404)299-6149. Fax (404)297-6651. E-mail: BoncaH@aol.com. Call/e-mail. GE/LC/GH/SP/theology. Does A/SS/N/NB/QL/JN/BS/E/D. Charges $20/hr for reading/critiquing or proofreading; $25/hr for editing, $35/hr for rewriting. Has Ph.D. in English; 10 years teaching college-level English; 16 years experience as editor; has ghost-written books; and authored 14 books.

LAMBLIGHTERS LITERARY SERVICE/CISI MORROW-SMITH, 1056 Sawgrass Ct., Lilburn GA 30047-1864. (770)978-9129. E-mail: cmorows@ bellsouth.net. Call/E-mail. GE/LC/GH/CA/B/NL/SP/tutors writing (child or adult). Does A/SS/F/N/NB/BP/QL/JN/PB/BS/TM/E/D/S. Phone consultation $35 (initial hour free). Charges $35/hr, $35 minimum; long-term projects negotiable. Has BA in Journalism/Creative Writing; 25 years experience.

POSITIVE DIFFERENCE COMMUNICATIONS/ROSS WEST, 100 Martha Dr., Rome GA 30165-4138. (706)232-9325. Fax (706)235-2716. E-mail: drrwest@ aol.com. Call/write/e-mail. GE/LC/GH. Does A/NB/BS. Charges by the page or provides a project cost estimate. Published professional; author of two books and several articles; more than 20 yrs editing experience.

*****SANDRA A. HUTCHESON**, 210 Montrose Dr., McDonough GA 30253-4239. (770)507-6665. Fax (770)474-8880. Call. GE/LC/CA/B/NL/SP. Does A/SS/F/ N/NB/BP/ JN/PB/BS/TM/E/D. Charges $25/hr ($25 min.), plus expenses (telephone, research, postage).

ILLINOIS

*****DEBORAH CHRISTENSEN**, PO Box 354, Addison IL 60101. (630)665-3044. E-mail: christen@stametinc.net. Send with $20 deposit. GE/LC/B/NL. Does A/SS/F/N/NB/JN/D. Charges $20/hour.

*****JOY LITERARY AGENCY**, 3 Golf Center, Ste. 141, Hoffman Estates IL 60195-3710. (847)310-0003. Fax (847)310-0893. E-mail: joyco2@juno.com. Write. GE/LC. Does A/SS/N/NB/JN. Charges $1.50/pg for line editing; $15/hr for reading & critique.

THE WRITER'S EDGE, PO Box 1266, Wheaton IL 60189. E-mail: writersedge @usa.net. Website: members.xoom.com/WRITERSEDGE. No phone calls. A manuscript screening service for 55 cooperating Christian publishers. Charges $59 to evaluate a book proposal and if publishable, they will send a synopsis of it to 55 publishers who might be interested. If not publishable they will tell how to improve it. If interested, send an SASE for guidelines and a Book Information Form; request a form via e-mail or copy from Website. The Writer's Edge now handles previously published books that are out of print and available for reprint. Requires a different form, but cost is the same. Reviews novels, nonfiction books, juvenile novels, Bible studies, devotionals, biography, and theology.

INDIANA

DENEHEN, INC./DR. DENNIS E. HENSLEY, 6824 Kanata Ct., Fort Wayne IN

46815-6388. Phone/Fax (219)485-9891 (Fax 10 a.m-6 p.m., M-F). E-mail: DENEHEN@aol.com. Write/e-mail. GE/LC/GH. Does A/SS/N/NB/JN/BS/E/ D/academic articles/editorials/op-ed pieces/columns/speeches/interviews. Rate sheet for SASE. Author of 31 books; Ph.D. in English; college English professor.

+JAMES C. HENDRIX, 2597 Stardale Dr., Fort Wayne IN 46816-1478. (219)447-2482. Fax (219)446-0275. E-mail: JMHendrix_2002@yahoo. com. E-mail. GE/LC/CA/B/NL/SP. Does A/SS/F/N/NB/BP/QL/JN/PB/BS/TM/E/ D/S. Published writer. Negotiable prices.

#CYNTHIA L. JACOBS, 222 Ardennes Ave., Mishawaka IN 46545-3927. (219)259-7634. E-mail: ejac@michianatoday.com. Website: www.helpfor writers.com. Call/write/e-mail. GE/LC/Market research. Does A/SS/F/NB/ BP/QL/E/D. Associate degree in writing; over 50 published articles; asst. editor on college newspaper.

JAMES N. WATKINS, PO Box 117, LaOtto IN 46763-0117. (219)897-4121. (219)897-3700. E-mail: watkins@fwi.com. Website: www2.fwi.com/ ~watkins. Write/$25 deposit or e-mail. GE. Does A/NB/D. Charges $25 to critique up to 2,000 wds; book proposals with one sample chapter. Awarded four Evangelical Press Assn. awards for editing, former editorial director, recipient of Amy Award, author of 14 books and 1,500 articles.

WRITING AND CREATIVE SERVICES/STEPHEN R. CLARK, 108 Glenwood Ln., Fishers IN 46038-1129. (317)841-1856. E-mail: stephen@Epiphany Lane.com. Website: www.EpiphanyLane.com. Call/write/e-mail. LC/GH/ CA/B/NL/SP. Does A/SS/N/NB/BS/TM/E/D. Charges by the hour or project. Base is $95/hr. Writer/editor for 20+ years.

IOWA

+THE WRITE WAY BUSINESS COMMUNICATIONS/MIRIAM MORONES, PO Box 174, Johnston IA 50131-0174. (515)727-4287. E-mail: writeway4u @aol.com. Website: www.writeway4u.com. Call/e-mail/write. GE/LC/GH/ B/NL/SP/grant writing/desktop publishing. Does A/SS/N/NB/BP/TM/E. Charges $25/hr to edit; $50/hr to compose or design. Seven years as a professional and judge for writing competitions.

KANSAS

+PAM GASTINEAU, 8125 E. Orme, Wichita KS 67207. (316)683-9411. Manuscript typing services.

LASTING IMPRESSIONS, GRAPHIC DESIGN & EDITORIAL SERVICES/ DAVID J. SWISHER, 2047 SW Central Park Ave., Topeka KS 66604-3093. (785)234-8329. Fax (785)234-9345. E-mail: djsnl@juno.com. Write/e-mail. GE/LC/GH/B/NL/SP/typesetting/graphic design/page layout. Does A/NB/ BS/booklets/pamphlets/brochures/fliers/newsletters. Charges $25/hr for editing; $30-50/hr for pre-press (design/layout), marketing/publicity, ghostwriting. Info & rate sheet available for SASE or by fax. Specializes in helping pastors and ministry leaders self- & subsidy-publish their books and booklets from consultation through publication, any or all aspects.

Familiar with ISBN, copyright, and print production processes. Marketing/publicity 10 yrs; author of 3 self-published books; experienced editor and ghostwriter.

KENTUCKY

+**BETTY L. WHITWORTH**, 15763 Leitchfield Rd., Leitchfield KY 42754. (270)257-2461. E-mail: Blwhit@bbtel.com. Call/e-mail/write. GE/SP. Does A/SS/N/NB/BP/QL/JN/BS/E/D. Typing, $2-4/pg; proofreading/moderate corrections .35-.75/pg; Extensive editing .75-$1.50/pg. Retired language arts teacher, newspaper columnist and feature writer.

LOUISIANA

*****INSPIRATION COVE PRESS/NINA HARRIS**, 605 Bass Haven Resort Dr., Anacoco LA 71403. (318)286-5307. Write/ send material/$25 deposit (will send copy of her book, *Creative Writing Made Easy*). GE/LC/GH. Does A/SS/P/F/N/NB/BP/QL/JN/E/D/humorous anecdotes. Complete literary services. Overall evaluation of manuscripts up to 200 pages for $100; line edit $2/pg; rewrite $5/pg; query/proposal $25; market consultation $25. Ghostwriting (200 pgs, nonfiction) $10,000. Ghostwriting (200 pgs fiction) $10,000. A writer for 25 years, with 3 books and over 150 articles.

MARYLAND

*****OWEN-SMITH & ASSOCIATES, INC./RHONDA OWEN-SMITH**, 34 Market Place, Ste. 317, Baltimore MD 21202. (410)659-2247. Fax (410)659-9758. E-mail: mapreos@aol.com. Does GH/CA/B/NL/SP/BP/Biographies/Market Analysis/Marketing & PR Plans/Potential Publisher Identification/Press Kits/Interview Scheduling/Book Signings. Will consider other requests. Charges a flat fee or hourly rate based upon the project.

MASSACHUSETTS

WORD PRO/BARBARA A. ROBIDOUX, 127 Gelinas Dr., Chicopee MA 01020-4813. (413)592-4386. Fax (413)594-8375. E-mail: Ebwordpro@aol.com. Call. GE/LC/GH/B/NL. Does A/SS/F/ NB/BP/QL/TM/E/D. Charges $20/hr. BA in English; 15 years as freelancer.

MICHIGAN

#**THE LITTFIN PRATT AGENCY/VALINDA LITTFIN/LONNI COLLINS PRATT**, 518 W. Nepessing, Ste. 201, Lapeer MI 48446-2196. (810)245-8572. Fax (810)664-1267. E-mail: lcollpr@tir.com. Website: www.littfin pratt.com. Write/e-mail/send with $25 deposit. GE/SP/BCE/publicist. Does A/N/NB/BP/QL/D. Charges $50 for 500-1,500 wds, $100 for 1,500-3,000 words; call for longer manuscripts. Send for complete list of services and fees. Also offers mentoring programs for serious new or intermediate writers (must have access to e-mail). Send for application information. National Press Assn. Awards, author of 12 books and over 1,500 articles, writers' conference instructor.

*LONNIE HULL DUPONT & ASSOCIATES, PO Box 142, Moscow MI 49257. (517)849-0100. Fax (517)849-7288. E-mail: Lonniehd@aol.com. Call/write/e-mail; don't send material without OK. GE/SP/condensing. Does N/NB/BP/QL. Charges by the hour. Editing and marketing books since 1983, in both CBA and ABA markets.

MINNESOTA

+ALICE 'N INK, 121 Washington St. S., #802, Minneapolis MN 55401-2127. Phone/fax (612)339-5081. E-mail: apeppler@aol.com. Website: www.jpeppler.com. Call/e-mail/write. GE/LC/B/NL. Does A/SS/P/F/N/NB/BP/JN/PB/QL/D. Three-chapter book proposal, including market analysis $85; additional editing $25/hr. Publishing experience of 25 years. Quality work; quick turn around.

PTL TRANSCRIPTION/SECRETARIAL SERVICES/CONNIE PETTERSEN, R 4 Box 289, Aitkin MN 56431. (218)927-6176. E-mail: Pett289@mlecmn.net. Website: www.mlecmn.net/~pett289. Call/write. Manuscript typing; edit for punctuation/spelling/grammar, etc. Published freelance writer; 27 years secretarial/Dictaphone experience. IBM compatible computer, WordPerfect 5 & 6, Corel 7.0 and Microsoft Word 97 software; micro-cassette transcriber. Fees: Negotiable, plus postage. Free estimates. Internet/e-mail/fax access. Confidentiality guaranteed.

*SARA WALDORF, RR #2, Box 114, Warren MN 56762-9567. (218)745-4346. E-mail: lynn.kathy@juno.com. Write/e-mail/send with $15 deposit. GE/LC/proofreading/rewriting. Does A/SS/N/NB/JN/BS/E/D. General editing $15/hr; copyediting $1.50/pg. Negotiable rates on longer projects. Rewriting $25-30/hr. Quality service for reasonable rates.

MISSISSIPPI

#WRITER'S CORNER EDITORIAL SERVICES/WILLA CANTU, 206 Jefferson St., New Albany MS 38652-4026. (662)539-0409. Fax (662)539-0480. Call/write. GE/LC/GH. Does A/SS/P/F/N/NB/QL/E/D. Word processing/typing, $1.25/pg; critique, $2/pg; editing $3/pg; typesetting, $5/pg; and rewriting/typing, $5/pg. Twenty-plus years experience in publishing, as editor, reporter, journalist and columnist.

MISSOURI

+ABACUS MANUSCRIPT SERVICES/SHAWNEE MCCARTY FLEENOR, 1428 N. Ash, Nevada MO 67442. (417)667-9452. E-mail: RSFleenor@juno.com. Call/write/e-mail. GE/LC/GH. Does A/SS/P/F/QL/E/D. Charges $10 for up to 1,000 words, $5 for each additional 1,000 words. Full report and market recommendations. Author of nearly 200 published articles, short stories, and poems; former marketing columnist.

*PRO WORD WRITING & EDITORIAL SERVICES/MARY R. RUTH, PO Box 155, Labadie MO 63055-0155. (636)742-3663. E-mail: prowordusa@juno. com. Call/write. GE/LC/SP/manuscript or script typing, scan hard copy to disk, proofreading, indexing. Does A/SS/N/NB/BP/JN/BS/TM/E/D/S/biographies/textbooks. Call to discuss your project. Reasonable rates/professional results. MC/Visa available.

NEW HAMPSHIRE

AMDG ENTERPRISES/SALLY WILKINS, Box 273, Amherst NH 03031-0393. (603)673-9331. E-mail: SEDWilkins@aol.com. Write. GE/LC. Does A/F/JN/ PB/ BS/TM. Rate sheet for SASE.

+DIRECT PATH MINISTRIES/THE WRITE CONNECTION/ELIZABETH M. HOEKSTRA, PO Box 103, Dublin NH 03444. (603)563-9202. Fax (603) 563-7739. E-mail: hoekstra@directpath.org. Website: www.DirectPath. org. E-mail. GE. Does A/NB/BP/QL/E/D. Rate sheet for SASE; reasonable rates, quick service. Author of 9 books; workshop leader.

NEW JERSEY

DAYSTAR WRITING & EDITORIAL SERVICES/DR. MARY ANN DIORIO, Box 405, Millville NJ 08332-0405. (856)327-1231. Fax (856)327-0291. E-mail: daystar405@aol.com. Website: www.daystarministries.com. E-mail/ write. GE/LC. Does A/SS/QL/D/copy for ads and PR material/résumés/business letters; also translations in French, Italian, and Spanish. Rate sheet for SASE. Freelance writer, 22 yrs; editor, 11 yrs; former college instructor; Ph.D. in literature/language.

NEW YORK

*ELIZABETH CRISPIN, Box 134 Schulyer Rd., Oswegatchie NY 13670-3126. (315)848-7401. Fax (315)848-9860. E-mail: Ecrispin@juno.com. E-mail, write, or send with $25 deposit and SASE. GE/LC/CA/NL. Does A/P/F/D. Charges $5-15/pg for copy editing, $10/hr for articles or newsletters (nontechnical), $5/pg for poetry or devotionals; $5-15/pg for fillers.

*LAST WORD OFFICE WORKS/MARY A. LACLAIR, PO Box 435, Vernon NY 13476-0435. (315)829-3356. Fax (315)829-3356 (auto switch). E-mail: mlaclair1@juno.com. Write; send material with $25 deposit. GE/LC. Does A/SS/N/JN/BS/D. Estimates for projects, about $2-5/pg or $10-20/hr (depending on amount of editing needed). Published writer; op-ed guest column in NY and FL newspapers.

NORTH CAROLINA

*ANNA W. FISHEL, 3416 Hunting Creek Dr., Pfafftown NC 27040. (336)924-5880. Fax (336)924-5881. E-mail: awfishgw2@aol.com. Call/write/e-mail. GE/LC/CA. Does SS/N/NB/JN/TM. Charges variable rates depending on job. Freelance editor with major Christian publishing house for over 10 years; published author.

PREP PUBLISHING/ANNE MCKINNEY, 3528 Turnberry Cir., Fayetteville NC 28303. (910)483-6611. Fax (910)483-2439. E-mail: preppub@aol.com. Website: www.prep-pub.com. GE/LC/SP/BCE. Does A/SS/F/BP/QL/JN/PB/ TM/E/S. Writes résumés and cover letters. Send SASE for rate sheet. Author of 10 books, MBA from Harvard Business School and BA in English.

OHIO

*****BOB HOSTETLER**, 2336 Gardner Rd., Hamilton OH 45013-9317. Phone/fax (513)737-1102. E-mail: BobHoss@compuserve.com. Call/write. GE/LC/ GH/ CA/B/N. Does A/SS/P/N/NB/BP/JN/PB. Rate sheet available for SASE.

ADRIENNE MIKLOVIC, 5741 Acres Rd., Sylvania OH 43560. Phone/fax (419) 882-0278. E-mail: AMM@aol.com. Call/e-mail. GE/LC/NL. Does A/SS/N/ NB/JN/BS/TM. Rates vary according to project. Editing for 15 years; writer; advertising writing experience.

OKLAHOMA

EPISTLEWORKS CREATIONS/JOANN RENO WRAY, 812 W Glenwood St., Broken Arrow OK 74011-6419. (918)451-4017. Fax (918)451-4417. E-mail: epistle@webzone.net. Website: www.epistleworks.com. Call/write/ e-mail (preferred); send material with $25 deposit. GE/LC/GH/CA/B/NL/ SP/research. Does A/SS/P/F/N/NB/BP/D. Charges $18/hr. (price list on Website). Offers e-mail classes on writing. Trained and experienced artist and writer, former editor.

+WINGS UNLIMITED/CRISTINE BOLLEY, PO Box 691532, Tulsa OK 74169-1532. (918)250-9239. E-mail: WingsUnlimited@aol.com.

THE WRITE WORD/IRENE MARTIN, PO Box 300332, Midwest City OK 73140-5641. E-mail: write/word@aol.com. Write. GE/LC/GH. Does A/SS/ N/JN/PB. For fee schedule send SASE/query letter detailing project. Charges $3/pg or $15/hr. Has MA in English-Creative Writing; published novelist; writing teacher.

OREGON

*****BESTSELLER CONSULTANTS/URSULA BACON**, PO Box 922, Wilsonville OR 97070. (503)682-3235. Fax (503)682-2057. Call. GE/LC/GH/full pre-press services. Does N/NB/BP. Fees are quoted on a per project basis before work commences. Ms evaluation for 250-325 pgs starts at $550. Full report and chapter-by-chapter recommendations included. Secular, but handles Christian books. Thirty years experience as writers/book doctors.

CONNIE'S EASY WRITER SERVICE/CONNIE SOTH, 4890 SW Menlo Dr., Beaverton OR 97005-2612. (503)644-4972. Call/Write. GE/LC/SP/book doctoring & guidance. Does A/N/NB/BP/JN/PB/E/D. Charges $10/hr.

MARION DUCKWORTH, 2495 Maple NE, Salem OR 97303. (503)364-9570.

E-mail: marion.duckworth@bbs.chemek.cc.or.us. Call/e-mail/write. GE. Does A/SS/F/N/NB/BP/QL/BS. Charges $30/hr. for critique or consultation. Negotiates on longer projects. Author of 20 books and 50 articles.

*EXQUISITE EDITING/SKIP SELLERS, 12700 SW Sara Dr., Gaston OR 97119-8547. (503)985-7281. Skip@bignetwork.com. Website: www. bignetwork.com. E-mail. LC. Does A/F/NB/BS/TM/E/D. Charges about $30/hr, plus .01/wd. Bachelor's degree in Journalism & English; creative writer and editor.

*BONNIE LEON, PO Box 774, Glide OR 97443. (541)496-3787. Fax (541) 496-3139. E-mail: leon@rosenet.net. Call/e-mail. GE/LC/NL. Does A/SS/N/ BP/QL/JN. Charges $25/hr ($25 minimum); larger projects negotiated. Weekend workshop—$250, plus expenses. Author of 7 novels (including a bestseller); writer's conference instructor.

LIT.DOC/KRISTEN JOHNSON INGRAM, 955 S. 59th St., Springfield OR 97478. (541)726-8320. Fax (541)988-9126. Pager: (541)710-3764. E-mail: writerlady@juno.com. Website: www.litdoc.com. Call/write/e-mail. GE/ LC/GH/CA/B/NL/SP. Does A/SS/F/N/NB/BP/QL/JN/BS/TM/E/D. Charges $40/ hr, or negotiates on longer manuscripts. Books on disk only. Author of 14 books, 2,000 articles, many short stories and poems; MA.

*MANUSCRIPT MARKETING/WILLIAM KERCHER, PO Box 1474, Gresham OR 97030. (503)661-2031. Fax (503)492-4104. E-mail: Mmsubmit@aol. com. This is a manuscript submission service. Contact for details on services available.

+MARCIA A. MITCHELL, 4427 Rodeo Dr. NE, Salem OR 97305-4704. (503)588-0372. Fax (503)375-8406. E-mail: marciaamitchell@home.com. Call/e-mail/write. GE/LC/GH/CA/B/NL. Does A/SS/F/N/NB/D. Charges $20/ hr. Published writer.

+PICKY, PICKY INK/SUE MIHOLER, 1075 Willow Lake Road N., Salem OR 97303.(503) 393-3356. E-mail: miholer@viser.net. Call/write/e-mail. $20 an hour or negotiable by job. GE/LC. Does A/F/NB/D. Manuscript preparation available. Freelance writer and copyeditor for several publishers. "Helping you write it right," whether it's a post card or a doctoral dissertation.

'LEEN POLLINGER, 14945 SW Rim Rd., Crooked River Rance OR 97760-9352. (541)548-2799. Fax (541)548-2674 (contact first). E-mail: leen@ transport.com. Write/e-mail. GE/LC. Does A/SS/F/N/NB/BS/D. Charges $20-35/hr depending on work done. Fee schedule available for SASE. Copy edited for 3 years for Aglow Publishing; 2 years experience in critiquing manuscripts.

+PRINT PREVIEW, INC./PAT JOHNSON, 10214 SW 36th Ct., Portland OR 97219-6100. (503)244-4460. Fax (503)244-4153. E-mail: djpj@world accessnet.com. Call/e-mail/write. LC/NL/SP. Does A/SS/F/N/NB/BP/QL/JN/ PB/BS/TM/D/S/typing. Charges $15/hr; $30 minimum. Editing, proofreading experience.

+ANNA LLOYD STONE, PO Box 2251, Lake Oswego OR 97035. (503)638-3811. Fax (503)638-6131. E-mail: mizanna@hotmail.com. Call/e-mail. LC. Does A/SS/F/N/NB/BP/JN/BS/TM/E/D/S. Charges $30/hr (1 hr min). Send ms/SASE or can edit by e-mail. Freelance writer/editor for 17 yrs.

SALLY STUART, 1647 SW Pheasant Dr., Aloha OR 97006. (503)642-9844. Fax

(503)848-3658. E-mail: stuartcwmg@aol.com. Website: www.stuartmarket. com. Call/write/e-mail. GE. Does A/SS/N/NB/BP/JN/PB/E. Charges $30/hr. for critique; $40/hr. for consultations. Comprehensive publishing contract evaluation $75-100. Author of 29 books, and over 34 years experience as a writer, teacher, marketing expert.

#THE WRITE CONNECTION/MARY HAMPTON, 8305 SE Lorry Ave., Vancouver WA 98664-2208. Offers help in promoting your published book. Will help you develop a marketing plan to help get the best exposure for you and your book. Send an SASE for details.

WRITING CONSULTS/DARLENE STAFFELBACH, 6950 SW Hampton, Ste. 107, Tigard OR 97223-8329. (503)684-5228. E-mail: writingconsults@ juno.com. Call. GE/SP. Does A/NB/TM/E. Assists writers with idea clarification and development; literature synthesis; integration of critical thinking. Specializes in scholarly writing such as theses and dissertations; letters and correspondence; formulation and review of reports and manuscripts; development of teaching syllabi and other presentation materials. Call for rates.

PENNSYLVANIA

*IMPACT COMMUNICATIONS/DEBRA PETROSKY, 11331 Tioga Rd., N. Huntingdon PA 15642-2445. Phone/fax (724)863-5906. E-mail: Editing4U @aol.com. Call/e-mail. GE/LC/B/NL. Does NB/BP. Charges $20/hr. Satisfied self-publishers endorse our typesetting services. Very reasonable rates.

SPREAD THE WORD/MAURCIA DELEAN HOUCK, 106 Danny Rd., Sanatoga PA 19464. (215)659-2912. E-mail: mhouck@voicenet.com. E-mail/write. GE/LC/BC. Does A/SS/F/N/NB/BP/QL/BS. Charges $1.75/pg. (double-spaced), or as quoted. Discount for over 200 pgs. Author of 2 books and over 1,500 articles and former newspaper editor.

WRITE HIS ANSWER MINISTRIES/MARLENE BAGNULL, Litt.D, 316 Blanchard Rd, Drexel Hill PA 19026-3507. Phone/fax: (610)626-6833. E-mail: mbagnull@aol.com. Website: www.writehisanswer.com. Call/write. GE/ LC/typesetting. Does A/SS/N/NB/BP/JN/BS/D. Charges $25/hr; estimates given. Call or write for information on At-Home Writing Workshops, a correspondence study program. Over 1,000 sales to Christian periodicals, 7 books.

SOUTH CAROLINA

NANCY KOESY PARKER WRITING & EDITING SERVICES, 3 Ben St., Greenville SC 29601. (864)232-1705. E-mail: NKPediting@aol.com. Call/e-mail. GE/LC/GH/B/NL/SP. Does A/SS/N/NB/BP/QL/JN/PB/BS/E/D. Send representative sample and return SASE for free critique and fee quote. Quote based on project scope and editing required. Will provide info sheet and references. Six years experience; edited 16 books.

#JULIE SALE, 212 Ridge Spring Dr., Columbia SC 29229-9080.

TENNESSEE

CHRISTIAN WRITERS INSTITUTE MANUSCRIPT CRITIQUE SERVICE, PO Box 110390, Nashville TN 37222. (800)21-WRITE. Website: www.ECPA. org/ACW. Call/write. GE/LC/GH/CA/SP/BC. Does A/SS/P/F/N/NB/BP/JN/PB/ BS/TM/E/D/S. Send SASE for rate sheet and submission slip.

DENNIS L. PETERSON EDITING & WRITING SERVICES, 7909 Tressa Circle, Powell TN 37849-3534. Phone/fax (865)947-0496. E-mail: wordworks1 @juno.com. Website: go.to/editing. Write/e-mail. GE/LC/proofreading/ workshops/seminars. Does A/SS/N/NB/BS. Proofreading $12-20/hr; copy-editing $12-25/hr; writing/rewriting $20-30/hr; send SASE for rate card. Published writer since 1981; former sr. tech editor with Lockheed Martin; 12 years teaching experience; 3 years+ full-time freelance editor.

#EDIT+/CHARLES STROHMER, PO Box 4325, Sevierville TN 37864. (865) 453-7120. Fax (865)428-0029. E-mail: livewise@esper.com. Call/e-mail. GE/LC/CA/NL/SP. Does A/NB/BP/QL/BS/TM/E/D. Charges $18-25/hr (nego-tiable on larger projects), plus expenses. Also does substantive editing, mentors new writers, and does phone consultations. More than 15 years experience as author and editor for major Christian publishers.

*JOHNSON LITERARY AND TALENT SERVICES/JOSEPH S. JOHNSON JR., 2915 Walnut Crest Dr., Antioch TN 37013-1337. Phone/fax (615)361-8627. Call. GE/LC/GH/CA/B/N/SP/BC/consultations. Does A/SS/P/F/N/NB/ BP/QL/JN/PB/BS/TM/E/D/S/advice on song writing. Reasonable rates; ne-gotiable. Fifty years experience as a professional writer.

*WRITEWAY COMMUNICATIONS/BEN JOBE, 931 Curdwood Blvd., Nash-ville TN 37216-2401. (615)226-7095. E-mail: jobeland@bellsouth.net. E-mail. LC/B. Does A/SS/N/NB/BP/JN/BS/E/D. Charges $10/hr for proofread-ing, or $1/pg; charges $12/hr for copyediting. Volume discounts available. Nine years experience as copyeditor for Broadman.

*THE YEOMAN'S SERVICE/VIRGINIA S. YOUMANS, 3227 Ella West Cir., Lynnville TN 38472-5228. Phone/fax (931)527-0101. E-mail: sergevirge@ netzero.net. Submit with $250 deposit. GE/LC. Does N/NB/BS/D. Charges $250 to evaluate manuscripts up to 300 double-spaced pages; additional $1/page over 300 pages. $20/hour to edit (min. $100 deposit).

TEXAS

SYLVIA BRISKEY, Dallas TX. (214)521-7507. Call. GE/LC. Does P/N/JN/PB/ children's stories/secular articles. Poetry, charges $5.60 plus $1/line; fic-tion $30 to 2,000 wds, $2.50/page thereafter. Writing teacher; writes chil-dren's books and poetry.

JAN E. KILBY, Ph.D., PO Box 171390, San Antonio TX 78217-8390. (210) 657-0171. Fax (210)657-0173. E-mail: jkilby@stic.net. Call. GE/LC. Does A/SS/P/F/N/NB/BP/JN/PB/TM/E/ D/S/speeches. Charges by the hour; call for prices/information.

PWC EDITING/PAUL W. CONANT, 527 Bayshore Pl., Dallas TX 75217-7755. (972)286-2882. Fax (972)286-7923. E-mail: paul@pwc-editing.com. E-mail. GE/LC/SP/BC/proofreading/word-processing/copyediting. Does A/ SS/P/F/N/NB/BS/TM/E/D/S. Writer, editor; proofreader for book publishers and magazines. Proofreading $25/hr.; word processing $21/hr; and copy-editing $30/hr. Projects by the hour.

*WORDS IN PROGRESS/CARRIE WOOD, 310 Lakewood Dr., Buda TX 78610. (512)295-2592. E-mail: pclwood@mciworld.com. Website: website. mciworld.com/~pclwood@mciworld.com. Call/write/e-mail. GE. Does A/ SS/N/NB/JN/BS/D. Charges $15-30/hr (negotiable), discount for CWFI members. Quick turn-around. Project estimates after evaluation of services needed. References available.

VIRGINIA

*HCI EDITORIAL SERVICES/DAVID HAZARD, PO Box 568, Round Hill VA 20142-0568. Write. GE. Does N/NB/BP. Works with agents and self-publishers. Fees on request.

SCRIVEN COMMUNICATIONS/KATHIE NEE SCRIVEN, 13371 Marie Dr., Manassas VA 20112. (703)791-2877. Fax (703)791-2701. E-mail: tbaum1210 @aol.com. Call/write. GE/LC. Does A/SS/P/F/N/NB/BP/QL/JN/PB/BS/E/D/S/ tracts/pamphlets/résumés/job application letters/biographical sketches. Charges $12-15/hr; 1/3 deposit. Brochure available for SASE. Has a BS in Mass Communication/Journalism; 13 years experience in print media. Specializes in spiritual growth books for ministers.

WASHINGTON

*MARY ARMSTRONG LITERARY SERVICES, 8018 38th Dr. NE, Marysville WA 98270. (360)653-6548. E-mail: bobnmarya@aol.com. Call, e-mail, write. GE/LC. Does A/SS/F/N/NB/BP/BS/E/D. No picture books. Line-editing $1.50/pg.; evaluations $25/hr.

BRISTOL SERVICES INTL./SANDRA E. HAVEN, PO Box 2109, Sequim WA 98382-2109. E-mail: services@bristolservicesintl.com. Website: www. bristolservicesintl.com. Write/$20 deposit. GE/LC/SP. Does A/SS/N/NB/BP/ QL/JN/BS/TM/E/D. Charges $2/pg for most services or gives project estimate for special projects. Fees and services fully explained at Website, or send SASE for rate sheet. Offers project overview for $20 for up to 20 manuscript pages for those unsure of services needed; $20 credit then applied to further services desired on the same manuscript. Editor of special interest publications since 1982; 30 years experience as a copy editor.

*DUE NORTH PUBLISHING/SCOTT R. ANDERSON, 7372 Guide Meridian, Lynden WA 98264. Phone/fax (360)354-0234 (call first for fax). E-mail: North_To_Alaska@hotmail.com. Write. GE/LC/GH/CA/B/NL/SP. Does A/ NB/BP/E. Charges $25/hr for copy and content editing or by the project (estimate given). Offers wide range of editorial & pre-press (design/layout) services, including layout and design for brochures.

+THE EDITORIAL (SERVICE) AGENCY/BRENDA WILBEE, 4514 Fir Tree Way, Bellingham WA 98226. E-mail: bwilbee@juno.com. E-mail/write/1/2 the fee. GE. Does N/NB/BP. Charges $500 for market analysis; $750 for review & critique; $150 for book proposals; and $500, plus $2/page for substantive editing. MA Professional Writing; award-winning author of 9 books; writing instructor.

*KALEIDOSCOPE PRESS/PENNY LENT, 2507 94th Ave. E., Puyallup WA 98371-2203. Phone/Fax (253)848-1116. Call/write. GE/LC/GH/CA/B/NL/SP/BC. Does A/SS/F/N/NB/BP/JN/PB/E/D. Also market analysis. Line item editing $3/pg; other projects negotiated individually.

GLORIA KEMPTON, 2139 52nd Ave. SW, #B, Seattle WA 98116-1803. Phone/fax: (206)935-3075. E-mail: glokemp@earthlink.net. Call/write. GE. Does A/SS/F/N/NB/BP/JN/E. Free estimates; generally $25-50 for article/short story, $100-250 for book proposal.

AGNES C. LAWLESS, 13600 Kenwanda Dr., Snohomish WA 98296-8256. (360)668-7634. E-mail: agneslaw@aol.com. E-mail/write. GE/LC. Does A/SS/F/N/NB/BP/QL/JN/BS/TM/E/D. Charges $16.50/hr. Professional copy editor; former English teacher.

*MOODY LITERARY AGENCY/VIRGINIA A. MOODY, 17402 114th Pl. NE, Granite Falls WA 98252-9667. (360)691-5402. Call/write. GE/LC/GH/CA/BC. Does A/SS/F/N/NB/BP/JN/BS/D/S. Charges $2/pg or as agreed.

NANCY SWANSON, 10234 38th Ave. SW, Seattle WA 98146-1118. (206)932-2161. E-mail: sannanvan@earthlink.net. Call/write/e-mail. GE/LC/GH/CA/NL/SP. Does A/SS/N/NB/BS/E/D/S. Charges $1/pg or as agreed by project. Former English teacher; twenty-five years' experience editing.

WRITERS INFORMATION NETWORK/ELAINE WRIGHT COLVIN, Box 11337, Bainbridge Island WA 98110. (206)842-9103. Fax (206)842-0536. E-mail: writersinfonetwork@juno.com. Website: www.bluejaypub.com/win. Call/send material/ $150 deposit. GE/LC/GH/CA/B/NL/SP. Does N/NB/BP/QL/BS. Send SASE for rate sheet & list of all services. Christian writers consultant for 24 years; author, co-author, ghostwriter of 30 books; editor; marketing expert.

WISCONSIN

*BETHESDA LITERARY SERVICE/MARGARET L. BEEN, South 63 West 35530 Piper Rd., Eagle WI 53119-9726. (414)392-9761. Call/write/send with $10 deposit/SASE. GE. Does A/SS/P/E/D. Charges reasonable and negotiable fees. Also does devotional & inspirational readings. Teaches writers' classes/poetry seminars for all ages, with emphasis on classical literature. Many years experience editing and teaching literary arts. Note: When submitting, be specific about what editorial services you want, what your goals are, etc.

MARGARET HOUK, West 2355 Valleywood Ln., Appleton WI 54915-8712. (920)687-0559. Fax (920)687-0259. E-mail: marghouk@juno.com. Call/write. GE/LC. Does A/SS/F/N/NB/BP/QL/BSE/D (all for teens or adults). Charges $20/hr; estimates given (no charge). Author of 3 books and 700 articles; has taught writing for years.

WYOMING

WORD-KRAFT/WADE KRAFT, PO Box 1423, Lusk WY 82225-1423. (307)334-0172. Fax (307)334-0187. E-mail: luwkraft@coffey.com. Write/$20 deposit. GE/LC/typesetting/word processing. Does A/SS/N/NB/JN/BS/TM/E/D/commentaries. Charges $1.50/pg for proofreading or typesetting; $2/pg for copyediting. Estimates given. Has MA in Journalism; freelance work for Broadman & Holman; author.

CANADA

BERYL HENNE, 52 Moira St. W., Belleville ON K8P 1S3 Canada (U.S. address: Box 40, Pt. Roberts WA 98281-0040). (613)961-1791. Fax (613)691-1792. Write or e-mail. GE/LC/ B/NL/SP. Does A/SS/NB/BS/TM/E/D. Charges $20/hr.

WRITING SERVICES INSTITUTE (WSI)/MARSHA L. DRAKE, #109—4351 Rumble St., Burnaby BC V5J 2A2, Canada. Phone/fax (604)321-3555. E-mail: write@telus.net. Website: www3.telus.net/WRITE. Call/e-mail/write. GE/LC/GH/CA/B; also book reviews, biographies, résumés, or company history. Does A/SS/F/N/NB/BP/QL/D. Offers correspondence course: Write for Fun and Profit. Charges negotiable fees. Write for details and information on correspondence course.

CHRISTIAN LITERARY AGENTS

The references in these listings to "published authors" refer to those who have had one or more books published by royalty publishers, or who have been published regularly in periodicals. If a listing indicates that the agent is "recognized in the industry," it means they have worked with the Christian publishers long enough that they are recognized (by the editors) as credible agents.

Note: Visit this Website to find information on agents or agents other writers have found less than desirable: www.agentresearch.com, or contact Professor Jim Fisher, Criminal Justice Dept., Edinboro University of Pennsylvania, Edinboro PA 16444, (814)732-2409, e-mail: Jfisher@edinboro.edu. Another such site, www.sfwa.org/beware/agents.html, is sponsored by the Association of Author's Representatives, www.bookwire.com/AAR (on this site you will find a list of agents who don't charge fees, except for office expenses). You may also send for their list of approved agents (send $7 with a #10 SAE/1 stamp) to: PO Box 237201, Ansonia Station, New York NY 10003. I also suggest that you check out any potential agent at their local Better Business Bureau or local attorney general's office. For a database of over 500 agencies, go to: www.literaryagent.com.; additional agent sites: www.writers.net/agentdir/dbmB.cgi?a+Specialization+FRL+25.

(*) Indicates that agent did not return questionnaire
(#) Indicates that listing was updated from guidelines or other sources
(+) Indicates new listing

AGENT RESEARCH & EVALUATION, INC., 334 E. 30th St., New York, New York 10016. Phone/fax (212)481-5721. E-mail: info@agentresearch.com. Website: www.agentresearch.com.This is not an agency, but a service that tracks the public record of literary agents, and helps authors use the data to obtain effective literary representation. Charges fees for this service. Also offers a newsletter about agents, called Talking Agents, $39/yr.

ALIVE COMMUNICATIONS, 7680 Goddard St., Ste. 200, Colorado Springs CO 80920. (719)260-7080. Fax (719)260-8223. Website: www.alivecom. com. Agents: Rick Christian, Greg Johnson, Kathryn Helmers, Chip MacGregor. Well known in the industry. Estab. 1989. Represents 100+ clients. Open to unpublished authors occasionally. Occasionally open to new clients. Handles any material except poetry, for all ages. Deals in both Christian (70%) and general market (30%).

   Contact: Query with letter, previous history and future ideas (no calls)/ SASE.
   Commission: 15%

Fees: Only extraordinary costs with client's pre-approval; no review/ reading fee.

*AUTHOR AID ASSOCIATES, 7542 Bear Canyon Rd. NE, Albuquerque NM 87109-3847. Agent: Arthur Orrmont. Not known in industry but expanding Christian/religious client list. Estab. 1967. Represents 10 Christian clients. Open to unpublished authors. Handles novels for all ages, nonfiction for all ages, and scripts.

    Contact: By mail or phone.

    Commission: 15%.

    Fees: Evaluation fees for new/unpublished authors.

#LORETTA BARRETT BOOKS, INC., 101—5th Ave., New York NY 10003. (212)242-3420. Fax (212)691-9418. E-mail: lbarbooks@aol.com. Agents: Loretta Barrett and Kirsten Lundell. Estab. 1991. Represents 70 clients. Open to unpublished authors & new clients. Handles adult novels and nonfiction: scholarly, sophisticated, religious, philosophy.

    Contact: Letter by mail only with SASE.

    Commission: 15%; 20% foreign.

    Fees: For office expenses only.

BIG SCORE PRODUCTIONS, INC., PO Box 4575, Lancaster PA 17604. (717)293-0247. Fax (717)293-1945. E-mail: bigscore@starburstpublishers .com. Website: www.starburstpublishers.com/bigscore. Agent: David A. Robie. Recognized in industry. Estab. 1995. Represents 2-5 clients. Open to unpublished or new clients. Handles adult fiction and nonfiction, gift books, secular cross-over books, health, self-help, and inspiration.

    Contact: Query or proposal. See Website for guidelines.

    Commission: 15%, foreign 20%.

    Fees: Photocopying, overnight, etc. No reading fees.

    Tips: "Very open to taking on new clients. Submit a well-prepared proposal that will take minimal fine tuning for presentation to publishers. Nonfiction writers must be highly marketable and media savvy—the more established in speaking or your profession, the better."

BOOKS & SUCH/JANET KOBOBEL GRANT, 4788 Carissa Ave., Santa Rosa CA 95405 (707)538-4184. E-mail: jkgbooks@aol.com. Agent: Janet Kobobel Grant. Recognized in industry. Estab. 1997. Represents 30 clients. Open to new or unpublished authors (with recommendation only). Handles fiction and nonfiction for all ages, picture books, gift books.

    Contact: Letter or e-mail.

    Commission: 15%.

    Fees: Photocopying and phone calls.

    Tips: "Especially looking for children's, teen nonfiction and women's nonfiction. Also fiction that depicts everyday life and everyday faith struggles. Always interested in a strong nonfiction manuscript."

BRANDENBURGH & ASSOCIATES LITERARY AGENCY, 24555 Corte Jaramillo, Murrieta CA 92562. (909)698-5200. E-mail: donbrand@ murrieta.net. Agent: Don Brandenburgh. Recognized in industry. Estab. 1986. Represents 5 clients. No unpublished authors. No new clients at this time. Handles adult nonfiction for the religious market only. Books only.

   Contact: Query/SASE (or no response).
   Commission: 15%; 20% for foreign or dramatic rights.
   Fees: $35 for mailing/materials when contract is signed.
MARIE BROWN ASSOCIATES, INC., 412 W 154th St, New York NY 10032-6302. (212)939-9725. Fax (212)939-9728. E-mail: mbrownlit@aol.com. Agent: Marie Brown. Estab. 1984. Represents 3 clients. Open to unpublished authors and 2-3 new clients/yr. Especially open to African-American and cultural writers. Handles novels for all ages, picture books, adult nonfiction (including religious/inspirational), and secular/crossover books.

   Contact: Letter e-mail. Responds in 10 wks.
   Commission: 15%; foreign 25%.
   Fees: Charges for excessive office expenses (i.e., foreign postage, copying, etc.).
PEMA BROWNE LTD., Pine Rd., HCR Box 104B, Neversink NY 12765. (914) 985-2936. Fax (914)985-7635. Website: www.geocities.com/~pema browneltd. Agents: Perry Browne & Pema Browne. Recognized in industry. Estab. 1966. Represents 10 clients. Open to unpublished authors and new clients. Handles novels & nonfiction for all ages; picture books/novelty books, gift books, crossover books, romance, limited number of scripts/screenplays. Only accepts mss not previously sent to publishers.

   Contact: Letter query with credentials & SASE; no fax or e-mail.
   Commission: 15%; 20% foreign.
   Fees: None.
   Tips: Check at the library in reference section, in *Books in Print,* for books similar to yours. Have good literary skills, neat presentation. Know what has been published and research the genre that interests you.
CAMBRIDGE LITERARY ASSOCIATES, Riverfront Landing, 150 Merrimac St., Ste. 301, Newburyport MA 01950. Phone/fax (978)499-0374. E-mail: MrMV@aol.com. Website: members.aol.com/MrMV/index.html. Agent: Michael Valentino. Represents 20 clients. Open to unpublished authors & new clients. Open to adult and teen religious fiction and nonfiction, screenplays, TV/movie scripts, and secular/crossover books.

   Contact: Letter query.
   Commission: 15%; 20% foreign.
   Fees: Only for pitching screenplays; $180 for 6 mos.
   Tips: "Only well-researched projects written by knowledgable people."
*CARLISLE & COMPANY, 24 E. 64th St., New York NY 10021. (212)813-1881. Fax (212)813-9567. E-mail: mvc@carlisleco.com. Agent: Michael Carlisle. Estab. 1998. Represents 70 clients. Open to few unpublished authors & new clients. Handles some adult religious/inspirational nonfiction, usually of an intellectual nature.

   Contact: Prefers e-query. Responds in 2-3 wks.
   Commission: 15%; foreign 20%.

CASTIGLIA LITERARY AGENCY, 1155 Camino del Mar, PMB 510, Del Mar CA 92014. (858)755-8761. Fax (858)755-7063. Agent: Julie Castiglia. Estab. 1993. Recognized in the industry. Represents 40 clients. Open to unpublished authors (with credentials) & selected new clients. Handles adult nonfiction and secular crossover books.

    Contact: Letter/SASE.

    Commission: 15%; 25% foreign.

    Fees: None.

    Tips: "I do not look at unsolicited manuscripts."

CLAUSEN, MAYS & TAHAN, LLC, 249 W. 43rd St., Ste. 605, New York NY 10001-2815. (212)239-4343. Fax (212)239-5248. Agent: Stedman Mays, Mary M. Tahan. Estab. 1976. Open to some unpublished authors & new clients. Handles adult religious nonfiction.

    Contact: Query or proposal. Responds in 1 month.

    Commission: 15%; foreign 20%.

    Fees: Charges office expenses.

*CVK INTERNATIONAL, 277 Smith St., New York NY 11231. (718)237-4570. Fax (718)237-4571. Agent: Cynthia Neeseman. Handles adult fiction and nonfiction; screenplays; and seeks foreign sales for translations of books published in the US.

    Contact: Query.

+DONE DEAL ENTERTAINMENT, INC., 139 Emily Ave., Elmont NY 11003-4223. (516)355-0928. (877)350-6760. Fax (516)328-6809. E-mail: donedeal@angelfire.com. Websites: www.sisterbetty.com, or www.pat GorgeWalker.com. Agent: Pat G'Orge-Walker. Recognized in industry. Estab. 1992. Represents 2 clients. Open to unpublished and new clients. Handles articles, short stories, secular/crossover books, Gospel comedy, and Christian fiction.

    Contact: Letter, e-mail, fax, or phone.

    Commission: 15%; foreign can be negotiated.

    Fees: Mailing fees. Also offers editing services, proofreading, or storyline editing, for which fees are charged.

    Comments: "We work hand-in-hand with Milligan Books Literary Services. Especially interested in Christian humor."

JANE DYSTEL LITERARY MANAGEMENT, INC., 1 Union Square W, Ste. 904, New York NY 10003. (212)627-9100. Fax (212)627-9313. Website: www.dystel.com. Agents: Jane Dystel, Miriam Goderich and Todd Keithley. Estab. 1994. Recognized in the industry. Represents 5-10 clients. Open to unpublished authors & new clients. Handles fiction & nonfiction for all ages, picture books, gift books, secular/crossover books.

    Contact: Query letter.

    Commission: 15%; foreign 19%.

    Fees: Photocopying is author's responsibility.

*ECLIPSE EDITORIAL SERVICES/TRACI MULLINS, 5110 Golden Hills Ct., Colorado Springs CO 80919. (719)265-5741. Fax (719)265-5752. E-mail: tlmullins@earthlink.net. Does some agenting.

ETHAN ELLENBERG LITERARY AGENCY, 548 Broadway, Ste. 5E, New York NY 10012. (212)431-4554. Fax (212)941-4652. E-mail: Ellenbergagent@

aol.com. Website: www.EthanEllenberg.com. Agent: Ethan Ellenberg. Estab. 1984. Building reputation in the industry. Represents 3 religious clients. Open to unpublished authors & new clients. Handles fiction and nonfiction for all ages, picture books, gift books and secular crossover books.

Contact: Letter only/SASE.

Commission: 15%; foreign 10-20%; co-agent in foreign country 10%.

Fees: Copying and postage expense only.

Tips: "Submit synopsis and first three chapters with SASE in initial query. Mainly interested in compelling fiction."

*JOYCE FARRELL AND ASSOCIATES, 669 Grove St., Upper Montclair NJ 07043. (973)746-6248. Fax (973)746-7348. Agent: Joyce Farrell. Recognized in the industry. Estab. 1985. Represents 20-25 clients. Open to unpublished authors; selectively open to new clients. Handles fiction and nonfiction for children and adults. No fantasy novels. In nonfiction, prefers issue books, or books with historical, scientific, psychological or theological orientation.

Contact: Prefers phone or fax. If by mail, send query letter, author bio, synopsis and SASE.

Commission: 15%.

Fees: Reading fee: up to 50 pgs, $35; complete manuscript $65 additional. Author provides copies for multiple submissions.

Tips: "Check the marketplace to see what is currently available, and whether your treatment of a subject presents a fresh, somewhat different angle than books already published. If not, choose another subject."

+THE FOGELMAN LITERARY AGENCY, 7515 Greenville Ave., Ste. 712, Dallas TX 75231; and 599 Lexington Ave., Ste. 2300, New York NY 10020. (214)361-9956. Fax (214)361-9553. Email: info@fogelman.com. Website: www.fogelman.com. Agent: Evan M. Fogelman. Estab. 1989. Recognized in the industry. Represents 10-15 clients. Open to unpublished authors & new clients. Handles adult novels and nonfiction, women's fiction and nonfiction, gift books, secular/crossover books.

Contact: E-mail or letter.

Commission: 10%; foreign 10%.

Fees: None.

*SARA A. FORTENBERRY LITERARY AGENCY, 1001 Halcyon Ave., Nashville TN 37204. (615)385-9074. Recognized in the industry. Estab. 1995. Represents 40 clients. Open to unpublished authors or new clients only by referral. Handles adult nonfiction and novels, picture books, gift books, and secular crossover books.

Contact: Unpublished authors query by mail; published authors by phone or mail. Query letters should be accompanied by referral, book proposal, and SASE.

Commission: 15%; foreign 10%, plus sub-agent commission.

Fees: Standard expenses directly related to specific projects (copies, messenger, overnight shipping, and postage).

Tips: "For my purposes, a published author is one who has had a book published by a commercial publisher."

*FOUR EMERALDS LITERARY SERVICES/AGENCY, PO Box 438, Vernon NY 13476-0438. (315)829-3356. Fax (315)829-3356 (auto switch). E-mail: MLaClair1@juno.com. Agent: Mary Adele LaClair. Estab 1995. Establishing reputation. Represents 4 clients. Open to unpublished authors; no new clients at this time. Handles adult novels and nonfiction, teen/young adult novels; children's novels and nonfiction; poetry books, gift books; articles, short stories and poetry. Christian books only; no New Age.

    Contact: Letter or e-mail.

    Commission: 10%.

    Fees: Office expenses.

    Tips: "Don't send original or only copy. If on computer, send disk with hard copy indicating software program and version used."

THE FRANKLIN LITERARY AGENCY, 310 Pine Burr St., Ste. B, Vidor TX 77662-6527. Phone/fax (409)769-7938. E-mail: franklinlit@msn.com. Website: www.geocities.com/flagency. Agent: Larry V. Franklin. Recognized in industry. Estab. 1996. Represents 28 clients/14 religious. Open to new and unpublished clients. Handles adult fiction and nonfiction; teen/young adult fiction and nonfiction; secular/crossover books. No textbooks, no biography.

    Contact: Query with short synopsis.

    Commission: 15%; foreign 18%.

    Fees: Representation fees charged to represent contracts (some waived by agency). No reading fees.

    Tips: "Send cover/query letters with SASE for replies. Avoid justified right margins."

SAMUEL FRENCH, INC., 45 W. 25th St., New York NY 10010-2751. (212)206-8990. Fax (212)206-1429. Agent: Lawrence Harbison. Estab. 1830. Handles religious/inspirational stage plays. Open to new clients.

    Contact: Query or send complete manuscript.

    Commission: 10% professional production royalties.

    Fees: None.

GENESIS CREATIVE GROUP, 28126 Peacock Ridge, Ste. 104, Rancho Palos Verdes CA 90275. (310)541-9232. Fax (310)541-9532. E-mail: KenRUnger @aol.com. Agent: Ken Unger. Estab. 1998; developing recognition in industry. Represents 5 clients. Open to unpublished authors and new clients. Handles screenplays, TV/movie scripts.

    Contact: Send one-page query with personal information, project description and target market, by mail or e-mail only. No phone calls; no unsolicited manuscripts.

    Commission: 15%; may vary by type of project.

    Fees: Office fees for long distance calls and postage only.

    Tips: "We formed this company to represent material to film and television community, no books. We want material that presents values based on Judeo-Christian tradition. In nonfiction we have no interest in rehashed dogma."

*GOOD NEWS LITERARY SERVICE, Box 587, Visalia CA 93279. Phone/fax (209)627-6241 (call first for fax). Agent: Cynthia A. Wachner. Recognized in industry. Estab. 1986. Represents 6 clients. Not open to unpublished authors (must have one published title). Open to new clients. Handles fiction and nonfiction for all ages, picture books, screenplays, TV/movie scripts, photos and games.

    Contact: Mail; query first. Short phone queries OK.

    Commission: Varies according to project.

    Fees: Requires $250 retainer fee. Charges for editorial services, when needed. Query for rates.

    Tips: "Believe your message. Work hard. Write eloquently. Package professionally to sell."

*STEPHEN GRIFFITH, PO Box 939, Leicester NC 28748. Unlisted phone. Fax (704)683-2851. Recognized in industry. Estab. 1990. Not open to unpublished authors. Open only to referrals from existing clients. Handles novels for all ages and adult nonfiction.

    Contact: By mail or fax.

    Commission: 15% (10% on reprinted books).

    Fees: None.

GROSVENOR LITERARY AGENCY, 5510 Grosvenor Ln., Bethesda MD 20814. (301)564-6231. Fax (301)581-9401. E-mail: dcgrosveno@aol.com. Agent: Deborah Grosvenor. Estab. 1995. Represents 30 clients. Open to few unpublished authors & new clients. Handles adult religious/inspirational nonfiction.

    Contact: Letter. Responds in 1-2 mos.

    Commission: 15%; foreign 20%.

    Fees: None.

HARTLINE LITERARY AGENCY, 123 Queenston Dr., Pittsburgh PA 15235. (412)829-2483 or (412)829-2495. Fax (412)829-2450. E-mail: jachart@aol.com, or jahart@Hartlinemarketing.com. Website: www.hartlinemarketing.com. Agent: Joyce A. Hart. Recognized in industry. Estab. 1992. Represents 12 clients. Published authors preferred. Open to published authors (or selected unpublished). Handles adult novels and nonfiction,secular/crossover books. No science fiction or poetry.

    Contact: Phone, letter, fax, e-mail.

    Commission: 15%.

    Fees: Office expenses; no reading fee for published authors.

    Tips: "Please ask for our literary guidelines if you have questions about preparing proposals. Working together we can make sure your manuscript gets the exposure and attention it deserves."

*JEFF HERMAN AGENCY, 332 Bleecker St., New York NY 10014. (212)941-0540. Fax (212)941-0614. Agents: Jeff Herman and Deborah Levine. Estab. 1986. Recognized in the industry. Represents 100 clients. Open to unpublished authors and new clients. Handles adult nonfiction (spirituality) and gift books.

    Contact: Query by mail.

    Commission: 15%.

    Fees: No reading or management fees.

    Tips: "I love a good book from the heart."

+HIS IMAGE PUBLISHERS AGENCY, 6310 Ranch Mission Rd., Ste. 339, San Diego CA 92108-1904. Phone/fax (619)282-7738. E-mail: kiplon-taylor@

juno.com. Website: my.websitenow.com/web5/00461/kman40. Agent: Kiplon L. Taylor. Estab. 1984. Recognized in the industry. Represents 1 client. Open to unpublished authors and new clients. Handles fiction and nonfiction for all ages, poetry books, gift books.

Contact: Query letter with manuscript.

Commission: 15%; foreign 15%+.

Fees: None.

Tips: "Maximum of 300 pages on all novels (special circumstances will be negotiable). You must include return postage with all submissions."

*HOLUB & ASSOCIATES, 24 Old Colony Rd., North Stonington CT 06359. (203)535-0689. Agent: William Holub. Recognized by Catholic publishers. Estab. 1966. Open to unpublished authors. Handles adult nonfiction; possibly picture books; Christian living in secular society.

Contact: Query with outline, 2 sample chapters, intended audience, and bio.

Commission: 15%.

Fees: Postage and photocopying.

*JOY S. LITERARY AGENCY, PO Box 957856, Hoffman Estates IL 60195. (847)310-0003. Fax (847)310-0893. E-mail: joyco2@juno.com. Agent: Carol S. Joy. Recognized in industry. Estab. 1996. Represents 15 clients. Open to unpublished authors. No new clients at this time. Handles adult novels and nonfiction. Always include SASE. Proofread your work carefully.

Contact: Letter.

Commission: 15%.

Fees: Charges only for extra editorial services.

NATASHA KERN LITERARY AGENCY INC., PO Box 2908, Portland OR 97208-2908. (503)297-6190. Fax (503)297-8241. Website: www.natasha kern.com. Agent: Natasha Kern. Recognized in the industry. Estab. 1986. Represents 5 clients. Open to unpublished authors and new clients. Handles adult fiction and nonfiction, crossover books.

Contact: Accepts queries by letter or online queries through their Website.

Commission: 15%; 20% foreign (includes foreign-agent commission).

Fees: No reading fee.

Tips: "We represent commercial properties only; adult only."

THE KNIGHT AGENCY, PO Box 550648, Atlanta GA 30355. Fax (404)237-3439. E-mail: Deidremk@aol.com. Website: www.knightagency.net. Agent: Deidre Knight. Recognized in industry. Estab. 1996. Represents 40 clients. Open to unpublished and new clients (very selective). Handles adult fiction & nonfiction, gift books, secular/crossover books.

Contact: Letter; no phone or fax.

Commission: 15%; 20-25% on foreign & film rights (includes subagent commission).

Fees: Charges only for office expenses.

Tips: "We're always looking for strong nonfiction, particularly with crossover appeal to the ABA. In children's or young adult, we're only considering authors who have published previously. In fiction, we're no longer accepting mystery or action-adventure submissions."

THE LITERARY GROUP INTL., 270 Lafayette St., #1505, New York NY 11204. (212)274-1616. Fax (212)274-9876. E-mail: Litgrpfw@hotmail. com. Website: www.theliterarygroup.com. Agent: Frank Weimann. Estab. 1986. Represents 10 clients. Open to new and unpublished authors. Handles adult & teen fiction & nonfiction, children's novels and picture books (over age 6), cookbooks, secular/crossover, gift books & short stories.

    Contact: Letter.

    Commission: 15%; foreign 20%.

    Fees: Extraordinary expenses, including copying & overnight shipping.

    Tips: "Looking for fresh, original spiritual fiction and nonfiction. We offer a written contract which may be canceled after 30 days."

DONALD MAASS LITERARY AGENCY, 157 W. 57th St., Ste. 703, New York NY 10019. (212)757-7755. Website: www.javanet.com/~nephilim/study. html. Agents: Donald Maass and Jennifer Jackson. Estab. 1980. Represents 100 clients. Open to unpublished authors and new clients. Handles religious fiction.

    Contact: One-page query letter/SASE, by mail only.

    Commission: 15%; foreign 20%.

    Fees: May charge office expenses.

MARANATHA MINISTRIES INTERNATIONAL, INC., 3800 Scarlet Oak Ln., Lexington KY 40514. (606)296-4377. E-mail: dhuddleston@maranatha ministriesintl.org. Website: www.MaranathaMinistriesIntl.org. Agent: Dr. David W. Huddleston. Recognized in the industry. Estab. 1998. Handles 12 clients. Open to unpublished authors; no new clients. Handles fiction & nonfiction for all ages; poetry books, gift books.

    Contact: E-mail.

    Commission: 15%; 15% foreign.

MARCH MEDIA, INC., 1114 Oman Dr., Brentwood TN 37027. (615)377-1146. Fax (615)373-1705. E-mail: marchmed@bellsouth.net. Agents: Etta Wilson & Cathey Clark. Estab. 1989. Recognized in the industry. Represents 17 clients. Open to new clients only if she sees a ready market for their writing. Handles teen/YA and children's novels and nonfiction, picture books, and gift books.

    Contact: Letter or e-mail.

    Commission: 15%.

    Fees: Only if agreed on in contract.

    Tips: "I prefer humor, tight plotting, and strong Christian values."

MULTIMEDIA PRODUCT DEVELOPMENT, INC., 410 S. Michigan Ave., Ste 724, Chicago IL 60615. (312)922-3063. Fax (312)922-1905. E-mail: mpdinc@aol.com. Agent: Jane Jordan Browne. Recognized in the industry. Estab. 1971. Represents 15 clients. Open to unpublished authors and new clients if talented and professional. Handles fiction and nonfiction for all ages, picture books, gift books, and secular/crossover books.

Contact: Query letter/SASE only.

Commission: 15%, foreign 20%.

Fees: No reading fees; charges for photocopies, and also foreign phone, fax, and postage.

BK NELSON LITERARY AGENCY, 84 Woodland Rd., Pleasantville NY 10570 and 1276 N Palm Canyon Dr., Palm Springs CA 92262-4411. (914)741-1322 (NY) and (310)858-7006 (CA). Fax (914)741-1324 and (310)858-7967. E-mail: bknelson4@cs.com. Website: www.bknelson.com. Agents: B.K. Nelson, Leonard Ashback. Recognized in the industry. Estab. 1980. Represents 4 clients. Open to unpublished authors and new clients. Handles adult, children's and teen fiction, adult and children's nonfiction, picture books, TV/movie scripts, screenplays, gift books, crossover books, and educational. Also CD-ROM, audio tapes and lecturers.

Contact: Query by letter first.

Commission: 20%, foreign 25%.

Fees: $350 reading fee for complete mss or $2/pg for proposals with sample chapters. Non-refundable. SASE required. Takes two weeks to read.

Comments: "Our success with first-book authors is outstanding. Work with us. Listen and follow agency guidelines to insure a good presentation. We'll do the business part—you write the bestsellers."

A PICTURE OF YOU AGENCY, 1176 Elizabeth Dr., Hamilton OH 45013. Phone/fax (513)863-1108. E-mail: apoy1@aol.com. Agent: Lenny Minelli. Estab. 1995. Branching out into Christian market. Represents 3 clients. Open to unpublished authors & new clients. Handles novels and nonfiction for all ages, screenplays, TV/movie scripts.

Contact: Query with proposal.

Commission: 10%; 15% foreign.

Fees: Postage and phone calls only.

Tips: "Make sure your material is the best it can be before seeking an agent. Always enclose an SASE."

*REYNOLDS COMPANIES, 321 N 46th Ave. W, Duluth MN 55807-1450. (218)624-1669. E-mail: reygen@uslink.net. Agent: Thomas Reynolds. Open to new clients. Handles religious fiction. Specializes in marketing books to the movie and television industry.

#DAMARIS ROWLAND AGENCY, 510 E. 23rd St., #8-G, New York NY 10010-5020. (212)475-8942. Fax (212)358-9411. Agents: Damaris Rowland and Steve Axelrod. Estab. 1994. Represents 50 clients. Open to unpublished authors & new clients. Handles religious/inspirational nonfiction.

Contact: Outline/proposal.

Commission: 15%; foreign 20%.

Fees: Some office expenses.

SCHIAVONE LITERARY AGENCY, INC., 236 Trails End, West Palm Beach FL 33413-2135. Phone/fax (561)966-9294. E-mail: profschia@aol.com. Website: www.freeyelow.com/members8/schiavone/index.html. Agent: James Schiavone, Ed.D. Recognized in the industry. Estab. 1997. Represents 6 clients. Open to unpublished and new clients. Handles adult, teen and children's fiction and nonfiction; picture books; screenplays; TV/movie scripts; celebrity biography; secular/crossover books.

Contact: Query letter/SASE; one-page e-mail query (no attachments).

Commission: 15%, foreign 20%.

Fees: No reading fees; office expenses only.

Tips: Works primarily with published authors; will consider first-time authors with excellent material. Actively seeking books on spirituality, major religions, and alternative health. Very selective on first novels.

SEDGEBAND LITERARY ASSOCIATES, 7312 Martha Ln., Fort Worth TX 76112-5336. (817)496-3652. Fax (425)952-9518. E-mail: Sedgeband@ aol.com. Website: members.home.net/sedgeband. Agent: Ginger Norton. Estab. 1997. Recognized in the industry. Represents 3 clients with religious books. Open to unpublished authors & new clients. Handles religious fiction & nonfiction, secular/crossover books. Manuscripts must be at least 70,000 wds.

Contact: E-mail or letter; fax if necessary.

Commission: 15%; foreign 20%.

Fees: Office expenses only.

Tips: Make your query as good as it can be. First impressions of your writing can be the ticket to retaining an agent. Do not be rude or egotistical.

THE SEYMOUR AGENCY/MARYSUE SEYMOUR, 475 Miner St. Rd., Canton NY 13617. (315)386-1831. Fax (315)386-1037. E-mail: mseymour@slic. com. Website: www.pages.slic.com/mseymour. Agent: Mary Sue Seymour. Estab. 1992. Recognized in the industry. Represents 15 religious clients. Open to unpublished authors & new clients. Handles novels and nonfiction for all ages.

Contact: Query letter with first 50 pages of mss.

Commission: 15%; 12½% for published authors; foreign 12 1/2%.

Fees: None for published authors. For unpublished: charges $3 per publisher for postage costs; refundable if book sells. Sometimes offers to edit first 50 pages for $50 and asks to see rewrite for consideration.

Tips: Mary Sue is a New York State certified (but retired) teacher. Former Sunday school teacher and superintendent.

THE SEYMOUR AGENCY/MIKE SEYMOUR, 475 Miner St. Rd., Canton NY 13617. (315)379-0028. Fax (315)386-1036. E-mail: mseymour@slic.com. Website: www.slic.com/mseymour. Agent: Mike Seymour. Estab. 1992. Not yet recognized in the industry. Represents 10 religious clients. Open to unpublished authors & new clients. Handles novels and nonfiction for teens and adults; nonfiction for children; secular/crossover books.

Contact: Query letter with first 50 pages of ms.

Commission: 15%; 12½% for published authors.

Fees: None.

Tips: "Will look at Christian romance novels and nonfiction proposals with mass appeal."

*****THE SHEPARD AGENCY**, Pawling Savings Bank Bldg., Ste. 3, Southeast Plaza, Rt. 22, Brewster NY 10509. (914)279-2900/3236. Fax (914)279-3239. Agents: Jean or Lance Shepard. Recognized in the industry. Estab.

1986. Represents 8 clients. Open to unpublished authors. Handles fiction and nonfiction for all ages; no picture books; especially business, reference, professional, self-help, cooking and crafts. Books only.

Contact: Query letter and sample material.

Commission: 15%.

Fees: None except long-distance calls and copying.

SOUTHEAST LITERARY AGENCY, PO Box 910, Sharpes FL 32959. (321)632-5019. Agent: Debbie Fine. Recognized in the industry. Estab. 1996. Represents 10 clients. Open to new clients and unpublished authors. Handles fiction and nonfiction for all ages, few picture books, secular/crossover books, some poetry books.

Contact: Query letter with overview, postage for return, and SASE for correspondence. Disposable complete manuscript with synopsis preferred.

Commission: 10%, foreign 20%.

Fees: Only for out-of-pocket expenses for postage, packaging, long-distance calls and copying.

Tips: Include return postage and packaging if you want submissions returned, and keep calls to a minimum.

*THE THORNTON LITERARY AGENCY, 1431 SE Knight, Portland OR 97202. (503)232-8729. Fax (503)233-8633. E-mail: roxy@thornlit.com. Website: www.thornlit.com. Agent: Roxann Caraway. Estab. 1997. Not recognized in the industry. Represents 2 clients. Open to unpublished authors and actively seeking new clients. Handles fiction and nonfiction for all ages, picture books, poetry books, anthologies.

Contact: Query by e-mail, if possible.

Commission: 15%.

Fees: None.

Tips: "We are a very young agency, but are aggressively marketing manuscripts. Please pay close attention to the technical merit of manuscripts."

+CHARLOTTE TREJOS LITERARY CONSULTANT, 510 Copper Basin Rd., Lot 15, Prescott AZ 86303-4637.

#SCOTT WAXMAN AGENCY, INC., 1650 Broadway, Ste. 1011, New York NY 10019. (212)262-2388. Fax (212)262-0119. E-mail: gracem@swagency.net. Agent: Scott Waxman and Grace Madamba. Recognized in the industry. Estab. 1996 (5 years' experience). Represents 60 clients. Open to unpublished authors and new clients. Handles adult fiction and nonfiction.

Contact: Query letter or e-mail.

Commission: 15%.

Fees: Office expenses.

WILLIAM PENS, PO Box 6426, Longmont CO 80501-2078. (303)485-5851. Fax (303)485-5864. E-mail: Wmpens@aol.com. Agent: William D. Watkins. Estab. 1986. Recognized in the industry. Represents about 50 clients. Very open to unpublished authors and new clients. Handles adult and teen novels and nonfiction, gift books, secular/crossover books, and academic books.

Contact: Query by letter, fax or e-mail.

Commission: 15%; foreign 20%.

Fees: Rates available upon request.

WILLIAMS' LITERARY AGENCY, RR 1 Box 109H, Kosciusko MS 39090-9706. (888)241-5616. E-mail: williamsagency@geocities.com. Website: www. geocities.com/williamsagency. Agent: Sheri Homan. Estab. 1997. Recognized in the industry. Represents 40+ clients. Open to unpublished authors & new clients (currently backlogged on requests, allow 3-8 weeks for response). Handles novels and nonfiction for all ages, picture books, poetry books, gift books, articles/short stories/poetry.

> **Contact:** Letter or e-mail.
>
> **Commission:** 15%; 10% foreign.
>
> **Fees: None.**
>
> **Tips:** "On articles and short stories, query first with samples and writing history."

+WINGS UNLIMITED/CRISTINE BOLLEY, 712 N. Sweet Gum Ave., Broken Arrow OK 74012-2156. (918)250-9239. E-mail: WingsUnlimited@aol.com.

WOLGEMUTH & ASSOCIATES, INC., 8600 Crestgate Circle, Orlando FL 32819. (407)909-9445. Fax (407)909-9446. E-mail: wolgemuth@earthlink. net. Agent: Robert D. Wolgemuth. Well recognized in the industry. Estab. 1992. Represents 18 clients. No new clients or unpublished authors. Handles mostly adult nonfiction, most other types of books handled only for current clients.

> **Contact:** By letter.
>
> **Commission:** 15%.
>
> **Fees:** None.
>
> **Tips:** "We work with authors who are either best-selling authors or potentially best-selling authors. Consequently, we want to represent clients with broad market appeal."

WOMACK PUBLISHING AGENCY, 468 W. Esperanza Blvd., Green Valley AZ 85614-2711. (520)625-9392 or (520)241-3884. E-mail: davewomack@aol. com. Website: www.dwomack.com. Agent: David A. Womack.

> **Contact:** Prefers e-mail.

THE WRITER'S EDGE—See listing under Editorial Services—Illinois.

+WRITERS HOUSE, 21 West 26th St., New York NY 10010. (212)685-2400. Fax (212)685-1781. E-mail: ksolem@writershouse.com. Agent: Karen Solem. Recognized in the industry. Handles religious fiction & nonfiction; romance novels, mysteries, thrillers, animals & nature, gardening, cookbooks, and style.

> **Contact:** Query with or without sample material; e-query OK.
>
> **Commission:** 15% on adult; 10% on yg. adult & children; 20% foreign.
>
> **Fees:** No reading fees.

YATES & YATES, LLP, 505 S. Main St., Ste. 100, Orange CA 92868. (714)835-3742. Fax (714)543-0858. Website: www.yates-yates.com. Estab. 1989. Recognized in the industry. Represents 50 clients. Not currently open to unpublished authors & new clients. Handles novels and nonfiction for all ages, picture books, poetry books, gift books, and secular/crossover books.

Contact: Letter or fax.
Commission: 15%.
Fees: No fees.
Tips: "The law firm of Yates & Yates, LLP, in addition to providing traditional literary agenting services, also serves the legal needs of its author clients, having extensive experience in intellectual property law (including copyright and trademark), entertainment law, tax law, estate planning and business law."

*THE YEOMAN'S SERVICE, 3227 Ella West Cir., Lynnville TN 38472-5228. Phone/fax (931)527-0101. E-mail: sergevirge@netzero.net. Agent: Virginia S. Youman. Note: Spelling difference is correct.

+ALAN YOUNGREN, LITERARY AGENT, 1243 Hawthorne, Downers Grove IL 60515. (630)964-7027. Fax (530)905-5978. E-mail: Ayoungren@worldnet.att.net. Estab. 1998. Recognized in the industry. Represents 8 clients. Open to unpublished authors and new clients. Handles adult fiction & nonfiction, secular/crossover books.
   Contact: Letter, fax, or e-mail (no phone calls).
   Commission: 15%; 20% foreign.
   Fees: No reading fees.

ADDITIONAL AGENTS

NOTE: The following agents did not return a questionnaire but have been identified as secular agents who handle religious manuscripts. Be sure to send queries first if you wish to submit to them. Always check out an agent thoroughly before committing to work with him or her. Ask for references and a list of books represented, check with the Better Business Bureau, and ask your writing friends.

*ABBEY HOUSE LITERARY AGENCY, 2301 John Matich Dr., Colton CA 92324-9550. Agent: L. Steven Hattendorf. Estab. 1995. Open to unpublished authors & new clients. Handles religious fiction.
   Contact: Visit Website for query and submission information.
   Tips: "This agency is headed by an attorney, and we're actively seeking writers."

ALLRED AND ALLRED LITERARY AGENTS, 7834 Alabama Ave., Canoga Park CA 91304-4905. (818)346-4313. Agent: Robert Allred. Estab. 1991. Represents 1 client. Open to unpublished authors & new clients. Handles religious/inspirational fiction and nonfiction.
   Contact: Query. Responds in 3 wks to 2 mos.
   Commission: 10%; foreign 10%.
   Fees: None.

*A.L.P. LITERARY AGENCY (Author's Launching Pad), PO Box 5069, Redwood City CA 94063. Phone/fax (415)326-6918. Agent: Devorah B. Harris. Estab. 1997. Represents 8-12 clients. Open to unpublished authors & new clients. Handles adult religious/inspirational novels; any adult nonfiction.
   Contact: Outline/1-2 chapters. Responds in 2-4 wks.
   Fees: Charges office expenses, $300 limit.

*ANGELIC ENTERTAINMENT LITERARY AGENCY, 555 W. Beech St., Ste. 525, San Diego CA 92101. (619)238-8234. Agent: Mark Maine. Estab. 1999. Motion pictures. 2000.

*AUTHORS ALLIANCE INC., 25 Claremont Ave., Ste. 3C, New York NY 10027. Phone/fax (212)662-9788. Agent: Chris Crane. Represents 25 clients. Open to unpublished authors & new clients. Handles religious/inspirational nonfiction.

    Contact: Outline/3 chapters. Responds in 2-5 wks.

    Commission: 15%; foreign 10%.

    Fees: Charges office expenses.

*BARBARA BAUER LITERARY AGENCY, 179 Washington Ave., Matawan NJ 07747-2944. (732)566-1213. E-mail: cannoliq@msn.com. Agent: Barbara Bauer. Estab. 1984. Handles religious fiction and nonfiction; picture books; poetry books.

+JENNY BENT, GRAYBILL & ENGLISH, L.L.C., 1920 N St. NW, #620, Washington DC 20036. Fax (202)457-0662. E-mail: jenlbent @aol.com. Agent: Jenny Bent. Estab. 1997. Secular agent who handles religious/inspirational books. Represents 40 clients. Open to unpublished authors & new clients. Handles adult novels and nonfiction.

    Contact: Query with outline and proposal; e-query OK.

    Commission: 15%; foreign 25%.

    Fees: Office expenses.

#PAM BERNSTEIN & ASSOCIATES, INC., 790 Madison Ave., Ste. 310, New York NY 10021. (212)288-1700. Fax (212)288-3054. Agents: Pam Bernstein and Donna Downing. Estab. 1992. Represents 50 clients. Open to unpublished authors & new clients. Handles religious nonfiction.

    Contact: Query.

    Commission: 15%; 20% foreign.

    Fees: Postage & photocopying only.

+BLEEKER STREET ASSOCIATES, INC., 532 LaGuardia Pl., New York NY 10012. (212)677-4492. Fax (212)388-0001. Agent: Agnes Birnbaum. Estab. 1984. Secular agent who handles religious/inspirational books. Represents 60 clients. Open to unpublished authors & new clients. Handles adult novels and nonfiction.

    Contact: Query by mail only.

    Commission: 15%; foreign 15-25%.

    Fees: Office fees to $150 max.

*THE BOSTON LITERARY GROUP, 156 Mount Auburn St., Cambridge MA 02138-4875. (617)547-0800. Fax (617)876-8474. E-mail: agent@boston literary.com. Agent: Elizabeth Mack. Estab. 1994. Represents 30 clients. Open to unpublished authors & new clients. Handles nonfiction books (mostly), novels and scripts; including religious/inspirational.

    Contact: Query. Responds in 6 wks.

    Commission: 15%; foreign 10%.

    Fees: Office expenses. Makes referrals to editing services.

BRUCE BARBOUR LITERARY AGENCY. Phone/fax (615)790-4180. Website: www.Brucebarbour.com. Agent: Bruce Barbour.

*CHARISMA COMMUNICATIONS, LTD., 210 E. 39th St., New York NY

10016. (212)832-3020. Fax (212)867-6906. Agent: James W. Grau. Estab. 1972. Represents 10 clients. Open to unpublished authors & new clients. Handles adult religious/inspirational novels.

    Contact: Proposal. Responds in 1-2 mos.

    Commission: 15%; foreign commission varies.

    Fees: None.

*CATHERINE CRONIN LITERARY AGENCY, PO Box 618, Bible School Park NY 13737-0618. E-mail: stuckart@spectra.net. Website: www.elit.com. Agent: Catherine Cronin. Open to new clients. Handles religious fiction, screenplays.

    Contact: See Website.

*ERICA BOOKS LITERARY AGENCY, PO Box 1109, Frederick MD 21702. (301)631-0747. Fax (301)631-1922. Agent: Erica Feberwee. Open to unpublished U.S. authors & new clients. Handles religious fiction and nonfiction.

    Contact: By mail or e-mail (no attached files).

    Fees: No fees for in-house editing.

FIRST LOOK TALENT AND LITERARY AGENCY, 511 Avenue of the Americas, Ste. 3000, New York NY 10011. (212)216-9522. Or, 264 S. La Cienega, Ste. 1068, Beverly Hills CA 90211. (310)967-5761. E-mail: firstlookny@firstlookagency.com or firstlookla@firstlookagency.com. Website: www.firstlookagency.com. Agent: Burt Avalon. Estab. 1997. Open to unpublished authors & new clients. Handles religious fiction and scripts. Specializes in movie, TV and play scripts.

*SARAH JANE FREYMANN LITERARY AGENCY, 59 W. 71st St., New York NY 10023. (212)362-9277. Fax (212)501-8240. Agent: Sarah Jane Freymann. Represents 100 clients. Open to unpublished authors & new clients. Handles religious/inspirational nonfiction.

    Contact: Query.

    Commission: 15%, 20% foreign.

    Fees: Charges office expenses.

+SHERYL B. FULLERTON ASSOCIATION, 1095 Amito Dr., Berkeley CA 94705. E-mail: sfullerton@aol.com.

*SUSAN HERNER RIGHTS AGENCY, PO Box 303, Scarsdale NY 10583-0303. (914)725-8967. Fax 914)725-8969. Agents: Susan Herner & Sue Yuen. Estab. 1987. Represents 100 clients. Very open to unpublished authors & new clients. Handles adult religious/inspirational nonfiction.

    Contact: Proposal. Responds in one month.

    Commission: 15%; foreign 20%.

    Fees: Charges office expenses.

*THE NED LEAVITT AGENCY, 70 Wooster St., #4F, New York NY 10012. (212)334-0999. Agent: Ned Leavitt. Handles religious fiction and nonfiction.

#MARGRET MCBRIDE LITERARY AGENCY, 7744 Fay Ave., Ste 201, La Jolla CA 92037. (858)454-1550. Fax (858)454-2156. Agent: Margret McBride. Estab. 1980. Represents 50 clients. Open to unpublished authors & new clients. Handles religious/inspirational nonfiction.

    Contact: Query with synopsis.

Commission: 15%; 10% dramatic sales; foreign 25%.

Fees: Office expenses.

THE MIDWEST LITERARY AND ENTERTAINMENT MANAGEMENT GROUP, 2545 Hilliard-Rome Rd., Ste. 320, Hilliard OH 43026. E-mail: Midwestlit@aol.com. Website: www.hwei.com. Agent: Vivian Hall. Handles religious fiction, and can negotiate film, music, and TV production rights.

Commission: 15%; foreign 20%.

Fees: Charges $450 on acceptance of new client. No reading fee.

+WILLIAM MORRIS LITERARY AGENCY, 2100 West End Ave., #1000, Nashville TN 37203. (615)963-3000. Agents: Claudia Cross and Matt Bialer.

*NEW WRITING LITERARY AGENCY, Box 1812, Amherst NY 14226. (716)834-1067. E-mail: wordfellow@aol.com. Agent: Mason Deitz. Open to unpublished authors & new clients. Handles religious fiction and non-fiction, picture books, poetry books, gift books.

Contact: Complete ms (if available), reading fee and SASE.

Commission: 12½%; foreign 18½%.

Fees: $40 reading fee and office expenses.

KATHI J. PATON LITERARY AGENCY, 19 W. 55th St., New York NY 10019-4907. (212)265-6586. E-mail: KjpLitBiz@aol.com. Agent: Kathi Paton. Estab. 1987. Handles adult religious/inspirational nonfiction.

Contact: Proposal/1 chapter for nonfiction; first 40 pages/summary for fiction.

Commission: 15%; foreign 20%.

Fees: For photocopying.

*STEPHEN PEVNER, INC., 248 W. 73rd St., Second Floor, New York NY 10023. (212)496-0474 or (323)464-5546. Fax (212)496-0796. Agent: Stephen Pevner. Estab. 1991. Represents under 50 clients. Open to unpublished authors & new clients. Handles religious/inspirational nonfiction.

Contact: Query/outline/proposal.

Commission: 10%; foreign 10%.

Fees: Commission only.

+THE GAIL ROSSMAN LITERARY AGENCY, 1666 Connecticut Ave. NW #500, Washington DC 20009. (202)328-3282. Fax (202)328-9162. Agent: Jennifer Manguera. Estab. 1988. Represents 200 clients. Open to unpublished authors & new clients. Handles adult religious/inspirational novels & nonfiction.

Contact: Query/SASE.

Commission: 15%; foreign 25%.

Fees: Office expenses.

+CAROL SUSAN ROTH, LITERARY REPRESENTATION, 1824 Oak Creek Dr., Palo Alto CA 94304. E-mail: carol@AUTHORBEST.com.

+SUSAN SCHULMAN—A LITERARY AGENCY, 454 W. 44TH St., New York NY 10036. E-mail: schulman@aol.com.

+JACQUELINE SIMENAUER LITERARY AGENCY, PO Box 1039, Barnegat NJ 08005-4039.

+UNITED TRIBES/JAN-ERIK GUERTH, 240 W. 35th St., #500, New York NY

10001. (212)534-7646. E-mail: janguerth@aol.com. Website: www.united tribes.com. Agent: Jan Erik-Guerth. Estab. 1998. Represents 40 clients. Open to few unpublished authors. Handles adult religious/inspirational novels & nonfiction. Specializes in "Spirituality of the Everyday Life" and comparative religions.

Contact: Send outline/3 chapters; e-query OK.

Commission: 15%; foreign 20%.

Fees: No information on fees.

+**STEPHANIE VON HIRSCHBERG LITERARY AGENCY,** 767 Third Ave., 39th Floor, New York NY 10017.

+**KARL WEBER LITERARY,** 2 Tanglewild Rd., Chappaqua NY 10514. E-mail: KWeberLit@aol.com.

*****WESTCHESTER LITERARY AGENCY,** 2533 Egret Lake Dr., West Palm Beach FL 33413. (561)642-2908. Fax (561)439-2228. E-mail: neilagency@msn. com. Agent: Neil McCluskey. Estab. 1991. Open to unpublished authors & new clients. Handles religious fiction and nonfiction.

CONTESTS

Note: Below is a listing of all the contests mentioned throughout this guide, plus additional contests that will be of interest. Some are sponsored by book publishers or magazines, some by conferences or writers' groups. For all but the additional contests at the end, you will find full listings for each of these sponsors elsewhere in the book. Look up the publishers in the index; the conferences and groups will be listed in those sections by state. Send an SASE to each one you are interested in to obtain a copy of their contest rules and guidelines. To determine if a contest is legitimate or just a scam, go to: www.sfwa.org/beware/contests.html.

SPONSORED BY BOOK PUBLISHERS

MARGUERITE DE ANGELI PRIZE. Sponsored by Bantam Doubleday Dell Books for Young Readers. Open to U.S. and Canadian authors who have not previously published a book for middle-grade readers. Submissions must be contemporary or historical fiction for ages 7-10 (40-144 manuscript pages) that examine the diversity of the American experience. Deadline: April 1 - June 30th. Winner receives a $1,500 cash prize and book contract with a $3,500 advance. For rules, send SASE to: Marguerite de Angeli Prize, Bantam Doubleday Dell BFYR, 1540 Broadway, New York NY 10036. (212)782-9000.

READ 'N RUN BOOKS, PO Box 294, Rhododendron OR 97049. (503)622-4798. Fax (503)658-6233. Crumb Elbow Publishing. Michael P. Jones, pub.
    Contest: Poetry contest. Send SASE for information.

WORD FOR WORD PUBLISHING CO., 44 Court St., Ste. 1210, Brooklyn NY 11201. (718)852-2222. Fax (718)875-5398. E-mail: Word4wrd@aol.com. Website: www.Come.To/WordForWord. Carolyn M. Davis, pres.
    Contest: Annual Writing Contest for Young Christian Writers.

YALE UNIVERSITY PRESS, 302 Temple St., New Haven CT 06520. (203)432-0960. Fax (203)432-0948. Website: http://www.yale.edu/yup. Charles Grench, ed-in-chief/religion.
    Contest: Yale's Series of Younger Poets Competition. Open to poets under 40 who have not had a book of poetry published. Submit manuscripts of 48-64 pages in February. Entry fee $15. Send SASE for guidelines.

SPONSORED BY ADULT PERIODICALS

THE BREAKTHROUGH INTERCESSOR, PO Box 121, Lincoln VA 20160. (540)338-4131. Fax (540)338-1934. E-mail: breakthrough@intercessors. org. Website: www.intercessors.org.

Contest: Pays $25 for article with most reader impact.

*BRIDAL GUIDES, PO Box 1264, Huntington WV 25714. (304)523-2162. Tellstar Productions/Interdenominational. Shannon Bridget Murphy, ed. **Contest:** Send SASE for contest information.

#CATHOLIC DIGEST, 2115 Summit Ave., St. Paul MN 55105-1081. (651)962-6739. Fax (651)962-6758. E-mail: cdigest@stthomas.edu. Website: www.CatholicDigest.org.
　　Contest: See Website for current contest or send an SASE.

#CHRISTIAN PARENTING TODAY, 465 Gundersen Dr., Carol Stream IL 60188-2498. (630)260-6200. Fax (630)260-0114. E-mail: CPTmag@aol.com. Website: www.Christianparenting.net.
　　Contest: Sponsors several per year.

CHRISTIAN READER, 465 Gundersen Dr., Carol Stream IL 60188-2498. (630)260-6200. Fax (630)260-0114. E-mail: creditoria@aol.com. Website: www.christianreader.net. Christianity Today, Inc. Bonne Steffen, ed.
　　Contest: Annual contest, March 1 deadline. Prizes $1,000, $500, $250. Articles to 1,250 words. Send SASE for contest fact sheet.

CHRISTIANITY AND THE ARTS, PO Box 118088, Chicago IL 60611. (312) 642-8606. Fax (312)266-7719. E-mail: CHRNARTS@aol.com. Website: www.christianarts.net.
　　Contest: Poetry contests with cash prizes. Deadlines vary. Entry fee is discounted subscription to the magazine at $15.

CREATION ILLUSTRATED, PO Box 7955, Auburn CA 95604. (530)269-1424. Fax (530)269-1428. E-mail: creation@foothill.net. Website: www.creation illustrated.com. Tom Ish, ed/pub.
　　Contest: Photography contest in each issue for best nature, animal and creation shots.

FAITH TODAY, M.I.P. Box 3745, Markham ON L3R 0Y4 Canada. (905)479-5885. Fax (905)479-4742. E-mail: ft@efc-canada.com. Website: www.efc-canada.com. Evangelical Fellowship of Canada. Larry Matthews, mng ed.
　　Contest: The Annual God Uses Ink Writer's Contest is open to work published in 2000, until February 7, 2001. Contest guidelines and entry forms available from *Faith Today.* Recognizes best writing of Canadian authors (must be Canadian citizen—can live anywhere). Prizes are $250 for best books, $150 for best short story, essay and third-person, nonfiction article. New category this year: Internet publication. Entry fees: $25 for books, $15 for articles (can be submitted by publishers). More information on Website.

#GRIT, 1503 SW 42nd St., Topeka KS 66609. (785)274-4300. Fax (785)274-4305. E-mail: grit@cjnetworks.com. Website: www.grit.com.
　　Contest: Sponsors various contests throughout the year: Christmas photo contest, holiday contests, TrueGrit Awards—annually in November issue (unsung heroes).

GUIDEPOSTS, 16 E 34th St., New York NY 10016. (212)251-8100. Website: www.guideposts.org. Interfaith. Submit to The Editor.
　　Contest: Writers Workshop Contest held on even years with a late June deadline. True, first-person stories (yours or someone else's),

1,500 words. Needs one spiritual message, with scenes, drama and characters. Winners attend a week-long seminar (all expenses paid) on how to write for Guideposts. Also Young Writers Contest; $36,000 in college scholarships; best stories to 1,200 wds; deadline November 29.

HOME TIMES, 3676 Collins Dr., #16, West Palm Beach FL 33406. (561)439-3509. Fax (561)968-1758. E-mail: hometimes2@aol.com. Website: www. hometimes.org. Neighbor News, Inc. Dennis Lombard, ed/pub.

Contest: Planning a contest for local, wannabe journalists within the next year.

JOURNAL OF CHRISTIAN NURSING, PO Box 1650, Downers Grove IL 60515-1650. (630)734-4030. Fax (630)734-4200. E-mail: jcn@ivpress. com. Website: www.ncf-jcn.org. Nurses Christian Fellowship of Inter-Varsity Christian Fellowship. Melodee Yohe, mng ed.

Contest: Sponsors an occasional contest. None planned for now.

A NEW SONG, PO Box 629 W.B.B., Dayton OH 45409-0629. (937)294-4552. E-mail: NSongPress@aol.com. New Song Press. Susan Jelus, ed. Contemporary poetry that addresses all aspects of life in faith.

Contest: Annual poetry chapbook contest. Deadline: July 1. Cash prize, plus publication and copies.

*NEW WRITING MAGAZINE, Box 1812, Amherst NY 14226-7812. (716)834-1067. E-mail: info@newwriting.com. Website: www.newwriting.com. New Writing Agency. Richard Lynch, co-ed.

Contest: "We run a writing contest and literary agency. Visit: www. newwriting.com."

THE PLOWMAN, Box 414, Whitby ON L1N 4G7 Canada. (905)668-7803. The Plowman Ministries/Christian. Tony Scavetta, ed/pub. Poetry and prose of social commentary; any topics.

Contest: Sponsors monthly poetry contests; $2/poem entry fee.

SHORT STORIES BIMONTHLY, 5713 Larchmont Dr., Erie PA 16509. Phone/fax (814)866-2543. E-mail: 75562.670@compuserve.com. Website: www. thepoetryforum.com. Poetry Forum. Gunvor Skogsholm, ed. Poetry and prose that takes an honest look at the human condition.

Contest: Chapbook contest, $12 entry fee. Prize: publication and 20 copies. Send SASE for information. December 15 deadline (may vary).

SILVER WINGS MAYFLOWER PULPIT, PO Box 1000, Pearblossom CA 93553-1000. (661)264-3726. E-mail: poetwing@yahoo.com. Poetry on Wings. Jackson Wilcox, ed. Christian understanding and uplift through poetry.

Contest: Annual poetry contest; send SASE for details.

STEPPING OUT OF THE DARKNESS, PO Box 712, Hingham MA 02043. (781)878-5531 (no calls). Puritan emphasis. Sharon White, ed.

Contest: Puritan History Day Contest. Deadline January 15, 2001. Fiction and articles on Puritan living in the present (see guidelines for specifics). Open to subscribers only. Contact for information on future contests.

THE STORYTELLER, 2442 Washington Rd., Maynard AR 72444. (870)647-2137. Fax (870)647-2137. E-mail: storyteller1@cox-internet.com. Fossil Creek Publishing. Regina Cook Williams, ed/pub.

Contest: Each quarter the magazine has a contest and the published works of that quarter are automatically entered. Winners in fiction, nonfiction, essays and poetry receive a free copy of the magazine.

STUDIO, A Journal of Christians Writing, 727 Peel St., Albury NSW 2640 Australia. Phone/fax (+61)2 6021 1135. E-mail: pgrover@bigpond.com. Submit to Studio Editor.

Contest: See copy of Studio for details.

TIME OF SINGING, A Magazine of Christian Poetry, PO Box 149, Conneaut Lake PA 16316. Fax(814)382-7159. E-mail: timesing@toolcity.net. Lora Zill, ed.

Contest: Sponsors 1-2 annual poetry contests on specific themes or forms ($2 entry fee/poem) with cash prizes (send SASE for rules).

*2-SOAR, 222 S. Falcon, South Bend IN 46619. (219)289-8760. Church of God in Christ (Pentecost). Izola Bird, pub.

Contest: Spring poetry contest; entry fee $10. Send SASE for details.

+WINSOME WIT, 12971 Fieldstone Rd., Milaca MN 56353. (320)983-5910. E-mail: jbeuoy@winsomewit.com. Website: www.winsomewit.com. Nondenominational. Jay Beuoy, ed. We write to persuade the unbeliever through the use of satire, from a Christian worldview. Online e-zine.

Contest: Details on Website.

SPONSORED BY CHILDREN'S PERIODICALS

AMERICAN GIRL, 8400 Fairway Pl., Middleton WI 53562. (608)836-4848. Fax (608)831-7089. E-mail: im_agmag_editor@pleasantco.com. Website: www. americangirl.com. Pleasant Company Publications. Submit to Magazine Department Assistant. Secular; for girls ages 8 and older to recognize and celebrate girls' achievements yesterday and today, inspire their creativity, and nurture their hopes and dreams.

Contest: Contests vary from issue to issue.

+HIGHLIGHTS FOR CHILDREN, 803 Church St., Honesdale PA 18431.

Contest: Highlights for Children Fiction Contest. Offers 3 prizes of $1,000 each for stories up to 900 words for children. Stories for beginning readers to 500 words. Send SASE for guidelines. No crime, violence, or derogatory humor. No entry fee or form required. Entries must be postmarked between January 1 and February 28.

J.A.M. (JUNIOR APOSTLES MAGAZINE), PMB 366, 3402 Edgemont Ave., Brookhaven PA 19015. (610)485-3512. E-mail: chuckjoy@bellatlantic.net. Website: jamag.org. Nondenominational. Joy Kieffer, ed; Devon Sitaris, articles ed; Brandon Hopkins, fiction ed. Written by young people, 8-18 yrs.

Contest: Sponsors several; see magazine or Website.

POCKETS, PO Box 340004, Nashville TN 37203-0004. (615)340-7333. Fax (615)340-7267. E-mail: pockets@upperroom.org. Website: www.upper room.org/pockets. United Methodist. Janet Knight, ed; submit to Lynn W. Gilliam, assoc ed.

Contest: Fiction-writing contest; submit between 3/1 & 8/15 every yr. Prize $1,000. Length 1,000-1,600 wds. Must be unpublished and not historical fiction. Previous winners not eligible. Send to Pockets

Fiction Contest at previous address, designating "Fiction Contest" on outside of envelope. Send an SASE for return and response.

SKIPPING STONES, A Multicultural Magazine, PO Box 3939, Eugene OR 97403. Phone/fax (541)342-4956. E-mail: skipping@efn.org. Website: www.nonviolence.org/skipping. Not specifically Christian. Arun N. Toké, ed. A multicultural awareness and nature appreciation magazine for young people 7-17, world-wide.

Contest: Annual Book Awards for Published Books and Authors; Annual Youth Honor Awards. June 20 deadline for students 7-17. Send SASE for guidelines.

SPONSORED BY MUSIC PERIODICALS

CONTEMPORARY SONGWRITER MAGAZINE (formerly Songwriter Magazine), PO Box 25879, Colorado Springs CO 80936-5879. (719)232-4489. Fax (303)223-1638. E-mail: contemposong@yahoo.com. Website: www.angelfire.com/co2/contempo. Roberta Redford, ed.

Contest: Monthly lyric contest, plus a major songwriting contest each year.

THE HYMN: A Journal of Congregational Song, School of Theology, Boston University, 745 Commonwealth Ave., Boston MA 02215-1401. (800) THEHYMN. E-mail: hymneditor@att.net. Website: www.bu.edu/sth/hymn/ www.hymnsociety.org. Hymn Society in the US & Canada. Carol A. Pemberton, ed, Box 46485, Eden Prairie MN 55344.

Contest: Hymn text and tune contests for special occasions or themes.

SPONSORED BY PASTORS/LEADERS PERIODICALS

***CELEBRATION**, 207 Hillsboro Dr., Silver Spring MD 20902-3125. William J. Freburger, ed.

Contest: Monthly contest on different themes, usually worship ideas for specific occasions (New Year, Easter, etc.).

MINISTRY & LITURGY, 160 E. Virginia St., #290, San Jose CA 95112. (408)286-8505. Fax (408)287-8748. E-mail: mdrnlitrgy@aol.com. Resource Publications, Inc. Nick Wagner, ed director.

Contest: Visual Arts Awards.

SHARING THE PRACTICE, 8919 Clemsonville Rd., Union Bridge MD 21791-7413. (301)694-6338. E-mail: darryl.zoller@juno.com Website: www.apclergy.org. Academy of Parish Clergy/Ecumenical/Interfaith. Rev. Darryl Zoller, ed-in-chief.

Contest: Book of the Year Award ($100+), Top Ten Books of the Year list, Parish Pastor of the Year award ($200+). Inquire by e-mail to: DIELPADRE@aol.com.

SPONSORED BY TEEN/YOUNG ADULT PERIODICALS

GUIDEPOSTS FOR TEENS, PO Box 638, Chesterton IN 46304. (219)929-

4429. Fax (219)926-3839. E-mail: gp4t@guideposts.org. Website: www. guideposts.org. Guideposts, Inc. Betsy Kohn, mng ed.

> **Contest:** Laws of Life essay contest for teens, 13-18. Prizes of $5,000, $3,000 and $2,000. Send SASE for guidelines.

INSIGHT, 55 W. Oak Ridge Dr., Hagerstown MD 21740-7301. (301)393-4037. Fax (301)393-4055. E-mail: insight@rhpa.org. Website: www.insight magazine.org. Review and Herald/Seventh-Day Adventist.

> **Contest:** Sponsors a nonfiction & poetry contest; includes a category for students under 21. Prizes to $250. May or June deadline (may vary). Send SASE for rules.

> **Contest:** Sponsors contests throughout the year. Send SASE for details.

YOUNG SALVATIONIST, PO Box 269, Alexandria VA 22313. (703)684-5500. Fax (703)684-5539. E-mail: ys@usn.salvationarmy.org. Website: publications. salvationarmyusa.org.

> **Contest:** Sponsors a contest for fiction, nonfiction, poetry, original art and photography. Send SASE for details.

SPONSORED BY WOMENS' PERIODICALS

+WOMEN WHO MINISTER TO WOMEN (WWM2W) EZINE, 2217 Lake Park Dr., Longmont CO 80503. (303)772-2035. Fax (303)678-0260. E-mail: RightToTheHeart@aol.com. Website: www.righttotheheart.org. Straight From the Heart. Amy Unger, ed. For Christian women in leadership and ministry (women's directors, authors, speakers, Bible teachers, etc.).

> **Contest:** Send 150 word nominations for Woman's Minister of the Year, and Women's Ministry of the Year.

SPONSORED BY WRITERS' PERIODICALS

AREOPAGUS MAGAZINE (UK), Mrs. P. Lindsay, 107 Coopers Green, Bicester OXON OX6 9US, United Kingdom. E-mail for UK: areo@ bigfoot.com. E-mail for US: AreopagUSA@aol.com. Website: www. churchnet.org.uk/areopagus/index.html. Areopagus Publications. Julian Barritt, ed. For amateur and semi-professional Christian writers, producing both secular and Christian writing.

> **Contest:** Sponsors a quarterly, subscribers-only, writing competition (fiction, nonfiction or poetry theme) with a prize of 10 pounds.

BYLINE, Box 130596, Edmond OK 73013-0001. Phone/fax (405)348-5591. E-mail: ByLineMP@aol.com. Website: www.BylineMag.com. Secular. Marcia Preston, ed; Carolyn Wall, fiction ed.

> **Contest:** Sponsors many contests year round; details included in magazine, and large listing of contests on their Website.

CANADIAN WRITER'S JOURNAL, White Mountain Publications, Box 5180, New Liskeard ON P0J 1P0 Canada. (705)647-5424. Fax (705)647-8366. E-mail: cwj@ntl.sympatico.ca. Deborah Ranchuk, ed.

> **Contest:** Sponsors semi-annual short fiction contest (March 31 and

September 30 deadlines); to 1,200 wds. Entry fee $5. Prizes $100, $50, $25. All fiction needs are filled by this contest.

*COCHRAN'S CORNER, 1003 Tyler Ct., Waldorf MD 20602-2964. (361)876-1664. Jeannie Saunders, exec ed.

Contest: Sponsors a short-story contest quarterly.

FELLOWSCRIPT, 121 Morin Maze, Edmonton AB T6K 1V1 Canada. Fax (403)461-1809. E-mail: nharms@oanet.com. Inscribe Christian Writers' Fellowship. Nathan Harms, ed.

Contest: Sponsors two a year, one in March for members, one in August that is open. Send #10 SAE/$1 to "Contest Info."

+FICTION WRITER ONLINE LITERARY MAGAZINE. E-mail: submissions@ thefictionwriter.com. Website: www.thefictionwriter.com. Secular. Joyce Siedler, mng ed. Online mag.

Contest: Sponsors a short fiction contest. No entry fee. Prizes $100, $75, $50. Stories 4,000-8,000 wds. Details on Website. May not be sponsored every year.

THE POETRY CONNECTION, 13455 SW 16th Ct., #F-405/CWM, Pembroke Pines FL 33027. (954)431-3016.Fax (509)351-7401. E-mail: poetryconnect @webtv.net. Sylvia Shichman, ed/pub.

Contests: Lists contests in newsletter; also sells *The Avisson Book of Contests & Prize Competitions for Poets.*

TICKLED BY THUNDER, 14076 86A Ave., Surrey BC V3W 0V9 Canada. Phone/fax (604)591-6095. E-mail: thunder@istar.ca. Website: home.istar. ca/thunder. Larry Lindner, ed. For writers wanting to better themselves.

Contest: For fiction (February 15 annual deadline) and poetry (February 15, May 15, August 15, and October 15 annual dealines). Article contests for subscribers only (February 15, May 15, August 15, and October 15 deadlines). Send SASE for guidelines.

WE!, 100 Upper Glen Dr., Blythewood SC 29016. E-mail: Eboone@aol.com. Website: members.aol.com/WriterNet. R.S.V.P. Press. Eugene Boone, ed.

Contest: Quarterly poetry contest; send SASE for rules.

WRITER'S DIGEST, 1507 Dana Ave., Cincinnati OH 45207. (513)531-2222. Fax (513)531-1843. E-mail: writersdig@fwpubs.com. Website: www. writersdigest.com. Secular/F & W Publications. Melanie Rigney, ed; submit to Katie Dumont, assoc ed.

Contest: Sponsors annual contest for articles, short stories, poetry and scripts; May 31 deadline (may vary). More than $25,000 in prizes. Also The National Self-Publishing Book Awards with $3,000 in prizes, including $1,000 grand prize. Send SASE for rules, or visit Website: www.writersdigest.com/novalearn.asp. Plus National Zine Publishing Awards.

*WRITER'S INK, PO Box 93156, Henderson NV 89009-3156. (800)974-8465. Panabaker Publications. Darla R. Panabaker, ed.

Contest: 2001 Poetry Competition. $100 grand prize. Deadline November 15. Send SASE for rules.

WRITER'S JOURNAL, PO Box 394, Perham MN 56573-0394. (218)346-7921. Fax (218)346-7924. E-mail: writersjournal@wadena.net. Website: www. writersjournal.com. Val-Tech Media/Secular. Leon Ogroske, ed.

Contest: Runs several contests each year. Prizes $300. Categories are: short story, horror/ghost, romance, travel writing, and fiction; 3 poetry; photo.

*WRITING WORLD, 44 Tarleton Rd., Newton MA 02159. Submit to The Editor.

Contest: Occasionally; see sample issues.

SPONSORED BY WRITERS' CONFERENCES/GROUPS

+CAPITAL CHRISTIAN WRITERS. Vienna. Leader: Betsy Dill, PO Box 873, Centreville VA 20122. Phone/fax (703)803-9447. E-mail: ccwriters@juno. com. Website: www.ccwriters.org. Sponsors a spring contest.

*CEHUC SPANISH CHRISTIAN WRITERS GROUP. El Cajon. Contact: Magdalena Latorre, 9802 Quail Canyon Rd., El Cajon CA 92021-6000. Phone/fax (619)390-3747. Fax (619)561-6172. Sponsors a contest open to non-members.

CHRISTIAN WRITERS FELLOWSHIP OF ORANGE COUNTY. Various groups meeting throughout the county. Contact: Bonnie Compton Hanson and Beverly Bush Smith, PO Box 538, Lake Forest CA 92630. (949) 768-3891. Sponsors contests open to nonmembers.

+CHRISTIAN WRITERS OF IDAHO. Boise. Contact: Diana James, 393 W. Willowbrook Dr., Meridian ID 83642-1689. (208)288-0983. Fax (208)288-2574. E-mail: DianaJames@aol.com. Website: www.idahochristianwriters. com. Sponsors a contest open to nonmembers.

EIGHTH ANNUAL CHRISTIAN WRITERS' CONFERENCE. China Lake Conference Center, August 16-18, 2001. Contact: Dr. Ken Parker, Minister of Conferencing & Camping, China Lake Conference Center, PO Box 149, China ME 04926. (207)968-2101. Fax (207)968-2434. E-mail: jvschad@ larck.net. Sponsors Dorothy Templeton Writer's Contest.

#FAITH, HOPE & LOVE is the inspirational chapter of Romance Writers of America. Dues for the chapter are $15/yr, but you must also be a member of RWA to join (dues $65/yr). Chapter offers these services: online list service for members, including an annual contest. Contest is open to members who do not have a novel published. To join, contact RWA National Office, 3707 FM 1960 West, Ste. 550, Houston TX 77068. (281)440-6885. Fax (281)440-7510. Website: www.rwanational.com. Or go to FHL Website: www.webpak.net/robinlee/FHL/info.html. New Inspirational Readers Choice Contest; deadline February 14, 2001; no cash prizes. Send SASE for guidelines.

FELLOWSHIP OF CHRISTIAN WRITERS (formerly Tulsa Christian Writers). Contact: JoAnn R. Wray, 812 W. Glenwood St., Broken Arrow OK 74011-6419. (918)451-4017. Fax (918)451-4417. E-mail: epistle@web zone.net. Quarterly contests (for members) and workshops. Planning a contest open to members and nonmembers during 2001.

GLORIETA CHRISTIAN WRITERS' CONFERENCE. Glorieta NM (18 mile N. of Santa Fe); October 2001. Speakers 2001 include: Barbara Nicolosi. Sponsors a writing contest. Contact: Glorieta Conference Center at (800)797-4222 or Mona Hodgson, PO Box 999, Cottonwood AZ 86326-

0999. (505)757-6161. Fax (505)757-6149. E-mail: mona@sedona.net. Website: www.desertcritters.com.

GREATER PHILADELPHIA CHRISTIAN WRITERS' FELLOWSHIP. Broomall PA. Contact: Marlene Bagnull, 316 Blanchard Rd., Drexel Hill PA 19026. Phone/fax (610)626-6833. E-mail: mbagnull@aol.com. Website: www. writehisanswer.com. Sponsors contest open to nonmembers.

*****INSCRIBE CHRISTIAN WRITERS' FELLOWSHIP** (formerly Alberta Christian Fellowship—Canada-wide) Calgary & Edmonton. Contact: Elsie Montgomery, pres, 333 Hunter's Run, Edmonton AB T6R 2N9, Canada. (780)988-5622. Fax (780)430-0139. E-mail: emontgom@compusmart. ab.ca. Website under construction. Sponsors 2 contests, spring & fall (fall open to non-members).

INSPIRATIONAL WRITERS ALIVE! Groups meet in Houston, Amarillo, Pasadena, Humble, and Jacksonville TX. Contact: Martha Rogers, 6038 Greenmont, Houston TX 77092-2332. (713)686-7209. Sponsors annual contest (November 1-April 1).

*****INTERNATIONAL BLACK WRITERS.** Chicago & New York. Contact: Mable Terrell, PO Box 1030, Chicago IL 60690-1030. (312)409-2292. Sponsors a contest open to nonmembers.

*****INTERNATIONAL NETWORK OF COMMUNICATORS & THE ARTS.** Contact: Sheri Stone, Box 1754, Post Falls ID 83854-1754. Phone/fax (208)667-9730. Sponsors a contest.

KANSAS CITY CHRISTIAN WRITERS' NETWORK. Kansas City Metro area. Contact: Teresa Vining, 1438 N Lucy Montgomery Way, Olathe KS 66061-6706. Phone/fax: (913)764-4610. E-mail: KCCWN@aol.com. Sponsors a contest for those who attend one of their seminars.

MINNESOTA CHRISTIAN WRITERS GUILD. Minneapolis. Contact: Jane Kise, 5504 Grove St., Edina MN 55436. (612)926-4343. E-mail: jagkise@ aol.com. Sponsors a contest open to nonmembers.

*****NORTHWEST CHRISTIAN WRITERS ASSN.** Bellevue WA. Contact: John Blanchard or Lorinda Newton, 10663 NE 133rd Pl., Kirkland WA 98034-2030. (425)821-6647. Fax (425)823-8590. E-mail: newton@integrityol. .com. Sponors a contest open to members.

OREGON CHRISTIAN WRITERS. Contact: Debbie Hedstrom, pres., 5490—8th Ave. SE, Salem OR 97306-1591. (503)370-9153. Fax (503)365-1801. E-mail: dhdstrom@wbc.edu. Website: cs.georgefox.edu/~rzempel/ocw. Sponsors a contest from time to time.

PITTSBURG CHRISTIAN WRITERS FELLOWSHIP. Gerard. Contact: Carol Russell, Walkertown 894—165th St., Fort Scott KS 66701. (316)547-2472. E-mail: rlrussell@ckt.net. Sponsors a contest open to nonmembers.

THE PRESBYTERIAN WRITERS GUILD. Contact: Nancy Regensburger, 615 Wightman St., Vassar MI 48768. Sponsors contests for members each year.

+RICHMOND (VA) ASSN. OF CHRISTIANS WHO WRITE. Contact: Thomas Lacy, 12114 Walnut Hill Dr., Rockville VA 23146-1854. (804)749-4050. Fax (804)749-4939. E-mail: RevTCL@aol.com. Membership (15) open. Sponsors a contest open to non-members.

SAN DIEGO COUNTY CHRISTIAN WRITERS' GUILD. Contact: Robert

Gillespie, 17041 Palacio Pl., San Diego CA 92027. Phone/fax (858)673-3921. E-mail: riters@adnc.com. Sponsors contest for members.

SILOAM SPRINGS WRITERS. Contact: Margaret Weathers, 716 N. University, Siloam Springs AR 72761-2658. (501)524-6598. Sponsoring a contest open to non-members.

+SOUTHWEST WRITERS ANNUAL CONFERENCE. Albuquerque, September 20-23, 2001. Contact: Stephanie Dooley, 8200 Mountain Rd. NE, Ste. 106, Albuquerque NM 87110-7835. (505)265-9485. Fax (505)265-9483. E-mail: SWriters@aol.com. Website: www.southwestwriters.org. Young Writers Contest (for New Mexico teens only).

*STATE OF MAINE WRITERS' CONFERENCE. Ocean Park; August 2001. Contact: Richard F. Burns, PO Box 7146, Ocean Park ME 04063-7146. (207)934-9806. Contest announcement available March 1; brochure available June 1.

*TEXAS CHRISTIAN WRITERS FORUM. Houston/First Baptist Church; August 2002 (first Saturday in August in even-numbered years). Contact: Martha Rogers, 6038 Greenmont, Houston TX 77092-2332. (713)686-7209. E-mail: mrogers353@aol.com. Sponsors a contest.

*WEST-DAYTON CHRISTIAN WRITERS GUILD. Contact: Tina V. Toles, PO Box 251, Englewood OH 45322-2049. Phone/fax (937)832-0541. E-mail: Poet11@ix.netcom.com. Sponsors a contest open to non-members.

ADDITIONAL CONTESTS

+ADAMS MEDIA INSPIRING TRUE STORY CONTEST, PO Box 863, Eugene OR 97440. $1,000 First Prize; $100 for each story accepted for publication. No entry fee. Write for current contest guidelines.

+ALL POETS: POETRY FOR EVERYONE. Website: www.allpoets.com. Good resource site for poets. Sponsors a poetry contest on their Website.

+AMAZON.COM. Lists current contests and information on several well-known literary awards. Website: www.amazon.com.

THE AMY FOUNDATION sponsors the Amy Writing Awards, which is a call to present spiritual truth reinforced with biblical references in secular, non-religious publications. First prize is $10,000 with a total of $34,000 given annually. The Amy Writing Awards is designed to recognize creative, skillful writing that presents in a sensitive, thought-provoking manner a biblical position on issues affecting the world today. To be eligible, submitted articles must be published in a secular, non-religious publication and must be reinforced with at least one passage of Scripture. For details on The Amy Writing Awards and a copy of last year's winning entries, contact: The Amy Foundation, PO Box 16091, Lansing MI 48901-6091. (517)323-6233. Website: www.amyfound.org.

+ANNIE DILLARD AWARD FOR NONFICTION. Essays on any subject to 10,000 wds. Entries must be postmarked between January 4, 2001 and March 4, 2001. Entry fee $10. Prizes of $1,000, $250, and $100. Unpublished works only. Send manuscripts to: Annie Dillard Award for Nonfiction, Mail Stop 9053, Western Washington University, Bellingham WA 98225.

*ARTS & LIFE PRIZE FOR RELIGION. International Literary Society, PO Box 3735, Anaheim CA 92803-3735. (206)890-4422. Fax (425)487-2633. E-mail: swhalen@mcwe.com. Steve Whalen, director. November 30 deadline each year. For 1,500 word stories of a spiritual journey or testimony; prefers nonfiction, but will accept fiction. Entry fee: $18. First prize $1,000; second prize $150. Send SASE for guidelines.

+AUTHOR LINK FICTION CONTEST. Website: www.authorlink.com. Sponsored a contest in 2000; check Website for current contest.

+BLUE UNICORN 20TH POETRY CONTEST. Deadline February 15 (postmarked). Three prizes from $50-100, plus the James A. Garvey Award of $250 for the best poem on specified topic. Entry fee of $6 for first poem and $3 for each additional. Any style or subject, to 40 lines (5 entries maximum). Original & unpublished. No identification on poem; include a 3x5 card with each entry that includes: name, address, title of poem, and first line of poem, with SASE. Send entries and check (to Blue Unicorn) to: Hal Bosworth, Contest Chair, 921 Ensenada Ave., Berkeley CA 94707.

+BOSTON REVIEW 4TH ANNUAL POETRY CONTEST. Deadline is June 1. First prize is $1,000, plus publication. Submit up to 5 published poems; $15 entry fee (includes a subscription to Boston Review). Submit manuscripts in duplicate with cover note. Send manuscript & fee to: Poetry Contest, Boston Review, E53-407 MIT, Cambridge MA 02139.

THE BROSE PRIZE, Lake Forest College, 555 N. Sheridan, Lake Forest IL 60045. (847)735-5169. E-mail: rmiller@lfc.edu. Professor Ron Miller, contact person. Offered only every 10 years; last one in 2000. Prizes vary, and winning entries become the property of the college. Open to a book or treatise on the relationship between any discipline or topic and the Christian religion.

BULWER-LYTTON FICTION CONTEST. For the worst opening line to a novel. www.bulwer-lytton.com. Rules on Website.

+CATHERINE MARSHALL CHRISTIAN FICTION AWARDS OF EXCELLENCE/CHRISTY AWARDS. Named after Marshall's book "Christy" that was made into a popular TV series. Donna Kehow, Administrator, 1571 Glastonbury Rd., Ann Arbor MI 48103. Phone/fax (734)663-7931. E-mail: CA2000DK@aol.com. Awards in 7 fiction genres: allegory, contemporary/general, futuristic, historical, romance, suspense/mystery, and western. Nominations are submitted by the book publishers.

THE E.F.S. RELIGIOUS FICTION WRITING COMPETITION. E.F.S. Enterprises, 2844—8th Ave., Ste. 6E, New York NY 10039. (212)283-8899. Website: www.efs-enterprises.com. Zeretha Jenkins, contest director. June 30 deadline. Entry fee $15. Prizes $100 (and online publishing contract); & $50. For unpublished religious fiction, short or book-length.

+49TH PARALLEL POETRY CONTEST. Poems in any style or on any subject. Entries must be postmarked between October 1, 2001 and December 1, 2001. Entry fee $10 for up to three poems. Prizes of $1,000, $250, and $100. Unpublished works only. Send manuscripts to: 49th Parallel Poetry Award, Mail Stop 9053, Western Washington University, Bellingham WA 98225.

GLIMMER TRAIN PRESS SHORT STORY AWARD FOR NEW WRITERS. Secular. Must be postmarked between February 1 and March 31. Also sponsors a fall contest with deadline between August 1 and September 30. Open to any writer who hasn't been published in a national magazine with a circulation over 5,000; unpublished stories 1,200-7,500 words; no children's stories; prizes $1,200, $500, and $300; staple pages together with name, address and phone on first page, no SASE (will not be returned); $12 reading fee. Send to: Short-Story Award, Glimmer Train Press, 710 SW Madison St., Ste. 504, Portland OR 97205. Results announced on July 1.

+**INTERNATIONAL LITERARY PROJECT LIVRET 2001 CONTEST**. For poetry and haiku. November 15 deadline. Prizes of $1,500, $500, and $150 for poetry; $500, $250, and $50 for haiku. Entry fee $10 for poetry, $5 for haiku. Website: www.literaryproject.com. Register online or mail to: The Intl. Literary Project, PMB 261, 16781 Chagrin Blvd., Shaker Heights OH 44120. Guidelines on Website.

"IN THE BEGINNING WAS THE WORD..." LITERARY ARTS CONTEST 2001. Sponsored by the Lake Oswego, Oregon, United Church of Christ. Categories include short fiction, creative nonfiction, or poetry; previously unpublished; to 4,000 words. One submission per person. Deadline September 1, 2001. Prizes of $500, $250, and $100 for first three places. Send SASE for official entry form to: Lake Oswego United Church of Christ, 1111 SW Country Club Rd., Lake Oswego OR 97034, or e-mail: loucc@teleport.com.

+**THE MILTON CENTER AWARD FOR EXCELLENCE IN WRITING**. Award is given for a single poem in English that elevates the human spirit. Three prizes: $1,000, $500, $250. Entry fee $15 (payable to the Milton Center). Submissions must be postmarked between March 1 and October 13 (may vary each year). For guidelines, contact: Program Director, The Milton Center, Newman University, 3100 McCormick Ave., Wichita KS 67213-2097. (316)942-4291x326. Fax (316)942-4483. Or download from: www.newmanu.edu/MiltonCenter/award for excellence, or www.angelfire.com/ks2/miltoncenter/MiltonAwardGuidelines.

*NATIONAL PUBLISHERS FREEDOM AWARDS**. Sponsored by the American Self-Publisher Association and BooksAmerica.com. For self-published authors only. Entries accepted in 20 categories, including religious. Winners receive trophies, cash prizes of $100-200. Entries must be published during the current year. For details call 1-800-929-7889. This contest was held first for 1999. Check to be sure it will be repeated in 2001.

*NOVELADVICE CONTESTS (SEMI-ANNUAL)**. Short stories and creative nonfiction (categories will vary). Entry fee $10. Prizes $50, $100, and $150. Guidelines and Contest Form available on Website. www.noveladvice.com.

*ONGOING HAIKU POETRY CONTEST**. Secular. www.toastpoints.com/haiku. No prizes, but it's a good way to learn this specialized form, and winning entries are printed on the Website.

+**REDBOOK'S 2001 NONFICTION WRITING CONTEST**. Secular. September 30 deadline. Offers $1,000 grand prize and two $250 runners-up. Details in *Redbook* magazine or write: Redbook Nonfiction Writing Contest, 224 W. 57th St., New York NY 10019.

*REMLEY'S CHRISTIAN POETRY CONTEST. Has two deadlines a year: June 30 and December 31. Five prizes ranging from $10 to $100. No fee. Must have Christian content or religious theme; to 30 lines; limit three entries per author. Send entries to: Remley Literary Agency, PO Box 240, Oldsmar FL 34677-0289, rem5326@gte.net, or submit online.

THE PLEASANT T. ROWLAND PRIZE FOR FICTION, Pleasant Company Publications, 8400 Fairway Pl., Middleton WI 53562. Annual prize. September 1 deadline. Prize is $10,000, plus publication. For unpublished fiction that captures the spirit of contemporary American girls.

+SCI-FI WRITERS OF CHRISTIANITY QUARTERLY AWARDS. Send submissions to jaycarper@zdnetonebox.com by the 15th of the last month of each quarter (March 15, June 15, September 15, and December 15). Must be 12,000 wds or less. Go to Website for details and copies of winning entries: carper.freeserver.com/sfwc.

THE THIRD ANNUAL BK NELSON SEARCH FOR TALENT CONTEST. Sponsored by the BK Nelson Literary Agency, 84 Woodland Rd., Pleasantville NY 10570 and 139 S. Beverly Dr., Beverly Hills CA 90212. (914)741-1322 (NY) and (310)858-7006 (CA). Fax (914)741-1324 and (310)858-7967. E-mail: bknelson@compuserve.com. Website: www.cmonline.com/bknelson. Deadline for entries is December 15, 2001. Prize is a car and 6 months representation. Send SASE for guidelines or copy from their Website.

+SOUL-MAKING LITERARY COMPETITION. November 30 deadline. Submit up to 3 poems, one per page. First prize $100; 5 entry fee. For complete guidelines, send SASE to: Soul-Making Literary Competition, Webhallow House, 1544 Sweetwood Dr., Colma CA 95015-2029; or e-mail: PenNobHill@aol.com.

*SOWING SEEDS FOURTH ANNUAL WRITING CONTEST 2001. Soliciting entries in three categories: Devotions (600-750 wds); Sermons (to 2,000 wds); and Poetry. Winner in each category gets $100, plus publication on their Webpage. Winners will also be submitted to other publications. Entries must be postmarked by June 30, 2001. Entry fee is $15 per submission. For details and sample entries, go to their Website at: www. sowingseedsoffaith.com/writing.htm. Send submissions to: Sowing Seeds Ministry, PO Box 22, Keysville VA 23947.

SPS STUDIOS POETRY CONTEST, PO Box 1007, Dept. E, Boulder CO 80306-1007. (303)449-0536. Fax (303)447-0939. E-mail: bma@rmi.net. Web site: www. bluemountainarts.com. General card publisher. Sponsors a tri-annual poetry card contest online. Prizes of $300, $150, and $50. Details and entry form on their Website.

+TOBIAS WOLFF AWARD FOR FICTION. Short story or novel excerpt to 10,000 wds. Entries must be postmarked between January 4, 2001 and March 4, 2001. Entry fee $10/story or chapter. Prizes of $1,000, $250, and $100. Unpublished works only. Send manuscripts to: The Tobias Wolff Award for Fiction, Mail Stop 9053, Western Washington University, Bellingham WA 98225.

RESOURCES FOR CONTESTS

+**BYLINE MAGAZINE CONTEST LISTINGS**. www.bylinemag.com/contests. htm.

CONTESTS LINK PAGE. www.billyates.com/cww/links.html.

+**FREELANCE WRITING: WEBSITE FOR TODAY'S WORKING WRITER.** www.freelancewriting.com/contests.html.

INKSPOTS CONTEST WEBSITE. Secular. www.inkspot.com/market/contests. html.

WRITER'S DIGEST WEBSITE FOR CONTESTS. www.writersdigest.com/ catalog/contest_frame.html.

DENOMINATIONAL LISTING OF BOOK PUBLISHERS AND PERIODICALS

An attempt has been made to divide publishers into appropriate denominational groups. However, due to the extensive number of denominations included, and sometimes incomplete denominational information, some publishers inadvertently may have been included in the wrong list. Additions and corrections are welcome.

ANTIOCHIAN ORTHODOX

Book Publishers:
Conciliar Press
Periodicals:
Again
The Handmaiden

ASSEMBLIES OF GOD

Book Publishers:
Gospel Publishing House
Logion Press
Periodicals:
American Horizon
CE Counselor
Club Connection
Discovery Trails
Enrichment
High Adventure
Live
Paraclete
Pentecostal Evangel
Testimony (Canada)
Resource (Canada)
Teen Life
Woman's Touch
Youth Leader

BAPTIST, SOUTHERN

Book Publishers:
Baylor Univ. Press
Broadman & Holman
New Hope Publishers
Southern Baptist Press
Periodicals:
Baptist History & Heritage
Believe
Church Administration
Church Media Library
Church Musician

Crusader
Experiencing God
Glory Songs
HomeLife
Journey
Let's Worship
Light
Living With Teenagers
Mature Living
Minister's Family
Music Makers
Music Time
National Drama Service
On Mission
ParentLife
Proclaim
Senior Musician
Stand Firm

BAPTIST, OTHER

Book Publishers:
Baptist Publishing House
Judson Press (American)
Mercer University Press
   (Baptist)
National Baptist
   (Missionary)
Periodicals:
African American Pulpit
   (American)
American Baptist in
   Missions
Certainty (Regular)
Challenge (Regular)
Co-Laborer (Free Will)
Conquest
Courage (Regular)
E Street (GA Baptist)
Friends Journal
Fundamentalist Journal

God's Special People
   (Independent)
Heartbeat (Free Will)
LIGHT...For/Christian Walk
   (Independent)
The Link (Fellowship/
   Canada)
Link & Visitor
Messenger (Pentecostal Free
   Will)
Messenger (Regular)
Moments with God (North
   American)
Primary Pal (Regular)
Secret Place (American)
Standard, The (General)
Writer's Forum

CATHOLIC

Book Publishers:
ACTA Publications
Alba House
American Catholic Press
Brown Publishing
Canticle Books
Catholic Book Publishing
Catholic University of America
   Press
Cistercian Publications
Cross Cultural Publications
Dimension Books
HarperSanFrancisco (Cath.
   bks)
ICS Publications
Libros Liguori
Liguori Publications
Liturgical Press
Loyola Press
Thomas More
Oregon Catholic Press
OSL Publications

Our Sunday Visitor
Pauline Books
Paulist Press
Regnery Publishing
St. Anthony Messenger
Sheed & Ward
Periodicals:
America
Annals of St. Anne
Arkansas Catholic
Arlington Catholic Herald
Bread of Life
Canticle
Caravan
Catechist
Catechumenate
Catholic Answer
Catholic Courier
Catholic Digest
Catholic Forester
Catholic Insight
Catholic Library World
Catholic Near East
Catholic New Times
Catholic New York
Catholic Parent
Catholic Peace Voice
Catholic Rural Life
Catholic Sentinel
Catholic Servant
Catholic Telegraph
Catholic Twin Circle
Celebration
CGA World
Columbia
Commonweal
Companion
Conscience
Culture Wars
Diocesan Dialogue
Early Childhood News
Environment & Art
Emmanuel
Eucharistic Minister
Family Digest
Forefront
Good News for Children
Immaculate Heart
    Messenger
Interim
Leaves
Liguorian
Living Words
Marian Helpers Bulletin
Messenger/Sacred Heart
Messenger (KY)
Messenger/St. Anthony
Miraculous Medal

Montana Catholic
My Friend
National Catholic Reporter
New Covenant
New Freeman
Notre Dame
N.A. Voice of Fatima
Oblates
Oblate World
Our Family
Our Sunday Visitor
Parish Liturgy
Pastoral Life
Prairie Messenger
Priest
Queen of All Hearts
Religion Teacher's Journal
Review for Religious
St. Anthony Messenger
St. Joseph's Messenger
St. Willibrord Journal
Seeds
Share
Social Justice Review
Spirit
Spiritual Life
Sursum Corda!
This Rock
Today's Catholic Teacher
Today's Parish
U.S. Catholic
Visions
Way of St. Francis
YOU! Magazine

CHRISTIAN CHURCH/ CHURCH OF CHRIST

Book Publishers:
CBP Press (Disciples of
    Christ)
Chalice Press (Disciples of
    Christ)
College Press (Church of
    Christ)
Pilgrim Press (United Church
    of Christ)
Periodicals:
Christian Standard
Disciple (Disciples of
    Christ)
Encounter
Four and Five
Kidz Chat
Lookout
Teenage Christian (Church
    of Christ)
Weekly Bible Reader

CHURCH OF GOD (Anderson, IN)

Book Publisher:
Warner Press
Periodicals:
Pathways to God

CHURCH OF GOD (Cleveland, TN)

Book Publisher:
Editorial Evangelica
Periodicals:
Church of God EVANGEL
So All May Hear
Youth and CE Leadership

CHURCH OF GOD (holiness)

Periodicals:
Beginner's Friend
Church Herald and Holiness
    Banner
Gems of Truth
Junior Companion
Primary Pal (KS)
Youth Compass

CHURCH OF GOD, OTHER

Periodicals:
Bible Advocate (Seventh-
    Day)
Church Advocate
Gem
Now What? (Seventh-Day)
Spirit (Pentecostal Church of
    God)
2 Soar (Church of God in
    Christ)

CHURCH OF THE NAZARENE

Book Publishers:
Lillenas (music)
Beacon Hill Press
Periodicals:
Celebrate
Children's Church Exch.
Discoveries
Herald of Holiness
Power and Light
Preacher's Magazine
Resource
Standard
Teens Today

Together Time
Wonder Time

EPISCOPAL/ANGLICAN

Book Publishers:
Alban Institute
Forward Movement
Morehouse Publishing
Periodicals:
Cathedral Age
Episcopal Life
Interchange
Living Church
Sewanee Theological
  Review

FREE METHODIST

Book Publishers:
Light and Life
  Communications
Periodicals:
Evangel
Light and Life
World Mission People

FREE WILL BAPTIST

Periodicals:
CoLaborer
Heartbeat

LUTHERAN

Book Publishers:
Concordia
Langmarc Publishing
Openbook Publishers
Periodicals:
Canada Lutheran (ELCC)
Cresset
Esprit (ELCC)
Evangelism (MO Synod)
Lutheran (ELCA)
Lutheran Digest
Lutheran Educ. (MO Synod)
Lutheran Forum
Lutheran Journal
Lutheran Parent
Lutheran Parent's
  Wellspring
Lutheran Partners (ELCA)
Lutheran Witness (MO
  Synod)
Lutheran Woman's Quarterly
  (MO Synod)

Lutheran Woman Today
  (ELCA)
Northwestern Lutheran
Parenting Treasures (MO
  Synod)
Parish Teacher (ELCA)
Word & World (ELCA)
Teachers Inter. (MO Synod)

MENNONITE

Book Publishers:
Kindred Press
Periodicals:
Canadian Mennonite
Christian Leader
Christian Living
Companions
Mennonite Brethren Herald
Mennonite Historian
Mennonite Weekly Review
On the Line
Partners
Purpose
Story Friends
Story Mates
With

MISSIONARY CHURCH

Periodicals:
Emphasis/Faith & Living

PENTECOSTAL HOLINESS CHURCH

Periodicals:
CE Connection
Helping Hand
Worldorama

PRESBYTERIAN

Book Publishers:
Canon Press
P & R Publishing
Westminster John Knox
Periodicals:
About Such Things (PCA)
Connection (EPC)
Covenanter Witness
Horizons (USA)
PCA Messenger
Presbyterian Layman (USA)
Presbyterian Outlook (USA)
Presbyterian Record
Presbyterian Today
Reflections (EPC)

QUAKER/FRIENDS

Book Publishers:
Barclay Press
Friends United Press
Periodicals:
Fruit of the Vine

REFORMED CHURCHES

Periodicals:
Perspectives
Reformed Worship
Vision (MI)

SEVENTH-DAY ADVENTIST

Book Publishers:
Pacific Press
Review and Herald
Periodicals:
GUIDE Magazine
Insight (MD)
Journal/Adventist Ed
Kids' Ministry Ideas
Liberty
Listen
Message
Ministry
Our Little Friend
Primary Treasure
Sabbath School Leadership
Signs of the Times
Vibrant Life
Young and Alive

UNITED METHODIST

Book Publishers:
Abingdon Press
Cokesbury
Dimensions for Living
United Methodist Publishing
  House
Upper Room Books
Periodicals:
alive now!
Christian Social Action
Good News
Kaleidoscope
Leader/Church School Today
Magazine/Christian Youth!
Mature Years
Methodist History
Michigan Christian Advocate
New World Outlook
Pockets
Quarterly Review

Upper Room

UNITED PENTECOSTAL

Periodicals:
Conqueror
Preserving Christian Homes
Vision

WESLEYAN CHURCH

Book Publishers:
Wesleyan Publishing House
Periodicals:
Changing Lives
Friend
In Touch
Wesleyan Advocate

Wesleyan World

MISCELLANEOUS DENOMINATIONS

Armenian Holy Apostolic
Pourastan
Christian Reformed
The Banner
Christian & Missionary Alliance
Christian Publications
Evangelical Covenant Church
Cornerstone
Covenant Companion
Evangelical Free Church
Evangelical Beacon

Pursuit
Fellowship of Evangelical Bible Churches
Gospel Tidings
Foursquare Gospel Church
Foursquare World Advance
Greek Orthodox
Holy Cross Orthodox Press
Open Bible Standard Churches
MESSAGE of the Open Bible
United Church of Canada
United Church Publishing House
United Church Observer
United Church of Christ
United Church Press

LIST OF BOOK PUBLISHERS AND PERIODICALS BY CORPORATE GROUP

Following is a listing of book publishers and periodicals that belong to the same group or family of publications.

CCM COMMUNICATIONS

CCM (Contemporary
    Christian Music)
Worship Leader
Youthworker
The CCM Update

CHRISTIAN BOOKSELLERS ASSN.

CBA Frontline
CBA Marketplace

CHRISTIANITY TODAY, INTL.

Books & Culture
Campus Life
Christian Computing
Christian History
Christianity Today
Christian Parenting Today
Christian Reader
Computing Today
Leadership Journal
Marriage Partnership
Men of Integrity
Today's Christian Woman
Your Church

CHRISTIAN MEDIA

Christian Media (books)
The Apocalypse Chronicles
Christian Media

COOK COMMUNICATIONS MINISTRIES

Chariot Books
Chariot Victor Books
Lion Publishing (books)
Counselor
I.D.
Power for Living

Primary Days
Quiet Hour
Real Time
The Rock
Single Adult Ministries
    Journal

FOCUS ON THE FAMILY

Focus on the Family (books)
Boundless Webzine
Breakaway
Brio
Citizen
Clubhouse
Clubhouse Jr.
Focus on the Family
Lifewise
Physician
Plugged-In
Single-Parent Family
Teachers in Focus

GROUP PUBLICATIONS, INC.

Children's Ministry
Group Publishing, Inc.
    (books)
Group Magazine
Group's Faithweaver Bible
    Curriculum

GUIDEPOSTS

Guideposts Books
Angels on Earth
Clarity
Guideposts
Guideposts for Kids
Guideposts for Teens
Plus

HARPERCOLLINS

HarperSanFrancisco

Zonderkidz
Zondervan Publishing House

THOMAS NELSON PUBLISHERS

J. Countryman
Thomas Nelson Publishers
    (books)
Tommy Nelson (books)
Word (books)

THE SALVATION ARMY

Faith & Friends
Horizons
War Cry
Young Salvationist

STANDARD PUBLISHING

Standard Publishing (books)
Christian Standard
Encounter
Kidz Chat
The Lookout
Seek

STRANG COMMUNICATIONS

Creation House (books)
Charisma & Christian Life
Christian Retailing
Ministries Today
New Man
Vida Cristiana

THE UPPER ROOM

Upper Room Books
alive now!
Devo'Zine
The Upper Room
Weavings

GLOSSARY OF TERMS

NOTE: This is not intended to be an exhaustive glossary of terms. It includes primarily those terms you will find within the context of this market guide.

Advance. Amount of money a publisher pays to an author up front, against future royalties. The amount varies greatly from publisher to publisher, and is often paid in two or three installments (on signing contract, on delivery of manuscript, and on publication).

All rights. An outright sale of your material. Author has no further control over it.

Anecdote. A short, poignant, real-life story, usually used to illustrate a single thought.

Assignment. When an editor asks a writer to write a specific piece for an agreed-upon price.

Avant-garde. Experimental; ahead of the times.

Backlist. A publisher's previously published books that are still in print a year after publication.

Bar code. Identification code and price on the back of a book read by a scanner at checkout counters.

Bible Versions. GNB—Good News Bible; ICB—International Children's Bible; KJV—King James Version; NAS—New American Standard; NJB—New Jerusalem Bible; NIV—New International Version; NKJV—New King James Version; NRSV—New Revised Standard Version; RSV—Revised Standard Version.

Bimonthly. Every two months.

Biweekly. Every two weeks.

Bluelines. Printer's proofs used to catch errors before a book is printed.

Book proposal. Submission of a book idea to an editor; usually includes a cover letter, thesis statement, chapter-by-chapter synopsis, market survey, and 1-3 sample chapters.

Byline. Author's name printed just below the title of a story, article, etc.

Camera-ready copy. The text and artwork for a book that are ready for the press.

Circulation. The number of copies sold or distributed of each issue of a publication.

Clips. See "Published Clips."

Column. A regularly appearing feature, section, or department in a periodical using the same heading; written by the same person or a different freelancer each time.

Contributor's copy. Copy of an issue of a periodical sent to the author whose work appears in it.

Copyright. Legal protection of an author's work.

Cover letter. A letter that accompanies some manuscript submissions. Usually needed only if you have to tell the editor something specific or to give your credentials for writing a piece of a technical nature. Also use to remind the editor that a manuscript was requested or expected.

Critique. An evaluation of a piece of writing.

Devotional. A short piece that shares a personal spiritual discovery, inspires to worship, challenges to commitment or action, or encourages.

Editorial guidelines. See "Writer's guidelines."

Electronic submission. The submission of a proposal or article to an editor by electronic means, such as by e-mail or on disk.

Endorsements. Flattering comments about a book; usually carried on the back cover or in promotional material.

EPA/Evangelical Press Assn. A professional trade organization for periodical publishers and associate members.

E-proposals. Proposals sent via e-mail.

E-queries. Queries sent via e-mail.

Eschatology. The branch of theology that is concerned with the last things, such as death, judgment, heaven and hell.

Essay. A short composition usually expressing the author's opinion on a specific subject.

Evangelical. A person who believes that one receives God's forgiveness for sins through Jesus Christ, and believes the Bible is an authoritative guide for daily living.

Exegesis. Interpretation of the Scripture.

Feature article. In-depth coverage of a subject, usually focusing on a person, an event, a process, an organization, a movement, a trend or issue; written to explain, encourage, help, analyze, challenge, motivate, warn, or entertain—as well as to inform.

Filler. A short item used to "fill" out the page of a periodical. It could be a timeless news item, joke, anecdote, light verse or short humor, puzzle, game, etc.

First rights. Editor buys the right to publish your piece for the first time.

Foreign rights. Selling or giving permission to translate or reprint published material in a foreign country.

Foreword. Opening remarks in a book introducing the book and its author.

Freelance. As in 50% freelance: means that 50% of the material printed in the publication is supplied by freelance writers.

Freelancer or freelance writer. A writer who is not on salary but sells his material to a number of different publishers.

Free verse. Poetry that flows without any set pattern.

Genre. Refers to type or classification, as in fiction or poetry. Such types as westerns, romances, mysteries, etc., are referred to as genre fiction.

Glossy. A black-and-white photo with a shiny, rather than matte, finish.

Go-ahead. When a publisher tells you to go ahead and write up or send your article idea.

Haiku. A Japanese lyric poem of a fixed 17-syllable form.

Hard copy. A typed manuscript, as opposed to one on disk or in an e-mail.

Holiday/seasonal. A story, article, filler, etc., that has to do with a specific holiday or season. This material must reach the publisher the stated number of months prior to the holiday/season.

Homiletics. The art of preaching.

Humor. The amusing or comical aspects of life that add warmth and color to an article or story.

Interdenominational. Distributed to a number of different denominations.

International Postal Reply Coupon. See "IRC."

Interview article. An article based on an interview with a person of interest to a specific readership.

IRC or IPRC. International Postal Reply Coupon: can be purchased at your local post office and should be enclosed with a manuscript sent to a foreign publisher.

ISBN number. International Standard Book Number; an identification code needed for every book.

Journal. A periodical presenting news in a particular area.

Kill fee. A fee paid for a completed article done on assignment that is subsequently not published. Amount is usually 25-50% of original payment.

Libel. To defame someone by an opinion or a misquote and put his or her reputation in jeopardy.

Light verse. Simple, light-hearted poetry.

Little/Literary. Small circulation publications whose focus is providing a forum for the literary writer, rather than on making money. Often do not pay, or pay in copies.

Mainstream fiction. Other than genre fiction, such as romance, mystery or science fiction. Stories of people and their conflicts handled on a deeper level.

Mass Market. Books intended for a wide, general market, rather than a specialized market. These books are produced in a smaller format, usually with smaller type, and are sold at a lower price. The expectation is that their sales will be higher.

Ms. Abbreviation for manuscript.

Mss. Abbreviation for more than one manuscript.

Multiple Submissions. Submitting more than one piece at a time to the same publisher, usually reserved for poetry, greeting cards, or fillers—not articles.

NASR. Abbreviation for North American serial rights.

Newsbreak. A newsworthy event or item sent to a publisher who might be interested in publishing it because it would be of interest to his particular readership.

Nondenominational. Not associated with a particular denomination.

Not copyrighted. Publication of your piece in such a publication will put it into public domain and it is not then protected. Ask that the publisher carry your copyright notice on your piece when it is printed.

On acceptance. Periodical or publisher pays a writer at the time manuscript is accepted for publication.

On assignment. Writing something at the specific request of an editor.

On publication. Publisher pays a writer when his/her manuscript is published.

On speculation/On spec. Writing something for an editor with the agreement that he will buy it only if he likes it.

One-time rights. Selling the right to publish a story one time to any number of publications (usually refers to publishing for a non-overlapping readership).

Overrun. The extra copies of a book printed during the initial print run.

Over the transom. Unsolicited articles that arrive at a publisher's office.

Payment on acceptance. See "On acceptance."

Payment on publication. See "On publication."

Pen name/Pseudonym. Using a name other than your legal name on an article or book in order to protect your identity or the identity of people included, or when the author wishes ro remain anonymous. Put the pen name in the byline under the title, and your real name in the upper, left-hand corner.

Permissions. Asking permission to use the text or art from a copyrighted source.

Personal experience story. A story based on a real-life experience.

Personality profile. A feature article that highlights a specific person's life or accomplishments.

Photocopied submission. Sending an editor a photocopy of your manuscript, rather than an original. Some editors prefer an original.

Piracy. To take the writings of others just as they were written and put your name on them as the author.

Plagiarism. To steal and use the ideas or writings of another as your own, rewriting them to make them sound like your own.

Press kit. A compilation of promotional materials on a particular book or author, usually organized in a folder, used to publicize a book.

Public domain. Work that has never been copyrighted, or on which the copyright has expired. Subtract 75 from the current year, and anything copyrighted prior to that is in public domain.

Published clips. Copies of actual articles you have had published, from newspapers or magazines.

Quarterly. Every three months.

Query letter. A letter sent to an editor telling about an article you propose to write and asking if he or she is interested in seeing it.

Reporting time. The number of weeks or months it takes an editor to get back to you about a query or manuscript you have sent in.

Reprint rights. Selling the right to reprint an article that has already been published elsewhere. You must have sold only first or one-time rights originally, and wait until it has been published the first time.

Review copies. Books given to book reviewers or buyers for chains.

Royalty. The percentage an author is paid by a publisher on the sale of each copy of a book.

SAE. Self-addressed envelope (without stamps).

SAN. Standard Account Number, used to identify libraries, book dealers, or schools.

SASE. Self-addressed, stamped envelope. Should always be sent with a manuscript or query letter.

SASP. Self-addressed, stamped postcard. May be sent with a manuscript submission to be returned by publisher indicating it arrived safely.

Satire. Ridicule that aims at reform.

Second serial rights. See "Reprint rights."

Semiannual. Issued twice a year.

Serial. Refers to publication in a periodical (such as first serial rights).

Sidebar. A short feature that accompanies an article and either elaborates on the human interest side of the story or gives additional information on the topic. It is often set apart by appearing within a box or border.

Simultaneous rights. Selling the rights to the same piece to several publishers simultaneously. Be sure everyone is aware that you are doing so.

Simultaneous submissions. Sending the same manuscript to more than one publisher at the same time. Usually done with non-overlapping markets (such as denominational or newspapers) or when you are writing on a timely subject. Be sure to state in a cover letter that it is a simultaneous submission and why.

Slanting. Writing an article so that it meets the needs of a particular market.

Slush pile. The stack of unsolicited manuscripts that have arrived at a publisher's office.

Speculation. See "On speculation."

Staff-written material. Material written by the members of a magazine staff.

Subsidiary rights. All those rights, other than book rights, included in a book contract—such as paperback, book club, movie, etc.

Subsidy publisher. A book publisher who charges the author to publish his book, as opposed to a royalty publisher who pays the author.

Synopsis. A brief summary of work—from one paragraph to several pages long.

Tabloid. A newspaper-format publication about half the size of a regular newspaper.

Take-home paper. A periodical sent home from Sunday school each week (usually) with Sunday school students, children through adults.

Think piece. A magazine article that has an intellectual, philosophical, or provocative approach to a subject.

Third World. Reference to underdeveloped countries of Asia and Africa.

Transparencies. Positive color slides, not color prints.

Trade magazine. A magazine whose audience is in a particular trade or business.

Traditional verse. One or more verses with an established pattern that is repeated throughout the poem.

Unsolicited manuscript. A manuscript an editor didn't specifically ask to see.

Vanity publisher. See "Subsidy publisher."

Vitae/Vita. An outline of one's personal history and experience.

Work-for-hire. Signing a contract with a publisher stating that a particular piece of writing you are doing for him is "work-for-hire." In the agreement you give the publisher full ownership and control of the material.

Writers' guidelines. An information sheet provided by a publisher which gives specific guidelines for writing for the publication. Always send an SASE with your request for guidelines.

GENERAL INDEX

This index includes periodicals, books, and greeting cards/specialty markets, as well as some of the various organizations and specialty lists you may need to find quickly. Conferences, groups, and editorial services are listed alphabetically by state; agents are listed alphabetically by the name of the agency. Check the Table of Contents for the location of supplementary listings.

Note: Due to the many changes in the market, and to help you determine the current status of any publisher you might be looking for, all markets will be listed in this index. If they are not viable markets, their current status will be indicated here, rather than in separate listings as they have been in previous years. The following codes will be used: (ABD)—asked to be deleted, (BA)—bad address or phone number, (ED)—editorial decision, (NF)—no freelance, (NR)—no recent response, (OB)—out of business. These changes will be noted in this listing for 5 years before being dropped altogether.

Worship Leader, 456
Write Now Publications, 173
Writer, 491
Writer Online, 491
Writer's Billboard, 491
Writer's Chronicle, 491
Writers Connection (OB)
Writer's Digest, 492
Writers Edge, 25
Writer's Exchange (see WE!)
Writer's Forum, 492
Writer's Guidelines & News
  (OB)
Writers Guild of America East,
  32
Writers Guild of America West,
  32
Writers Information Network, 32
Writer's Ink, 492
Writers' Intl. Forum (OB)
Writer's Journal, 493

Writer's Lifeline, 493
Writer's News (NF)
Writer's Nook News (OB)
Writer's Potpourri, 493
Writer's Resource (OB)
Writers' Union of Canada, 32
Writer's World (OB)
Writes of Passage, 493
Write Touch, 494
Writing & Surfing (BA)
Writing Right (OB)
Writing World, 494
WRS Publishing (ABD)
Yale University Press, 173
YES Intl. Publishers, 174
Yesterday's Family (OB)
You!, 467
Young Adult Today, 467
Young and Alive, 467
Young Christian (OB)
Young Musicians (OB)

Young Reader's Christian
  Library, 174
Young Salvationist, 468
Your Church, 456
Youth & CE Leadership, 420
Youth Challenge, 468
Youth Compass, 468
Youth Focus (BA)
Youth Illustrated (NF)
Youth 98 (see Campus Life)
Youth Life Creations, 513
Youth Specialties, 174
Youth Update (ABD)
YouthGuide (NF)
Youthwalk, 469
Youthworker, 457
Youth World (OB)
YWAM Publishing, 174
Zelos (NF)
ZonderKidz, 174
Zondervan, 175